CONSTITUTIONAL
LAW
AND POLITICS

VOLUME TWO

Other Books by David M. O'Brien

CONSTITUTIONAL LAW AND POLITICS

VOLUME TWO

Civil Rights and Civil Liberties

DAVID M. O'BRIEN

UNIVERSITY OF VIRGINIA

W · W · NORTON & COMPANY · *New York*

Printed in the United States of America.

The text of this book is composed in New Baskerville,
with the display set in New Baskerville.
Composition by Arcata Graphics/Kingsport.
Manufacturing by Arcata Graphics/Halliday.
Book design by Jacques Chazaud.

First Edition.
Library of Congress Cataloging-in-Publication Data

O'Brien, David M.
    Constitutional law and politics/David M. O'Brien.
      p. cm.
    Includes indexes.
    Contents: v. 1. Struggles for power and governmental
accountability—v. 2. Civil rights and civil liberties.
      1. United States—Constitutional law—Interpretation and
construction—History—Cases. 2. United States—Constitutional
history—Cases. 3. Political questions and judicial power—United
States—History—Cases. 4. Civil rights—United States—History—
Cases. 5. United States—Politics and government. I. Title.
KF4541.A7027 1991
342.73—dc20
[347.302]   90–7878

ISBN 0-393-96035-8

W. W. Norton & Company, Inc., 500 Fifth Avenue, New York, N.Y. 10110
W. W. Norton & Company, Ltd., 10 Coptic Street, London WC1A 1PU

1 2 3 4 5 6 7 8 9 0

For
Claudine, Benjamin, and Sara

CONTENTS

Cases within brackets are discussed and extensively quoted in the topic introductions.

Chapter 11. *The Right of Privacy* *1146*

ILLUSTRATIONS

PREFACE

Because there is no dearth of casebooks, the introduction of a new one perhaps needs a defense, or at least an explanation of how it differs from others. What distinguishes this casebook is its treatment and incorporation of material on constitutional history and American politics. Few casebooks pay adequate attention to the forces of history and politics on the course of constitutional law. Yet constitutional law, history, and politics are intimately intertwined.

The Constitution and Bill of Rights, of course, are political documents. Rooted in historic struggles and based on political compromises, their provisions and guarantees continue to invite competing interpretations and political contests over, for example, the separation of powers between Congress and the president, federalism, and civil rights and liberties. Because the Constitution says nothing about *who* should interpret it or about *how* it should be interpreted, constitutional law is animated by the politics of interpretation and the interpretation of politics. Neither do we have a single accepted theory of constitutional interpretation, nor do the justices write on a clean slate. Instead, we face constitutional choices and competing judicial and political philosophies.

The Supreme Court's decisions do not occur in a political vacuum, standing apart from history and the political struggles within the Court and the country. Virtually every major political controversy raises questions of constitutional law, no less than do technological changes and social movements and economic forces. The development and direction of constitutional law also shifts (more or less quickly) with the Court's changing composition. Members of the Court, just as other citizens, differ in their readings of the Constitution. Moreover, major confrontations in constitutional law and politics, such as those over the powers of the national government, or slavery, school desegregation, and abortion, involve continuing struggles that run from one generation to another. In the course of those struggles, constitutional law evolves with changes in the Court and the country. The Constitution and the Bill of Rights bind the Court, other political institutions, and the people in an ongoing dialogue over the exercise of and limitations on governmental power.

By providing the historical context and explaining the political contests among the justices and between the Court and the country, this casebook aims to make constitutional law more accessible for students. History and politics are also important for students' analyzing particular decisions and their relation to developments and changes in constitutional law and politics. They are crucial as well for students trying to critically evaluate competing interpretations and to appreciate the political consequences of alternative interpretations. And they are essential if students are to engage in the dialogue of constitutional law, confront constitutional choices, and come to terms with their and others' views of the Constitution and the Bill of Rights.

This casebook is different in several ways. First, it comes in two volumes. Volume I, *Struggles for Power and Governmental Accountability,* deals with separation of powers, federalism, and the democratic process. Volume II, *Civil Rights and Civil Liberties* is devoted to the enduring struggles to limit governmental power and guarantee civil rights and liberties. As a two-volume set, it is more comprehensive in its coverage than other casebooks. This permits both more introductory background material and a larger selection of cases. Instructors, therefore, have greater flexibility when assigning cases, and students will find useful the additional cases and guides to other cases and resources.

Second, two chapters dealing with the politics of constitutional interpretation and Supreme Court decision making contain material not usually found in casebooks. Chapter 1 goes beyond dealing with the establishment of the power of judicial review, and political criticisms of the Court's exercise of that power, to examining rival theories of constitutional interpretation. Students are introduced to differing judicial and political philosophies and referred to cases and opinions found in subsequent chapters that illustrate these different positions on constitutional interpretation. Chapter 2 combines an introduction to jurisdictional matters, such as standing, with a discussion of how the Court operates as an institution and in relation to other political institutions, which may help promote compliance with and implementation of its rulings, or thwart and even reverse them. In short, Chapter 1 prepares students for critically evaluating competing interpretations of constitutional provisions in subsequent chapters. And Chapter 2 prepares them for understanding the political struggles that take place within the Court as well as between the Court and other political institutions over its decisions. While the volumes are designed for a two-semester course, both of these chapters are included in each volume for the convenience of teachers and students who have only a one-semester course in constitutional law.

As already noted, each chapter and subsection contains a lengthy introductory essay. These essays focus on particular provisions of the Constitution and the Bill of Rights, why they took the form they did, and what controversies surround them during the Founding period and later. Most begin with the debates at the Constitutional Convention of 1787 and those between the Federalists and Anti-Federalists during the ratification period, and then review subsequent cases and controversies. Besides providing a historical and political context for the cases in each chapter, the essays highlight the continuity and changes in the debates over constitutional law and politics that run from the Founding period to recent rulings of the Rehnquist Court.

Something should also be said about the case excerpts. Most are preceded by "headnotes," short explanations of the facts and why the case was appealed to the Court. But, unlike the brief (and usually dry) headnotes typically found in casebooks, these reveal something about the personal and political struggles of those who appeal to the Court. Throughout, there is an attempt to help students understand the judicial and political process and appreciate how questions of constitutional law are embedded in everyday life. For this reason, students will also find excerpts from oral arguments before the Court and other materials bearing on the political struggles that they represent. Along with excerpts of the opinion announcing the decision of the Court, students will frequently encounter excerpts from separate concurring and dissenting opinions. These are included to help students appreciate the choices that the Court and they must make when interpreting the Constitution and the Bill of Rights.

In addition, each volume contains three types of boxes, which include materials that further place constitutional interpretation and law in historical and political perspective. One set of boxes, *Constitutional History,* presents important background material, such as excerpts from John Locke on the connection between property and liberty and explanatory notes on the "Watergate crisis" and the battle over the Equal Rights Amendment. Another set, *The Development of Law,* shows changes and patterns in constitutional law and refers students to other cases on topics of special interest. The third, *Inside the Court,* illustrates the internal dynamics of the Court when engaged in the process of constitutional interpretation and deciding cases. These boxes are indicated by ☐ in the contents.

Finally, each volume begins with the Constitution of the United States. What follows will, it is hoped, enrich students' understanding of constitutional law, politics, and history, as well as open them to the possibilities in interpreting the Constitution and the Bill of Rights. But the Constitution is where students should begin their study, and it is assuredly where they will return again and again.

D. M. O.

ACKNOWLEDGMENTS

I am indebted to my students and colleagues, but I owe a larger debt to Claudine, my wife, for giving me the freedom to work as I do and to enjoy life's pleasures with Benjamin and Sara. I continue to be grateful for the inspiration and support of my teacher C. Herman Pritchett, University of California, Santa Barbara, and my colleague at the University of Virginia Henry J. Abraham. They along with Ira Carmen, University of Illinois; Phillip Cooper, SUNY at Albany; Jerome Hanus, The American University; and Gerald Rosenberg, University of Chicago, read and made very helpful suggestions on various parts of the manuscript for which I am grateful. Also, I thank Thomas Baker, Texas Tech University; Sue Davis, University of Delaware; Susan Fino, Wayne State University; Christine Harrington, New York University; and H. N. Hirsch, University of California, San Diego, for offering comments that helped shape the project early on in its development. The generous support of the American Philosophical Society and the Earhart Foundation contributed to this project as well. Stephen Bragaw was a faithful and meticulous research assistant; Candace Levy copyedited the manuscript with the utmost care. Once again, I appreciate the understanding and assistance of Donald Fusting, a patient and wise editor at Norton.

I am grateful as well for permission to reproduce materials here granted by the following individuals and organizations:

Justices William J. Brennan, Jr., Lewis F. Powell, and Antonin Scalia; Ronald K. L. Collins; the curator of the Supreme Court of the United States; Peter Galie; the Library of Congress; Justice Hans Linde of the Oregon State Supreme Court; the Supreme Court Historical Society; the National Portrait Gallery/Smithsonian Institution; *The New York Times;* the Roosevelt Library; Sygma/*New York Times Magazine;* Paula Okamoto; and Wide World Photos.

CONSTITUTIONAL
LAW
AND POLITICS

VOLUME TWO

THE UNITED STATES CONSTITUTION AND AMENDMENTS

W E THE PEOPLE of the United States, in Order to form a more perfect Union, establish Justice, insure domestic Tranquility, provide for the common defence, promote the general Welfare, and secure the Blessings of Liberty to ourselves and our Posterity, do ordain and establish this Constitution for the United States of America.

ARTICLE I

SECTION 1. All legislative Powers herein granted shall be vested in a Congress of the United States, which shall consist of a Senate and House of Representatives.

SECTION 2. The House of Representatives shall be composed of Members chosen every second Year by the People of the several States, and the Electors in each State shall have the Qualifications requisite for Electors of the most numerous Branch of the State Legislature.

No Person shall be a Representative who shall not have attained to the Age of twenty five Years, and been seven Years a Citizen of the United States, and who shall not, when elected, be an Inhabitant of that State in which he shall be chosen.

[Representatives and [direct Taxes] shall be apportioned

among the several States [which may be included within this Union,] according to their respective Numbers, which shall be determined by adding to the whole Number of free Persons, including those bound to Service for a Term of Years, and excluding Indians not taxed, three fifths of all other Persons. *(This clause was changed by section 2 of the Fourteenth Amendment.)*] The actual Enumeration shall be made within three Years after the first Meeting of the Congress of the United States, and within every subsequent Term of ten Years, in such Manner as they shall by Law direct. The Number of Representatives shall not exceed one for every thirty Thousand, but each State shall have at Least one Representative; and until such enumeration shall be made, the State of New Hampshire shall be entitled to chuse three, Massachusetts eight, Rhode-Island and Providence Plantations one, Connecticut five, New-York six, New Jersey four, Pennsylvania eight, Delaware one, Maryland six, Virginia ten, North Carolina five, South Carolina five, and Georgia three.

When vacancies happen in the Representation from any State, the Executive Authority thereof shall issue Writs of Election to fill such Vacancies.

The House of Representatives shall chuse their Speaker and other Officers; and shall have the sole Power of Impeachment.

SECTION 3. The Senate of the United States shall be composed of two Senators from each State, [chosen by the Legislature thereof, *(This provision was changed by section 1 of the Seventeenth Amendment.)*] for six Years; and each Senator shall have one Vote.

Immediately after they shall be assembled in Consequence of the first Election, they shall be divided as equally as may be into three Classes. The Seats of the Senators of the first Class shall be vacated at the Expiration of the second Year, of the second Class at the Expiration of the fourth Year, and of the third Class at the Expiration of the sixth Year, so that one third may be chosen every second Year; [and if Vacancies happen by Resignation, or otherwise, during the Recess of the Legislature of any State, the Executive thereof may make temporary Appointments until the next Meeting of the Legislature, which shall then fill such Vacancies. *(This clause was changed by section 2 of the Seventeenth Amendment.)*]

No Person shall be a Senator who shall not have attained to the Age of thirty Years, and been nine Years a Citizen of the United States, and who shall not, when elected, be an Inhabitant of that State for which he shall be chosen.

The Vice President of the United States shall be President of the Senate, but shall have no Vote, unless they be equally divided.

The Senate shall chuse their other Officers, and also a President pro tempore, in the Absence of the Vice President, or when he shall exercise the Office of President of the United States.

The Senate shall have the sole Power to try all Impeachments. When sitting for that Purpose, they shall be on Oath or Affirmation. When the President of the United States is tried, the Chief Justice shall preside: And no Person shall be convicted without the Concurrence of two thirds of the Members present.

Judgment in Cases of Impeachment shall not extend further than to removal from Office, and disqualification to hold and enjoy any Office of honor, Trust or Profit under the United States: but the Party convicted shall nevertheless be liable and subject to Indictment, Trial, Judgment and Punishment, according to Law.

SECTION 4. The Times, Places and Manner of holding Elections for Senators and Representatives, shall be prescribed in each State by the Legislature thereof; but the Congress may at any time by Law make or alter such Regulations, except as to the Places of chusing Senators.

The Congress shall assemble at least once in every Year, and such Meeting shall be [on the first Monday in December, *(This provision was changed by section 2 of the Twentieth Amendment.)*] unless they shall by Law appoint a different Day.

SECTION 5. Each House shall be the Judge of the Elections, Returns and Qualifications of its own Members, and a Majority of each shall constitute a Quorum to do Business; but a smaller Number may adjourn from day to day, and may be authorized to compel the Attendance of absent Members, in such Manner, and under such Penalties as each House may provide.

Each House may determine the Rules of its Proceedings, punish its Members for disorderly Behaviour, and, with the Concurrence of two thirds, expel a Member.

Each House shall keep a Journal of its Proceedings, and from time to time publish the same, excepting such Parts as may in their Judgment require Secrecy; and the Yeas and Nays of the Members of either House on any question shall, at the Desire of one fifth of those Present, be entered on the Journal.

Neither House, during the Session of Congress, shall, without the Consent of the other, adjourn for more than three days, nor to any other Place than that in which the two Houses shall be sitting.

SECTION 6. The Senators and Representatives shall receive a Compensation for their Services, to be ascertained by Law, and paid out of the Treasury of the United States. They shall in all Cases, except Treason, Felony and Breach of the Peace, be privileged from Arrest during their Attendance at the Session of their respective Houses, and in going to and returning from the same; and for any Speech or Debate in either House, they shall not be questioned in any other Place.

No Senator or Representative shall, during the Time for which he was elected, be appointed to any civil Office under the Authority of the United States, which shall have been created, or the Emoluments whereof shall have been encreased during such time; and no Person holding any Office under the United States, shall be a Member of either House during his Continuance in Office.

SECTION 7. All Bills for raising Revenue shall originate in the House of Representatives; but the Senate may propose or concur with Amendments as on other Bills.

Every Bill which shall have passed the House of Representatives and the Senate, shall, before it become a Law, be presented to the President of the United States; If he approve he shall sign it, but if not he shall return it, with his Objections to that House in which it shall have originated, who shall enter the Objections at large on their Journal, and proceed to reconsider it. If after such Reconsideration two thirds of that House shall agree to pass the Bill, it shall be sent, together with the Objections, to the other House, by which it shall likewise be reconsidered, and if approved by two thirds of that House, it shall become a Law. But in all such Cases the Votes of both Houses shall be determined by yeas and Nays, and the Names of the Persons voting for and against the Bill shall be entered on the Journal of each House respectively. If any bill shall not be returned by the President within ten Days (Sundays excepted) after it shall have been presented to him, the Same shall be a Law, in like Manner as if he had signed it, unless the Congress by their Adjournment prevent its Return, in which Case it shall not be a Law.

Every Order, Resolution, or Vote to which the Concurrence of the Senate and House of Representatives may be necessary (except on a question of Adjournment) shall be presented to the President of the United States; and before the Same shall take Effect, shall be approved by him, or being disapproved by him, shall be repassed by two thirds of the Senate and House of Representatives, according to the Rules and Limitations prescribed in the Case of a Bill.

SECTION 8. The Congress shall have Power To lay and collect Taxes, Duties, Imposts and Excises, to pay the Debts and provide for the common Defence and general Welfare of the United

States; but all Duties, Imposts and Excises shall be uniform throughout the United States;

To borrow Money on the credit of the United States;

To regulate Commerce with foreign Nations, and among the several States, and with the Indian tribes;

To establish an uniform Rule of Naturalization, and uniform Laws on the subject of Bankruptcies throughout the United States;

To coin Money, regulate the Value thereof, and of foreign Coin, and fix the Standard of Weights and Measures;

To provide for the Punishment of counterfeiting the Securities and current Coin of the United States;

To establish Post Offices and post Roads;

To promote the Progress of Science and useful Arts, by securing for limited Times to Authors and Inventors the exclusive Right to their respective Writings and Discoveries;

To constitute Tribunals inferior to the supreme Court;

To define and punish Piracies and Felonies committed on the high Seas, and Offences against the Law of Nations;

To declare War, grant Letters of Marque and Reprisal, and make Rules concerning Captures on Land and Water;

To raise and support Armies, but no Appropriation of Money to that Use shall be for a longer Term than two Years;

To provide and maintain a Navy;

To make Rules for the Government and Regulation of the land and naval Forces;

To provide for calling forth the Militia to execute the Laws of the Union, suppress Insurrections and repel Invasions;

To provide for organizing, arming, and disciplining, the Militia, and for governing such Part of them as may be employed in the Service of the United States, reserving to the States respectively, the Appointment of the Officers, and the Authority of training the Militia according to the discipline prescribed by Congress;

To exercise exclusive Legislation in all Cases whatsoever, over such District (not exceeding ten Miles square) as may, by Cession of particular States, and the Acceptance of Congress, become the Seat of the Government of the United States, and to exercise like Authority over all Places purchased by the Consent of the Legislature of the State in which the Same shall be, for the Erection of Forts, Magazines, Arsenals, dock-Yards, and other needful Buildings;—And

To make all Laws which shall be necessary and proper for carrying into Execution the foregoing Powers, and all other Powers vested by this Constitution in the Government of the United States, or in any Department or Officer thereof.

SECTION 9. The Migration or Importation of such Persons as any of the States now existing shall think proper to admit, shall not be prohibited by the Congress prior to the Year one thousand eight hundred and eight, but a Tax or duty may be imposed on such Importation, not exceeding ten dollars for each Person.

The Privilege of the Writ of Habeas Corpus shall not be suspended, unless when in Cases of Rebellion or Invasion the public Safety may require it.

No Bill of Attainder or ex post facto Law shall be passed.

No Capitation, or other direct, Tax shall be laid, unless in Proportion to the Census or Enumeration herein before directed to be taken.

No Tax or Duty shall be laid on Articles exported from any State.

No Preference shall be given by any Regulation of Commerce or Revenue to the Ports of one State over those of another: nor shall Vessels bound to, or from, one State, be obliged to enter, clear, or pay Duties in another.

No Money shall be drawn from the Treasury, but in Consequence of Appropriations made by Law; and a regular Statement and Account of the Receipts and Expenditures of all public Money shall be published from time to time.

No Title of Nobility shall be granted by the United States: And no Person holding any Office of Profit or Trust under them, shall, without the Consent of the Congress, accept of any present, Emolument, Office, or Title, of any kind whatever, from any King, Prince, or foreign State.

SECTION 10. No State shall enter into any Treaty, Alliance, or Confederation; grant Letters of Marque and Reprisal; coin Money; emit Bills of Credit; make any Thing but gold and silver Coin a Tender in Payment of Debts; pass any Bill of Attainder, ex post facto Law, or Law impairing the Obligation of Contracts, or grant any Title of Nobility.

No State shall, without the Consent of the Congress, lay any Imposts or Duties on Imports or Exports, except what may be absolutely necessary for executing it's inspection Laws: and the net Produce of all Duties and Imposts, laid by any State on Imports or Exports, shall be for the Use of the Treasury of the United States; and all such Laws shall be subject to the Revision and Controul of the Congress.

No State shall, without the Consent of Congress, lay any Duty of Tonnage, keep Troops, or Ships of War in time of Peace, enter into any Agreement or Compact with another State, or with a foreign Power, or engage in War, unless actually invaded, or in such imminent Danger as will not admit of delay.

ARTICLE II

SECTION 1. The executive Power shall be vested in a President of the United States of America. He shall hold his Office during the Term of four Years, and, together with the Vice President, chosen for the same Term, be elected, as follows

Each State shall appoint, in such Manner as the Legislature thereof may direct, a Number of Electors, equal to the whole Number of Senators and Representatives to which the State may be entitled in the Congress: but no Senator or Representative, or Person holding an Office of Trust or Profit under the United States, shall be appointed an Elector.

[The Electors shall meet in their respective States, and vote by Ballot for two Persons, of whom one at least shall not be an inhabitant of the same State with themselves. And they shall make a List of all the Persons voted for, and of the Number of Votes for each; which List they shall sign and certify, and transmit sealed to the Seat of the Government of the United States, directed to the President of the Senate. The President of the Senate shall, in the Presence of the Senate and House of Representatives, open all the Certificates, and the Votes shall then be counted. The Person having the greatest Number of Votes shall be the President, if such Number be a Majority of the whole Number of Electors appointed; and if there be more than one who have such Majority, and have an equal Number of Votes, then the House of Representatives shall immediately chuse by Ballot one of them for President; and if no Person have a Majority, then from the five highest on the List the said House shall in like Manner chuse the President. But in chusing the President, the Votes shall be taken by States, the Representation from each State having one Vote; A quorum for this purpose shall consist of a Member or Members from two thirds of the States, and a Majority of all the States shall be necessary to a Choice. In every Case, after the Choice of the President, the Person having the greatest Number of Votes of the Electors shall be the Vice President. But if there should remain two or more who have equal Votes, the Senate shall chuse from them by Ballot the Vice President. *(This clause was superseded by the Twelfth Amendment.)*]

The Congress may determine the Time of chusing the Electors, and the Day on which they shall give their Votes; which Day shall be the same throughout the United States.

No Person except a natural born Citizen, or a Citizen of the United States, at the time of the Adoption of this Constitution, shall be eligible to the Office of President; neither shall any Person be eligible to that Office who shall not have attained to the Age of thirty five Years, and been fourteen Years a Resident within the United States.

[In Case of the Removal of the President from Office, or of his Death, Resignation, or Inability to discharge the Powers and Duties of the said Office, the Same shall devolve on the Vice President, and the Congress may by Law provide for the Case of Removal, Death, Resignation or Inability, both of the President and Vice President, declaring what Officer shall then act as President, and such Officer shall act accordingly, until the Disability be removed, or a President shall be elected. *(This clause was modified by the Twenty-Fifth Amendment.)*]

The President shall, at stated Times, receive for his Services, a Compensation, which shall neither be encreased nor diminished during the Period for which he shall have been elected, and he shall not receive within that Period any other Emolument from the United States, or any of them.

Before he enter on the Execution of his Office, he shall take the following Oath or Affirmation:—"I do solemnly swear (or affirm) that I will faithfully execute the Office of President of the United States, and will to the best of my Ability, preserve, protect and defend the Constitution of the United States."

SECTION 2. The President shall be Commander in Chief of the Army and Navy of the United States, and of the Militia of the several States, when called into the actual Service of the United States; he may require the Opinion, in writing, of the principal Officer in each of the executive Departments, upon any Subject relating to the Duties of their respective Offices, and he shall have Power to grant Reprieves and Pardons for Offences against the United States, except in Cases of Impeachment.

He shall have Power, by and with the Advice and Consent of the Senate, to make Treaties, provided two thirds of the Senators present concur; and he shall nominate, and by and with the Advice and Consent of the Senate, shall appoint Ambassadors, other public Ministers and Consuls, Judges of the supreme Court, and all other Officers of the United States, whose Appointments are not herein otherwise provided for, and which shall be established by Law: but the Congress may by Law vest the Appointment of such inferior Officers, as they think proper, in the President alone, in the Courts of Law, or in the Heads of Departments.

The President shall have Power to fill up all Vacancies that may happen during the Recess of the Senate, by granting Commissions which shall expire at the End of their next Session.

SECTION 3. He shall from time to time give to the Congress Information of the State of the Union, and recommend to their Consideration such Measures as he shall judge necessary and expedient; he may, on extraordinary Occasions, convene both Houses, or either of them, and in Case of Disagreement between them, with Respect to the Time of Adjournment, he may adjourn them to such Time as he shall think proper; he shall receive Ambassadors and other public Ministers; he shall take Care that the Laws be faithfully executed, and shall Commission all the Officers of the United States.

SECTION 4. The President, Vice President and all civil Officers of the United States, shall be removed from Office on Impeachment for, and Conviction of, Treason, Bribery, or other high Crimes and Misdemeanors.

ARTICLE III

SECTION 1. The judicial Power of the United States, shall be vested in one supreme Court, and in such inferior Courts as the Congress may from time to time ordain and establish. The Judges, both of the supreme and inferior Courts, shall hold their Offices during good Behaviour, and shall, at stated Times receive for their Services, a Compensation, which shall not be diminished during their Continuance in Office.

SECTION 2. The judicial Power shall extend to all Cases, in Law and Equity, arising under this Constitution, the Laws of the United States, and Treaties made, or which shall be made, under their Authority;—to all Cases affecting Ambassadors, other public Ministers and Consuls;—to all Cases of admiralty and maritime Jurisdiction;—to Controversies to which the United States shall be a Party;—to Controversies between two or more States;—between a State and Citizens of another State;—between Citizens of different States,—between Citizens of the same State claiming Lands under Grants of different States, and between a State, or the Citizens thereof, and foreign States, Citizens or Subjects.

In all Cases affecting Ambassadors, other public Ministers and Consuls, and those in which a State shall be Party, the supreme Court shall have original Jurisdiction. In all the other Cases before mentioned, the supreme Court shall have appellate Jurisdiction, both as to Law and Fact, with such Exceptions, and under such Regulations as the Congress shall make.

The Trial of all Crimes, except in Cases of Impeachment,

shall be by Jury; and such Trial shall be held in the State where the said Crimes shall have been committed; but when not committed within any State, the Trial shall be at such Place or Places as the Congress may by Law have directed.

SECTION 3. Treason against the United States, shall consist only in levying War against them, or in adhering to their Enemies, giving them Aid and Comfort. No Person shall be convicted of Treason unless on the Testimony of two Witnesses to the same overt Act, or on Confession in open Court.

The Congress shall have Power to declare the Punishment of Treason, but no Attainder of Treason shall work Corruption of Blood, or Forfeiture except during the Life of the Person attainted.

ARTICLE IV

SECTION 1. Full Faith and Credit shall be given in each State to the public Acts, Records, and judicial Proceedings of every other State; And the Congress may by general Laws prescribe the Manner in which such Acts, Records and Proceedings shall be proved, and the Effect thereof.

SECTION 2. The Citizens of each State shall be entitled to all Privileges and Immunities of Citizens in the several States.

A Person charged in any State with Treason, Felony, or other Crime, who shall flee from Justice, and be found in another State, shall on Demand of the executive Authority of the State from which he fled, be delivered up, to be removed to the State having Jurisdiction of the Crime.

[No Person held to Service or Labour in one State, under the Laws thereof, escaping into another, shall, in Consequence of any Law or Regulation therein, be discharged from such Service or Labour, but shall be delivered up on Claim of the Party to whom such Service or Labour may be due. *(This clause was superseded by the Thirteenth Amendment.)*]

SECTION 3. New States may be admitted by the Congress into this Union; but no new State shall be formed or erected within the Jurisdiction of any other State; nor any State be formed by the Junction of two or more States, or Parts of States, without the Consent of the Legislatures of the States concerned as well as of the Congress.

The Congress shall have Power to dispose of and make all needful Rules and Regulations respecting the Territory or other Property belonging to the United States; and nothing in this

Constitution shall be so construed as to Prejudice any Claims of the United States, or of any particular State.

Section 4. The United States shall guarantee to every State in this Union a Republican Form of Government, and shall protect each of them against Invasion; and on Application of the Legislature, or of the Executive (when the Legislature cannot be convened) against domestic Violence.

ARTICLE V

The Congress, whenever two thirds of both Houses shall deem it necessary, shall propose Amendments to this Constitution, or, on the Application of the Legislatures of two thirds of the several States, shall call a Convention for proposing Amendments, which, in either Case, shall be valid to all Intents and Purposes, as Part of this Constitution, when ratified by the legislatures of three fourths of the several States, or by Conventions in three fourths thereof, as the one or the other Mode of Ratification may be proposed by the Congress; Provided that no Amendment which may be made prior to the Year One thousand eight hundred and eight shall in any Manner affect the first and fourth Clauses in the Ninth Section of the first Article; and that no State, without its Consent, shall be deprived of it's equal Suffrage in the Senate.

ARTICLE VI

All Debts contracted and Engagements entered into, before the Adoption of this Constitution, shall be as valid against the United States under this Constitution, as under the Confederation.

This Constitution, and the Laws of the United States which shall be made in Pursuance thereof; and all Treaties made, or which shall be made, under the Authority of the United States, shall be the supreme Law of the Land; and the Judges in every State shall be bound thereby, any Thing in the Constitution or Laws of any State to the Contrary notwithstanding.

The Senators and Representatives before mentioned, and the Members of the several State Legislatures, and all executive and judicial Officers, both of the United States and of the several States, shall be bound by Oath or Affirmation, to support this Constitution; but no religious Test shall ever be required as a Qualification to any Office or public Trust under the United States.

ARTICLE VII

The Ratification of the Conventions of nine States, shall be sufficient for the Establishment of this Constitution between the States so ratifying the Same.

DONE in Convention by the Unanimous Consent of the States present the Seventeenth Day of September in the Year of our Lord one thousand seven hundred and Eighty seven and of the Independance of the United States of America the Twelfth.

IN WITNESS whereof We have hereunto subscribed our Names.

AMENDMENT I

[The first ten amendments (the Bill of Rights) were ratified December 15, 1791.]

Congress shall make no law respecting an establishment of religion, or prohibiting the free exercise thereof; or abridging the freedom of speech, or of the press, or the right of the people peaceably to assemble, and to petition the Government for a redress of grievances.

AMENDMENT II

A well regulated Militia, being necessary to the security of a free State, the right of the people to keep and bear Arms, shall not be infringed.

AMENDMENT III

No Soldier shall, in time of peace be quartered in any house, without the consent of the Owner, nor in time of war, but in a manner to be prescribed by law.

AMENDMENT IV

The right of the people to be secure in their persons, houses, papers, and effects, against unreasonable searches and seizures, shall not be violated, and no Warrants shall issue, but upon probable cause, supported by Oath or affirmation, and particularly describing the place to be searched, and the persons or things to be seized.

AMENDMENT V

No person shall be held to answer for a capital, or otherwise infamous crime, unless on a presentment or indictment of a Grand Jury, except in cases arising in the land or naval forces, or in the Militia, when in actual service in time of War or public danger; nor shall any person be subject for the same offence to be twice put in jeopardy of life or limb, nor shall be compelled in any criminal case to be a witness against himself, nor be deprived of life, liberty, or property, without due process of law; nor shall private property be taken for public use, without just compensation.

AMENDMENT VI

In all criminal prosecutions, the accused shall enjoy the right to a speedy and public trial, by an impartial jury of the State and district wherein the crime shall have been committed; which district shall have been previously ascertained by law, and to be informed of the nature and cause of the accusation; to be confronted with the witnesses against him; to have compulsory process for obtaining Witnesses in his favor, and to have the assistance of counsel for his defence.

AMENDMENT VII

In Suits at common law, where the value in controversy shall exceed twenty dollars, the right of trial by jury shall be preserved, and no fact tried by a jury, shall be otherwise re-examined in any Court of the United States, than according to the rules of the common law.

AMENDMENT VIII

Excessive bail shall not be required, nor excessive fines imposed, nor cruel and unusual punishments inflicted.

AMENDMENT IX

The enumeration in the Constitution, of certain rights, shall not be construed to deny or disparage others retained by the people.

AMENDMENT X

The powers not delegated to the United States by the Constitution, nor prohibited by it to the States, are reserved to the States respectively, or to the people.

AMENDMENT XI

[Ratified February 7, 1795.]

The Judicial power of the United States shall not be construed to extend to any suit in law or equity, commenced or prosecuted against one of the United States by Citizens of another State, or by Citizens or Subjects of any Foreign State.

AMENDMENT XII

[Ratified June 15, 1804.]

The Electors shall meet in their respective states, and vote by ballot for President and Vice-President, one of whom, at least, shall not be an inhabitant of the same state with themselves; they shall name in their ballots the person voted for as President, and in distinct ballots the person voted for as Vice-President, and they shall make distinct lists of all persons voted for as President, and of all persons voted for as Vice-President, and of the number of votes for each, which lists they shall sign and certify, and transmit sealed to the seat of the government of the United States, directed to the President of the Senate;—The President of the Senate shall, in the presence of the Senate and House of Representatives, open all the certificates and the votes shall then be counted;—The person having the greatest number of votes for President, shall be the President, if such number be a majority of the whole number of Electors appointed; and if no person have such majority, then from the persons having the highest numbers not exceeding three on the list of those voted for as President, the House of Representatives shall choose immediately, by ballot, the President. But in choosing the President, the votes shall be taken by states, the representation from each state having one vote; a quorum for this purpose shall consist of a member or members from two-thirds of the states, and a majority of all the states shall be necessary to a choice. [And if the House of Representatives shall not choose a President whenever the right of choice shall devolve upon them, before the fourth day of March next following, then the Vice-

President shall act as President, as in the case of the death or other constitutional disability of the President— *(This clause was superseded by section 3 of the Twentieth Amendment.)*]. The person having the greatest number of votes as Vice-President, shall be the Vice-President, if such number be a majority of the whole number of Electors appointed, and if no person have a majority, then from the two highest numbers on the list, the Senate shall choose the Vice-President; a quorum for the purpose shall consist of two-thirds of the whole number of Senators, and a majority of the whole number shall be necessary to a choice. But no person constitutionally ineligible to the office of President shall be eligible to that of Vice-President of the United States.

AMENDMENT XIII

[Ratified December 6, 1865.]

SECTION 1. Neither slavery nor involuntary servitude, except as a punishment for crime whereof the party shall have been duly convicted, shall exist within the United States, or any place subject to their jurisdiction.

SECTION 2. Congress shall have power to enforce this article by appropriate legislation.

AMENDMENT XIV

[Ratified July 9, 1868.]

SECTION 1. All persons born or naturalized in the United States, and subject to the jurisdiction thereof, are citizens of the United States and of the State wherein they reside. No State shall make or enforce any law which shall abridge the privileges or immunities of citizens of the United States; nor shall any State deprive any person of life, liberty, or property, without due process of law; nor deny to any person within its jurisdiction the equal protection of the laws.

SECTION 2. Representatives shall be apportioned among the several States according to their respective numbers, counting the whole number of persons in each State, excluding Indians not taxed. But when the right to vote at any election for the choice of electors for President and Vice President of the United States, Representatives in Congress, the Executive and Judicial officers of a State, or the members of the Legislature thereof, is denied to any of the male inhabitants of such State, being twenty-one years of age, and citizens of the United States, or in any way abridged, except for participation in rebellion, or other crime, the basis of representation therein shall be reduced in the proportion which the number of such male citizens shall bear to the whole number of male citizens twenty-one years of age in such State.

SECTION 3. No person shall be a Senator or Representative in Congress, or elector of President and Vice President, or hold any office, civil or military, under the United States, or under any State, who, having previously taken an oath, as a member of Congress, or as an officer of the United States, or as a member of any State legislature, or as an executive or judicial officer of any State, to support the Constitution of the United States, shall have engaged in insurrection or rebellion against the same, or given aid or comfort to the enemies thereof. But Congress may by a vote of two-thirds of each House, remove such disability.

SECTION 4. The validity of the public debt of the United States, authorized by law, including debts incurred for payment of pensions and bounties for services in suppressing insurrection or rebellion, shall not be questioned. But neither the United States nor any State shall assume or pay any debt or obligation incurred in aid of insurrection or rebellion against the United States, or any claim for the loss or emancipation of any slave; but all such debts, obligations and claims shall be held illegal and void.

SECTION 5. The Congress shall have power to enforce, by appropriate legislation, the provisions of this article.

AMENDMENT XV

[Ratified February 3, 1870.]

SECTION 1. The right of citizens of the United States to vote shall not be denied or abridged by the United States or by any State on account of race, color, or previous condition of servitude.

SECTION 2. The Congress shall have power to enforce this article by appropriate legislation.

AMENDMENT XVI

[Ratified February 3, 1913.]

The Congress shall have power to lay and collect taxes on incomes, from whatever source derived, without apportionment among the several States, and without regard to any census or enumeration.

AMENDMENT XVII

[Ratified April 8, 1913.]

The Senate of the United States shall be composed of two Senators from each State, elected by the people thereof, for six years; and each Senator shall have one vote. The electors in each State shall have the qualifications requisite for electors of the most numerous branch of the State legislatures.

When vacancies happen in the representation of any State in the Senate, the executive authority of such State shall issue writs of election to fill such vacancies: *Provided,* That the legislature of any State may empower the executive thereof to make temporary appointments until the people fill the vacancies by election as the legislature may direct.

This amendment shall not be so construed as to affect the election or term of any Senator chosen before it becomes valid as part of the Constitution.

AMENDMENT XVIII

[Ratified January 16, 1919.]

SECTION 1. After one year from the ratification of this article the manufacture, sale, or transportation of intoxicating liquors within, the importation thereof into, or the exportation thereof from the United States and all territory subject to the jurisdiction thereof for beverage purposes is hereby prohibited.

SECTION 2. The Congress and the several States shall have concurrent power to enforce this article by appropriate legislation.

SECTION 3. This article shall be inoperative unless it shall have been ratified as an amendment to the Constitution by the legislatures of the several States, as provided in the Constitution, within seven years from the date of the submission hereof to the States by the Congress.

AMENDMENT XIX

[Ratified August 18, 1920.]

The right of citizens of the United States to vote shall not be denied or abridged by the United States or by any State on account of sex.

Congress shall have power to enforce this article by appropriate legislation.

AMENDMENT XX

[Ratified January 23, 1933.]

SECTION 1. The terms of the President and Vice President shall end at noon on the 20th day of January, and the terms of Senators and Representatives at noon on the 3d day of January, of the years in which such terms would have ended if this article had not been ratified; and the terms of their successors shall then begin.

SECTION 2. The Congress shall assemble at least once in every year, and such meeting shall begin at noon on the 3d day of January, unless they shall by law appoint a different day.

SECTION 3. If, at the time fixed for the beginning of the term of the President, the President elect shall have died, the Vice President elect shall become President. If a President shall not have been chosen before the time fixed for the beginning of his term, or if the President elect shall have failed to qualify, then the Vice President elect shall act as President until a President shall have qualified; and the Congress may by law provide for the case wherein neither a President elect nor a Vice President elect shall have qualified, declaring who shall then act as President, or the manner in which one who is to act shall be selected, and such person shall act accordingly until a President or Vice President shall have qualified.

SECTION 4. The Congress may by law provide for the case of the death of any of the persons from whom the House of Representatives may choose a President whenever the right of choice shall have devolved upon them, and for the case of the death of any of the persons from whom the Senate may choose a Vice President whenever the right of choice shall have devolved upon them.

SECTION 5. Sections 1 and 2 shall take effect on the 15th day of October following the ratification of this article.

SECTION 6. This article shall be inoperative unless it shall have been ratified as an amendment to the Constitution by the legislatures of three-fourths of the several States within seven years from the date of its submission.

AMENDMENT XXI

[Ratified December 5, 1933.]

SECTION 1. The eighteenth article of amendment to the Constitution of the United States is hereby repealed.

SECTION 2. The transportation or importation into any State, Territory, or possession of the United States for delivery or use therein of intoxicating liquors, in violation of the laws thereof, is hereby prohibited.

SECTION 3. This article shall be inoperative unless it shall have been ratified as an amendment to the Constitution by conventions in the several States, as provided in the Constitution, within seven years from the date of the submission hereof to the States by the Congress.

AMENDMENT XXII

[Ratified February 27, 1951.]

SECTION 1. No person shall be elected to the office of the President more than twice, and no person who has held the office of President, or acted as President, for more than two years of a term to which some other person was elected President shall be elected to the office of the President more than once. But this Article shall not apply to any person holding the office of President when this Article was proposed by the Congress, and shall not prevent any person who may be holding the office of President, or acting as President, during the term within which this Article becomes operative from holding the office of President or acting as President during the remainder of such term.

SECTION 2. This article shall be inoperative unless it shall have been ratified as an amendment to the Constitution by the legislatures of three-fourths of the several States within seven years from the date of its submission to the States by the Congress.

AMENDMENT XXIII

[Ratified March 29, 1961.]

SECTION 1. The District constituting the seat of Government of the United States shall appoint in such manner as the Congress may direct:

A number of electors of President and Vice President equal to the whole number of Senators and Representatives in Congress to which the District would be entitled if it were a State, but in no event more than the least populous State; they shall be in addition to those appointed by the States, but they shall be considered, for the purposes of the election of President and Vice President, to be electors appointed by a State; and they shall meet in the District and perform such duties as provided by the twelfth article of amendment.

SECTION 2. The Congress shall have power to enforce this article by appropriate legislation.

AMENDMENT XXIV

[Ratified January 23, 1964.]

SECTION 1. The right of citizens of the United States to vote in any primary or other election for President or Vice President, for electors for President or Vice President, or for Senator or Representatives in Congress, shall not be denied or abridged by the United States or any State by reason of failure to pay any poll tax or other tax.

SECTION 2. The Congress shall have power to enforce this article by appropriate legislation.

AMENDMENT XXV

[Ratified February 10, 1967.]

SECTION 1. In case of the removal of the President from office or of his death or resignation, the Vice President shall become President.

SECTION 2. Whenever there is a vacancy in the office of the Vice President, the President shall nominate a Vice President who shall take office upon confirmation by a majority vote of both Houses of Congress.

SECTION 3. Whenever the President transmits to the President pro tempore of the Senate and the Speaker of the House of Representatives his written declaration that he is unable to discharge the powers and duties of his office, and until he transmits to them a written declaration to the contrary, such powers and duties shall be discharged by the Vice President as Acting President.

SECTION 4. Whenever the Vice President and a majority of either the principal officers of the executive departments or of such other body as Congress may by law provide, transmit to the President pro tempore of the Senate and the Speaker of the House of Representatives their written declaration that the President is unable to discharge the powers and duties of his office, the Vice President shall immediately assume the powers and duties of the office as Acting President.

Thereafter, when the President transmits to the President pro tempore of the Senate and the Speaker of the House of Representatives his written declaration that no inability exists, he shall resume the powers and duties of his office unless the Vice President and a majority of either the principal officers of the executive department or of such other body as Congress may by law provide, transmit within four days to the President pro tempore of the Senate and the Speaker of the House of Representatives their written declaration that the President is unable to discharge the powers and duties of his office. Thereupon Congress shall decide the issue, assembling within forty-eight hours for that purpose if not in session. If the Congress, within twenty-one days after receipt of the latter written declaration, or, if Congress is not in session, within twenty-one days after Congress is required to assemble, determines by two-thirds vote of both Houses that the President is unable to discharge the powers and duties of his office, the Vice President shall continue to discharge the same as Acting President; otherwise, the President shall resume the powers and duties of his office.

AMENDMENT XXVI

[Ratified July 1, 1971.]

SECTION 1. The right of citizens of the United States, who are eighteen years of age or older, to vote shall not be denied or abridged by the United States or by any State on account of age.

SECTION 2. The Congress shall have power to enforce this article by appropriate legislation.

1

THE SUPREME COURT, JUDICIAL REVIEW, AND CONSTITUTIONAL POLITICS

J UDICIAL REVIEW IS one of the greatest and most controversial contributions of the Constitution to the law and politics of government. Article III of the Constitution simply provides that "[t]he judicial Power of the United States, shall be vested in one supreme Court, and in such inferior Courts as the Congress may from time to time ordain and establish." Remarkably, that power is not further defined in the Constitution. But in the course of constitutional politics, *judicial review* has come to be the power of the Supreme Court and the federal judiciary to consider and overturn any congressional and state legislation or other official governmental action deemed inconsistent with the Constitution, Bill of Rights, or federal law.

Like other provisions of the Constitution, the three brief sections in Article III register compromises forged during the Constitutional Convention; the Constitution, as the renowned historian and editor of *The Records of the Federal Convention of 1787*, Max Farrand, observed, is "a bundle of compromises."[1] The first section of Article III makes clear that the Supreme Court is the only federal court constitutionally required. The convention left it for the First Congress to establish a system of lower federal courts, which it did with the Judiciary Act of 1789. Both the convention and the First Congress rejected proposals that would have left the administration of justice entirely in the hands of state courts (with appeals to the Supreme Court). Also rejected was a proposal to join justices and executive branch officials in a "council of revision" with a veto power over congressional legislation. Agreement on the importance of guaranteeing judicial independence resulted in the first section of Article III also providing that federal judges "hold their Offices during good Behaviour," subject only to impeachment, and forbidding the diminution of their salaries. That guarantee reflects colonial opposition to royalist judges under the English Crown. One of the grievances listed in the Declaration of Independence as a justification for the Revolutionary War was that King George III had "made Judges dependent on his Will alone."[2] The two remaining sections of Article III specify the kinds of cases and controversies that the federal judiciary may hear (that is, jurisdiction) (see Chapter 2) and empower Congress to punish individuals for treason.

The Framers, it is fair to say, failed to think through the power of judicial review and its ramifications for constitutional politics. "[T]he framers anticipated some sort of judicial review," noted political scientist Edward S. Corwin, but he added that "it is equally without question that the ideas generally current in 1787 were far from presaging the present role of the Court."[3] In a letter to Corwin, Max Farrand also concluded that "[t]he framers of the Constitution did not realize it themselves [how markedly different their conceptions of judicial review were]: they were struggling to express an idea and their experience was as yet insufficient."[4]

The Constitutional Convention left the power of the judiciary (and much else set forth in the Constitution) to be worked out in practice. As John Mercer, a delegate to the Constitutional Convention from Maryland, observed, "It is a great mistake to suppose that the paper we are to propose will govern the United States. It is the men whom it will bring into the government and interest in maintaining it that is to govern them. The paper will only mark out the mode and the form."[5] The Constitution, of course, is not self-interpreting and crucial principles—such as judicial review, separation of powers, and federalism—are presupposed rather than spelled out. Moreover, in creating separate institutions that share specific and delegated powers, the Constitution amounts to a prescription for political struggle and an invitation for an ongoing debate about enduring constitutional principles.

Almost immediately following the convention in 1787, controversy erupted over the powers granted the national government and in particular to the federal judiciary. Those opposed to the states' ratification of the Constitution, the Anti-Federalists, warned that "[t]here are no well defined limits of the Judiciary Powers, they seem to be left as a boundless ocean."[6] Fears that "the powers of the judiciary may be extended to any degree short of Almighty" were echoed by Thomas Tredwell, among others, during New York's convention.[7] Robert Yates, one of the most articulate Anti-Federalists writing under the name of Brutus, attacked both the independence and the power of federal judges:

There is no authority that can remove them, and they cannot be controuled by the laws of the legislature. In short, they are independent of the people, of the legislature, and of every power under heaven. Men placed in this situation will generally soon feel themselves independent of heaven itself. . . .

And in their decisions they will not confine themselves to any fixed or established rules, but will determine, according to what appears to them, the reason and spirit of the constitution. The opinions of the supreme court, whatever they may be, will have the force of law; because there is no power provided in the constitution, that can correct their errors, or controul their adjudiciations. From this court there is no appeal.[8]

"This power in the judicial," charged Brutus, "will enable them to mould the government, into almost any shape they please."

Defenders of the Constitution countered that "the powers given the Supreme Court are not only safe, but constitute a wise and valuable part of the system."[9] In North Carolina's convention, Governor Johnston observed that "[i]t is obvious to every one that there ought to be one Supreme Court for national purposes."[10] During the fight for New York's ratification, Alexander Hamilton provided the classic defense of the judiciary as "the least dangerous branch." Responding to Brutus in *The Federalist*, No. 78, Hamilton argued,

Whoever attentively considers the different departments of power must perceive, that in a government in which they are separated from each other, the judiciary, from the nature of its functions, will always be the least dangerous to the political rights of the constitution; because it will be least in a capacity to annoy or injure them. The executive not only dispenses the honors, but holds the sword of the community. The legislature not only commands the purse, but prescribes the rules by which the duties and rights of every citizen are to be regulated. The judiciary on the contrary has no influence over either the sword or the purse, no direction either of the strength or of the wealth of the society, and can take no active resolution whatever. It may truly be said to have neither Force nor Will, but merely judgment; and must ultimately depend upon the aid of the executive arm even for the efficacy of its judgments.

If it be said that the legislative body are themselves the constitutional judges of their own powers, and that the construction they put upon them is conclusive upon other departments, it may be answered, that this cannot be the natural presumption, where it is not to be collected from any particular provisions in the constitution. It is not otherwise to be supposed that the constitution could intend to enable the representatives of the people to substitute their *will* to that of their constituents. It is far more rational to suppose that the courts were designed to be an intermediate body between the people and the legislature, in order, among other things, to keep the latter within the limits assigned to their authority. The interpretation of the laws is the proper and peculiar province of the courts. A constitution is in fact, and must be, regarded by the judges as a fundamental law. It therefore belongs to them as to ascertain its meaning as well as the meaning of any particular act proceeding from the legislative body. If there should happen to be an irreconcilable variance between the two, that which has the superior obligation and validity ought of course to be preferred; or in other words, the constitution ought to be preferred to the statute, the intention of the people to the intention of their agents.

Nor does this conclusion by any means suppose a superiority of the judicial to the legislative power. It only supposes that the power of the people is superior to both; and that where the will of the legislature declared in its statutes, stands in opposition to that of the people declared in the constitution, the judges ought to be governed by the latter, rather than the former. . . .

If then the courts of justice are to be considered as the bulwarks of a limited constitution against legislative encroachments, this consideration will afford a strong argument for the permanent tenure of judicial offices, since nothing will contribute so much as this to that independent spirit in the judges, which must be essential to the faithful performance of so arduous a duty.

The Federalists' interpretation of Article III was advanced by others in the effort to win ratification. In Pennsylvania's convention, James Wilson, who was one of the first justices appointed by President George Washington, argued that

under this Constitution, the legislature may be restrained, and kept within its prescribed bounds, by the interposition of the judicial department. . . . [T]he power of the Constitution [is] paramount to the power of the legislature acting under that Constitution; for it is possible that the legislature, when acting in that capacity, may transgress the bounds assigned to it, and an act may pass, in the usual *mode,* notwithstanding that transgression; but when it comes to be discussed before *the judges,—* when they consider its principles, and find it to be incompatible with the superior power of the Constitution,—it is their duty to pronounce it *void.*[11]

In Connecticut, Oliver Ellsworth, another who was later appointed to the Court, declared, "If the general legislature should at any time overleap their limits, the judicial department is a constitutional check."[12]

Even among the Federalists, however, there were differing

views of the judiciary's power. Alexander Hamilton and James Madison agreed that the Court would exercise some checking power over the states. The Court, in Madison's words, was "the surest expositor of . . . the [constitutional] boundaries . . . between the Union and its members."[13] But they were in less agreement on whether the Court had the power to check coequal branches, the Congress and the president. In *The Federalist*, Madison called the judiciary an "auxiliary precaution" against the possible domination of one branch of government over another.

HOW TO LOCATE DECISIONS OF THE SUPREME COURT

The decisions of the Supreme Court are published in the *United States Reports* by the U.S. Government Printing Office. Each decision is referred to by the names of the appellant, the person bringing the suit, and the appellee, the respondent: hence, *McCulloch v. Maryland*. After the name of the case is the volume number in which it appears in the *United States Reports* and the page number on which the Court's opinion begins, followed by the year of the decision. *McCulloch v. Maryland*, 17 U.S. 316 (1819), thus may be found in volume 17 of the *United States Reports* beginning on page 316.

Prior to the publication of the *United States Reports* in 1875, the Court's opinions used to be cited according to the name of the reporter of the Court, who published the Court's opinions at his own expense. Decisions thus would originally be cited as follows:

1789–1800	Dallas	(1–4 Dall., 1–4 U.S.)
1801–1815	Cranch	(1–9 Cr., 5–13 U.S.)
1816–1827	Wheaton	(1–12 Wheat., 14–25 U.S.)
1828–1842	Peters	(1–16 Pet., 26–41 U.S.)
1843–1860	Howard	(1–24 How., 42–65 U.S.)
1861–1862	Black	(1–2 Bl., 66–67 U.S.)
1863–1874	Wallace	(1–23 Wall., 68–90 U.S.)
1875–		(91– , U.S.)

The full citation for *McCulloch v. Maryland* is 4 Wheat. (17 U.S.) 316 (1819). But with volume 91 in 1875, the reporters' names were dropped, and decisions were then cited only by the volume number and the designation "U.S."

In addition, two companies print editions of the Court's decisions. There is the *Lawyers' Edition*, published by the Lawyer's Cooperative, and *The Supreme Court Reporter*, published by West Publishing Company. The *Lawyers' Edition* is cited as L.Ed. (e.g., 91 L.Ed. 575), and *The Supreme Court Reporter* is cited as S.Ct. (e.g., 104 S.Ct. 3005).

Later, during a debate in the First Congress in 1789, he observed that "in the ordinary course of Government, . . . the exposition of the laws and Constitution devolves upon the Judiciary." Still, Madison doubted that the Court's interpretation of the Constitution was superior to that given by Congress. "Nothing has been offered to invalidate the [view]," he argued, "that the meaning of the Constitution may as well be ascertained by the legislative as by the judicial authority."[14] The Court stood as a forum of last resort, Madison explained, but "this resort must necessarily be deemed the last in relation to the authorities of the other departments of the government; not in relation to the rights of the parties to the constitutional compact, from which the judicial, as well as the other departments, hold their delegated trusts."[15]

From the initial debate in the Constitutional Convention in 1787 to those between the Federalists and the Anti-Federalists over state ratification of the Constitution and into the First Congress, the power of judicial review and the meaning of other key provisions and principles of the Constitution has remained a continuing source of controversy in constitutional politics. And the Supreme Court has remained, as Justice Oliver Wendell Holmes observed, a "storm center" of political controversy.

A. ESTABLISHING AND CONTESTING THE POWER OF JUDICIAL REVIEW

In its first decade, the Supreme Court had little business, frequent turnover in personnel, no chambers or staff, no fixed customs, and no institutional identity. When the Court initially convened on February 1, 1790, only Chief Justice John Jay and two other justices arrived at the Exchange Building in New York City. They adjourned until the next day when Justice John Blair arrived; the two other justices never arrived. With little to do other than admit attorneys to practice before its bar, the Court concluded its first sessions in less than two weeks.

When the capital moved from New York City to Philadelphia in the winter of 1790, the Court met in Independence Hall and in the Old City Hall, until the capital again moved to Washington, D.C., in 1800. Most of the first justices' time was spent riding circuit. That is, each would travel throughout a particular area, or circuit, in the country. Under the Judiciary Act of 1789, they were required twice a year to hold court, in the company of local district judges, in a circuit to hear appeals from the federal district courts. Hence, the justices resided primarily in their circuits, rather than in Washington, and felt a greater allegiance to their circuits than to the Court.

The Court's uncertain status was reflected in the first justices' exercise of their power of judicial review. Although in its initial years the Court had few important cases, *Chisholm v. Georgia,* 2 Dall. (2 U.S.) 419 (1793) (see Vol. 1, Ch. 7), precipitated the country's first constitutional crisis. In that case, Justice James Wilson, who had been a delegate to the Constitutional Convention and Pennsylvania's ratifying convention, ruled that citizens of one state could sue another state in federal courts. That provoked an angry dissent from Justice James Iredell, a southerner who had attended North Carolina's ratifying convention and a strong proponent of "states' rights." His dissent invited the adoption by Congress of the Eleventh Amendment in 1795, overturning *Chisholm* and guaranteeing sovereign immunity for states from lawsuits brought by citizens of other states. The outcry over *Chisholm* convinced Chief Justice John Jay that the Court would remain "the least dangerous branch." He resigned in 1795 to become an envoy to England and later declined reappointment as chief justice.

The Court, though, in *Ware v. Hylton,* 3 Dall. (3 U.S.) 199 (1796), upheld the provisions of a federal treaty, the 1783 peace treaty with England, over state law. And *Hylton v. United States,* 3 Dall. (3 U.S.) 171 (1796), affirmed, over objections raised by the states, Congress's power to levy a carriage tax (and thus implicitly asserted the Court's power to nullify acts of Congress).

Still, two years later, *Calder v. Bull,* 3 Dall. (3 U.S.) 386 (1798) illustrates how uncertain and divided the justices were about exercising their power of judicial review. There the Court declined to assert its power when ruling that conflicts between state laws and state constitutions are matters for state, not federal, courts to resolve. But Justice Iredell maintained that a state law might run against principles of "natural justice" and the Court still have no power to strike it down. By contrast, Justice Samuel Chase contended that the Court had the power to overturn laws that violate fundamental principles, explaining,

I cannot subscribe to the omnipotence of a State legislature, or that it is absolute and without controul; although its authority should not be expressly restrained by the Constitution, or fundamental laws of the State. The people of the United States erected their Constitution . . . to establish justice, to promote the general welfare, to secure the blessings of liberty; and to protect their persons and property from violence. . . . There are acts which the Federal, or State, Legislature cannot do. . . . It is against all reason and justice to entrust a Legislature with SUCH [despotic] powers; and therefore, it cannot be presumed that they have done it. The genius, the nature, and the spirit of our State Governments, amount to a prohibition of such [unlimited] acts of legislation; and the general principles of law and reason forbid them.

The uncertainty and controversy over the power of judicial review was further underscored in 1798 with the passage of the Virginia and Kentucky Resolutions (see p. 41), in response to Congress's enactment of the Alien and Sedition Acts. Drafted by James Madison and Thomas Jefferson, the Virginia and Kentucky Resolutions not only contended that Congress had violated the First Amendment but claimed that state legislatures had the power to judge the constitutionality of federal laws. Jefferson went so far as to assert that states could nullify federal laws that they deemed unconstitutional. The "sovereign and independent" states, in his words, "have the unquestionable right to judge . . . and, that a nullification [by] those sovereignties, of all unauthorized acts done under the color of that instrument is the rightful remedies."

Jefferson remained opposed to the power of judicial review and the view that the Supreme Court's interpretation of the Constitution was binding on the other branches of government. In a 1819 letter to Spencer Roane, a Virginia state judge, Jefferson explained,

My construction of the Constitution is . . . that each department is truly independent of the others, and has an equal right to decide for itself what is the meaning of the Constitution in the cases submitted to its action most especially where it is to act ultimately and without appeal. . . . Each of the three departments has equally the right to decide for itself what is its duty under the Constitution, without any regard to what the others may have decided for themselves under a similar question.[16]

Although less strident than Jefferson, Madison thought that the "true and safe construction" of the Constitution would emerge with the "uniform sanction of successive legislative bodies; through a period of years and under the varied ascendency of parties."[17]

Chief Justice John Marshall provided the classic justification for the power of judicial review in the landmark ruling in *Marbury v. Madison* (1803) (see p. 45). Notice that Marshall's arguments draw on both general principles and the text of the Constitution and are not unassailable. In an otherwise unimportant state case, *Eakin v. Raub* (Pa., 1825) (see p. 55), for example, Pennsylvania Supreme Court Justice John Gibson expressly refutes Marshall's arguments. It does not inexorably follow from Marshall's claim that the Constitution created a limited government that *only* the judiciary should enforce those limitations. No more persuasive is the argument that judges have the power to authoritatively interpret the Constitution based on their taking an oath to uphold the document, because all federal and state officers take an oath to support the Constitution. Like Madison and Jefferson, Justice Gibson rejects *Marbury*'s implication that the judiciary has a monopoly (or supremacy) over interpretating the Constitution or, as Chief Justice Charles Evans Hughes's later put it, "We are under a Constitution but the Constitution is what the judges say it is."[18] In providing a rationale for judicial self-restraint, Gibson embraces a theory of *tripartie* constitutional interpretation—namely, that each branch has the authority to interpret the Constitution.

Chief Justice Marshall's arguments based on the text of the Constitution fare better. In specifying that the "judicial Power shall extend to" cases and controversies "arising under this Constitution," Article III implies that constitutional questions may be decided by the judiciary. And, as Marshall points out, the Supremacy Clause of Article III makes it clear that the Constitution is "the supreme Law of the Land." Judicial review is thus a logical implication of the Constitution, for as Justice Joseph Story observed,

> The laws and treaties, and even the constitution, of the United States, would become a dead letter with out it. Indeed, in a complicated government, like ours, where there is an assemblage of republics, combined under a common head, the necessity of some controlling judicial power, to ascertain and enforce the powers of the Union is, if possible, still more striking. The laws of the whole would otherwise be in continual danger of being contravened by the laws of the parts. The national government would be reduced to a servile dependence upon the states; and the same scenes would be again acted over in solemn mockery, which began in the neglect, and ended in the ruin, of the confederation.[19]

Still and undeniably, the power of judicial review is not expressly provided for in the Constitution and its exercise remains a continuing source of controversy.

The immediate political controversy over the exercise of judicial review in *Marbury* in striking down a section of the Judiciary Act of 1789 was defused by Chief Justice Marshall's conclusion that the Court had no power to order the delivery of Marbury's commission. Though outraged by Marshall's assertion of judicial review, Madison and Jefferson had not been compelled by the Court to do anything. Jefferson continued to maintain that each branch of government could interpret the Constitution and to deny that the Court's interpretations were binding on the president's exercise of executive powers. In a letter to Mrs. John Adams in 1804, explaining his decision to pardon those tried and convicted under the Sedition Act of 1798, Jefferson wrote,

> The Judges, believing the law constitutional, had a right to pass a sentence of fine and imprisonment; because that power was placed in

A. *Establishing and Contesting the Power of Judicial Review*

their hands by the Constitution. But the Executive, believing the law to be unconstitutional, was bound to remit the execution of it; because that power has been confided to him by the Constitution. The instrument meant that its co-ordinate branches should be checks on each other. But the opinion which gives to the Judges the right to decide what Laws are constitutional, and what not, not only for themselves in their own sphere of action, but for the Legislative and Executive also in their spheres, would make the Judiciary a despotic branch.[20]

Jefferson was not the last president to contest the authority of the Court. An irate President Andrew Jackson, on hearing of the decision in *Worcester v. Georgia,* 31 U.S. 515 (1832), holding that states could not pass laws affecting federally recognized Indian nations, reportedly declared, "John Marshall has made his decision, now let him enforce it."[21] Jackson elaborated his view in his Veto Message of 1832 (see p. 60), explaining his vetoing of legislation recharting the national bank (see Vol. 1, Ch. 6). Besides contending that *McCulloch v. Maryland,* 17 U.S. 316 (1819) (see Vol. 1, Ch. 6) was not binding on his actions, Jackson reiterated the position that

[t]he Congress, the Executive, and the Court must each for itself be guided by its own opinion of the Constitution. Each public officer who takes an oath to support the Constitution swears that he will support it as he understands it, and not as it is understood by others. . . . The opinion of the judges has no more authority over Congress than the opinion of Congress has over the judges, and on that point the President is independent of both.[22]

Jackson's Veto Message drew an impassioned response from Senator Daniel Webster, who thundered in the halls of Congress that

[t]he President is as much bound by the law as any private citizen. . . . He may refuse to obey the law, and so may a private citizen; but both do it at their own peril, and neither of them can settle the question of its validity. The President may say a law is unconstitutional, but he is not the judge. . . . If it were otherwise, there would be no government of laws; but we should all live under the government, the rule, the caprices of individuals. . . .

[President Jackson's] message . . . converts a constitutional limitation of power into mere matters of opinion, and then strikes the judicial department, as an efficient department, out of our system. . . .

[The message] denies first principles. It contradicts truths heretofore received as indisputable. It denies to the judiciary the interpretation of law.

Controversy over judicial review continues, but it bears emphasizing that Jefferson, Jackson, and subsequent presidents concede that the Court's rulings are binding for the actual cases decided and handed down. Technically, a decision of the Court is final only for the parties involved in the case. Yet, because the justices in their opinions give general principles for deciding a case and because they generally adhere to precedents (or tend to do so until the composition of the bench markedly changes), the Court's rulings are usually considered controlling for other similar cases and the larger political controversy they represent. But in major confrontations in constitutional politics—like those over the creation of a national bank, slavery, school desegregation, and abortion—the Court alone cannot lay those controversies to rest.

What presidents, Congress, the states, and others occasionally deny is *judicial supremacy* or the finality of the Court's interpretation of broad constitutional principles for resolving major political controversies. In his famous debates with Stephen Douglas, for instance, Abraham Lincoln denounced the Court's ruling in *Dred Scott v. Sandford,* 60 U.S. 393 (1857) (see Vol. 2, Ch. 12), that blacks were not citizens of the United States. While Lincoln doubted that "we, as a mob, will decide [Dred Scott] to be free," he exclaimed that

we nevertheless do oppose that decision as a political rule which shall be binding on the voter, to vote for nobody who thinks it wrong, which shall be binding on the members of Congress or the President to favor no measure that does not actually concur with the principles of that decision. . . . We propose so resisting it as to have it reversed if we can, and a new judicial rule established upon this subject.[23]

Later, in his first Inaugural Address in 1861, Lincoln elaborated,

I do not forget the position assumed by some, that constitutional questions are to be decided by the Supreme Court; nor do I deny that such decisions must be binding in any case, upon the parties to a suit, as to the object of that suit, while they are also entitled to a very high respect and consideration, in all parallel cases, by all other departments of government. And while it is obviously possible that such decision may be erroneous in any given case, still the evil effect following it, being limited to that particular case, with the chance that it may be over-ruled, and never become a precedent for other cases, can better be borne than could the evils of a different practice. At the same time the candid citizen must confess that if the policy of the government, upon vital questions, affecting the whole people, is to be irrevocably fixed by the decisions of the Supreme Court, the instant they are made, in ordinary litigation between parties, in personal actions, the people will have ceased, to be their own rulers, having to that extent, practically resigned their government, into the hands of that eminent tribunal. Nor is there, in this view, any assault upon the court, or the judges. It is a duty, from which they may not shrink, to decide cases properly brought before them; and it is no fault of theirs, if others seek to turn their decisions to political purposes.

In major confrontations with the Court, other presidents have taken similar positions to that of President Lincoln. During the constitutional crisis of 1937, resulting from the Court's invalidation of much of the early New Deal progressive economic legislation, President Franklin D. Roosevelt proposed that Congress expand the size of the Court from nine to fifteen justices, and thereby enable him to secure a majority sympathetic to his programs and policies. And in a "Fireside Chat" in March 1937 (see p. 63), FDR followed the footsteps of Jefferson, Jackson, and Lincoln in attacking the Court for becoming a "super-legislature."

Judicial supremacy over interpreting the Constitution remains controversial. In *Marbury*, however, Chief Justice Marshall did not lay claim to judicial supremacy, only that the Court, no less than the president and Congress, has the authority and duty to interpret the Constitution.[24] By contrast, in this century justices have often asserted the supremacy of their decisions. In *United States v. Butler*, 297 U.S. 1 (1936), Justice (and later Chief Justice) Harlan Stone claimed that "While unconstitutional exercise of power by the executive and legislative branches of government is subject to judicial restraint, the only check upon our own exercise of power is our own sense of self-restraint." In the wake of massive resistence to the Court's watershed ruling on school desegregation, in *Brown v. Board of Education*, 347 U.S. 483 (1954) (see Vol. 2, Ch. 12), all nine justices took the unusual step of signing the opinion announcing *Cooper v. Aaron*, 358 U.S. 1 (1958) (see Vol. 2, Ch. 12), which ordered the desegregation of schools in Little Rock, Arkansas. And they interpreted *Marbury* to have

declared the basic principle that the federal judiciary is supreme in the exposition of the law of the Constitution. . . . It follows that the interpretation of the Fourteenth Amendment enunciated by this Court in the *Brown* case is the supreme law of the land, and Article VI of the Constitution makes it binding effect on the States. . . . Every state legislator and executive and judicial officer is solemnly committed by oath taken pursuant to Article VI, 3 "to support this Constitution."

The Court likewise proclaimed itself the "ultimate interpreter of the Constitution" in *Baker v. Carr*, 369 U.S. 186 (1962) (see page 131), when holding that courts could decide disputes over the malapportionment of state legislatures. And again citing *Marbury* in *Powell v. McCormack*, 395 U.S. 486 (1969) (see Vol. 1, Ch. 5), involving a controversy over the House of Representatives' exclusion of a duely elected representative, the Court declared that "it is the responsibility of this Court to act as the ultimate interpreter of the Constitution."

Despite the Court's occasional claims of judicial supremacy, the president, Congress, and the states may in various ways undercut and thwart compliance with, if not ultimately overturn, the Court's rulings (see Chapter 2). By deciding only immediate cases, the Court infuses constitutional meaning into the larger surrounding political controversies by bringing them within the language, structure, and spirit of the Constitution. The Court may thus raise a controversial issue, as it did with school desegregation in *Brown* and with the right to abortion in *Roe*, to the national political agenda. But by itself the Court cannot lay those controversies to rest because its power, in Chief Justice Edward White's words, rests "solely upon the approval of a free people."[25] In areas of major and continuing political controversy, constitutional law is a kind of dialogue between the Court and the country over the meaning of the Constitution, and judicial review is more provisional than final.[26]

Even more than Chief Justice Marshall's arguments in *Marbury*, the establishment of judicial review turned on public acceptance and the forces of history. That is not to gainsay Marshall's contributions. He had a keen understanding of the malleable nature of the young republic and the important role that the first generation would play in establishing the power of the national government. Marshall's long tenure (1801–1835) and that of others who served with him may have contributed as well. After *Marbury*, moreover, the Court did not again strike down another act of Congress or challenge a coequal branch of government until the 1857 ill-fated ruling in *Dred Scott*, which left the Court at low ebb for two decades. Instead, the Marshall Court buttressed its own power by defending the interests of the national government against the states and striking down state laws.

Finally, social forces have shaped the Court's role in the kinds of cases and controversies brought to it for review. As already noted, the Court had little important business during its first decade. Over 40 percent of its business consisted in admiralty and prize cases (disputes over captured property at sea). About 50 percent raised issues of common law, and the remaining 10 percent dealt with matters like equity, including one probate case. By the late nineteenth century, the Court's business gradually changed in response to developments in American society. The number of admiralty cases, for instance, had by 1882 dwindled to less than 4 percent of the total. Almost 40 percent of the Court's decisions still dealt with either disputes of common law or questions of jurisdiction and procedure in federal courts. More than 43 percent of the Court's business, however, involved interpreting congressional statutes. Less than 4 percent of the cases raised issues of constitutional interpretation. The decline in admiralty and common law litigation and the increase in statutory interpretation reflected the impact of the Industrial Revolution and the growing governmental regulation of social and economic relations. In the twentieth century, the trend has continued. In the 1980s, about 47 percent of the cases annually decided by the Court involved matters of constitutional law. Another 38 percent dealt with the interpretation of congressional legislation. The remaining 15 percent resolved issues of administrative law, taxation, patents, and claims.

The Court is no longer "the least dangerous branch" or primarily concerned with correcting the errors of lower courts. In response to growing and changing litigation, the Court more frequently overturns prior rulings, congressional legislation, and state and local laws. The Court takes only "hard cases," involving major issues of legal policy and "not primarily to preserve the rights of the litigants," in the words of Chief Justice William Howard Taft: "The Supreme Court's function is for the purpose of expounding and stabilizing principles of law for the benefit of the people of the country, passing upon constitutional questions and other important questions of law for the public benefit."[27]

The Court and the country have changed with constitutional politics. From 1789 to the Civil War, the major controversies confronting the Court involved disputes between the national government and the states, and the Court employed its power to preserve the Union (see Vol. 1, Ch. 6 and 7). Between 1865 and 1937, during the Reconstruction and the Industrial Revolution, the dominant political controversy revolved around balancing regulatory interests and those of businesses, and the Court defended the interests of American capitalism and private enterprise (see Vol. 2, Ch. 3). Only after 1937 did the Court begin to assume the role of "a guardian for civil liberties and civil rights" in defending the rights of minorities (see Vol. 2, Chs. 4–12). The Court's role has changed with constitutional politics, as Harvard Law School professor Paul Freund nicely expressed by analogy, "As Hamlet is to one generation a play of revenge, to another a conflict between will and conscience, and to another a study in mother-fixation, so the Constitution has been to one generation a means of cementing the Union, to another a protectorate of burgeoning property, and to another a safeguard of basic human rights and equality before the law."[28]

CONSTITUTIONAL HISTORY

Decisions of the Supreme Court Overruled and Acts of Congress Held Unconstitutional, and State Laws and Municipal Ordinances Overturned, 1789–1989*

Year	Supreme Court Decision Overruled	Acts of Congress Overturned	State Laws Overturned	Ordinances Overturned
1789–1800, Pre-Marshall				
1801–1835, Marshall Court	3	1	18	
1836–1864, Taney Court	6	1	21	
1865–1873, Chase Court	3	10	33	
1874–1888, Waite Court	11	9	7	
1889–1910, Fuller Court	4	14	73	15
1910–1921, White Court	6	12	107	18
1921–1930, Taft Court	5	12	131	12
1930–1940, Hughes Court	14	14	78	5
1941–1946, Stone Court	24	2	25	7
1947–1952, Vinson Court	11	1	38	7
1953–1969, Warren Court	46	25	150	16
1969–1986, Burger Court	50	34	192	15
1986– , Rehnquist Court	5	4	31	4

* Note that in *Immigration and Naturalization Service v. Chadha* (1983), the Burger Court struck down a provision for a "one-house" legislative veto in the Immigration and Naturalization Act but effectively declared all one- and two-house legislative vetoes unconstitutional. While 212 statutes containing provisions for legislative vetoes were implicated by the Court's decision, *Chadha* is here counted as a single declaration of the unconstitutionality of congressional legislation. Note also that the Court's ruling in *Texas v. Johnson* (1989), striking down a Texas law making it a crime to desecrate the American flag, invalidated laws in forty-eight states and a federal statute. It is counted here, however, only once.

NOTES

1. See Max Farrand, *The Framing of the Constitution* (New Haven, CT: Yale University Press, 1913); Max Farrand, ed., *The Records of the Federal Convention of 1787,* 4 vols. (New Haven, CT: Yale University Press, 1911); and John P. Roche, "The Founding Fathers: A Reform Caucus in Action," 55 *American Political Science Review* 799 (1961).

2. The Supreme Court has enforced the tenure and salary provisions

in *Ex parte Milligan,* 4 Wall. 2 (1867) (see Vol. 1, Ch. 3), holding that civilians cannot be tried before military tribunals; in *O'Donoghue v. United States,* 289 U.S. 516 (1933), holding that judicial salaries cannot be reduced, even during the Great Depression; and *Northern Pipe Line Construction Co. v. Marathon Pipe Line Co.,* 458 U.S. 50 (1982), striking down a statute expanding the power of bankruptcy judges.

3. Edward S. Corwin, "The Constitution as Instrument and as Symbol," 30 *American Political Science Review* 1078 (1936).

4. Letter from Max Farrand to Edward Corwin, Jan. 3, 1939, in Edward Samuel Corwin Papers, Box 3, Princeton University Library, Princeton, NJ.

5. Quoted in James Madison, *Notes of Debates in the Federal Convention of 1787* (Athens: Ohio University Press, 1966), 455–456.

6. A Columbia Patriot, in *The Complete Anti-Federalist,* Vol. 4, ed. Herbert J. Storing (Chicago: University of Chicago Press, 1981), 276.

7. Thomas Tredwell, in *The Debates in the Several State Conventions on the Adoption of the Federal Constitution,* Vol. 4, ed., Jonathan Elliot (New York: Burt Franklin, 1974), 401.

8. Brutus, in *The Complete Anti-Federalist,* Vol. 2, ed. Storing, 438–439, 420, 422.

9. James Wilson, in *The Debates,* Vol. 2, ed. Elliot, 494.

10. Governor Johnston, in *The Debates,* Vol. 4, ed. Elliot, 142.

11. James Wilson, in *The Debates,* Vol. 2, ed. Elliot, 445–446.

12. Oliver Ellsworth, in *The Debates,* Vol. 2, ed. Elliot, 196.

13. Letter from James Madison to an unidentified person, Aug. 1834, reprinted in *Letters and Other Writings of James Madison,* Vol. 4 (Philadelphia, 1865), 350.

14. James Madison, in *Annals of Congress,* Vol. 1 (Washington, DC: Gales & Seaton, 1789), 500, 546–547.

15. James Madison, "Report on the Virginia Resolutions," in *The Debates,* Vol. 5, ed. Elliot, 549.

16. Thomas Jefferson, *The Works of Thomas Jefferson,* Vol. 12, ed. Paul Ford (New York: G. P. Putnam's Sons, 1904–1905), 137–138.

17. Quoted in Robert J. Morgan, *James Madison on the Constitution and the Bill of Rights* (Westport, CT: Greenwood Press, 1988), 196. For more on Jefferson's and Madison's views, see the discussion of the controversy over Congress's creating a national bank and *McCulloch v. Maryland,* 17 U.S. 316 (1819) (see page 447).

18. Charles Evans Hughes, *Address and Papers of Charles Evans Hughes* (New York: Columbia University Press, 1908), 139.

19. Joseph Story, *Commentaries on the Constitution,* (Durham, NC: Carolina Academic Press, 1987), reprint of 1833 ed.

20. Thomas Jefferson, Letter to John Adams, Sept. 11, 1804, as quoted in Charles Warren, *The Supreme Court in United States History,* Vol. 1 (Boston: Little, Brown, 1922), 265.

21. Quoted in Edward Corwin, *The Doctrine of Judicial Review* (Princeton, NJ: Princeton University Press, 1914), 22.

22. President's Veto Message (July 10, 1832), *A Compilation of the Messages and Papers of the Presidents,* Vol. 2, ed. J. Richardson (New

York: Bureau of National Literature, 1917), 582.

23. Abraham Lincoln, *The Collected Works of Abraham Lincoln,* Vol. 2, ed. Roy Basler (New Brunswick, NJ: Rutgers University Press, 1953), 401.

24. See David M. O'Brien, "Judicial Review and Constitutional Politics: Theory and Practice," 48 *University of Chicago Law Review* 1070 (1981).

25. Quoted in David M. O'Brien, *Storm Center: The Supreme Court in American Politics,* 2nd ed. (New York: W. W. Norton, 1990), 22.

26. See Paul Diamond, *The Supreme Court and Judicial Choice* (Ann Arbor: University of Michigan Press, 1989).

27. William H. Taft, *Hearings before the House Committee on the Judiciary,* 67th Cong., 2d sess., 1922, 2.

28. Paul Freund, "My Philosophy of Law," 39 *Connecticut Bar Journal* 220 (1965).

SELECTED BIBLIOGRAPHY

Cannon, Mark, and O'Brien, David, eds. *Views from the Bench: The Judiciary and Constitutional Politics.* Chatham, NJ: Chatham House, 1985.

Corwin, Edward S. *The Doctrine of Judicial Review.* Princeton, NJ: Princeton University Press, 1914.

———. *Constitutional Revolution, Ltd.* Claremont, CA: Claremont Colleges, 1941.

Diamond, Paul R. *The Supreme Court & Judicial Choice.* Ann Arbor: University of Michigan, 1989.

Fisher, Louis. *Constitutional Dialogues.* Princeton, NJ: Princeton University Press, 1988.

Freund, Paul A. *The Supreme Court of the United States.* Cleveland, OH: World Publishing, 1961.

Lasser, William. *The Limits of Judicial Power.* Chapel Hill: University of North Carolina Press, 1988.

Levy, Leonard, ed. *American Constitutional History.* New York: Macmillan, 1989.

———. *Judicial Review, History and Democracy.* New York: Harper & Row, 1967.

Nagel, Robert F. *Constitutional Cultures.* Berkeley: University of California, 1989.

Steamer, Robert. *The Supreme Court in Crisis: A History of Conflict.* Amherst: University of Massachusetts Press, 1971.

Warren, Charles. *The Supreme Court in United States History,* 3 vols. Boston: Little, Brown, 1922.

The Virginia and Kentucky
Resolutions of 1798

In the spring of 1798, President John Adams and his Federalist-dominated Congress enacted the Alien and Sedition Acts, regulating immigration and making criticism of the government a crime of seditious libel. The laws aimed at silencing partisan criticism of the Adams's administration's pro-British policies by Jeffersonian-Republicans. Although Jeffersonian-Republicans were prosecuted under the laws, often receiving stiff penalties, no court ruled on the constitutionality of the laws or whether they violated the First Amendment's guarantee for freedom of speech and press. The Kentucky legislature adopted a resolution secretly written by Thomas Jefferson, and Virginia adopted a similar resolution drafted by James Madison. Prosecutions for seditious libel ended in 1801, when the laws expired and Jefferson became president. Over 160 years later, the Supreme Court in a landmark ruling on libel, in The *New York Times Company v. Sullivan*, 376 U.S. 254 (1964) (see Vol. 2, Ch. 5), declared the Sedition Act and seditious libel unconstitutional and inconsistent with the First Amendment.

VIRGINIA RESOLUTIONS, DECEMBER 21, 1798

1. *Resolved,* That the General Assembly of Virginia doth unequivocally express a firm resolution to maintain and defend the Constitution of the United States, and the Constitution of this State, against every aggression, either foreign or domestic, and that it will support the government of the United States in all measures warranted by the former. . . .

3. That this Assembly doth explicitly and peremptorily declare that it views the powers of the Federal Government as resulting from the compact to which the States are parties, as limited by the plain sense and intention of the instrument constituting that compact; as no further valid than they are authorized by the grants enumerated in that compact; and that in case of a deliberate, palpable, and dangerous exercise of other powers not granted by the said compact, the States, who are the parties thereto, have the right, and are in duty bound, to interpose for arresting the progress of the evil, and for maintaining within their respective limits, the authorities, rights, and liberties appertaining to them.

4. That the General Assembly doth also express its deep regret that a spirit has in sundry instances been manifested by the Federal Government, to enlarge its powers by forced constructions of the constitutional charter which defines them; and that indications have appeared of a design to expound certain general phrases

(which, having been copied from the very limited grant of powers in the former articles of confederation, were the less liable to be misconstrued), so as to destroy the meaning and effect of the particular enumeration, which necessarily explains and limits the general phrases, and so as to consolidate the States by degrees into one sovereignty, the obvious tendency and inevitable result of which would be to transform the present republican system of the United States into an absolute, or at best, a mixed monarchy.

5. That the General Assembly doth particularly protest against the palpable and alarming infractions of the Constitution, in the two late cases of the "alien and sedition acts," passed at the last session of Congress, the first of which exercises a power nowhere delegated to the Federal Government; and which by uniting legislative and judicial powers to those of executive, subverts the general principles of free government, as well as the particular organization and positive provisions of the federal Constitution; and the other of which acts exercises in like manner a power not delegated by the Constitution, but on the contrary expressly and positively forbidden by one of the amendments thereto; a power which more than any other ought to produce universal alarm, because it is levelled against that right of freely examining public characters and measures, and of free communication among the people thereon, which has ever been justly deemed the only effectual guardian of every other right.

6. That this State having by its convention which ratified the federal Constitution, expressly declared, "that among other essential rights, the liberty of conscience and of the press cannot be cancelled, abridged, restrained, or modified by any authority of the United States," and from its extreme anxiety to guard these rights from every possible attack of sophistry or ambition, having with other States recommended an amendment for that purpose, which amendment was in due time annexed to the Constitution, it would mark a reproachful inconsistency and criminal degeneracy, if an indifference were now shown to the most palpable violation of one of the rights thus declared and secured, and to the establishment of a precedent which may be fatal to the other.

KENTUCKY RESOLUTIONS, NOVEMBER 10, 1798

1. *Resolved,* That the several states composing the United States of America, are not united on the principle of unlimited submission to their general government; but that by compact, under the style and title of a Constitution for the United States, and of amendments thereto, they constituted a general government for special purposes, delegated to that government certain definite powers, reserving, each state to itself, the residuary mass of right to their own self-government; and that whensoever the general government assumes undelegated powers, its acts are unauthorita-

tive, void, and of no force: That to this compact each state acceded as a state, and is an integral party, its co-states forming as to itself, the other party: That the government created by this compact was not made the exclusive or final *judge* of the extent of the powers delegated to itself; since that would have made its discretion, and not the Constitution, the measure of its powers; but that, as in all other cases of compact among parties having no common judge, each party has an equal right to judge for itself, as well of infractions, as of the mode and measure of redress.

2. *Resolved,* That the Constitution of the United States having delegated to Congress a power to punish treason, counterfeiting the securities and current coin of the United States, piracies and felonies committed on the high seas, and offences against the laws of nations, and no other crimes whatever, . . . all other [of] their acts which assume to create, define, or punish crimes other than those enumerated in the Constitution, are altogether void, and of no force, and that the power to create, define, and punish such other crimes is reserved, and of right appertains, solely and exclusively, to the respective states, each within its own territory.

3. *Resolved,* That it is true as a general principle, and is also expressly declared by one of the amendments to the Constitution, that "the powers not delegated to the United States by the Constitution, nor prohibited by it to the states, are reserved to the states respectively, or to the people"; and that no power over the freedom of religion, freedom of speech, or freedom of the press, being delegated to the United States by the Constitution, nor prohibited by it to the states, all lawful powers respecting the same did of right remain, and were reserved to the states, or to the people; that thus was manifested their determination to retain to themselves the right of judging how far the licentiousness of speech and of the press may be abridged without lessening their useful freedom, and how far those abuses which cannot be separated from their use, should be tolerated rather than the use be destroyed; and thus also they guarded against all abridgment by the United States of the freedom of religious opinions and exercises, and retained to themselves the right of protecting the same, as this state by a law passed on the general demand of its citizens, had already protected them from all human restraint or interference: and that in addition to this general principle and express declaration, another and more special provision has been made by one of the amendments to the Constitution, which expressly declares, that "Congress shall make no law respecting an establishment of religion, or prohibiting the free exercise thereof, or abridging the freedom of speech, or of the press," thereby guarding in the same sentence, and under the same words, the freedom of religion, of speech, and of the press, insomuch, that whatever violates either, throws down the sanctuary which

covers the others, and that libels, falsehoods, and defamations, equally with heresy and false religion, are withheld from the cognizance of federal tribunals: that therefore the act of the Congress of the United States, passed on the 14th day of July, 1798, entitled, "an act in addition to the act for the punishment of certain crimes against the United States," which does abridge the freedom of the press, is not law, but is altogether void and of no effect.

4. *Resolved,* That alien-friends are under the jurisdiction and protection of the laws of the state wherein they are; that no power over them has been delegated to the United States, nor prohibited to the individual states distinct from their power over citizens; and it being true as a general principle, and one of the amendments to the Constitution having also declared, that "the powers not delegated to the United States by the Constitution, nor prohibited by it to the states, are reserved to the states respectively, or to the people," the act of the Congress of the United States, passed on the 22d day of June, 1798, entitled "an act concerning aliens," which assumes power over alien-friends not delegated by the Constitution, is not law, but is altogether void and of no force. . . .

6. *Resolved,* That the imprisonment of a person under the protection of the laws of this commonwealth, on his failure to obey the simple *order* of the President, to depart out of the United States, as is undertaken by the said act, entitled "an act concerning aliens," is contrary to the Constitution, one amendment to which has provided, that "no person shall be deprived of liberty without due process of law," and that another having provided, "that in all criminal prosecutions, the accused shall enjoy the right to a public trial by an impartial jury, to be informed of the nature and cause of the accusation, to be confronted with the witnesses against him, to have compulsory process for obtaining witnesses in his favour, and to have the assistance of counsel for his defence," the same act undertaking to authorize the President to remove a person out of the United States, who is under the protection of the law, on his own suspicion, without accusation, without jury, without public trial, without confrontation of the witnesses against him, without having witnesses in his favour, without defence, without counsel, is contrary to these provisions, also, of the Constitution, is therefore not law, but utterly void and of no force.

That transferring the power of judging any person who is under the protection of the laws, from the courts to the President of the United States, as is undertaken by the same act, concerning aliens, is against the article of the Constitution which provides, that "the judicial power of the United States shall be vested in courts, the judges of which shall hold their offices during good behaviour," and that the said act is void for that reason also;

and it is further to be noted, that this transfer of judiciary power is to that magistrate of the General Government, who already possesses all the executive, and a qualified negative in all the legislative powers.

Marbury v. Madison
1 Cr. (5 U.S.) 137 (1803)

This case grew out of one of the great early struggles over the course of constitutional politics. Shortly after the ratification of the Constitution, two rival political parties emerged with widely different views of the Constitution and governmental power. The Federalists who, since the Constitutional Convention, supported a strong national government, including the power of the federal courts to interpret the Constitution. Their opponents, the Anti-Federalists and later the Jeffersonian-Republicans (who after the 1832 election became known as Democrats), remained distrustful of the national government and continued to favor the states and state courts. The struggle between the Federalists and the Jeffersonian-Republicans finally came to a head with the election of 1800. The Jeffersonians defeated the Federalists, who had held office since the creation of the republic and feared what the Jeffersonian-Republicans might do once in office.

Before leaving office, President John Adams and his Federalist-dominated Congress vindictively created a number of new judgeships and appointed all Federalists in the hope that they would counter the Jeffersonians once in office. But with time running out before the inauguration of Thomas Jefferson as president in 1801, not all of the commissions for the new judgeships were delivered. John Marshall, whom Adams had just appointed as chief justice, continued to work as secretary of state, delivering the commissions. But he failed to deliver seventeen commissions before Adams's term expired and left them for his successor as secretary of state, James Madison, to deliver. The Federalists' attempt to pack the courts infuriated the Jeffersonian-Republicans. And President Jefferson instructed Madison not to deliver the rest of the commissions.

William Marbury was one whose commission went undelivered. He decided to sue to force Madison to give him his commission. Specifically, he sought a *writ of mandamus,* which is simply a court order directing a government official (Madison) to perform a certain act (hand over the commission). Marbury argued that Section 13 of the Judiciary Act of 1789 had authorized the Supreme Court to issue such writs. He saw this as a way of getting back his commission and for the Marshall Court to take a stand against the Jeffersonians.

Marbury v. Madison was a politically explosive case for the Court and the country over the still-untested power of judicial review. The Court faced a major dilemma. On the one hand, if the Marshall Court ordered Marbury's commission, it was likely that Jefferson would refuse to comply. The Court would then be powerless, perhaps permanently. On the other hand, if the Court refused to issue the writ, it would appear weak and that would confirm the Jeffersonian argument that the courts had no power to intrude on the executive branch. Chief Justice Marshall's opinion, handed down on February 24, 1803, however, shrewdly asserted the power of judicial review and for the first time overturned part of an act of Congress, but gave Jefferson no opportunity to retaliate and thus helped to defuse the political controversy surrounding the case. While Jeffersonians fervently disagreed with Marshall's ruling, there was little for them to do because Marshall had not ordered the delivery of Marbury's commission.

Chief Justice MARSHALL delivers the opinion of the Court.

At the last term on the affidavits then read and filed with the clerk, a rule was granted in this case, requiring the secretary of state to show cause why a mandamus should not issue, directing him to deliver to William Marbury his commission as a justice of the peace for the county of Washington, in the District of Columbia.

No cause has been shown, and the present motion is for a *mandamus.* The peculiar delicacy of this case, the novelty of some of its circumstances, and the real difficulty attending the points which occur in it, require a complete exposition of the principles on which the opinion to be given by the court is founded.

These principles have been, on the side of the applicant very ably argued at the bar. In rendering the opinion of the court, there will be some departure in form, though not in substance, from the points stated in that argument.

In the order in which the court has viewed this subject, the following questions have been considered and decided.

1st. Has the applicant a right to the commission he demands?

2d. If he has a right, and that right has been violated, do the laws of his country afford him a remedy?

3d. If they do afford him a remedy, is it a *mandamus* issuing from this court?

The first object of inquiry is,

1st. Has the applicant a right to the commission he demands?

His right originates in an act of congress passed in February, 1801, concerning the District of Columbia.

After dividing the district into two counties, the 11th section of this law enacts, "that there shall be appointed in and for each of the said counties, such number of discreet persons to be justices of the peace as the president of the United States shall, from time to time, think expedient, to continue in office for five years."

It appears, from the affidavits, that in compliance with this law, a commission for William Marbury, as a justice of the peace for the county of Washington, was signed by John Adams, then President of the United States; after which the seal of the United States was affixed to it; but the commission has never reached the person for whom it was made out.

In order to determine whether he is entitled to this commission, it becomes necessary to inquire whether he has been appointed to the office. For if he has been appointed, the law continues him in office for five years, and he is entitled to the possession of those evidences of office, which, being completed, became his property.

The 2d section of the 2d article of the constitution declares, that "the president shall nominate, and, by and with the advice and consent of the senate, shall appoint, ambassadors, other public ministers and consuls, and all other officers of the United States, whose appointments are not otherwise provided for."

The 3d section declares, that "he shall commission all the officers of the United States."

An act of congress directs the secretary of state to keep the seal of the United States, "to make out and record, and affix the said seal to all civil commissions to officers of the United States, to be appointed by the president, by and with the consent of the senate, or by the president alone; provided, that the said seal shall not be affixed to any commission before the same shall have been signed by the President of the United States."

These are the clauses of the constitution and laws of the United States, which affect this part of the case. They seem to contemplate three distinct operations:

1st. The nomination. This is the sole act of the president, and is completely voluntary.

2d. The appointment. This is also the act of the president, and is also a voluntary act, though it can only be performed by and with the advice and consent of the senate.

3d. The commission. To grant a commission to a person appointed, might, perhaps, be deemed a duty enjoined by the constitution. "He shall," says that instrument, "commission all the officers of the United States." . . .

The last act to be done by the president is the signature of the commission. He has then acted on the advice and consent of the senate to his own nomination. The time for deliberation has then passed. He has decided. His judgment, on the advice and consent of the senate concurring with his nomination, has been made, and the officer is appointed. . . .

It is . . . decidedly the opinion of the court, that when a commission has been signed by the president, the appointment is made; and that the commission is complete when the seal of the United States has been affixed to it by the secretary of state.

Where an officer is removable at the will of the executive, the circumstance which completes his appointment is of no concern; because the act is at any time revocable; and the commission may be arrested, if still in the office. But when the officer is not removable at the will of the executive, the appointment is not revocable, and cannot be annulled. It has conferred legal rights which cannot be resumed. . . .

Mr. Marbury, then, since his commission was signed by the president, and sealed by the secretary of state, was appointed; and as the law creating the office, gave the officer a right to hold for five years, independent of the executive, the appointment was not revocable, but vested in the officer legal rights, which are protected by the laws of his country.

To withhold his commission, therefore, is an act deemed by the court not warranted by law, but violative of a vested legal right.

This brings us to the second inquiry; which is,

2d. If he has a right, and that right has been violated, do the laws of this country afford him a remedy?

The very essence of civil liberty certainly consists in the right of every individual to claim the protection of the laws, whenever he receives an injury. One of the first duties of government is to afford that protection. In Great Britain the king himself is sued in the respectful form of a petition, and he never fails to comply with the judgment of his court. . . .

By the constitution of the United States, the president is invested with certain important political powers, in the exercise of which he is to use his own discretion, and is accountable only to his country in his political character and to his own conscience. To aid him in the performance of these duties, he is authorized to appoint certain officers, who act by his authority, and in conformity with his orders.

In such cases, their acts are his acts; and whatever opinion may be entertained of the manner in which executive discretion may be used, still there exists, and can exist, no power to control that discretion. The subjects are political. They respect the nation, not individual rights, and being intrusted to the executive, the decision of the executive is conclusive. . . .

But when the legislature proceeds to impose on that officer other duties; when he is directed peremptorily to perform certain acts; when the rights of individuals are dependent on the performance of those acts; he is so far the officer of the law; is amenable to the laws for his conduct; and cannot at his discretion sport away the vested rights of others.

The conclusion from this reasoning is, that where the heads of departments are the political or confidential agents of the executive, merely to execute the will of the president, or rather to act in cases in which the executive possesses a constitutional or legal discretion, nothing can be more perfectly clear than that their acts are only politically examinable. But where a specific duty is assigned by law, and individual rights depend upon the performance of that duty, it seems equally clear that the individual who considers himself injured, has a right to resort to the laws of his country for a remedy. . . .

It is, then, the opinion of the Court,

1st. That by signing the commission of Mr. Marbury, the President of the United States appointed him a justice of peace for the county of Washington, in the District of Columbia; and that the seal of the United States, affixed thereto by the secretary of state, is conclusive testimony of the verity of the signature, and of the completion of the appointment; and that the appointment conferred on him a legal right to the office for the space of five years.

2d. That, having this legal title to the office, he has a consequent right to the commission; a refusal to deliver which is a plain violation of that right, for which the laws of his country afford him a remedy.

It remains to be inquired whether,

3d. He is entitled to the remedy for which he applies. This depends on,

1st. The nature of the writ applied for; and,

2d. The power of this court.

1st. The nature of the writ. . . .

[T]o render the *mandamus* a proper remedy, the officer to whom it is to be directed, must be one to whom, on legal principles, such writ may be directed; and the person applying for it must be without any other specific and legal remedy.

1st. With respect to the officer to whom it would be directed. The intimate political relation subsisting between the President of the United States and the heads of departments, necessarily renders any legal investigation of the acts of one of those high officers peculiarly irksome, as well as delicate; and excites some hesitation with respect to the propriety of entering into such investigation. Impressions are often received without much reflection or examination, and it is not wonderful that in such a case as this the assertion, by an individual, of his legal claims in a court of justice, to which claims it is the duty of that court to attend, should at first view be considered by some, as an attempt to intrude into the cabinet, and to intermeddle with the prerogatives of the executive.

It is scarcely necessary for the court to disclaim all pretensions to such jurisdiction. An extravagance, so absurd and excessive, could not have been entertained for a moment. The province of the court is, solely, to decide on the rights of individuals, not to inquire how the executive, or executive officers, perform duties in which they have a discretion. Questions in their nature political, or which are, by the constitution and laws, submitted to the executive, can never be made in this court.

But, if this be not such a question; if, so far from being an intrusion into the secrets of the cabinet, it respects a paper which, according to law, is upon record, and to a copy of which the law gives a right. . . .

If one of the heads of departments commits any illegal act, under colour of his office, by which an individual sustains an injury, it cannot be pretended that his office alone exempts him from being sued in the ordinary mode of proceeding, and being compelled to obey the judgment of the law. How, then, can his office exempt him from this particular mode of deciding on the legality of his conduct if the case be such a case as would, were any other individual the party complained of, authorize the process?

It is not by the office of the person to whom the writ is directed, but the nature of the thing to be done, that the propriety or impropriety of issuing a *mandamus* is to be determined. . . .

This, then, is a plain case for a *mandamus*, either to deliver the commission, or a copy of it from the record; and it only remains to be inquired,

Whether it can issue from this court.

The act to establish the judicial courts of the United States authorizes the Supreme Court "to issue writs of *mandamus* in cases warranted by the principles and usages of law, to any courts appointed, or persons holding office, under the authority of the United States."

The secretary of state, being a person holding an office under the authority of the United States, is precisely within the letter of the description, and if this court is not authorized to issue a writ of mandamus to such an officer, it must be because the law is unconstitutional, and therefore absolutely incapable of conferring the authority, and assigning the duties which its words purport to confer and assign.

The constitution vests the whole judicial power of the United States in one supreme court, and such inferior courts as congress shall, from time to time, ordain and establish. This power is expressly extended to all cases arising under the laws of the United States; and, consequently, in some form, may be exercised over the present case; because the right claimed is given by a law of the United States.

In the distribution of this power it is declared that "the supreme court shall have original jurisdiction in all cases affecting ambassadors, other public ministers and consuls, and those in which a state shall be a party. In all other cases, the supreme court shall have appellate jurisdiction."

It has been insisted, at the bar, that as the original grant of jurisdiction, to the supreme and inferior courts, is general, and the clause, assigning original jurisdiction to the supreme court, contains no negative or restrictive words, the power remains to the legislature, to assign original jurisdiction to that court in other cases than those specified in the article which has been recited; provided those cases belong to the judicial power of the United States.

If it had been intended to leave it in the discretion of the legislature to apportion the judicial power between the supreme and inferior courts according to the will of that body, it would certainly have been useless to have proceded further than to have defined the judicial power, and the tribunals in which it should be vested. The subsequent part of the section is mere surplusage, is entirely without meaning, if such is to be the construction. If congress remains at liberty to give this court appellate jurisdiction, where the constitution has declared their jurisdiction shall be original; and original jurisdiction where the constitution has declared it shall be appellate; the distribution of jurisdiction, made in the constitution, is form without substance.

Affirmative words are often, in their operation, negative of other objects than those affirmed; and in this case, a negative or exclusive sense must be given to them, or they have no operation at all.

It cannot be presumed that any clause in the constitution is intended to be without effect; and, therefore, such a construction is inadmissible, unless the words require it.

If the solicitude of the convention, respecting our peace with foreign powers, induced a provision that the supreme court should take original jurisdiction in cases which might be supposed to affect them; yet the clause would have proceeded no further than to provide for such cases, if no further restriction on the powers of congress had been intended. That they should have appellate jurisdiction in all other cases, with such exceptions as congress might make, is no restriction; unless the words be deemed exclusive of original jurisdiction.

When an instrument organizing fundamentally a judicial system, divides it into one supreme, and so many inferior courts as the legislature may ordain and establish; then enumerates its powers, and proceeds so far to distribute them, as to define the jurisdiction of the supreme court by declaring the cases in which it shall take original jurisdiction, and that in others it shall take appellate jurisdiction; the plain import of the words seems to be, that in one class of cases its jurisdiction is original, and not appellate; in the other it is appellate, and not original. If any other construction would render the clause inoperative, that is an additional reason for rejecting such other construction, and for adhering to their obvious meaning.

To enable this court, then, to issue a *mandamus*, it must be shown to be an exercise of appellate jurisdiction, or to be necessary to enable them to exercise appellate jurisdiction.

It has been stated at the bar that the appellate jurisdiction may be exercised in a variety of forms, and that if it be the will of the legislature that a *mandamus* should be used for that purpose, that will must be obeyed. This is true, yet the jurisdiction must be appellate, not original.

It is the essential criterion of appellate jurisdiction, that it revises and corrects the proceedings in a cause already instituted, and does not create that cause. Although, therefore, a mandamus may be directed to courts, yet to issue such a writ to an officer for the delivery of a paper, is in effect the same as to sustain an original action for that paper, and, therefore, seems not to belong to appellate, but to original jurisdiction. Neither is it necessary in such a case as this, to enable the court to exercise its appellate jurisdiction.

The authority, therefore, given to the supreme court, by the act establishing the judicial courts of the United States, to issue writs of *mandamus* to public officers, appears not to be warranted by the constitution; and it becomes necessary to inquire whether a jurisdiction so conferred can be exercised.

The question, whether an act, repugnant to the constitution, can become the law of the land, is a question deeply interesting to the United States; but, happily, not of an intricacy proportioned to its interest. It seems only necessary to recognize certain principles, supposed to have been long and well established, to decide it.

That the people have an original right to establish, for their future government, such principles, as, in their opinion, shall most conduce to their own happiness is the basis on which the whole American fabric has been erected. The exercise of this original right is a very great exertion; nor can it, nor ought it, to be frequently repeated. The principles, therefore, so established, are deemed fundamental. And as the authority from which they proceed is supreme, and can seldom act, they are designed to be permanent.

This original and supreme will organizes the government, and assigns to different departments their respective powers. It may either stop here, or establish certain limits not to be transcended by those departments.

The government of the United States is of the latter description. The powers of the legislature are defined and limited; and that those limits may not be mistaken, or forgotten, the constitution is written. To what purpose are powers limited, and to what purpose is that limitation committed to writing, if these limits may, at any time, be passed by those intended to be restrained? The distinction between a government with limited and unlimited powers is abolished, if those limits do not confine the persons on whom they are imposed, and if acts prohibited and acts allowed, are of equal obligation. It is a proposition too plain to be contested, that the constitution controls any legislative act repugnant to it; or, that the legislature may alter the constitution by an ordinary act.

Between these alternatives there is no middle ground. The constitution is either a superior paramount law, unchangeable by ordinary means, or it is on a level with ordinary legislative acts, and, like other acts, is alterable when the legislature shall please to alter it.

If the former part of the alternative be true, then a legislative act contrary to the constitution is not law: if the latter part be true, then written constitutions are absurd attempts, on the part of the people, to limit a power in its own nature illimitable.

Certainly all those who have framed written constitutions contemplate them as forming the fundamental and paramount law of the nation, and, consequently, the theory of every such government must be, that an act of the legislature, repugnant to the constitution, is void.

This theory is essentially attached to a written constitution, and, is consequently, to be considered, by this court, as one of the fundamental principles of our society. It is not therefore to be lost sight of in the further consideration of this subject.

If an act of the legislature, repugnant to the constitution, is void, does it, notwithstanding its invalidity, bind the courts, and oblige them to give it effect? Or, in other words, though it be not law, does it constitute a rule as operative as if it was a law? This would be to overthrow in fact what was established in theory; and would seem, at first view, an absurdity too gross to be insisted on. It shall, however, receive a more attentive consideration.

It is emphatically the province and duty of the judicial department to say what the law is. Those who apply the rule to particular cases, must of necessity expound and interpret that rule. If two laws conflict with each other, the courts must decide on the operation of each.

So if a law be in opposition to the constitution; if both the law and the constitution apply to a particular case, so that the court must either decide that case conformably to the law, disregarding the constitution; or conformably to the constitution, disregarding the law; the court must determine which of these conflicting rules governs the case. This is of the very essence of judicial duty.

If, then, the courts are to regard the constitution, and the constitution is superior to any ordinary act of the legislature, the constitution, and not such ordinary act, must govern the case to which they both apply.

Those, then, who controvert the principle that the constitution is to be considered, in court, as a paramount law, are reduced to the necessity of maintaining that courts must close their eyes on the constitution, and see only the law.

This doctrine would subvert the very foundation of all written constitutions. It would declare that an act which, according to the principles and theory of our government, is entirely void, is yet, in practice, completely obligatory. It would declare that if the legislature shall do what is expressly forbidden, such act, notwithstanding the express prohibition, is in reality effectual. It would be given to the legislature a practical and real omnipotence, with the same breath which professes to restrict their powers within narrow limits. It is prescribing limits, and declaring that those limits may be passed at pleasure.

That it thus reduces to nothing what we have deemed the greatest improvement on political institutions, a written constitution, would of itself be sufficient, in America, where written constitutions have been viewed with so much reverence, for rejecting the construction. But the peculiar expressions of the constitution of the United States furnish additional arguments in favour of its rejection.

The judicial power of the United States is extended to all cases arising under the constitution.

Could it be the intention of those who gave this power, to say that in using it the constitution should not be looked into? That a case arising under the constitution should be decided without examining the instrument under which it arises?

This is too extravagant to be maintained.

In some cases, then, the constitution must be looked into by the judges. And if they can open it at all, what part of it are they forbidden to read or to obey?

There are many other parts of the constitution which serve to illustrate this subject.

It is declared that "no tax or duty shall be laid on articles exported from any state." Suppose a duty on the export of cotton, of tobacco, or of flour; and a suit instituted to recover it. Ought judgment to be rendered in such a case? Ought the judges to close their eyes on the constitution, and only see the law?

The constitution declares "that no bill of attainder or *ex post facto* law shall be passed."

If, however, such a bill should be passed, and a person should be prosecuted under it; must the court condemn to death those victims whom the constitution endeavors to preserve?

"No person," says the constitution, "shall be convicted of treason unless on the testimony of two witnesses to the same overt act, or on confession in open court."

Here the language of the constitution is addressed especially to the courts. It prescribes, directly for them, a rule of evidence not to be departed from. If the legislature should change that rule, and declare one witness, or a confession out of court, sufficient for conviction, must the constitutional principle yield to the legislative act?

From these, and many other selections which might be made, it is apparent, that the framers of the constitution contemplated that instrument as a rule for the government of courts, as well as of the legislature.

Why otherwise does it direct the judges to take an oath to support it? This oath certainly applies in an especial manner, to their conduct in their official character. How immoral to impose it on them, if they were to be used as the instruments, and the knowing instruments, for violating what they swear to support!

The oath of office, too, imposed by the legislature, is completely demonstrative of the legislative opinion on this subject. It is in these words: "I do solemnly swear that I will administer justice without respect to persons, and do equal right to the poor and to the rich; and that I will faithfully and impartially discharge all the duties incumbent on me as ———, according to the best of my abilities and understanding agreeably to the constitution and laws of the United States."

Why does a judge swear to discharge his duties agreeably to the constitution of the United States, if that constitution forms no rule for his government? if it is closed upon him, and cannot be inspected by him?

If such be the real state of things, this is worse than solemn mockery. To prescribe, or to take this oath, becomes equally a crime.

It is also not entirely unworthy of observation, that in declaring what shall be the *supreme law* of the land, *the constitution* itself is first mentioned; and not the laws of the United States generally, but those only which shall be made in *pursuance* of the constitution, have that rank.

Thus, the particular phraseology of the constitution of the United States confirms and strengthens the principle, supposed to be essential to all written constitutions, that a law repugnant to the constitution is void; and that *courts,* as well as other departments, are bound by that instrument.

The rule must be discharged.

Eakin v. Raub

12 Sargeant & Rawle 330 (Pa., 1825)

In this case involving the power of the Pennsylvania Supreme Court to invalidate a state law, Justice John Bannister Gibson wrote a dissenting opinion aimed at refuting Chief Justice John Marshall's arguments for judicial review in *Marbury v. Madison*

(1803) (see p. 45). Note that Justice Gibson's criticism of *Marbury* was limited to the exercise of judicial review over coequal branches of government. While he contended that state courts had no power to overturn state laws deemed to violate the state constitution, Justice Gibson did not deny that state courts could strike down state laws that were inconsistent with federal law or the Constitution. Moreover, twenty years later, Justice Gibson repudiated the position taken in his opinion here. In *Norris v. Clymer*, 2 Pa. 277 (1845), he explained his change in "opinion for two reasons. The late convention (which drafted Pennsylvania's state constitution), by their silence, sanctioned the pretensions of the courts to deal freely with the Acts of the Legislature; and from experience of the necessity of the case."

Justice GIBSON dissenting.

I am aware, that a right [in the judiciary] to declare all unconstitutional acts void . . . is generally held as a professional dogma, but, I apprehend, rather as a matter of faith than of reason. I admit that I once embraced the same doctrine, but without examination, and I shall therefore state the arguments that impelled me to abandon it, with great respect for those by whom it is still maintained. But I may premise, that it is not a little remarkable, that although the right in question has all along been claimed by the judiciary, no judge has ventured to discuss it, except Chief Justice MARSHALL, and if the argument of a jurist so distinguished for the strength of his ratiocinative powers be found inconclusive, it may fairly be set down to the weakness of the position which he attempts to defend. . . .

I begin, then, by observing that in this country, the powers of the judiciary are divisible into those that are POLITICAL and those that are purely civil. Every power by which one organ of the government is enabled to control another, or to exert an influence over its acts, is a political power. . . .

The constitution and the right of the legislature to pass the act, may be in collision. But is that a legitimate subject for judicial determination? If it be, the judiciary must be a peculiar organ, to revise the proceedings of the legislature, and to correct its mistakes; and in what part of the constitution are we to look for this proud pre-eminence? Viewing the matter in the opposite direction, what would be thought of an act of assembly in which it should be declared that the supreme court had, in a particular case, put a wrong construction on the constitution of the United States, and that the judgment should therefore be reversed? It would doubtless be thought a usurpation of judicial power. But it is by no means clear, that to declare a law void which has been enacted according to the forms prescribed in the constitution, is not a usurpation of legislative power. . . .

But it has been said to be emphatically the business of the judiciary, to ascertain and pronounce what the law is; and that this necessarily involves a consideration of the constitution. It does so: but how far? If the judiciary will inquire into anything besides the form of enactment, where shall it stop? . . .

In theory, all the organs of the government are of equal capacity; or, if not equal, each must be supposed to have superior capacity only for those things which peculiarly belong to it; and as legislation peculiarly involves the consideration of those limitations which are put on the law-making power, and the interpretation of the laws when made, involves only the construction of the laws themselves, it follows that the construction of the constitution in this particular belongs to the legislature, which ought therefore to be taken to have superior capacity to judge of the constitutionality of its own acts. But suppose all to be of equal capacity in every respect, why should one exercise a controlling power over the rest? That the judiciary is of superior rank, has never been pretended, although it has been said to be co-ordinate. It is not easy, however, to comprehend how the power which gives law to all the rest, can be of no more than equal rank with one which receives it, and is answerable to the former for the observance of its statutes. Legislation is essentially an act of sovereign power; but the execution of the laws by instruments that are governed by prescribed rules and exercise no power of volition, is essentially otherwise. . . . It may be said, the power of the legislature, also, is limited by prescribed rules. It is so. But it is nevertheless, the power of the people, and sovereign as far as it extends. It cannot be said, that the judiciary is co-ordinate merely because it is established by the constitution. If that were sufficient, sheriffs, registers of wills, and recorders of deeds, would be so too. Within the pale of their authority, the acts of these officers will have the power of the people for their support; but no one will pretend, they are of equal dignity with the acts of the legislature. Inequality of rank arises not from the manner in which the organ has been constituted, but from its essence and the nature of its functions; and the legislative organ is superior to every other, inasmuch as the power to will and to command, is essentially superior to the power to act and to obey. . . .

Everyone knows how seldom men think exactly alike on ordinary subjects; and a government constructed on the principle of assent by all its parts, would be inadequate to the most simple operations. The notion of a complication of counter checks has been carried to an extent in theory, of which the framers of the constitution never dreamt. When the entire sovereignty was separated into its elementary parts, and distributed to the appropriate branches, all things incident to the exercise of its powers were committed to each branch exclusively. The negative which each part of the legislature may exercise, in regard to the acts of the other, was thought sufficient to prevent material infractions of the restraints which were put on the power of the whole; for, had it been intended to interpose the judiciary as an additional barrier, the matter would surely not have been left in doubt. The judges would not have been left to stand on the insecure and ever shifting ground of public opinion as to constructive powers; they would have been placed on the impregnable ground of an express grant. They would not have been compelled to resort to debates in the convention, or the opinion that was generally entertained at the time. . . .

The power is said to be restricted to cases that are free from doubt or difficulty. But the abstract existence of a power cannot depend on the clearness or obscurity of the case in which it is to be exercised; for that is a consideration that cannot present itself, before the question of the existence of the power shall have been determined; and, if its existence be conceded, no considerations of policy arising from the obscurity of the particular case, ought to influence the exercise of it. . . .

To say, therefore, that the power is to be exercised but in perfectly clear cases, is to betray a doubt of the propriety of exercising it at all. Were the same caution used in judging of the existence of the power that is inculcated as to the exercise of it, the profession would perhaps arrive at a different conclusion. The grant of a power so extraordinary ought to appear so plain, that he who should run might read. . . .

What I have in view in this inquiry, is the supposed right of the judiciary to interfere, in cases where the constitution is to be carried into effect through the instrumentality of the legislature, and where that organ must necessarily first decide on the constitutionality of its own act. The oath to support the constitution is not peculiar to the judges, but is taken indiscriminately by every officer of the government, and is designed rather as a test of the political principles of the man, than to bind the officer in the discharge of his duty; otherwise it is difficult to determine what operation it is to have in the case of a recorder of deeds, for instance, who, in the execution of his office, has nothing to do with the constitution. But granting it to relate to the official conduct of the judge, as well as every other officer, and not to his political principles, still it must be understood in reference to supporting the constitution, *only as far as that may be involved in his official duty;* and, consequently, if his official duty does not comprehend an inquiry into the authority of the legislature, neither does his oath. . . .

But do not the judges do a positive act in violation of the constitution, when they give effect to an unconstitutional law? Not if the law has been passed according to the forms established in the constitution. The fallacy of the question is, in supposing that the judiciary adopts the acts of the legislature as its own; whereas the enactment of a law and the interpretation of it are not concurrent acts, and as the judiciary is not required to concur in the enactment, neither is it in the breach of the constitution which may be the consequence of the enactment. The fault is imputable to the legislature, and on it the responsibility exclusively rests. . . .

But it has been said, that this construction would deprive the citizen of the advantages which are peculiar to a written constitution, by at once declaring the power of the legislature in practice to be illimitable. . . . But there is no magic or inherent power in parchment and ink, to command respect and protect principles from violation. In the business of government a recurrence to first principles answers the end of an observation at sea with a view to correct the dead reckoning; and for this purpose, a written constitution is an instrument of inestimable value. It is of inestimable value, also, in rendering its first principles familiar to the mass of people; for, after all, there is no effectual guard against legislative usurpation but public opinion, the force of which, in this country is inconceivably great. . . . Once let public opinion be so corrupt as to sanction every misconstruction of the constitution and abuse of power which the temptation of the moment may dictate, and the party which may happen to be predominant, will laugh at the puny efforts of a dependent power to arrest it in its course.

For these reasons, I am of [the] opinion that it rests with the people, in whom full and absolute sovereign power resides, to correct abuses in legislation, by instructing their representatives to repeal the obnoxious act. What is wanting to plenary power in the government, is reserved by the people for their own immediate use; and to redress an infringement of their rights in this respect, would seem to be an accessory of the power thus reserved. It might, perhaps, have been better to vest the power in the judiciary; as it might be expected that its habits of deliberation, and the aid derived from the arguments of counsel, would more frequently lead to accurate conclusions. On the other hand, the judiciary is not infallible; and an error by it would admit of no remedy but a more distinct expression of the public will, through the extraordinary medium of a convention; whereas, an error by the legislature admits of a remedy by an exertion of the same will, in the ordinary exercise of the right of suffrage—a mode better calculated to attain the end, without popular excitement. It may be said, the people would probably not notice an error of their representatives. But they would as probably do so, as notice an error of the judiciary; and, besides, it is a postulate in the theory of our government, and the very basis of the superstructure, that the people are wise, virtuous, and competent to manage their own affairs; and if they are not so, in fact, still every question of this sort must be determined according to the principles of the constitution, as it came from the hands of the framers, and the existence of a defect which was not foreseen, would not justify those who administer the government, in applying a corrective in practice, which can be provided only by convention. . . .

But in regard to an act of [a state] assembly, which is found to be in collision with the constitution, laws, or treaties of the *United States*, I take the duty of the judiciary to be exactly the reverse. By becoming parties to the federal constitution, the states have agreed to several limitations of their individual sovereignty, to enforce which, it was thought to be absolutely necessary to prevent them from giving effect to laws in violation of those limitations, through the instrumentality of their own judges. Accordingly, it is declared in the sixth article and second section of the federal constitution, that "This constitution, and the laws of the *United States* which shall be made in pursuance thereof, and all treaties made, or which shall be made under the authority of the *United States,* shall be the *supreme* law of the land; and the *judges* in every *state* shall be BOUND thereby: anything in the *laws* or *constitution* of any *state* to the contrary notwithstanding."

President Jackson's Veto Message of 1832

President Andrew Jackson distrusted banks and, as a westerner, opposed the policies of the Bank of the United States which limited credit for land speculation. When Congress rechartered the Bank in 1832, Jackson vetoed the bill with this message,[*] drafted by Secretary of Treasury (and later appointed as chief justice) Roger B. Taney. The controversy over the establishment of the national bank and its importance in shaping constitutional politics is dealt with further in Vol. 1, Ch. 6.

To the Senate:

The bill "to modify and continue" the act entitled "An act to incorporate the subscribers to the Bank of the United States" was presented to me on the 4th July instant. Having considered it with that solemn regard to the principles of the Constitution which the day was calculated to inspire, and come to the conclusion that it ought not to become a law, I herewith return it to the Senate, in which it originated, with my objections.

---

[*] From James D. Richardson, ed., *A Compilation of the Messages and Papers of the Presidents,* (Washington, DC: Bureau of National Literature and Act, 1908), Vol. 2, 581–582.

It is maintained by the advocates of the bank that its constitutionality in all its features ought to be considered as settled by precedent and by the decision of the Supreme Court. To this conclusion I can not assent. Mere precedent is a dangerous source of authority, and should not be regarded as deciding questions of constitutional power except where the acquiescence of the people and the States can be considered as well settled. So far from this being the case on this subject, an argument against the bank might be based on precedent. One Congress, in 1791, decided in favor of a bank; another in 1811, decided against it. One Congress, in 1815, decided against a bank, another, in 1816, decided in its favor. Prior to the present Congress, therefore, the precedents drawn from that source were equal. If we resort to the States, the expressions of legislative, judicial, and executive opinions against the bank have been probably to those in its favor as 4 to 1. There is nothing in precedent, therefore, which, if its authority were admitted, ought to weigh in favor of the act before me.

If the opinion of the Supreme Court covered the whole ground of this act, it ought not to control the coordinate authorities of this Government. The Congress, the Executive, and the Court must each for itself be guided by its own opinion of the Constitution. Each public officer who takes an oath to support the Constitution swears that he will support it as he understands it, and not as it is understood by others. It is as much the duty of the House of Representatives, of the Senate, and of the President to decide upon the constitutionality of any bill or resolution which may be presented to them for passage or approval as it is of the supreme judges when it may be brought before them for judicial decision. The opinion of the judges has no more authority over Congress than the opinion of Congress has over the judges, and on that point the President is independent of both. The authority of the Supreme Court must not, therefore, be permitted to control the Congress or the Executive when acting in their legislative capacities, but to have only such influence as the force of their reasoning may deserve.

But in the case relied upon the Supreme Court have not decided that all the features of this corporation are compatible with the Constitution. It is true that the court have said that the law incorporating the bank is a constitutional exercise of power by Congress; but taking into view the whole opinion of the court and the reasoning by which they have come to that conclusion, I understand them to have decided that inasmuch as a bank is an appropriate means for carrying into effect the enumerated powers of the General Government, therefore the law incorporating it is in accordance with that provision of the Constitution which declares that Congress shall have power "to make all laws which shall be necessary and proper for carrying those powers into execution."

Having satisfied themselves that the word *"necessary"* in the Constitution means *"needful," "requisite," "essential," "conducive to,"* and that "a bank" is a convenient, a useful, and essential instrument in the prosecution of the Government's "fiscal operations," they conclude that to "use one must be within the discretion of Congress" and that "the act to incorporate the Bank of the United States is a law made in pursuance of the Constitution"; "but," say they, *"where the law is not prohibited and is really calculated to effect any of the objects intrusted to the Government, to undertake here to inquire into the degree of its necessity would be to pass the line which circumscribes the judicial department and to tread on legislative ground."*

The principle here affirmed is that the "degree of its necessity," involving all the details of a banking institution, is a question exclusively for legislative consideration. A bank is constitutional, but it is the province of the Legislature to determine whether this or that particular power, privilege, or exemption is "necessary and proper" to enable the bank to discharge its duties to the Government, and from their decision there is no appeal to the courts of justice. Under the decision of the Supreme Court, therefore, it is the exclusive province of Congress and the President to decide whether the particular features of this act are *necessary* and *proper* in order to enable the bank to perform conveniently and efficiently the public duties assigned to it as a fiscal agent, and therefore constitutional, or *unnecessary* and *improper*, and therefore unconstitutional. . . .

The bank is professedly established as an agent of the executive branch of the Government, and its constitutionality is maintained on that ground. Neither upon the propriety of present action nor upon the provisions of this act was the Executive consulted. It has had no opportunity to say that it neither needs nor wants an agent clothed with such powers and favored by such exemptions. There is nothing in its legitimate functions which makes it necessary or proper. Whatever interest or influence, whether public or private, has given birth to this act, it can not be found either in the wishes or necessities of the executive department, by which present action is deemed premature, and the powers conferred upon its agent not only unnecessary, but dangerous to the Government and country. . . .

Nor is our Government to be maintained or our Union preserved by invasions of the rights and powers of the several States. In thus attempting to make our General Government strong we make it weak. Its true strength consists in leaving individuals and States as much as possible to themselves—in making itself felt, not in its power, but in its beneficence; not in its control, but in its protection; not in binding the States more closely to the center, but leaving each to move unobstructed in its proper orbit.

Experience should teach us wisdom. Most of the difficulties

our Government now encounters and most of the dangers which impend over our Union have sprung from an abandonment of the legitimate objects of Government by our national legislation, and the adoption of such principles as are embodied in this act. Many of our rich men have not been content with equal protection and equal benefits, but have besought us to make them richer by act of Congress. By attempting to gratify their desires we have in the results of our legislation arrayed section against section, interest against interest, and man against man, in a fearful commotion which threatens to shake the foundations of our Union. It is time to pause in our career to review our principles, and if possible revive that devoted patriotism and spirit of compromise which distinguished the sages of the Revolution and the fathers of our Union. If we can not at once, in justice to interests vested under improvident legislation, make our Government what it ought to be, we can at least take a stand against all new grants of monopolies and exclusive privileges, against any prostitution of our Government to the advancement of the few at the expense of the many, and in favor of compromise and gradual reform in our code of laws and system of political economy.

I have now done my duty to my country. If sustained by my fellow-citizens, I shall be grateful and happy; if not, I shall find in the motives which impel me ample grounds for contentment and peace.

President Roosevelt's Radio Broadcast, March 9, 1937

During President Franklin D. Roosevelt's first term (1933–1937), the Supreme Court by a vote of five to four invalidated much of his New Deal program and plan for the country's economic recovery from the Great Depression. After his landslide reelection in November 1936, FDR proposed in February 1937 that Congress expand the size of the Court from nine to fifteen justices, and thereby give him the chance to secure a majority sympathetic to his policies. On March 9, 1937, the Democratic president made the following radio address in an effort to marshal public support for his "Court-packing plan." But that same month, while the Senate Judiciary Committee was considering his proposal, Justice Owen Roberts, who had previously cast the crucial vote for overturning progressive economic legislation, switched sides and voted to uphold New Deal legislation. The Court's proverbial

---

* From 1937 *Public Papers and Addresses of Franklin D. Roosevelt* (1941), 122.

"switch-in-time-that-saved-nine" then contributed to the Democrat-dominated Senate's defeat of FDR's proposal. The constitutional crisis that loomed over the Court and the country in 1937 is discussed further in Vol. 1, Ch. 6 and in Vol. 2, Ch. 3.

Tonight, sitting at my desk in the White House, I make my first radio report to the people in my second term of office.

I am reminded of that evening in March, four years ago, when I made my first radio report to you. We were then in the midst of the great banking crisis.

Soon after, with the authority of the Congress, we asked the Nation to turn over all of its privately held gold, dollar for dollar, to the Government of the United States.

Today's recovery proves how right that policy was.

But when, almost two years later, it came before the Supreme Court its constitutionality was upheld only by a five-to-four vote. The change of one vote would have thrown all the affairs of this great Nation back into hopeless chaos. In effect, four Justices ruled that the right under a private contract to exact a pound of flesh was more sacred than the main objectives of the Constitution to establish an enduring Nation.

In 1933 you and I knew that we must never let our economic system get completely out of joint again—that we could not afford to take the risk of another great depression.

We also became convinced that the only way to avoid a repetition of those dark days was to have a government with power to prevent and to cure the abuses and the inequalities which had thrown that system out of joint.

We then began a program of remedying those abuses and inequalities—to give balance and stability to our economic system—to make it bomb-proof against the causes of 1929.

Today we are only part-way through that program—and recovery is speeding up to a point where the dangers of 1929 are again becoming possible, not this week or month perhaps, but within a year or two.

National laws are needed to complete that program. Individual or local or state effort alone cannot protect us in 1937 any better than ten years ago.

It will take time—and plenty of time—to work out our remedies administratively even after legislation is passed. To complete our program of protection in time, therefore, we cannot delay one moment in making certain that our National Government has power to carry through.

Four years ago action did not come until the eleventh hour. It was almost too late.

If we learned anything from the depression we will not allow ourselves to run around in new circles of futile discussion and debate, always postponing the day of decision.

The American people have learned from the depression. For in the last three national elections an overwhelming majority of them voted a mandate that the Congress and the President begin the task of providing that protection—not after long years of debate, but now.

The Courts, however, have cast doubts on the ability of the elected Congress to protect us against catastrophe by meeting squarely our modern social and economic conditions.

We are at a crisis in our ability to proceed with that protection. It is a quiet crisis. There are no lines of depositors outside closed banks. But to the far-sighted it is far-reaching in its possibilities of injury to America.

I want to talk with you very simply about the need for present action in this crisis—the need to meet the unanswered challenge of one-third of a Nation ill-nourished, ill-clad, ill-housed.

Last Thursday I described the American form of Government as a three horse team provided by the Constitution to the American people so that their field might be plowed. The three horses are, of course, the three branches of government—the Congress, the Executive and the Courts. Two of the horses are pulling in unison today; the third is not. Those who have intimated that the President of the United States is trying to drive that team, overlook the simple fact that the President, as Chief Executive, is himself one of the three horses.

It is the American people themselves who are in the driver's seat.

It is the American people themselves who want the furrow plowed.

It is the American people themselves who expect the third horse to pull in unison with the other two.

I hope that you have re-read the Constitution of the United States. Like the Bible, it ought to be read again and again.

It is an easy document to understand when you remember that it was called into being because the Articles of Confederation under which the original thirteen States tried to operate after the Revolution showed the need of a National Government with power enough to handle national problems. In its Preamble, the Constitution states that it was intended to form a more perfect Union and promote the general welfare; and the powers given to the Congress to carry out those purposes can be best described by saying that they were all the powers needed to meet each and every problem which then had a national character and which could not be met by merely local action.

But the framers went further. Having in mind that in succeeding generations many other problems then undreamed of would become national problems, they gave to the Congress the ample broad powers "to levy taxes . . . and provide for the common defense and general welfare of the United States."

That, my friends, is what I honestly believe to have been the clear and underlying purpose of the patriots who wrote a Federal Constitution to create a National Government with national power, intended as they said, "to form a more perfect union . . . for ourselves and our posterity."

For nearly twenty years there was no conflict between the Congress and the Court. Then, in 1803, Congress passed a statute which the Court said violated an express provision of the Constitution. The Court claimed the power to declare it unconstitutional and did so declare it. But a little later the Court itself admitted that it was an extraordinary power to exercise and through Mr. Justice Washington laid down this limitation upon it: "It is but a decent respect due to the wisdom, the integrity and the patriotism of the Legislative body, by which any law is passed, to presume in favor of its validity until its violation of the Constitution is proved beyond all reasonable doubt."

But since the rise of the modern movement for social and economic progress through legislation, the Court has more and more often and more and more boldly asserted a power to veto laws passed by the Congress and State Legislatures in complete disregard of this original limitation.

In the last four years the sound rule of giving statutes the benefit of all reasonable doubt has been cast aside. The Court has been acting not as a judicial body, but as a policy-making body.

When the Congress has sought to stabilize national agriculture, to improve the conditions of labor, to safeguard business against unfair competition, to protect our national resources, and in many other ways, to serve our clearly national needs, the majority of the Court has been assuming the power to pass on the wisdom of these Acts of the Congress—and to approve or disapprove the public policy written into these laws.

That is not only my accusation. It is the accusation of most distinguished Justices of the present Supreme Court. I have not the time to quote to you all the language used by dissenting Justices in many of these cases. But in the case holding the Railroad Retirement Act unconstitutional, for instance, Chief Justice Hughes said in a dissenting opinion that the majority opinion was "a departure from sound principles," and placed "an unwarranted limitation upon the commerce clause." And three other Justices agreed with him.

In the case holding the A.A.A. unconstitutional, Justice Stone said of the majority opinion that it was a "tortured construction of the Constitution." And two other Justices agreed with him.

In the case holding the New York Minimum Wage Law unconstitutional, Justice Stone said that the majority were actually reading into the Constitution their own "personal economic predilections," and that if the legislative power is not left free to choose the methods of solving the problems of poverty, subsistence and health of large numbers in the community, then "government is to be rendered impotent." And two other Justices agreed with him.

In the face of these dissenting opinions, there is no basis for the claim made by some members of the Court that something in the Constitution has compelled them regretfully to thwart the will of the people.

In the face of such dissenting opinions, it is perfectly clear, that as Chief Justice Hughes has said: "We are under a Constitution but the Constitution is what the Judges say it is."

The Court in addition to the proper use of its judicial functions has improperly set itself up as a third House of the Congress— a super-legislature, as one of the Justices has called it—reading into the Constitution words and implications which are not there, and which were never intended to be there.

We have, therefore, reached the point as a Nation where we must take action to save the Constitution from the Court and the Court from itself. We must find a way to take an appeal from the Supreme Court to the Constitution itself. We want a Supreme Court which will do justice under the Constitution— not over it. In our Courts we want a government of laws and not of men.

I want—as all Americans want—an independent judiciary as proposed by the framers of the Constitution. That means a Supreme Court that will enforce the Constitution as written—that will refuse to amend the Constitution by the arbitrary exercise of judicial power—amendment by judicial say-so. It does not mean a judiciary so independent that it can deny the existence of facts universally recognized.

How then could we proceed to perform the mandate given us? It was said in last year's Democratic platform "If these problems cannot be effectively solved within the Constitution, we shall seek such clarifying amendment as will assure the power to enact those laws, adequately to regulate commerce, protect public health and safety, and safeguard economic security." In other words, we said we would seek an amendment only if every other possible means by legislation were to fail.

When I commenced to review the situation with the problem squarely before me, I came by a process of elimination to the conclusion that short of amendments the only method which was clearly constitutional, and would at the same time carry out other much needed reforms, was to infuse new blood into all our Courts. We must have men worthy and equipped to carry out impartial justice. But, at the same time, we must have Judges who will bring to the Courts a present-day sense of the Constitution—Judges who will retain in the Courts the judicial functions of a court, and reject the legislative powers which the Courts have today assumed. . . .

What is my proposal? It is simply this: whenever a Judge or Justice of any Federal Court has reached the age of seventy and does not avail himself of the opportunity to retire on a pension, a new member shall be appointed by the President then in office, with the approval, as required by the Constitution, of the Senate of the United States.

That plan has two chief purposes. By bringing into the Judicial system a steady and continuing stream of new and younger blood, I hope, first, to make the administration of all Federal justice speedier and, therefore, less costly; secondly, to bring to the decision of social and economic problems younger men who have had personal experience and contact with modern facts and circumstances under which average men have to live and work. This plan will save our national Constitution from hardening of the judicial arteries.

The number of Judges to be appointed would depend wholly on the decision of present Judges now over seventy, or those who would subsequently reach the age of seventy.

If, for instance, any one of the six Justices of the Supreme Court now over the age of seventy should retire as provided under the plan, no additional place would be created. Consequently, although there never can be more than fifteen, there may be only fourteen, or thirteen, or twelve. And there may be only nine.

There is nothing novel or radical about this idea. It seeks to maintain the Federal bench in full vigor. It has been discussed and approved by many persons of high authority ever since a similar proposal passed the House of Representatives in 1869.

Why was the age fixed at seventy? Because the laws of many States, the practice of the Civil Service, the regulations of the Army and Navy, and the rules of many of our Universities and of almost every great private business enterprise, commonly fix the retirement age at seventy years or less.

The statute would apply to all the Courts in the Federal system. There is general approval so far as the lower Federal courts are concerned. The plan has met opposition only so far as the Supreme Court of the United States itself is concerned. If such a plan is good for the lower courts it certainly ought to be equally good for the highest Court from which there is no appeal.

Those opposing this plan have sought to arouse prejudice and fear by crying that I am seeking to "pack" the Supreme Court and that a baneful precedent will be established.

What do they mean by the words "packing the Court"?

Let me answer this question with a bluntness that will end all *honest* misunderstanding of my purposes.

If by that phrase "packing the Court" it is charged that I wish to place on the bench spineless puppets who would disregard the law and would decide specific cases as I wished them to be decided, I make this answer—that no President fit for his office would appoint, and no Senate of honorable men fit for their office would confirm, that kind of appointees to the Supreme Court.

But if by that phrase the charge is made that I would appoint and the Senate would confirm Justices worthy to sit beside present members of the Court who understand those modern conditions— that I will appoint Justices who will not undertake to override the judgment of the Congress on legislative policy—that I will appoint Justices who will act as Justices and not as legislators— if the appointment of such Justices can be called "packing the Courts," then I say that I and with me the vast majority of the American people favor doing just that thing—now.

Is it a dangerous precedent for the Congress to change the number of the Justices? The Congress has always had, and will have, that power. The number of Justices has been changed several times before—in the Administrations of John Adams and Thomas Jefferson,—both signers of the Declaration of Independence—Andrew Jackson, Abraham Lincoln and Ulysses S. Grant.

I suggest only the addition of Justices to the bench in accordance with a clearly defined principle relating to a clearly defined age limit. Fundamentally, if in the future, America cannot trust the Congress it elects to refrain from abuse of our Constitutional usages, democracy will have failed far beyond the importance to it of any kind of precedent concerning the Judiciary. . . .

It is the clear intention of our public policy to provide for a constant flow of new and younger blood into the Judiciary. Normally every President appoints a large number of District and Circuit Judges and a few members of the Supreme Court. Until my first term practically every President of the United States had appointed at least one member of the Supreme Court. President Taft appointed five members and named a Chief Justice— President Wilson three—President Harding four including a Chief Justice—President Coolidge one—President Hoover three including a Chief Justice.

Such a succession of appointments should have provided a Court well-balanced as to age. But chance and the disinclination of individuals to leave the Supreme bench have now given us a Court in which five Justices will be over seventy-five years of age before next June and one over seventy. Thus a sound public policy has been defeated.

I now propose that we establish by law an assurance against any such ill-balanced Court in the future. I propose that hereafter, when a Judge reaches the age of seventy, a new and younger Judge shall be added to the Court automatically. In this way I propose to enforce a sound public policy by law instead of leaving the composition of our Federal Courts, including the highest, to be determined by chance or the personal decision of individuals.

If such a law as I propose is regarded as establishing a new precedent—is it not a most desirable precedent?

Like all lawyers, like all Americans, I regret the necessity of this controversy. But the welfare of the United States, and indeed of the Constitution itself, is what we all must think about first. Our difficulty with the Court today rises not from the Court as an institution but from human beings within it. But we cannot yield our constitutional destiny to the personal judgment of a few men who, being fearful of the future, would deny us the necessary means of dealing with the present.

This plan of mine is no attack on the Court; it seeks to restore the Court to its rightful and historic place in our system of Constitutional Government and to have it resume its high task of building anew on the Constitution "a system of living law."

B. THE POLITICS OF CONSTITUTIONAL INTERPRETATION

Constitutional interpretation and law, Justice Felix Frankfurter observed, "is not at all a science, but applied politics."[1] The Constitution, of course, is a political document and as a written document is not self-interpreting; its interpretation is political. *How* the Constitution should be interpreted is thus as controversial as the ongoing debate over *who* should interpret it.

For much of the nineteenth century, theories of constitutional interpretation were generally not debated.[2] The Court's interpretation of the Constitution, of course, remained politically controversial. Yet, the great debates between Jeffersonian-Republicans and Federalists centered on disagreements over fundamental principles of constitutional politics (the power and structure of government and guarantees for civil rights and liberties), rather than competing interpretative theories. Their struggle was over rival political philosophies and interpretations of the political system created by the Constitution. That struggle continues except that contemporary debates, within the Court and the legal community, tend to be more complex and linked to rival theories of constitutional interpretation that aim to justify or criticize the Court's exercise of judicial review.

In 1833, for example, Justice Joseph Story in his influential *Commentaries on the Constitution of the United States* saw no need to offer a theory of constitutional interpretation, explaining that,

[t]he reader must not expect to find in these pages any novel views and novel constructions of the Constitution. I have not the ambition to be the author of any new plan of interpreting the theory of the Constitution, or of enlarging or narrowing its powers by ingenious subtleties and learned doubts. . . . Upon subjects of government, it has always appeared to me, that metaphysical refinements are out of place. A constitution of government is addressed to the common sense of the people, and never was designed for trials of logical skill or visionary speculation.[3]

Story assumed that "The first and fundamental rule in the interpretation of all instruments is, to construe them according to the sense of the terms and the intention of the parties."[4] This "plain meaning rule" was set forth by Chief Justice John Marshall in *Sturges v. Crowninshield*, 17 U.S. 122 (1819):

[A]lthough the spirit of an instrument, especially of a constitution, is to be respected not less than its letter, yet the spirit is to be collected chiefly from its words. . . . [I]f, in any case, the plain meaning of a provision, not contradicted by any other provision in the same instrument, is to be disregarded, because we believe the framers of that instrument could not intend what they say, it must be one in which the absurdity and injustice of applying the provision to the case, would be so monstrous that all mankind would, without hesitation, unite in rejecting the application.

While the plain meaning of the Constitution for Story and Marshall was derived from a commonsense, rather than a literal, reading of the Constitution, Jeffersonian-Republicans nevertheless charged them with distorting the plain meaning of the document to advance their nationalistic political vision.

One reason political struggles in the nineteenth century did not invite debates over competing theories of constitutional interpretation is that Federalists and Jeffersonian-Republicans largely professed acceptance of the English declaratory theory of law. This theory, or philosophy, of legal positivism holds that judges have no discretion, make no law, but simply discover and "declare" the law.[5] According to one of the most widely read English jurists, Sir William Blackstone, in his *Commentaries on the Laws of England* (1765–1768), judges were merely the "depositories of the laws; the living oracles" of law. Hamilton and Marshall considered themselves Blacktonians; judges, Hamilton wrote in *The Federalist*, No. 78, "may truly be said to have neither FORCE nor WILL, but merely judgment."

By the late nineteenth century, the Blackstonian theory of law was under sharp attack. Oliver Wendell Holmes (1841–1935) was one of the first to debunk the idea that law is "a brooding omnipresence in the sky."[6] In his words, "The life of the law has not been logic; it has been experience. The felt necessities of the time, the prevalent moral and political theories, intuitions of public policy, avowed or unconscious, even the prejudices which judges share with their fellow-men, have had a good deal more to do than the syllogism in determining the rules by which men should be governed."[7] Holmes took it for granted that judges make law and pointed toward the empirical study of law: "The prophecies of what the courts will do in fact, and nothing more pretentious, are what I mean by the law."[8] Nor was Holmes alone in the revolt against legal formalism and the "mechanical jurisprudence" associated with the declaratory theory of judicial decision making.[9] Roscoe Pound (1870–1964), the founder of "sociological jurisprudence" and dean of Harvard Law School, encouraged the use of sociology and the study of law in relation to changing social forces. Unlike Holmes, though, Pound also encouraged judges to creatively mold law to the needs of society; judges should become "social engineers."[10]

One immediate consequence of this revolt against legal formalism was the innovation in legal argumentation that became known as "the Brandeis brief," after its author, a progressive legal reformer and later justice, Louis D. Brandeis. In 1908, in support of Oregon's law limiting working hours for women, Brandeis filed a brief in *Muller v. Oregon,* 208 U.S. 412 (1908), which included only two pages of legal argumentation, followed by ninety-seven pages of statistics and other social science data documenting the health risks for women working long hours. Drawing on social science in legal argumentation was necessary, claimed Brandeis, if law was to keep "pace with the rapid development of our political, economic, and social ideals."[11]

In the 1920s and 1930s a diverse group of law professors, political scientists, economists and sociologists, emerged calling themselves "American legal realists."[12] They further questioned the determinancy of formal legal rules and the facts of cases for judicial decision making, thereby underscoring that judges interpret (and manipulate) both legal rules and the facts when deciding cases.[13] Karl Llewellyn, one of the most influential legal realists, brought these insights to bear on constitutional interpretation when calling for a "jurisprudence of a living Constitution":

A "written constitution" is a system of unwritten practices in which the Document in question, by virtue of men's attitudes, has *a little influence. Where it makes no important difference which way the decision goes,* the Text—in the absence of countervailing practice—is an excellent traffic light. . . . The view advanced here *sounds* unorthodox. It sounds unorthodox only because it puts into words the *tacit* doing of the Court, and draws from that doing conclusions not to be avoided by a candid child. . . . Whatever the Court has *said,* it has repeatedly turned to established governmental practice in search of norms. What the Court has *said*, it has shaped the living Constitution to the needs of the day as it felt them. The whole expansion of the due process clause has been an enforcement of the majority's ideal of government-as-it-should-be, running free of the language of the Document.[14]

The Supreme Court was not immune from this change in legal thinking. On the bench sat Holmes (1902–1932), Brandeis (1916–1939), Benjamin Cardozo (1932–1938),[15] and Felix Frankfurter (1939–1962), among other legal progressives. More-over, even judicial conservatives on the Court no longer denied that the process of interpreting the Constitution involves making law. As Chief Justice Harlan F. Stone, a political and judicial conservative, reflected in a letter to Edward Corwin, "I always thought the real villain in the play was Blackstone, who gave to both lawyers and judges artificial notions of the law which, when applied to constitutional interpretation made the Consti-tutional a mechanical and inadequate instrument of govern-ment."[16] Justice Frankfurter, a former liberal professor at Harvard Law School who became an advocate of judicial self-restraint on the bench, elaborated his view in a letter to Justice Hugo Black:

I think one of the evil features, a very evil one, about all this assumption that judges only find the law and don't make it, often becomes the evil of a lack of candor. By covering up the law-making function of judges, we miseducate the people and fail to bring out into the open the real responsibility of judges for what they do. . . .

That phrase "judicial legislation" has become ever since a staple of a term of condemnation. I, too, am opposed to judicial legislation in its invidious sense; but I deem equally mischievous—because founded on an untruth and an impossible aim—the notion that judges merely an-nounce the law which they find and do not themselves inevitably have a share in the law-making. Here, as elsewhere, the difficulty comes from arguing in terms of absolutes when the matter at hand is con-ditioned by circumstances, is contingent upon the everlasting prob-lem of how far is too far and how much is too much. Judges as you well know, cannot escape the responsibility of filling in gaps which the finitude of even the most imaginative legislation renders inevi-table. . . .

So the problem is not whether judges make the law, but when and how and how much. Holmes put it in his highbrow way, that "they can do so only interstitially; they are confined from molar to molecular motions." I used to say to my students that legislatures make law whole-sale, judges retail.[17]

Once constitutional interpretation was candidly conceded to be a lawmaking process, the Court and its commentators squarely faced what has been called the Madisonian dilemma and "the countermajoritarian difficulty" for judicial review. As former judge and unsuccessful 1987 Supreme Court nominee Robert Bork explains,

The United States was founded as what we now call a Madisonian system, one which allows majorities to rule in wide areas of life simply because they are majorities, but which also holds that individuals have some freedoms that must be exempt from majority control. The dilemma is that neither the majority nor the minority can be trusted to define the proper spheres of democratic authority and individual liberty. The first would court tyranny by the majority; the second tyranny by the minority.[18]

When overturning legislation, the Court exercises a countermajoritarian power and substitutes its interpretation of the Constitution for that of elected representatives. Theories or rationalizations of the Court's interpretation of the Constitution thus appear necessary to justify the Court's countermajoritarian role in American politics, especially in the last fifty years as the Court increasingly overturned legislation in defense of civil rights and liberties.

In addition, in the aftermath of the American legal realist movement, legal scholarship became more pluralistic and interdisciplinary. Again quoting Judge Bork:

The fact is that the law has little intellectual or structural resistence to outside influences, influences that should properly remain outside. The striking, and peculiar, fact . . . is that the law possesses very little theory about itself. . . . This theoretical emptiness at its center makes law, particularly constitutional law, unstable, a ship with a great deal of sail but a very shallow keel, vulnerable to the winds of intellectual or moral fashion, which it then validates as the commands of our most basic compact.[19]

Since World War II, legal scholars have turned not only toward moral and political philosophy as a guide for constitutional interpretation and the Court's exercise of judicial review, they have also called for the development of a "political jurisprudence," combining normative theory with empirical studies;[20] an economic approach to law, which would make rights turn on cost-risk-benefit analysis;[21] and drawn on theories of literary criticism.[22] Still others in the Critical Legal Studies movement attack theories of liberal legalism in an effort to deconstruct legal reasoning and law to show its drawbacks for minorities, women, and the poor.[23]

The rest of this section surveys and illustrates various theories of constitutional interpretation in terms of two broad approaches that have come to be known as *interpretivism* and *noninterpretivism*. Broadly speaking, interpretivists hold that constitutional interpretation should be limited solely to the text and historical context of particular provisions of the Constitution and Bill of Rights. By contrast, noninterpretivists maintain that constitutional interpretation frequently requires going beyond the text and historical context of specific provisions to articulate and apply broader principles of constitutional politics. Neither approach is inextricably linked to either a liberal or a conservative political philosophy; for example, a predominately conservative Court in the late nineteenth century invented and wrote into constitutional law a "liberty of contract" to strike down progressive economic legislation (see Vol. 2, Ch. 3), while in the twentieth century a more liberal Court proclaimed and enforced a "right of privacy" to overturn legislation restricting the use of contraceptives and the availability of abortions (see Vol. 2, Ch. 11).

NOTES

1. Felix Frankfurter, in *Law and Politics,* ed. E. Prichard, Jr., and Archibald Macleish (New York: Harcourt, Brace, 1939), 6.

2. See Robert H. Bork, "Styles in Constitutional Theory," 1984 *Supreme Court Historical Society Yearbook* 53 (1985).

3. Joseph Story, *Commentaries on the Constitution of the United States* (Durham, NC: Carolina Academic Press, 1987), vi, reprint of 1833 ed.

4. Ibid., 135.

5. See, generally, Lord Lloyd, *Lloyd's Introduction to Jurisprudence,* 5th ed. (London: Stevens & Sons, 1985); H. L. A. Hart, *Essays in Jurisprudence and Philosophy* (Oxford, UK: Claredon Press, 1983), Chs. 1–5, 13; William Nelson, *Americanization of the Common Law* (Cambridge: Harvard University Press, 1975); and Morton Horwitz, *The Transformation of American Law, 1780–1860* (Cambridge: Harvard University Press, 1977).

6. *Southern Pacific Co. v. Jensen,* 244 U.S. 205 (1916).

7. Oliver W. Holmes, *The Common Law* (Boston: Little, Brown, 1881), 1.

8. Oliver W. Holmes, "The Path of Law," 10 *Harvard Law Review* 39 (1897).

9. See, generally, Morton White, *Social Thought in America: The Revolt against Formalism* (New York: Viking Press, 1949); and Benjamin Twiss, *Lawyers and the Constitution* (Princeton, NJ: Princeton University Press, 1942).

10. See Roscoe Pound, *An Introduction to the Philosophy of Law* (New Haven, CT: Yale University Press, 1922).

11. Louis Brandeis, "The Living Law," 10 *Illinois Law Review* 461 (1916).

12. See Wilfred Rumble, *American Legal Realism* (Ithica, NY: Cornell University Press, 1968).

13. See Jerome Frank, *Law and the Modern Mind* (New York: Coward-McCann, 1930), and *Courts on Trial* (Princeton, NJ: Princeton University Press, 1949).

14. Karl Llewellyn, "The Constitution As an Institution," 34 *Columbia Law Review* 39–40 (1934).

15. See Benjamin Cardozo's highly acclaimed *The Nature of the Judicial Process* (New York: Yale University Press, 1921).

16. Letter to E. Corwin, November 5, 1942, in Harlan F. Stone Papers, Box 10, Library of Congress, Washington, DC

17. Letter to Justice Black, December 15, 1939, in Stone Papers, Box 13.

18. Bork, "Styles in Constitutional Theory," 53.

19. Robert H. Bork, "Tradition and Morality in Constitutional Law," in *Views from the Bench: The Judiciary and Constitutional Politics*, ed. Mark Cannon and David M. O'Brien (Chatham, NJ: Chatham House, 1985), 166.

20. See Martin Shapiro, "Political Jurisprudence," 52 *Kentucky Law Review* 294 (1964); Harry Stumpf, Martin Shapiro, David Danelski, Austin Sarat, and David O'Brien, "Whither Political Jurisprudence?: A Symposium," 36 *Western Political Quarterly* 533 (1984); and Rogers Smith, "Political Jurisprudence, The 'New Institutionalism,' and the Future of Public Law," 82 *American Political Science Review* 89 (1988).

21. See, for example, Richard Posner, *Economic Analysis of Law*, 2d ed. (Boston: Little, Brown, 1977).

22. See William Bishin and Christopher Stone, *Law, Language and Ethics* (Mineola, NY: Foundation Press, 1972); John Brigham, *Constitutional Language* (Westport, CT: Greenwood Press, 1978); Leif Carter, *Contemporary Constitutional Lawmaking* (New York: Pergamon, 1985); James White, *The Legal Imagination* (Chicago: University of Chicago Press, 1973); James White, *When Words Lose Their Meaning* (Chicago: Chicago University Press, 1984); Richard Posner, *Law and Literature: A Misunderstood Relation* (Cambridge: Harvard University Press, 1988); and James White, *Justice as Translation* (Chicago: University of Chicago Press, 1990).

23. See David Kairys, ed., *The Politics of Law* (New York: Pantheon, 1982); and Editors of the Harvard Law Review, *Essays on Critical Legal Studies* (Cambridge: Harvard Law Review Association, 1986).

(1) The Text and Historical Context

The Supreme Court has been criticized by presidents from Thomas Jefferson to Ronald Reagan and George Bush for departing from a "strict" or "literal" interpretation of the Constitution. During the 1968 presidential election campaign, for instance, Republican nominee Richard Nixon attacked the "liberal jurisprudence" of the Warren Court (1953–1969) and promised to appoint only strict constructionists to the bench. *Strict constructionists* hold that constitutional interpretation should be confined to the "four corners" of the document, the literal language of the text of the Constitution.

Within the Court, Chief Justice Roger Taney expressed a strong version of strict constructionism in *Dred Scott v. Sandford,* 60 U.S. 393 (1857) (see Vol. 2, Ch. 12), when holding that blacks were not citizens of the United States within the meaning of "citizens" in Article III:

No one, we presume, supposes that any change in public opinion or feeling, in relation to this unfortunate race [of blacks], in the civilized nations of Europe or in this country, should induce the court to give to the words of the Constitution a more liberal construction in their favor than they were intended to bear when the instrument was framed and adopted. . . .

It [the Constitution] speaks not only in the same words, but with the same meaning and intent with which it spoke when it came from the hands of its framers, and was voted on and adopted by the people of the United States. Any other rule of construction would abrogate the judicial character of this Court and make it the mere reflex of the popular opinion or passion of the day.

This version of strict constructionism unrealistically (or disingenuously) denies the basic choices involved in constitutional interpretation. For example, much turns on whether the Court analyzes church-state controversies from the perspective of the First Amendment's free exercise clause or its establishment clause (see Vol. 2, Ch. 6). When applying the Fourth Amendment's guarantee against "unreasonable searches and seizures," the Warren Court chose to enforce strictly the requirements specified in that amendment's warrants and probable cause clauses. By contrast, the Burger Court (1969–1986), and the Rehnquist Court (1986–), tended to give less force to those requirements by relying instead on the justices' reading of what is "reasonable" under the amendment's reasonableness clause. Whether the Fourth Amendment is enforced primarily in terms of its reasonableness clause or its warrants and probable cause clauses represents a basic constitutional choice with important consequences for individual rights and law enforcement interests (see Vol. 2, Ch. 7).

Justice Hugo Black claimed to be an "absolutist," a "literalist." In his words:

My view is, without deviation, without exception, without any if's, but's, or whereas, that freedom of speech means that government shall not do anything to people, or, in the words of the Magna Carta, move against people, either for the views they have or the views they express or the words they speak or write. Some people would have you believe that this is a very radical position, and maybe it is. But all I am doing is following what to me is the clear wording of the First Amendment that "Congress shall make no law . . . abridging the freedom of speech or of the press."[1]

However, Justice Black acknowledged that the Constitution presents some interpretive problems and constitutional choices. In the controversy over the Court's application of the Bill of Rights to the states under the Fourteenth Amendment, for instance, Black became convinced that those guarantees were included in the amendment's privileges or immunities clause, whereas other justices contended that they were included in the Fourteenth Amendment's due process clause (see Vol. 2, Ch. 4).

Justice Black's absolutism was in response to the Court's *balancing* of First Amendment freedoms against governmental interests in national security in cases like *Dennis v. United States,* 341 U.S. 494 (1951) (see Vol. 2, Ch. 5), under the guise of the "clear and present danger" test. He opposed the Court's invention and use of such tests and metaphors. Still, much of constitutional law consists in metaphors created by the Court when explaining and applying constitutional provisions; consider the debates over executive privilege (see Vol. 1, Ch. 4), states' sovereignty (see Vol. 1, Ch. 4), the liberty of contract (see Vol. 2, Ch. 3), the high wall of separation between church and state (see Vol. 2, Ch. 6), or the controversy over whether the Constitution is colorblind (see Vol. 2, Ch. 12).

Interpretivism is usually only the beginning, not the end, of constitutional interpretation. The most frequently contested guarantees of the Constitution are neither unambiguous nor amenable to a literal or strict interpretation. What is the literal meaning of the reasonableness clause of the Fourth Amendment or of the due process and equal protection clauses of the Fourteenth Amendment? Nor do interpretivists, like Justice Black, deny First Amendment protection for posters and songs on the ground that they are not strictly speaking "speech"; although Black drew a line at extending protection to speech-plus-conduct and "symbolic speech" (see Vol. 2, Ch. 5).

Crucial provisions in the Constitution have what philosophers call an "open texture."[2] They are framed in general terms that are nonexhaustive of all future applications and have an essential incompleteness in dictating unforeseeable applications. The commerce clause in Article I, for example, gives Congress the power to regulate interstate commerce but fails to define *interstate commerce.* No one today, though, contends that interstate commerce should include only the methods of transportation available in 1787 or exclude modes of commerce, such as telecommunications, that were unforeseen by the Constitutional Convention.

These are only some of the problems with strict constructionism, as federal court of appeals Judge Richard Posner notes in an essay titled, "What Am I? A Potted Plant? The Case against

Strict Constructionism." Moreover, Posner underscores that nothing in the Constitution commands the Court to construe either "strictly" or "broadly" the document:

Even the decision to read the Constitution narrowly, and thereby "restrain" judicial interpretation, is not a decision that can be read directly from the text. The Constitution does not say, "Read me broadly," "Read me narrowly." That decision must be made a matter of political theory, and will depend on such things as one's view of the springs of judicial legitimacy and of the relative competence of courts and legislatures in dealing with particular types of issues.[3]

Strict constructionism is incomplete as a theory of interpretation and inadequately deals with the fact that the Constitution was framed in generalities in order to express general principles. Because this is so, interpretivists often turn to the historical context of the Constitution. Consider, for example, the 1985 call for a *jurisprudence of original intention* by Ronald Reagan's attorney general, Edwin Meese III:

As the "faithful guardians of the Constitution," the judges were expected to resist any political effort to depart from the literal provisions of the Constitution. The test of the document and the original intention of those who framed it would be the judicial standard in giving effect to the Constitution. . . . [But] it seems fair to conclude that far too many of the court's opinions are, on the whole, more policy choices than articulations of constitutional principle. The voting blocs, the arguments, all reveal a greater allegiance to what the court thinks constitutes sound public policy than a deference to what the Constitution—its text and intention—demand.[4]

Meese was not the first to contend that the text and the Framers' intent should solely guide constitutional interpretation.[5] Nonetheless, he sparked considerable debate and provoked Justice William J. Brennan to respond in a speech, observing,

In its most doctrinaire incarnation, this view demands that Justices discern exactly what the Framers thought about the question under consideration and simply follow that intention in resolving the case before them. It is a view that feigns self-effacing deference to the specific judgments of those who forged our original social compact. But in truth it is little more than arrogance cloaked as humility. It is arrogant to pretend that from our vantage we can gauge accurately the intent of the Framers on application of principle to specific, contemporary questions. All too often, sources of potential enlightenment such as records of the ratification debates provide sparse or ambiguous evidence of the original intention. Typically, all that can be gleaned is that the Framers themselves did not agree about the application or meaning of particular constitutional provisions, and hid their differences in cloaks of generality. Indeed, it is far from clear whose intention is relevant— that of the drafters, the congressional disputants, or the ratifiers in the states?—or even whether the idea of an original intention is a coherent way of thinking about a jointly drafted document drawing its authority from a general assent of the states. And apart from the problematic nature of the sources, our distance of two centuries cannot but work as a prism refracting all we perceive. . . .

We current Justices read the Constitution in the only way that we can: as Twentieth Century Americans. We look to the history of the time of framing and to the intervening history of interpretation. But the ultimate question must be, what do the words of the text mean in our time. For the genius of the Constitution rests not in any static meaning it might have had in a world that is dead and gone, but in the adaptability of its great principles to cope with current problems and current needs. What the Constitution's fundamentals meant to the wisdom of other times cannot be their measure to the vision of our time. Similarly, what those fundamentals mean for us, our descendants will learn, cannot be the measure to the vision of their time.[6]

As Justice Brennan suggests, there are methodological difficulties with a "jurisprudence of original intention." For one thing, determining "intent" is a subjective enterprise; it proposes to discover what the Framers had in mind when drafting and ratifying the Constitution. But as already noted, the Framers often disagreed and were forced to compromise on the language of the Constitution. At best, this approach considers the intentions of the drafters and ratifiers of the Constitution. And, who are "the Framers"? Should the views of only the thirty-nine signers of the document be considered, or should those of the other sixteen delegates who left before the Constitutional Convention concluded or refused to sign the document be considered as well? There are also compelling reasons for including the views of delegates to the thirteen state ratifying conventions, for as a result of those conventions the Bill of Rights was immediately added to the Constitution (see Vol. 2, Ch. 4).

Problems with discovering the intentions of the Framers also arise because the proceedings of the Constitutional Convention were conducted in secrecy and records of that convention and those in the states are far from complete and reliable. Moreover, it is debatable that the Framers intended their intentions to limit or guide constitutional interpretation.[7] Not until 1819 were speeches, resolutions, and votes of the delegates to the Constitutional Convention published. Almost another decade passed before Jonathan Elliot began publishing his collection of the debates in the state ratifying conventions. James Madison, who took notes of the debates at the Constitutional Convention and whose notes provide the only full record, refused to allow the publication of his notes until 1840, after his death. Madison insisted that the intent and literal reading of the text would be a "hard rule of construction." Instead, among the "obvious and just guides applicable to the Constn. of the U.S.," he listed:

1. the evils & defects for curing which the Constitution was called for & introduced. 2. The comments prevailing at the times it was adopted. 3. The early, deliberate & continued practice under the Constitution as preferable to constructions adopted on the spur of occasions, and subject to the vicissitudes of party or personal considerations.[8]

In addition, it bears noting that in its first fifty years the Supreme Court infrequently cited works such as *The Federalist Papers* in its opinions. Between 1790 and 1839, *The Federalist Papers* were cited in only fifteen decisions; by comparison, between 1950 and 1984 they were cited in 108 cases.[9]

Because of these difficulties, Chief Justice William Rehnquist, Justice Antonin Scalia, Judge Bork, and others associated with interpretivism and the "originalist" approach to constitutional interpretation more modestly contend that the Court should remain faithful to the "original understanding" or "original meaning"[10] of the governing principles or political philosophy of the Framers. They do not claim to be uncovering the Framers' subjective intentions but rather limiting the interpretation of constitutional provisions to those principles that the Framers might be fairly said to have embraced when drafting and ratifying the Constitution. Judge Bork explains that

[a] major problem with the idea of original intention is that the Framers articulated their principles in light of the world they knew, a world very different in important respects from that in which judges must decide cases today. . . . In order to protect the freedoms the Framers envisaged, the judge must discern a principle in the applications the Framers thought of and then apply that principle to circumstances they did not foresee.[11]

Nor do Chief Justice Rehnquist, Justice Scalia, and Judge Bork claim that originalism eliminates the burden of making basic constitutional choices. Rather, they argue that this approach is superior to other noninterpretativist approaches because it ostensibly sharply limits the exercise of judicial review and thus proves more responsive to criticisms of the Court's countermajoritarian power. In Justice Scalia words,

The principal theoretical defect of nonoriginalism, in my view, is its incompatibility with the very principle that legitimizes judicial review of constitutionality. Nothing in the text of the Constitution confers upon the courts the power to inquire into, rather than passively assume, the constitutionality of federal statutes. . . . Quite to the contrary, the legislature would seem a much more appropriate expositor of social values, and *its* determination that a statute is compatible with the Constitution should, as in England, prevail.[12]

Justice Scalia concedes that originalism poses methodological problems in practice, but nonetheless claims that it is "the lesser evil" in constitutional interpretation:

[It] *is* true that it is often exceedingly difficult to plumb the original understanding of an ancient text. Properly done, the task requires the consideration of an enormous mass of material—in the case of the Constitution and its Amendments, for example, to mention only one element, the records of the ratifying debates in all the states. Even beyond that, it requires an evaluation of the reliability of that material—many of the reports of the ratifying debates, for example, are thought to be quite unreliable. And further still, it requires immersing oneself in the political and intellectual atmosphere of the time—somehow placing out of mind knowledge that we have which an earlier age did not, and putting on beliefs, attitudes, philosophies, prejudices and loyalties that are not those of our day. It is, in short, a task sometimes better suited to the historian than the lawyer. . . .

I can be much more brief in describing what seems to me the second most serious objection to originalism. In its undiluted form, at least, it is medicine that seems too strong to swallow. Thus, almost every originalist would adulterate it with the doctrine of *stare decisis* [which holds that prior decisions should be respected]. . . . But *stare decisis* alone is not enough to prevent originalism from being what many would consider too bitter a pill. What if some state should enact a new law providing public lashing, or branding of the right hand, as punishment for certain criminal offenses? Even if it could be demonstrated unequivocally that these were not cruel and unusual measures [which are forbidden under the Eighth Amendment] in 1791, and even though no prior Supreme Court decision has specifically disapproved them, I doubt whether any federal judge—even among the many who consider themselves originalists—would sustain them against an eighth amendment challenge. It may well be . . . that this cannot legitimately be reconciled with originalist philosophy—that it represents the unrealistic view of the Constitution as a document intended to create a perfect society for all ages to come, whereas in fact it was a political compromise that did not pretend to create a perfect society even for its own age (as its toleration of slavery, which a majority of the founding generation recognized as an evil, well enough demonstrates). Even so, I am confident that public flogging and hand-branding would not be sustained by our courts, and any espousal of originalism as a practical theory of exegesis must somehow come to terms with that reality.[13]

Justice Scalia's discussion of public flogging and the Eighth Amendment is revealing not only in indicating that he is (in his words) "a faint-hearted originalist," because he would hold public flogging unconstitutional despite the fact that the Framers permitted that practice. The original understanding of constitutional guarantees, as Justice Anthony Kennedy observed during his 1987 Senate confirmation hearings, is a "necessary starting point," not an "adequate methodology" or "mechanical process" that "tells us how to decide a case."

What Scalia's discussion also points out is that crucial *concepts* in the Constitution give rise to competing *conceptions* and political philosophies.[14] Scalia would not limit the concept of cruel and unusual punishment in the Eighth Amendment to the Framers' conception of that punishment in 1791. Nor would Scalia go as far as Justice Brennan in interpreting the Eighth Amendment to bar capital punishment based on his "constitutional vision of human dignity" (see Vol. 2, Ch. 10). But, why not? What divides justices like Scalia and Brennan is their underlying judicial and political philosophies of the Constitution and the exercise of judicial review. So too, just as the Federalists and Anti-Federalists had competing political visions of the separation of powers and federalism, for example, even originalists such as Chief Justice Rehnquist and Justice Scalia may have rival conceptions and interpretations of the separation of powers; see, for instance, *Morrison v. Olson*, 108 S.Ct. 2597 (1988) (see Vol. 1, Ch. 4).

An underlying problem for interpretivists and noninterpretivists is how broadly or narrowly they conceive and express the concept or principle of a constitutional provision. Consider, for example, the constitutional choices presented in interpreting and applying the Fourth Amendment and the equal protection clause of the Fourteenth Amendment.

The Fourth Amendment guarantees the people a right "to be secure in their persons, houses, papers, and effects against unreasonable searches and seizures." That guarantee was interpreted in *Olmstead v. United States*, 277 U.S. 438 (1928) (see Vol. 2, Ch. 7), not to cover wiretaps because a majority of the Court limited the amendment's application to Framers' conception of "unreasonable searches and seizures," giving the lowest level of generality to the amendment's principle, so as to bar only actual physical trespass by police. By contrast, dissenting Justice Louis Brandeis argued for a broader conception of the amendment and a more general principle of privacy in the home that would have extended the guarantees of the amendment to cover electronic surveillance. Almost forty years later, in *Katz v. United States*, 389 U.S. 347 (1967) (see Vol. 2, Ch. 7), the Court finally embraced the broader principle of Fourth Amendment–protected privacy.

The Fourteenth Amendment guarantees "the equal protection of the laws." The principle of equality embodied there might be interpreted to bar only discrimination against blacks, because in the historical context of the post–Civil War period the Thirty-ninth Congress was indisputably primarily concerned with ensuring that states did not deny certain rights of newly freed blacks. However, the principle of equality has been given broader application and a higher level of generality so as to bar other kinds of racial discrimination against, for example, Hispanics and Asians. Even more broadly (as further discussed in Vol. 2, Ch. 12), the amendment has been construed to forbid forms of nonracial discrimination against women, children, and aliens. But how and on what basis may this broader application of the equal protection clause be defended and the Court's exercise of judicial review in this way justified?

In sum and in Judge Bork's words, "The question is always the level of generality the judge chooses when he states the idea or object of the Framers."[15] Interpretivists, no less than noninterpretivists, cannot evade making basic constitutional choices in their conceptions and formulations of the underlying principles of constitutional provisions.

NOTES

1. Hugo Black, *A Constitutional Faith* (New York: Knopf, 1968), 45.

2. See H. L. A. Hart, *The Concept of Law* (Oxford, UK: Clarendon Press, 1961), 124–132.

3. Richard Posner, "What Am I? A Potted Plant?" *The New Republic*, Sept. 28, 1987, 23.

4. Edwin Meese, "The Attorney General's View of the Supreme Court: Toward a Jurisprudence of Original Intention," in *Special Issue, Law and Public Affairs*, ed. Charles Wise and David O'Brien, 45 *Public Administration Review* 701 (1985).

5. See also Raoul Berger, *Government by Judiciary* (Cambridge: Harvard University Press, 1977); and Walter Berns, *Taking the Constitution Seriously* (New York: Simon & Schuster, 1987).

6. William J. Brennan, Jr., "The Constitution of the United States: Contemporary Ratification," Georgetown University, Washington, DC (Oct. 12, 1985).

7. See H. Jefferson Powell, "The Original Understanding of Original Intent," 98 *Harvard Law Review* 885 (1985); and James Hutson, "The Creation of the Constitution: The Integrity of the Documentary Record," 65 *Texas Law Review* 1 (1986).

8. Quoted in Robert Morgan, *James Madison on the Constitution and the Bill of Rights* (Westport, CT: Greenwood Press, 1988), 196–197.

9. See James Wilson, "The Most Sacred Text: The Supreme Court's Use of *The Federalist Papers*," 1985 *Brigham Young University Law Review* 65 (1985).

10. See Antonin Scalia, "Originalism: The Lesser Evil," 57 *Cincinnati Law Review* 849 (1989).

11. Robert Bork, "Foreword" to Gary McDowell, *The Constitution and Contemporary Constitutional Theory* (Cumberland, VA: Center for Judicial Studies, 1985), x.

12. Scalia, "Originalism," 854.

13. Scalia, "Originalism," 856–857.

14. On the distinction between concepts and conceptions, see Ronald Dworkin, *Taking Rights Seriously* (Cambridge: Harvard University Press, 1977), 135–137.

15. Bork, "Foreword," x.

SELECTED BIBLIOGRAPHY

Berger, Raoul. *Government by Judiciary: The Transformation of the Fourteenth Amendment.* Cambridge: Harvard University Press, 1977.

Berns, Walter. *Taking the Constitution Seriously.* New York: Simon & Schuster, 1987.

Bickel, Alexander. *The Morality of Consent.* New Haven, CT: Yale University Press, 1975.

Black, Hugo. *A Constitutional Faith.* New York: Knopf, 1968.

Bork, Robert. *The Tempting of America.* New York: Free Press, 1989.

Gabin, Sanford. *Judicial Review and the Reasonable Doubt Test.* Port Washington, NY: Kennikat Press, 1980.

Jacobson, Gary. *Pragmatism, Statesmanship, and the Supreme Court.* Ithaca, NY: Cornell University Press, 1977.

Levy, Leonard. *Original Intent and The Framers' Constitution.* New York: Macmillan, 1988.

Nagel, Robert. *Constitutional Cultures.* Berkeley: University of California Press, 1989.

Thayer, Bradley. *Thayer's Legal Essays.* Boston: Boston Book Company, 1908.

(2) In and Beyond the Text

Noninterpretivism differs from interpretivism in the sources and kinds of argumentation marshaled in support of giving broader scope or higher levels of generality to constitutional principles. Whereas interpretivists confine analysis to the text and historical context of a provision, noninterpretivists tend to formulate more broadly the underlying principle of a constitutional provision. Noninterpretivists may turn to history and social science, for example, or appeal to natural law, natural rights, and moral or political philosophy, or call on process-oriented theories of judicial review and arguments about the structure of the Constitution.

Historical, economic, technological, and political changes are obviously relevant to constitutional interpretation. Yet, when and how should the Court use *history*? The Sixth Amendment, for instance, guarantees criminal defendants the right to a jury trial but does not define *jury*. When confronted with the question of whether juries must consist of twelve members, in *Thompson v. Utah*, 170 U.S. 343 (1882), the Court simply ruled that the Sixth Amendment incorporated the traditional common-law practice of twelve-member juries because that practice was firmly rooted in English history and familiar to the Framers of the Bill of Rights. The Court may also take *judicial notice* of historical events without the benefit of their being adjudicated, such as the fact that there was an economic depression in the 1930s. Chief Justice Morrison Waite drew heavily on history as a guide when upholding under the commerce clause the power of Congress, over that of the states, to regulate interstate telegraph lines, in *Pensacola Telegraph Co. v. Western Union Telegraph, Co.,* 96 U.S. 1 (1877):

> The powers thus granted are not confined to the instrumentalities of commerce . . . known or in use when the Constitution was adopted, but they keep pace with the progress of the country, and adapt themselves to the new developments of time and circumstance. They extend from the horse with its rider to the stage-coach, from the sailing-vessel to the steamboat . . . and from the railroad to the telegraph, as these new agencies are successively brought into use to meet the demands of increasing population and wealth. . . . As they were intrusted to the general government for the good of the nation, it is not only the right, but the duty, of Congress to see to it that intercourse among the States and the transmission of intelligence are not obstructed or unnecessarily encumbered by State legislation.

Justice Holmes took an even more expansive view of the use of history in the famous case dealing with the national government's treaty-making power. In *Missouri v. Holland,* 252 U.S. 416 (1920) (see Vol. 1, Ch. 3). Note his observation that "[t]he case before us must be considered in light of our whole experience and not merely in that of what was said a hundred years ago."

The Court's reliance on history is not unproblematic, however.[1] Justices are not trained as historians and they may confront problems in evaluating different schools of history and the works of revisionist historians. More fundamentally, Chief Justice William Rehnquist, among others, cautions against turning to history because it encourages the notion that the "Constitution is a living document" and that the Court ought to keep the Constitution in "tune with the times." In Rehnquist's view, there are three serious flaws with the notion of a living Constitution:

> First, it misconceives the nature of the Constitution, which was designed to enable the popularly elected branches of government, not the judicial branch, to keep the country abreast of the times. Second, [it] ignores the Supreme Court's disasterous experiences when in the past it embraced contemporary, fashionable notions of what a living Constitution should contain. Third, however socially desirable the goals to be advanced, . . . advancing them through a free-wheeling, non-elected judiciary is quite unacceptable in a democratic society.[2]

Social science may prove a no less controversial source of support for the Court's decisions. In the landmark school desegregation ruling in *Brown v. Board of Education,* 347 U.S. 483 (1954) (see Vol. 2, Ch. 12), for example, the Court cited in footnote 11 several social science studies in support of overturning the racial doctrine of "separate but equal facilities." Among those studies was the Swedish economist and sociologist Gunner Myrdal's book *An American Dilemma* (1944), the premier work on race relations in America. The Court's mention of *An American Dilemma* intensified the antagonism of powerful southerners, such as the South Carolina governor and former Supreme Court justice James F. Byrnes and Mississippi senator James O. Eastland. They and others attacked the Court for citing the work of "foreign sociologists," bad social science research, and, most of all, for drawing on social science in the first place, instead of simply sticking to the text and historical context of the Constitution.

The Court's use of social science materials may raise questions about judicial competence and the legitimacy of basing decisions on social science evidence.[3] Consider *Williams v. Florida,* 399 U.S. 78 (1970) (see Vol. 2, Ch. 9), upholding juries composed of less than twelve members, despite history and the ruling in *Thompson v. Utah* that the Sixth Amendment jury consisted "as it was at common law, of twelve persons, neither more nor less." *Williams* proved controversial because the Court held on the basis of psychological and sociological studies of small-group behavior that juries of less than twelve members were "functionally equivalent" to traditional twelve-member juries.

Natural law and *natural rights,* or what Edward Corwin termed, the "higher law" background of the Constitution, is an older tradition and source of constitutional interpretation.[4] The Framers took seriously natural law and natural rights in maintaining that individuals enjoy certain rights prior to the establishment of government and which may not be denied by government. Federalists, though, contended that the Constitution adequately safeguarded natural rights by creating a government of limited and specifically delegated powers. But the Anti-Federalists pushed for the addition of a bill of rights containing a statement of natural rights (see Vol. 2, Ch. 4).

Although the natural rights tradition runs throughout much of constitutional law, controversy has ensnarled appeals to natural law and rights ever since Justices Iredell and Chase debated, in *Calder v. Bull,* 3 Dall. 398, (1798), whether the Court has the power to strike down legislation based on principles of natural justice. Chief Justice John Marshall faced the problem of enforcing his own acceptance of natural rights against the claims of Spanish and Portuguese slave traders in *The Antelope Case,* 23 U.S. 66 (1825). Slaves had been seized by pirates, who were later captured by an American naval ship, and the slave traders and owners sued to recover their "property." Of slavery and the slave trade, Chief Justice Marshall observed "[t]hat it is contrary to the law of nature will scarcely be denied. That every man has a natural right to the fruits of his own labor, is generally admitted, and [that] no other person can rightfully deprive him of those fruits, and appropriate them against his will, seems to be the necessary result of this admission." But Marshall concluded that

[w]hatever might be the answer of a moralist to this question, a jurist must search for its legal solution, in those principles of action which are sanctioned by the usages, the national acts, and the general assent, of that portion of the world of which he considers himself as a part, and to whose law the appeal is made. If we resort to this standard as the test of international law, the question . . . is decided in favor of the legality of the [slave] trade.

Other members of the Court, though, have sided with Justice Chase's position in *Calder* that with respect to "certain vital principles . . . [a]n act of the Legislature (for I cannot call it a *law*) contrary to the *great first principles* of the social compact, cannot be considered a *rightful exercise* of legislative authority" and, therefore, must be overturned. Consider the debate over fundamental rights and the formulations and standards used by the Court when interpreting the Fourteenth Amendment's due process clause (see Vol. 2, Ch. 4). In *Hurtado v. California*, 110 U.S. 516 (1884) (see Vol. 2, Ch. 4), for example, Justice Stanley Matthews speaks of the "wellsprings of justice." In *Adamson v. California*, 332 U.S. 46 (1947) (see Vol. 2, Ch. 4), and *Rochin v. California*, 342 U.S. 165 (1952) (see Vol. 2, Ch. 4), Justice Frankfurter invokes "the shocks the conscience test" and "fundamental fairness standard" for determining what process is due under the due process clause.

The principal criticism of "natural law formulations" is levied in opinions by Justice Hugo Black, particularly in his dissent from the Court's recognition of a right of privacy in *Griswold v. Connecticut*, 381 U.S. 481 (1965) (see Vol. 2, Ch. 4), where he observes that

[o]ne of the most effective ways of diluting or expanding a constitutionally guaranteed right is to substitute for the crucial word or words of a constitutional guarantee another word for the word or words, more or less flexible and more or less restricted in meaning. . . . Use of any such broad, unbounded judicial authority would make this Court's members a day-to-day constitutional convention.

This criticism of the Court for imposing its own substantive value choices applies as well to those arguing that the Court should draw on *moral* and *political philosophy*. Yet Professor Ronald Dworkin and other contemporary legal scholars call for "a fusion of constitutional law and moral theory" or political philosophy.[5] Contemporary legal scholarship is indeed marked by a proliferation of expressly normative theories that would rationalize and guide constitutional interpretation according to "abstract beliefs about morality and justice,"[6] the "voice of reason,"[7] "a moral patrimony" implicit in "our common heritage,"[8] "the circumstances and values of the present generation,"[9] "conventional morality,"[10] "public morality,"[11] "constitutional morality,"[12] "fundamental values,"[13] and the "essential principles of justice,"[14] or "the idea of progress."[15] But this movement toward more specialized and abstract theories of constitutional interpretation raises the ante for reaching consensus within the Supreme Court and the country.[16]

Interpretivists counter that the turn to moral and political philosophy only exacerbates the problems of constitutional interpretation and the countermajoritarian difficulty of judicial review. As Stanford University Law School professor John Hart Ely cleverly put it, "The Constitution may follow the flag, but is it really supposed to keep up with the *New York Review of Books?*"[17] Judge Bork raises other concerns:

> The abstract, universalistic style of legal thought has a number of dangers. For one thing, it teaches disrespect for the actual institutions of the American polity. These institutions are designed to achieve compromise, to slow change, to dilute absolutisms. They embody wholesome inconsistencies. They are designed, in short, to do things that abstract generalizations about the just society tend to bring into contempt.[18]

Interpreting the Constitution, nevertheless, presupposes a judicial and political philosophy and poses inescapable questions of substantive value choices. As Justice Brennan explains,

> Faith in democracy is one thing, blind faith quite another. Those who drafted our Constitution understood the difference. One cannot read the text without admitting that it embodies substantive choices; it places certain values beyond the power of any legislature. . . .

> To remain faithful to the content of the Constitution, therefore, an approach to interpreting the text must account for the existence of these substantive value choices, and must accept the ambiguity inherent in the effort to apply them to modern circumstances. The Framers discerned fundamental principles through struggles against particular malefactions of the Crown; the struggle shapes the particular contours of the articulated principles. But our acceptance of the fundamental principles has not and should not bind us to those precise, at times anachronistic, contours. Successive generations of Americans have continued to respect these fundamental choices and adopt them as their

own guide to evaluating quite different historical practices. Each generation has the choice to overrule or add to the fundamental principles enunciated by the Framers; the Constitution can be amended or it can be ignored. Yet with respect to its fundamental principles, the text has suffered neither fate. . . .

The Constitution on its face is, in large measure, a structuring text, a blueprint for government. And when the text is not prescribing the form of the government it is limiting the powers of that government. The original document, before addition of any of the amendments, does not speak primarily of the rights of man, but of the abilities and disabilities of government. When one reflects upon the text's preoccupation with the scope of government as well as its shape, however, one comes to understand that what this text is about is the relationship of the individual and the state. The text marks the metes and bounds of official authority and individual autonomy. When one studies the boundary that the text marks out, one gets a sense of the vision of the individual embodied in the Constitution.

As augmented by the Bill of Rights and the Civil War Amendments, this text is a sparking vision of the supremacy of the human dignity of every individual. This vision is reflected in the very choice of democratic self-governance: the supreme value of a democracy is the presumed worth of each individual. . . . It is a vision that has guided us as a people throughout our history, although the precise rules by which we have protected fundamental human dignity have been transformed over time in response to both transformations of social conditions and evolution of our concepts of human dignity.[19]

Neither do alternative theories and modes of constitutional interpretation elude a dependence on political philosophy. Interpreting the Constitution frequently requires, as Professor Charles L. Black, Jr., argues, "inference from the structure and relationships created by the constitution in all its parts or in some principal part."[20] Chief Justice Marshall's watershed opinion in *McCulloch v. Maryland,* 4 Wheat. (17 U.S.) 316 (1819) (see Vol. 1, Ch. 6), illustrates the role of *structural analysis* of the Constitution. There, Marshall upheld the constitutionality of the national bank as a necessary and proper exercise of Congress's powers based on inferences from the structure of federalism, instead of relying on the necessary and proper clause per se. Still, Jeffersonian-Republicans disagreed with the infusion of Marshall's nationalistic political philosophy into constitutional law. Moreover, differences rooted in rival political philosophies over the structure of federalism persist in the Court and the country (see Vol. 1, Ch. 6).

Nor do attempts to reconcile the exercise of the Court's power with majoritarian democracy in terms of what has become known as *process-oriented theory of judicial review* fare much better.[21] Justice Harlan Stone initially suggested that the Court's role ought to be limited to policing the political process and ensuring that it does not discriminate against "discrete insular minorities," in footnote 4 of *United States v. Carolene Products Co.*, 304 U.S. 144 (1938) (see Vol. 2, Ch. 12). In a book titled *Democracy and Distrust*, Professor Ely further developed the theory that the Court's role should be limited to policing the democratic process and facilitating the representation of minorities in the electoral process: "[T]he general theory is one that bounds judicial review under the Constitution's open-ended provisions by insisting that it can appropriately concern itself only with questions of participation, and not with the substantive merits of the political choice under attack."[22] In this way, Ely aims to justify the Court's supervision of the electoral process (see Vol. 1, Ch. 8) and reconcile judicial review with democratic theory. But Ely fails to provide a general theory in saying nothing about how the Court should handle cases involving disputes over presidential power and federalism, for example.[23] Moreover, the process-oriented theory of judicial review has criticized for too sharply limiting the Court's role in protecting civil liberties and civil rights. As Justice Robert Jackson in *West Virginia State Board of Education v. Barnette*, 319 U.S. 624 (1943) (see Vol. 2, Ch. 6), observes, "The very purpose of a Bill of Rights was to withdraw certain subjects from the vicissitudes of political controversy, to place them beyond the reach of majorities and officials and to establish them as legal principles to be applied by the courts" (see also Vol. 2, Ch. 4).

Ultimately, what divides the justices, and sometimes the Court and the country, has less to do with interpretivism and noninterpretivism than fundamentally rival political philosophies and views of the role of the Court in American politics. It is not just that constitutional interpretation draws on the text, structure, history, doctrines, practices, and moral and political philosophy that is important, but how these sources and modes of analysis are employed. Admittedly, as Justice Scalia has noted, there may be a "sense of dissatisfaction" with finding that we "do not yet have an agreed-upon theory" of constitutional interpretation. "But it should come as no surprise."[24] Indeed, in constitutional politics there are no simple solutions but instead an invitation for reflection and enduring political struggles.

NOTES

1. See Willard Hurst, "The Role of History," in *Supreme Court and Supreme Law*, ed. Edmond Cahn, *(New York: Clarion Book, 1971);* and Charles Miller, *The Supreme Court and the Uses of History* (Cambridge: Harvard University Press, 1969).

2. William Rehnquist, "The Notion of a Living Constitution," in

Views from the Bench: The Judiciary and Constitutional Politics, ed. Mark Cannon and David O'Brien (Chatham, NJ: Chatham House, 1985), 191.

3. See Paul Rosen, *The Supreme Court and Social Science* (Urbana: University of Illinois Press, 1972); Wallace Loh, ed., *Social Research in the Judicial Process* (New York: Russell Sage Foundation, 1984); and David O'Brien, "The Seduction of the Judiciary: Social Science and the Courts," 64 *Judicature* 8 (1980).

4. See Edward S. Corwin, *The "Higher Law" Background of American Constitutional Law* (Ithaca, NY: Cornell University Press, 1955); Thomas Grey, "Do We Have an Unwritten Constitution," 27 *Stanford Law Review* 703 (1975); Robert Goldwin and William Schambra, eds., *How Does the Constitution Secure Rights?* (Washington, DC: American Enterprise Institute, 1985); Morton White, *The Philosophy of the American Revolution* (New York: Oxford University Press, 1978); and Symposium, "The Framers' Intent: An Exchange," 10 *University of Puget Sound Law Review* 343–369 (1987).

5. See Ronald Dworkin, *Taking Rights Seriously* (Cambridge: Harvard University Press, 1977), 149; Ronald Dworkin, *A Matter of Principle* (Harvard University Press, 1985); and Ronald Dworkin, *Law's Empire* (Cambridge: Harvard University Press, 1986).

6. See G. Edward White, "Reflections on the Role of the Supreme Court: The Contemporary Debate and the Lessons of History," 63 *Judicature* 162 (1979); and Philip Bobbit, *Constitutional Fate* (New York: Oxford University Press, 1982).

7. Henry Hart, "Foreword: The Time Chart of the Justices," 73 *Harvard Law Review* 84 (1959).

8. Charles Black, "Old and New Ways in Judicial Review," address given at Bowdoin College, 1957.

9. Terrance Sandalow, "Constitutional Interpretation," 79 *Michigan Law Review* 1033 (1981). See also Joseph Grano, "Judicial Review and a Written Constitution in a Democratic Society," 28 *Wayne Law Review* 1 (1981); and Paul Brest, "The Misconceived Quest for the Original Understanding," 60 *Boston University Law Review* 204 (1980).

10. Harry Wellington, "Common Law Rules and Constitutional Double Standards: Some Notes on Adjudication," 83 *Yale Law Journal* 221 (1973). See also Michael Perry, *The Constitution, the Courts, and Human Rights* (New Haven, CT: Yale University Press, 1982); and Michael Perry, *Morality, Politics & Law* (New York: Oxford University Press, 1988).

11. Owen Fiss, "Objectivity and Interpretation," 34 *Stanford Law Review* 739 (1982).

12. Dworkin, *Taking Rights Seriously,* 149.

13. Kenneth Karst, "The Freedom of Intimate Association," 89 *Yale Law Journal* 624 (1980); and Richard Richards, "Human Rights As the Unwritten Constitution: The Problem of Change and Stability in Constitutional Interpretation," 4 *University of Dayton Law Review* 295 (1979).

14. Michael Michelman, "In Pursuit of Constitutional Welfare Rights: One View of Rawl's Theory of Justice," 121 *University of Pennsylvania Law Review* 962 (1979).

15. Alexander Bickel, *The Supreme Court and the Idea of Progress* (New York: Harper & Row, 1970).

16. See David O'Brien, " 'The Imperial Judiciary:' Of Paper Tigers and Socio-Legal Indicators," 2 *Journal of Law & Politics* 1 (1985); and William Van Alstyne, "Interpreting *This* Constitution: The Unhelpful Contributions of Special Theories of Judicial Review," 35 *University of Florida Law Review* 209 (1983).

17. John Ely, *Democracy and Distrust* (Cambridge: Harvard University Press, 1980), 58.

18. Robert Bork, "Tradition and Morality in Constitutional Law," in *Views from the Bench*, ed. Cannon and O'Brien, 169.

19. William Brennan, Jr., "The Constitution of the United States: Contemporary Ratification," speech given at Georgetown University, Oct. 12, 1985.

20. Charles Black, Jr., *Structure and Relationship in Constitutional Law* (Baton Rouge: Louisiana University Press, 1969).

21. See Laurence Tribe, "The Puzzling Persistence of Process-Based Constitutional Theories," 89 *Yale Law Journal* 1063 (1980); and Mark Tushnet, "Darkness on the Edge of Town: The Contributions of John Hart Ely," 89 *Yale Law Journal* 1037 (1980).

22. Ely, *Democracy and Distrust*, 181.

23. See David O'Brien, "Judicial Review and Constitutional Politics: Theory and Practice," 48 *University of Chicago Law Review* 1052 (1981).

24. Antonin Scalia, "Originalism: The Lesser Evil," 57 *Cincinnati Law Review* 850 (1989), 865.

SELECTED BIBLIOGRAPHY

Barber, Sotirios. *On What the Constitution Means*. Baltimore, MD: Johns Hopkins University Press, 1984.

Bickel, Alexander. *The Supreme Court and the Idea of Progress*. New York: Harper & Row, 1970.

———. *The Least Dangerous Branch*. New York: Bobbs-Merrill, 1961.

Black, Charles, Jr. *Decision According to Law*. New York: W. W. Norton, 1981.

———. *Structure and Relationship in Constitutional Law*. Baton Rouge: Louisiana State University Press, 1969.

Bobbitt, Philip. *Constitutional Fate*. New York: Oxford University Press, 1982.

Carter, Leif. *Contemporary Constitutional Lawmaking*. New York. Pergamon, 1985.

Choper, Jesse. *Judicial Review and the National Political Process*. Chicago: University of Chicago Press, 1980.

Corwin, Edward. *The "Higher Law" Background of American Constitutional Law*. Ithaca, NY: Cornell University Press, 1955.

Dworkin, Ronald. *Taking Rights Seriously*. Cambridge: Harvard University Press, 1977.

———. *Law's Empire*. Cambridge: Harvard University Press, 1986.

Ely, John. *Democracy and Distrust.* Cambridge: Harvard University Press, 1980.

Harmon, M. Judd, ed., *Essays on the Constitution of the United States.* Port Washington, NY: Kennikat Press, 1978.

Kairys, David. *The Politics of Law.* New York: Pantheon Books, 1982.

Levinson, Sanford. *Constitutional Faith.* Princeton, NJ: Princeton University Press, 1988.

Loh, Wallace, ed., *Social Research in the Judicial Process.* New York: Russell Sage Foundation, 1984.

Lusky, Louis. *By What Right? A Commentary on the Supreme Court's Power to Revise the Constitution,* Charlottesville, VA: Michie, 1975.

Miller, Charles. *The Supreme Court and the Uses of History,* Cambridge: Harvard University Press, 1969.

Perry, Michael. *Morality, Politics & Law.* New York: Oxford University Press, 1988.

———. *The Constitution, the Courts, and Human Rights.* New Haven, CT: Yale University Press, 1982.

Posner, Richard. *The Problems of Jurisprudence.* Cambridge: Harvard University Press, 1990.

Rosen, Paul. *The Supreme Court and Social Science.* Urbana: University of Illinois Press, 1972.

Smith, Rogers. *Liberalism and American Constitutional Law.* Cambridge: Harvard University Press, 1985.

Tribe, Laurence. *Constitutional Choices.* Cambridge: Harvard University Press, 1985.

Tushnet, Mark. *Red, White, and Blue: A Critical Analysis of Constitutional Law.* Cambridge: Harvard University Press, 1988.

White, James. *Justice as Translation.* Chicago: University of Chicago Press, 1990.

———. *When Words Lose Their Meaning.* Chicago: University of Chicago Press, 1984.

2

LAW AND POLITICS IN THE SUPREME COURT: JURISDICTION AND DECISION-MAKING PROCESS

THE SUPREME COURT is the only federal court in the United States to have complete power to decide what to decide, that is, which cases to hear. This power enables the Court to set its own agenda as well as to manage its docket. Like other courts, the Supreme Court, however, must await issues brought by lawsuits; it does not initiate its own. Also, like other social institutions, it is affected by social change. One hundred and fifty years ago, the Court's docket did not include issues of personal privacy raised by electronic surveillance and computer data banks, for instance, or controversies over abortion and the patenting of organic life-forms. As technology develops and society changes, courts respond. Law evolves more or less quickly in response to social change. Another change occurring over the past several decades has been a substantial increase in the number of cases, the caseload, sent to the Court. Unable to hear them all, the Court assumed the power to pick which issues it will decide. The Court now functions like a roving commission in responding to social forces.

A. JURISDICTION AND JUSTICIABLE CONTROVERSIES

Jurisdiction is the authorized power of a court to hear a case and to exercise judicial review. The Court's jurisdiction derives from three sources: (1) Article III of the Constitution, which defines the Court's original jurisdiction; (2) congressional legislation, providing the basis for hearing appeals of lower courts' decisions, or appellate jurisdiction; and (3) the Court's own interpretation of 1 and 2 together with its own rules for accepting cases.

Article III of the Constitution provides that the judicial power extends to all federal questions, that is, "all Cases, in Law and Equity, arising under this Constitution, the Laws of the United States, and Treaties." The Court also has original jurisdiction over specific kinds of "cases or controversies": those affecting ambassadors and other public ministers and consuls, disputes to which the United States is a party, disputes between two or more states, disputes between a state and a citizen of another state, and disputes between a state (or its citizens) and foreign countries. The Court today has only about ten cases each term (the first Monday in October through June) coming on original jurisdiction. Most involve states suing each other over land and water rights, and they tend to be rather complex and carried over for several terms before they are finally decided.

Congress establishes (and may change) the appellate jurisdiction of the federal judiciary, including the Supreme Court. Most cases used to come as direct appeals, requiring obligatory review. But as the caseload increased, Congress expanded the Court's discretionary jurisdiction by replacing appeals with petitions for *certiorari* (a petition asking a court to inspect the proceedings and decision of a lower court), which the Court may in its discretion grant or deny. Prior to the Judiciary Act of 1925, which broadened the Court's discretionary jurisdiction, appeals amounted to 80 percent of the docket and petitions for *certiorari*, less than 20 percent. Today, well over 95 percent of the docket comes on *certiorari*.

Although most cases now come as *certiorari* (*cert.*) petitions, Congress provides that appellate courts may submit a writ of certification to the Court, requesting the justices to clarify or "make more certain" a point of federal law. The Court receives only a handful of such cases each term. Congress also gave the Court the power to issue certain extraordinary writs, or orders. In a few cases, the Court may issue writs of *mandamus* and prohibition, ordering lower courts or public officials to either do something or refrain from some action. In addition, the Court has the power to grant writs of *habeas corpus* ("produce the body"), enabling it to review cases by prisoners who claim that their constitutional rights have been violated and they are unlawfully imprisoned.

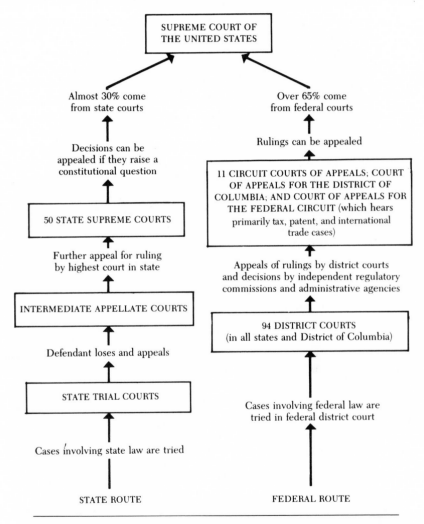

FIGURE 2.1

Avenues of appeal:
The two main routes to the Supreme Court.

Note: In addition, some cases come directly to the Supreme Court from trial courts when they involve reapportionment or civil rights disputes. Appeals from the Court of Military Appeals also go directly to the Supreme Court. A few cases come on "original jurisdiction" and involve disputes between state governments.

Congress also established the practice of giving the poor, or the indigent, the right to file without the payment of fees. When filing an appeal or petition for certiorari, indigents may file an affidavit requesting that they be allowed to proceed *in forma pauperis* ("in the manner of a pauper,") without the usual filing fees and forms. The Court sets both the rules governing filing fees and the form that appeals, cert. petitions, and other documents must take. Except for indigents, the Court requires $200 for filing any case and another $100 if a case is granted oral argument. Indigents are exempt as well from the Court's rules specifying particular colors and lengths of paper for various kinds of filings. All cert. petitions, for instance, must have a white color, whereas opposing briefs are light orange. Any document filed by the federal government has a gray cover. No petition or appeal may exceed thirty pages, and for those few cases granted oral argument, briefs on the merits of cases are limited to fifty pages.

The Constitution and Congress thus stipulate the kinds of cases and controversies the Court may consider. Yet, as Charles Evans Hughes, who later became chief justice (1930–1941), candidly remarked, "We are under the Constitution, but the Constitution is what the Judges say it is."[1] The Court has developed its own doctrines for denying a large number of case reviews and for setting its own agenda. Specifically, the Court considers whether it has jurisdiction over a "case or controversy," and then whether that dispute is justiciable, or capable of judicial resolution. Justices thus may, or may not, deny a case if it (1) lacks adverseness or (2) is brought by parties who lack "standing to sue," or poses issues that either (3) are not "ripe," (4) have become "moot," or (5) involve a "political question." What all this means is discussed below.

Adverseness and Advisory Opinions

The Court generally maintains that litigants, those involved in a lawsuit, must be real and adverse in seeking a decision that will resolve their dispute and not some hypothetical issue. The requirement of real and adverse parties means that the Court will not decide so-called friendly suits, (when the parties do not have adverse interests in the outcome of a case). Nor will the Court give "advisory opinions" on issues not raised in an actual lawsuit. The Jay Court denied two requests for advisory opinions: one in 1790 by Secretary of Treasury Alexander Hamilton on the national government's power to assume state Revolutionary War debts, and the other in 1793 by Secretary of State Thomas Jefferson for an interpretation of certain treaties and international law. Chief Justice John Jay held that it would be improper for the Court to judge such matters, because the president may call on cabinet heads for advice. The Court continues to maintain that it is inappropriate "to give opinions in the nature of advice concerning legislative action, a function never conferred upon it by the Constitution and against the exercise of which this court has steadily set its face from the beginning."[2]

Historically, justices have nevertheless extrajudicially advised attorneys, congressmen, and presidents. They occasionally even accuse each other of including in opinions *dicta* (statements of personal opinion or philosophy not necessary to the decision handed down) that is tantamount to "giving legal advice."[3] The Court, furthermore, upheld the constitutionality of the Declaratory Judgment Act authorizing federal courts to declare, or make clear, rights and legal relationships even before a legislature has mandated a law to take effect, although only in "cases of actual controversy."[4]

Standing to Sue

Standing, like adverseness, is a threshold requirement for getting into court. "Generalizations about standing to sue," as Justice William O. Douglas discouragingly, but candidly, put it, "are largely worthless as such."[5] Nonetheless, the basic requirement is that individuals show injury to a legally protected interest or right and demonstrate that other opportunities for defending that claim (before an administrative tribunal or a lower court) have been exhausted. The claim of an injury "must be of a personal and not official nature" and of "some specialized interest of [the individual's] own to vindicate, apart from political concerns which belong to it."[6] The interest must be real as opposed to speculative or hypothetical.

The injuries and legal interests claimed traditionally turned on a showing of personal or proprietary damage. Typically, plaintiffs had suffered some "pocketbook" or monetary injury. But in the last thirty years, individuals have sought standing to represent nonmonetary injuries and "the public interest."

The law of standing is a combination of judge-made law and congressional legislation, as interpreted by the Court. During Earl Warren's tenure as chief justice (1953–1969) the Court substantially lowered the threshold for standing and permitted more litigation of public policy issues. *Frothingham v. Mellon*, 262 U.S. 447 (1923), was the leading case on taxpayer suits until it was overturned in *Flast v. Cohen* (1968) (see page 116). In *Frothingham*, the Taft Court had denied taxpayers standing to challenge the constitutionality of federal legislation. Mrs. Frothingham, a tax-

Figure 2.2

Jurisdictional map of the U.S. courts of appeal and U.S. district courts.

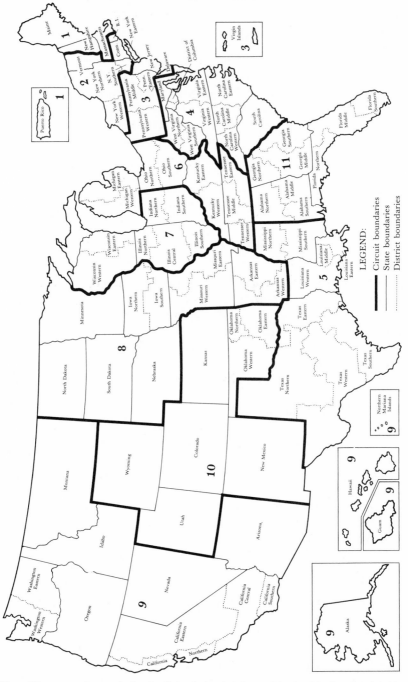

Note: The court of appeals for the federal circuit is located in the District of Columbia.
Source: Administrative Office of the U.S. Courts, Washington, D.C.

payer, had attacked Congress's appropriation of federal funds
to the states for a maternal and infant care program. She claimed
that Congress exceeded its power and intruded on "the reserved
rights of the states" under the Tenth Amendment of the Constitution. Writing for the Court, Justice George Sutherland avoided
confronting the merits of her claim by denying standing. He
did so on the grounds that an individual taxpayer's interest in
the financing of federal programs is "comparatively minute and
indeterminable," when viewed in light of all taxpayers. Frothingham's "injury" was neither direct nor immediate and the issue
raised was basically "political, not judicial." As Sutherland put
it,

[T]he relation of a taxpayer of the United States to the Federal Government is very different [from that relationship with state and local govern-
ments]. His interest in the moneys of the Treasury—partly realized
from taxation and partly from other sources—is shared with millions
of others; is comparatively minute and indeterminable; and the effect
upon future taxation, or any payment out of the funds, so remote,
fluctuating and uncertain, that no basis is afforded for an appeal to
the preventive powers of a court of equity.

To gain standing, according to Sutherland, a taxpayer "must
be able to show not only that the statute is invalid but that he
has sustained . . . some direct injury as the result of its enforcement, and not merely that he suffers in some indefinite way in
common with people generally."

Frothingham's "direct injury" test was met in *Pierce v. Society
of Sisters*, 268 U.S. 510 (1925). There, a religious school won a
court order barring the enforcement of Oregon's 1922 constitutional amendment requiring children between the ages of eight
and sixteen to attend public schools. The Court affirmed on
the grounds that the law directly damages the business and property interests of the school and because it "unreasonably interferes with the liberty of parents and guardians to direct the
upbringing and education of children under their control."

The federal government relied on *Frothingham* to provide an
absolute barrier to subsequent taxpayer suits until the Warren
Court repudiated that view in *Flast v. Cohen* (1968) (see page
116). In his opinion for the Court, Chief Justice Warren created
a two-pronged standard for granting standing to taxpayers: Taxpayers must show a logical relationship between their status as
taxpayers and the challenged legislative statute as well as a connection between that status and the "precise nature of the constitutional infringement alleged."

The Burger Court (1969–1986) and the current Rehnquist
Court tightened the requirements for standing in some cases,
but relaxed it in others. In 1972, in two sharply divided decisions,

CONSTITUTIONAL HISTORY

Major Legislation Affecting the Jurisdiction and Business of the Supreme Court

Legislation	Commentary
Judiciary Act of 1789	Provided basic appellate jurisdiction; a 3-tier judiciary system staffed by justices and district court judges; and required circuit riding.
Acts of 1793, 1801, 1802, and 1803	Provided rotation system for circuit riding, then eliminated the responsibilities, only to have Jeffersonians reinstate circuit-riding duties.
Act of 1807	Added 7th circuit and justice.
Act of 1837	Divided country into 9 circuits and brought number of justices to 9. (Court's jurisdiction was also expanded to include appeals from new states and territories in 1825, 1828, and 1848.)
Acts of 1855 and 1863	California added as 10th circuit and 10th justice added to the Court.
Acts of 1866, 1867, 1869, and 1871	Expanded federal jurisdiction over civil rights; reorganized country into 9 circuits and reduced number of justices to 7, and later fixed the number at 9; as well as expanded jurisdiction over habeas corpus and state court decisions.
Act of 1875	Greatly expanded jurisdiction over civil disputes, and gave power to review of writs of error, and granted full federal question review from state courts.
Act of 1887	Curbed access by raising amount of dispute in diversity cases; and provided writ of error in all capital cases.
Circuit Court of Appeals Act of 1891	Established 9 circuit courts, and judgeships; broadened review of criminal cases and provided for limited discretionary review via writs of *certiorari*.

Legislation	Commentary
Act of 1892	Provided for *in forma pauperis* filings.
Act of 1893	Created District of Columbia Circuit.
Acts of 1903 and 1907	Provided direct appeal under antitrust and interstate commerce acts; granted government right of direct appeal in dismissals of criminal prosecutions.
Acts of 1910, 1911, and 1913	Altered federal injunctive power; established 3-judge courts because of abuses by single judges in enjoining state economic regulation; and later extended the jurisdiction of 3-judge courts and direct appeals to the Court.
Acts of 1914, 1915, and 1916	Jurisdiction over some state cases made discretionary and eliminated right to review in bankruptcy, trademark, and Federal Employer's Liability Act (FELA).
Judiciary Act of 1925	Greatly extended the Court's discretionary jurisdiction by replacing mandatory appeals with petitions for certiorari.
Act of 1928	Appeals became the sole method of mandatory appellate review.
Act of 1939	Expanded review of decisions by Court of Claims over both law and fact.
Act of 1948	Judicial code revised, codified, and enacted into law; 11th circuit established.
Act of 1950 (Hobbes Act)	Eliminated 3-judge court requirement in certain areas.
Voting Rights Act of 1965	Provided direct appeal over decisions of 3-judge courts in area of voting rights.
Acts of 1970, 1971, 1974, 1975, and 1976	Reorganized District of Columbia courts; expanded Court's discretionary review; repealed direct government appeals under Act of 1907; eliminated direct appeals in antitrust and Interstate Commerce Commission (ICC) cases; further cut back jurisdiction and direct appeals from 3-judge courts, with the exception of areas of voting rights and reapportionment.

Legislation	Commentary
Federal Courts Improvement Act of 1982	Created Court of Appeals for the Federal Circuit, by joining the court of claims with the court of customs and patent appeals.
Act to Improve the Administration of Justice of 1988	Eliminated virtually all of the Court's non-discretionary appellate jurisdiction, except for appeals in reapportionment cases, cases under the Civil Rights Act and Voting Rights Act, antitrust laws, and the Presidential Election Campaign Fund Act.

the Burger Court denied standing to a group challenging military surveillance of lawful political protests in public places and to the Sierra Club when challenging the construction of a ski resort in Mineral King National Park. In both *Laird v. Tatum,* 408 U.S. 1 (1972), and *Sierra Club v. Morton,* 405 U.S. 727 (1972), a bare majority found that the groups failed to show a "personal stake in the outcome" of the litigation. The following year, however, standing was granted to a group of law students attacking a proposed surcharge on railroad freight. The students contended that the surcharge would discourage the recycling of bottles and cans, and thus contribute to environmental pollution. In *United States v. Students Challenging Regulatory Agency Procedure (SCRAP),* 412 U.S. 669 (1973), the Burger Court granted standing, observing that "[a]esthetic and environmental well-being, like economic well-being, are important ingredients of the quality of life in our society, and the fact that particular environmental interests are shared by the many rather than the few does not make them less deserving of legal protection through the judicial process."

Plaintiffs, those bringing suit, must still claim a personal injury, but they now can act as surrogates for special interest groups. The personal injuries claimed thus embrace a public injury. Congress at the same time expanded the principle even more by providing that any individual "adversely affected or aggrieved" may challenge administrative decisions. Health, safety, and environmental legislation passed in the 1970s mandated such "citizen suits" and right to judicial review of regulatory action. Even when legislation does not provide for the citizen suits, individuals may claim personal injuries, or a "private cause of action," to gain access to the courts and to force agency compliance with the law.

The more conservative Burger and Rehnquist courts have restricted standing requirements in several ways. First, they have refused to recognize new interests and injuries in granting standing. In *Linda R. S. v. Richard D.*, 410 U.S. 614 (1973), an unwed mother sought enforcement of child support under the Texas Penal Code because the local prosecutor refused to enforce the statute against fathers of illegitimate children. A majority of the Court ruled that she had no recognizable injury and no standing because she could not prove that payments stopped because that particular statute was unenforced. Justices Byron White and William Douglas, in dissent, argued that unwed mothers and illegitimate children were thus rendered nonpersons: "Texas prosecutes fathers of legitimate children on the complaint of the mother asserting nonsupport and refuses to entertain like complaints from the mother of an illegitimate child. [We] see no basis for saying that the latter mother has no standing to demand that the discrimination be ended, one way or another."

In *Paul v. Davis*, 424 U.S. 693 (1976), the Court's majority rejected a claim of injury to personal reputation by an individual who objected to the circulation of a flyer to local merchants that carried his photograph along with that of other alleged "active shoplifters." Rehnquist dismissed the claim out-of-hand. But, Justice William Brennan in dissent responded that, "The Court by mere fiat and with no analysis wholly excludes personal interest in reputation from the ambit of 'life, liberty, or property' under the Fifth and Fourteenth Amendments, thus rendering due process concerns *never* applicable to the official stigmatization, however, arbitrary." The Court went even further with its reinterpretation of the application of *Flast*'s test for taxpayer suits in *Valley Forge Christian College v. Americans United for Separation of Church and State, Inc.* (1982) (see page 125).

Ripeness and Mootness

With these doctrines the Court wields a double-edged sword. Appellants, those appealing a lower court ruling, may discover that a case is dismissed because it was brought too early or because the issues are moot and the case was brought too late. Cases are usually rejected as not ripe if the injury claimed has not yet been realized, or if other avenues of appeal have not yet been exhausted. Alternatively, a case may be dismissed if pertinent facts or laws change so that there is no longer real adverseness or an actual case or controversy. The issue becomes moot because "there is no subject matter on which the judgement of the court can operate," and hence a ruling would not prove "conclusive" and final.[7] In practice both doctrines bend to the Court's will, because the requirement of ripeness permits the Court to avoid or delay deciding certain issues.

THE DEVELOPMENT OF LAW
Other Important Recent Rulings on Standing

Case	Vote	Ruling
Schlesinger v. Reservists Committee to Stop the War, 418 U.S. 208 (1974)	6:3	Members of an organization of present and past members of the military reserves opposed to the Vietnam War had no standing to file a class action suit against the secretary of defense, attacking the constitutionality of members of Congress holding commissions in the reserves and voting on appropriations for the war, as an alleged violation of Article I, Section 6, Clause 2, which declares that "no person holding any office under the United States, shall be a Member of either House during his continuance in office."
United States v. Richardson, 418 U.S. 166 (1974)	5:4	Denied taxpayer standing to bring suit against Congress's secret funding for the Central Intelligence Agency, as an alleged violation of Article I, Section 9, Clause 7, which provides that "no Money shall be drawn from the Treasury, but in Consequence of Appropriations made by Law; and a regular Statement of Account of the Receipts and Expenditures of all public money shall be published from time to time."
Warth v. Seldin, 422 U.S. 490 (1975)	5:4	Denied standing to various organizations in Rochester, New York, seeking to sue officials of the suburban town of Penfield, claiming that the latter's zoning ordinance excluded low- and moderate-income persons from living in the town and violated their rights under the Bill of Rights. The Court held that the individuals and organizations failed to show that they had been "personally" injured.

Case	Vote	Ruling
Simon v. Eastern Kentucky Welfare Rights Organization, 426 U.S. 26 (1976)	9:0	Denied standing to indigents seeking to challenge federal tax regulations reducing the amount of free medical care hospitals must provide in order to receive certain tax benefits.
City of Los Angeles v. Lyons, 461 U.S. 95 (1983)	5:4	Held that an arrestee had standing to sue the city for damages incurred as a result of police subjecting him to a "choke hold," but that he had no standing to seek an injunction against the police practice of using choke holds, because he failed to show that he might ever be subjected to a choke hold again.
Allen v. Wright, 468 U.S. 737 (1984)	5:3	Denied standing to parents of black children, attending public schools in districts around the country that were in the process of desegregation, to sue various government officials and present their contention that the IRS failed to fulfill its obligation under the law to deny tax-exempt status to private schools engaged in racial discrimination.

A finding of mootness likewise enables the Court to avoid, if not escape, deciding controversial political issues. *DeFunis v. Odegaard*, 416 U.S. 312 (1974), for example, involved a white student, who was denied admission to the University of Washington Law School. The student claimed that the school's affirmative action program discriminated against him and allowed the entrance of minorities with lower LSAT test scores. After the trial judge ruled in his favor, he was admitted into law school but by the time his case reached the Supreme Court he was completing his final year and assured of graduation. Over four dissenters, the majority held that the case was moot. Yet, as the dissenters predicted, the issue would not go away. Within four years, the Burger Court reconsidered the issue of reverse discrimination in university affirmative action programs in *Regents of the University of California v. Bakke*, 438 U.S. 265 (1978) (see Vol. 2, Ch. 12). In *Bakke*, Justice Lewis Powell held that quota systems for minorities in college admissions are unconstitutional, but also that the Constitution is not "color-blind" and affirmative action programs are permissible to achieve a diverse student body in colleges and universities.

THE DEVELOPMENT OF LAW
Class Action Suits

The Federal Rules of Civil Procedure provide for "class action" suits—suits filed by an individual for himself and for all others who have suffered the same injury. This rule enables individuals who have suffered small monetary damages to bring lawsuits that they might not otherwise have because of the prohibitively high cost of litigation. Specifically, Rule 23 provides in that,

One or more members of a class may use or be sued as representative parties on behalf of all only if (1) the class is so numerous that joinder of all members is impracticable, (2) there are questions of law or fact common to the class, (3) the claims or defenses of the representative parties are typical of the claims or defenses of the class, and (4) the representative parties will fairly and adequently protect the interests of the class. . . .

In any class action maintained under [this Rule], the court shall direct to the members of the class the best notice practicable under the circumstances, including individual notice to all members who can be identified.

The scope of this rule, however, was limited by *Eisen v. Carlisle & Jacquelin*, 417 U.S. 156 (1974), holding that when a representative of a class action suit refuses to pay the cost of giving actual notice to all reasonably identiable class members, federal courts are required to dismiss the suit. Here, representatives would have had to notify 2,250,000 class members at a cost of $225,000.

The issue of mootness could have presented a problem when the Burger Court ruled on abortion in *Roe v. Wade,* 410 U.S. 113 (1973) (see Vol. 2, Ch. 11). There the Court struck down Texas's criminal statute prohibiting abortions, except when necessary to save a mother's life. When defending the law, the state's attorney general argued that the plaintiff was a single woman whose pregnancy had already resulted in birth by the time the case reached the Court, and hence her claim was moot. However, Justice Harry Blackmun, writing for the Court, rejected that view out of hand:

[W]hen, as here, pregnancy is a significant fact in the litigation, the normal 266-day human gestation period is so short that the pregnancy will come to term before the usual appellate process is complete. If that termination makes a case moot, pregnancy litigation seldom will survive much beyond the trial stage, and appellate review will be effectively denied. Our law should not be that rigid. Pregnancy often comes more than once to the same woman, and in the general population, if man is to survive, it will always be with us. Pregnancy provides a classic justification for a conclusion of nonmootness. It truly could be "capable of repetition, yet evading review."

INSIDE THE COURT

Standing and the Connecticut Birth Control Cases

Between 1943 and 1965, the Court continually refused standing to individuals attacking the constitutionality of a late nineteenth-century Connecticut statute. The law prohibited virtually all single and married individuals from using contraceptives and physicians from giving advice about their use. In *Tileston v. Ullman*, 318 U.S. 44 (1943), a doctor sued charging that the statute prevented him from giving information to patients. But the Court ruled that he had no real interest or personal injury because he had not been arrested, observing that

[w]e are of the opinion that the proceedings in the state courts present no constitutional question which appellant has standing to assert. The sole constitutional attack upon the statutes under the Fourteenth Amendment is confined to their deprivation of life—obviously not appellant's but his patients'. There is no allegation or proof that appellant's life is in danger. His patients are not parties to this proceeding and there is no basis on which we can say that has standing to secure an adjudication of his patient's constitutional right to life, which they do not assert in their own behalf.

More than a decade later in *Poe v. Ullman*, 367 U.S. 497 (1961), a doctor, Buxton, and a patient were likewise denied standing on the ground that the law had not been enforced for more than eighty years, even though the state had begun to close birth control clinics. This time the justices split five to four and only Chief Justice Warren and Justices Clark and Whittaker joined Justice Frankfurter's opinion for the Court (Justice Brennan concurred in the decision but not in the opinion). There, Frankfurter observed that

[t]he Connecticut law prohibiting the use of contraceptives has been on the State's books since 1879. . . . During more than three-quarters of a century since its enactment, a prosecution for its violation seems never to have been initiated, save in [one] case. . . . Neither counsel nor our own researches have discovered any other attempt to enforce the prohibition of distribution or use of contraceptive devices by criminal process. The unreality of these law suits is illuminated by another circumstance. We were advised by counsel for appellants that contraceptives are commonly and notoriously sold in Connecticut drug stores. Yet no prosecutions are recorded. . . .

The restriction of our jurisdiction to cases and controversies within the meaning of Article III of the Constitution . . . is not the sole limitation on the exercise of our appellate powers, especially in cases raising constitutional questions. . . .

The various doctrines of "standing," "ripeness," and "mootness," which this Court has evolved with particular, though not exclusive, reference to such cases are but several manifestations—each having its own "varied application"—of the primary conception that federal judicial power is to be exercised to strike down legislation, whether state or federal, only at the instance of one who is himself immediately harmed, or immediately threatened with harm, by the challenged action. . . .

Nor does the allegation by the Poes and Doe that they are unable to obtain information concerning contraceptive devices from Dr. Buxton, "for the sole reason that the delivery and use of such information and advice may or will be claimed by the defendant's State's Attorney to constitute offenses," disclose a necessity for present constitutional decision. It is true that this Court has several times passed upon criminal statutes challenged by persons who claimed that the effects of the statutes were to deter others from maintaining profitable or advantageous relations with the complainants. . . . But in these cases the deterrent effect complained of was one which was grounded in a realistic fear of prosecution. We cannot agree that if Dr. Buxton's compliance with these statutes is uncoerced by the risk of their enforcement, his patients are entitled to a declaratory judgment concerning the statute's validity.

Finally, after Dr. Buxton and Estelle Griswold, executive director of Planned Parenthood League of Connecticut, were found guilty of prescribing contraceptives to a married couple, the Court in *Griswold v. Connecticut* (1965) (see Vol. 2, Ch. 3) struck down what Justice Potter Stewart called Connecticut's "uncommonly silly law." In his opinion announcing the Court's ruling, Justice Douglas explained why Griswold and Buxton were now being granted standing:

They gave information, instruction, and medical advice to *married persons* as to the means of preventing conception. They examined the wife and prescribed the best contraceptive device or material for her use. Fees were usually charged, although some couples were serviced free. . . .

The appellants were found guilty as accessories and fined $100 each, against the claim that the accessory statute as so applied violated the Fourteenth Amendment. . . .

We think that appellants have standing to raise the constitutional rights of the married people with whom they had a professional relationship. *Tileston v. Ullman,* is different, for there the plaintiff seeking to represent others asked for a declaratory judgment. In that situation, we thought that the requirements of standing should be strict, lest the standards of "case or controversy" in Article III of the Constitution become blurred. Here those doubts are removed by reason of a criminal conviction for serving married couples in violation of an aiding-and-abetting statute. Certainly the accessory should have standing to assert that the offense which he is charged with assisting is not, or cannot constitutionally be a crime.

Griswold was limited to the privacy and marital decisions of couples. Consequently, in *Eisenstadt v. Baird,* 405 U.S. 438 (1972), to gain standing to claim that single individuals also have a right to acquire and use contraceptives, a doctor arranged to be arrested after delivering a public lecture on contraceptives and handing out samples to single women in the audience. The Court accepted the case and ruled that single women also have the right to acquire and use contraceptives.

Political Questions

Even when the Court has jurisdiction over a properly framed suit, it may decline to rule because it decides that a case raises a "political question" that should be resolved by other political branches. Like other jurisdictional doctrines, the political question doctrine means what the justices say it means.

The doctrine has its origin in Chief Justice Marshall's observation in *Marbury v. Madison*, 5 U.S. 137 (1803) (see Chapter 1), that "[t]he province of the Court, is, solely, to decide on the rights of individuals. . . . Questions in the nature political, or which are, by the constitution and laws, submitted to the executive can never be made in this Court." Yet as the French commentator Alexis de Tocqueville noted in the 1830s, "Scarcely any political question arises in the United States that is not resolved, sooner or later, into a judicial question."[8] Litigation that reaches the Court is political, and the justices for political reasons decide what and how to decide cases on their docket.

The Taney Court first developed the doctrine in *Luther v. Borden*, 7 How. [48 U.S.] 1 (1849). There, the Court held that whether Rhode Island had a "republican form of government," as guaranteed by Article IV of the Constitution, was a question for Congress, not the Court, to decide. Subsequent rulings elaborated other reasons for the doctrine besides deference to separation of powers. The Court may lack information and resources needed for a ruling. In some areas, as in foreign policy and international relations, the Court lacks both adequate standards for resolving disputes and the means to enforce its decisions.

For many decades the Court relied on the doctrine to avoid entering the "political thicket" of state representation and apportionment, that is, the ways by which a state is divided geographically as a basis for representation in state and federal elections. When declining to rule on the malapportionment of Illinois's congressional districts in *Colegrove v. Green*, 328 U.S. 549 (1946), Justice Felix Frankfurter explained,

We are of opinion that the petitioners ask of this Court what is beyond its competence to grant. This is one of those demands on judicial power which cannot be met by verbal fencing about "jurisdiction." It must be resolved by considerations on the basis of which this Court, from time to time, has refused to intervene in controversies. It has refused to do so because due regard for the effective working of our Government revealed this issue to be of a peculiarly political nature and therefore not meet for judicial determination.

This is not an action to recover for damages because of the discriminatory exclusion of a plaintiff from rights enjoyed by other citizens. The basis for the suit is not a private wrong, but a wrong suffered by Illinois as a polity. . . . In effect this is an appeal to the federal courts to reconstruct the electoral process of Illinois in order that it may be adequately represented in the councils of the Nation. Because the Illinois legislature has failed to revise its Congressional Representative districts in order to reflect great changes, during more than a generation, in the distribution of its population, we are asked to do this, for Illinois. . . .

Of course no court can affirmatively remap the Illinois districts so as to bring them more in conformity with the standards of fairness for a representative system. At best we could only declare the existing electoral system invalid. The result would be to leave Illinois undistricted and to bring into operation, if the Illinois legislature chose not to act, the choice of members for the House of Representatives on a state-wide ticket. The last stage may be worse than the first. . . .

Nothing is clearer than that this controversy concerns matters that bring courts into immediate and active relations with party contests. From the determination of such issues this Court has traditionally held aloof. It is hostile to the democratic system to involve the judiciary in the politics of the people. And it is not less pernicious if such judicial intervention in an essentially political contest be dressed up in the abstract phrases of the law.

The one stark fact that emerges from the study of the history of Congressional apportionment is its enrollment in politics, in the sense of party contests and party interests. The Constitution enjoins upon Congress the duty of apportioning Representatives "among the several States . . . according to their respective Numbers. . . ." Article I, Sec. 2. Yet, Congress has at times been heedless of this command and not apportioned according to the requirements of the Census. It never occurred to anyone that this Court could issue mandamus to compel Congress to perform its mandatory duty to apportion.

Still, blacks and other minorities in urban areas were often denied equal representation until the Court reversed itself in *Baker v. Carr* (1962) (see page 131).

In *Goldwater v. Carter* (1979) (see page 145), the Court issued an order vacating (overturning) a lower court decision in a dispute between several congressmen, headed by conservative Senator Barry Goldwater, and Democratic President James Carter over the termination of a defense treaty with Taiwan. There, Justices Lewis F. Powell and William Rehnquist took quite different views of the application of the "political questions" doctrine in controversies between Congress and the president.

The doctrine's logic is admittedly circular. "Political questions are matters not soluble by the judicial process; matters not soluble by the judicial process are political questions. As an early dictionary explained," political scientist John Roche says, "violins are small cellos, and cellos are large violins."[9] Still, Columbia Law professor Louis Henkin points out, even when denying review because of a political question, "the court does not refuse judicial review; it exercises it. It is not dismissing the case or the issue as nonjusticiable; it adjudicates it. It is not refusing to pass on the power of the political branches; it passes upon it, only to affirm that they had the power which had been challenged and that nothing in the Constitution prohibited the particular exercise of it."[10]

Stare Decisis and Other Policies

The justices occasionally rely on other self-denying policies to avoid reaching issues as well. They, for example, may invoke what has been called the doctrine of *strict necessity*, and thereupon formulate and decide only the narrowest possible issue.

Another doctrine, *stare decisis* ("let the prior decision stand"), is also not a mechanical formula. It is rather a judicial policy that promotes "the certainty, uniformity, and stability of the law." Even conservative Justice George Sutherland recognized that members of the Court "are not infallible, and when convinced that a prior decision was not originally based on, or that conditions have so changed as to render the decision no longer in accordance with, sound reason, [they] should not hesitate to say so."[11] "*Stare decisis* is usually the wise policy," Justice Louis Brandeis remarked, "because in most matters it is more important that the applicable rule of law be settled than that it be settled right."[12] On constitutional matters, however, Justice Douglas among others emphasizes, "*stare decisis*—that is, established law—was really no sure guideline because what did . . . the judges who sat there in 1875 know about, say, electronic surveillance? They didn't know anything about it."[13] At the time of his ill-fated nomination to the Court in 1987, former Court of Appeals Judge Robert Bork agreed and raised serious questions about the value of judicial precedents, although for somewhat different reasons than Douglas. Bork contended that "the real meaning of the Constitution ought to prevail over a prior mistake by the Court" and "the Court ought to be always open to rethink constitutional problems." But he also maintained that "certain precedents [are] so fixed, some issues so settled, that regardless of how you felt about them you shouldn't vote to overrule them." Bork gave as an example nineteenth-century cases dealing with Congress's power under the commerce clause, which however wrongly decided should be upheld. By contrast, he did "not include *Roe v. Wade* in that category."[14] Even without Bork on the high bench, the Rehnquist Court has made clear that it pays much less deference to decisions handed down by the Warren and Burger courts in the area of civil liberties and civil rights.

In sum, *stare decisis* and the precedential value of the Court's jurisdictional doctrines and policies, as Justice Jackson in half-jest quipped, "are accepted only at their current valuation and have a mortality rate as high as their authors."[15]

Formal Rules and Practices

Except for government attorneys and members of the practicing bar, few people pay any attention to the technical Rules of the Court. Yet, they are an exercise of political power and determine the nation's access to justice. The rules govern the admission and activities of attorneys in filing appeals, petitions, and motions, and conducting oral arguments. They stipulate the fees, forms, and length of filings. Most important, they explain the Court's formal grounds for granting and disposing of cases.

To expedite the process of deciding what to decide, the Court periodically revises its rules. For example, even after the Judiciary Act of 1925 expanded the Court's discretionary jurisdiction, the justices still felt burdened by mandatory appeals. Accordingly, in 1928 the Court required the filing of a jurisdictional statement, explaining the circumstances of an appeal, the questions presented, and why the Court should grant review. The requirement also allowed the justices to screen appeals just like petitions for *certiorari*.

One of the reasons for granting *certiorari* given in the Court's rules is whether "a federal court of appeals has rendered a decision in conflict with the decision of another federal court of appeals on the same matter." This rule is especially advantageous for the federal government. The Department of Justice has a relitigation policy. If it receives an adverse ruling from circuit court of appeals, it will relitigate the issue in other circuits to obtain favorable decisions and generate a conflict among the circuits, which then may be brought to the Court. One function of the Court, in Chief Justice Fred Vinson's words, has become the resolution of "conflicts of opinion on federal questions that have arisen among lower courts."[16] The rule for granting circuit conflicts, however important, does not control the justices' actual practice of granting *certiorari*. The government and individuals often allege circuit conflicts simply in an effort to get their cases accepted. But most circuit conflicts are "tolerable" and need not be immediately decided. The justices often feel that conflicts should percolate in the circuits before they take them. Sometimes, a majority may want to avoid or delay addressing an issue that has created a conflict among the circuits. Most crucial in granting *certiorari* is simply the majority's agreement on the importance of the issue presented.

NOTES

1. Charles E. Hughes, *Addresses of Charles Evans Hughes* (New York: Putnam's, 1916), 185–186.
2. *Muskrat v. United States*, 219 U.S. 346 (1911).
3. See *Duke Power Co. v. Carolina Environmental Study Group*, 438 U.S. 59 (1978); and *Bellotti v. Baird*, 443 U.S. 622 (1979).
4. *Aetna Life Insurance Co. v. Haworth*, 300 U.S. 277 (1937).
5. *Data Processing Service v. Camp*, 397 U.S. 150, 151 (1970).
6. *Braxton County Court v. West Virginia*, 208 U.S. 192 (1908); and *Coleman v. Miller*, 307 U.S. 433 (1931) (Frankfurter, J., dissenting opinion).
7. *Ex parte Baez*, 177 U.S. 378 (1900).
8. Alexis de Tocqueville, *Democracy in America*, Vol. 1, ed. P. Bradley (New York: Vintage, 1945), 288.
9. John Roche, "Judicial Self-Restraint," 49 *American Political Science Review* 768 (1955).
10. Louis Henkin, "Is There a 'Political Question' Doctrine?" 85 *Yale Law Journal* 606 (1976).
11. Draft of an opinion, George Sutherland Papers, Manuscript Room, Library of Congress.
12. *Burnet v. Coronado Oil*, 285 U.S. 393 (1932) (Brandeis, J., dissenting opinion).
13. William O. Douglas, interview on *CBS Reports*, Sept. 6, 1972, CBS News, transcript p. 13.
14. See Ronald Collins and David M. O'Brien, "Just Where Does Judge Bork Stand?" *The National Law Journal* 13 (Sept. 7, 1987).
15. Robert Jackson, "The Task of Maintaining Our Liberties: The Role of the Judiciary," 39 *American Bar Association Journal* 962 (1953).
16. Fred Vinson, address before the American Bar Association, Sept. 7, 1949, reprinted in 69 S.Ct. vi (1949).

SELECTED BIBLIOGRAPHY

Cannon, Mark, and O'Brien, David M. *Views from the Bench: The Judiciary and Constitutional Politics*. Chatham, NJ: Chatham House, 1985.

Carp, Robert. *Policymaking and Politics in the Federal District Courts*. Knoxville: University of Tennessee Press, 1983.

Goldman, Sheldon, and Sarat, Austin, eds. *American Court Systems*, 2nd ed. New York: Longman's, 1989.

Howard, J. Woodford. *Courts of Appeals in the Federal Judicial System*. Princeton, N.J.: Princeton University Press, 1981.

Stern, Robert, and Gressman, Eugene *Supreme Court Practice*, 6th ed. Washington, DC: Bureau of National Affairs, 1987.

Strum, Philippa. *The Supreme Court and "Political Questions": A Study in Judicial Evasion*. Birmingham: University of Alabama Press, 1974.

Flast v. Cohen
392 U.S. 83, 88 S.Ct. 1942 (1968)

Florance Flast and several other taxpayers sought standing to challenge the constitutionality of the Elementary and Secondary Education Act of 1965. The act provided funding for the instruction and purchase of textbooks for religious schools. Flast contended that the act violated the First Amendment's ban on the establishment of religion and guarantee for the free exercise of religion. In a federal district court in New York, she filed suit against Wilbur Cohen, the secretary of health, education, and welfare, to enjoin the spending of funds authorized for religious schools. The district court denied standing and Flast appealed to the Supreme Court.

Chief Justice WARREN delivers the opinion of the Court.

In *Frothingham v. Mellon* [262 U.S. 447] (1923), this Court ruled that a federal taxpayer is without standing to challenge the constitutionality of a federal statute. That ruling has stood for 45 years as an impenetrable barrier to suits against Acts of Congress brought by individuals who can assert only the interest of federal taxpayers. In this case, we must decide whether the *Frothingham* barrier should be lowered when a taxpayer attacks a federal statute on the ground that it violates the Establishment and Free Exercise Clauses of the First Amendment. . . .

This Court first faced squarely the question whether a litigant asserting only his status as a taxpayer has standing to maintain a suit in a federal court in *Frothingham v. Mellon,* supra, and that decision must be the starting point for analysis in this case. The taxpayer in *Frothingham* attacked as unconstitutional the Maternity Act of 1921, 42 Stat. 224, which established a federal program of grants to those States which would undertake programs to reduce maternal and infant mortality. . . . The Court noted that a federal taxpayer's "interest in the moneys of the Treasury . . . is comparatively minute and indeterminable" and that "the effect upon future taxation, of any payment out of the [Treasury's] funds, . . . [is] remote, fluctuating and uncertain." As a result, the Court ruled that the taxpayer had failed to allege the type of "direct injury" necessary to confer standing.

Although the barrier *Frothingham* erected against federal taxpayer suits has never been breached, the decision has been the source of some confusion and the object of considerable criticism. The confusion has developed as commentators have tried to determine whether *Frothingham* establishes a constitutional bar to taxpayer suits or whether the Court was simply imposing a rule of self restraint which was not constitutionally compelled. The conflicting viewpoints are reflected in the arguments made to this Court by the parties in this case. The Government has pressed upon us the view that *Frothingham* announced a constitutional rule, compelled by the Article III limitations on federal court jurisdiction and grounded in considerations of the doctrine of separation of powers. Appellants, however, insist that *Frothingham* expressed no more than a policy of judicial self-restraint which can be disregarded when compelling reasons for assuming jurisdiction over a taxpayer's suit exist. The opinion delivered in *Frothingham* can be read to support either position. . . .

To the extent that *Frothingham* has been viewed as resting on policy considerations, it has been criticized as depending on assumptions not consistent with modern conditions. For example, some commentators have pointed out that a number of corporate taxpayers today have a federal tax liability running into hundreds of millions of dollars, and such taxpayers have a far greater monetary stake in the Federal Treasury than they do in any municipal treasury. To some degree, the fear expressed in *Frothingham* that allowing one taxpayer to sue would inundate the federal courts with countless similar suits has been mitigated by the ready availability of the devices of class actions and joinder under the Federal Rules of Civil Procedure, adopted subsequent to the decision in *Frothingham*. . . .

The jurisdiction of federal courts is defined and limited by Article III of the Constitution. In terms relevant to the question for decision in this case, the judicial power of federal courts is constitutionally restricted to "cases" and "controversies." As is so often the situation in constitutional adjudication, those two words have an iceberg quality, containing beneath their surface simplicity submerged complexities which go to the very heart of our constitutional form of government. Embodied in the words "cases" and "controversies" are two complementary but somewhat different limitations. In part those words limit the business of federal courts to questions presented in an adversary context and in a form historically viewed as capable of resolution through the judicial process. And in part those words define the role assigned to the judiciary in a tripartite allocation of power to assure that the federal courts will not intrude into areas committed to the other branches of government. Justiciability is the term of art employed to give expression to this dual limitation placed upon federal courts by the case-and-controversey doctrine.

Justiciability is itself a concept of uncertain meaning and scope. Its reach is illustrated by the various grounds upon which questions sought to be adjudicated in federal courts have been held not to be justiciable. Thus, no justiciable controversy is presented when the parties seek adjudication of only a political question, when the parties are asking for an advisory opinion, when the question sought to be adjudicated has been mooted by subsequent developments, and when there is no standing to maintain the action. Yet it remains true that "[j]usticiability is . . . not a legal concept with a fixed content or susceptible of scientific verification. Its utilization is the resultant of many subtle pressures," *Poe v. Ullman* [367 U.S. 497 (1961)].

Part of the difficulty in giving precise meaning and form to the concept of justiciability stems from the uncertain historical antecedents of the case-and-controversy doctrine. For example, Justice FRANKFURTER twice suggested that historical meaning could be imparted to the concepts of justiciability and case and controversy by reference to the practices of the courts of Westminster when the Constitution was adopted. . . .

However, the power of English judges to deliver advisory opinions was well established at the time the Constitution was drafted. And it is quite clear that "the oldest and most consistent thread in the federal law of justiciability is that the federal courts will not give advisory opinions." Thus, the implicit policies embodied in Article III, and not history alone, impose the rule against advisory opinions on federal courts. When the federal judicial power is invoked to pass upon the validity of actions by the Legislative and Executive Branches of the Government, the rule against advisory opinions implements the separation of powers prescribed by the Constitution and confines federal courts to the role assigned them by Article III. However, the rule against advisory opinions also recognizes that such suits often "are not pressed before the Court with that clear concreteness provided when a question emerges precisely framed and necessary for decision from a clash of adversary argument exploring every aspect of a multifaced situation embracing conflicting and demanding interests." Consequently, the Article III prohibition against advisory opinions reflects the complementary constitutional considerations expressed by the justiciability doctrine: Federal judicial power is limited to those disputes which confine federal courts to a rule consistent with a system of separated powers and which are traditionally thought to be capable of resolution through the judicial process.

Additional uncertainty exists in the doctrine of justiciability because that doctrine has become a blend of constitutional requirements and policy considerations. And a policy limitation is "not always clearly distinguished from the constitutional limitation.". . . The "many subtle pressures" which cause policy considerations to blend into the constitutional limitations of Article III make the justiciability doctrine one of uncertain and shifting contours.

It is in this context that the standing question presented by this case must be viewed and that the Government's argument on that question must be evaluated. As we understand it, the Government's position is that the constitutional scheme of separation of powers, and the deference owed by the federal judiciary to the other two branches of government within that scheme, present an absolute bar to taxpayer suits challenging the validity of federal spending programs. The Government views such suits as involving no more than the mere disagreement by the taxpayer "with the uses to which tax money is put." According to the Government, the resolution of such disagreements is committed to other branches of the Federal Government and not to the judiciary. Consequently, the Government contends that, under no circumstances, should standing be conferred on federal taxpayers to challenge a federal taxing or spending program. An analysis of the function served by standing limitations compels a rejection of the Government's position.

Standing is an aspect of justiciability and, as such, the problem of standing is surrounded by the same complexities and vagaries that inhere in justiciability. . . .

Despite the complexities and uncertainties, some meaningful form can be given to the jurisdictional limitations placed on federal court power by the concept of standing. The fundamental aspect of standing is that it focuses on the party seeking to get his complaint before a federal court and not on the issues he wishes to have adjudicated. The "gist of the question of standing" is whether the party seeking relief has "alleged such a personal stake in the outcome of the controversy as to assure that concrete adverseness which sharpens the presentation of issues upon which the court so largely depends for illumination of difficult constitutional questions." *Baker v. Carr,* [369 U.S. 186] (1962). In other words, when standing is placed in issue in a case, the question is whether the person whose standing is challenged is a proper party to request an adjudication of a particular issue and not whether the issue itself is justiciable. Thus, a party may have standing in a particular case, but the federal court may nevertheless decline to pass on the merits of the case because, for example, it presents a political question. A proper party is demanded so that federal courts will not be asked to decide "ill-defined controversies over constitutional issues," *United Public Workers of America v. Mitchell,* 330 U.S. 75, (1947), or a case which is of "a hypothetical or abstract character," . . . So stated, the standing requirement is closely related to, although more general than, the rule that federal courts will not entertain friendly suits. . . .

When the emphasis in the standing problem is placed on whether the person invoking a federal court's jurisdiction is a proper party to maintain the action, the weakness of the Government's argument in this case becomes apparent. The question whether a particular person is a proper party to maintain the action does not, by its own force, raise separation of powers problems related to improper judicial interference in areas committed to other branches of the Federal Government. Such problems arise, if at all, only from the substantive issues the individual seeks to have adjudicated. Thus, in terms of Article III limitations on federal court jurisdiction, the question of standing is related only to whether the dispute sought to be adjudicated will be presented in an adversary context and in a form historically viewed as capable of judicial resolution. It is for that reason that the emphasis in standing problems is on whether the party invoking federal court jurisdiction has "a personal stake in the outcome of the controversy," *Baker v. Carr,* and whether the dispute touches upon "the legal relations of parties having adverse legal interests." A taxpayer may or may not have the requisite personal stake in the outcome, depending upon the circumstances of the particular case. Therefore, we find no absolute bar in Article III to suits by federal taxpayers challenging allegedly unconstitutional federal taxing and spending programs. There remains, however, the problem of determining the circumstances under which a federal taxpayer will be deemed to have the personal stake and interest that impart the necessary concrete adverseness to such litigation so that standing can be conferred on the taxpayer *qua* taxpayer consistent with the constitutional limitations of Article III. . . .

Whether such individuals have standing to maintain that form of action turns on whether they can demonstrate the necessary stake as taxpayers in the outcome of the litigation to satisfy Article III requirements.

The nexus demanded of federal taxpayers has two aspects to it. First, the taxpayer must establish a logical link between that status and the type of legislative enactment attacked. Thus, a taxpayer will be a proper party to allege the unconstitutionality only of exercises of congressional power under the taxing and spending clause of Art. I, § 8, of the Constitution. It will not be sufficient to allege an incidental expenditure of tax funds in the administration of an essentially regulatory statute. . . . Secondly, the taxpayer must establish a nexus between that status and the precise nature of the constitutional infringement alleged. Under this requirement, the taxpayer must show that the challenged enactment exceeds specific constitutional limitations imposed upon the exercise of the congressional taxing and spending power and not simply that the enactment is generally beyond the powers delegated to Congress by Art. I, § 8. When both nexuses are established, the litigant will have shown a taxpayer's stake in the outcome of the controversy and will be a proper and appropriate party to invoke a federal court's jurisdiction.

The taxpayer-appellants in this case have satisfied both nexuses to support their claim of standing under the test we announce today. Their constitutional challenge is made to an exercise by Congress of its power under Art. I, § 8, to spend for the general welfare, and the challenged program involves a substantial expenditure of federal tax funds. In addition, appellants have alleged that the challenged expenditures violate the Establishment and

Free Exercise Clauses of the First Amendment. Our history vividly illustrates that one of the specific evils feared by those who drafted the Establishment Clause and fought for its adoption was that the taxing and spending power would be used to favor one religion over another or to support religion in general. James Madison, who is generally recognized as the leading architect of the religion clauses of the First Amendment, observed in his famous Memorial and Remonstrance Against Religious Assessments that "the same authority which can force a citizen to contribute three pence only of his property for the support of any one establishment, may force him to conform to any other establishment in all cases whatsoever." 2 Writings of James Madison 183, 186 (Hunt ed. 1901). The concern of Madison and his supporters was quite clearly that religious liberty ultimately would be the victim if government could employ its taxing and spending powers to aid one religion over another or to aid religion in general. The Establishment Clause was designed as a specific bulwark against such potential abuses of governmental power, and that clause of the First Amendment operates as a specific constitutional limitation upon the exercise by Congress of the taxing and spending power conferred by Art. I, § 8.

The allegations of the taxpayer in *Frothingham v. Mellon*, supra, were quite different from those made in this case, and the result in *Frothingham* is consistent with the test of taxpayer standing announced today. The taxpayer in *Frothingham* attacked a federal spending program and she, therefore, established the first nexus required. However, she lacked standing because her constitutional attack was not based on an allegation that Congress, in enacting the Maternity Act of 1921, had breached a specific limitation upon its taxing and spending power. The taxpayer in *Frothingham* alleged essentially that Congress, by enacting the challenged statute, had exceeded the general powers delegated to it by Art. I, § 8, and that Congress had thereby invaded the legislative province reserved to the States by the Tenth Amendment. To be sure, Mrs. Frothingham made the additional allegation that her tax liability would be increased as a result of the allegedly unconstitutional enactment, and she framed that allegation in terms of a deprivation of property without due process of law. However, the Due Process Clause of the Fifth Amendment does not protect taxpayers against increases in tax liability, and the taxpayer in *Frothingham* failed to make any additional claim that the harm she alleged resulted from a breach by Congress of the specific constitutional limitations imposed upon an exercise of the taxing and spending power. In essence, Mrs. Frothingham was attempting to assert the States' interest in their legislative prerogatives and not a federal taxpayer's interest in being free of taxing and spending in contravention of specific constitutional limitations imposed upon Congress' taxing and spending power.

We have noted that the Establishment Clause of the First Amendment does specifically limit the taxing and spending power conferred by Art. I, § 8. Whether the Constitution contains other specific limitations can be determined only in the context of future cases. However, whenever such specific limitations are found, we believe a taxpayer will have a clear stake as a taxpayer in assuring that they are not breached by Congress. Consequently, we hold that a taxpayer will have standing consistent with Article III to invoke federal judicial power when he alleges that congressional action under the taxing and spending clause is in derogation of those constitutional provisions which operate to restrict the exercise of the taxing and spending power. The taxpayer's allegation in such cases would be that his tax money is being extracted and spent in violation of specific constitutional protections against such abuses of legislative power. Such an injury is appropriate for judicial redress, and the taxpayer has established the necessary nexus between his status and the nature of the allegedly unconstitutional action to support his claim of standing to secure judicial review. Under such circumstances, we feel confident that the questions will be framed with the necessary specificity, that the issues will be contested with the necessary adverseness and that the litigation will be pursued with the necessary vigor to assure that the constitutional challenge will be made in a form traditionally thought to be capable of judicial resolution. We lack that confidence in cases such as *Frothingham* where a taxpayer seeks to employ a federal court as a forum in which to air his generalized grievances about the conduct of government or the allocation of power in the Federal System.

Justice DOUGLAS concurring.

While I have joined the opinion of the Court, I do not think that the test it lays down is a durable one for the reasons stated by my Brother HARLAN. . . . It would therefore be the part of wisdom, as I see the problem, to be rid of *Frothingham* here and now. . . .

Most laws passed by Congress do not contain even a ghost of a constitutional question. The "political" decisions, as distinguished from the "justiciable" ones, occupy most of the spectrum of congressional action. The case or controversy requirement comes into play only when the Federal Government does something that affects a person's life, his liberty, or his property. The wrong may be slight or it may be grievous. . . .

We have a Constitution designed to keep government out of private domains. But the fences have often been broken down; and *Frothingham* denied effective machinery to restore them. The Constitution even with the judicial gloss it has acquired plainly is not adequate to protect the individual against the growing bureaucracy in the Legislative and Executive Branches. He faces a formidable opponent in government, even when he is endowed with funds and with courage. The individual is almost certain to be plowed under, unless he has a well-organized active political group to speak for him. The church is one. The press is another. The union is a third. But if a powerful sponsor is lacking, individual liberty withers—in spite of glowing opinions and resounding constitutional phrases.

I would not be niggardly therefore in giving private attorneys general standing to sue. I would certainly not wait for Congress to give its blessing to our deciding cases clearly within our Article III jurisdiction. To wait for a sign from Congress is to allow important constitutional questions to go undecided and personal liberty unprotected.

Justice STEWART concurring.

I join the judgment and opinion of the Court, which I understand to hold only that a federal taxpayer has standing to assert that a specific expenditure of federal funds violates the Establishment Clause of the First Amendment. Because that clause plainly prohibits taxing and spending in aid of religion, every taxpayer can claim a personal constitutional right not to be taxed for the support of a religious institution. The present case is thus readily distinguishable from *Frothingham v. Mellon,* where the taxpayer did not rely on an explicit constitutional prohibition but instead questioned the scope of the powers delegated to the national legislature by Article I of the Constitution. . . .

In concluding that the appellants therefore have standing to sue, we do not undermine the salutary principle, established by *Frothingham* and reaffirmed today, that a taxpayer may not "employ a federal court as a forum in which to air his generalized grievances about the conduct of government or the allocation of power in the Federal System."

Justice FORTAS concurring.

I would confine the ruling in this case to the proposition that a taxpayer may maintain a suit to challenge the validity of a federal expenditure on the ground that the expenditure violates the Establishment Clause. As the Court's opinion recites, there is enough in the constitutional history of the Establishment Clause to support the thesis that this Clause includes a *specific* prohibition upon the use of the power to tax to support an establishment of religion. There is no reason to suggest, and no basis in the logic of this decision for implying, that there may be other types of congressional expenditures which may be attacked by a litigent solely on the basis of his status as a taxpayer.

Justice HARLAN dissenting.

The problems presented by this case are narrow and relatively abstract, but the principles by which they must be resolved involve nothing less than the proper functioning of the federal courts, and so run to the roots of our constitutional system. The nub of my view is that the end result of *Frothingham v. Mellon* was correct, even though, like others, I do not subscribe to all of its reasoning and premises. Although I therefore agree with certain of the conclusions reached today by the Court, I cannot accept the standing doctrine that it substitutes for *Frothingham,* for it seems to me that this new doctrine rests on premises that do not withstand analysis. Accordingly, I respectfully dissent. . . .

The lawsuits here and in *Frothingham* are fundamentally different. They present the question whether federal taxpayers *qua* taxpayers may, in suits in which they do not contest the validity of their previous or existing tax obligations, challenge the constitutionality of the uses for which Congress has authorized the expenditure of public funds. These differences in the purposes of the cases are reflected in differences in the litigants' interests. An action brought to contest the validity of tax liabilities assessed to the plaintiff is designed to vindicate interests that are personal and proprietary. The wrongs alleged and the relief sought by such a plaintiff are unmistakably private; only secondarily are his interests representative of those of the general population. I take it that the Court, although it does not pause to examine the question, believes that the interests of those who as taxpayers challenge the constitutionality of public expenditures may, at least in certain circumstances, be similar. Yet this assumption is surely mistaken. . . .

Presumably the Court recognizes at least certain . . . hazards, else it would not have troubled to impose limitations upon the situations in which, and purposes for which, such suits may be brought. Nonetheless, the limitations adopted by the Court are, as I have endeavored to indicate, wholly untenable. This is the more unfortunate because there is available a resolution of this problem that entirely satisfies the demands of the principle of separation of powers. This Court has previously held that individual litigants have standing to represent the public interest, despite their lack of economic or other personal interests, if Congress has appropriately authorized such suits. Any hazards to the proper allocation of authority among the three branches of the Government would be substantially diminished if public actions had been pertinently authorized by Congress and the President. I appreciate that this Court does not ordinarily await the mandate of other branches of the Government, but it seems to me that the extraordinary character of public actions, and of the mischievous, if not dangerous, consequences they involve for the proper functioning of our constitutional system, and in particular of the federal courts, makes such judicial forbearance the part of wisdom. It must be emphasized that the implications of these questions of judicial policy are of fundamental significance for the other branches of the Federal Government.

Such a rule could readily be applied to this case. Although various efforts have been made in Congress to authorize public actions to contest the validity of federal expenditures in aid of religiously affiliated schools and other institutions, no such authorization has yet been given.

This does not mean that we would, under such a rule, be enabled to avoid our constitutional responsibilities, or that we would confine to limbo the First Amendment or any other constitutional command. The question here is not, despite the Court's unarticulated premise, whether the religious clauses of the First Amendment are hereafter to be enforced by the federal courts; the issue is simply whether plaintiffs of an *additional* category, heretofore excluded from those courts, are to be permitted to maintain suits. The recent history of this Court is replete with illustrations, including even one announced today that questions involving the religious clauses will not, if federal taxpayers are prevented from contesting federal expenditures, be left "unacknowledged, unresolved, and undecided."

Accordingly, for the reasons contained in this opinion, I would affirm the judgment of the District Court.

Valley Forge Christian College v. Americans United for Separation of Church and State, Inc.
454 U.S. 464, 102 S.Ct. 752 (1982)

Americans United for Separation of Church and State, an organization dedicated to the separation of religion from government, filed a suit in federal district court in Pennsylvania to stop the Department of Health, Education and Welfare (now the Department of Education) from conveying as "surplus property" a closed and former army hospital to Valley Forge Christian College. Under the Federal Property and Administrative Services Act of 1949, the department has authority to sell surplus government property for educational use to nonprofit, tax-exempt educational institutions. Congress has the power to "dispose of and make all needful Rules and Regulations respecting the . . . Property belonging to the United States," under Article IV, Section 3, Clause 2. But Americans United for Separation of Church and State contended that the department's conveyance here abridged its members First Amendment rights to religious freedom and "deprived [them] of the fair and constitutional use of [their] tax dollars." The district court dismissed the suit but the Court of Appeals for the Third Circuit reversed. Thereupon, Valley Forge Christian College appealed to the Supreme Court.

Justice REHNQUIST delivers the opinion of the Court.

We need not mince words when we say that the concept of "Art. III standing" has not been defined with complete consistency in all of the various cases decided by this Court which have discussed it, nor when we say that this very fact is probably proof that the concept cannot be reduced to a one-sentence or one-paragraph definition. But of one thing we may be sure: Those who do not possess Art. III standing may not litigate as suitors in the courts of the United States. Article III, which is every bit as important in its circumscription of the judicial power of the United States as in its granting of that power, is not merely a troublesome hurdle to be overcome if possible so as to reach the "merits" of a lawsuit which a party desires to have adjudicated; it is a part of the basic charter promulgated by the Framers of the Constitution at Philadelphia in 1787, a charter which created a general government, provided for the interaction between that government and the governments of the several States, and was later amended so as to either enhance or limit its authority with respect to both States and individuals. . . .

[I]n *Flast v. Cohen*, [392 U.S. 83 (1968)], [t]he Court developed a two-part test to determine whether the plaintiffs had standing to sue. First, because a taxpayer alleges injury only by virtue of his liability for taxes, the Court held that "a taxpayer will be a proper party to allege the unconstitutionality only of exercises of congressional power under the taxing and spending clause of Art. I, § 8, of the Constitution." Second, the Court required the taxpayer to "show that the challenged enactment exceeds specific constitutional limitations upon the exercise of the taxing and spending power and not simply that the enactment is generally beyond the powers delegated to Congress by Art. I, § 8."

Unlike the plaintiffs in *Flast*, respondents fail the first prong of the test for taxpayer standing. Their claim is deficient in two respects. First, the source of their complaint is not a congressional action, but a decision by HEW to transfer a parcel of federal property. *Flast* limited taxpayer standing to challenges directed "only [at] exercises of congressional power." See *Schlesinger v. Reservists Committee to Stop the War*, [418 U.S. 208 (1974)] (denying standing because the taxpayer plaintiffs "did not challenge an enactment under Art. I, § 8, but rather the action of the Executive Branch").

Second, and perhaps redundantly, the property transfer about which respondents complain was not an exercise of authority conferred by the Taxing and Spending Clause of Art. I, § 8. The authorizing legislation, the Federal Property and Administrative Services Act of 1949, was an evident exercise of Congress' power under the Property Clause, Art. IV, § 3, cl. 2. Respondents do not dispute this conclusion, and it is decisive of any claim of taxpayer standing under the *Flast* precedent.

Justice BRENNAN, with whom Justice MARSHALL and Justice BLACKMUN join, dissenting.

The opinion of the Court is a stark example of this unfortunate trend of resolving cases at the "threshold" while obscuring the nature of the underlying rights and interests at stake. The Court waxes eloquent on the blend of prudential and constitutional considerations that combine to create our misguided "standing" jurisprudence. *But not one word is said about the Establishment Clause right that the plaintiff seeks to enforce.* And despite its pat recitation of our standing decisions, the opinion utterly fails, except by the sheerest form of *ipse dixit*, to explain why this case is unlike *Flast v. Cohen* (1968), and is controlled instead by *Frothingham v. Mellon* (1923). . . .

It is at once apparent that the test of standing formulated by the Court in *Flast* sought to reconcile the developing doctrine of taxpayer "standing" with the Court's historical understanding that the Establishment Clause was intended to prohibit the Federal Government from using tax funds for the advancement of religion, and thus the constitutional imperative of taxpayer standing in certain cases brought pursuant to the Establishment Clause. The two-pronged "nexus" test offered by the Court, despite its general language, is best understood as "a determinant of standing of plaintiffs alleging only injury as taxpayers who challenge alleged violations of the Establishment and Free Exercise Clauses of the First Amendment," and not as a general statement of standing principles. The test explains what forms of governmental action may be attacked by someone alleging *only* taxpayer status, and, without ruling out the possibility that history might reveal another similarly founded provision, explains why an Establishment Clause claim is treated differently from any other assertion that the Federal Government has exceeded the bounds of the law in allocating its largesse. . . .

The nexus test that the Court "announced," sought to maintain necessary continuity with prior cases, and set forth principles to guide future cases involving taxpayer standing. But *Flast* did not depart from the principle that no judgment about standing should be made without a fundamental understanding of the rights at issue. The two-part *Flast* test did not supply the rationale for the Court's decision, but rather is exposition: That rationale was supplied by an understanding of the nature of the restrictions on government power imposed by the Constitution and the intended beneficiaries of those restrictions.

It may be that Congress can tax for *almost* any reason, or for no reason at all. There is, so far as I have been able to discern, but one constitutionally imposed limit on that authority. Congress cannot use tax money to support a church, or to encourage religion. That is "*the* forbidden exaction." *Everson v. Board of Education* [330 U.S. 1 (1947)]. In absolute terms the history of the Establishment Clause of the First Amendment makes this clear. History also makes it clear that the federal taxpayer is a singularly "proper and appropriate party to invoke a federal court's jurisdiction" to challenge a federal bestowal of largesse as a violation of the Establishment Clause. Each, and indeed every, federal taxpayer suffers precisely the injury that the Establishment Clause guards against when the Federal Government directs that funds be taken from the pocketbooks of the citizenry and placed into the coffers of the ministry.

A taxpayer cannot be asked to raise his objection to such use of his funds at the time he pays his tax. Apart from the unlikely circumstance in which the Government announced in advance that a particular levy would be used for religious subsidies, taxpayers could hardly assert that they were being injured until the Government actually lent its support to a religious venture. Nor would it be reasonable to require him to address his claim to those officials charged with the collection of federal taxes. Those officials would be without the means to provide appropriate redress—there is no practical way to segregate the complaining taxpayer's money from that being devoted to the religious purpose. Surely, then, a taxpayer must have standing at the time that he learns of the Government's alleged Establishment Clause violation to seek equitable relief in order to halt the continuing and intolerable burden on his pocketbook, his conscience, and his constitutional rights.

Blind to history, the Court attempts to distinguish this case from *Flast* by wrenching snippets of language from our opinions, and by perfunctorily applying that language under color of the first prong of *Flast*'s two-part nexus test. The tortuous distinctions thus produced are specious, at best: at worst, they are pernicious to our constitutional heritage.

First, the Court finds this case different from *Flast* because here the "source of [plaintiffs'] complaint is not a *congressional* action, but a decision by HEW to transfer a parcel of federal property." This attempt at distinction cannot withstand scrutiny. *Flast* involved a challenge to the actions of the Commissioner of Education, and other officials of HEW, in disbursing funds under the Elementary and Secondary Education Act of 1965 to "religious and sectarian" schools. Plaintiffs disclaimed "any intent[ion] to challenge . . . all programs under . . . the Act." Rather, they claimed that defendant-administrators' approval of such expenditures was not authorized by the Act, or alternatively, to the extent the expenditures were authorized, the Act was "unconstitutional and void." In the present case, respondents challenge HEW's grant of property pursuant to the Federal Property and Administrative Services Act of 1949, seeking to enjoin HEW "from making a grant of this and other property to the [defendant] so long as such a grant will violate the Establishment Clause." It may be that the Court is concerned with the adequacy of respondents' pleading; respondents have not, in so many words, asked for a declaration that the "Federal Property and Administrative Services Act is unconstitutional and void to the extent that it authorizes HEW's actions." I would not construe their complaint so narrowly.

More fundamentally, no clear division can be drawn in this context between actions of the Legislative Branch and those of the Executive Branch. To be sure, the First Amendment is phrased as a restriction on Congress' legislative authority; this is only natural since the Constitution assigns the authority to legislate and appropriate only to the Congress. But it is difficult to conceive of an expenditure for which the last governmental actor, either implementing directly the legislative will, or acting within the scope of legislatively delegated authority, is not an Executive Branch official. The First Amendment binds the Government as a whole, regardless of which branch is at work in a particular instance.

The Court's second purported distinction between this case and *Flast* is equally unavailing. The majority finds it "decisive" that the Federal Property and Administrative Services Act of 1949 "was an evident exercise of Congress' power under the Property Clause, Art. IV, § 3, cl. 2," while the Government action in *Flast* was taken under Art. I, § 8. The Court relies on *United States v. Richardson*, 418 U.S. [166] (1974), and *Schlesinger v. Reservists Committee to Stop the War*, 418 U.S. 208 (1974), to support the distinction between the two Clauses, noting that those cases involved alleged deviations from the requirements of Art. I, § 9, cl. 7, and Art. I, § 6, cl. 2, respectively. The standing defect in each case was *not*, however, the failure to allege a violation of the Spending Clause; rather, the taxpayers in those cases had not complained of the distribution of Government largesse, and thus failed to meet the essential requirement of taxpayer standing recognized in *Doremus* [*v. Board of Education*, 342 U.S. 429 (1952)].

It can make no constitutional difference in the case before us whether the donation to the petitioner here was in the form of a cash grant to build a facility, see *Tilton v. Richardson*, 403 U.S. 672 (1971), or in the nature of a gift of property including a facility already built. That this is a meaningless distinction is illustrated by *Tilton*. In that case, taxpayers were afforded standing to object to the fact that the Government had not received adequate assurance that if the property that it financed for use as an educational facility was later converted to religious uses, it would receive full value for the property, as the Constitution requires. The complaint here is precisely that, although the property at issue is actually being used for a sectarian purpose, the Government has not received, nor demanded, full value payment. Whether undertaken pursuant to the Property Clause or the Spending Clause, the breach of the Establishment Clause, and the relationship of the taxpayer to that breach, is precisely the same.

Plainly hostile to the Framers' understanding of the Establishment Clause, and *Flast*'s enforcement of that understanding, the Court vents that hostility under the guise of standing, "to slam the courthouse door against plaintiffs who [as the Framers intended] are entitled to full consideration of their [Establishment Clause] claims on the merits." *Barlow v. Collins*, 397 U.S. 159 (1970) (BRENNAN, J., concurring in result and dissenting). Therefore, I dissent.

Justice STEVENS dissenting.

For the Court to hold that plaintiffs' standing depends on whether the Government's transfer was an exercise of its power to spend money, on the one hand, or its power to dispose of tangible property, on the other, is to trivialize the standing doctrine. . . .

Today the Court holds, in effect, that the Judiciary has no greater role in enforcing the Establishment Clause than in enforcing other "norm[s] of conduct which the Federal Government is bound to honor," such as the Accounts Clause, *United States v. Richardson*, and the Incompatibility Clause, *Schlesinger v. Reservists Committee to Stop the War*. Ironically, however, its decision rests on the premise that the difference between a disposition of funds pursuant to the Spending Clause and a disposition of realty pursuant to the Property Clause is of fundamental jurisprudential significance. With all due respect, I am persuaded that the essential holding of *Flast v. Cohen* attaches special importance to the Establishment Clause and does not permit the drawing of a tenuous distinction between the Spending Clause and the Property Clause.

Baker v. Carr
369 U.S. 186, 82 S.Ct. 691 (1962)

In 1901, the Tennessee legislature apportioned both houses and provided for subsequent reapportionment every ten years on the basis of the number of voters in each of the state's counties as reported in the census. But for more than sixty years proposals to redistribute legislative seats failed to pass, while the state's population shifted from rural to urban areas. Charles Baker and several other citizens and urban residents sued various Tennessee officials. Baker claimed that as an urban resident he was being denied the equal protection of the law under the Fourteenth Amendment. He asked the court to order state officials to either hold an at-large election or an election in which legislators would be selected from constituencies in accordance with the 1960 federal census. The federal district court dismissed the suit, conceding that Baker's civil rights were being denied but holding that the court could offer no remedy. Baker made a further appeal to the Supreme Court.

When the Supreme Court granted review in *Baker v. Carr,* it faced two central issues: first, whether the malapportionment of a state legislature is a "political question" for which courts have no remedy and second, the merits of Baker's claim that individuals have a right to equal votes and equal representation. With potentially broad political consequences, the case was divisive for the Court and was carried over and reargued for a term. Allies on judicial self-restraint, Justices Frankfurter and Harlan were committed to their view, expressed in *Colegrove v. Green,* 328 U.S. 549 (1948), that the "Court ought not to enter this political thicket." At conference, Justices Clark and Whittaker supported their view that the case presented a nonjusticiable political question. By contrast, Chief Justice Warren and Justices Black, Douglas, and Brennan thought that the issue was justiciable. They were also prepared to address the merits of the case. The pivotal justice, Potter Stewart, considered the issue justiciable, but he refused to address the merits of the case. He voted to reverse the lower court ruling only if the Court's decision was limited to holding that courts have jurisdiction to decide such disputes. He did not want the Court to take on the merits of reapportionment in this case.

Assigned the task of drafting the opinion, Brennan had to hold on to Stewart's vote and dissuade Black and Douglas from writing opinions on the merits that would threaten the loss of the crucial fifth vote. After circulating his draft and incorporating suggested changes, he optimistically wrote Black, "Potter Stewart was satisfied with all of the changes. The Chief also is agreed. It, therefore, looks as though we have a court agreed upon this as circulated." It appeared that the decision would come down on the original five to four vote.

Clark, however, had been pondering the fact that in this case the population ratio for the urban and rural districts in Tennessee was more than nineteen to one. As he put it, "city slickers" had been "too long deprive[d] of a constitutional form of government." Clark concluded that citizens denied equal voting power had no political recourse; their only recourse was to the federal judiciary. Clark thus wrote an opinion abandoning Frankfurter and going beyond the majority to address the merits of the claim.

Brennan faced the dilemma of how to bring in Clark without losing Stewart, and thereby enlarge the consensus. Further negotiations were necessary but limited. Brennan wrote his brethren:

> The changes represent the maximum to which Potter will subscribe. We discussed much more elaborate changes which would have taken over a substantial part of Tom Clark's opinion. Potter felt that if they were made it would be necessary for him to dissent from that much of the revised opinion. I therefore decided it was best not to press for the changes but to hope that Tom will be willing to join the Court opinion but say he would go further as per his separate opinion.

Even though there were five votes for deciding the merits, the final opinion was limited to the jurisdictional question. Douglas refrained from addressing the merits in his concurring opinion. Stewart joined with an opinion emphasizing how limited he deemed the ruling. Clark filed his opinion discussing the merits of the case. Whittaker withdrew from the case, retiring from the Court two weeks later because of poor health. Only Frankfurter and Harlan were left dissenting, resulting in a six-to-two majority.*

Justice BRENNAN delivers the opinion of the Court.

[W]e hold today only (a) that the court possessed jurisdiction of the subject matter: (b) that a justiciable cause of action is stated upon which appellants would be entitled to appropriate relief; and (c) because appellees raise the issue before this Court, that the appellants have standing to challenge the Tennessee apportionment statutes. Beyond noting that we have no cause at this

---

* Sources of quotations are internal Court memos, located in the William J. Brennan, Jr., Papers, Library of Congress; and the Tom C. Clark Papers, University of Texas Law School.

stage to doubt the District Court will be able to fashion relief if violations of constitutional rights are found, it is improper now to consider what remedy would be most appropriate if appellants prevail at the trial.

JURISDICTION OF THE SUBJECT MATTER

The District Court was uncertain whether our cases withholding federal judicial relief rested upon a lack of federal jurisdiction or upon the inappropriateness of the subject matter for judicial consideration—what we have designated "nonjusticiability." The distinction between the two grounds is significant. In the instance of nonjusticiability, consideration of the cause is not wholly and immediately foreclosed: rather, the Court's inquiry necessarily proceeds to the point of deciding whether the duty asserted can be judicially identified and its breach judicially determined, and whether protection for the right asserted can be judicially molded. In the instance of lack of jurisdiction the cause either does not "arise under" the Federal Constitution, laws or treaties (or fall within one of the other enumerated categories of Art. III, § 2), or is not a "case or controversy" within the meaning of that section; or the cause is not one described by any jurisdictional statute. Our conclusion that this cause presents no nonjusticiable "political question" settles the only possible doubt that it is a case or controversy. . . .

The appellees refer to *Colegrove v. Green,* 328 U.S. 549 [1946], as authority that the District Court lacked jurisdiction of the subject matter. Appellees misconceive the holding of that case. The holding was precisely contrary to their reading of it. Seven members of the Court participated in the decision. Unlike many other cases in this field which have assumed without discussion that there was jurisdiction, all three opinions filed in Colegrove discussed the question. Two of the opinions expressing the views of four of the Justices, a majority, flatly held that there was jurisdiction of that subject matter. Justice BLACK joined by Justice DOUGLAS and Justice MURPHY stated: "It is my judgment that the District Court had jurisdiction. . . ." Justice RUTLEDGE, writing separately, expressed agreement with this conclusion. . . . Indeed, it is even questionable that the opinion of Justice FRANK-FURTER, joined by Justices REED and BURTON, doubted jurisdiction of the subject matter. . . .

JUSTICIABILITY

In holding that the subject matter of this suit was not justiciable, the District Court relied on *Colegrove v. Green,* supra, and subsequent *per curiam* cases. The court stated: "From a review of these decisions there can be no doubt that the federal rule . . . is that the federal courts . . . will not intervene in cases of this type to compel legislative reapportionment." We understand the District

Court to have read the cited cases as compelling the conclusion that since the appellants sought to have a legislative apportionment held unconstitutional, their suit presented a "political question" and was therefore nonjusticiable. We hold that this challenge to an apportionment presents no nonjusticiable "political question." The cited cases do not hold the contrary.

Of course the mere fact that the suit seeks protection of a political right does not mean it presents a political question. Such an objection "is little more than a play upon words." Rather, it is argued that apportionment cases, whatever the actual wording of the complaint, can involve no federal constitutional right except one resting on the guaranty of a republican form of government, and that complaints based on that clause have been held to present political questions which are nonjusticiable.

We hold that the claim pleaded here neither rests upon nor implicates the Guaranty Clause and that its justiciability is therefore not foreclosed by our decisions of cases involving that clause. . . . To show why we reject the argument based on the Guaranty Clause, we must examine the authorities under it. But because there appears to be some uncertainty as to why those cases did present political questions, and specifically as to whether this apportionment case is like those cases, we deem it necessary first to consider the contours of the "political question" doctrine.

Our discussion, even at the price of extending this opinion, requires review of a number of political question cases, in order to expose the attributes of the doctrine—attributes which, in various settings, diverge, combine, appear, and disappear in seeming disorderliness. . . .

We have said that "In determining whether a question falls within [the political question] category, the appropriateness under our system of government of attributing finality to the action of the political departments and also the lack of satisfactory criteria for a judicial determination are dominant considerations." *Coleman v. Miller* [307 U.S. 433 (1939)]. The nonjusticiability of a political question is primarily a function of the separation of powers. Much confusion results from the capacity of the "political question" label to obscure the need for case-by-case inquiry. Deciding whether a matter has in any measure been committed by the Constitution to another branch of government, or whether the action of that branch exceeds whatever authority has been committed, is itself a delicate exercise in constitutional interpretation, and is a responsibility of this Court as ultimate interpreter of the Constitution. To demonstrate this requires no less than to analyze representative cases and to infer from them the analytical threads that make up the political question doctrine. We shall then show that none of those threads catches this case.

Foreign relations: There are sweeping statements to the effect that all questions touching foreign relations are political questions. Not only does resolution of such issues frequently turn on standards that defy judicial application, or involve the exercise of a discretion demonstrably committed to the executive or legislature; but many such questions uniquely demand single-voiced statement of the Government's views. Yet it is error to suppose that every case or controversy which touches foreign relations lies beyond judicial cognizance. Our cases in this field seem invariably to show a discriminating analysis of the particular question posed, in terms of the history of its management by the political branches, of its susceptibility to judicial handling in the light of its nature and posture in the specific case, and of the possible consequences of judicial action. . . .

Dates of duration of hostilities: Though it has been stated broadly that the power which declared the necessity is the power to declare its cessation, and what the cessation requires," *Commercial Trust Co. v. Miller,* 262 U.S. 51 [1923], here too analysis reveals isolable reasons for the presence of political questions, underlying this Court's refusal to review the political departments' determination of when or whether a war has ended. Dominant is the need for finality in the political determination, for emergency's nature demands "A prompt and unhesitating obedience." *Martin v. Mott,* 12 Wheat. [(256 U.S.) 19 (1827)] [Calling up of militia.] . . . Further, clearly definable criteria for decision may be available. In such case the political question barrier falls away. . . .

Validity of enactments: In *Coleman v. Miller,* supra, this Court held that the questions of how long a proposed amendment to the Federal Constitution remained open to ratification, and what effect a prior rejection had on a subsequent ratification, were committed to congressional resolution and involved criteria of decision that necessarily escaped the judicial grasp. Similar considerations apply to the enacting process: "The respect due to coequal and independent departments," and the need for finality and certainty about the status of a statute contribute to judicial reluctance to inquire whether, as passed, it complied with all requisite formalities. *Field v. Clark,* 143 U.S. 649 [1892]. . . .

Republican form of government: Luther v. Borden, 7 How. 1 [1848], though in form simply an action for damages for trespass was, as Daniel Webster said in opening the argument for the defense, "an unusual case." The defendants, admitting an otherwise tortious breaking and entering, sought to justify their action on the ground that they were agents of the established lawful government of Rhode Island, which State was then under martial law to defend itself from active insurrection; that the plaintiff was engaged in that insurrection; and that they entered under orders to arrest the plaintiff. The case arose "out of the unfortunate political differences which agitated the people of Rhode Island in 1841 and 1842," and which had resulted in a situation wherein two groups laid competing claims to recognition as the lawful government. . . .

Chief Justice TANEY's opinion for the Court reasoned as follows: (1) If a court were to hold the defendants' acts unjustified because the charter government had no legal existence during the period in question, it would follow that all of that government's actions—laws enacted, taxes collected, salaries paid, accounts settled, sentences passed—were of no effect; and that "the officers who carried their decisions into operation [were]answerable as trespassers, if not in some cases as criminals." There was, of course, no room for application of any doctrine of *de facto* status to uphold prior acts of an officer not authorized *de jure,* for such would have defeated the plaintiff's very action. A decision for the plaintiff would inevitably have produced some significant measure of chaos, a consequence to be avoided if it could be done without abnegation of the judicial duty to uphold the Constitution.

(2) No state court had recognized as a judicial responsibility settlement of the issue of the locus of state governmental authority. Indeed, the courts of Rhode Island had in several cases held that "it rested with the political power to decide whether the charter government had been displaced or not," and that that department had acknowledged no change.

(3) Since "[t]he question relates, altogether, to the constitution and laws of [the] . . . State," the courts of the United States had to follow the state courts' decisions unless there was a federal constitutional ground for overturning them.

(4) No provision of the Constitution could be or had been invoked for this purpose except Art. IV, § 4, the Guaranty Clause. Having already noted the absence of standards whereby the choice between governments could be made by a court acting independently, Chief Justice TANEY now found further textual and practical reasons for concluding that, if any department of the United States was empowered by the Guaranty Clause to resolve the issue, it was not the judiciary:

"Under this article of the Constitution it rests with Congress to decide what government is the established one in a State. For as the United States guarantee to each State a republican government, Congress must necessarily decide what government is established in the State before it can determine whether it is a republican or not. And when the senators and representatives of a State are admitted into the councils of the Union, the authority of the government under which they are appointed, as well as its republican character, is recognized by the proper constitutional authority. And its decision is binding on every other department of the government, and could not be questioned in a judicial tribunal. It is true that the contest in this case did not last long enough to bring the matter to this issue; and . . . Congress was not called upon to decide the controversy. Yet the right to decide is placed there, and not in the courts.

"So, too, as relates to the clause in the above-mentioned article of the Constitution, providing for cases of domestic violence. It rested with Congress, too, to determine upon the means proper to be adopted to fulfill this guarantee. . . . [B]y the act of February 28, 1795, [Congress] provided, that, 'in case of an insurrection in any State against the government thereof, it shall be lawful for the President of the United States, on application of the legislature of such State or of the executive (when the legislature cannot be convened) to call forth such number of the militia of any other State or States, as may be applied for, as he may judge sufficient to suppress such insurrection.'

"By this act, the power of deciding whether the exigency had arisen upon which the government of the United States is bound to interfere, is given to the President" [*Luther v. Borden*].

Clearly, several factors were thought by the Court in *Luther* to make the question there "political": the commitment to the other branches of the decision as to which is the lawful state government; the unambiguous action by the President, in recognizing the charter government as the lawful authority; the need for finality in the executive's decision; and the lack of criteria by which a court could determine which form of government was republican. . . .

But the only significance that *Luther* could have for our immediate purposes is in its holding that the Guaranty Clause is not a repository of judicially manageable standards which a court could utilize independently in order to identify a State's lawful government. The Court has since refused to resort to the Guaranty Clause—which alone had been invoked for the purpose—as the source of a constitutional standard for invalidating state action. . . .

We come, finally, to the ultimate inquiry whether our precedents as to what constitutes a nonjusticiable "political question" bring the case before us under the umbrella of that doctrine. A natural beginning is to note whether any of the common characteristics which we have been able to identify and label descriptively are present. We find none: The question here is the consistency of state action with the Federal Constitution. We have no question decided, or to be decided, by a political branch of government coequal with this Court. Nor do we risk embarrassment of our government abroad, or grave disturbance at home if we take issue with Tennessee as to the constitutionality of her action here challenged. Nor need the appellants, in order to succeed in this action, ask the Court to enter upon policy determinations for which judicially manageable standards are lacking. Judicial standards under the Equal Protection Clause are well developed and familiar, and it has been open to courts since the enactment of the Fourteenth Amendment to determine, if on the particular facts they must, that a discrimination reflects *no* policy, but simply arbitrary and capricious action.

This case does, in one sense, involve the allocation of political power within a State, and the appellants might conceivably have added a claim under the Guaranty Clause. Of course, as we have seen, any reliance on that clause would be futile. But because any reliance on the Guaranty Clause could not have succeeded it does not follow that appellants may not be heard on the equal protection claim which in fact they tender. . . .

We conclude that the complaint's allegations of a denial of equal protection present a justiciable constitutional cause of action upon which appellants are entitled to a trial and a decision. The right asserted is within the reach of judicial protection under the Fourteenth Amendment.

The judgment of the District Court is reversed and the cause is remanded for further proceedings consistent with this opinion.

Reversed and remanded.

Justice WHITTAKER did not participate in the decision of this case.

Justice DOUGLAS concurring.

While I join the opinion of the Court and, like the Court, do not reach the merits, a word of explanation is necessary. I put to one side the problems of "political" questions involving the distribution of power between this Court, the Congress, and the Chief Executive. We have here a phase of the recurring problem of the relation of the federal courts to state agencies. More particularly, the question is the extent to which a State may weight one person's vote more heavily than it does another's.

So far as voting rights are concerned, there are large gaps in the Constitution. Yet the right to vote is inherent in the republican form of government envisaged by Article IV, Section 4 of the Constitution. . . .

Race, color, or previous condition of servitude is an impermissible standard by reason of the Fifteenth Amendment, and that alone is sufficient to explain *Gomillion v. Lightfoot,* 364 U.S. 339 [1960].

Sex is another impermissible standard by reason of the Nineteenth Amendment.

There is a third barrier to a State's freedom in prescribing qualifications of voters and that is the Equal Protection Clause of the Fourteenth Amendment, the provision invoked here. And so the question is, may a State weight the vote of one county or one district more heavily than it weights the vote in another?

The traditional test under the Equal Protection Clause has been whether a State has made "an invidious discrimination," as it does when it selects "a particular race or nationality for oppressive treatment." Universal equality is not the test; there is room for weighting. . . .

I agree with my Brother CLARK that if the allegations in the complaint can be sustained a case for relief is established. We are told that a single vote in Moore County, Tennessee, is worth 19 votes in Hamilton County, that one vote in Stewart or in Chester County is worth nearly eight times a single vote in Shelby or Knox County. The opportunity to prove that an "invidious discrimination" exists should therefore be given the appellants.

Justice CLARK concurring.

One emerging from the rash of opinions with their accompanying clashing of views may well find himself suffering a mental blindness. The Court holds that the appellants have alleged a cause of action. However, it refuses to award relief here—although the facts are undisputed—and fails to give the District Court any guidance whatever. One dissenting opinion, bursting with words that go through so much and conclude with so little, contemns the majority action as "a massive repudiation of the experience of our whole past." Another describes the complaint as merely asserting conclusory allegations that Tennessee's apportionment is "incorrect," "arbitrary," "obsolete," and "unconstitutional." I believe it can be shown that this case is distinguishable from earlier cases dealing with the distribution of political power by a State, that a patent violation of the Equal Protection Clause of the United States Constitution has been shown, and that an appropriate remedy may be formulated. . . .

The truth is that—although this case has been here for two years and has had over six hours' argument (three times the ordinary case) and has been most carefully considered over and over again by us in Conference and individually—no one, not even the State nor the dissenters, has come up with any rational basis for Tennessee's apportionment statute. . . .

Although I find the Tennessee apportionment statute offends the Equal Protection Clause, I would not consider intervention by this Court into so delicate a field if there were any other relief available to the people of Tennessee. But the majority of the people of Tennessee have no "practical opportunities for exerting their political weight at the polls" to correct the existing "invidious discrimination." Tennessee has no initiative and referendum. I have searched diligently for other "practical opportunities" present under the law. I find none other than through the federal courts. The majority of the voters have been caught up in a legislative strait jacket. Tennessee has an "informed, civically militant electorate" and "an aroused popular conscience," but it does not sear "the conscience of the people's representatives." This is because the legislative policy has riveted the present seats in the Assembly to their respective constituencies, and by the votes of their incumbents a reapportionment of any kind is prevented. The people have been rebuffed at the hands of the Assembly; they have tried the constitutional convention route, but since the call must originate in the Assembly it, too, has been fruitless. They have tried Tennessee courts with the same result, and Governors have fought the tide only to flounder. It is said that there is recourse in Congress and perhaps that may be, but from a practical standpoint this is without substance. To date Congress has never undertaken such a task in any State. We therefore must conclude that the people of Tennessee are stymied and without judicial intervention will be saddled with the present discrimination in the affairs of their state government.

Justice STEWART concurring.

The separate writings of my dissenting and concurring Brothers stray so far from the subject of today's decision as to convey, I think, a distressingly inaccurate impression of what the Court decides. For that reason, I think it appropriate, in joining the opinion of the Court, to emphasize in a few words what the opinion does and does not say.

The Court today decides three things and no more: "(a) that the court possessed jurisdiction of the subject matter; (b) that a justiciable cause of action is stated upon which appellants would be entitled to appropriate relief; and (c) . . . that the appellants have standing to challenge the Tennessee apportionment statutes.". . .

Justice FRANKFURTER, with whom Justice HARLAN joins, dissenting.

The Court today reverses a uniform course of decision established by a dozen cases, including one by which the very claim now sustained was unanimously rejected only five years ago. The impressive body of rulings thus cast aside reflected the equally uniform course of our political history regarding the relationship between population and legislative representation—a wholly different matter from denial of the franchise to individuals because of race, color, religion or sex. Such a massive repudiation of the experience of our whole past in asserting destructively novel judicial power demands a detailed analysis of the role of this Court in our constitutional scheme. Disregard of inherent limits in the effective exercise of the Court's "judicial Power" not only presages the futility of judicial intervention in the essentially political conflict of forces by which the relation between population and representation has time out of mind been and now is determined. It may well impair the Court's position as the ultimate organ of "the supreme Law of the Land" in that vast range of legal problems, often strongly entangled in popular feeling, on which this Court must pronounce. The Court's authority—possessed of neither the purse nor the sword—ultimately rests on sustained public confidence in its moral sanction. Such feeling must be nourished by the Court's complete detachment, in fact and in appearance, from political entanglements and by abstention from injecting itself into the clash of political forces in political settlements.

A hypothetical claim resting on abstract assumptions is now for the first time made the basis for affording illusory relief for a particular evil even though it foreshadows deeper and more pervasive difficulties in consequence. The claim is hypothetical and the assumptions are abstract because the Court does not vouchsafe the lower courts—state and federal—guidelines for formulating specific, definite, wholly unprecedented remedies for the inevitable litigations that today's umbrageous disposition is bound to stimulate in connection with politically motivated reapportionments in so many States. In such a setting, to promulgate jurisdiction in the abstract is meaningless. It is as devoid of reality as "a brooding omnipresence in the sky," for it conveys no intimation what relief, if any, a District Court is capable of affording that would not invite legislatures to play ducks and drakes with the judiciary. For this Court to direct the District Court to enforce a claim to which the Court has over the years consistently found itself required to deny legal enforcement and at the same time to find it necessary to withhold any guidance to the lower court how to enforce this turnabout, new legal claim, manifests an odd—indeed an esoteric—conception of judicial propriety. One of the Court's supporting opinions, as elucidated by commentary, unwittingly affords a disheartening preview of the mathematical quagmire (apart from divers judicially inappropriate and elusive determinants) into which this Court today catapults the lower courts of the country without so much as adumbrating the basis for a legal calculus as a means of extrication. Even assuming the indispensable intellectual disinterestedness on the part of judges in such matters, they do not have accepted legal standards or criteria or even reliable analogies to draw upon for making judicial judgments. To charge courts with the task of accommodating the incommensurable factors of policy that underlie these mathematical puzzles is to attribute, however flatteringly, omnicompetence to judges. . . .

We were soothingly told at the bar of this Court that we need not worry about the kind of remedy a court could effectively fashion once the abstract constitutional right to have courts pass on a state-wide system of electoral districting is recognized as a matter of judicial rhetoric, because legislatures would heed the Court's admonition. This is not only a euphoric hope. It implies a sorry confession of judicial impotence in place of a frank acknowledgment that there is not under our Constitution a judicial remedy for every political mischief, for every undesirable exercise of legislative power. The Framers carefully and with deliberate forethought refused so to enthrone the judiciary. In this situation, as in others of like nature, appeal for relief does not belong here. Appeal must be to an informed, civically militant electorate. In a democratic society like ours, relief must come through an aroused popular conscience that sears the conscience of the people's representatives. In any event there is nothing judicially more unseemly nor more self-defeating than for this Court to make *in terrorem* pronouncements, to indulge in merely empty rhetoric, sounding a word of promise to the ear, sure to be disappointing to the hope. . . .

From its earliest opinions this Court has consistently recognized a class of controversies which do not lend themselves to judicial standards and judicial remedies. To classify the various instances as "political questions" is rather a form of stating this conclusion than revealing of analysis. Some of the cases so labelled have no relevance here. But from others emerge unifying considerations that are compelling.

1. The cases concerning war or foreign affairs, for example, are usually explained by the necessity of the country's speaking with one voice in such matters. While this concern alone undoubtedly accounts for many of the decisions, others do not fit the pattern. It would hardly embarrass the conduct of war were this Court to determine, in connection with private transactions between litigants, the date upon which war is to be deemed terminated. But the Court has refused to do so. A controlling factor in such cases is that, decision respecting these kinds of complex matters of policy being traditionally committed not to courts but to the political agencies of government for determination by criteria of political expediency, there exists no standard ascertainable by settled judicial experience or process by reference to which a political decision affecting the question at issue between the parties can be judged. . . .

2. The Court has been particularly unwilling to intervene in matters concerning the structure and organization of the political institutions of the States. The abstention from judicial entry into such areas has been greater even than that which marks the Court's ordinary approach to issues of state power challenged under broad federal guarantees. . . .

3. The cases involving Negro disfranchisement are no exception to the principle of avoiding federal judicial intervention into matters of state government in the absence of an explicit and clear constitutional imperative. For here the controlling command of Supreme Law is plain and unequivocal. An end of discrimination against the Negro was the compelling motive of the Civil War Amendments. . . .

4. The Court has refused to exercise its jurisdiction to pass on "abstract questions of political power, of sovereignty, of government." *Massachusetts v. Mellon,* 262 U.S. 447 [1923]. The "political question" doctrine, in this aspect, reflects the policies underlying the requirement of "standing": that the litigant who would challenge official action must claim infringement of an interest particular and personal to himself, as distinguished from a cause of dissatisfaction with the general frame and functioning of government—a complaint that the political institutions are awry. . . . What renders cases of this kind non-justiciable is not necessarily the nature of the parties to them, for the Court has resolved other issues between similar parties; nor is it the nature of the legal question involved, for the same type of question has been adjudicated when presented in other forms of controversy. The crux of the matter is that courts are not fit instruments of decision where what is essentially at stake is the composition of those large contests of policy traditionally fought out in non-judicial forums, by which governments and the actions of governments are made and unmade. . . .

5. The influence of these converging considerations—the caution not to undertake decision where standards meet for judicial judgment are lacking, the reluctance to interfere with matters of state government in the absence of an unquestionable and effectively enforceable mandate, the unwillingness to make courts arbiters of the broad issues of political organization historically committed to other institutions and for whose adjustment the judicial process is ill-adapted—has been decisive of the settled line of cases, reaching back more than a century, which holds that Art. IV, § 4, of the Constitution, guaranteeing to the States "a Republican Form of Government," is not enforceable through the courts. . . .

The present case involves all of the elements that have made the Guarantee Clause cases non-justiciable. It is, in effect, a Guarantee Clause claim masquerading under a different label. But it cannot make the case more fit for judicial action that appellants invoke the Fourteenth Amendment rather than Art. IV, § 4, where, in fact, the gist of their complaint is the same—unless it can be found that the Fourteenth Amendment speaks with greater particularity to their situation. We have been admonished to avoid "the tyranny of labels." Art. IV, § 4, is not committed by express constitutional terms to Congress. It is the nature of the controversies arising under it, nothing else, which has made it judicially unenforceable. Of course, if a controversy falls within judicial power, it depends "on how he [the plaintiff] casts his action," whether he brings himself within a jurisdictional statute. But where judicial competence is wanting, it cannot be created by invoking one clause of the Constitution rather than another. . . .

Appellants invoke the right to vote and to have their votes counted. But they are permitted to vote and their votes are counted. They go to the polls, they cast their ballots, they send their representatives to the state councils. Their complaint is simply that the representatives are not sufficiently numerous or powerful—in short, that Tennessee has adopted a basis of representation with which they are dissatisfied. . . . What is actually asked of the Court in this case is to choose among competing bases of representation—ultimately, really, among competing theories of political philosophy—in order to establish an appropriate frame of government for the State of Tennessee and thereby for all the States of the Union. . . .

To find such a political conception legally enforceable in the broad and unspecific guarantee of equal protection is to rewrite the Constitution. See *Luther v. Borden,* supra. Certainly, "equal protection" is no more secure a foundation for judicial judgment of the permissibility of varying forms of representative government than is "Republican Form.". . .

The notion that representation proportioned to the geographic spread of population is so universally accepted as a necessary element of equality between man and man that it must be taken to be the standard of a political equality preserved by the Fourteenth Amendment—that it is, in appellants' words "the basic principle of representative government"—is, to put it bluntly, not true. However desirable and however desired by some among the great political thinkers and framers of our government, it has never been generally practiced, today or in the past. It was not the English system, it was not the colonial system, it was not the system chosen for the national government by the Constitution, it was not the system exclusively or even predominantly practiced by the States at the time of adoption of the Fourteenth Amendment, it is not predominantly practiced by the States today. Unless judges, the judges of this Court, are to make their private views of political wisdom the measure of the Constitution—views which in all honesty cannot but give the appearance, if not reflect the reality, of involvement with the business of partisan politics so inescapably a part of apportionment controversies—the Fourteenth Amendment, "itself a historical product," *Jackman v. Rosenbaum Co.,* 260 U.S. 22 [1922], provides no guide for judicial oversight of the representation problem.

Justice HARLAN, with whom Justice FRANKFURTER joins, dissenting.

I can find nothing in the Equal Protection Clause or elsewhere in the Federal Constitution which expressly or impliedly supports the view that state legislatures must be so structured as to reflect with approximate equality the voice of every voter. Not only is that proposition refuted by history, as shown by my Brother FRANKFURTER, but it strikes deep into the heart of our federal system. Its acceptance would require us to turn our backs on the regard which this Court has always shown for the judgment of state legislatures and courts on matters of basically local concern.

In the last analysis, what lies at the core of this controversy is a difference of opinion as to the function of representative government. It is surely beyond argument that those who have the responsibility for devising a system of representation may permissibly consider that factors other than bare numbers should be taken into account. The existence of the United States Senate is proof enough of that. To consider that we may ignore the Tennessee Legislature's judgment in this instance because that body was the product of an asymmetrical electoral apportionment would in effect be to assume the very conclusion here disputed. Hence we must accept the present form of the Tennessee Legislature as the embodiment of the State's choice," or, more realistically, its compromise, between competing political philosophies. The federal courts have not been empowered by the Equal Protection Clause to judge whether this resolution of the State's internal political conflict is desirable or undesirable, wise or unwise.

Goldwater v. Carter
444 U.S. 996, 100 S.Ct. 533 (1979)

In 1979, Senator Barry Goldwater and several other senators filed suit against President James ("Jimmy") Carter, challenging the constitutionality of Carter's termination of a defense treaty with Taiwan without the approval of the Senate. Underlying the case was the enduring support that the nation's conservative leadership extended toward Taiwan. A tiny island, Taiwan housed the Chinese nationalist government after it was forced out of the China mainland by the new communist government. Granting a petition for *certiorari* but without hearing oral arguments, the Court vacated a court of appeals ruling and remanded the case to a federal district court with directions to dismiss the complaint. In separate concurring opinions, Justice Powell rejects the application of the "political questions" doctrine here, while Justice Rehnquist contends that it applies here and in other controversies over foreign policy. In his dissenting opinion, Justice Brennan rejects the idea that the question presented here is "political" and further discusses the scope of the judicial power.

Justice POWELL concurring.

Although I agree with the result reached by the Court, I would dismiss the complaint as not ripe for judicial review.

This Court has recognized that an issue should not be decided if it is not ripe for judicial review. Prudential considerations persuade me that a dispute between Congress and the President is not ready for judicial review unless and until each branch has taken action asserting its constitutional authority. Differences between the President and the Congress are commonplace under our system. The differences should, and almost invariably do, turn on political rather than legal considerations. The Judicial Branch should not decide issues affecting the allocation of power between the President and Congress until the political branches reach a constitutional impasse. Otherwise, we would encourage small groups or even individual Members of Congress to seek judicial resolution of issues before the normal political process has the opportunity to resolve the conflict.

In this case, a few Members of Congress claim that the President's action in terminating the treaty with Taiwan has deprived them of their constitutional role with respect to a change in the supreme law of the land. Congress has taken no official action. In the present posture of this case, we do not know whether there ever will be an actual confrontation between the Legislative and Executive Branches. Although the Senate has considered a resolution declaring that Senate approval is necessary for the termination of any mutual defense treaty, no final vote has been taken on the resolution. Moreover, it is unclear whether the resolution would have retroactive effect. It cannot be said that either the Senate or the House has rejected the President's claim. If the Congress chooses not to confront the President, it is not our task to do so. I therefore concur in the dismissal of this case.

Justice REHNQUIST suggests, however, that the issue presented by this case is a nonjusticiable political question which can never be considered by this Court. I cannot agree. In my view, reliance upon the political-question doctrine is inconsistent with our precedents. As set forth in the seminal case of *Baker v. Carr*, [369 U.S. 186] (1962), the doctrine incorporates three inquiries: (i) Does the issue involve resolution of questions committed by the text of the Constitution to a coordinate branch of Government? (ii) Would resolution of the question demand that a court

move beyond areas of judicial expertise? (iii) Do prudential considerations counsel against judicial intervention? In my opinion the
answer to each of these inquiries would require us to decide
this case if it were ready for review. . . .

In my view, the suggestion that this case presents a political
question is incompatible with this Court's willingness on previous
occasions to decide whether one branch of our Government has
impinged upon the power of another. Under the criteria enunciated in *Baker v. Carr,* we have the responsibility to decide whether
both the Executive and Legislative Branches have constitutional
roles to play in termination of a treaty. If the Congress, by appropriate formal action, had challenged the President's authority to
terminate the treaty with Taiwan, the resulting uncertainty could
have serious consequences for our country. In that situation, it
would be the duty of this Court to resolve the issue.

JUSTICE REHNQUIST, with whom the Chief Justice, Justice
STEWART, and Justice STEVENS join, concurring.

I am of the view that the basic question presented by the petitioners in this case is "political" and therefore nonjusticiable because
it involves the authority of the President in the conduct of our
country's foreign relations and the extent to which the Senate
or the Congress is authorized to negate the action of the President.
In *Coleman v. Miller,* 307 U.S. 433 (1939), a case in which members
of the Kansas Legislature brought an action attacking a vote of
the State Senate in favor of the ratification of the Child Labor
Amendment, Chief Justice HUGHES wrote in what is referred
to as the "Opinion of the Court":

> We think that . . . the question of the efficacy of ratifications
> by state legislatures, in the light of previous rejection or at-
> tempted withdrawal, should be regarded as a political question
> pertaining to the political departments, with the ultimate au-
> thority in the Congress in the exercise of its control over the
> promulgation of the adoption of the Amendment.

> The precise question as now raised is whether, when the
> legislature of the State, as we have found, has actually ratified
> the proposed amendment, the Court should restrain the state
> officers from certifying the ratification to the Secretary of State,
> because of an earlier rejection, and thus prevent the question
> from coming before the political departments. We find no basis
> in either Constitution or statute for such judicial action. Article
> V, speaking solely of ratification, contains no provision as to
> rejection.

Thus, Chief Justice HUGHES' opinion concluded that "Congress
in controlling the promulgation of the adoption of a constitutional

amendment has the final determination of the question whether by lapse of time its proposal of the amendment had lost its vitality prior to the required ratifications.". . .

I believe it follows a *fortiori* from *Coleman* that the controversy in the instant case is a nonjusticiable political dispute that should be left for resolution by the Executive and Legislative Branches of the Government. Here, while the Constitution is express as to the manner in which the Senate shall participate in the ratification of a treaty, it is silent as to that body's participation in the abrogation of a treaty. . . .

I think that the justification for concluding that the question here is political in nature are even more compelling than in *Coleman* because it involves foreign relations—specifically a treaty commitment to use military force in the defense of a foreign government if attacked. In *United States v. Curtiss-Wright Corp.*, 299 U.S. 304 (1936), this Court said:

> Whether, if the Joint Resolution had related solely to internal affairs it would be open to the challenge that it constituted an unlawful delegation of legislative power to the Executive, we find it unnecessary to determine. The whole aim of the resolution is to affect a situation entirely external to the United States, and falling within the category of foreign affairs.

The present case differs in several important respects from *Youngstown Sheet & Tube Co. v. Sawyer*, 343 U.S. 579 (1952), cited by petitioners as authority both for reaching the merits of this dispute and for reversing the Court of Appeals. In *Youngstown*, private litigants brought a suit contesting the President's authority under his war powers to seize the Nation's steel industry, an action of profound and demonstrable domestic impact. Here, by contrast, we are asked to settle a dispute between coequal branches of our Government, each of which has resources available to protect and assert its interests, resources not available to private litigants outside the judicial forum. Moreover, as in *Curtiss-Wright*, the effect of this action, as far as we can tell, is "entirely external to the United States, and [falls] within the category of foreign affairs." Finally, as already noted, the situation presented here is closely akin to that presented in *Coleman*, where the Constitution spoke only to the procedure for ratification of an amendment, not to its rejection.

Justice BLACKMUN, with whom Justice WHITE joins, dissenting in part.

In my view, the time factor and its importance are illusory; if the President does not have the power to terminate the treaty (a substantial issue that we should address only after briefing and oral argument), the notice of intention to terminate surely has no legal effect. It is also indefensible, without further study, to pass on the issue of justiciability or on the issues of standing or ripeness. While I therefore join in the grant of the petition for certiorari, I would set the case for oral argument and give it the plenary consideration it so obviously deserves.

Justice BRENNAN dissenting.

I respectfully dissent from the order directing the District Court to dismiss this case, and would affirm the judgment of the Court of Appeals insofar as it rests upon the President's well-established authority to recognize, and withdraw recognition from, foreign governments.

In stating that this case presents a non-justiciable "political question," Justice REHNQUIST, in my view, profoundly misapprehends the political-question principle as it applies to matters of foreign relations. Properly understood, the political-question doctrine restrains courts from reviewing an exercise of foreign policy judgment by the coordinate political branch to which authority to make that judgment has been "constitutional[ly] commit[ted]." *Baker v. Carr.* But the doctrine does not pertain when a court is faced with the *antecedent* question whether a particular branch has been constitutionally designated as the repository of political decisionmaking power. The issue of decisionmaking authority must be resolved as a matter of constitutional law, not political discretion; accordingly, it falls within the competence of the courts.

The constitutional question raised here is prudently answered in narrow terms. Abrogation of the defense treaty with Taiwan was a necessary incident to Executive recognition of the Peking Government, because the defense treaty was predicated upon the now-abandoned view that the Taiwan Government was the only legitimate political authority in China. Our cases firmly establish that the Constitution commits to the President alone the power to recognize, and withdraw recognition from, foreign regimes. That mandate being clear, our judicial inquiry into the treaty rupture can go no further.

B. THE COURT'S DOCKET AND SCREENING CASES

The justices' interpretation of their jurisdiction and rules governs access to the Court. But they also need flexible procedures for screening cases and deciding what to decide. This is because the Court's docket has grown phenomenally (see Figure 2.3).

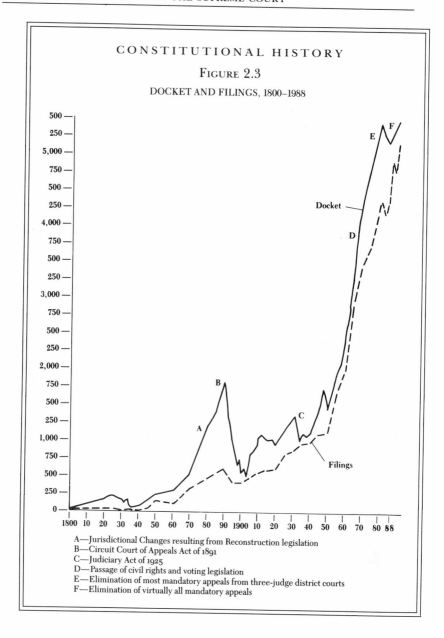

CONSTITUTIONAL HISTORY

FIGURE 2.3

DOCKET AND FILINGS, 1800–1988

A—Jurisdictional Changes resulting from Reconstruction legislation
B—Circuit Court of Appeals Act of 1891
C—Judiciary Act of 1925
D—Passage of civil rights and voting legislation
E—Elimination of most mandatory appeals from three-judge district courts
F—Elimination of virtually all mandatory appeals

When any appeal or cert. petition arrives at the Court it immediately goes to the clerk's office. Staff look at whether it satisfies
requirements as to form, length, and fees and if the filing is
from an indigent whether there is an affidavit stating that the
petitioner is too poor to pay fees. All unpaid cases are assigned

a number, in the order they arrive, and placed on what is called the Miscellaneous Docket. Paid cases are also assigned a number, but placed on the Appellate Docket. The clerk then notifies the other party, or respondent, in each case that they must file a brief in response within thirty days. After receiving briefs from respondents, the clerk circulates to the justices' chambers a list of cases ready for consideration and a set of briefs for each case.

For much of the Court's history every justice was responsible for reviewing each case. The justices did not work by panels or delegate responsibility for screening cases to others. That is no longer true. In 1972 the *"cert. pool"* was established. Seven of the justices now share their collective law clerks' memos on all paid and unpaid cases. The memos explain the facts, issues raised, and lower court ruling as well as recommend whether the case should be granted or denied. Those justices not joining the pool— Marshall and Stevens—receive copies of unpaid cases along with other filings. Brennan examined each case himself, when he had time to do so. Stevens has his clerks screen all the cases and write memos on only those they think are important enough for him to consider.

C. THE RULE OF FOUR AND AGENDA SETTING

When Congress gave the Court discretionary jurisdiction in the Judiciary Act of 1925, by substituting petitions for *certiorari* for mandatory appeals, the justices developed the informal "rule of four" to decide which petitions they would grant. During conference, at least four justices must agree that a case warrants oral argument and consideration by the full Court.

The rule of four operates in a fraction of cases due to the increasing caseload, which is a result of a number of factors. Most important, institutional norms promote a shared conception of the role of the Court as a tribunal for resolving only issues of national importance. Justices agree that the overwhelming proportion of cases are "frivolous," and that there is a limited number of cases to which they may give full consideration. "As a rule of thumb," Byron White, among others on the current Court, said, "the Court should not be expected to produce more than 150 opinions per term in argued cases."[1]

The caseload and institutional norms push toward limiting the operation of the rule of four. But the rule remains useful, particularly if there is a bloc of justices who share the same ideological orientation. The rule of four thus enables a bloc of justices to work together in picking cases they want the Court to rule on.

Denial of *certiorari* is an important technique for managing the Court's caseload. But its meaning in particular cases may be far from clear. The Court has few fixed rules and even the rule of four is not "an absolutely inflexible rule."[2] In two capital punishment cases, *Drake v. Zant* and *Westbrook v. Balkcom*, 449 U.S. 999 (1980), *four* justices issued dissenting opinions from the denial of review of both cases. Each justice indicated but for one more vote, they would have granted the case, vacated the ruling below, and remanded the case to the lower court.

Although enabling the Court to manage its business, denials invite confusion and the suspicion, as Justice Jackson once observed, "that this Court no longer respects impersonal rules of law but is guided in these matters by personal impression which from time to time may be shared by a majority of the justices."[3]

NOTES

1. Byron White, "The Work of the Supreme Court: Nuts and Bolts Description," 54 *New York State Bar Journal* 346 (1982).
2. Potter Stewart, "Inside the Supreme Court," *The New York Times*, Oct. 1, 1979, p. 17A, col. 2.
3. *Brown v. Allen*, 344 U.S. 443, 535 (1953) (Jackson, J., concurring opinion).

D. SUMMARILY DECIDED CASES

Even before the 1988 Act to Improve the Administration of Justice, which eliminated virtually all mandatory appeals, the distinction between mandatory and discretionary review of appeals and *cert.* petitions had largely disappeared in the Court's process of deciding what to decide. The Court annually received only about 250 appeals and the overwhelming majority were summarily decided (without hearing oral arguments and full consideration). They simply dismissed them for want of jurisdiction or failure to present a substantial federal question, or they ordered the lower court ruling affirmed or reversed.

Summarily decided cases enable the Court to cut down on its workload. But they also engender confusion among the lower courts. Summary decisions take the form of rather cryptic orders or *per curiam* (unsigned) opinions. Like denials of *cert.* petitions, they invite confusion over how the Court views the merits of a case and the lower court ruling. The problem is one of the Court's own making. The Court holds that summarily decided cases do not have the same precedential weight as plenary decisions, but they are nonetheless binding on lower courts "until such time as the Court informs [them] that [they] are not."[1]

Another problem is that occasionally cases that some justices think deserve full consideration are summarily decided. "No specter of increasing caseload can possibly justify today's summary disposition of this case," Brennan charged in *Roe v. Locke*, 423 U.S. 48 (1975), holding a Tennessee statute forbidding "crimes against nature" was not vague as claimed by an individual convicted of forcibly performing cunnilingus. Stewart sounded the refrain the next term in *United States v. Jacobs*, 429 U.S. 909 (1975). "While our heavy caseload necessarily leads us sometimes to dispose of cases summarily, it must never lead us to dispose of any case irresponsibly. Yet I fear precisely that has happened here." These are the words of dissenters in cases that they thought merited full consideration, but were outvoted by a majority who simply did not want to bother with hearing oral arguments and giving cases full consideration. *Goldwater v. Carter* (1979) (see page 145) is another example. There, Justices Blackmun and White viewed the majority's summary disposition and decision "indefensible" in failing to "set the case for oral argument and giv[ing] it the plenary consideration it so obviously deserved." Later that term, Stevens, Brennan, and Marshall dissented in *Snepp v. United States* (1980) (see page 154), which they thought raised important First Amendment issues. *Florida v. Meyers* (1984) (see page 156) illustrates the Court's continued practice of summarily deciding cases, even those that come as petitions for *certiorari*, when a majority wants to decide a case but does not want to bother with hearing oral arguments on the case.

NOTE

1. *Hicks v. Miranda*, 422 U.S. 322 (1975).

Snepp v. United States
444 U.S. 507, 100 S.Ct. 763 (1980)

The United States government sought an injunction (an order) against Frank Snepp, a former agent for the Central Intelligence Agency (CIA), requiring him to submit all of his future fiction and nonfiction writings for prepublication review by the CIA and ordering the creation of a government trust from the royalties he earned from his book *Decent Interval,* which he published without CIA approval as required in his CIA contract. The district court decided for the government and Snepp appealed, contending that the CIA's prepublication review and the lower court's ruling abridged his First Amendment freedoms of speech and press. Without hearing oral arguments, the Court in a *per curiam* opinion held that Snepp had breached his fiduciary obligations by failing to submit his manuscript for review and upheld the lower court's ruling denying him royalties from his book. Justice Stevens's dissenting opinion discusses some additional facts and objects to the Court's summary disposition of this case.

Justice STEVENS, with whom Justice BRENNAN and Justice MARSHALL join, dissenting.

In this case Snepp admittedly breached his duty to submit the manuscript of his book, Decent Interval, to the CIA for prepublication review. However, the Government has conceded that the book contains no classified, nonpublic material. Thus, by definition, the interest in confidentiality that Snepp's contract was designed to protect has not been compromised. Nevertheless, the Court today grants the Government unprecedented and drastic relief in the form of a constructive trust over the profits derived by Snepp from the sale of the book. Because that remedy is not authorized by any applicable law and because it is most inappropriate for the Court to dispose of this novel issue summarily on the Government's conditional cross-petition for certiorari, I respectfully dissent. . . .

The Court's decision to dispose of this case summarily on the Government's conditional cross-petition for certiorari is just as unprecedented as its disposition of the merits.

Snepp filed a petition for certiorari challenging the Fourth Circuit's decision insofar as it affirmed the entry of an injunction requiring him to submit all future manuscripts for prepublication review and remanded for a determination of whether punitive damages would be appropriate for his failure to submit Decent Interval to the Agency prior to its publication. The Government filed a brief in opposition as well as a cross petition for certiorari, the Government specifically stated, however, that it was cross-petitioning only to bring the entire case before the Court in the event that the Court should decide to grant Snepp's petition. The Government explained that "[b]ecause the contract remedy provided by the court of appeals appears to be sufficient in this case to protect the Agency's interest, the government has not independently sought review in this Court.". . .

Given the Government's position, it would be highly inappropriate, and perhaps even beyond this Court's jurisdiction, to grant the Government's petition while denying Snepp's. Yet that is in essence what has been done. The majority obviously does not believe that Snepp's claims merit this Court's consideration, for they are summarily dismissed in a footnote. . . .

It is clear that Snepp's petition would not have been granted on its own merits.

The Court's opinion is a good demonstration of why this Court should not reach out to decide a question not necessarily presented to it, as it has done in this case. Despite the fact that the Government has specifically stated that the punitive damages remedy is "sufficient" to protect its interests, the Court forges ahead and summarily rejects that remedy on the grounds that (a) it is too speculative and thus would not provide the Government with a "reliable deterrent against similar breaches of security." and (b) it might require the Government to reveal confidential information in court, the Government might forego damages rather than make such disclosures, and the Government might thus be left with "no remedy at all." It seems to me that the Court is foreclosed from relying upon either ground by the Government's acquiescence in the punitive damages remedy. Moreover, the second rationale is entirely speculative and, in this case at least, almost certainly wrong. The Court states that

> [p]roof of the tortious conduct necessary to sustain an award of punitive damages might force the Government to disclose some of the very confidences that Snepp promised to protect. . . .

Yet under the Court of Appeals' opinion the Government would be entitled to punitive damages simply by proving that Snepp deceived it into believing that he was going to comply with his duty to submit the manuscript for prepublication review and that the Government relied on these misrepresentations to its detriment. I fail to see how such a showing would require the Government to reveal any confidential information or to expose itself to "probing discovery into the Agency's highly confidential affairs.". . .

The uninhibited character of today's exercise in lawmaking is highlighted by the Court's disregard of two venerable principles that favor a more conservative approach to this case.

First, for centuries the English-speaking judiciary refused to grant equitable relief unless the plaintiff could show that his remedy at law was inadequate. Without waiting for an opportunity to appraise the adequacy of the punitive damages remedy in this case, the Court has jumped to the conclusion that equitable relief is necessary.

Second, and of greater importance, the Court seems unaware of the fact that its drastic new remedy has been fashioned to enforce a species of prior restraint on a citizen's right to criticize his government. Inherent in this prior restraint is the risk that the reviewing agency will misuse its authority to delay the publication of a critical work or to persuade an author to modify the contents of his work beyond the demands of secrecy. The character of the covenant as a prior restraint on free speech surely imposes an especially heavy burden on the censor to justify the remedy it seeks. It would take more than the Court has written to persuade me that that burden has been met.

I respectfully dissent.

Florida v. Meyers
466 U.S. 380, 104 S.Ct. 1852 (1984)

The pertinent facts are discussed in the *per curiam* opinion announcing the Court's decision. Justice Stevens's dissenting opinion raises issues about the Court's summary disposition of cases.

Per Curiam.

Respondent was charged with sexual battery. At the time of his arrest, police officers searched his automobile and seized several items. The vehicle was then towed to Sunny's Wrecker, where it was impounded in a locked, secure area. Approximately eight hours later, a police officer went to the compound and, without obtaining a warrant, searched the car for a second time. Additional evidence was seized. At the subsequent trial, the court denied respondent's motion to suppress the evidence seized during the second search, and respondent was convicted.

On appeal, the Florida District Court of Appeal for the Fourth District reversed the conviction, holding that even though respondent conceded that the initial search of the automobile was valid, the second search violated the Fourth Amendment. . . . The Florida Supreme Court denied the State's petition for discretionary review, and the State filed the present petition for certiorari. We reverse.

The District Court of Appeal either misunderstood or ignored our prior rulings with respect to the constitutionality of the warrantless search of an impounded automobile. In *Michigan v. Thomas*, 458 U.S. 259 (1982), we upheld a warrantless search of an automobile even though the automobile was in police custody and even though a prior inventory search had already been made. That ruling controls the disposition of this case. . . . The petition for certiorari is therefore granted, the judgment of the District Court of Appeal is reversed, and the case is remanded to that court for further proceedings not inconsistent with this opinion.

It is so ordered.

Justice STEVENS, with whom Justice BRENNAN and Justice MARSHALL join, dissenting.

No judicial system is perfect. In this case the Florida District Court of Appeal for the Fourth District appears to have made an error. In the exercise of its discretion, the Florida Supreme Court elected not to correct that error. No reasons were given for its denial of review and since the record is not before us, we cannot know what discretionary factors may have prompted the Florida Supreme Court's decision. This Court, however, finds time to correct the apparent error committed by the intermediate appellate court, acting summarily without benefit of briefs on the merits or argument. . . .

For three other reasons I believe the Court should deny certiorari in cases of this kind. First, our pronouncements concerning our confidence in the ability of the state judges to decide Fourth Amendment questions, are given a hollow ring when we are found peering over their shoulders after every misreading of the Fourth Amendment. Second, our ability to perform our primary responsibilities can only be undermined by enlarging our self-appointed role as supervisors of the administration of justice in the state judicial systems. Dispositions such as that today can only encourage prosecutors to file in increasing numbers petitions for certiorari in relatively routine cases, and if we take it upon ourselves to review and correct every incorrect disposition of a federal question by every intermediate state appellate court, we will soon become so busy that we will either be unable to discharge our primary responsibilities effectively, or else be forced to make still another adjustment in the size of our staff in order to process cases effectively. We should focus our attention on methods of using our scarce resources wisely rather than laying another course of bricks in the building of a federal judicial bureaucracy.

Third, and perhaps most fundamental, this case and cases like it pose disturbing questions concerning the Court's conception of its role. Each such case, considered individually, may be regarded as a welcome step forward in the never-ending war against crime. Such decisions are certain to receive widespread approbation, particularly by members of society who have been victimized by lawless conduct. But we must not forget that a central purpose of our written Constitution, and more specifically of its unique creation of a life-tenured federal judiciary, was to ensure that certain rights are firmly secured *against* possible oppression by the Federal or State Governments. As I wrote last Term: "I believe that in reviewing the decisions of state courts, the primary role of this Court is to make sure that persons who seek to *vindicate* federal rights have been fairly heard." *Michigan v. Long*, 463 U.S. 1032 (1983) (emphasis in original) (dissenting opinion). Yet the Court's recent history indicates that, at least with respect to its summary dispositions, it has been primarily concerned with vindicating the will of the majority and less interested in its role as protector of the individual's constitutional rights. Since the beginning of the October 1981 Term, the Court has decided in summary fashion 19 cases, including this one, concerning the constitutional rights of persons accused or convicted of crime. All 19 were decided on the petition of the warden or prosecutor, and in all he was successful in obtaining reversal of a decision upholding a claim of constitutional right. I am not saying that none of these cases should have been decided summarily. But I am saying that this pattern of results, and in particular the fact that in its last two and one-half Terms the Court has been unwilling in even a single criminal case to employ its discretionary power of summary disposition in order to uphold a claim of constitutional right, is quite striking. It may well be true that there have been times when the Court overused its power of summary disposition to protect the citizen against government overreaching. Nevertheless, the Court must be ever mindful of its primary role as the protector of the citizen and not the warden or the prosecutor. The Framers surely feared the latter more than the former.

I respectfully dissent.

E. THE ROLE OF ORAL ARGUMENT

The Court grants a full hearing—that is, oral argument—to less than 180 of the more than 5,000 cases on the docket each term. When cases are granted full consideration, attorneys for each side submit briefs setting forth their arguments and how they think the case should be decided. The clerk of the Court circulates the briefs to each chamber and sets a date for the attorneys to orally argue their views before the justices. After hearing oral arguments, in private conference the justices vote on how to decide the issues presented in a case.

For fourteen weeks each term, from the first Monday in October until the end of April, the Court hears arguments from ten to twelve o'clock and from one to three o'clock on Monday, Tuesday, and Wednesday about every two weeks. The importance of oral argument, Chief Justice Hughes observed, lies in the fact that often "the impression that a judge has at the close of a full oral argument accords with the conviction which controls his final vote."[1] The justices hold conference and take their initial, often decisive, vote on cases within a day or two after hearing arguments. Oral arguments come at a crucial time. They focus the minds of the justices and present the possibility for fresh perspectives on a case. It is the only opportunity for attorneys to communicate directly with the justices. Two basic factors appear to control the relative importance of oral argument. As Justice Wiley Rutledge observed, "One is brevity. The other is the preparation with which the judge comes to it."[2] When the Court revised its rules in 1980, the justices underscored that *"[t]he Court looks with disfavor on any oral argument that is read from a prepared text."* Central to preparation and delivery is a bird's-eye view of the case, the issues and facts, and the reasoning behind legal developments. Crisp, concise, and conversational presentations are what the justices want. An attorney must never forget, in Chief Justice Rehnquist's words, that "[h]e is not, after all, presenting his case to some abstract, platonic embodiment of appellate judges as a class, but . . . nine flesh and blood men and women." Oral argument is definitely not a "brief with gestures."[3]

NOTES

1. Charles E. Hughes, *The Supreme Court of the United States* (New York: Columbia University Press, 1928), 61.
2. Wiley Rutledge, "The Appellate Brief," 28 *American Bar Association Journal* 251 (1942).
3. William Rehnquist, "Oral Advocacy: A Disappearing Art," Brainerd Currie Lecture, Mercer University School of Law, Oct. 20, 1983, msp. 4.

F. CONFERENCE DELIBERATIONS

The justices meet alone in conference to decide which cases to accept and to discuss the merits of those few cases on which they hear oral arguments. Throughout the term during the weeks in which the Court hears oral arguments, conferences are held on Wednesday afternoons to take up the four cases argued on Monday, and then on Fridays to discuss new filings and the eight cases for which oral argument was heard on Tuesday and Wednesday. In May and June, when the Court does not hear oral arguments, conferences are held on Thursdays, from ten in the morning until four or four-thirty in the afternoon, with the justices breaking for a forty-five-minute lunch around twelve-thirty. A majority may vote to hold a special session during the summer months, when extraordinarily urgent cases arise.

Summoned by a buzzer five minutes before the hour, the justices meet in the conference room, located directly behind the courtroom itself and next to the chief justice's chamber. The oak-paneled room is lined with *United States Reports* (containing the Court's decisions). Over the mantle of an exquisite fireplace at one end hangs a portrait of Chief Justice Marshall. Next to the fireplace stands a large rectangular table where the justices sit. The chief justice sits at the one end and the senior associate justice at the other. Along the right-hand side of the chief justice, next to the fireplace, sit Marshall, Blackmun, and Stevens; on the left-hand side, sit O'Connor, Scalia, Kennedy, and Souter, the most junior justice. The seating of the justices traditionally has been on the basis of seniority. But variations occur due to individual justices' preferences.

Members of the Burger Court, in the tradition begun by Chief Justice Melville Fuller, shaking hands in the robing room prior to going on the bench to hear oral arguments. *Yoichi Okamoto*

Two conference lists are circulated to each chamber by noon on Wednesday prior to the Friday conference. They structure conference discussion and enable the justices to get through their caseload. On the first list—Special List I, or the Discuss List—are jurisdictional statements, petitions for certiorari and motions that are ready and worth discussing. The Discuss List typically includes between forty and fifty cases for each conference. Attached is a second list—Special List II or what was called the Dead List—containing those cases considered unworthy of discussion. Any justice may request that a case be put on the Discuss List, and only after the chief's conference secretary has heard from all chambers do the lists become final. Over 70 percent of the cases on the conference lists are automatically denied without discussion and most of those that do make the Discuss List are denied as well. The conference lists are an important

---

INSIDE THE COURT
On the Tentativeness of Votes and the Importance of Opinion Writing

In two other controversial cases, involving claims by the press to a First Amendment right of access to visit and interview prisoners, Burger switched his vote after conference. During the conference discussion of *Pell v. Procunier* 417 U.S. 817 (1974) and *Saxbe v. Washington Post* 417 U.S. 843 (1974), the vote went five to four for recognizing that the press has a First Amendment right of access. But Burger later changed his mind and explained that the final outcome of the cases depended on how the opinions were written:

This difficult case has few very clear cut and fixed positions but my further study over the weekend leads me to see my position as closer for those who would sustain the authority of the corrections administrators than those who would not! I would therefore reverse in 73–754, affirm in 73–918 and reverse in 73–1265.

This is another one of those cases that will depend a good deal on "how it is written." The solution to the problem must be allowed time for experimentation and I fear an "absolute" constitutional holding adverse to administrators will tend to "freeze" progress.

The Court ultimately divided five to four, but held that the press does not have a First Amendment right of access to interview inmates of prisons. Like *Roe v. Wade* 410 U.S. 113 (1973), these examples illustrate how important postconference deliberations and communications among the chambers have become for the Court's decision making.

Source: William J. Brennan, Jr., Papers, Manuscripts Room, Library of Congress.

technique for saving time and focusing attention on the few cases deemed worthy of consideration.

The significance of conference discussions has changed with the increasing caseload. Conference discussions do not play the role that they once did. When the docket was smaller in the nineteenth century, conferences were integral to the justices' collective deliberations. As the caseload grew, conferences became largely symbolic of past collective deliberations. They now serve only to discover consensus. There is no longer time to reach agreement and compromise on opinions for the Court. "In fact," Justice Antonin Scalia claims, "to call our discussion of a case a conference is really something of a misnomer. It's much more a statement of the views of each of the nine Justices."[1] More discussion, however, he admits would probably not contribute much or lead justices to change their minds when voting on cases. This is because the justices confront similar issues year after year and, as Chief Justice Rehnquist notes, "it would be surprising if [justices] voted differently than they had the previous time."[2]

The justices' votes are always tentative until the day the Court hands down its decision and opinion. Before, during, and after conference justices may use their votes in strategic ways to influence the disposition of a case.

NOTES

1. Antonin Scalia, comments at George Washington National Law Center, Feb. 16, 1988, quoted in "Ruling Fixed Opinions," *The New York Times*, Feb. 22, 1988, p. 16A.

2. William H. Rehnquist, quoted in David M. O'Brien, *Storm Center: The Supreme Court in American Politics*, 2d ed., (New York: W. W. Norton, 1990).

G. POSTCONFERENCE WRITING AND CIRCULATION OF OPINIONS

Opinions justify or explain votes at conference. The opinion for the Court is the most important and most difficult to write because it represents a collective judgment. Because conference votes are tentative, the assignment, drafting, and circulation of opinions is crucial to the Court's rulings. At each stage justices compete for influence in determining the Court's final decision and opinion.

By tradition, when the chief justice is in the majority, he assigns the Court's opinion. If the chief justice did not vote with the majority, then the senior associate justice who was in the majority either writes the opinion or assigns it to another. Chief justices may keep cases for themselves. This is in the tradition of Chief Justice Marshall, but as modified by the workload and other justices' expectations of equitable opinion assignments. In unanimous decisions and landmark cases the chief justice often self-assigns the Court's opinion.

Parity in opinion assignment now generally prevails. But the practice of immediately assigning opinions after conference as Hughes did, or within a day or two as Stone did, was gradually abandoned by the end of Vinson's tenure as chief justice. Warren and Burger adopted the practice of assigning opinions after each two-week session of oral arguments and conferences. With more assignments to make at any given time, they thus acquired greater flexibility in distributing the workload. They also enhanced their own opportunities for influencing the final outcome of cases through their assignment of opinions.

Writing opinions is the most difficult and time-consuming task of the justices. Justices differ in their styles and approaches to opinion writing. They now more or less delegate responsibility to their clerks for assisting in the preparation of opinions. Chief Justice Rehnquist, for example, usually has one of his clerks do a first draft, without bothering about style, and gives him about ten days to prepare it. Before having the clerk begin work, Rehnquist goes over the conference discussion with the clerk and explains how he thinks "an opinion can be written supporting the result reached by the majority."

Only after a justice is satisfied with an initial draft does the opinion circulate to the other justices for their reactions. The practice of circulating draft opinions is pivotal in the Court's decision-making process because all votes are tentative until the final opinion is handed down.

Final published opinions for the Court are the residue of conflicts and compromises among the justices. But they also reflect changing institutional norms. In historical perspective, changes in judicial norms have affected trends in opinion writing, the value of judicial opinions and the Court's contributions to public law.

"The business of the Court," Justice Stewart once observed, "is to give institutional opinions for its decisions." The opinion for the Court serves to communicate an institutional decision. For much of the Court's history, there were few concurring opinions (those in which a justice agrees with the Court's ruling but not the reasons given in its opinion) and dissenting opinions (those in which justices disagree with the Court's ruling and give an alternative interpretation). It was also rare for a justice to write a separate opinion in which he or she concurred and dissented from parts of the opinion for the Court. But in the last forty years there has been a dramatic increase in the total number of opinions issued each term, as depicted in Figure 2.4.

The increase in the number of opinions reflects in part that the justices are now more interested in merely the tally of votes than arriving at an institutional decision and opinion. The number of cases decided by a bare majority has thus grown in the

CONSTITUTIONAL HISTORY
Comparison of Dissent Rates

Justice	Number of Dissenting Opinions	Average Per Term
The Great Dissenters		
W. Johnson (1804–1834)	30	1.0
J. Catron (1837–1865)	26	0.9
N. Clifford (1858–1881)	60	2.6
J. Harlan (1877–1911)	119	3.5
O. Holmes (1902–1932)	72	2.4
L. Brandeis (1915–1939)	65	2.9
H. Stone (1925–1946)	93	4.6
H. Black (1937–1971)	310	9.1
F. Frankfurter (1939–1962)	251	10.9
J. Harlan (1955–1971)	242	15.1
The Burger and Rehnquist Courts		
W. Douglas (1969–1974)	231	38.5
J. Stevens (1975–1990)	318	21.2
W. Brennan, Jr. (1969–1990)	379	18.0
T. Marshall (1969–1990)	322	15.3
W. Rehnquist (1971–1990)	250	13.1
P. Stewart (1969–1981)	130	10.8
B. White (1969–1990)	217	10.6
H. Blackmun (1971–1990)	203	10.5
A. Scalia (1986–1990)	32	8.3
L. Powell, Jr. (1971–1987)	159	9.9
S. O'Connor (1981–1990)	64	7.0
W. Burger (1969–1986)	111	6.5
A. Kennedy (1987–1990)	17	5.6

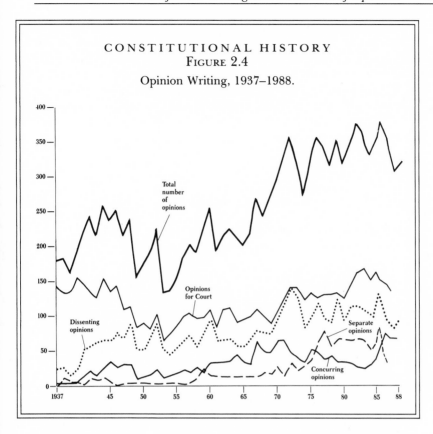

CONSTITUTIONAL HISTORY
FIGURE 2.4

Opinion Writing, 1937–1988.

Total number of opinions

Opinions for Court

Dissenting opinions

Separate opinions

Concurring opinions

last few decades. In addition, sometimes a bare majority for deciding a case a certain way cannot agree on an opinion for the Court's decision and the author of the opinion announcing the Court's decision must write for only a plurality.

In contrast to the author of an opinion for the Court, a justice writing separate concurring or dissenting opinions does not carry the burden of massing other justices. Dissenting opinions are more understandable and defensible. Dissenting opinions in the view of Chief Justice Charles Evans Hughes, who rarely wrote dissents, appeal "to the brooding spirit of the law, to the intelligence of a future day, when a later decision may possibly correct the error into which the dissenting judge believes the Court to have been betrayed."[1] The first Justice John M. Harlan's dissent from the doctrine of "separate but equal" in *Plessy v. Ferguson*, 163 U.S. 537 (1896) (see Vol. 2, Ch. 12) was eventually vindicated in *Brown v. Board of Education* (1954). Dissents may also appeal for more immediate legislative action: Justice James Iredell's dissent in *Chisholm v. Georgia*, 2 U.S. 419 (1793), invited the adoption of the Eleventh Amendment overturning the Court's decision; and the dissenters' arguments in *Dred Scott v. Sandford*, 60 U.S. 393 (1857) (see Vol. 2, Ch. 12), lent support to the passage of the Thirteenth, Fourteenth, and Fifteenth Amendments after the Civil War. A dissenting opinion is a way of undercutting the Court's decision and opinion. The threat of a dissent may thus be useful when trying to persuade the majority to narrow its holding or tone down the language of its opinion.

NOTE

1. Charles Evans Hughes, *The Supreme Court of the United States* (New York: Columbia University Press, 1928).

H. OPINION DAYS AND COMMUNICATING DECISIONS

The justices announce their decisions in the courtroom, typically crowded with reporters, anxious attorneys, and curious spectators. When several decisions are to be handed down, the justices delivering the Court's opinions make their announcements in reverse order of seniority. Authors of concurring or dissenting opinions are free to give their views orally as well. By tradition there is no prior announcement as to when cases will be handed down. Most opinions are now announced in two to four minutes with justices merely stating the result in each case. In especially controversial cases, for example, *Webster v. Reproductive Health Services* (1989) (see Vol. 2, Ch. 11) concerning restrictions on abortion, justices may read portions of their opinions and, sometimes, dissents.

Justices appreciate that compliance with their decisions depends on public understanding of their opinions. And media coverage of the Court has grown in the last thirty years. On "Opinion Days," journalists now receive copies of the headnotes—prepared by the reporter of decisions—summarizing the main points of a decision. The Court now has a public information office as well. The office serves primarily reporters (not members of the general public, whose inquiries are typically handled by the offices of the clerk, marshal, or curator) and provides space for a pressroom with sixteen assigned cubicles. The public information officer makes available all filings and briefs for cases on the docket, the Court's conference lists and final opinions, and speeches made by the justices.

The justices' private conference room. *Supreme Court Historical Society.*

I. THE IMPACT OF SUPREME COURT DECISIONS: COMPLIANCE AND IMPLEMENTATION

"By itself," political scientist Robert Dahl observed, "the Court is almost powerless to affect the course of national policy."[1] This is because the Court's rulings are not self-executing. Enforcement and implementation required the cooperation and coordination of all three branches of government.

Brown v. Board of Education (1954) (see Vol. 2, Ch. 12), the public school desegregation case, dramatically altered the course of American life, but also reflected the justices' awareness that their decisions are not self-executing. When striking down the "separate but equal" doctrine, which was practised in segregated public school systems, the Warren Court waited a year after *Brown I* (1954) before issuing in *Brown II* its mandate for "all deliberate speed" in ending racial segregation in public education. The Court knew that there would be substantial public resistence to the social policy announced in *Brown I*. A rigid time table for desegregation would have only intensified opposition. President Dwight Eisenhower refused to endorse the ruling for some time. Hence, implementation of *Brown* was deliberately slow and uneven. The Department of Justice had little role in ending school segregation before the passage of the Civil Rights

Act of 1964 during Lyndon B. Johnson's presidency. For over three decades problems of implementing and achieving compliance with *Brown* persisted. Litigation by civil rights groups forced change, but it was piecemeal, costly, and modest. The judiciary alone could not achieve desegregation.

Public opinion serves to curb the Court when it threatens to go too far or too fast in its rulings. The Court has usually been in line with major political movements, except during transitional periods or critical elections.[2] Life in the marble temple is not immune from shifts in public opinion. But justices deny being directly influenced by public opinion. The Court's prestige rests on preserving the public's view that justices base their decisions on interpretations of the law, rather than on their personal policy preferences. Yet complete indifference to public opinion would be the height of judicial arrogance.

Most of the Court's decisions do not attract widespread public attention. Most people find the Court remote and confusing or identify with its institutional symbols. The public perceives the Court as a temple of law rather than of politics—impartial and removed from the pressures of special partisan interests.[3] Issues such as school desegregation, school prayer, and abortion focus public attention and may mobilize public support or opposition for the Court. But those issues are also the most divisive within the country as well. Public opinion, therefore, tends to be diffuse and indirectly expressed by public officials and elected representatives.

Less concerned about public opinion than elected public officials, justices are sensitive to the attitudes of the Court's immediate constituents: the solicitor general, the attorney general and the Department of Justice, counsel for federal agencies, states' attorneys general, and the legal profession. Their responses to the Court's rulings help shape public understanding and determine the extent of compliance.

The solicitor general, attorney general, and agency counsel interpret the Court's decisions and advise the White House and agencies on compliance. Justices may find a favorable or unfavorable reception from the executive branch. The solicitor general decides which and what kinds of cases to take to the Court. In selecting cases he tries to offer the Court (or a majority) opportunities for pursuing their policy goals and those of the president.

The attorney general, cabinet heads, and agency counsel may likewise extend or thwart the Court's policies. They do so through their advisory opinions, litigation strategies, and development of agency policy and programs. The reactions of the fifty state attorneys general are no less important. Each has a pivotal role in advising governors, mayors, police chiefs, and others in his or her state. Their responses tend to reflect state and local reactions to the Court's rulings. Regional differences were evident in responses to the 1962 and 1963 school prayer decisions. In upholding separation of church and state, the Court struck down a state-composed prayer in *Engel v. Vitale*, 370 U.S. 421 (1962), and the reciting of the Lord's Prayer in public schools in *Abington School District v. Schempp*, 374 U.S. 203 (1963) (see Vol. 2, Ch. 6). Long-standing practices of school prayer in the East and South were not to be easily relinquished. Voluntary school prayer, silent meditation, and "the objective study of the Bible and of religion" were viewed as still permissible. Where school prayer received support in state constitutions or legislation, state and local officials denied the legitimacy of the Court's decrees and refused to obey.

The justices do consider anticipated reactions of the immediate audience of the Court's rulings. One example is that of Chief Justice Warren's opinion in *Miranda v. Arizona*, 384 U.S. 436 (1966) (see Vol. 2, Ch. 8), which held that police must read suspects their rights, granted them by the Fifth and Sixth Amendments, to remain silent and to consult and have the presence of an attorney during police questioning. A former attorney general in California, Chief Justice Warren knew full well that not all state attorneys general and police supported the Court's rulings on criminal procedure. He, therefore, strove to outline in *Miranda* a code for police procedures governing the interrogation of criminal suspects that police could not easily evade.

The Court's decisions have traditionally applied retroactively, permitting individuals to have retrials. In *Linkletter v. Walker* (1965) (see page 178), however, the Court refused to apply retroactively its controversial ruling in *Mapp v. Ohio*, 367 U.S. 643 (1961) (see Vol. 2, Ch. 7), which extended to the states the Fourth Amendment exclusionary rule, forbidding the use at trial of evidence obtained in violation of the requirements for a proper search and seizure. The Court subsequently developed what became known as its *ambulatory-retroactively doctrine* in other areas of criminal law as well. "That doctrine," Justice Harlan explained, "was the product of the Court's disquietude with the impacts of its fast-moving pace in constitutional innovation in the criminal field." But he also objected that the doctrine merely rationalizes the Court's freedom "to act, in effect, like a legislature, making its new constitutional rules wholly or partially retroactive or only prospective as it deems wise."[4] In *Griffith v. Kentucky* (1987) (see page 183), Justice Blackmun further explains the Court's application of the doctrine of ambulatory retroactivity.

The Court directly and indirectly encourages interest groups and the government to litigate issues of public policy. The Court selects and decides "only those cases which present questions whose resolution will have immediate importance far beyond the particular facts and parties involved." Attorneys whose cases are accepted by the Court, Chief Justice Fred Vinson emphasized, "are, in a sense, prosecuting or defending class actions; that you represent your clients, but [more crucially] tremendously important principles, upon which are based the plans, hopes and aspirations of a great many people throughout the country."[5]

Interest groups from the entire political spectrum look to the Court to decide issues of public policy: from business organizations and corporations in the late nineteenth century to the Jehovah's Witnesses in the 1930s, to the ACLU and NAACP in the 1950s and 1960s, and to "liberal" women's rights groups and consumer and environmental protection groups—like the National Organization of Women (NOW), Common Cause, "Nader's Raiders," the Sierra Club, the Environmental Defense Fund, and the Natural Resources Defense Council—as well as to a growing number of conservative "public interest" law firms like the Pacific Legal Foundation, the Mountain States Legal Foundation, and the Washington Legal Foundation. "This is government by lawsuit," Justice Robert Jackson declared, "these constitutional lawsuits are the stuff of power politics in America."[6]

Interest group activities and public interest law firms offer a number of advantages for litigating policy disputes. They command greater financial resources than the average individual. A single suit may settle a large number of claims, and the issues are not as likely to be compromised or settled out of court. Interest group law firms typically specialize in particular kinds of lawsuits. They are, therefore, able to litigate more skillfully and over a longer period of time. There are also tactical opportunities. Litigants may be chosen to bring test cases, and those cases may be coordinated with other litigation and the activities of other organizations.

The Court is an instrument of political power, but the justices remain dependent on the attitudes and actions of their immediate constitutents, elected officials, and the dynamics of pressure-group politics and public opinion. Implementation and compliance largely depends on lower courts, Congress, and the president.

Compliance with the Court's decisions by lower courts is invariably uneven. They may extend or limit decisions in anticipation of later rulings by the high Court. Following the watershed ruling on privacy in *Griswold v. Connecticut,* 381 U.S. 479 (1965) (see Vol. 2, Ch. 4), lower courts interpreted the newfound constitutional right of privacy to strike down a wide range of laws, from those limiting the length of male employees' and students' hair to ones forbidding certain sexual acts between consenting adults and the use of marijuana, to laws requiring psychological tests of applicants for government jobs, and to laws governing access to financial and medical records. The Court reversed or would not approve the extension of the right of privacy in many of these areas.

A simple model of compliance is not very useful: Decisions handed down by the Court are not necessarily or readily applied by lower courts. Ambiguity and plurality or five-to-four decisions invite lower courts to pursue their own policy goals. Crucial language in an opinion may be treated as *dicta*. Differences between the facts on which the Court ruled and the circumstances of a case at hand may be emphasized so as to distinguish or reach the opposite result of the Court's decision. Lower courts may thus effectively delay implementation and compliance.

Open defiance is infrequent but not unprecedented. *Jaffree v. Board of School Commissioners* (1983) (see page 187) is extreme but illustrative of lower court defiance. There, a federal district court judge in Alabama directly challenged the legitimacy of the Court in its public school prayer rulings. A majority of the Court rebuffed the lower court when it decided an appeal of the ruling and struck down the "moment of silence" law in *Wallace v. Jaffree*, 472 U.S. 38 (1985) (see Vol. 2, Ch. 6).

Major confrontations between Congress and the Court have occurred a number of times. With the election of Thomas Jefferson in 1800, Republicans gained control of Congress. Defeated President John Adams and the outgoing Federalists in Congress passed the Judiciary Act of 1801, creating new circuit court judgeships and stipulating that when the next vacancy on the Court occurred it should go unfilled. That attempt to maintain influence in the judiciary was quickly countered. In 1802, the Republican Congress repealed the Act of 1801, abolishing the judgeships and returning the number of justices to six. Congress also postponed the Court's next term to preclude it from immediately hearing a challenge, in *Stuart v. Laird*, 5 U.S. 299 (1803), to its repealing legislation. When the Court decided *Stuart*, it upheld Congress's power to repeal the Judiciary Act of 1801. The Jeffersonian-Republicans then impeached Justice Samuel Chase for expounding federalist doctrine. Although the Senate acquitted him, it would not confirm nominees for federal judgeships unless they were Republicans.

The Marshall Court approved the expansion of national governmental power, but in response Congress in the 1820s and 1830s threatened to remove the Court's jurisdiction over disputes involving states' rights. After the Civil War, Congress succeeded in repealing the Court's jurisdiction over certain denials of writs of *habeas corpus*—orders commanding that a prisoner be brought before a judge and cause shown for his imprisonment. In *Ex parte McCardle,* 74 U.S. 506 (1869), the Court upheld the repeal of its jurisdiction and thus avoided deciding a controversial case attacking the constitutionality of Reconstruction legislation.

At the turn of the century, Progressives in Congress unsuccessfully sought to pressure the Court—dominated at the time by advocates of laissez-faire social and economic policy. They proposed requiring a two-thirds vote by the justices when striking down federal statutes and permitting Congress to overrule the Court's decisions by a two-thirds majority. The confrontation escalated with the Court's invalidation of President Franklin D. Roosevelt's early New Deal program passed by Congress in the 1930s. FDR retaliated by attempting to pack the Court by increasing the number of justices. Even though it was upset by the Court's invalidation of the New Deal, Congress would not accept FDR's Court-packing plan. It did, though pass legislation allowing justices to retire, after ten years of service at age seventy, with full- rather than half-salary. Congress thus made retirement more financially attractive and gave FDR opportunities to appoint justices who shared his political philosophy.

Congress may pressure the Court in a number of ways. The Senate may try to influence judicial appointments and justices may be impeached. More often, institutional and jurisdictional changes are used as weapons against the Court. Congress has tried to pressure the Court when setting its terms and size, and when authorizing appropriations for salaries, law clerks, secretaries, and office technology. Only once, in 1802 when repealing the Judiciary Act of 1801 and abolishing a session for a year, did Congress actually set the Court's term to delay and influence a particular decision.

The size of the Court is not preordained and changes generally reflect attempts to control the Court. The Jeffersonian-Republicans' quick repeal of the act passed by the Federalists in 1801, reducing the number of justices, was the first of several attempts to influence the Court. Presidents James Madison, James Monroe, and John Adams all claimed that the country's geographical expansion warranted enlarging the size of the Court. But Congress refused to do so until the last day of Andrew Jackson's term in 1837. During the Civil War, the number of justices increased to ten ostensibly due to the creation of a tenth circuit in the West. This gave Abraham Lincoln his fourth appointment and a chance to secure a pro-Union majority on the bench. Antagonism toward President Andrew Johnson's Reconstruction policies following the Civil War led to a reduction from ten to seven justices. After General Ulysses S. Grant was elected president, Congress again authorized nine justices—the number that has prevailed. In the nineteenth century at least, Congress rather successfully denied presidents additional appointments to preserve the Court's policies and increased the number of justices as a way to change the ideological composition of the Court.

Although Article III of the Constitution forbids reducing justices' salaries, Congress may withhold salary increases as punishment, especially in times of high inflation. More direct attacks are possible. Under Article III, Congress is authorized "to make exceptions" to the appellate jurisdiction of the Court. That authorization has been viewed as a way of denying the Court review of certain kinds of cases. But Congress succeeded only once, with the 1868 repeal of jurisdiction over writs of *habeas corpus,* which the Court upheld in *Ex parte McCardle,* 7 Wall. (74 U.S.) 506 (1869).

Court-curbing legislation is not a very viable weapon. Rather than limiting judicial review, Congress has given the Court the power to set its own agenda and decide major issues of public law and policy—precisely the kinds of issues that Congress then seeks to deny the Court review. The Court has also suggested that it would not approve repeals of its jurisdiction that are merely attempts to dictate how particular kinds of cases should be decided.[7] Most proposals to curb the Court, of course, are simply that. During the McCarthy era, for instance, Republican Senator William Jenner spearheaded a drive to forbid review of cases challenging legislative committees investigating un-American activities. Another unsuccessful attempt was made in 1968 to amend the Omnibus Crime Control and Safe Streets Act so as to prevent the Court from reviewing state criminal cases raising *Miranda* issues.

Congress has had somewhat greater success in reversing the Court by constitutional amendment. Congress must pass a constitutional amendment that three-fourths of the states must then ratify. The process is cumbersome and thousands of amendments to overrule the Court have failed. But four decisions have been overturned by constitutional amendment. *Chisholm v. Georgia,* 2 U.S. 419 (1793), holding that citizens of one state could sue in federal courts another state, was reversed by the Eleventh Amendment, guaranteeing sovereign immunity for states from suits by citizens of another state. The Thirteenth and Fourteenth Amendments, abolishing slavery and making blacks citizens of the United States, technically overturned the ruling in *Dred Scott v. Sanford* (1857) that blacks were not persons under the Constitution. With the ratification in 1913 of the Sixteenth Amendment, Congress reversed *Pollock v. Farmers' Loan and Trust Company,* 157 U.S. 429 (1895), which had invalidated a federal income tax. In 1970 an amendment to the Voting Rights Act of 1965 lowered the voting age to eighteen years for all elections. Although signing the act into law, President Richard Nixon had his attorney general challenge the validity of lowering the voting age by simple legislation, rather than by constitutional amendment. Within six months in *Oregon v. Mitchell,* 400 U.S. 112 (1970), a bare majority of the Court held that Congress exceeded its power by lowering the voting age for state and local elections. Less than a year later the Twenty-sixth Amendment was ratified extending the franchise to eighteen year olds in all elections.

More successful than Court-curbing and amending the Constitution are congressional enactments and rewriting of legislation in response to the Court's rulings. Congressional reversals usually relate to nonstatutory matters involving administrative policies. *Zurcher v. The Stanford Daily,* 436 U.S. 547 (1978) (see Vol. 2, Ch. 5), held that there was no constitutional prohibition against police searching newsrooms for "mere evidence," photographs, of a crime. Congress subsequently reversed that holding by passing the Privacy Protection Act of 1980 prohibiting unannounced searches of newsrooms and requiring that such evidence be obtained by a subpoena.

Congress cannot overturn the Court's interpretations of the Constitution by mere legislation. But Congress can enhance or thwart compliance with the Court's rulings. After the Warren Court's landmark decision in *Gideon v. Wainwright,* 372 U.S. 335 (1963) (see Vol. 2, Ch. 9), that indigents have a right to counsel, Congress provided attorneys for indigents charged with federal offenses. By contrast, in the Crime Control and Safe Streets Act of 1968, Congress permitted federal courts to use evidence obtained from suspects who had not been read their *Miranda* rights, if their testimony appeared voluntary based on the "totality of the circumstances" surrounding their interrogation. Congress thus attempted to return to a pre-*Miranda* standard for police questioning of criminal suspects.

Congress indubitably has the power to delay and undercut implementation of the Court's rulings. On major issues of public policy Congress is likely to prevail or, at least, temper the impact of the Court's rulings. But the Court forges public policy not only when invalidating federal legislation. No less importantly, the Court makes policy by overturning state and local laws and practices. The continuing controversies over decisions striking down state laws on school desegregation, school prayer, and abortion are a measure of the Court's influence on American life.

Charged with the responsibility of taking "care that the laws be faithfully executed," the president is the chief executive officer under the Constitution. As the only nationally elected public official, the president represents the views of the dominant national political coalition. A president's obligation to faithfully execute the laws, including decisions of the Court, thus may collide with his own perceived electorial mandate.

The Court has often been the focus of presidential campaigns and power struggles. But presidents rarely openly defy particular decisions by the Court. Presidential defiance is, perhaps, symbolized by the famous remark attributed to Andrew Jackson: "John Marshall has made his decision, now let him enforce it." Jackson's refusal to enforce the decision in *Worcester v. Georgia,* 31 U.S. 515 (1832), which denied state courts jurisdiction over crimes committed on Indian lands, in fact simply left enforcement problems up to the courts and legislatures. During the Civil War however, Lincoln ordered his military commanders to refuse to obey writs of habeas corpus issued by Chief Justice Taney.

In major confrontations, presidents generally yield to the Court. Richard Nixon complied with the ruling in *New York Times Co. v. United States,* 403 U.S. 713 (1971) (see Vol. 1, Ch. 4) (page 273), which struck down, as a prior restraint on freedom of the press, an injunction against the publication of the Pentagon Papers—a top secret report detailing the history of America's involvement in Vietnam. Then, during the Watergate scandal in 1974, Nixon submitted to the Court's decision in *United States v. Nixon,* 418 U.S. 683 (1974) (see Vol. 1, Ch. 4) (page 273) ordering the release of White House tape recordings pertinent to the trial of his former attorney general John Mitchell and other presidential aides for conspiracy and obstruction of justice.

Although seldom directly defying the Court, in the short and long run they may undercut Supreme Court policymaking. By contradictory directives to federal agencies and assigning low priority for enforcement by the Department of Justice, presidents may limit the Court's decisions. Presidents may also make broad moral appeals in response to the Court's rulings, and those appeals may transcend their limited time in office. The Court put school desegregation and abortion on the national agenda. But President John F. Kennedy's appeal for civil rights captivated a generation and encouraged public acceptance of the Court's rulings. Similarly, President Ronald Reagan's opposition to abortion focused attention on "traditional family values" and served to legitimate resistence to the Court's decisions.

Presidential influence over the Court in the long run remains contingent on appointments to the Court. Vacancies occur on the average of one every twenty-two months. Four presidents—including Jimmy Carter—had no opportunity to appoint members of the Court. There is no guarantee how a justice will vote or whether that vote will prove sufficient in limiting or reversing past rulings with which a president disagrees. But through their appointments presidents may leave their mark on Supreme Court policymaking and possibly align the Court and the country or precipitate later confrontations.

For much of the Court's history, the work of the justices has not involved major issues of public policy. In most areas of public law and policy, the fact that the Court decides an issue is more important than what it decides. Relatively few of the major issues of public policy that arise in government reach the Court. When the Court does decide major questions of public policy, its rulings decide only the instant case and not the larger surrounding political controversies. Major confrontations in constitutional politics, like those over school desegregation and abortion, are determined as much by what is possible in a system of free government and pluralistic society as by what the Court says about the meaning of the Constitution. And on those controversial issues of public policy, constitutional law frames the political debate in the ongoing dialogue between the Court and the country. The Court's rulings and interpretation of the Constitution rests, in Chief Justice Edward White's words, "solely upon the approval of a free people."[8]

NOTES

1. Robert Dahl, "Decision-Making in a Democracy: The Supreme Court as a National Policy-Maker," 6 *Journal of Public Law* 293 (1957).

2. See Richard Funston, "The Supreme Court and Critical Elections," 69 *American Political Science Review* 795 (1975).

3. See, for example, Walter Murphy, J. Tananhaus and D. Kastner, *Public Evaluations of Constitutional Courts* (Beverly Hills, CA: Sage, 1973).

4. Williams v. United States, 401 U.S. 675 (1971).

5. Fred Vinson, speech given before the American Bar Association, Sept. 7, 1949, reprinted in 69 S.Ct. vi (1949).

6. Robert Jackson, *The Struggle for Judicial Supremacy* (New York: Knopf, 1951), 287.

7. *United States v. Klein,* 80 U.S. 128 (1872).

8. Edward White, "The Supreme Court of the United States," 7 *American Bar Association Journal* 341 (1921).

SELECTED BIBLIOGRAPHY

Abraham, Henry J. *The Judicial Process*, 6th ed. New York: Oxford University Press, 1991.

Baum, Lawrence. *The Supreme Court*. Washington, DC, Congressional Quarterly, 1989.

Becker, Ted, and Feeley, Malcolm, eds. *The Impact of Supreme Court Decisions*, 2nd ed. New York: Oxford University Press, 1973.

Blandford, Linda, and Evans, Patricia. *Supreme Court of the United States 1789–1980: An Index to Opinions Arranged by Justice*, 2 vols. New York: Kraus International, 1983.

Cannon, Mark, and O'Brien, David M. *Views from the Bench: The Judiciary and Constitutional Politics*. Chatham: Chatham House, 1985.

Cardozo, Benjamin. *The Nature of the Judicial Process*. New Haven, CT: Yale University Press, 1921.

Cooper, Phillip. *Hard Judicial Choices*. New York: Oxford University Press, 1988.

Friedman, Leon, and Israel, Fred. *The Justices of the United States Supreme Court 1789–1978: Their Lives and Major Opinions*, 5 vols. New York: Chelsea House, 1980.

Goldman, Sheldon, and Jahnige, Thomas P. *The Federal Courts as a Political System*, 3rd ed. New York: Harper & Row, 1985.

Horwitz, Donald. *The Courts and Social Policy*. Washington, DC: Brookings Institution, 1977.

Johnson, Charles, and Canon, Bradley. *Judicial Policies: Implementation and Impact*. Washington, DC: Congressional Quarterly, 1984.

Lawrence, Susan. *The Poor in Court*. Princeton, NJ: Princeton University Press, 1990.

Murphy, Walter. *Elements of Judicial Strategy*. Chicago: University of Chicago Press, 1964.

Murphy, Walter, and Pritchett, C. Herman, eds. *Courts, Judges, and Politics*, 4th ed. New York: Random House, 1985.

O'Brien, David M. *Storm Center: The Supreme Court in American Politics*, 2nd ed. New York: W. W. Norton, 1990.

O'Connor, Karen, and Epstein, Lee. *Woman's Organizations' Use of the Courts*. Lexington, MA: Lexington Books, 1980.

Pritchett, C. Herman. *The Roosevelt Court*. New York: Macmillan, 1947.

Provine, Doris. *Case Selection in the United States Supreme Court*. Chicago: University of Chicago Press, 1980.

Schubert, Glendon. *The Judicial Mind*. Chicago: Northwestern University Press, 1965.

————, ed. *Judicial Behavior: A Reader in Theory and Research*. Chicago: Rand McNally, 1964.

————. *The Constitutional Polity*. Boston: Boston University, 1970.

————. *Judicial Policymaking*, 2nd ed. New York: Scott, Foresman, 1974.

Shapiro, Martin. *Law and Politics in the Supreme Court*. New York: Free Press, 1964.

Sheldon, Charles. *The Judicial Process: Models and Approaches.* New York: Dodd, Mead, 1974.

Supreme Court Historical Society. *Yearbook.* Washington, DC: SCHS, 1976–present.

Linkletter v. Walker
381 U.S. 618, 85 S.Ct. 1731 (1965)

Victor Linkletter was tried and convicted in state court on evidence illegally obtained by police prior to *Mapp v. Ohio,* 367 U.S. 643 (1961) (see Vol. 2, Ch. 7), which barred states from using illegally obtained evidence at trial under the Fourth Amendment's exclusionary rule. Linkletter contended that *Mapp* should apply retroactively and he should be retried with the illegally obtained evidence excluded. A federal district court disagreed and after a court of appeals affirmed that ruling, Linkletter appealed to the Supreme Court.

Justice CLARK delivers the opinion of the Court.

In *Mapp v. Ohio,* 367 U.S. 643 (1961), we held that the exclusion of evidence seized in violation of the search and seizure provisions of the Fourth Amendment was required of the States by the Due Process Clause of the Fourteenth Amendment. In so doing we overruled *Wolf v. People of State of Colorado,* 338 U.S. 25 (1949), to the extent that it failed to apply the exclusionary rule to the States. This case presents the question of whether this requirement operates retrospectively upon cases finally decided in the period prior to *Mapp.* The Court of Appeals for the Fifth Circuit held that it did not, and we granted certiorari in order to settle what has become a most troublesome question in the administration of justice. We agree with the Court of Appeals. . . .

At common law there was no authority for the proposition that judicial decisions made law only for the future. Blackstone stated the rule that the duty of the court was not to "pronounce a new law, but to maintain and expound the old one." 1 Blackstone, Commentaries 69 (15th ed. 1809). . . .

In the case of the overruled decision, *Wolf v. People of State of Colorado,* supra, here, it was thought to be only a failure at true discovery and was consequently never the law; while the overruling one, Mapp, was not "new law but an application of what is, and theretofore had been, the true law.". . .

On the other hand, [the late-nineteenth century legal philosopher John] Austin maintained that judges do in fact do something more than discover law; they make it interstitially by filling in with judicial interpretation the vague, indefinite, or generic statutory or common-law terms that alone are but the empty crevices of the law. Implicit in such an approach is the admission when a case is overruled that the earlier decision was wrongly decided. However, rather than being erased by the later overruling decision it is considered as an existing juridical fact until overruled, and intermediate cases finally decided under it are not to be disturbed.

The Blackstonian view ruled English jurisprudence and cast its shadow over our own. . . . However, some legal philosophers continued to insist that such a rule was out of tune with actuality largely because judicial repeal ofttime did "work hardship to those who [had] trusted to its existence." Cardozo, Address to the N. Y. Bar Assn. (1932). . . .

It is true that heretofore, without discussion, we have applied new constitutional rules to cases finalized before the promulgation of the rule. Petitioner contends that our method of resolving those prior cases demonstrates that an absolute rule of retroaction prevails in the area of constitutional ad judication. However, we believe that the Constitution neither prohibits nor requires retrospective effect. As Justice CARDOZO said, "We think the Federal Constitution has no voice upon the subject.". . .

Once the premise is accepted that we are neither required to apply, nor prohibited from applying, a decision retrospectively, we must then weigh the merits and demerits in each case by looking to the prior history of the rule in question, its purpose and effect, and whether retrospective operation will further or retard its operation. We believe that this approach is particularly correct with reference to the Fourth Amendment's prohibitions as to unreasonable searches and seizures. Rather than "disparaging" the Amendment we but apply the wisdom of Justice HOLMES that "[t]he life of the law has not been logic: it has been experience." Holmes, The Common Law 5 (Howe ed. 1963).

Since *Weeks v. United States,* 232 U.S. 383 (1914) this Court has adhered to the rule that evidence seized by federal officers in violation of the Fourth Amendment is not admissible at trial in a federal court. In 1949 in *Wolf v. People of State of Colorado,* supra, the Court decided that while the right to privacy—"the core of the Fourth Amendment"—was such a basic right as to be implicit in "the concept of ordered liberty" and thus enforceable against the States through the Fourteenth Amendment, "the ways of enforcing such a basic right raise questions of a different order. How such arbitrary conduct should be checked, what remedies against it should be afforded, the means by which the right should be made effective, are all questions that are not to be so dogmatically answered as to preclude the varying solutions which spring from an allowable range of judgment on issues not susceptible of quantitative solution."

Mapp was announced in 1961. The Court in considering "the current validity of the factual grounds upon which Wolf was based" pointed out that prior to *Wolf* "almost two-thirds of the States were opposed to the use of the exclusionary rule, now, despite the *Wolf* case, more than half of those since passing upon it . . . have wholly or partly adopted or adhered to the *Weeks* rule.". . .

We believe that the existence of the *Wolf* doctrine prior to *Mapp* is "an operative fact and may have consequences which cannot justly be ignored. The past cannot always be erased by a new judicial declaration." The thousands of cases that were finally decided on *Wolf* cannot be obliterated. The "particular conduct, private and official," must be considered. Here "prior determinations deemed to have finality and acted upon accordingly" have "become vested." And finally, "public policy in the light of the nature both of the [*Wolf* doctrine] and of its previous application" must be given its proper weight. In short, we must look to the purpose of the *Mapp* rule; the reliance placed upon the *Wolf* doctrine; and the effect on the administration of justice of a retrospective application of *Mapp*.

It is clear that the *Wolf* Court, once it had found the Fourth Amendment's unreasonable Search and Seizure Clause applicable to the States through the Due Process Clause of the Fourteenth Amendment, turned its attention to whether the exclusionary rule was included within the command of the Fourth Amendment. This was decided in the negative. It is clear that based upon the factual considerations heretofore discussed the *Wolf* Court then concluded that it was not necessary to the enforcement of the Fourth Amendment for the exclusionary rule to be extended to the States as a requirement of due process. *Mapp* had as its prime purpose the enforcement of the Fourth Amendment through the inclusion of the exclusionary rule within its rights. This, it was found, was the only effective deterrent to lawless police action. Indeed, all of the cases since *Wolf* requiring the exclusion of illegal evidence have been based on the necessity for an effective deterrent to illegal police action. We cannot say that this purpose would be advanced by making the rule retrospective. The misconduct of the police prior to *Mapp* has already occurred and will not be corrected by releasing the prisoners involved. Nor would it add harmony to the delicate state-federal relationship of which we have spoken as part and parcel of the purpose of *Mapp*. Finally, the ruptured privacy of the victims' homes and effects cannot be restored. Reparation comes too late. . . .

Finally, there are interests in the administration of justice and the integrity of the judicial process to consider. To make the rule of *Mapp* retrospective would tax the administration of justice to the utmost. Hearings would have to be held on the excludability of evidence long since destroyed, misplaced or deteriorated. If it is excluded, the witnesses available at the time of the original trial will not be available or if located their memory will be dimmed. To thus legitimate such an extraordinary procedural weapon that has no bearing on guilt would seriously disrupt the administration of justice. . . .

All that we decide today is that though the error complained of might be fundamental it is not of the nature requiring us to overturn all final convictions based upon it. After full consideration of all the factors we are not able to say that the *Mapp* rule requires retrospective application.

Affirmed.

Justice BLACK, with whom Justice DOUGLAS joins, dissenting.

The Court offers no defense based on any known principle of justice for discriminating among defendants who were similarly convicted by use of evidence unconstitutionally seized. It certainly cannot do so as between Linkletter and Miss Mapp. The crime with which she was charged took place more than a year before his, yet the decision today seems to rest on the fanciful concept that the Fourth Amendment protected her 1957 offense against conviction by use of unconstitutional evidence but denied its protection to Linkletter for his 1958 offense. In making this ruling the Court assumes for itself the virtue of acting in harmony with a comment of Justice HOLMES that "[t]he life of the law has not been logic: it has been experience." Justice HOLMES was not there talking about the Constitution; he was talking about the evolving judge-made law of England and of some of our States whose judges are allowed to follow in the common law tradition. It should be remembered in this connection that no member of this Court has ever more seriously criticized it than did Justice HOLMES for reading its own predilections into the "vague contours" of the Due Process Clause. But quite apart from that, there is no experience of the past that justifies a new Court-made rule to perpetrate a grossly invidious and unfair discrimination against Linkletter simply because he happened to be prosecuted in a State that was evidently well up with its criminal court docket. If this discrimination can be excused at all it is not because of experience but because of logic—sterile and formal at that—not, according to Justice HOLMES, the most dependable guide in lawmaking. . . .

As the Court concedes, this is the first instance on record where this Court, having jurisdiction, has ever refused to give a previously convicted defendant the benefit of a new and more expansive Bill of Rights interpretation. I am at a loss to understand why those who suffer from the use of evidence secured by a search and seizure in violation of the Fourth Amendment should be treated differently from those who have been denied other guarantees of the Bill of Rights. . . .

One reason—perhaps a basic one—put forward by the Court for its refusal to give Linkletter the benefit of the search and seizure exclusionary rule is the repeated statement that the purpose of that rule is to deter sheriffs, policemen, and other law officers from making unlawful searches and seizures. The inference I gather from these repeated statements is that the rule is not a right or privilege accorded to defendants charged with crime but is a sort of punishment against officers in order to keep them from depriving people of their constitutional rights. In passing I would say that if that is the sole purpose, reason, object and effect of the rule, the Court's action in adopting it sounds more like law making than construing the Constitution. . . . [T]he undoubted implication of today's opinion that the rule is not a safeguard for defendants but is a mere punishing rod to be applied to law enforcement officers is a rather startling departure from many past opinions, and even from *Mapp* itself. *Mapp* quoted from the Court's earlier opinion in *Weeks v. United States,* supra, certainly not with disapproval, saying that the Court "in that case clearly stated that use of the seized evidence involved 'a denial of the constitutional rights of the accused.' " I have read and reread the *Mapp* opinion but have been unable to find one word in it to indicate that the exclusionary search and seizure rule should be limited on the basis that it was intended to do nothing in the world except to deter officers of the law. . . .

The Court says that the exclusionary rule's purpose of preventing law enforcement officers from making lawless searches and seizures "will not at this late date be served by the wholesale release of the guilty victims." It has not been the usual thing to cut down trial protections guaranteed by the Constitution on the basis that some guilty persons might escape. There is probably no one of the rights in the Bill of Rights that does not make it more difficult to convict defendants. But all of them are based on the premise, I suppose, that the Bill of Rights' safeguards should be faithfully enforced by the court without regard to a particular judge's judgment as to whether more people could be convicted by a refusal of courts to enforce the safeguards. Such has heretofore been accepted as a general maxim. . . .

The plain facts here are that the Court's opinion cuts off many defendants who are now in jail from any hope of relief from unconstitutional convictions. . . . No State should be considered to have a vested interest in keeping prisoners in jail who were convicted because of lawless conduct by the State's officials. Careful analysis of the Court's opinion shows that it rests on the premise that a State's assumed interest in sustaining convictions obtained under the old, repudiated rule outweighs the interests both of that State and of the individuals convicted in having wrongful convictions set aside. It certainly offends my sense of justice to say that a State holding in jail people who were convicted by unconstitutional methods has a vested interest in keeping them there that outweighs the right of persons adjudged guilty of crime to challenge their unconstitutional convictions at any time. . . .

Griffith v. Kentucky
479 U.S. 314, 107 S.Ct. 708 (1987)

Justice Blackmun's opinion for the Court discusses the issues presented here.

Justice BLACKMUN delivers the opinion of the Court.

These cases, one state and one federal, concern the retrospective application of *Batson v. Kentucky,* [476 U.S. 79] (1986).

In *Batson,* this Court ruled that a defendant in a state criminal trial could establish a prima facie case of racial discrimination violative of the Fourteenth Amendment, based on the prosecution's use of peremptory challenges to strike members of the defendant's race from the jury venire, and that, once the defendant had made the prima facie showing, the burden shifted to the prosecution to come forward with a neutral explanation for those challenges. In the present cases we consider whether that ruling is applicable to litigation pending on direct state or federal review or not yet final when *Batson* was decided. We answer that question in the affirmative. . . .

Twenty-one years ago, this Court adopted a three-pronged analysis for claims of retroactivity of new constitutional rules of criminal procedure. See *Linkletter v. Walker,* 381 U.S. 618 (1965). In *Linkletter,* the Court held that *Mapp v. Ohio* [367 U.S. 643 (1961)], which extended the Fourth Amendment exclusionary rule to the States, would not be applied retroactively to a state conviction that had become final before *Mapp* was decided. The Court explained that "the Constitution neither prohibits nor requires retrospective effect" of a new constitutional rule, and that a determination of retroactivity must depend on "weigh[ing] the merits and demerits in each case." The Court's decision not to apply *Mapp* retroactively was based on "the purpose of the *Mapp* rule; the reliance placed upon the [previous] doctrine; and the effect on the administration of justice of a retrospective application of *Mapp.*". . . .

Shortly after the decision in *Linkletter*, the Court held that the three-pronged analysis applied both to convictions that were final and to convictions pending on direct review. . . .

In *United States v. Johnson*, 457 U.S. 537 (1982), however, the Court shifted course. In that case, we reviewed at some length the history of the Court's decisions in the area of retroactivity and concluded, in the words of Justice HARLAN: " '[R]etroactivity' must be rethought." Specifically, we concluded that the retroactivity analysis for convictions that have become final must be different from the analysis for convictions that are not final at the time the new decision is issued. We observed that, in a number of separate opinions since *Linkletter*, various Members of the Court "have asserted that, at a minimum, all defendants whose cases were still pending on direct appeal at the time of the law-changing decision should be entitled to invoke the new rule." The rationale for distinguishing between cases that have become final and those that have not, and for applying new rules retroactively to cases in the latter category, was explained at length by Justice HARLAN in *Desist v. United States*, 394 U.S. [244 (1969)] (dissenting opinion), and in *Mackey v. United States*, 401 U.S. 667 (1971) (opinion concurring in judgments). In *United States v. Johnson*, we embraced to a significant extent the comprehensive analysis presented by Justice HARLAN in those opinions.

In Justice HARLAN's view, and now in ours, failure to apply a newly declared constitutional rule to criminal cases pending on direct review violates basic norms of constitutional adjudication. First, it is a settled principle that this Court adjudicates only "cases" and "controversies." See U.S. Const., Art. III, § 2. Unlike a legislature, we do not promulgate new rules of constitutional criminal procedure on a broad basis. Rather, the nature of judicial review requires that we adjudicate specific cases, and each case usually becomes the vehicle for announcement of a new rule. But after we have decided a new rule in the case selected, the integrity of judicial review requires that we apply that rule to all similar cases pending on direct review. . . .

As a practical matter, of course, we cannot hear each case pending on direct review and apply the new rule. But we fulfill our judicial responsibility by instructing the lower courts to apply the new rule retroactively to cases not yet final. . . .

Second, selective application of new rules violates the principle of treating similarly situated defendants the same. . . .

In *United States v. Johnson*, our acceptance of Justice HARLAN's views led to the holding that "subject to [certain exceptions], a decision of this Court construing the Fourth Amendment is to be applied retroactively to all convictions that were not yet final at the time the decision was rendered." The exceptions to which we referred related to three categories in which we concluded that existing precedent established threshold tests for the retroactivity analysis. In two of these categories, the new rule already was retroactively applied: (1) when a decision of this Court did nothing more than apply settled precedent to different factual situations, and (2) when the new ruling was that a trial court lacked authority to convict a criminal defendant in the first place. . . .

The third category—where a new rule is a "clear break" with past precedent—is the one at issue in these cases. . . .

Under this exception, a new constitutional rule was not applied retroactively, even to cases on direct review, if the new rule explicitly overruled a past precedent of this Court, or disapproved a practice this Court had arguably sanctioned in prior cases, or overturned a longstanding practice that lower courts had uniformly approved. . . .

For the same reasons that persuaded us in *United States v. Johnson* to adopt different conclusions as to convictions on direct review from those that already had become final, we conclude that an engrafted exception based solely upon the particular characteristics of the new rule adopted by the Court is inappropriate.

First, the principle that this Court does not disregard current law, when it adjudicates a case pending before it on direct review, applies regardless of the specific characteristics of the particular new rule announced. . . .

Second, the use of a "clear break" exception creates the same problem of not treating similarly situated defendants the same. . . .

We therefore hold that a new rule for the conduct of criminal prosecutions is to be applied retroactively to all cases, state or federal, pending on direct review or not yet final, with no exception for cases in which the new rule constitutes a "clear break" with the past. Accordingly, in No. 85–5221, the judgment of the Supreme Court of Kentucky is reversed, and the case is remanded to that court for further proceedings not inconsistent with this opinion. In No. 85–5731, the judgment of the United States Court of Appeals for the Tenth Circuit is reversed, and the case is remanded to that court for further proceedings consistent with this opinion.

Justice POWELL concurring.

I join the Court's opinion, and consider it an important step toward ending the confusion that has resulted from applying *Linkletter v. Walker* on a case by case basis.

Chief Justice REHNQUIST dissenting.

In Justice HARLAN's view, new constitutional rules governing criminal prosecutions should apply retroactively for cases pending on direct appeal when the rule is announced, and, with narrow exceptions, should not apply in collateral proceedings challenging convictions that become final before the rule is announced. The majority today adopts only a portion of this approach. I therefore join Justice WHITE's dissent. . . .

Justice WHITE, with whom the Chief Justice and Justice O'CONNOR join, dissenting.

Last Term this Court decided that the rule announced in *Batson v. Kentucky* (1986), should not apply on collateral review of convictions that became final before the decision in *Batson* was announced. *Allen v. Hardy* [478 U.S. 255] (1986). In reaching this judgment, the Court weighed the three factors that it has traditionally considered in deciding the retroactivity of a new rule of criminal procedure: " '(a) the purpose to be served by the new standards, (b) the extent of the reliance by law enforcement authorities on the old standards, and (c) the effect on the administration of justice of a retroactive application of the new standards.' " No Justice suggested that this test is unworkable. The question, then, is why the Court feels constrained to fashion a different rule for cases on direct review. The reasons the Court offers are not new, and I find them as unpersuasive today as I have in the past. . . .

The Court has already recognized that *Batson* constitutes "an explicit and substantial break with prior precedent," and that "prosecutors, trial judges, and appellate courts throughout our state and federal systems justifiably have relied on the standard of *Swain.*" *Allen v. Hardy.* The reasons that the Court gave in *Allen v. Hardy* for concluding that "retroactive application of the *Batson* rule on collateral review of final convictions would seriously disrupt the administration of justice" apply equally to retroactive application of the *Batson* rule on direct review.

The majority knows that it is penalizing justifiable reliance on *Swain,* and in doing so causing substantial disruption in the administration of justice; yet the majority acts as if it has no principled alternative.

Jaffree v. Board of School Commissioners of Mobile County

554 F.Supp. 1104 (1983)

Ishmael Jaffree challenged the constitutionality of Alabama's law authorizing teachers to lead students in a moment of "silent mediation or voluntary prayer" as a violation of the First Amendment guarantees for religious freedom. Federal District Court Judge Brevard Hand rejected Jaffree's complaint in an opinion sharply critical of the Supreme Court's rulings on the First Amendment establishment clause. His ruling was subsequently appealed by Jaffree and overturned by a court of appeals. Governor George Wallace then appealed that ruling to the Supreme Court in *Wallace v. Jaffree*, 472 U.S. 38 (1985) (see Vol. 2, Ch. 6).

MEMORANDUM OPINION

Chief Judge BREVARD HAND.

The United States Supreme Court has previously addressed itself in many cases to the practice of prayer and religious services in the public schools. As courts are wont to say, this court does not write upon a clean slate when it addresses the issue of school prayer.

Viewed historically, three decisions have lately provided general rules for school prayer. In *Engel v. Vitale*, 370 U.S. 421 [1962], *Abington v. Schempp*, 374 U.S. 203 (1963), and *Murray v. Curlett*, 374 U.S. 203 (1963) the Supreme Court established the basic considerations. As stated, the rule is that "[t]he First Amendment has erected a wall between church and state. That wall must be kept high and impregnable. We could not approve the slightest breach." *Everson v. Board of Education*, 330 U.S. 1 (1947).

The principles enunciated in *Engel v. Vitale, Abington v. Schempp*, and *Murray v. Curlett* have been distilled to this: "To pass muster under the Establishment Clause, the governmental activity must, first, reflect a clearly secular governmental purpose; second, have a primary effect that neither advances nor inhibits religion; and third, avoid excessive government entanglement with religion. *Committee for Public Education & Religious Liberty v. Nyquist*, 413 U.S. 756 (1973)."...

In sum, under present rulings the use of officially-authorized prayers or Bible readings for motivational purposes constitutes a direct violation of the establishment clause. Through a series of decisions, the courts have held that the establishment clause was designed to avoid any official sponsorship or approval of religious beliefs. Even though a practice may not be coercive, active support of a particular belief raises the danger, under the rationale of the Court, that state-approved religious views may be eventually established. . . .

In the face of this precedent the defendants argue that school prayers as they are employed are constitutional. The historical argument which they advance takes two tacks. First, the defendants urge that the first amendment to the U.S. Constitution was intended only to prohibit the *federal government* from establishing a *national* religion. Read in its proper historical context, the defendants contend that the first amendment has no application to the states. The intent of the drafters and adoptors of the first amendment was to prevent the establishment of a national church or religion, and to prevent any single religious sect or denomination from obtaining a preferred position under the auspices of the federal government. . . .

Second, the defendants argue that whatever prohibitions were initially placed upon the federal government by the first amendment that those prohibitions were not incorporated against the states when the fourteenth amendment became law on July 19, 1868. The defendants have introduced the Court to a mass of historical documentation which all point to the intent of the Thirty-ninth Congress to narrowly restrict the scope of the fourteenth amendment. In particular, these historical documents, according to the defendants, clearly demonstrate that the first amendment was never intended to be incorporated through the fourteenth amendment to apply against the states. The Court [subsequently] examine[d] each historical argument in turn. . . .

[The Court concluded that] the establishment clause, as ratified in 1791, was intended only to prohibit the federal government from establishing a national religion. The function of the establishment clause was two-fold. First, it guaranteed to each individual that Congress would not impose a national religion. Second, the establishment clause guaranteed to each state that the states were free to define the meaning of religious establishment under their own constitutions and laws.

The historical record clearly establishes that when the fourteenth amendment was ratified in 1868 that its ratification did not incorporate the first amendment against the states. . . .

What is a court to do when faced with a direct challenge to settled precedent? In most types of cases "it is more important that the applicable rule of law be settled than that it be settled right." *Burnet v. Coronado Oil & Gas Co.*, 285 U.S. 393 (1932) (BRANDEIS, J., dissenting). This general rule holds even where the court is persuaded that it has made a serious error of interpretation in cases involving a statute. However, in cases involving the federal constitution, where correction through legislative action is practically impossible, a court should be willing to examine earlier precedent and to overrule it if the court is persuaded that the earlier precedent was wrongly decided. . . .

"[T]he ultimate touchstone of constitutionality is the Constitution itself and not what we have said about it." *Graves v. O'Keefe,* 306 U.S. 466 (1939) (FRANKFURTER, J., concurring). "By placing a premium on 'recent cases' rather than the language of the Constitution, the Court makes it dangerously simple for future Courts using the technique of interpretation to operate as a 'continuing Constitutional Convention.' " *Coleman v. Alabama,* 399 U.S. 1 (1970) (BURGER, C.J.). . . .

This Court's review of the relevant legislative history surrounding the adoption of both the first amendment and of the fourteenth amendment, together with the plain language of those amendments, leaves no doubt that those amendments were not intended to forbid religious prayers in the schools which the states and their political subdivisions mandate. . . .

If the appellate courts disagree with this Court in its examination of history and conclusion of constitutional interpreation thereof, then this Court will look again at the record in this case and reach conclusions which it is not now forced to reach.

3

ECONOMIC RIGHTS AND AMERICAN CAPITALISM

P RIVATE PROPERTY is not mentioned in the Constitution even though its protection was one of the central purposes of the Constitution. Sections 8 and 10 of Article I and Section 1 of Article IV govern various matters related to private property—taxes, duties, imposts, excises, commerce, bankruptcies, bills of credit, debts, the impairment of contracts, and the rights of authors and inventors. Yet private property did not receive specific protection until the ratification in 1791 of the Fifth Amendment. The due process and takings clauses of that amendment provide that "No person shall . . . be deprived of life, liberty, or property without due process of law; nor shall private property be taken for public use without just compensation."

Liberty and property were, nevertheless, closely tied together in the minds of the Framers of the Constitution. Property conditioned suffrage and was closely linked with representation (see Vol. 1, Chs. 5 and 8). When defending the Constitution in *The Federalist*, Alexander Hamilton sought to show that it would provide security "to liberty and to property." Noah Webster, a prominent New York publisher, even more bluntly claimed "that *property* is the basis of *power*," when differentiating America from England and Europe, where property was concentrated in the hands of a few:

[I]n America, and here alone, we have gone at once to the *foundation of liberty*, and raised the people to their true dignity. Let the lands be possessed by the people in fee-simple, let the fountain be kept pure, and the streams will be pure of course. Our jealousy of *trial by jury, the liberty of the press,* &c., is totally groundless. Such rights are inseparably connected with the *power* and *dignity* of the people, which rest on their *property.* They cannot be abridged. All *other* [free] nations have wrested *property* and *freedom* from *barons* and *tyrants; we* begin our empire with full possession of property and all its attending rights.[1]

The Framers took to heart the teaching of the English philosopher John Locke, in his *Second Treatise of Government,* that property is a natural right—a right preceeding the establishment of government—and its preservation one of the chief ends of government. On Locke's labor theory of value, property was but an extension of liberty. "The *labour* that was mine, removing [objects] out of that common state [of nature] they were in, hath *fixed* my *Property* in them," argued Locke. "Thus the Grass my Horse has bit; the Turfs my Servant has cut; and the Ore I have digg'd in any place where I have a right to them in common with others, become my *Property.*"[2] No less influential than Locke on the Framers was Sir William Blackstone, who also maintained in his *Commentaries on the Laws of England* that property was an "absolute right, inherent in every Englishman."[3]

Given this background and understanding of the fundamental nature of property, it is perhaps not surprising that the Supreme Court emerged within a generation of the ratification of the Constitution as a defender of property rights and economic liberty. Through an expansive interpretation of the contract clause in the early nineteenth century, and the creation of a "liberty of contract" in the latter part of that century, the Court laid the basis in constitutional law for the growth of American capitalism.

NOTES

1. Noah Webster, "An Examination into the Leading Principles of the Federal Constitution" (Oct. 10, 1787), in *The Founders' Constitution,* Vol. 1, ed. Philip Kurland and Ralph Lerner (Chicago: University of Chicago Press, 1987), 596–597.

2. John Locke, "Second Treatise of Government" (1689), in *Two Treatises of Government,* ed. Peter Laslett (New York: Mentor Books, 1960), 330.

3. Sir William Blackstone, *Commentaries on the Laws of England* (1765–1769) (Chicago: University of Chicago, 1979).

SELECTED BIBLIOGRAPHY

Levy, Leonard. "Property as a Human Right." 5 *Constitutional Commentary* 169 (1988).

Goldwin, Robert A., and Schambra, William, A., eds. *How Capitalistic Is the Constitution?* Washington, D.C.: American Enterprise Institute, 1982.

Pennock, J. Roland, and Chapman, John, eds. *Property.* New York: New York University Press, 1980.

A. THE CONTRACT CLAUSE AND VESTED INTERESTS IN PROPERTY

Article I, Section 10 forbids the states from "impairing the Obligation of Contracts." That provision was ostensibly aimed at preventing the states from reneging on private contracts (such as loans made by banks) and passing laws favoring debtors, as was done in the 1780s in the aftermath of the Revolutionary War. As such, the guarantee presumably covered only private contracts. But in a series of rulings, the Marshall Court (1801–1836) broadly interpreted the contract clause to apply to public contracts (that is, contracts between a governmental agency and private individuals) and to safeguard vested interests in private property.

The famous *"Yazoo case," Fletcher v. Peck* (1810) (see page 196) was the first important ruling of the Marshall Court in which the contract clause was turned into a guarantee for public contracts, in addition to a limitation on states' powers over private contracts. Notice that besides broadly construing the contract clause, Chief Justice Marshall notes that Georgia's law revoking its earlier land grants contravened "general principles, which are common to our free institutions, or by the particular provisions of the constitution of the United States." Chief Justice Marshall pushed his theory further two years later in *New Jersey v. Wilson*, 7 Cr. 164 (11 U.S.) (1812). New Jersey had made Indian lands tax-exempt, but when the land was sold to a non-Indian the state sought to tax the new owner. However, the Marshall Court ruled that the original contract with the Indians was still valid and the state could not tax the land. In one of the few cases involving private contracts, *Sturges v. Crowninshield*, 4 Wheat. (17 U.S.) 122 (1819), Chief Justice Marshall struck down a New York bankruptcy law as applied to a contract made before the law was passed. However, he found himself in the minority in *Ogden v. Sauders*, 12 Wheat. (25 U.S.) 213 (1827), when the Court upheld another bankruptcy law that had been enacted before a contested contract was made.

Next to *Fletcher v. Peck*, the second most important Marshall

CONSTITUTIONAL HISTORY

John Locke on the Ends of Political Society and Government

123. If Man in the State of Nature be so free, as has been said; If he be absolute Lord of his own Person and Possessions, equal to the greatest, and subject to no Body, why will he part with his Freedom? Why will he give up this Empire, and subject himself to the Dominion and Controul of any other Power? To which 'tis obvious to Answer, that though in the state of Nature he hath such a right, yet the Enjoyment of it is very uncertain, and constantly exposed to the Invasion of others. For all being Kings as much as he, every Man his Equal, and the greater part no strict Observers of Equity and Justice, the enjoyment of the property he has in this state is very unsafe, very unsecure. This makes him willing to quit a Condition, which however free, is full of fears and continual dangers: And 'tis not without reason, that he seeks out, and is willing to joyn in Society with others who are already united, or have a mind to unite for the mutual *Preservation* of their Lives, Liberties and Estates, which I call by the general Name, *Property*.

124. The great and *chief end* therefore, of Mens uniting into Commonwealths, and putting themselves under Government, *is the Preservation of their Property*. To which in the state of Nature there are many things wanting.

First, There wants an *establish'd*, settled, known *Law*, received and allowed by common consent to be the Standard of Right and Wrong, and the common measure to decide all Controversies between them. For though the Law of Nature be plain and intelligible to all rational Creatures; yet Men being biassed by their Interest, as well as ignorant for want of study of it, are not apt to allow of it as a Law binding to them in the application of it to their particular Cases.

125. *Secondly*, In the State of Nature there wants a *known and indifferent Judge*, with Authority to determine all differences according to the established Law. For every one in that state being both Judge and Executioner of the Law of Nature, Men being partial to themselves, Passion and Revenge is very apt to carry them too far, and with too much heat, in their own Cases; as well as negligence, and unconcernedness, to make them too remiss, in other Mens.

126. *Thirdly*, In the state of Nature there often wants *Power* to back and support the Sentence when right, and to *give* it due *Execution*. They who by any Injustice offended, will seldom fail, where they are able, by force to make good their Injustice: such resistance many times makes the punishment dangerous, and frequently destructive, to those who attempt it.

Source: John Locke, "Second Treatise of Government," in *Two Treatises of Government*, ed. Peter Laslett (New York: Mentor Books, 1960), ch. 5.

Court ruling on the contract clause is *Trustees of Dartmouth College v. Woodward* (1819) (see page 200). Again, the clause was expansively read to protect the vested interests in a corporate charter granted by the English Crown in 1769, prior to the Revolutionary War.

The Marshall Court's interpretation of the contract clause was controversial and was viewed as a severe limitation on states' regulatory powers. Yet it remained the dominant feature in the early development of constitutional law and the vehicle by which the power of judicial review was asserted and established. Indeed, political scientist Benjamin Wright found that the contract clause was used in almost 40 percent of the cases challenging state legislation before 1889 and that the Court and lower federal courts used it to strike down some seventy-five state laws.[1]

The Court under Chief Justice Roger Taney (1836–1864) maintained respect for proprietary interests but was more deferential to the powers of states. In its leading ruling on the contract clause, *Charles River Bridge Co. v. Warren Bridge Co.* (1837) (see page 205), notice that Chief Justice Taney emphasizes that "[w]hile the rights of private property are sacredly guarded, we must not forget that the community also have rights, and that the happiness and well-being of every citizen depends on their faithful preservation." Taney thus established the principle that public contracts were to be strictly construed on the recognition that states have an important role in promoting the general welfare and technological advances in the public interest.

Despite the expansive interpretation given the contract clause in the early and mid-nineteenth century, its protection for proprietary interests did not override state police powers or the power of eminent domain (the government's taking of private property for public use without just compensation) (see section C, in this chapter). Nor did it foreclose the possibility of state regulations aimed at promoting public morals, health, safety, and welfare. In *Stone v. Mississippi*, 101 U.S. 814 (1880), for instance, the Court unanimously upheld state police power over John Stone's claim of vested property rights. Stone had been granted by the Mississippi legislature a twenty-five-year franchise to sell lottery tickets, but two years later the state adopted a new constitution prohibiting the sale of lottery tickets. When Stone sought to evade prosecution for selling lottery tickets, the Court rejected his invocation of the contract clause, just as it did when state prohibition laws were attacked for infringing on contracts for the sale of beer,[2] and when employment contracts were superceded by workmen's compensation laws.[3] As Justice Mahlon Pitney, in *Atlantic Coastline Railroad Co. v. City of Goldsboro*, 232 U.S. 548 (1914), explained for a unanimous Court, when affirming that states may delegate to cities the power to regulate health, safety, and welfare:

[I]t is settled that neither the "contract" clause nor the "due process" clause has the effect of overriding the power of the state to establish all regulations that are reasonably necessary to secure the health, safety, good order, comfort, or general welfare of the community; that this power can neither be abdicated nor bargained away, and is inalienable even by express grant; and that all contract and property rights are held subject to its faire exercise.

Justice Pitney expressed the modern view of the contract clause. *Home Building & Loan Association v. Blasidell* (1934) (see page 214) illustrates how far the Court in the twentieth century has moved away from its earlier application of the contract clause. There a bare majority of the Hughes Court upheld Minnesota's law, passed during the Great Depression, preventing the repossession of mortgaged property. *Blaisdell* established, according to Justice Felix Frankfurter in *East New York Savings Bank v. Hahn*, 326 U.S. 230 (1945), that "[w]hen a widely diffused public interest has become enmeshed in a network of multitudinous private arrangements, the authority of the State 'to safeguard the vital interests of the people'. . . is not to be gainsaid by abstracting one such arrangement from its public context and treating it as though it were an isolated private contract constitutionally immune from impairment." The principle of judicial deference to legislative regulation of private contracts asserted in *Blaisdell* was reaffirmed in *City of El Paso v. Simmons* (1965) (see page 220). However, *United States Trust Co. of New York v. State of New Jersey* (1977) (see page 223) indicates that the Court gives heightened scrutiny and greater weight to claims under the contract clause in controversies involving a state's impairment of its own contracts.

Why did the Court's reliance on and enforcement of the contract clause decline in the late nineteenth and twentieth centuries? There are a number of reasons. For one thing, the Industrial Revolution brought a growth in the number of corporations and economic problems that could not be accommodated even with a broad reading of the contract clause. Second, the Court developed its contract clause jurisprudence in the absence of congressional legislation. But in the late nineteenth century Congress responded to the social and economic pressures that accompanied industrialization and urbanization. Finally, as discussed below, the Court invented and enforced a "liberty of contract" under the Fourteenth Amendment's due process clause in defense of vested property rights against progressive economic legislation.

NOTES

1. Benjamin Wright, *The Contract Clause of the Constitution* (Cambridge, MA: Harvard University Press, 1938), 95.

2. See Boston Beer Co. v. Massachusetts, 97 U.S. 25 (1878).
3. New York Central R. Co. v. White, 243 U.S. 188 (1917).

SELECTED BIBLIOGRAPHY

Ackerman, Bruce. *Private Property and the Constitution.* New Haven, CT: Yale University Press, 1977.
Kutler, Stanley I. *Privilege and Creative Destruction: The Charles River Bridge Case.* 2nd ed. Baltimore, MD: Johns Hopkins University Press, 1990.
Magrath, C. Peter. *Yazoo: The Case of Fletcher v. Peck,* New York: W. W. Norton & Co., 1967.
Stites, Francis. *Private Interest and Public Gain: The Dartmouth College Case.* Amherst: University of Massachusetts, 1972.
Wright, Benjamin. *The Contract Clause of the Constitution.* Cambridge, MA: Harvard University Press, 1938.

Fletcher v. Peck

6 Cr. (10 U.S.) 87 (1810)

Robert Fletcher sued John Peck for the breach of a covenant on land that Peck had sold him. The land was part of a larger land grant in 1795 of the Georgia legislature to four land-holding companies, which had bribed several members of the legislature to win passage of the land grant. The next year, however, the state enacted legislation declaring the 1795 law and all rights and claims to it null and void. Peck had acquired the land in 1800 and sold it three years later to Fletcher, at which time he claimed that all past sales of the land had been lawful. Fletcher, though, contended that because the original sale of the land had been declared invalid by the Georgia legislature Peck could not legally sell the land and was guilty of breach of contract. A federal circuit court found in favor of Peck, and Fletcher appealed directly to the Supreme Court.

Chief Justice MARSHALL delivers the opinion of the Court.

The pleadings being now amended, this cause comes on again to be heard on sundry demurrers, and on a special verdict.

The suit was instituted on several covenants contained in a deed made by John Peck, the defendant in error, conveying to Robert Fletcher, the plaintiff in error, certain lands which were part of a large purchase made by James Gunn and others, in the year 1795, from the state of Georgia, the contract for which was made in the form of a bill passed by the legislature of that state. . . .

Titles which, according to every legal test, are perfect, are acquired with that confidence which is inspired by the opinion that the purchaser is safe. If there be any concealed defect, arising from the conduct of those who had held the property long before he acquired it, of which he had no notice, that concealed defect cannot be set up against him. He has paid his money for a title good at law, he is innocent, whatever may be the guilt of others, and equity will not subject him to the penalties attached to that guilt. All titles would be insecure, and the intercourse between man and man would be very seriously obstructed, if this principle be overturned. . . .

If the legislature felt itself absolved from those rules of property which are common to all the citizens of the United States, and from those principles of equity which are acknowledged in all our courts, its act is to be supported by its power alone, and the same power may devest any other individual of his lands, if it shall be the will of the legislature so to exert it.

It is not intended to speak with disrespect of the legislature of Georgia, or of its acts. Far from it. The question is a general question and is treated as one. For although such powerful objections to a legislative grant, as are alleged against this, may not again exist, yet the principle, on which alone this rescinding act is to be supported, may be applied to every case to which it shall be the will of any legislature to apply it. The principle is this: that a legislature may, by its own act, devest the vested estate of any man whatever, for reasons which shall, by itself, be deemed sufficient. . . .

Is the power of the legislature competent to the annihilation of such title, and to a resumption of the property thus held?

The principle asserted is, that one legislature is competent to repeal any act which a former legislature was competent to pass; and that one legislature cannot abridge the powers of a succeeding legislature.

The correctness of this principle, so far as respects general legislation, can never be controverted. But, if an act be done under a law, a succeeding legislature cannot undo it. The past cannot be recalled by the most absolute power. Conveyances have been made; those conveyances have vested legal estates, and, if those estates may be seized by the sovereign authority, still, that they originally vested is a fact, and cannot cease to be a fact.

When, then, a law is in its nature a contract, when absolute rights have vested under that contract; a repeal of the law cannot devest those rights; and the act of annulling them, if legitimate, is rendered so by a power applicable to the case of every individual in the community. . . .

It is the peculiar province of the legislature to prescribe general rules for the government of society; the application of those rules to individuals in society would seem to be the duty of other departments. How far the power of giving the law may involve every other power, in cases where the constitution is silent, never has been, and perhaps never can be, definitely stated.

The validity of this rescinding act, then, might well be doubted, were Georgia a single sovereign power. But Georgia cannot be viewed as a single, unconnected, sovereign power, on whose legislature no other restrictions are imposed than may be found in its own constitution. She is a part of a large empire; she is a member of the American Union; and that Union has a constitution the supremacy of which all acknowledge, and which imposes limits to the legislatures of the several states, which none claim a right to pass. The constitution of the United States declares that no state shall pass any bill of attainder, ex post facto law or law impairing the obligation of contracts.

Does the case now under consideration come within this prohibitory section of the constitution?

In considering this very interesting question, we immediately ask ourselves what is a contract? Is a grant a contract?

A contract is a compact between two or more parties, and is either executory or executed. An executory contract is one in which a party binds himself to do, or not to do, a particular thing; such was the law under which the conveyance was made by the governor. A contract executed is one in which the object of contract is performed; and this, says Blackstone, differs in nothing from a grant. The contract between Georgia and the purchasers was executed by the grant. A contract executed, as well as one which is executory, contains obligations binding on the parties. A grant, in its own nature, amounts to an extinguishment of the right of the grantor, and implies a contract not to re-assert that right. A party is, therefore, always estopped by his own grant.

Since, then, in fact, a grant is a contract executed, the obligation of which still continues, and since the constitution uses the general term contract, without distinguishing between those which are executory and those which are executed, it must be construed to comprehend the latter as well as the former. A law annulling conveyances between individuals, and declaring that the grantors should stand seized of their former estates, notwithstanding those grants, would be as repugnant to the constitution as a law discharging the vendors of property from the obligation of executing their contracts by conveyances. It would be strange if a contract to convey was secured by the constitution, while an absolute conveyance remained unprotected.

If, under a fair construction of the constitution, grants are comprehended under the term contracts, is a grant from the state excluded from the operation of the provision? Is the clause to be considered as inhibiting the state from impairing the obligation of contracts between two individuals, but as excluding from that inhibition contracts made with itself?

The words themselves contain no such distinction. They are general, and are applicable to contracts of every description. . . .

It is, then, the unanimous opinion of the court, that, in this case, the estate having passed into the hands of a purchaser for a valuable consideration, without notice, the state of Georgia was restrained, either by general principles, which are common to our free institutions, or by the particular provisions of the constitution of the United States, from passing a law whereby the estate of the plaintiff in the premises so purchased could be constitutionally and legally impaired and rendered null and void. . . .

Justice JOHNSON delivering a separate opinion.

In this case I entertain . . . an opinion different from that which has been delivered by the court. . . .

[My] opinion . . . is not founded on the provision in the constitution of the United States, relative to laws impairing the obligation of contracts. It is much to be regretted that words of less equivocal signification had not been adopted in that article of the constitution. There is reason to believe, from the letters of Plubius, which are well known to be entitled to the highest respect, that the object of the convention was to afford a general protection to individual rights against the acts of the state legislatures. Whether the words, "acts impairing the obligation of contracts," can be construed to have the same force as must have been given to the words "obligation and effect of contracts," is the difficulty in my mind.

There can be no solid objection to adopting the technical definition of the word "contract," given by Blackstone. The etymology, the classical signification, and the civil law idea of the word, will all support it. But the difficulty arises on the word "obligation," which certainly imports an existing moral or physical necessity. Now, a grant or conveyance by no means necessarily implies the continuance of an obligation beyond the moment of executing it. . . .

I enter with great hesitation upon this question, because it involves a subject of the greatest delicacy and much difficulty. The states and the United States are continually legislating on the subject of contracts, prescribing the mode of authentication, the time within which suits shall be prosecuted for them, in many cases affecting existing contracts by the laws which they pass, and declaring them to cease or lose their effect for want of compliance, in the parties, with such statutory provisions. All these acts appear to be within the most correct limits of legislative powers, and most beneficially exercised, and certainly could not have been intended to be affected by this constitutional provision; yet where to draw the line, or how to define or limit the words, "obligation of contracts," will be found a subject of extreme difficulty.

To give it the general effect of a restriction of the state powers in favor of private rights, is certainly going very far beyond the obvious and necessary import of the words, and would operate to restrict the states in the exercise of that right which every community must exercise, of possessing itself of the property of the individual, when necessary for public uses; a right which a magnanimous and just government will never exercise without amply indemnifying the individual, and which perhaps amounts to nothing more than a power to oblige him to sell and convey, when the public necessities require it.

Trustees of Dartmouth College v. Woodward
4 Wheat. (17 U.S.) 518 (1819)

Dartmouth College was incorporated in 1769 under a charter granted by the English Crown, which authorized a twelve-member board of trustees to govern the college and to appoint their successors. The New Hampshire legislature, however, amended the charter in 1816 with legislation increasing the size of the board of trustees to twenty-one, establishing a board of overseers, and authorizing the governor to appoint new trustees and members of the board of overseers. The incumbant trustees refused to recognize the legislation as binding and sued William Woodward, the college's treasurer, to recover corporate property that was temporarily entrusted to him under the legislation. A trial court failed to resolve the question of the constitutionality of the legislation, but it was upheld by a state superior court. The trustees of Dartmouth College then appealed to the Supreme Court. As was the practice through most of the nineteenth century, they hired a member of the Supreme Court's bar, Daniel Webster, to argue their case. As was also the practice, attorneys for both sides were given unlimited time to present their arguments. Webster was one of the greatest orators and rather dramatically concluded his argument before the bench, observing,

Sir, you may destroy this little institution. It is weak. It is in your hands! I know it is one of the lesser lights in the literary horizon of the country. You may put it out. But if you do so, you must carry through your work. You must extinguish, one after another, all those great lights of science which, for more than a century, have thrown their radiance over our land.

It is, Sir, as I have said, a small college and yet, there are those who love it. . . .

Sir, I care not how others may feel, but, for myself, when I see my Alma Mater surrounded, like Caesar in the senate-house, by those who are reinterating stab on stab, I would not, for this right hand, have her turn to me, and say *et tu quoque, mi fili!*

Chief Justice MARSHALL delivers the opinion of the Court.

It can require no argument to prove that the circumstances of this case constitute a contract. An application is made to the crown for a charter to incorporate a religious and literary institution. In the application, it is stated that large contributions have been made for the object, which will be conferred on the corporation as soon as it shall be created. The charter is granted, and on its faith the property is conveyed. Surely in this transaction every ingredient of a complete and legitimate contract is to be found.

The points for consideration are:

1. Is this contract protected by the constitution of the United States?

2. Is it impaired by the acts under which the defendant holds?

1. On the first point it . . . becomes, then, the duty of the court most seriously to examine this charter, and to ascertain its true character. . . .

From [a] review of the charter, it appears that Dartmouth College is an eleemosynary institution, incorporated for the purpose of perpetuating the application of the bounty of the donors, to the specified objects of that bounty; that its trustees or governors were originally named by the founder, and invested with the power of perpetuating themselves; that they are not public officers, nor is it a civil institution, participating in the administration of government; but a charity school, or a seminary of education, incorporated for the preservation of its property, and the perpetual application of that property to the objects of its creation.

Yet a question remains to be considered, of more real difficulty, on which more doubt has been entertained than on all that have been discussed. The founders of the college, at least those whose contributions were in money, have parted with the property bestowed upon it, and their representatives have no interest in that property. The donors of land are equally without interest, so long as the corporation shall exist. Could they be found, they are unaffected by any alteration in its constitution, and probably regardless of its form, or even of its existence. The students are fluctuating, and no individual among our youth has a vested interest in the institution, which can be asserted in a court of justice. Neither the founders of the college nor the youth for whose benefit it was founded, complain of the alteration made in its charter, or thing themselves injured by it. The trustees alone complain, and the trustees have no beneficial interest to be protected. Can this be such a contract as the constitution intended to withdraw from the power of state legislation? Contracts, the parties to which have a vested beneficial interest, and those only, it has been said, are the objects about which the constitution is solicitous, and to which its protection is extended.

The court has bestowed on this argument the most deliberate consideration, and the result will be stated. Dr. Wheelock, acting for himself, and for those who, at his solicitation, had made contributions to his school, applied for this charter, as the instrument which should enable him, and them, to perpetuate their beneficent intention. It was granted. An artificial, immortal being, was created by the crown, capable of receiving and distributing forever, according to the will of the donors, the donations which should be made to it. On this being, the contributions which had been collected were immediately bestowed. These gifts were made, not, indeed, to make a profit for the donors, or their posterity, but for something in their opinion of inestimable value; for something which they deemed a full equivalent for the money with which it was purchased. The consideration for which they stipulated, is the perpetual application of the fund to its object, in the mode prescribed by themselves. Their descendants may take no interest in the preservation of this consideration. But in this respect their descendants are not their representatives. They are represented by the corporation. The corporation is the assignee of their rights, stands in their place, and distributes their bounty, as they would themselves have distributed it, had they been immortal. So with respect to the students who are to derive learning from this source. The corporation is a trustee for them also. Their potential rights, which, taken distributively, are imperceptible, amount collectively to a most important interest. These are, in the aggregate, to be exercised, asserted and protected, by the corporation. They were as completely out of the donors, at the instant of their being vested in the corporation, and as incapable of being asserted by the students, as at present. . . .

This is plainly a contract to which the donors, the trustees, and the crown (to whose rights and obligations New Hampshire succeeds), were the original parties. It is a contract made on a valuable consideration. It is a contract for the security and disposition of property. It is a contract, on the faith of which real and personal estate has been conveyed to the corporation. It is then a contract within the letter of the constitution, and within its spirit also, unless the fact that the property is invested by the donors in trustees for the promotion of religion and education, for the benefit of persons who are perpetually changing, though the objects remain the same, shall create a particular exception, taking this case out of the prohibition contained in the constitution.

It is more than possible that the preservation of rights of this description was not particularly in the view of the framers of the constitution when the clause under consideration was introduced into that instrument. It is probable that interferences of more frequent recurrence, to which the temptation was stronger, and of which the mischief was more extensive, constituted the great motive for imposing this restriction on the state legislatures. But although a particular and a rare case may not, in itself, be of sufficient magnitude to induce a rule, yet it must be governed by the rule, when established unless some plain and strong reason for excluding it can be given. It is not enough to say that this particular case was not in the mind of the convention when the article was framed, nor of the American people when it was adopted. It is necessary to go farther, and to say that, had this particular case been suggested, the language would have been so varied, as to exclude it, or it would have been made a special exception. The case being within the words of the rule, must be within its operation likewise, unless there be something in the literal construction so obviously absurd, or mischievous, or repugnant to the general spirit of the instrument, as to justify those who expound the constitution in making it an exception.

On what safe and intelligible ground can this exception stand. There is no exception in the constitution, no sentiment delivered by its contemporaneous expounders, which would justify us in making it. In the absence of all authority of this kind, is there, in the nature and reason of the case itself, that which would sustain a construction of the constitution, not warranted by its words? Are contracts of this description of a character to excite so little interest that we must exclude them from the provisions of the constitution, as being unworthy of the attention of those who framed the instrument? Or does public policy so imperiously demand their remaining exposed to legislative alteration, as to compel us, or rather permit us to say that these words, which were introduced to give stability to contracts, and which in their plain import comprehend this contract, must yet be so construed as to exclude it?

Almost all eleemosynary corporations, those which are created for the promotion of religion of charity, or of education, are of the same character. The law of this case is the law of all. . . .

The opinion of the court, after mature deliberation, is, that this is a contract, the obligation of which cannot be impaired without violating the constitution of the United States. This opinion appears to us to be equally supported by reason, and by the former decisions of this court.

2. We next proceed to the inquiry whether its obligation has been impaired by those acts of the legislature of New Hampshire to which the special verdict refers.

From the review of this charter, which has been taken, it appears that the whole power of governing the college, of appointing and removing tutors, of fixing their salaries, of directing the course of study to be pursued by the students, and of filling up vacancies created in their own body, was vested in the trustees. On the part of the crown it was expressly stipulated that this corporation, thus constituted, should continue forever; and that the number of trustees should forever consist of twelve, and no more. By this contract the crown was bound, and could have made no violent alteration in its essential terms, without impairing its obligation. . . .

It has been already stated that the act "to amend the charter, and enlarge and improve the corporation of Dartmouth College," increases the number of trustees to twenty-one, gives the appointment of the additional members to the executive of the state, and creates a board of overseers, to consist of twenty-five persons, of whom twenty-one are also appointed by the executive of New Hampshire, who have power to inspect and control the most important acts of the trustees. . . .

The whole power of governing the college is transferred from trustees appointed according to the will of the founder, expressed in the charter, to the executive of New Hampshire. The management and application of the funds of this eleemosynary institution, which are placed by the donors in the hands of trustees named in the charter, and empowered to perpetuate themselves, are placed by this act under the control of the government of the state. The will of the state is substituted for the will of the donors in every essential operation of the college. This is not an immaterial change. The founders of the college contracted, not merely for the perpetual application of the funds which they gave, to the objects for which those funds were given; they contracted also to secure that application by the constitution of the corporation. They contracted for a system which should, as far as human foresight can provide, retain forever the government of the literary institution they had formed, in the hands of persons approved by themselves. This system is totally changed. The charter of 1769 exists no longer. It is reorganized; and re-organized in such a manner as to convert a literary institution, moulded according to the will of its founders, and placed under the control of private literary men, into a machine entirely subservient to the will of government. This may be for the advantage of this college in particular, and may be for the advantage of literature in general, but it is not according to the will of the donors, and is subversive of that contract, on the faith of which their property was given. . . .

It results from this opinion, that the acts of the legislature of New Hampshire, which are stated in the special verdict found in this cause, are repugnant to the constitution of the United

States; and that the judgment on this special verdict ought to have been for the plaintiffs. The judgment of the State Court must therefore be reversed.

Justice WASHINGTON and Justice STORY concurred in separate opinions.

Justice DUVALL dissented.

Charles River Bridge Co. v. Warren Bridge Co.
11 Pet. (36 U.S) 420 (1837)

In 1785, the Massachusetts legislature incorporated the Charlestown Bridge Company and authorized it to build a toll bridge over the Charles River. The company was obligated to pay Harvard College £200 annually as compensation in lieu of its right to operate a ferry that had been granted the college in 1650. In 1792, the charter was extended for another seventy years. But in 1832 the legislature incorporated the Warren Bridge Company and authorized it to build a bridge for free public use just 275 yards away from the Charles River Bridge. That prompted the owners of Charles River Bridge Company to seek an injunction against the construction of the Warren Bridge. The Massachusetts Supreme Judicial Court dismissed the complaint and Charles River Bridge Company appealed to the Supreme Court.

Chief Justice TANEY delivers the opinion of the court.

[On] what ground can the plaintiffs in error contend that the ferry rights of the college have been transferred to the proprietors of the bridge? If they have been thus transferred, it must be by some mode of transfer known to the law, and the evidence relied on to prove it can be pointed out in the record. How was it transferred? It is not suggested that there ever was in point of fact, a deed of conveyance executed by the college to the bridge company. Is there any evidence in the record from which such a conveyance may, upon legal principle, be presumed? The testimony before the court, so far from laying the foundation for such a presumption, repels it in the most positive terms. The petition to the Legislature in 1785, on which the charter was granted, does not suggest an assignment, nor any agreement or consent on the part of the college; and the petitioners do not appear to have regarded the wishes of that institution, as by any means necessary to insure their success. They place their application entirely on considerations of public interest and public convenience, and the superior advantages of a communication across Charles River by a bridge instead of a ferry. The Legislature, in granting the charter, show, by the language of the law, that they acted on the principles assumed by the petitioners. The preamble recites that the bridge "will be of great public utility;" and that is the only reason they assign for passing the law which incorporates this company. The validity of the charter is not made to depend on the consent of the college, nor of any assignment or surrender on their part; and the Legislature deal with the subject, as if it were one exclusively within their own power, and as if the ferry right were not to be transferred to the bridge company, but to be extinguished; and they appear to have acted on the principle that the State, by virtue of its sovereign powers and eminent domain, had a right to take away the franchise of the ferry; because in their judgment, the public interest and convenience would be better promoted by a bridge in the same place; and upon that principle they proceed to make a pecuniary compensation to the college for the franchise thus taken away. . . .

It does not, by any means, follow that because the legislative power in Massachusetts, in 1650, may have granted to a justly favored seminary of learning, the exclusive right of ferry between Boston and Charlestown, they would, in 1785, give the same extensive privilege to another corporation, who were about to erect a bridge in the same place. The fact that such a right was granted to the college cannot, by any sound rule of construction, be used to extend the privileges of the bridge company beyond what the words of the charter naturally and legally import. Increased population longer experienced in legislation, the different character of the corporations which owned the ferry from that which owned the bridge, might well have induced a change in the policy of the State in this respect; and as the franchise of the ferry and that of the bridge are different in their nature. . . .

[T]here is no rule of legal interpretation which would authorize the court to associate these grants together, and to infer that any privilege was intended to be given to the bridge company, merely because it had been conferred on the ferry. The charter to the bridge is a written instrument which must speak for itself, and be interpreted by its own terms.

This brings us to the Act of the Legislature of Massachusetts of 1785, by which the plaintiffs were incorporated by the name of "The Proprietors of the Charles River Bridge;" and it is here, and in the law of 1792, prolonging their charter, that we must look for the extent and nature of the franchise conferred upon the plaintiffs. . . .

This, like many other cases, is a bargain between a company of adventurers and the public, the terms of which are expressed in the statute; and the rule of construction in all such cases, is now fully established to be this—that any ambiguity in the terms of the contract, must operate against the adventurers, and in favor of the public, and the plaintiffs can claim nothing that is not clearly given them by the act." And the doctrine thus laid down is abundantly sustained by the authorities referred to, in this decision. . . .

[T]he object and end of all government is to promote the happiness and prosperity of the community by which it is established, and it can never be assumed that the government intended to diminish its power of accomplishing the end for which it was created. And in a country like ours, free, active and enterprising, continually advancing in numbers and wealth; new channels of communication are daily found necessary, both for travel and trade, and are essential to the comfort, convenience, and prosperity of the people. A State ought never to be presumed to surrender this power, because, like the taxing power, the whole community have an interest in preserving it undiminished. And when a corporation alleges that a State has surrendered for seventy years its power of improvement and public accommodation, in a great and important line of travel, along which a vast number of its citizens must daily pass; the community have a right to insist, in the language of this court above quoted, "that its abandonment ought not to be presumed, in a case in which the deliberate purpose of the State to abandon it does not appear." The continued existence of a government would be of no great value, if by implications and presumptions, it was disarmed of the powers necessary to accomplish the ends of its creation, and the functions it was designed to perform, transferred to the hands of privileged corporations. The rule of construction announced by the court was not confined to the taxing power, nor is it so limited in the opinion delivered. On the contrary, it was distinctly placed on the ground that the interests of the community were concerned in preserving, undiminished, the power then in question; and whenever any power of the State is said to be surrendered or diminished, whether it be the taxing power or any other affecting the public interest, the same principle applies, and the rule of construction must be the same. No one will question that the interests of the great body of the people of the State, would, in this instance, be affected by the surrender of this great line of travel to a single corporation, with the right to exact toll, and exclude competition for seventy years. While the rights of private property are sacredly guarded, we must not forget that the community also have rights, and that the happiness and well being of every citizen depends on their faithful preservation.

Adopting the rule of construction above stated as the settled one, we proceed to apply it to the charter of 1785, to the proprietors of the Charles River Bridge. This act of incorporation is in the usual form, and the privileges such as are commonly given to corporations of that kind. It confers on them the ordinary faculties of a corporation, for the purpose of building the bridge; and establishes certain rates of toll, which the company are authorized to take. This is the whole grant. There is no exclusive privilege given to them over the waters of Charles River, above or below their bridge. No right to erect another bridge themselves, nor to prevent other persons from erecting one. No engagement from the State that another shall not be erected, and no undertaking not to sanction competition, nor to make improvements that may diminish the amount of its income. Upon all these subjects the charter is silent, and nothing is said in it about a line of travel, so much insisted on in the argument, in which they are to have exclusive privileges. No words are used from which an intention to grant any of these rights can be inferred. If the plaintiff is entitled to them, it must be implied simply from the nature of the grant, and cannot be inferred from the words by which the grant is made.

The relative position of the Warren Bridge has already been described. It does not interrupt the passage over the Charles River Bridge, nor make the way to it or from it less convenient. None of the faculties or franchises granted to that corporation have been revoked by the Legislature; and its right to take the tolls granted by the charter remains unaltered. In short, all the franchises and rights of property enumerated in the charter, and there mentioned to have been granted to it, remain unimpaired. But its income is destroyed by the Warren Bridge; which, being free, draws off the passengers and property which would have gone over it, and renders their franchise of no value. This is the gist of the complaint. For it is not pretended that the erection of the Warren Bridge would have done them any injury, or in any degree affected their right of property, if it had not diminished the amount of their tolls. In order, then, to entitle themselves to relief, it is necessary to show that the Legislature contracted not to do the act of which they complain; and that they impaired, or in other words violated, that contract, by the erection of the Warren Bridge.

The inquiry then is, does the charter contain such a contract on the part of the State? Is there any such stipulation to be found in that instrument? It must be admitted on all hands, that there is none—no words that even relate to another bridge, or to the diminution of their tolls, or to the line of travel. If a contract on that subject can be gathered from the charter, it must be by implication, and cannot be found in the words used. Can such an agreement be implied? The rule of construction before stated is an answer to the question. In charters of this description, no rights are taken from the public or given to the corporation, beyond those which the words of the charter, by their natural and proper construction, purport to convey. There are no words which import such a contract as the plaintiffs in error contend for, and none can be implied. . . .

Indeed, the practice and usage of almost every State in the Union, old enough to have commenced the work of internal improvement, is opposed to the doctrine contended for on the part of the plaintiffs in error. Turnpike roads have been made in succession, on the same line of travel; the latter ones interfering materially with the profits of the first. These corporations have, in some instances, been utterly ruined by the introduction of newer and better modes of transportation and traveling. In some cases railroads have rendered the turnpike roads on the same line of travel so entirely useless, that the franchise of the turnpike corporation is not worth preserving. Yet in none of these cases have the corporations supposed that their privileges were invaded, or any contract violated on the part of the State. . . .

If this court should establish the principles now contended for, what is to become of the numerous railroads established on the same line of travel with turnpike companies; and which have rendered the franchises of the turnpike corporations of no value? Let it once be understood that such charters carry with them these implied contracts, and give this unknown and undefined property in a line of traveling, and you will soon find the old turnpike corporations awakening from their sleep, and calling upon this court to put down the improvements which have taken their place. The millions of property which have been invested in railroads and canals, upon lines of travel which had been before occupied by turnpike corporations, will be put in jeopardy. We shall be thrown back to the improvements of the last century, and obliged to stand still until the claims of the old turnpike corporations shall be satisfied, and they shall consent to permit these States to avail themselves of the lights of modern science, and to partake of the benefit of those improvements which are now adding to the wealth and prosperity, and the convenience and comfort, of every other part of the civilized world. . . .

The judgment of the Supreme Judicial Court of the Commonwealth of Massachusetts, dismissing the plaintiffs' bill, must, therefore, be affirmed with costs.

Justice M'LEAN concurred in a separate opinion.

Justice STORY dissenting.

I admit that where the terms of a grant are to impose burdens upon the public, or to create a restraint injurious to the public interest, there is sound reason for interpreting the terms, if ambiguous, in favor of the public. But at the same time, I insist that there is not the slightest reason for saying, even in such a case, that the grant is not to be construed favorably to the grantee, so as to secure him in the enjoyment of what is actually granted. . . .

This charter is not . . . any restriction upon the legislative power, unless it be true that because the Legislature cannot grant again what it has already granted, the legislative power is restricted. If so, then every grant of the public land is a restriction upon that power; a doctrine that has never yet been established, nor (as far as I know) ever contended for. Every grant of a franchise is, so far as that grant extends, necessarily exclusive; and cannot be resumed, or interfered with. All the learned judges in the State court admitted that the franchise of Charles River Bridge, whatever it be, could not be resumed or interfered with. The Legislature could not recall its grant or destroy it. It is a contract, whose obligation cannot be constitutionally impaired. In this respect, it does not differ from a grant of lands. In each case, the particular land, or the particular franchise, is withdrawn from the legislative operation. . . .

Then, again, how is it established that this is a grant in derogation of the rights and interests of the people? No individual citizen has any right to build a bridge over navigable waters; and consequently he is deprived of no right, when a grant is made to any other persons for that purpose. Whether it promotes or injures the particular interest of an individual citizen, constitutes no ground for judicial or legislative interference, beyond what his own rights justify. When, then, it is said that such a grant is in derogation of the rights and interests of the people, we must understand that reference is had to the rights and interests common to the whole people, as such (such as the right of navigation), or belonging to them as a political body; or, in other words, the rights and interests of the State. Now, I cannot understand how any grant of a franchise is a derogation from the rights of the people of the State, any more than a grant of public land. The right, in each case, is gone to the extent of the thing granted, and so far may be said to derogate from, that is to say, to lessen the rights of the people, or of the State. But that is not the sense in which the argument is pressed; for, by derogation, is here meant an injurious or mischievous detraction from the sovereign rights of the State. On the other hand, there can be no derogation from the rights of the people, as such, except it applies to rights common there before; which the building of a bridge over navigable waters certainly is not. If it had been said that the grant of this bridge was in derogation of the common right of navigating the Charles River, by reason of its obstructing, pro tanto, a free and open passage, the ground would have been intelligible. So, if it had been an exclusive grant of the navigation of that stream. But, if at the same time, equivalent public rights of a different nature, but of greater public accommodation and use, had been obtained; it could hardly have been said, in a correct sense, that there was any derogation from the rights of the people, or the rights of the State. It would be a mere exchange of one public right for another. . . .

No sound lawyer will, I presume, assert that the grant of a right to erect a bridge over a navigable stream, is a grant of a common right. Before such grant, had all the citizens of the State a right to erect bridges over navigable streams? Certainly they had not; and, therefore, the grant was no restriction of any common right. It was neither a monopoly, nor, in a legal sense, had it any tendency to a monopoly. It took from no citizen what he possessed before, and had no tendency to take it from him. It took, indeed, from the Legislature the power of granting the same identical privilege or franchise to any other persons. But this made it no more a monopoly than the grant of the public stock or funds of a State for a valuable consideration. Even in cases of monopolies, strictly so called, if the nature of the grant be such that it is for the public good, as in cases of patents for inventions, the rule has always been to give them a favorable construction in support of the patent. . . .

I have thus endeavored to answer, and I think I have successfully answered all the arguments (which indeed run into each other) adduced to justify a strict construction of the present charter. I go farther, and maintain not only that it is not a case for strict construction, but that the charter upon its very face, by its terms, and for its professed objects, demands from the court, upon undeniable principles of law, a favorable construction for the grantees. In the first place, the Legislature has declared that the erecting of the bridge will be of great public utility; and this exposition of its own motives for the grant requires the court to give a liberal interpretation, in order to promote, and not to destroy an enterprise of great public utility. In the next place, the grant is a contract for a valuable consideration, and a full and adequate consideration. The proprietors are to lay out a large sum of money (and in those times it was a very large outlay of capital) in erecting a bridge; they are to keep it in repair during the whole period of forty years; they are to surrender it in good repair at the end of that period to the State, as its own property; they are to pay, during the whole period, an annuity of two hundred pounds to Harvard College; and they are to incur other heavy expenses and burdens, for the public accommodation. In return for all these charges, they are entitled to no more than the receipt of the tolls during the forty years, for their re-imbursement of capital, interest and expenses. With all this they are to take upon themselves the chances of success; and if the enterprise fails, the loss is exclusively their own. Nor let any man imagine that there was not, at the time when this charter was granted, much solid ground for doubting success. In order to entertain a just view of this subject, we must go back to that period of general bankruptcy, and distress and difficulty. The Constitution of the United States was not only not then in existence, but it was not then even dreamed of. The union of the States was crumbling into ruins, under the old confederation. Agriculture, manufactures and commerce were at their lowest ebb. There was infinite danger to all the States from local interests and jealousies, and from the apparent impossibility of a much longer adherence to that shadow of a government the Continental Congress. And even four years afterwards, when every evil had been greatly aggravated, and civil war was added to other calamities, the Constitution of the United States was all but shipwrecked in passing through the State conventions. It was adopted by very slender majorities. These are historical facts which required no coloring to give them effect, and admitted of no concealment to seduce men into schemes of future aggrandizement. I would even now put it to the common sense of every man, whether, if the Constitution of the United States had not been adopted, the charter would have been worth a forty years' purchase of the tolls. . . .

Now, I put it to the common sense of every man, whether if at the moment of granting the charter the Legislature had said to the proprietors—you shall build the bridge; you shall bear the burdens; you shall be bound by the charges; and your sole re-imbursement shall be from the tolls of forty years: and yet we will not even guaranty you any certainty of receiving any tolls. On the contrary, we reserve to ourselves the full power and authority to erect other bridges, toll or free bridges, according to our own free will and pleasure, contiguous to yours, and having the same termini with yours; and if you are successful we may thus supplant you, divide, destroy your profits, and annihilate your tolls, without annihilating your burdens: if, I say, such had been the language of the Legislature, is there a man living of ordinary discretion or prudence, who would have accepted such a charter upon such terms? I fearlessly answer no. . . .

Yet, this is the very form and pressure of the present case. It is not an imaginary and extravagant case. Warren Bridge has been erected, under such a supposed reserved authority, in the immediate neighborhood of Charles River Bridge; and with the same termini, to accommodate the same line of travel. For a half dozen years it was to be a toll bridge for the benefit of the proprietors, to re-imburse them for their expenditures. At the end of that period, the bridge is to become the property of the State, and free of toll, unless the Legislature should hereafter impose one. In point of fact, it has since become, and now is, under the sanction of the act of incorporation, and other subsequent acts, a free bridge without the payment of any tolls for all persons. So that, in truth, here now is a free bridge, owned by and erected under the authority of the Commonwealth, which necessarily takes away all the tolls from Charles River Bridge, while its prolonged charter has twenty years to run. And yet the act of the Legislature establishing Warren Bridge is said to be no violation of the franchise granted to the Charles River Bridge. . . .

To sum up, then, the whole argument on this head, I maintain that, upon the principles of common reason and legal interpretation, the present grant carries with it a necessary implication that the Legislature shall do no act to destroy or essentially to impair the franchise: that (as one of the learned judges of the State court expressed it) there is an implied agreement that the State will not grant another bridge between Boston and Charlestown, so near as to draw away the custom from the old one: and (as another learned judge expressed it) that there is an implied agreement of the State to grant the undisturbed use of the bridge and its tolls, so far as respects any acts of its own, or of any persons acting under its authority. In other words, the State, impliedly, contracts not to resume its grant, or to do any act to the prejudice or destruction of its grant.

Justice THOMPSON concurred in the dissenting opinion.

Home Building & Loan Association v. Blaisdell
290 U.S. 398, 54 S.Ct. 231 (1934)

In response to the social pressures arising from the economic depression in the early 1930s, Minnesota's legislature passed the Minnesota Moratorium Act of 1934. The law authorized state courts to postpone the payments of homeowners and farmers on mortgages to prevent their foreclosures. Under the act, John Blaisdell sought an extension of time on the payment of his mortgage to Home Building & Loan Association. But a trial court granted a motion to dismiss Blaisdell's petition. The Minnesota Supreme Court reversed and the trial court subsequently granted Blaisdell an extension of time on his mortgage payments. Home Building & Loan Association appealed, contending that Minnesota's moratorium law violated state and federal protections for private contracts and the taking of property without the due process of law.

"Hooverville," named after President Herbert Hoover, in New York City during the Great Depression. Hoover was president from 1928 to 1932, when he lost the presidential election to Democratic Franklin D. Roosevelt. The economic collapse that began in Hoover's first year as president led to the Great Depression. *Bettmann.*

Chief Justice HUGHES delivers the opinion of the Court.

In determining whether the provision for this temporary and conditional relief exceeds the power of the state by reason of the clause in the Federal Constitution prohibiting impairment of the obligations of contracts, we must consider the relation of emergency to constitutional power, the historical setting of the contract clause, the development of the jurisprudence of this Court in the construction of that clause, and the principles of construction which we may consider to be established.

Emergency does not create power. Emergency does not increase granted power or remove or diminish the restrictions imposed upon power granted or reserved. The Constitution was adopted

in a period of grave emergency. Its grants of power to the federal
government and its limitations of the power of the States were
determined in the light of emergency, and they are not altered
by emergency. What power was thus granted and what limitations
were thus imposed are questions which have always been, and
always will be, the subject of close examination under our constitutional system.

While emergency does not create power, emergency may furnish the occasion for the exercise of power. . . . The constitutional question presented in the light of an emergency is whether
the power possessed embraces the particular exercise of it in
response to particular conditions. . . .

In the construction of the contract clause, the debates in the
Constitutional Convention are of little aid. But the reasons which
led to the adoption of that clause, and of the other prohibitions
of section 10 of article 1, are not left in doubt, and have frequently
been described with eloquent emphasis. The widespread distress
following the revolutionary period and the plight of debtors had
called forth in the States an ignoble array of legislative schemes
for the defeat of creditors and the invasion of contractual obligations. Legislative interferences had been so numerous and extreme
that the confidence essential to prosperous trade had been undermined and the utter destruction of credit was threatened. "The
sober people of America" were convinced that some "thorough
reform" was needed which would "inspire a general prudence
and industry, and give a regular course to the business of society."
The Federalist, No. 44. It was necessary to interpose the restraining power of a central authority in order to secure the foundations
even of "private faith." The occasion and general purpose of
the contract clause are summed up in the terse statement of
Chief Justice MARSHALL in *Ogden v. Saunders,* 12 Wheat. 213
[1827]. "The power of changing the relative situation of debtor
and creditor, of interfering with contracts, a power which comes
home to every man, touches the interest of all, and controls the
conduct of every individual in those things which he supposes
to be proper for his own exclusive management, had been used
to such an excess by the state legislatures, as to break in upon
the ordinary intercourse of society, and destroy all confidence
between man and man. This mischief had become so great, so
alarming, as not only to impair commercial intercourse, and
threaten the existence of credit, but to sap the morals of the
people, and destroy the sanctity of private faith. To guard against
the continuance of the evil, was an object of deep interest with
all the truly wise, as well as the virtuous, of this great community,
and was one of the important benefits expected from a reform
of the government.". . .

The obligation of a contract is the law which binds the parties
to perform their agreement. This Court has said that "the laws

which subsist at the time and place of the making of a contract, and where it is to be performed, enter into and form a part of it, as if they were expressly referred to or incorporated in its terms." This principle embraces alike those which affect its validity, construction, discharge, and enforcement. . . .

Not only is the constitutional provision qualified by the measure of control which the state retains over remedial processes, but the state also continues to possess authority to safeguard the vital interests of its people. It does not matter that legislation appropriate to that end "has the result of modifying or abrogating contracts already in effect." Not only are existing laws read into contracts in order to fix obligations as between the parties, but the reservation of essential attributes of sovereign power is also read into contracts as a postulate of the legal order. The policy of protecting contracts against impairment presupposes the maintenance of a government by virtue of which contractual relations are worth while,—a government which retains adequate authority to secure the peace and good order of society. This principle of harmonizing the constitutional prohibition with the necessary residuum of state power has had progressive recognition in the decisions of this Court. . . .

The question is not whether the legislative action affects contracts incidentally, or directly or indirectly, but whether the legislation is addressed to a legitimate end and the measures taken are reasonable and appropriate to that end. . . .

Undoubtedly, whatever is reserved of state power must be consistent with the fair intent of the constitutional limitation of that power. The reserved power cannot be construed so as to destroy the limitation, nor is the limitation to be construed to destroy the reserved power in its essential aspects. They must be construed in harmony with each other. This principle precludes a construction which would permit the state to adopt as its policy the repudiation of debts or the destruction of contracts or the denial of means to enforce them. But it does not follow that conditions may not arise in which a temporary restraint of enforcement may be consistent with the spirit and purpose of the constitutional provision and thus be found to be within the range of the reserved power of the state to protect the vital interests of the community. It cannot be maintained that the constitutional prohibition should be so construed as to prevent limited and temporary interpositions with respect to the enforcement of contracts if made necessary by a great public calamity such as fire, flood, or earthquake. . . .

Where, in earlier days, it was thought that only the concerns of individuals or of classes were involved, and that those of the state itself were touched only remotely, it has later been found that the fundamental interests of the state are directly affected; and that the question is no longer merely that of one party to a contract as against another, but of the use of reasonable means to safeguard the economic structure upon which the good of all depends.

It is no answer to say that this public need was not apprehended a century ago, or to insist that what the provision of the Constitution meant to the vision of that day it must mean to the vision of our time. If by the statement that what the Constitution meant at the time of its adoption it means to-day, it is intended to say that the great clauses of the Constitution must be confined to the interpretation which the framers, with the conditions and outlook of their time, would have placed upon them, the statement carries its own refutation. It was to guard against such a narrow conception that Chief Justice Marshall uttered the memorable warning: "We must never forget, that it is *a constitution* we are expounding" (*McCulloch v. Maryland,* 4 Wheat. 316 [1819]) "a constitution intended to endure for ages to come, and, consequently, to be adapted to the various *crises* of human affairs." . . . When we are dealing with the words of the Constitution, said this Court in *Missouri v. Holland,* 252 U.S. 416 [1920], "we must realize that they have called into life a being the development of which could not have been foreseen completely by the most gifted of its begetters. . . . The case before us must be considered in the light of our whole experience and not merely in that of what was said a hundred years ago."

Nor is it helpful to attempt to draw a fine distinction between the intended meaning of the words of the Constitution and their intended application. When we consider the contract clause and the decisions which have expounded it in harmony with the essential reserved power of the states to protect the security of their peoples, we find no warrant for the conclusion that the clause has been warped by these decisions from its proper significance or that the founders of our government would have interpreted the clause differently had they had occasion to assume that responsibility in the conditions of the later day. The vast body of law which has been developed was unknown to the fathers, but it is believed to have preserved the essential content and the spirit of the Constitution. With a growing recognition of public needs and the relation of individual right to public security, the court has sought to prevent the perversion of the clause through its use as an instrument to throttle the capacity of the states to protect their fundamental interests. This development is a growth from the seeds which the fathers planted. It is a development forecast by the prophetic words of Justice Johnson in *Ogden v. Saunders,* already quoted. And the germs of the later decisions are found in the early cases of the *Charles River Bridge* [11 Pet. 420 (1837)] and the *West River Bridge* [*Co. v. Dix,* 6 How. (47 U.S.) 506 (1848)], which upheld the public right against strong insistence upon the contract clause. The principle of this development is, as we have seen, that the reservation of the reasonable exercise of the protective power of the state is read into all contracts, and there is no greater reason for refusing to apply this principle to Minnesota mortgages. . . .

Applying the criteria established by our decisions, we conclude:

1. An emergency existed in Minnesota which furnished a proper occasion for the exercise of the reserved power of the state to protect the vital interests of the community. The declarations of the existence of this emergency by the Legislature and by the Supreme Court of Minnesota cannot be regarded as a subterfuge or as lacking in adequate basis. . . .

2. The legislation was addressed to a legitimate end; that is, the legislation was not for the mere advantage of particular individuals but for the protection of a basic interest of society.

3. In view of the nature of the contracts in question—mortgages of unquestionable validity—the relief afforded and justified by the emergency, in order not to contravene the constitutional provision, could only be of a character appropriate to that emergency, and could be granted only upon reasonable conditions.

4. The conditions upon which the period of redemption is extended do not appear to be unreasonable. . . .

5. The legislation is temporary in operation. It is limited to the exigency which called it forth. While the postponement of the period of redemption from the foreclosure sale is to May 1, 1935, that period may be reduced by the order of the court under the statute, in case of a change in circumstances, and the operation of the statute itself could not validly outlast the emergency or be so extended as virtually to destroy the contracts.

We are of the opinion that the Minnesota statute as here applied does not violate the contract clause of the Federal Constitution. Whether the legislation is wise or unwise as a matter of policy is a question with which we are not concerned.

Justice SUTHERLAND dissenting.

Few questions of greater moment than that just decided have been submitted for judicial inquiry during this generation. He simply closes his eyes to the necessary implications of the decision who fails to see in it the potentiality of future gradual but ever-advancing encroachments upon the sanctity of private and public contracts. . . .

A provision of the Constitution, it is hardly necessary to say, does not admit of two distinctly opposite interpretations. It does not mean one thing at one time and an entirely different thing at another time. If the contract impairment clause, when framed and adopted, meant that the terms of a contract for the payment of money could not be altered in invitum by a state statute enacted for the relief of hardly pressed debtors to the end and with the effect of postponing payment or enforcement during and because of an economic or financial emergency, it is but to state the obvious to say that it means the same now. . . .

[W]e are here dealing, not with a power granted by the Federal Constitution, but with the state police power, which exists in its own right. Hence the question is, not whether an emergency furnishes the occasion for the exercise of that state power, but whether an emergency furnishes an occasion for the relaxation of the restrictions upon the power imposed by the contract impairment clause; and the difficulty is that the contract impairment clause forbids state action under any circumstances, if it have the effect of impairing the obligation of contracts. That clause restricts every state power in the particular specified, no matter what may be the occasion. It does not contemplate that an emergency shall furnish an occasion for softening the restriction or making it any the less a restriction upon state action in that contingency than it is under strictly normal conditions.

The Minnesota statute either impairs the obligation of contracts or it does not. If it does not, the occasion to which it relates becomes immaterial, since then the passage of the statute is the exercise of a normal, unrestricted, state power and requires no special occasion to render it effective. If it does, the emergency no more furnishes a proper occasion for its exercise than if the emergency were nonexistent. And so, while, in form, the suggested distinction seems to put us forward in a straight line, in reality it simply carries us back in a circle, like bewildered travelers lost in a wood, to the point where we parted company with the view of the state court.

If what has now been said is sound, as I think it is, we come to what really is the vital question in the case: Does the Minnesota statute constitute an impairment of the obligation of the contract now under review? . . .

It is quite true . . . that "the reservation of essential attributes of sovereign power is also read into contracts"; and that the Legislature cannot "bargain away the public health or the public morals." General statutes to put an end to lotteries, the sale or manufacture of intoxicating liquors, the maintenance of nuisances, to protect the public safety, etc., although they have the indirect effect of absolutely destroying private contracts previously made in contemplation of a continuance of the state of affairs then in existence but subsequently prohibited, have been uniformly upheld as not violating the contract impairment clause. The distinction between legislation of that character and the Minnesota statute, however, is readily observable. . . .

[T]he statute denies appellant for a period of two years the ownership and possession of the property—an asset which, in any event, is of substantial character, and which possibly may turn out to be of great value. The statute, therefore, is not merely a modification of the remedy; it effects a material and injurious change in the obligation.

City of El Paso v. Simmons
379 U.S. 497, 85 S.Ct. 577 (1965)

Since 1876, Texas offered land for sale to raise funds for public schools and to settle the state. Under its law, land could be bought with a down payment of one-fourth of the purchase price and the annual payment of 3 percent interest. If a purchaser missed an interest payment, the land was forfeited to the state unless the purchaser paid the interest before a third party obtained title to the land. Under this program, Greenberry Simmons bought some forfeited land which he in turn forfeited to the state in 1947. Two days and five years later, however, Simmons offered to pay the interest and applied to have his land reinstated. The state denied his request, citing a 1941 amendment to its law barring the reinstatement of forfeited land after five years from the date of forfeiture. Texas then sold the land to the City of El Paso in 1955. And Simmons sued in federal district court for the return of the land title, claiming that Texas's 1941 amendment to its law violated the contract clause of the Constitution. A district court judge decided for the city but a federal appellate court reversed. The City of El Paso then appealed to the Supreme Court.

Justice WHITE delivers the opinion of the Court.

The City seeks to bring this case within the long line of cases recognizing a distinction between contract obligation and remedy and permitting a modification of the remedy as long as there is no substantial impairment of the value of the obligation.

We do not pause to consider further whether the Court of Appeals correctly ascertained the Texas law at the time these contracts were made, or to chart again the dividing line under federal law between "remedy" and "obligation," or to determine the extent to which this line is controlled by state court decisions, decisions often rendered in contexts not involving Contract Clause considerations. For it is not every modification of a contractual promise that impairs the obligation of contract under federal law, any more than it is every alteration of existing remedies that violates the Contract Clause. . . .

The decisions "put it beyond question that the prohibition is not an absolute one and is not to be read with literal exactness like a mathematical formula," as Chief Justice Hughes said in *Home Building & Loan Assn. v. Blaisdell,* 290 U.S. 398 [1934], The Blaisdell opinion, which amounted to a comprehensive restatement of the principles underlying the application of the Contract Clause, makes it quite clear that "[n]ot only is the constitutional provision qualified by the measure of control which the state retains over remedial processes, but the state also continues to possess authority to safeguard the vital interests of its people. It does not matter that legislation appropriate to that end 'has the result of modifying or abrogating contracts already in effect.' ". . .

Of course, the power of a State to modify or affect the obligation of contract is not without limit. . . . But we think the objects of the Texas statute make abundantly clear that it impairs no protected right under the Contract Clause. . . .

The circumstances behind the 1941 amendment are well described in the Reports of the Commissioner of the General Land Office. The general purpose of the legislation enacted in 1941 was to restore confidence in the stability and integrity of land titles and to enable the State to protect and administer its property in a businesslike manner. . . .

The State's policy of quick resale of forfeited lands did not prove entirely successful; forfeiting purchasers who repurchased the lands again defaulted and other purchasers bought without any intention of complying with their contracts unless mineral wealth was discovered. The market for land contracted during the depression. These developments hardly to be expected or foreseen, operated to confer considerable advantages on the purchaser and his successors and a costly and difficult burden on the State. . . .

Laws which restrict a party to those gains reasonably to be expected from the contract are not subject to attack under the Contract Clause, notwithstanding that they technically alter an obligation of a contract. The five-year limitation allows defaulting purchasers with a bona fide interest in their lands a reasonable time to reinstate. It does not and need not allow defaulting purchasers with a speculative interest in the discovery of minerals to remain in endless default while retaining a cloud on title. . . .

The measure taken to induce defaulting purchasers to comply with their contracts, requiring payment of interest in arrears within five years, was a mild one indeed, hardly burdensome to the purchaser who wanted to adhere to his contract of purchase, but nonetheless an important one to the State's interest. The Contract Clause does not forbid such a measure.

The judgment is reversed.

Justice BLACK dissenting.

I have previously had a number of occasions to dissent from judgments of this Court balancing away the First Amendment's unequivocally guaranteed rights of free speech, press, assembly and petition. In this case I am compelled to dissent from the Court's balancing away the plain guarantee of Art. 1. § 10, that

"No State shall . . . pass any . . . Law impairing the Obligation of Contracts . . . ,"

a balancing which results in the State of Texas' taking a man's private property for public use without compensation in violation of the equally plain guarantee of the Fifth Amendment, made applicable to the States by the Fourteenth, that

". . . private property [shall not] be taken for public use, without just compensation."

The respondent, Simmons, is the loser and the treasury of the State of Texas the ultimate beneficiary of the Court's action.

I do not believe that any or all of the things set out above on which the Court relies are reasons for relieving Texas of the unconditional duty of keeping its contractual obligations as required by the Contract Clause. At most the Court's reasons boil down to the fact that Texas' contracts, perhaps very wisely made a long time ago, turned out when land soared in value, and particularly after oil was discovered, to be costly to the State. As the Court euphemistically puts it, the contracts were "not wholly effectual to serve the objectives of the State's land program many decades later. Settlement was no longer the objective, but revenues . . ." among other things were. In plainer language, the State decided it had made a bad deal and wanted out. There is nothing unusual in this. It is a commonplace that land values steadily rise when population increases and rise sharply when valuable minerals are discovered, and that many sellers would be much richer and happier if when lands go up in value they were able to welch on their sales. No plethora of words about state school funds can conceal the fact that to get money easily without having to tax the whole public Texas took the easy way out and violated the Contract Clause of the Constitution as written and as applied up to now. If the values of these lands and of valid contracts to buy them have increased, that increase belongs in equity as well as in sound constitutional interpretation not to Texas, but to the many people who agreed to these contracts under what now turns out to have been a mistaken belief that Texas would keep the obligations it gave to those who dealt with it.

All this for me is just another example of the delusiveness of calling "balancing" a "test." With its deprecatory view of the equities on the side of Simmons and other claimants and its remarkable sympathy for the State, the Court through its balancing process states the case in a way inevitably destined to bypass the Contract

Clause and let Texas break its solemn obligation. As the Court's opinion demonstrates, constitutional adjudication under the balancing method becomes simply a matter of this Court's deciding for itself which result in a particular case seems in the circumstances the more acceptable governmental policy and then stating the facts in such a way that the considerations in the balance lead to the result. Even if I believed that we as Justices of this Court had the authority to rely on our judgment of what is best for the country instead of trying to interpret the language and purpose of our written Constitution, I would not agree that Texas should be permitted to do what it has done here. But more importantly, I most certainly cannot agree that constitutional law is simply a matter of what the Justices of this Court decide is not harmful for the country, and therefore is "reasonable." James Madison said that the Contract Clause was intended to protect people from the "fluctuating policy" of the legislature. The Federalist, No. 44. Today's majority holds that people are not protected from the fluctuating policy of the legislature, so long as the legislature acts in accordance with the fluctuating policy of this Court.

United States Trust Co. of New York v. State of New Jersey
431 U.S. 1, 97 S.Ct. 1505 (1977)

In 1962, New York and New Jersey made an interstate compact limiting the Port Authority's ability to subsidize mass transit through bonds. But during the 1974 energy crisis the New York and New Jersey legislatures repealed the covenant. The United States Trust Company of New York, a trustee and bondholder of the Port Authority, contended that repealing the covenant violated the contract clause and filed a lawsuit which a state court dismissed. The New Jersey Supreme Court affirmed and United States Trust Company of New York appealed to the Supreme Court.

Justice BLACKMUN delivers the opinion of the Court.

This case presents a challenge to a New Jersey statute as violative of the Contract Clause of the United States Constitution. That statute, together with a concurrent, and parallel New York statute repealed a statutory covenant made by the two States in 1962 that had limited the ability of The Port Authority of New York and New Jersey to subsidize rail passenger transportation from revenues and reserves. . . .

The trial court concluded that repeal of the 1962 covenant was a valid exercise of New Jersey's police power because repeal served important public interests in mass transportation, energy conservation, and environmental protection. Yet the Contract Clause limits otherwise legitimate exercises of state legislative authority, and the existence of an important public interest is not always sufficient to overcome that limitation. . . .

Of course, to say that the financial restrictions of the 1962 covenant were valid when adopted does not finally resolve this case. The Contract Clause is not an absolute bar to subsequent modification of a State's own financial obligations. As with laws impairing the obligations of private contracts, an impairment may be constitutional if it is reasonable and necessary to serve an important public purpose. In applying this standard, however, complete deference to a legislative assessment of reasonableness and necessity is not appropriate because the State's self-interest is at stake. A governmental entity can always find a use for extra money, especially when taxes do not have to be raised. If a State could reduce its financial obligations whenever it wanted to spend the money for what it regarded as an important public purpose, the Contract Clause would provide no protection at all. . . .

Mass transportation, energy conservation, and environmental protection are goals that are important and of legitimate public concern. Appellees contend that these goals are so important that any harm to bondholders from repeal of the 1962 covenant is greatly outweighed by the public benefit. We do not accept this invitation to engage in a utilitarian comparison of public benefit and private loss. Contrary to Justice BLACK's fear expressed in sole dissent in *El Paso v. Simmons* [379 U.S. 497 (1965)], the Court has not "balanced away" the limitation on state action imposed by the Contract Clause. Thus a State cannot refuse to meet its legitimate financial obligations simply because it would prefer to spend the money to promote the public good rather than the private welfare of its creditors. We can only sustain the repeal of the 1962 covenant if that impairment was both reasonable and necessary to serve the admittedly important purposes claimed by the State.

The more specific justification offered for the repeal of the 1962 covenant was the States' plan for encouraging users of private automobiles to shift to public transportation. The States intended to discourage private automobile use by raising bridge and tunnel tolls and to use the extra revenue from those tolls to subsidize improved commuter railroad service. Appellees contend that repeal of the 1962 covenant was necessary to implement this plan because the new mass transit facilities could not possibly be self-supporting and the covenant's "permitted deficits" level had already been exceeded. We reject this justification because the repeal was neither necessary to achievement of the plan nor reasonable in light of the circumstances.

The determination of necessity can be considered on two levels. First, it cannot be said that total repeal of the covenant was essential; a less drastic modification would have permitted the contemplated plan without entirely removing the covenant's limitations on the use of Port Authority revenues and reserves to subsidize commuter railroads. Second, without modifying the covenant at all, the States could have adopted alternative means of achieving their twin goals of discouraging automobile use and improving mass transit. . . .

We also cannot conclude that repeal of the covenant was reasonable in light of the surrounding circumstances. In this regard a comparison with *El Paso v. Simmons, supra,* again is instructive. There a 19th century statute had effects that were unforeseen and unintended by the legislature when originally adopted. As a result speculators were placed in a position to obtain windfall benefits. The Court held that adoption of a statute of limitation was a reasonable means to "restrict a party to those gains reasonably to be expected from the contract" when it was adopted. . . .

By contrast, in the instant case the need for mass transportation in the New York metropolitan area was not a new development, and the likelihood that publicly owned commuter railroads would produce substantial deficits was well known. As early as 1922, over a half century ago, there were pressures to involve the Port Authority in mass transit. It was with full knowledge of these concerns that the 1962 covenant was adopted. . . .

During the 12-year period between adoption of the covenant and its repeal, public perception of the importance of mass transit undoubtedly grew because of increased general concern with environmental protection and energy conservation. But these concerns were not unknown in 1962, and the subsequent changes were of degree and not of kind. We cannot say that these changes caused the covenant to have a substantially different impact in 1974 than when it was adopted in 1962. And we cannot conclude that the repeal was reasonable in the light of changed circumstances.

We therefore hold that the Contract Clause of the United States Constitution prohibits the retroactive repeal of the 1962 covenant. The judgment of the Supreme Court of New Jersey is reversed.

It is so ordered.

Justice STEWART did not participate in the decision of this case.

Justice POWELL did not participate in the consideration or decision of this case.

Chief Justice BURGER concurred in a separate opinion.

Justice BRENNAN, with whom Justice WHITE and Justice MARSHALL join, dissenting.

Decisions of this Court for at least a century have construed the Contract Clause largely to be powerless in binding a State to contracts limiting the authority of successor legislatures to enact laws in furtherance of the health, safety, and similar collective interests of the polity. In short, those decisions established the principle that lawful exercises of a State's police powers stand paramount to private rights held under contract. Today's decision, in invalidating the New Jersey Legislature's 1974 repeal of its predecessor's 1962 covenant, rejects this previous understanding and remolds the Contract Clause into a potent instrument for overseeing important policy determinations of the state legislature. At the same time, by creating a constitutional safe haven for property rights embodied in a contract, the decision substantially distorts modern constitutional jurisprudence governing regulation of private economic interests. . . .

One of the fundamental premises of our popular democracy is that each generation of representatives can and will remain responsive to the needs and desires of those whom they represent. Crucial to this end is the assurance that new legislators will not automatically be bound by the policies and undertakings of earlier days. In accordance with this philosophy, the Framers of our Constitution conceived of the Contract Clause primarily as protection for economic transactions entered into by purely private parties, rather than obligations involving the State itself. The Framers fully recognized that nothing would so jeopardize the legitimacy of a system of government that relies upon the ebbs and flows of politics to "clean out the rascals" than the possibility that those same rascals might perpetuate their policies simply by locking them into binding contracts.

Following an early opinion of the Court, however, that took the first step of applying the Contract Clause to public undertakings, *Fletcher v. Peck,* 6 Cranch 87 (1810), later decisions attempted to define the reach of the Clause consistently with the demands of our governing processes. The central principle developed by these decisions, beginning at least a century ago, has been that Contract Clause challenges such as that raised by appellant are to be resolved by according unusual deference to the lawmaking authority of state and local governments. . . .

This theme of judicial self-restraint and its underlying premise that a State always retains the sovereign authority to legislate in behalf of its people was commonly expressed by the doctrine that the Contract Clause will not even recognize efforts of a State to enter into contracts limiting the authority of succeeding legislators to enact laws in behalf of the health, safety, and similar collective interests of the polity—in short, that that State's police power is inalienable by contract. . . .

I would not want to be read as suggesting that the States should blithely proceed down the path of repudiating their obligations, financial or otherwise. Their credibility in the credit market obviously is highly dependent on exercising their vast lawmaking powers with self-restraint and discipline, and I, for one, have little doubt that few, if any, jurisdictions would choose to use their authority "so foolish[ly] as to kill a goose that lays golden eggs for them," *Erie R. Co. v. Public Util. Comm'rs.*, [254 U.S. 394 (1921)]. But in the final analysis, there is no reason to doubt that appellant's financial welfare is being adequately policed by the political processes and the bond marketplace itself. The role to be played by the Constitution is at most a limited one. For this Court should have learned long ago that the Constitution— be it through the Contract or Due Process Clause—can actively intrude into such economic and policy matters only if my Brethren are prepared to bear enormous institutional and social costs. Because I consider the potential dangers of such judicial interference to be intolerable, I dissent.

B. THE DEVELOPMENT AND DEMISE OF A "LIBERTY OF CONTRACT"

Ratification of the Fourteenth Amendment in 1868 provided the Supreme Court with a new basis for protecting economic rights. The amendment overturned the Taney Court's ruling in *Dred Scott v. Sandford*, 60 U.S. 393 (1857) (see Ch. 12), that blacks were not citizens of the United States. Section 1 of the amendment aimed at ensuring that states would not deny blacks of their citizenship by providing that "[n]o State shall make or enforce any law which shall abridge the privileges or immunities of citizens of the United States; nor shall any State deprive any person of life, liberty, or property, without due process of law; nor deny to any person within its jurisdiction the equal protection of the laws." The drafters of the amendment in the Thirty-ninth Congress thought that the privileges or immunities clause was the most important guarantee, because it expressly prohibited states from denying the privileges and immunities of being a citizen of the United States. Its importance is underscored by its almost literal repetition of the privileges and immunities clause of Article IV, Section 2, which provides that "[t]he Citizens of each State shall be entitled to all Privileges and Immunities of Citizens in the several States."

What counted among the privileges and immunities, however, was far from certain. In *Dred Scott*, Chief Justice Taney construed Article IV to protect only the privileges and immunities of citizens of states who were also citizens of the United States and who were temporarily in a state other than their own. The Fourteenth Amendment overturned this interpretation by extending citizenship to blacks, but offered no further clarification.

An obvious, although narrow, view is that the privileges or immunities clause simply forbids states from discriminating against citizens of other states.[1] Yet during the House and Senate debates on the amendment's adoption a frequently cited opinion was that of Justice Bushrod Washington. While sitting on a circuit court, he had interpreted the privileges and immunities clause in *Corfield v. Coryell*, 6 Fed. Cases 3230 (1825), upholding a New Jersey statute prohibiting nonresidents from gathering oysters in the state. Gathering oysters was not among the privileges and immunities of citizenship, but Washington added that citizens were guaranteed those rights "which are, in their nature, fundamental; which belong of right, to the citizens of all free governments." He listed (notably without mentioning the Bill of Rights) a rather wide-ranging set of fundamental rights; among others, he included the right to possess property, to travel from one state to another, to be protected by the government, to be exempt from higher taxes than paid by other citizens, and the right to bring suits in courts of law.

Whatever potential the Fourteenth Amendment's privileges or immunities clause had was soon dashed in *Butchers' Benevolent Association v. Cresent City Livestock Landing & Slaughterhouse Co.* (1873) (see page 240). When upholding a Louisiana law that created a monopoly on the operation of slaughterhouses, Justice Samuel Miller construed citizenship in the states and the United States to be distinct and separate and the Fourteenth Amendment to apply only to national citizenship. The independent butchers who opposed the legislative creation of a monopoly thus could not claim protection under the Fourteenth Amendment.

Four dissenters in *The Slaughterhouse* Cases disagreed. Justice Stephen Field rejected the majority's notion of dual citizenship, while Justice Joseph Bradley contended that the butchers had a right to practice their profession under the due process clauses of the Fifth and Fourteenth Amendment. Bradley was the only one to accept the interpretation of the amendment advanced by the butchers' attorney, John Campbell, a former member of the Court who resigned when his state succeeded from the Union.

Campbell had argued that the Fourteenth Amendment had a grander purpose than just guaranteeing the rights of former slaves. Its due process clause guaranteed individual freedom, free enterprise, and laissez-faire individualism. His argument was an invitation for the Court to interpret the due process clause as something more than a mere procedural guarantee. Although Campbell failed to carry the day, his argument proved prophetic of what would come.

Due process was generally understood to mean "the law of the land," but the law of the land and due process were on the brink of transformation. The due process clauses of the Fifth and Fourteenth Amendments were rooted in the English common law, running back to the Magna Carta of 1215. The Magna Carta granted that "[n]o freeman shall be arrested, or imprisoned, or disseized, or outlawed, or exiled, or in any way molested; not will [the Crown] proceed against him, unless by lawful judgment of his peers or by the law of the land." That guarantee was reaffirmed and reformed in the Petition of Right in 1628, which specified that freemen could "be imprisoned or detained only by the law of the land, or by due process of law, and not by the King's special command without any charge." Later, colonial charters and state constitutions incorporated this provision as well.

The Court's first opportunity to interpret the Fifth Amendment's due process clause had come in 1856. *Murray's Lessee v. Hoboken Land & Improvement Company,* 18 How. (59 U.S.) 272 (1856), upheld a congressional statute authorizing the Treasury Department to issue administrative warrants (without prior judicial approval) for the property of revenue collectors found to be indebted to the United States. The Taney Court rejected the claim that this amounted to the taking of property without due process because it found no conflict between this procedure and any guarantee of the Bill of Rights or settled common-law practices.

The following year in *Dred Scott,* Chief Justice Taney relied in part on the Fifth Amendment's due process clause when upholding slaveowners' proprietary interests in slaves. Taney thereby suggested that the due process of law included substantive rights as well as procedural guarantees. Moreover, state courts were beginning to acknowledge protection for property rights and economic liberties as a matter of due process of law. In *Wynehamer v. New York,* 13 N.Y. 378 (1856), New York's highest court struck down a law prohibiting the possession of liquor as a denial of due process of law.[2]

Campbell's due process argument and Justice Bradley's dissent in *The Slaughterhouse* Cases were thus early manifestations of the legal movement toward extending greater protection to economic liberties under constitutional guarantees other than that of the contract clause. In 1870, the Legal Tender Act of 1862 was invalidated, partially on the grounds that it deprived creditors of property without the due process of law, in *Hepburn v. Griswold*, 8 Wall. 608 (1870). Five years later, in *Loan Association v. Topeka*, 20 Wall. (87 U.S.) 655 (1875), a Kansas tax designed to help local industries was overturned, in Justice Miller's words, as an "unauthorized invasion of [the] private right [of property which grows] . . . out of the essential nature of free government."

By 1877, the Court under Chief Justice Morrison Waite (1874–1888) was prepared to acknowledge the due process clause's substantive protection for economic liberty. Although upholding Illinois's law regulating grain elevators as "clothed with the public interest" in *Munn v. Illinois* (1877) (see page 245), Waite conceded that economic legislation might constitute the taking of property without due process of law. And while he cautioned that "[f]or protection against abuses by legislatures, the people must resort to the polls, not to the courts," *Munn* signaled that the Court might be persuaded to supervise legislation regulating economic activities. In any event, the Court faced a growing stream of litigation attacking legislation on due process grounds. In *Davidson v. New Orleans*, 96 U.S. 97 (1878), Justice Miller was thus moved to complain that

the docket of this court is crowded with cases in which we are asked to hold that State courts and State legislatures have deprived their own citizens of life, liberty, or property without due process of law. There is here abundant evidence that there exists some strange misconception of the scope of this provision as found in the Fourteenth Amendment. In fact, it would seem, from the character of many of the cases before us, and the arguments made in them, that the clause under consideration is looked upon as means of bringing to the test of the decision of this court the abstract opinions of every unsuccessful litgant in a State court of justice of the decision against him, and of the merits of the legislation on which such a decision may be founded.

"The great tides and currents which engulf the rest of men," as Justice Benjamin Cardozo observed, "do not turn aside in their course, and pass the judges by."[3] The country's economic expansion in the late nineteenth century was reinforced by the intellectual currents of Conservative Social Darwinism—the philosophy of the survival of the fittest as applied to social and economic relations and perpetuating the myth of rugged individualism and laissez-faire capitalism.

The Court was gradually infused with this philosophy of laissez-faire capitalism, as its composition changed between 1877 and 1890 with the elevation of corporate lawyers to the ranks

Cartoon depicting the Supreme Court's backlog of cases in 1883 due to the growing amount of litigation challenging government regulations. *Puck magazine/Library of Congress.*

of justices.[4] And its assumption of the guardianship of economic liberty manifest itself in various ways. Notably, in an otherwise uninteresting tax case, *Santa Clara County v. Southern Pacific Railroad Company*, 118 U.S. 398 (1886), corporations were proclaimed to be "legal persons" entitled to full protection of the Fourteenth Amendment. Chief Justice Waite evidently thought this was so self-evident that he did not bother to emphasize it in his opinion, and the reporter of the Court's decisions decided on his own initiative that it merited special note in the headnotes accompanying the Court's opinion. The significance of that ruling, of course, was not lost on lawyers for railroads, corporations, and other businesses attacking government regulations.

One year after *Santa Clara County*, the Court explicitly held that the Fourteenth Amendment due process clause protects the "liberty of contract." *Allgeyer v. Louisiana*, 165 U.S. 578 (1897), invalidated a Louisiana law restricting the issuance of insurance policies and imposing a $1,000 fine on anyone having an illegal policy. Allgeyer & Company had a maritime insurance policy with a New York insurance firm in violation with Louisiana's law and appealed a ruling of that state's supreme court upholding the law and a fine on Allgeyer. When striking down the law,

Justice Rufus Peckham boldly announced the doctrine of a liberty of contract:

The "liberty" mentioned in [the Fourteenth] Amendment means not only the right of the citizen to be free from the mere physical restraint of his person, as by incarceration, but the term is deemed to embrace the right of the citizen to be free in the enjoyment of all his faculties; to be free to use them in all lawful ways; to live and work where he will; to earn his livelihood by any lawful calling; to pursue any livelihood or avocation, and for that purpose to enter into all contracts which may be proper, necessary and essential to his carrying out to a successful conclusion the purposes above mentioned.

Allgeyer ushered in what became known as the *Lochner* era, after one of the most notorious rulings on the liberty of contract, *Lochner v. New York* (1905) (see page 249). There, speaking for a bare majority, Justice Peckham struck down New York's labor law limiting the number of hours bakers could work as an interference with their liberty of contract. And in one of his most famous dissenting opinions, Justice Oliver Wendell Holmes sharply criticized his brethren for reading their own conservative economic philosophy into the Constitution. Under the guise of a liberty of contract and its substantive due process analysis, Holmes charged, the Court had become a superlegislature in overseeing economic regulations.

For four decades (from 1887 to 1937) the philosophy of laissez-faire capitalism held sway with a majority of the Court under Chief Justices Waite, Melville Fuller (1888–1910), Edward White (1910–1921), William Howard Taft (1921–1930), and Charles Evans Hughes (1930–1941). Never before or since were economic regulations more severely scrutinized. Close to 200 state and federal laws were overturned during the *Lochner* era.

The Court did not strike down all legislation, however. Where legislation sought to enforce health, safety, or moral standards with little or no impact on economic liberty, the Court deferred to the states and Congress. In *Mugler v. Kansas*, 123 U.S. 623 (1887), for instance, when sustaining a state prohibition law, Justice John Harlan explained that

[t]here is no justification for holding that the State, under the guise merely of police regulation, is here aiming to deprive the citizen of his constitutional rights; for we cannot shut out of view the fact, within the knowledge of all, that the public health, the public morals, and the public safety, may be endangered by the general use of intoxicating drinks; nor the fact, established by statistics accessible to everyone, that the idleness, disorder, pauperism, and crime existing in the country are, in some degree at least, traceable to this evil.

But Harlan also cautioned that not every law enacted for the promotion of public welfare would survive or

> be accepted as a legitimate exertion of the police powers of the State. There are, of necessity, limits beyond which legislation cannot rightfully go. . . . The courts are not bound by mere forms, nor are they to be misled by mere pretenses. They are at liberty—indeed, are under a solemn duty—to look at the substance of things, whenever they enter upon the inquiry whether the legislature has transcended the limits of its authority. If, therefore, a statute purporting to have been enacted to protect the public health, the public morals, or the public safety, has no real or substantial relation to those objects, or is a palpable invasion of rights secured by the fundamental law, it is the duty of the courts to so adjudge, and thereby give affect to the Constitution.

On this reasoning, the Court also upheld federal laws prohibiting the sale of liquor[5] and state laws banning sales and advertisements for cigarettes,[6] as well as zoning and land-use laws.[7]

The extent to which the Court was predisposed to defer to states when regulations had no direct economic impact is underscored in two further rulings during the *Lochner* era. In *Jacobson v. Massachusetts*, 197 U.S. 11 (1905), the Court refused to question the basis for a state law requiring smallpox vaccinations. In Justice Harlan's words:

> We must assume that when the statute in question was passed, the legislature of Massachusetts was not unaware of . . . opposing theories [of the effectiveness of vaccinations], and was compelled, of necessity, to choose between them. It was not compelled to commit a matter involving the public health and safety to the final decision of a court or jury. It is no part of the function of a court or a jury to determine which one of two modes was likely to be the most effective for the protection of the public against disease. That was for the legislative department to determine in the light of all the information it had or could obtain.

Nor was the Court inclined to scrutinize the basis for Virginia's law, passed in response to the eugenics movement, requiring the sterilization of those who were mentally defective or afflicted with epilepsy. It affirmed the compulsory sterilization of Carrie Buck, a seventeen-year-old, "feebleminded" female in a state mental institution, whose mother had also been an inmate and who had already given birth to a mentally defective child. Justice Holmes's opinion for the Court revealed not only his deference to legislatures but his acceptance of the tooth and claw of Social Darwinism. In *Buck v. Bell*, 274 U.S. 200 (1927), he observed that

[w]e have seen more than once that the public welfare may call upon the best citizens for their lives. It would be strange if it could not call upon those who already sap the strength of the State for these lesser sacrifices, often not felt to be such by those concerned, in order to prevent our being swamped with incompetence. It is better for all the world, if instead of waiting to execute degenerate offspring for crime, or to let them starve for the imbecility, society can prevent those who are manifestly unfit from continuing their kind. The principle that sustains compulsory vaccination is broad enough to cover cutting the Fallopian tubes. . . . Three generations of imbeciles are enough.

When legislation aimed at promoting health, safety, or welfare *and* directly affected economic activities, the Court did not automatically strike it down. But the Court had to be convinced of the reasonableness of the regulations. In *Holden v. Hardy*, 169 U.S. 366 (1898), with only Justices Peckham and David Brewer dissenting, the Court upheld Utah's law limiting the number of hours in a day miners could work in mines and smelters to eight.

In *Muller v. Oregon*, 208 U.S. 412 (1908), the Court unanimously approved a state law limiting the workday for women in industries to ten hours per day. There the Court was persuaded by what became known as "the Brandeis brief." When defending Oregon's law, the progressive and highly regarded labor lawyer, Louis Brandies filed an extraordinary brief, containing only two pages of legal argument and more than a hundred pages of statistics and social science studies showing how long hours of labor endangered the health of women and thus the reasonableness of the state's law. Acknowledging its debt to "the brief field by Mr. Louis D. Brandeis," the Court ruled that a "woman's physical structure, and the functions she performs in consequence thereof, justify special legislation restricting or qualifying the conditions under which she should be permitted to toil."[8] (Notably, after Brandeis was named to the Court in 1916, he never cited social science materials when writing an opinion for the Court upholding state legislation. Instead, he only cited these materials when writing dissenting opinions, criticizing the majority for overturning state laws and showing the reasonableness of the legislation.)

Although upholding state regulations in cases like *Muller* and *Bunting v. Oregon*, 243 U.S. 426 (1917), sustaining a labor law limiting workdays to ten hours a day for men and women, the Court's prevailing practice was nevertheless to strike down economic regulations. The problem for the Court and the country was that while the development of the doctrine of a liberty of contract may have been in response, in Holmes's classic phrase, "to the felt necessities of the time," it ran against the political currents of the early twentieth century. Reform Social Darwinism had replaced Conservative Social Darwinism in teaching that humans not only adapt to the environment but may change it as well.[9] Under pressure from reformers, labor unions, and the progressive movement, legislatures were passing new laws in response to the plight of workers in sweatshops, child labor, and generally dismal working conditions as depicted in novels by Upton Sinclair. The justices were no longer in tune with the times. The Court and the country were on a collision course in constitutional politics.

In *Adair v. United States*, 208 U.S. 161 (1908), for example, the Court, with only Justices Holmes and Joseph McKenna dissenting, struck down a section of a congressional labor-relations law banning yellow-dog contracts—contracts signed by workers promising they would not join labor unions—and forbidding the firing of employees who belonged to unions. When approving of Adair's firing of O. B. Coppage from the Louisville & Nashville Railroad Company because he was a union member, Justice Harlan disabused any thought of abandoning the liberty of contract:

> While . . . the right of liberty and property guaranteed by the Constitution against deprivation without due process of law is subject to such reasonable restraints as the common good or the general welfare may require, it is not within the functions of government—at least, in the absence of contract between the parties—to compel any person, in the course of his business and against his will, to accept or retain the personal services of another, or to compel any person, against his will, to perform personal services for another. The right of a person to sell his labor upon such terms as he deems proper is, in its essence, the same as the right of the purchaser of labor to prescribe the conditions upon which he will accept such labor from the person offering to sell it. So the right of the employee to quit the service of the employer, for whatever reason, is the same as the right of the employer, for whatever reason, to dispense with the services of such employee. It was the legal right of the defendant Adair,—however unwise such a course might have been,—to discharge Coppage because of this being a member of a labor organization, as it was the legal right of Coppage, if he saw fit to do so,—however unwise such a course on his part might have been,—to quit the service in which he was engaged, because the defendant employed some persons who were not members of a labor organization. In all such particulars the employer and the employee have equality of right, and any legislation that disturbs that equality is an arbitrary interference with the liberty of contract which no government can legally justify in a free land.

In *Coppage v. Kansas*, 236 U.S. 1 (1915), with Justices Holmes, Rufus Day, and Charles Evans Hughes dissenting, the Court struck down a state law outlawing yellow-dog contracts. The Kansas state supreme court had upheld the law and the conviction of T. B. Coppage for firing a switchman for the St. Louis &

San Francisco Railway Company because the employee refused to give up his union membership. In another vintage expression of the doctrine of a liberty of contract, Justice Mahlon Pitney explained that

it is said by the Kansas supreme court to be a matter of common knowledge that "employees, as a rule, are not financially able to be as independent in making contracts for the sale of their labor as are employers in making a contract of purchase thereof." No doubt; wherever the right of private property exists, there must and will be inequalities of fortune; and thus it naturally happens that parties negotiating about a contract are not equally unhampered by circumstances. This applies to all contracts, and not merely to that between employer and employee. Indeed, a little reflection will show that wherever the right of private property and the right of a free contract coexist, each party when contracting is inevitably more or less influenced by the question whether he has much property, or little, or none; for the contract is made to the very end that each may gain something that he needs or desires more urgently than that which he proposes to give in exchange. And, since it is self-evident that, unless all things are held in common, some persons must have more property than others, it is from the nature of things impossible to uphold freedom of contract and the right of private property without at the same time recognizing as legitimate those inequalities of fortune that are the necessary result of the exercise of those rights. But the 14th Amendment, in declaring that a state shall not "deprive any person of life, liberty, or property without due process of law," gives to each of these an equal sanction; it recognizes "liberty" and "property" as coexistent human rights, and debars the states from any unwarranted interference with either.

And since a state may not strike them down directly, it is clear that it may not do so indirectly, as by declaring in effect that the public good requires the removal of those inequalities that are but the normal and inevitable result of their exercise. . . . The police power is broad, and not easily defined, but it cannot be given the wide scope that is here asserted for it, without in effect nullifying the constitutional guaranty.

In the 1920s the Court's defense of the liberty of contract reached the high-water mark and the controversy was exacerbated by the Great Depression. In *Adkins v. Children's Hospital*, 261 U.S. 525 (1923), a bare majority struck down the District of Columbia's minimum wage law for women and again made clear that *Lochner* was still alive. The minimum wage law, according to Justice Arthur Sutherland, was "simply and exclusively a price-fixing law." "Women," he added, "are legally as capable of contracting for themselves as men." In dissent, Chief Justice Taft maintained that *Muller*, not *Lochner*, should control the decision and questioned whether *Lochner* had not been "overruled *sub silentio*," that is, overruled without expressly saying so. But *Wolf Packing Co. v. Court of Industrial Relations*, 262 U.S. 522 (1923), with none other than Taft delivering the Court's opinion, underscored that economic liberty was a "preferred freedom," when striking down Kansas's law creating an industrial-relations court to handle labor-management disputes. And there remained a die-hard majority on the Court into the 1930s for defending the vestiges of laissez-faire capitalism. In *Morehead v. Tipaldo,* 298 U.S. 587 (1936), the four remaining justices from *Adkins*'s majority—Sutherland, Pierce Butler, Willis Van Devanter, and James McReynolds—were thus joined by Owen Roberts in overturning New York's minimum wage law.

The controversy over the Court finally erupted into the most serious crisis in constitutional politics since *Dred Scott.* During President Franklin D. Roosevelt's first term, the Court invalidated most of his early New Deal programs thereby thwarting his plans for the country's recovery from the Great Depression. After FDR's landslide reelection in 1936, he boldly proposed judicial reforms that would allow him to expand the size of the Court to fifteen by appointing a new member for every justice over seventy years of age. Then in the spring of 1937 when the Senate Judiciary Committee was debating his Court-packing plan, the Court abruptly upheld major pieces of the New Deal legislation. The Court had become badly split five to four in striking down progressive New Deal legislation. Sutherland, McReynolds, Butler, and Van Devanter—the "Four Hoursemen"—voted as a bloc against economic legislation for violating economic liberty, while Stone and Cardozo followed Brandeis in supporting progressive legislation. Hughes and Roberts were the swing votes, although the latter, more conservative justice, had cast the crucial fifth vote to strike down FDR's programs. Roberts, however, was persuaded by Hughes to change his mind. In March he abandoned the Four Housemen in *West Coast Hotel Co. v. Parrish* (1937) (see page 254) to uphold Washington state's minimum wage law. Two weeks later, in *National Labor Relations Board v. Jones & Laughlin Steel Corporation,* 301 U.S. 1 (1937) (see Vol. 1, Ch. 4), Roberts again switched sides to affirm a major piece of New Deal legislation, the National Labor Relations Act.

The Court's "switch in time that saved nine" was widely speculated to have been due to FDR's Court-packing plan. But even though the rulings did not come down until the spring, Roberts had switched his vote at conference in December 1936, two months before FDR announced his plan. The reversal of the Court's position nonetheless contributed to the Senate Judiciary Committee's rejection of FDR's proposal in May. Then Van Devanter—one of the president's stauchest opponents—told the president that he would resign at the end of the next term. FDR had the first of eight appointments in the next six years to infuse his own political philosophy into the Court.

The Court's about-face in 1937 ended a constitutional crisis and an era. With the Court's abandonment of the liberty of contract and turning its back on substantive due process, came a virtual abdication of judicial supervision of economic regulations. *Lincoln Federal Labor Union v. Northwestern Iron & Metal Co.* (1949) (see page 257), which expressly repudiated *Adair* and *Coppage*, is illustrative. As FDR's first appointee to the Court, Justice Hugo Black, in *Ferguson v. Skrupa*, 372 U.S. 726 (1963), exclaimed, "it is up to legislatures, not courts, to decide on the wisdom and utility of legislation."[10] The Burger Court, when upholding a state law requiring employees to be compensated when on jury duty by their employers, in *Dean v. Gadsden Times Publishing Corporation*, 412 U.S. 543 (1973), underscored that "[i]f our recent cases mean anything, they leave debatable issues as respects business, economic, and social affairs to legislative decision. We could strike down this law only if we returned to the philosophy of *Lochner, Coppage,* and *Adkins* cases."

Since the 1937 revolution in constitutional politics, the Court has evolved a proverbial double standard: it gives economic regulation only minimal scrutiny, requiring only that it have some rational basis, while giving that affecting civil liberties heightened scrutiny, often upholding legislation only if the government's interest in regulation is compelling. And since 1937 the Court has assumed a special role in overseeing voting rights and access to the political process (see Vol. 1, Ch. 8); the freedom of speech, press, and association (see Chapter 5); and invidious forms of racial and nonracial discrimination (see Chapter 12).

But Court watchers, such as political scientist Robert McCloskey, have questioned why the "liberty of economic choice . . . [is] less dispensable to the 'openness' of a society than freedom of expression."[11] Indeed, in the 1980s some scholars and judges appointed during the era of the Ronald Reagan's presidency have called for the resurrection of protection for economic liberty.[12]

It appears highly unlikely that the Court will once again heightened its scrutiny of economic legislation under the due process clause, let alone return to the days of the liberty of contract. Justice William Rehnquist, for example, in *United States Railroad Retirement Board v. Fritz*, 449 U.S. 166 (1980), rebuffed a due process attack on legislation eliminating railroad retirees' social security and retirement benefits with the observation that "[t]he plain language [of the statute] marks the beginning and end of our inquiry."

Finally, it bears noting that although the Court turned its back on the doctrine of a liberty of contract in 1937, it did not abandon reading substantive guarantees into the due process clause of the Fourteenth Amendment, as further discussed in Chapter 4 and Chapter 10.

NOTES

1. For further discussion, see Charles Fairman, "Does the Fourteenth Amendment Incorporate the Bill of Rights?" 2 *Stanford Law Review* 5 (1949); and William Crosskey, "Charles Fairman, 'Legislative History,' and the Constitutional Limitations on State Authority," 22 *University of Chicago Law Review* 1 (1954).

2. See Edward Corwin, *Liberty against Government: The Rise, Flowering and Decline of a Famous Judicial Concept* (Baton Rouge: Louisiana State University Press, 1948).

3. Benjamin Cardozo, *The Nature of the Judicial Process* (New Haven, CT: Yale University Press, 1921), 168.

4. For further discussion, see Benjamin Twiss, *Lawyers and the Constitution: How Laissez Faire Came to the Supreme Court* (Princeton, NJ: Princeton University Press, 1942); Robert McCloskey, *American Conservatism in the Age of Enterprise* (Cambridge, MA: Harvard University Press, 1951); and James Willard Hurst, *Law and the Conditions of Freedom in the Nineteenth-Century United States* (Madison, WI: University of Wisconsin, 1956).

5. *Hamilton v. Kentucky Distilleries and Warehouse Co.*, 251 U.S. 146 (1919).

6. See *Austin v. Tennessee*, 179 U.S. 343 (1900); and *Packer Corporation v. Utah*, 285 U.S. 105 (1932).

7. A leading case is *Euclid v. Ambler Realty Co.*, 272 U.S. 365 (1926). See also *Welch v. Swasey*, 214 U.S. 91 (1909); *Cusack v. Chicago*, 242 U.S. 526 (1917); and *Berman v. Parker*, 348 U.S. 26 (1954).

8. Other rulings upholding labor laws for women include *Cotting v. Godard*, 183 U.S. 79 (1901); *German Alliance Insurance Co. v. Lewis*, 233 U.S. 389 (1914); and *Townsend v. Yeomans*, 301 U.S. 441 (1937).

9. For further discussion, see Morton White, *Social Thought in America: The Revolt against Formalism* (New York: Viking Press, 1949).

10. See also *Williamson v. Lee Optical of Oklahoma*, 348 U.S. 483 (1955); *Olsen v. Nebraska*, 313 U.S. 236 (1952); and Richard Funston, "The Double Standard of Constitutional Protection in the Era of the Welfare State," 90 *Political Science Quarterly* 261 (1975).

11. Robert McCloskey, "Economic Due Process and the Supreme Court," in *The Supreme Court Review: 1962*, ed. Philip Kurland (Chicago: University of Chicago Press, 1962), 34–62.

12. See, for example, Bernard H. Siegan, *Economic Liberties and the Constitution* (Chicago: University of Chicago Press, 1980).

SELECTED BIBLIOGRAPHY

Miller, Arthur S. *The Supreme Court and American Capitalism*. New York: Free Press, 1968.

Paul, Arnold. *Conservative Crisis and the Rule of Law: Attitudes of Bench and Bar, 1887–1895.* Ithaca, NY: Cornell University Press, 1960.

Pritchett, C. Herman. *The Roosevelt Court.* New York: Macmillan Co., 1948.

Seigan, Bernard. *Economic Liberties and the Constitution.* Chicago: University of Chicago Press, 1980.

Twiss, Benjamin. *Lawyers and the Constitution: How Laissez Faire Came to the Supreme Court.* Princeton, NJ: Princeton University Press, 1942.

Butchers' Benevolent Association v. Cresent City Livestock Landing & Slaughterhouse Co. (The Slaughterhouse Cases)
16 Wall. (83 U.S.) 36 (1873)

In 1869 due to the pollution and the spread of cholera, the Louisiana legislature passed a law aimed at cleaning up the Mississippi River by prohibiting all slaughtering of livestock in the City of New Orleans and surrounding parishes except at one slaughterhouse, which was given an exclusive franchise for twenty-five years. The Butchers' Benevolent Association, a group of independent slaughterers, challenged the constitutionality of the legislation on the grounds that it violated the Thirteen and Fourteenth Amendments by depriving them of their livelihood. A state court and the Louisiana State Supreme Court upheld the law, and the Butchers' Benevolent Association appealed to the Supreme Court.

Justice MILLER delivers the opinion of the Court.

The plaintiffs . . . allege that the statute is a violation of the Constitution of the United States in these several particulars:

That it creates an involuntary servitude forbidden by the 13th article of amendment;

That it abridges the privileges and immunities of citizens of the United States;

That it denies to the plaintiffs the equal protection of the laws; and,

That it deprives them of their property without due process of law; contrary to the provisions of the 1st section of the 14th article of amendment.

This court is thus called upon for the first time to give construction to these articles. . . .

The most cursory glance at these articles discloses a unity of purpose, when taken in connection with the history of the times, which cannot fail to have an important bearing on any question of doubt concerning their true meaning. . . .

[N]o one can fail to be impressed with the one pervading purpose found in [the 13th, 14th and 15th Amendments], lying at the foundation of each, and without which none of them would have been even suggested; we mean the freedom of the slave race, the security and firm establishment of that freedom, and the protection of the newly made freemen and citizen from the oppressions of those who had formerly exercised unlimited dominion over him. It is true that only the 15th Amendment, in terms, mentions the negro by speaking of his color and his slavery. But it is just as true that each of the other articles was addressed to the grievances of that race, and designed to remedy them as the fifteenth.

We do not say that no one else but the negro can share in this protection. Both the language and spirit of these articles are to have their fair and just weight in any question of construction. Undoubtedly, while negro slavery alone was in the mind of the Congress which proposed the 13th article, it forbids any other kind of slavery, now or hereafter. . . .

The next observation is more important in view of the arguments of counsel in the present case. It is that the distinction between citizenship of the United States and citizenship of a state is clearly recognized and established. Not only may a man be a citizen of the United States without being a citizen of a state, but an important element is necessary to convert the former into the latter. He must reside within the state to make him a citizen of it, but it is only necessary that he should be born or naturalized in the United States to be a citizen of the Union.

It is quite clear, then, that there is a citizenship of the United States and a citizenship of a state, which are distinct from each other and which depend upon different characteristics or circumstances in the individual.

We think this distinction and its explicit recognition in this Amendment of great weight in this argument, because the next paragraph of this same section, which is the one mainly relied on by the plaintiffs in error, speaks only of privileges and immunities of citizens of the United States, and does not speak of those of citizens of the several states. The argument, however, in favor of the plaintiffs, rests wholly on the assumption that the citizenship is the same and the privileges and immunities guaranteed by the clause are the same.

The language is: "No state shall make or enforce any law which shall abridge the privileges or immunities of citizens of the United States." It is a little remarkable, if this clause was intended as a protection to the citizen of a state against the legislative power of his own state, that the words "citizen of the state" should be left out when it is so carefully used, and used in contradistinction to "citizens of the United States" in the very sentence which precedes it. It is too clear for argument that the change in phraseology was adopted understandingly and with a purpose.

Of the privileges and immunities of the citizens of the United States, and of the privileges and immunities of the citizen of the state, and what they respectively are, we will presently consider; but we wish to state here that it is only the former which are placed by this clause under the protection of the Federal Constitution, and that the latter, whatever they may be, are not intended to have any additional protection by this paragraph of the Amendment.

If, then, there is a difference between the privileges and immunities belonging to a citizen of the United States as such, and those belonging to the citizen of the state as such, the latter must rest for their security and protection where they have heretofore rested; for they are not embraced by this paragraph of the Amendment. . . .

In the Constitution of the United States, which superseded the Articles of Confederation, the corresponding provision is found in section two of the 4th article, in the following words: The citizens of each state shall be entitled to all the privileges and immunities of citizens of the several states.

There can be but little question that the purpose of both these provisions is the same, and that the privileges and immunities intended are the same in each. In the Article of the Confederation we have some of these specifically mentioned, and enough perhaps to give some general idea of the class of civil rights meant by the phrase. . . .

The constitutional provision there alluded to did not create those rights, which it called privileges and immunities of citizens of the states. It threw around them in that clause no security for the citizen of the state in which they were claimed or exercised. Nor did it profess to control the power of the state governments over the rights of its own citizens.

Its sole purpose was to declare to the several states, that whatever those rights, as you grant or establish them to your own citizens, or as you limit or qualify, or impose restrictions on their exercise, the same, neither more nor less, shall be the measure of the rights of citizens of other states within your jurisdiction. . . .

The argument has not been much pressed in these cases that the defendant's charter deprives the plaintiffs of their property without due process of law, or that it denies to them the equal protection of the law. The first of these paragraphs has been in the Constitution since the adoption of the 5th Amendment, as a restraint upon the Federal power. It is also to be found in some form of expression in the constitutions of nearly all the states, as a restraint upon the power of the states. This law, then, has practically been the same as it now is during the existence of the government, except so far as the present Amendment may place the restraining power over the states in this matter in the hands of the Federal government.

We are not without judicial interpretation, therefore, both state and national, of the meaning of this clause. And it is sufficient to say that under no construction of that provision that we have ever seen, or any that we deem admissible, can the restraint imposed by the state of Louisiana upon the exercise of their trade by the butchers of New Orleans be held to be a deprivation of property within the meaning of that provision.

"Nor shall any state deny to any person within its jurisdiction the equal protection of the laws."

In the light of the history of these amendments, and the pervading purpose of them, which we have already discussed, it is not difficult to give a meaning to this clause. The existence of laws in the states where the newly emancipated negroes resided, which discriminated with gross injustice and hardship against them as a class, was the evil to be remedied by this clause, and by it such laws are forbidden.

Justice FIELD dissenting.

The question presented is . . . nothing less than the question whether the recent Amendments to the Federal Constitution protect the citizens of the United States against the deprivation of their common rights by state legislation. In my judgment the 14th Amendment does afford such protection, and was so intended by the Congress which framed and the states which adopted it.

The counsel for the plaintiffs in error have contended, with great force, that the act in question is also inhibited by the 13th Amendment.

That Amendment prohibits slavery and involuntary servitude, except as a punishment for crime, but I have not supposed it was susceptible of a construction which would cover the enactment in question. I have been so accustomed to regard it as intended to meet that form of slavery which had previously prevailed in this country, and to which the recent Civil War owed its existence, that I was not prepared, nor am I yet, to give to it the extent and force ascribed by counsel. Still it is evident that the language of the Amendment is not used in a restrictive sense. It is not confined to African slavery alone. It is general and universal in its application. Slavery of white men as well as of black men is prohibited, and not merely slavery in the strict sense of the term, but involuntary servitude in every form. . . .

The first clause of the fourteenth amendment . . . recognizes in express terms, if it does not create, citizens of the United States, and it makes the citizenship dependent upon the place of the birth, or the fact of their adoption, and not upon the Constitution or laws of any state or the condition of their ancestry. A citizen of a state is now only a citizen of the United States residing in that state. The fundamental rights, privileges, and immunities which belong to him as a free man and a free citizen, now belong to him as a citizen of the United States, and are not dependent upon his citizenship of any state. . . .

The Amendment does not attempt to confer any new privileges or immunities upon citizens or to enumerate or define those already existing. It assumes that there are such privileges and immunities which belong of right to citizens as such, and ordains that they shall not be abridged by state legislation. If this inhibition has no reference to privileges and immunities of this character, but only refers, as held by the majority of the court in their opinion, to such privileges and immunities as were before its adoption specially designated in the Constitution or necessarily implied as belonging to citizens of the United States, it was a vain and idle enactment, which accomplished nothing, and most unnecessarily excited Congress and the people on its passage. With privileges and immunities thus designated no state could ever have interfered by its laws, and no new constitutional provision was required to inhibit such interference. The supremacy of the Constitution and the laws of the United States always controlled any state legislation of that character. But if the Amendment refers to the natural and inalienable rights which belong to all citizens, the inhibition has a profound significance and consequence.

What, then, are the privileges and immunities which are secured against abridgement by state legislation? . . .

The privileges and immunities designated are those which of right belong to the citizens of all free governments. Clearly among these must be placed the right to pursue a lawful employment in a lawful manner, without other restraint than such as equally affects all persons. . . .

This equality of right, with exemption from all disparaging and partial enactments, in the lawful pursuits of life, throughout the whole country, is the distinguishing privilege of citizens of the United States. To them, everywhere, all pursuits, all professions, all avocations are open without other restrictions than such as are imposed equally upon all others of the same age, sex and condition. The state may prescribe such regulations for every pursuit and calling of life as will promote the public health, secure the good order and advance the general prosperity of society, but when once prescribed, the pursuit or calling must be free to be followed by every citizen who is within the conditions designated, and will conform to the regulations. This is the fundamental idea upon which our institutions rest, and unless adhered to in the legislation of the country our government will be a Republic only in name. The 14th Amendment, in my judgment, makes it essential to the validity of the legislation of every state that this equality of right should be respected. . . .

I am authorized by Chief Justice Chase, Justice Swayne and Justice Bradley, to state that they concur with me in this dissenting opinion.

Justice BRADLEY dissenting.

In my view, a law which prohibits a large class of citizens from adopting a lawful employment, or from following a lawful employment previously adopted, does deprive them of liberty as well as property, without due process of law. Their right of choice is a portion of their liberty; their occupation is their property. Such a law also deprives those citizens of the equal protection of the laws, contrary to the last clause of the section. . . .

It is futile to argue that none but persons of the African race are intended to be benefited by this Amendment. They may have been the primary cause of the Amendment, but its language is general, embracing all citizens, and I think it was purposely so expressed.

Justice SWAYNE dissenting.

These Amendments are a new departure, and mark an important epoch in the constitutional history of the country. They trench directly upon the power of the states, and deeply affect those bodies. They are in this respect, at the opposite pole from the first eleven. . . .

Fairly construed, these Amendments may be said to rise to the dignity of a new Magna Charta.

Munn v. Illinois
4 Otto (94 U.S.) 113, 24 L.Ed. 77 (1877)

In 1871 in response to the Granger movement—a movement to promote the interests of independent farmers in midwest states—and pressures to stop the exploitation of farmers by grain-elevator operators, Illinois's legislature enacted a law requiring operating licenses and setting the maximum rates that grain warehouses and elevators could charge for the storage of grain.

Ira Munn was found in violation of the law and attacked its constitutionality as a violation of the commerce clause and the due process clause of the Fourteenth Amendment. The Illinois State Supreme court, however, upheld Munn's conviction and Munn appealed to the Supreme Court.

Chief Justice WAITE delivers the opinion of the Court.

Every statute is presumed to be constitutional. The courts ought not to declare one to be unconstitutional, unless it is clearly so. If there is doubt, the expressed will of the Legislature should be sustained.

The Constitution contains no definition of the word "deprive," as used in the 14th Amendment. To determine its signification, therefore, it is necessary to ascertain the effect which usage has given it, when employed in the same or a like connection.

While this provision of the Amendment is new in the Constitution of the United States as a limitation upon the powers of the States, it is old as a principle of civilized government. It is found in Magna Charta, and, in substance if not in form, in nearly or quite all the constitutions that have been from time to time adopted by the several States of the Union. By the 5th Amendment, it was introduced into the Constitution of the United States as a limitation upon the powers of the National Government, and by the 14th, as a guaranty against any encroachment upon an acknowledged right of citizenship by the Legislatures of the States. . . .

This Act was passed at a time when Magna Charta had been recognized as the fundamental law of England for hundreds of years.

This great charter embodied the principle that no person shall be deprived of life, liberty or property, but by the judgment of his peers or the law of the land, which is an equivalent for the modern phrase, "due process of law.". . .

[I]t is apparent that, down to the time of the adoption of the 14th Amendment, it was not supposed that statutes regulating the use, or even the price of the use, of private property necessarily deprived an owner of his property without due process of law. Under some circumstances they may, but not under all. The Amendment does not change the law in this particular; it simply prevents the States from doing that which will operate as such a deprivation.

This brings us to inquire as to the principles upon which this power of regulation rests, in order that we may determine what is within and what without its operative effect. Looking, then, to the common law, from whence came the right which the Constitution protects, we find that when private property is "affected with a public interest, it ceases to be juris privati only." This was said by Lord Chief Justice Hale more than two hundred years ago, in his treatise De Portibus Maris, 1 Harg. I. Tr., 78, and has been accepted without objection as an essential element in the law of property ever since. Property does become clothed with a public interest when used in a manner to make it of public consequence, and affect the community at large. When, therefore, one devotes his property to a use in which the public has an interest, he, in effect, grants to the public an interest in that use, and must submit to be controlled by the public for the common good, to the extent of the interest he has thus created. He may withdraw his grant by discontinuing the use; but, so long as he maintains the use, he must submit to the control. . . .

It remains only to ascertain whether the warehouses of these plaintiffs in error, and the business which is carried on there, come within the operation of this principle. . . .

[I]t is difficult to see why, if the common carrier, or the miller, or the ferryman, or the innkeeper, or the wharfinger, or the baker, or the cartman, or the hackney-coachman, pursues a public employment and exercises "a sort of public office," these plaintiffs in error do not. They stand, to use again the language of their counsel, in the very "gateway of commerce," and take toll from all who pass. Their business most certainly "tends to a common charge, and is become a thing of public interest and use." Every bushel of grain for its passage "pays a toll, which is a common charge," and, therefore, according to Lord Hale, every such warehouseman "ought to be under public regulation, viz.: that he . . . take but reasonable toll." Certainly, if any business can be clothed "with a public interest, and cease to be juris privati only," this has been. It may not be made so by the operation of the Constitution of Illinois or this statute, but it is by the facts. . . .

We know that this is a power which may be abused; but that is no argument against its existence. For protection against abuses by Legislatures the people must resort to the polls; not to the courts. . . .

We come now to consider the effect upon this statute of the power of Congress to regulate commerce. . . . The warehouses of these plaintiffs in error are situated and their business carried on exclusively within the limits of the State of Illinois. They are used as instruments by those engaged in State as well as those engaged in interstate commerce, but they are no more necessarily a part of commerce itself than the dray or the cart by which, but for them, grain would be transferred from one railroad station to another. Incidentally they may become connected with interstate commerce, but not necessarily so. Their regulation is a thing of domestic concern and, certainly, until Congress acts in reference to their interstate relations, the State may exercise all the powers of government over them, even though in so doing it may indirectly operate upon commerce outside its immediate jurisdiction. We do not say that a case may not arise in which it will be found that a State, under the form of regulating its own affairs, has encroached upon the exclusive domain of Congress in respect to interstate commerce, but we do say that, upon the facts as they are represented to us in this record, that has not been done. . . .

The judgment is affirmed.

Justice FIELD dissenting.

I am compelled to dissent from the decision of the court in this case, and from the reasons upon which that decision is founded. The principle upon which the opinion of the majority proceeds is, in my judgment, subversive of the rights of private property, heretofore believed to be protected by constitutional guaranties against legislative interference, and is in conflict with the authorities cited in its support. . . .

There is nothing in the character of the business of the defendants as warehousemen which called for the interference complained of in this case. Their buildings are not nuisances; their occupation of receiving and storing grain infringes upon no rights of others, disturbs no neighborhood, infects not the air, and in no respect prevents others from using and enjoying their property as to them may seem best. The legislation in question is nothing less than a bold assertion of absolute power by the State to control, at its discretion, the property and business of the citizen, and fix the compensation he shall receive. . . .

The business of a warehouseman was, at common law, a private business, and is so in its nature. It has no special privileges connected with it, nor did the law ever extend to it any greater protection than it extended to all other private business. No reason can be assigned to justify legislation interfering with the legitimate profits of that business, that would not equally justify an intermeddling with the business of every man in the community, so soon, at least, as his business became generally useful.

I am of opinion that the judgment of the Supreme Court of Illinois should be reversed.

Justice STRONG concurred in the dissent.

Joseph Lochner in his bakery. *Dante Tranquille. Collection of Joseph Lochner, Jr.*

Lochner v. New York
198 U.S. 45, 25 S.Ct. 539 (1905)

Joseph Lochner was found guilty and fined $50 for violating an 1897 New York law prohibiting employers from having their employees work more than sixty hours a week in a bakery. Lochner's conviction was affirmed by two state courts and he applied for a writ of error from the Supreme Court.

Justice PECKHAM delivers the opinion of the Court.

The mandate of the statute, that "no employee shall be required or permitted to work," is the substantial equivalent of an enactment that "no employee shall contract or agree to work," more than ten hours per day; and, as there is no provision for special emergencies, the statute is mandatory in all cases. It is not an act merely fixing the number of hours which shall constitute a legal day's work, but an absolute prohibition upon the employer permitting, under any circumstances, more than ten hours' work to be done in his establishment. The employee may desire to earn the extra money which would arise from his working more than the prescribed time, but this statute forbids the employer from permitting the employee to earn it.

The statute necessarily interferes with the right of contract between the employer and employees, concerning the number of hours in which the latter may labor in the bakery of the employer. The general right to make a contract in relation to his business is part of the liberty of the individual protected by the 14th Amendment of the Federal Constitution. *Allgeyer v. Louisiana,* 165 U.S. 578 [1897]. Under that provision no state can deprive any person of life, liberty, or property without due process of law. The right to purchase or to sell labor is part of the liberty protected by this amendment, unless there are circumstances which exclude the right. There are, however, certain powers, existing in the sovereignty of each state in the Union, somewhat vaguely termed police powers, the exact description and limitation of which have not been attempted by the courts. Those powers, broadly stated, and without, at present, any attempt at a more specific limitation, relate to the safety, health, morals, and general welfare of the public. Both property and liberty are held on such reasonable conditions as may be imposed by the governing power of the state in the exercise of those powers, and with such conditions the 14th Amendment was not designed to interfere. . . .

The state, therefore, has power to prevent the individual from making certain kinds of contracts, and in regard to them the Federal Constitution offers no protection. If the contract be one which the state, in the legitimate exercise of its police power, has the right to prohibit, it is not prevented from prohibiting it by the 14th Amendment. Contracts in violation of a statute, either of the Federal or state government, or a contract to let one's property for immoral purposes, or to do any other unlawful act, could obtain no protection from the Federal Constitution, as coming under the liberty of person or of free contract. Therefore, when the state, by its legislature, in the assumed exercise of its police powers, has passed an act which seriously limits the right to labor or the right of contract in regard to their means of livelihood between persons who are *sui juris* (both employer and employee), it becomes of great importance to determine which shall prevail,—the right of the individual to labor for such time as he may choose, or the right of the state to prevent the individual from laboring, or from entering into any contract to labor, beyond a certain time prescribed by the state.

This court has recognized the existence and upheld the exercise of the police powers of the states in many cases which might fairly be considered as border ones, and it has, in the course of its determination of questions regarding the asserted invalidity of such statutes, on the ground of their violation of the rights secured by the Federal Constitution, been guided by rules of a very liberal nature, the application of which has resulted, in numerous instances, in upholding the validity of state statutes thus assailed. . . .

It must, of course, be conceded that there is a limit to the valid exercise of the police power by the state. . . . Otherwise the 14th Amendment would have no efficacy and the legislatures of the states would have unbounded power, and it would be enough to say that any piece of legislation was enacted to conserve the morals, the health, or the safety of the people; such legislation would be valid, no matter how absolutely without foundation the claim might be. The claim of the police power would be a mere pretext,—become another and delusive name for the supreme sovereignty of the state to be exercised free from constitutional restraint. . . . In every case that comes before this court, therefore, where legislation of this character is concerned, and where the protection of the Federal Constitution is sought, the question necessarily arises: Is this a fair, reasonable, and appropriate exercise of the police power of the state, or is it an unreasonable, unnecessary, and arbitrary interference with the right of the individual to his personal liberty, or to enter into those contracts in relation to labor which may seem to him appropriate or necessary for the support of himself and his family? Of course the liberty of contract relating to labor includes both parties to it. The one has as much right to purchase as the other to sell labor.

This is not a question of substituting the judgment of the court for that of the legislature. If the act be within the power of the state it is valid, although the judgment of the court might be totally opposed to the enactment of such a law. . . .

The question whether this act is valid as a labor law, pure and simple, may be dismissed in a few words. There is no reasonable ground for interfering with the liberty of person or the right of free contract, by determining the hours of labor, in the occupation of a baker. There is no contention that bakers as a class are not equal in intelligence and capacity to men in other trades or manual occupations, or that they are not able to assert their rights and care for themselves without the protecting arm of the state, interfering with their independence of judgment and of action. They are in no sense wards of the state. Viewed in the light of a purely labor law, with no reference whatever to the question of health, we think that a law like the one before us involves neither the safety, the morals, nor the welfare, of the public, and that the interest of the public is not in the slightest degree affected by such an act. The law must be upheld, if at all, as a law pertaining to the health of the individual engaged in the occupation of a baker. It does not affect any other portion of the public than those who are engaged in that occupation.

Clean and wholesome bread does not depend upon whether the baker works but ten hours per day or only sixty hours a week. The limitation of the hours of labor does not come within the police power on that ground.

It is a question of which of two powers or rights shall prevail,— the power of the state to legislate or the right of the individual to liberty of person and freedom of contract. The mere assertion that the subject relates, though but in a remote degree, to the public health, does not necessarily render the enactment valid. The act must have a more direct relation, as a means to an end, and the end itself must be appropriate and legitimate, before an act can be held to be valid which interferes with the general right of an individual to be free in his person and in his power to contract in relation to his own labor. . . .

We think that there can be no fair doubt that the trade of a baker, in and of itself, is not an unhealthy one to that degree which would authorize the legislature to interfere with the right to labor, and with the right of free contract on the part of the individual, either as employer or employee. In looking through statistics regarding all trades and occupations, it may be true that the trade of a baker does not appear to be as healthy as some other trades, and is also vastly more healthy than still others. To the common understanding the trade of a baker has never been regarded as an unhealthy one. . . .

It seems to us that the real object and purpose were simply to regulate the hours of labor between the master and his employees (all being men, *sui juris*), in a private business, not dangerous in any degree to morals, or in any real and substantial degree to the health of the employees. Under such circumstances the freedom of master and employee to contract with each other in relation to their employment, and in defining the same, cannot be prohibited or interfered with, without violating the Federal Constitution.

Justice HOLMES dissenting.

This case is decided upon an economic theory which a large part of the country does not entertain. If it were a question whether I agreed with that theory, I should desire to study it further and long before making up my mind. But I do not conceive that to be my duty, because I strongly believe that my agreement or disagreement has nothing to do with the right of a majority to embody their opinions in law. It is settled by various decisions of this court that state constitutions and state laws may regulate life in many ways which we as legislators might think as injudicious, or if you like as tyrannical, as this, and which equally with this, interfere with the liberty to contract. Sunday laws and usury laws are ancient examples. A more modern one is the prohibition of lotteries. The liberty of the citizen to do as he likes so long as he does not interfere with the liberty of others to do the same, which has been a shibboleth for some well-known writers, is interfered with by school laws, by the Postoffice, by every state or municipal institution which takes his money for purposes thought desirable, whether he likes it or not. The 14th Amendment does not enact Mr. Herbert Spencer's Social Statics. The other day we sustained the Massachusetts vaccination law. *Jacobson v. Massachusetts,* 197 U.S. 11 [1905]. United States and state statutes and decisions cutting down the liberty to contract by way of combination are familiar to this court. *Northern Securities Co. v. United States,* 193 U.S. 197 [(1904)]. Two years ago we upheld the prohibition of sales of stock on margins, or for future delivery, in the Constitution of California. *Otis v. Parker,* 187 U.S. 606 [1903]. The decision sustaining an eight-hour law for miners is still recent. *Holden v. Hardy* [169 U.S. 366 [1898)]. Some of these laws embody convictions or prejudices which judges are likely to share. Some may not. But a Constitution is not intended to embody a particular economic theory, whether of paternalism and the organic relation of the citizen to the state or of *laissez faire.* It is made for people of fundamentally differing views, and the accident of our finding certain opinions natural and familiar, or novel, and even shocking, ought not to conclude our judgment upon the question whether statutes embodying them conflict with the Constitution of the United States.

General propositions do not decide concrete cases. The decision will depend on a judgment or intuition more subtle than any articulate major premise. But I think that the proposition just stated, if it is accepted, will carry us far toward the end. Every opinion tends to become a law. I think that the word "liberty," in the 14th Amendment, is perverted when it is held to prevent the natural outcome of a dominant opinion, unless it can be said that a rational and fair man necessarily would admit that the statute proposed would infringe fundamental principles as they have been understood by the traditions of our people and our law. It does not need research to show that no such sweeping condemnation can be passed upon the statute before us. A reasonable man might think it a proper measure on the score of health. Men whom I certainly could not pronounce unreasonable would uphold it as a first instalment of a general regulation of the hours of work. Whether in the latter aspect it would be open to the charge of inequality I think it unnecessary to discuss.

Justice HARLAN, with whom Justice WHITE and Justice DAY joined, dissented in a separate opinion.

West Coast Hotel Co. v. Parrish
300 U.S. 379, 57 S.Ct. 578 (1937)

An employee of the West Coast Hotel Company, Elsie Parrish, sued to recover the difference between her wage and the minimum wage of $14.50 per forty-eight hour week as set the Industrial Welfare Committee of Washington State. In 1913, Washington's legislature passed legislation to protect the health and welfare of women and minors by setting a minimum wage. But the trial court denied Parrish's claim. When the Washington Supreme Court reversed, attorneys for West Coast Hotel Company appealed to the Supreme Court, arguing that the law ran afoul of the Fourteenth Amendment's due process clause.

Chief Justice HUGHES delivers the opinion of the Court.

This case presents the question of the constitutional validity of the minimum wage law of the state of Washington. . . .

The appellant conducts a hotel. The appellee Elsie Parrish was employed as a chambermaid and (with her husband) brought this suit to recover the difference between the wages paid her and the minimum wage fixed pursuant to the state law. The minimum wage was $14.50 per week of 48 hours. The appellant challenged the act as repugnant to the due process clause of the Fourteenth Amendment of the Constitution of the United States. The Supreme Court of the state, reversing the trial court, sustained the statute and directed judgment for the plaintiffs. *Parrish v. West Coast Hotel Co.,* 185 Wash. 581, 55 P.(2d) 1083 [(1936)]. The case is here on appeal.

The appellant relies upon the decision of this Court in *Adkins v. Children's Hospital,* 261 U.S. 525 [1923], which held invalid the District of Columbia Minimum Wage Act (40 Stat. 960) which was attacked under the due process clause of the Fifth Amendment. . . .

The recent case of *Morehead v. New York ex rel. Tipaldo,* 298 U.S. 587 [1936]. came here on certiorari to the New York court which had held the New York minimum wage act for women to be invalid. A minority of this Court thought that the New York statute was distinguishable in a material feature from that involved in the *Adkins* Case and that for that and other reasons the New York statute should be sustained. But the Court of Appeals of New York had said that it found no material difference between the two statutes and this Court held that the "meaning of the statute" as fixed by the decision of the state court "must be accepted here as if the meaning had been specifically expressed in the enactment." That view led to the affirmance by this Court of the judgment in the *Morehead* Case, as the Court considered that the only question before it was whether the *Adkins* Case was distinguishable and that reconsideration of that decision had not been sought. . . .

We think that the question which was not deemed to be open in the *Morehead* Case is open and is necessarily presented here. . . .

The principle which must control our decision is not in doubt. The constitutional provision invoked is the due process clause of the Fourteenth Amendment governing the states, as the due process clause invoked in the *Adkins* Case governed Congress. In each case the violation alleged by those attacking minimum wage regulation for women is deprivation of freedom of contract. What is this freedom? The Constitution does not speak of freedom of contract. It speaks of liberty and prohibits the deprivation of liberty without due process of law. In prohibiting that deprivation, the Constitution does not recognize an absolute and uncontrollable liberty. Liberty in each of its phases has its history and connotation. But the liberty safe-guarded is liberty in a social organization which requires the protection of law against the evils which menace the health, safety, morals, and welfare of the people. Liberty under the Constitution is thus necessarily subject to the restraints of due process, and regulation which is reasonable in relation to its subject and is adopted in the interests of the community is due process.

This essential limitation of liberty in general governs freedom of contract in particular. More than twenty-five years ago we set forth the applicable principle in these words, after referring to the cases where the liberty guaranteed by the Fourteenth Amendment had been broadly described. . . .

This power under the Constitution to restrict freedom of contract has had many illustrations. That it may be exercised in the public interest with respect to contracts between employer and employee is undeniable. Thus statutes have been sustained limiting employment in underground mines and smelters to eight hours a day; in requiring redemption in cash of store orders or other evidences of indebtedness issued in the payment of wages; in forbidding the payment of seamen's wages in advance; in making it unlawful to contract to pay miners employed at quantity rates upon the basis of screened coal instead of the weight of the coal as originally produced in the mine; in prohibiting contracts limiting liability for injuries to employees; in limiting hours of work of employees in manufacturing establishments; and in maintaining workmen's compensation laws. In dealing with the relation of employer and employed, the Legislature has necessarily a wide field of discretion in order that there may be suitable protection of health and safety, and that peace and good order may be promoted through regulations designed to insure wholesome conditions of work and freedom from oppression. . . .

This array of precedents and the principles they applied were thought by the dissenting Justices in the *Adkins* Case to demand that the minimum wage statute be sustained. The validity of the distinction made by the Court between a minimum wage and a maximum of hours in limiting liberty of contract was especially challenged. That challenge persists and is without any satisfactory answer. . . .

We think that the views thus expressed are sound and that the decision in the *Adkins* Case was a departure from the true application of the principles governing the regulation by the state of the relation of employer and employed. . . .

There is an additional and compelling consideration which recent economic experience has brought into a strong light. The exploitation of a class of workers who are in an unequal position with respect to bargaining power and are thus relatively defenseless against the denial of a living wage is not only detrimental to their health and well being, but casts a direct burden for their support upon the community. What these workers lose in wages the tax-payers are called upon to pay. The bare cost of living must be met. We may take judicial notice of the unparalleled demands for relief which arose during the recent period of depression and still continue to an alarming extent despite the degree of economic recovery which has been achieved. It is unnecessary to cite official statistics to establish what is of common knowledge through the length and breadth of the land. While in the instant case no factual brief has been presented, there is no reason to doubt that the state of Washington has encountered the same social problem that is present elsewhere. The community is not bound to provide what is in effect a subsidy for unconscionable employers. The community may direct its law-making power to correct the abuse which springs from their selfish disregard of the public interest. . . .

Our conclusion is that the case of *Adkins v. Children's Hospital, supra,* should be, and it is, overruled. The judgment of the Supreme Court of the state of Washington is affirmed.

Affirmed.

Justice SUTHERLAND

Justice VAN DEVANTER, Justice MCREYNOLDS, Justice BUTLER, and I think the judgment of the court below should be reversed.

It is urged that the question involved should now receive fresh consideration, among other reasons, because of "the economic conditions which have supervened"; but the meaning of the Constitution does not change with the ebb and flow of economic events. We frequently are told in more general words that the Constitution must be construed in the light of the present. If by that it is meant that the Constitution is made up of living words that apply to every new condition which they include, the statement is quite true. But to say, if that be intended, that the words of the Constitution mean today what they did not mean when written—that is, that they do not apply to a situation now to which they would have applied then—is to rob that instrument of the essential element which continues it in force as the people have made it until they, and not their official agents, have made it otherwise. . . .

The judicial function is that of interpretation; it does not include the power of amendment under the guise of interpretation. To miss the point of difference between the two is to miss all that the phrase "supreme law of the land" stands for and to convert what was intended as inescapable and enduring mandates into mere moral reflections.

If the Constitution, intelligently and reasonably construed in the light of these principles, stands in the way of desirable legislation, the blame must rest upon that instrument, and not upon the court for enforcing it according to its terms. The remedy in that situation—and the only true remedy—is to amend the Constitution. . . .

In the *Adkins* Case we . . . said that while there was no such thing as absolute freedom of contract, but that it was subject to a great variety of restraints, nevertheless, freedom of contract was the general rule and restraint the exception; and that the power to abridge that freedom could only be justified by the existence of exceptional circumstances. This statement of the rule has been many times affirmed; and we do not understand that it is questioned by the present decision.

Lincoln Federal Labor Union v. Northwestern Iron & Metal Co.

335 U.S. 525, 69 S.Ct. 251 (1949)

In 1946, Nebraska's constitution was amended to provide that

[n]o person shall be denied employment because of membership in or affiliation with, or resignation or expulsion from a labor organization or because of refusal to join or affiliate with a labor organization; nor shall any individual or corporation or association of any kind enter

into any contract, written or oral, to exclude persons from employment because of membership in or nonmembership in a labor organization.

Several labor unions challenged the constitutionality of this and other state right to work laws, claiming that they infringed on the First Amendment freedoms of speech and assembly and the Fourteenth Amendment's due process clause. The Nebraska State Supreme Court rejected their claims and the Lincoln Federal Labor Union appealed to the Supreme Court of the United States.

Justice BLACK delivers the opinion of the Court.

Many cases are cited by appellants in which this Court has said that in some instances the due process clause protects the liberty of persons to make contracts. But none of these cases, even those according the broadest constitutional protection to the making of contracts, ever went so far as to indicate that the due process clause bars a state from prohibiting contracts to engage in conduct banned by a valid state law. So here, if the provisions in the state laws against employer discrimination are valid, it follows that the contract prohibition also is valid. We therefore turn to the decisive question under the due process contention, which is: Does the due process clause forbid a state to pass laws clearly designed to safeguard the opportunity of non-union members to get and hold jobs, free from discrimination against them because they are non-union workers?

There was a period in which labor union members who wanted to get and hold jobs were the victims of widespread employer discrimination practices. Contracts between employers and their employees were used by employers to accomplish this anti-union employment discrimination. Before hiring workers, employers required them to sign agreements stating that the workers were not and would not become labor union members. Such anti-union practices were so obnoxious to workers that they gave these required agreements the name of "yellow dog contracts." This hostility of workers also prompted passage of state and federal laws to ban employer discrimination against union members and to outlaw yellow dog contracts. . . .

The *Allgeyer-Lochner-Adair-Coppage* constitutional doctrine was for some years followed by this Court. It was used to strike down laws fixing minimum wages and maximum hours in employment, laws fixing prices, and laws regulating business activities. . . .

This Court beginning at least as early as 1934, when the *Nebbia* [*v. New York*, 291 U.S. 902 (1931)] case was decided, has steadily rejected the due process philosophy enunciated in the *Adair-Coppage* line of cases. In doing so it has consciously returned closer and closer to the earlier constitutional principle that states have power to legislate against what are found to be injurious practices in their internal commercial and business affairs, so long as their laws do not run afoul of some specific federal constitutional prohibition, or of some valid federal law. Under this constitutional doctrine the due process clause is no longer to be so broadly construed that the Congress and state legislatures are put in a strait jacket when they attempt to suppress business and industrial conditions which they regard as offensive to the public welfare.

Appellants now ask us to return, at least in part, to the due process philosophy that has been deliberately discarded. Claiming that the Federal Constitution itself affords protection for union members against discrimination, they nevertheless assert that the same Constitution forbids a state from providing the same protection for non-union members. Just as we have held that the due process clause erects no obstacle to block legislative protection of union members, we now hold that legislative protection can be afforded non-union workers.

Affirmed.

Justice FRANKFURTER and Justice RUTLEDGE concurred in separate opinions.

C. THE "TAKINGS CLAUSE" AND JUST COMPENSATION

A final source for the Court's protection of proprietary interests is the Fifth Amendment's provision that "private property [shall not] be taken for public use, without just compensation." It is also one area of constitutional law in which there appears to be an emerging trend on the Rehnquist Court toward giving somewhat greater protection for property rights; *First English Evangelical Lutheran Church v. County of Los Angeles* (1987) (see page 263), *Nollan v. California Coastal Commission* (1987) (see page 267), and the table on page 261 are illustrative. Also relevant is *Dames & Moore v. Regan,* 453 U.S. 654 (1981) (see Vol. 1, Ch. 3).

The takings clause broadly guarantees government the power of eminent domain—the power to take private property for public purposes—subject to the just compensation of the owners. But what is a "public purpose"? What constitutes the "taking" of property? And what amounts to "just" compensation?

The requirement that government put private property to public use has been rather loosely interpreted. The only limitations appear to be that government may not take property for the sole purpose of making money for itself or for a private enterprise. However, government may take property and then resell it to private companies for such purposes as urban renewal, the development of industrial parks, or shopping centers, and for the use by (even privately owned) public utilities. In *Hawaii Housing Authority v. Midkiff,* 467 U.S. 229 (1984), for example, the Burger Court approved a state land reform act. As a vestige of Hawaiian feudalism, 96 percent of the state was owned by seventy-two landowners or else state and federal governments. In 1967, Hawaii's legislature authorized the use of the power of eminent domain to condemn residential lots and to sell and transfer ownership to existing tenants on the land. The Court unanimously rejected the contention that this program constituted a taking of private property for private, not public, purposes.

General benefit to the public, not public ownership, is what matters, and the Court tends to be highly deferential to legislatures as to what benefits the public. "Subject to specific constitutional limitations," as the Court observed in *Berman v. Parker,* 348 U.S. 26 (1954), "when the legislature has spoken, the public interest has been declared in terms wellnigh conclusive."

Private property does not have to be physically taken by the government for an individual to win compensation. However, *Loretto v. Teleprompter Manhattan CATV,* 458 U.S. 419 (1982), held that permanent physical occupation of property by the government is per se taking and *First English Evangelical Lutheran Church* ruled that temporary land-use laws may constitute a taking of private property.

In the classic case of *United States v. Causby,* 328 U.S. 258 (1946), the Court upheld a demand for compensation by a farmer whose land was adjacent to a military airport. The noise of airplane flights over the farm rendered it virtually worthless and the Court upheld the farmer's claim that the government was using his farmland as an extension of its runway and had to pay for it.

Not everyone next to an airport or highway, however, may demand compensation because of the accompanying noise or, for that matter, inconvenience of government regulations. Instead, for property to be "taken" in a constitutional sense an owner must show a nearly total loss of the use of the property. In *Pennsylvania Coal Co. v. Mahon,* 260 U.S. 393 (1922), Justice Holmes formulated a practical rule, when holding that "property may be regulated to a certain extent, [but] if regulation goes too far it will be recognized as a taking." There is no "brightline rule" but rather the burden is placed on the property owner of showing a virtually complete loss of the use of his or her property to win compensation.

THE DEVELOPMENT OF LAW
Other Recent Rulings on the Takings Clause

Case	Vote	Ruling
Andrus v. Allard, 444 U.S. 51 (1979)	9:0	When Congress passed the Eagle Protection Act and Migratory Bird Treaty Act, it authorized the secretary of the interior to prohibit commercial transactions of parts of the birds, even those legally killed prior to the act, the constitutionality of the prohibitions was challenged by sellers of Indian artifacts, which were composed of feathers from birds that existed prior to the laws enactment. The Court held that the artifacts need not be surrendered, but also that the prohibition on commercial transactions did not violate Fifth Amendment property rights.
Agins v. City of Tiburon, 447 U.S. 255 (1980)	9:0	Relying on *Village of Euclid v. Ambler Realty Co.*, 272 U.S. 365 (1926), the Court approved a San Francisco zoning ordinance requiring the construction of single-family homes on a minimum of one-acre lots, over the objections of owners of five acres of undeveloped land of great value because of its view of the San Francisco Bay. The owners had contended the zoning restriction amounted to a taking of their property.
Loretto v. Teleprompter Manhattan CATV Corporation, 458 U.S. 419 (1982)	6:3	Affirmed a takings clause challenge of a New York law prohibiting landlords from interfering with cable companies' installation of cables and boxes in their buildings and specifying that property owners may not demand compensation in excess of a limit set by a state commission. When so holding, the Court observed that "Teleprompter's cable installation on appellant's building constitutes a taking under the traditional test. The installation involved a direct physical

Case	Vote	Ruling
		attachment of plates, boxes, wires, bolts and screws to the building, completely occupying space immediately above and upon the roof and along the building's exterior wall."
Keystone Bituminous Coal Association v. DeBenedictis, 480 U.S. 470 (1987)	5:4	Rejected the claims of a coal company attacking the constitutionality of a Pennsylvania law limiting the mining of more than 50 percent of the coal beneath government and commercial buildings, private residences, and cemeteries to ensure surface support.
Pennell v. City of San Jose, 485 U.S. 1 (1988)	6:2	Rejected an attack by landlords on a city rent control ordinance limiting rent increases to 18 percent and allowing tenants to demand a hearing as to whether a rent increase was "reasonable under the circumstances"—circumstances that included the tenant's hardship.
Dupuesne Light Co. v. Barasch, 109 S.Ct. 609 (1989)	8:1	Held that states may protect consumers by barring utilities from building into their rate structures the costs of abandoned nuclear power plants and rejected the claims of utility companies that such laws constituted taking of property.
Presault v. I.C.C., 110 S.Ct. 914 (1990)	9:0	Upheld the Interstate Commerce Commission's rulings on the transfer of a railroad's right of way and held that the Fifth Amendment does not require that just compensation be paid in advance or even contemporaneously with a taking of private property.

In another important ruling in *Penn Central Transportation Co. v. New York*, 438 U.S. 104 (1978), the Burger Court affirmed an historic preservation law prohibiting the owners of Grand Central Station in New York City from building a high-rise office tower above the station.

Finally, the Court largely avoided controversies over whether a property owner has received just compensation. In general, just compensation means what, in the absence of the government's acquisition of the property, a willing buyer would pay, or the fair market value. As the Court observed in *Backus v. Fort Street Union Depot Co.*, 169 U.S. 557 (1898): "All that is essential is that in some appropriate way, before some properly constituted tribunal, inquiry shall be made as to the amount of compensation, and when this has been provided there is that due process of law which is required by the Federal Constitution."

SELECTED BIBLIOGRAPHY

Ackerman, Bruce. *Private Property and the Constitution.* New Haven, CT: Yale University Press, 1977.
Epstein, Richard. *Takings: Private Property and the Power of Eminent Doman.* Chicago: University of Chicago Press, 1985.

First English Evangelical Lutheran Church v. County of Los Angeles
482 U.S. 304, 107 S.Ct. 2378 (1987)

In 1978 a flood destroyed the buildings on a campground owned by the First English Evangelical Lutheran Church. The next year, the County of Los Angeles passed an ordinance prohibiting the construction or reconstruction of buildings on certain land affected by the flood, including the church's campground. Church attorneys immediately filed a complaint in the Superior Court of California, claiming that the ordinance amounted to a reverse condemnation and taking of property. The court denied the complaint and an appellate court and the California Supreme Court affirmed. First English Evangelical Lutheran Church appealed to the Supreme Court.

Chief Justice REHNQUIST delivers the opinion of the Court.

Consideration of the compensation question must begin with direct reference to the language of the Fifth Amendment, which provides in relevant part that "private property [shall not] be taken for public use, without just compensation." As its language indicates, and as the Court has frequently noted, this provision does not prohibit the taking of private property, but instead places a condition on the exercise of that power.

This basic understanding of the Amendment makes clear that it is designed not to limit the governmental interference with property rights *per se,* but rather to secure *compensation* in the event of otherwise proper interference amounting to a taking. Thus, government action that works a taking of property rights necessarily implicates the "constitutional obligation to pay just compensation.". . .

It has also been established doctrine at least since Justice HOLMES' opinion for the Court in *Pennsylvania Coal Co. v. Mahon,* 260 U.S. 393 (1922) that "[t]he general rule at least is, that while property may be regulated to a certain extent, if regulation goes too far it will be recognized as a taking." While the typical taking occurs when the government acts to condemn property in the exercise of its power of eminent domain, the entire doctrine of inverse condemnation is predicated on the proposition that a taking may occur without such formal proceedings. In *Pumpelly v. Green Bay Co.,* 13 Wall. 166 (1872), construing a provision in the Wisconsin Constitution identical to the Just Compensation Clause, this Court said:

> "It would be a very curious and unsatisfactory result if . . . it shall be held that if the government refrains from the absolute conversion of real property to the uses of the public it can destroy its value entirely, can inflict irreparable and permanent injury to any extent, can, in effect, subject it to total destruction without making any compensation, because, in the narrowest sense of that word, it is not *taken* for the public use."

But we have not resolved whether abandonment by the government requires payment of compensation for the period of time during which regulations deny a landowner all use of his land.

In considering this question, we find substantial guidance in cases where the government has only temporarily exercised its right to use private property. In *United States v. Dow* [357 U.S. 17 (1958)], though rejecting a claim that the Government may not abandon condemnation proceedings, the Court observed that abandonment "results in an alteration in the property interest taken—from [one of] full ownership to one of temporary use and occupation. . . . In such cases compensation would be measured by the principles normally governing the taking of a right to use property temporarily. . . ."

[That and other] cases reflect the fact that "temporary" takings which, as here, deny a landowner all use of his property, are not different in kind from permanent takings, for which the Constitution clearly requires compensation. It is axiomatic that the Fifth Amendment's just compensation provision is "designed to bar Government from forcing some people alone to bear public burdens which, in all fairness and justice, should be borne by the public as a whole.". . .

In the present case the interim ordinance was adopted by the county of Los Angeles in January 1979, and became effective immediately. Appellant filed suit within a month after the effective date of the ordinance and yet when the Supreme Court of California denied a hearing in the case on October 17, 1985, the merits of appellant's claim had yet to be determined. The United States has been required to pay compensation for leasehold interests of shorter duration than this. The value of a leasehold interest in property for a period of years may be substantial, and the burden on the property owner in extinguishing such an interest for a period of years may be great indeed. Where this burden results from governmental action that amounted to a taking, the Just Compensation Clause of the Fifth Amendment requires that the government pay the landowner for the value of the use of the land during this period.

Nothing we say today is intended to abrogate the principle that the decision to exercise the power of eminent domain is a legislative function, " 'for Congress and Congress alone to determine.' " Once a court determines that a taking has occurred, the government retains the whole range of options already available—amendment of the regulation, withdrawal of the invalidated regulation, or exercise of eminent domain. . . .

We also point out that the allegation of the complaint which we treat as true for purposes of our decision was that the ordinance in question denied appellant all use of its property. We limit our holding to the facts presented, and of course do not deal with the quite different questions that would arise in the case of normal delays in obtaining building permits, changes in zoning ordinances, variances, and the like which are not before us. We realize that even our present holding will undoubtedly lessen to some extent the freedom and flexibility of land-use planners and governing bodies of municipal corporations when enacting land-use regulations. But such consequences necessarily flow from any decision upholding a claim of constitutional right; many of the provisions of the Constitution are designed to limit the flexibility and freedom of governmental authorities and the Just Compensation Clause of the Fifth Amendment is one of them. . . .

Here we must assume that the Los Angeles County ordinances have denied appellant all use of its property for a considerable period of years, and we hold that invalidation of the ordinance without payment of fair value for the use of the property during this period of time would be a constitutionally insufficient remedy. The judgment of the California Court of Appeals is therefore reversed, and the case is remanded for further proceedings not inconsistent with this opinion.

It is so ordered.

Justice STEVENS, with whom Justice BLACKMUN and Justice O'CONNOR join, dissenting.

One thing is certain. The Court's decision today will generate a great deal of litigation. Most of it, I believe, will be unproductive. But the mere duty to defend the actions that today's decision will spawn will undoubtedly have a significant adverse impact on the land-use regulatory process. The Court has reached out to address an issue not actually presented in this case, and has then answered that self-imposed question in a superficial and, I believe, dangerous way.

Four flaws in the Court's analysis merit special comment. First, the Court unnecessarily and imprudently assumes that appellant's complaint alleges an unconstitutional taking of Lutherglen. Second, the Court distorts our precedents in the area of regulatory takings when it concludes that all ordinances which would constitute takings if allowed to remain in effect permanently, necessarily also constitute takings if they are in effect for only a limited period of time. Third, the Court incorrectly assumes that the California Supreme Court has already decided that it will never allow a state court to grant monetary relief for a temporary regulatory taking, and then uses that conclusion to reverse a judgment which is correct under the Court's own theories. Finally, the Court errs in concluding that it is the Takings Clause, rather than the Due Process Clause, which is the primary constraint on the use of unfair and dilatory procedures in the land-use area. . . .

There is no dispute about the proposition that a regulation which goes "too far" must be deemed a taking. When that happens, the Government has a choice: it may abandon the regulation or it may continue to regulate and compensate those whose property it takes. In the usual case, either of these options is wholly satisfactory. Paying compensation for the property is, of course, a constitutional prerogative of the sovereign. Alternatively, if the sovereign chooses not to retain the regulation, repeal will, in virtually all cases, mitigate the overall effect of the regulation so substantially that the slight diminution in value that the regulation caused while in effect cannot be classified as a taking of property. . . .

A temporary interference with an owner's use of his property may constitute a taking for which the Constitution requires that compensation be paid. At least with respect to physical takings, the Court has so held. . . .

But our cases also make it clear that regulatory takings and physical takings are very different in this, as well as other, respects. While virtually all physical invasions are deemed takings, a regulatory program that adversely affects property values does not constitute a taking unless it destroys a major portion of the property's value. This diminution of value inquiry is unique to regulatory takings. Unlike physical invasions, which are relatively rare and easily identifiable without making any economic analysis, regulatory programs constantly affect property values in countless ways, and only the most extreme regulations can constitute takings. Some dividing line must be established between everyday regulatory inconveniences and those so severe that they constitute takings. The diminution of value inquiry has long been used in identifying that line. As Justice Holmes put it: "Government hardly could go on if to some extent values incident to property could not be diminished without paying for every such change in the general law." It is this basic distinction between regulatory and physical takings that the Court ignores today. . . .

The cases that the Court relies upon for the proposition that there is no distinction between temporary and permanent takings are inapposite, for they all deal with physical takings—where the diminution of value test is inapplicable. . . .

Until today, we have repeatedly rejected the notion that all temporary diminutions in the value of property automatically activate the compensation requirement of the Takings Clause. . . .

The policy implications of today's decision are obvious and, I fear, far reaching. Cautious local officials and land-use planners may avoid taking any action that might later be challenged and thus give rise to a damage action. Much important regulation will never be enacted, even perhaps in the health and safety area. Were this result mandated by the Constitution, these serious implications would have to be ignored. But the loose cannon the Court fires today is not only unattached to the Constitution, but it also takes aim at a long line of precedents in the regulatory takings area. It would be the better part of valor simply to decide the case at hand instead of igniting the kind of litigation explosion that this decision will undoubtedly touch off.

I respectfully dissent.

Nollan v. California Coastal Commission
483 U.S. 825, 107 S.Ct. 3141 (1987)

James Nollan and several other owners of beachfront property filed a suit against the California Coastal Commission in 1982. They contended that its regulations governing the construction and reconstruction of buildings on beachfront property were unconstitutional. Specifically, they argued its requirement, as a condition of receiving a building permit, that property owners transfer to the public an easement across their property constituted a taking of property under the Fifth and Fourteenth Amendments. The California Superior Court agreed but a state appellate court reversed, and Nollan appealed to the Supreme Court of the United States.

Justice SCALIA delivers the opinion of the court.

We have long recognized that land use regulation does not effect a taking if it "substantially advance[s] legitimate state interests" and does not "den[y] an owner economically viable use of his land." *Agins v. Tiburon*, 447 U.S. 255 (1980). . . . Our cases have not elaborated on the standards for determining what constitutes a "legitimate state interest" or what type of connection between the regulation and the state interest satisfies the requirement that the former "substantially advance" the latter. They have made clear, however, that a broad range of governmental purposes and regulations satisfies these requirements. See *Agins v. Tiburon, supra,* (scenic zoning; *Penn Central Transportation Co. v. New York City* (landmark preservation); *Euclid v. Ambler Realty Co.*, 272 U.S. 365 (1926) (residential zoning); Laitos and Westfall, Government Interference with Private Interests in Public Resources, 11 Harv.Envtl.L.Rev. 1, 66 (1987). The Commission argues that among these permissible purposes are protecting the public's ability to see the beach, assisting the public in overcoming the "psychological barrier" to using the beach created by a developed shorefront, and preventing congestion on the public beaches. We assume, without deciding, that this is so—in which case the Commission unquestionably would be able to deny the Nollans their permit outright if their new house (alone, or by reason of the cumulative impact produced in conjunction with other construction) would substantially impede these purposes, unless the denial would interfere so drastically with the Nollans use of their property as to constitute a taking.

The Commission argues that a permit condition that serves the same legitimate police-power purpose as a refusal to issue the permit should not be found to be a taking if the refusal to issue the permit would not constitute a taking. We agree. . . . Although such a requirement, constituting a permanent grant of continuous access to the property, would have to be considered a taking if it were not attached to a development permit, the Commission's assumed power to forbid construction of the house in order to protect the public's view of the beach must surely include the power to condition construction upon some concession by the owner, even a concession of property rights, that serves the same end. If a prohibition designed to accomplish that purpose would be a legitimate exercise of the police power rather than a taking, it would be strange to conclude that providing the owner an alternative to that prohibition which accomplishes the same purpose is not.

The evident constitutional propriety disappears, however, if the condition substituted for the prohibition utterly fails to further the end advanced as the justification for the prohibition. When that essential nexus is eliminated, the situation becomes the same as if California law forbade shouting fire in a crowded theater, but granted dispensations to those willing to contribute $100 to the state treasury. While a ban on shouting fire can be a core exercise of the State's police power to protect the public safety, and can thus meet even our stringent standards for regulation of speech, adding the unrelated condition alters the purpose to one which, while it may be legitimate, is inadequate to sustain the ban. Therefore, even though, in a sense, requiring a $100 tax contribution in order to shout fire is a lesser restriction on speech than an outright ban, it would not pass constitutional muster. Similarly here, the lack of nexus between the condition and the original purpose of the building restriction converts that purpose to something other than what it was. The purpose then becomes, quite simply, the obtaining of an easement to serve some valid governmental purpose, but without payment of compensation. Whatever may be the outer limits of "legitimate state interests" in the takings and land use context, this is not one of them. In short, unless the permit condition serves the same governmental purpose as the development ban, the building restriction is not a valid regulation of land use but "an out-and-out plan of extortion.". . .

It is quite impossible to understand how a requirement that people already on the public beaches be able to walk across the Nollans' property reduces any obstacles to viewing the beach created by the new house. It is also impossible to understand how it lowers any "psychological barrier" to using the public beaches, or how it helps to remedy any additional congestion on them caused by construction of the Nollans' new house. We therefore find that the Commission's imposition of the permit condition cannot be treated as an exercise of its land use power for any of these purposes. . . .

Justice BRENNAN aruges that imposition of the access requirement is not irrational. In his version of the Commission's argument, the reason for the requirement is that in its absence, a person looking toward the beach from the road will see a street of residential structures including the Nollans' new home and conclude that there is no public beach nearby. If, however, that person sees people passing and repassing along the dry sand behind the Nollans' home, he will realize that there is a public beach somewhere in the vicinity. The Commission's action, however, was based on the opposite factual finding that the wall of houses completely blocked the view of the beach and that a person looking from the road would not be able to see it at all. . . .

We are left, then, with the Commission's justification for the access requirement unrelated to land use regulation:

"Finally, the Commission notes that there are several existing provisions of pass and repass lateral access benefits already given by past Faria Beach Tract applicants as a result of prior coastal permit decisions. The access required as a condition of this permit is part of a comprehensive program to provide continuous public access along Faria Beach as the lots undergo development or redevelopment."

That is simply an expression of the Commission's belief that the public interest will be served by a continuous strip of publicly accessible beach along the coast. The Commission may well be right that it is a good idea, but that does not establish that the Nollans (and other coastal residents) alone can be compelled to contribute to its realization. Rather, California is free to advance its "comprehensive program," if it wishes, by using its power of eminent domain for this "public purpose," see U.S Const., Amdt. V; but if it wants an easement across the Nollans' property, it must pay for it.

Reversed.

Justice BRENNAN, with whom Justice MARSHALL joins, dissenting.

The Court's conclusion that the permit rendition imposed on appellants is unreasonable cannot withstand analysis. First, the Court demands a degree of exactitude that is inconsistent with our standard for reviewing the rationality of a state's exercise of its police power for the welfare of its citizens. Second, even if the nature of the public access condition imposed must be identical to the precise burden on access created by appellants, this requirement is plainly satisfied. . . .

Imposition of the permit condition in this case represents the State's reasonable exercise of its police power. The Coastal Commission has drawn on its expertise to preserve the balance between private development and public access, by requiring that any project that intensifies development on the increasingly crowded California coast must be offset by gains in public access. Under the normal standard for review of the police power, this provision is eminently reasonable. Even accepting the Court's novel insistence on a precise *quid pro quo* of burdens and benefits, there is a reasonable relationship between the public benefit and the burden created by appellants' development. The movement of development closer to the ocean creates the prospect of encroachment on public tidelands, because of fluctuation in the mean high tide line. The deed restriction ensures that disputes about the boundary between private and public property will not deter the public from exercising its right to have access to the sea.

Furthermore, consideration of the Commission's action under

traditional takings analysis underscores the absence of any viable takings claim. The deed restriction permits the public only to pass and repass along a narrow strip of beach, a few feet closer to a seawall at the periphery of appellants' property. Appellants almost surely have enjoyed an increase in the value of their property even with the restriction, because they have been allowed to build a significantly larger new home with garage on their lot. Finally, appellants can claim the disruption of no expectation interest, both because they have no right to exclude the public under state law, and because, even if they did, they had full advance notice that new development along the coast is conditioned on provisions for continued public access to the ocean. . . .

I dissent.

Justice BLACKMUN dissenting.

I disagree with the Court's rigid interpretation of the necessary correlation between a burden created by development and a condition imposed pursuant to the State's police power to mitigate that burden. The land-use problems this country faces require creative solutions. These are not advanced by an "eye for an eye" mentality. The close nexus between benefits and burdens that the Court now imposes on permit conditions creates an anomaly in the ordinary requirement that a State's exercise of its police power need be no more than rationally based. In my view, the easement exacted from appellants and the problems their development created are adequately related to the governmental interest in providing public access to the beach. Coastal development by its very nature makes public access to the shore generally more difficult. Appellants' structure is part of that general development and, in particular, it diminishes the public's visual access to the ocean and decreases the public's sense that it may have physical access to the beach. These losses in access can be counteracted, at least in part, by the condition on appellants' construction permitting public passage that ensures access along the beach.

Traditional takings analysis compels the conclusion that there is no taking here. The governmental action is a valid exercise of the police power, and, so far as the record reveals, has a nonexistent economic effect on the value of appellants' property. No investment-backed expectations were diminished. It is significant that the Nolans had notice of the easement before they purchased the property and that public use of the beach had been permitted for decades.

For these reasons, I respectfully dissent.

Justice STEVENS, with whom Justice BLACKMUN joined, dissented in a separate opinion.

4

THE NATIONALIZATION
OF THE BILL OF RIGHTS

This chapter examines the constitutional basis for civil liberties and civil rights and the controversy over the nationalization of the Bill of Rights—that is, the Supreme Court's extension of those guarantees as limitations on the states. The original Constitution contained few explicit guarantees for civil liberties and civil rights. But with the adoption of the Bill of Rights, the first ten amendments to the Constitution, the basis for civil liberties and civil rights was laid. The Bill of Rights, however, only limited the powers of the national government, not the states. With the ratification of the Fourteenth Amendment in 1868, though, there was a new basis for applying the Bill of Rights to the states. Its due process clause provides that "No state shall . . . deprive any person of life, liberty, or property without due process of law." This chapter examines the controversy over the Supreme Court's reading into the Fourteenth Amendment's due process clause guarantees of the Bill of Rights to make them applicable to the states. Subsequent chapters examine how the Supreme Court has interpreted and applied specific provisions of the Bill of Rights. Chapter 5 considers the First Amendment's guarantees for free speech, press, and association and Chapter 6, its provisions for religious freedom. Chapters 7 through 10 then examine guarantees for the rights of the accused in the criminal justice system. Chapter 11 takes up the right of privacy and Chapter 12, the Fourteenth Amendment's guarantee for the equal protection of the laws.

Unamended, the Constitution contains only five provisions for civil liberties. Article 1 forbids Congress and the states from passing *ex post facto* laws (laws making some activity retroactively a crime) and bills of attainder (legislation punishing specific individuals or members of a group without a trial). It also provides that Congress may not, except in times of rebellion or invasion, suspend writs of *habeas corpus*. A writ of *habeas corpus* is an ancient order (which is Latin for "you should have the body") aimed at safeguarding against unlawful arrests and imprisonment of individuals. (A prisoner in jail may petition a court for a writ of *habeas corpus* that then requires the government to explain to a judge why the prisoner is being held, of what crimes he or she is accused, and the basis for continuing imprisonment.) In addition (as dealt with in Chapter 3), states are also forbidden in Article I from "impairing the Obligation of Contract," and in Article IV from denying the privileges and immunities of citizenship.

The Constitution was itself deemed to be a bill of rights, at least by the Federalists. James Wilson and Alexander Hamilton, among others, argued that civil rights and civil liberties would remain secure because the powers of the national government are limited to those expressly granted, and the states would continue to safeguard individuals' civil rights and liberties.

Those opposing the Constitution, the Anti-Federalists, were unpersuaded. They feared that the national government's power was too great and would further expand at the expense of the powers of (and the protections for individual liberty afforded by) the states. A leading New York Anti-Federalist, Brutus, for example, warned that the federal judiciary would "extend the limits of the general government gradually, and by insensible degrees . . . facilitate the abolition of the state governments."[1] Nor did the Anti-Federalists trust Congress, let alone the executive branch, to respect civil rights and liberties. As Richard Henry Lee wrote to Samuel Adams in 1787:

The corrupting nature of power, and its insatiable appetite for increase, hath proved the necessity, and procured the adoption of the strongest and most express declarations of that *Residuum* of natural rights, which is not intended to be given up to Society; and which indeed is not necessary to be given for any good social purpose. In a government therefore, when the power of judging what shall be for the *general welfare,* which goes to every object of human legislation; and where the laws of such Judges shall be the *supreme Law of the Land:* it seems to be of the last consequence to declare in most explicit terms the reservations above alluded to.[2]

Although the Anti-Federalists unsuccessfully fought against the Constitution's ratification, they succeeded in insisting on the addition of the Bill of Rights. Delaware unanimously ratified the document on December 7, 1787. Within weeks Pennsylvania, New Jersey, Georgia, and Connecticut gave their approval. Massachusetts followed in February 1788, but with a closely divided vote of 187 to 168. In the spring, Maryland and South Carolina gave their overwhelming endorsements. Then in June, close votes in New Hampshire and Virginia secured the requisite nine states for ratification. But the battle in the New York convention was fierce and crucial, for this large commercial state separated New England from the Southern states. It was largely due to the leadership of Hamilton, a Federalist, that New York finally voted in favor. The price of winning ratification there and in Massachusetts and Virginia, however, was agreement that the First Congress would adopt a declaration of rights and promptly send it to the states for ratification. North Carolina did not ratify until November 1789 and Rhode Island held out until May 1790.

During the debate over New York's ratification, Hamilton tried to popularize the counter arguments to those made by the Anti-Federalists. "[T]he Constitution itself, in every rational sense, and to every useful purpose, is a bill of rights," he insisted in *Federalist* No. 84, when contending that the addition of a declaration of rights was "not only unnecessary . . . but would even be dangerous." In arguing that a bill of rights was unnecessary, Hamilton pointed to the Preamble of the Constitution:

We the people of the United States, to secure the blessings of liberty to ourselves and our posterity, do *ordain* and *establish* this constitution for the United States of America." Here is a better recognition of popular rights than volumes of those aphorisms which make the principal figure in several of our state bills of rights, and which would sound much better in a treatise of ethics than in a constitution of government.

A bill of rights might also prove dangerous, Hamilton contended, because it

would contain various exceptions to powers which are not granted; and on this very account, would afford a colourable pretext to claim more than were granted. For why declare that things shall not be done which there is no power to do? Why for instance, should it be said, that the liberty of the press shall not be restrained, when no power is given by which restrictions may be imposed? I will not contend that such a provision would confer a regulating power; but it is evident that it would furnish, to men disposed to usurp, a plausible pretence for claiming that power. They might urge with a semblance of reason, that the constitution ought not to be charged with the absurdity of providing against the abuse of an authority, which was not given, and that provision against restraining the liberty of press afforded a clear implication, that a power to prescribe proper regulations concerning it, was intended to be vested in the national government.

Furthermore, Hamilton suggested the problems of which rights to include and exclude and how to define those rights specified in a declaration of rights:

On the subject of the liberty of the press, as much has been said, I cannot forbear adding a remark or two: In the first place, I observe that there is not a syllable concerning it in the constitution of this state [New York], and in the next I contend that whatever has been said about it in that of any other state, amounts to nothing. What signifies a declaration that "the liberty of the press shall be inviolably preserved?" What is the liberty of the press? Who can give it any definition which would not leave the utmost latitude for evasion? I hold it to be impracticable; and from this, I infer, that its security, whatever fine declarations may be inserted in any constitution respecting it, must altogether depend on public opinion, and on the general spirit of the people and of the government.

Despite their success in securing the ratification of the Constitution, the Federalists failed to turn the tide of public opinion running in favor of a bill of rights. As Thomas Jefferson noted in a letter to James Madison on December 20, 1787, "a bill of rights is what the people are entitled to against every government on earth, general or particular, and what no just government should refuse, or rest on inference."[3] Madison was not initially inclined toward the addition of a declaration of rights.

In a letter to Jefferson, Madison gave four reasons for his ambivalence. First, he accepted the Federalists' argument that "the rights in question are reserved by the manner in which the federal powers are granted." Second, he feared "that a positive declaration of some of the most essential rights could not be obtained in the requisite latitude." In particular, "the rights of Conscience" might be narrowed by any formal-legal definition. Third, republican liberty was guarded against Congress by its constitutionally "limited powers" and "the jealousy" of the states. Finally, he maintained that "experience proves the inefficacy of a bill of rights on those occasions when its controul is most needed."[4]

Madison came to side with Jefferson and the Anti-Federalists and provided some of the strongest arguments for a bill of rights. They, too, worried about what to include and exclude in a bill of rights. In 1788, Madison explained that he had not viewed a bill of rights "in an important light . . . [b]ecause there is great reason to fear that a positive declaration of some of the most essential rights could not be obtained in the requisite latitude."[5] But Jefferson responded that "Half a loaf is better than no bread. If we cannot secure all our rights, let's secure what we can."[6] He and Madison, furthermore, came to view a bill of rights as putting into "the hands of the judiciary" an additional check on the coercive powers of government. "This is a body," observed Jefferson, "which if rendered independent, and kept strictly to their own department merits great confidence for their learning and integrity."[7]

In the First Congress in 1789, as a member of the House of Representatives Madison championed the cause of adding a declaration of rights to the Constitution. His aim was "to satisfy the public mind that their liberties will be perpetual, and this without endangering any part of the constitution."[8] With parliamental skill, Madison steered the amendments through Congress and the Bill of Rights was ratified by the states in 1791. Madison, however, was forced to compromise and failed to achieve two goals. He had proposed that the amendments be incorporated into the body of the original Constitution, because he did not want them to be perceived as inferior or less important than the document itself. But he was defeated on that as well as on proposing that the amendments bind the states along with the national government.

NOTES

1. Brutus, in *New York Journal*, in *The Complete Anti-Federalist*, Vol. 2, ed. Herbert Storing (Chicago: University of Chicago Press, 1981), 441.

2. Richard Henry Lee to Samuel Adams (Oct. 5, 1787), in *The Founders' Constitution*, Vol. 1, ed. Philip Kurland and Ralph Lerner (Chicago: University of Chicago Press, 1987), 448.

3. Thomas Jefferson, *The Papers of Thomas Jefferson*, Vol. 12, ed. Julian Boyd (Princeton, NJ: Princeton University Press, 1950–), 440.

4. James Madison, *The Papers of James Madison*, Vol. 11, ed. R. Rutland (Charlottesville: University Press of Virginia, 1977), 295–298.

5. *Ibid.*

6. Jefferson, *The Papers of Thomas Jefferson*, Vol. 14, 659.

7. *Ibid.*

8. Madison, *The Papers of James Madison*, Vol. 12, 196–209.

SELECTED BIBLIOGRAPHY

Abraham, Henry. *Freedom and the Court: Civil Liberties and Civil Rights in the United States*, 5th ed. New York: Oxford University Press, 1988.

Gillespie, Michael, and Lienesch, Michael, eds. *Ratifying the Constitution.* Lawrence: University Press of Kansas, 1989.

Goldwin, Robert A., and Schambra, William, eds. *How Does the Constitution Secure Rights?* Washington, DC: American Enterprise Institution, 1985.

Levy, Leonard W. *Original Intent and the Framers' Constitution.* New York: Macmillan, 1988.

Rutland, Robert. *The Birth of the Bill of Rights, 1776–1791.* Chapel Hill: University of North Carolina Press, 1955.

Schwartz, Bernard, ed. *The Roots of the Bill of Rights,* 5 vols. New York: Chelsea House, 1980.

A. THE SELECTIVE NATIONALIZATION OF GUARANTEES OF THE BILL OF RIGHTS PLUS OTHER FUNDAMENTAL RIGHTS

The Bill of Rights did not limit the powers of the states until this century. The Supreme Court's nationalization—or application to the states—of the Bill of Rights and its interpretative basis for doing so remains controversial. The prevailing view of the Bill of Rights in the last century was well stated in 1833 by Chief Justice John Marshall. In *Barron v. The Mayor and City Council of Baltimore* (1833) (see page 286), after reviewing the history of the Bill of Rights, Marshall concluded there was "no expression indicating an intention to apply [guarantees of the Bill of the Rights] to the State governments. This court cannot so apply them."

Barron was reaffirmed in *Permoli v. New Orleans,* 3 How. (44 U.S.) 589 (1845), and in *Mattox v. United States,* 156 U.S. 237 (1894). As late as 1922 the Court maintained that "the Constitution of the United States imposes upon the states no obligation to confer upon those within its jurisdiction . . . the right to free speech" in *Prudential Insurance Company v. Cheek,* 259 U.S. 530 (1922). Indeed, despite the Court's eventual nationalization of most of the guarantees of the Bill of Rights, *Barron* has never been expressly overturned.

Ratification of the Fourteenth Amendment in 1868, however, changed the constitutional landscape and laid a new basis for applying the Bill of Rights to the states. It specifically denied the states the power to "make or enforce any law which shall abridge the privileges or immunities of citizens of the United States . . . [or] deprive any person of life, liberty, or property, without due process of law . . . [or] deny to any person within its jurisdiction the equal of the laws." Two of the principal leaders in the Thirty-ninth Congress proposing the amendment, Ohio

Representative John A. Bingham and Michigan Senator Jacob M. Howard, suggested during floor debates that an objective was the extension of the Bill of Rights to the states (thereby overturning *Barron*). The Fourteenth Amendment, Senator Howard claimed, would bar the states from denying citizens their privileges and immunities guaranteed by the Constitution, including "the personal rights guaranteed and secured by the first eight amendments of the Constitution."[1]

Whether Congress intended the Fourteenth Amendment to incorporate and apply guarantees of the Bill of Rights to the states, however, is a long-running controversy. The record of the Thirty-ninth Congress and of the states' ratification of the Fourteenth Amendment is far from complete and unambiguous.[2] Justices, historians, and legal scholars are unlikely to agree on the historical basis for the Court's reading provisions of the Bill of Rights into the Fourteenth Amendment. Justices Felix Frankfurter and (the second) John Harlan, as well as some law professors, maintain that the amendment was not intended to apply the Bill of Rights to the states.[3] By contrast, Justices Hugo Black and William Douglas, along with other leading historians and legal scholars, championed an interpretation of the legislative record pointing in the opposite direction.[4] And it seems fair to conclude, as John Hart Ely put it, that "the legislative argument is one neither side can win."[5]

History, though, is not all that divided the Court when interpretating the Fourteenth Amendment. No less important are the politics of interpretation and rival judicial and political philosophies. And those differences, as much as different readings of history, account for the continuing controversy over turning the Fourteenth Amendment into a vehicle for nationalizating the Bill of Rights.

When initially confronted with the question of extending the Bill of Rights to the states in *The Slaughterhouse Cases* (1873) (see page 240), the justices split five to four. The majority rejected the view that the Fourteenth Amendment's privileges or immunities clause incorporated the Bill of Rights. Yet the four dissenters (Chief Justice Chase and Justices Bradley, Field, and Swayne) took the opposite view. The Court's narrow reading of the amendment, in Swayne's words, turned "what was meant for bread into stone."

The Slaughterhouse Cases, as dissenting Justice Field remarked, rendered the Fourteenth Amendment "a vain and idle enactment, which accomplished nothing, and most unnecessarily excited Congress and the people on its passage." The majority's opinion, however, dealt primarily with the privileges and immunities clause. And that left open the possibility that the Court might eventually be persuaded to incorporate or absorb the Bill of Rights into the amendment's due process clause.

With two exceptions in the late nineteenth century, the Court remained unmoved from its interpretation in *The Slaughterhouse Cases*. Both rulings involved the Fifth Amendment's prohibition against the taking of private property for public use without just compensation, and registered the Court's embrace of laissez-faire capitalism and the priority given to economic liberties, see the table on page 280 and, there, *Missouri Pacific Railway Co. v. Nebraska* and *Chicago, Burlington & Quincy Railway Co. v. Chicago*.

Despite refusing to nationalize the Bill of Rights, the Court could not escape responsibility for giving meaning to the Fourteenth Amendment's due process clause. That meant coming up with standards or tests for determining what state practices and procedures denied individuals their rights under the Fourteenth Amendment due process clause. So long as the Court held that the due process clause did not include the guarantees afforded by the Bill of Rights, the justices had to create their own standards and rationalizations for what process is due under the Fourteenth Amendment.

The Court faced the question of what process is due in *Hurtado v. California* (1884) (see page 289). In holding that states need not honor the Fifth Amendment's requirement that individuals be indicted by a grand jury before being tried for a crime, Justice Mathews proclaimed the states free to experiment with their own criminal justice procedures. They, he said, were free "to draw on the wells of justice, so long as they don't go too far." On this standard, each case would have to be considered on its own merits. But as dissenting Justice John Marshall Harlan suggested, whether states ran afoul of the due process clause also turned on each justice's conception of what process is due, rather than on enumerated guarantees. In Harlan's opinion the Bill of Rights were incorporated lock, stock, and barrel into the due process clause. His position of *total incorporation*, nevertheless, failed to command a majority. Accordingly, state practices and procedures falling short of the requirements of the Bill of Rights were upheld. In *Maxwell v. Dow*, 176 U.S. 581 (1900), for example, the Court ruled that states were free to convict individuals before juries composed of less than twelve members and on less than a unanimous verdict. And *Twining v. New Jersey*, 211 U.S. 78 (1908), held that states need not honor an accused's Fifth Amendment's privilege against self-incrimination.

Forty years passed before the Court was prepared to extend guarantees of the Bill of Rights to the states. Then when confronted with a spate of litigation challenging state laws punishing

THE DEVELOPMENT OF LAW

The Selective Nationalization of the Bill of Rights Plus Other Fundamental Rights

Guarantee/Right	Amend-ment	Year	Case
Public use and just compensation provisions condition the taking of private property by the government	5	1896 1897	*Missouri Pacific Railway Co. v. Nebraska,* 164 U.S. 403 *Chicago, Burlington & Quincy Railway Co. v. Chicago,* 166 U.S. 226
Freedom of speech	1	1927	*Fiske v. Kansas,* 274 U.S. 380 (also earlier in *dictum: Gitlow v. New York,* 268 U.S. 652 (1925); and *Gilbert v. Minnesota,* 254 U.S. 325)(1920)
Freedom of the press	1	1931	*Near v. Minnesota,* 283 U.S. 697
Fair trial and right to counsel in capital cases	6	1932	*Powell v. Alabama,* 287 U.S. 45
Freedom of religion	1	1934	*Hamilton v. Regents of the University of California,* 293 U.S. 245 (in *dictum*)
Freedom of assembly (and implicitly freedom to petition for redress of grievances)	1	1937	*De Jonge v. Oregon,* 299 U.S. 353
Free exercise of religion	1	1940	*Cantwell v. Connecticut,* 310 U.S. 296
Separation of church and state	1	1947	*Everson v. Board of Education,* 330 U.S. 1
Right to a public trial	6	1948	*In re Oliver,* 333 U.S. 257
Right against unreasonable searches and seizures	4	1949	*Wolf v. Colorado,* 338 U.S. 25
Freedom of association	1	1958	*NAACP v. Alabama,* 357 U.S. 449
Exclusionary rule	4	1961	*Mapp v. Ohio,* 367 U.S. 643
Ban against cruel and unusual punishments	8	1962	*Robinson v. California,* 370 U.S. 660

Guarantee/Right	Amend-ment	Year	Case
Right to counsel in all felony cases	6	1963	*Gideon v. Wainwright,* 372 U.S. 335
Right against self-incrimination	5	1964	*Malloy v. Hogan,* 378 U.S. 1
Right to confront witness (and by implication the right to be informed of the nature and cause of the accusation)	6	1965	*Pointer v. Texas,* 380 U.S. 400
Right to privacy	penumbra of 1, 3, 4, 5, and 9	1965	*Griswold v. Connecticut,* 381 U.S. 479
Right to impartial jury	6	1966	*Parker v. Gladden,* 385 U.S. 363
Right to speedy trial	6	1967	*Klopfer v. North Carolina,* 386 U.S. 213
Right to compulsory process for obtaining witnesses	6	1967	*Washington v. Texas,* 388 U.S. 14
Right to jury trial in nonpetty cases	6	1968	*Duncan v. Louisiana,* 391 U.S. 145
Right against double jeopardy	5	1969	*Benton v. Maryland,* 395 U.S. 784
Right to counsel in all criminal cases involving a jail term	6	1972	*Argersinger v. Hamlin,* 407 U.S. 25

subversive speech, the Court merely assumed (in spite of its previous denials) that the First Amendment freedoms of speech and press limited the states, no less than the national government. In *Gilbert v. Minnesota,* 254 U.S. 652 (1920), the Court granted that individuals might challenge the constitutionality of state laws making it a crime to falsely or maliciously criticize the government. In *Gitlow v. New York,* 268 U.S. 652 (1925) (see Chapter 5), Justice Edward Sanford noted in *dictum* that "[w]e may and do assume that freedom of speech and of the press . . . are among the fundamental rights and liberties protected . . . from impairment by the states." By the 1940s, the other First Amendment freedoms were construed to be so fundamental as to constrain the states as well.

Still, in the area of criminal procedure, the Court remained reluctant to impose the guarantees of the Fourth through the

Eighth Amendments on the states. Indicative of the Court's deference to the states is the infamous *Scottsboro Case, Powell v. Alabama,* 287 U.S. 32 (1932) (see Chapter 9). There seven black teenagers were tried and convicted for raping a white woman (a capital offense), without the representation of counsel, before an all-white jury in Scottsboro, Alabama. In ordering that they be retried and appointed an attorney, the Court ruled that they had been denied due process and subjected to a fundamentally unfair trial. But it declined to make the Fifth and Sixth Amendments applicable to the states. Instead, the Court relied on general principles of "natural justice" and "ordered liberty," as it also did in *Norris v. Alabama,* 294 U.S. 587 (1935), holding jury trials are required in criminal cases and *Brown v. Mississippi,* 297 U.S. 278 (1936), holding that confessions coerced by third-degree police tactics violate due process.

In *Palko v. Connecticut* (1937) (see page 294), Justice Benjamin Cardozo rationalized the selective application of some but not all guarantees of the Bill of Rights. According to his theory of *selective incorporation,* some rights are "so rooted in the traditions and conscience of our people as to be ranked as fundamental" and "implicit in the concept of ordered liberty." Among those he deemed applicable to the states were the First Amendment freedoms, the Fifth Amendment's eminent domain provision, and the Sixth Amendment right to counsel in capital cases. Other guarantees of the Bill of Rights were simply formal rights not binding on the states. Cardozo's honor roll of preferred freedoms thus created a constitutional double standard for enforcing the Bill of Rights.

Cardozo's theory of selective incorporation stood for almost twenty-five years, until the 1960s when the Warren Court forged a constitutional revolution in criminal procedure by extending virtually all of the guarantees of the Fourth through the Eighth Amendments to the states. In the 1940s and 1950s, the Court remained sharply divided over whether and how to nationalize the Bill of Rights.

The divisiveness within the Court arising from the debate over the nationalization of the Bill of Rights and the politics of interpretation is exemplified by *Adamson v. California* (1947) (see page 298). There Justice Reed, writing for the majority, adhered to the theory of selective incorporation. But concurring Justice Frankfurter maintained that the requirements of the due process clause in the Fifth Amendment and those of the due process clause in the Fourteenth Amendment were completely independent and that when enforcing the latter the justices should balance the rights of the accused against the interests of the states in prosecuting crime. When balancing these competing interests,

Frankfurter urged the Court to look at what *fundamental fairness* requires in each case. Dissenting Justices Black and Douglas, however, countered that that standard was no improvement over the theory of selective incorporation; it was as ambiguous as other natural law formulations in giving the Court unbridled power. For that reason, along with his own reading of the history of the Fourteenth Amendment, Black continued to press for total incorporation. The two other dissenters in *Adamson*, Justices Frank Murphy and Wiley Rutledge, went further in advancing an even broader libertarian position, that of *total incorporation plus* other any other fundamental rights not enumerated in the Bill of Rights.

In response to Justice Black's criticisms, Justice Frankfurter in *Rochin v. California* (1952) (see page 303), invented a "shocks-the-conscience" test for determining when police practices violate the due process clause. Yet as Black pointed out, it was no less subjective or unproblematic in application. Two years after *Rochin*, in Chief Justice Earl Warren's first term, the Court again relied on the test. But in *Irvine v. California*, 347 U.S. 128 (1954), the majority failed to find police bugging of an entire house for over a month, without obtaining a search warrant, to either violate the Fourth Amendment or shock their consciences.

The Warren Court remained until the 1960s split between Frankfurter's approach and Black's insistence on total incorporation. That intellectual struggle would not be decisively settled until the Court's composition changed. In *Mapp v. Ohio*, 367 U.S. 643 (1961) (see Chapter 7), the Court finally agreed to extend to the states the Fourth Amendment's exclusionary rule, requiring that illegally obtained evidence be excluded from use at trial. Then the following year Justices Frankfurter and Whittaker retired. With their replacements, Justices Byron White and Arthur Goldberg, there was finally a solid majority supporting the nationalization of the major guarantees of the Bill of Rights.

By the end of Chief Justice Warren's tenure in 1969, nearly all of the guarantees of the Bill of Rights were applied to the states. In addition, in *Griswold v. Connecticut*, (1965) (see page 308), the Court created out of whole constitutional cloth a right of privacy, which Justice Douglas found in the penumbras, or shadows, of the First, Third, Fourth, Fifth, and Ninth Amendments, and made applicable to the states by the Fourteenth Amendment. While joining the decision announced in Douglas's opinion, concurring Justice Goldberg, joined by Chief Justice Warren and Justice Brennan, stakes out yet another theory of incorporation—that of *selective incorporation plus* other fundamental yet unenumerated rights. The Court in *Griswold* went too

---

CONSTITUTIONAL HISTORY
Guarantees of the Bill of Rights That Have Not Been Applied to the States

Second Amendment "right of the people to keep and bear Arms."
Third Amendment limitation on the quartering of soldiers in a person's house.
Fifth Amendment right to indictment by a grand jury.
Seventh Amendment right to a jury trial in civil cases.
Eighth Amendment right against excessive fines and bail.

---

far for Justices Black and Stewart. In dissent, Black again warns that whenever the justices substitute their own interpretative language for that of the Constitution, they threaten to become "a day-to-day constitutional convention."

The controversy over the nationalization of the Bill of Rights continues. The divisions among the justices are further evident in the opinions issued in *Duncan v. Louisiana* (1968) (see page 319). This ruling held that defendants charged in state courts with serious crimes are entitled to a trial by jury under the Sixth Amendment. Subsequently, the Burger Court in *Williams v. Florida*, 399 U.S. 78 (1970) (see Chapter 9) and *Apodaca v. Oregon*, 406 U.S. 404 (1972), respectively, ruled, that despite *Duncan*, states were free to use juries composed of less than the traditional twelve jurors, and to depart from the requirement that juries reach unanimous verdicts. In other areas, the more conservative Burger and Rehnquist Courts cut back and shifted the direction in which the Warren Court had pushed constitutional in nationalizing the Bill of Rights.[6]

The Court's interpretative politics changed in the 1970s and 1980s with its changing composition. The Court's rulings extending to the states the rights of the accused afforded in the Bill of Rights made for a larger struggle in constitutional politics. They effectively raised the issue of "law and order" and "crime control" to the national political agenda as well. During their presidential campaigns, Richard Nixon, Ronald Reagan, and George Bush effectively criticized the Court for being soft on criminals. Subsequently, they appointed more conservative justices, which in turn changed the internal dynamics of the Court. The Rehnquist Court, though, appears unlikely to turn back the constitutional clock on the incorporation of the Bill of Rights. Rather than disincorporate those guarantees, the Court (as further discussed in later chapters) has limited their reach and carved out exceptions for state compliance with the commands of the Bill of Rights.[7]

CONSTITUTIONAL HISTORY

Approaches to Nationalization of the Bill of Rights under the Fourteenth Amendment

Total incorporation of all guarantees—Justice Harlan's opinion, dissenting in *Hurtado v. California* (1884).

Selective incorporation of "preferred freedoms" and those rights "implicit in the concept of ordered liberty"—Justice Benjamin Cardozo's opinion in *Palko v. Connecticut* (1937).

Fundamental fairness and the selective application on a case-by-case basis—Justice Felix Frankfurter, concurring in *Adamson v. California* (1947).

Total incorporation plus other fundamental rights not expressly granted in the Bill of Rights—Justice Frank Murphy and Wiley Rutledge, dissenting in *Adamson v. California* (1947).

Selective incorporation plus other fundamental rights not expressly granted in the Bill of Rights—Justices Arthur Goldberg, Chief Justice Earl Warren, and Justice William J. Brennan, concurring in *Griswold v. Connecticut* (1965).

NOTES

1. *Congressional Globe,* 39th Cong., 1st sess., 1865–1866, 2765.

2. For further discussion see, Howard J. Graham, "The 'Conspiracy Theory' of the Fourteenth Amendment," 47 *Yale Law Journal* 371 (1938); and Walter F. Murphy, "Constitutional Interpretation: The Art of the Historian, Magician, or Statesman?" 87 *Yale Law Journal* 1752 (1978).

3. Besides the cases discussed and reprinted here see, Felix Frankfurter, "Memorandum on 'Incorporation' of the Bill of Rights into the Due Process Clause of the Fourteenth Amendment," 78 *Harvard Law Review* 746 (1965); Charles Fairman, "Does the Fourteenth Amendment Incorporate the Bill of Rights?" 2 *Stanford Law Review* 1 (1949); Charles Fairman, "A Reply to Professor Crosskey," 22 *University of Chicago Law Review* 145 (1954); Raoul Berger, *Government by Judiciary: The Transformation of the Fourteenth Amendment* (Cambridge, MA: Harvard University Press, 1977).

4. See Hugo Black, "The Bill of Rights," 35 *New York University Law Review* 865 (1960); Alfred Avins, "Incorporation of the Bill of Rights: The Crosskey-Fairman Debates Revisited," 6 *Harvard Journal on Legislation* 1 (1968); William Crosskey, "Charles Gariman, 'Legislative History,' and the Constitutional Limitations on State Authority," 22 *University*

of *Chicago Law Review* 1 (1954); Horace Flack, *The Adoption of the Fourteenth Amendment* (Baltimore, MD: Johns Hopkins University Press, 1908); and Jacobus tenBroek, *Equal Under Law* (London: Collier Books, 1965).

5. John Hart Ely, *Democracy and Distrust: A Theory of Judicial Review* (Cambridge, MA: Harvard University Press, 1981), 27.

6. See, for example, *Argersinger v. Hamlin,* 407 U.S. 25 (1972) in Chapter 9.

7. However, see Rehnquist's dissenting opinion in *Wallace v. Jaffree,* 472 U.S. 38 (1985) (see Chapter 6). raising questions about the Court's extension of the First Amendment establishment clause to the states.

SELECTED BIBLIOGRAPHY

Berger, Roaul. *Government by Judiciary: The Transformation of the Fourteenth Amendment.* Cambridge, MA: Harvard University Press, 1977.

Cortner, Richard C. *The Supreme Court and the Second Bill of Rights: The Fourteenth Amendment and the Nationalization of Civil Liberties.* Madison: University of Wisconsin Press, 1981.

Flack, Horace. *The Adoption of the Fourteenth Amendment.* Baltimore, MD: Johns Hopkins University Press, 1908.

Graham, Howard. *Everyman's Constitution: Historical Essays on the Fourteenth Amendment, the "Conspiracy Theory," and American Constitutionalism.* Madison, WI: State Historical Society of Madison, 1968.

Israel, Jerold H. "Selective Incorporation: Revisited." 71 *Georgetown Law Journal* 253 (1982).

tenBroek, Jacobus. *The Antislavery Origins of the Fourteenth Amendment.* Berkeley: University of California Press, 1951.

Barron v. The Mayor and City of Baltimore
7 Pet. (32 U.S.) 243, 8 L.Ed. 672 (1833)

John Barron inherited and was coowner of a wharf in the eastern harbor of Baltimore. The wharf had been highly profitable because it was surrounded by some of the deepest water in the harbor. But city improvements (the diversion of certain streams and the paving of streets) resulted in large deposits of sand accumulating around the wharf. The waters became too shallow for ships to gain access to the wharf and Barron faced a major financial loss.

Barron sued the mayor and city council of Baltimore for damages in county court. He did so on the grounds that the Fifth Amendment forbid the states as well as the national government from taking private property for public use without just compensation. The trial court agreed and awarded Barron $4,500 in damages. That decision was reversed by an appellate court, and Barron appealed to the Supreme Court. When Barron's attorney appeared before the high bench, Chief Justice Marshall asked him to confine his argument to whether the Fifth Amendment was applicable to the states and thus gave the Court jurisdiction over the case. After hearing his arguments, the chief justice announced that the Court need not bother hearing the attorneys representing the city of Baltimore. Shortly thereafter Chief Justice Marshall announced the unanimous decision of the Court.

Chief Justice MARSHALL delivers the opinion of the court.

The question thus presented is, we think, of great importance, but not of much difficulty.

The Constitution was ordained and established by the people of the United States for themselves, for their own government, and not for the government of the individual States. Each State established a constitution for itself, and in that constitution provided such limitations and restrictions on the powers of its particular government as its judgment dictated. The people of the United States framed such a government for the United States as they supposed best adapted to their situation, and best calculated to promote their interests. The powers they conferred on this government were to be exercised by itself; and the limitations on power, if expressed in general terms, are naturally, and, we think, necessarily applicable to the government created by the instrument. They are limitations of power granted in the instrument itself; not of distinct governments, framed by different persons and for different purposes.

If these propositions be correct, the fifth amendment must be understood as restraining the power of the general government, not as applicable to the States. In their several constitutions they have imposed such restrictions on their respective governments as their own wisdom suggested; such as they deemed most proper for themselves. It is a subject on which they judge exclusively, and with which others interfere no farther than they are supposed to have a common interest.

The counsel for the plaintiff in error insists that the Constitution was intended to secure the people of the several States against the undue exercise of power by their respective State governments; as well as against that which might be attempted by their general government. In support of this argument he relies on the inhibitions contained in the tenth section of the first article.

We think that section affords a strong if not a conclusive argument in support of the opinion already indicated by the court.

The preceding section contains restrictions which are obviously intended for the exclusive purpose of restraining the exercise of power by the departments of the general government. Some of them use language applicable only to Congress, others are expressed in general terms. The third clause, for example, declares that "no bill of attainder or ex post facto law shall be passed." No language can be more general; yet the demonstration is complete that it applies solely to the government of the United States. . . .

If the original Constitution, in the ninth and tenth sections of the first article, draws this plain and marked line of discrimination between the limitations it imposes on the powers of the general government and on those of the States; if in every inhibition intended to act on State power, words are employed which directly express that intent, some strong reason must be assigned for departing from this safe and judicious course in framing the amendments, before that departure can be assumed.

We search in vain for that reason. . . .

Had the framers of these amendments intended them to be limitations on the powers of the State governments they would have imitated the framers of the original Constitution, and have expressed that intention. Had Congress engaged in the extraordinary occupation of improving the constitutions of the several States by affording the people additional protection from the exercise of power by their own governments in matters which concerned themselves alone, they would have declared this purpose in plain and intelligible language.

But it is universally understood, it is a part of the history of the day, that the great revolution which established the Constitution of the United States was not effected without immense opposition. Serious fears were extensively entertained that those powers which the patriot statesmen who then watched over the interests of our country, deemed essential to union, and to the attainment of those invaluable objects for which union was sought, might be exercised in a manner dangerous to liberty. In almost every convention by which the Constitution was adopted, amendments to guard against the abuse of power were recommended. These amendments demanded security against the apprehended encroachments of the general government—not against those of the local governments.

In compliance with a sentiment thus generally expressed, to quiet fears thus extensively entertained, amendments were proposed by the required majority in Congress, and adopted by the States. These amendments contain no expression indicating an intention to apply them to the State governments. This court cannot so apply them.

We are of opinion that the provision in the fifth amendment to the Constitution, declaring that private property shall not be taken for public use without just compensation, is intended solely as a limitation on the exercise of power by the government of the United States, and is not applicable to the legislation of the States. . . .

This court, therefore, has no jurisdiction of the cause, and is dismissed.

The Slaughterhouse Cases
16 Wall. (83 U.S.) 36, 21 L.Ed. 394 (1873)

See Chapter 3, where these cases are discussed (page 227) and reprinted (page 240), in part.

Hurtado v. California
110 U.S. 516, 4 S.Ct. 111 (1884)

On Saturday, February 4, 1882, Joseph Hurtado assaulted Jose Estuardo in a saloon brawl in Sacramento, California. He was arrested and scheduled for trial the following Monday. But the city attorney was unable to appear, the trial was postponed, and Hurtado released. He headed for a nearby bar. Later, Hurtado saw Estuardo approaching the bar and walked out and shot him in the chest. As Estuardo tried to flee, Hurtado shot him again in the back, and a third time as Estuardo lay on the ground. Hurtado was arrested and subsequently tried and convicted for murder, and sentenced to death.

If Hurtado had been tried in federal court, he would have been indicted by a grand jury before being tried for his crime. The Fifth Amendment requires indictment by a grand jury before a person accused of a capital offense may be tried. By contrast, the California Constitution of 1879 provided that prosecutions of criminal defendants could proceed on a prosecutor's filing a statement of information (a formal statement of accusation of the crimes committed, but not submitted to a grand jury). On appeal, Hurtado's attorney challenged the constitutionality of this procedure as a violation of the Fifth Amendment and the due process clause of the Fourteenth Amendment. After two state courts upheld his conviction, Hurtado petitioned the Supreme Court for a writ of error, claiming that the state had denied him of his rights under the Bill of Rights. But the justices rejected that plea, only Justice Harlan dissented.

Justice MATTHEWS delivers the opinion of the Court.

It is claimed on behalf of the prisoner that the conviction and sentence are void, on the ground that they are repugnant to that clause of the fourteenth article of amendment to the constitution of the United States, which is in these words: "Nor shall any state deprive any person of life, liberty, or property without due process of law." The proposition of law we are asked to affirm is that an indictment or presentment by a grand jury, as known to the common law of England, is essential to that "due process of law," when applied to prosecutions for felonies, which is secured and guaranteed by this provision of the constitution of the United States, and which accordingly it is forbidden to the states, respectively, to dispense with in the administration of criminal law. . . .

[I]t is maintained that the phrase "due process of law" is equivalent to "law of the land," as found in the twenty-ninth chapter of *Magna Charta;* that by immemorial usage it has acquired a fixed, definite, and technical meaning; that it refers to and includes, not only the general principles of public liberty and private right, which lie at the foundation of all free government, but the very institutions which, venerable by time and custom, have been tried by experience and found fit and necessary for the preservation of those principles, and which, having been the birthright and inheritance of every English subject, crossed the Atlantic with the colonists and were transplanted and established in the fundamental laws of the state; that, having been originally introduced into the constitution of the United States as a limitation upon the powers of the government, brought into being by that instrument, it has now been added as an additional security to the individual against oppression by the states themselves; that one of these institutions is that of the grand jury, an indictment or presentment by which against the accused in cases of alleged felonies is an essential part of due process of law, in order that he may not be harassed and destroyed by prosecutions founded only upon private malice or popular fury.

It is urged upon us, however, in argument, that the claim made in behalf of the plaintiff in error is supported by the decision of this court in *Murray's Lessee v. Hoboken Land & Imp. Co.* [18 How. (59 U.S.) 272 (1856)]. There, Justice CURTIS, delivering the opinion of the court, after showing that due process of law must mean something more than the actual existing law of the land, for otherwise it would be no restraint upon legislative power, proceeds as follows: "To what principle, then, are we to resort to ascertain whether this process, enacted by congress, is due process? To this the answer must be twofold. We must examine the constitution itself to see whether this process be in conflict with any of its provisions. If not found to be so, we must look to those settled usages and modes of proceeding existing in the common and statute law of England before the emigration of our ancestors, and which are shown not to have been unsuited to their civil and political condition by having been acted on by them after the settlement of this country.". . .

We are to construe this phrase in the fourteenth amendment by the *usus loquendi* of the constitution itself. The same words are contained in the fifth amendment. That article makes specific and express provision for perpetuating the institution of the grand jury, so far as relates to prosecutions for the more aggravated crimes under the laws of the United States. It declares that "no person shall be held to answer for a capital or otherwise infamous crime, unless on a presentment or indictment of a grand jury, except in cases arising in the land or naval forces, or in the militia when in actual service in time of war or public danger; nor shall any person be subject for the same offense to be twice put in jeopardy of life or limb; nor shall he be compelled in any criminal case to be a witness against himself." It then immediately adds: "nor be deprived of life, liberty, or property without due process of law." According to a recognized canon of interpretation, especially applicable to formal and solemn instruments of constitutional law, we are forbidden to assume, without clear reason to the contrary, that any part of this most important amendment is superfluous. The natural and obvious inference is that, in the sense of the constitution, "due process of law" was not meant or intended to include, *ex vi termini,* the institution and procedure of a grand jury in any case. The conclusion is equally irresistible, that when the same phrase was employed in the fourteenth amendment to restrain the action of the states, it was used in the same sense and with no greater extent; and that if in the adoption of that amendment it had been part of its purpose to perpetuate the institution of the grand jury in all the states, it would have embodied, as did the fifth amendment, express declarations to that effect. Due process of law in the latter refers to that law of the land which derives its authority from the legislative powers conferred upon congress by the constitution of the United States, exercised within the limits therein prescribed, and interpreted according to the principles of the common law. In the fourteenth amendment, by parity of reason, it refers to that law of the land in each state which derives its authority from the inherent and reserved powers of the state, exerted within the limits of those fundamental principles of liberty and justice which lie at the base of all our civil and political institutions.

But it is not to be supposed that these legislative powers are absolute and despotic, and that the amendment prescribing due process of law is too vague and indefinite to operate as a practical restraint. It is not every act, legislative in form, that is law. Law is something more than mere will exerted as an act of power. It must be not a special rule for a particular person or a particular case, but, in the language of Mr. Webster, in his familiar definition, "the general law, a law which hears before it condemns, which proceeds upon inquiry, and renders judgment only after trial," so "that every citizen shall hold his life, liberty, property, and immunities under the protection of the general rules which govern society," and thus excluding, as not due process of law, acts of attainder, bills of pains and penalties, acts of confiscation, acts reversing judgments, and acts directly transferring one man's estate to another, legislative judgments and decrees, and other similar special, partial, and arbitrary exertions of power under the forms of legislation. Arbitrary power, enforcing its edicts to the injury of the persons and property of its subjects, is not law, whether manifested as the decree of a personal monarch or of an impersonal multitude. And the limitations imposed by our constitutional law upon the action of the governments, both state and national, are essential to the preservation of public and private rights, notwithstanding the representative character of our political institutions. The enforcement of these limitations by judicial process is the device of self-governing communities to protect the rights of individuals and minorities, as well against the power of numbers, as against the violence of public agents transcending the limits of lawful authority, even when acting in the name and wielding the force of the government. . . .

Tried by these principles, we are unable to say that the substitution for a presentment or indictment by a grand jury of the proceeding by information after examination and commitment by a magistrate, certifying to the probable guilt of the defendant, with the right on his part to the aid of counsel, and to the cross-examination of the witnesses produced for the prosecution, is not due process of law. It is, as we have seen, an ancient proceeding at common law, which might include every case of an offense of less grade than a felony, except misprision of treason; and in every circumstance of its administration, as authorized by the statute of California, it carefully considers and guards the substantial interest of the prisoner. It is merely a preliminary proceeding, and can result in no final judgment, except as the consequence of a regular judicial trial, conducted precisely as in cases of indictments. . . .

For these reasons, finding no error therein, the judgment of the supreme court of California is affirmed.

Justice HARLAN dissenting.

It seems to me that too much stress is put upon the fact that the framers of the Constitution made express provision for the security of those rights which at common law were protected by the requirement of due process of law, and, in addition, declared, generally, that no person shall "be deprived of life, liberty or property without due process of law." The rights, for the security of which these express provisions were made, were of a character so essential to the safety of the people that it was deemed wise to avoid the possibility that Congress, in regulating the processes of law, would impair or destroy them. Hence, their specific enumeration in the earlier amendments of the Constitution, in connection with the general requirement of due process of law, the latter itself being broad enough to cover every right of life, liberty or property secured by the settled usages and modes of proceeding existing under the common and statute law of England at the time our government was founded. . . .

[I]t is a fact of momentous interest in this discussion, that, when the Fourteenth Amendment was submitted and adopted, the Bill of Rights and the constitutions of twenty-seven States expressly forbade criminal prosecutions, by information, for capital cases; while, in the remaining ten States, they were impliedly forbidden by a general clause declaring that no person should be deprived of life otherwise than by "the judgment of his peers or the law of the land," or "without due process of law." It may be safely affirmed that, when that Amendment was adopted, a criminal prosecution, by information, for a crime involving life, was not permitted in any one of the States composing the Union. So that the court, in this case, while conceding that the requirement of due process of law protects the fundamental principles of liberty and justice, adjudges, in effect, that an immunity or right, recognized at the common law to be essential to personal security, jealously guarded by our national Constitution against violation by any tribunal or body exercising authority under the general government, and expressly or impliedly recognized, *when the Fourteenth Amendment was adopted,* in the Bill of Rights or Constitution of every State in the Union, is, yet, not a fundamental principle in governments established, as those of the States of the Union are, to secure to the citizen liberty and justice, and, therefore, is not involved in that due process of law required in proceedings conducted under the sanction of a State. My sense of duty constrains me to dissent from this interpretation of the supreme law of the land.

Justice FIELD did not participate in the decision of this case.

Roughly one year before his death, Justice Cardozo (left) joined Chief Justice Charles Evans Hughes at the opening session of the American Law Institute's annual meeting in 1937. Justice Cardozo's opinion in *Palko v. Connecticut* (1937) set the stage for the Court's selective nationalization of the Bill of Rights. Chief Justice Hughes is regarded as one of the best chief justices in the twentieth century. During his tenure as chief justice (1930–1941), the Court survived FDR's Court-packing plan and made the "shift in time that saved nine" in 1937 and gradually assumed a vote as a guardian of civil liberties and civil rights. *Collection of the Supreme Court of the United States.*

Palko v. Connecticut
302 U.S. 319, 58 S.Ct. 149 (1937)

Frank Jacob Palko was a man wanted for killing two police officers in Bridgeport, Connecticut, in September 1935. He had been stopped by them for questioning about the burglary of a music store and when confronted shot them both and then escaped. A month later, he was arrested in New York and confessed to the Bridgeport murders. Plako was subsequently indicted by a grand jury on the charge of first-degree premeditated murder; tried before a jury, which found him guilty of second-degree murder; and sentenced to life imprisonment.

After his trial, the prosecution persisted in seeking the death penalty and appealed Palko's trial and sentence. Under Connecticut law, a criminal sentence could be appealed by the state if the trial judge made errors prejudicial to the prosecution and the judge granted his permission for an appeal. The prosecution objected to the judge's orders forbidding the use of Palko's confession as evidence and of certain questioning during the trial, as well as the judge's characterization of what constitutes premeditated murder in his instructions to the jury on the difference between first- and second-degree murder. The state supreme court of errors agreed the trial judge had erred, reversed Palko's conviction, and ordered a retrial.

At Palko's second trial, his attorney objected that retrial violated the Fifth Amendment guarantee against holding a person in double jeopardy for the same offense. The trial judge overruled that objection. Palko was convicted for first-degree murder and sentenced to be electrocuted. After unsuccessfully appealing to the state supreme court, Palko's attorney petitioned the Supreme Court. In claiming that Palko's retrial violated the double jeopardy clause of the Fifth Amendment, he argued that historical evidence showed that the Bill of Rights were applicable to the states under the Fourteenth Amendment. Once again the Court rejected that argument, with only Justice Pierce Butler dissenting without filing an opinion.

Justice CARDOZO delivers the opinion of the Court.

The . . . appellant [contends] that whatever is forbidden by the Fifth Amendment is forbidden by the Fourteenth also. The Fifth Amendment, which is not directed to the States, but solely to the federal government, creates immunity from double jeopardy. No person shall be "subject for the same offense to be twice put in jeopardy of life or limb." The Fourteenth Amendment ordains, "nor shall any State deprive any person of life, liberty, or property, without due process of law." To retry a defendant, though under one indictment and only one, subjects him, it is said, to double jeopardy in violation of the Fifth Amendment, if the prosecution is one on behalf of the United States. From this the consequence is said to follow that there is a denial of life or liberty without due process of law, if the prosecution is one on behalf of the people of a state. . . .

We have said that in appellant's view the Fourteenth Amendment is to be taken as embodying the prohibitions of the Fifth. His thesis is even broader. Whatever would be a violation of the original bill of rights (Amendments 1 to 8) if done by the federal government is now equally unlawful by force of the Fourteenth Amendment if done by a state. There is no such general rule.

The Fifth Amendment provides, among other things, that no person shall be held to answer for a capital or otherwise infamous crime unless on presentment or indictment of a grand jury. This court has held that, in prosecutions by a state, presentment or indictment by a grand jury may give way to informations at the instance of a public officer. *Hurtado v. California,* 110 U.S. 516 [1884]. The Fifth Amendment provides also that no person shall be compelled in any criminal case to be a witness against himself. This court has said that, in prosecutions by a state, the exemption will fail if the state elects to end it. The Sixth Amendment calls for a jury trial in criminal cases and the Seventh for a jury trial in civil cases at common law where the value in controversy shall exceed $20. This court has ruled that consistently with those amendments trial by jury may be modified by a state or abolished altogether. . . .

On the other hand, the due process clause of the Fourteenth Amendment may make it unlawful for a state to abridge by its statutes the freedom of speech which the First Amendment safeguards against encroachment by the Congress (*De Jonge v. Oregon,* 299 U.S. 353 [1937]) or the like freedom of the press (*Grosjean v. American Press Co.,* 297 U.S. 233 [1936]; *Near v. Minnesota,* 283 U.S. 697 [1931]), or the free exercise of religion (*Hamilton v. Regents of University,* 293 U.S. 245 [1934]), or the right of peaceable assembly, without which speech would be unduly trammeled . . . or the right of one accused of crime to the benefit of counsel (*Powell v. Alabama,* 287 U.S. 45 [1932]). In these and other situations immunities that are valid as against the federal government by force of the specific pledges of particular amendments have been found to be implicit in the concept of ordered liberty, and thus, through the Fourteenth Amendment, become valid as against the states.

The line of division may seem to be wavering and broken if there is a hasty catalogue of the cases on the one side and the other. Reflection and analysis will induce a different view. There emerges the perception of a rationalizing principle which gives to discrete instances a proper order and coherence. The right to trial by jury and the immunity from prosecution except as the result of an indictment may have value and importance. Even so, they are not of the very essence of a scheme of ordered liberty. To abolish them is not to violate a "principle of justice so rooted in the traditions and conscience of our people as to be ranked as fundamental." What is true of jury trials and indictments is true also, as the cases show, of the immunity from compulsory self-incrimination. *Twining v. New Jersey* [211 U.S. 78 (1908)]. This too might be lost, and justice still be done. . . .

We reach a different plane of social and moral values when we pass to the privileges and immunities that have been taken over from the earlier articles of the Federal Bill of Rights and brought within the Fourteenth Amendment by a process of absorption. These in their origin were effective against the federal government alone. If the Fourteenth Amendment has absorbed them, the process of absorption has had its source in the belief that neither liberty nor justice would exist if they were sacrificed. This is true, for illustration, of freedom of thought and speech. Of that freedom one may say that it is the matrix, the indispensable condition, of nearly every other form of freedom. With rare aberrations a pervasive recognition of that truth can be traced in our history, political and legal. So it has come about that the domain of liberty, withdrawn by the Fourteenth Amendment from encroachment by the states, has been enlarged by latter-day judgments to include liberty of the mind as well as liberty of action. The extension became, indeed, a logical imperative when once it was recognized, as long ago it was, that liberty is something more than exemption from physical restraint, and that even in the field of substantive rights and duties the legislative judgment, if oppressive and arbitrary, may be overridden by the courts. Fundamental too in the concept of due process, and so in that of liberty, is the thought that condemnation shall be rendered only after trial. The hearing, moreover, must be a real one, not a sham or a pretense. For that reason, ignorant defendants in a capital case were held to have been condemned unlawfully when in truth, though not in form, they were refused the aid of counsel. *Powell v. Alabama.* The decision did not turn upon the fact that the benefit of counsel would have been guaranteed to the defendants by the provisions of the Sixth Amendment if they had been prosecuted in a federal court. The decision turned upon the fact that in the particular situation laid before us in the evidence the benefit of counsel was essential to the substance of a hearing.

Our survey of the cases serves, we think, to justify the statement that the dividing line between them, if not unfaltering throughout its course, has been true for the most part to a unifying principle. On which side of the line the case made out by the appellant has appropriate location must be the next inquiry and the final one. Is that kind of double jeopardy to which the statute has subjected him a hardship so acute and shocking that our polity will not endure it? Does it violate those "fundamental principles of liberty and justice which lie at the base of all our civil and political institutions"? The answer surely must be "no." What the answer would have to be if the state were permitted after a trial free from error to try the accused over again or to bring another case against him, we have no occasion to consider. We deal with the statute before us and no other. The state is not attempting to wear the accused out by a multitude of cases with accumulated trials. It asks no more than this, that the case against him shall go on until there shall be a trial free from the corrosion of substantial legal error. This is not cruelty at all, nor even vexation in any immoderate degree. . . .

The judgment is affirmed.

Justice BUTLER dissented.

Adamson v. California
332 U.S. 46, 67 S.Ct. 1672 (1947)

Admiral Dewey Adamson, a forty-three-year-old black man with a prior criminal record, was arrested and tried for breaking into the Los Angeles apartment of a sixty-four-year-old widow and then murdering her. At his trial, Adamson refused to testify in his own defense because of his prior criminal record. If he had, the prosecution could impeach his credibility as a witness based on his previous convictions for robbery and burglary. The Fifth Amendment guarantees the accused a right against self-incrimination and being "compelled in any criminal case to be a witness against himself." But California's state constitution permitted prosecutors to comment on a defendant's failure to testify. At Adamson's trial, the district attorney told the jury that Adamson's refusal to testify stripped him of a presumption of innocence. He told the jury in summation, "Counsel asked you to find this defendant not guilty. But does the Defendant get on the stand and say, under oath, 'I am not guilty'? Not one word from him, and not one word from a single witness. I leave the case in your hands." The jury convicted Adamson on both counts. He was sentenced, as a habitual criminal, to life imprisonment on the burglary count and to death in the gas chamber on the murder count. Adamson's attorney appealed unsuccessfully to the state supreme court and then to the Supreme Court.

Adamson's attorney asked the Supreme Court to strike down California's law permitting prosecutorial comment. It penalized the defendant for exercising his Fifth Amendment rights which, he also argued, were applicable to the states under the Fourteenth Amendment's privileges or immunities clause and due process clause. That meant overturning *Twining v. New Jersey*, 211 U.S. 78 (1908), which upheld New Jersey's practice of allowing juries to draw unfavorable inferences from a defendant's failure to testify. But Adamson's attorney urged the Court to reconsider and adopt dissenting Justice Harlan's opinion there and in *Hurtado*. At conference, the justices voted five to three to affirm

Adamson's conviction, with Justice Black initially passing because he was unsure prosecutorial comments violated the Fifth Amendment, although he was certain that the amendment and others of the Bill of Rights should apply to the states. In the end, Black joined the dissenters writing one of his major opinions disputing the majority's reading of the history and purposes of the Bill of Rights and the Fourteenth Amendment. Justice Reed's opinion for the majority paid little attention to privileges or immunities claim and concentrated instead on the due process claim.

Justice REED delivers the opinion of the Court.

[The appellant contends that] the due process clause of the Fourteenth Amendment protects his privilege against self-incrimination. The due process clause of the Fourteenth Amendment, however, does not draw all the rights of the federal Bill of Rights under its protection. That contention was made and rejected in *Palko v. Connecticut* [302 U.S. 319 (1937)]. Palko held that such provisions of the Bill of Rights as were "implicit in the concept of ordered liberty" became secure from state interference by the clause. But it held nothing more. . . .

For a state to require testimony from an accused is not necessarily a breach of a state's obligation to give a fair trial. Therefore, we must examine the effect of the California law applied in this trial to see whether the comment on failure to testify violates the protection against state action that the due process clause does grant to an accused. The due process clause forbids compulsion to testify by fear of hurt, torture or exhaustion. It forbids any other type of coercion that falls within the scope of due process. California follows Anglo-American legal tradition in excusing defendants in criminal prosecutions from compulsory testimony. That is a matter of legal policy and not because of the requirements of due process under the Fourteenth Amendment. So our inquiry is directed, not at the broad question of the constitutionality of compulsory testimony from the accused under the due process clause, but to the constitutionality of the provision of the California law that permits comment upon his failure to testify. . . .

Generally, comment on the failure of an accused to testify is forbidden in American jurisdictions. . . . California, however, is one of a few states that permit limited comment upon a defendant's failure to testify. That permission is narrow. . . . This does not involve any presumption, rebuttable or irrebuttable, either of guilt or of the truth of any fact, that is offered in evidence.

It allows inferences to be drawn from proven facts. Because of this clause, the court can direct the jury's attention to whatever evidence there may be that a defendant could deny and the prosecution can argue as to inferences that may be drawn from the accused's failure to testify. . . . California has prescribed a method for advising the jury in the search for truth. However sound may be the legislative conclusion that an accused should not be compelled in any criminal case to be a witness against himself, we see no reason why comment should not be made upon his silence. It seems quite natural that when a defendant has opportunity to deny or explain facts and determines not to do so, the prosecution should bring out the strength of the evidence by commenting upon defendant's failure to explain or deny it. The prosecution evidence may be of facts that may be beyond the knowledge of the accused. If so, his failure to testify would have little if any weight. But the facts may be such as are necessarily in the knowledge of the accused. In that case a failure to explain would point to an inability to explain.

Justice FRANKFURTER concurring.

For historical reasons a limited immunity from the common duty to testify was written into the Federal Bill of Rights, and I am prepared to agree that, as part of that immunity, comment on the failure of an accused to take the witness stand as forbidden in federal prosecutions. . . .

But to suggest that such a limitation can be drawn out of "due process" in its protection of ultimate decency in a civilized society is to suggest that the Due Process Clause fastened fetters of unreason upon the States. . . .

Between the incorporation of the Fourteenth Amendment into the Constitution and the beginning of the present membership of the Court—a period of 70 years—the scope of that Amendment was passed upon by 43 judges. Of all these judges, only one, who may respectfully be called an eccentric exception, ever indicated the belief that the Fourteenth Amendment was a shorthand summary of the first eight Amendments theretofore limiting only the Federal Government, and that due process incorporated those eight Amendments as restrictions upon the powers of the States. . . .

The notion that the Fourteenth Amendment was a covert way of imposing upon the States all the rules which it seemed important to Eighteenth Century statesmen to write into the Federal Amendments, was rejected by judges who were themselves witnesses of the process by which the Fourteenth Amendment became part of the Constitution. Arguments that may now be adduced to prove that the first eight Amendments were concealed within the historic phrasing of the Fourteenth Amendment were not unknown at the time of its adoption. A surer estimate of their bearing was possible for judges at the time than distorting distance is likely to vouchsafe. Any evidence of design or purpose not contemporaneously known could hardly have influenced those who ratified the Amendment. Remarks of a particular proponent of the Amendment, no matter how influential, are not to be deemed part of the Amendment. What was submitted for ratification was his proposal, not his speech. Thus, at the time of the ratification of the Fourteenth Amendment the constitutions of nearly half of the ratifying States did not have the rigorous requirements of the Fifth Amendment for instituting criminal proceedings through a grand jury. It could hardly have occurred to these States that by ratifying the Amendment they uprooted their established methods for prosecuting crime and fastened upon themselves a new prosecutorial system. . . .

It may not be amiss to restate the pervasive function of the Fourteenth Amendment in exacting from the States observance of basic liberties. The Amendment neither comprehends the specific provisions by which the founders deemed it appropriate to restrict the federal government nor is it confined to them. The Due Process Clause of the Fourteenth Amendment has an independent potency, precisely as does the Due Process Clause of the Fifth Amendment in relation to the Federal Government. It ought not to require argument to reject the notion that due process of law meant one thing in the Fifth Amendment and another in the Fourteenth. The Fifth Amendment specifically prohibits prosecution of an "infamous crime" except upon indictment; it forbids double jeopardy; it bars compelling a person to be a witness against himself in any criminal case; it precludes deprivation of "life, liberty, or property, without due process of law." Are Madison and his contemporaries in the framing of the Bill of Rights to be charged with writing into it a meaningless clause? To consider "due process of law" as merely a shorthand statement of other specific clauses in the same amendment is to attribute to the authors and proponents of this Amendment ignorance of, or indifference to, a historic conception which was one of the great instruments in the arsenal of constitutional freedom which the Bill of Rights was to protect and strengthen. . . .

And so, when, as in a case like the present, a conviction in a State court is here for review under a claim that a right protected by the Due Process Clause of the Fourteenth Amendment has been denied, the issue is not whether an infraction of one of the specific provisions of the first eight Amendments is disclosed by the record. The relevant question is whether the criminal proceedings which resulted in conviction deprived the accused of the due process of law to which the United States Constitution entitled him. Judicial review of that guaranty of the Fourteenth Amendment inescapably imposes upon this Court an exercise of judgment upon the whole course of the proceedings in order to ascertain whether they offend those canons of decency and fairness which express the notions of justice of English-speaking peoples even toward those charged with the most heinous offenses. These standards of justice are not authoritatively formulated anywhere as though they were prescriptions in a pharmacopoeia. But neither does the application of the Due Process Clause imply that judges are wholly at large. The judicial judgment in applying the Due Process Clause must move within the limits of accepted notions of justice and is not to be based upon the idiosyncrasies of a merely personal judgement.

Justice MURPHY, with whom Justice RUTLEDGE joins, dissenting.

While in substantial agreement with the views of Justice BLACK, I have one reservation and one addition to make.

I agree that the specific guarantees of the Bill of Rights should be carried over intact into the first section of the Fourteenth Amendment. But I am not prepared to say that the latter is entirely and necessarily limited by the Bill of Rights. Occasions may arise where a proceeding falls so far short of conforming to fundamental standards of procedure as to warrant constitutional condemnation in terms of a lack of due process despite the absence of a specific provision in the Bill of Rights.

Justice BLACK dissenting.

My study of the historical events that culminated in the Fourteenth Amendment, and the expressions of those who sponsored and favored, as well as those who opposed its submission and passage, persuades me that one of the chief objects that the provisions of the Amendment's first section, separately, and as a whole, were intended to accomplish was to make the Bill of Rights, applicable to the states. With full knowledge of the import of the *Barron* [*v. Baltimore* (1833)] decision, the framers and backers of the Fourteenth Amendment proclaimed its purpose to be to overturn the constitutional rule that case had announced. This historical purpose has never received full consideration or exposition in any opinion of this Court interpreting the Amendment. . . .

For this reason, I am attaching to this dissent, an appendix which contains a resumé, by no means complete, of the Amendment's history. In my judgment that history conclusively demonstrates that the language of the first section of the Fourteenth Amendment, taken as a whole, was thought by those responsible for its submission to the people, and by those who opposed its submission, sufficiently explicit to guarantee that thereafter no state could deprive its citizens of the privileges and protections of the Bill of Rights. Whether this Court ever will, or whether it now should, in the light of past decisions, give full effect to what the Amendment was intended to accomplish is not necessarily essential to a decision here. However that may be, our prior decisions, including *Twining* [*v. New Jersey*, 211 U.S. 78 (1908)], do not prevent our carrying out that purpose, at least to the extent of making applicable to the states, not a mere part, as the Court has, but the full protection of the Fifth Amendment's provision against compelling evidence from an accused to convict him of crime. And I further contend that the "natural law" formula which the Court uses to reach its conclusion in this case should be abandoned as an incongruous excrescence on our Constitution. I believe that formula to be itself a violation of our Constitution, in that it subtly conveys to courts, at the expense of legislatures, ultimate power over public policies in fields where no specific provision of the Constitution limits legislative power. . . .

I cannot consider the Bill of Rights to be an outworn 18th Century "strait jacket" as the *Twining* opinion did. Its provisions may be thought outdated abstractions by some. And it is true that they were designed to meet ancient evils. But they are the same kind of human evils that have emerged from century to century wherever excessive power is sought by the few at the expense of the many. In my judgment the people of no nation can lose their liberty so long as a Bill of Rights like ours survives and its basic purposes are conscientiously interpreted, enforced and respected so as to afford continuous protection against old, as well as new, devices and practices which might thwart those purposes. I fear to see the consequences of the Court's practice of substituting its own concepts of decency and fundamental justice for the language of the Bill of Rights as its point of departure in interpreting and enforcing that Bill of Rights. If the choice must be between the selective process of the *Palko* decision applying some of the Bill of Rights to the States, or the *Twining* rule applying none of them, I would choose the *Palko* selective process. But rather than accept either of these choices, I would follow what I believe was the original purpose of the Fourteenth Amendment—to extend to all the people of the nation the complete protection of the Bill of Rights.

Justice DOUGLAS joined in this opinion.

Rochin v. California
342 U.S. 165, 72 S.Ct. 205 (1952)

Antonio Richard Rochin was sitting in his bedroom when three Los Angeles county deputy sheriffs crashed through the door, armed, without a search or arrest warrant. He quickly grabbed and swallowed two morphine capsules lying on a nightstand. The deputies immediately tried to force him to vomit the pills by choking and sticking their fingers down his throat. When that failed, they rushed Rochin to a hospital, where a doctor inserted a tube and an emetic solution down his throat. At that, he finally vomited the pills into a pail. Rochin was later charged, tried, and convicted for violating a state narcotics law. His conviction was upheld on appeal by a state appellate court, and the California State Supreme Court denied a further appeal. Rochin's attorney petitioned the Supreme Court on the ground that the police denied Rochin's rights under the Fourth and Fifth Amendments and the due process clause of the Fourteenth Amendment. The petition was granted and the Court reversed the two California State court rulings.

Justice FRANKFURTER delivers the opinion of the Court.

In our federal system the administration of criminal justice is predominantly committed to the care of the States. The power to define crimes belongs to Congress only as an appropriate means of carrying into execution its limited grant of legislative powers. U.S.Const. Art. I, § 8, cl. 18. Broadly speaking, crimes in the United States are what the laws of the individual States make them, subject to the limitations of Art. I, § 10, cl. 1, in the original Constitution, prohibiting bills of attainder and *ex post facto* laws, and of the Thirteenth and Fourteenth Amendments.

These limitations, in the main, concern not restrictions upon the powers of the States to define crime, except in the restricted area where federal authority has pre-empted the field, but restrictions upon the manner in which the States may enforce their penal codes. Accordingly, in reviewing a State criminal conviction under a claim of right guaranteed by the Due Process Clause of the Fourteenth Amendment, from which is derived the most far-reaching and most frequent federal basis of challenging State criminal justice, "we must be deeply mindful of the responsibilities of the States for the enforcement of criminal laws, and exercise with due humility our merely negative function in subjecting convictions from state courts to the very narrow scrutiny which the Due Process Clause of the Fourteenth Amendment authorizes." . . .

However, this Court too has its responsibility. Regard for the requirements of the Due Process Clause "inescapably imposes upon this Court an exercise of judgment upon the whole course of the proceedings [resulting in a conviction] in order to ascertain whether they offend those canons of decency and fairness which express the notions of justice of English-speaking peoples even toward those charged with the most heinous offenses." These standards of justice are not authoritatively formulated anywhere as though they were specifics. Due process of law is a summarized constitutional guarantee of respect for those personal immunities which, as Justice CARDOZO twice wrote for the Court, are "so rooted in the tradition and conscience of our people as to be ranked as fundamental," or are "implicit in the concept of ordered liberty." *Palko v. State of Connecticut* [302 U.S. 319 (1937)].

The Due Process Clause places upon this Court the duty of exercising a judgment, within the narrow confines of judicial power in reviewing State convictions, upon interests of society pushing in opposite directions.

Due process of law thus conceived is not to be derided as resort to a revival of "natural law." To believe that this judicial exercise of judgment could be avoided by freezing "due process of law" at some fixed stage of time or thought is to suggest that the most important aspect of constitutional adjudication is a function for inanimate machines and not for judges, for whom the independence safeguarded by Article III of the Constitution was designed and who are presumably guided by established standards of judicial behavior. Even cybernetics has not yet made that haughty claim. To practice the requisite detachment and to achieve sufficient objectivity no doubt demands of judges the habit of self-discipline and self-criticism, incertitude that one's own views are incontestable and alert tolerance toward views not shared. But these are precisely the presuppositions of our judicial process. They are precisely the qualities society has a right to expect from those entrusted with ultimate judicial power.

Restraints on our jurisdiction are self-imposed only in the sense that there is from our decisions no immediate appeal short of impeachment or constitutional amendment. But that does not make due process of law a matter of judicial caprice. The faculties of the Due Process Clause may be indefinite and vague, but the mode of their ascertainment is not self-willed. In each case "due process of law" requires an evaluation based on a disinterested inquiry pursued in the spirit of science, on a balanced order of facts exactly and fairly stated, on the detached consideration of conflicting claims, on a judgment not *ad hoc* and episodic but duly mindful of reconciling the needs both of continuity and of change in a progressive society.

Applying these general considerations to the circumstances of the present case, we are compelled to conclude that the proceedings by which this conviction was obtained do more than offend some fastidious squeamishness or private sentimentalism about combatting crime too energetically. This is conduct that shocks the conscience. Illegally breaking into the privacy of the petitioner, the struggle to open his mouth and remove what was there, the forcible extraction of his stomach's contents—this course of proceeding by agents of government to obtain evidence is bound to offend even hardened sensibilities. They are methods too close to the rack and the screw to permit of constitutional differentiation. . . .

On the facts of this case the conviction of the petitioner has been obtained by methods that offend the Due Process Clause. The judgment below must be reversed.

Reversed.

Justice MINTON did not participate in the consideration or decision of this case.

Justice BLACK concurring.

Adamson v. People of State of California, 332 U.S. 46 [1947], sets out reasons for my belief that state as well as federal courts and law enforcement officers must obey the Fifth Amendment's command that "No person . . . shall be compelled in any criminal case to be a witness against himself." I think a person is compelled to be a witness against himself not only when he is compelled to testify, but also when as here, incriminating evidence is forcibly taken from him by a contrivance of modern science. . . .

In the view of a majority of the Court, however, the Fifth Amendment imposes no restraint of any kind on the states. They nevertheless hold that California's use of this evidence violated the Due Process Clause of the Fourteenth Amendment. Since they hold as I do in this case, I regret my inability to accept their interpretation without protest. But I believe that faithful adherence to the specific guarantees in the Bill of Rights insures a more permanent protection of individual liberty than that which can be afforded by the nebulous standards stated by the majority.

What the majority hold is that the Due Process Clause empowers this Court to nullify any state law if its application "shocks the conscience," offends "a sense of justice" or runs counter to the "decencies of civilized conduct.". . . We are further admonished to measure the validity of state practices, not by our reason, or by the traditions of the legal profession, but by "the community's sense of fair play and decency"; by the "traditions and conscience of our people"; or by "those canons of decency and fairness which express the notions of justice of English-speaking peoples." These canons are made necessary, it is said, because of "interests of society pushing in opposite directions.". . .

[O]ne may well ask what avenues of investigation are open to discover "canons" of conduct so universally favored that this Court should write them into the Constitution? All we are told is that the discovery must be made by an evaluation based on a disinterested inquiry pursued in the spirit of science, on a balanced order of facts.". . .

I long ago concluded that the accordion-like qualities of this philosophy must inevitably imperil all the individual liberty safeguards specifically enumerated in the Bill of Rights.

Justice DOUGLAS concurring.

I think that words taken from [Rochin's] lips, capsules taken from his stomach, blood taken from his veins are all inadmissible provided they are taken from him without his consent. They are inadmissible because of the command of the Fifth Amendment.

That is an unequivocal, definite and workable rule of evidence for state and federal courts. But we cannot in fairness free the state courts from that command and yet excoriate them for flouting the "decencies of civilized conduct" when they admit the evidence. That is to make the rule turn not on the Constitution but on the idiosyncrasies of the judges who sit here.

INSIDE THE COURT
The Theory and Drafting of Justice Douglas's Opinion in *Griswold v. Connecticut*

After the justices' conference, Chief Justice Earl Warren assigned Justice Douglas the task of drafting an opinion to announce the Court's decision in *Griswold v. Connecticut*. His initial draft, however, did not develop the theory that a constitutional right of privacy was based on penumbrae of various guarantees of the Bill of Rights, as eventually announced in *Griswold*. Rather, Douglas sought to justify the decision based on earlier cases recognizing a First Amendment right of associational privacy. The analogy and precedents, he admitted, "do not decide this case. . . . Marriage does not fit precisely any of the categories of First Amendment rights. But it is a form of association as vital in the life of a man or a woman as any other, and perhaps more so."

Both Black and Brennan strongly objected to Douglas's extravagant reliance on First Amendment precedents. In a three-page letter, Brennan detailed an alternative approach, as the following excerpt indicates:

> I have read your draft opinion in *Griswold v. Connecticut*, and, while I agree with a great deal of it, I should like to suggest a substantial change in emphasis for your consideration. It goes without saying, of course, that your rejection of any approach based on *Lochner v. New York* is absolutely right. [In *Lochner*, a majority read into the Fourteenth Amendment a "liberty of contract" to strike down economic legislation. Although the Court later abandoned the doctrine of a liberty of contract, *Lochner* continues to symbolize the original sin of constitutional interpretation—that is, the Court's creation and enforcement of unenumerated rights.] And I agree that the association of husband and wife is not mentioned in the Bill of Rights, and that that is the obstacle we must hurdle to effect a reversal in this case.

> But I hesitate to bring the husband-wife relationship within the right to association we have constructed in the First Amendment context. . . . In the First Amendment context, in situations like *NAACP v. Alabama,* privacy is necessary to protect the capacity of an association for fruitful advocacy. In the present context, it seems to me that we are really interested in the privacy of married couples quite apart from any interest in advocacy. . . . Instead of expanding the First Amendment right of association to include marriage, why not say that what has been done for the First Amendment can also be done for some of the other fundamental guarantees of the Bill of Rights? In other words, where fundamentals are concerned, the Bill of Rights guarantees are but expressions or examples of those rights, and do not preclude applications or extensions of those rights to situations unanticipated by the Framers.

The restriction on the dissemination and use of contraceptives, Brennan explained, "would, on this reasoning, run afoul of a right to privacy created out of the Fourth Amendment and the self-incrimination clause of the Fifth, together with the Third, in much the same way as the right of association has been created out of the First. Taken together, those amendments indicate a fundamental concern with the sanctity of the home and the right of the individual to be alone." "With this change of emphasis," Brennan concluded, the opinion "would be most attractive to me because it would require less departure from the specific guarantees and because I think there is a better chance it will command a Court."

Douglas subsequently revised his opinion and based the right of privacy on the penumbrae of the First, Third, Fourth, Fifth, Ninth, and Fourteenth Amendments. In the end, his opinion was joined by only a plurality of the Court. Justice Goldberg, joined by Chief Justice Warren and Justice Brennan, wrote a separate concurring opinion, as did Justices Harlan and White. Justices Black and Stewart each wrote separate dissenting opinions.

Source: William J. Brennan, Jr., Letter of April 24, 1965, in William J. Brennan, Jr., Papers, Library of Congress.

Griswold v. Connecticut
391 U.S. 145, 85 S. Ct. 1678 (1968)

Estelle Griswold, executive director of the Planned Parenthood League of Connecticut, and Dr. C. Lee Buxton were part of a movement to repeal Connecticut's 1879 law prohibiting the dissemination of information about and the use of contraceptives. In the 1940s, after unsuccessfully seeking a repeal of the law by the state legislature, the league turned to the courts for a declaratory judgment finding the law unconstitutional. When the state supreme court upheld the law, a doctor appealed its ruling to the Supreme Court. In *Tileston v. Ullman*, 318 U.S. 44 (1943) (discussed in Chapter 2), however, the Court ruled that the doctor had no standing alone, without his patients, to challenge the constitutionality of the law under the Fourteenth Amendment. Almost twenty years later, Dr. Buxton and two of his female patients, both of whom had previously experienced difficult pregnancies, decided to again ask the Court for a declaratory judgment striking down the law. Once again, in *Poe v. Ullman*, 367 U.S. 497 (1961) (discussed in Chapter 2), a majority of the Court denied standing, largely because the law (with one exception) had gone unenforced for more than three-quarters of a century. But four justices dissented and the next year two of the justices in the majority, Justices Frankfurter and Whittaker, retired. Because Justice Frankfurter's opinion in *Poe* had stressed the unenforceability of the law, Griswold and Buxton decided that they would have to get arrested to gain standing to challenge Connecticut's law. They opened a birth control clinic, ten days later were arrested, and subsequently convicted in state courts. They thereupon made another appeal to the Supreme Court, which granted review.

Justice DOUGLAS delivers the opinion of the Court.

[W]e are met with a wide range of questions that implicate the Due Process Clause of the Fourteenth Amendment. Overtones of some arguments suggest that *Lochner v. State of New York*, 198 U.S. 45 [1905], should be our guide. But we decline that invitation as we did in *West Coast Hotel Co. v. Parrish*, 300 U.S. 379 [1937]; *Olsen v. State of Nebraska*, 313 U.S. 236 [1941]; *Lincoln Federal Labor Union v. Northwestern Co.*, 335 U.S. 525 [1949]; *Williamson v. Lee Optical Co.*, 348 U.S. 483 [1955]; [and] *Giboney v. Empire Storage Co.*, 336 U.S. 490 [1949]. We do not sit as a super-legislature to determine the wisdom, need, and propriety of laws that touch economic problems, business affairs, or social conditions. This law, however, operates directly on an intimate relation of husband and wife and their physician's role in one aspect of that relation.

The association of people is not mentioned in the Constitution nor in the Bill of Rights. The right to educate a child in a school of the parents' choice—whether public or private or parochial—is also not mentioned. Nor is the right to study any particular subject or any foreign language. Yet the First Amendment has been construed to include certain of those rights.

By *Pierce v. Society of Sisters*, [268 U.S. 510 (1925)], the right to educate one's children as one chooses is made applicable to the States by the force of the First and Fourteenth Amendments. By *Meyer v. State of Nebraska*, [262 U.S. 390 (1923)] the same dignity is given the right to study the German language in a private school. In other words, the State may not, consistently with the spirit of the First Amendment, contract the spectrum of available knowledge. The right of freedom of speech and press includes not only the right to utter or to print, but the right to distribute, the right to receive, the right to read; and freedom of inquiry, freedom of thought, and freedom to teach—indeed the freedom of the entire university community. *Sweezy v. State of New Hampshire*, 354 U.S. 234 [1957]. Without those peripheral rights the specific rights would be less secure. And so we reaffirm the principle of the Pierce and the Meyer cases.

In *NAACP v. State of Alabama* [357 U.S. 44 (1958)], we protected the "freedom to associate and privacy in one's associations," noting that freedom of association was a peripheral First Amendment right. Disclosure of membership lists of a constitutionally valid association, we held, was invalid "as entailing the likelihood of a substantial restraint upon the exercise by petitioner's members of their right to freedom of association." In other words, the First Amendment has a penumbra where privacy is protected from governmental intrusion. In like context, we have protected forms of "association" that are not political in the customary sense but pertain to the social, legal, and economic benefit of the members. . . .

Those cases involved more than the "right of assembly"—a right that extends to all irrespective of their race or idealogy. . . . The right of "association" like the right of belief (*West Virginia State Board of Education v. Barnette*, 319 U.S. 624 [1943]), is more than the right to attend a meeting; it includes the right to express one's attitudes or philosophies by membership in a group or by affiliation with it or by other lawful means. Association in that context is a form of expression of opinion; and while it is not expressly included in the First Amendment its existence is necessary in making the express guarantees fully meaningful.

The foregoing cases suggest that specific guarantees in the Bill of Rights have penumbras, formed by emanations from those guarantees that help give them life and substance. See *Poe v. Ullman*, 367 U.S. 497 [1961] (dissenting opinion). Various guarantees create zones of privacy. The right of association contained in the penumbra of the First Amendment is one, as we have seen. The Third Amendment in its prohibition against the quartering of soldiers "in any house" in time of peace without the consent of the owner is another facet of that privacy. The Fourth Amendment explicitly affirms the "right of the people to be secure in their persons, houses, papers, and effects, against unreasonable searches and seizures." The Fifth Amendment in its Self-Incrimination Clause enables the citizen to create a zone of privacy which government may not force him to surrender to his detriment. The Ninth Amendment provides: "The enumeration in the Constitution, of certain rights, shall not be construed to deny or disparage others retained by the people."

The Fourth and Fifth Amendments were described in *Boyd v. United States,* 116 U.S. 616 [1886], as protection against all governmental invasions "of the sanctity of a man's home and the privacies of life."

We recently referred in *Mapp v. Ohio,* 367 U.S. 643 [1961], to the Fourth Amendment as creating a "right to privacy, no less important than any other right carefully and particularly reserved to the people.". . .

We have had many controversies over these penumbral rights of "privacy and repose." These cases bear witness that the right of privacy which presses for recognition here is a legitimate one.

The present case, then, concerns a relationship lying within the zone of privacy created by several fundamental constitutional guarantees. And it concerns a law which, in forbidding the *use* of contraceptives rather than regulating their manufacture or sale, seeks to achieve its goals by means having a maximum destructive impact upon that relationship. Such a law cannot stand in light of the familiar principle, so often applied by this Court, that a "governmental purpose to control or prevent activities constitutionally subject to state regulation may not be achieved by means which sweep unnecessarily broadly and thereby invade the area of protected freedoms." NAACP v. Alabama. . . . Would we allow the police to search the sacred precincts of marital bedrooms for telltale signs of the use of contraceptives? The very idea is repulsive to the notions of privacy surrounding the marriage relationship.

We deal with a right of privacy older than the Bill of Rights—older than our political parties, older than our school system. Marriage is a coming together for better or for worse, hopefully enduring, and intimate to the degree of being sacred. It is an association that promotes a way of life, not causes; a harmony in living, not political faiths; a bilateral loyalty, not commercial or social projects. Yet it is an association for as noble a purpose as any involved in our prior decisions.

Reversed.

Justice GOLDBERG, with whom the CHIEF JUSTICE and Justice BRENNAN join, concurring.

I agree with the Court that Connecticut's birth-control law unconstitutionally intrudes upon the right of marital privacy, and I join in its opinion and judgment. Although I have not accepted the view that "due process" as used in the Fourteenth Amendment includes all of the first eight Amendments (see my concurring opinion in *Pointer v. Texas*, 380 U.S. 400 [1965], and the dissenting opinion of Justice BRENNAN in *Cohen v. Hurley*, 366 U.S. 117 [1961]. I do agree that the concept of liberty protects those personal rights that are fundamental, and is not confined to the specific terms of the Bill of Rights. My conclusion that the concept of liberty is not so restricted and that it embraces the right of marital privacy though that right is not mentioned explicitly in the Constitution is supported both by numerous decisions of this Court, referred to in the Court's opinion, and by the language and history of the Ninth Amendment. In reaching the conclusion that the right of marital privacy is protected, as being within the protected penumbra of specific guarantees of the Bill of Rights, the Court refers to the Ninth Amendment. I add these words to emphasize the relevance of that Amendment to the Court's holding. . . .

The language and history of the Ninth Amendment reveal that the Framers of the Constitution believed that there are additional fundamental rights, protected from governmental infringement, which exist alongside those fundamental rights specifically mentioned in the first eight constitutional amendments.

The Ninth Amendment reads, "The enumeration in the Constitution, of certain rights, shall not be construed to deny or disparage others retained by the people." The Amendment is almost entirely the work of James Madison. It was introduced in Congress by him and passed the House and Senate with little or no debate and virtually no change in language. It was proffered to quiet expressed fears that a bill of specifically enumerated rights could not be sufficiently broad to cover all essential rights and that the specific mention of certain rights would be interpreted as a denial that others were protected.

In presenting the proposed Amendment, Madison said:

> "It has been objected also against a bill of rights, that, by enumerating particular exceptions to the grant of power, it would disparage those rights which were not placed in that enumeration; and it might follow by implication, that those rights which were not singled out, were intended to be assigned into the hands of the General Government, and were consequently insecure. This is one of the most plausible arguments I have ever heard urged against the admission of a bill of rights into this system; but, I conceive, that it may be guarded against. I have attempted it, as gentlemen may see by turning to the last clause of the fourth resolution [the Ninth Amendment]." I Annals of Congress 439 (Gales and Seaton ed. 1834). . . .

While this Court has had little occasion to interpret the Ninth Amendment, "[i]t cannot be presumed that any clause in the constitution is intended to be without effect." *Marbury v. Madison,* 1 Cranch 137 [1803]. To hold that a right so basic and fundamental and so deep-rooted in our society as the right of privacy in marriage may be infringed because that right is not guaranteed in so many words by the first eight amendments to the Constitution is to ignore the Ninth Amendment and to give it no effect whatsoever. . . .

I do not mean to imply that the Ninth Amendment is applied against the States by the Fourteenth. Nor do I mean to state that the Ninth Amendment constitutes an independent source of rights protected from infringement by either the States or the Federal Government. Rather, the Ninth Amendment shows a belief of the Constitution's authors that fundamental rights exist that are not expressly enumerated in the first eight amendments and an intent that the list of rights included there not be deemed exhaustive. . . . The Ninth Amendment simply shows the intent of the Constitution's authors that other fundamental personal rights should not be denied such protection or disparaged in any other way simply because they are not specifically listed in the first eight constitutional amendments. . . .

In determining which rights are fundamental, judges are not left at large to decide cases in light of their personal and private notions. Rather, they must look to the "traditions and [collective] conscience of our people" to determine whether a principle is "so rooted [there] . . . as to be ranked as fundamental." *Snyder v. Com. of Massachusetts,* 291 U.S. 97 [1934]. The inquiry is whether a right involved "is of such a character that it cannot be denied without violating those 'fundamental principles of liberty and justice which lie at the base of all our civil and political institutions' . . ." *Powell v. State of Alabama,* 287 U.S. 45 [1932]. . . .

The entire fabric of the Constitution and the purposes that clearly underlie its specific guarantees demonstrate that the rights to marital privacy and to marry and raise a family are of similar order and magnitude as the fundamental rights specifically protected.

Although the Constitution does not speak in so many words of the right of privacy in marriage, I cannot believe that it offers these fundamental rights no protection. The fact that no particular provision of the Constitution explicitly forbids the State from disrupting the traditional relation of the family—a relation as old and as fundamental as our entire civilization—surely does not show that the Government was meant to have the power to do so. Rather, as the Ninth Amendment expressly recognizes, there are fundamental personal rights such as this one, which are protected from abridgment by the Government though not specifically mentioned in the Constitution. . . .

The logic of the dissents would sanction federal or state legislation that seems to me even more plainly unconstitutional than the statute before us. Surely the Government, absent a showing of a compelling subordinating state interest, could not decree that all husbands and wives must be sterilized after two children have been born to them. Yet by their reasoning such an invasion of marital privacy would not be subject to constitutional challenge because, while it might be "silly," no provision of the Constitution specifically prevents the Government from curtailing the marital right to bear children and raise a family. While it may shock some of my Brethren that the Court today holds that the Constitution protects the right of marital privacy, in my view it is far more shocking to believe that the personal liberty guaranteed by the Constitution does not include protection against such totalitarian limitation of family size, which is at complete variance with our constitutional concepts. . . .

In a long series of cases this Court has held that where fundamental personal liberties are involved, they may not be abridged by the States simply on a showing that a regulatory statute has some rational relationship to the effectuation of a proper state purpose. "Where there is a significant encroachment upon personal liberty, the State may prevail only upon showing a subordinating interest which is compelling," *Bates v. City of Little Rock,* 361 U.S. 516 [1960]. . . .

Although the Connecticut birth-control law obviously encroaches upon a fundamental personal liberty, the State does not show that the law serves any "subordinating [state] interest which is compelling" or that it is "necessary . . . to the accomplishment of a permissible state policy." The State, at most, argues that there is some rational relation between this statute and what is admittedly a legitimate subject of state concern—the discouraging of extra-marital relations. It says that preventing the use of birth-control devices by married persons helps prevent the indulgence by some in such extra-marital relations. The rationality of this justification is dubious, particularly in light of the admitted widespread availability to all persons in the State of Connecticut, unmarried as well as married, of birth-control devices for the prevention of disease, as distinguished from the prevention of conception. . . . But, in any event, it is clear that the state interest in safeguarding marital fidelity can be served by a more discriminately tailored statute, which does not, like the present one, sweep unnecessarily broadly, reaching far beyond the evil sought to be dealt with and intruding upon the privacy of all married couples. . . . The law must be shown "necessary, and not merely rationally related to, the accomplishment of a permissible state policy." . . .

In sum, I believe that the right of privacy in the marital relation is fundamental and basic—a personal right "retained by the people" within the meaning of the Ninth Amendment. Connecticut cannot constitutionally abridge this fundamental right, which is protected by the Fourteenth Amendment from infringement by the States. I agree with the Court that petitioners' convictions must therefore be reversed.

Justice HARLAN concurring.

I fully agree with the judgment of reversal, but find myself unable to join the Court's opinion. The reason is that it seems to me to evince an approach to this case very much like that taken by my Brothers BLACK and STEWART in dissent, namely: the Due Process Clause of the Fourteenth Amendment does not touch this Connecticut statute unless the enactment is found to violate some right assured by the letter or penumbra of the Bill of Rights.

In other words, what I find implicit in the Court's opinion is that the "incorporation" doctrine may be used to *restrict* the reach of Fourteenth Amendment Due Process. For me this is just as unacceptable constitutional doctrine as is the use of the "incorporation" approach to *impose* upon the States all the requirements of the Bill of Rights as found in the provisions of the first eight amendments and in the decisions of this Court interpreting them.

In my view, the proper constitutional inquiry in this case is whether this Connecticut statute infringes the Due Process Clause of the Fourteenth Amendment because the enactment violates basic values "implicit in the concept of ordered liberty," *Palko v. State of Connecticut,* 302 U.S. 319 [1937]. For reasons stated at length in my dissenting opinion in *Poe v. Ullman,* [367 U.S. 497 (1961)], I believe that it does. While the relevant inquiry may be aided by resort to one or more of the provisions of the Bill of Rights, it is not dependent on them or any of their radiations. The Due Process Clause of the Fourteenth Amendment stands, in my opinion, on its own bottom. . . .

While I could not more heartily agree that judicial "self re-straint" is an indispensable ingredient of sound constitutional adjudication, I do submit that the formula suggested for achieving it is more hollow than real. "Specific" provisions of the Constitution, no less than "due process," lend themselves as readily to "personal" interpretations by judges whose constitutional outlook is simply to keep the Constitution in supposed "tune with the times.". . .

Judicial self-restraint will not, I suggest, be brought about in the "due process" area by the historically unfounded incorporation formula long advanced by my Brother BLACK, and now in part espoused by my Brother STEWART. It will be achieved in this area, as in other constitutional areas, only by continual insistence upon respect for the teachings of history, solid recognition of the basic values that underlie our society, and wise appreciation of the great roles that the doctrines of federalism and separation of powers have played in establishing and preserving American freedoms. . . . Adherence to these principles will not, of course, obviate all constitutional differences of opinion among judges, nor should it. Their continued recognition will, however, go farther toward keeping most judges from roaming at large in the constitutional field than will the interpolation into the Constitution of an artificial and largely illusory restriction on the content of the Due Process Clause.

Justice WHITE concurring.

In my view this Connecticut law as applied to married couples deprives them of "liberty" without due process of law as that concept is used in the Fourteenth Amendment. I therefore concur in the judgment of the Court reversing these convictions under Connecticut's aiding and abetting statute.

Justice BLACK, with whom Justice STEWART joins, dissenting.

The Court talks about a constitutional "right of privacy" as though there is some constitutional provision or provisions forbidding any law ever to be passed which might abridge the "privacy" of individuals. But there is not. There are, of course, guarantees in certain specific constitutional provisions which are designed in part to protect privacy at certain times and places with respect to certain activities. Such, for example, is the Fourth Amendment's guarantee against "unreasonable searches and seizures." But I think it belittles that Amendment to talk about it as though it protects nothing but "privacy.". . .

One of the most effective ways of diluting or expanding a constitutionally guaranteed right is to substitute for the crucial word or words of a constitutional guarantee another word or words, more or less flexible and more or less restricted in meaning. This fact is well illustrated by the use of the term "right of privacy" as a comprehensive substitute for the Fourth Amendment's guarantee against "unreasonable searches and seizures." "Privacy" is a broad, abstract and ambiguous concept which can easily be shrunken in meaning but which can also, on the other hand, easily be interpreted as a constitutional ban against many things other than searches and seizures. I have expressed the view many times that First Amendment freedoms, for example, have suffered from a failure of the courts to stick to the simple language of the First Amendment in construing it, instead of invoking multitudes of words substituted for those the Framers used. For these reasons I get nowhere in this case by talk about a constitutional "right or privacy" as an emanation from one or more constitutional provisions. I like my privacy as well as the next one, but I am nevertheless compelled to admit that government has a right to invade it unless prohibited by some specific constitutional provision. For these reasons I cannot agree with the Court's judgment and the reasons it gives for holding this Connecticut law unconstitutional. . . .

I think that if properly construed neither the Due Process Clause nor the Ninth Amendment, nor both together, could under any circumstances be a proper basis for invalidating the Connecticut law. I discuss the due process and Ninth Amendment arguments together because on analysis they turn out to be the same thing—merely using different words to claim for this Court and the federal judiciary power to invalidate any legislative act which the judges find irrational, unreasonable or offensive.

The due process argument which my Brothers HARLAN and WHITE adopt here is based, as their opinions indicate, on the premise that this Court is vested with power to invalidate all state laws that it considers to be arbitrary, capricious, unreasonable, or oppressive, or this Court's belief that a particular state law under scrutiny has no "rational or justifying" purpose, or is offensive to a "sense of fairness and justice." If these formulas based on "natural justice," or others which mean the same thing, are to prevail, they require judges to determine what is or is not constitutional on the basis of their own appraisal of what laws are unwise or unnecessary. The power to make such decisions is of course that of a legislative body. . . . I do not believe that we are granted power by the Due Process Clause or any other constitutional provision or provisions to measure constitutionality by our belief that legislation is arbitrary, capricious or unreasonable, or accomplishes no justifiable purpose, or is offensive to our own notions of "civilized standards of conduct." Such an appraisal of the wisdom of legislation is an attribute of the power to make laws, not of the power to interpret them. . . .

My Brother GOLDBERG has adopted the recent discovery that the Ninth Amendment as well as the Due Process Clause can be used by this Court as authority to strike down all state legislation which this Court thinks violates "fundamental principles of liberty and justice," or is contrary to the "traditions and [collective] conscience of our people." He also states, without proof satisfactory to me, that in making decisions on this basis judges will not consider "their personal and private notions." One may ask how they can avoid considering them. Our Court certainly has no machinery with which to take a Gallup Poll. . . .

I realize that many good and able men have eloquently spoken and written, sometimes in rhapsodical strains, about the duty of this Court to keep the Constitution in tune with the times. The idea is that the Constitution must be changed from time to time and that this Court is charged with a duty to make those changes.

For myself, I must with all deference reject that philosophy. The Constitution makers knew the need for change and provided for it. Amendments suggested by the people's elected representatives can be submitted to the people or their selected agents for ratification. That method of change was good for our Fathers, and being somewhat old-fashioned I must add it is good enough for me. And so, I cannot rely on the Due Process Clause or the Ninth Amendment or any mysterious and uncertain natural law concept as a reason for striking down this state law. The Due Process Clause with an "arbitrary and capricious" or "shocking to the conscience" formula was liberally used by this Court to strike down economic legislation in the early decades of this century, threatening, many people thought, the tranquility and stability of the Nation. See, e. g., *Lochner v. State of New York,* 198 U.S. 45 [1905]. That formula, based on subjective considerations of "natural justice," is no less dangerous when used to enforce this Court's views about personal rights than those about economic rights. I had thought that we had laid that formula, as a means for striking down state legislation, to rest once and for all in cases like *West Coast Hotel Co. v. Parrish,* [300 U.S. 379 (1937)], and many other opinions.

Justice STEWART, whom Justice BLACK joins, dissenting.

Since 1879 Connecticut has had on its books a law which forbids the use of contraceptives by anyone. I think this is an uncommonly silly law. . . . But we are not asked in this case to say whether we think this law is unwise, or even asinine. We are asked to hold that it violates the United States Constitution. And that I cannot do.

In the course of its opinion the Court refers to no less than six Amendments to the Constitution: the First, the Third, the Fourth, the Fifth, the Ninth, and the Fourteenth. But the Court does not say which of these Amendments, if any, it thinks is infringed by this Connecticut law.

We *are* told that the Due Process Clause of the Fourteenth Amendment is not, as such, the "guide" in this case. With that much I agree. . . .

As to the First, Third, Fourth, and Fifth Amendments, I can find nothing in any of them to invalidate this Connecticut law, even assuming that all those Amendments are fully applicable against the States. . . .

[And] to say that the Ninth Amendment has anything to do with this case is to turn somersaults with history. The Ninth Amendment, like its companion the Tenth, which this Court held "states but a truism that all is retained which has not been surrendered," *United States v. Darby,* 312 U.S. 100 [1941], was framed by James Madison and adopted by the States simply to make clear that the adoption of the Bill of Rights did not alter the plan that the *Federal* Government was to be a government of express and limited powers, and that all rights and powers not delegated to it were retained. . . .

What provision of the Constitution, then, does make this state law invalid? The Court says it is the right of privacy "created by several fundamental constitutional guarantees." With all deference, I can find no such general right of privacy in the Bill of Rights, in any other part of the Constitution, or in any case ever before decided by this Court.

Duncan v. Louisiana
391 U.S. 145, 88 S.Ct. 1444 (1968)

Gary Duncan, a nineteen-year-old black, was driving in Plaquemines Parish, Louisiana, a community in which racial tensions ran high and opposition to school desegregation remained heated in 1966. He saw four white boys confronting two of his younger cousins and stopped to pick his cousins up. At that point, there apparently was some sort of exchange in which Duncan "touched" or "slapped" the arm of one of the white boys, Herman Landry, and then drove away. The head of a private school, established in opposition to the desegregation of the local public schools, saw the incident and called the sheriff. Duncan was intercepted and questioned by a deputy sheriff, but allowed to leave. Three days later, he was arrested on a charge of cruelty to minors. Believing that the arrest was racial harassment, Duncan's parents sought help from the Lawyers Constitutional Defense Committee (LCDC), an organization providing attorneys for civil rights litigation. While the LCDC was initially reluctant to take what appeared to be a minor case, further developments led to an important ruling by the Supreme Court.

At Duncan's preliminary hearing, his attorney Richard Sobol moved to quash the charge since Louisiana's law governing cruelty to minors applied only to those with parental control or responsibility over an abused minor (which clearly did not apply to Duncan). Before the judge ruled on that motion, however, Landry's parents signed an affidavit charging Duncan with assault and battery. Duncan was rearrested and scheduled for another trial on the battery charge, which carried a maximum sentence of two years in prison. This time, Sobol asked the judge for a jury trial on the grounds that the Sixth Amendment provision for jury trials applied to the states and that jury trials were required whenever an accused faces a serious charge and the possibility of being sentenced to six months or more in jail. That request was also denied by the trial judge. The basis was thus laid for a test case for determining whether the Sixth Amendment applied to the states. Duncan was convicted for battery, fined $150, and sentenced to sixty days in prison. Sobol appealed Duncan's conviction to the supreme court of Louisiana, which upheld the lower court, and then to the Supreme Court. The fundamental issue in this case, as Duncan's attorney told the Court, is "whether the Due Process Clause of the Fourteenth Amendment secures the right to trial by jury in state criminal cases."

Justice WHITE delivers the opinion of the Court.

The Fourteenth Amendment denies the States the power to "deprive any person of life, liberty, or property, without due process of law." In resolving conflicting claims concerning the meaning of this spacious language, the Court has looked increasingly to the Bill of Rights for guidance; many of the rights guaranteed by the first eight Amendments to the Constitution have been held to be protected against state action by the Due Process Clause of the Fourteenth Amendment. That clause now protects the right to compensation for property taken by the State; the rights of speech, press, and religion covered by the First Amendment; the Fourth Amendment rights to be free from unreasonable searches and seizures and to have excluded from criminal trials any evidence illegally seized; the right guaranteed by the Fifth Amendment to be free of compelled self-incrimination; and the Sixth Amendment rights to counsel, to a speedy and public trial, to confrontation of opposing witnesses, and to compulsory process for obtaining witnesses.

The test for determining whether a right extended by the Fifth and Sixth Amendments with respect to federal criminal proceedings is also protected against state action by the Fourteenth Amendment has been phrased in a variety of ways in the opinions of this Court. The question has been asked whether a right is among those " 'fundamental principles of liberty and justice which lie at the base of all our civil and political institutions' "; whether it is "basic in our system of jurisprudence"; and whether it is "a fundamental right, essential to a fair trial.". . . Because we believe that trial by jury in criminal cases is fundamental to the American scheme of justice, we hold that the Fourteenth Amendment guarantees a right of jury trial in all criminal cases which—were they to be tried in a federal court—would come within the Sixth Amendment's guarantee. . . .

We are aware of prior cases in this Court in which the prevailing opinion contains statements contrary to our holding today that the right to jury trial in serious criminal cases is a fundamental right and hence must be recognized by the States as part of their obligation to extend due process of law to all persons within their jurisdiction. . . . Respectfully, we reject the prior dicta regarding jury trial in criminal cases.

The guarantees of jury trial in the Federal and State Constitutions reflect a profound judgment about the way in which law should be enforced and justice administered. A right to jury trial is granted to criminal defendants in order to prevent oppression by the Government. Those who wrote our constitutions knew from history and experience that it was necessary to protect against unfounded criminal charges brought to eliminate enemies and against judges too responsive to the voice of higher authority. The framers of the constitutions strove to create an independent judiciary but insisted upon further protection against arbitrary action. Providing an accused with the right to be tried by a jury of his peers gave him an inestimable safeguard against the corrupt or overzealous prosecutor and against the compliant, biased, or eccentric judge. If the defendant preferred the common-sense judgment of a jury to the more tutored but perhaps less sympathetic reaction of the single judge, he was to have it. Beyond this, the jury trial provisions in the Federal and State Constitutions reflect a fundamental decision about the exercise of official power—a reluctance to entrust plenary powers over the life and liberty of the citizen to one judge or to a group of judges. Fear of unchecked power, so typical of our State and Federal Governments in other respects, found expression in the criminal law in this insistence upon community participation in the determination of guilt or innocence. The deep commitment of the Nation to the right of jury trial in serious criminal cases as a defense against arbitrary law enforcement qualifies for protection under the Due Process Clause of the Fourteenth Amendment, and must therefore be respected by the States. . . .

Louisiana's final contention is that even if it must grant jury trials in serious criminal cases, the conviction before us is valid and constitutional because here the petitioner was tried for simple battery and was sentenced to only 60 days in the parish prison. We are not persuaded. It is doubtless true that there is a category of petty crimes or offenses which is not subject to the Sixth Amendment jury trial provision and should not be subject to the Fourteenth Amendment jury trial requirement here applied to the States. Crimes carrying possible penalties up to six months do not require a jury trial if they otherwise qualify as petty offenses.

But the penalty authorized for a particular crime is of major relevance in determining whether it is serious or not and may in itself, if severe enough, subject the trial to the mandates of the Sixth Amendment. . . .

We need not, however, settle in this case the exact location of the line between petty offenses and serious crimes. It is sufficient for our purposes to hold that a crime punishable by two years in prison is, based on past and contemporary standards in this country, a serious crime and not a petty offense.

Justice BLACK, with whom Justice DOUGLAS joins, concurring.

With this holding I agree for reasons given by the Court. I also agree because of reasons given in my dissent in *Adamson v. People of State of California* [322 U.S. 46 (1947)]. In that dissent I took the position that the Fourteenth Amendment made all of the provisions of the Bill of Rights applicable to the States. And I am very happy to support this selective process through which our Court has since the *Adamson* case held most of the specific Bill of Rights' protections applicable to the States to the same extent they are applicable to the Federal Government. Among these are the right to trial by jury decided today, the right against compelled self-incrimination, the right to counsel, the right to compulsory process for witnesses, the right to confront witnesses, the right to a speedy and public trial, and the right to be free from unreasonable searches and seizures. . . .

I want to emphasize that I believe as strongly as ever that the Fourteenth Amendment was intended to make the Bill of Rights applicable to the States. I have been willing to support the selective incorporation doctrine, however, as an alternative, although perhaps less historically supportable than complete incorporation. The selective incorporation process, if used properly, does limit the Supreme Court in the Fourteenth Amendment field to specific Bill of Rights' protections only and keeps judges from roaming at will in their own notions of what policies outside the Bill of Rights are desirable and what are not. And, most importantly for me, the selective incorporation process has the virtue of having already worked to make most of the Bill of Rights' protections applicable to the States.

Justice FORTAS concurring.

[A]lthough I agree with the decision of the Court, I cannot agree with the implication that the tail must go with the hide: that when we hold, influenced by the Sixth Amendment, that "due process" requires that the States accord the right of jury trial for all but petty offenses, we automatically import all of the ancillary rules which have been or may hereafter be developed incidental to the right to jury trial in the federal courts. I see no reason whatever, for example, to assume that our decision today should require us to impose federal requirements such as unanimous verdicts or a jury of 12 upon the States. We may well conclude that these and other features of federal jury practice are by no means fundamental—that they are not essential to due process of law—and that they are not obligatory on the States.

I would make these points clear today. Neither logic nor history nor the intent of the draftsmen of the Fourteenth Amendment can possibly be said to require that the Sixth Amendment or its jury trial provision be applied to the States together with the total gloss that this Court's decisions have supplied. The draftsmen of the Fourteenth Amendment intended what they said, not more or less: that no State shall deprive any person of life, liberty, or property without due process of law. It is ultimately the duty of this Court to interpret, to ascribe specific meaning to this phrase. There is no reason whatever for us to conclude that, in so doing, we are bound slavishly to follow not only the Sixth Amendment but all of its bag and baggage, however securely or insecurely affixed they may be by law and precedent to federal proceedings. To take this course, in my judgment, would be not only unnecessary but mischievous because it would inflict a serious blow upon the principle of federalism. The Due Process Clause commands us to apply its great standard to state court proceedings to assure basic fairness. It does not command us rigidly and arbitrarily to impose the exact pattern of federal proceedings upon the 50 States. On the contrary, the Constitution's command, in my view, is that in our insistence upon state observance of due process, we should, so far as possible, allow the greatest latitude for state differences. It requires, within the limits of the lofty basic standards that it prescribes for the States as well as the Federal Government, maximum opportunity for diversity and minimal imposition of uniformity of method and detail upon the States. Our Constitution sets up a federal union, not a monolith.

Justice HARLAN whom Justice STEWART joins, dissenting.

The question in this case is whether the State of Louisiana, which provides trial by jury for all felonies, is prohibited by the Constitution from trying charges of simple battery to the court alone. In my view, the answer to that question, mandated alike by our constitutional history and by the longer history of trial by jury, is clearly "no.". . .

I have raised my voice many times before against the Court's continuing undiscriminating insistence upon fastening on the

States federal notions of criminal justice, and I must do so again in this instance. With all respect, the Court's approach and its reading of history are altogether topsy-turvy.

I believe I am correct in saying that every member of the Court for at least the last 135 years has agreed that our Founders did not consider the requirements of the Bill of Rights so fundamental that they should operate directly against the States. They were wont to believe rather that the security of liberty in America rested primarily upon the dispersion of governmental power across a federal system. The Bill of Rights was considered unnecessary by some but insisted upon by others in order to curb the possibility of abuse of power by the strong central government they were creating.

The Civil War Amendments dramatically altered the relation of the Federal Government to the States. The first section of the Fourteenth Amendment imposes highly significant restrictions on state action. But the restrictions are couched in very broad and general terms: citizenship; privileges and immunities; due process of law; equal protection of the laws. . . . The question has been, Where does the Court properly look to find the specific rules that define and give content to such terms as "life, liberty, or property" and "due process of law"?

A few members of the Court have taken the position that the intention of those who drafted the first section of the Fourteenth Amendment was simply, and exclusively, to make the provisions of the first eight Amendments applicable to state action. This view has never been accepted by this Court. In my view, often expressed elsewhere, the first section of the Fourteenth Amendment was meant neither to incorporate nor to be limited to, the specific guarantees of the first eight Amendments. The overwhelming historical evidence demonstrates, to me conclusively, that the Congressmen and state legislators who wrote debated, and ratified the Fourteenth Amendment did not think they were "incorporating" the Bill of Rights.

Although I therefore fundamentally disagree with the total incorporation view of the Fourteenth Amendment, it seems to me that such a position does at least have the virtue, lacking in the Court's selective incorporation approach of internal consistency: we look to the Bill of Rights, word for word, clause for clause, precedent for precedent because it is said, the men who wrote the Amendment wanted it that way. . . .

Apart from the approach taken by the absolute incorporationists, I can see only one method of analysis that has an internal logic. That is to start with the words "liberty" and "due process of law" and attempt to define them in a way that accords with American traditions and our system of government. This approach, involving a much more discriminating process of adjudication than does "incorporation," is, albeit difficult, the one that was followed through out the 19th and most of the present century. It entails a "gradual progress of judicial inclusion and exclusion," seeking, with due recognition of constitutional tolerance for state experimentation and disparity, to ascertain those "immutable principles . . . of justice which inhere in the very idea of free government which no member of the Union may disregard.". . .

The relationship of the Bill of Rights to this "gradual process" seems to me to be twofold. In the first place it has long been clear that the Due Process Clause imposes some restrictions on state action that parallel Bill of Rights restrictions on federal action. Second, and more important than this accidental overlap, is the fact that the Bill of Rights is evidence, at various points, of the content Americans find in the term "liberty" and of American standards of fundamental fairness. . . .

Today's Court still remains unwilling to accept the total incorporationists' view of the history of the Fourteenth Amendment. This, if accepted, would afford a cogent reason for applying the Sixth Amendment to the States. The Court is also, apparently, unwilling to face the task of determining whether denial of trial by jury in the situation before us, or in other situations, is fundamentally unfair. Consequently, the Court has compromised on the ease of the incorporationist position, without its internal logic. It has simply assumed that the question before us is whether the Jury Trial Clause of the Sixth Amendment should be incorporated into the Fourteenth, jot-for-jot and case-for-case, or ignored. Then the Court merely declares that the clause in question is "in" rather than "out."

The Court has justified neither its starting place nor its conclusion. If the problem is to discover and articulate the rules of fundamental fairness in criminal proceedings, there is no reason to assume that the whole body of rules developed in this Court constituting Sixth Amendment jury trial must be regarded as a unit. The requirement of trial by jury in federal criminal cases has given rise to numerous subsidiary questions respecting the exact scope and content of the right. It surely cannot be that every answer the Court has given, or will give, to such a question is attributable to the Founders; or even that every rule announced carries equal conviction of this Court; still less can it be that every such subprinciple is equally fundamental to ordered liberty.

Examples abound. I should suppose it obviously fundamental to fairness that a "jury" means an "impartial jury." I should think it equally obvious that the rule, imposed long ago in the federal courts, that "jury" means "jury of exactly twelve," is not fundamental to anything: there is no significance except to mystics in the number 12. Again, trial by jury has been held to require a unanimous verdict of jurors in the federal courts, although unanimity has not been found essential to liberty in Britain, where the requirement has been abandoned. . . .

The argument that jury trial is not a requisite of due process is quite simple. The central proposition of *Palko* [*v. Connecticut,* 302 U.S. 319 (1937)], . . . is that "due process of law" requires only that criminal trials be fundamentally fair. As stated above, apart from the theory that it was historically intended as a mere shorthand for the Bill of Rights, I do not see what else "due process of law" can intelligibly be thought to mean. If due process of law requires only fundamental fairness, then the inquiry in each case must be whether a state trial process was a fair one. The Court has held, properly I think, that in an adversary process it is a requisite of fairness, for which there is no adequate substitute, that a criminal defendant be afforded a right to counsel and to cross-examine opposing witnesses. But it simply has not been demonstrated, nor, I think, can it be demonstrated, that trial by jury is the only fair means of resolving issues of fact. . . .

In sum, there is a wide range of views on the desirability of trial by jury, and on the ways to make it most effective when it is used; there is also considerable variation from State to State in local conditions such as the size of the criminal caseload, the ease or difficulty of summoning jurors, and other trial conditions bearing on fairness. We have before us, therefore, an almost perfect example of a situation in which the celebrated dictum of Justice BRANDEIS should be invoked. It is, he said, "one of the happy incidents of the federal system that a single courageous state may, if its citizens choose, serve as a laboratory. . . ." *New State Ice Co. v. Liebmann,* 285 U.S. 262 [1932]. This Court, other courts, and the political process are available to correct any experiments in criminal procedure that prove fundamentally unfair to defendants. That is not what is being done today: instead, and quite without reason, the Court has chosen to impose upon every State one means of trying criminal cases; it is a good means, but it is not the only fair means, and it is not demonstrably better than the alternatives States might devise.

I would affirm the judgment of the Supreme Court of Louisiana.

B. THE RISE AND RETREAT OF THE "DUE PROCESS REVOLUTION"

The due process revolution forged during the Warren Court years by extending the major guarantees of the Bill of Rights to the states took on a life of its own. In the early 1970s, the Burger Court continued to expand the protection of the due process clause to require trial-type hearings prior to the infringement of individuals' rights and entitlements. Notably, in *Goldberg v. Kelly*, 397 U.S. 254 (1970), the Court held that the due process clause of the Fourteenth Amendment requires a trial-type hearing for recipients of Aid to Families with Dependent Children (AFDC) prior to the termination of their benefits under the AFDC program.

The Court subsequently extended due process–based requirements in *Wisconsin v. Constantineau*, 400 U.S. 208 (1971), for the public posting of the names of people deemed unfit to consume alcoholic beverages; *Richardson v. Wright*, 405 U.S. 208 (1972), requiring the opportunity to offer oral evidence and to cross-examine witnesses in a hearing before the termination of disability benefits; *Morrissey v. Brewer*, 408 U.S. 471 (1972), requiring a hearing before the revocation of parole; *Gibson v. Berryhill*, 411 U.S. 609 (1973), requiring an impartial hearing by officers on a state optometry board; *Weinberger v. Hynson, Westcott & Dunning, Inc.*, 412 U.S. 609 (1973), requiring a hearing prior to the Food and Drug Administration's withdrawal of new drug applications; and *Arnett v. Kennedy*, 416 U.S. 134 (1974), holding that federal employees must be accorded minimal procedural guarantees as afforded by federal law before having their employment terminated.

In Justice William O' Douglas's last term after more than thirty-six years on the bench, a bare majority of the Court signaled that the due process revolution was coming to an end in *Goss v. Lopez*, 419 U.S. 565 (1975). There President Nixon's four appointees—Chief Justice Burger and Justices Blackmun, Powell, and Rehnquist—dissented from the majority's view that due process requires a conversation, and not a hearing, prior to the temporary suspension of students from school and that they must receive at least notice of the charges against them, an explanation of the evidence authorities have, and an opportunity to tell their side of the story. In Justice Byron White's words for the majority:

Even truncated trial-type procedures might well overwhelm administrative facilities in many places and, in diverting resources, cost more than it would save in educational effectiveness. Moreover, further formalizing the suspension process and escalating its formality and adversary nature may not only make it too costly as a regular disciplinary tool but also destroy its effectiveness as part of the teaching process. On the other hand, requiring effective notice and informal hearing permitting the student to give his version of the events will provide a meaningful hedge against erroneous action.

The Burger Court's rulings on the substantive and procedural rights of individuals committed to mental institutions further illustrate its movement away from an expansive reading of the constitutional protection afforded by the due process clause. Along with *Goss v. Lopez* in 1975, the Burger Court held, in *O'Connor v. Donaldson*, 422 U.S. 563 (1975), that individuals who are not dangerous to others may not be confined in institutions against their will, if they can survive outside with the aid of relatives or friends and are not receiving special therapy. At the same time, the Court refused to embrace a constitutional "right to treatment." Kenneth Donaldson was confined to the Florida State Hospital, following commitment proceedings initiated by his father who said that he suffered from delusions. For almost fifteen years, Donaldson repeatedly requested to be released, claiming that he was not receiving any special treatment justifying his confinement and that he could survive outside of the institution with the help of friends and relatives. But, the hospital superintendent, Dr. J. B. O'Connor, denied his release. Finally, Donaldson filed a lawsuit charging that O'Connor was depriving him of his constitutional right to liberty under the Fourteenth Amendment. Following a trial, a jury agreed and awarded damages. O'Connor appealed but the Court of Appeals for the Fifth Circuit affirmed, holding that Donaldson had "a constitutional right to receive such individual treatment as will give him a reasonable opportunity to be cured or to improve his mental health." O'Connor then made a further appeal to the Supreme Court.

Although declining to read a substantive "right to treatment" into the Fourteenth Amendment due process clause in *O'Connor v. Donaldson*, Justice Potter Stewart ruled that "a State cannot constitutionally confine without more a nondangerous individual who is capable of surviving safely in freedom by himself or with the help of willing and responsible family members or friends." Justice Stewart further explained that

The jury found that Donaldson was neither dangerous to himself nor dangerous to others, and also found that, if mentally ill, Donaldson had not received treatment. That verdict based on abundant evidence, makes the issue before the Court a narrow one. We need not decide whether, when, or by what procedures, a mentally ill person may be confined by the State on any of the grounds which, under contemporary statutes, are generally advanced to justify involuntary confinement of such a person—to prevent injury to the public, to ensure his own survival or safety, or to alleviate or cure his illness. For the jury found that none of the above grounds for continued confinement was present in Donaldson's case.

Given the jury's findings, what was left as justification for keeping Donaldson in continued confinement? The fact that state law may have authorized confinement of the harmless mentally ill does not itself establish a constitutionally adequate purpose for the confinement. Nor is it enough that Donaldson's original confinement was founded upon a constitutionally adequate basis, if in fact it was, because even if his involuntary confinement was initially permissible, it could not constitutionally continue after that basis no longer existed.

A finding of "mental illness" alone cannot justify a State's locking a person up against his will and keeping him indefinitely in simple custodial confinement. Assuming that that term can be given a reasonably precise content and that the "mentally ill" can be identified with reasonable accuracy, there is still no constitutional basis for confining such persons involuntarily if they are dangerous to no one and can live safely in freedom.

In a concurring opinion, Chief Justice Burger hastened to underscore the rejection of the lower court's holding that the due process clause embraces an unenumerated constitutional "right to treatment":

I cannot accept the reasoning of the Court of Appeals and can discern no basis for equating an involuntarily committed mental patient's unquestioned constitutional right not to be confined without due process of law with a constitutional right to *treatment*. . . . Nor can I accept the theory that a State may lawfully confine an individual thought to need treatment and justify that deprivation of liberty solely by providing some treatment. Our concepts of due process would not tolerate such a "trade-off." Because the Court of Appeals' analysis could be read as authorizing those results, it should not be followed.

Subsequently, the Burger Court held that due process requires a standard of proof in civil commitment proceedings greater than the "preponderance of the evidence" standard used in other civil proceedings, but less rigorous than the "beyond a reasonable doubt" standard used in criminal cases. *Addington v. Texas,* 441 U.S. 418 (1979), created a new (middle level) standard requiring clear and convincing evidence to justify an individual's involuntary hospitalization. In cases involving the commitment of children to mental health institutions, the Court also held that a commitment hearing before a "neutral fact finder" (who, however, need not be legally trained) is required under the due process clause.[1] Notice, a hearing, and the opportunity to call and cross-examine witnesses before a neutral fact finder, are also required before inmates in a state prison may be transferred to a mental institution.[2] Moreover, although the Burger Court in a six-to-three decision interpeted the Developmentally Disabled Assistance and Bill of Rights Act not to create any substantive rights for the developmentally disabled or to impose affirmative obligations on states to provide certain servies for those in their care,[3] *Youngberg v. Romeo,* 457 U.S. 307 (1982), held that mentally retarded individuals still enjoy certain constitutionally protected liberty interests. In *Youngberg,* the Court unanimously ruled that individuals confined to state mental institutions may assert under the Fourteenth Amendment due process clause "constitutionally protected interests in the conditions of reasonable care and safety, reasonably nonrestrictive confinement conditions, and such training as may be required by these interests." Thus while *O'Connor v. Donaldson* declined to embrace a broad right to treatment under the due process clause, the Burger Court nevertheless held that individuals have some constitutionally protected procedural and substantive liberty interests in commitment proceedings and in the conditions of their hospitalization.

With the Senate's confirmation of Justice Douglas's successor, Justice John Paul Stevens, the Burger Court took a more restrictive, less expansive view of what process is due under the due process clause. In *Mathews v. Elridge,* 424 U.S. 319 (1976), the Court held that an evidentiary hearing is not required prior to the termination of disability benefits. In a number of other cases, the Burger Court denied claims to procedural guarantees under the due process clause: *Meachum v. Fano,* 427 U.S. 215 (1976), rejected a due process argument for a hearing prior to the transfer of a prisoner from one prison to another. *Bishop v. Wood,* 426 U.S. 341 (1976), approved the dismissal of a city police officer without a pretermination hearing. *Codd v. Velger,* 429 U.S. 624 (1977), held that a hearing need not be held for the dismissal of policemen who challenged materials placed in their files as damaging. *Dixon v. Love,* 431 U.S. 105 (1977) upheld Illinois's summary revocation of drivers' licenses for repeated traffic violations, holding that Eldridge does not require a pretermination hearing. And in *Ingraham v. Wright,* 430 U.S. 651 (1977), the justices split five to four when holding that no hearing is necessary prior to the "paddling" of students in public schools. In *Board of Curators of University of Missouri v. Horowitz,* 435 U.S. 78 (1978), a bare majority of the Court affirmed that the dismissal of a medical student did not require an elaborate procedural hearing before the school's decision-making body. *Greenholtz v. Inmates,* 442 U.S. 1 (1979), ruled that an oral hearing for parole decisions was not needed and that a parole board could rely simply on the files on an inmate. *Barry v. Barchi,* 443 U.S. 55 (1979) upheld the summary dismissal of harness racing trainers.

The Burger Court, however, upheld claims for procedural due process in a few cases. In *Memphis Light, Gas & Water Division v. Craft,* 436 U.S. 1 (1978), for example, the Court held that the due process clause requires public utilities to establish an administrative procedure for hearing complaints before disconnecting gas, water, and electric services. And *Vitek v. Jones,* 445 U.S. 480 (1980), ruled that a hearing was required before the transfer of prisoners to state mental health institution for involuntary commitment. *Cleveland Board of Education v. Loudermill,* 470 U.S. 532 (1985), also held that in the dismissal of an employee for cause the state must afford a hearing on the charges during the pretermination process.

The Burger and Rehnquist Courts, nevertheless, have tended to cut back on further readings of substantive rights into the due process clause. The due process clause has been interpreted only to prevent government "from abusing [its] power, or employing it as an instrument of oppression."[4]

As Chief Justice Rehnquist explains, in *DeShaney v. Winnebago County Department of Social Services,* 109 S.Ct. 998 (1989), "the Due Process Clauses generally confer no affirmative right to governmental aid, even where such aid may be necessary to secure life, liberty, or property interests of which the government itself may not deprive the individual." *Harris v. McRae,* 448 U.S. 297 (1980), thus held that the right of privacy does not entail governmental funding of abortions or medical services. *Lindsey v. Normet,* 405 U.S. 56 (1972), dismissed a due process claim to adequate housing. "As a general matter," observed the Court in *Youngberg v. Romero,* 457 U.S. 307 (1982), "a State is under no constitutional duty to provide substantive services for those within its border."

In *DeShaney* (with Justices Brennan, Blackmun, and Marshall dissenting) the Rehnquist Court held that

> In the substantive due process analysis, it is the State's affirmative act of restraining the individual's freedom to act on his own behalf—through incarceration, institutionalization, or other similar restrain of personal liberty—which is the "deprivation of liberty" triggering the protections of the Due Process Clause, not its failure to act to protect his liberty interests against harms inflicted by other means.

In that case, Chief Justice Rehnquist rejected the claim of Melody DeShaney that welfare workers were liable for the repeated beatings by the natural father of her son, Joshua, which left the four-year-old boy brain damaged. As Chief Justice Rehnquist observed,

> [T]he harms Joshua suffered did not occur while he was in the State's custody, but while he was in the custody of his natural father, who was in no sense a state actor. While the State may have been aware of the dangers that Joshua faced in the free world, it played no part in their creation, nor did it do anything to render him any more vulnerable to them. That the State once took temporary custody of Joshua does not alter the analysis, for when it returned him to his father's custody,

it placed him in no worse position than that in which he would have been had it not acted at all; the State does not become the permanent guarantor of an individual's safety by having once offered him shelter. Under these circumstances, the State had no constitutional duty to protect Joshua. . . .

The people of Wisconsin may well prefer a system of liability which would place upon the State and its officials the responsibility for failure to act in situations such as the present one. They may create such a system, if they do not have it already, by changing the tort law of the State in accordance with the regular law-making process. But they should not have it thrust upon them by this Court's expansion of the Due Process Clause of the Fourteenth Amendment.

In another decision handed down in 1989, *Michael H. v. Gerald D.*, 109 S.Ct. 2333 (1989), the Rehnquist Court split five to four in rejecting the substantive due process argument that the natural (unwed) father of the child of a married woman had a right to file to establish paternity and for visitation rights. Under California law, which the majority upheld, the legal husband of a married woman who bears a child is presumptively the legal father. Writing for a bare majority, Justice Antonin Scalia explained that

[i]n an attempt to limit and guide interpretation of the [Due Process] Clause, we have insisted not merely that the interest denominated as a "liberty" be "fundamental" (a concept that, in isolation, is hard to objectify), but also that it be an interest traditionally protected by our society. As we have put it, the Due Process Clause affords only those protections "so rooted in the traditions and conscience of our people as to be ranked as fundamental." *Snyder v. Massachusetts*, 291 U.S. 97 (1934). Our cases reflect "continual insistence upon respect for the teachings of history [and] solid recognition of the basic values that underlie our society. . . ." [Quoting *Griswold v. Connecticut.*]

[T]he legal issue in the present case reduces to whether the relationship between persons in the situation of Michael and Victoria has been treated as a protected family unit under the historic practices of our society, or whether on any other basis it has been accorded special protection. We think it impossible to find that it has. In fact, quite to the contrary, our traditions have protected the marital family. . . .

The presumption of legitimacy was a fundamental principle of the common law. . . .

[W]hat is at issue here is not entitlement to a state pronouncement that Victoria was begotten by Michael. It is no conceivable denial of constitutional right for a State to decline to declare facts unless some legal consequence hinges upon the requested declaration. What Michael asserts here is a right to have himself declared the natural father *and thereby to obtain parental prerogatives*. What he must establish, therefore, is not that our society has traditionally allowed a natural father in his circumstances to establish paternity, but that it has traditionally accorded such a father parental rights, or at least has not traditionally denied them. Even if the law in all States had always been that the entire world could challenge the marital presumption and obtain a declaration as to who was the natural father, that would not advance Michael's claim. Thus, it is ultimately irrelevant, even for purposes of determining *current* social attitudes towards the alleged substantive right Michael asserts, that the present law in a number of States appears to allow the natural father—including the natural father who has not established a relationship with the child—the theoretical power to rebut the marital presumption.

By contrast, dissenting Justice Brennan argued that

it would be comforting to believe that a search for "tradition" involves nothing more idiosyncratic or complicated than poring through dusty volumes on American history. . . . "What the deeply rooted traditions of the country are is arguable." Indeed, wherever I would begin to look for an interest "deeply rooted in the country's traditions," one thing is certain: I would not stop (as does the plurality) at Bracton, or Blackstone, or Kent, or even the American Law Reports in conducting my search. Because reasonable people can disagree about the content of particular traditions, and because they can disagree even about which traditions are relevant to the definition of "liberty," the plurality has not found the objective boundary that it seeks.

Even if we could agree, moreover, on the content and significance of particular traditions, we still would be forced to identify the point at which a tradition becomes firm enough to be relevant to our definition of liberty and the moment at which it becomes too obsolete to be relevant any longer. The plurality supplies no objective means by which we might make these determinations. Indeed, as soon as the plurality sees signs that the tradition upon which it bases its decision (the laws denying putative fathers like Michael standing to assert paternity) is crumbling, it shifts ground and says that the case has nothing to do with that tradition, after all. "What is at issue here," the plurality asserts after canvassing the law on paternity suits, "is not entitlement to a state pronouncement that Victoria was begotten by Michael." But that is precisely what is at issue here, and the plurality's last-minute denial of this fact dramatically illustrates the subjectivity of its own analysis.

It is ironic that an approach so utterly dependent on tradition is so indifferent to our precedents. Citing barely a handful of this Court's numerous decisions defining the scope of the liberty protected by the Due Process Clause to support its reliance on tradition, the plurality acts as though English legal treatises and the American Law Reports always have provided the sole source for our constitutional principles. They have not. Just as common-law notions no longer define the "property" that the Constitution protects, see *Goldberg v. Kelly,* 397 U.S. 254 [1970], neither do they circumscribe the "liberty" that it guarantees. On the contrary, " '[l]iberty' and 'property' are broad and majestic terms. . . ."

The plurality's interpretive method is more than novel; it is misguided. It ignores the good reasons for limiting the role of "tradition" in interpreting the Constitution's deliberately capacious language. In the plurality's constitutional universe, we may not take notice of the fact that the original reasons for the conclusive presumption of paternity are out of place in a world in which blood tests can prove virtually beyond a shadow of a doubt who sired a particular child and in which the fact of illegitimacy no longer plays the burdensome and stigmatizing role it once did. Nor, in the plurality's world, may we deny "tradition" its full scope by pointing out that the rationale for the conventional rule has changed over the years; instead, our task is simply to identify a rule denying the asserted interest and not to ask whether the basis for that rule—which is the true reflection of the values undergirding it—has changed too often or too recently to call the rule embodying that rationale a "tradition." Moreover, by describing the decisive question as whether Michael and Victoria's interest is one that has been "tradition-ally *protected by* our society," (emphasis added), rather than one that society traditionally has thought important (with or without protecting it), and by suggesting that our sole function is to "*discern* the society's views," (emphasis added), the plurality acts as if the only purpose of the Due Process Clause is to confirm the importance of interests already protected by a majority of the States. Transforming the protection afforded by the Due Process Clause into a redundancy mocks those who, with care and purpose, wrote the Fourteenth Amendment.

In construing the Fourteenth Amendment to offer shelter only to those interests specifically protected by historical practice, moreover, the plurality ignores the kind of society in which our Constitution exists. We are not an assimilative, homogeneous society, but a facilitative, pluralistic one, in which we must be willing to abide someone else's unfamiliar or even repellant practice because the same tolerant impulse protects our own idiosyncracies. Even if we can agree, therefore, that "family" and "parenthood" are part of the good life, it is absurd to assume that we can agree on the content of those terms and destructive to pretend that we do. In a community such as ours, "liberty" must include the freedom not to conform. The plurality today squashes this freedom by requiring specific approval from history before protecting anything in the name of liberty.

The document that the plurality construes today is unfamiliar to me. It is not the living charter that I have taken to be our Constitution; it is instead a stagnant, archaic, hidebound document steeped in the prejudices and superstitions of a time long past. *This* Constitution does not recognize that times change, does not see that sometimes a practice or rule outlives its foundations. I cannot accept an interpretive method that does such violence to the charter that I am bound by oath to uphold.

The question before us . . . is whether California has an interest so powerful that it justifies granting Michael *no* hearing before terminating his parental rights. . . .

Make no mistake: to say that the State must provide Michael with a hearing to prove his paternity is not to express any opinion of the ultimate state of affairs between Michael and Victoria and Carole and Gerald. In order to change the current situation among these people, Michael first must convince a court that he is Victoria's father, and even if he is able to do this, he will be denied visitation rights if that would be in Victoria's best interests. It is elementary that a determination that a State must afford procedures before it terminates a given right is not a prediction about the end result of those procedures.

In a separate dissenting opinion, Justice White observed

California plainly denies Michael [due process] protection, by refusing him the opportunity to rebut the State's presumption that the mother's husband is the father of the child. California law not only deprives Michael H. of a legal parent-child relationship with his daughter Victoria but even denies him the opportunity to introduce blood-test evidence to rebut the demonstrable fiction that Gerald is Victoria's father. . . .

"The emphasis of the Due Process Clause is on 'process.' " *Moore v. East Cleveland,* 431 U.S. 494 (1977) (White, J., dissenting). I fail to see the fairness in the process established by the State of California and endorsed by the Court today. Michael H. has evidence which demonstrates that he is the father of young Victoria. Yet he is blocked by the State from presenting that evidence to a court. As a result, he is foreclosed from establishing his paternity and is ultimately precluded, by the State, from developing a relationship with his child. "A fundamental requirement of due process is 'the opportunity to be heard.' *Grannis v. Ordean,* 234 U.S. 385 (1914)]. It is an opportunity which must be granted at a meaningful time and in a meaningful manner." *Armstrong v. Manzo,* 380 U.S. 545 (1965). I fail to see how appellant was granted any meaningful opportunity to be heard when he was precluded at the very outset from introducing evidence which would support his assertion of paternity. Michael H. has never been afforded an opportunity to present his case in any meaningful manner.

In a further ruling in *Washington v. Harper,* 110 S.Ct. 1028 (1990), the Rehnquist Court held that mentally ill prison inmates may be treated with antipsychotic drugs against their will and without a prior judicial proceeding. In his opinion for the Court, Justice Kennedy held that such treatment does not violate substantive due process where the prisoner is deemed to be dangerous to himself or others and the treatment is in the prisoner's medical interest. Justice Kennedy also held that the due process clause does not require a judicial hearing prior to such treatment of prisoners. The requirements of "procedural due process," according to Justice Kennedy, are satisfied by prison policies requiring administrative panels, composed of corrections officials and medical professionals, to review decisions to treat prisoners with antipsychotic drugs. Justices Stevens, joined by Justices Brennan and Marshall, dissented.

NOTES

1. See *Parham v. J. R.,* 442 U.S. 584 (1979).
2. See *Vitek v. Jones,* 445 U.S. 480 (1980).
3. See *Pennhurst State School and Hospital v. Halderman,* 451 U.S. 1 (1981).
4. *Davidson v. Cannon,* 474 U.S. 344 (1986). See also *Parratt v. Taylor,* 451 U.S. 527 (1981).

SELECTED BIBLIOGRAPHY

Chemerinsky, Erwin. "Foreword: The Vanishing Constitution." 103 *Harvard Law Review* 43 (1989).

Donaldson, Kenneth. *Insanity Inside Out,* New York: Crown Publishers, 1976.

Stauss, David. "Due Process, Government Inaction, and Private Wrongs." In Gerhard Casper, and Dennis Hutchinson, eds., *The Supreme Court Review* (*1989*) (Chicago: University of Chicago Press, 1990), 53.

Tribe, Laurence. "The Curvature of Constitutional Space: What Lawyers Can Learn from Modern Physics." 103 *Harvard Law Review* 1 (1989).

5

FREEDOM OF EXPRESSION AND ASSOCIATION

A CONNECTION BETWEEN freedom of speech, press, and association and the exigencies of a self-governing society was acknowledged by the colonists and the Framers of the Constitution and Bill of Rights. Yet in the seventeenth and eighteenth centuries those freedoms were more circumscribed than today and were still emerging from a protracted struggle that began in England in the Middle Ages.

Government censorship stems from the 1275 enactment of *De Scandalis Magnatum,* imposing penalties for any false talk about the king.[1] The law punished what a later amendment in 1559 termed "seditious words" (criticism of the government subject to criminal penalties) for contributing to public disorder and lawlessness. In the sixteenth and seventeenth centuries, censorship expanded with the enforcement of *Scandalum Magnatum* by the King's Council, which sat in the "starred chambre" at Westminster and became infamously known as the Star Chamber. The Star Chamber was especially merciless in cases such as that of the *Trial of William Prynn.*[2] Prynn had published a book expressing disdain for actors and acting, which was viewed as an attack on the queen, who had recently appeared in a play, and, therefore, as seditious libel against the government. Prynn was fined £10,000, sentenced to life imprisonment, branded on the forehead, and had his nose slit and ears cut off!

The Star Chamber left a legacy of human tragedy and an

imprint on the English heritage from which the drafters of the Bill of Rights drew their principles of free government. The Star Chamber was abolished in 1641, but its precedents continued to be applied by common-law courts. Criminal liability for slander remained a question of law, not of fact for juries to decide, and the truth or falsity of a publication was immaterial as a defense against prosecution. Partisan political publications (especially in the colonies) were discouraged both by the Licensing Act of 1662 and a tax on all newspapers imposed by the Stamp and Advertising Act of 1711.

By 1776 freedom of speech and press basically meant the absence of prior restraints or censorship. As the most influential eighteenth century legal commentator, Sir William Blackstone, authoritatively observed:

The liberty of the press is indeed essential to the nature of a free state; but this consists in laying no *previous* restraints upon publications, and not in freedom from censure for criminal matter when published. Every freeman has an undoubted right to lay what sentiments he pleases before the public; but if he publishes what is improper, mischievous, or illegal, he must take the consequences of his own termerity.[3]

Blackstone assumed that the Parliament could punish licentious speech and press, and offered no principle or standard for protecting speakers and publishers from subsequent punishment for what they said or published.

In England and in the colonies, differences over what constituted liberty and licentiousness, truth and falsehood, and good motives and criminal intent, perpetuated a tumultuous struggle for freedom of speech and press. In 1792, with the Fox Libel Act, English juries were finally given the power to determine the cuplability of allegedly libelous publications, rather than being confined to deciding whether an individual had in fact published allegedly libelous materials. Not until Lord Campbell's Act in 1843 was truth accepted as a defense against libel indictments, and only after 1855 was the Stamp and Advertising Act abandoned.

Colonial governments could be just as suppressive as the English Crown and Parliament. Indeed restrictions on speech and press articulated in English common law were largely incorporated into colonial common law. "Colonial America was an open society dotted with closed enclaves," as political scientist John P. Roche concluded, "and one could generally settle in with his co-believers in safety and comfort and exercise the right of oppression."[4]

While objecting to the prior censorship of the press, English and colonial libertarians did not seriously question the propriety of punishing seditious libel and licentious publications. Thus although poet John Milton exalted freedom of speech and press in *Areopagitica*, he refused to recognize such freedom for Protestants and deplored libel of Parliament.[5] So too, John Locke, whose writings were so influential for the Framers, in *A Letter Concerning Toleration*, urged that "no opinions contrary to human society, or to those moral rules which are necessary to the preservation of civil society, are to be tolerated by the magistrate."[6]

Widely read in the colonies were the letters of two English Whig political journalists, John Trenchard and Thomas Gordon, who wrote under the pseudonym of "Cato." Benjamin Franklin, who himself ran a printing house, first published Cato's essays in 1721. When proclaiming freedom of speech and press as "the great bulwark of Liberty," Cato observed:

The Administration of Government, is nothing else but the Attendance of the Trustees of the People upon the Interest, and Affairs of the People. And it is the Part and Business of the People, for whose sake alone all publick Matters are or ought to be transacted, to see whether they be well or ill transacted; so it is the Interest, and ought to be Ambition of all honest Magistrates, to have their Deeds openly examined and publickly scanned.

Freedom of Speech is ever the Symptom as well as the Effect of good Government.[7]

Although giving expression to the eighteenth-century libertarian vision of free speech and press, *Cato's Letters* did not challenge the common law rejection of truth as a defense in libel actions. Like Milton and Locke, Cato accepted the common law proscription of seditious libel. Even Cato's colonial protégé, John Peter Zenger, failed to repudiate the common law of seditious libel when defending an unbridled freedom of the press to criticize government.

The struggle for freedom of speech and press during the colonial period largely revolved around the application of accepted common law principles as articulated by Blackstone. By the time of the ratification of the Constitution, however, libertarians, like James Madison, broke with Alexander Hamilton and others who continued to embrace the Blackstonian understanding of free speech and press.

In 1789, when the First Congress entertained amendments to the Constitution, Madison endeavored to give constitutional effect to his rejection of common-law principles. He urged the adoption of the following provision: "The people shall not be deprived or abridged of their right to speak, to write, or to publish their sentiments; and the freedom of the press, as one

CONSTITUTIONAL HISTORY
The 1735 Trial of John Zenger and Free Speech in the Colonies

Undoubtedly, the *cause célèbre* of colonial prosecutions was the trial of John Peter Zenger, publisher of *The New York Weekly Journal*. The *Journal*, like other colonial newspapers, was a partisan publication, and Zenger, poorly educated and neither an editor or writer for his paper, was part of political faction that lost power when William Cosby became governor of New York. In 1734, Zenger published, along with several of Cato's essays, a series of satirical ballads attacking Governor Cosby. A year later, Zenger was tried for printing "many things tending to raise factions and tumults among the people of this province, inflaming their minds with contempt for his majesty's government, and greatly disturbing the peace thereof." In the penultimate trial before royal judges, Zenger's initial lawyers, James Alexander and William Smith, sought to use the trial to further discredit Cosby's administration, and went so far as to attack the chief justice for presiding at the trial. They were promptly disbarred from practicing law in the colony. An acclaimed Quaker attorney, Andrew Hamilton, came unsolicited from Philadelphia to Zenger's defense with an unprecedented challenge of the common law principles governing freedom of speech and press. Hamilton contended that Zenger's publications were true and that if he was not permitted to demonstrate their truth as a defense, then the jury should acquit Zenger. The jury, already critical of Cosby's administration and the chief justice, found Zenger not guilty.

Zenger's trial popularized for colonists the struggle against governmental censorship in the form of prosecutions for sedition. Both sides of the Zenger controversy, however, accepted the common-law principle that freedom of speech and press did not permit licentiousness and seditious libel. What divided them was the issue of when and where to draw a line between permissible political commentary and licentious criticism of the government.

Sources: See Livingston Rutherford, *John Peter Zenger, His Press, His Trial, and a Bibliography of Zenger Imprints* (New York: Dodd, Mead, & Co., 1904); and Leonard Levy, ed., *Freedom of the Press from Zenger to Jefferson* (New York: Bobbs-Merrill, 1966).

of the great bulwarks of liberty, shall be inviolable." Madison argued that "freedom of the press and the rights of conscience, those choicest privileges of the people, are unguarded in the British constitution." In England, Parliament was trusted to guard the people against the sovereign's unlawful acts. By contrast, Madison pointed out, in the United States the people are sovereign and their rights, therefore, had to be guaranteed against both the executive and the legislature. For these reasons, Madison not only rejected the application of Blackstonian common law principles to freedom of speech and press, but proposed as another constitutional amendment that "No State shall violate the equal rights of conscience, or the freedom of the press."

Madison advanced perhaps the broadest possible view of free speech and press. Considering a vigorous press essential to free government, he rejected the imposition of any sanctions for the licentiousness accompanying the exercise of free speech and press. In Madison's words:

Among those principles deemed sacred in America, among those sacred rights considered as forming the bulwark of liberty, which the Government contemplates with awful reverence and would approach only with the most cautious circumspection, there is no one of which the importance is more deeply impressed on the public mind than the liberty of the press. That this *liberty* is often carried to excess; that it has sometimes degenerated into *licentiousness,* is seen and lamented, *but the remedy has* not yet been discovered. Perhaps it is an evil inseparable from the good with which it is allied; perhaps it is a shoot which cannot be stripped from the stalk without wounding vitally the plant from which it is torn. However desirable those measures might be which might correct without enslaving the press, they have never yet been devised in America.[8]

Still, as Madison acknowledged, his understanding of freedom of speech and press was not representative of that in the founding period.[9] Colonial experiences with censorship by the Crown had fostered agreement that free speech and press should be protected. Also, there was little debate in the First Congress on adopting a provision guaranteeing the freedom of speech and press. But those, including Thomas Jefferson, who feared the abuse of these freedoms also expected the states to continue common law restrictions on libel and other licentious publications.

Madison's proposal for expressly prohibiting the states from limiting the freedom of speech and press did not survive. Ratified on December 15, 1791, the First Amendment provides, "Congress shall make no law respecting an establishment of religion, or prohibiting the exercise thereof; or abridging the freedom of speech, or of the press; or the right of the people peaceably to assemble." The amendment was thought to protect only against prior restraint by the national government; it did not provide absolute immunity for what speakers or publishers might utter or print. Thus the First Amendment was in Hamiltonian terms superfluous (because the Constitution did not give Congress the power to regulate speech and press in the first place), whereas from Madison's vantage point it did not sufficiently safeguard individuals' freedom (particularly from state regulation), and from Jefferson's perspective, the amendment simply reaffirmed both the limits of the national government's power and the reserved powers of the states.

Less than a decade later, a constitutional crisis over the First Amendment arose when Congress passed the Alien and Sedition Acts of 1798. The Sedition Act imposed criminal sanctions for "any false, scandalous writing against the government of the United States." It was passed by the Federalist Congress to censure political criticism and turn public opinion against the Jeffersonian-Republicans. The ensuing controversy revealed, once again, that the predominant view of freedom of speech and press was that the First Amendment incorporated traditional Blackstonian common law principles, rather than broader libertarian principles.

The congressional reports on the repeal of the Sedition Act on February 25, 1799, amply illustrate the acceptance of Blackstonian principles. The constitutionality of the act was defended in the majority's report to Congress on four grounds. First, punishment of seditious libel did not constitute an abridgement of freedom of speech and press, because those freedoms never included "a license for every man to publish what he pleases without being liable to punishment." Second, although little more than a restatement of the first point, the laws of the states and national government never extended "to the publication of false, scandalous, and malicious writings against the Government." Third, the Sedition Act was "merely declaratory of the common law, and useful for rendering that law more generally known, and more easily understood." Fourth, the committee drew a distinction between the religious and the speech and press freedoms protected by the First Amendment. The amendment provides that "*Congress shall make no law respecting* an establishment of religion, *or prohibiting* the free exercise thereof," implying that the national government is absolutely barred from legislating on religious matters. By comparison, the amendment forbids Congress only from passing laws "*abridging* the freedom of speech, or of the press." From that language, the committee surmised that Congress was not precluded from passing legislation *respecting* speech and press.[10]

In the House of Representatives, Albert Gallatin and others had argued against the constitutionality of the Sedition Act on the grounds that "The States have complete power on the subject." Likewise, Thomas Jefferson, in the Kentucky Resolutions of 1798 and 1799 (see Chapter 1), insisted that the states alone possessed the power to initiate libel actions. But the minority report filed in Congress on the repeal of the Sedition Act drew on Madison's understanding of the importance of political speech and guaranteeing the freedom of political debate and criticism:

The most important and necessary information for the people to receive is, of the misconduct of the Government; because their good deeds, although they will produce affection and gratitude to public officers, will only confirm the existing confidence, and will, therefore, make no change in the conduct of the people. The question, whether the Government ought to have control over the persons who alone can give information throughout the country, is nothing more than this, whether men interested in suppressing information necessary for the people to have, ought to be entrusted with the power, or whether they ought to have a power which their personal interest leads to the abuse of?[11]

On this basis, Jeffersonian-Republicans and libertarians, who were a minority in Congress, rejected the majority's report on the constitutionality of the Sedition Act. But their arguments proved unpersuasive, in part because they were neither in complete agreement nor consistent in their views of the scope of freedom of speech and press. The Jeffersonian-Republicans waxed and waned in maintaining that the only permissible restrictions on speech and press could come from the states. And the continued prosecutions for seditious libel after the Sedition Act expired underscores how deeply rooted was the common law understanding of the freedom of speech and press.

There were no prosecutions under the Sedition Act after 1801, when the act expired and Thomas Jefferson became president. But seditious libel remained a crime in common law. In 1804, President Jefferson wrote to Mrs. John Adams and explained his pardoning of those convicted under the Sedition Act, insisting that the "law [was] a nullity as absolute and as papable as if Congress had ordered us to fall down and worship a golden image." Eloquent in describing his rage against the Federalists' prosecutions under the act, Jefferson was no less vengeful in recommending prosecutions by the states of Federalist editors![12] In New York courts, in *People v. Croswell*, 3 Johnson's (N.Y.) Cases 336 (1804), Republicans prosecuted a Federalist editor for seditious libel against President Jefferson. Three years later, they were still relying on state and federal courts to try individuals for seditious libel against the president. Not until 1812, in another action for libel against the president, did the Supreme Court finally rule that there was no federal common law of crimes, including the crime of seditious libel. *United States v. Hudson and Goodwin*, 1 Cr. 21 (1812).

In 1833, the most widely read commentator on the Constitution within a generation of the founding period and a Supreme Court justice, Joseph Story, observed that "There is a good deal of loose reasoning on the subject of the liberty of the press, as if its inviolability were constitutionally such." Story endorsed Blackstone's view of free speech and press, remained uncertain whether the First Amendment prohibited Congress from "punishing the licentiousness of the press," and had no doubt that the states could punish individuals for libelous and "other mischievous publications."[13]

By the late nineteenth century, another influential authority on the Constitution, Thomas Cooley, acknowledged that the press had assumed an increasingly important role in society as a result of technological innovations and urbanization. Cooley agreed with Madison that "Repression of full and free discussion is dangerous in any government resting upon the will of the people." However, like Story, Cooley continued to view the First Amendment in terms of common law principles and practices. The amendment, as he put it, guaranteed "a right to freely utter and publish whatever the citizen may please, and to be protected against any responsibility for so doing, except so far as such publications, from their blasphemy, obscenity, or scandalous character, may be a public offense, or as by their falsehood and malice they may injuriously affect the standing, reputation, or pecuniary interests of individuals."[14]

From the founding period and throughout the nineteenth century, the First Amendment was thus comprehended in terms of developing common law principles and practices. That meant that Blackstone's definition of free speech and press served as the touchstone for understanding those freedoms. As we saw earlier, Blackstone's view was that liberty of speech and press meant the absence of prior restraints but also the permissibility of subsequent punishment for speech or print that was deemed "improper, mischievous or illegal." While Blackstone distinguished between liberty and licentiousness—or protected and unprotected communications—he failed to articulate the criteria for determining what and when speech and print constituted an abuse of liberty, assuming that common law judges would defer to legislatures when defining the nature of licentiousness.

In the absence of constitutional restraints imposed by the Supreme Court under the First Amendment, the struggle for free speech and press became a legacy of suppression. In the nineteenth century, lower courts, legislatures, government officials, and ultimately the shifting tides of public opinion enjoyed broad power to punish speech and press and thereby the power to deprive the rights of minorities to express unpopular views.

After the public outcry against the Sedition Act, the national government in the first half of the nineteenth century largely left the suppression of licentious publications to the states. Beginning in the 1830s, the dissemination of information about slavery was punished in the North and the South by enthusiasts both of abolition and of the institution of slavery. In the North, crusading vigilantes fomented mob action, leading to the tarring and feathering, clubbing, whipping, and shooting of abolitionists. William Lloyd Garrison, for one, was stripped half-naked and paraded through the streets of Boston. In Illinois, Elijah Lovejoy died at the hands of a mob, while resisting the destruction of his printing press. In the South, legislation punished abolitionist sentiments as "incendiary," "inflammatory," and "provoking servile insurrection." That legislation was reinforced by censorship of the mails. Censorship of the mails began in 1835 with the refusal of a Charleston, South Carolina, postmaster to deliver abolitionist mail in the South. The postmaster general, along with President Andrew Jackson and John C. Calhoun, endeavored to get Congress to pass a law authorizing such actions. Congress refused and passed a law to the contrary, at the urging of Daniel Webster and Henry Clay that such legislation would abridge free of speech and press. But states effectively nullified federal law. During the Civil War, major newspapers in the North and the South criticized President Abraham Lincoln's conduct of the war, and Lincoln reluctantly ordered the New York *World* and the New York *Journal of Commerce* closed and their editors arrested.

While abolitionist sentiments sparked government censorship in the early nineteenth century, allegedly lewd and obscene materials were the object of censorship in the latter part of the century. In 1865, Congress authorized punishment for purveyors of obscenity and further expanded the law with the Comstock Act of 1873, named after Anthony Comstock, a tireless crusader against impure and lustful publications. Into this century, federal courts upheld congressional power to suppress obscene materials. Likewise, state courts affirmed bans against publishing, importing, mailing, and purchasing of pornographic materials, as well as supposed objectionable books by noted authors Honoré Balzac, Gustav Flaubert, James Joyce, and D. H. Lawrence, as well as Theodore Dreiser's *An American Tragedy!*

Along with a growing number of obscenity prosecutions, actions for criminal libel increased in the last quarter of the nineteenth century, with more than 100 prosecutions between 1890 and 1900. By the turn of the century, public opinion was aroused by the doctrines of socialism, anarachism, syndicalism, and the specter of violent revolution raised by radical political groups, especially Communists. The assassination of President William McKinley by a reputed anarchist dramatized for the public the dangers of such doctrines. Consequently, there was resumption of legislation punishing seditious libel. By the end of World War I, no less thirty-two states had laws against criminal syndicalism or sedition; more than 1,900 individuals were prosecuted for seditious libel and more than 100 newspapers, pamphlets, and other periodicals were censored.[15]

The Espionage Act of 1917 was the primary source of federal restrictions on speech and press in the early twentieth century. That act rested on the traditional dichotomy of liberty versus licentiousness in imposing criminal liability on any individual who, when the country was at war, would "make or convey false reports or false statements with the intent to interfere with the operations or success of the military or naval forces of the United States or to promote the success of its enemies," or to "willfully cause or attempt to cause insubordination, disloyalty, mutiny, or refusal of duty, in the military or naval forces of the United States," or to "willfully obstruct the recruiting or enlistment service of the United States, to the injury of the service of the United States."[16]

When challenges to the Espionage Act and other state laws punishing dissident and subversive individual and groups finally reached the Supreme Court, the justices faced the vexing responsibility of giving meaning to the First Amendment by developing standards and tests for determining the scope of constitutionally protected free speech and press.

NOTES

1. See Fredrick Siebert, *Freedom of the Press in England, 1476–1776* (Urbana: University of Illinois, 1965).

2. *Trial of William Prynn*, 3 Howell's State Trials 561 (1632).

3. Sir William Blackstone, *Commentaries on the Laws of England*, Vol. 4 (Oxford, UK: Clarendon Press, 1766), 151–152.

4. John P. Roche, *Shadow and Substance* (New York: Macmillan, 1964), 11.

5. John Milton, *Areopagitica*, in *The Works of John Milton*, Vol. 4, ed. William Haller (New York: Columbia University Press, 1931); and see William Clyde, *The Struggle for the Freedom of the Press from Caxton to Cromwell* (London: Oxford University Press, 1934).

6. John Locke, "A Letter Concerning Toleration," in *The Works of John Locke*, Vol. 4, 11th ed. (London: W. Otridge, 1905–1907), 45–46.

7. Cato, "Reflections on Libelling," in *Freedom of the Press from Zenger to Jefferson* ed. Leonard Levy (New York: Bobbs-Merrill, 1966), 12.

8. *Annals of Congress: First Congress, 1798–1791*, Vol. 1 (Washington, DC: Gales and Seaton, 1834), 453; and James Madison, *The Writings*

of James Madison, Vol. 6, ed. Haillard Hunt (New York: Putnam's Sons, 1906–1910), 336.

9. See James Madison to Edward Everett (Aug. 28, 1830), in Madison, *The Writings of James Madison*, Vol. 9, 383.

10. "Majority Report on Repeal of the Sedition Act," *Annals of Congress*, 5th Cong., 3d Sess., Feb. 25, 1799, 2987–2990.

11. *Ibid.*, 3003–3014.

12. Letters from Thomas Jefferson to Abigal Adams (Sept. 11, 1804), and to Thomas LcKean (Feb. 19, 1803) in *The Writings of Thomas Jefferson*, Vol. 8, ed. Paul Ford (New York: Putnam's Sons, 1892–1899), 310 and 218–219.

13. Joseph Story, *Commentaries on the Constitution of the United States* (Boston: Little, Brown, 1833), 735.

14. Thomas Cooley, *A Treatise on the Constitutional Limitations*, Vol. 2 (Boston: Little, Brown, 1868), 886 and 931–940.

15. See Fredrick Siebert, *The Rights and Privileges of the Press* (New York: D. Appleton-Century, 1934), 271; and James Paul and Murrary Schwartz, *Federal Censorship: Obscenity in the Mail* (New York: Free Press, 1961), 17–24.

16. The Espionage Act of June 15, 1917, 40 Stat. 217. See also Act of May 16, 1918, 40 Stat. 553.

SELECTED BIBLIOGRAPHY

Chafee, Zechariah, Jr. *Free Speech in the United States*. Cambridge, MA: Harvard University Press, 1941.

Levy, Leonard, ed. *Freedom of Press from Zenger to Jefferson*. New York: Bobbs-Merrill, 1966.

Levy, Leonard, *Emergence of a Free Press*. New York: Oxford University Press, 1985.

Meiklejohn, Alexander. *Political Freedom: The Constitutional Powers of the People*. New York: Harper & Row, 1948.

Nelson, Harold, ed. *Freedom of the Press from Hamilton to the Warren Court*. New York: Bobbs-Merrill, 1967.

Smith, James M. *Freedom's Fetters: The Alien and Sedition Laws and American Civil Liberties*. Ithaca, New York: Cornell University Press, 1956.

A. JUDICIAL APPROACHES TO THE FIRST AMENDMENT

When First Amendment challenges to state and federal sedition laws reached the Supreme Court in the aftermath of World War I, the convictions were upheld. This litigation, however, forced the Court to confront two long-avoided tasks: first, deciding whether the First Amendment applied equally against the states and the national government and, second, articulating standards for defining the scope of constitutionally protected free speech and press. Once the Court held the First Amendment applied to the states (see Chapter 3), it could no longer avoid the even more difficult task of giving constitutional meaning to the amendment. Initially, the Court took for granted that Blackstone's common law principles governed the First Amendment's guarantees for free speech and press. But gradually members of the Court pressed for the development of constitutional principles that would define the scope of protected speech and press. By 1936, in *Grosjean v. American Press Co.*, 297 U.S. 233 (1936), Justice George Sutherland finally noted, as Madison more than a century before had urged, that constitutional principles (not the English common law) governed the scope of protected speech and press. In Sutherland's words,

It is impossible to concede that by the words "freedom of the press" the framers of the amendment intended to adopt merely the narrow view then reflected by the law of England that such freedom consisted only in immunity from previous censorship. . . . Undoubtedly, the range of a constitutional provision phrased in terms of the common law sometimes may be fixed by recourse to the applicable rules of law. But the doctrine which justifies such recourse, like other canons of construction, must yield to more compelling reasons whenever they exist.

Still, it took decades for the Court to respond to those "more compelling reasons" for breaking away from common law principles and articulating the constitutional principles that now govern the application of the First Amendment. For the justices that meant reconciling rival interpretative approaches to the First Amendment and a political struggle within the Court, as well as between the Court and the country over the freedoms of speech and press.

(1) Fifty Years of "Clear and Present Danger"

The surge of litigation challenging convictions under the Espionage Act and state sedition laws necessitated that the Court develop its own interpretative standards for protecting the freedom of speech and press. In *Schenck v. United States* (1919) (see page 355), Justice Oliver Wendell Holmes initially intimated what would become one of the best-known tests for defining the scope of constitutionally protected free speech and press: "the clear and present danger" test—"whether the words used are used in such circumstances and are of such a nature as to create a clear and present danger that they will bring about the substantive evils that Congress has a right to prevent." However, Holmes retreated and based his opinion on the old common law presumption of the "reasonableness of legislation" and whether the proscribed speech had a "bad tendency"—"whether the statements contained in the [communication] had a natural tendency to produce the forbidden consequences."[1] Within a week, in two more unanimous rulings, Holmes again upheld convictions under the Espionage Act on the bad tendency standard.[2]

But in a fourth case in 1919, *Abrams v. United States*, 250 U.S. 616 (1919), Holmes broke with the majority over using the clear and present danger test as an alternative to the bad tendency test. *Abrams* involved the conviction of five individuals under the Espionage Act for distributing leaflets condemning the government's war effort and intervention in Russia and calling for a general strike of workers in protest. When rejecting the majority's reliance on the bad tendency test, in dissent with Justice Louis Brandeis, Holmes proclaimed that "Only the emergency that makes it immediately dangerous to leave the correction of evil counsels to time warrants making any exception to the sweeping command, 'Congress shall make no law . . . abridging the freedom of speech." His dissent in *Abrams* was followed by four other biting dissents and one concurring opinion, establishing the foundations for evolution of this most famous of judicial approaches to the First Amendment.[3]

In the 1920s, the Court continued to hold that the First Amendment did not protect speech and press that might have pernicious effects on society. *Gitlow v. People of the State of New York* (1920) (see page 357), is illustrative. There Justice Sanford reaffirmed the traditional common law principles governing the punishment of subversive speech:

Such utterance, by their very nature, involve danger to the public peace and to the security of the State. They threaten breaches of the peace and ultimate revolution. And the immediate danger is none the less real and substantial, because the effect of a given utterance cannot be accurately foreseen. The State cannot reasonably be required to measure the danger from every such utterance in the nice balance of a jeweler's scale. A single revolutionary spark may kindle a fire that, smoldering for a time, may burst into a sweeping and destructive confragration.

In another illustrious dissent in *Gitlow*, Holmes reiterated his clear and present danger test. Two years later, in *Whitney v. California*, 274 U.S. 357 (1927), involving the conviction of a Communist under a state syndicalism act, Brandeis endeavored to further sharpen the clear and present danger test. Even in the face of legislation, the First Amendment forbids restrictions

Justices Oliver Wendell Holmes (left) and Louis D. Brandeis. In the 1920s, Justices Brandeis and Holmes dissented from the Court's upholding the convictions of individuals for expressing unpopular, and what was considered subversive, political ideas. In an effort to extend First Amendment protection for free speech, Justice Holmes invented the clear and present danger test. *Collection of the Supreme Court of the United States.*

short of demonstrating an *imminent* clear and present danger; in Brandeis's words, "Only an emergency can justify repression."

In the two decades following *Abrams,* the clear and present danger test was virtually abandoned. Under the leadership of Chief Justice Charles Evans Hughes in the 1930s, however, the Court also substantially undermined reliance on the reasonableness of legislation and bad tendency approach. A series of rulings extended First Amendment protection to pamphlets and leaflets,[4] and peaceful picketing,[5] because its guarantees were construed to safeguard "the liberty to discuss publicly and truthfully all matters of public concern without previous restraint or fear of subsequent punishment."[6]

In the 1940s, the clear and present danger test enjoyed a kind of renaissance, buttressed by the Hughes Court's precedents expanding the scope of the First Amendment. The test, though, was also fundamentally transformed during the tenures of Chief Justices Harlan Stone and Fred Vinson (respectively, 1941–1946 and 1946–1953).

Holmes and Brandeis formulated the clear and present danger

test as an evidentiary rule for determining the permissibility of applying statutory prohibitions in particular circumstances; it did not purport to establish a standard for reviewing the constitutionality of legislation per se. Moreover, they invoked the test only in cases involving alleged threats to national security.

By contrast, in the 1940s the Court turned the clear and present danger test into a standard for judging both the application and constitutionality per se of statutes. It also became a basis for reviewing a wide range of restrictions on speech and press, including state laws restricting or prohibiting handbill distributions and solicitations,[7] and requiring compulsory saluting of the American flag,[8] as well as contempt-of-court convictions and individuals' speeches before public assemblies.[9]

As the scope of the First Amendment expanded in the 1940s, some justices pushed for an even more libertarian approach. Chief Justice Stone and Justices Black, Douglas, Murphy, and Rutledge claimed the amendment enjoyed a "preferred position," virtually foreclosing the possibility of upholding any restrictions on free speech and press. As Stone observed, "The First Amendment is not confined to safeguarding freedom of speech and freedom of religion against discriminatory attempts to wipe them out. On the contrary, the Constitution, by virtue of the First and Fourteenth Amendments, has put those freedoms in a *preferred position.*"[10]

The reformulation of the clear and present danger test and articulation of the preferred position approach toward the First Amendment was not without opposition from within the Court. Throughout his twenty-three years on the bench (1939–1962), Justice Frankfurter criticized his colleagues for their "idle play on words" and "perversion" of the Holmesian-Brandeis formulation and ridiculed those embracing a "preferred position" for devising a "deceptive formula . . . [that] makes for mechanical jurisprudence."[11]

Divisions within the Court were further exacerbated by the political currents in the 1940s and 1950s. Beginning in the early 1940s, political passions again swept the country with dire warnings about fascism and communism. In 1940, Congress enacted the Alien Registration Act, or Smith Act, the first federal peacetime sedition act since the Alien and Sedition Acts of 1798. Less restrictive than the Sedition Act, the Smith Act made it a crime to advocate or to belong to any organization that advocated the forceful overthrow of the government. Subsequently, Congress required loyalty oaths and statements of non-Communist affiliation from public and private sector employees, with the Labor-Management Relations Act of 1947. The paranoia over Communists continued through the 1950s. Over President Harry

Truman's veto, Congress passed the Internal Security Act of 1950, also known as the McCarran Act, which required members of the Communist party to register with the U.S. attorney general. Senator Joseph McCarthy's subcommittee and the Special House Committee on Un-American Activities as well as numerous legislative committees, held hearings and investigations of individuals' loyalty.

Bitterly divided, the Court affirmed the constitutionality of both the Smith Act and the McCarran Act in, respectively, *Dennis v. United States* (1951) (see page 362), and *Communist Party v. Subversive Activities Control Board,* 367 U.S. 203 (1961). *Dennis* remains the watershed case in which the Vinson Court's reformulation of the clear and present danger test rendered futile further reliance on the test.

Dennis was presaged Chief Justice Vinson's opinion in *American Communications Association v. Douds,* 339 U.S. 382 (1950), upholding a requirement for the filing on non-Communist affidavits in the Labor-Management Relations Act. In their briefs before the Court, the unions argued that it was difficult "to conceive how the expression of belief, or the joining of a political party, without more, could ever constitute [a clear and present] danger." Chief Justice Vinson thought otherwise: The threat of communism was substantial, considerably greater than when Holmes proposed his clear and present danger test and, therefore, justified congressional action. No less important, Vinson indicated that the clear and present danger test was not a mechanical rule, but rather a balancing technique:

[E]ven harmful conduct cannot justify restrictions upon speech unless substantial interests of society are at stake. But in suggesting that the substantive evil must be serious and substantial, it was never the intention of this Court to lay down an absolutist test measured in terms of danger to the Nation. When the effect of a statute or ordinance upon the exercise of First Amendment freedoms is relatively small and the public interest to be protected is substantial, it is obvious that a rigid test requiring a showing of imminent danger to the security of the Nation is an absurdity.

In Vinson's hands, the clear and present danger test became a balancing technique for rationalizing restrictions on speech and press.[12]

The opinions in *Dennis* reveal the internal politics of the Vinson Court and the competing interpretative approaches toward the First Amendment. When a second opportunity to interpret the Smith Act arose with *Yates v. United States,* 354 U.S. 178 (1957), it was anticipated that the result would be different from that in *Dennis.* Oleta Yates and thirteen other second-string functionaries of the Communist party were prosecuted shortly after *Dennis* was announced; each was guilty, fined $10,000, and sentenced to five years in prison. By the time their appeal was granted in 1955, Vinson and his three supporters in *Dennis* were gone. President Dwight Eisenhower in 1953 had appointed Earl Warren as chief justice, and Justices Reed, Jackson, and Minton had been replaced by Whittaker, Harlan, and Brennan. Still, the Warren Court (with newly appointed Justices Whittaker and Brennan not participating) declined to strike down the Smith Act in *Yates*. However, it reversed five of the convictions and ordered retrials for the others, setting forth certain conditions for applying the Smith Act that made future convictions exceedingly difficult.

Justice Harlan's opinion for the Court in *Yates* abandoned the clear and present danger test and substituted instead a *balancing approach* on which First Amendment freedoms were weighed against society's right of self-preservation. He claimed that was the essense of *Dennis* in distinguishing between advocacy of abstract doctrines (which receives First Amendment protection) and the advocacy of violence and unlawful action. Two years later, he again provided the voice for a bare majority and reasserted his balancing approach to the First Amendment in *Barenblatt v. United States*, 360 U.S. 109 (1959) (see Vol. 1, Ch. 5).

By the 1960s, the clear and present danger test had evolved into a rhetorial technique and then gave way to Harlan's explicit balancing of First Amendment freedoms against legislative restrictions. Harlan's balancing approach, however, enjoyed the support only of a bare majority of the Court. In the early 1960s, the Warren Court was split five to four over balancing First Amendment freedoms, with Justice Potter Stewart as the swing vote. A bare majority, in *Scales v. United States*, 367 U.S. 203 (1961), upheld the Smith Act's prohibition on membership in subversive organizations, and in *Communist Party of the United States v. Subversives Activities Control Board (SACB)*, 367 U.S. 1 (1961), the registration requirements for all members of subversive organization, as established by the Internal Security Act of 1950. In *Scales*, Harlan upheld the membership clause by distinguishing between mere, passive members (the "foolish, deluded, or perhaps merely optimistic") and those knowing, active members whose intent was "to bring about the overthrow of the government as speedily as circumstances would permit." Over the four dissenters' objections that the Court had legitimated "guilt by association," Harlan's opinion for the majority concluded that there was enough evidence that Scales was an "active" member engaged in illegal advocacy. In the second case upholding the SCAB, Frankfurter performed the delicate task of writing an opinion for another bare majority. In both cases, Chief Justice Warren and Justices Black, Douglas, and Brennan dissented. One week later, though, Justice Stewart swung over to the dissenters side to form a majority for reversing the conviction of an individual found in contempt for refusing to answer questions before a subcommittee of the House Committee on Un-American Activities, *Deutch v. United States*, 367 U.S. 456 (1961).

Following *Scales*, prosecutions for subversive activities under the Smith Act sharply declined, and by the mid-1960s (with the appointments of Abe Fortas and Thurgood Marshall as associate justices) there was a solid majority on the Warren Court for striking down portions of the McCarran Act. Because Congress refused to appropriate funds, the SACB was finally shut down in 1973, over the objections of President Richard Nixon, who as a congressman in 1950 had been one of its sponsors. A year later, the Special House Committee on Un-American Activities was abolished and its duties transferred to the House Judicial Committee.

In Chief Justice Earl Warren's last term, the Court handed down a *per curiam* opinion in *Brandenburg v. Ohio* (1969) (see page 376), finally laying to rest the long line of cases upholding convictions for so-called subversive speech and activities advocating unpopular political doctrines. Justices Black and Douglas gave their final requiem for the clear and present danger test in brief concurring opinions.

NOTES

1. *Pierce v. United States*, 252 U.S. 239 (1920).

2. *Debs v. United States*, 249 U.S. 211 (1919); and *Frowerk v. United States*, 249 U.S. 204 (1919).

3. See *Schaefer v. United States*, 251 U.S. 466 (1920); *Pierce v. United States*, 252 U.S. 239 (1920); *Gilbert v. Minnesota*, 254 U.S. 235 (1920); *Gitlow v. New York*, 268 U.S. 652 (1925); and *Whitney v. California*, 274 U.S. 357 (1927).

4. See *Lovell v. City of Griffin*, 303 U.S. 444 (1938); *Schneider v. New Jersey*, 308 U.S. 147 (1939); *Marsh v. Alabama*, 326 U.S. 296 (1940); *Cantwell v. Connecticut*, 310 U.S. 296 (1940); and *Cox v. New Hampshire*, 312 U.S. 569 (1941).

5. *Cantwell v. Connecticut*, 310 U.S. 296 (1940).

6. *Thornhill v. Alabama*, 310 U.S. 102 (1940).

7. See *Cantwell v. Connecticut*, 310 U.S. 296 (1940); *Douglas v. City of Jeanette*, 319 U.S. 157 (1943); *Jones v. Opelika*, 319 U.S. 103 (1943); *Murdock v. Pennsylvania*, 319 U.S. 105 (1943); and *Follet v. Town of McCormick*, 321 U.S. 573 (1944).

8. See and compare *Minersville School District v. Gobitis*, 310 U.S. 586 (1940), with *West Virginia Board of Education v. Barnette*, 319 U.S. 624 (1943).

9. *Bridges v. California*, 314 U.S. 252 (1941); *Pennekamp v. Florida*, 328 U.S. 331 (1946); *Craig v. Harney*, 331 U.S. 367 (1947) (contempt-of-court citations for publications concerning pending trials); and *Terminello v. Chicago*, 337 U.S. 1 (1949) (conviction for public speech).

10. *Jones v. Opelika*, 316 U.S. 584, 608 (1902) (Stone, J., dissenting opinion), adopted on rehearing, *Jones v. Opelika*, 319 U.S. 103 (1943).

11. See *Bridges v. California*, 314 U.S. 252, 295 (1941); *Craig v. Harney*, 331 U.S. 367, 391 (1947); and *Kovacs v. Cooper*, 336 U.S. 77, 96 (1949).

12. See *Niemotko v. Maryland*, 340 U.S. 268 (1951); and *Feiner v. New York*, 340 U.S. 315 (1951).

SELECTED BIBLIOGRAPHY

Bollinger, Lee. *The Tolerant Society: Freedom of Speech and Extremist Speech in America.* New York: Oxford University Press, 1986.

Polenberg, Richard. *Fighting Faiths: The Abrams Case, the Supreme Court, and Free Speech.* New York: Viking, 1987.

Strong, Frank B. "Fifty Years of 'Clear and Present Danger': From Schenck to Brandenburg—and Beyond." In *Free Speech and Association,* edited by Philip Kurland. Chicago: University of Chicago Press, 1975.

Schenck v. United States
249 U.S. 47, 39 S.Ct. 247 (1919)

As secretary of the Socialist party, Schenck was responsible for the printing, distributing, and mailing to men eligible for the draft, leaflets that advocated opposition to the government's involvement in World War I and urged them to resist conscription. He was arrested, tried, and convicted in federal courts for violating the Espionage Act of 1917. That act was passed amid the so-called Red (Communist) scare, prompted by economic dislocations due to the war and growing distrust of aliens and foreign-born radicals because of the Bolshevik revolution in Russia. Schenck's appeal was the first of several cases challenging the Espionage Act to reach the Supreme Court.

Justice HOLMES delivers the opinion of the Court.

The document in question upon its first printed side recited the first section of the Thirteenth Amendment, said that the idea embodied in it was violated by the conscription act and that a conscript is little better than a convict. In impassioned language it intimated that conscription was despotism in its worst form and a monstrous wrong against humanity in the interest of Wall Street's chosen few. It said, "Do not submit to intimidation," but in form at least confined itself to peaceful measures such as a petition for the repeal of the act. The other and later printed side of the sheet was headed "Assert Your Rights." It stated reasons for alleging that any one violated the Constitution when he refused to recognize "your right to assert your opposition to the draft," and went on, "If you do not assert and support your rights, you are helping to deny or disparage rights which it is the solemn duty of all citizens and residents of the United States to retain." It described the arguments on the other side as coming from cunning politicians and a mercenary capitalist press, and even silent consent to the conscription law as helping to support an infamous conspiracy. It denied the power to send our citizens away to foreign shores to shoot up the people of other lands, and added that words could not express the condemnation such cold-blooded ruthlessness deserves, &c., &c., winding up, "You must do your share to maintain, support and uphold the rights of the people of this country." Of course the document would not have been sent unless it had been intended to have some effect, and we do not see what effect it could be expected to have upon persons subject to the draft except to influence them to obstruct the carrying of it out. The defendants do not deny that the jury might find against them on this point.

But it is said, suppose that that was the tendency of this circular, it is protected by the First Amendment to the Constitution. Two of the strongest expressions are said to be quoted respectively from well-known public men. It well may be that the prohibition of laws abridging the freedom of speech is not confined to previous restraints, although to prevent them may have been the main purpose, as intimated in *Patterson v. Colorado*, 205 U. S. 454 [(1907)]. We admit that in many places and in ordinary times the defendants in saying all that was said in the circular would have been within their constitutional rights. But the character of every act depends upon the circumstances in which it is done. *Aikens v. Wisconsin*, 195 U. S. 194 [(1904)]. The most stringent protection of free speech would not protect a man in falsely shouting fire in a theatre and causing a panic. It does not even protect a man from an injunction against uttering words that may have all the effect of force. The question in every case is whether the words used are used in such circumstances and are of such a nature as to create a clear and present danger that they will bring about the substantive evils that Congress has a right to prevent. It is a question of proximity and degree. When a nation is at war many things that might be said in time of peace are such a hindrance to its effort that their utterance will not be endured so long as men fight and that no Court could regard them as protected by any constitutional right. It seems to be admitted that if an actual obstruction of the recruiting service were proved, liability for words that produced that effect might be enforced. The statute of 1917 in section 4 (Comp. St. 1918, § 10212d) punishes conspiracies to obstruct as well as actual obstruction. If the act, (speaking, or circulating a paper,) its tendency and the intent with which it is done are the same, we perceive no ground for saying that success alone warrants making the act a crime. . . .

Judgments affirmed.

Gitlow v. People of the State of New York
268 U.S. 652, 45 S.Ct. 625 (1925)

On November 8, 1919, police arrested Benjamin Gitlow, a twenty-eight-year-old son of Russian-Jewish immigrants, who a year before was elected to the New York legislature as a Socialist and who was well known as a leader of the left-wing faction of the Socialist party—which would later form the American Communist party. Gitlow was arrested and tried under the New York Criminal Anarchy Act of 1902, prohibiting the advocacy of criminal anarchy—"the doctrine that organized governments should be overthrown by force or violence, or by the assassination of the executive head or of any of the executive officials of government, or by any unlawful means." Gitlow's crime was publishing a pamphlet, *Left Wing Manifesto*, proclaiming the inevitability of a proletarian revolution. Although no evidence was introduced at trial that his publication had led to any unlawful action, Gitlow was convicted by a jury and given the maximum sentence of five to ten years in prison. Gitlow unsuccessfully appealed his conviction in state courts on the grounds that the New York law was unconstitutional under the First and Fourteenth Amendments. The recently formed American Civil Liberties Union (ACLU) then came to Gitlow's defense and appealed his case to the Supreme Court.

Justice SANFORD delivers the opinion of the Court.

Benjamin Gitlow was indicted in the Supreme Court of New York, with three others, for the statutory crime of criminal anarchy. He was separately tried, convicted, and sentenced to imprisonment. . . .

The contention here is that the statute, by its terms and as applied in this case, is repugnant to the due process clause of the Fourteenth Amendment. Its material provisions are: . . .

"Sec. 161. *Advocacy of Criminal Anarchy.* Any person who:

"1. By word of mouth or writing advocates, advises or teaches the duty, necessity or propriety of overthrowing or overturning organized government by force or violence, or by assassination of the executive head or of any of the executive officials of government, or by any unlawful means; or,

"2. Prints, publishes, edits, issues or knowingly circulates, sells, distributes or publicly displays any book, paper, document, or written or printed matter in any form, containing or advocating, advising or teaching the doctrine that organized government should be overthrown by force, violence or any unlawful means, . . .

"Is guilty of a felony and punishable" by imprisonment or fine, or both. . . .

The defendant is a member of the Left Wing Section of the Socialist Party, a dissenting branch or faction of that party formed in opposition to its dominant policy of "moderate Socialism." Membership in both is open to aliens as well as citizens. The Left Wing Section was organized nationally at a conference in New York City in June, 1919, attended by ninety delegates from twenty different States. The conference elected a National Council, of which the defendant was a member, and left to it the adoption of a "Manifesto." This was published in The Revolutionary Age, the official organ of the Left Wing. The defendant was on the board of managers of the paper and was its business manager. He arranged for the printing of the paper and took to the printer the manuscript of the first issue which contained the Left Wing Manifesto, and also a Communist Program and a Program of the Left Wing that had been adopted by the conference. Sixteen thousand copies were printed, which were delivered at the premises in New York City used as the office of the Revolutionary Age and the headquarters of the Left Wing, and occupied by the defendant and other officials. . . .

There was no evidence of any effect resulting from the publication and circulation of the Manifesto.

No witnesses were offered in behalf of the defendant. . . .

The sole contention here is, essentially, that as there was no evidence of any concrete result flowing from the publication of the Manifesto or of circumstances showing the likelihood of such result, the statute as construed and applied by the trial court penalizes the mere utterance, as such, of "doctrine" having no quality of incitement, without regard either to the circumstances of its utterance or to the likelihood of unlawful consequences. . . .

The statute does not penalize the utterance or publication of abstract "doctrine" or academic discussion having no quality of incitement to any concrete action. It is not aimed against mere historical or philosophical essays. It does not restrain the advocacy of changes in the form of government by constitutional and lawful means. What it prohibits is language advocating, advising or teaching the overthrow of organized government by unlawful means. These words imply urging to action. . . .

The Manifesto, plainly, is neither the statement of abstract doctrine nor, as suggested by counsel, mere prediction that industrial disturbances and revolutionary mass strikes will result spontaneously in an inevitable process of evolution in the economic system. It advocates and urges in fervent language mass action which shall progressively foment industrial disturbances and through political mass strikes and revolutionary mass action overthrow and destroy organized parliamentary government. It concludes with a call to action in these words:

> "The proletariat revolution and the Communist reconstruction of society—*the struggle for these*—is now indispensable. . . . The Communist International calls the proletariat of the world to the final struggle!"

This is not the expression of philosophical abstraction, the mere prediction of future events; it is the language of direct incitement. . . .

For present purposes we may and do assume that freedom of speech and of the press—which are protected by the First Amendment from abridgment by Congress—are among the fundamental personal rights and "liberties" protected by the due process clause of the Fourteenth Amendment from impairment by the States. . . .

It is a fundamental principle, long established, that the freedom of speech and of the press which is secured by the Constitution, does not confer an absolute right to speak or publish, without responsibility, whatever one may choose, or an unrestricted and unbridled license that gives immunity for every possible use of language and prevents the punishment of those who abuse this freedom. . . .

That a State in the exercise of its police power may punish those who abuse this freedom by utterances inimical to the public welfare, tending to corrupt public morals, incite to crime, or disturb the public peace, is not open to question. . . .

By enacting the present statute the State has determined, through its legislative body, that utterances advocating the overthrow of organized government by force, violence and unlawful means, are so inimical to the general welfare and involve such danger of substantive evil that they may be penalized in the exercise of its police power. That determination must be given great weight. Every presumption is to be indulged in favor of the validity of the statute. *Mugler v. Kansas*. . . . And the case is to be considered "in the light of the principle that the State is primarily the judge of regulations required in the interest of public safety and welfare"; and that its police "statutes may only be declared unconstitutional where they are arbitrary or unreasonable attempts to exercise authority vested in the State in the public interest." *Great Northern Ry. v. Clara City* [246 U.S. 434 (1918)]. That utterances inciting to the overthrow of organized government by unlawful means, present a sufficient danger of substantive evil to bring their punishment within the range of legislative discretion, is clear. Such utterances, by their very nature, involve danger to the public peace and to the security of the State. They threaten breaches of the peace and ultimate revolution. And the immediate danger is none the less real and substantial, because the effect of a given utterance cannot be accurately foreseen. The State cannot reasonably be required to measure the danger from every such utterance in the nice balance of a jeweler's scale. A single revolutionary spark may kindle a fire that, smouldering for a time, may burst into a sweeping and destructive conflagration. It cannot be said that the State is acting arbitrarily or unreasonably when in the exercise of its judgment as to the measures necessary to protect the public peace and safety, it seeks to extinguish the spark without waiting until it has enkindled the flame or blazed into the conflagration. It cannot reasonably be required to defer the adoption of measures for its own peace and safety until the revolutionary utterances lead to actual disturbances of the public peace or imminent and immediate danger of its own destruction; but it may, in the exercise of its judgment, suppress the threatened danger in its incipiency. . . .

We cannot hold that the present statute is an arbitrary or unreasonable exercise of the police power of the State unwarrantably infringing the freedom of speech or press; and we must and do sustain its constitutionality.

This being so it may be applied to every utterance—not too trivial to be beneath the notice of the law—which is of such a character and used with such intent and purpose as to bring it within the prohibition of the statute. . . .

In other words, when the legislative body has determined generally, in the constitutional exercise of its discretion, that utterances of a certain kind involve such danger of substantive evil that they may be punished, the question whether any specific utterance coming within the prohibited class is likely, in and of itself, to bring about the substantive evil, is not open to consideration. It is sufficient that the statute itself be constitutional and that the use of the language comes within its prohibition.

It is clear that the question in such cases is entirely different from that involved in those cases where the statute merely prohibits certain acts involving the danger of substantive evil, without any reference to language itself, and it is sought to apply its provisions to language used by the defendant for the purpose of bringing about the prohibited results. There, if it be contended that the statute cannot be applied to the language used by the defendant because of its protection by the freedom of speech or press, it must necessarily be found, as an original question, without any previous determination by the legislative body, whether the specific language used involved such likelihood of bringing about the substantive evil as to deprive it of the constitutional protection. In such case it has been held that the general provisions of the statute may be constitutionally applied to the specific utterance of the defendant if its natural tendency and probable effect was to bring about the substantive evil which the legislative body might prevent. *Schenck v. United States,* [249 U.S. 47 (1919)]; *Debs v. United States,* [249 U.S. 211 (1919)]. And the general statement in the *Schenck* Case, [249 U.S. 47 (1919)], that the "question in every case is whether the words used are used in such circumstances and are of such a nature as to create a clear and present danger that they will bring about the substantive evils,"—upon which great reliance is placed in the defendant's argument—was manifestly intended, as shown by the context, to apply only in cases of this class, and has no application to those like the present, where the legislative body itself has previously determined the danger of substantive evil arising from utterances of a specified character. . . .

Affirmed.

Justice HOLMES dissenting.

Justice BRANDEIS and I are of opinion that this judgment should be reversed. The general principle of free speech, it seems to me, must be taken to be included in the Fourteenth Amendment, in view of the scope that has been given to the word "liberty" as there used, although perhaps it may be accepted with a somewhat larger latitude of interpretation than is allowed to Congress by the sweeping language that governs or ought to govern the laws of the United States. If I am right then I think that the criterion sanctioned by the full Court in *Schenck v. United States,* applies:

> "The question in every case is whether the words used are used in such circumstances and are of such a nature as to create a clear and present danger that they will bring about the substantive evils that [the State] has a right to prevent.". . .

If what I think the correct test is applied it is manifest that there was no present danger of an attempt to overthrow the government by force on the part of the admittedly small minority who shared the defendant's views. It is said that this manifesto was more than a theory, that it was an incitement. Every idea is an incitement. It offers itself for belief and if believed it is acted on unless some other belief outweighs it or some failure of energy stifles the movement at its birth. The only difference between the expression of an opinion and an incitement in the narrower sense is the speaker's enthusiasm for the result. Eloquence may set fire to reason. But whatever may be thought of the redundant discourse before us it had no chance of starting a present conflagration. If in the long run the beliefs expressed in proletarian dictatorship are destined to be accepted by the dominant forces of the community, the only meaning of free speech is that they should be given their chance and have their way.

If the publication of this document had been laid as an attempt to induce an uprising against government at once and not at some indefinite time in the future it would have presented a different question. The object would have been one with which the law might deal, subject to the doubt whether there was any danger that the publication could produce any result, or in other words, whether it was not futile and too remote from possible consequences. But the indictment alleges the publication and nothing more.

Dennis v. United States
341 U.S. 494, 71 S.Ct. 857 (1951)

Eugene Dennis and ten other leaders of the American Communist party were indicted under the Smith Act of 1940 for willfully and knowingly conspiring to teach and advocate the forceful and violent overthrow and destruction of the government. After a nine-month trial, Dennis and the others were found guilty and, thereafter, appealed their convictions in a federal appeals court. That court upheld their convictions with a scholarly opinion written by prominent Judge Learned Hand. Reviewing the evolution of the clear and present danger test since *Schenck,* Hand concluded that it was no more than a balancing technique. But he also ventured to give the test greater precision by adding that courts must consider "whether the gravity of the 'evil.' discounted by its improbability, justifies such invasion of free speech as is necessary to avoid the danger." According to Hand, restrictions on speech and press were permissible only if they posed a clear and, not merely present but, imminent and probable danger. As refashioned, the clear and present danger test was sharper than Justice Holmes's initial formulation, yet it permitted changing political circumstances to determine the scope of the

First Amendment. Turning to international events and the threat of communism, Judge Hand could not imagine "a more probable danger, unless one must wait till the actual eve of hostilities." Dennis's attorneys promptly appealed Judge Hand's ruling to the Supreme Court. The Court granted review (with newly appointed Justice Tom Clark recusing himself, because he had been attorney general when the government began prosecuting Dennis).

Chief Justice VINSON, with whom Justice REED, Justice BURTON, and Justice MINTON join, delivers the opinion of the Court.

Petitioners were indicted in July, 1948, for violation of the conspiracy provisions of the Smith Act, 54 Stat. 671, 18 U.S.C. (1946 ed.) § 11, during the period of April, 1945, to July, 1948. . . . A verdict of guilty as to all the petitioners was returned by the jury on October 14, 1949. The Court of Appeals affirmed the convictions. We granted certiorari [to decide] . . . the following two questions: (1) Whether either § 2 or § 3 of the Smith Act, inherently or as construed and applied in the instant case, violates the First Amendment and other provisions of the Bill of Rights; (2) whether either § 2 or § 3 of the Act, inherently or as construed and applied in the instant case, violates the First and Fifth Amendments because of indefiniteness.

Sections 2 and 3 of the Smith Act provide as follows:

"Sec. 2.
"(a) It shall be unlawful for any person—
"(1) to knowingly or willfully advocate, abet, advise, or teach the duty, necessity, desirability, or propriety of overthrowing or destroying any government in the United States by force or violence, or by the assassination of any officer of any such government. . . ."
"Sec. 3. It shall be unlawful for any person to attempt to commit, or to conspire to commit, any of the acts prohibited by the provisions of . . . this title."

The indictment charged the petitioners with wilfully and knowingly conspiring (1) to organize as the Communist Party of the United States of America a society, group and assembly of persons who teach and advocate the overthrow and destruction of the Government of the United States by force and violence, and (2) knowingly and wilfully to advocate and teach the duty and necessity of overthrowing and destroying the Government of the United States by force and violence. . . .

The trial of the case extended over nine months, six of which were devoted to the taking of evidence, resulting in a record of

16,000 pages. Our limited grant of the writ of certiorari has removed from our consideration any question as to the sufficiency of the evidence to support the jury's determination that petitioners are guilty of the offense charged. Whether on this record petitioners did in fact advocate the overthrow of the Government by force and violence is not before us, and we must base any discussion of this point upon the conclusions stated in the opinion of the Court of Appeals, which treated the issue in great detail. That court held that the record in this case amply supports the necessary finding of the jury that petitioners, the leaders of the Communist Party in this country, were unwilling to work within our framework of democracy, but intended to initiate a violent revolution whenever the propitious occasion appeared. . . .

The obvious purpose of the statute is to protect existing Government, not from change by peaceable, lawful and constitutional means, but from change by violence, revolution and terrorism. That it is within the *power* of the Congress to protect the Government of the United States from armed rebellion is a proposition which requires little discussion. Whatever theoretical merit there may be to the argument that there is a "right" to rebellion against dictatorial governments is without force where the existing structure of the government provides for peaceful and orderly change. We reject any principle of governmental helplessness in the face of preparation for revolution, which principle, carried to its logical conclusion, must lead to anarchy. No one could conceive that it is not within the power of Congress to prohibit acts intended to overthrow the Government by force and violence. The question with which we are concerned here is not whether Congress has such *power*, but whether the *means* which it has employed conflict with the First and Fifth Amendments to the Constitution. . . .

[The petitioners attack] the statute on the grounds that by its terms it prohibits academic discussion of the merits of Marxism-Leninism, that it stifles ideas and is contrary to all concepts of a free speech and a free press. . . .

The very language of the Smith Act negates the interpretation which petitioners would have us impose on that Act. It is directed at advocacy, not discussion. Thus, the trial judge properly charged the jury that they could not convict if they found that petitioners did "no more than pursue peaceful studies and discussions or teaching and advocacy in the realm of ideas.". . . Congress did not intend to eradicate the free discussion of political theories, to destroy the traditional rights of Americans to discuss and evaluate ideas without fear of governmental sanction. Rather Congress was concerned with the very kind of activity in which the evidence showed these petitioners engaged.

But although the statute is not directed at the hypothetical cases which petitioners have conjured, its application in this case has resulted in convictions for the teaching and advocacy of the overthrow of the Government by force and violence, which, even though coupled with the intent to accomplish that overthrow, contains an element of speech. For this reason, we must pay special heed to the demands of the First Amendment marking out the boundaries of speech. . . .

The rule we deduce from [*Schenck v. United States* and the other Espionage Act] cases is that where an offense is specified by a statute in nonspeech or nonpress terms, a conviction relying upon speech or press as evidence of violation may be sustained only when the speech or publication created a "clear and present danger" of attempting or accomplishing the prohibited crime, e.g., interference with enlistment. The dissents, in emphasizing the value of speech, were addressed to the argument of the sufficiency of the evidence. . . .

Although no case subsequent to *Whitney* [*v. California*, 274 U.S. 421 (1927)] and *Gitlow* [*v. New York* (1925)] has expressly overruled the majority opinions in those cases, there is little doubt that subsequent opinions have inclined toward the Holmes-Brandeis rationale. . . . But . . . neither Justice HOLMES nor Justice BRANDEIS ever envisioned that a shorthand phrase should be crystallized into a rigid rule to be applied inflexibly without regard to the circumstances of each case. Speech is not an absolute, above and beyond control by the legislature when its judgment, subject to review here, is that certain kinds of speech are so undesirable as to warrant criminal sanction. . . .

In this case we are squarely presented with the application of the "clear and present danger" test, and must decide what that phrase imports. We first note that many of the cases in which this Court has reversed convictions by use of this or similar tests have been based on the fact that the interest which the State was attempting to protect was itself too insubstantial to warrant restriction of speech. . . . Overthrow of the Government by force and violence is certainly a substantial enough interest for the Government to limit speech. . . . If, then, this interest may be protected, the literal problem which is presented is what has been meant by the use of the phrase "clear and present danger" of the utterances bringing about the evil within the power of Congress to punish.

Obviously, the words cannot mean that before the Government may act, it must wait until the *putsch* is about to be executed, the plans have been laid and the signal is awaited. If Government is aware that a group aiming at its overthrow is attempting to indoctrinate its members and to commit them to a course whereby they will strike when the leaders feel the circumstances permit, action by the Government is required. The argument that there is no need for Government to concern itself, for Government is strong, it possesses ample powers to put down a rebellion, it may defeat the revolution with ease needs no answer. For that is not the question. Certainly an attempt to overthrow the Government by force, even though doomed from the outset because of inadequate numbers or power of the revolutionists, is a sufficient evil for Congress to prevent. The damage which such attempts create both physically and politically to a nation makes it impossible to measure the validity in terms of the probability of success, or the immediacy of a successful attempt. In the instant case the trial judge charged the jury that they could not convict unless they found that petitioners intended to overthrow the Government "as speedily as circumstances would permit." This does not mean, and could not properly mean, that they would not strike until there was certainty of success. What was meant was that the revolutionists would strike when they thought the time was ripe. We must therefore reject the contention that success or probability of success is the criterion.

The situation with which Justices HOLMES and BRANDEIS were concerned in *Gitlow* was a comparatively isolated event, bearing little relation in their minds to any substantial threat to the safety of the community. . . . They were not confronted with any situation comparable to the instant one—the development of an apparatus designed and dedicated to the overthrow of the Government, in the context of world crisis after crisis.

Chief Judge Learned Hand, writing for the majority below, interpreted the phrase as follows: "In each case [courts] must ask whether the gravity of the 'evil,' discounted by its improbability, justifies such invasion of free speech as is necessary to avoid the danger." We adopt this statement of the rule. As articulated by Chief Judge Hand, it is as succinct and inclusive as any other we might devise at this time. It takes into consideration those factors which we deem relevant, and relates their significances. More we cannot expect from words.

Likewise, we are in accord with the court below, which affirmed the trial court's finding that the requisite danger existed. The mere fact that from the period 1945 to 1948 petitioners' activities did not result in an attempt to overthrow the Government by force and violence is of course no answer to the fact that there was a group that was ready to make the attempt. The formation by petitioners of such a highly organized conspiracy, with rigidly disciplined members subject to call when the leaders, these petitioners, felt that the time had come for action, coupled with the inflammable nature of world conditions, similar uprisings in other countries, and the touch-and-go nature of our relations with countries with whom petitioners were in the very least ideologically attuned, convince us that their convictions were justified on this score. And this analysis disposes of the contention that a conspiracy to advocate, as distinguished from the advocacy itself, cannot be constitutionally restrained, because it comprises only the prepara-

tion. It is the existence of the conspiracy which creates the danger.
. . . If the ingredients of the reaction are present, we cannot bind the Government to wait until the catalyst is added. . . .

When facts are found that establish the violation of a statute, the protection against conviction afforded by the First Amendment is a matter of law. The doctrine that there must be a clear and present danger of a substantive evil that Congress has a right to prevent is a judicial rule to be applied as a matter of law by the courts. The guilt is established by proof of facts. Whether the First Amendment protects the activity which constitutes the violation of the statute must depend upon a judicial determination of the scope of the First Amendment applied to the circumstances of the case. . . .

[I]n the very case in which the phrase was born, *Schenck,* this Court itself examined the record to find whether the requisite danger appeared, and the issue was not submitted to a jury. And in every later case in which the Court has measured the validity of a statute by the "clear and present danger" test, that determination has been by the court, the question of the danger not being submitted to the jury.

The question in this case is whether the statute which the legislature has enacted may be constitutionally applied. In other words, the Court must examine judicially the application of the statute to the particular situation, to ascertain if the Constitution prohibits the conviction. We hold that the statute may be applied where there is a "clear and present danger" of the substantive evil which the legislature had the right to prevent.

Justice CLARK did not participate in the consideration or decision of this case.

Justice FRANKFURTER concurring.

Just as there are those who regard as invulnerable every measure for which the claim of national survival is invoked, there are those who find in the Constitution a wholly unfettered right of expression. Such literalness treats the words of the Constitution as though they were found or a piece of outworn parchment instead of being words that have called into being a nation with a past to be preserved for the future. The soil in which the Bill of Rights grew was not a soil of arid pedantry. The historic antecedents of the First Amendment preclude the notion that its purpose was to give unqualified immunity to every expression that touched on matters within the range of political interest. . . .

The demands of free speech in a democratic society as well as the interest in national security are better served by candid and informed weighing of the competing interests, within the confines of the judicial process, than by announcing dogmas too inflexible for the non-Euclidian problems to be solved.

But how are competing interests to be assessed? Since they are not subject to quantitative ascertainment, the issue necessarily resolves itself into asking, who is to make the adjustment?—who is to balance the relevant factors and ascertain which interest is in the circumstances to prevail? Full responsibility for the choice cannot be given to the courts. Courts are not representative bodies. They are not designed to be a good reflex of a democratic society. Their judgment is best informed, and therefore most dependable, within narrow limits. Their essential quality is detachment, founded on independence. History teaches that the independence of the judiciary is jeopardized when courts become embroiled in the passions of the day and assume primary responsibility in choosing between competing political, economic and social pressures.

Primary responsibility for adjusting the interests which compete in the situation before us of necessity belongs to the Congress. . . . We are to set aside the judgment of those whose duty it is to legislate only if there is no reasonable basis for it. . . .

"Great cases," it is appropriate to remember, "like hard cases make bad law. For great cases are called great, not by reason of their real importance in shaping the law of the future, but because of some accident of immediate overwhelming interest which appeals to the feelings and distorts the judgment. These immediate interests exercise a kind of hydraulic pressure which makes what previously was clear seem doubtful, and before which even well settled principles of law will bend." Justice HOLMES, dissenting in *Northern Securities Co. v. United States,* 193 U.S. 197. [(1904)].

This is such a case. Unless we are to compromise judicial impartiality and subject these defendants to the risk of an *ad hoc* judgment influenced by the impregnating atmosphere of the times, the constitutionality of their conviction must be determined by principles established in cases decided in more tranquil periods. . . .

First. Free-speech cases are not an exception to the principle that we are not legislators, that direct policy-making is not our province. How best to reconcile competing interests is the business of legislatures, and the balance they strike is a judgment not to be displaced by ours, but to be respected unless outside the pale of fair judgment. . . .

Second. A survey of the relevant decisions indicates that the results which we have reached are on the whole those that would ensue from careful weighing of conflicting interests. . . .

Third. Not every type of speech occupies the same position on the scale of values. There is no substantial public interest in permitting certain kinds of utterances: "the lewd and obscene, the profane, the libelous, and the insulting or 'fighting' words—those which by their very utterance inflict injury or tend to incite an immediate breach of the peace." *Chaplinsky v. State of New Hampshire*, 315 U.S. 568. [(1942)]. It is pertinent to the decision before us to consider where on the scale of values we have in the past placed the type of speech now claiming constitutional immunity.

The defendants have been convicted of conspiring to organize a party of persons who advocate the overthrow of the Government by force and violence. The jury has found that the object of the conspiracy is advocacy as "a rule or principle of action," "by language reasonably and ordinarily calculated to incite persons to such action," and with the intent to cause the overthrow "as speedily as circumstances would permit."

On any scale of values which we have hitherto recognized, speech of this sort ranks low. . . .

But there is underlying validity in the distinction between advocacy and the interchange of ideas, and we do not discard a useful tool because it may be misused. That such a distinction could be used unreasonably by those in power against hostile or unorthodox views does not negate the fact that it may be used reasonably against an organization wielding the power of the centrally controlled international Communist movement. The object of the conspiracy before us is so clear that the chance of error in saying that the defendants conspired to advocate rather than to express ideas is slight. Justice DOUGLAS quite properly points out that the conspiracy before us is not a conspiracy to overthrow the Government. But it would be equally wrong to treat it as a seminar in political theory.

These general considerations underlie decision of the case before us.

On the one hand is the interest in security. The Communist Party was not designed by these defendants as an ordinary political party. For the circumstances of its organization, its aims and methods, and the relation of the defendants to its organization and aims we are concluded by the jury's verdict. The jury found that the Party rejects the basic premise of our political system—that change is to be brought about by nonviolent constitutional process. The jury found that the Party advocates the theory that there is a duty and necessity to overthrow the Government by force and violence. It found that the Party entertains and promotes this view, not as a prophetic insight or as a bit of unworldly speculation, but as a program for winning adherents and as a policy to be translated into action. . . .

On the other hand is the interest in free speech. The right to exert all governmental powers in aid of maintaining our institutions and resisting their physical overthrow does not include intolerance of opinions and speech that cannot do harm although opposed and perhaps alien to dominant, traditional opinion. . . .

A public interest is not wanting in granting freedom to speak their minds even to those who advocate the overthrow of the Government by force. For, as the evidence in this case abundantly illustrates, coupled with such advocacy is criticism of defects in our society. . . . Suppressing advocates of overthrow inevitably will also silence critics who do not advocate overthrow but fear that their criticism may be so construed. No matter how clear we may be that the defendants now before us are preparing to overthrow our Government at the propitious moment, it is self-delusion to think that we can punish them for their advocacy without adding to the risks run by loyal citizens who honestly believe in some of the reforms these defendants advance. It is a sobering fact that in sustaining the convictions before us we can hardly escape restriction on the interchange of ideas. . . .

It is not for us to decide how we would adjust the clash of interests which this case presents were the primary responsibility for reconciling it ours. Congress has determined that the danger created by advocacy of overthrow justifies the ensuing restriction on freedom of speech. . . .

To make validity of legislation depend on judicial reading of events still in the womb of time—a forecast, that is, of the outcome of forces at best appreciated only with knowledge of the topmost secrets of nations—is to charge the judiciary with duties beyond its equipment.

Justice JACKSON concurring.

The Communist Party . . . does not seek its strength primarily in numbers. Its aim is a relatively small party whose strength is in selected, dedicated, indoctrinated, and rigidly disciplined members. From established policy it tolerates no deviation and no debate. It seeks members that are, or may be, secreted in strategic posts in transportation, communications, industry, government, and especially in labor unions where it can compel employers to accept and retain its members. It also seeks to infiltrate and control organizations of professional and other groups. Through these placements in positions of power it seeks a leverage over society that will make up in power of coercion what it lacks in power of persuasion.

The Communists have no scruples against sabotage, terrorism, assassination, or mob disorder; but violence is not with them, as with the anarchists, an end in itself. The Communist Party advocates force only when prudent and profitable. Their strategy of stealth precludes premature or uncoordinated outbursts of violence, except, of course, when the blame will be placed on shoulders other than their own. They resort to violence as to truth, not as a principle but as an expedient. Force or violence, as they would resort to it, may never be necessary, because infiltration and deception may be enough. . . .

The foregoing is enough to indicate that, either by accident or design, the Communist strategem outwits the anti-anarchist pattern of statute aimed against "overthrow by force and violence" if qualified by the doctrine that only "clear and present danger" of accomplishing that result will sustain the prosecution.

The "clear and present danger" test was an innovation by Justice HOLMES in the *Schenck* case, reiterated and refined by him and Justice BRANDEIS in later cases, all arising before the era of World War II revealed the subtlety and efficacy of modernized revolutionary techniques used by totalitarian parties. In those cases, they were faced with convictions under so-called criminal syndicalism statutes aimed at anarchists but which, loosely construed, had been applied to punish socialism, pacifism, and left-wing ideologies, the charges often resting on far-fetched inferences which, if true, would establish only technical or trivial violations. They proposed "clear and present danger" as a test for the sufficiency of evidence in particular cases.

I would save it, unmodified, for application as a "rule of reason" in the kind of case for which it was devised. When the issue is criminality of a hot-headed speech on a street corner, or circulation of a few intendiary pamphlets, or parading by some zealots behind a red flag, or refusal of a handful of school children to salute our flag, it is not beyond the capacity of the judicial process to gather, comprehend, and weigh the necessary materials for decision whether it is a clear and present danger of substantive evil or a harmless letting off of steam. It is not a prophecy, for the danger in such cases has matured by the time of trial or it was never present. The test applies and has meaning where a conviction is sought to be based on a speech or writing which does not directly or explicitly advocate a crime but to which such tendency is sought to be attributed by construction or by implication from external circumstances. The formula in such cases favors freedoms that are vital to our society, and, even if sometimes applied too generously, the consequences cannot be grave. But its recent expansion has extended, in particular to Communists, unprecedented immunities. Unless we are to hold our Government captive in a judge-made verbal trap, we must approach the problem of a well-organized, nation-wide conspiracy, such as I have described, as realistically as our predecessors faced the trivialities that were being prosecuted until they were checked with a rule of reason.

I think reason is lacking for applying that test to this case.

If we must decide that this Act and its application are constitutional only if we are convinced that petitioner's conduct creates a "clear and present danger" of violent overthrow, we must appraise imponderables, including international and national phenomena which baffle the best informed foreign offices and our most experienced politicians. We would have to foresee and predict the effectiveness of Communist propaganda, opportunities for infiltration, whether, and when, a time will come that they consider propitious for action, and whether and how fast our existing government will deteriorate. And we would have to speculate as to whether an approaching Communist *coup* would not be anticipated by a nationalistic fascist movement. No doctrine can be sound whose application requires us to make a prophecy of that sort in the guise of a legal decision. The judicial process simply is not adequate to a trial of such far-flung issues. The answers given would reflect our own political predilections and nothing more.

The authors of the clear and present danger test never applied it to a case like this, nor would I. If applied as it is proposed here, it means that the Communist plotting is protected during its period of incubation; its preliminary stages of organization and preparation are immune from the law; the Government can move only after imminent action is manifest, when it would, of course, be too late.

The highest degree of constitutional protection is due to the individual acting without conspiracy. But even an individual cannot claim that the Constitution protects him in advocating or teaching overthrow of government by force or violence. I should suppose no one would doubt that Congress has power to make such attempted overthrow a crime. But the contention is that one has the constitutional right to work up a public desire and will to do what it is a crime to attempt. I think direct incitement by speech or writing can be made a crime, and I think there can be a conviction without also proving that the odds favored its success by 99 to 1, or some other extremely high ratio. . . .

Of course, it is not always easy to distinguish teaching or advocacy in the sense of incitement from teaching or advocacy in the sense of exposition or explanation. It is a question of fact in each case.

What really is under review here is a conviction of conspiracy, after a trial for conspiracy, on an indictment charging conspiracy, brought under a statute outlawing conspiracy. With due respect to my colleagues, they seem to me to discuss anything under the sun except the law of conspiracy. . . .

The Constitution does not make conspiracy a civil right. The Court has never before done so and I think it should not do so now. . . .

The reasons underlying the doctrine that conspiracy may be a substantive evil in itself, apart from any evil it may threaten, attempt or accomplish, are peculiarly appropriate to conspiratorial Communism. . . .

I do not suggest that Congress could punish conspiracy to advocate something, the doing of which it may not punish. Advocacy or exposition of the doctrine of communal property ownership, or any political philosophy unassociated with advocacy of its imposition by force or seizure of government by unlawful means could not be reached through conspiracy prosecution. But it is not forbidden to put down force or violence, it is not forbidden to punish its teaching or advocacy, and the end being punishable, there is no doubt of the power to punish conspiracy for the purpose.

Justice BLACK dissenting.

At the outset I want to emphasize what the crime involved in this case is, and what it is not. These petitioners were not charged with an attempt to overthrow the Government. They were not charged with overt acts of any kind designed to overthrow the Government. They were not even charged with saying anything or writing anything designed to overthrow the Government. The charge was that they agreed to assemble and to talk and publish certain ideas at a later date: The indictment is that they conspired to organize the Communist Party and to use speech or newspapers and other publications in the future to teach and advocate the forcible overthrow of the Government. No matter how it is worded, this is a virulent form of prior censorship of speech and press, which I believe the First Amendment forbids. I would hold § 3 of the Smith Act authorizing this prior restraint unconstitutional on its face and as applied. . . .

[T]he other opinions in this case show that the only way to affirm these convictions is to repudiate directly or indirectly the established "clear and present danger" rule. This the Court does in a way which greatly restricts the protections afforded by the First Amendment. The opinions for affirmance indicate that the chief reason for jettisoning the rule is the expressed fear that advocacy of Communist doctrine endangers the safety of the Republic. Undoubtedly, a governmental policy of unfettered communication of ideas does entail dangers. To the Founders of this Nation, however, the benefits derived from free expression were worth the risk. They embodied this philosophy in the First Amendment's command that "Congress shall make no law . . . abridging the freedom of speech, or of the press. . . ." I have always believed that the First Amendment is the keystone of our Government, that the freedoms it guarantees provide the best insurance against destruction of all freedom. At least as to speech in the realm of public matters I believe that the "clear and present danger" test does not "mark the furthermost constitutional boundaries of protected expression" but does "no more than recognize a minimum compulsion of the Bill of Rights." *Bridges v. State of California*, 314 U.S. 252 [(1941)]. . . .

So long as this Court exercises the power of judicial review of legislation, I cannot agree that the First Amendment permits us to sustain laws suppressing freedom of speech and press on the basis of Congress' or our own notions of mere "reasonableness." Such a doctrine waters down the First Amendment so that it amounts to little more than an admonition to Congress. . . .

Public opinion being what it now is, few will protest the conviction of these Communist petitioners. There is hope, however, that in calmer times, when present pressures, passions and fears subside, this or some later Court will restore the First Amendment liberties to the high preferred place where they belong in a free society.

Justice DOUGLAS dissenting.

If this were a case where those who claimed protection under the First Amendment were teaching the techniques of sabotage, the assassination of the President, the filching of documents from public files, the planting of bombs, the art of street warfare, and the like, I would have no doubts. The freedom to speak is not absolute; the teaching of methods of terror and other seditious conduct should be beyond the pale along with obscenity and immorality. This case was argued as if those were the facts. . . . But the fact is that no such evidence was introduced at the trial. There is a statute which makes a seditious conspiracy unlawful. Petitioners, however, were not charged with a "conspiracy to overthrow" the Government. They were charged with a conspiracy to form a party and groups and assemblies of people who teach and advocate the overthrow of our Government by force or violence and with a conspiracy to advocate and teach its overthrow by force and violence. It may well be that indoctrination in the techniques of terror to destroy the Government would be indictable under either statute. But the teaching which is condemned here is of a different character.

So far as the present record is concerned, what petitioners did was to organize people to teach and themselves teach the Marxist-Leninist doctrine contained chiefly in four books: Foundations of Leninism by Stalin (1924); The Communist Manifesto by Marx and Engels (1848); State and Revolution by Lenin (1917); History of the Communist Party of the Soviet Union (B.) (1939).

Those books are to Soviet Communism what Mein Kampf was to Nazism. If they are understood, the ugliness of Communism is revealed, its deceit and cunning are exposed, the nature of its activities becomes apparent, and the chances of its success less likely. That is not, of course, the reason why petitioners chose these books for their classrooms. They are fervent Communists to whom these volumes are gospel. They preached the creed with the hope that some day it would be acted upon.

The opinion of the Court does not outlaw these texts nor condemn them to the fire, as the Communists do literature offensive to their creed. But if the books themselves are not outlawed, if they can lawfully remain on library shelves, by what reasoning does their use in a classroom become a crime? It would not be a crime under the Act to introduce these books to a class, though that would be teaching what the creed of violent overthrow of the Government is. The Act, as construed, requires the element of intent—that those who teach the creed believe in it. The crime then depends not on what is taught but on who the teacher is. That is to make freedom of speech turn not on *what is said,* but on the *intent* with which it is said. Once we start down that road we enter territory dangerous to the liberties of every citizen. . . .

Intent, of course, often makes the difference in the law. An act otherwise excusable or carrying minor penalties may grow to an abhorrent thing if the evil intent is present. We deal here, however, not with ordinary acts but with speech, to which the Constitution has given a special sanction. . . .

There comes a time when even speech loses its constitutional immunity. Speech innocuous one year may at another time fan such destructive flames that it must be halted in the interests of the safety of the Republic. That is the meaning of the clear and present danger test. When conditions are so critical that there will be no time to avoid the evil that the speech threatens, it is time to call a halt. Otherwise, free speech which is the strength of the Nation will be the cause of its destruction.

Yet free speech is the rule, not the exception. The restraint to be constitutional must be based on more than fear, on more than passionate opposition against the speech, on more than a revolted dislike for its contents. There must be some immediate injury to society that is likely if speech is allowed. The classic statement of these conditions was made by Justice BRANDEIS in his concurring opinion in *Whitney v. People of State of California,* 274 U.S. 357 [(1927)].

"Fear of serious injury cannot alone justify suppression of free speech and assembly. Men feared witches and burnt women. It is the function of speech to free men from the bondage of irrational fears. To justify suppression of free speech there must be reasonable ground to fear that serious evil will result if free speech is practiced. There must be reasonable ground to believe that the danger apprehended is imminent. There must be reasonable ground to believe that the evil to be prevented is a serious one. Every denunciation of existing law tends in some measure to increase the probability that there will be violation of it. Condonation of a breach enhances the probability. Expressions of approval add to the probability. Propagation of the criminal state of mind by teaching syndicalism increases it. Advocacy of law-breaking heightens it still further. But even advocacy of violation, however reprehensible morally, is not a justification for denying free speech where the advocacy falls short of incitement and there is nothing to indicate that the advocacy would be immediately acted on. The wide difference between advocacy and incitement, between preparation and attempt, between assembling and conspiracy, must be borne in mind. In order to support a finding of clear and present danger it must be shown either that immediate serious violence was to be expected or was advocated, or that the past conduct furnished reason to believe that such advocacy was then contemplated."

Brandenburg v. Ohio
395 U.S. 444, 89 S.Ct. 1827 (1969)

Charles Brandenburg, the leader of a Ku Klux Klan group, was arrested, tried, and convicted under the Ohio Criminal Syndicalism statute for "advocat[ing] . . . the duty, necessity, or propriety of crime, sabotage, violence, or unlawful methods of terrorism as a means of accomplishing industrial or political reform" and for "voluntarily assembl[ing] with any society, group, or assemblage or persons formed to teach or advocate the doctrines of criminal syndicalism." He had addressed a small rally of hooded men, some of whom carried firearms, standing before a burning cross and declared, among other things, that if the president, Congress, and the Court continued "to suppress the white, Caucasian race, it's possible that there might have to be revengenance [sic] taken." The major evidence introduced against Brandenburg at trial were two films of his speeches at rallies. Brandenburg unsuccessfully appealed his conviction in a state appellate court and then to the state supreme Court, which denied review. On further appeal to the Supreme Court, Brandenburg's case was granted review. At conference, the justices unanimously voted to overturn his conviction. Subsequently, Chief Justice Warren assigned Justice Abe Fortas to draft an opinion for the Court. But Justice Fortas was pressed into resigning in May, and hence the Court's opinion came on June 9 as an unsigned (*per curiam*) opinion.

PER CURIAM.

The appellant, a leader of a Ku Klux Klan group, was convicted under the Ohio Criminal Syndicalism statute for "advocat[ing] . . . the duty, necessity, or propriety of crime, sabotage, violence, or unlawful methods of terrorism as a means of accomplishing industrial or political reform" and for "voluntarily assembl[ing] with any society, group, or assemblage of persons formed to teach or advocate the doctrines of criminal syndicalism." Ohio Rev. Code Ann. § 2923.13. He was fined $1,000 and sentenced to one to 10 years' imprisonment. The appellant challenged the constitutionality of the criminal syndicalism statute under the First and Fourteenth Amendments to the United States Constitution, but the intermediate appellate court of Ohio affirmed his conviction without opinion. . . . We reverse.

The record shows that a man, identified at trial as the appellant, telephoned an announcer-reporter on the staff of a Cincinnati television station and invited him to come to a Ku Klux Klan "rally" to be held at a farm in Hamilton County. With the cooperation of the organizers, the reporter and a cameraman attended the meeting and filmed the events. Portions of the films were later broadcast on the local station and on a national network. . . .

One film showed 12 hooded figures, some of whom carried firearms. They were gathered around a large wooden cross, which they burned. No one was present other than the participants and the newsmen who made the film. Most of the words uttered during the scene were incomprehensible when the film was projected, but scattered phrases could be understood that were derogatory of Negroes and, in one instance, of Jews. . . .

The second film showed six hooded figures one of whom, later identified as the appellant, repeated a speech very similar to that recorded on the first film. The reference to the possibility of "revengeance" was omitted, and one sentence was added: "Personally, I believe the nigger should be returned to Africa, the Jew returned to Israel." Though some of the figures in the films carried weapons, the speaker did not. . . .

[The Court's] decisions have fashioned the principle that the constitutional guarantees of free speech and free press do not permit a State to forbid or proscribe advocacy of the use of force or of law violation except where such advocacy is directed to inciting or producing imminent lawless action and is likely to incite or produce such action. As we said in *Noto v. United States,* 367 U.S. 290 (1961), "the mere abstract teaching . . . of the moral propriety or even moral necessity for a resort to force and violence, is not the same as preparing a group for violent action and steeling it to such action." A statute which fails to draw this distinction impermissibly intrudes upon the freedoms guaranteed by the First and Fourteenth Amendments. It sweeps within its condemnation speech which our Constitution has immunized from governmental control.

Measured by this test, Ohio's Criminal Syndicalism Act cannot be sustained. The Act punishes persons who "advocate or teach the duty, necessity, or propriety" of violence "as a means of accomplishing industrial or political reform"; or who publish or circulate or display any book or paper containing such advocacy; or who "justify" the commission of violent acts "with intent to exemplify, spread or advocate the propriety of the doctrines of criminal syndicalism"; or who "voluntarily assemble" with a group formed "to teach or advocate the doctrines of criminal syndicalism." Neither the indictment nor the trial judge's instructions to the jury in any way refined the statute's bald definition of the crime in terms of mere advocacy not distinguished from incitement to imminent lawless action.

Accordingly, we are here confronted with a statute which, by its own words and as applied, purports to punish mere advocacy and to forbid, on pain of criminal punishment, assembly with others merely to advocate the described type of action. Such a statute falls within the condemnation of the First and Fourteenth Amendments. The contrary teaching of *Whitney v. California,* [274 U.S. 357 (1927)], cannot be supported, and that decision is therefore overruled.

Reversed.

Justice BLACK concurring.

I agree with the views expressed by Justice DOUGLAS in his concurring opinion in this case that the "clear and present danger" doctrine should have no place in the interpretation of the First Amendment.

Justice DOUGLAS concurring.

While I join the opinion of the Court, I desire to enter a *caveat.* . . .

I see no place in the regime of the First Amendment for any "clear and present danger" test, whether strict and tight as some would make it, or free-wheeling as the Court in *Dennis* [*v. United States* (1951)] rephrased it.

When one reads the opinions closely and sees when and how the "clear and present danger" test has been applied, great misgivings are aroused. First, the threats were often loud but always puny and made serious only by judges so wedded to the *status quo* that critical analysis made them nervous. Second, the test was so twisted and perverted in *Dennis* as to make the trial of those teachers of Marxism an all-out political trial which was part and parcel of the cold war that has eroded substantial parts of the First Amendment. . . .

The line between what is permissible and not subject to control and what may be made impermissible and subject to regulation is the line between ideas and overt acts.

The example usually given by those who would punish speech is the case of one who falsely shouts fire in a crowded theatre. This is, however, a classic case where speech is brigaded with action. They are indeed inseparable and a prosecution can be launched for the overt acts actually caused. Apart from rare instances of that kind, speech is, I think, immune from prosecution.

(2) Judicial Line Drawing: *Ad Hoc* and Definitional Balancing

The internal struggle within the Court over rival interpretative approaches to the First Amendment registered not merely differences over the history and principles of free speech and press. There were profound differences as well in judicial self-perception and philosophy over the role of the Court in a constitutional democracy. How deferential should the Court be to legislative majorities in defining the line between constitutionally protected and unprotected speech and press? What standards and principles should guide the Court's line drawing?

The clear and present danger test was initially formulated as an alternative to the traditional presumption of the reasonableness of legislation and the bad tendency test, which was used by the Court to rationalize legislative restrictions on speech and press. Although potentially a basis for protecting free speech and press, the clear and present danger test gradually evolved into a balancing technique for upholding restrictions on speech and press. After fifty years, the clear and present danger test was laid to rest in *Brandenburg v. Ohio* (1969) (see page 376), and since then survives primarily in *dicta*.[1] A majority of the Warren Court also eventually repudiated the *ad hoc* or case-by-case balancing approach advanced by Justice Harlan. Two years before *Brandenburg*, in a six-to-two decision (with Harlan and White in dissent and newly appointed Justice Thurgood Marshall not participating), Chief Justice Warren struck down as unconstitutional a provision of the McCarran Act, forbidding any member of the Communist party to be employed in a defense facility. Joined by Black, Douglas, Stewart, Fortas, and Brennan in *United States v. Robel*, 389 U.S. 258, 268 n.20 (1967), Warren used the occasion to expressly reject *ad hoc* balancing of First Amendment freedoms:

Faced with a clear conflict between a federal statute enacted in the interests of national security and an individual's exercise of his First Amendment rights, we have confined our analysis to whether Congress has adopted a constitutional means in achieving its concededly legitimate legislative goal. In making this determination we have found it necessary to measure the validity of the means adopted by Congress against both the goal it has sought to achieve and the specific prohibitions of the First Amendment. But we have in no way "balanced" those respective interests. We have ruled only that the Constitution requires that the conflict between congressional power and individual rights be accommodated by legislation drawn more narrowly to avoid the conflict.

Ad hoc balancing, whether under the clear and present danger test or as advocated by Harlan, was widely criticized within and without the Court for three principal reasons: (1) it was ambiguous and unpredictable in application, (2) it failed to establish a constitutional standard for adjudicating claims in a principled fashion, and (3) it tended to legitimate restrictions on speech and press because First Amendment claims were construed as simply private interests to be juxtaposed with public interests in self-preservation and punishing licentiousness.[2]

During his more than thirty years on the high bench, Justice Black remained one of the sharpest critics of balancing First Amendment freedoms and championed an "absolutist-literalist" interpretation. As he summarized his approach in 1968, when giving the James Carpenter Lectures at Columbia University School of Law,

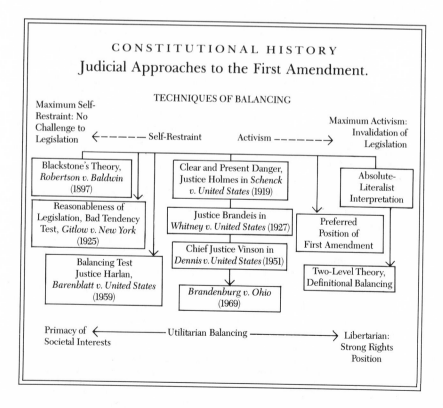

CONSTITUTIONAL HISTORY
Judicial Approaches to the First Amendment.

TECHNIQUES OF BALANCING

Maximum Self-Restraint: No Challenge to Legislation ← − − − − − Self-Restraint   Activism − − − − − − → Maximum Activism: Invalidation of Legislation

Blackstone's Theory, *Robertson v. Baldwin* (1897)

Clear and Present Danger, Justice Holmes in *Schenck v. United States* (1919)

Absolute-Literalist Interpretation

Reasonableness of Legislation, Bad Tendency Test, *Gitlow v. New York* (1925)

Justice Brandeis in *Whitney v. United States* (1927)

Preferred Position of First Amendment

Chief Justice Vinson in *Dennis v. United States* (1951)

Balancing Test Justice Harlan, *Barenblatt v. United States* (1959)

Brandenburg v. Ohio (1969)

Two-Level Theory, Definitional Balancing

Primacy of ← −−−−−−−− Utilitarian Balancing −−−−−−− → Libertarian: Societal Interests   Strong Rights Position

My view is, without deviation, without exception, without any ifs, buts, or whereas, that freedom of speech means that government shall not do anything to people, or, in the words of the Magna Carta, move against people, either for the views they have or the views they express or the words they speak or write. Some people would have you believe that this is a very radical position, and maybe it is. But all I am doing is following what to me is the clear wording of the First Amendment that "Congress shall make no law . . . abridging the freedom of speech[,] or of the press."[3]

The Court's abandonment of *ad hoc* balancing is a measure of Black's contribution to the constitutional politics of the First Amendment. Still a majority of the Court has never been persuaded to embrace his absolutist-literalist position.

Instead of *ad hoc* balancing and Black's absolutism, the Court gradually developed a "principled, or definitional, balancing" approach to the First Amendment—that is, the Court has defined certain categories of speech as protected or unprotected per se. The Court's definitional-balancing approach to, or two-level theory of, the First Amendment was initially intimated by Justice Murphy, when writing for a unanimous Court in *Chaplinksy v. New Hampshire,* 315 U.S. 568 (1942). There the Court upheld the conviction under a statute forbidding the use of offensive or derisive language in public. Chaplinsky, at the time of his arrest for creating a public disturbance, called the arresting office "a Goddamned racketeer" and "a damned Fascist." In contemplating these "fighting words," Murphy held that the First Amendment provides no protection for such language because they "are no essential part of any exposition of ideas." Certain categories of speech—the insulting or fighting words, the obscene, and libelous—have minimal, if any, social value and, therefore, are not worthy of constitutional protection. In Justice Murphy's words:

There are certain well-defined and narrowly limited classes of speech, the prevention and punishment of which has never been thought to raise any constitutional problem. These include the lewd and the obscene, the profane, the libelous, and the insulting or "fighting words"— those which by their very utterance inflict injury or tend to incite an immediate breach of the peace. It has been observed that such utterances are no essential part of any exposition of ideas, and are of such slight social value as a step to truth that any benefit that may be derived from them is clearly outweighed by the social interest in law and order.

Justice Murphy thus implied a two-level theory of the First Amendment: The amendment safeguards communications that have social value, but not those categories of (unprotected) speech that are "clearly outweighed by the social interest in order and morality."

Definitional balancing remains no less problematic than *ad hoc* balancing, because the Court must with some precision define the categories of and the standards for determining unprotected speech (fighting words, obscenity, libel, and commercial speech). Because of the Court's preoccupation with subversive political speech in the early part of the twentieth century and due to its deference to legislative and common law proscriptions on speech and press, the task of further defining these categories of unprotected speech was largely avoided until the era of the Warren Court. Since then the Burger and Rehnquist Courts have faced the problems of refining and defining the tests for those narrow categories of speech that fall outside the scope of First Amendment protection. It is those and other problems of judicial line drawing that the following sections of this chapter address.

Justice Hugo Black in his chambers. Black was President Roosevelt's first appointee to the Court and a leader of liberals on the Court. Justice Black is also known for his view that the First Amendment is absolute, that "Congress shall make no law . . . abridging the freedom of speech, or of the press" means what it says. *Supreme Court Historical Society/National Geographic Society.*

NOTES

1. See, for example, *Detroit Edison Company v. National Labor Relations Board*, 440 U.S. 301 (1979); *Federal Communications Commission v. Pacifica Foundation*, 438 U.S. 726 (1978); *Landmark Communications, Inc. v. Virginia*, 435 U.S. 829 (1977); *Nebraska Press Association v. Stuart*, 427 U.S. 539 (1976); *Greer v. Spock*, 424 U.S. 828 (1976); *Pell v. Procunier*, 417 U.S. 817 (1974); *Cohen v. California*, 403 U.S. 15 (1971); and *Younger v. Harris*, 401 U.S. 37 (1971).

2. For criticism of the *ad hoc* balancing approach, see Thomas I. Emerson, "Toward a General Theory of the First Amendment," 72 *Yale Law Journal* 854 (1963); Laurent Frantz, "The First Amendment in the Balance," 71 *Yale Law Journal* 1424 (1962); Robert McKay, "The Preference for Freedom," 34 *New York University Law Review* 1182 (1959); Samuel Krislov, "From Ginzburg to Ginsberg: The Unhurried Children's Hour in Obscenity Litigation," in *Supreme Court Review*, ed. Philip Kurland (Chicago: University of Chicago Press, 1968); and Harry Kalven, "Uninhibited, Robust, and Wide-Open—A Note on Free Speech and the Warren Court," 67 *Minnesota Law Review* 289 (1968). For defenses of balancing, see Wallace Mendelson, "On the Meaning of the First Amendment: Absolutes in the Balance," 50 *California Law Review* 821 (1962); and Dean Alfange, Jr., "The Balancing of Interests in Free Speech Cases: In Defense of an Abused Doctrine," 2 *Law in Transition Quarterly* 35 (1965).

3. Hugo L. Black, *A Constitutional Faith* (New York: Alfred Knopf, 1969), 45.

SELECTED BIBLIOGRAPHY

Berns, Walter. *Freedom Virtue and the First Amendment*. Baton Rouge: Louisiana State University Press, 1957.

Berns, Walter. *The First Amendment and the Future of American Democracy*. New York: Basic Books, 1976.

Emerson, Thomas. *The System of Freedom of Expression*. New York: Random House, 1970.

Haiman, Franklyn S. *Speech and Law in a Free Society*. Chicago: University of Chicago Press, 1981.

Meiklejohn, Alexander. *Political Freedom: The Constitutional Powers of the People*. New York: Harper & Row, 1965.

Shapiro, Martin. *Freedom of Speech: The Supreme Court and Judicial Review*. Englewood Cliffs, NJ: Prentice Hall, 1966.

B. OBSCENITY, PORNOGRAPHY, AND OFFENSIVE SPEECH

The problem of defining and dealing with obscenity, pornography, and other offensive speech is a continuing controversy in the constitutional politics of interpreting the First Amendment. Perhaps, as political scientist Harry Clor proposed:

> In the ideal system of legal control . . . wise men would solemnly weigh three considerations: the moral evils of obscenity, the virtues of art, and the requirements of public consensus in a regime of rational liberty. Each consideration would be given its full weight in the light of the common good. No work which is grossly obscene would ever be publicly circulated in society. No work which is not obscene would ever be censored.[1]

But such an "ideal system," as Clor concedes, "cannot be achieved among us." In a pluralistic society, people disagree over what is obscene, pornographic, and offensive; no consensus is likely. "One man's vulgarity is another man's lyric," as Justice Harlan put it in *Cohen v. California*, (1971) (see page 428). Or as Justice Stewart quipped in *Jacobellis v. Ohio*, 378 U.S. 476 (1964), "I know it [pornography] when I see it." Yet, for that very reason, Justice Black and Harvard Law School professor Alan Dershowitz, among others, argued, "To deny constitutional protection to a genre of speech that is incapable of precise definition is to endanger all freedom of expression. . . . Pornography should be included within the protection of the First Amendment, if no other reason than by excluding it we give too much definitional power to the voracious censor."[2]

The Supreme Court in maintaining that obscenity, pornography, and fighting words fall outside the scope of First Amendment protection continues to confront the vexing definitional problems presented by its own line drawing. So too, as the Court's composition has changed, the tests and boundaries drawn defining *obscenity* and other forms of constitutionally unprotected offensive speech have evolved.

(1) Obscenity and Pornography

From the late nineteenth to the twentieth century, federal courts upheld congressional and state power to suppress allegedly obscene materials by applying the extremely restrictive English common law test set forth in *Regina v. Hicklin*, L.R. 2 Q.B. 360 (1868). The so-called *Hicklin* test was "whether the tendency of the matter charged as obscenity is to deprive and corrupt those whose minds are open to such immoral influences and into whose hands a publication of this sort might fall." Under this test, books by Honoré Balzac, Gustav Flaubert, James Joyce, D. H. Lawrence, and Arthur Miller were banned based on isolated passages and the influence they might have on the weakest members of society (children and the mentally impaired). As Justice

Frankfurter was moved to observe, "the incidence of this standard is to reduce the adult population of [the country] to reading only what is fit for children."[3]

Not until *Roth v. United States* and its companion case, *Alberts v. California* (1957) (see page 390) was the *Hicklin* test finally repudiated. There with Justices Black, Douglas, and Harlan in dissent over the holding that obscenity is "utterly without redeeming social value" and without First Amendment protection, Justice Brennan proposed a constitutional test for obscenity— "whether to the average person, applying contemporary community standards, the dominant theme of the material taken as a whole appeals to the prurient interests." As the opinions of the dissenters point out, though, the *Roth* test was problematic. Who is an "average person," what are "contemporary community standards," how and where are those standards to be determined, and, finally, what is "prurient interest"?

The Warren Court subsequently expanded the *Roth* test in three other important rulings. In *Kingsley International Corporation v. Regents of University of New York*, 360 U.S. 684 (1959), overturning the denial of a license to exhibit the movie *Lady Chatterly's Lover*, Justice Stewart held that books and films could not be banned for "thematic obscenity"—their dealing primarily with sexual themes. In *Manual Enterprises, Inc. v. Day*, 370 U.S. 478 (1962), Justice Harlan interpreted the prurient interest element of *Roth* to require that materials appeal to prurient interests in a "patently offensive way." Again writing for the Court in *Jacobellis v. State of Ohio*, 378 U.S. 184 (1964), Justice Brennan reversed the convictions of the makers and distributors of a film *The Lovers* and added to the *Roth* test the requirement that a book or film must be shown to lack "redeeming social importance" according to "national contemporary standards." Finally, in *A Book Named "John Cleland's Memoirs of a Woman of Pleasure" v. Massachusetts*, 383 U.S. 413 (1966), Justice Brennan combined all three of the above requirements in holding that obscene materials were excluded from First Amendment protection only if they fail all three requirements—that is, they (1) have a prurient interest that (2) appeals in a patently offensive way and (3) lack social redeeming value.

As a result of the Warren Court's rulings only hard-core pornography fell outside of the scope of protected speech. This encouraged the proliferation of sexually oriented publications during the 1960s, the decade of the sexual revolution, and, in turn, elevated pornography to an issue in national politics. In 1968, for example, one of the charges made against Justice Fortas during his ill-fated nomination to be chief justice was that he had sided with the majority on the Warren Court in expansively reading the protection afforded by the First Amendment. Richard Nixon then made an issue of pornography in his 1968 presidential election campaign, pledging to return law and order to the country and appoint only "strict constructionists" to the Court.[4]

The Warren Court responded to the increased legislation and law enforcement efforts to control the "explosion" in the dissemination of sexually oriented and pornographical materials. The Court, for instance, upheld the conviction of Ralph Ginzburg for pandering by advertising the sale and mailing of his magazine *Eros* from such places as Middlesex, New Jersey; Blue Balls, Montana; and Intercourse, Pennsylvania, in *Ginzburg v. United States*, 383 U.S. 463 (1966). Selective prosecutions and bans on the sales of sexually oriented magazines to minors were also upheld in *Ginsberg v. New York*, 390 U.S. 629 (1968), sustaining the conviction of Sam Ginsberg for selling two "girlie" magazines to a sixteen-year-old boy. In addition, permit systems and local censorship boards for screening sexually oriented films were approved so long as they afforded the film's distributors due process and abided by the Court's standards for determining what is obscene.[5]

However, even in Chief Justice Earl Warren's last term, the Court stood by its expansive reading of the First Amendment. *Stanley v. Georgia* (1969) (see page 395) struck down a statute prohibiting the possession of obscene materials, even in an individual's own house; as Justice Marshall put it, "Whatever may be the justifications for other statutes regulating obscenity, we do not think they reach into the privacy of one's home."

The year after *Stanley,* however, President Nixon's first appointee, Chief Justice Warren Burger, came to the Court. Already critical of the Warren Court's rulings on obscenity, he quickly tried to persuade his colleagues that the *Roth* line of rulings should be reconsidered. Initially unsuccessful, Burger was forced to voice his disagreement in dissenting opinions, questioning the propriety of "the national community standard" for obscenity in *Hoyt v. Minnesota*, 399 U.S. 524 (1970), and criticizing the Court for becoming a "super-censorship board" in *Cain v. Kentucky*, 387 U.S. 319 (1970), and *Walker v. Ohio*, 398 U.S. 434 (1970).

By 1973, Nixon's last two appointees, Justices Lewis Powell and William Rehnquist, were on the Court. And Burger finally got a bare majority to agree on a new test for obscenity, giving states and localities greater flexibility and control over sexually oriented materials. In *Miller v. California* (1973) (see page 398), Burger set out more concrete rules for obscenity prosecutions. While maintaining the prurient interest test, he redefined it as "whether the work depicts or describes, in a patently offensive way sexual conduct specifically defined by state law," thus inviting states to precisely define obscenity in legislation. He also rejected as too broad the utterly without redeeming social value test and devised his own more precise test—"whether the work, taken as a whole, lacks serious literary, artistic, political or scientific value." Finally, the contemporary community standards test was reinterpreted to mean local, not national standards.

Ten companion cases coming down on a five-to-four vote with *Miller* buttressed the Burger Court's renewed deference to states and localities in controlling sexually oriented materials. *Paris Adult Theatre I v. Slaton* (1973) (see page 403), for example, limited the ruling in *Stanley v. Georgia,* by upholding state regulation of adult movie houses. Prior to *Paris Adult Theatre I,* the Court had held that the First Amendment and the right of privacy did not preclude searches of luggage for obscene materials by U.S. customs officials at airports in *United States v. 37-Photographs,* 402 U.S. 363 (1971). Subsequently, in *United States v. 12-1200 Foot Reels of Super 8Mm Film,* 413 U.S. 123 (1973), the Court held that an individual does not have a First Amendment or privacy right to purchase obscene materials.

The test for obscenity announced in *Miller* was problematic and the four dissenters remained adamant in their opposition. But the politics of the Court had changed. As Justice Stevens, in an unusual concurring opinion to the denial of review of an appeal of one of the hundreds of obscenity convictions following *Miller,* explained, "[T]here is no reason to believe that the majority of the Court which decided *Miller v. California* . . . is any less adamant than the minority. Accordingly, regardless of how I might vote on the merits after full argument, it would be pointless to grant certiorari in case after case of this character only to have *Miller* reaffirmed time after time."[6]

The most troubling problems with *Miller* arose because obscenity prosecutions under the ruling turned on varying local community standards. At the federal level this allowed prosecutors to "forum shop," that is, they could initiate prosecutions in a district court in a geographical area with the most restrictive community standards. The Court declined to review this practice. For example, it refused to hear *Novick, Haim and Unique Specialities, Inc. v. U.S. District Court,* 423 U.S. 911 (1975), challenging an obscenity prosecution in Louisiana for materials produced in California and mailed to New York, but which passed through (and were seized) en route in Louisiana. At the state level, materials deemed obscene in one state might not be obscene in another. Consequently, the Court frequently cannot avoid rendering a final decision on the matter, notwithstanding that obscenity under

388 FREEDOM OF EXPRESSION AND ASSOCIATION

Miller is determined according to local community standards. The Court thus held, in *Jenkins v. Georgia*, 413 U.S. 496 (1973), that the movie *Carnal Knowledge* was not obscene, despite lower court rulings to the contrary.

The Burger and Rehnquist Courts tried to clarify some of the ambiguous aspects of *Miller*. *Pinkus v. United States*, 436 U.S. 293 (1978), held that children are not part of the "community," but "sensitive persons" and deviant groups are and should be considered in determining whether sexually oriented materials run afoul of local community standards. In *Pope v. Illinois*, 481 U.S. 497 (1987), the Court ruled that *Miller*'s third prong— requiring the showing that a work lacks serious literary, artistic, political, or scientific value—be applied based on standards set by a "reasonable" person, not an "ordinary" person. In addition, in *New York v. Ferber* (1982) (see page 410) the Court unanimously, although with four separate concurring opinions, upheld New York's ban on child pornography. Subsequently, in *Osborne v. Ohio*, 110 S.Ct. 1691 (1990), the Rehnquist Court upheld Ohio's statute banning the possession and viewing of child pornography. Dissenting Justice Brennan, joined by Justices Marshall and Stevens, however, protested that the law was overly broad and that the majority's ruling severely limited the Court's prior decision in *Stanley v. Georgia* (1969) (see page 395).

Besides trying to clarify the application of *Miller*'s tests for obscenity, the Burger and Rehnquist Court's have been more receptive to restrictions on the availability of sexually oriented materials. Over First Amendment objections, for example, restrictions on the mailing of obscene materials have been upheld. *Rowan v. U.S. Post Office Department*, 397 U.S. 728 (1970), sustained a federal obscenity statute allowing individuals to request that the post office not deliver unsolicited mailings to their homes of materials they find offensive. *United States v. Reidel*, 402 U.S. 351 (1971) upheld a federal obscenity statute prohibiting the mailing of certain pornographic materials, but *Bolger v. Youngs Drug Product Corp.*, 463 U.S. 60 (1983), struck down another statute as applied to the unsolicited mailing of advertisements for contraceptives.

Restrictions on adult bookstores, nude dancing, and other forms of live sexually oriented entertainment have also been approved. *California v. LaRue*, 409 U.S. 109 (1972), sustained California's law prohibiting sexually explicit live entertainment and films in bars. Although striking down a law prohibiting nude dancers in places of adult-only entertainment in *Schad v. Borough of Mount Ephraim*, 452 U.S. 61 (1981), the Court upheld New York's prohibition on nude dancing on the basis of the state's power to regulate liquor under the Twenty-first

Amendment.[7] *Arcara v. Cloud Books, Inc.*, 478 U.S. 697 (1986), also allowed the closing of an adult bookstore where its premises are used for the purpose of soliciting for prostitution. And in *FW/PBS, Inc. v. City of Dallas*, 110 S.Ct. 602 (1990), the Rehnquist Court unanimously upheld a portion of zoning and licensing ordinance that prohibited motels from renting rooms for less than ten hours, observing that "it is reasonable to believe that [a] shorter rental time period indicate[s] that the motels foster prostitution."

One of the principal ways that cities and localities control and regulate adult theaters and nightclubs is through exclusionary zoning, that is, restricting the operation of such businesses to certain areas of a community. In *Young v. American Mini Theatres*, 327 U.S. 50 (1976), the justices (five to four) upheld the barring of adult theaters from within 1,000 feet of each other or 500 feet from a residential area. *Larkin v. Grendel's Den, Inc.*, 459 U.S. 116 (1982), however, struck down a Massachusetts statute giving the power to churches to veto applications for liquor licenses for running afoul of the First Amendment establishment clause. *City of Renton v. Playtime Theatres, Inc.* (1986) (see page 415) is the Court's most recent pronouncement on the use of exclusionary zoning and the First Amendment.

NOTES

1. Harry Clor, *Obscenity and Public Morality* (Chicago: University of Chicago Press, 1969), 272.
2. Alan Dershowitz, "What Is Porn?" *ABA Journal* 36 (Nov. 1, 1986).
3. Butler v. Michigan, 352 U.S. 380 (1957).
4. See David M. O'Brien, *Storm Center: The Supreme Court in American Politics*, 2nd ed., (New York: Norton, 1990), Ch. 2; and Bruce Murphy, *Fortas: The Rise and Ruin of a Supreme Court Justice* (New York: Morrow, 1988).
5. See, for example, *Kingsley Books v. Brown*, 354 U.S. 436 (1957) (city may get injunction against sale of indecent books with appeal and trial within two days); *Times Film Corporation v. City of Chicago*, 365 U.S. 43 (1961) (no absolute right to exhibit, even once, any and every kind of film; no prior censorship of permit system); *Bantam Books, Inc. v. Sullivan*, 372 U.S. 58 (1963) (held Rhode Island Committee on Morality constituted prior restraint in providing no hearing on books banned for youths); *A Quantity of Copies of Books v. Kansas*, 378 U.S. 205 (1964) (procedure for impoundment of books was unconstitutional); *Freedman v. Maryland*, 380 U.S. 51 (1965) (held state motion picture censorship statute failed to provide adequate safeguards against undue repression of speech); *Teitel Film Corporation v. Cusack*, 390 U.S. 139

(1968) (held censorship board for review of films was unconstitutional, where fifty days passed before completion of administrative process and no provision was made for prompt judicial decision); *Rabe v. Washington*, 405 U.S. 313 (1972) (held state's obscenity statute, proscribing showing of pictures at drive-ins, which could be shown in adult theaters, was unconstitutional and vague); *Heller v. New York*, 413 U.S. 483 (1973) (held because judge saw entire film before issuing warrant for seizure for obscene film, no adversary hearing prior to seizure was required); *Roaden v. Kentucky*, 413 U.S. 496 (1973) (holding seizure of film in public distribution without warrant was prior restraint and violated Fourth Amendment); *Southern Promotions, Ltd. v. Conrad*, 420 U.S. 546 (1975) (held denial of city-leased theater for production of *Hair* was prior restraint because it was imposed without procedural safeguards); *Vance v. Universal Amusement Co.*, 445 U.S. 308 (1980) (struck down as prior restraint restriction on an exhibition of obscene motion pictures).

6. *Lies v. Oregon*, 425 U.S. 963 (1976).

7. *New York State Liquor Authority v. Bellanca*, 452 U.S. 714 (1981); reaffirmed in *City of Newport, Kentucky v. Iacobucci*, 479 U.S. 92 (1986).

SELECTED BIBLIOGRAPHY

Clor, Harry. *Obscenity and Public Morality*. Chicago: University of Chicago Press, 1969.

Clor, Harry, ed. *Censorship and Freedom of Expression: Essays on Obscenity and the Law*. New York: Rand McNally, 1971.

Rembar, Charles. *The End of Obscenity*. New York: Random House, 1968.

Schaver, Frederick. *Free Speech: A Philosophical Inquiry*. Cambridge, UK: Cambridge University Press, 1982.

Roth v. United States and *Alberts v. California*
354 U.S. 476, 77 S.Ct. 1304 (1957)

Samuel Roth was charged with violating a federal statute making it a crime to send "obscene, lewd, lascivious, or filthy" materials or advertisements through the mail. He was convicted for advertising and selling a quarterly publication, *American Aphrodite*, dealing with literary erotica and containing nude photographs, but acquitted on the charge that the photographs were obscene. David Alberts was indicted and convicted under California's obscenity law for publishing pictures of "nude and scantily-clad women"; his works made no claim to literary aspirations. On appeal of their convictions to the Supreme Court, their cases were consolidated in the Warren Court's landmark ruling and opinion by Justice Brennan, who was still in his freshman year having arrived at the Court only nine months before.

Justice BRENNAN delivers the opinion of the Court.

Roth conducted a business in New York in the publication and sale of books, photographs and magazines. He used circulars and advertising matter to solicit sales. He was convicted by a jury in the District Court for the Southern District of New York upon 4 counts of a 26-count indictment charging him with mailing obscene circulars and advertising, and an obscene book, in violation of the federal obscenity statute. His conviction was affirmed by the Court of Appeals for the Second Circuit. . . .

Alberts conducted a mail-order business from Los Angeles. He was convicted . . . under a misdemeanor complaint which charged him with lewdly keeping for sale obscene and indecent books, and with writing, composing and publishing an obscene advertisement of them, in violation of the California Penal Code. The conviction was affirmed by the Appellate Department of the Superior Court of the State of California in and for the County of Los Angeles. . . .

The dispositive question is whether obscenity is utterance within the area of protected speech and press. . . .

All ideas having even the slightest redeeming social importance—unorthodox ideas, controversial ideas, even ideas hateful to the prevailing climate of opinion—have the full protection of the guaranties, unless excludable because they encroach upon the limited area of more important interests. But implicit in the history of the First Amendment is the rejection of obscenity as utterly without redeeming social importance. This rejection for that reason is mirrored in the universal judgment that obscenity should be restrained, reflected in the international agreement of over 50 nations, in the obscenity laws of all of the 48 States, and in the 20 obscenity laws enacted by the Congress from 1842 to 1956. This is the same judgment expressed by this Court in *Chaplinsky v. New Hampshire* [315 U.S. 568 (1942)]. We hold that obscenity is not within the area of constitutionally protected speech or press. . . .

[S]ex and obscenity are not synonymous. Obscene material is material which deals with sex in a manner appealing to prurient interest. The portrayal of sex, *e.g.,* in art, literature and scientific works, is not itself sufficient reason to deny material the constitutional protection of freedom of speech and press. Sex, a great and mysterious motive force in human life, has indisputably been a subject of absorbing interest to mankind through the ages; it is one of the vital problems of human interest and public concern. . . .

It is therefore vital that the standards for judging obscenity safeguard the protection of freedom of speech and press for material which does not treat sex in a manner appealing to prurient interest.

The early leading standard of obscenity allowed material to be judged merely by the effect of an isolated excerpt upon particularly susceptible persons. *Regina v. Hicklin,* [1868] L.R. 3 Q.B. 360. Some American courts adopted this standard but later decisions have rejected it and substituted this test: whether to the average person, applying contemporary community standards, the dominant theme of the material taken as a whole appeals to prurient interest. The *Hicklin* test, judging obscenity by the effect of isolated passages upon the most susceptible persons, might well encompass material legitimately treating with sex, and so it must be rejected as unconstitutionally restrictive of the freedoms of speech and press. On the other hand, the substituted standard provides safeguards adequate to withstand the charge of constitutional infirmity.

Both trial courts below sufficiently followed the proper standard. Both courts used the proper definition of obscenity. . . .

In summary, then, we hold that these statutes, applied according to the proper standard for judging obscenity, do not offend constitutional safeguards against convictions based upon protected material, or fail to give men in acting adequate notice of what is prohibited.

Chief Justice WARREN, concurring.

The line dividing the salacious or pornographic from literature or science is not straight and unwavering. Present laws depend largely upon the effect that the materials may have upon those who receive them. It is manifest that the same object may have a different impact varying according to the part of the community it reached. But there is more to these cases. It is not the book that is on trial; it is a person. The conduct of the defendant is the central issue, not the obscenity of a book or picture. The nature of the materials is, of course, relevant as an attribute of the defendant's conduct, but the materials are thus placed in context from which they draw color and character. A wholly different result might be reached in a different setting.

Justice HARLAN, concurring in part and dissenting in part.

In final analysis, the problem presented by these cases is how far, and on what terms, the state and federal government have power to punish individuals for disseminating books considered to be undesirable because of their nature of supposed deleterious effect upon human conduct. Proceeding from the premise that "no issue is presented in either case concerning the obscenity of the material involved," the Court finds the "dispositive question" to be "whether obscenity is utterance within the area of protected speech and press," and then holds that "obscenity" is not so protected because it is "utterly without redeeming social importance." This sweeping formula appears to me to beg the very question before us. The Court seems to assume that "obscenity" is a peculiar *genus* of "speech and press," which is as distinctly recognizable, and classifiable as poison ivy is among other plants. On this basis the *constitutional* question before us simply becomes, as the Court says, whether "obscenity," as an abstraction is protected by the First and Fourteenth Amendments, and the question whether a *particular* book may be suppressed becomes a mere matter of classification, of "fact," to be entrusted to a fact-finder and insulated from independent constitutional judgment. But surely the problem cannot be solved in such a generalized fashion. Every communication has an individuality and "value" or its own. The suppression of a particular writing or other tangible form of expression is, therefore, an *individual* matter, and in the nature of things every such suppression raises an individual constitutional problem, in which a reviewing court must determine for *itself* whether the attacked expression is suppressable within constitutional standards. Since those standards do not readily lend themselves to generalized definitions, the constitutional problem in the last analysis becomes one of particularized judgments which appellate courts must make for themselves. . . .

I concur in the judgment of the Court in No. 61, *Alberts v. People of State of California.*

The question in this case is whether the defendant was deprived of liberty without due process of law when he was convicted for selling certain materials found by the judge to be obscene because they would have a "tendency to deprave or corrupt its readers by exciting lascivious thoughts or arousing lustful desire.". . .

Since the domain of sexual morality is pre-eminently a matter of state concern, this Court should be slow to interfere with state legislation calculated to protect that morality. It seems to me that nothing in the broad and flexible command of the Due Process Clause forbids California to prosecute one who sells books whose dominant tendency might be to "deprave or corrupt" a reader. I agree with the Court, of course, that the books must be judged as a whole and in relation to the normal adult reader.

What has been said, however, does not dispose of the case. It still remains for us to decide whether the state court's determination that this material should be suppressed is consistent with the Fourteenth Amendment; and that, of course, presents a federal question as to which we, and not the state court, have the ultimate responsibility. And so, in the final analysis, I concur in the judgment because, upon an independent perusal of the material involved, and in light of the considerations discussed above, I cannot say that its suppression would so interfere with the communication of "ideas" in any proper sense of that term that it would offend the Due Process Clause. I therefore agree with the Court that appellant's conviction must be affirmed.

I dissent in No. 582, *Roth v. United States.*

We are faced here with the question whether the federal obscenity statute, as construed and applied in this case, violates the First Amendment to the Constitution. To me, this question is of quite a different order than one where we are dealing with state legislation under the Fourteenth Amendment. I do not think it follows that state and federal powers in this area are the same, and that just because the State may suppress a particular utterance, it is automatically permissible for the Federal Government to do the same. . . .

The Federal Government has, for example, power to restrict seditious speech directed against it, because that Government certainly has the substantive authority to protect itself against revolution. But in dealing with obscenity we are faced with the converse situation, for the interests which obscenity statutes purportedly protect are primarily entrusted to the care, not of the Federal Government, but of the States. Congress has no substantive power over sexual morality. Such powers as the Federal Government has in this field are but incidental to its other powers, here the postal power, and are not of the same nature as those possessed by the States, which bear direct responsibility for the protection of the local moral fabric. . . .

Not only is the federal interest in protecting the Nation against pornography attenuated, but the dangers of federal censorship in this field are far greater than anything the States may do. It has often been said that one of the great strengths of our federal system is that we have, in the forty-eight States, forty-eight experimental social laboratories. Different States will have different attitudes toward the same work of literature. The same book which is freely read in one State might be classed as obscene in another. And it seems to me that no overwhelming danger to our freedom to experiment and to gratify our tastes in literature is likely to result from the suppression of a borderline book in one of the States, so long as there is no uniform nation-wide suppression of the book, and so long as other States are free to experiment with the same or bolder books.

Quite a different situation is presented, however, where the Federal Government imposes the ban. The danger is perhaps not great if the people of one State, through their legislature, decide that "Lady Chatterley's Lover" goes so far beyond the acceptable standards of candor that it will be deemed offensive and non-sellable, for the State next door is still free to make its own choice. At least we do not have one uniform standard. But the dangers to free thought and expression are truly great if the Federal Government imposes a blanket ban over the Nation on such a book. The prerogative of the States to differ on their ideas of morality will be destroyed, the ability of States to experiment will be stunted. The fact that the people of one State cannot read some of the works of D. H. Lawrence seems to me, if not wise or desirable, at least acceptable. But that no person in the United States should be allowed to do so seems to me to be intolerable, and violative of both the letter and spirit of the First Amendment.

I judge this case, then, in view of what I think is the attenuated federal interest in this field, in view of the very real danger of a deadening uniformity which can result from nation-wide federal censorship, and in view of the fact that the constitutionality of this conviction must be weighed against the First and not the Fourteenth Amendment. So viewed, I do not think that this conviction can be upheld.

Justice DOUGLAS, with whom Justice BLACK joins, dissenting.

I do not think that the problem can be resolved by the Court's statement that "obscenity is not expression protected by the First Amendment." . . . I reject too the implication that problems of freedom of speech and of the press are to be resolved by weighing against the values of free expression, the judgment of the Court that a particular form of that expression has "no redeeming social importance." The First Amendment, its prohibition in terms absolute, was designed to preclude courts as well as legislatures from weighing the values of speech against silence. The First Amendment puts free speech in the preferred position.

Stanley v. Georgia
394 U.S. 561, 89 S.Ct. 1243 (1969)

Robert Eli Stanley was charged in Fulton County, Georgia, for violating the state's law making it a crime to possess obscene materials. His arrest arose from a search of his home by police who had a warrant to seize evidence of bookmaking activities, but discovered in a desk drawer in Stanley's bedroom three reels of 8-millimeter film. After viewing the films in his living room, the police arrested Stanley, and he was later convicted for the possession of allegedly obscene materials in a state superior court. Stanley appealed a decision by the state supreme court upholding his conviction to the Supreme Court, which granted certiorari.

Justice MARSHALL delivers the opinion of the Court.

Appellant argues here, and argued below, that the Georgia obscenity statute, insofar as it punishes mere private possession of obscene matter, violates the First Amendment, as made applicable to the States by the Fourteenth Amendment. For reasons set forth below, we agree that the mere private possession of obscene matter cannot constitutionally be made a crime. . . .

[The] appellant is asserting . . . the right to read or observe what he pleases—the right to satisfy his intellectual and emotional needs in the privacy of his own home. He is asserting the right to be free from state inquiry into the contents of his library. Georgia contends that appellant does not have these rights, that there are certain types of materials that the individual may not read or even possess. Georgia justifies this assertion by arguing that the films in the present case are obscene. But we think that mere categorization of these films as "obscene" is insufficient justification for such a drastic invasion of personal liberties guaranteed by the First and Fourteenth Amendments. Whatever may be the justifications for other statutes regulating obscenity, we do not think they reach into the privacy of one's own home. If the First Amendment means anything, it means that a State has no business telling a man, sitting alone in his own house, what books he may read or what films he may watch. Our whole constitutional heritage rebels at the thought of giving government the power to control men's minds. . . .

We hold that the First and Fourteenth Amendments prohibit making mere private possession of obscene material a crime. *Roth* [*v. United States* (1957)] and the cases following that decision are not impaired by today's holding. As we have said, the States retain broad power to regulate obscenity; that power simply does not extend to mere possession by the individual in the privacy of his own home. Accordingly, the judgment of the court below is reversed and the case is remanded for proceedings not inconsistent with this opinion.

Justice BLACK concurred.

Justice STEWART, with whom Justice BRENNAN and Justice WHITE joined, concurred in a separate opinion.

INSIDE THE COURT
Letter from Justice Black to Justice Harlan, December 10, 1969.

Because the Supreme Court held that obscene materials fall outside of the protection of the First Amendment, when hearing appeals of convictions under state and federal obscenity laws, the justices had to examine the evidence in each case, including screening sexually explicit films in a room in the basement of the Court. Because of Justice Hugo Black's absolutist interpretation of the First Amendment, he declined to join the other justices in screening allegedly obscene films, as the following letter indicates.

Supreme Court of the United States
Washington, D. C. 20543

CHAMBERS OF
JUSTICE HUGO L. BLACK

December 10, 1969

Dear John,

I have your note advising that arrangements have been made for the Court to see "I, a Woman" and "I Am Curious (Yellow)" at 11 A.M. next Monday morning. I cannot see that looking at the pictures would change my view that the First Amendment would be violated by barring the showing of these pictures. Consequently I shall not be present.

Sincerely,

Hugo

Mr. Justice Harlan

cc: Members of the Conference

Source: Justice William J. Brennan, Jr., *Papers,* Box 201, Manuscripts Room, Library of Congress, Washington, DC. *Photo source:* Library of Congress.

Miller v. California
413 U.S. 15, 93 S.Ct. 2607 (1973)

By the 1970s, as a result of the *Roth* line of cases, there was a proliferation of sexually oriented materials and renewed attempts by states and localities to regulate and ban obscene and pornographical materials. That in turn meant a large number of appeals of obscenity convictions coming to the Supreme Court. In 1971–1972, there were more than sixty such cases on the Court's docket and the justices heard oral arguments in eight cases in the 1972 term. One of these cases involved the conviction of Marvin Miller for violating California's obscenity law. He was found guilty of mailing unsolicited materials advertising adult books and films, which included pictures of men and women engaged in sexual acts and displaying their genitals.

When the justices discussed *Miller* and other obscenity cases in May and June, 1972, they were dissatisfied with *Roth* yet pulled in opposite directions. In particular, Chief Justice Burger and Justice Brennan each wanted to take the Court in a different direction on the obscenity problem.

Chief Justice Burger had come to the Court in 1969 believing that the *Roth* line of cases were mistaken; they were too permissive and failed to give states and localities enough power over sexually explicit materials. He urged a reconsideration of *Roth* and tougher standards. "In short," as he put in a June 14, 1974 memorandum, "a little 'chill' will do some of the 'pornos' no great harm and it might be good for the country."

Justice Brennan, who authored *Roth* and other opinions in this area for the Warren Court, was no less concerned and had come to revaluate his earlier position in *Roth*. In his view, however, *Roth* was mistaken in not going far enough; it allowed too much censorship. As he explained in a memorandum for the justices on May 22, 1972:

With all respect, the Chief Justice's proposed solution to the obscenity quagmire will, in my view, worsen an already intolerable mess. I've been thinking for some time that only a drastic change in applicable constitutional principles promises a way out. I've decided that I shall use this case as a vehicle for saying that I'm prepared to make that change. I'll write in effect that it has proved impossible to separate expression concerning sex, called obscenity, from other expression concerning sex, whether the material takes the form of words, photographs or film; . . . that we should treat obscenity not as expression concerning sex except from First Amendment speech but as expression, although constituting First Amendment speech, that is regulable to the extent of legislating against its offensive exposure to unwilling adults and dissemination to juveniles.

Both Burger and Brennan began working on draft opinions in the hope of winning a majority over to their side. That proved impossible so late in the term and *Miller* was carried over for reargument in the October 1972 term. Both continued to compete for votes but in the end, on June 21, 1973, a bare majority accepted Burger's analysis and more restrictive tests for obscenity based on local community standards. Nixon's three other appointees, Justices Blackmun, Powell, and Rehnquist, joined along with Justice White, who had sided with Brennan in *Roth* but would go no further. Brennan's draft became a dissenting opinion.

Chief Justice BURGER delivers the opinion of the Court.

This is one of a group of "obscenity-pornography" cases being reviewed by the Court in a re-examination of standards enunciated in earlier cases involving what Justice HARLAN called "the intractable obscenity problem.". . .

Appellant conducted a mass mailing campaign to advertise the sale of illustrated books, euphemistically called "adult" material. After a jury trial, he was convicted of violating California Penal Code § 311.2(a), a misdemeanor, by knowingly distributing obscene matter, and the Appellate Department, Superior Court of California, County of Orange, summarily affirmed the judgment without opinion. Appellant's conviction was specifically based on his conduct in causing five unsolicited advertising brochures . . . [containing] pictures and drawings very explicitly depicting men and women in groups of two or more engaging in a variety of sexual activities, with genitals often prominently displayed.

This case involves the application of a State's criminal obscenity statute to a situation in which sexually explicit materials have been thrust by aggressive sales action upon unwilling recipients who had in no way indicated any desire to receive such materials. . . .

[O]bscene material is unprotected by the First Amendment. . . . We acknowledge, however, the inherent dangers of undertaking to regulate any form of expression. State statutes designed to regulate obscene materials must be carefully limited. As a result, we now confine the permissible scope of such regulation to works which depict or describe sexual conduct. That conduct must be specifically defined by the applicable state law, as written or authoritatively construed. A state offense must also be limited to works which, taken as a whole, appeal to the prurient interest in sex, which portray sexual conduct in a patently offensive way, and which, taken as a whole, do not have serious literary, artistic, political, or scientific value.

The basic guidelines for the trier of fact must be: (a) whether "the average person, applying contemporary community standards" would find that the work, taken as a whole, appeals to the prurient interest; (b) whether the work depicts or describes, in a patently offensive way, sexual conduct specifically defined by the applicable state law; and (c) whether the work, taken as a whole, lacks serious literary, artistic, political, or scientific value. We do not adopt as a constitutional standard the *"utterly* without redeeming social value" test of *Memoirs v. Massachusetts* [383 U.S. 413 (1966)].

We emphasize that it is not our function to propose regulatory schemes for the States. That must await their concrete legislative efforts. It is possible, however, to give a few plain examples of what a state statute could define for regulation under part (b) of the standard announced in this opinion, *supra:*

(a) Patently offensive representations or descriptions of ultimate sexual acts, normal or perverted, actual or simulated.

(b) Patently offensive representation or descriptions of masturbation, excretory functions, and lewd exhibition of the genitals.

Sex and nudity may not be exploited without limit by films or pictures exhibited or sold in places of public accommodation any more than live sex and nudity can be exhibited or sold without limit in such public places. At a minimum, prurient, patently offensive depiction or description of sexual conduct must have serious literary, artistic, political, or scientific value to merit First Amendment protection. . . . For example, medical books for the education of physicians and related personnel necessarily use graphic illustrations and descriptions of human anatomy. In resolving the inevitably sensitive questions of fact and law, we must continue to rely on the jury system, accompanied by the safeguards that judges, rules of evidence, presumption of innocence, and other protective features provide, as we do with rape, murder, and a host of other offenses against society and its individual members.

Justice BRENNAN has abandoned his former position and now maintains that no formulation of this Court, the Congress, or the States can adequately distinguish obscene-material unprotected by the First Amendment from protected expression. . . .

[But under] the holdings announced today, no one will be subject to prosecution for the sale or exposure of obscene materials unless these materials depict or describe patently offensive "hard core" sexual conduct specifically defined by the regulating state law, as written or construed. We are satisfied that these specific prerequisites will provide fair notice to a dealer in such materials that his public and commercial activities.

Justice BRENNAN also emphasizes "institutional stress" in justification of his change of view. Noting that "[t]he number of obscenity cases on our docket gives ample testimony to the burden that has been placed upon this Court," he quite rightly remarks that the examination of contested materials "is hardly a source of edification to the members of this Court." He also notes, and we agree, that "uncertainty of the standards creates a continuing source of tension between state and federal courts. . . ."

But today, for the first time since *Roth* was decided in 1957, a majority of this Court has agreed on concrete guidelines to isolate "hard core" pornography from expression protected by the First Amendment. Now we may abandon the casual practice of *Redrup v. New York*, 386 U.S. 767 (1967), and attempt to provide positive guidance to federal and state courts alike.

This may not be an easy road, free from difficulty. But no amount of "fatigue" should lead us to adopt a convenient "institutional" rationale—an absolutist, "anything goes" view of the First Amendment—because it will lighten our burdens. . . .

Under a National Constitution, fundamental First Amendment limitations on the powers of the States do not vary from community to community, but this does not mean that there are, or should or can be, fixed, uniform national standards of precisely what appeals to the "prurient interest" or is "patently offensive." These are essentially questions of fact, and our Nation is simply too big and too diverse for this Court to reasonably expect that such standards could be articulated for all 50 States in a single formulation, even assuming the prerequisite consensus exists. When triers of fact are asked to decide whether "the average person, applying contemporary community standards" would consider certain materials "prurient," it would be unrealistic to require that the answer be based on some abstract formulation. The adversary system, with lay jurors as the usual ultimate fact-finders in criminal prosecutions, has historically permitted triers of fact to draw on the standards of their community, guided always by limiting instructions on the law. To require a State to structure obscenity proceedings around evidence of a *national* "community standard" would be an exercise in futility. . . .

We conclude that neither the state's alleged failure to offer evidence of "national standards," nor the trial court's charge that the jury consider state community standards, were constitutional errors. Nothing in the First Amendment requires that a jury must consider hypothetical and unascertainable "national standards" when attempting to determine whether certain materials are obscene as a matter of fact. . . . It is neither realistic nor constitutionally sound to read the First Amendment as requiring that the people of Maine or Mississippi accept public depiction of conduct found tolerable in Las Vegas, or New York City. . . . People in different States vary in their tastes and attitudes, and this diversity is not to be strangled by the absolutism of imposed uniformity. . . . We hold that the requirement that the jury evaluate the materials with reference to "contemporary standards of the State of California" serves this protection purpose and is constitutionally adequate. . . .

In sum, we (a) reaffirm the *Roth* holding that obscene material is not protected by the First Amendment; (b) hold that such material can be regulated by the States, subject to the specific safeguards enunciated above, without a showing that the material is "*utterly* without redeeming social value"; and (c) hold that obscenity is to be determined by applying "contemporary community standards," . . . not "national standards.". . .

Vacated and remanded.

Justice DOUGLAS dissenting.

Today the Court retreats from the earlier formulations of the constitutional test and undertakes to make new definitions. This effort, like the earlier ones, is earnest and well intentioned. The difficulty is that we do not deal with constitutional terms, since "obscenity" is not mentioned in the Constitution or Bill of Rights. And the First Amendment makes no such exception from "the press" which it undertakes to protect nor, as I have said on other occasions, is an exception necessarily implied, for there was no recognized exception to the free press at the time the Bill of Rights was adopted which treated "obscene" publications differently from other types of papers, magazines, and books. So there are no constitutional guidelines for deciding what is and what is not "obscene." The Court is at large because we deal with tastes and standards of literature. What shocks me may be sustenance for my neighbor. What causes one person to boil up in rage over one pamphlet or movie may reflect only his neurosis, not shared by others. We deal here with a regime of censorship which, if adopted, should be done by constitutional amendment after full debate by the people. . . .

The idea that the First Amendment permits government to ban publications that are "offensive" to some people puts an ominous gloss on freedom of the press. That test would make it possible to ban any paper or any journal or magazine in some benighted place. . . . The idea that the First Amendment permits punishment for ideas that are "offensive" to the particular judge or jury sitting in judgment is astounding. No greater leveler of speech or literature has ever been designed. . . .

I do not think we, the judges, were ever given the constitutional power to make definitions of obscenity. If it is to be defined, let the people debate and decide by a constitutional amendment what they want to ban as obscene and what standards they want the legislatures and the courts to apply. Perhaps the people will decide that the path towards a mature, integrated society requires that all ideas competing for acceptance must have no censor.

Perhaps they will decide otherwise. Whatever the choice, the courts will have some guidelines. Now we have none except our own predilections.

Justice BRENNAN, with whom Justice STEWART and Justice MARSHALL join, dissenting.

In my dissent in *Paris Adult Theatre I v. Slaton,* 413 U.S. 49 [1973], I noted that I had no occasion to consider the extent of state power to regulate the distribution of sexually oriented material to juveniles or the offensive exposure of such material to unconsenting adults. . . . I need not now decide whether a statute might be drawn to impose, within the requirements of the First Amendment, criminal penalties for the precise conduct at issue here. For it is clear that under my dissent in *Paris Adult Theatre I,* the statute under which the prosecution was brought is unconstitutionally overbroad, and therefore invalid on its face.

Paris Adult Theatre I v. Slaton
413 U.S. 49, 93 S.Ct. 2628 (1973)

This ruling came down on June 21, 1973 with *Miller v. California* and three other obscenity decisions. The case originated with Atlanta's district attorney, Lewis Slaton, seeking an injunction against the showing of two allegedly obscene movies, *Magic Mirror* and *It All Comes Out in the End,* by Paris Adult Theatre I. The trial judge refused to issue an injunction on the ground that showing such movies to consenting adults in a commercial theater was constitutionally permissible under the First Amendment. On appeal, the Georgia state supreme court reversed on finding the movies to be hard-core pornography. The owners of Paris Adult Theatre I appealed to the Supreme Court.

Chief Justice BURGER delivers the opinion of the Court.

We categorically disapprove the theory, apparently adopted by the trial judge, that obscene, pornographic films acquire constitutional immunity from state regulation simply because they are exhibited for consenting adults only. . . . Although we have often pointedly recognized the high importance of the state interest in regulating the exposure of obscene materials to juveniles and unconsenting adults, . . . this Court has never declared these to be the only legitimate state interests permitting regulation of obscene material. . . . In particular, we hold that there are legitimate state interests at stake in stemming the tide of commercialized obscenity, even assuming it is feasible to enforce effective safeguards against exposure to juveniles and to passersby. Rights and interests "other than those of the advocates are involved." These include the interest of the public in the quality of life and the total community environment, the tone of commerce in the great city centers, and, possibly, the public safety itself. The Hilllink Minority Report of the Commission on Obscenity and Pornography indicates that there is at least an arguable correction between obscene material and crime. Quite apart from sex crimes, however, there remains one problem of large proportions aptly described by Professor Bickel:

> "It concerns the tone of the society, the mode, or to use terms that have perhaps greater currency, the style and quality of life, now and in the future. A man may be entitled to read an obscene book in his room, or expose himself indecently there. . . . We should protect his privacy. But if he demands a right to obtain the books and pictures he wants in the market, and to foregather in public places—discreet, if you will, but accessible to all—with others who share his tastes, *then to grant him his right is to affect the world about the rest of us, and to impinge on other privacies.* Even supposing that each of us can, if he wishes, effectively avert the eye and stop the ear (which, in truth, we cannot), what is commonly read and seen and heard and done intrudes upon us all, want it or not." 22 The Public Interest 25–26 (Winter 1971). (Emphasis added.)

As Chief Justice WARREN stated, there is a "right of the Nation and of the States to maintain a decent society. . . ."

But, it is argued, there are no scientific data which conclusively demonstrate that exposure to obscene material adversely affects men and women or their society. It is urged on behalf of the petitioners that, absent such a demonstration, any kind of state regulation is "impermissible." We reject this argument. It is not for us to resolve empirical uncertainties underlying state legislation, save in the exceptional case where that legislation plainly impinges upon rights protected by the Constitution itself. . . . Although there is no conclusive proof of a connection between antisocial behavior and obscene material, the legislature of Georgia could quite reasonably determine that such a connection does or might exist. In deciding *Roth*, this Court implicitly accepted that a legislature could legitimately act on such a conclusion to protect *"the social interest in order and morality."*. . .

If we accept the unprovable assumption that a complete education requires the reading of certain books, and the well nigh universal belief that good books, plays, and art lift the spirit, improve the mind, enrich the human personality, and develop character, can we then say that a state legislature may not act on the corollary assumption that commerce in obscene books, or public exhibitions focused on obscene conduct, have a tendency to exert a corrupting and debasing impact leading to antisocial behavior? . . .

It is asserted, however, that . . . state regulation of access by consenting adults to obscene material violates the constitutionally protected right to privacy enjoyed by petitioners' customers. Even assuming that petitioners have vicarious standing to assert potential customers' rights, it is unavailing to compare a theater, open to the public for a fee, with the private home of *Stanley v. Georgia* [394 U.S. 557 (1969)], and the marital bedroom of *Griswold v. Connecticut* [381 U.S. 479 (1965)].

Our prior decisions recognizing a right to privacy guaranteed by the Fourteenth Amendment included "only personal rights that can be deemed 'fundamental' or 'implicit in the concept of ordered liberty.'. . . "This privacy right encompasses and protects the personal intimacies of the home, the family, marriage, motherhood, procreation, and child rearing. Nothing, however, in this Court's decisions intimates that there is any "fundamental" privacy right "implicit in the concept of ordered liberty" to watch obscene movies in places of public accommodation. . . .

It is also argued that the State has no legitimate interest in "control [of] the moral content of a person's thoughts," and we need not quarrel with this. But we reject the claim that the State of Georgia is here attempting to control the minds or thoughts of those who patronize theaters. Preventing unlimited display or distribution of obscene material, which by definition lacks any serious literary, artistic, political, or scientific value as communication, is distinct from a control of reason and the intellect. . . .

Finally, petitioners argue that conduct which directly involves "consenting adults" only has, for that sole reason, a special claim to constitutional protection. Our Constitution establishes a broad range of conditions on the exercise of power by the States, but for us to say that our Constitution incorporates the proposition that conduct involving consenting adults only is always beyond state regulation, is a step we are unable to take. Commercial exploitation of depictions, descriptions, or exhibitions of obscene conduct on commercial premises open to the adult public falls within a State's broad power to regulate commerce and protect the public environment. The issue in this context goes beyond whether someone, or even the majority, considers the conduct depicted as "wrong" or "sinful." The States have the power to make a morally neutral judgment that public exhibition of obscene material, or commerce in such material, has a tendency to . . . endanger the public safety, or to jeopardize in Chief Justice WARREN's words, the States' "right . . . to maintain a decent society."

Justice BRENNAN, with whom Justice STEWART and Justice MARSHALL join, dissenting.

Our experience with the *Roth* approach has certainly taught us that the outright suppression of obscenity cannot be reconciled with the fundamental principles of the First and Fourteenth Amendments. For we have failed to formulate a standard that sharply distinguishes protected from unprotected speech, and out of necessity, we have resorted to . . . disposing of these cases through summary reversal or denial of certiorari [and] we have deliberately and effectively obscured the rationale underlying the decisions. It comes as no surprise that judicial attempts to follow our lead conscientiously have often ended in hopeless confusion. . . .

[A]fter 16 years of experimentation and debate I am reluctantly forced to the conclusion that none of the available formulas, including the one announced today, can reduce the vagueness to a tolerable level while at the same time striking an acceptable balance between the protections of the First and Fourteenth Amendments, on the one hand, and on the other the asserted state interest in regulating the dissemination of certain sexually oriented materials. Any effort to draw a constitutionally acceptable boundary on state power must resort to such indefinite concepts as "prurient interest," "patent offensiveness," "serious literary value," and the like. The meaning of these concepts necessarily varies with the experience, outlook, and even idiosyncrasies of the person defining them. Although we have assumed that obscenity does exist and that we "know it when [we] see it," *Jacobellis v. Ohio* [378 U.S. 184 (1964)] (STEWART, J., concurring), we are manifestly unable to describe it in advance except by reference to concepts so elusive that they fail to distinguish clearly between protected and unprotected speech. . . .

The severe problems arising from the lack of fair notice, from the chill on protected expression, and from the stress imposed on the state and federal judicial machinery persuade me that a significant change in direction is urgently required. I turn, therefore, to the alternatives that are now open.

1. The approach requiring the smallest deviation from our present course would be to draw a new line between protected and unprotected speech, still permitting the States to suppress all material on the unprotected side of the line. In my view, clarity cannot be obtained pursuant to this approach except by drawing a line that resolves all doubt in favor of state power and against the guarantees of the First Amendment. We could hold, for example, that any depiction or description of human sexual organs, irrespective of the manner or purpose of the portrayal, is outside the protection of the First Amendment and therefore open to suppression by the States. That formula would, no doubt, offer much fairer notice of the reach of any state statute

drawn at the boundary of the State's constitutional power. And it would also, in all likelihood, give rise to a substantial probability of regularity in most judicial determinations under the standard. But such a standard would be appallingly overbroad, permitting the suppression of a vast range of literary, scientific, and artistic masterpieces. Neither the First Amendment nor any free community could possibly tolerate such a standard. Yet short of that extreme it is hard to see how any choice of words could reduce the vagueness problem to tolerable proportions, so long as we remain committed to the view that some class of materials is subject to outright suppression by the State.

2. The alternative adopted by the Court today recognizes that a prohibition against any depiction or description of human sexual organs could not be reconciled with the guarantees of the First Amendment. But the Court does retain the view that certain sexually oriented material can be considered obscene and therefore unprotected by the First and Fourteenth Amendments. To describe that unprotected class of expression, the Court adopts a restatement of the *Roth-Memoirs* definition of obscenity: "The basic guidelines for the trier of fact must be: (a) whether 'the average person, applying contemporary community standards' would find that the work, taken as a whole, appeals to the prurient interest. . . (b) whether the work depicts or describes, in a patently offensive way, sexual conduct specifically defined by the applicable state law, and (c) whether the work, taken as a whole, lacks serious literary, artistic, political, or scientific value." *Miller v. California.* In apparent illustration of "sexual conduct," as that term is used in the test's second element, the Court identifies "(a) Patently offensive representations or descriptions of ultimate sexual acts, normal or perverted, actual or simulated," and "(b) Patently offensive representations or descriptions of masturbation, excretory functions, and lewd exhibition of the genitals." . . .

In my view, the restatement [of *Roth*'s standards] leaves unresolved the very difficulties that compel our rejection of the underlying *Roth* approach, while at the same time contributing substantial difficulties of its own. . . . And today's restatement will likely have the effect, whether or not intended, of permitting far more sweeping suppression of sexually oriented expression, including expression that would almost surely be held protected under our current formulation. . . .

It is beyond dispute that the [Court's new] approach can have no ameliorative impact on the cluster of problems that grow out of the vagueness of our current standards. Indeed, even the Court makes no argument that the reformulation will provide fairer notice to booksellers, theater owners, and the reading and viewing public. Nor does the Court contend that the approach will provide clearer guidance to law enforcement officials or reduce the chill on protected expression. Nor, finally, does the Court suggest that the approach will mitigate to the slightest degree the institutional problems that have plagued this Court and the state and federal judiciary as a direct result of the uncertainty inherent in any definition of obscenity.

Of course, the Court's restated *Roth* test does limit the definition of obscenity to depictions of physical conduct and explicit sexual acts. . . . But, just as the agreement in *Roth* on an abstract definition of obscenity gave little hint of the extreme difficulty that was to follow in attempting to apply that definition to specific material, the mere formulation of a "physical conduct" test is no assurance that it can be applied with any greater facility. . . .

If the application of the "physical conduct" test to pictorial material is fraught with difficulty, its application to textual material carries the potential for extraordinary abuse. Surely we have passed the point where the mere written description of sexual conduct is deprived of First Amendment protection. Yet the test offers no guidance to us, or anyone else, in determining which written descriptions of sexual conduct are protected, and which are not. . . .

I am convinced that a definition of obscenity in terms of physical conduct cannot provide sufficient clarity to afford fair notice, to avoid a chill on protected expression, and to minimize the institutional stress, so long as that definition is used to justify the outright suppression of any material that is asserted to fall within its terms.

3. I have also considered the possibility of reducing our own role, and the role of appellate courts generally, in determining whether particular matter is obscene. Thus, we might conclude that juries are best suited to determine obscenity *vel non* and that jury verdicts in this area should not be set aside except in cases of extreme departure from prevailing standards. . . . [Yet] the First Amendment requires an independent review by appellate courts of the constitutional fact of obscenity. That result is required by principles applicable to the obscenity issue no less than to any other area involving free expression. . . .

4. Finally, I have considered the view, urged so forcefully since 1957 by our Brothers BLACK and DOUGLAS, that the First Amendment bars the suppression of any sexually oriented expression. That position would effect a sharp reduction, although perhaps not a total elimination, of the uncertainty that surrounds our current approach. Nevertheless, I am convinced that it would achieve that desirable goal only by stripping the States of power to an extent that cannot be justified by the commands of the Constitution, at least so long as there is available an alternative approach that strikes a better balance between the guarantee of free expression and the States' legitimate interests.

Our experience since *Roth* requires us not only to abandon the effort to pick out obscene materials on a case-by-case basis, but also to reconsider a fundamental postulate of *Roth:* that there exists a definable class of sexually oriented expression that may be totally suppressed by the Federal and State Governments. Assuming that such a class of expression does in fact exist, I am forced to conclude that the concept of "obscenity" cannot be defined with sufficient specificity and clarity to provide fair notice to persons who create and distribute sexually oriented materials, to prevent substantial erosion of protected speech as a byproduct of the attempt to suppress unprotected speech, and to avoid very costly institutional harms. Given these inevitable side effects of state efforts to suppress what is assumed to be *unprotected* speech, we must scrutinize with care the state interest that is asserted to justify the suppression. For in the absence of some very substantial interest in suppressing such speech, we can hardly condone the ill effects that seem to flow inevitably from the effort. . . .

The opinions in *Redrup* [*v. New York* (1967)] and *Stanley* [*v. Georgia* (1969)] reflected our emerging view that the state interests in protecting children and in protecting unconsenting adults may stand on a different footing from the other asserted state interests. . . .

But, whatever the strength of the state interests in protecting juveniles and unconsenting adults from exposure to sexually oriented materials, those interests cannot be asserted in defense of the holding of the Georgia Supreme Court in this case. That court assumed for the purposes of its decision that the films in issue were exhibited only to persons over the age of 21 who viewed them willingly and with prior knowledge of the nature of their contents. And on that assumption the state court held that the films could still be suppressed. The justification for the suppression must be found, therefore, in some independent interest in regulating the reading and viewing habits of consenting adults. . . .

In *Stanley* we pointed out that "[t]here appears to be little empirical basis for" the assertion that "exposure to obscene materials may lead to deviant sexual behavior or crimes of sexual violence." In any event, we added that "if the State is only concerned about printed or filmed materials inducing antisocial conduct, we believe that in the context of private consumption of ideas and information we should adhere to the view that '[a]mong free men, the deterrents ordinarily to be applied to prevent crime are education and punishment for violations of the law. . . .'"

Moreover, in *Stanley* we rejected as "wholly inconsistent with the philosophy of the First Amendment," the notion that there is a legitimate state concern in the "control [of] the moral content of a person's thoughts," and we held that a State "cannot constitutionally premise legislation on the desirability of controlling a person's private thoughts." That is not to say, of course, that a State must remain utterly indifferent to—and take no action bearing on—the morality of the community. The traditional description of state police power does embrace the regulation of morals as well as the health, safety, and general welfare of the citizenry. . . . But the State's interest in regulating morality by suppressing obscenity, while often asserted, remains essentially unfocused and ill defined. And, since the attempt to curtail unprotected speech necessarily spills over into the area of protected speech, the effort to serve this speculative interest through the suppression of obscene material must tread heavily on rights protected by the First Amendment. . . .

In short, while I cannot say that the interests of the State— apart from the question of juveniles and unconsenting adults— are trivial or nonexistent, I am compelled to conclude that these interests cannot justify the substantial damage to constitutional rights and to this Nation's judicial machinery that inevitably results from state efforts to bar the distribution even of unprotected material to consenting adults. I would hold, therefore, that at least in the absence of distribution to juveniles or obtrusive exposure to unconsenting adults, the First and Fourteenth Amendments prohibit the State and Federal Governments from attempting wholly to suppress sexually oriented materials on the basis of their allegedly "obscene" contents. Nothing in this approach precludes those governments from taking action to serve what may be strong and legitimate interests through regulation of the manner of distribution of sexually oriented material.

Justice DOUGLAS dissenting.

I am sure I would find offensive most of the books and movies charged with being obscene. But in a life that has not been short, I have yet to be trapped into seeing or reading something that would offend me. I never read or see the materials coming to the Court under charges of "obscenity," because I have thought the First Amendment made it unconstitutional for me to act as a censor. I see ads in bookstores and neon lights over theaters that resemble bait for those who seek vicarious exhilaration. As a parent or a priest or as a teacher I would have no compunction in edging my children or wards away from the books and movies that did no more than excite man's base instincts. But I never supposed that government was permitted to sit in judgment on one's tastes or beliefs—save as they involved action within the reach of the police power of government.

New York v. Ferber
458 U.S. 747, 102 S.Ct. 3348 (1982)

Paul Ferber, the proprietor of a Manhattan adult bookstore, sold to an undercover police officer two films almost exclusively showing young boys masturbating. He was arrested, tried and convicted under New York's law prohibiting anyone from knowingly promoting a sexual performance by a child under the age of sixteen by distributing materials depicting such activities. The New York Court of Appeals, however, overturned the conviction and found the statute overly broad and afoul of the First Amendment. The state, thereupon, appealed to the Supreme Court.

Justice WHITE delivers the opinion of the Court.

At issue in this case is the constitutionality of a New York criminal statute which prohibits persons from knowingly promoting sexual performances by children under the age of 16 by distributing material which depicts such performances. . . .

In *Miller v. California* [1973], a majority of the Court agreed that "a state offense must also be limited to works which, taken as a whole, appeal to the prurient interest in sex, which portray sexual conduct in a patently offensive way, and which, taken as a whole, do not have serious literary, artistic, political, or scientific value." Over the past decade, we have adhered to the guidelines expressed in *Miller*, which subsequently has been followed in the regulatory schemes of most states.

The *Miller* standard, like its predecessors, was an accommodation between the state's interests in protecting the "sensibilities of unwilling recipients" from exposure to pornographic material and the dangers of censorship inherent in unabashedly content-based laws. Like obscenity statutes, laws directed at the dissemination of child pornography run the risk of suppressing protected expression by allowing the hand of the censor to become unduly heavy. For the following reasons, however, we are persuaded that the States are entitled to greater leeway in the regulation of pornographic depictions of children.

First. It is evident beyond the need for elaboration that a state's interest in "safeguarding the physical and psychological well being of a minor" is "compelling.". . .

The legislative judgment, as well as the judgment found in the relevant literature, is that the use of children as subjects of pornographic materials is harmful to the physiological, emotional, and mental health of the child. That judgment, we think, easily passes muster under the First Amendment.

Second. The distribution of photographs and films depicting sexual activity by juveniles is intrinsically related to the sexual abuse of children in at least two ways. First, the materials produced are a permanent record of the children's participation and the harm to the child is exacerbated by their circulation. Second, the distribution network for child pornography must be closed if the production of material which requires the sexual exploitation of children is to be effectively controlled. . . .

Third. The advertising and selling of child pornography provides an economic motive for and is thus an integral part of the production of such materials, an activity illegal throughout the nation. . . . We note that were the statutes outlawing the employment of children in these films and photographs fully effective, and the constitutionality of these laws have not been questioned, the First Amendment implications would be no greater than that presented by laws against distribution: enforceable production laws would leave no child pornography to be marketed.

Fourth. The value of permitting live performances and photographic reproductions of children engaged in lewd sexual conduct is exceedingly modest, if not *de minimis*. We consider it unlikely that visual depictions of children performing sexual acts or lewdly exhibiting their genitals would often constitute an important and necessary part of a literary performance or scientific or educational work. As the trial court in this case observed, if it were necessary for literary or artistic value, a person over the statutory age who perhaps looked younger could be utilized. Simulation outside of the prohibition of the statute could provide another alternative. Nor is there is any question here of censoring a particular literary theme or portrayal of sexual activity. The First Amendment interest is limited to that of rendering the portrayal somewhat more "realistic" by utilizing or photographing children.

Fifth. Recognizing and classifying child pornography as a category of material outside the protection of the First Amendment is not incompatible with our earlier decisions. . . .

[I]t is not rare that a content-based classification of speech has been accepted because it may be appropriately generalized that within the confines of the given classification, the evil to be restricted so overwhelmingly outweighs the expressive interests, if any, at stake, that no process of case-by-case adjudication is required. When a definable class of material, such as that covered by § 263.15, bears so heavily and pervasively on the welfare of children engaged in its production, we think the balance of competing interests is clearly struck and that it is permissible to consider these materials as without the protection of the First Amendment.

There are, of course, limits on the category of child pornography which, like obscenity, is unprotected by the First Amendment. As with all legislation in this sensitive area, the conduct to be prohibited must be adequately defined by the applicable state law, as written or authoritatively construed. Here the nature of the harm to be combatted requires that the state offense be limited to works that *visually* depict sexual conduct by children below a specified age. The category of "sexual conduct" proscribed must also be suitably limited and described.

The test for child pornography is separate from the obscenity standard enunciated in *Miller,* but may be compared to it for purpose of clarity. The *Miller* formulation is adjusted in the following respects: A trier of fact need not find that the material appeals to the prurient interest of the average person; it is not required that sexual conduct portrayed be done so in a patently offensive manner; and the material at issue need not be considered as a whole. We note that the distribution of descriptions of other depictions of sexual conduct, not otherwise obscene, which do not involve live performance or photographic or other visual reproduction of live performances, retain First Amendment protection. . . .

It is therefore clear that there is nothing unconstitutionally "underinclusive" about a statute that singles out this category of material for proscription. It also follows that the State is not barred by the First Amendment from prohibiting the distribution of unprotected materials produced outside the State.

It remains to address the claim that the New York statute is unconstitutionally overbroad because it would forbid the distribution of material with serious literary, scientific or educational value or material which does not threaten the harms sought to be combatted by the State. . . .

The scope of the First Amendment overbreadth doctrine, like most exceptions to established principles, must be carefully tied to the circumstances in which facial invalidation of a statute is truly warranted. Because of the wide-reaching effects of striking a statute down on its face at the request of one whose own conduct may be punished despite the First Amendment, we have recognized that the overbreadth doctrine is "strong medicine" and have employed it with hesitation, and then "only as a last resort." We have, in consequence, insisted that the overbreadth involved be "substantial" before the statute involved will be invalidated on its face. . . .

The requirement of substantial overbreadth is directly derived from the purpose and nature of the doctrine. While a sweeping statute, or one incapable of limitation, has the potential to repeatedly chill the exercise of expressive activity by many individuals, the extent of deterrence of protected speech can be expected to decrease with the declining reach of the regulation. This observation appears equally applicable to the publication of books and films as it is to activities, such as picketing or participation in election campaigns, which have previously been categorized as involving conduct plus speech. . . .

Applying these principles, § 263.15 is not substantially overbroad. We consider this the paradigmatic case of a state statute whose legitimate reach dwarfs its arguably impermissible applications. . . . While the reach of the statute is directed at the hard core of child pornography, the Court of Appeals was understandably concerned that some protected expression, ranging from medical textbooks to pictorials in National Geographic would fall prey to the statute. How often, if ever, it may be necessary to employ children to engage in conduct clearly within the reach of the § 263.15 in order to produce educational, medical or artistic works cannot be known with certainty. Yet we seriously doubt, and it has not been suggested, that these arguably impermissible applications of the statute amount to more than a tiny fraction of the materials within the statute's reach. . . .

As applied to Paul Ferber and to others who distribute similar material, the statute does not violate the First Amendment as applied to the States through the Fourteenth. The decision of the New York Court of Appeals is reversed and the case is remanded to that Court for further proceedings not inconsistent with this opinion.

Justice BLACKMUN concurred.

Justice O'CONNOR concurring.

Although I join the Court's opinion, I write separately to stress that the Court does not hold that New York must except "material with serious literary, scientific or educational value," from its statute. The Court merely holds that, even if the First Amendment shelters such material, New York's current statute is not sufficiently overbroad to support respondent's facial attack. The compelling interests identified in today's opinion, suggest that the Constitution might in fact permit New York to ban knowing distribution of works depicting minors engaged in explicit sexual conduct, regardless of the social value of the depictions.

Justice BRENNAN, with whom Justice MARSHALL joins, concurring.

I agree with much of what is said in the Court's opinion. . . .

But in my view application of § 263.15 or any similar statute to depictions of children that in themselves do have serious literary, artistic, scientific or medical value, would violate the First Amendment. As the Court recognizes, the limited classes of speech, the suppression of which does not raise serious First Amendment concerns, have two attributes. They are of exceedingly "slight social value," and the State has a compelling interest in their regulation. See *Chaplinsky v. New Hampshire* [315 U.S. 568] (1942). The First Amendment value of depictions of children that are in themselves serious contributions to art, literature or science, is, by definition, simply not *"de minimis."* At the same time, the State's interest in suppression of such materials is likely to be far less compelling. For the Court's assumption of harm to the child resulting from the "permanent record" and "circulation" of the child's "participation," lacks much of its force where the depiction is a serious contribution to art or science.

Justice STEVENS concurred in a separate opinion.

City of Renton v. Playtime Theatres, Inc.

475 U.S. 41, 106 S.Ct. 925 (1986)

This case involves a city's zoning regulations, which restricted the location of adult movie houses. The facts in this case are stated at the outset of Justice Rehnquist's opinion for the Court.

Justice REHNQUIST delivers the opinion of the Court.

This case involves a constitutional challenge to a zoning ordinance, enacted by appellant, the city of Renton, Washington, that prohibits adult motion picture theaters from locating within 1,000 feet of any residential zone, single- or multiple-family dwelling, church, park, or school. Appellees, Playtime Theatres, Inc., and Sea-First Properties, Inc., filed an action in the United States District Court for the Western District of Washington seeking a declaratory judgment that the Renton ordinance violated the First and Fourteenth Amendments and a permanent injunction against its enforcement. The District Court ruled in favor of Renton and denied the permanent injunction, but the Court of Appeals for the Ninth Circuit reversed and remanded for reconsideration. We . . . now reverse the judgment of the Ninth Circuit. . . .

In our view, the resolution of this case is largely dictated by our decision in *Young v. American Mini Theatres, Inc,* [327 U.S. 50] (1976). There, although five Members of the Court did not agree on a single rationale for the decision, we held that the city of Detroit's zoning ordinance, which prohibited locating an adult theater within 1,000 feet of any two other "regulated uses" or within 500 feet of any residential zone, did not violate the First and Fourteenth Amendments. The Renton ordinance, like the one in *American Mini Theatres,* does not ban adult theaters altogether, but merely provides that such theaters may not be located within 1,000 feet of any residential zone, single- or multiple-family dwelling, church, park, or school. The ordinance is therefore properly analyzed as a form of time, place, and manner regulation. . . .

At first glance, the Renton ordinance, like the ordinance in *American Mini Theatres,* does not appear to fit neatly into either the "content-based" or the "content-neutral" category. To be sure, the ordinance treats theaters that specialize in adult films differently from other kinds of theaters. Nevertheless, as the District Court concluded, the Renton ordinance is aimed not at the *content* of the films shown at "adult motion picture theatres," but rather at the *secondary effects* of such theaters on the surrounding community. . . .

The District Court's finding as to "predominate" intent, left undisturbed by the Court of Appeals, is more than adequate to establish that the city's pursuit of its zoning interests here was unrelated to the suppression of free expression. The ordinance by its terms is designed to prevent crime, protect the city's retail trade, maintain property values, and generally "protec[t] and preserv[e] the quality of [the city's] neighborhoods, commercial districts, and the quality of urban life," not to suppress the expression of unpopular views. . . .

The appropriate inquiry in this case, then, is whether the Renton ordinance is designed to serve a substantial governmental interest and allows for reasonable alternative avenues of communication. It is clear that the ordinance meets such a standard. As a majority of this Court recognized in *American Mini Theatres,* a city's "interest in attempting to preserve the quality of urban life is one that must be accorded high respect.". . .

We hold that Renton was entitled to rely on the experiences of Seattle and other cities, and in particular on the "detailed findings" summarized in the Washington Supreme Court's *Northend Cinema* opinion, in enacting its adult theater zoning ordinance. The First Amendment does not require a city, before enacting such an ordinance, to conduct new studies or produce evidence independent of that already generated by other cities, so long as whatever evidence the city relies upon is reasonably believed to be relevant to the problem that the city addresses. That was the case here. Nor is our holding affected by the fact that Seattle ultimately chose a different method of adult theater zoning than that chosen by Renton, since Seattle's choice of a different remedy to combat the secondary effects of adult theaters does not call into question either Seattle's identification of those secondary effects or the relevance of Seattle's experience to Renton.

We also find no constitutional defect in the method chosen by Renton to further its substantial interests. Cities may regulate adult theaters by dispersing them, as in Detroit, or by effectively concentrating them, as in Renton.

Justice BLACKMUN concurred.

Justice BRENNAN, with whom Justice MARSHALL joins, dissenting.

The Court asserts that the ordinance is "aimed not at the *content* of the films shown at 'adult motion picture theatres,' but rather at the *secondary effects* of such theatres on the surrounding community" (emphasis in original), and thus is simply a time, place, and manner regulation. This analysis is misguided. . . .

The fact that adult movie theaters may cause harmful "secondary" land use effects may arguably give Renton a compelling reason to regulate such establishments; it does not mean, however, that such regulations are content-neutral. Because the ordinance imposes special restrictions on certain kinds of speech on the basis of *content,* I cannot simply accept, as the Court does, Renton's claim that the ordinance was not designed to suppress the content of adult movies. . . .

The ordinance discriminates on its face against certain forms of speech based on content. Movie theaters specializing in "adult motion pictures" may not be located within 1,000 feet of any residential zone, single- or multiple-family dwelling, church, park, or school. Other motion picture theaters, and other forms of "adult entertainment," such as bars, massage parlors, and adult bookstores, are not subject to the same restrictions. This selective treatment strongly suggests that Renton was interested not in controlling the "secondary effects" associated with adult businesses, but in discriminating against adult theaters based on the content of the films they exhibit. . . .

In this case, the city has not justified treating adult movie theaters differently from other adult entertainment businesses. The ordinance's underinclusiveness is cogent evidence that it was aimed at the *content* of the films shown in adult movie theaters. . . .

The Court holds that Renton was entitled to rely on the experiences of cities like Detroit and Seattle, which had enacted special zoning regulations for adult entertainment businesses after studying the adverse effects caused by such establishments. However, even assuming that Renton was concerned with the same problems as Seattle and Detroit, it never actually reviewed any of the studies conducted by those cities. Renton had no basis for determining if any of the "findings" made by these cities were relevant to *Renton's* problems or needs. Moreover, since Renton ultimately adopted zoning regulations different from either Detroit or Seattle, these "studies" provide no basis for assessing the effectiveness of the particular restrictions adopted under the ordinance. Renton cannot merely rely on the general experiences of Seattle or Detroit, for it must "justify its ordinance in the context of *Renton's* problems—not Seattle's or Detroit's problems.". . .

In sum, the circumstances here strongly suggest that the ordinance was designed to suppress expression, even that constitutionally protected, and thus was not to be analyzed as a content-neutral time, place, and manner restriction. The Court allows

Renton to conceal its illicit motives, however, by reliance on the fact that other communities adopted similar restrictions. The Court's approach largely immunizes such measures from judicial scrutiny, since a municipality can readily find other municipal ordinances to rely upon, thus always retrospectively justifying special zoning regulations for adult theaters. Rather than speculate about Renton's motives for adopting such measures, our cases require that the ordinance, like any other contentbased restriction on speech, is constitutional "only if the [city] can show that [it] is a precisely drawn means of serving a compelling [governmental] interest." Only this strict approach can insure that cities will not use their zoning powers as a pretext for suppressing constitutionally protected expression.

Applying this standard to the facts of this case, the ordinance is patently unconstitutional. Renton has not shown that locating adult movie theaters in proximity to its churches, schools, parks, and residences will necessarily result in undesirable "secondary effects," or that these problems could not be effectively addressed by less intrusive restrictions.

(2) Fighting Words and Offensive Speech

Although fighting words is a category of unprotected First Amendment speech, the Court so narrowly applies the category as to virtually eliminate it. Fighting words, observed Stanford Law School professor John Ely, are "no longer to be understood as a euphemism for either controversial or dirty talk but requires instead an unambiguous invitation to a brawl."[1] Even an invitation to a brawl no longer appears excluded from First Amendment protection. The Court, for example, reversed the conviction of a black man who while being arrested rather unambiguously invited a fight by calling a white police officer a son of a bitch and threatened to kill him.[2] *Lewis v. New Orleans*, 415 U.S. 130 (1974), struck down an ordinance prohibiting the cursing of policemen, and in *City of Houston, Texas v. Hill*, 107 S.Ct. 2502 (1987), invalidated a law that made it unlawful to interfer with police officer while performing his duties.

Offensive speech may convey a political statement and hence be entitled to protection. In *Watts v. United States*, 395 U.S. 705 (1969), for instance, the Court overturned the conviction of an individual who, at a protest rally against the Vietnam War, shouted, "If they ever make me carry a rifle, the first man I want to get is LBJ [President Lyndon Johnson]." The justices agreed (six to three) that the federal statute criminalizing threats against the life of the president must be strictly construed and the statement here was an expression of political views, rather an actual threat. The Rehnquist Court, however, was more sharply split in *Rankin v. McPherson* (1987) (see page 422), holding that an employee could not be fired for remarking during a private conversation, after hearing of the 1981 assassination attempt on President Reagan, "If they go for him again, I hope they get him." Dissenting Justice Scalia, joined by Chief Justice Rehnquist and Justices O'Connor and White, contended that such speech conveys no "public concerns" entitled to First Amendment protection.

The landmark ruling in *Cohen v. California* (1969) (see page 428) held that four-letter words, however offensive, are not per se excluded from First Amendment protection. Over the objections of three dissenters, Justice Harlan rejected arguments that privacy interests justified the conviction, under California's penal code punishing disturbances of the peace and offensive conduct, of an individual who wore a jacket embazoned with the words *Fuck the Draft* in the corridor of a Los Angeles County courthouse. Notice that Harlan weighs the competing claims of privacy and free speech not on the basis of the content of the speech (whether some individuals regard certain speech as obscene or offensive), but in terms of the manner of the intrusion and the context in which individuals claim that they have reasonable expectations of privacy against being made a "captive audience" for offensive speech.

When weighing free speech claims against interests in privacy and safeguards against offensive intrusions, the Court considers the context and relative intrusiveness of different modes of communication. Justice Brandeis in *Packer Corporation v. Utah*, 285 U.S. 105 (1932), suggested this approach when upholding a statute forbidding all advertising of cigarettes on billboards and streetcar signs, but permitting such ads in newspapers, magazines, and storefront windows:

> Billboards, street car signs, and placards and such are in a class by themselves. . . . [They] are constantly before the eyes of observers on the streets and in street cars to be seen without the exercise of choice or violation on their part. Other forms of advertising are ordinarily seen as a matter of choice on the part of the observer. The young people as well as the adults have the message of the billboard thrust upon them by all the arts and devices that skill can produce. In the case of newspapers and magazines, there must be some seeking by the one who is to see and read the advertisement. The radio can be turned off, but not so the billboard or street car placard.

In the *Handbills Cases* of 1939, however, the Court ruled that Jehovah's Witnesses and others seeking to engage in religious or political canvassing could not be barred from ringing doorbells and knocking on the doors of private residencies.[3] As the Court, in *Martin v. City of Struthers*, 319 U.S. 141 (1943), observed, "[T]he ordinance was designed to protect a legitimate interest, that of privacy in the home, but in balancing the interests, the considerations of free speech and the free exercise of religion out-weighed this interest." Subsequently, the owners of a company town were forbidden from prohibiting the door-to-door circulation of religious and political literature.[4]

By contrast, *Kovacs v. Cooper*, 336 U.S. 77 (1949), upheld an ordinance outlawing sound trucks emitting "loud and raucous noises" because their intrusiveness was such that an individual "is practically helpless to escape this interference with his privacy by loudspeakers." Two years later, *Breard v. Alexandria*, 341 U.S. 622 (1951), sustained a prohibition on solicitors, peddlers, and transient vendors of merchandise from going onto private property without the owner's permission. There the Court distinguished the solicitations for religious purposes from that of the door-to-door salesmen in finding that the latter did not outweigh the intrusion on individuals' privacy in their homes.

As in *Cohen*, the Court in *Public Utilities Commission v. Pollak*, 343 U.S. 451 (1952), ruled that individuals have greater privacy interests against offensive intrusions in their homes than in public places. There the Court sustained a privately owned transit company's use of radio loudspeakers in its streetcars and buses for the purpose of providing "music as you ride." In rejecting the arguments of patrons who found the music offensive and intrusive on their privacy, Justice Burton observed,

The Court below has emphasized the claim that the radio programs are an invasion of the constitutional rights of privacy of the passengers. . . . This position wrongly assumes that . . . each passenger on a public vehicle regulated by the Federal Government [has] a right of privacy substantially equal to the privacy to which he is entitled in his own home. However complete his right of privacy may be at home, it is substantially limited by the rights of others when its possessor travels on a public thoroughfare or rides in a public conveyance.

Still, balancing free speech claims against interests in privacy and freedom from offensive speech is often difficult for the Court. Over the dissent of Chief Justice Burger and Justices White and Rehnquist, *Erzoznik v. City of Jacksonville*, 422 U.S. 205 (1975), struck down an ordinance making it a public nuisance to show any motion picture containing nudity in a drive-in theater where the screen was visible from a public street. In rejecting the privacy claims of homeowners who could see the movie screen from their backyards and of drivers of cars passing by on a highway, Justice Powell reasoned that

[t]his discrimination cannot be justified as a means of preventing significant intrusions on privacy. The ordinance seeks to keep these films from being seen from public streets and places where the offended viewer can avert his eyes. In short, the screen of a drive-in theater is not "so unobtrusive as to make it impossible for an unwilling individual to avoid exposure to it." . . . Thus, we conclude that the limited privacy interest of persons on the public streets cannot justify this censorship of otherwise protected speech on the basis of its content.

Compare the reasoning in cases such as *Cohen* and *Erzoznik* with that in Justice Stevens's plurality opinion and the dissenters' opinions in *Federal Communications Commission v. Pacifica Foundation* (1976) (see page 433). There a bare majority upheld the Federal Communication Commission's regulations banning indecent, but not obscene, speech on the radio, in a case arising from a twelve-minute monologue by satiric humorist George Carlin on seven dirty words that cannot be said on the radio or television. However, in *Sable Communications v. Federal Communications Commission,* 109 S.Ct. 2829 (1989), the Rehnquist Court unanimously struck down a 1988 congressional statute banning indecent telephone "dial-a-porn" services when holding that only hard-core obscene messages may be outlawed.

Controversy over indecent and offensive speech has also led to some important rulings on the rights of students in primary and secondary schools.[5] In *Board of Education, Island Trees Union Free School District v. Pico,* 457 U.S. 853 (1985), the Court ruled that local school boards could not *remove* books from school libraries because they were deemed offensive. Although not addressing the power of school boards to select books for its libraries, Justice Brennan emphasized that "[o]ur Constitution does not permit the official suppression of *ideas.* . . . [L]ocal school boards may not remove books from school library shelves simply because they dislike the ideas contained in those books and seek by their removal to "prescribe what shall be orthodox in politics, nationalism, religion, or other matters of opinion.'" In dissent, Chief Justice Burger, along with Justices O'Connor, Powell, and Rehnquist, rebutted the implication that students have a "right to receive information." As he explained, "I agree with the fundamental proposition that 'students do not "shed their rights to freedom of speech or expression at the schoolhouse gate.'. . . Here, however, no restraints of any kind are placed on the students. They are free to read the books in question, which are available at public libraries and bookstores; they are free to discuss them in the classroom or elsewhere."

In *Bethel School District No. 403 v. Fraser* (1986) (see page 441), however, the Court (voting seven to two) upheld the authority of a principal to discipline a student for using suggestive (possibly indecent, but not obscene) language in a speech at a student rally. Consider the opinions in this case with those in *Tinker v. Des Moines Independent Community School District*, 393 U.S. 503 (1969) (see section H, in this chapter). Following *Bethel*, the Rehnquist Court upheld over First Amendment objections a high-school principal's censorship of articles on teenage pregnancy scheduled to appear in a student newspaper.[6]

NOTES

1. John Ely, "Flag Desecration," 88 *Harvard Law Review* 1482, 1493 (1975).
2. *Gooding v. Wilson*, 405 U.S. 518 (1972).
3. *Schneider v. New Jersey*, 308 U.S. 147 (1939).
4. *Marsh v. Alabama*, 326 U.S. 501 (1946).
5. In *Papish v. Board of Curators*, 410 U.S. 15 (1973), the Court held that a graduate student could not be expelled from a university for distributing a publication that included a cartoon of the Statue of Liberty with the word *motherfucker*.
6. *Hazelwood School District v. Kuhlmeier*, 482 U.S. 260 (1988).

Rankin v. McPherson
483 U.S. 378, 107 S.Ct. 2891 (1987)

This case involves the First Amendment claim of a public employee who was fired for remarking, after hearing of an assassination attempt on President Reagan, that next time she hoped that they would get him. The facts in this case are set out in Justice Marshall's opinion for the Court.

Justice MARSHALL delivers the opinion of the Court.

The issue in this case is whether a clerical employee in a county constable's office was properly discharged for remarking, after hearing of an attempt on the life of the President, "If they go for him again, I hope they get him."

On January 12, 1981, respondent Ardith McPherson was appointed a deputy in the office of the constable of Harris County, Texas. The constable is an elected official who functions as a law enforcement officer. At the time of her appointment, McPherson, a black woman, was 19 years old and had attended college for a year, studying secretarial science. Her appointment was conditional for a 90-day probationary period.

Although McPherson's title was "deputy constable," this was the case only because all employees of the constable's office, regardless of job function, were deputy constables. She was not a commissioned peace officer, did not wear a uniform, and was not authorized to make arrests or permitted to carry a gun. McPherson's duties were purely clerical. . . .

On March 30, 1981, McPherson and some fellow employees heard on an office radio that there had been an attempt to assassinate the President of the United States. Upon hearing that report, McPherson engaged a co-worker, Lawrence Jackson, who was apparently her boyfriend, in a brief conversation, which according to McPherson's uncontroverted testimony went as follows:

> "Q: What did you say?
> "A: I said I felt that that would happen sooner or later.
> "Q: Okay. And what did Lawrence say?
> "A: Lawrence said, yeah, agreeing with me.
> "Q: Okay. Now, when you—after Lawrence spoke, then what was your next comment?
> "A: Well, we were talking—it's a wonder why they did that. I felt like it would be a black person that did that, because I feel like most of my kind is on welfare and CETA, and they use medicaid, and at the time, I was thinking that's what it was.
> ". . . But then after I said that, and then Lawrence said, yeah, he's cutting back medicaid and food stamps. And I said, yeah, welfare and CETA. I said, shoot, if they go for him again, I hope they get him."

McPherson's last remark was overheard by another deputy constable, who, unbeknownst to McPherson, was in the room at the time. The remark was reported to Constable Rankin, who summoned McPherson. McPherson readily admitted that she had made the statement, but testified that she told Rankin, upon being asked if she made the statement, "Yes, but I didn't mean anything by it." After their discussion, Rankin fired McPherson.

McPherson brought suit in the United States District Court for the Southern District of Texas under 42 U.S.C. § 1983, alleging that petitioner Rankin, in discharging her, had violated her constitutional rights under color of state law. She sought reinstatement, back pay, costs and fees, and other equitable relief. . . .

[T]he District Court held . . . that the statements were not protected speech. . . . [T]he Court of Appeals concluded that the Government's interest did not outweigh the First Amendment interest in protecting McPherson's speech. Given the nature of McPherson's job and the fact that she was not a law enforcement officer, was not brought by virtue of her job into contact with the public, and did not have access to sensitive information, the Court of Appeals deemed her "duties . . . so utterly ministerial and her potential for undermining the office's mission so trivial" as to forbid her dismissal for expression of her political opinions. "However ill-considered Ardith McPherson's opinion was," the Court of Appeals concluded, "it did not make her unfit" for the job she held in Constable Rankin's office. . . .

We . . . now affirm. . . .

The determination whether a public employer has properly discharged an employee for engaging in speech requires "a balance between the interests of the [employee], as a citizen, in commenting upon matters of public concern and the interest of the State, as an employer, in promoting the efficiency of the public services it performs through its employees." This balancing is necessary in order to accommodate the dual role of the public employer as a provider of public services and as a government entity operating under the constraints of the First Amendment. On one hand, public employers are *employers,* concerned with the efficient function of their operations; review of every personnel decision made by a public employer could, in the long run, hamper the performance of public functions. On the other hand, "the threat of dismissal from public employment is . . . a potent means of inhibiting speech." Vigilance is necessary to ensure that public employers do not use authority over employees to silence discourse, not because it hampers public functions but simply because superiors disagree with the content of employees' speech.

The threshold question in applying this balancing test is whether McPherson's speech may be "fairly characterized as constituting speech on a matter of public concern." "Whether an employee's speech addresses a matter of public concern must be determined by the content, form, and context of a given statement, as revealed by the whole record." The District Court apparently found that McPherson's speech did not address a matter of public concern. The Court of Appeals rejected this conclusion, finding that "the life and death of the President are obviously matters of public concern.". . .

Considering the statement in context discloses that it plainly dealt with a matter of public concern. The statement was made in the course of a conversation addressing the policies of the President's administration. . . . While a statement that amounted to a threat to kill the President would not be protected by the First Amendment, the District Court concluded, and we agree, that McPherson's statement did not amount to a threat punishable under 18 U.S.C. § 871(a) or 18 U.S.C. § 2385, or, indeed, that could properly be criminalized at all. The inappropriate or controversial character of a statement is irrelevant to the question whether it deals with a matter of public concern. . . .

Because McPherson's statement addressed a matter of public

concern . . . we [must] balance McPherson's interest in making her statement against "the interest of the State, as an employer, in promoting the efficiency of the public services it performs through its employees." The State bears a burden of justifying the discharge on legitimate grounds. . . .

[T]he very nature of the balancing test make[s] apparent that the state interest element of the test focuses on the effective functioning of the public employer's enterprise. Interference with work, personnel relationships, or the speaker's job performance can detract from the public employer's function; avoiding such interference can be a strong state interest. From this perspective, however, petitioner fails to demonstrate a state interest that outweighs McPherson's First Amendment rights. While McPherson's statement was made at the workplace, there is no evidence that it interfered with the efficient functioning of the office. . . .

While the facts underlying Rankin's discharge of McPherson are, despite extensive proceedings in the District Court, still somewhat unclear, it is undisputed that he fired McPherson based on the *content* of her speech. Evidently because McPherson had made the statement, and because the constable believed that she "meant it," he decided that she was not a suitable employee to have in a law enforcement agency. But in weighing the State's interest in discharging an employee based on any claim that the content of a statement made by the employee somehow undermines the mission of the public employer, some attention must be paid to the responsibilities of the employee within the agency. The burden of caution employees bear with respect to the words they speak will vary with the extent of authority and public accountability the employee's role entails. Where, as here, an employee serves no confidential, policymaking, or public contact role, the danger to the agency's successful function from that employee's private speech is minimal. We cannot believe that every employee in Constable Rankin's office, whether computer operator, electrician, or file clerk, is equally required, on pain of discharge, to avoid any statement susceptible of being interpreted by the Constable as an indication that the employee may be unworthy of employment in his law enforcement agency. At some point, such concerns are so removed from the effective function of the public employer that they cannot prevail over the free speech rights of the public employee.

This is such a case. McPherson's employment-related interaction with the Constable was apparently negligible. Her duties were purely clerical and were limited solely to the civil process function of the constable's office. There is no indication that she would ever be in a position to further—or indeed to have any involvement with—the minimal law enforcement activity engaged in by the constable's office. Given the function of the agency, McPherson's position in the office, and the nature of her statement, we are not persuaded that Rankin's interest in discharging her outweighed her rights under the First Amendment.

Justice POWELL concurring.

It is not easy to understand how this case has assumed constitutional dimensions and reached the Supreme Court of the United States. The fact that the case is here, however, illustrates the uniqueness of our Constitution and our system of judicial review: courts at all levels are available and receptive to claims of injustice, large and small, by any and every citizen of this country. . . .

In my view, however, the case is hardly as complex as might be expected in a dispute that now has been considered five separate times by three different federal courts. The undisputed evidence shows that McPherson made an ill-considered—but protected—comment during a private conversation, and the Constable made an instinctive, but intemperate, employment decision on the basis of this speech. I agree that on these facts, McPherson's private speech is protected by the First Amendment.

I join the opinion of the Court.

Justice SCALIA, with whom the CHIEF JUSTICE, Justice WHITE, and Justice O'CONNOR join, dissenting.

I agree with the proposition, felicitously put by Constable Rankin's counsel, that no law enforcement agency is required by the First Amendment to permit one of its employees to "ride with the cops and cheer for the robbers." The issue in this case is whether Constable Rankin, a law enforcement official, is prohibited by the First Amendment from preventing his employees from saying of the attempted assassination of President Reagan—on the job and within hearing of other employees—"If they go for him again, I hope they get him." The Court holds that McPherson's statement was protected by the First Amendment because (1) it "addressed a matter of public concern," and (2) McPherson's interest in making the statement outweighs Rankin's interest in suppressing it. In so doing, the Court significantly and irrationally expands the definition of "public concern"; it also carves out a new and very large class of employees—*i.e.,* those in "nonpolicymaking" positions—who, if today's decision is to be believed, can never be disciplined for statements that fall within the Court's expanded definition. Because I believe the Court's conclusions rest upon a distortion of both the record and the Court's prior decisions, I dissent. . . .

[S]peech on matters of public concern is that speech which lies "at the heart of the First Amendment's protection." If, but only if, an employee's speech falls within this category, a public employer seeking to abridge or punish it must show that the employee's interest is outweighed by the government's interest, "as an employer, in promoting the efficiency of the public services it performs through its employees."

McPherson fails this threshold requirement. The statement for which she was fired—and the only statement the Constable heard—was, "If they go for him again, I hope they get him.". . .

The District Judge rejected McPherson's argument that her statement was "mere political hyperbole," finding, to the contrary, that it was, "in context," "violent words." "This is not," he said, "the situation where one makes an idle threat to kill someone for not picking them [*sic*] up on time, or not picking up their [*sic*] clothes. It was more than that." He ruled against McPherson at the conclusion of the second hearing because "I don't think it is a matter of public concern to approve even more to [*sic*] the second attempt at assassination.". . .

McPherson's statement . . . is only one step removed from statements that we have previously held entitled to no First Amendment protection even in the nonemployment context—including assassination threats against the President (which are illegal under 18 U.S.C. § 871) " 'fighting' words," epithets or personal abuse, and advocacy of force or violence. A statement lying so near the category of completely unprotected speech cannot fairly be viewed as lying within the "heart" of the First Amendment's protection; it lies within that category of speech that can neither be characterized as speech on matters of public concern nor properly subject to criminal penalties. Once McPherson stopped explicitly criticizing the President's policies and expressed a desire that he be assassinated, she crossed the line.

The Court reaches the opposite conclusion only by distorting the concept of "public concern." It does not *explain* how a statement expressing approval of a serious and violent crime—assassination of the President—can possibly fall within that category. It simply rehearses the "context" of McPherson's statement, and then concludes that because of that context, and because the statement "came on the heels of a news bulletin regarding what is certainly a matter of heightened public attention: an attempt on the life of the President," the statement "plainly dealt with a matter of public concern." I cannot respond to this progression of reasoning except to say I do not understand it. . . .

Even if I agreed that McPherson's statement was speech on a matter of "public concern," I would still find it unprotected. It is important to be clear on what the issue is in this part of the case. . . . We are asked to determine whether, given the interests of this law enforcement office, McPherson had a *right* to say what she did—so that she could not only not be fired for it, but could

not be formally reprimanded for it, or even prevented from repeating it endlessly into the future. It boggles the mind to think
that she has such a right.

Cohen v. California
403 U.S. 15, 91 S.Ct. 1780 (1971)

Justice Harlan's opinion for the Court recounts the facts that
led to this important ruling announcing the First Amendment
principle that four-letter words are not obscene per se and may
express political ideas as well. His position was controversial
within the Court, however. In a circulated but unpublished dissenting opinion, Chief Justice Burger protested, "that this Court's
limited resources of time should be devoted to such a case as
this. It is a measure of a lack of a sense of priorities. . . . It is
nothing short of absurd nonsense that juvenile delinquents and
their emotionally unstable outbursts should command the attention of this Court. The appeal should be dismissed for failure
to present a substantial federal question." By the time the decision
came down, Burger decided to withhold his draft and to join
with Justice Black in a dissenting opinion filed by Justice Blackmun.

Justice HARLAN delivers the opinion of the Court.

This case may seem at first blush too inconsequential to find
its way into our books, but the issue it presents is of no small
constitutional significance.

Appellant Paul Robert Cohen was convicted in the Los Angeles
Municipal Court of violating that part of California Penal Code
§ 415 which prohibits "maliciously and willfully disturb[ing] the
peace or quiet of any neighborhood or person . . . by . . . offensive conduct. . . ." He was given 30 days' imprisonment. The
facts upon which his conviction rests are detailed in the opinion
of the Court of Appeal of California, Second Appellate District,
as follows:

> "On April 26, 1968, the defendant was observed in the
> Los Angeles County Courthouse in the corridor outside of
> division 20 of the municipal court wearing a jacket bearing
> the words 'Fuck the Draft' which were plainly visible. There
> were women and children present in the corridor. The defen-
> dant was arrested. The defendant testified that he wore the

jacket knowing that the words were on the jacket as a means of informing the public of the depth of his feelings against the Vietnam War and the draft.

"The defendant did not engage in, nor threaten to engage in, nor did anyone as the result of his conduct in fact commit or threaten to commit any act of violence. The defendant did not make any loud or unusual noise, nor was there any evidence that he uttered any sound prior to his arrest.". . .

In order to lay hands on the precise issue which this case involves, it is useful first to canvass various matters which this record does *not* present.

The conviction quite clearly rests upon the asserted offensiveness of the *words* Cohen used to convey his message to the public. The only "conduct" which the State sought to punish is the fact of communication. Thus, we deal here with a conviction resting solely upon "speech.". . .

[T]he state certainly lacks power to punish Cohen for the underlying content of the message the inscription conveyed. At least so long as there is no showing of an intent to incite disobedience to or disruption of the draft, Cohen could not, consistently with the First and Fourteenth Amendments, be punished for asserting the evident position on the inutility or immorality of the draft his jacket reflected. . . .

In the second place, as it comes to us, this case cannot be said to fall within those relatively few categories of instances where prior decisions have established the power of government to deal more comprehensively with certain forms of individual expression simply upon a showing that such a form was employed. This is not, for example, an obscenity case. Whatever else may be necessary to give rise to the States' broader power to prohibit obscene expression, such expression must be, in some significant way, erotic. *Roth v. United States,* 354 U.S. 476 (1957). It cannot plausibly be maintained that this vulgar allusion to the Selective Service System would conjure up such psychic stimulation in anyone likely to be confronted with Cohen's crudely defaced jacket.

This Court has also held that the States are free to ban the simple use, without a demonstration of additional justifying circumstances, of so-called "fighting words," those personally abusive epithets which, when addressed to the ordinary citizen, are, as a matter of common knowledge, inherently likely to provoke violent reaction. *Chaplinsky v. New Hampshire,* 315 U.S. 568 (1942). While the four-letter word displayed by Cohen in relation to the draft is not uncommonly employed in a personally provocative fashion, in this instance it was clearly not "directed to the person of the hearer." No individual actually or likely to be present could reasonably have regarded the words on appellant's jacket as a direct personal insult. Nor do we have here an instance of the exercise of the State's police power to prevent a speaker from intentionally provoking a given group to hostile reaction.

There is, as noted above, no showing that anyone who saw Cohen was in fact violently aroused or that appellant intended such a result.

Finally, in arguments before this Court much has been made of the claim that Cohen's distasteful mode of expression was thrust upon unwilling or unsuspecting viewers, and that the State might therefore legitimately act as it did in order to protect the sensitive from otherwise unavoidable exposure to appellant's crude form of protest. Of course, the mere presumed presence of unwitting listeners or viewers does not serve automatically to justify curtailing all speech capable of giving offense. While this Court has recognized that government may properly act in many situations to prohibit intrusion into the privacy of the home of unwelcome views and ideas which cannot be totally banned from the public dialogue, e.g., Rowan v. United States Post Office Dept., 397 U.S. 728 (1970), we have at the same time consistently stressed that "we are often 'captives' outside the sanctuary of the home and subject to objectionable speech." The ability of government, consonant with the Constitution, to shut off discourse solely to protect others from hearing it is, in other words, dependent upon a showing that substantial privacy interests are being invaded in an essentially intolerable manner. Any broader view of this authority would effectively empower a majority to silence dissidents simply as a matter of personal predilections.

In this regard, persons confronted with Cohen's jacket were in a quite different posture than, say, those subjected to the raucous emissions of sound trucks blaring outside their residences. Those in the Los Angeles courthouse could effectively avoid further bombardment of their sensibilities simply by averting their eyes. And, while it may be that one has a more substantial claim to a recognizable privacy interest when walking through a courthouse corridor than, for example, strolling through Central Park, surely it is nothing like the interest in being free from unwanted expression in the confines of one's own home. Given the subtlety and complexity of the factors involved, if Cohen's "speech" was otherwise entitled to constitutional protection, we do not think the fact that some unwilling "listeners" in a public building may have been briefly exposed to it can serve to justify this breach of the peace conviction where, as here, there was no evidence that persons powerless to avoid appellant's conduct did in fact object to it, and where that portion of the statute upon which Cohen's conviction rests evinces no concern, either on its face or as construed by the California courts with the special plight of the captive auditor, but, instead, indiscriminately sweeps within its prohibitions all "offensive conduct" that disturbs "any neighborhood or person.". . .

Against this background, the issue flushed by this case stands out in bold relief. It is whether California can excise, as "offensive conduct," one particular scurrilous epithet from the public discourse, either upon the theory of the court below that its use is inherently likely to cause violent reaction or upon a more general assertion that the States, acting as guardians of public morality, may properly remove this offensive word from the public vocabulary.

The rationale of the California Court is plainly untenable. At most it reflects an "undifferentiated fear or apprehension of disturbance [which] is not enough to overcome the right to freedom of expression." *Tinker v. Des Moines Indep. Community School Dist.*, 393 U.S. 503 (1969). We have been shown no evidence that substantial numbers of citizens are standing ready to strike out physically at whoever may assault their sensibilities with execrations like that uttered by Cohen. There may be some persons about with such lawless and violent proclivities, but that is an insufficient base upon which to erect, consistently with constitutional values, a governmental power to force persons who wish to ventilate their dissident views into avoiding particular forms of expression. . . .

Admittedly, it is not so obvious that the First and Fourteenth Amendments must be taken to disable the States from punishing public utterance of this unseemingly expletive in order to maintain what they regard as a suitable level of discourse within the body politic. We think, however, that examination and reflection will reveal the shortcomings of a contrary viewpoint.

At the outset, we cannot overemphasize that, in our judgment, most situations where the State has a justifiable interest in regulating speech will fall within one or more of the various established exceptions, discussed above but not applicable here, to the usual rule that governmental bodies may not prescribe the form or content of individual expression. Equally important to our conclusion is the constitutional backdrop against which our decision must be made. The constitutional right of free expression is powerful medicine in a society as diverse and populous as ours. It is designed and intended to remove governmental restraints from the arena of public discussion, putting the decision as to what views shall be voiced largely into the hands of each of us, in the hope that use of such freedom will ultimately produce a more capable citizenry and more perfect polity and in the belief that no other approach would comport with the premise of individual dignity and choice upon which our political system rests. . . .

To many, the immediate consequence of this freedom may often appear to be only verbal tumult, discord, and even offensive utterance. These are, however, within established limits, in truth necessary side effects of the broader enduring values which the process of open debate permits us to achieve. That the air may at times seem filled with verbal cacophony is, in this sense not a sign of weakness but of strength. . . .

Against this perception of the constitutional policies involved, we discern certain more particularized considerations that peculiarly call for reversal of this conviction. First, the principle contended for by the State seems inherently boundless. How is one to distinguish this from any other offensive word? Surely the State has no right to cleanse public debate to the point where it is grammatically palatable to the most squeamish among us. Yet no readily ascertainable general principle exists for stopping short of that result were we to affirm the judgment below. For, while the particular four-letter word being litigated here is perhaps more distasteful than most others of its genre, it is nevertheless often true that one man's vulgarity is another's lyric. Indeed, we think it is largely because governmental officials cannot make principled distinctions in this area that the Constitution leaves matters of taste and style so largely to the individual.

Additionally, we cannot overlook the fact, because it is well illustrated by the episode involved here, that much linguistic expression serves a dual communicative function: it conveys not only ideas capable of relatively precise, detached explication, but otherwise inexpressible emotions as well. In fact, words are often chosen as much for their emotive as their cognitive force. We cannot sanction the view that the Constitution, while solicitous of the cognitive content of individual speech has little or no regard for that emotive function which practically speaking, may often be the more important element of the overall message sought to be communicated. . . .

Finally, and in the same vein, we cannot indulge the facile assumption that one can forbid particular words without also running a substantial risk of suppressing ideas in the process. Indeed, governments might soon seize upon the censorship of particular words as a convenient guise for banning the expression of unpopular views. We have been able, as noted above, to discern little social benefit that might result from running the risk of opening the door to such grave results.

It is, in sum, our judgment that absent a more particularized and compelling reason for its actions, the State may not, consistently with the First and Fourteenth Amendments, make the simple public display here involved of this single four-letter expletive a criminal offense. Because that is the only arguably sustainable rationale for the conviction here at issue, the judgment below must be reversed.

Reversed.

Justice BLACKMUN, with whom the CHIEF JUSTICE and Justice BLACK join.

I dissent [because] . . . Cohen's absurd and immature antics, in my view, was mainly conduct and little speech. . . . Further, the case appears to me to be well within the sphere of *Chaplinsky v. New Hampshire,* where Justice Murphy, a known champion of First Amendment freedoms, wrote for an unanimous bench. As a consequence, this Court's agonizing over First Amendment values seems misplaced and unnecessary.

Federal Communications Commission v. Pacifica Foundation
438 U.S. 726, 98 S.Ct. 3026 (1978)

Justice Stevens explains the facts in this case, involving satiric humorist George Carlin and the FCC's regulation of indecent language on radio and television, at the outset of his plurality opinion announcing the decision of the Court.

Justice STEVENS delivers the opinion of the Court, with whom the CHIEF JUSTICE and Justice REHNQUIST join.

This case requires that we decide whether the Federal Communications Commission has any power to regulate a radio broadcast that is indecent but not obscene.

A satiric humorist named George Carlin recorded a 12-minute monologue entitled "Filthy Words" before a live audience in a California theater. He began by referring to his thoughts about "the words you couldn't say on the public, ah, airwaves, um, the ones you definitely wouldn't say, ever." He proceeded to list those words and repeat them over and over again in a variety of colloquialisms. The transcript of the recording, which is appended to this opinion, indicates frequent laughter from the audience. [The words that Carlin said could not be said on television or the radio, were "shit, piss, fuck, cunt, cocksucker, motherfucker, and tits."]

At about 2 o'clock in the afternoon on Tuesday, October 30, 1973, a New York radio station, owned by respondent Pacifica Foundation, broadcast the "Filthy Words" monologue. A few weeks later a man, who stated that he had heard the broadcast while driving with his young son, wrote a letter complaining to the Commission. . . .

The complaint was forwarded to the station for comment. In its response, Pacifica explained that the monologue had been played during a program about contemporary society's attitude toward language and that, immediately before its broadcast, listeners had been advised that it included "sensitive language which might be regarded as offensive to some." Pacifica characterized George Carlin as "a significant social satirist" who "like Twain and Sahl before him, examines the language of ordinary people. . . . Carlin is not mouthing obscenities, he is merely using words to satirize as harmless and essentially silly our attitudes towards those words." Pacifica stated that it was not aware of any other complaints about the broadcast.

On February 21, 1975, the Commission issued a declaratory order granting the complaint and holding that Pacifica "could have been the subject of administrative sanctions." 56 F.C.C.2d 94, 99. The Commission did not impose formal sanctions, but it did state that the order would be "associated with the station's license file, and in the event that subsequent complaints are received, the Commission will then decide whether it should utilize any of the available sanctions it has been granted by Congress.". . .

The Commission characterized the language used in the Carlin monologue as "patently offensive," though not necessarily obscene, and expressed the opinion that it should be regulated by principles analogous to those found in the law of nuisance where the "law generally speaks to *channeling* behavior more than actually prohibiting it. . . . [T]he concept of 'indecent' is intimately connected with the exposure of children to language that describes, in terms patently offensive as measured by contemporary community standards for the broadcast medium, sexual or excretory activities and organs at times of the day when there is a reasonable risk that children may be in the audience.". . .

The United States Court of Appeals for the District of Columbia reversed. . . . [We now reverse that ruling and uphold the F.C.C.'s action.]

The question in this case is whether a broadcast of patently offensive words dealing with sex and excretion may be regulated because of its content. Obscene materials have been denied the protection of the First Amendment because their content is so offensive to contemporary moral standards. *Roth v. United States*, 354 U.S. 476 [1957]. But the fact that society may find speech offensive is not a sufficient reason for suppressing it. Indeed, if it is the speaker's opinion that gives offense, that consequence is a reason for according it constitutional protection. For it is a central tenet of the First Amendment that the government must remain neutral in the marketplace of ideas. If there were any reason to believe that the Commission's characterization of the Carlin monologue as offensive could be traced to its political content—or even to the fact that it satirized contemporary attitudes about four-letter words—First Amendment protection might be required. But that is simply not this case. These words offend for the same reasons that obscenity offends. Their place in the hierarchy of First Amendment values was aptly sketched by Justice MURPHY when he said: "Such utterances are no essential part of any exposition of ideas, and are of such slight social value as a step to truth that any benefit that may be derived from them is clearly outweighed by the social interest in order and morality." *Chaplinsky v. New Hampshire* [315 U.S. 568 (1942)]. . . .

Although these words ordinarily lack literary, political, or scientific value, they are not entirely outside the protection of the First Amendment. Some uses of even the most offensive words are unquestionably protected. See, *e.g., Hess v. Indiana,* 414 U.S. 105 [1973]. Indeed, we may assume, *arguendo,* that this monologue would be protected in other contexts. Nonetheless, the constitutional protection accorded to a communication containing such patently offensive sexual and excretory language need not be the same in every context. It is a characteristic of speech such as this that both its capacity to offend and its "social value," to use Justice MURPHY's term, vary with the circumstances. Words that are commonplace in one setting are shocking in another. To paraphrase Justice HARLAN, one occasion's lyric is another's vulgarity. Cf. *Cohen v. California,* [403 U.S. 15 (1971)].

In this case it is undisputed that the content of Pacifica's broadcast was "vulgar," "offensive," and "shocking." Because content of that character is not entitled to absolute constitutional protection under all circumstances, we must consider its context in order to determine whether the Commission's action was constitutionally permissible.

We have long recognized that each medium of expression presents special First Amendment problems. And of all forms of communication, it is broadcasting that has received the most limited First Amendment protection. Thus, although other speakers cannot be licensed except under laws that carefully define and narrow official discretion, a broadcaster may be deprived of his license and his forum if the Commission decides that such an action would serve "the public interest, convenience, and necessity." Similarly, although the First Amendment protects newspaper publishers from being required to print the replies of those whom they criticize, *Miami Herald Publishing Co. v. Tornillo,* 418 U.S. 241 [1974], it affords no such protection to broadcasters; on the contrary, they must give free time to the victims of their criticism. *Red Lion Broadcasting Co. v. FCC,* 395 U.S. 367 [1969].

The reasons for these distinctions are complex, but two have relevance to the present case. First, the broadcast media have established a uniquely pervasive presence in the lives of all Americans. Patently offensive, indecent material presented over the airwaves confronts the citizen, not only in public, but also in the privacy of the home, where the individual's right to be left alone plainly outweighs the First Amendment rights of an intruder. *Rowan v. Post Office Dept.*, 397 U.S. 728. [1970]. Because the broadcast audience is constantly tuning in and out, prior warnings cannot completely protect the listener or viewer from unexpected program content. To say that one may avoid further offense by turning off the radio when he hears indecent language is like saying that the remedy for an assault is to run away after the first blow. One may hang up on an indecent phone call, but that option does not give the caller a constitutional immunity or avoid a harm that has already taken place.

Second, broadcasting is uniquely accessible to children, even those too young to read. Although Cohen's written message might have been incomprehensible to a first grader, Pacifica's broadcast could have enlarged a child's vocabulary in an instant. Other forms of offensive expression may be withheld from the young without restricting the expression at its source. Bookstores and motion picture theaters, for example, may be prohibited from making indecent material available to children. We held in *Ginsberg v. New York*, 390 U.S. 629 [1968], that the government's interest in the "well-being of its youth" and in supporting "parents' claim to authority in their own household" justified the regulation of otherwise protected expression. The ease with which children may obtain access to broadcast material, coupled with the concerns recognized in *Ginsberg*, amply justify special treatment of indecent broadcasting.

It is appropriate, in conclusion, to emphasize the narrowness of our holding. This case does not involve a two-way radio conversation between a cab driver and a dispatcher, or a telecast of an Elizabethan comedy. We have not decided that an occasional expletive in either setting would justify any sanction or, indeed, that this broadcast would justify a criminal prosecution. The Commission's decision rested entirely on a nuisance rationale under which context is all-important. The concept requires consideration of a host of variables. The time of day was emphasized by the Commission. The content of the program in which the language is used will also affect the composition of the audience, and differences between radio, television, and perhaps closed-circuit transmissions, may also be relevant. As Justice SUTHERLAND wrote a "nuisance may be merely a right thing in the wrong place,—like a pig in the parlor instead of the barnyard." *Euclid v. Ambler Realty Co.*, 272 U.S. 365 [1926]. We simply hold that when the Commission finds that a pig has entered the parlor, the exercise of its regulatory power does not depend on proof that the pig is obscene.

The judgment of the Court of Appeals is reversed.

It is so ordered.

Justice POWELL, with whom Justice BLACKMUN joins, concurring in part.

The issue . . . is whether the Commission may impose civil sanctions on a licensee radio station for broadcasting the monologue at two o'clock in the afternoon. The Commission's primary concern was to prevent the broadcast from reaching the ears of unsupervised children who were likely to be in the audience at that hour. In essence, the Commission sought to "channel" the monologue to hours when the fewest unsupervised children would be exposed to it. In my view, this consideration provides strong support for the Commission's holding.

The Court has recognized society's right to "adopt more stringent controls on communicative materials available to youths than on those available to adults." This recognition stems in large part from the fact that "a child . . . is not possessed of that full capacity for individual choice which is the presupposition of First Amendment guarantees." . . . At the same time, such speech may have a deeper and more lasting negative effect on a child than on an adult. . . . The Commission properly held that the speech from which society may attempt to shield its children is not limited to that which appeals to the youthful prurient interest. The language involved in this case is as potentially degrading and harmful to children as representations of many erotic acts.

In most instances, the dissemination of this kind of speech to children may be limited without also limiting willing adults' access to it. Sellers of printed and recorded matter and exhibitors of motion pictures and live performances may be required to shut their doors to children, but such a requirement has no effect on adults' access. The difficulty is that such a physical separation of the audience cannot be accomplished in the broadcast media. . . .

In my view, the Commission was entitled to give substantial weight to this difference in reaching its decision in this case.

A second difference, not without relevance, is that broadcasting—unlike most other forms of communication—comes directly into the home, the one place where people ordinarily have the right not to be assaulted by uninvited and offensive sights and sounds. . . . The Commission also was entitled to give this factor appropriate weight in the circumstances of the instant case. This is not to say, however, that the Commission has an unrestricted license to decide what speech, protected in other media, may be banned from the airwaves in order to protect unwilling adults from momentary exposure to it in their homes. Making the sensitive judgments required in these cases is not easy. But this responsibility has been reposed initially in the Commission, and its judgment is entitled to respect. . . .

In short, I agree that on the facts of this case, the Commission's order did not violate respondent's First Amendment rights. . . .

In my view, the result in this case does not turn on whether Carlin's monologue, viewed as a whole, or the words that constitute it, have more or less "value" than a candidate's campaign speech. This is a judgment for each person to make, not one for the judges to impose upon him.

The result turns instead on the unique characteristics of the broadcast media, combined with society's right to protect its children from speech generally agreed to be inappropriate for their years, and with the interest of unwilling adults in not being assaulted by such offensive speech in their homes. Moreover, I doubt whether today's decision will prevent any adult who wishes to receive Carlin's message in Carlin's own words from doing so, and from making for himself a value judgment as to the merit of the message and words.

Justice BRENNAN, with whom Justice MARSHALL joins, dissenting.

Without question, the privacy interests of an individual in his home are substantial and deserving of significant protection. In finding these interests sufficient to justify the content regulation of protected speech, however, the Court commits two errors. First, it misconceives the nature of the privacy interests involved where an individual voluntarily chooses to admit radio communications into his home. Second, it ignores the constitutionally protected interests of both those who wish to transmit and those who desire to receive broadcasts that many—including the FCC and this Court—might find offensive. . . .

Even if an individual who voluntarily opens his home to radio communications retains privacy interests of sufficient moment to justify a ban on protected speech if those interests are "invaded in an essentially intolerable manner," *Cohen v. California*, [403 U.S. 15 [1971], the very fact that those interests are threatened only by a radio broadcast precludes any intolerable invasion of privacy; for unlike other intrusive modes of communication, such as sound trucks, "[t]he radio can be turned off," *Lehman v. Shaker Heights*, 418 U.S. 298 (1974)—and with a minimum of effort. . . . Whatever the minimal discomfort suffered by a listener who inadvertently tunes into a program he finds offensive during the brief interval before he can simply extend his arm and switch stations or flick the "off" button, it is surely worth the candle to preserve the broadcaster's right to send, and the right of those interested to receive, a message entitled to full First Amendment protection. . . .

The Court's balance, of necessity, fails to accord proper weight to the interests of listeners who wish to hear broadcasts the FCC deems offensive. It permits majoritarian tastes completely to preclude a protected message from entering the homes of a receptive, unoffended minority. No decision of this Court supports such a result. Where the individuals constituting the offended majority may freely choose to reject the material being offered, we have never found their privacy interests of such moment to warrant the suppression of speech on privacy grounds. . . .

Most parents will undoubtedly find understandable as well as commendable the Court's sympathy with the FCC's desire to prevent offensive broadcasts from reaching the ears of unsupervised children. Unfortunately, the facial appeal of this justification for radio censorship masks its constitutional insufficiency. . . .

Because the Carlin monologue is obviously not an erotic appeal to the prurient interests of children, the Court, for the first time, allows the government to prevent minors from gaining access to materials that are not obscene, and are therefore protected, as to them. It thus ignores our recent admonition that "[s]peech that is neither obscene as to youths nor subject to some other legitimate proscription cannot be suppressed solely to protect the young from ideas or images that a legislative body thinks unsuitable for them." The Court's refusal to follow its own pronouncements is especially lamentable since it has the anomalous subsidiary effect, at least in the radio context at issue here, of making completely unavailable to adults material which may not constitutionally be kept even from children. This result violates in spades the principle of *Butler v. Michigan,* [352 U.S. 380 (1957)]. *Butler* involved a challenge to a Michigan statute that forbade the publication, sale, or distribution of printed material "tending to incite minors to violent or depraved or immoral acts, manifestly tending to the corruption of the morals of youth." Although *Roth v. United States* [357 U.S. 476 (1957)], had not yet been decided, it is at least arguable that the material the statute in *Butler* was designed to suppress could have been constitutionally denied to children. Nevertheless, this Court found the statute unconstitutional. Speaking for the Court, Justice FRANK-FURTER reasoned:

> "The incidence of this enactment is to reduce the adult population of Michigan to reading only what is fit for children. It thereby arbitrarily curtails one of those liberties of the individual, now enshrined in the Due Process Clause of the Fourteenth Amendment, that history has attested as the indispensable conditions for the maintenance and progress of a free society.". . .

Where, as here, the government may not prevent the exposure of minors to the suppressed material, the principle of *Butler* applies a *fortiori.* . . .

[N]either of the factors relied on by both the opinion of my Brother POWELL and the opinion of my Brother Stevens—the intrusive nature of radio and the presence of children in the listening audience—can, when taken on its own terms, support the FCC's disapproval of the Carlin monologue. These two asserted justifications are further plagued by a common failing: the lack of principled limits on their use as a basis for FCC censorship. No such limits come readily to mind, and neither of the opinions constituting the Court serve to clarify the extent to which the FCC may assert the privacy and children-in-the-audience rationales as justification for expunging from the airways protected communications the Commission finds offensive. Taken to their logical extreme, these rationales would support the cleansing of public radio of any "four-letter words" whatsoever, regardless of their context. The rationales could justify the banning from radio of a myriad of literary works, novels, poems, and plays by the likes of Shakespeare, Joyce, Hemingway, Ben Jonson, Henry Fielding, Robert Burns, and Chaucer; they could support the suppression of a good deal of political speech, such as the Nixon tapes; and they could even provide the basis for imposing sanctions for the broadcast of certain portions of the Bible. . . .

To insure that the FCC's regulation of protected speech does not exceed these bounds, my Brother POWELL is content to rely upon the judgment of the Commission while my Brother STEVENSs deems it prudent to rely on this Court's ability accurately to assess the worth of various kinds of speech. For my own part, even accepting that this case is limited to its facts, I would place the responsibility and the right to weed worthless and offensive communications from the public airways where it belongs and where, until today, it resided: in a public free to choose those communications worthy of its attention from a marketplace unsullied by the censor's hand. . . .

[T]here runs throughout the opinions of my Brothers POWELL and STEVENS another vein I find equally disturbing: a depressing inability to appreciate that in our land of cultural pluralism, there are many who think, act, and talk differently from the Members of this Court, and who do not share their fragile sensibilities. It is only an acute ethnocentric myopia that enables the Court to approve the censorship of communications solely because of the words they contain. . . .

Today's decision will thus have its greatest impact on broadcasters desiring to reach, and listening audiences composed of, persons who do not share the Court's view as to which words or expressions are acceptable and who, for a variety of reasons, including a conscious desire to flout majoritarian conventions, express themselves using words that may be regarded as offensive by those from different socio-economic backgrounds. In this context, the Court's decision may be seen for what, in the broader perspective, it really is: another of the dominant culture's inevitable efforts to force those groups who do not share its mores to conform to its way of thinking, acting, and speaking.

Justice STEWART, with whom Justice BRENNAN, Justice WHITE, and Justice MARSHALL join, dissenting.

I think that "indecent" should properly be read as meaning no more than "obscene." Since the Carlin monologue concededly was not "obscene," I believe that the Commission lacked statutory authority to ban it. Under this construction of the statute, it is unnecessary to address the difficult and important issue of the Commission's constitutional power to prohibit speech that would be constitutionally protected outside the context of electronic broadcasting.

Bethel School District No. 403 v. Fraser

478 U.S. 675, 106 S.Ct. 3159 (1986)

The facts in this case involving lewd speech at a school assembly are given in Chief Justice Burger's opinion for the Court, Justice Brennan's concurring opinion, and Justice Steven's dissenting opinion. Notice how each emphasizes particular facts and views differently the context and circumstances that gave rise to this case.

Chief Justice BURGER delivers the opinion of the Court.

We granted certiorari to decide whether the First Amendment prevents a school district from disciplining a high school student for giving a lewd speech at a school assembly.

On April 26, 1983, respondent Matthew N. Fraser, a student at Bethel High School in Bethel, Washington, delivered a speech nominating a fellow student for student elective office. Approximately 600 high school students, many of whom were 14-year-olds, attended the assembly. Students were required to attend the assembly or to report to the study hall. The assembly was part of a school-sponsored educational program in self-government. Students who elected not to attend the assembly were required to report to study hall. During the entire speech, Fraser referred to his candidate in terms of an elaborate, graphic, and explicit sexual metaphor.

Two of Fraser's teachers, with whom he discussed the contents of his speech in advance, informed him that the speech was "inappropriate and that he probably should not deliver it," and that his delivery of the speech might have "severe consequences.". . .

A Bethel High School disciplinary rule prohibiting the use of obscene language in the school provides:

> "Conduct which materially and substantially interferes with the educational process is prohibited, including the use of obscene, profane language or gestures."

The morning after the assembly, the Assistant Principal called Fraser into her office and notified him that the school considered his speech to have been a violation of this rule. . . . Fraser served two days of his suspension, and was allowed to return to school on the third day. . . .

This Court acknowledged in *Tinker v. Des Moines Independent Community School Dist.*, [393 U.S. 503 (1969)], that students do not "shed their constitutional rights to freedom of speech or expression at the schoolhouse gate." The Court of Appeals read that case as precluding any discipline of Fraser for indecent speech and lewd conduct in the school assembly. That court appears to have proceeded on the theory that the use of lewd and obscene speech in order to make what the speaker considered to be a point in a nominating speech for a fellow student was essentially the same as the wearing of an armband in *Tinker* as a form of protest or the expression of a political position.

The marked distinction between the political "message" of the armbands in *Tinker* and the sexual content of respondent's speech in this case seems to have been given little weight by the Court of Appeals. In upholding the students' right to engage in a nondisruptive, passive expression of a political viewpoint in *Tinker,* this Court was careful to note that the case did "not concern speech or action that intrudes upon the work of the schools or the rights of other students.". . .

It is against this background that we turn to consider the level of First Amendment protection accorded to Fraser's utterances and actions before an official high school assembly attended by 600 students.

The role and purpose of the American public school system was well described by two historians, saying "public education must prepare pupils for citizenship in the Republic. . . . It must inculcate the habits and manners of civility as values in themselves conducive to happiness and as indispensable to the practice of self-government in the community and the nation.". . .

These fundamental values of "habits and manners of civility" essential to a democratic society must, of course, include tolerance of divergent political and religious views, even when the views expressed may be unpopular. But these "fundamental values" must also take into account consideration of the sensibilities of others, and, in the case of a school, the sensibilities of fellow students. The undoubted freedom to advocate unpopular and controversial views in schools and classrooms must be balanced against the society's countervailing interest in teaching students the boundaries of socially appropriate behaviour. Even the most heated political discourse in a democratic society requires consideration for the personal sensibilities of the other participants and audiences. . . .

Surely it is a highly appropriate function of public school education to prohibit the use of vulgar and offensive terms in public discourse. Indeed, the "fundamental values necessary to the maintenance of a democratic political system" disfavor the use of terms of debate highly offensive or highly threatening to others. Nothing in the Constitution prohibits the states from insisting that certain modes of expression are inappropriate and subject to sanctions. The inculcation of these values is truly the "work of the schools." The determination of what manner of speech in the classroom or in school assembly is inappropriate properly rests with the school board. . . .

This Court's First Amendment jurisprudence has acknowledged limitations on the otherwise absolute interest of the speaker in reaching an unlimited audience where the speech is sexually explicit and the audience may include children. . . .

We hold that petitioner School District acted entirely within its permissible authority in imposing sanctions upon Fraser in response to his offensively lewd and indecent speech. Unlike the sanctions imposed on the students wearing armbands in *Tinker*, the penalties imposed in this case were unrelated to any political viewpoint. The First Amendment does not prevent the school officials from determining that to permit a vulgar and lewd speech such as respondent's would undermine the school's basic educational mission. A high school assembly or classroom is no place for a sexually explicit monologue directed towards an unsuspecting audience of teenage students. Accordingly, it was perfectly appropriate for the school to disassociate itself to make the point to the pupils that vulgar speech and lewd conduct is wholly inconsistent with the "fundamental values" of public school education.

Justice BLACKMUN concurred.

Justice BRENNAN concurring.

Respondent gave the following speech at a high school assembly in support of a candidate for student government office:

> " 'I know a man who is firm—he's firm in his pants, he's firm in his shirt, his character is firm—but most . . . of all, his belief in you, the students of Bethel, is firm.

> " 'Jeff Kuhlman is a man who takes his point and pounds it in. If necessary, he'll take an issue and nail it to the wall.

He doesn't attack things in spurts—he drives hard, pushing and pushing until finally—he succeeds.' "

Jeff is a man who will go to the very end—even the climax, for each and every one of you.

" 'So vote for Jeff for A.S.B. vice-president—he'll never come between you and the best our high school can be.' " App. 47.

The Court, referring to these remarks as "obscene," "vulgar," "lewd," and "offensively lewd," concludes that school officials properly punished respondent for uttering the speech. Having read the full text of respondent's remarks, I find it difficult to believe that it is the same speech the Court describes. To my mind, the most that can be said about respondent's speech—and all that need be said—is that in light of the discretion school officials have to teach high school students how to conduct civil and effective public discourse, and to prevent disruption of school educational activities, it was not unconstitutional for school officials to conclude, under the circumstances of this case, that respondent's remarks exceeded permissible limits. Thus, while I concur in the Court's judgment, I write separately to express my understanding of the breadth of the Court's holding. . . .

In the present case, school officials sought only to ensure that a high school assembly proceed in an orderly manner. There is no suggestion that school officials attempted to regulate respondent's speech because they disagreed with the views he sought to express. Nor does this case involve an attempt by school officials to ban written materials they consider "inappropriate" for high school students, or to limit what students should hear, read, or learn about. Thus, the Court's holding concerns only the authority that school officials have to restrict a high school student's use of disruptive language in a speech given to a high school assembly.

Justice MARSHALL dissenting.

I agree with the principles that Justice BRENNAN sets out in his opinion concurring in the judgment. I dissent from the Court's decision, however, because in my view the school district failed to demonstrate that respondent's remarks were indeed disruptive.

Justice STEVENS dissenting.

"Frankly, my dear, I don't give a damn."

When I was a high school student, the use of those words in a public forum shocked the Nation. Today Clark Gable's four-letter expletive is less offensive than it was then. Nevertheless, I assume that high school administrators may prohibit the use of that word in classroom discussion and even in extracurricular activities that are sponsored by the school and held on school premises. For I believe a school faculty must regulate the content as well as the style of student speech in carrying out its educational mission. It does seem to me, however, that if a student is to be punished for using offensive speech, he is entitled to fair notice of the scope of the prohibition and the consequences of its violation. The interest in free speech protected by the First Amendment and the interest in fair procedure protected by the Due Process Clause of the Fourteenth Amendment combine to require this conclusion.

This respondent was an outstanding young man with a fine academic record. The fact that he was chosen by the student body to speak at the school's commencement exercises demonstrates that he was respected by his peers. This fact is relevant for two reasons. It confirms the conclusion that the discipline imposed on him—a three-day suspension and ineligibility to speak at the school's graduation exercises—was sufficiently serious to justify invocation of the School District's grievance procedures. More importantly, it indicates that he was probably in a better position to determine whether an audience composed of 600 of his contemporaries would be offended by the use of a four-letter word—or a sexual metaphor—than is a group of judges who are at least two generations and 3,000 miles away from the scene of the crime.

The fact that the speech may not have been offensive to his audience—or that he honestly believed that it would be inoffensive—does not mean that he had a constitutional right to deliver it. For the school—not the student—must prescribe the rules of conduct in an educational institution. But it does mean that he should not be disciplined for speaking frankly in a school assembly if he had no reason to anticipate punitive consequences.

One might conclude that respondent should have known that he would be punished for giving this speech on three quite different theories: (1) It violated the "Disruptive Conduct" rule published in the student handbook; (2) he was specifically warned by his teachers; or (3) the impropriety is so obvious that no specific notice was required. . . .

The fact that respondent reviewed the text of his speech with three different teachers before he gave it does indicate that he must have been aware of the possibility that it would provoke an adverse reaction, but the teachers' responses certainly did not give him any better notice of the likelihood of discipline than did the student handbook itself. In my opinion, therefore, the most difficult question is whether the speech was so obviously offensive that an intelligent high school student must be presumed to have realized that he would be punished for giving it. . . .

It seems fairly obvious that respondent's speech would be inappropriate in certain classroom and formal social settings. On the other hand, in a locker room or perhaps in a school corridor the metaphor in the speech might be regarded as rather routine comment. If this be true, and if respondent's audience consisted almost entirely of young people with whom he conversed on a daily basis, can we—at this distance—confidently assert that he must have known that the school administration would punish him for delivering it?

For three reasons, I think not. First, it seems highly unlikely that he would have decided to deliver the speech if he had known that it would result in his suspension and disqualification from delivering the school commencement address. Second, I believe a strong presumption in favor of free expression should apply whenever an issue of this kind is arguable. Third, because the Court has adopted the policy of applying contemporary community standards in evaluating expression with sexual connotations, this Court should defer to the views of the district and circuit judges who are in a much better position to evaluate this speech than we are.

C. LIBEL

Libel is defamation of character by print or visual presentation; slander is defamation by oral presentation. Libel prosecutions may be either criminal or civil. Criminal prosecutions for libel against the government and groups repair and maintain the peace and order of a community; whereas, civil suits brought by victims of libel are for monetary damages.

English common law permitted prosecutions for seditious libel (libel of the government and government officials), as did the Alien and Sedition Act in 1798. But in the landmark libel ruling *New York Times v. Sullivan* (1964) (see page 453), the Court had occasion to declare the Sedition Act and seditious libel unconstitutional and inconsistent with the First Amendment.

Some states also provided criminal penalties for group libel, attacks on groups. In *Beauharnas v. Illinois*, 343 U.S. 250 (1952), the Court upheld an Illinois law making it unlawful to publish, or exhibit any writing or picture portraying the "depravity, criminality, unchastly, or lack of virtue of a class of citizens, of any race, color, creed or religion." Beauharnis, head of the White Circle League, had circulated on the streets of Chicago a leaflet containing derogatory statements about blacks and urging the police to protect whites from their "rapes, knives, guns, and marijuana." But dissenting Justice Douglas warned that "Today a white man stands convicted for protesting in unseemly language against our decisions invalidating restrictive convenants. Tomorrow a Negro will be hauled before a court for denouncing lynch law in heated terms." Indeed, *Beauharnais* was widely criticized for failing to consider the close relationship between group libel and seditious libel, and allowing an important area of public discussion—the role of interest groups in American politics—to fall outside of First Amendment protection. Finally, in *Ashton v. Kentucky*, 384 US 195 (1966), Justice Douglas proclaimed criminal libel law unconstitutional.

Civil libel suits may seek two kinds of damages: (1) compensatory damages as reimbursement for an individual's actual financial loss resulting from, for example, loss of employment or reputation as a result of being libeled; and (2) punitive damages awarded as compensation for mental suffering due to a libelous attack.

Awards for libel *by* public officials are virtually impossible to win. Members of Congress enjoy absolute immunity under the speech and debate clause, subject to the ruling in *Hutchinson v. Proxmire*, 443 U.S. 111 (1979) (see Vol. 1, Ch. 5). In *Barr v. Matteo*, 360 U.S. 564 (1959), the Court extended immunity to all federal administrative officials for statements made within the "outer perimeter" of their official duties.

Not until *New York Times v. Sullivan* (1964) did the Court set down a constitutional standard for determining libel *of* public officials and "public figures." There Justice Brennan declared that public officials may win libel suits only on showing "actual malice," that is, "with knowledge that it was false or with reckless disregard of whether it was false or not."

The *New York Times* ruling proved controversial and makes it exceedingly difficult for public officials and public figures to win libel suits. Some critics, following Justices Black and Douglas in their concurring opinion in *New York Times*, argue that the Court did not go far enough toward safeguarding First Amendment freedoms and predicted problems in applying the test. Other critics counter that the *New York Times* rule renders public officials defenseless against all but the most vicious attacks. As Justice Fortas observed in *St. Amant v. Thompson*, 390 U.S. 727 (1968), "The First Amendment does not require that we license shotgun attacks on public officials in virtually unlimited open-season. The occupation of public officeholder does not forfeit one's membership in the human race."

Following *New York Times*, the Court confronted the problems in defining "public officials" and "public figures" and over whether the actual malice test should apply to both. In *Rosenblatt v. Baer*, 383 U.S. 75 (1966), the Court held that a former ski instructor and county commissioner was a public figure, who had to prove actual malice in a libel suit over reports alleging his involvement in city corruption. A year later in two cases, *Associated Press v. Walker,* 388 U.S. 130 (1967), and *Curtis Publishing Company v. Butts,* 388 U.S. 130 (1967), both involving public figures, the Warren Court split five to four, with the chief justice as the swing vote.

In the *Associated Press* case, Edwin A. Walker, a well-known, retired, right-wing general, sought libel damages for a news report that he personally "took command" of a violent crowd protesting the enrollment of James Meredith, a black, at the University of Mississippi. Walker claimed to have been libeled as a private individual and won a jury award of $500,000 in compensatory damages and $300,000 in punitive damages. However, the trial judge found no malice in the publication and struck down the latter award, which an appellate court affirmed. The Supreme Court unanimously reversed, but disagreed on the standard to be applied. Justices Brennan, Douglas, Black, and White, along with the chief justice, thought that the actual malice test should apply. But Justices Clark, Stewart, and Fortas joined an opinion by Justice Harlan allowing public figures (unlike public officials) to recover damages on showing only a "highly unreasonable conduct constituting an extreme departure from the standards of investigation and reporting ordinarily adhered to by responsible publishers." However, in *Curtis Publishing Company,* Harlan and three supporters in *Walker* were joined by Chief Justice Warren in upholding Wally Butts's libel award of $460,000 for an article in *The Saturday Evening Post,* alleging that Butts, a coach at the University of Georgia, conspired to rig a football game between his team and the University of Alabama. Although Butts, like Walker, was found to be a public figure, Harlan reasoned that here the publication was not "hot news" and, therefore, his standard of highly unreasonable conduct in the investigation and reporting of the story should apply. Although Chief Justice Warren concurred, he nevertheless agreed with the four dissenters that the actual malice test should apply to both public officials and public figures.

The Warren Court failed to reach complete agreement on the application of the actual malice test and, moreover, never found a private individual who was not a public figure.[1] Finally, in *Gertz v. Robert Welch, Inc.* (1974) (see page 461), the Burger Court found a "private individual" and announced a new libel standard for that category of persons—private individuals must prove only that a publisher was negligent in failing to exercise normal care in reporting. Two years later in *Time Inc. v. Firestone,* 424 U.S. 448 (1976), Justice Rehnquist reaffirmed that ruling in holding that a divorcée of the heir to the fortune of the Firestone Corporation was not a public figure, even though she had held news conferences about her divorce. *Time* magazine mistakenly referred to her as an "adulteress," when the divorce decree had not specifically found that she had committed adultery.[2]

In *Gertz*, Justice Powell emphasized that "Under the First Amendment there is no such thing as a false idea. However pernicious an opinion may seem, we depend for its correction not on the conscience of judges and juries but on the competition of other ideas. But there is no constitutional value in false statements of fact." He, thereby, suggested that statements of "opinion" might be exempt from state libel laws. But in *Milkovich v. Lorain Journal Co.*, 110 S.Ct. 2695 (1990), the Rehnquist Court rejected that implication. Michael Milkovich, Sr., a high-school wrestling coach, sued a small daily newspaper, owned by the Lorain Journal Company, for an article that asserted that he had lied under oath during an investigation of a melee in the school's gymnasium. The newspaper contended that its sportswriter was merely stating an "opinion" for which under *Gertz* he could not be held libel. Writing for the Court, however, Chief Justice Rehnquist rejected that interpretation of *Gertz:*

[W]e do not think this passage from *Gertz* was intended to create a wholesale defamation exemption for anything that might be labeled "opinion." . . . Not only would such an interpretation be contrary to the tenor and context of the passage, but it would also ignore the fact that expressions of "opinion" may often imply an assertion of objective fact. . . .

If a speaker says, "In my opinion John Jones is a liar," he implies a knowledge of facts which lead to the conclusion that Jones told an untruth. Even if the speaker states the facts upon which he bases his opinion, if those facts are either incorrect or incomplete, or if his assessment of them is erroneous, the statement may still imply a false assertion of fact. Simply couching such statements in terms of opinion does not dispel these implications; and the statement, "In my opinion Jones is a liar," can cause as much damage to reputation as the statement, "Jones is a liar.". . .

Apart from their reliance on the *Gertz* dictum, respondents do not really contend that a statement such as, "In my opinion John Jones is a liar," should be protected by a separate privilege for "opinion" under the First Amendment. But they do contend that in every defamation case the First Amendment mandates an inquiry into whether a statement is "opinion" or "fact," and that only the latter statements may be actionable.

They propose that a number of factors developed by the lower courts (in what we hold was a mistaken reliance on the *Gertz* dictum) be considered in deciding which is which. But we think the "breathing space" which "freedoms of expression require in order to survive," [*Philadelphia Newspapers, Inc. v.*] *Hepps*, [475 U.S. 767 (1986)], (quoting *New York*

Times), is adequately secured by existing constitutional doctrine without the creation of an artifical dichotomy between "opinion" and "fact."

Foremost, we think *Hepps* stands for the proposition that a statement on matters of public concern must be provable as false before there can be liability under state defamation law, at least in situations, like the present, where a media defendant is involved.

Thus, unlike the statement, "In my opinion Mayor Jones is a liar," the statement, "In my opinion Mayor Jones shows abysmal ignorance by accepting the teachings of Marx and Lenin," would not be actionable. *Hepps* insures that a statement of opinion relating to matters of public concern which does not contain a provably false factual connotation will receive full constitutional protection.

Although agreeing with much of the Court's analysis, dissenting Justice Brennan, joined by Justice Marshall, rejected its application to the facts in the case at hand and contended the statements made about Milkovich were entitled to "full constitutional protection." In his view:

[A]s long as it is clear to the reader that he is being offered conjecture and not solid information, danger to reputation is one we have chosen to tolerate in pursuit of individual liberty and the common quest for truth and the vitality of society as a whole. . . .

Readers are as capable of independently evaluating the merits of such speculative conclusions as they are of evaluating the merits of pure opprobrium. Punishing such conjecture protects reputation only at the cost of expunging a genuinely useful mechanism for public debate.

In other recent rulings the Court has made it somewhat easier for public officials and public figures, while somewhat more difficult for private individuals, to win libel awards. *Herbert v. Lando* (1979) (see page 470) held that at trial attorneys could probe the editorial process, questioning editors and reporters, to prove actual malice; members of the press have no privilege from testifying in libel cases and answering questions about editorial prepublication decisions. In *Philadelphia Newspapers, Inc. v. Hepps* (1986) (see page 475), a bare majority agreed that private individuals bringing libel actions have the burden of showing the falsity in reports or stories that touch on matters of public concern.

The Court, however, continues to refuse to recognize in its First Amendment jurisprudence the difference between libel actions and suits over invasion of privacy. In tort law and common law, individuals may sue for basically four kinds of privacy interests: (1) intrusions into their private affairs, causing mental distress; (2) public disclosure of embarrassing facts damaging to their reputation; (3) publicity placing them in a false light; and (4) appropriation of their name or likeness without their permission.[3] In suits for invasion of privacy, unlike those for libel, truth is no defense; indeed, that is the basic difference between the two—truth is always a defense against libel, whereas in private suits it is the actual intrusion on, and truthful disclosure of, privacy affairs per se that causes mental suffering and injury to reputation.

In giving priority to First Amendment freedoms, the Court applies its tests for libel in cases involving invasion of privacy as well. As the Court explained, in *Time, Inc. v. Hill,* 385 U.S. 374 (1967), "We create a risk of serious impairment of the indispensable service of a free press in a free society if we saddle the press with the impossible burden of verifying to a certainty the facts associated with news articles with a person's name, picture, or portrait, particularly as related to nondefamatory matter." In this case, the Hill sued *Life* magazine for a pictorial essay on the opening of a play, *The Desperate Hours,* which was based on the Hill family's experiences as hostages of three escaped convicts. The *Life* account, though, failed to differentiate between the truth and fiction in the play, and the Hills sued for invasion of privacy and portrayal of them in false light. The Court (with only Justice Fortas dissenting) reversed a lower court's award to the Hills on the grounds that the opening of the play was a matter of public interest.

Seven years later, in *Cantrell v. Forest City Publishing Company,* 419 U.S. 245 (1974), Margaret Cantrell and her children brought an invasion of privacy suit against the Forest City Publishing Company for a follow-up story on a bridge disaster that a year before had claimed the life of her husband. The story inaccurately portrayed the Cantrells as destitute after the bridge collapsed, and Mrs. Cantrell sued for invasion of privacy and misrepresentation. At trial, the judge instructed the jury to find the publisher liable on the *New York Times* actual malice test. On appeal, the Court refused to consider whether states may constitutionally apply more relaxed standards of liability for invasion of privacy than for libel.

In *Cox Broadcasting Corporation v. Cohn* (1975) (see page 478), however, the Court struck down a privacy statute, making it a misdemeanor to name or identify a rape victim, in a case brought by the father of a deceased rape victim against Cox Broadcasting Corporation for identifying his daughter as a rape victim in a television broadcast.[4] On a vote of six to three in *The Florida Star v. B.J.F.,* 109 S.Ct. 2603 (1989), the justices also overturned a civil award against a newspaper for truthfully reporting, in violation of a state statute, the name of a rape victim. But there the Court suggested that *Cohn* was limited to actual public records and that a majority may eventually emerge on the Rehnquist Court for overturning *Cohn.*

THE DEVELOPMENT OF LAW
Other Important Rulings on Libel

Case	Vote	Holding
Keeton v. Hustler Magazine, Inc., 465 U.S. 770 (1984)	6:3	Libel suits may be brought in any jurisdiction in which a magazine is sold; allowing forum shopping.
Bose Corporation v. Consumers Union, 466 U.S. 485 (1984)	6:3	Actual malice test applies in libel suit against consumer magazine for review of loudspeakers.
Dun & Bradstreet, Inc. v. Greenmoss Builders, Inc., 472 1 U.S. 749 (1985)	6:3	Contractor need not prove actual malice in a suit against a credit reporting agency for issuing a false credit report to a bank.
Anderson v. Liberty Lobby 477 U.S. 242 (1986)	6:3	Libel actions should go to trial only if there is clear and convincing evidence of actual malice.
Hustler Magazine v. Falwell, 485 U.S. 46 (1988)	9:0	Public figure forbidden from recovering damages for emotional distress due to advertisement parody.
Harte-Hanks v. Connaughton, 109 S.Ct. 2678 (1989)	9:0	Upheld a $200,000 libel judgment for a lawyer who was a judicial candidate against a newspaper.
Milkovich v. Lorain Journal Co., 110 S.Ct. 2695 (1990)	7:2	Held that there is no exception in the application of libel laws for statements of opinion, although defendants may not be held liable for statements that cannot be proved true or false. The First Amendment, in Chief Justice Rehnquist's words, does not create "a wholesale defamation exemption for anything that might be labeled opinion."

NOTES

1. See *Greenbelt Coop. v. Bresler,* 398 U.S. 6 (1970) (use of term *blackmail* when characterizing the conduct of a real estate developer, who was deemed to be a public figure, seeking zoning variances was not libel); *Monitor Patriot Co. v. Roy,* 401 U.S. 265, (1971) (held candidates for elective office were public officials or public figures subject to actual malice test); *Rosenbloom v. Metromedia,* 403 U.S. 29 (1971) (held that a distributor of nudist magazines, who was called a "smut peddler," but was later acquitted of obscenity charges, had to prove actual malice).
2. See also *Wolston v. Reader's Digest,* 443 US 157 (1979) (holding alleged KGB spy not a public figure).
3. See William Prosser, "Privacy," 48 *California Law Review* 383 (1960).
4. See, however, *Zacchini v. Scripps-Howard Broadcasting Corporation,* 433 U.S. 562 (1977) (holding five to four that the First Amendment does not immunize news media from a suit brought by a "human cannon-ball" for appropriation of names and likeness in media coverage of the stunt that arguably diminished its value).

SELECTED BIBLIOGRAPHY

Forer, Louis. *A Chilling Effect: The Mounting Threat of Libel and Invasion of Privacy Actions to the First Amendment.* New York: Norton, 1987.
Lewis, Anthony. *"New York Times v. Sullivan* Reconsidered: Time to Return to 'The Central Meaning of the First Amendment.' " 83 *Columbia Law Review* 603 (1983).
Smolla, Rodney. *Suing the Press: Libel, the Media, & Power.* New York: Oxford University Press, 1986.
Smolla, Rodeny. *Jerry Falwell v. Larry Flynt: The First Amendment on Trial.* New York: St. Martins, 1988.

The New York Times Company v. Sullivan
376 U.S. 254, 84 S.Ct. 710 (1964)

Justice Brennan sets forth the pertinent facts at the outset of his opinion for the Court. The advertisement that gave rise to the litigation leading to this landmark ruling is reprinted here.

Justice BRENNAN delivers the opinion of the Court.

We are required in this case to determine for the first time the extent to which the constitutional protections for speech and press limit a State's power to award damages in a libel action brought by a public official against critics of his official conduct.

Respondent L. B. Sullivan is one of the three elected Commissioners of the City of Montgomery, Alabama. . . . He brought this civil libel action against the four individual petitioners, who are Negroes and Alabama clergymen, and against petitioner the New York Times Company, a New York corporation which publishes the New York Times, a daily newspaper. . . .

Respondent's complaint alleged that he had been libeled by statements in a full-page advertisement that was carried in the New York Times on March 29, 1960. Entitled "Heed Their Rising Voices," the advertisement began by stating that "As the whole world knows by now, thousands of Southern Negro students are engaged in widespread non-violent demonstrations in positive affirmation of the right to live in human dignity as guaranteed by the U.S. Constitution and the Bill of Rights." . . . The text concluded with an appeal for funds for three purposes: support of the student movement, "the struggle for the right-to-vote," and the legal defense of Dr. Martin Luther King, Jr., leader of the movement, against a perjury indictment then pending in Montgomery. . . .

Of the 10 paragraphs of text in the advertisement, the third and a portion of the sixth were the basis of respondent's claim of libel. They read as follows:

Third paragraph:

"In Montgomery, Alabama, after students sang 'My Country, 'Tis of Thee' on the State Capitol steps, their leaders were expelled from school, and truckloads of police armed with shotguns and tear-gas ringed the Alabama State College Campus. When the entire student body protested to state authorities by refusing to re-register, their dining hall was padlocked in an attempt to starve them into submission."

Sixth paragraph:

"Again and again the Southern violators have answered Dr. King's peaceful protests with intimidation and violence. They have bombed his home almost killing his wife and child. They have assaulted his person. They have arrested him seven times—for 'speeding,' 'loitering' and similar 'offenses.' And now they have charged him with 'perjury'—a *felony* under which they could imprison him for *ten years.* . . ."

Although neither of these statements mentions respondent by name, he contended that the word "police" in the third paragraph referred to him as the Montgomery Commissioner who supervised the Police Department, so that he was being accused of "ringing" the campus with police. He further claimed that the paragraph would be read as imputing to the police, and hence to him, the padlocking of the dining hall in order to starve the students into submission. As to the sixth paragraph, he contended that since arrests are ordinarily made by the police, the statement "They have arrested [Dr. King] seven times" would be read as referring to him. . . .

It is uncontroverted that some of the statements contained in the two paragraphs were not accurate descriptions of events which occurred in Montgomery. Although Negro students staged a demonstration on the State Capital steps, they sang the National Anthem and not "My Country, 'Tis of Thee." Although nine students were expelled by the State Board of Education, this was not for leading the demonstration at the Capitol, but for demanding service at a lunch counter in the Montgomery County Courthouse on another day. Not the entire student body, but most of it, had protested the expulsion, not by refusing to register, but by boycotting classes on a single day; virtually all the students did register for the ensuing semester. . . . Although the police were deployed near the campus in large numbers on three occasions, they did not at any time "ring" the campus, and they were not called to the campus in connection with the demonstration on the State Capitol steps, as the third paragraph implied. Dr. King had not been arrested seven times, but only four. . . .

Respondent made no effort to prove that he suffered actual pecuniary loss as a result of the alleged libel.[*] . . .

The trial judge submitted the case to the jury under instructions that the statements in the advertisement were "libelous per se" and were not privileged, so that petitioners might be held liable if the jury found that they had published the advertisement and that the statements were made "of and concerning" respondent. The jury was instructed that, because the statements were libelous *per se,* "the law . . . implies legal injury from the bare fact of publication itself," "falsity and malice are presumed," "general damages need not be alleged or proved but are presumed," and "punitive damages may be awarded by the jury even though the amount of actual damages is neither found nor shown." [The jury found for the respondent and awarded $500,000 in damages.] . . .

We reverse the judgment. We hold that the rule of law applied by the Alabama courts is constitutionally deficient for failure to provide the safeguards for freedom of speech and of the press that are required by the First and Fourteenth Amendments in a libel action brought by a public official against critics of his official

---

[*]   Approximately 394 copies of the edition of the Times containing the advertisement were circulated in Alabama. Of these, about 35 copies were distributed in Montgomery County. The total circulation of the Times for that day was approximately 650,000 copies.

conduct. We further hold that under the proper safeguards the evidence presented in this case is constitutionally insufficient to support the judgment for respondent.

I.

We may dispose at the outset of two grounds asserted to insulate the judgment of the Alabama courts from constitutional scrutiny. The first is the proposition relied on by the State Supreme Court— that "The Fourteenth Amendment is directed against State action and not private action." That proposition has no application to this case. Although this is a civil lawsuit between private parties, the Alabama courts have applied a state rule of law which petitioners claim to impose invalid restrictions on their constitutional freedoms of speech and press. . . .

The second contention is that the constitutional guarantees of freedom of speech and of the press are inapplicable here, at least so far as the Times is concerned, because the allegedly libelous statements were published as part of a paid, "commercial" advertisement. The argument relies on *Valentine v. Chrestensen,* 316 U.S. 52 [1942], where the Court held that a city ordinance forbidding street distribution of commercial and business advertising matter did not abridge the First Amendment freedoms, even as applied to a handbill having a commercial message on one side but a protest against certain official action on the other. The reliance is wholly misplaced. . . .

The publication here was not a "commercial" advertisement in the sense in which the word was used in Chrestensen. It communicated information, expressed opinion, recited grievances, protested claimed abuses, and sought financial support on behalf of a movement whose existence and objectives are matters of the highest public interest and concern. . . . That the Times was paid for publishing the advertisement is as immaterial in this connection as is the fact that newspapers and books are sold. Any other conclusion would discourage newspapers from carrying "editorial advertisements" of this type, and so might shut off an important outlet for the promulgation of information and ideas by persons who do not themselves have access to publishing facilities—who wish to exercise their freedom of speech even though they are not members of the press. . . .

II.

Respondent relies heavily, as did the Alabama courts, on statements of this Court to the effect that the Constitution does not protect libelous publications. Those statements do not foreclose our inquiry here. None of the cases sustained the use of libel laws to impose sanctions upon expression critical of the official conduct of public officials. In deciding the question now, we are compelled by neither precedent nor policy to give any more weight to the epithet "libel" than we have to other "mere labels" of state law. . . . Like insurrection, contempt, advocacy of unlawful acts, breach of the peace, obscenity, solicitation of legal business, and the various other formulae for the repression of expression that have been challenged in this Court, libel can claim no talismanic immunity from constitutional limitations. It must be measured by standards that satisfy the First Amendment. . . .

[W]e consider this case against the background of a profound national commitment to the principle that debate on public issues should be uninhibited, robust, and wide-open, and that it may well include vehement, caustic, and sometimes unpleasantly sharp attacks on government and public officials. The present advertisement, as an expression of grievance and protest on one of the major public issues of our time, would seem clearly to qualify for the constitutional protection. The question is whether it forfeits that protection by the falsity of some of its factual statements and by its alleged defamation of respondent.

Authoritative interpretations of the First Amendment guarantees have consistently refused to recognize an exception for any test of truth—whether administered by judges, juries, or administrative officials—and especially one that puts the burden of proving truth on the speaker. The constitutional protection does not turn upon "the truth, popularity, or social utility of the ideas and beliefs which are offered." . . . That erroneous statement is inevitable in free debate, and that it must be protected if the freedoms of expression are to have the "breathing space" that they "need . . . to survive.". . .

Injury to official reputation error affords no more warrant for repressing speech that would otherwise be free than does factual error. Where judicial officers are involved, this Court has held that concern for the dignity and reputation of the courts does not justify the punishment as criminal contempt of criticism of the judge or his decision. This is true even though the utterance contains "half-truths" and "misinformation." Such repression can be justified, if at all, only by a clear and present danger of the obstruction of justice. . . .

If neither factual error nor defamatory content suffices to remove the constitutional shield from criticism of official conduct, the combination of the two elements is no less inadequate. This is the lesson to be drawn from the great controversy over the Sedition Act of 1798, 1 Stat. 596, which first crystallized a national awareness of the central meaning of the First Amendment. . . .

Although the Sedition Act was never tested in this Court, the attack upon its validity has carried the day in the court of history. Fines levied in its prosecution were repaid by Act of Congress on the ground that it was unconstitutional. Jefferson, as President, pardoned those who had been convicted and sentenced under the Act and remitted their fines. . . .

There is no force in respondent's argument that the constitutional limitations implicit in the history of the Sedition Act apply only to Congress and not to the States. It is true that the First Amendment was originally addressed only to action by the Federal Government. . . . But this distinction was eliminated with the adoption of the Fourteenth Amendment and the application to the States of the First Amendment's restrictions.

What a State may not constitutionally bring about by means of a criminal statute is likewise beyond the reach of its civil law of libel. The fear of damage awards under a rule such as that invoked by the Alabama courts here may be markedly more inhibiting than the fear of prosecution under a criminal statute. Alabama, for example, has a criminal libel law which subjects to prosecution "any person who speaks, writes, or prints of and concerning another any accusation falsely and maliciously importing the commission by such person of a felony, or any other indictable offense involving moral turpitude," and which allows as punishment upon conviction a fine not exceeding $500 and a prison sentence of six months. Presumably a person charged with violation of this statute enjoys ordinary criminal-law safeguards such as the requirements of an indictment and of proof beyond a reasonable doubt. These safeguards are not available to the defendant in a civil action. The judgment awarded in this case—without the need for any proof of actual pecuniary loss—was one thousand times greater than the maximum fine provided by the Alabama criminal statute, and one hundred times greater than that provided by the Sedition Act. . . . Whether or not a newspaper can survive a succession of such judgments, the pall of fear and timidity imposed upon those who would give voice to public criticism is an atmosphere in which the First Amendment freedoms cannot survive. . . .

The state rule of law is not saved by its allowance of the defense of truth. . . . A rule compelling the critic of official conduct to guarantee the truth of all his factual assertions—and to do so on pain of libel judgments virtually unlimited in amount—leads to a comparable "self-censorship." Allowance of the defense of truth, with the burden of proving it on the defendant, does not mean that only false speech will be deterred. . . . Under such a rule, would-be critics of official conduct may be deterred from voicing their criticism, even though it is believed to be true and even though it is in fact true, because of doubt whether it can be proved in court or fear of the expense of having to do so. They tend to make only statements which "steer far wider of the unlawful zone." The rule thus dampens the vigor and limits the variety of public debate. It is inconsistent with the First and Fourteenth Amendments.

The constitutional guarantees require, we think, a federal rule that prohibits a public official from recovering damages for a defamatory falsehood relating to his official conduct unless he proves that the statement was made with "actual malice"—that is, with knowledge that it was false or with reckless disregard of whether it was false or not. . . .

Such a privilege for criticism of official conduct is appropriately analogous to the protection accorded a public official when *he* is sued for libel by a private citizen. In *Barr v. Matteo*, 360 U.S. 564 [1959], this Court held the utterance of a federal official to be absolutely privileged if made "within the outer perimeter" of his duties. The States accord the same immunity to statements of their highest officers, although some differentiate their lesser officials and qualify the privilege they enjoy. But all hold that all officials are protected unless actual malice can be proved. The reason for the official privilege is said to be that the threat of damage suits would otherwise "inhibit the fearless, vigorous, and effective administration of policies of government" and "dampen the ardor of all but the most resolute, or the most irresponsible, in the unflinching discharge of their duties." Analogous considerations support the privilege for the citizen-critic of government. It is as much his duty to criticize as it is the official's duty to administer. As Madison said, "the censorial power is in the people over the Government, and not in the Government over the people." It would give public servants an unjustified preference over the public they serve, if critics of official conduct did not have a fair equivalent of the immunity granted to the officials themselves.

We conclude that such a privilege is required by the First and Fourteenth Amendments.

III.

We hold today that the Constitution delimits a State's power to award damages for libel in actions brought by public officials against critics of their official conduct. Since this is such an action, the rule requiring proof of actual malice is applicable. . . .

Since respondent may seek a new trial, we deem that considerations of effective judicial administration require us to review the evidence in the present record to determine whether it could constitutionally support a judgment for respondent. . . .

[T]he proof presented to show actual malice lacks the convincing clarity which the constitutional standard demands, and hence that it would not constitutionally sustain the judgment for respondent under the proper rule of law. . . .

We also think the evidence was constitutionally defective in another respect: it was incapable of supporting the jury's finding that the allegedly libelous statements were made "of and concerning" respondent. . . . There was no reference to respondent in the advertisement, either by name or official position. A number of the allegedly libelous statements—the charges that the dining hall was padlocked and that Dr. King's home was bombed, his person assaulted, and a perjury prosecution instituted against him—did not even concern the police; despite the ingenuity of the arguments which would attach this significance to the word "They," it is plain that these statements could not reasonably be read as accusing respondent of personal involvement in the acts in question. . . .

The judgment of the Supreme Court of Alabama is reversed and the case is remanded to that court for further proceedings not inconsistent with this opinion.

Reversed and remanded.

Justice BLACK, with whom Justice DOUGLAS joins, concurring.

I base my vote to reverse on the belief that the First and Fourteenth Amendments not merely "delimit" a State's power to award damages to "public officials against critics of their official conduct" but completely prohibit a State from exercising such a power. The Court goes on to hold that a State can subject such critics to damages if "actual malice" can be proved against them. "Malice," even as defined by the Court, is an elusive, abstract concept, hard to prove and hard to disprove. The requirement that malice be proved provides at best an evanescent protection for the right critically to discuss public affairs and certainly does not measure up to the sturdy safeguard embodied in the First Amendment. Unlike the Court, therefore, I vote to reverse exclusively on the ground that the Times and the individual defendants had an absolute, unconditional constitutional right to publish in the Times advertisement their criticisms of the Montgomery agencies and officials.

Justice GOLDBERG, with whom Justice DOUGLAS joins, concurring.

In my view, the First and Fourteenth Amendments to the Constitution afford to the citizen and to the press an absolute, unconditional privilege to criticize official conduct despite the harm which may flow from excesses and abuses. The prized American right "to speak one's mind" about public officials and affairs needs "breathing space to survive." The right should not depend upon a probing by the jury of the motivation of the citizen or press. The theory of our Constitution is that every citizen may speak his mind and every newspaper express its view on matters of public concern and may not be barred from speaking or publishing because those in control of government think that what is said or written is unwise, unfair, false, or malicious. In a democratic society, one who assumes to act for the citizens in an executive, legislative, or judicial capacity must expect that his official acts will be commented upon and criticized. Such criticism cannot, in my opinion, be muzzled or deterred by the courts at the instance of public officials under the label of libel. . . .

The conclusion that the Constitution affords the citizen and the press an absolute privilege for criticism of official conduct does not leave the public official without defenses against unsubstantiated opinions or deliberate misstatements. . . . The public official certainly has equal if not greater access than most private citizens to media of communication. In any event, despite the possibility that some excesses and abuses may go unremedied, we must recognize that "the people of this nation have ordained in the light of history, that, in spite of the probability of excesses and abuses, [certain] liberties are, in the long view, essential to enlightened opinion and right conduct on the part of the citizens of a democracy." *Cantwell v. Connecticut*, 310 U.S. 296. [(1940)]. As Justice BRANDEIS correctly observed, "sunlight is the most powerful of all disinfectants."

Gertz v. Robert Welch, Inc.

418 U.S. 323, 94 S.Ct. 2997 (1974)

Elmer Gertz was a Chicago lawyer hired to sue a policeman by a family whose son had been killed by the officer. The John Birch Society in its magazine *American Opinion* charged that Gertz was a "Leninist" and "Communist-fronter" and that the lawsuit against the policeman was part of a nationwide communist conspiracy to discredit law enforcement. Gertz sued Robert Welch, publisher of the magazine, for libel in federal district court. That court held for the publisher on applying the *New York Times v. Sullivan* actual malice rule. Gertz appealed to the United States Court of Appeals for the Seventh Circuit, which affirmed the lower court's ruling, and finally to the Supreme Court.

Justice POWELL delivers the opinion of the Court.

The principal issue in this case is whether a newspaper or broadcaster that publishes defamatory falsehoods about an individual who is neither a public official nor a public figure may claim a constitutional privilege against liability for the injury inflicted by those statements. . . .

We begin with the common ground. Under the First Amendment there is no such thing as a false idea. However pernicious an opinion may seem, we depend for its correction not on the conscience of judges and juries but on the competition of other ideas. But there is no constitutional value in false statements of fact. Neither the intentional lie nor the careless error materially advances society's interest in "uninhibited, robust, and wide-open" debate on public issues. *New York Times Co. v. Sullivan,* [376 U.S. 254 (1964)]. They belong to that category of utterances which "are no essential part of any exposition of ideas, and are of such slight social value as a step to truth that any benefit that may be derived from them is clearly outweighed by the social interest in order and morality." *Chaplinsky v. New Hampshire* [315 U.S. 568] (1942).

Although the erroneous statement of fact is not worthy of constitutional protection, it is nevertheless inevitable in free debate. . . . And punishment of error runs the risk of inducing a cautious and restrictive exercise of the constitutionally guaranteed freedoms of speech and press. Our decisions recognize that a rule of strict liability that compels a publisher or broadcaster to guarantee the accuracy of his factual assertions may lead to intolerable self-censorship. . . . The First Amendment requires that we protect some falsehood in order to protect speech that matters.

The need to avoid self-censorship by the news media is, however, not the only societal value at issue. If it were, this Court would have embraced long ago the view that publishers and broadcasters enjoy an unconditional and indefeasible immunity from liability for defamation.

The legitimate state interest underlying the law of libel is the compensation of individuals for the harm inflicted on them by defamatory falsehood. We would not lightly require the State to abandon this purpose, for, as Justice STEWART has reminded us, the individual's right to the protection of his own good name

"reflects no more than our basic concept of the essential dignity and worth of every human being—a concept at the root of any decent system of ordered liberty. The protection of private personality, like the protection of life itself, is left primarily to the individual States under the Ninth and Tenth Amendments. But this does not mean that the right is entitled to any less recognition by this Court as a basic of our constitutional system." *Rosenblatt v. Baer,* 383 U.S. 75 (1966) (concurring opinion). . . .

The *New York Times* standard defines the level of constitutional protection appropriate to the context of defamation of a public person. . . . For the reasons stated below, we conclude that the state interest in compensating-injury to the reputation of private individuals requires that a different rule should obtain with respect to them. . . .

[W]e have no difficulty in distinguishing among defamation plaintiffs. The first remedy of any victim of defamation is self-help—using available opportunities to contradict the lie or correct the error and thereby to minimize its adverse impact on reputation. Public officials and public figures usually enjoy significantly greater access to the channels of effective communication and hence have a more realistic opportunity to counteract false statements then private individuals normally enjoy. Private individuals are therefore more vulnerable to injury, and the state interest in protecting them is correspondingly greater.

More important than the likelihood that private individuals will lack effective opportunities for rebuttal, there is a compelling normative consideration underlying the distinction between public and private defamation plaintiffs. An individual who decides to seek governmental office must accept certain necessary consequences of that involvement in public affairs. He runs the risk of closer public scrutiny than might otherwise be the case. . . .

Those classed as public figures stand in a similar position. Hypothetically, it may be possible for someone to become a public figure through no purposeful action of his own, but the instances of truly involuntary public figures must be exceedingly rare. For the most part those who attain this status have assumed roles of especial prominence in the affairs of society. Some occupy positions of such persuasive power and influence that they are deemed public figures for all purposes. More commonly, those classed as public figures have thrust themselves to the forefront of particular public controversies in order to influence the resolution of the issues involved. In either event, they invite attention and comment.

Even if the foregoing generalities do not obtain in every instance, the communications media are entitled to act on the assumption that public officials and public figures have voluntarily exposed themselves to increased risk of injury from defamatory falsehood concerning them. No such assumption is justified with respect to a private individual. He has not accepted public office or assumed an "influential role in ordering society." He has relinquished no part of his interest in the protection of his own good name, and consequently he has a more compelling call on the courts for redress of injury inflicted by defamatory falsehood. Thus, private individuals are not only more vulnerable to injury than public officials and public figures: they are also more deserving of recovery.

For these reasons we conclude that the States should retain substantial latitude in their efforts to enforce a legal remedy for defamatory falsehood injurious to the reputation of a private individual. The extension of the *New York Times* test . . . would abridge this legitimate state interest to a degree that we find unacceptable. And it would occasion the additional difficulty of forcing state and federal judges to decide on an *ad hoc* basis which publications address issues of "general or public interest" and which do not—to determine, in the words of Justice MAR-SHALL, "what information is relevant to self-government," *Rosenbloom v. Metromedia, Inc.,* [403 U.S. 29 (1971)]. We doubt the wisdom of committing this task to the conscience of judges. . . .

We hold that, so long as they do not impose liability without fault, the States may define for themselves the appropriate standard of liability for a publisher or broadcaster of defamatory falsehood injurious to a private individual. This approach provides a more equitable boundary between the competing concerns involved here. It recognizes the strength of the legitimate state interest in compensating private individuals for wrongful injury to reputation, yet shields the press and broadcast media from the rigors of strict liability for defamation. At least this conclusion obtains where, as here, the substance of the defamatory statement "makes substantial danger to reputation apparent." This phrase places in perspective the conclusion we announce today. . . .

Our accommodation of the competing values at stake in defamation suits by private individuals allows the States to impose liability on the publisher or broadcaster of defamatory falsehood on a less demanding showing than that required by *New York Times.* This conclusion is not based on a belief that the considerations which prompted the adoption of the *New York Times* privilege for defamation of public officials and its extension to public figures are wholly inapplicable to the context of private individuals. Rather, we endorse this approach in recognition of the strong and legitimate state interest in compensating private individuals for injury to reputation. But this countervailing state interest extends no further than compensation for actual injury. For the reasons stated below, we hold that the States may not permit recovery of presumed or punitive damages, at least when liability is not based on a showing of knowledge of falsity or reckless disregard for the truth.

The common law of defamation is an oddity of tort law, for it allows recovery of purportedly compensatory damages without evidence of actual loss. Under the traditional rules pertaining to actions for libel, the existence of injury is presumed from the fact of publication. Juries may award substantial sums as compensation for supposed damage to reputation without any proof that such harm actually occurred. The largely uncontrolled discretion of juries to award damages where there is no loss unnecessarily compounds the potential of any system of liability for defamatory falsehood to inhibit the vigorous exercise of First Amendment freedoms. Additionally, the doctrine of presumed damages invites juries to punish unpopular opinion rather than to compensate individuals for injury sustained by the publication of a false fact. More to the point, the States have no substantial interest in securing for plaintiffs such as this petitioner gratuitous awards of money damages far in excess of any actual injury.

We would not, of course, invalidate state law simply because we doubt its wisdom, but here we are attempting to reconcile state law with a competing interest grounded in the constitutional command of the First Amendment. It is therefore appropriate to require that state remedies for defamatory falsehood reach no farther than is necessary to protect the legitimate interest involved. It is necessary to restrict defamation plaintiffs who do not prove knowledge of falsity or reckless disregard for the truth to compensation for actual injury. We need not define "actual injury," as trial courts have wide experience in framing appropriate jury instructions in tort actions. Suffice it to say that actual injury is not limited to out-of-pocket loss. Indeed, the more customary types of actual harm inflicted by defamatory falsehood include impairment of reputation and standing in the community, personal humiliation, and mental anguish and suffering. Of course, juries must be limited by appropriate instructions, and all awards must be supported by competent evidence concerning the injury, although there need be no evidence which assigns an actual dollar value to the injury.

We also find no justification for allowing awards of punitive damages against publishers and broadcasters held liable under state-defined standards of liability for defamation. In most jurisdictions jury discretion over the amounts awarded is limited only by the gentle rule that they not be excessive. Consequently, juries assess punitive damages in wholly unpredictable amounts bearing no necessary relation to the actual harm caused. And they remain free to use their discretion selectively to punish expressions of unpopular views. Like the doctrine of presumed damages, jury discretion to award punitive damages unnecessarily exacerbates the danger of media self-censorship, but, unlike the former rule, punitive damages are wholly irrelevant to the state interest that justifies a negligence standard for private defamation actions. They are not compensation for injury. Instead, they are private fines levied by civil juries to punish reprehensible conduct and to deter its future occurrence. In short, the private defamation plaintiff who establishes liability under a less demanding standard than that stated by *New York Times* may recover only such damages as are sufficient to compensate him for actual injury.

Notwithstanding our refusal to extend the *New York Times* privilege to defamation of private individuals, respondent contends that we should affirm the judgment below on the ground that petitioner is either a public official or a public figure. There is little basis for the former assertion. Several years prior to the present incident, petitioner had served briefly on housing committees appointed by the mayor of Chicago, but at the time of publication he had never held any remunerative governmental position. Respondent admits this but argues that petitioner's appearance at the coroner's inquest rendered him a "de facto public official."

Our cases recognized no such concept. Respondent's suggestion would sweep all lawyers under the *New York Times* rule as officers of the court and distort the plain meaning of the "public official" category beyond all recognition. We decline to follow it. . . .

Petitioner has long been active in community and professional affairs. He has served as an officer of local civic groups and of various professional organizations, and he has published several books and articles on legal subjects. Although petitioner was consequently well known in some circles, he had achieved no general fame or notoriety in the community. None of the prospective jurors called at the trial had ever heard of petitioner prior to this litigation, and respondent offered no proof that this response was atypical of the local population. We would not lightly assume that a citizen's participation in community and professional affairs rendered him a public figure for all purposes. Absent clear evidence of general fame or notoriety in the community, and pervasive involvement in the affairs of society, an individual should not be deemed a public personality for all aspects of his life. It is preferable to reduce the public-figure question to a more meaningful context by looking to the nature and extent of an individual's participation in the particular controversy giving rise to the defamation.

In this context it is plain that petitioner was not a public figure. He played a minimal role at the coroner's inquest, and his participation related solely to his representation of a private client. He took no part in the criminal prosecution of Officer Nuccio. Moreover, he never discussed either the criminal or civil litigation with the press and was never quoted as having done so. He plainly did not thrust himself into the vortex of this public issue, nor did he engage the public's attention in an attempt to influence its outcome. We are persuaded that the trial court did not err in refusing to characterize petitioner as a public figure for the purpose of this litigation.

We therefore conclude that the *New York Times* standard is inapplicable to this case and that the trial court erred in entering judgment for respondent. Because the jury was allowed to impose liability without fault and was permitted to presume damages without proof of injury, a new trial is necessary. We reverse and remand for further proceedings in accord with this opinion.

It is so ordered.

Justice BLACKMUN concurring.

The Court today refuses to apply *New York Times* to the private individual, as contrasted with the public official and the public figure. . . . I sense some illogic in this. . . . [Still] I am willing to join, and do join, the Court's opinion and its judgment for two reasons:

1. By removing the specters of presumed and punitive damages in the absence of *New York Times* malice, the Court eliminates significant and powerful motives for self-censorship that otherwise are present in the traditional libel action. . . . By so doing, the Court leaves what should prove to be sufficient and adequate breathing space for a vigorous press. What the Court has done, I believe, will have little, if any, practical effect on the functioning of responsible journalism.

2. The Court was sadly fractionated in *Rosenbloom* [*v. Metromedia, Inc.*, 403 U.S. 29 (1971)]. A result of that kind inevitably leads to uncertainty. I feel that it is of profound importance for the Court to come to rest in the defamation area and to have a clearly defined majority position that eliminates the unsureness engendered by *Rosenbloom's* diversity. If my vote were not needed to create a majority, I would adhere to my prior view. A definitive ruling, however, is paramount.

Chief Justice BURGER dissenting.

I am frank to say I do not know the parameters of a "negligence" doctrine as applied to the news media. Conceivably this new doctrine could inhibit some editors, as the dissents of Justice DOUGLAS and Justice BRENNAN suggest. But I would prefer to allow this area of law to continue to evolve as it has up to now with respect to private citizens rather than embark on a new doctrinal theory which has no jurisprudential ancestry.

Justice DOUGLAS dissenting.

The Court describes this case as a return to the struggle of "defin[ing] the proper accommodation between the law of defamation and the freedoms of speech and press protected by the First Amendment." It is indeed a struggle, once described by Justice BLACK as "the same quagmire" in which the Court "is now helplessly struggling in the field of obscenity." I would suggest that the struggle is a quite hopeless one, for, in light of the command of the First Amendment, no "accommodation" of its freedoms can be "proper" except those made by the Framers themselves.

Justice BRENNAN dissenting.

I cannot agree . . . that free and robust debate—so essential to the proper functioning of our system of government—is permitted adequate "breathing space," when, as the Court holds, the States may impose all but strict liability for defamation if the defamed party is a private person and "the substance of the defamatory statement 'makes substantial danger to reputation apparent.' " I adhere to my view expressed in *Rosenbloom v. Metromedia, Inc., supra,* that we strike the proper accommodation between avoidance of media self-censorship and protection of individual reputations only when we require States to apply the *New York Times Co. v. Sullivan* knowing-or-reckless-falsity standard in civil libel actions concerning media reports of the involvement of private individuals in events of public or general interest. . . .

Although acknowledging that First Amendment values are of no less significance when media reports concern private persons' involvement in matters of public concern, the Court refuses to provide, in such cases, the same level of constitutional protection that has been afforded the media in the context of defamation of public persons. The accommodation that this Court has established between free speech and libel laws in cases involving public officials and public figures—that defamatory falsehood be shown by clear and convincing evidence to have been published with knowledge of falsity or with reckless disregard of truth—is not apt, the Court holds, because the private individual does not have the same degree of access to the media to rebut defamatory comments as does the public person and he has not voluntarily exposed himself to public scrutiny.

While these arguments are forcefully and eloquently presented, I cannot accept them, for the reasons I stated in *Rosenbloom:*

"The *New York Times* standard was applied to libel of a public official or public figure to give effect to the [First] Amendment's function to encourage ventilation of public issues, not because the public official has any less interest in protecting his reputation than an individual in private life. While the argument that public figures need less protection because they can command media attention to counter criticism may be true for some very prominent people, even then it is the rare case where the denial overtakes the original charge. Denials, retractions, and corrections are not 'hot' news, and rarely receive the prominence of the original story. When the public official or public figure is a minor functionary, or has left the position that put him in the public eye, . . . the argument loses all of its force. In the vast majority of libels involving public officials or public figures, the ability to respond through the media will depend on the same complex factor on which the ability of a private individual depends: the unpredictable event of the media's continuing interest in the story. Thus the unproved, and highly improbable, generalization that an as yet [not fully defined] class of 'public figures' involved in matters of public concern will be better able to respond through the media than private individuals also involved in such matters seems too insubstantial a reed on which to rest a constitutional distinction.". . .

Moreover, the argument that private persons should not be required to prove *New York Times* knowing-or-reckless falsity because they do not assume the risk of defamation by freely entering the public arena "bears little relationship either to the values protected by the First Amendment or to the nature of our society." Social interaction exposes all of us to some degree of public view. . . . "Thus, the idea that certain 'public' figures have voluntarily exposed their entire lives to public inspection, while private individuals have kept theirs carefully shrouded from public view is, at best, a legal fiction."

Justice WHITE dissenting.

For some 200 years—from the very founding of the Nation—the law of defamation and right of the ordinary citizen to recover for false publication injurious to his reputation have been almost exclusively the business of state courts and legislatures. Under typical state defamation law, the defamed private citizen had to prove only a false publication that would subject him to hatred, contempt, or ridicule. Given such publication, general damage to reputation was presumed, while punitive damages required proof of additional facts. The law governing the defamation of private citizens remained untouched by the First Amendment because until relatively recently, the consistent view of the Court was that libelous words constitute a class of speech wholly unprotected by the First Amendment, subject only to limited exceptions carved out since 1964.

But now, using that Amendment as the chosen instrument, the Court, in a few printed pages, has federalized major aspects of libel law by declaring unconstitutional in important respects the prevailing defamation law in all or most of the 50 States. . . .

These are radical changes in the law and severe invasions of the prerogatives of the States. They should at least be shown to be required by the First Amendment or necessitated by our present circumstances. Neither has been demonstrated. . . .

Scant, if any, evidence exists that the First Amendment was intended to abolish the common law of libel, at least to the extent of depriving ordinary citizens of meaningful redress against their defamers. . . .

[T]he law has heretofore put the risk of falsehood on the publisher where the victim is a private citizen and no grounds of special privilege are invoked. The Court would now shift this risk to the victim, even though he has done nothing to invite the calumny, is wholly innocent of fault, and is helpless to avoid his injury. I doubt that jurisprudential resistance to liability without fault is sufficient ground for employing the First Amendment to revolutionize the law of libel, and in my view, that body of legal rules poses no realistic threat to the press and its service to the public. The press today is vigorous and robust. To me, it is quite incredible to suggest that threats of libel suits from private citizens are causing the press to refrain from publishing the truth. I know of no hard facts to support that proposition, and the Court furnishes none. . . .

In any event, if the Court's principal concern is to protect the communications industry from large libel judgments, it would appear that its new requirements with respect to general and punitive damages would be ample protection. Why it also feels compelled to escalate the threshold standard of liability I cannot fathom, particularly when this will eliminate in many instances the plaintiff's possibility of securing a judicial determination that the damaging publication was indeed false, whether or not he is entitled to recover money damages. Under the Court's new rules, the plaintiff must prove not only the defamatory statement but also some degree of fault accompanying it. The publication may be wholly false and the wrong to him unjustified, but his case will nevertheless be dismissed for failure to prove negligence or other fault on the part of the publisher. I find it unacceptable to distribute the risk in this manner and force the wholly innocent victim to bear the injury: for, as between the two, the defamer is the only culpable party. It is he who circulated a falsehood that he was not required to publish.

Herbert v. Lando
441 U.S. 153, 99 S.Ct. 1635 (1979)

This case involves a libel action brought by a former military officer against CBS for a documentary on the Vietnam War. The facts are further recounted by Justice White in his opinion for the Court.

Justice WHITE delivers the opinion of the Court.

Petitioner, Anthony Herbert, is a retired Army officer who had extended war-time service in Vietnam and who received widespread media attention in 1969–1970 when he accused his superior officers of covering up reports of atrocities and other war crimes. Three years later, on February 4, 1973, respondent Columbia Broadcasting System, Inc. (CBS), broadcast a report on petitioner and his accusations. The program was produced and edited by respondent Barry Lando and was narrated by respondent Mike Wallace. Lando later published a related article in Atlantic Monthly magazine. Herbert then sued Lando, Wallace, CBS, and Atlantic Monthly for defamation. . . . In his complaint, Herbert alleged that the program and article falsely and maliciously portrayed him as a liar and a person who had made war-crimes charges to explain his relief from command, and he requested substantial damages for injury to his reputation and to the literary value of a book he had just published recounting his experiences.

Although his cause of action arose under New York State defamation law, Herbert conceded that because he was a "public figure" the First and Fourteenth Amendments precluded recovery absent proof that respondents had published a damaging falsehood "with 'actual malice'—that is, with knowledge that it was false or with reckless disregard of whether it was false or not.". . . .

In preparing to prove his case in light of these requirements, Herbert deposed Lando at length and sought an order to compel answers to a variety of questions to which response was refused on the ground that the First Amendment protected against inquiry into the state of mind of those who edit, produce or publish, and into the editorial process. . . . The District Court rejected the claim of constitutional privilege. . . .

A divided panel reversed the District Court. . . . [The appellate court] concluded that the First Amendment lent sufficient protection to the editorial processes to protect Lando from inquiry about his thoughts, opinions, and conclusions with respect to the material gathered by him and about his conversations with his editorial colleagues. The privilege not to answer was held to be absolute. We granted certiorari because of the importance of the issue involved. . . . We have concluded that the Court of Appeals misconstrued the First and Fourteenth Amendments and accordingly reverse its judgment. . . .

To be liable, the alleged defamer of public officials or of public figures must know or have reason to suspect that his publication is false. In other cases proof of some kind of fault; negligence perhaps, is essential to recovery. Inevitably, unless liability is to be completely foreclosed, the thoughts and editorial processes of the alleged defamer would be open to examination. . . .

[L]ong before *New York Times* was decided, certain qualified privileges had developed to protect a publisher from liability for libel unless the publication was made with malice. Malice was defined in numerous ways, but in general depended upon a showing that the defendant acted with improper motive. This showing in turn hinged upon the intent or purpose with which the publication was made, the belief of the defendant in the truth of his statement, or upon the ill will which the defendant might have borne towards the defendant. . . .

[C]ontrary to the views of the Court of Appeals, according an absolute privilege to the editorial process of a media defendant in a libel case is not required, authorized or presaged by our prior cases, and would substantially enhance the burden of proving actual malice. . . .

Of course, if inquiry into editorial conclusions threatens the suppression not only of information known or strongly suspected to be unreliable but also of truthful information, the issue would be quite different. But as we have said, our cases necessarily contemplate examination of the editorial process to prove the necessary awareness of probable falsehood, and if indirect proof of this element does not stifle truthful publication and is consistent with the First Amendment, as respondents seem to concede, we do not understand how direct inquiry with respect to the ultimate issue would be substantially more suspect. . . .

[I]f the publisher in fact had serious doubts about accuracy, but published nevertheless, no undue self-censorship will result from permitting the relevant inquiry. Only knowing or reckless error will be discouraged; and unless there is to be an absolute First Amendment privilege to inflict injury by knowing or reckless conduct, which respondents do not suggest, constitutional values will not be threatened.

It is also urged that frank discussion among reporters and editors will be dampened and sound editorial judgment endangered if such exchanges, oral or written, are subject to inquiry by defamation plaintiffs. We do not doubt the direct relationship between consultation and discussion on the one hand and sound decisions on the other; but whether or not there is liability for the injury, the press has an obvious interest in avoiding the infliction of harm by the publication of false information, and it is not unreasonable to expect the media to invoke whatever procedures that may be practicable and useful to that end. Moreover, given exposure to liability when there is knowing or reckless error, there is ever more reason to resort to prepublication precautions, such as a frank interchange of fact and opinion. Accordingly, we find it difficult to believe that error-avoiding procedures will be terminated or stifled simply because there is liability for culpable error and because the editorial process will itself be examined in the tiny percentage of instances in which error is claimed and litigation ensues. Nor is there sound reason to believe that editorial exchanges and the editorial process are so subject to distortion and to such recurring misunderstanding that they should be immune from examination in order to avoid erroneous judgments in defamation suits. The evidentiary burden Herbert must carry to prove at least reckless disregard for the truth is substantial indeed, and we are unconvinced that his chances of winning an undeserved verdict are such that an inquiry into what Lando learned or said during editorial process must be foreclosed. . . .

The judgment of the Court of Appeals is reversed.

Justice POWELL concurred in a separate opinion.

Justice BRENNAN dissenting in part.

The Court today rejects respondents' claim that an "editorial privilege" shields from discovery information that would reveal respondents' editorial processes. I agree with the Court that no such privilege insulates factual matters that may be sought during discovery, and that such a privilege should not shield respondents' "mental processes." I would hold, however, that the First Amendment requires predecisional communication among editors to be protected by an editorial privilege, but that this privilege must yield if a public figure plaintiff is able to demonstrate to the prima facie satisfaction of a trial judge that the libel in question constitutes defamatory falsehood. . . .

Although the various senses in which the First Amendment serves democratic values will in different contexts demand distinct emphasis and development, they share the common characteristic of being instrumental to the attainment of social ends. It is a great mistake to understand this aspect of the First Amendment solely through the filter of individual rights. . . .

In recognition of the social values served by the First Amendment, we stated that the guarantees of the First Amendment "are not for the benefit of the press so much as for the benefit of all of us. A broadly defined freedom of the press assures the maintenance of our political system and an open society." The editorial privilege claimed by respondents must be carefully analyzed to determine whether its creation would significantly further these social values recognized by our prior decisions. . . .

Through the editorial process expression is composed; to regulate the process is therefore to regulate the expression. The autonomy of the speaker is thereby compromised, whether that speaker is a large urban newspaper or an individual pamphleteer. The print and broadcast media, however, because of their large organizational structure, cannot exist without some form of editorial process. The protection of the editorial process of these institutions thus becomes a matter of particular First Amendment concern.

There is in this case, however, no direct government regulation of respondents' editorial process. But it is clear that disclosure of the editorial process of the press will increase the likelihood of large damage judgments in libel actions, and will thereby discourage participants in that editorial process. . . .

To the extent coverage of such figures becomes fearful and inhibited, to the extent the accuracy, effectiveness, and thoroughness of such coverage is undermined, the social values protected by the First Amendment suffer abridgment.

I find compelling these justifications for the existence of an editorial privilege. The values at issue are sufficiently important to justify some incidental sacrifice of evidentiary material. . . .

I fully concede that my reasoning is essentially paradoxical. For the sake of more accurate information, an editorial privilege would shield from disclosure the possible inaccuracies of the press; in the name of a more responsible press, the privilege would make more difficult of application the legal restraints by which the press is bound. The same paradox, however, inheres in the concept of an execution privilege: so as to enable the government more effectively to implement the will of the people, the people are kept in ignorance of the workings of their government. The paradox is unfortunately intrinsic to our social condition. Judgment is required to evaluate and balance these competing perspectives. . . .

In the area of libel, the balance struck by *New York Times* between the values of the First Amendment and society's interest in preventing and redressing attacks upon reputation must be preserved. This can best be accomplished if the privilege functions to shield the editorial process from general claims of damaged reputation. If, however, a public figure plaintiff is able to establish, to the prima facie satisfaction of a trial judge, that the publication at issue constitutes defamatory falsehood, the claim of damaged reputation becomes specific and demonstrable, and the editorial privilege must yield. Contrary to the suggestion of the Court, an editorial privilege so understood would not create "a substantial interference with the ability of a defamation plaintiff to establish the ingredients of malice as required by *New York Times*.". . . Requiring a public figure plaintiff to make a prima facie showing of defamatory falsehood will not constitute an undue burden, since he must eventually demonstrate these elements as part of his case-in-chief. And since editorial privilege protects only deliberative and policymaking processes and not factual material, discovery should be adequate to acquire the relevant evidence of falsehood. A public figure plaintiff will thus be able to redress attacks on his reputation, and at the same time the editorial process will be protected in all but the most necessary cases.

Justice STEWART dissenting.

As I understand the constitutional rule of *New York Times v. Sullivan* . . . inquiry into the broad "editorial process" is simply not relevant in a libel suit brought by a public figure against a publisher. And if such an inquiry is not relevant, it is not permissible. . . .

Under the constitutional restrictions imposed by *New York Times* and its progeny, a plaintiff who is a public official or public figure can recover from a publisher for a defamatory statement upon convincingly clear proof of the following elements:

(1) the statement was published by the defendant,

(2) the statement defamed the plaintiff,

(3) the defamation was untrue,

(4) and the defendant knew the defamatory statement was untrue, or published it in reckless disregard of its truth or falsity. . . .

The gravamen of such a lawsuit thus concerns that which was in fact published. What was *not* published has nothing to do with the case. And liability ultimately depends upon the publisher's state of knowledge of the falsity of what he published, not at all upon his motivation in publishing it—not at all, in other words, upon actual malice as those words are ordinarily understood. . . .

Once . . . it is firmly recognized that publisher's motivation in a case such as this is irrelevant, there is clearly no occasion for inquiry into the editorial process as conceptualized in this case. . . .

By the time this case went to the Court of Appeals, the deposition of the respondent Lando alone had lasted intermittently for over a year and had filled 2,903 pages of transcript, with an additional 240 exhibits. The plaintiff had, in Chief Judge Kauffman's words, "already discovered what Lando knew, saw, said and wrote during his investigation." That, it seems to me, was already more than sufficient. . . .

Like the Court of Appeals, I would remand this case to the District Court, but with directions to measure each of the proposed questions strictly against the constitutional criteria of *New York Times* and its progeny. Only then can it be determined whether invasion of the editorial process is truly threatened.

Justice MARSHALL dissenting.

I would foreclose discovery in defamation cases as to the substance of editorial conversation. Shielding this limited category of evidence from disclosure would be unlikely to preclude recovery by plaintiffs with valid defamation claims. For there are a variety of other means to establish deliberate or reckless disregard for the truth, such as absence of verification, inherent implausibility, obvious reasons to doubt the veracity of accuracy of information, and concessions or inconsistent statements by the defendant.

Philadelphia Newspapers, Inc. v. Hepps
475 U.S. 767, 106 S.Ct. 1558 (1986)

Maurice Hepps was the principal owner of a corporation franchising Thrifty stores, which sold primarily beer, soft drinks, and snacks. During 1975–1976, the *Philadelphia Inquirer* ran a series of articles linking Hepps to organized crime and alleging that he used those connection to influence state government. Hepps sued the publishers of the *Inquirer* in state court and, after a lengthy trial, the jury found in favor of the newspaper. The jury, however, was instructed by the judge that under Pennsylvania law Hepps bore the burden of proving that the articles were false. Hepps appealed to the Pennsylvania Supreme Court, which reversed the lower court and ordered a new trial. Based on its reading of the ruling in *Gertz v. Robert Welch, Inc.,* 418 U.S. 323 (1974) (see p. 461), the state supreme court held that burden of showing the truth of its publications rested with the newspaper. An appeal of that ruling was then made to the Supreme Court, which reversed the decision of the state supreme court.

Justice O'CONNOR delivers the opinion of the Court.

This case requires us once more to "struggl[e] . . . to define the proper accommodation between the law of defamation and the freedoms of speech and press protected by the First Amendment." *Gertz v. Robert Welch, Inc.* In *Gertz,* the Court held that a private figure who brings a suit for defamation cannot recover without some showing that the media defendant was at fault in publishing the statements at issue. Here, we hold that, at least where a newspaper publishes speech of public concern, a private-figure plaintiff cannot recover damages without also showing that the statements at issue are false. . . .

When the speech is of public concern and the plaintiff is a public official or public figure, the Constitution clearly requires the plaintiff to surmount a much higher barrier before recovering damages from a media defendant than is raised by the common law. When the speech is of public concern but the plaintiff is a private figure, as in *Gertz,* the Constitution still supplants the standards of the common law, but the constitutional requirements are, in at least some of their range, less forbidding than when the plaintiff is a public figure and the speech is of public concern. When the speech is of exclusively private concern and the plaintiff is a private figure, as in *Dun & Bradstreet,* [*Inc. v. Greenmoss Builders, Inc.,* 472 U.S. 749 (1985)], the constitutional requirements do not necessarily force any change in at least some of the features of the common-law landscape.

Our opinions to date have chiefly treated the necessary showings of fault rather than of falsity. Nonetheless, as one might expect given the language of the Court in *New York Times* [*v. Sullivan* (1964)], a public-figure plaintiff must show the falsity of the statements at issue in order to prevail on a suit for defamation. . . .

Here, as in *Gertz,* the plaintiff is a private figure and the newspaper articles are of public concern. In *Gertz*, as in *New York Times*, the common-law rule was superseded by a constitutional rule. We believe that the common law's rule on falsity—that the defendant must bear the burden of proving truth—must similarly fall here to a constitutional requirement that the plaintiff bear the burden of showing falsity, as well as fault, before recovering damages.

There will always be instances when the factfinding process will be unable to resolve conclusively whether the speech is true or false, it is in those cases that the burden of proof is dispositive. Under a rule forcing the plaintiff to bear the burden of showing falsity, there will be some cases in which plaintiffs cannot meet their burden despite the fact that the speech is in fact false. The plaintiff's suit will fail despite the fact that, in some abstract sense, the suit is meritorious. Similarly, under an alternative rule placing the burden of showing truth on defendants, there would be some cases in which defendants could not bear their burden despite the fact that the speech is in fact true. Those suits would succeed despite the fact that, in some abstract sense, those suits are unmeritorious. Under either rule, then, the outcome of the suit will sometimes be at variance with the outcome that we would desire if all speech were either demonstrably true or demonstrably false.

This dilemma stems from the fact that the allocation of the burden of proof will determine liability for some speech that is true and some that is false, but *all* of such speech is *unknowably* true or false. Because the burden of proof is the deciding factor only when the evidence is ambiguous, we cannot know how much of the speech affected by the allocation of the burden of proof is true and how much is false. . . . To ensure that true speech on matters of public concern is not deterred, we hold that the common-law presumption that defamatory speech is false cannot stand when a plaintiff seeks damages against a media defendant for speech of public concern. . . .

We recognize that requiring the plaintiff to show falsity will insulate from liability some speech that is false, but unprovably so. Nonetheless, for true speech on matters of public concern, the Court has been willing to insulate even *demonstrably* false speech from liability, and has imposed additional requirements of fault upon the plaintiff in a suit for defamation. We therefore do not break new ground here in insulating speech that is not even demonstrably false.

Justice BRENNAN, with whom Justice BLACKMUN joined, concurred.

Justice STEVENS, with whom the CHIEF JUSTICE, Justice WHITE, and Justice REHNQUIST join, dissenting.

The issue the Court resolves today will make a difference in only one category of cases—those in which a private individual can prove that he was libeled by a defendant who was at least negligent. For unless such a plaintiff can overcome the burden imposed by *Gertz v. Robert Welch, Inc.*, 418 U.S. 323 (1974), he cannot recover regardless of how the burden of proof on the issue of truth or falsity is allocated. By definition, therefore, the only litigants—and the only publishers—who will benefit from today's decision are those who act negligently or maliciously. . . .

I do not agree that our precedents require a private individual to bear the risk that a defamatory statement—uttered either with a mind toward assassinating his good name or with careless indifference to that possibility—cannot be proven false. By attaching no weight to the state's interest in protecting the private individual's good name, the Court has reached a pernicious result. . . .

In my opinion deliberate, malicious character assassination is not protected by the First Amendment to the United States Constitution. That Amendment does require the target of a defamatory statement to prove that his assailant was at fault, and I agree that it provides a constitutional shield for truthful statements. I simply do not understand, however, why a character assassin should be given an absolute license to defame by means of statements that can be neither verified nor disproven. The danger of deliberate defamation by reference to unprovable facts is not a merely speculative or hypothetical concern. Lack of knowledge about third parties, the loss of critical records, an uncertain recollection about events that occurred long ago, perhaps during a period of special stress, the absence of eyewitnesses—a host of factors—may make it impossible for an honorable person to disprove malicious gossip about his past conduct, his relatives, his friends, or his business associates. . . .

In my view, as long as publishers are protected by the requirement that the plaintiff has the burden of proving fault, there can be little, if any, basis for a concern that a significant amount of true speech will be deterred unless the private person victimized by a malicious libel can also carry the burden of proving falsity. The Court's decision trades on the good names of private individuals with little First Amendment coin to show for it.

I respectfully dissent.

Cox Broadcasting Corporation v. Cohn
420 U.S. 469, 95 S.Ct. 1029 (1975)

In August 1971, Martin Cohn's seventeen-year-old daughter was raped and died as result of the incident. Subsequently, a television report on the incident and the arrest of six youths charged with her rape and murder identified Cohn's daughter as the victim, based on police reports and other public records. Cohn, thereupon, sued the owner of the television station, Cox Broadcasting Corporation, under a Georgia privacy statute making it a misdemeanor to broadcast the name or identity of a rape victim. The trial judge rejected arguments of Cox Broadcasting Corporation that its broadcast was protected under the First and Fourteenth Amendments. On appeal, the state supreme court upheld Georgia's statute as a legitimate limitation on the First Amendment. Cox Broadcasting Corporation subsequently appealed that ruling to the Supreme Court.

Justice WHITE delivers the opinion of the Court.

The issue before us in this case is whether, consistently with the First and Fourteenth Amendments, a State may extend a cause of action for damages for invasion of privacy caused by the publication of the name of a deceased rape victim which was publicly revealed in connection with the prosecution of the crime. . . .

Georgia stoutly defends both § 26–9901 and the State's common-law privacy action challenged here. Its claims are not without force, for powerful arguments can be made, and have been made, that however it may be ultimately defined, there *is* a zone of privacy surrounding every individual, a zone within which the State may protect him from intrusion by the press, with all its attendant publicity. Indeed, the central thesis of the root article by Warren and Brandeis, The Right to Privacy, 4 Harv.L.Rev. 193, 196 (1890), was that the press was overstepping its prerogatives by publishing essentially private information and that there should be a remedy for the alleged abuses.

More compellingly, the century has experienced a strong tide running in favor of the so-called right of privacy. In 1967, we noted that "[i]t has been said that a 'right of privacy' has been recognized at common law in 30 States plus the District of Columbia and by statute in four States." *Time, Inc. v. Hill*, 385 U.S. 374 [1967].

These are impressive credentials for a right of privacy, but we should recognize that we do not have at issue here an action for the invasion of privacy involving the appropriation of one's name or photograph, a physical or other tangible intrusion into a private area, or a publication of otherwise private information that is also false although perhaps not defamatory. The version of the privacy tort now before us—termed in Georgia "the tort of public disclosure."—is that in which the plaintiff claims the right to be free from unwanted publicity about his private affairs, which, although wholly true, would be offensive to a person of ordinary sensibilities. Because the gravamen of the claimed injury is the publication of information, whether true or not, the dissemination of which is embarrassing or otherwise painful to an individual, it is here that claims of privacy most directly confront the constitutional freedoms of speech and press. The face-off is apparent, and the appellants urge upon us the broad holding that the press may not be made criminally or civilly liable for publishing information that is neither false nor misleading but absolutely accurate, however damaging it may be to reputation or individual sensibilities. . . .

In this sphere of collision between claims of privacy and those of the free press, the interests on both sides are plainly rooted in the traditions and significant concerns of our society. Rather than address the broader question whether truthful publications may ever be subjected to civil or criminal liability consistently with the First and Fourteenth Amendments, or to put it another way, whether the State may ever define and protect an area of privacy free from unwanted publicity in the press, it is appropriate to focus on the narrower interface between press and privacy that this case presents, namely, whether the State may impose sanctions on the accurate publication of the name of a rape victim obtained from public records—more specifically, from judicial records which are maintained in connection with a public prosecution and which themselves are open to public inspection. We are convinced that the State may not do so.

In the first place, in a society in which each individual has but limited time and resources with which to observe at first hand the operations of his government, he relies necessarily upon the press to bring to him in convenient form the facts of those operations. Great responsibility is accordingly placed upon the news media to report fully and accurately the proceedings of government, and official records and documents open to the public are the basic data of governmental operations. Without the information provided by the press most of us and many of our representatives would be unable to vote intelligently or to register opinions on the administration of government generally. With respect to judicial proceedings in particular, the function of the press serves to guarantee the fairness of trials and to bring to bear the beneficial effects of public scrutiny upon the administration of justice. . . .

Appellee has claimed in this litigation that the efforts of the press have infringed his right to privacy by broadcasting to the world the fact that his daughter was a rape victim. The commission of crime, prosecutions resulting from it, and judicial proceedings arising from the prosecutions, however, are without question events of legitimate concern to the public and consequently fall within the responsibility of the press to report the operations of government. . . .

The developing law surrounding the tort of invasion of privacy recognizes a privilege in the press to report the events of judicial proceedings. The Warren and Brandeis article, *supra*, noted that the proposed new right would be limited in the same manner as actions for libel and slander where such a publication was a privileged communication: "the right to privacy is not invaded by any publication made in a court of justice . . . and (at least in many jurisdictions) reports of any such proceedings would in some measure be accorded a like privilege.". . .

Thus even the prevailing law of invasion of privacy generally recognizes that the interests in privacy fade when the information involved already appears on the public record. The conclusion is compelling when viewed in terms of the First and Fourteenth Amendments and in light of the public interest in a vigorous press. The Georgia cause of action for invasion of privacy through public disclosure of the name of a rape victim imposes sanctions on pure expression—the content of a publication—and not conduct or a combination of speech and nonspeech elements that might otherwise be open to regulation or prohibition. The publication of truthful information available on the public record contains none of the indicia of those limited categories of expression, such as "fighting" words, which "are no essential part of any exposition of ideas, and are of such slight social value as a step to truth that any benefit that may be derived from them is clearly outweighed by the social interest in order and morality." *Chaplinsky v. New Hampshire*, 315 U.S. 568 (1942) (footnote omitted).

By placing the information in the public domain on official court records, the State must be presumed to have concluded that the public interest was thereby being served. Public records by their very nature are of interest to those concerned with the administration of government, and a public benefit is performed by the reporting of the true contents of the records by the media. The freedom of the press to publish that information appears to us to be of critical importance to our type of government in which the citizenry is the final judge of the proper conduct of public business. In preserving that form of government the First and Fourteenth Amendments command nothing less than that the States may not impose sanctions on the publication of truthful information contained in official court records open to public inspection.

We are reluctant to embark on a course that would make public records generally available to the media but forbid their publication if offensive to the sensibilities of the supposed reasonable man. Such a rule would make it very difficult for the media to inform citizens about the public business and yet stay within the law. The rule would invite timidity and self-censorship and very likely lead to the suppression of many items that would otherwise be published and that should be made available to the public. At the very least, the First and Fourteenth Amendments will not allow exposing the press to liability for truthfully publishing information released to the public in official court records. If there are privacy interests to be protected in judicial proceedings, the States must respond by means which avoid public documentation or other exposure of private information. Their political institutions must weigh the interests in privacy with the interests of the public to know and of the press to publish. Once true information is disclosed in public court documents open to public inspection, the press cannot be sanctioned for publishing it. In this instance as in others reliance must rest upon the judgment of those who decide what to publish or broadcast.

Appellant Wassell based his televised report upon notes taken during the court proceedings and obtained the name of the victim from the indictments handed to him at his request during a recess in the hearing. Appellee has not contended that the name was obtained in an improper fashion or that it was not on an official court document open to public inspection. Under these circumstances, the protection of freedom of the press provided by the First and Fourteenth Amendments bars the State of Georgia from making appellants' broadcast the basis of civil liability.

Reversed.

Chief Justice BURGER concurred.

Justice POWELL and Justice DOUGLAS concurred in separate opinions.

Justice REHNQUIST dissented.

D. COMMERCIAL SPEECH

In contrast with the toughening of obscenity standards in the 1970s and 1980s, the Court moved in the direction of extending greater protection to commercial speech, although not without sharp criticism from Chief Justice Rehnquist. Commercial speech involves the advertising of goods and services, such as the costs of toothpaste or attorney's fees, as well as that of corporations and businesses that aim at influencing public policy.

That commercial speech should be "less protected" than other kinds of speech was first suggested in *Valentine v. Chrestensen,*

316 U.S. 52 (1942). There the Court upheld a New York ordinance prohibiting the distribution of "commercial and business advertising matter." Lewis Chrestensen was convicted under the ordinance for distributing handbills that on one side advertised his submarine and, on the other, printed the First Amendment as a protest against the ordinance. The justices unanimously held there was no "restraint on the government as respects purely commercial advertising." It remained unclear, though, whether commercial speech was unprotected per se (like obscenity) or simply less protected, and why it fell outside of First Amendment protection—was it the commercial motive, the content, or the method of distribution?

The problems with *Valentine* became more apparent in later cases. When confronted with the issue of whether the ad, "Heed Their Rising Voices," in *New York Times v. Sullivan* (1964) (see page 453) fell under the commercial speech doctrine, Justice Brennan ducked the issue, observing that (unlike Christensen's handbill), *The New York Times* ad "communicated information, expressed opinion, recited grievances, protested claimed abuses, and sought financial support on behalf of a movement whose existence and objectives are matters of the highest public interest and concern. . . . That the *Times* was paid for publishing the advertisement is as immaterial in this connection as is the fact that newspapers and books are sold." In *New York Times v. Sullivan,* Brennan thus implied that the motive of a publisher might be used to define the scope of the First Amendment. But in *Pittsburgh Press v. Pittsburgh Commission* on Human Rights, 413 U.S. 376 (1973), the Court went the opposite way, suggesting that editorial motives may diminish a publication's status and First Amendment protection as well. There the *Pittsburgh Press* was found in violation of an ordinance against discriminatory hiring on the basis of gender, due to its carrying help-wanted advertisements in gender-designated columns. The publishers contended the First Amendment protected their editorial judgments; they had a right to decide whether to accept an ad in the first place and, once accepted, where to place it in the newspaper. A majority of the Court (with Chief Justice Burger and Justice Douglas dissenting) rejected that argument. Justice Powell, writing for the majority, found no impairment of editorial freedom and emphasized that, "The advertisements, as embroidered by their placement, signaled that the advertisers were likely to show an illegal sex preference in their hiring decisions."

In *Bigelow v. Virginia* (1976) (see page 487) the Court finally limited *Valentine,* in holding that the "commercial aspects" and "publisher's motives of financial gain" in advertisements do not "negate all First Amendment guarantees." Compare the rationale for extending First Amendment protection to commercial speech given in Justice Blackmun's opinion with the competing arguments of Justice Rehnquist in his dissenting opinion.

One year after *Bigelow*, a ban on lawyer advertising of routine legal services was struck down in *Bates v. State Bar of Arizona* (1977) (see page 491). But the Court did not end the controversy over lawyer advertising in *Bates*. *In re Primus*, 436 U.S. 412 (1978), held that the First Amendment protects lawyers who solicit clients for a nonprofit organization (there, the American Civil Liberties Union), but in *Ohralik v. Ohio State Bar Association*, 436 U.S. 447 (1978), the Court upheld disciplining an attorney for ambulance chasing and soliciting clients on a contingency basis (that is, if a lawyer wins the case for his client, he gets a percentage of the award). More recently, *In re R.M.J.*, 455 U.S. 191 (1982), reaffirmed First Amendment protection for lawyer advertising so long as it is not misleading. In *Zauderer v. Office of Disciplinary Counsel of Supreme Court of Ohio*, 471 U.S. 626 (1985), when holding that lawyers may not be disciplined for advertising in newspapers, the Court ruled that advertisements for contingency-fee services must disclose the difference between legal fees and costs (the latter are paid by the client regardless of the outcome of a case). *Shapero v. Kentucky Bar Association*, 486 U.S. 466 (1988), held that direct-mail solicitation by an attorney was protected First Amendment-commercial speech, and that a state bar association could not prevent the lawyer from soliciting clients in this way. With an unsigned opinion in *Oring v. California*, 489 U.S. 1092 (1989), however, the Rehnquist Court let stand a California ban on lawyer advertisements using client testimonials and endorsements.

The Court's expansion of First Amendment protection for commercial speech based on a public interest rationale came with strong opposition from Chief Justice Rehnquist. As Justice Blackmun explained in *Virginia State Board of Pharmacy v. Virginia Citizen Consumer Council*, 425 U.S. 748 (1976), "So long as we preserve a predominantly free enterprise economy, the allocation of our resources in large measure will be made through numerous private economic decisions. It is a matter of public interest that those decisions in the aggregate, be intelligent and well informed. To this end, the free flow of commercial information is indispensible." But, dissenting from that ruling, Rehnquist retorted, "I cannot distinguish between the public's right to know the price of drugs and its right to know the price of title searches or physical examinations or other professional services for which standardized fees are charged."

Although Rehnquist failed to carry the Court, he massed a bare majority in *Posados de Puerto Rico v. Tourism Company of*

Puerto Rico (1986) (see page 498), upholding Puerto Rico's ban on advertisements for casino gambling. Whether the Court now moves in the direction of Rehnquist's position on commercial speech remains to be seen. In *Meyer v. Grant,* 486 U.S. 414 (1988), the Court struck down a Colorado law prohibiting paid circulators of initiative and referendum petitions, advocating a state constitutional amendment to deregulate trucking. In finding the law to violate the First Amendment, Justice Stevens, writing for a unanimous Court, declared that the state's reliance on Rehnquist's opinion in *Posados* was misplaced.

DEVELOPMENT OF LAW

Other Important Rulings on Commercial Speech and the First Amendment

Case	Vote	Holding
Virginia State Board of Pharmacy v. Virginia Citizen Consumer Council, 425 U.S. 748 (1976)	8:1	Upheld advertising of prescription drug prices.
First National Bank of Boston v. Bellotti, 435 U.S. 765 (1978)	5:4	Held corporations enjoy First Amendment protection in publicizing their views on an income tax referendum.
Friedman v. Rogers, 440 U.S. 1 (1979)	7:2	Upheld ban on advertising of optometrists under trade names.
Consolidated Edison Company v. Public Service Commission, 447 U.S. 530 (1980)	7:2	Upheld insertion of handbills on nuclear energy with billing statements.
Central Hudson v. Public Service Commission, 447 U.S. 557 (1980)	8:1	Upheld promotional ads of a public utility and electrical monopoly.
Metromedia, Inc. v. San Diego, 453 U.S. 490 (1981)	6:3	Held the city must explain ban on commercial billboards when noncommercial billboards are permitted.
Bolger v. Youngs Drug Products Corporation, 463 U.S. 60 (1983)	9:0	Held unconstitutional a statute barring unsolicited mailings of ads for contraceptives.
Pacific Gas & Electric v. Public Utilities Commission of California, 475 U.S. 1 (1986)	5:4	A state may not force a public utility company to include in its newsletter the material of a third party.

Case	Vote	Holding
San Francisco Arts & Athletics, Inc. (SFAA) v. United States Olympic Committee, 483 U.S. 522 (1987)	5:4	Held that the SFAA was prohibited from promoting "Gay Olympic Games" because the use of the word "Olympic" was under the Lanham Act exclusively reserved for the United States Olympic Committee.
Board of Trustees of the State University of New York v. Fox, 109 S.Ct. 3028 (1989)	6:3	Held that officials of a university did not violate students' First Amendment free speech rights by banning Tupperware parties in dormitories; commercial speech need not meet the least drastic means test that applies when reviewing regulations of noncommercial speech.
Peel v. Attorney Registration and Disciplinary Commission of Illinois, 110 S.Ct. 2281 (1990)	5:4	In a plurality opinion, Justice Stevens held that Illinois had improperly censured an attorney for printing on his letterhead that he was a certified civil trial specialist, because the letterhead was nondeceptive and protected commercial speech. Justices White, O'Connor, and Scalia, along with Chief Justice Rehnquist, dissented.

SELECTED BIBLIOGRAPHY

Baker, C. Edwin. "Commercial Speech: A Problem in the Theory of Freedom." 62 *Iowa Law Review* 1 (1976).

Colloquy. "The First Amendment and the Paratroopers' Paradox." 68 *Texas Law Review* 1087 (1990).

Jackson, Thomas H., and Jeffries, John, Jr. "Commercial Speech: Economic Due Process and the First Amendment." 65 *Virginia Law Review* 1 (1979).

Bigelow v. Virginia
421 U.S. 809, 95 S.Ct. 2222 (1975)

Justice Blackmun in his opinion for the Court sets forth the facts in this case involving a Virginia State prohibition against advertising the availability of abortion services and clinics, even those in other states.

Justice BLACKMUN delivered the opinion of the Court.

An advertisement carried in appellant's newspaper led to his conviction for a violation of a Virginia statute that made it a misdemeanor, by the sale or circulation of any publication, to encourage or prompt the procuring of an abortion. The issue here is whether the editor-appellant's First Amendment rights were unconstitutionally abridged by the statute. . . .

The Virginia Weekly was a newspaper published by the Virginia Weekly Associates of Charlottesville. . . . Jeffrey C. Bigelow, was a director and the managing editor and responsible officer of the newspaper.

On February 8, 1971, the Weekly's Vol. V, No. 6, was published and circulated under the direct responsibility of the appellant. On page 2 of that issue was the following advertisement:

> "UNWANTED PREGNANCY
> LET US HELP YOU
> Abortions are now legal in New York
> There are no residency requirements.
> FOR IMMEDIATE PLACEMENT IN
> ACCREDITED HOSPITALS AND
> CLINICS AT LOW COST
> Contact
> WOMEN'S PAVILION
> 515 Madison Avenue
> New York, N.Y. 10022
> or call any time
> (212) 371–6670 or (212) 371–6650
> AVAILABLE 7 DAYS A WEEK
> STRICTLY CONFIDENTIAL. We
> will make all arrangements for you
> and help you with information and
> counseling."

It is to be observed that the advertisement announced that the Women's Pavilion of New York City would help women with unwanted pregnancies to obtain "immediate placement in accredited hospitals and clinics at low cost" and would "make all arrangements" on a "strictly confidential" basis; that it offered "information and counseling"; that it gave the organization's address and telephone numbers; and that it stated that abortions "are now legal in New York" and there "are no residency requirements." Although the advertisement did not contain the name of any licensed physician, the "placement" to which it referred was to "accredited hospitals and clinics."

Bigelow was charged with [and convicted for] violating . . . [a statute that provided]:

"If any person, by publication, lecture, advertisement, or by the sale or circulation of any publication, or in any other manner, encourage or prompt the procuring of abortion or miscarriage, he shall be guilty of a misdemeanor."

[The Supreme Court of Virginia upheld Bigelow's conviction.] . . .

The central assumption made by the Supreme Court of Virginia was that the First Amendment guarantees of speech and press are inapplicable to paid commercial advertisements. Our cases, however, clearly establish that speech is not stripped of First Amendment protection merely because it appears in that form. . . .

The appellee, as did the Supreme Court of Virginia, relies on *Valentine v. Chrestensen,* 316 U.S. 52 (1942), where a unanimous Court, in a brief opinion, sustained an ordinance which had been interpreted to ban the distribution of a handbill advertising the exhibition of a submarine. The handbill solicited customers to tour the ship for a fee. The promoter-advertiser had first attempted to distribute a single-faced handbill consisting only of the advertisement, and was denied permission to do so. He then had printed, on the reverse side of the handbill, a protest against official conduct refusing him the use of wharfage facilities. The Court found that the message of asserted "public interest" was appended solely for the purpose of evading the ordinance and therefore did not constitute an "exercise of the freedom of communicating information and disseminating opinion.". . .

But the holding is distinctly a limited one: the ordinance was upheld as a reasonable regulation of the manner in which commercial advertising could be distributed. The fact that it had the effect of banning a particular handbill does not mean that *Chrestensen* is authority for the proposition that all statutes regulating commercial advertising are immune from constitutional challenge. The case obviously does not support any sweeping proposition that advertising is unprotected *per se.*

This Court's cases decided since *Chrestensen* clearly demonstrate as untenable any reading of that case that would give it so broad an effect. In *New York Times Co. v. Sullivan,* [376 U.S. 254 (1964)], a city official instituted a civil libel action against four clergymen and the New York Times. The suit was based on an advertisement carried in the newspaper criticizing police action against members of the civil rights movement and soliciting contributions for the movement. The Court held that this advertisement, although containing factually erroneous defamatory content, was entitled to the same degree of constitutional protection as ordinary speech. . . .

The principle that commercial advertising enjoys a degree of First Amendment protection was reaffirmed in *Pittsburgh Press Co. v. Human Rel. Comm'n,* 413 U.S. 376 (1973). There, the Court, although divided sustained an ordinance that had been construed to forbid newspapers to carry help-wanted advertisements in sex-designated columns except where based upon a bona fide occupational exemption. The Court did describe the advertisements at issue as "classic examples of commercial speech," for each was "no more than a proposal of possible employment." But the Court indicated that the advertisements would have received some degree of First Amendment protection if the commercial proposal had been legal. . . .

The legitimacy of appellant's First Amendment claim in the present case is demonstrated by the important differences between the advertisement presently at issue and those involved in *Chrestensen* and in *Pittsburgh Press.* The advertisement published in appellant's newspaper did more than simply propose a commercial transaction. It contained factual material of clear "public interest." Portions of its message, most prominently the lines, "Abortions are now legal in New York. There are no residency requirements," involve the exercise of the freedom of communicating information and disseminating opinion.

Viewed in its entirety, the advertisement conveyed information of potential interest and value to a diverse audience—not only to readers possibly in need of the services offered, but also to those with a general curiosity about, or genuine interest in, the subject matter or the law of another State and its development, and to readers seeking reform in Virginia. . . .

Advertising, like all public expression, may be subject to reasonable regulation that serve a legitimate public interest. To the extent that commercial activity is subject to regulation, the relationship of speech to that activity may be one factor, among others, to be considered in weighing the First Amendment interest against the governmental interest alleged. Advertising is not thereby stripped of all First Amendment protection. The relationship of speech to the marketplace of products or of services does not make it valueless in the marketplace of ideas. . . .

If . . . this statute were upheld . . . Virginia might exert the power sought here over a wide variety of national publications or interstate newspapers carrying advertisements similar to the one that appeared in Bigelow's newspaper or containing articles on the general subject matter to which the advertisement referred. Other States might do the same. The burdens thereby imposed on publications would impair, perhaps severely, their proper functioning. We know from experience that "liberty of the press is in peril as soon as the government tries to compel what is to go into a newspaper." The policy of the First Amendment favors dissemination of information and opinion, and "[t]he guarantees of freedom of speech and press were not designed to prevent "the censorship of the press merely, but any action of the government by means of which it might prevent such free and general discussion of public matters as seems absolutely essential. . . .

We conclude that Virginia could not apply Va.Code Ann. § 18.1–63 (1960), as it read in 1971, to appellant's publication of the advertisement in question without unconstitutionally infringing upon his First Amendment rights. The judgment of the Supreme Court of Virginia is therefore reversed.

Justice REHNQUIST, with whom Justice WHITE joins, dissenting.

Since the Court concludes, apparently from two lines of the advertisement, that it conveyed information of value to those interested in the "subject matter or the law of another State and its development" and to those "seeking reform in Virginia," and since the ad relates to abortion, elevated to constitutional stature by the Court, it concludes that this advertisement is entitled to something more than the limited constitutional protection traditionally accorded commercial advertising. Although recognizing that "[a]dvertising, like all public expression, may be subject to reasonable regulation that serves a legitimate public interest," the Court for reasons not entirely clear to me concludes that Virginia's interest is of "little, if any, weight.". . .

If the Court's decision does, indeed, turn upon its conclusion that the advertisement here in question was protected by the First and Fourteenth Amendments, the subject of the advertisement ought to make no difference. It will not do to say, as the Court does, that this advertisement conveyed information about the "subject matter or the law of another State and its development" to those "seeking reform in Virginia," and that it related to abortion, as if these factors somehow put it on a different footing from other commercial advertising. This was a proposal to furnish services on a commercial basis, and since we have always refused to distinguish for First Amendment purposes on the basis of content, it is no different from an advertisement for a bucket shop operation or a Ponzi scheme which has its headquarters in New York. If Virginia may not regulate advertising of commercial abortion agencies because of the interest of those seeking to reform Virginia's abortion laws, it is difficult to see why it is not likewise precluded from regulating advertising for an out-of-state bucket shop on the ground that such information might be of interest to those interested in repealing Virginia's "blue sky" laws. . . .

[T]he advertisement appears to me, as it did to the courts below, to be a classic commercial proposition directed toward the exchange of services rather than the exchange of ideas. . . . Whatever slight factual content the advertisement may contain and whatever expression of opinion may be laboriously drawn from it does not alter its predominantly commercial content. . . . I am unable to perceive any relationship between the instant advertisement and that for example in issue in *New York Times Co. v. Sullivan.* . . .

Assuming *arguendo* that this advertisement is something more than a normal commercial proposal, I am unable to see why Virginia does not have a legitimate public interest in its regulation. The Court apparently concedes . . . that the States have a strong interest in the prevention of commercial advertising in the health field—both in order to maintain high ethical standards in the medical profession and to protect the public from unscrupulous practices.

Without denying the power of either New York or Virginia to prohibit advertising such as that in issue where both publication of the advertised activity and the activity itself occur in the same State, the Court instead focuses on the multistate nature of this transaction. . . .

The source of this rigid territorial limitation on the power of the States in our federal system to safeguard the health and welfare of their citizens is not revealed. . . . [W]e have consistently recognized that irrespective of a State's power to regulate extraterritorial commercial transactions in which its citizens participate it retains an independent power to regulate the business of commercial solicitation and advertising within its borders.

Were the Court's statements taken literally, they would presage a standard of the lowest common denominator for commercial ethics and business conduct. . . . Loan sharks might well choose States with unregulated small loan industries, luring the unwary with immune commercial advertisements. And imagination would place the only limit on the use of such a "no-man's land" together with artificially created territorial contacts to bilk the public and circumvent long-established state schemes of regulation.

Bates v. State Bar of Arizona
433 U.S. 350, 97 S.Ct. 2691 (1977)

This case involves the application of the commercial speech doctrine to advertisements for legal services. Justice Blackmun further sets forth the facts in his opinion for the Court.

Justice BLACKMUN delivers the opinion of the Court.

As part of its regulation of the Arizona Bar, the Supreme Court of that State has imposed and enforces a disciplinary rule that restricts advertising by attorneys. This case presents [the issue of] . . . whether the operation of the rule violates the First Amendment, made applicable to the State through the Fourteenth. . . .

Appellants John R. Bates and Van O'Steen are attorneys licensed to practice law in the State of Arizona. . . .

In March 1974, [they] . . . opened a law office, which they call a "legal clinic," in Phoenix. Their aim was to provide legal services at modest fees to persons of moderate income who did not qualify for governmental legal aid.

In order to achieve this end, they would accept only routine matters, such as uncontested divorces, uncontested adoptions, simple personal bankruptcies, and changes of name, for which costs could be kept down by extensive use of paralegals, automatic typewriting equipment, and standardized forms and office procedures. More complicated cases, such as contested divorces, would not be accepted. Because appellants set their prices so as to have a relatively low return on each case they handled, they depended on substantial volume.

After conducting their practice in this manner for two years, appellants concluded that their practice and clinical concept could not survive unless the availability of legal services at low cost was advertised and in particular, fees were advertised. . . .

Last Term, in *Virginia Pharmacy Board v. Virginia Consumer Council*, 425 U.S. 748 (1976), the Court considered the validity under the First Amendment of a Virginia statute declaring that a pharmacist was guilty of "unprofessional conduct" if he advertised prescription drug prices. The pharmacist would then be subject to a monetary penalty or the suspension or revocation of his license. The statute thus effectively prevented the advertising of prescription drug price information. We recognized that the pharmacist who desired to advertise did not wish to report any particularly newsworthy fact or to comment on any cultural, philosophical, or political subject; his desired communication was characterized simply: " 'I will sell you the X prescription drug at the Y price.' " Nonetheless, we held that commercial speech of that kind was entitled to the protection of the First Amendment. . . .

[A] consideration of competing interests reinforced our view that such speech should not be withdrawn from protection merely because it proposed a mundane commercial transaction. Even though the speaker's interest is largely economic, the Court has protected such speech in certain contexts. The listener's interest is substantial: the consumer's concern for the free-flow of commercial speech often may be far keener than his concern for urgent political dialogue. Moreover, significant societal interests are served by such speech. Advertising, though entirely commercial, may often carry information of import to significant issues of the day. And commercial speech serves to inform the public of the availability, nature, and prices of products and services, and thus performs an indispensable role in the allocation of resources in a free enterprise system. In short, such speech serves individual and societal interests in assuring informed and reliable decision-making. . . .

The heart of the dispute before us today is whether lawyers also may constitutionally advertise the *prices* at which certain routine services will be performed. Numerous justifications are proffered for the restriction of such price advertising. We consider each in turn:

1. The Adverse Effect on Professionalism. . . . The key to professionalism, it is argued, is the sense of pride that involvement in the discipline generates. It is claimed that price advertising will bring about commercialization, which will undermine the attorney's sense of dignity and self-worth. . . . Advertising is also said to erode the client's trust in his attorney: once the client perceives that the lawyer is motivated by profit, his confidence that the attorney is acting out of a commitment to the client's welfare is jeopardized. And advertising is said to tarnish the dignified public image of the profession. . . .

At its core, the argument presumes that attorneys must conceal from themselves and from their clients the real-life fact that lawyers earn their livelihood at the bar. We suspect that few attorneys engage in such self-deception.

Moreover, the assertion that advertising will diminish the attorney's reputation in the community is open to question. Bankers and engineers advertise, and yet these professions are not regarded as undignified. . . .

2. The Inherently Misleading Nature of Attorney Advertising. It is argued that advertising of legal services inevitably will be misleading (a) because such services are so individualized with regard to content and quality as to prevent informed comparison on the basis of an advertisement, (b) because the consumer of legal services is unable to determine in advance just what services he needs, and (c) because advertising by attorneys will highlight irrelevant factors and fail to show the relevant factor of skill.

We are not persuaded that restrained professional advertising by lawyers inevitably will be misleading. Although many services performed by attorneys are indeed unique, it is doubtful that any attorney would or could advertise fixed prices for services of that type. The only services that lend themselves to advertising are the routine ones: the uncontested divorce, the simple adoption, the uncontested personal bankruptcy, the change of name, and the like—the very services advertised by appellants. . . .

The second component of the argument—that advertising ignores the diagnostic role—fares little better. It is unlikely that many people go to an attorney merely to ascertain if they have a clean bill of legal health. Rather, attorneys are likely to be employed to perform specific tasks. . . .

The third component is not without merit: advertising does not provide a complete foundation on which to select an attorney. But it seems peculiar to deny the consumer, on the ground that the information is incomplete, at least some of the relevant information needed to reach an informed decision. The alternative— the prohibition of advertising—serves only to restrict the information that flows to consumers. . . .

3. The Adverse Effect on the Administration of Justice. . . . Advertising, it is argued, serves to encourage the assertion of legal rights in the courts, thereby undesirably unsettling societal repose. . . .

But advertising by attorneys is not an unmitigated source of harm to the administration of justice. It may offer great benefits. Although advertising might increase the use of the judicial machinery, we cannot accept the notion that it is always better for a person to suffer a wrong silently than to redress it by legal action. As the bar acknowledges, "the middle 70% of our population is not being reached or served adequately by the legal profession.". . . Among the reasons for this underutilization is fear of the cost, and an inability to locate a suitable lawyer. . . . Advertising can help to solve this acknowledged problem: advertising is the traditional mechanism in a free-market economy for a supplier to inform a potential purchaser of the availability and terms of exchange. . . .

4. The Undesirable Economic Effects of Advertising. It is claimed that advertising will increase the overhead costs of the profession, and that these costs then will be passed along to consumers in the form of increased fees. Moreover, it is claimed that the additional cost of practice will create a substantial entry barrier, deterring or preventing young attorneys from penetrating the market and entrenching the position of the bar's established members.

These two arguments seem dubious at best. Neither distinguishes lawyers from others, and neither appears relevant to the First Amendment. . . .

5. The Adverse Effect of Advertising on the Quality of Service. It is argued that the attorney may advertise a given "package" of service at a set price, and will be inclined to provide, by indiscriminate use, the standard package regardless of whether it fits the client's needs.

Restraints on advertising, however, are an ineffective way of deterring shoddy work. An attorney who is inclined to cut quality will do so regardless of the rule on advertising. And the advertisement of a standardized fee does not necessarily mean that the services offered are undesirably standardized. Indeed, the assertion that an attorney who advertises a standard fee will cut quality is substantially undermined by the fixed fee schedule of appellee's own prepaid Legal Services Program. Even if advertising leads to the creation of "legal clinics" like that of appellants'—clinics that emphasize standardized procedures for routine problems—it is possible that such clinics will improve service by reducing the likelihood of error.

6. *The Difficulties of Enforcement.* Finally, it is argued that the wholesale restriction is justified by the problems of enforcement if any other course is taken. Because the public lacks sophistication in legal matters, it may be particularly susceptible to misleading or deceptive advertising by lawyers. . . .

It is at least somewhat incongruous for the opponents of advertising to extol the virtues and altruism of the legal profession at one point, and, at another, to assert that its members will seize the opportunity to mislead and distort. We suspect that, with advertising, most lawyers will behave as they always have: they will abide by their solemn oaths to uphold the integrity and honor of their profession and of the legal system. For every attorney who overreaches through advertising, there will be thousands of others who will be candid and honest and straightforward. And, of course, it will be in the latters' interest, as in other cases of misconduct at the bar, to assist in weeding out those few who abuse their trust.

In sum, we are not persuaded that any of the proffered justifications rises to the level of an acceptable reason for the suppression of all advertising by attorneys. . . .

In holding that advertising by attorneys may not be subjected to blanket suppression, and that the advertisement at issue is protected, we, of course, do not hold that advertising by attorneys may not be regulated in any way. We mention some of the clearly permissible limitations on advertising not foreclosed by our holding.

Advertising that is false, deceptive, or misleading of course is subject to restraint. . . .

[W]e recognize that many of the problems in defining the boundary between deceptive and nondeceptive advertising remain to be resolved, and we expect that the bar will have a special role to play in assuring that advertising by attorneys flows both freely and cleanly.

As with other varieties of speech, it follows as well that there may be reasonable restrictions on the time, place, and manner of advertising. Advertising concerning transactions that are themselves illegal obviously may be suppressed. And the special problems of advertising on the electronic broadcast media will warrant special consideration. . . .

The constitutional issue in this case is only whether the State may prevent the publication in a newspaper of appellants' truthful advertisement concerning the availability and terms of routine legal services. We rule simply that the flow of such information may not be restrained, and we therefore hold the present application of the disciplinary rule against appellants to be violative of the First Amendment.

Chief Justice BURGER concurring in part and dissenting in part.

To be sure, the public needs information concerning attorneys, their work and their fees. At the same time, the public needs protection from the unscrupulous or the incompetent practitioner anxious to prey on the uninformed. It seems to me that these twin goals can best be served by permitting the organized bar to experiment with, and perfect programs which would announce to the public the probable *range* of fees for specifically defined services and thus give putative clients some idea of potential cost liability when seeking out legal assistance. However, even such programs should be confined to the known and knowable, *e. g.,* the truly "routine" uncontested divorce which is defined to exclude any dispute over alimony, property rights, child custody or support, and should make clear to the public that the actual fee charged in any given case will vary according to the individual circumstances involved.

Justice POWELL, with whom Justice STEWART joins, concurring in part and dissenting in part.

I cannot join the Court's holding that under the First Amendment "truthful" newspaper advertising of a lawyer's prices for "routine legal services" may not be restrained. . . . [I]t is clear that within undefined limits today's decision will effect profound changes in the practice of law, viewed for centuries as a learned profession. The supervisory power of the courts over members of the bar, as officers of the courts, and the authority of the respective States to oversee the regulation of the profession have been weakened. Although the Court's opinion professes to be framed narrowly, and its reach is subject to future clarification, the holding is explicit and expansive with respect to the advertising of undefined "routine legal services." In my view, this result is neither required by the First Amendment, nor in the public interest. . . .

Even the briefest reflection on the tasks for which lawyers are trained and the variation among the services they perform should caution against facile assumptions that legal services can be classified into the routine and the unique. In most situations it is impossible—both for the client and the lawyer—to identify with reasonable accuracy in advance the nature and scope of problems that may be encountered even when handling a matter that at the outset seems routine. Neither quantitative nor qualitative measurement of the service actually needed is likely to be feasible in advance. . . .

The area into which the Court now ventures has, until today, largely been left to self-regulation by the profession within the framework of canons or standards of conduct prescribed by the respective States and enforced where necessary by the courts. . . .

In this context, the Court's imposition of hard and fast constitutional rules as to price advertising is neither required by precedent nor likely to serve the public interest. One of the great virtues of federalism is the opportunity it affords for experimentation and innovation, with freedom to discard or amend that which proves unsuccessful or detrimental to the public good. The constitutionalizing—indeed the affirmative encouraging—of competitive price advertising of specified legal services will substantially inhibit the experimentation that has been underway and also will limit the control heretofore exercised over lawyers by the respective States.

Justice REHNQUIST dissenting.

I continue to believe that the First Amendment speech provision, long regarded by this Court as a sanctuary for expressions of public importance or intellectual interest, is demeaned by invocation to protect advertisements of goods and services. I would hold quite simply that the appellants' advertisement, however truthful or reasonable it may be, is not the sort of expression that the Amendment was adopted to protect. . . .

[O]nce the Court took the first step down the "slippery slope" in *Virginia Pharmacy Board*, [*v. Virginia Citizen Consumer Council*, 425 U.S. 748 (1976)], the possibility of understandable and workable differentiations between protected speech and unprotected speech in the field of advertising large evaporated. Once the exception of commercial speech from the protection of the First Amendment which had been established by *Valentine v. Chrestensen*, [316 U.S. 52 (1942)], was abandoned, the shift to case-by-case adjudication of First Amendment claims of advertisers was a predictable consequence. . . .

The *Valentine* distinction was constitutionally sound and practically workable, and I am still unwilling to take even one step down the slippery slope away from it.

Posadas de Puerto Rico Associates v. Tourism Company of Puerto Rico
479 U.S. 328, 106 S.Ct. 2968 (1986)

Posadas de Puerto Rico Associates and Condado Holiday Inn, operators of a gambling casino, sought a declaratory judgment that Puerto Rico's statute and regulations restricting the advertising of casino gambling to residents of Puerto Rico violated their First Amendment rights. The Puerto Rico Superior Court narrowly construed the statute and upheld its restrictions on the advertising of casino gambling. After another appeal to that court was dismissed, an appeal was made to the Supreme Court, which granted review.

Justice REHNQUIST delivers the opinion of the Court.

In this case we address the facial constitutionality of a Puerto Rico statute and regulations restricting advertising of casino gambling aimed at the residents of Puerto Rico. . . . Appellant sought a declaratory judgment that the statute and regulations, both facially and as applied by the Tourism Company, impermissibly suppressed commercial speech in violation of the First Amendment and the equal protection and due process guarantees of the United States Constitution. . . .

In 1948, the Puerto Rico Legislature legalized certain forms of casino gambling. The Games of Chance Act of 1948, Act No. 221 of May 15, 1948 (Act), authorized the playing of roulette, dice, and card games in licensed "gambling rooms." § 2, codified, as amended, at P.R.Laws Ann., Tit. 15, § 71 (1972). Bingo and slot machines were later added to the list of authorized games of chance under the Act. . . . The Act also provided that "[n]o gambling room shall be permitted to advertise or otherwise offer their facilities to the public of Puerto Rico.". . .

Because this case involves the restriction of pure commercial speech which does "no more than propose a commercial transaction," *Virginia Pharmacy Board v. Virginia Citizens Consumer Council, Inc.*, 425 U.S. 748 (1976), our First Amendment analysis is guided by the general principles identified in *Central Hudson Gas & Electric Corp. v. Public Service Comm'n*, 447 U.S. 557 (1980). See *Zauderer v. Office of Disciplinary Counsel*, 471 U.S. 626 (1985). Under *Central Hudson*, commercial speech receives a limited form of First Amendment protection so long as it concerns a lawful activity and is not misleading or fraudulent. Once it is determined that the First Amendment applies to the particular kind of commercial speech at issue, then the speech may be restricted only if the government's interest in doing so is substantial, the restrictions directly advance the government's asserted interest, and the restrictions are no more extensive than necessary to serve that interest. . . .

The particular kind of commercial speech at issue here, namely, advertising of casino gambling aimed at the residents of Puerto Rico, concerns a lawful activity and is not misleading or fraudulent, at least in the abstract. We must therefore proceed to the three remaining steps of the *Central Hudson* analysis in order to determine whether Puerto Rico's advertising restrictions run afoul of the First Amendment. The first of these three steps involves an assessment of the strength of the government's interest in restricting the speech. The interest at stake in this case, as determined by the Superior Court, is the reduction of demand for casino gambling by the residents of Puerto Rico. Appellant acknowledged the existence of this interest in its February 24, 1982, letter to the Tourism Company. See App. to Juris. Statement 2h ("The legislators wanted the tourists to flock to the casinos to gamble, but not our own people"). The Tourism Company's brief before this Court explains the legislature's belief that "[e]xcessive casino gambling among local residents . . . would produce serious harmful effects on the health, safety and welfare of the Puerto Rican citizens, such as the disruption of moral and cultural patterns, the increase in local crime, the fostering of prostitution, the development of corruption, and the infiltration of organized crime." These are some of the very same concerns, of course, that have motivated the vast majority of the 50 States to prohibit casino gambling. We have no difficulty in concluding that the Puerto Rico Legislature's interest in the health, safety, and welfare of its citizens constitutes a "substantial" governmental interest. Cf. *Renton v. Playtime Theatres, Inc.*[475 U.S. 41] (1986) (city has substantial interest in "preserving the quality of life in the community at large").

The last two steps of the *Central Hudson* analysis basically involve a consideration of the "fit" between the legislature's ends and the means chosen to accomplish those ends. Step three asks the question whether the challenged restrictions on commercial speech "directly advance" the government's asserted interest. In the instant case, the answer to this question is clearly "yes.". . .

Appellant argues, however, that the challenged advertising restrictions are underinclusive because other kinds of gambling such as horse racing, cockfighting, and the lottery may be advertised to the residents of Puerto Rico. Appellant's argument is misplaced for two reasons. First, whether other kinds of gambling are advertised in Puerto Rico or not, the restrictions on advertising of casino gambling "directly advance" the legislature's interest in reducing demand for games of chance. . . . Second, the legislature's interest, as previously identified, is not necessarily to reduce demand for all games of chance, but to reduce demand for casino gambling. According to the Superior Court, horse racing, cock-fighting, "picas," or small games of chance at fiestas, and the lottery "have been traditionally part of the Puerto Rican's roots," so that "the legislator could have been more flexible than in authorizing more sophisticated games which are not so widely sponsored by the people." In other words, the legislature felt that for Puerto Ricans the risks associated with casino gambling were significantly greater than those associated with the more traditional kinds of gambling in Puerto Rico. In our view, the legislature's separate classification of casino gambling, for purposes of the advertising ban, satisfies the third step of the *Central Hudson* analysis.

We also think it clear beyond peradventure that the challenged statute and regulations satisfy the fourth and last step of the *Central Hudson* analysis, namely, whether the restrictions on commercial speech are no more extensive than necessary to serve the government's interest. . . .

In short, we conclude that the statute and regulations at issue in this case, as construed by the Superior Court, pass muster under each prong of the *Central Hudson* test. We therefore hold that the Supreme Court of Puerto Rico properly rejected appellant's First Amendment claim.

Appellant argues, however, that the challenged advertising restrictions are constitutionally defective under our decisions in *Carey v. Population Services Int'l*, 431 U.S. 678 (1977), and *Bigelow v. Virginia*, 421 U.S. 809 (1975). In *Carey*, this Court struck down a ban on any "advertisement or display" of contraceptives, and in *Bigelow*, we reversed a criminal conviction based on the advertisement of an abortion clinic. We think appellant's argument ignores a crucial distinction between the *Carey* and *Bigelow* decisions and the instant case. In *Carey* and *Bigelow*, the underlying conduct that was the subject of the advertising restrictions was constitutionally protected and could not have been prohibited by the State. Here, on the other hand, the Puerto Rico Legislature surely could have prohibited casino gambling by the residents of Puerto Rico altogether. In our view, the greater power to completely ban casino gambling necessarily includes the lesser power to ban advertising of casino gambling, and *Carey* and *Bigelow* are hence inapposite.

Appellant also makes the related argument that, having chosen to legalize casino gambling for residents of Puerto Rico, the First Amendment prohibits the legislature from using restrictions on advertising to accomplish its goal of reducing demand for such gambling. We disagree. In our view, appellant has the argument backwards. As we noted in the preceding paragraph, it is precisely *because* the government could have enacted a wholesale prohibition of the underlying conduct that it is permissible for the government to take the less intrusive step of allowing the conduct, but reducing the demand through restrictions on advertising. It would surely be a Pyrrhic victory for casino owners such as appellant to gain recognition of a First Amendment right to advertise their casinos to the residents of Puerto Rico, only to thereby force the legislature into banning casino gambling by residents altogether. It would just as surely be a strange constitutional doctrine which would concede to the legislature the authority to totally ban a product or activity, but deny to the legislature the authority to forbid the stimulation of demand for the product or activity through advertising on behalf of those who would profit from such increased demand. Legislative regulation of products or activities deemed harmful, such as cigarettes, alcoholic beverages, and prostitution, has varied from outright prohibition on the one hand, see, *e.g.,* Cal. Penal Code Ann. § 647(b) (West Supp. 1986) (prohibiting soliciting or engaging in act of prostitution), to legalization of the product or activity with restrictions on stimulation of its demand on the other hand, see, *e.g.,* Nev.Rev.Stat. §§ 244.345(1), (8) (1986) (authorizing licensing of houses of prostitution except in counties with more than 250,000 population), §§ 201.430, 201.440 (prohibiting advertising of houses of prostitution "[i]n any public theater, on the public streets of any city or town, or on any public highway," or "in [a] place of business"). To rule out the latter, intermediate kind of response would require more than we find in the First Amendment. . . .

For the foregoing reasons, the decision of the Supreme Court of Puerto Rico that, as construed by the Superior Court, § 8 of the Games of Chance Act of 1948 and the implementing regulations do not facially violate the First Amendment or the due process or equal protection guarantees of the Constitution, is affirmed.

Justice BRENNAN, with whom Justice MARSHALL and Justice BLACKMUN join, dissenting.

I see no reason why commercial speech should be afforded less protection than other types of speech where, as here, the government seeks to suppress commercial speech in order to deprive consumers of accurate information concerning lawful activity. Commercial speech is considered to be different from other kinds of protected expression because advertisers are particularly well suited to evaluate "the accuracy of their messages and the lawfulness of the underlying activity," *Central Hudson,* and because "commercial speech, the offspring of economic self-interest, is a hardy breed of expression that is not 'particularly susceptible to being crushed by overbroad regulation.'" These differences, we have held, "justify a more permissive approach to regulation of the manner of commercial speech for the purpose of protecting consumers from deception or coercion, and these differences explain why doctrines designed to prevent 'chilling' of protected speech are inapplicable to commercial speech." *Central Hudson*. However, no differences between commercial and other kinds of speech justify protecting commercial speech less extensively where, as here, the government seeks to manipulate private behavior by depriving citizens of truthful information concerning lawful activities. . . .

Accordingly, I believe that where the government seeks to suppress the dissemination of nonmisleading commercial speech relating to legal activities, for fear that recipients will act on the information provided, such regulation should be subject to strict judicial scrutiny. . . .

The Court nevertheless sustains Puerto Rico's advertising ban because the legislature *could* have determined that casino gambling would seriously harm the health, safety, and welfare of the Puerto Rican citizens. This reasoning is contrary to this Court's long established First Amendment jurisprudence. When the government seeks to place restrictions upon commercial speech, a court may not, as the Court implies today, simply speculate about valid reasons that the government might have for enacting such restrictions. Rather, the government ultimately bears the burden of justifying the challenged regulation, and it is incumbent upon the government to *prove* that the interests it seeks to further are real and substantial. In this case, appellee has not shown that "serious harmful effects" will result if Puerto Rico residents gamble in casinos, and the legislature's decision to legalize such activity suggests that it believed the opposite to be true. In short, appellees have failed to show that a substantial government interest supports Puerto Rico's ban on protected expression. . . .

The Court fails even to acknowledge the wide range of effective alternatives available to Puerto Rico, and addresses only appellant's claim that Puerto Rico's legislature might choose to reduce the demand for casino gambling among residents by "promulgating additional speech designed to discourage it." The Court rejects this alternative, asserting that "it is up to the legislature to decide whether or not such a 'counterspeech' policy would be as effective in reducing the demand for casino gambling as a restriction on advertising." This reasoning ignores the commands of the First Amendment. Where the government seeks to restrict speech in order to advance an important interest, it is not, contrary to what the Court has stated, "up to the legislature" to decide whether or not the government's interest might be protected adequately by less intrusive measures. Rather, it is incumbent upon the government to *prove* that more limited means are not sufficient to protect its interests, and for a *court* to decide whether or not the government has sustained this burden. In this case, nothing suggests that the Puerto Rico Legislature ever considered the efficacy of measures other than suppressing protected expression. More importantly, there has been no showing that alternative measures would inadequately safeguard the Commonwealth's interest in controlling the harmful effects allegedly associated with casino gambling. Under these circumstances, Puerto Rico's ban on advertising clearly violates the First Amendment.

Justice STEVENS, with whom Justice MARSHALL and Justice BLACKMUN join, dissenting.

The Court concludes that "the greater power to completely ban casino gambling necessarily includes the lesser power to ban advertising of casino gambling." Whether a State may ban all advertising of an activity that it permits but could prohibit—such as gambling, prostitution, or the consumption of marijuana or liquor—is an elegant question of constitutional law. It is not, however, appropriate to address that question in this case because Puerto Rico's rather bizarre restraints on speech are so plainly forbidden by the First Amendment.

Puerto Rico does not simply "ban advertising of casino gambling." Rather, Puerto Rico blatantly discriminates in its punishment of speech depending on the publication, audience, and words employed. Moreover, the prohibitions, as now construed by the Puerto Rico courts, establish a regime of prior restraint and articulate a standard that is hopelessly vague and unpredictable.

With respect to the publisher, in stark, unabashed language, the Superior Court's construction favors certain identifiable publications and disfavors others. If the publication (or medium) is from outside Puerto Rico, it is very favored indeed. "Within the ads of casinos allowed by this regulation figure . . . movies, television, radio, newspapers, and trade magazines which may be published, taped, or filmed in the exterior for tourism promotion in the exterior even though they may be exposed or incidentally circulated in Puerto Rico. For example: an advertisement in the New York Times, an advertisement in CBS which reaches us through Cable TV, whose main objective is to reach the potential tourist." App. to Juris. Statement 38b–39b. If the publication is native to Puerto Rico, however—the San Juan Star, for instance—it is subject to a far more rigid system of restraints and controls regarding the manner in which a certain form of speech (casino ads) may be carried in its pages. Unless the Court is prepared to uphold an Illinois regulation of speech that subjects The New York Times to one standard and The Chicago Tribune to another, I do not understand why it is willing to uphold a Puerto Rico regulation that applies one standard to The New York Times and another to the San Juan Star.

With respect to the audience, the newly construed regulations plainly discriminate in terms of the intended listener or reader. Casino advertising must be "addressed to tourists." It must not "invite the residents of Puerto Rico to visit the casino." The regulation thus poses what might be viewed as a reverse Privileges and Immunities problem: Puerto Rico's residents are singled out for disfavored treatment in comparison to all other Americans. But nothing so fancy is required to recognize the obvious First Amendment problem in this kind of audience discrimination. I cannot imagine that this Court would uphold an Illinois regulation that forbade advertising "addressed" to Illinois residents while allowing the same advertiser to communicate his message to visitors and commuters; we should be no more willing to uphold a Puerto Rico regulation that forbids advertising "addressed" to Puerto Rico residents.

With respect to the message, the regulations now take one word of the English language—"casino"—and give it a special opprobrium. Use of that suspicious six letter word is permitted only "where the trade name of the hotel is used even though it may contain a reference to the casino." The regulations explicitly include an important provision—"that the word casino is never used alone nor specified." (The meaning of "specified"—perhaps italicization, or bold-face, or all capital letters—is presumably left to subsequent case-by-case adjudication). Singling out the use of a particular word for official sanctions raises grave First Amendment concerns, and Puerto Rico has utterly failed to justify the disfavor in which that particular six-letter word is held. . . .

The general proposition advanced by the majority today—that a State may prohibit the advertising of permitted conduct if it may prohibit the conduct altogether—bears little resemblance to the grotesquely flawed regulation of speech advanced by Puerto Rico in this case. The First Amendment surely does not permit Puerto Rico's frank discrimination among publications, audiences, and words. Nor should sanctions for speech be as unpredictable and haphazardous as the roll of dice in a casino.

I respectfully dissent.

E. FREEDOM OF THE PRESS

The Supreme Court articulated constitutional principles for freedom of the press based on the recognition that "speech concerning public affairs . . . is the essence of self-government."[1] Consistent with "the assumption that the widest possible dissemination of information from diverse and antagonistic sources is essential to the welfare of the public," in *Associated Press v. United States,* 326 U.S. 1 (1945), the Court reaffirmed that "Any system of prior restraint of expression . . . [bears] a heavy presumption against its constitutional validity" in *New York Times v. United States*, 403 U.S. 713 (1971).

At the same time, First Amendment protection for the press also extends to various modes of disseminating information— pamphlets, leaflets, signs, magazines, advertisements, books, motion pictures, and radio and television broadcasts.[2] Accordingly, the "lonely pamphleter" and the "citizen-critic" are protected along with the "institutional press." This is because the speech and press clauses have traditionally been viewed as inseparable, coterminous, and thus a constitutional redundancy. As the Court in *Thornhill v. Alabama*, 310 U.S. 88 (1940), observed,

The freedom of speech and of the press guaranteed by the Constitution embraces at least the liberty to discuss publicly and truthfully all matters of public concern without previous restraint or fear of subsequent punishment. The exigencies of the colonial period and the efforts to secure freedom from oppressive administration developed a broadened conception of these liberties as adequate to supply the public need for information and education with respect to the significant issues of the times. . . . Freedom of discussion, if it would fulfill its historical function in this nation, must embrace all issues about which information is needed or appropriate to enable the members of society to cope with the exigencies of their period.

In the last two decades, though, there has been a movement to ostensibly further enlarge the scope of the First Amendment by recognizing the "institutional status" of the press, including affirmative rights to acquire information and special press privileges shielding reporters from indirect restraints on their freedom. Justice Stewart, among others, argued that the First Amendment "is, in essence, a *structural* provision of the Constitution" that confers preferred constitutional status on "the organized press" and "the daily newspapers and other established news media." The "primary purpose" of the amendment, in his words, "was to create a fourth institution outside the Government as an additional check on the three official branches. . . . The publishing business is, in short, the only organized private business that is given explicit constitutional protection."[3]

Contrary to Justice Stewart's interpretation, however, professor Robert Sack argues that "What [the First Amendment] should protect is not the *institution*, but the *role* of the press: To afford a vehicle of information and opinion, to inform and educate the public, to offer criticism, to provide a forum for discussion and debate, and to act as a surrogate to obtain for readers news and information that individual citizens could not or would not gather on their own."[4] Likewise, *New York Times* contributor Anthony Lewis lamented, "The Press does itself no good when it claims special privileges under the Constitution" and the strategy of the press to use the politics of constitutional adjudication to secure "different and better treatment under the Constitution [is a] fundamental mistake."[5]

A dilemma posed by a structuralist interpretation of the First Amendment and special privileges for the institutional press lies in how to define *the press*. As Justice White notes in *Branzburg v. Hayes* (1972) (see page 531), press privileges "present practical and conceptual difficulties of a high order." The Court could fashion constitutional press privileges by following the lines drawn by some legislatures in drafting press shield laws (which, in some instances, protect reporters from having to reveal their sources), either defining members of the institutional press according to their employer, work schedule, or publication record. Alternatively, immunity could be given for all who write professionally. But both approaches threaten to deny constitutional protection for the citizen-critic, and broader definitions of "the press" might prove so overinclusive as to render meaningless special privileges carved out for the press in the first place.

Is the First Amendment guarantee against "abridging the freedom of speech, or of the press" redundant? Should the press be accorded special constitutional status? These are some of the underlying issues confronting the Court in cases arising from direct and indirect restraints on press freedom.

NOTES

1. *Garrison v. Louisiana*, 379 U.S. 64 (1964).

2. See *Lovell v. City of Griffin*, 303 U.S. 444 (1938) (pamphlets); *Schneider v. New Jersey*, 308 U.S. 147 (1939) (leaflets); *Thornhill v. Alabama*, 310 U.S. 88 (1940) (signs); *Roth v. United States*, 354 U.S. 376 (1957) (*dicta*, books); *Joseph Burstyn, Inc. v. Wilson*, 343 U.S. 495 (1952) (motion pictures); *New York Times Co. v. Sullivan*, 376 U.S. 254 (1964) (noncommercial advertisements); *Virginia State Board of Pharmacy v. Virginia Citizens Consumer Council*, 425 U.S. 748 (1976) (commercial advertisements); *Greenbelt Cooperative Publishing Association v. Bresler*, 398 U.S. 6 (1970) (newspapers); *Time, Inc. v. Hill*, 385 U.S. 374 (1967) (magazines); *Red Lion Broadcasting Co. v. Federal Communications Commission*, 395 U.S. 367 (1969) (radio); and *Estes v. Texas*, 381 U.S. 532 (1965) (*dicta*, television).

3. Potter Stewart, "Or of the Press," 26 *Hastings Law Journal* 631 (1975). See also Randall Bezanson, "The New Free Press Guarantee," 63 *Virginia Law Review* 731 (1977); John Paul Stevens, "Some Thoughts about a General Rule," 21 *Arizona Law Review* 599 (1979); and Floyd Abrams, "The Press *Is* Different: Reflections on Justice Stewart and the Autonomous Press," 7 *Hofstra Law Review* 559 (1979).

4. Robert Sack, "Reflections on the Wrong Question: Special Constitutional Privilege for the Institutional Press," 7 *Hofstra Law Review* 629 (1979).

5. Anthony Lewis, "A Preferred Position for Journalism," 7 *Hofstra Law Review* 595 (1979). See also Anthony Lewis, "A Public Right to Know about Public Institutions: The First Amendment as Sword," in *The Supreme Court Review*, Vol. 1, ed. Philip Kurland and Gerhard Casper (Chicago: University of Chicago Press, 1981).

(1) The Doctrine of No Prior Restraint

The doctrine of no prior restraint was the touchstone for freedom of the press in English common law and generally assumed to be incorporated into the First Amendment. As Justice Holmes observed, "[T]he main purpose of [the Free Speech and Press] provisions is to 'prevent all such *previous restraints* upon publications as had been practiced by other governments,' and they do not prevent the subsequent punishment of such as may be deemed contrary to the public welfare."[1]

In *Near v. State of Minnesota ex rel. Olson* (1931) (see page 507), Chief Justice Hughes wrote the doctrine into the developing law of the First Amendment. Subsequently, *Grosjean v. American Press Company*, 297 U.S. 233 (1936), held that taxes may not impose a discriminatory burden on newspapers. There, Governor Huey Long and his political machine in the Louisiana legislature passed a license tax of 2 percent of the gross income of newspapers selling more than 2,000 copies a week, to stifle their opponents. The principle that taxes may not operate as a prior restraint was reaffirmed in *Minneapolis Star and Tribune v. Minnesota Commissioner of Revenue* (1983) (see page 512), but compare Justice O'Connor's opinion for the Court with Rehnquist's dissenting opinion. Chief Justice Rehnquist, joined by Justice Scalia, again dissented from the Court's striking down a law imposing a sales tax on magazines, but not newspapers, in *Arkansas Writers' Project v. Ragland*, 481 U.S. 221 (1987).

Under the doctrine of no prior restraint, *Mills v. Alabama*, 384 U.S. 214 (1966), invalidated a law barring editorial comments on election days. In *Landmark Communications, Inc. v. Virginia*, 435 U.S. 829 (1978), the Court struck down a Virginia law forbidding the disclosure of confidential information about the proceedings of the state's Judicial Inquiry and Review Commission. So too in *Smith v. Daily Mail Publishing Company* (1979) (see page 516) a statute barring the disclosure of the names of juveniles arrested by police was struck down as a prior restraint. And *Butterworth v. Smith*, 110 S.Ct. 1376 (1990), overturned a Florida statute barring witnesses before grand juries from later disclosing their testimony.

Notice that Chief Justice Hughes in *Near v. Minnesota* does not deny that "a government might prevent actual obstruction of the sailing dates of transports or the number or location of troops," implying that there might be a "national security" exception to the First Amendment doctrine of no prior restraint. "On similar grounds," he also notes that "the primary requirements of decency may be enforced against obscene publications" and "[t]he security of the community life may be protected against incitements to acts of violence." In these areas there remains controversy over the application of the doctrine of no prior restraint. In *New York Times Co. v. United States*, 403 U.S. 713 (1971) (see page 518) the Court denied as a prior restraint the government's attempt to enjoin the publication of the "Pentagon Papers." In *Southeastern Promotions v. Conrad*, 420 U.S. 546 (1975), the Court required the municipal board of Chattanooga, Tennessee, to make its city Memorial Auditorium available for the stage production of *Hair*, a theatrical performance that includes nudity, simulated sex, and vulgar language. Over Rehnquist's dissent that there was no real issue of prior restraint (because scheduling limitations for the auditorium precluded the presentation of every production), the majority concluded that denying the use of the facility constituted a prior restraint. In reaffirming that "a system of prior restraint 'avoids constitutional infirmity only if it takes place under procedural safeguards designed to obviate the dangers of a censorship system,' " the Court indicated that local governments bear a burden of instituting judicial proceedings and of proving that materials or productions are unprotected expression under the First Amendment.

NOTE

1. *Patterson v. Colorado*, 205 U.S. 454 (1907).

SELECTED BIBLIOGRAPHY

Friendly, Fred. *Minnesota Rag: The Dramatic Story of the Landmark Supreme Court That Gave New Meaning to Freedom of the Press.* New York: Random House, 1981.

Lofton, John. *The Press as Guardian of the First Amendment.* Columbia: University of South Carolina Press, 1980.

O'Brien, David. *The Public's Right to Know: The Supreme Court and the First Amendment.* New York: Praeger, 1981.

Near v. State of Minnesota ex rel. Olson
283 U.S. 697, 51 S.Ct. 625 (1930)

Jay Near was the editor of a muckraking newspaper, the *Saturday Press*, that gave vent to his anti-Semitic, antiblack, anti-Catholic, and antilabor views. In 1927, his newspaper was closed under a 1925 Minnesota abatement statute for any newspaper, magazine, or periodical creating a public nuisance by "malicious, scandalous and defamatory" publication. Under the law, Near could be permanently enjoined from publishing, with a penalty of $1,000 as a fine or a year in jail for violating the injunction against publishing. Near contended the law was unconstitutional, but the state supreme court disagreed, and subsequently a district court and the state supreme court upheld the closing of Near's newspaper. But Near's case came to be championed by Colonel Robert McCormick, the publisher of the Chicago *Tribune*, who paid for an appeal to the Supreme Court.

Chief Justice HUGHES delivers the opinion of the Court.

Chapter 285 of the Session Laws of Minnesota for the year 1925 provides for the abatement, as a public nuisance, of a "malicious, scandalous and defamatory newspaper, magazine or other periodical." Section 1 of the act is as follows:

> "Section 1. Any person who, as an individual, or as a member or employee of a firm, or association or organization, or as an officer, director, member or employee of a corporation, shall be engaged in the business of regularly or customarily producing, publishing or circulating, having in possession, selling or giving away.
>
> "(a) an obscene, lewd and lascivious newspaper, magazine, or other periodical, or
>
> "(b) a malicious, scandalous and defamatory newspaper, magazine or other periodical,

> —is guilty of a nuisance, and all persons guilty of such nuisance may be enjoined, as hereinafter provided. . . .

Under this statute (section 1, clause (b), the county attorney of Hennepin county brought this action to enjoin the publication of what was described as a "malicious, scandalous and defamatory newspaper, magazine or other periodical," known as The Saturday Press, published by the defendants in the city of Minneapolis. . . .

Without attempting to summarize the contents of the voluminous exhibits attached to the complaint, we deem it sufficient to say that the articles charged, in substance, that a Jewish gangster was in control of gambling, bootlegging, and racketeering in Minneapolis, and that law enforcing officers and agencies were not energetically performing their duties. . . .

If we cut through mere details of procedure, the operation and effect of the statute in substance is that public authorities may bring the owner or publisher of a newspaper or periodical before a judge upon a charge of conducting a business of publishing scandalous and defamatory matter—in particular that the matter consists of charges against public officers of official dereliction—and, unless the owner or publisher is able and disposed to bring competent evidence to satisfy the judge that the charges are true and are published with good motives and for justifiable ends, his newspaper or periodical is suppressed and further publication is made punishable as a contempt. This is of the essence of censorship.

The question is whether a statute authorizing such proceedings in restraint of publication is consistent with the conception of the liberty of the press as historically conceived and guaranteed. In determining the extent of the constitutional protection, it has been generally, if not universally, considered that it is the chief purpose of the guaranty to prevent previous restraints upon publication. The struggle in England, directed against the legislative power of the licenser, resulted in renunciation of the censorship of the press. The liberty deemed to be established was thus described by Blackstone: "The liberty of the press is indeed essential to the nature of a free state; but this consists in laying no *previous* restraints upon publications, and not in freedom from censure for criminal matter when published. Every freeman has an undoubted right to lay what sentiments he pleases before the public; to forbid this, is to destroy the freedom of the press; but if he publishes what is improper, mischievous or illegal, he must take the consequence of his own temerity." 4 Bl. Com. 151, 152. See Story on the Constitution, §§ 1884, 1889. The distinction was early pointed out between the extent of the freedom with respect to censorship under our constitutional system and that enjoyed in England. Here, as Madison said, "the great and essential rights of the people are secured against legislative as well as against executive ambition. They are secured, not by laws paramount to prerogative, but by constitutions paramount to laws. This security of the freedom of the press requires that it should be exempt not only from previous restraint by the Executive, as in Great Britain, but from legislative restraint also." Report on the Virginia Resolutions, Madison's Works, vol. IV, p. 543. . . .

The criticism upon Blackstone's statement has not been because immunity from previous restraint upon publication has not been regarded as deserving of special emphasis, but chiefly because that immunity cannot be deemed to exhaust the conception of the liberty guaranteed by State and Federal Constitutions. . . .

[I]t is recognized that punishment for the abuse of the liberty accorded to the press is essential to the protection of the public, and that the common-law rules that subject the libeler to responsibility for the public offense, as well as for the private injury, are not abolished by the protection extended in our Constitutions. The law of criminal libel rests upon that secure foundation. There is also the conceded authority of courts to punish for contempt when publications directly tend to prevent the proper discharge of judicial functions. In the present case, we have no occasion to inquire as to the permissible scope of subsequent punishment. For whatever wrong the appellant has committed or may commit, by his publications, the state appropriately affords both public and private redress by its libel laws. As has been noted, the statute in question does not deal with punishments; it provides for no punishment, except in case of contempt for violation of the court's order, but for suppression and injunction—that is, for restraint upon publication.

The objection has also been made that the principle as to immunity from previous restraint is stated too broadly, if every such restraint is deemed to be prohibited. That is undoubtedly true; the protection even as to previous restraint is not absolutely unlimited. But the limitation has been recognized only in exceptional cases. "When a nation is at war many things that might be said in time of peace are such a hindrance to its effort that their utterance will not be endured so long as men fight and that no Court could regard them as protected by any constitutional right." *Schenck v. United States.* [249 U.S. 47 (1919)]. No one would question but that a government might prevent actual obstruction to its recruiting service or the publication of the sailing dates of transports or the number and location of troops. On similar grounds, the primary requirements of decency may be enforced against obscene publications. The security of the community life may be protected against incitements to acts of violence and the overthrow by force of orderly government. The constitutional guaranty of free speech does not "protect a man from an injunction against uttering words that may have all the effect of force. *Gompers v. Buck's Stove & Range Co.,* 221 U.S. 418 [1911]. . . ." *Schenck v. United States, supra.* These limitations are not applicable here. . . .

The fact that for approximately one hundred and fifty years there has been almost an entire absence of attempts to impose previous restraints upon publications relating to the malfeasance of public officers is significant of the deep-seated conviction that such restraints would violate constitutional right. Public officers, whose character and conduct remain open to debate and free discussion in the press, find their remedies for false accusations in actions under libel laws providing for redress and punishment, and not in proceedings to restrain the publication of newspapers and periodicals. The general principle that the constitutional guaranty of the liberty of the press gives immunity from previous restraints has been approved in many decisions under the provisions of state constitutions. . . .

For these reasons we hold the statute, so far as it authorized the proceedings in this action under clause (b) of section 1, to be an infringement of the liberty of the press guaranteed by the Fourteenth Amendment.

Justice BUTLER dissenting.

The decision of the Court in this case . . . gives to freedom of the press a meaning and a scope not heretofore recognized, and construes "liberty" in the due process clause of the Fourteenth Amendment to put upon the states a federal restriction that is without precedent. . . .

The Minnesota statute does not operate as a *previous* restraint on publication within the proper meaning of that phrase. It does not authorize administrative control in advance such as was formerly exercised by the licensers and censors, but prescribes a remedy to be enforced by a suit in equity. In this case there was previous publication made in the course of the business of regularly producing malicious, scandalous, and defamatory periodicals. The business and publications unquestionably constitute an abuse of the right of free press. The statute denounces the things done as a nuisance on the ground, as stated by the state Supreme Court, that they threaten morals, peace, and good order. There is no question of the power of the state to denounce such transgressions. The restraint authorized is only in respect of continuing to do what has been duly adjudged to constitute a nuisance.

Justice VAN DEVANTER, Justice McREYNOLDS. and Justice SUTHERLAND concurred.

Minneapolis Star and Tribune Company v. Minnesota Commissioner of Revenue
460 U.S. 575, 103 S.Ct. 1365 (1983)

Justice O'Connor presents the facts in this case concerning state taxation of the press in her opinion announcing the decision of the Court.

Justice O'CONNOR delivers the opinion of the Court.

This case presents the question of a State's power to impose a special tax on the press and, by enacting exemptions, to limit its effect to only a few newspapers. . . .

The appellant, Minneapolis Star and Tribune Company "Star Tribune," is the publisher of a morning newspaper and an evening newspaper in Minneapolis. From 1967 until 1971, it enjoyed an exemption from the sales and use tax provided by Minnesota for periodic publications. In 1971, however, while leaving the exemption from the sales tax in place, the legislature amended the scheme to impose a "use tax" on the cost of paper and ink products consumed in the production of a publication. . . . In 1974, the legislature again amended the statute, this time to exempt the first $100,000 worth of ink and paper consumed by a publication in any calendar year, in effect giving each publication an annual tax credit of $4,000. . . .

After the enactment of the $100,000 exemption, 11 publishers, producing 14 of the 388 paid circulation newspapers in the State, incurred a tax liability in 1974. Star Tribune was one of the 11, and, of the $893,355 collected, it paid $608,634, or roughly two-thirds of the total revenue raised by the tax. In 1975, 13 publishers, producing 16 out of 374 paid circulation papers, paid a tax. That year, Star Tribune again bore roughly two-thirds of the total receipts from the use tax on ink and paper.

Star Tribune instituted this action to seek a refund of the use taxes it paid from January 1, 1974 to May 31, 1975. It challenged the imposition of the use tax on ink and paper used in publications as a violation of the guarantees of freedom of the press and equal protection in the First and Fourteenth Amendments. The Minnesota Supreme Court upheld the tax against the federal constitutional challenge. . . . We . . . now reverse. . . .

Clearly, the First Amendment does not prohibit all regulation of the press. It is beyond dispute that the States and the Federal Government can subject newspapers to generally applicable economic regulations without creating constitutional problems. Minnesota, however, has not chosen to apply its general sales and use tax to newspapers. Instead, it has created a special tax that applies only to certain publications protected by the First Amendment. . . .

We then must determine whether the First Amendment permits such special taxation. A tax that burdens rights protected by the First Amendment cannot stand unless the burden is necessary to achieve an overriding governmental interest. . . .

There is substantial evidence that differential taxation of the press would have troubled the Framers of the First Amendment. The role of the press in mobilizing sentiment in favor of independence was critical to the Revolution. When the Constitution was proposed without an explicit guarantee of freedom of the press, the Antifederalists objected. Proponents of the Constitution, relying on the principle of enumerated powers, responded that such a guarantee was unnecessary because the Constitution granted Congress no power to control the press. . . .

The fears of the Antifederalists were well-founded. A power to tax differentially, as opposed to a power to tax generally, gives a government a powerful weapon against the taxpayer selected. When the State imposes a generally applicable tax, there is little cause for concern. We need not fear that a government will destroy a selected group of taxpayers by burdensome taxation if it must impose the same burden on the rest of its constituency. When the State singles out the press, though, the political constraints that prevent a legislature from passing crippling taxes of general applicability are weakened, and the threat of burdensome taxes becomes acute. That threat can operate as effectively as a censor to check critical comment by the press, undercutting the basic assumption of our political system that the press will often serve as an important restraint on government. . . .

Minnesota's ink and paper tax violates the First Amendment not only because it singles out the press, but also because it targets a small group of newspapers. The effect of the $100,000 exemption enacted in 1974 is that only a handful of publishers pay any tax at all, and even fewer pay any significant amount of tax. The State explains this exemption as part of a policy favoring an "equitable" tax system, although there are no comparable exemptions for small enterprises outside the press. Again, there is no legislative history supporting the State's view of the purpose of the amendment. Whatever the motive of the legislature in this case, we think that recognizing a power in the State not only to single out the press but also to tailor the tax so that it singles out a few members of the press presents such a potential for abuse that no interest suggested by Minnesota can justify the scheme.

Justice WHITE concurred in part and dissented in part.

Justice REHNQUIST dissenting.

While the Court purports to rely on the intent of the "Framers of the First Amendment," I believe it safe to assume that in 1791 "abridge" meant the same thing it means today: to diminish or curtail. Not until the Court's decision in this case, nearly two centuries after adoption of the First Amendment has it been read to prohibit activities which in no way diminish or curtail the freedoms it protects. . . .

The Court recognizes in several parts of its opinion that the

State of Minnesota could avoid constitutional problems by imposing on newspapers the 4% sales tax that it imposes on other retailers. Rather than impose such a tax, however, the Minnesota legislature decided to provide newspapers with an exemption from the sales tax and impose a 4% use tax on ink and paper; thus, while both taxes are part of one "system of sales and use taxes," newspapers are classified differently within that system. The problem the Court finds too difficult to deal with is whether this difference in treatment results in a significant burden on newspapers.

The record reveals that in 1974 the Minneapolis Star & Tribune had an average daily circulation of 489,345 copies. . . . Thus, total sales revenues in 1974 would be $46,498,738. Had a 4% sales tax been imposed, the Minneapolis Star & Tribune would have been liable for $1,859,950 in 1974. The same "complexities of factual economic proof" can be analyzed for 1975. . . . Total sales revenues in 1975 would be $45,628,544; at a 4% rate, the sales tax for 1975 would be $1,825,142. Therefore, had the sales tax been imposed, as the Court agrees would have been permissible, the Minneapolis Star & Tribune's liability, for 1974 and 1975 would have been $3,685,092.

The record further indicates that the Minneapolis Star & Tribune paid $608,634 in use taxes in 1974 and $636,113 in 1975—a total liability of $1,244,747. We need no expert testimony from modern day Euclids or Einsteins to determine that the $1,224,747 paid in use taxes is significantly less burdensome than the $3,685,092 that could have been levied by a sales tax. *A fortiori*, the Minnesota taxing scheme which singles out newspapers for "differential treatment" has benefited, not burdened, the "freedom of speech, [and] of the press."

Ignoring these calculations, the Court concludes that "differential treatment" alone in Minnesota's sales and use tax scheme requires that the statutes be found "presumptively unconstitutional" and declared invalid "unless the State asserts a counterbalancing interest of compelling importance that it cannot achieve without differential taxation." The "differential treatment" standard that the Court has conjured up is unprecedented and unwarranted. To my knowledge this Court has never subjected governmental action to the most stringent constitutional review solely on the basis of "differential treatment" of particular groups. . . .

[In my view] the State is required to show [merely] that its taxing scheme is rational. But in this case that showing can be made easily. . . . [N]ewspapers are commonly sold in a different way than other goods. The legislature could have concluded that paper boys, corner newsstands, and vending machines provide an unreliable and unsuitable means for collection of a sales tax. Must everyone buying a paper put 26¢ in the vending machine rather than 25¢; or should the price of a paper be raised to

30¢, giving the paper 4¢ more profit; or should the price be kept at 25¢ with the paper absorbing the tax? In summary, so long as the State can find another way to collect revenue from the newspapers, imposing a sales tax on newspapers would be to no one's advantage; not the newspaper and its distributors who would have to collect the tax, not the State who would have to enforce collection, and not the consumer who would have to pay for the paper in odd amounts. The reasonable alternative Minnesota chose was to impose the use tax on ink and paper. . . .

To collect from newspapers their fair share of taxes under the sales and use tax scheme and at the same time avoid abridging the freedoms of speech and press, the Court holds today that Minnesota must subject newspapers to millions of additional dollars in sales tax liability. Certainly this is a hollow victory for the newspapers and I seriously doubt the Court's conclusion that this result would have been intended by the "Framers of the First Amendment."

Smith v. Daily Mail Publishing Company
443 U.S. 97, 99 S.Ct. 2667 (1979)

The facts in this case, involving the publication of the names of minors arrested for criminal offenses, are stated by Chief Justice Burger in his opinion announcing the decision of the Court.

Chief Justice BURGER delivers the opinion of the Court.

We granted certiorari to consider whether a West Virginia statute violates the First and Fourteenth Amendments of the United States Constitution by making it a crime for a newspaper to publish, without the written approval of the juvenile court, the name of any youth charged as a juvenile offender. . . .

On February 9, 1978, a 15-year-old student was shot and killed at Hayes Junior High School in St. Albans, W. Va., a small community located about 13 miles outside of Charleston, W. Va. The alleged assailant, a 14-year-old classmate, was identified by seven different eye witnesses and was arrested by police soon after the incident.

The Charleston Daily Mail and the Charleston Daily Gazette, respondents here, learned of the shooting by monitoring routinely the police band radio frequency; they immediately dispatched reporters and photographers to the Junior High School. The reporters for both papers obtained the name of the alleged assailant simply by asking various witnesses, the police and an assistant prosecuting attorney who were at the school.

The staffs of both newspapers prepared articles for publication about the incident. The Daily Mail's first article appeared in its February 9 afternoon edition. The article did not mention the alleged attacker's name. The editorial decision to omit the name was made because of the statutory prohibition against publication, without prior court approval.

The Daily Gazette made a contrary editorial decision and published the juvenile's name and picture in an article about the shooting that appeared in the February 10 morning edition of the paper. In addition, the name of the alleged juvenile attacker was broadcast over at least three different radio stations on February 9 and 10. Since the information had become public knowledge, the Daily Mail decided to include the juvenile's name in an article in its afternoon paper on February 10. . . .

Our recent decisions demonstrate that state action to punish the publication of truthful information seldom can satisfy constitutional standards. In *Landmark Communications* [*v. Virginia,* 435 U.S. 829 (1978)], we declared unconstitutional a Virginia statute making it a crime to publish information regarding confidential proceedings before a state judicial review commission that heard complaints about alleged disabilities and misconduct of state court judges. In declaring that statute unconstitutional, we concluded:

> "[T]he publication Virginia seeks to punish under its statute lies near the core of the First Amendment, and the Commonwealth's interests advanced by the imposition of criminal sanctions are insufficient to justify the actual and potential encroachments on freedom of speech and of the press which follow therefrom." *Id.*

In *Cox Broadcasting Corp. v. Cohn,* [420 U.S. 469 (1975)] we held that damages could not be recovered against a newspaper for publishing the name of a rape victim. The suit had been based on a state statute that made it a crime to publish the name of the victim; the purpose of the statute was to protect the privacy right of the individual and the family. The name of the victim had become known to the public through official court records dealing with the trial of the rapist. In declaring the statute unconstitutional, the Court, speaking through Justice WHITE, reasoned:

> "By placing the information in the public domain on official court records, the State must be presumed to have concluded that the public interest was thereby being served. . . . States may not impose sanctions on the publication of truthful information contained in official court records open to public inspection."

If the information is lawfully obtained, as it was here, the State may not punish its publication except when necessary to further an interest more substantial than is present here. . . .

Accordingly, the judgment of the West Virginia Supreme Court of Appeals is Affirmed.

Justice POWELL did not participate in the consideration or decision of this case.

Justice REHNQUIST concurring.

In my view, a State's interest in preserving the anonymity of its juvenile offenders—an interest that I consider to be, in the words of the Court, of the "highest order"—far outweighs any minimal interference with freedom of the press that a ban on publication of the youth's names entails. . . .

Although I disagree with the Court that a state statute punishing publication of the identity of a juvenile offender can never serve an interest of the "highest order" and thus pass muster under the First Amendment, I agree with the Court that West Virginia's statute "does not accomplish its stated purpose." The West Virginia statute prohibits only newspapers from printing the names of youths charged in juvenile proceedings. Electronic media and other forms of publication can announce the young person's name with impunity. In fact, in this case three radio stations broadcast the alleged assailant's name before it was published by The Charleston Daily Mail. This statute thus largely fails to achieve its purpose. . . .

I, therefore, join in the Court's judgment striking down the West Virginia law. But for the reasons previously stated, I think that a generally effective ban on publication that applied to all forms of mass communication, electronic and print media alike, would be constitutional.

New York Times Company v. United States
403 U.S. 670, 91 S.Ct. 2140 (1971)

In 1971, amid growing opposition to the undeclared Vietnam War, the Nixon administration sought to enjoin the *New York Times* and the *Washington Post* from publishing a series of articles based on a forty-seven-volume study, *History of U.S. Decision Making Process on Vietnam Policy*. The study was prepared in 1968 and was classified "Top Secret—Sensitive." The *New York Times* received copies of the study from Daniel Ellsberg, who had secretly copied them while working for a think tank and after his unsuccessful efforts to persuade leading politicians to publicize the study.

After several months of reviewing the documents, the *New York Times* commenced publication of selected items on June 13, 1971. Following the third installment the Department of Justice sought an injunction against publication of the balance of the series, and obtained a temporary restraining order prohibiting further publication until June 19. On June 18 the *Washington Post* also printed two articles based on the study and by five o'clock that day the government had filed a similar suit against its further publication of the material.

The next morning a district court denied the government's request for a preliminary injunction, but later in the day a circuit court judge extended the temporary restraining order until noon, June 21, to give a panel of the circuit court the opportunity to consider the government's application. On June 22, the circuit court remanded the case to the district court to determine whether any of the other materials posed such grave and immediate danger to the security of the country as to warrant prior restraint and a continued stay on publication until June 25. The *New York Times* promptly appealed to the Supreme Court to vacate the stay on publication and to expedite consideration of the case. On June 25 the Court granted certiorari and heard arguments the next day. Remarkably, four days later the Court issued no less than ten opinions. In a brief *per curiam* opinion, the Court held that the government's injunction constituted a prior restraint on the press. Six justices wrote concurring opinions; and three, dissenting opinions.

Per Curiam

We granted certiorari in these cases in which the United States seeks to enjoin the New York Times and the Washington Post from publishing the contents of a classified study entitled "History of U.S. Decision-Making Process on Viet Nam Policy."

"Any system of prior restraints of expression comes to this Court bearing a heavy presumption against its constitutional validity." *Bantam Books, Inc. v. Sullivan,* 372 U.S. 58 (1963); see also *Near v. Minnesota ex rel. Olson,* 283 U.S. 697 (1931). The Government "thus carries a heavy burden of showing justification for the imposition of such a restraint." *Organization for a Better Austin v. Keefe,* 402 U.S. 415 (1971). The District Court for the Southern District of New York in the *New York Times* case, 328 F.Supp. 324, and the District Court for the District of Columbia and the Court of Appeals for the District of Columbia Circuit, 446 F.2d

1327, in the *Washington Post* case held that the Government had not met that burden. We agree.

The judgment of the Court of Appeals for the District of Columbia Circuit is therefore affirmed. The order of the Court of Appeals for the Second Circuit is reversed and the case is remanded with directions to enter a judgment affirming the judgment of the District Court for the Southern District of New York. The stays entered June 25, 1971, by the Court are vacated.

Justice BLACK, with whom Justice DOUGLAS joins, concurring.

I believe that every moment's continuance of the injunctions against these newspapers amounts to a flagrant, indefensible, and continuing violation of the First Amendment. . . . In my view it is unfortunate that some of my Brethren are apparently willing to hold that the publication of news may sometimes be enjoined. Such a holding would make a shambles of the First Amendment. . . .

In seeking injunctions against these newspapers and in its presentation to the Court, the Executive Branch seems to have forgotten the essential purpose and history of the First Amendment. When the Constitution was adopted, many people strongly opposed it because the document contained no Bill of Rights to safeguard certain basic freedoms. They especially feared that the new powers granted to a central government might be interpreted to permit the government to curtail freedom of religion, press, assembly, and speech. . . . Madison and the other Framers of the First Amendment, able men that they were, wrote in language they earnestly believed could never be misunderstood: "Congress shall make no law . . . abridging the freedom . . . of the press. . . ." Both the history and language of the First Amendment support the view that the press must be left free to publish news, whatever the source, without censorship, injunctions, or prior restraints. . . .

The Government's case here is based on premises entirely different from those that guided the Framers of the First Amendment. The Solicitor General has carefully and emphatically stated:

> "Now, Justice [BLACK], your construction of . . . [the First Amendment] is well known, and I certainly respect it. You say that no law means no law, and that should be obvious. I can only say, Mr. Justice, that to me it is equally obvious that 'no law' does not mean 'no law,' and I would seek to persuade the Court that that is true. . . . [T]here are other parts of the Constitution that grant powers and responsibilities to the Executive, and . . . the First Amendment was not intended to make it impossible for the Executive to function or to protect the security of the United States."

And the Government argues in its brief that in spite of the First Amendment, "[t]he authority of the Executive Department to protect the nation against publication of information whose disclosure would endanger the national security stems from two interrelated sources: the constitutional power of the President over the conduct of foreign affairs and his authority as Commander-in-Chief."

In other words, we are asked to hold that despite the First Amendment's emphatic command, the Executive Branch, the Congress, and the Judiciary can make laws enjoining publication of current news and abridging freedom of the press in the name of "national security." The Government does not even attempt to rely on any act of Congress. Instead it makes the bold and dangerously farreaching contention that the courts should take it upon themselves to "make" a law abridging freedom of the press in the name of equity, presidential power and national security. . . . To find that the President has "inherent power" to halt the publication of news by resort to the courts would wipe out the First Amendment and destroy the fundamental liberty and security of the very people the Government hopes to make "secure." No one can read the history of the adoption of the First Amendment without being convinced beyond any doubt that it was injunctions like those sought here that Madison and his collaborators intended to outlaw in this Nation for all time.

The word "security" is a broad, vague generality whose contours should not be invoked to abrogate the fundamental law embodied in the First Amendment. The guarding of military and diplomatic secrets at the expense of informed representative government provides no real security for our Republic. The Framers of the First Amendment, fully aware of both the need to defend a new nation and the abuses of the English and Colonial Governments, sought to give this new society strength and security by providing that freedom of speech, press, religion, and assembly should not be abridged.

Justice DOUGLAS, with whom Justice BLACK joins, concurring.

The Government says that it has inherent powers to go into court and obtain an injunction to protect the national interest, which in this case is alleged to be national security.

Near v. Minnesota ex rel. Olson, 283 U.S. 697 [1931], repudiated that expansive doctrine in no uncertain terms. . . .

Secrecy in government is fundamentally anti-democratic, perpetuating bureaucratic errors. Open debate and discussion of public issues are vital to our national health. On public questions there should be "uninhibited, robust, and wide-open" debate.

Justice BRENNAN concurring.

I write separately in these cases only to emphasize what should be apparent that our judgments in the present cases may not be taken to indicate the propriety, in the future, of issuing temporary stays and restraining orders to block the publication of material sought to be suppressed by the Government. So far as I can determine, never before has the United States sought to enjoin a newspaper from publishing information in its possession. The relative novelty of the questions presented, the necessary haste with which decisions were reached, the magnitude of the interests asserted, and the fact that all the parties have concentrated their arguments upon the question whether permanent restraints were proper may have justified at least some of the restraints heretofore imposed in these cases. . . . But even if it be assumed that some of the interim restraints were proper in the two cases before us, that assumption has no bearing upon the propriety of similar judicial action in the future. . . . More important, the First Amendment stands as an absolute bar to the imposition of judicial restraints in circumstances of the kind presented by these cases.

Justice STEWART, with whom Justice WHITE joins, concurring.

In the governmental structure created by our Constitution, the Executive is endowed with enormous power in the two related areas of national defense and international relations. This power, largely unchecked by the Legislative and Judicial branches, has been pressed to the very hilt since the advent of the nuclear missile age. For better or for worse, the simple fact is that a President of the United States possesses vastly greater constitutional independence in these two vital areas of power than does, say, a prime minister of a country with a parliamentary form of government.

In the absence of the governmental checks and balances present in other areas of our national life, the only effective restraint upon executive policy and power in the areas of national defense and international affairs may lie in an enlightened citizenry—in an informed and critical public opinion which alone can here protect the values of democratic government. For this reason, it is perhaps here that a press that is alert, aware, and free most vitally serves the basic purpose of the First Amendment. For without an informed and free press there cannot be an enlightened people.

Yet it is elementary that the successful conduct of international diplomacy and the maintenance of an effective national defense require both confidentiality and secrecy. Other nations can hardly deal with this Nation in an atmosphere of mutual trust unless they can be assured that their confidences will be kept. And within our own executive departments, the development of considered and intelligent international policies would be impossible if those charged with their formulation could not communicate with each other freely, frankly, and in confidence. In the area of basic national defense the frequent need for absolute secrecy is, of course, self-evident.

I think there can be but one answer to this dilemma, if dilemma it be. The responsibility must be where the power is. If the Constitution gives the Executive a large degree of unshared power in the conduct of foreign affairs and the maintenance of our national defense, then under the Constitution the Executive must have the largely unshared duty to determine and preserve the degree of internal security necessary to exercise that power successfully. It is an awesome responsibility, requiring judgment and wisdom of a high order. I should suppose that moral, political, and practical considerations would dictate that a very first principle of that wisdom would be an insistence upon avoiding secrecy for its own sake. For when everything is classified, then nothing is classified, and the system becomes one to be disregarded by the cynical or the careless, and to be manipulated by those intent on self-protection or self-promotion. I should suppose, in short, that the hallmark of a truly effective internal security system would be the maximum possible disclosure, recognizing that secrecy can best be preserved only when credibility is truly maintained. But be that as it may, it is clear to me that it is the constitutional duty of the Executive—as a matter of sovereign prerogative and not as a matter of law as the courts know law—through the promulgation and enforcement of executive regulations, to protect the confidentiality necessary to carry out its responsibilities in the fields of international relations and national defense.

This is not to say that Congress and the courts have no role to play. Undoubtedly Congress has the power to enact specific and appropriate criminal laws to protect government property and preserve government secrets. . . . Moreover, if Congress should pass a specific law authorizing civil proceedings in this field, the courts would likewise have the duty to decide the constitutionality of such a law as well as its applicability to the facts proved.

But in the cases before us we are asked neither to construe specific regulations nor to apply specific laws. We are asked, instead, to perform a function that the Constitution gave to the Executive, not the Judiciary. We are asked, quite simply, to prevent the publication by two newspapers of material that the Executive Branch insists should not, in the national interest, be published. I am convinced that the Executive is correct with respect to some of the documents involved. But I cannot say that disclosure of any of them will surely result in direct, immediate, and irreparable damage to our Nation or its people. That being so, there can under the First Amendment be but one judicial resolution of the issues before us. I join the judgments of the Court.

Justice WHITE, with whom Justice STEWART joins, concurring.

I concur in today's judgments, but only because of the concededly extraordinary protection against prior restraints enjoyed by the press under our constitutional system. I do not say that in no circumstances would the First Amendment permit an injunction against publishing information about government plans or operations. Nor, after examining the materials the Government characterizes as the most sensitive and destructive, can I deny that revelation of these documents will do substantial damage to public interests. Indeed, I am confident that their disclosure will have that result. But I nevertheless agree that the United States has not satisfied the very heavy burden that it must meet to warrant an injunction against publication in these cases, at least in the absence of express and appropriately limited congressional authorization for prior restraints in circumstances such as these.

The Government's position is simply stated: The responsibility of the Executive for the conduct of the foreign affairs and for the security of the Nation is so basic that the President is entitled to an injunction against publication of a newspaper story whenever he can convince a court that the information to be revealed threatens "grave and irreparable" injury to the public interest; and the injunction should issue whether or not the material to be published is classified, whether or not publication would be lawful under relevant criminal statutes enacted by Congress, and regardless of the circumstances by which the newspaper came into possession of the information.

At least in the absence of legislation by Congress, based on its own investigations and findings, I am quite unable to agree that the inherent powers of the Executive and the courts reach so far as to authorize remedies having such sweeping potential for inhibiting publications by the press. Much of the difficulty inheres in the "grave and irreparable danger" standard suggested by the United States. If the United States were to have judgment under such a standard in these cases, our decision would be of little guidance to other courts in other cases, for the material at issue here would not be available from the Court's opinion or from public records, nor would it be published by the press. Indeed, even today where we hold that the United States has not met its burden, the material remains sealed in court records and it is properly not discussed in today's opinions. Moreover, because the material poses substantial dangers to national interests and because of the hazards of criminal sanctions, a responsible press may choose never to publish the more sensitive materials. To sustain the Government in these cases would start the courts down a long and hazardous road that I am not willing to travel, at least without congressional guidance and direction.

Justice MARSHALL concurring.

The problem here is whether in these particular cases the Executive Branch has authority to invoke the equity jurisdiction of the courts to protect what it believes to be the national interest. See *In re Debs,* 158 U.S. 564 (1895). The Government argues that in addition to the inherent power of any government to protect itself, the President's power to conduct foreign affairs and his position as Commander in Chief give him authority to impose censorship on the press to protect his ability to deal effectively with foreign nations and to conduct the military affairs of the country. Of course, it is beyond cavil that the President has broad powers by virtue of his primary responsibility for the conduct of our foreign affairs and his position as Commander in Chief. . . .

It would, however, be utterly inconsistent with the concept of separation of powers for this Court to use its power of contempt to prevent behavior that Congress has specifically declined to prohibit. There would be a similar damage to the basic concept of these co-equal branches of Government if when the Executive Branch has adequate authority granted by Congress to protect "national security" it can choose instead to invoke the contempt power of a court to enjoin the threatened conduct. The Constitution provides that Congress shall make laws, the President execute laws, and courts interpret laws. It did not provide for government by injunction in which the courts and the Executive Branch can "make law" without regard to the action of Congress. It may be more convenient for the Executive Branch if it need only convince a judge to prohibit conduct rather than ask the Congress to pass a law, and it may be more convenient to enforce a contempt order than to seek a criminal conviction in a jury trial. Moreover, it may be considered politically wise to get a court to share the responsibility for arresting those who the Executive Branch has probable cause to believe are violating the law. But convenience and political considerations of the moment do not justify a basic departure from the principles of our system of government.

Chief Justice BURGER dissenting.

I suggest . . . these cases have been conducted in unseemly haste. . . .

Here, moreover, the frenetic haste is due in large part to the manner in which the Times proceeded from the date it obtained the purloined documents. It seems reasonably clear now that the haste precluded reasonable and deliberate judicial treatment of these cases and was not warranted. . . .

The newspapers make a derivative claim under the First Amendment; they denominate this right as the public "right to know"; by implication, the Times asserts a sole trusteeship of that right by virtue of its journalistic "scoop." The right is asserted as an absolute. Of course, the First Amendment right itself is not an absolute, as Justice HOLMES so long ago pointed out in his aphorism concerning the right to shout "fire" in a crowded theater if there was no fire. There are other exceptions, some of which Chief Justice HUGHES mentioned by way of example in *Near v. Minnesota ex rel. Olson*. There are no doubt other exceptions no one has had occasion to describe or discuss. . . .

It is not disputed that the Times has had unauthorized possession of the documents for three to four months, during which it has had its expert analysts studying them, presumably digesting them and preparing the material for publication. During all of this time, the Times, presumably in its capacity as trustee of the public's "right to know," has held up publication for purposes it considered proper and thus public knowledge was delayed. No doubt this was for a good reason; the analysis of 7,000 pages of complex material drawn from a vastly greater volume of material would inevitably take time and the writing of good news stories takes time. But why should the United States Government, from whom this information was illegally acquired by someone, along with all the counsel, trial judges, and appellate judges be placed under needless pressure? After these months of deferral, the alleged "right to know" has somehow and suddenly become a right that must be vindicated instanter.

Would it have been unreasonable, since the newspaper could anticipate the Government's objections to release of secret material, to give the Government an opportunity to review the entire collection and determine whether agreement could be reached on publication? Stolen or not, if security was not in fact jeopardized, much of the material could no doubt have been declassified, since it spans a period ending in 1968. With such an approach—one that great newspapers have in the past practiced and stated editorially to be the duty of an honorable press—the newspapers and Government might well have narrowed the area of disagreement as to what was and was not publishable, leaving the remainder to be resolved in orderly litigation, if necessary. To me it is hardly believable that a newspaper long regarded as a great institution in American life would fail to perform one of the basic and simple duties of every citizen with respect to the discovery or possession of stolen property or secret government documents. That duty, I had thought—perhaps naively—was to report forthwith, to responsible public officers. This duty rests on taxi drivers, Justices, and the New York Times. The course followed by the Times, whether so calculated or not, removed any possibility of orderly litigation of the issues. If the action of the judges up to now has been correct, that result is sheer happenstance.

Justice HARLAN, with whom THE CHIEF JUSTICE and Justice BLACKMUN join, dissenting.

With all respect, I consider that the Court has been almost irresponsibly feverish in dealing with these cases.

Both the Court of Appeals for the Second Circuit and the Court of Appeals for the District of Columbia Circuit rendered judgment on June 23. The New York Times' petition for certiorari, its motion for accelerated consideration thereof, and its application for interim relief were filed in this Court on June 24 at about 11 A.M. The application of the United States for interim relief in the *Post* case was also filed here on June 24 at about 7:15 P.M. This Court's order setting a hearing before us on June 26 at 11 A.M., a course which I joined only to avoid the possibility of even more peremptory action by the Court, was issued less than 24 hours before. The record in the *Post* case was filed with the Clerk shortly before 1 P.M. on June 25; the record in the *Times* case did not arrive until 7 or 8 o'clock that same night. The briefs of the parties were received less than two hours before argument on June 26.

This frenzied train of events took place in the name of the presumption against prior restraints created by the First Amendment. Due regard for the extraordinarily important and difficult questions involved in these litigations should have led the Court to shun such a precipitate timetable. In order to decide the merits of these cases properly, some or all of the following questions should have been faced:

1. Whether the Attorney General is authorized to bring these suits in the name of the United States. . . .

2. Whether the First Amendment permits the federal courts to enjoin publication of stories which would present a serious threat to national security. . . .

3. Whether the threat to publish highly secret documents is of itself a sufficient implication of national security to justify an injunction on the theory that regardless of the contents of the documents harm enough results simply from the demonstration of such a breach of secrecy.

4. Whether the unauthorized disclosure of any of these particular documents would seriously impair the national security.

5. What weight should be given to the opinion of high officers in the Executive Branch of the Government with respect to questions 3 and 4.

6. Whether the newspapers are entitled to retain and use the documents notwithstanding the seemingly uncontested facts that the documents, or the originals of which they are duplicates, were purloined from the Government's possession and that the newspapers received them with knowledge that they had been feloniously acquired. . . .

7. Whether the threatened harm to the national security or the Government's possessory interest in the documents justifies the issuance of an injunction against publication in light of—

a. The strong First Amendment policy against prior restraints on publication;

b. The doctrine against enjoining conduct in violation of criminal statutes; and

c. The extent to which the materials at issue have apparently already been otherwise disseminated.

These are difficult questions of fact, of law, and of judgment: the potential consequences of erroneous decision are enormous. The time which has been available to us, to the lower courts, and to the parties has been wholly inadequate for giving these cases the kind of consideration they deserve. It is a reflection on the stability of the judicial process that these great issues—as important as any that have arisen during my time on the Court— should have been decided under the pressures engendered by the torrent of publicity that has attended these litigations from their inception.

Forced as I am to reach the merits of these cases, I dissent from the opinion and judgments of the Court. . . .

It is plain to me that the scope of the judicial function in passing upon the activities of the Executive Branch of the Government in the field of foreign affairs is very narrowly restricted. This view is, I think, dictated by the concept of separation of powers upon which our constitutional system rests.

In a speech on the floor of the House of Representatives, Chief Justice John MARSHALL, then a member of that body, stated:

"The President is the sole organ of the nation in its external relations, and its sole representative with foreign nations." 10 Annals of Cong. 613.

From that time, shortly after the founding of the Nation, to this, there has been no substantial challenge to this description of the scope of executive power. . . . I agree that, in performance of its duty to protect the values of the First Amendment against political pressures, the judiciary must review the initial Executive determination to the point of satisfying itself that the subject matter of the dispute does lie within the proper compass of the President's foreign relations power. Constitutional considerations forbid "a complete abandonment of judicial control." Moreover the judiciary may properly insist that the determination that disclosure of the subject matter would irreparably impair the national security be made by the head of the Executive Department concerned—here the Secretary of State or the Secretary of Defense—after actual personal consideration by that officer. This safeguard is required in the analogous area of executive claims of privilege for secrets of state. . . .

But in my judgment the judiciary may not properly go beyond these two inquiries and redetermine for itself the probable impact of disclosure on the national security.

Justice BLACKMUN dissenting.

The country would be none the worse off were the cases tried quickly, to be sure, but in the customary and properly deliberative manner. The most recent of the material, it is said, dates no later than 1968, already about three years ago, and the Times itself took three months to formulate its plan of procedure and, thus, deprived its public for that period.

The First Amendment, after all, is only one part of an entire Constitution. Article II of the great document vests in the Executive Branch primary power over the conduct of foreign affairs and places in that branch the responsibility for the Nation's safety. Each provision of the Constitution is important, and I cannot subscribe to a doctrine of unlimited absolutism for the First Amendment at the cost of downgrading other provisions. First Amendment absolutism has never commanded a majority of this Court. . . .

What is needed here is a weighing, upon properly developed standards, of the broad right of the press to print and of the very narrow right of the Government to prevent.

(2) Indirect Prior Restraints

Besides direct prior restraints, the press may be subject to indirect restraints and requirements that arguably have a chilling effect on the exercise of free speech and press. In *Snepp v. United States,* 444 U.S. 507 (1980) (see Chapter 2), for example, the Court summarily dismissed a First Amendment challenge to the Central Intelligence Agency's requiring employees and former employees to submit for any (fiction or nonfiction) writings for prepublication review. In *Meese v. Keene,* 481 U.S. 465 (1987), over the objections of three dissenters (Justices Blackmun, Brennan, and Marshall), the Rehnquist Court upheld the labeling as "political propaganda" of three documentary films (dealing with acid rain and the environment) under the Foreign Agents Registration Act.

In three companion cases in 1972, *Branzburg v. Hayes, In re*

Pappas, and *United States v. Caldwell* (see page 531), a bare majority of the Court rejected reporters' claims that thè First Amendment guarantees them a testimonial privilege against discussing their sources before grand juries and at trials. Compare Justice White's opinion announcing the decision of the Court with the views expressed in the two dissenting opinions filed by Justice Stewart (with whom Justices Brennan and Marshall joined) and Justice Douglas. Justice White, again, wrote for the Court in *Zurcher v. The Stanford Daily* (1978) (see page 539), rejecting the dissenters interpretation of the First Amendment, in holding that newspaper offices are not exempt for searches by police for photographs and other mere evidence of crime. The ruling in *Zurcher,* however, was undercut by Congress's passing the Privacy Protection Act of 1980, which prohibits the unannounced searches of newsrooms by federal, state, and local law enforcement officers, except in certain narrowly defined circumstances. As discussed in section B of this chapter, the Rehnquist Court has also substantially cut back on the First Amendment freedoms of students and student newspapers in cases such as *Hazelwood School District v. Kuhlmeier,* 484 U.S. 260 (1988).

In the 1970s, members of the press also unsuccessfully sought to have the Court vindicate a First Amendment right of access to acquire information. In *dicta* in a number of rulings the Court had suggested that the amendment conveys a "right to receive" as a corollary of the freedom to disseminate information.[1] But a bare majority of the Court rebuffed a further expansion of the First Amendment when members of the press pushed for an "affirmative right of access" in challenging prohibitions of personal interviews between reporters and inmates in state and federal prisons, in *Pell v. Procunier,* 417 U.S. 817 (1974), and *Saxbe v. Washington Post,* 417 U.S. 843 (1974). There Justice Stewart reaffirmed that "the First Amendment does not guarantee the press a constitutional right of special access to information not available to the public generally." In dissent with Justices Brennan and Marshall, Justice Douglas argued that the First Amendment confers special privileges on the press so it may vindicate the public's interests in information about the operation of government. Justice Powell also dissented, finding that the prohibition "significantly impairs the right of the people to a free flow of information and ideas on the conduct of Government," and explained, "The underlying right is the right of the public generally. The press is the necessary representative of the public's interests in this context and the instrumentality which effects the public's rights." When the issue again arose in *Houchins v. KQED, Inc.* (1978) (see page 542), the Court remained sharply divided. However, see and compare *Globe Newspa-*

pers Co. v. Superior Court (1982) (see page 570) and the discussion in section G of this chapter.

NOTE

1. See *Martin v. City of Struthers*, 319 U.S. 141, 143 (1943); *Thomas v. Collins*, 323 U.S. 516 (1945); *Procunier v. Martinez*, 416 U.S. 396 (1974); and *Kleindienst v. Mandel*, 408 U.S. 753 (1972).

SELECTED BIBLIOGRAPHY

Barron, Jerome. *Freedom of the Press for Whom?* Bloomington: Indiana University Press, 1973.
Cross, Harold. *The People's Right to Know.* Morningside Heights, NY: Columbia University Press, 1953.
Van Gerpen, Maurice. *Privileged Communication and the Press.* Westport, CT: Greenwood Press, 1979.

Branzburg v. Hayes, In re Pappas, and *United States v. Caldwell*
408 U.S. 665, 92 S.Ct. 2646 (1972)

Paul Branzburg, Paul Pappas, and Earl Caldwell were reporters working for different newspapers and television stations on unrelated stories involving the production of hashish and the activities of the Black Panthers and other black militant groups. Each refused to reveal the sources of their stories and claimed a First Amendment reporter's privilege of confidentiality, for which each were found in contempt by a judge. On appeal to the Supreme Court, their cases were consolidated for oral argument and decided in a plurality opinion announcing the decision of the Court, and in which Justice White further discusses the facts in each case.

Justice WHITE delivers the opinion of the Court.

The issue in these cases is whether requiring newsmen to appear and testify before state or federal grand juries abridges the freedom of speech and press guaranteed by the First Amendment. We hold that it does not.

The writ of certiorari in No. 70–85, *Branzburg v. Hayes and Meigs*, brings before us two judgments of the Kentucky Court of Appeals, both involving petitioner Branzburg, a staff reporter for the Courier-Journal, a daily newspaper published in Louisville, Kentucky.

On November 15, 1969, the Courier-Journal carried a story under petitioner's by-line describing in detail his observations of two young residents of Jefferson County synthesizing hashish from marihuana, an activity which, they asserted, earned them about $5,000 in three weeks. The article included a photograph of a pair of hands working above a laboratory table on which was a substance identified by the caption as hashish. The article stated that petitioner had promised not to reveal the identity of the two hashish makers. Petitioner was shortly subpoenaed by the Jefferson County grand jury; he appeared, but refused to identify the individuals he had seen possessing marihuana or the persons he had seen making hashish from marihuana. A state trial court judge ordered petitioner to answer these questions and rejected his contention that the Kentucky reporters' privilege statute, the First Amendment of the United States Constitution, or §§ 1, 2 and 8 of the Kentucky Constitution authorized his refusal to answer. . . .

In re Pappas, No. 70–94, originated when petitioner Pappas, a television newsman-photographer working out of the Providence, Rhode Island, office of a New Bedford, Massachusetts, television station, was called to New Bedford on July 30, 1970, to report on civil disorders there which involved fires and other turmoil. He intended to cover a Black Panther news conference at that group's headquarters in a boarded-up store. Petitioner found the streets around the store barricaded, but he ultimately gained entrance to the area and recorded and photographed a prepared statement read by one of the Black Panther leaders at about 3 P.M. . . . As a condition of entry, Pappas agreed not to disclose anything he saw or heard inside the store except an anticipated police raid, which Pappas, "on his own," was free to photograph and report as he wished. . . . Two months later, petitioner was summoned before the Bristol County Grand Jury and appeared, answered questions as to his name, address, employment, and what he had seen and heard outside Panther headquarters, but refused to answer any questions about what had taken place inside headquarters while he was there, claiming that the First Amendment afforded him a privilege to protect confidential informants and their information. . . .

United States v. Caldwell, No. 70–57, arose from subpoenas issued by a federal grand jury in the Northern District of California to respondent Earl Caldwell, a reporter for the New York Times assigned to cover the Black Panther Party and other black militant groups. . . . [Caldwell maintained that to even appear before a grand jury, investigating violations of law, would destroy his relationship with the Panthers and violate his First Amendment rights.]

Petitioners Branzburg and Pappas and respondent Caldwell press First Amendment claims that may be simply put: that to gather news it is often necessary to agree either not to identify the source of information published or to publish only part of the facts revealed, or both; that if the reporter is nevertheless forced to reveal these confidences to a grand jury, the source so identified and other confidential sources of other reporters will be measurably deterred from furnishing publishable information, all to the detriment of the free flow of information protected by the First Amendment. Although the newsmen in these cases do not claim an absolute privilege against official interrogation in all circumstances, they assert that the reporter should not be forced either to appear or to testify before a grand jury or at trial until and unless sufficient grounds are shown for believing that the reporter possesses information relevant to a crime the grand jury is investigating, that the information the reporter has is unavailable from other sources, and that the need for the information is sufficiently compelling to override the claimed invasion of First Amendment interests occasioned by the disclosure. . . .

The heart of the claim is that the burden on news gathering resulting from compelling reporters to disclose confidential information outweighs any public interest in obtaining the information.

We do not question the significance of free speech, press, or assembly to the country's welfare. Nor is it suggested that news gathering does not qualify for First Amendment protection; without some protection for seeking out the news, freedom of the press could be eviscerated. But these cases involve no intrusions upon speech or assembly, no prior restraint or restriction on what the press may publish, and no express or implied command that the press publish what it prefers to withhold. . . .

The sole issue before us is the obligation of reporters to respond to grand jury subpoenas as other citizens do and to answer questions relevant to an investigation into the commission of crime. Citizens generally are not constitutionally immune from grand jury subpoenas; and neither the First Amendment nor any other constitutional provision protects the average citizen from disclosing to a grand jury information that he has received in confidence. . . .

It is clear that the First Amendment does not invalidate every incidental burdening of the press that may result from the enforcement of civil or criminal statutes of general applicability. . . .

It has generally been held that the First Amendment does not guarantee the press a constitutional right of special access to information not available to the public generally. In *Zemel v. Rusk,* [381 U.S. 1 (1965)] for example, the Court sustained the Government's refusal to validate passports to Cuba even though that restriction "render[ed] less than wholly free the flow of information concerning that country." The ban on travel was held constitutional, for "[t]he right to speak and publish does not carry with it the unrestrained right to gather information."

Despite the fact that news gathering may be hampered, the press is regularly excluded from grand jury proceedings, our own conferences, the meetings of other official bodies gathered in executive session, and the meetings of private organizations. Newsmen have no constitutional right of access to the scenes of crime or disaster when the general public is excluded, and they may be prohibited from attending or publishing information about trials if such restrictions are necessary to assure a defendant a fair trial before an impartial tribunal. . . .

The prevailing constitutional view of the newsman's privilege is very much rooted in the ancient role of the grand jury that has the dual function of determining if there is probable cause to believe that a crime has been committed and of protecting citizens against unfounded criminal prosecutions. . . . Because its task is to inquire into the existence of possible criminal conduct and to return only well-founded indictments, its investigative powers are necessarily broad. . . .

Until now the only testimonial privilege for unofficial witnesses that is rooted in the Federal Constitution is the Fifth Amendment privilege against compelled self-incrimination. We are asked to create another by interpreting the First Amendment to grant newsmen a testimonial privilege that other citizens do not enjoy. This we decline to do. Fair and effective law enforcement aimed at providing security for the person and property of the individual is a fundamental function of government, and the grand jury plays an important, constitutionally mandated role in this process. On the records now before us, we perceive no basis for holding that the public interest in law enforcement and in ensuring effective grand jury proceedings is insufficient to override the consequential, but uncertain, burden on news gathering that is said to result from insisting that reporters, like other citizens, respond to relevant questions put to them in the course of a valid grand jury investigation or criminal trial.

This conclusion itself involves no restraint on what newspapers may publish or on the type or quality of information reporters may seek to acquire, nor does it threaten the vast bulk of confidential relationships between reporters and their sources. . . . Only where news sources themselves are implicated in crime or possess information relevant to the grand jury's task need they or the reporter be concerned about grand jury subpoenas. Nothing before us indicates that a large number or percentage of *all* confidential news sources falls into either category and would in any way be deterred by our holding that the Constitution does not, as it never has, exempt the newsman from performing the citizen's normal duty of appearing and furnishing information relevant to the grand jury's task. . . .

Of course, the press has the right to abide by its agreement not to publish all the information it has, but the right to withhold news is not equivalent to a First Amendment exemption from the ordinary duty of all other citizens to furnish relevant information to a grand jury performing an important public function. Private restraints on the flow of information are not so favored by the First Amendment that they override all other public interests. . . .

Finally, as we have earlier indicated, news gathering is not without its First Amendment protections, and grand jury investigations if instituted or conducted other than in good faith, would pose wholly different issues for resolution under the First Amendment. Official harassment of the press undertaken not for purposes of law enforcement but to disrupt a reporter's relationship with his news sources would have no justification. Grand juries are subject to judicial control and subpoenas to motions to quash. We do not expect courts will forget that grand juries must operate within the limits of the First Amendment as well as the Fifth.

Justice POWELL concurring.

I add this brief statement to emphasize what seems to me to be the limited nature of the Court's holding. The Court does not hold that newsmen, subpoenaed to testify before a grand jury, are without constitutional rights with respect to the gathering of news or in safeguarding their sources. . . .

As indicated in the concluding portion of the opinion, the Court states that no harassment of newsmen will be tolerated. If a newsman believes that the grand jury investigation is not being conducted in good faith he is not without remedy. Indeed, if the newsman is called upon to give information bearing only a remote and tenuous relationship to the subject of the investigation, or if he has some other reason to believe that his testimony implicates confidential source relationships without a legitimate need of law enforcement, he will have access to the court on a motion to quash and an appropriate protective order may be entered. The asserted claim to privilege should be judged on its facts by the striking of a proper balance between freedom of the press and the obligation of all citizens to give relevant testimony with respect to criminal conduct. The balance of these vital constitutional and societal interests on a case-by-case basis accords with the tried and traditional way of adjudicating such questions.

In short, the courts will be available to newsmen under circumstances where legitimate First Amendment interests require protection.

Justice STEWART, with whom Justice BRENNAN and Justice MARSHALL join, dissenting.

The Court's crabbed view of the First Amendment reflects a disturbing insensitivity to the critical role of an independent press in our society. The question whether a reporter has a constitutional right to a confidential relationship with his source is of first impression here, but the principles that should guide our decision are as basic as any to be found in the Constitution. While Justice POWELL's enigmatic concurring opinion gives some hope of a more flexible view in the future, the Court in these cases holds that a newsman has no First Amendment right to protect his sources when called before a grand jury. The Court thus invites state and federal authorities to undermine the historic independence of the press by attempting to annex the journalistic profession as an investigative arm of government. . . .

The reporter's constitutional right to a confidential relationship with his source stems from the broad societal interest in a full and free flow of information to the public. It is this basic concern that underlies the Constitution's protection of a free press, because the guarantee is "not for the benefit of the press so much as for the benefit of all of us." *Time, Inc. v. Hill* [385 U.S. 374 (1967)].

The right to gather news implies, in turn, a right to a confidential relationship between a reporter and his source. This proposition follows as a matter of simple logic once three factual predicates are recognized: (1) newsmen require informants to gather news; (2) confidentiality—the promise or understanding that names or certain aspects of communications will be kept off the record—is essential to the creation and maintenance of a news-gathering relationship with informants; and (3) an unbridled subpoena power—the absence of a constitutional right protecting, in *any* way, a confidential relationship from compulsary process—will either deter sources from divulging information or deter reporters from gathering and publishing information. . . .

The impairment of the flow of news cannot, of course, be proved with scientific precision, as the Court seems to demand. . . . But we have never before demanded that First Amendment rights rest on elaborate empirical studies demonstrating beyond any conceivable doubt that deterrent effects exist; we have never before required proof of the exact number of people potentially affected by governmental action, who would actually be dissuaded from engaging in First Amendment activity.

Rather, on the basis of common sense and available information, we have asked, often implicitly, (1) whether there was a rational connection between the cause (the governmental action) and the effect (the deterrence or impairment of First Amendment activity), and (2) whether the effect would occur with some regularity, *i. e.,* would not be *de minimis.* . . . Once this threshold inquiry has been satisfied, we have then examined the competing interests in determining whether there is an unconstitutional infringement of First Amendment freedoms. . . .

To require any greater burden of proof is to shirk our duty to protect values securely embedded in the Constitution. We cannot await an unequivocal—and therefore unattainable—imprimatur from empirical studies. We can and must accept the evidence developed in the record, and elsewhere, that overwhelmingly supports the premise that deterrence will occur with regularity in important types of news-gathering relationships. . . .

In striking the proper balance between the public interest in the efficient administration of justice and the First Amendment guarantee of the fullest flow of information, we must begin with the basic proposition that because of their "delicate and vulnerable" nature, and their transcendent importance for the just functioning of our society, First Amendment rights require special safeguards. . . .

Thus, when an investigation impinges on First Amendment rights, the government must not only show that the inquiry is of "compelling and overriding importance" but it must also "convincingly" demonstrate that the investigation is "substantially related" to the information sought.

Governmental officials must, therefore, demonstrate that the information sought is *clearly* relevant to a *precisely* defined subject of governmental inquiry. They must demonstrate that it is reasonable to think the witness in question has that information. And they must show that there is not any means of obtaining the information less destructive of First Amendment liberties. . . .

I believe the safeguards developed in our decisions involving governmental investigations must apply to the grand jury inquiries in these cases. Surely the function of the grand jury to aid in the enforcement of the law is no more important than the function of the legislature, and its committees, to make the law. . . .

Accordingly, when a reporter is asked to appear before a grand jury and reveal confidences, I would hold that the government must (1) show that there is probable cause to believe that the newsman has information that is clearly relevant to a specific probable violation of law; (2) demonstrate that the information sought cannot be obtained by alternative means less destructive of First Amendment rights; and (3) demonstrate a compelling and overriding interest in the information.

Justice DOUGLAS dissenting.

Today's decision will impede the wide-open and robust dissemination of ideas and counterthought which a free press both fosters and protects and which is essential to the success of intelligent self-government. Forcing a reporter before a grand jury will have two retarding effects upon the ear and the pen of the press. Fear of exposure will cause dissidents to communicate less openly to trusted reporters. And, fear of accountability will cause editors and critics to write with more restrained pens.

I see no way of making mandatory the disclosure of a reporter's confidential source of the information on which he bases his news story. . . .

A reporter is no better than his source of information. Unless he has a privilege to withhold the identity of his source, he will be the victim of governmental intrigue or aggression. If he can be summoned to testify in secret before a grand jury, his sources will dry up and the attempted exposure, the effort to enlighten the public, will be ended. If what the Court sanctions today becomes settled law, then the reporter's main function in American society will be to pass on to the public the press releases which the various departments of government issue. . . .

When we deny newsmen that protection, we deprive the people of the information needed to run the affairs of the Nation in an intelligent way.

Madison said:

"A popular Government, without popular information, or the means of acquiring it, is but a Prologue to a Farce or a Tragedy; or, perhaps both. Knowledge will forever govern ignorance: And a people who mean to be their own Governors, must arm themselves with the power which knowledge gives." (To W. T. Barry, Aug. 4, 1822). 9 Writings of James Madison 103. (G. Hunt ed. 1910).

Today's decision is more than a clog upon news gathering. It is a signal to publishers and editors that they should exercise caution in how they use whatever information they can obtain. Without immunity they may be summoned to account for their criticism. Entrenched officers have been quick to crash their powers down upon unfriendly commentators. . . .

The intrusion of government into this domain is symptomatic of the disease of this society. As the years pass the power of government becomes more and more pervasive. It is a power to suffocate both people and causes. Those in power, whatever their politics, want only to perpetuate it. Now that the fences of the law and the tradition that has protected the press are broken down, the people are the victims. The First Amendment, as I read it, was designed precisely to prevent that tragedy.

Zurcher v. The Stanford Daily
436 U.S. 547, 98 S.Ct. 1970 (1978)

Justice White states the facts in this case, involving a police search for photographs in the editorial office of a student newspaper, at the outset of his opinion announcing the decision of the Court.

Justice WHITE delivers the opinion of the Court.

Late in the day on Friday, April 9, 1971, officers of the Palo Alto Police Department and of the Santa Clara County Sheriff's Department responded to a call from the director of the Stanford University Hospital requesting the removal of a large group of demonstrators who had seized the hospital's administrative offices and occupied them since the previous afternoon. After several futile efforts to persuade the demonstrators to leave peacefully, more drastic measures were employed. The demonstrators had barricaded the doors at both ends of a hall adjacent to the administrative offices. The police chose to force their way in at the west end of the corridor. As they did so, a group of demonstrators emerged through the doors at the east end and, armed with sticks and clubs, attacked the group of nine police officers stationed there. One officer was knocked to the floor and struck repeatedly on the head; another suffered a broken shoulder. All nine were injured. There were no police photographers at the east doors, and most bystanders and reporters were on the west side. The officers themselves were able to identify only two of their assailants, but one of them did see at least one person photographing the assault at the east doors.

On Sunday, April 11, a special edition of the Stanford Daily (Daily), a student newspaper published at Stanford University, carried articles and photographs devoted to the hospital protest and the violent clash between demonstrators and police. . . . The next day, the Santa Clara County District Attorney's Office secured a warrant from the municipal court for an immediate search of the Daily's offices for negatives, film and pictures showing the events and occurrences at the hospital on the evening of April 9. The warrant issued on a finding of "just, probable and reasonable cause for believing that: Negatives and photographs and films, evidence material and relevant to the identification of the perpetrators of felonies, to wit, Battery on a Peace Officer, and Assault with a Deadly Weapon, will be located [on the premises of the Daily.]". . .

The search pursuant to the warrant was conducted later that day by four police officers and took place in the presence of some members of the Daily staff. The Daily's photographic laboratories, filing cabinets, desks, and waste paper baskets were searched. Locked drawers and rooms were not opened. The officers apparently had opportunity to read notes and correspondence during the search; but contrary to claims of the staff, the officers denied that they had exceeded the limits of the warrant. They had not been advised by the staff that the areas they were searching contained confidential materials. The search revealed only the photographs that had already been published on April 11, and no materials were removed from the Daily's office. . . .

The issue here is how the Fourth Amendment is to be construed and applied to the "third party" search, the recurring situation where state authorities have probable cause, to believe that fruits, instrumentalities, or other evidence of crime is located on identified property but do not then have probable cause to believe that the owner or possessor of the property is himself implicated in the crime that has occurred or is occurring. . . .

The critical element in a reasonable search is not that the owner of the property is suspected of crime but that there is reasonable cause to believe that the specific "things" to be searched for and seized are located on the property to which entry is sought. . . .

[I]t is untenable to conclude that property may not be searched unless its occupant is reasonably suspected of crime and is subject to arrest. And if those considered free of criminal involvement may nevertheless be searched or inspected under civil statutes, it is difficult to understand why the Fourth Amendment would prevent entry onto their property to recover evidence of a crime not committed by them but by others. As we understand the structure and language of the Fourth Amendment and our cases expounding it, valid warrants to search property may be issued when it is satisfactorily demonstrated to the magistrate that fruits, instrumentalities, or evidence of crime is located on the premises. The Fourth Amendment has itself struck the balance between privacy and public need, and there is no occasion or justification for a court to revise the Amendment and strike a new balance by denying the search warrant in the circumstances present here and by insisting that the investigation proceed by subpoena *duces tecum,* whether on the theory that the latter is a less intrusive alternative, or otherwise. . . .

It is true that the struggle from which the Fourth Amendment emerged "is largely a history of conflict between the Crown and the press," *Stanford v. Texas,* 379 U.S. 476 (1965), and that in issuing warrants and determining the reasonableness of a search, state and federal magistrates should be aware that "unrestricted power of search and seizure could also be an instrument for stifling liberty of expression." *Marcus v. Search Warrant,* 367 U.S. 717 (1961). Where the materials sought to be seized may be protected by the First Amendment, the requirements of the Fourth Amendment must be applied with "scrupulous exactitude." *Stan-*

ford v. Texas, supra. Hence, in *Stanford v. Texas,* the Court invalidated a warrant authorizing the search of a private home for all books, records, and other materials relating to the Communist Party, on the ground that whether or not the warrant would have been sufficient in other contexts, it authorized the searchers to rummage among and make judgments about books and papers and was the functional equivalent of a general warrant, one of the principal targets of the Fourth Amendment. Where presumptively protected materials are sought to be seized, the warrant requirement should be administered to leave as little as possible to the discretion or whim of the officer in the field. . . .

Aware of the long struggle between Crown and press and desiring to curb unjustified official intrusions, the Framers took the enormously important step of subjecting searches to the test of reasonableness and to the general rule requiring search warrants issued by neutral magistrates. They nevertheless did not forbid warrants where the press was involved, did not require special showings that subpoenas would be impractical, and did not insist that the owner of the place to be searched, if connected with the press, must be shown to be implicated in the offense being investigated. . . .

We accordingly reject the reasons given by the District Court and adopted by the Court of Appeals for holding the search for photographs at the *Stanford Daily* to have been unreasonable within the meaning of the Fourth Amendment and in violation of the First Amendment. Nor has anything else presented here persuaded us that the Amendments forbade this search. It follows that the judgment of the Court of Appeals is reversed.

Justice BRENNAN did not participate in the consideration or decision of this case.

Justice POWELL concurred.

Justice STEWART with whom Justice MARSHALL joins, dissenting.

Believing that the search by the police of the offices of The Stanford Daily infringed the First and Fourteenth Amendments' guarantee of a free press, I respectfully dissent.

It seems to me self-evident that police searches of newspaper offices burden the freedom of the press. The most immediate and obvious First Amendment injury caused by such a visitation by the police is physical disruption of the operation of the newspaper. Policemen occupying a newsroom and searching it thoroughly for what may be an extended period of time will inevitably interrupt its normal operations, and thus impair or even temporarily prevent the processes of newsgathering, writing, editing, and publishing. By contrast, a subpoena would afford the newspaper itself an opportunity to locate whatever material might be requested and produce it.

But there is another and more serious burden on a free press imposed by an unannounced police search of a newspaper office: the possibility of disclosure of information received from confidential sources, or of the identity of the sources themselves. Protection of those sources is necessary to ensure that the press can fulfill its constitutionally designated function of informing the public, because important information can often be obtained only by an assurance that the source will not be revealed. . . .

A search warrant allows police officers to ransack the files of a newspaper, reading each and every document until they have found the one named in the warrant, while a subpoena would permit the newspaper itself to produce only the specific documents requested. A search, unlike a subpoena, will therefore lead to the needless exposure of confidential information completely unrelated to the purpose of the investigation. The knowledge that police officers can make an unannounced raid on a newsroom is thus bound to have a deterrent effect on the availability of confidential news sources. The end result, wholly inimical to the First Amendment, will be a diminishing flow of potentially important information to the public. . . .

Perhaps as a matter of abstract policy a newspaper office should receive no more protection from unannounced police searches than, say, the office of a doctor or the office of a bank. But we are here to uphold a Constitution. And our Constitution does not explicitly protect the practice of medicine or the business of banking from all abridgment by government. It does explicitly protect the freedom of the press.

For these reasons I would affirm the judgment of the Court of Appeals.

Justice STEVENS dissented in a separate opinion.

Houchins v. KQED, Inc.
438 U.S. 1, 98 S.Ct. 2588 (1978)

This case involves the claim of a radio station, KQED, to have a "right of access," under the First Amendment, to interview particular prisoners in a jail. Chief Justice Burger further discusses the facts in this case in his plurality opinion announcing the decision of the Court.

Chief Justice BURGER, with whom Justice WHITE and Justice REHNQUIST join, delivers the opinion of the Court.

The question presented is whether the news media have a constitutional right of access to a county jail, over and above that of other persons, to interview inmates and make sound recordings, films, and photographs for publication and broadcasting by newspapers, radio and television.

Petitioner Houchins, as Sheriff of Alameda County, Cal., controls all access to the Alameda County Jail at Santa Rita. Respondent KQED operates licensed television and radio broadcasting stations which have frequently reported newsworthy events relating to penal institutions in the San Francisco Bay Area. On March 31, 1975, KQED reported the suicide of a prisoner in the Greystone portion of the Santa Rita Jail. The report included a statement by a psychiatrist that the conditions at the Greystone facility were responsible for the illnesses of his patient-prisoners there, and a statement from petitioner denying that prison conditions were responsible for the prisoners' illnesses.

KQED requested permission to inspect and take pictures within the Greystone facility. After permission was refused, KQED and the Alameda and Oakland Branches of the National Association for the Advancement of Colored People (NAACP) filed suit under 42 U.S.C. § 1983. They alleged that petitioner had violated the First Amendment by refusing to permit media access and failing to provide any effective means by which the public could be informed of conditions prevailing in the Greystone facility or learn of the prisoners' grievances. Public access to such information was essential, they asserted, in order for NAACP members to participate in the public debate on jail conditions in Alameda County. They further asserted that television coverage of the conditions in the cells and facilities was the most effective way of informing the public of prison conditions. . . .

From the right to gather news and the right to receive information [the respondents] argue for an implied special right of access to government controlled sources of information. This right, they contend, compels access as a *constitutional* matter. . . . Respondents contend that public access to penal institutions is necessary to prevent officials from concealing prison conditions from the voters and impairing the public's right to discuss and criticize the prison system and its administration. . . .

Beyond question, the role of the media is important; acting as the "eyes and ears" of the public, they can be a powerful and constructive force, contributing to remedial action in the conduct of public business. They have served that function since the beginning of the Republic, but like all other components of our society media representatives are subject to limits. . . .

The public importance of conditions in penal facilities and

the media's role of providing information afford no basis for reading into the Constitution a right of the public or the media to enter these institutions, with camera equipment, and take moving and still pictures of inmates for broadcast purposes. This Court has never intimated a First Amendment guarantee of a right of access to all sources of information within government control. Nor does the rationale of the decisions upon which respondents rely lead to the implication of such a right. . . .

The respondents' argument is flawed, not only because it lacks precedential support and is contrary to statements in this Court's opinions, but also because it invites the Court to involve itself in what is clearly a legislative task which the Constitution has left to the political processes. Whether the government should open penal institutions in the manner sought by respondents is a question of policy which a legislative body might appropriately resolve one way or the other.

Justice MARSHALL and Justice BLACKMUN did not participate in the consideration or decision of this case.

Justice STEWART concurring.

The First and Fourteenth Amendments do not guarantee the public a right of access to information generated or controlled by government, nor do they guarantee the press any basic right of access superior to that of the public generally. The Constitution does no more than assure the public and the press equal access once government has opened its doors. Accordingly, I agree substantially with what the opinion of the CHIEF JUSTICE has to say on that score.

We part company, however, in applying these abstractions to the facts of this case. Whereas he appears to view "equal access" as meaning access that is identical in all respects, I believe that the concept of equal access must be accorded more flexibility in order to accommodate the practical distinctions between the press and the general public.

When on assignment, a journalist does not tour a jail simply for his own edification. He is there to gather information to be passed on to others, and his mission is protected by the Constitution for very specific reasons. . . .

That the First Amendment speaks separately of freedom of speech and freedom of the press is no constitutional accident, but an acknowledgement of the critical role played by the press in American society. The Constitution requires sensitivity to that role and to the special needs of the press in performing it effectively. A person touring Santa Rita Jail can grasp its reality with his own eyes and ears. But if a television reporter is to convey the jail's sights and sounds to those who cannot personally visit the place, he must use cameras and sound equipment. In short, terms of access that are reasonably imposed on individual members of the public may, if they impede effective reporting without sufficient justification, be unreasonable as applied to journalists who are there to convey to the general public what the visitors see.

Under these principles, KQED was clearly entitled to some form of preliminary injunctive relief. At the time of the District Court's decision, members of the public were permitted to visit most parts of the Santa Rita Jail, and the First and Fourteenth Amendments required the Sheriff to give members of the press *effective* access to the same areas. The Sheriff evidently assumed that he could fulfill this obligation simply by allowing reporters to sign up for tours on the same terms as the public. I think he was mistaken in this assumption, as a matter of constitutional law. . . .

In two respects, however, the District Court's preliminary injunction was overbroad. It ordered the Sheriff to permit reporters into the Little Greystone facility and it required him to let them interview randomly encountered inmates. In both these respects, the injunction gave the press access to areas and sources of information from which persons on the public tours had been excluded, and thus enlarged the scope of what the Sheriff and Supervisors had opened to public view. The District Court erred in concluding that the First and Fourteenth Amendments compelled this broader access for the press.

Justice STEVENS, with whom Justice BRENNAN and Justice POWELL join, dissenting.

The Court holds that the scope of press access to the Santa Rita jail required by the preliminary injunction issued against petitioner is inconsistent with the holding in *Pell v. Procunier,* [417 U.S. 817 (1974)], that "newsmen have no constitutional right of access to prisons or their inmates beyond that afforded the general public" and therefore the injunction was an abuse of the District Court's discretion. I respectfully disagree. . . .

For two reasons, which shall be discussed separately, the decisions in *Pell* and *Saxbe* [*v. Washington Post,* 417 U.S. 843 (1974)] do not control the propriety of the District Court's preliminary injunction. First, the unconstitutionality of petitioner's policies which gave rise to this litigation does not rest on the premise that the press has a greater right of access to information regarding prison conditions than do other members of the public. Second, relief tailored to the needs of the press may properly be awarded to a representative of the press which is successful in proving that it has been harmed by a constitutional violation and need not await the grant of relief to members of the general public who may also have been injured by petitioner's unconstitutional access policy but have not yet sought to vindicate their rights. . . .

In *Pell v. Procunier,* the Court stated that "newsmen have no constitutional right of access to prisons or their inmates beyond that afforded the general public." But the Court has never intimated that a nondiscriminatory policy of excluding entirely both the public and the press from access to information about prison conditions would avoid constitutional scrutiny. . . .

The preservation of a full and free flow of information to the general public has long been recognized as a core objective of the First Amendment to the Constitution. It is for this reason that the First Amendment protects not only the dissemination but also the receipt of information and ideas. . . .

In this case . . . "[r]espondents do not assert a right to force disclosure of confidential information or to invade in any way the decisionmaking processes of governmental officials." They simply seek an end to petitioner's policy of concealing prison conditions from the public. Those conditions are wholly without claim to confidentiality. While prison officials have an interest in the time and manner of public acquisition of information about the institutions they administer, there is no legitimate, penological justification for concealing from citizens the conditions in which their fellow citizens are being confined.

The reasons which militate in favor of providing special protection to the flow of information to the public about prisons relate to the unique function they perform in a democratic society. Not only are they public institutions, financed with public funds and administered by public servants; they are an integral component of the criminal justice system. The citizens confined therein are temporarily, and sometimes permanently, deprived of their liberty as a result of a trial which must conform to the dictates of the Constitution. By express command of the Sixth Amendment the proceeding must be a public trial." It is important not only that the trial itself be fair, but also that the community at large have confidence in the integrity of the proceeding. That public interest survives the judgment of conviction and appropriately carries over to an interest in how the convicted person is treated during his period of punishment and hoped-for rehabilitation. While a ward of the State and subject to its stern discipline, he retains constitutional protections against cruel and unusual punishment, a protection which may derive more practical support from access to information about prisons by the public than by occasional litigation in a busy court. . . .

In this case, the record demonstrates that both the public and the press had been consistently denied any access to the inner portions of the Santa Rita jail, that there had been excessive censorship of inmate correspondence, and that there was no valid justification for these broad restraints on the flow of information. An affirmative answer to the question whether respondent established a likelihood of prevailing on the merits did not depend, in final analysis, on any right of the press to special treatment beyond that accorded the public at large. Rather, the probable existence of a constitutional violation rested upon the special importance of allowing a democratic community access to knowledge about how its servants were treating some of its members who have been committed to their custody. An official prison policy of concealing such knowledge from the public by arbitrarily cutting off the flow of information at its source abridges the freedom of speech and of the press protected by the First and Fourteenth Amendments to the Constitution.

F. REGULATING THE BROADCAST MEDIA

Radio, television, cable, and other electronic media have posed special First Amendment problems. This is because they were considered a scarce public resource that should be licensed and regulated in "the public interest." In 1934, the Federal Communications Commission (FCC) was created to regulate broadcast and telecommunications systems based on considerations of "public interest, convenience and necessity." While the FCC is forbidden from exercising censorship per se, it has the authority to license every radio and television station, subject to renewal every three years, and to revoke or suspend those licenses for violations of its rules or other statutory requirements, including antitrust laws. Among the regulations imposed are those requiring "equal time" for opponents of political candidates who are given air time, a "family hour" on television (during which programs are shown that have little or no violence and suggestive sexual material), bans against broadcasting obscene and indecent language, and limitations on the coownership of newspapers and broadcasting systems.

In the 1970s and 1980s, however, regulations were gradually cut back. This was partially in response to technological developments, such as cable television and satellite transmissions. These advances increased the multiplicity of channels and held the potential for greater public access. This, in turn, undermined the traditional rationale for regulating radio and television as a scarce public resource, and exempted from First Amendment protection. In addition, beginning in Jimmy Carter's presidency and throughout that of Ronald Reagan, there was a movement toward deregulation to promote economic competition and efficiency. Because the radio market, for example, had grown and competition increased since the 1930s, the FCC relaxed some of its regulations and did away with others—such as requiring maximum time limits for commercials and minimum requirements for news and public affairs programming.

One of the most controversial requirements imposed on the broadcast media in 1949, and finally eliminated in 1987, was the "fairness doctrine," requiring stations to notify and provide air time for individuals personally attacked or made the subject of political editorials. When upholding the fairness doctrine in *Red Lion Broadcasting Co., Inc. v. Federal Communications Commission* (1969) (see page 550), Justice White reviews the rationales for treating the broadcast media differently from the print media in terms of the First Amendment. *Red Lion's* distinctions were underscored by the Court's striking down Florida's "right to reply" law, requiring newspapers to print the reply of any political candidate who was subject to a personal attack by a newspaper. In *Miami Herald Publishing Company v. Tornillo,* 418 U.S. 241 (1974), Justice White explained that "this [right to reply] law runs afoul of the elementary First Amendment proposition that government may not force a newspaper to print copy which, in its journalistic discretion, it chooses to leave on the newspaper floor."

In *Columbia Broadcasting System v. Democratic National Committee* (1973) (see page 553) the Court also ruled that the FCC was not required to ensure a "private right of access to the broadcast media," when sustaining CBS's policy of refusing paid editorial advertisements. But, compare the views expressed in Chief Justice Burger's plurality opinion with those in Justice Douglas's concurring opinion and Justice Brennan's dissenting opinion. In *CBS, Inc. v. FCC,* 453 U.S. 367 (1981), however, the Court affirmed a "right of access" for legally qualified candidates for federal office when ruling that CBS should not have refused to sell air time in 1979 to the Democratic National Committee for President Carter's reelection bid because it deemed it too early for the presidential campaign of 1980 to begin.

While the FCC abandoned the fairness doctrine, in 1987 it also moved to more strictly enforce its regulations against "indecent" broadcasts. This followed the ruling in *Federal Communications Commission v. Pacifica Foundation,* (1978) (see page 433), and from a change in the views of a majority of the commissioners, who were appointed by President Reagan. As a result, some new First Amendment controversies have arisen over the reading on the radio of literary works, such as Allen Ginsberg's poem "Howl."[1]

The Court upheld as well the FCC's rules banning the acquisition of radio and television stations by newspapers in *FCC v. National Citizens Committee*, 436 U.S. 775 (1978), and the FCC's decision not to consider changes in the entertainment format of radio stations when reviewing applications for renewal or transfer of broadcasting licenses in *FCC v. WNCN Listeners Guild*, 450 U.S. 582 (1981).

The Court moved in the direction of according greater First Amendment to electronic media because of the multiplicity of channels and greater access brought by the development of cable television and more satellite and telecommunications systems.[2] In *United States v. Midwest Video Corporation*, 406 U.S. 649 (1972), the justices (five to four) upheld the FCC's regulation of television antenna and cable systems. But in *FCC v. Midwest Video Corporation*, 440 U.S. 689 (1979), the Court (six to three) struck down the FCC's regulations requiring major cable systems (with twenty or more channel capacities) to provide up to four channels for free public expression and public affairs programming. "Under the [FCC's] rules," Justice White observed, "cable operators [were] deprived of all discretion regarding who may exploit their access channels and what may be transmitted over such channels."

Due to the Court's ruling in *Midwest Video Corporation* (II), the FCC has less jurisdiction over cable television systems than over radio and broadcast television. The Court, though, held the FCC's technical standards governing the quality of cable television signals to preempt those of states and localities. *City of New York v. FCC*, 486 U.S. 57 (1988). The powers of states and localities over cable television were also sharply limited in *Capital Cities Cable, Inc. v. Crisp*, 467 U.S. 691 (1984), overturning an Oklahoma law barring the broadcasting of advertisements for alcoholic beverages as applied to cable television operators. Without hearing oral arguments or issuing a written opinion, the Court also affirmed a lower federal court ruling striking down Utah's law restricting cable telecasts of nudity, sex acts, and other "indecent" images in *Wilkinson v. Jones*, 480 U.S. 926 (1987).

NOTES

1. See Richard Wiley, "Broadcasters Urged to Use Caution with New FCC Indecency Standard," *The National Law Journal* 24 (June 8, 1987).
2. See *City of Los Angeles v. Preferred Communications*, 476 U.S. 488 (1986) (noting that the First Amendment is implicated by cable operations).

SELECTED BIBLIOGRAPHY

Friendly, Fred W. *The Good Guys, the Bad Guys and the First Amendment.* New York: Random House, 1976.

Labunski, Richard. *The First Amendment under Siege: The Politics of Broadcast Regulation.* Westport, CT: Greenwood Press, 1981.

Powe, Lucas. *American Broadcasting and the First Amendment.* Berkeley: University of California Press, 1987.

Schmidt, Benno, Jr. *Freedom of the Press vs. Public Access.* New York: Praeger, 1976.

Simmons, Steven. *The Fairness Doctrine and the Media.* Berkeley: University of California, 1978.

Red Lion Broadcasting Co., Inc. v. Federal Communications Commission

395 U.S. 367, 89 S.Ct. 1794 (1969)

Justice White states the facts in this case, upholding the FCC's fairness doctrine, at the outset of his opinion for the Court. Although the FCC abandoned the fairness doctrine in 1987, Justice White's opinion remains important for its articulation of the traditional rationales for treating the print and broadcast media differently for First Amendment purposes.

Justice WHITE delivers the opinion of the Court.

The Red Lion Broadcasting Company is licensed to operate a Pennsylvania radio station, WGCB. On November 27, 1964, WGCB carried a 15-minute broadcast by the Reverend Billy James Hargis as part of a "Christian Crusade" series: A book by Fred J. Cook entitled "Goldwater—Extremist on the Right" was discussed by Hargis, who said that Cook had been fired by a newspaper for making false charges against city officials; that Cook had then worked for a Communist-affiliated publication; that he had defended Alger Hiss and attacked J. Edgar Hoover and the Central Intelligence Agency; and that he had now written a "book to smear and destroy Barry Goldwater." When Cook heard of the broadcast he concluded that he had been personally attacked and demanded free reply time, which the station refused. After an exchange of letters among Cook, Red Lion, and the FCC, the FCC declared that the Hargis broadcast constituted a personal attack on Cook; that Red Lion had failed to meet its obligation under the fairness doctrine. . . . On review in the Court of Appeals for the District of Columbia Circuit, the FCC's position was upheld as constitutional and otherwise proper. . . .

The broadcasters challenge the fairness doctrine and its specific manifestations in the personal attack and political editorial rules on conventional First Amendment grounds, alleging that the rules abridge their freedom of speech and press. Their contention is that the First Amendment protects their desire to use their allotted frequencies continuously to broadcast whatever they choose, and to exclude whomever they choose from ever using that frequency. No man may be prevented from saying or publishing what he thinks, or from refusing in his speech or other utterances to give equal weight to the views of his opponents. This right, they say, applies equally to broadcasters.

Although broadcasting is clearly a medium affected by a First Amendment interest, differences in the characteristics of new media justify differences in the First Amendment standards applied to them. . . .

Where there are substantially more individuals who want to broadcast than there are frequencies to allocate, it is idle to posit an unabridgeable First Amendment right to broadcast comparable to the right of every individual to speak, write, or publish. If 100 persons want broadcast licenses but there are only 10 frequencies to allocate, all of them may have the same "right" to a license; but if there is to be any effective communication by radio, only a few can be licensed and the rest must be barred from the airwaves. It would be strange if the First Amendment, aimed at protecting and furthering communications, prevented the Government from making radio communication possible by requiring licenses to broadcast and by limiting the number of licenses so as not to overcrowd the spectrum. . . .

By the same token, as far as the First Amendment is concerned those who are licensed stand no better than those to whom licenses are refused. A license permits broadcasting, but the licensee has no constitutional right to be the one who holds the license or to monopolize a radio frequency to the exclusion of his fellow citizens. There is nothing in the First Amendment which prevents the Government from requiring a licensee to share his frequency with others and to conduct himself as a proxy or fiduciary with obligations to present those views and voices which are representative of his community and which would otherwise, by necessity, be barred from the airwaves. . . .

Nor can we say that it is inconsistent with the First Amendment goal of producing an informed public capable of conducting its own affairs to require a broadcaster to permit answers to personal attacks occurring in the course of discussing controversial issues, or to require that the political opponents of those endorsed by the station be given a chance to communicate with the public. Otherwise, station owners and a few networks would have unfettered power to make time available only to the highest bidders, to communicate only their own views on public issues, people and candidates, and to permit on the air only those with whom they agreed. There is no sanctuary in the First Amendment for unlimited private censorship operating in a medium not open to all. . . .

It is strenuously argued, however, that if political editorials or personal attacks will trigger an obligation in broadcasters to afford the opportunity for expression to speakers who need not pay for time and whose views are unpalatable to the licensees, then broadcasters will be irresistibly forced to self-censorship and their coverage of controversial public issues will be eliminated or at least rendered wholly ineffective. Such a result would indeed be a serious matter, for should licensees actually eliminate their coverage of controversial issues, the purposes of the doctrine would be stifled.

At this point, however, as the Federal Communications Commission has indicated, that possibility is at best speculative. The communications industry, and in particular the networks, have taken pains to present controversial issues in the past, and even now they do not assert that they intend to abandon their efforts in this regard. It would be better if the FCC's encouragement were never necessary to induce the broadcasters to meet their responsibility. And if experience with the administration of those doctrines indicates that they have the net effect of reducing rather than enhancing the volume and quality of coverage, there will be time enough to reconsider the constitutional implications. The fairness doctrine in the past has had no such overall effect.

That this will occur now seems unlikely, however, since if present licensees should suddenly prove timorous, the Commission is not powerless to insist that they give adequate and fair attention to public issues. It does not violate the First Amendment to treat licensees given the privilege of using scarce radio frequencies as proxies for the entire community, obligated to give suitable time and attention to matters of great public concern. To condition the granting or renewal of licenses on a willingness to present representative community views on controversial issues is consistent with the ends and purposes of those constitutional provisions forbidding the abridgment of freedom of speech and freedom of the press. . . .

[T]he fact remains that existing broadcasters have often attained their present position because of their initial government selection in competition with others before new technological advances opened new opportunities for further uses. Long experience in broadcasting, confirmed habits of listeners and viewers, network affiliation, and other advantages in program procurement give existing broadcasters a substantial advantage over new entrants, even where new entry is technologically possible. These advantages are the fruit of a preferred position conferred by the Government. Some present possibility for new entry by competing stations is not enough, in itself, to render unconstitutional the Government's effort to assure that a broadcaster's programming ranges widely enough to serve the public interest.

In view of the scarcity of broadcast frequencies, the Government's role in allocating those frequencies, and the legitimate claims of those unable without governmental assistance to gain access to those frequencies for expression of their views, we hold the regulations and ruling at issue here are both authorized by statute and constitutional.

Justice DOUGLAS did not participate in the decision of this case.

Columbia Broadcasting System v. Democratic National Committee
412 U.S. 94, 93 S.Ct. 2080 (1973)

In 1970, the Democratic National Committee and the Business Executives' Move for Vietnam Peace requested a declaratory ruling from the Federal Communications Commission (FCC) that the Communications Act of 1934 or the First Amendment precluded Columbia Broadcasting System (CBS) from refusing to sell time to responsible entities to present their views on public issues. The Business Executives' Move for Vietnam Peace also filed a complaint with the FCC, alleging that CBS violated the First Amendment by refusing to sell it broadcast time for spot announcements of its views on the Vietnam War, and that CBS's coverage of antiwar views did not meet the requirements of the fairness doctrine. The FCC rejected the fairness doctrine challenge and ruled that CBS was not required to accept paid editorial advertisements. On appeal, the Court of Appeals for the District of Columbia Circuit reversed the commission, holding that "a flat ban on paid public issue announcements [was] in violation of the First Amendment." CBS then appealed to the Supreme Court.

Chief Justice BURGER, with whom Justice STEWART and Justice REHNQUIST join in part, delivers the opinion of the Court.

We granted the writs of certiorari in these cases to consider whether a broadcast licensee's general policy of not selling advertising time to individuals or groups wishing to speak out on issues they consider important violates the Federal Communications Act of 1934, or the First Amendment.

In two orders announced the same day, the Federal Communications Commission ruled that a broadcaster who meets his public obligation to provide full and fair coverage of public issues is not required to accept editorial advertisements . . . [expressing the views of the Democratic National Committee on the Vietnam War]. A divided Court of Appeals reversed the Commission, holding that a broadcaster's fixed policy of refusing editorial advertisements violates the First Amendment; the court remanded the cases to the Commission to develop procedures and guidelines for administering a First Amendment right of access. . . .

[U]nder the Fairness Doctrine broadcasters are responsible for providing the listening and viewing public with access to a balanced presentation of information on issues of public importance. The basic principle underlying that responsibility is "the right of the public to be informed, rather than any right on the part of the Government, any broadcast licensee or any individual member of the public to broadcast his own particular views on any matter. . . ." Report of Editorializing by Broadcast Licensees (1949). Consistent with that philosophy, the Commission on several occasions has ruled that no private individual or group has a right to command the use of broadcast facilities. . . .

With this background in mind, we next proceed to consider whether a broadcaster's refusal to accept editorial advertisements is governmental action violative of the First Amendment. . . .

The licensee policy challenged in this case is intimately related to the journalistic role of a licensee for which it has been given initial and primary responsibility by Congress. The licensee's policy against accepting editorial advertising cannot be examined as an abstract proposition, but must be viewed in the context of its journalistic role. It does not help to press on us the idea that editorial ads are "like" commercial ads, for the licensee's policy against editorial spot ads is expressly based on a journalistic judgment that 10- to 60-second spot announcements are ill-suited to intelligible and intelligent treatment of public issues; the broadcaster has chosen to provide a balanced treatment of controversial questions in a more comprehensive form. Obviously the licensee's evaluation is based on its own journalistic judgment of priorities and newsworthiness.

Moreover, the Commission has not fostered the licensee policy challenged here: it has simply declined to command particular action because it fell within the area of journalistic discretion. . . .

Were we to read the First Amendment to spell out governmental action in the circumstances presented here, few licensee decisions on the content of broadcasts or the processes of editorial evaluation would escape constitutional scrutiny. In this sensitive area so sweeping a concept of governmental action would go far in practical effect to undermine nearly a half century of unmistakable congressional purpose to maintain—no matter how difficult the task—essentially private broadcast journalism held only broadly accountable to public interest standards. . . .

There remains for consideration the question whether the "public interest" standard of the Communications Act requires broadcasters to accept editorial advertisements or, whether, assuming governmental action, broadcasters are required to do so by reason of the First Amendment. . . . [T]he question before us is whether the various interests in free expression of the public, the broadcaster, and the individuals require broadcasters to sell commercial time to persons wishing to discuss controversial issues. . . . The Commission was justified in concluding that the public interest in providing access to the marketplace of "ideas and experiences" would scarcely be served by a system so heavily weighted in favor of the financially affluent, or those with access to wealth. . . . Moreover, there is the substantial danger, as the Court of Appeals acknowledged . . . that the time allotted for editorial advertising could be monopolized by those of one political persuasion. . . .

[However, we cannot] accept the Court of Appeals' view that every potential speaker is "the best judge" of what the listening public ought to hear or indeed the best judge of the merits of his or her views. All journalistic tradition and experience is to the contrary. For better or worse editing is what editors are for; and editing is selection and choice of material. That editors—newspaper or broadcast—can and do abuse this power is beyond doubt, but that is no reason to deny the discretion Congress provided. Calculated risks of abuse are taken in order to preserve higher values. The presence of these risks is nothing new; the authors of the Bill of Rights accepted the reality that these risks were evils for which there was no acceptable remedy other than a spirit of moderation and a sense of responsibility—and civility—on the part of those who exercise the guaranteed freedoms of expression. . . .

[Moreover, under] a constitutionally commanded and Government supervised right-of-access system urged by respondents and mandated by the Court of Appeals, the Commission would be required to oversee far more of the day-to-day operations of broadcasters' conduct, deciding such questions as whether a particular individual or group has had sufficient opportunity to present its viewpoint and whether a particular viewpoint has already been sufficiently aired. Regimenting broadcasters is too radical a therapy for the ailment respondents complain of.

Justice STEWART concurred. Justice WHITE concurred in part and dissented in part.

Justice BLACKMUN, with whom Justice POWELL joined, concurred.

Justice DOUGLAS concurring.

My conclusion is that TV and radio stand in the same protected position under the First Amendment as do newspapers and magazines. The philosophy of the First Amendment requires that result, for the fear that Madison and Jefferson had of government intrusion is perhaps even more relevant to TV and radio than it is to newspapers and other like publications. That fear was founded not only on the spectre of a lawless government but of government under the control of a faction that desired to foist its views of the common good on the people. . . .

Both TV and radio news broadcasts frequently tip the news one direction or another and even try to turn a public figure into a character of disrepute. Yet so do the newspapers and the magazines and other segments of the press. The standards of TV, radio, newspapers, or magazines—whether of excellence or mediocrity—are beyond the reach of Government. Government—acting through courts—disciplines lawyers. Government makes criminal some acts of doctors and of engineers. But the First Amendment puts beyond the reach of Government federal regulation of news agencies save only business or financial practices which do not involve First Amendment rights. . . .

What kind of First Amendment would best serve our needs as we approach the 21st century may be an open question. But the old-fashioned First Amendment that we have is the Court's only guideline; and one hard and fast principle which it announces is that Government shall keep its hands off the press. That principle has served us through days of calm and eras of strife and I would abide by it until a new First Amendment is adopted. That means, as I view it, that TV and radio, as well as the more conventional methods for disseminating news, are all included in the concept of "press" as used in the First Amendment and therefore are entitled to live under the laissez-faire regime which the First Amendment sanctions.

Justice BRENNAN, with whom Justice MARSHALL joins, dissenting.

In my view, the principle at stake here is one of fundamental importance for it concerns the people's right to engage in and to hear vigorous public debate on the broadcast media. And balancing what I perceive to be the competing interests of broadcasters, the listening and viewing public, and individuals seeking to express their views over the electronic media, I can only conclude that the exclusionary policy upheld today can serve only to inhibit, rather than to further, our "profound national commitment to the principle that debate on public issues should be uninhibited, robust, and wide-open." I would therefore affirm the determination of the Court of Appeals that the challenged broadcaster policy is violative of the First Amendment. . . .

At the outset, it should be noted that both radio and television broadcasting utilize a natural resource, the electromagnetic spectrum that is part of the public domain. And, although broadcasters are granted the temporary use of this valuable resource for terminable three-year periods, "ownership" and ultimate control remain vested in the people of the United States. . . .

[W]e have explicitly recognized that, in light of the unique nature of the electronic media, the public have strong First Amendment interests in the reception of a full spectrum of views—presented in a vigorous and uninhibited manner—on controversial issues of public importance. And, as we have seen, it has traditionally been thought that the most effective way to insure this "uninhibited, robust, and wide-open" debate is by fostering a "free trade in ideas" by making our forums of communication readily available to all persons wishing to express their views. Although apparently conceding the legitimacy of these principles, the Court nevertheless upholds the absolute ban on editorial advertising because, in its view, the Commission's Fairness Doctrine, in and of itself, is sufficient to satisfy the First Amendment interests of the public. I cannot agree. . . .

Under the Fairness Doctrine, broadcasters decide what issues are "important," how "fully" to cover them, and what format, time, and style of coverage are "appropriate." The retention of such *absolute* control in the hands of a few Government licensees is inimical to the First Amendment, for vigorous, free debate can be attained only when members of the public have at least *some* opportunity to take the initiative and editorial control into their own hands. . . .

Moreover, a proper balancing of the competing First Amendment interests at stake in this controversy must consider, not only the interests of broadcasters and of the listening and viewing public, but also the independent First Amendment interest of groups and individuals in effective self-expression. . . . "[S]peech concerning public affairs . . . is the essence of self-government," *Garrison v. Louisiana,* 379 U.S. 64 (1964), and the First Amendment must therefore safeguard not only the right of the public to *hear* debate, but also the right of individuals to *participate* in that debate and to attempt to persuade others to their points of view. . . .

Here, of course, there can be no doubt that the broadcast frequencies allotted to the various radio and television licensees constitute appropriate "forums" for the discussion of controversial issues of public importance. Indeed, unlike the streets, parks, public libraries, and other "forums" that we have held to be appropriate for the exercise of First Amendment rights, the broadcast media are dedicated *specifically* to communication. And, since the expression of ideas—whether political, commercial, musical, or otherwise—is the exclusive purpose of the broadcast spectrum, it seems clear that the adoption of a limited scheme of editorial advertising would in no sense divert that spectrum from its intended use. . . .

This is not to say, of course, that broadcasters have *no* First Amendment interest in exercising journalistic supervision over the use of their facilities. On the contrary, such an interest does indeed exist, and it is an interest that must be weighed heavily in any legitimate effort to balance the competing First Amendment interests involved in this case. In striking such a balance, however, it must be emphasized that these cases deal *only* with the allocation of *advertising* time—air time that broadcasters regularly relinquish to others without the retention of significant editorial control. Thus, we are concerned here, not with the speech of broadcasters themselves, but, rather, with their "right" to decide which *other* individuals will be given an opportunity to speak in a forum that has already been opened to the public.

Viewed in this context, the *absolute* ban on editorial advertising seems particularly offensive because, although broadcasters refuse to sell any air time whatever to groups or individuals wishing to speak out on controversial issues of public importance, they make such air time readily available to those "commercial" advertisers who seek to peddle their goods and services to the public. Thus, as the system now operates, any person wishing to market a particular brand of beer, soap, toothpaste, or deodorant has direct, personal, and instantaneous access to the electronic media. He can present his own message, in his own words, in any format he selects, and at a time of his own choosing. Yet a similar individual seeking to discuss war, peace, pollution, or the suffering of the poor is denied this right to speak. . . .

The First Amendment values of individual self-fulfillment through expression and individual participation in public debate are central to our concept of liberty. If these values are to survive in the age of technology, it is essential that individuals be permitted at least *some* opportunity to express their views on public issues over the electronic media. Balancing those interests against the limited interest of broadcasters in exercising "journalistic supervision" over the mere allocation of *advertising* time that is already made available to some members of the public, I simply cannot conclude that the interest of broadcasters must prevail.

Federal Communications Commission v. Pacifica Foundation

438 U.S. 726, 98 S.Ct. 3026 (1978)

In this case, the Court upheld the FCC's power to ban indecent language on the radio. The case is reprinted in part on page 433.

G. FAIR TRIAL/FREE PRESS CONTROVERSIES

The development of television, along with newspapers, and their coverage of sensational trials led to a series of "fair trial/free press" controversies. Adverse, prejudicial pretrial and trial publicity ostensibly creates a conflict between the defendant's Sixth Amendment right to a fair trial and the First Amendment freedoms of speech and press, as well as the public's interests in information about the operation of the criminal justice system. But because constitutional rights are assertable only against the government, not other individuals, fair trial/free press controversies actually involve determining what process is due and how to reconcile governmental attempts to limit publicity or access to judicial proceedings with First Amendment principles.

The Sixth Amendment specifically provides that "In all criminal prosecutions the accused shall enjoy the right to a speedy and *public trial*" (emphasis added). A presumption of openness is rooted in common law practice, stemming from earlier Anglo-Saxon customs. Open, public trials have traditionally been viewed as an essential safeguard against judicial abuse of power and miscarriages of justice. Also, publicity may both educate people about the operation of the judiciary and provide an opportunity for members of the public to scrutinize the administration of justice.

Despite the language of the Sixth Amendment and generally accepted practice of having open trials, neither the press nor the public could compel openness. While acknowledging the public's interests in open trials, the Court maintained that the Sixth Amendment guarantees only the rights of the accused, not the public. However, the Court also noted that "although a defendant can, under some circumstances, waive his constitutional right to a public trial, he has no absolute right to compel a private trial" in *Singer v. United States,* 380 U.S. 24 (1965). In short, under the Sixth Amendment, members of the public have no constitutional claim to compel open trials, but neither do defendants have a right to a closed trial.

Because the Sixth Amendment guarantees an accused person's rights, and only secondarily the public's interests, judges may restrict public access and publicity to ensure due process and procedural fairness.[1] But as judges began to increasingly restrict media coverage of judicial proceedings, lawyers turned to the First Amendment claiming, as Justice Douglas once put it, "The trial is a public event. What transpires in the court room is public property."[2] Because the First Amendment, unlike the Sixth Amendment, comprehends the public's broad interests in freedom of information, it provides a basis for challenging restraints on publicity and access to trials.

Prior to the 1960s, the Court tended to overturn contempt charges of the press for editorials and news stories concerning pretrial and trial proceedings.[3] But extensive publicity and, in one case, the videotaping and playing of a confession on television prior to the accused's trial, led to the Court's reconsideration and insistence that judges exercise their powers to ensure fair trials.[4] Then in *Estes v. Texas*, 381 U.S. 532 (1965), when the Court first tackled the controversy over televising of criminal trials, the justices were deeply split. Justice Stewart's initial draft failed to command a majority. He was relegated to writing a dissenting opinion, joined by three others. Justice Tom Clark wrote the majority's opinion holding that cameras in the courtroom were too disruptive and denied the defendant's right to a fair trial.

The year after *Estes*, with an even more controversial ruling, in *Sheppard v. Maxwell*, 385 U.S. 333 (1966), the Warren Court overturned the conviction of Dr. Sam Sheppard for murdering his wife because the trial judge failed to ensure the decorum essential to a fair trial. There the press had what Justice Clark characterized as "a Roman holiday," with live broadcasting of the coroner's inquest from a high-school gymnasium. During the trial, the judge reserved three of the four rows of benches in the courtroom for news reporters and permitted the erection of a press table inside the bar of the courtroom, which allowed journalists to overhear all of Sheppard's conversations with his attorneys.

In *Sheppard*, Justice Clark's opinion for the Court suggested that in sensational trials judges should adopt rules governing reporters' access to the courtroom and insulating witnesses from journalists, as well as issue gag orders barring police, witnesses, and counsel from talking with reporters about trial proceedings. But this ruling only intensified the fair trial/free press controversy. Immediately, the American Bar Association adopted as part of its Canons of Professional Ethics rules limiting attorney's permissible statements about pending trials and recommendations that judges use their contempt power to inhibit prejudicial publicity. The American Newspaper Publishers Association countered that such interference with news reporting constituted a prior restraint.

Following *Sheppard,* trial courts' increasing reliance on gag orders was vigorously contested by the press as a prior restraint in violation of the First Amendment. The Court finally addressed the constitutionality of gag orders in *Nebraska Press Association v. Stuart* (1976) (see page 564). In striking down the gag order there, notice that Chief Justice Burger's opinion does not hold gag orders unconstitutional per se, which prompted Justice Brennan's concurring opinion expressing the view that all gag orders run afoul of the First Amendment. Notice also that Burger indicates alternatives to issuing gag orders, including changes of venue (that is, moving a trial to another locality where there is less public interest in or publicity about the trial), postponing trials to permit adverse publicity to die down, permitting rigorous examination of potential jurors to check against prejudice, instructing juries emphatically of their responsibility to consider admitted evidence only, and even sequestering juries. In addition, mistrials for adverse publicity may be granted and convictions overturned on appeal.

Although the Court in *Nebraska Press Association* did not rule out gag orders in all circumstances, it made them extremely difficult to defend against First Amendment challenges.[5] As a result when confronted with the difficulties of controlling for prejudicial publicity, trial judges simply closed pretrial hearings and trials. That generated a new controversy over the right of the press and the public to attend judicial proceedings under the First and Sixth Amendments.

When the Court initially confronted the issue of closed judicial proceedings in *Gannett Co. v. DePasquale,* 443 U.S. 368 (1979), involving the closure of a pretrial hearing, the justices split five to four, and even those in the majority were not in agreement on interpreting the First and Sixth Amendments. Justice Stewart's opinion announcing the decision upholding the closure there, moreover, further fueled the controversy, prompting five justices later to publicly try to explain the ruling.[6] Stewart expressly rejected the view that the Sixth Amendment embodies a right of the public to attend criminal trials and declined to decide "in the abstract . . . whether there is any such constitutional right" under the First Amendment. But because he also stated twelve times in his opinion that the public and press have no constitutional right of access to *either pretrial hearings or trials,* there was confusion over the scope of the Court's ruling. Concurring, Chief Justice Burger underlined that the ruling dealt only with pretrial hearings. Justice Powell's concurring opinion emphasized "the importance of the public's having accurate information concerning the operation of its criminal justice system" and expressed his view that reporters have, in some circumstances, a First Amendment right to access. By contrast, in another concurring opinion, Justice Rehnquist stressed that "the public does not have *any* Sixth Amendment right of access" and dismissed Powell's understanding of the First Amendment. In his view, "The First and Fourteenth Amendments do not guarantee the public a right of access to information generated or controlled by the government, nor do they guarantee the press any basic right of access superior to that of the public generally." The four dissenters, however, maintained that the Sixth Amendment guarantees the right of the public to attend pretrial hearings as well as trials.

Gannett's ambiguity and confusion had considerable impact on public and press access to judicial proceedings. In the year following the ruling, defendants, prosecutors, witnesses, and judges sought to close proceedings in thirteen federal courts and 259 state courts. Motions for closure were introduced in 214 preindictment and pretrial proceedings and in no less than forty-seven trials and eleven posttrial proceedings. Significantly, motions for closure were successful in 122 preindictment and pretrial hearings, and resulted in thirty-three closed trials and five posttrial arraignments.

One year after *Gannett,* the Court tried to clear up some of the confusion, but a majority of the justices still could not agree on the rationale for and scope of the Court's ruling in *Richmond Newspapers, Inc. v. Virginia,* 488 U.S. 555 (1980). Only Justices Stevens and White joined Chief Justice Burger's opinion announcing the Court's overturning the closure of a criminal trial. Both the First and Sixth Amendments, according to Burger, run together to make trials analogous to other "public forums" in which members of the press and public have historically enjoyed access, and distinguishable from places not generally recognized as open to the public (such as prisons, jails, and military bases). For this reason, Burger held that the press and public enjoy a "right of visitation" that precludes, except in extraordinary circumstances, the closing of criminal trials in contrast with pretrial hearings. But Burger did not go far enough for concurring Justices Brennan, Marshall, and Stevens, who contended that the First Amendment has an "affirmative side" requiring public access to pretrial hearings and trials in every circumstance.

Finally, three years after *Gannett,* Justice Brennan was able to mass a solid majority behind his opinion in *Globe Newspaper Company v. Superior Court for the County of Norfolk* (1982) (see page 570), holding that the First Amendment guarantees the press and the public access to pretrial hearings and trials. Subsequently, the Court reaffirmed the principle of openness when overturning the closure of *voir dire* examinations, in *Press-Enterprise Co. v. Superior Court of California*, 464 U.S. 501 (1984). In *Waller v. Georgia*, 467 U.S. 39 (1984), Justice Powell held, for an unanimous Court, that the entire closure of pretrial hearings on the suppression of evidence violated the Sixth Amendment. In another case, however, challenging a judge's protective order restricting access to information relating to donations to a religious organization, Justice Powell upheld the judge's order but emphasized its narrowness and the fact that it did not preclude the press from publishing the information if obtained from other sources.[7] Finally, *Press-Enterprise Co. v. Superior Court of California*, 477 U.S. 648 (1986), reaffirmed the First Amendment right of the press and the public to attend pretrial hearings in virtually all cases; Chief Justice Burger's opinion for the Court there was so sweeping that dissenting Justices Rehnquist and Stevens warned that the ruling could lead to the opening up of grand jury proceedings.

Controversies over ensuring both fair trials and freedom of the press evolved with the struggles within the Court over reaching agreement on the scope of the First Amendment. At the same time, though, television coverage of trials became more responsible and television technology became more sophisticated and less intrusive. In the 1970s, a number of states began once again allowing television coverage of state criminal trials. The Court reconsidered *Estes* and *Sheppard* in *Chandler v. Florida* (1981) (see page 574), upholding television coverage of criminal trials over the objections of the defendants.

NOTES

1. *Illinois v. Allen*, 397 U.S. 337 (1970).

2. *Craig v. Harney*, 331 U.S. 367 (1947).

3. See *Pennekamp v. Florida*, 328 U.S. 331 (1946); and *Craig v. Harney*, 331 U.S. 367 (1947).

4. See *Irvin v. Dowd*, 366 U.S. 717 (1961); and *Rideau v. Louisiana*, 373 U.S. 723 (1963) (videotaping and televising of confession denied due process).

5. See *Oklahoma Press Publishing Company v. District Court*, 430 U.S. 308 (1977) (striking down gag orders); and *Seattle Times Co. v. Rhinehart*,

467 U.S. 20 (1984) (upholding a protective order on pretrial discovery proceedings so long as it did not preclude dissemination of same information gathered from other sources).

6. See David M. O'Brien, "The Trials and Tribulations of Courtroom Secrecy and Judicial Craftsmanship: Reflections on Gannett and Richmond Newspapers," 3 *Communications and the Law* 3–33 (1981).

7. *Seattle Times Company v. Rhinehart*, 467 U.S. 20 (1984).

SELECTED BIBLIOGRAPHY

Brennan, Jr. William J., "Address." 32 *Rutgers Law Review* 137 (1979).
Siebert, Fredrick. *Free Press and Fair Trial.* Athens: University of Georgia, 1970.
Stevens, John Paul. "Some Thoughts about a General Rule." 21 *Arizona Law Review* 559 (1979).

Nebraska Press Association v. Stuart
427 U.S. 539, 96 S.Ct. 2791 (1976)

On the evening of October 18, 1975, police found six members of the Henry Kellie family murdered in their home in Sutherland, Nebraska, a community of 850 people. At the scene of the crime, reporters were given by the police the description of their suspect, Erwin Charles Simants. The following morning, Simants was arrested and arraigned.

Three days later, the county attorney and Simants's attorney joined in asking the trial judge to issue a restraining order on "matters that may or may not be publicly reported or disclosed to the public" because of the "mass coverage by the news media" and "the reasonable likelihood of prejudicial news which would make difficult, if not impossible, the impaneling of an impartial jury and tend to prevent a fair trial." The judge issued a restraining order on the coverage of five subjects:

(1) the existence or contents of a confession Simants had made to law enforcement officers, which had been introduced in open court at arraignment; (2) the fact or nature of statements Simants had made to other persons; (3) the contents of a note he had written the night of the crime; (4) certain aspects of the medical testimony at the preliminary hearing; and (5) the identity of the victims of the alleged sexual assault and the nature of the assault.

In addition, the judge's order set out a plan for attendance, seating, and courthouse traffic control during the trial.

Four days after the judge issued his restraining order, the Nebraska Press Association asked the court to stay its order and, at the same time, applied to the Nebraska Supreme Court for an expedited appeal from the order. The state supreme court upheld the constitutionality of the trial court's issuing restraining orders, but modified the order to prohibit the reporting on only three matters: "(a) the existence and nature of any confessions or admissions made by the defendant to law enforcement officers, (b) any confessions or admissions made to any third parties, except members of the press; and (c) other facts strongly implicative of the accused." The Nebraska Press Association subsequently challenged the constitutionality of these orders when appealing to the Supreme Court, which granted *certiorari.*

Chief Justice BURGER delivers the opinion of the Court.

The Sixth Amendment in terms guarantees "trial by an impartial jury . . ." in federal criminal prosecutions. Because "trial by jury in criminal cases is fundamental to the American scheme of justice," the Due Process Clause of the Fourteenth Amendment guarantees the same right in state criminal prosecutions. . . .

In the overwhelming majority of criminal trials, pretrial publicity presents few unmanageable threats to this important right. But when the case is a "sensational" one tensions develop between the right of the accused to trial by an impartial jury and the rights guaranteed others by the First Amendment. The relevant decisions of this Court, even if not dispositive, are instructive by way of background.

In *Irvin v. Dowd,* [366 U.S. 717] (1961), for example, the defendant was convicted of murder following intensive and hostile news coverage. The trial judge had granted a defense motion for a change of venue, but only to an adjacent county, which had been exposed to essentially the same news coverage. At trial, 430 persons were called for jury service; 268 were excused because they had fixed opinions as to guilt. Eight of the 12 who served as jurors thought the defendant guilty, but said they could nevertheless render an impartial verdict. On review the Court vacated the conviction and death sentence and remanded to allow a new trial for, "[w]ith his life at stake, it is not requiring too much that petitioner be tried in an atmosphere undisturbed by so huge a wave of public passion. . . ."

In *Sheppard v. Maxwell,* 384 U.S. 333 (1966), the Court focused sharply on the impact of pretrial publicity and a trial court's duty to protect the defendant's constitutional right to a fair trial.

With only Justice BLACK dissenting, and he without opinion, the Court ordered a new trial for the petitioner, even though the first trial had occurred 12 years before. Beyond doubt the press had shown no responsible concern for the constitutional guarantee of a fair trial; the community from which the jury was drawn had been inundated by publicity hostile to the defendant. But the trial judge "did not fulfill his duty to protect [the defendant] from the inherently prejudicial publicity which saturated the community and to control disruptive influences in the courtroom.". . .

[P]retrial publicity—even pervasive, adverse publicity—does not inevitably lead to an unfair trial. The capacity of the jury eventually impaneled to decide the case fairly is influenced by the tone and extent of the publicity, which is in part, and often in large part, shaped by what attorneys, police, and other officials do to precipitate news coverage. The trial judge has a major responsibility. What the judge says about a case, in or out of the courtroom, is likely to appear in newspapers and broadcasts. More important, the measures a judge takes or fails to take to mitigate the effects of pretrial publicity may well determine whether the defendant receives a trial consistent with the requirements of due process. That this responsibility has not always been properly discharged is apparent from the decisions just reviewed. . . .

The state trial judge in the case before us acted responsibly, out of a legitimate concern, in an effort to protect the defendant's right to a fair trial. What we must decide is not simply whether the Nebraska courts erred in seeing the possibility of real danger to the defendant's rights, but whether in the circumstances of this case the means employed were foreclosed by another provision of the Constitution. . . .

The thread running through [our rulings on the First Amendment] is that prior restraints on speech and publication are the most serious and the least tolerable infringement on First Amendment rights. A criminal penalty or a judgment in a defamation case is subject to the whole panoply of protections afforded by deferring the impact of the judgment until all avenues of appellate review have been exhausted. Only after judgment has become final, correct or otherwise, does the law's sanction become fully operative.

A prior restraint, by contrast and by definition, has an immediate and irreversible sanction. If it can be said that a threat of criminal or civil sanctions after publication "chills" speech, prior restraint "freezes" it at least for the time.

The damage can be particularly great when the prior restraint falls upon the communication of news and commentary on current events. Truthful reports of public judicial proceedings have been afforded special protection against subsequent punishment. . . . It is not asking too much to suggest that those who exercise First Amendment rights in newspapers or broadcasting enterprises direct some effort to protect the rights of an accused to a fair trial by unbiased jurors.

Of course, the order at issue . . . [here] does not prohibit but only postpones publication. Some news can be delayed and most commentary can even more readily be delayed without serious injury, and there often is a self-imposed delay when responsible editors call for verification of information. But such delays are normally slight and they are self-imposed. Delays imposed by governmental authority are a different matter. As a practical matter moreover, the element of time is not unimportant if press coverage is to fulfill its traditional function of bringing news to the public promptly. . . .

We turn now to the record in this case to . . . determine (a) the nature and extent of pretrial news coverage; (b) whether other measures would be likely to mitigate the effects of unrestrained pretrial publicity; (c) how effectively a restraining order would operate to prevent the threatened danger. . . . We must then consider whether the record supports the entry of a prior restraint on publication, one of the most extraordinary remedies known to our jurisprudence. . . .

Our review of the pretrial record persuades us that the trial judge was justified in concluding that there would be intense and pervasive pretrial publicity concerning this case. He could also reasonably conclude, based on common human experience, that publicity might impair the defendant's right to a fair trial. He did not purport to say more, for he found only "a clear and present danger that pretrial publicity could impinge upon the defendant's right to a fair trial.". . .

We find little in the record that goes to another aspect of our task, determining whether measures short of an order retraining all publication would have insured the defendant a fair trial. . . .

Most of the alternatives to prior restraint of publication in these circumstances were discussed with obvious approval in *Sheppard v. Maxwell*, (a) change of trial venue to a place less exposed to the intense publicity that seemed imminent in Lincoln County; (b) postponement of the trial to allow public attention to subside; (c) use of searching questioning of prospective jurors, as Chief Justice MARSHALL did in the [*United States v.*] *Burr*, [4 Cr. (8 U.S.) 469 (1807)] case, to screen out those with fixed opinions as to guilt or innocence; (d) the use of emphatic and clear instructions on the sworn duty of each juror to decide the issues only on evidence presented in open court. Sequestration of jurors is, of course, always available. Although that measure insulates jurors only after they are sworn, it also enhances the likelihood of dissipating the impact of pretrial publicity and emphasizes the elements of the jurors' oaths. . . .

We have noted earlier that pretrial publicity, even if pervasive and concentrated, cannot be regarded as leading automatically and in every kind of criminal case to an unfair trial. . . .

We have therefore examined this record to determine the probable efficacy of the measures short of prior restraint on the press and speech. There is no finding that alternative measures would not have protected Simants' rights, and the Nebraska Supreme Court did no more than imply that such measures might not be adequate. Moreover, the record is lacking in evidence to support such a finding.

We must also assess the probable efficacy of prior restraint on publication as a workable method of protecting Simants' right to a fair trial, and we cannot ignore the reality of the problems of managing and enforcing pretrial restraining orders. The territorial jurisdiction of the issuing court is limited by concepts of sovereignty. . . . The need for *in personam* jurisdiction also presents an obstacle to a restraining order that applies to publication atlarge as distinguished from restraining publication within a given jurisdiction. . . .

The Nebraska Supreme Court narrowed the scope of the restrictive order, and its opinion reflects awareness of the tensions between the need to protect the accused as fully as possible and the need to restrict publication as little as possible. The dilemma posed underscores how difficult it is for trial judges to predict what information will in fact undermine the impartiality of jurors, and the difficulty of drafting an order that will effectively keep prejudicial information from prospective jurors. When a restrictive order is sought, a court can anticipate only part of what will develop that may injure the accused. But information not so obviously prejudicial may emerge, and what may properly be published in these "gray zone" circumstances may not violate the restrictive order and yet be prejudicial.

Finally, we note that the events disclosed by the record took place in a community of 850 people. It is reasonable to assume that, without any news accounts being printed or broadcast, rumors would travel swiftly by word of mouth. One can only speculate on the accuracy of such reports, given the generative propensities of rumors; they could well be more damaging than reasonably accurate news accounts. But plainly a whole community cannot be restrained from discussing a subject intimately affecting life within it.

Given these practical problems, it is far from clear that prior restraint on publication would have protected Simants' rights. . . .

Of necessity our holding is confined to the record before us. But our conclusion is not simply a result of assessing the adequacy of the showing made in this case; it results in part from the problems inherent in meeting the heavy burden of demonstrating, in advance of trial, that without prior restraint a fair trial will be denied. The practical problems of managing and enforcing restrictive orders will always be present. In this sense, the record now before us is illustrative rather than exceptional. It is significant that when this Court has reversed a state conviction, because of prejudicial publicity, it has carefully noted that some course of action short of prior restraint would have made a critical difference. However difficult it may be, we need not rule out the possibility of showing the kind of threat to fair trial rights that would possess the requisite degree of certainty to justify restraint. This Court has frequently denied that First Amendment rights are absolute and has consistently rejected the proposition that a prior restraint can never be employed.

Justice WHITE concurring.

I should add, however, that for the reasons which the Court itself canvasses there is grave doubt in my mind whether orders with respect to the press such as were entered in this case would ever be justifiable.

Justice POWELL concurring.

In my judgment a prior restraint properly may issue only when it is shown to be necessary to prevent the dissemination of prejudicial publicity that otherwise poses a high likelihood of preventing, directly are irreparably, the impaneling of a jury meeting the Sixth Amendment requirement of impartiality. This requires a showing that (i) there is a clear threat to the fairness of trial, (ii) such a threat is posed by the actual publicity to be restrained, and (iii) no less restrictive alternatives are available. Not withstanding such a showing, a restraint may not issue unless it also is shown that previous publicity or publicity from unrestrained sources will not render the restraint inefficacious.

Justice BRENNAN, with whom Justice STEWART and Justice MARSHALL join, concurring.

I unreservedly agree with Justice BLACK that "free speech and fair trials are two of the most cherished policies of our civilization, and it would be a trying task to choose between them." *Bridges v. California*, 314 U.S. 252 (1961). But I would reject the notion that a choice is necessary, that there is an inherent conflict that cannot be resolved without essentially abrogating one right or the other. To hold that courts cannot impose any prior restraints on the reporting of or commentary upon information revealed in open court proceedings, disclosed in public documents, or divulged by other sources with respect to the criminal justice system is not, I must emphasize, to countenance the sacrifice of precious Sixth Amendment rights on the altar of the First Amendment. For although there may in some instances be tension between uninhibited and robust reporting by the press and fair trials for criminal defendants, judges possess adequate tools short of injunctions against reporting for relieving that tension. To be sure, these alternatives may require greater sensitivity and effort on the part of judges conducting criminal trials than would the stifling of publicity through the simple expedient of issuing a restrictive order on the press; but that sensitivity and effort is required in order to ensure the full enjoyment and proper accommodation of both First and Sixth Amendment rights.

There is, beyond peradventure, a clear and substantial damage to freedom of the press whenever even a temporary restraint is imposed on reporting of material concerning the operations of the criminal justice system, an institution of such pervasive influence in our constitutional scheme. And the necessary impact of reporting even confessions can never be so direct, immediate and irreparable that I would give credence to any notion that prior restraints may be imposed on that rationale. It may be that such incriminating material would be of such slight news value or so inflammatory in particular cases that responsible organs of the media, in an exercise of self-restraint, would choose not to publicize that material, and not make the judicial task of safeguarding precious rights of criminal defendants more difficult. Voluntary codes such as the Nebraska Bar-Press Guidelines are a commendable acknowledgement by the media that constitutional prerogatives bring enormous responsibilities, and I would encourage continuation of such voluntary cooperative efforts between the bar and the media. However, the press may be arrogant, tyrannical, abusive, and sensationalist, just as it may be incisive, probing, and informative. But at least in the context of prior restraints on publication, the decision of what, when, and how to publish is for editors, not judges. . . . Every restrictive order imposed on the press in this case was accordingly an unconstitutional prior restraint on the freedom of the press, and I would therefore reverse the judgment of the Nebraska Supreme Court and remand for further proceedings not inconsistent with this opinion.

Justice STEVENS concurred.

Globe Newspaper Company v. Superior Court for the County of Norfolk
457 U.S. 596, 102 S.Ct. 2613 (1982)

Under a Massachusetts statute, trial courts were required to exclude members of the press and public from the courtroom in cases involving certain sexual offenses and during the testimony of victims under the age of eighteen. Citing the statute, a trial judge excluded reporters from Globe Newspapers at a preliminary hearing for a person charged with raping three minor girls and ordered the trial closed. The newspaper moved to have the court revoke its order. When that failed, the newspaper immediately sought injunctive relief from the Supreme Judicial Court of Massachusetts, which was denied. Attorneys for Globe Newspapers, then, filed an appeal to the full court, but before its decision came down, the rape trial proceeded and the defendant was acquitted. Nine months later, the Supreme Judicial Court found the case moot but nevertheless proceeded to rule that the statute did not require the closure of entire trials, only the exclusion of the press and public during the testimony of a minor rape victim. Globe Newspapers Company appealed that ruling to the Supreme Court.

Justice BRENNAN delivers the opinion of the Court.

Section 16A of Chapter 278 of the Massachusetts General Laws, as construed by the Massachusetts Supreme Judicial Court, requires trial judges, at trials for specified sexual offenses involving a victim under the age of 18, to exclude the press and general public from the courtroom during the testimony of that victim. The question presented is whether the statute thus construed violates the First Amendment as applied to the States through the Fourteenth Amendment. . . .

The Court's recent decision in *Richmond Newspapers* [*Inc. v. Virginia*, 488 U.S. 555 (1980)], firmly established for the first time that the press and general public have a constitutional right of access to criminal trials. Although there was no opinion of the Court in that case, seven Justices recognized that this right of access is embodied in the First Amendment, and applied to the States through the Fourteenth Amendment. . . .

Of course, this right of access to criminal trials is not explicitly mentioned in terms in the First Amendment. But we have long eschewed any "narrow, literal conception" of the Amendment's terms, *NAACP v. Button*, 371 U.S. 415 (1963), for the Framers were concerned with broad principles, and wrote against a background of shared values and practices. The First Amendment is thus broad enough to encompass those rights that, while not unambiguously enumerated in the very terms of the Amendment, are nonetheless necessary to the enjoyment of other First Amendment rights. . . .

Two features of the criminal justice system, emphasized in the various opinions in *Richmond Newspapers*, together serve to explain why a right of access to *criminal trials* in particular is properly afforded protection by the First Amendment. First, the criminal trial historically has been open to the press and general public. "[A]t the time when our organic laws were adopted, criminal trials both here and in England had long been presumptively open." *Richmond Newspapers, Inc. v. Virginia, supra.* . . .

Second, the right of access to criminal trials plays a particularly significant role in the functioning of the judicial process and the government as a whole. Public scrutiny of a criminal trial enhances the quality and safeguards the integrity of the factfinding process, with benefits to both the defendant and to society as a whole. Moreover, public access to the criminal trial fosters an appearance of fairness, thereby heightening public respect for the judicial process. And in the broadest terms, public access to criminal trials permits the public to participate in and serve as a check upon the judicial process—an essential component in our structure of self-government. In sum, the institutional value of the open criminal trial is recognized in both logic and experience.

Although the right of access to criminal trials is of constitutional stature, it is not absolute. See *Richmond Newspapers, Inc. v. Virginia* (plurality opinion); *Nebraska Press Assn. v. Stuart,* 427 U.S. [539 (1976)]. But the circumstances under which the press and public can be barred from a criminal trial are limited; the State's justification in denying access must be a weighty one. Where, as in the present case, the State attempts to deny the right of access in order to inhibit the disclosure of sensitive information, it must be shown that the denial is necessitated by a compelling governmental interest, and is narrowly tailored to serve that interest. . . .

The state interests asserted to support § 16A, though articulated in various ways, are reducible to two: the protection of minor victims of sex crimes from further trauma and embarrassment; and the encouragement of such victims to come forward and testify in a truthful and credible manner. We consider these interests in turn.

We agree with appellee that the first interest—safeguarding the physical and psychological well-being of a minor—is a compelling one. But as compelling as that interest is, it does not justify a *mandatory* closure rule, for it is clear that the circumstances of the particular case may affect the significance of the interest. . . .

Nor can § 16A be justified on the basis of the Commonwealth's second asserted interest—the encouragement of minor victims of sex crimes to come forward and provide accurate testimony. The Commonwealth has offered no empirical support for the claim that the rule of automatic closure contained in § 16A will lead to an increase in the number of minor sex victims coming forward and cooperating with state authorities. Not only is the claim speculative in empirical terms, but it is also open to serious question as a matter of logic and common sense. Although § 16A bars the press and general public from the courtroom during the testimony of minor sex victims, the press is not denied access to the transcript, court personnel, or any other possible source that could provide an account of the minor victim's testimony. Thus § 16A cannot prevent the press from publicizing the substance of a minor victim's testimony, as well as his or her identity. . . .

For the foregoing reasons, we hold that § 16A, as construed by the Massachusetts Supreme Judicial Court, violates the First Amendment to the Constitution. Accordingly, the judgment of the Massachusetts Supreme Judicial Court is

Reversed.

Justice O'CONNOR concurred in separate opinion.

Justice STEVENS dissented in a separate opinion.

Chief Justice BURGER, with whom Justice REHNQUIST joins, dissenting.

Historically our society has gone to great lengths to protect minors *charged* with crime, particularly by prohibiting the release of the names of offenders, barring the press and public from juvenile proceedings, and sealing the records of those proceedings. Yet today the Court holds unconstitutional a state statute designed to protect not the *accused,* but the minor *victims* of sex crimes. In doing so, it advances a disturbing paradox. Although states are permitted, for example, to mandate the closure of all proceedings in order to protect a 17-year-old charged with rape, they are not permitted to require the closing of part of criminal proceedings in order to protect an innocent child who has been raped or otherwise sexually abused. . . .

I cannot agree with the Court's expansive interpretation of our decision in *Richmond Newspapers, Inc. v. Virginia* (1980), or its cavalier rejection of the serious interests supporting Massachusetts' mandatory closure rule. Accordingly, I dissent.

The Court seems to read our decision in *Richmond Newspapers, supra,* as spelling out a First Amendment right of access to all aspects of all criminal trials under all circumstances. That is plainly incorrect. In *Richmond Newspapers,* we examined "the right of access to places traditionally open to the public" and concluded that criminal trials were generally open to the public throughout this country's history and even before that in England. The opinions of a majority of the Justices emphasized the historical tradition of open criminal trials. . . .

Today Justice BRENNAN ignores the weight of historical practice. There is clearly a long history of exclusion of the public from trials involving sexual assaults, particularly those against minors. . . .

For me, it seems beyond doubt, considering the minimal impact of the law on First Amendment rights and the overriding weight of the Commonwealth's interest in protecting child rape victims, that the Massachusetts law is not unconstitutional. The Court acknowledges that the press and the public have prompt and full access to all of the victim's testimony. Their additional interest in actually being present during the testimony is minimal. While denying it the power to protect children, the Court admits that the Commonwealth's interest in protecting the victimized child is a compelling interest. . . .

There is, of course, "a presumption of openness [that] inheres in the very nature of a criminal trial under our system of justice." But we have consistently emphasized that this presumption is not absolute or irrebuttable. A majority of the Justices in *Richmond Newspapers* acknowledged that closure might be permitted under certain circumstances. Justice STEWART's separate opinion pointedly recognized that exclusion of the public might be justified to protect "the sensibilities of a youthful prosecution witness . . . in a criminal trial for rape." The Massachusetts statute has a relatively minor incidental impact on First Amendment rights and gives effect to the overriding state interest in protecting child rape victims. Paradoxically, the Court today denies the victims the kind of protection routinely given to juveniles who commit crimes. Many will find it difficult to reconcile the concern so often expressed for the rights of the accused with the callous indifference exhibited today for children who, having suffered the trauma of rape or other sexual abuse, are denied the modest protection the Massachusetts Legislature provided.

Chandler v. Florida
449 U.S. 560, 101 S.Ct. 802 (1981)

Two Miami Beach police officers, Noel Chandler and Robert Granger, were charged with breaking into and burglary of a well-known local restaurant. The prosecution's principal witness was John Sion, an amateur ham-radio operator, who by sheer chance overheard and recorded an incriminating conversation between the two officers over their walkie-talkie radios during the burglary.

Because of the circumstances of the case, there was considerable attention from the local media. In addition, the Florida Supreme Court had recently established a rule allowing electronic media to televise all judicial proceedings in state courts, subject to certain technical restrictions, such as permitting no more than one television camera in a courtroom at a time. And local television stations planned to televise portions of the trial.

Attorneys for Chandler and Granger filed a pretrial motion asking that the rule permitting television coverage of criminal trials be declared unconstitutional, but the trial court declined to do so. The only coverage shown on the television of the trial consisted in two minutes and fifty-five seconds of the prosecution's evidence; there was no coverage of Chandler's and Granger's defense. Both were found guilty and they promptly appealed their convictions, claiming they had been denied a fair trial and an impartial jury. A Florida appeals court upheld their convictions, and the state supreme court denied review of another appeal. Chandler and Granger then petitioned the Supreme Court for review.

Chief Justice BURGER delivers the opinion of the Court.

The question presented on this appeal is whether, consistent with constitutional guarantees, a state may provide for radio, television, and still photographic coverage of a criminal trial for public broadcast, notwithstanding the objection of the accused. . . .

Appellants rely chiefly on *Estes v. Texas,* 381 U.S. 532 (1964), and Chief Justice WARREN's separate concurring opinion in that case. They argue that the televising of criminal trials is inherently a denial of due process, and they read *Estes* as announcing a *per se* constitutional rule to that effect. . . .

[But] we conclude that *Estes* is not to be read as announcing a constitutional rule barring still photographic, radio and television coverage in all cases and under all circumstances. It does not stand as an absolute ban on state experimentation with an evolving technology, which, in terms of modes of mass communication, was in its relative infancy in 1964, and is, even now, in a state of continuing change.

Since we are satisfied that *Estes* did not announce a constitutional rule that all photographic or broadcast coverage of criminal trials is inherently a denial of due process, we turn to consideration, as a matter of first impression, of the petitioner's suggestion that we now promulgate such a *per se* rule. . . .

An absolute constitutional ban on broadcast coverage of trials cannot be justified simply because there is a danger that, in some cases, prejudicial broadcast accounts of pretrial and trial events may impair the ability of jurors to decide the issue of guilt or innocence uninfluenced by extraneous matter. The risk of juror prejudice in some cases does not justify an absolute ban on news coverage of trials by the printed media; so also the risk of such prejudice does not warrant an absolute constitutional ban on all broadcast coverage. A case attracts a high level of public attention because of its intrinsic interest to the public and the manner of reporting the event. The risk of juror prejudice is present in any publication of a trial, but the appropriate safeguard against such prejudice is the defendant's right to demonstrate that the media's coverage of his case—be it printed or broadcast—compromised the ability of the particular jury that heard the case to adjudicate fairly.

It is also significant that safeguards have been built into the experimental programs in state courts, and into the Florida program, to avoid some of the most egregious problems envisioned by the six opinions in the *Estes* case. Florida admonishes its courts to take special pains to protect certain witnesses—for example, children, victims of sex crimes, some informants, and even the very timid witness or party—from the glare of publicity and the tensions of being "on camera.". . .

The Florida guidelines place on trial judges positive obligations to be on guard to protect the fundamental right of the accused to a fair trial. The Florida statute, being one of the few permitting broadcast coverage of criminal trials over the objection of the accused, raises problems not present in the statutes of other states. Inherent in electronic coverage of a trial is a risk that the very awareness by the accused of the coverage and the contemplated broadcast may adversely affect the conduct of the participants and the fairness of the trial, yet leave no evidence of how the conduct or the trial's fairness was affected. Given this danger, it is significant that Florida requires that objections of the accused to coverage be heard and considered on the record by the trial court. In addition to providing a record for appellate review, a pretrial hearing enables a defendant to advance the basis of his objection to broadcast coverage and allows the trial court to define the steps necessary to minimize or eliminate the risks of prejudice to the accused. . . .

It is not necessary either to ignore or to discount the potential danger to the fairness of a trial in a particular case in order to conclude that Florida may permit the electronic media to cover trials in its state courts. Dangers lurk in this, as in most, experiments, but unless we were to conclude that television coverage under all conditions is prohibited by the Constitution, the states must be free to experiment. We are not empowered by the Constitution to oversee or harness state procedural experimentation; only when the state action infringes fundamental guarantees are we authorized to intervene. We must assume state courts will be alert to any factors that impair the fundamental rights of the accused.

Justice STEVENS did not participate in the decision of this case.

Justice STEWART concurring.

Although concurring in the judgment, I cannot join the opinion of the Court because I do not think the convictions in this case can be affirmed without overruling *Estes v. Texas*.

I believe now, as I believed in dissent then, that *Estes* announced a *per se* rule that the Fourteenth Amendment "prohibits all television cameras from a state courtroom whenever a criminal trial is in progress." Accordingly, rather than join what seems to me a wholly unsuccessful effort to distinguish that decision, I would now flatly overrule it.

Justice WHITE concurred in a separate opinion.

H. SYMBOLIC SPEECH AND SPEECH-PLUS-CONDUCT

Besides the First Amendment protection accorded pure speech (except, as discussed above, for those categories of unprotected speech), the Supreme Court has extended protection to "symbolic speech"—symbols, signs, and other means of expression—and to "speech-plus-conduct"—activities such as sit-ins, picketing, and demonstrating. The Court has done so because symbolic speech and speech-plus-conduct are, in Justice Harlan's words,

as much a part of the "free trade in ideas" . . . as in verbal expression, more commonly thought of as "speech." It, like speech, appeals to good sense and to "the power of reason as applied through public discussion" . . . just as much as, if not more than, a public oration delivered from a soapbox at a street corner. This Court has never limited the right to speak, a protected "liberty" under the Fourteenth Amendment . . . to mere verbal expression.[1]

Justice Harlan, however, also pointed out that it is often necessary to weigh these First Amendment claims against the competing interests and rights of property owners, for example, and the government's interests in preserving the public safety and order in public streets, parks, and buildings. In these cases, the Court must determine whether symbols or conduct in fact serve to express or communicate ideas; whether the government's interests in regulating or prohibiting expression is content neutral, rather than an effort to supress particular ideas; and how great of an inhibition particular ordinances and statutes impose on the exercise of First Amendment freedoms.

By extending First Amendment protection in these and other areas, the Court has created a complex "system of freedom of expression." As Yale Law professor Thomas I. Emerson summarizes:

At its core is a group of rights assured to individual members of the society. This set of rights, which makes up our present-day concept of free expression, includes the right to form and hold beliefs and opinions on any subject, and to communicate ideas, opinions, and information through any medium—in speech, writing, music, art, or in other ways. To some extent it involves the right to remain silent. For the obverse side it includes the right to hear the views of others and to listen to their version of the facts. It encompasses the right to inquire and, to a degree, the right of access to information. As a necessary corollary, it embraces the right to assemble and to form associations, that is, to combine with others in joint expression. . . . At the same time, the rights of all in freedom of expression must be reconciled with other individual and social interests.[2]

NOTES

1. Garner v. Louisiana, 368 U.S. 157 (1961).
2. Thomas Emerson, *The System of Freedom of Expression* (New York: Random House, 1970), at p. 3.

SELECTED BIBLIOGRAPHY

Downs, D. A. *Nazis in Skokie: Freedom, Communication, and the First Amendment*. Notre Dame, IN: Notre Dame University Press, 1985.

Emerson, Thomas. *The System of Freedom of Expression*. New York: Random House, 1970.

Fortas, Abe. *Concerning Dissent and Civil Disobedience*. New York: New American Library, 1968.

Kalven, Harry, Jr. *The Negro & The First Amendment*. Chicago: University of Chicago Press, 1965.

Shiffin, Steve. *The First Amendment, Democracy, and Romance*. Cambridge, MA: Harvard University Press, 1990.

(1) Symbolic Speech

The Court initially acknowledged that symbols and symbolic speech may receive First Amendment protection in *Stromberg v. California*, 283 U.S. 359 (1931). There Chief Justice Hughes struck down a state law prohibiting the display of a red flag as a symbol of opposition to the government and overturned the conviction of a director of a Communist youth camp who raised a red flag every morning as part of the camp's daily activities.

In *West Virginia State Board of Education v. Barnette* (1943) (see page 582), striking down a state law compelling schoolchildren to salute the American flag, the Court reaffirmed that nonverbal expressions receive First Amendment protection and that an individual may not be forced to participate in symbolic activities. In this case, compare Justice Jackson's interpretation of the First Amendment with Justice Frankfurter's impassioned dissenting opinion.

The Court underscored the principles announced in *Barnette* in *Wooley v. Maynard* (1977) (see page 593), when striking down New Hampshire's statute requiring passenger cars to carry license plates inscribed with the state's motto Live Free or Die. But note the issue of how far these principles should or should not extend that Justice Rehnquist raises in his dissenting opinion discussing an atheist's possible objections to the motto In God We Trust on U.S. coins and currency.

First Amendment protection for other symbols and nonverbal expression has been extended as well. *Tinker v. Des Moines Independent Community School District* (1969) (see page 596) upheld the right of children to wear black arm bands to school when protesting America's involvement in the Vietnam War. Compare the Court's opinion there, however, with the ruling and opinions in *Bethel School District No. 403 v. Fraser* (1986) (see page 441).

The Court also found, in *Brown v. Louisiana,* 383 U.S. 131 (1966), that the protest of a group of black students standing silently in a "whites-only" library to be constitutionally protected symbolic speech. But in *Clark v. Community for Creative Non-Violence,* 468 U.S. 288 (1984), over the objections of Justices Brennan and Marshall, the Court held that the National Park Service's regulations against camping in national parks not designated as campsites do not violate the First Amendment as applied to demonstrators who erected and slept in a tent city in Lafayette Park, Washington, D.C., as a way of dramatizing the plight of the needy and homeless. In reaffirming there that not all forms of symbolic speech and nonverbal expression are protected, the Court applied a test created in *United States v. O'Brien,* 391 U.S. 367 (1968).

In *United States v. O'Brien,* the Court held that burning draft cards at protest rallys against the Vietnam War was not protected symbolic speech. There Chief Justice Earl Warren set out certain guidelines for differentiating between protected and unprotected symbolic speech, explaining that

We cannot accept the view that an apparently limitless variety of conduct can be labelled "speech" whenever the person engaging in the conduct intends thereby to express an idea. . . . This Court has held that when "speech" and "nonspeech" elements are combined in the same course of conduct, a sufficiently important governmental interest in regulating the nonspeech element can justify incidental limitations on First Amendment freedoms. To characterize the quality of the governmental interest which must appear, the Court has employed a variety of descriptive terms: compelling; substantial; subordinating; paramount; cogent; strong. Whatever imprecision inheres in these terms, we think it clear that a government regulation is sufficiently justified if it is within the constitutional power of the Government; if it furthers an important or substantial governmental interest; if the governmental interest is unrelated to the suppression of free expression; and if the incidental restriction on alleged First Amendment freedoms is no greater than is essential to the furtherance of that interest.

One of the most potent national political symbols is the American flag and the Court has often faced controversies over not just the government's forcing individuals to participate in symbolic acts honoring the flag, as in *Barnette,* but over punishing individuals who use and abuse the flag as a way of expressing their political views. In *Street v. New York,* 394 U.S. 576 (1969), the justices split five to four when overturning the conviction of a protestor who burned the flag, in violation of a law making it a misdemeanor to publicly mutilate, deface, or cast contempt on the flag "by words or act."[1] There Chief Justice Warren and Justices Black, Fortas, and White dissented. Over the dissent of Chief Justice Burger and Justices Blackmun and Rehnquist, the Court, in *Smith v. Groguen,* 415 U.S. 566 (1974), overturned the conviction of an individual wearing a small United States flag on the seat of his pants. With those three justices in dissent again, *Spence v. Washington,* 418 U.S. 405 (1974), held that the First Amendment protected a student who hung the American flag upside down with a peace symbol attached on the window of his dormitory room. With the Court's composition substantially changed due to Nixon's and Reagan's appointments, the issue of flag burning was again confronted twenty years after *Street.*

In another surprising and controversial five to four decision, the Court once again upheld the First Amendment protection for symbolic speech in *Texas v. Johnson* (1989) (see page 599), prompting President George Bush and numerous congressmen to call for a constitutional amendment overturning that decision. Congress, however, passed instead the Federal Flag Protection Act of 1989, authorizing the prosecution of those who desecrate the American flag. That law was immediately challenged and was overturned by the Court. As in *Johnson,* the justices split five to four in holding that the federal statute "suffer[ed] from the same fundamental flaw" as the earlier state laws in aiming at "suppressing expression."[2] Following that ruling, a further attempt to overturn *Texas v. Johnson* by passing a constitutional amendment failed. The House of Representatives voted 254 in favor and 177 against the proposed amendment, 34 votes short of the required two-thirds needed to propose a constitutional amendment. The proposed constitutional amendment later fell 9 votes short of the required two-thirds majority needed in the Senate.

NOTES

1. In two other cases, however, the Court declined to review the convictions of individuals for mutilating and burning the American flag. *Sutherland v. Illinois,* 425 U.S. 947 (1976); and *Kime v. United States,* 459 U.S. 949 (1982).

2. *United States v. Eichman,* 110 S.Ct. 2404 (1990).

Gregory Johnson being arrested after setting fire to the American flag during a protest at the Republican party's 1984 national convention. His arrest and conviction was appealed and overturned in *Texas v. Johnson* (1989). *John Keating/Time Magazine.*

West Virginia State Board of Education v. Barnette
319 U.S. 624, 63 S.Ct. 1178 (1943)

During World War I and throughout World War II, patriotism and fear of communism, socialism, and fascism led states and localities to enact statutes requiring, among other things, students to salute the flag and recite the pledge of allegiance. When Jehovah's Witnesses challenged the constitutionality of a small Pennsylvanian town's 1914 ordinance compelling students to salute the American flag (in a manner similar to that in Nazi Germany, with right arm extended and the palm of the hand pointing upward), the Court upheld the flag-salute statute in *Minersville School District v. Gobitis,* 310 U.S. 586 (1940), with an opinion by Justice Frankfurter and only Justice Stone dissenting.

Following *Gobitis,* the West Virginia state legislature enacted a law requiring all schools to offer history and civics courses, and pursuant to that legislation the State Board of Education directed all teachers and students to salute the flag as part of the daily activities of the school. Failure to comply with this requirement could lead to students being expelled and parents were liable for prosecution with a penalty of thirty days in jail and a $50 fine.

Walter Barnette, a Jehovah's Witness, sought in federal district court an injunction against the enforcement of compulsory flag salutes in school on the grounds that it violated his and his children's religious belief that they should not worship any graven image and the First Amendment free exercise clause. The State Board of Education moved to dismiss the complaint, but a federal district judge granted the injunction. The State Board of Education appealed that decision to the Supreme Court.

By the time the justices heard *Barnette,* the Court's composition had changed from that when *Gobitis* was decided three years earlier. Chief Justice Hughes and Justice McReynolds retired in 1941, and President Franklin Roosevelt elevated Justice Stone to chief justice, appointed his attorney general, Robert Jackson, to fill Stone's seat as associate justice, and named James Byrnes to replace McReynolds. Justice Byrnes served only one year and was succeeded by FDR's last appointee, Wiley Rutledge. Moreover, FDR's three earlier appointees, Justices Black, Douglas, and Murphy, who had voted with the majority in *Gobitis,* switched their positions and voted with FDR's last three appointees in *Barnette.* Chief Justice Stone assigned Jackson to write the opinion for the Court striking down compulsory flag salutes as a violation of the First Amendment guarantee for free speech, instead of on the free exercise clause. Justices Black, Douglas, and Murphy wrote separate concurring opinions explaining their reversing of positions. Justice Frankfurter wrote an impassioned dissenting opinion and, along with Justices Reed and Roberts, maintained the views expressed in *Gobitis*.

Justice JACKSON delivers the opinion of the Court.

The freedom asserted by these appellees does not bring them into collision with rights asserted by any other individual. It is such conflicts which most frequently require intervention of the State to determine where the rights of one end and those of another begin. But the refusal of these persons to participate in the ceremony does not interfere with or deny rights of others to do so. Nor is there any question in this case that their behavior is peaceable and orderly. The sole conflict is between authority and rights of the individual. The State asserts power to condition access to public education on making a prescribed sign and profession and at the same time to coerce attendance by punishing both parent and child. The latter stand on a right of self-determination in matters that touch individual opinion and personal attitude.

As the present CHIEF JUSTICE said in dissent in the *Gobitis* case, the State may "require teaching by instruction and study of all in our history and in the structure and organization of our government, including the guaranties of civil liberty which tend to inspire patriotism and love of country." Here, however, we are dealing with a compulsion of students to declare a belief. They are not merely made acquainted with the flag salute so that they may be informed as to what it is or even what it means. The issue here is whether this slow and easily neglected route to aroused loyalties constitutionally may be short-cut by substituting a compulsory salute and slogan. . . .

There is no doubt that, in connection with the pledges, the flag salute is a form of utterance. Symbolism is a primitive but effective way of communicating ideas. The use of an emblem or flag to symbolise some system, idea, institution, or personality, is a short cut from mind to mind. Causes and nations, political parties, lodges and ecclesiastical groups seek to knit the loyalty of their followings to a flag or banner, a color or design. The State announces rank, function, and authority through crowns and maces, uniforms and black robes; the church speaks through the Cross, the Crucifix, the altar and shrine, and clerical raiment. Symbols of State, often convey political ideas just as religious symbols come to convey theological ones. Associated with many of these symbols are appropriate gestures of acceptance or respect: a salute, a bowed or barred head, a bended knee. A person gets from a symbol the meaning he puts into it, and what is one man's comfort and inspiration is another's jest and scorn.

Over a decade ago Chief Justice HUGHES led this Court in holding that the display of a red flag as a symbol of opposition by peaceful and legal means to organized government was protected by the free speech guaranties of the Constitution. *Stromberg v. California*, 283 U.S. 359 [1931]. Here it is the State that employs a flag as a symbol of adherence to government as presently organized. It requires the individual to communicate by word and sign his acceptance of the political ideas it thus bespeaks. Objection to this form of communication when coerced is an old one, well known to the framers of the Bill of Rights. . . .

[H]ere the power of compulsion is invoked without any allegation that remaining passive during a flag salute ritual creates a clear and present danger that would justify an effort even to muffle expression. To sustain the compulsory flag salute we are required to say that a Bill of Rights which guards the individual's right to speak his own mind, left it open to public authorities to compel him to utter what is not in his mind.

Whether the First Amendment to the Constitution will permit officials to order observance of ritual of this nature does not depend upon whether as a voluntary exercise we would think it to be good, bad or merely innocuous. . . .

Nor does the issue as we see it turn on one's possession of particular religious views or the sincerity with which they are held. While religion supplies appellees' motive for enduring the discomforts of making the issue in this case, many citizens who do not share these religious views hold such a compulsory rite to infringe constitutional liberty of the individual. It is not necessary to inquire whether non-conformist beliefs will exempt from the duty to salute unless we first find power to make the salute a legal duty.

The *Gobitis* decision, however, *assumed,* as did the argument in that case and in this, that power exists in the State to impose the flag salute discipline upon school children in general. The Court only examined and rejected a claim based on religious beliefs of immunity from an unquestioned general rule. The question which underlies the flag salute controversy is whether such a ceremony so touching matters of opinion and political attitude may be imposed upon the individual by official authority under powers committed to any political organization under our Constitution. We examine rather than assume existence of this power and, against this broader definition of issues in this case, re-examine specific grounds assigned for the *Gobitis* decision.

1. It was said that the flag-salute controversy confronted the Court with "the problem which Lincoln cast in memorable dilemma: 'Must a government of necessity be too *strong* for the

liberties of its people, or too *weak* to maintain its own existence?'" and that the answer must be in favor of strength. . . .

We think these issues may be examined free of pressure or restraint growing out of such considerations.

It may be doubted whether Mr. Lincoln would have thought that the strength of government to maintain itself would be impressively vindicated by our confirming power of the state to expel a handful of children from school. Such oversimplification, so handy in political debate, often lacks the precision necessary to postulates of judicial reasoning. If validly applied to this problem, the utterance cited would resolve every issue of power in favor of those in authority and would require us to override every liberty thought to weaken or delay execution of their policies. . . .

2. It was also considered in the *Gobitis* case that functions of educational officers in states, counties and school districts were such that to interfere with their authority "would in effect make us the school board for the country.". . .

The Fourteenth Amendment, as now applied to the States, protects the citizen against the State itself and all of its creatures—Boards of Education not excepted. These have, of course, important, delicate, and highly discretionary functions, but none that they may not perform within the limits of the Bill of Rights. That they are educating the young for citizenship is reason for scrupulous protection of Constitutional freedoms of the individual, if we are not to strangle the free mind at its source and teach youth to discount important principles of our government as mere platitudes. . . .

3. The *Gobitis* opinion reasoned that this is a field "where courts possess no marked and certainly no controlling competence," that it is committed to the legislatures as well as the courts to guard cherished liberties and that it is constitutionally appropriate to "fight out the wise use of legislative authority in the forum of public opinion and before legislative assemblies rather than to transfer such a contest to the judicial arena," since all the "effective means of inducing political changes are left free.". . .

The very purpose of a Bill of Rights was to withdraw certain subjects from the vicissitudes of political controversy, to place them beyond the reach of majorities and officials and to establish them as legal principles to be applied by the courts. One's right to life, liberty, and property, to free speech, a free press, freedom of worship and assembly, and other fundamental rights may not be submitted.

4. Lastly, and this is the very heart of the *Gobitis* opinion, it reasons that "National unity is the basis of national security," that the authorities have "the right to select appropriate means for its attainment," and hence reaches the conclusion that such

compulsory measures toward "national unity" are constitutional. Upon the verity of this assumption depends our answer in this case.

Struggles to coerce uniformity of sentiment in support of some end thought essential to their time and country have been waged by many good as well as by evil men. Nationalism is a relatively recent phenomenon but at other times and places the ends have been racial or territorial security, support of a dynasty or regime, and particular plans for saving souls. As first and moderate methods to attain unity have failed, those bent on its accomplishment must resort to an ever-increasing severity. As governmental pressure toward unity becomes greater, so strife becomes more bitter as to whose unity it shall be. Probably no deeper division of our people could proceed from any provocation than from finding it necessary to choose what doctrine and whose program public educational officials shall compel youth to unite in embracing. Ultimate futility of such attempts to compel coherence is the lesson of every such effort from the Roman drive to stamp out Christianity as a disturber of its pagan unity, the Inquisition, as a means to religious and dynastic unity, the Siberian exiles as a means to Russian unity, down to the fast failing efforts of our present totalitarian enemies. Those who begin coercive elimination of dissent soon find themselves exterminating dissenters. Compulsory unification of opinion achieves only the unanimity of the graveyard.

It seems trite but necessary to say that the First Amendment to our Constitution was designed to avoid these ends by avoiding these beginnings. There is no mysticism in the American concept of the State or of the nature or origin of its authority. We set up government by consent of the governed, and the Bill of Rights denies those in power any legal opportunity to coerce that consent. Authority here is to be controlled by public opinion, not public opinion by authority. . . .

If there is any fixed star in our constitutional constellation, it is that no official, high or petty, can prescribe what shall be orthodox in politics, nationalism, religion, or other matters of opinion or force citizens to confess by word or act their faith therein. If there are any circumstances which permit an exception, they do not now occur to us.

We think the action of the local authorities in compelling the flag salute and pledge transcends constitutional limitations on their power and invades the sphere of intellect and spirit which it is the purpose of the First Amendment to our Constitution to reserve from all official control.

Justice Roberts and Justice Reed adhere to the views expressed by the Court in *Minersville School District v. Gobitis,* and are of the opinion that the judgment below should be reversed.

Justice BLACK and Justice DOUGLAS concurring.

We are substantially in agreement with the opinion just read, but since we originally joined with the Court in the *Gobitis* case, it is appropriate that we make a brief statement of reasons for our change of view.

Reluctance to make the Federal Constitution a rigid bar against state regulation of conduct thought inimical to the public welfare was the controlling influence which moved us to consent to the Gobitis decision. Long reflection convinced us that although the principle is sound, its application in the particular case was wrong. We believe that the statute before us fails to accord full scope to the freedom of religion secured to the appellees by the First and Fourteenth Amendments. . . .

No well-ordered society can leave to the individuals an absolute right to make final decisions, unassailable by the State, as to everything they will or will not do. The First Amendment does not go so far. Religious faiths, honestly held, do not free individuals from responsibility to conduct themselves obediently to laws which are either imperatively necessary to protect society as a whole from grave and pressingly imminent dangers or which, without any general prohibition, merely regulate time, place or manner of religious activity. Decision as to the constitutionality of particular laws which strike at the substance of religious tenets and practices must be made by this Court. The duty is a solemn one, and in meeting it we cannot say that a failure, because of religious scruples, to assume a particular physical position and to repeat the words of a patriotic formula creates a grave danger to the nation. Such a statutory exaction is a form of test oath, and the test oath has always been abhorrent in the United States.

Justice MURPHY concurring.

Without wishing to disparage the purposes and intentions of those who hope to inculcate sentiments of loyalty and patriotism by requiring a declaration of allegiance as a feature of public education, or unduly belittle the benefits that may accrue therefrom, I am impelled to conclude that such a requirement is not essential to the maintenance of effective government and orderly society. . . . Official compulsion to affirm what is contrary to one's religious beliefs is the antithesis of freedom of worship.

Justice FRANKFURTER dissenting.

One who belongs to the most vilified and persecuted minority in history is not likely to be insensible to the freedoms guaranteed by our Constitution. Were my purely personal attitude relevant I should wholeheartedly associate myself with the general libertarian views in the Court's opinion, representing as they do the thought and action of a lifetime. But as judges we are neither Jew nor Gentile, neither Catholic nor agnostic. We owe equal attachment to the Constitution and are equally bound by our judicial obligations whether we derive our citizenship from the earliest or the latest immigrants to these shores. As a member of this Court I am not justified in writing my private notions of policy into the Constitution, no matter how deeply I may cherish them or how mischievous I may deem their disregard. The duty of a judge who must decide which of two claims before the Court shall prevail, that of a State to enact and enforce laws within its general competence or that of an individual to refuse obedience because of the demands of his conscience, is not that of the ordinary person. It can never be emphasized too much that one's own opinion about the wisdom or evil of a law should be excluded altogether when one is doing one's duty on the bench. The only opinion of our own even looking in that direction that is material is our opinion whether legislators could in reason have enacted such a law. In the light of all the circumstances, including the history of this question in this Court, it would require more daring than I possess to deny that reasonable legislators could have taken the action which is before us for review. Most unwillingly, therefore, I must differ from my brethren with regard to legislation like this. I cannot bring my mind to believe that the "liberty" secured by the Due Process Clause gives this Court authority to deny to the State of West Virginia the attainment of that which we all recognize as a legitimate legislative end, namely, the promotion of good citizenship, by employment of the means here chosen.

Not so long ago we were admonished that "the only check upon our own exercise of power is our own sense of self-restraint. For the removal of unwise laws from the statute books appeal lies, not to the courts, but to the ballot and to the processes of democratic government." We have been told that generalities do not decide concrete cases. But the intensity with which a general principle is held may determine a particular issue, and whether we put first things first may decide a specific controversy.

The admonition that judicial self-restraint alone limits arbitrary exercise of our authority is relevant every time we are asked to nullify legislation. The Constitution does not give us greater veto power when dealing with one phase of "liberty" than with another, or when dealing with grade school regulations than with college regulations that offend conscience, as was the case in *Hamilton v. Regents*, 293 U.S. 245 [1934]. In neither situation is our function comparable to that of a legislature or are we free to act as though we were a super-legislature. Judicial self-restraint is equally necessary whenever an exercise of political or legislative power is challenged. There is no warrant in the constitutional basis of this Court's authority for attributing different roles to it depending upon the nature of the challenge to the legislation. Our power does not vary according to the particular provision of the Bill of Rights which is invoked. The right not to have property taken without just compensation has, so far as the scope of judicial power is concerned, the same constitutional dignity as the right to be protected against unreasonable searches and seizures, and the latter has no less claim than freedom of the press or freedom of speech or religious freedom. In no instance is this Court the primary protector of the particular liberty that is invoked. . . .

When Justice HOLMES, speaking for this Court, wrote that "it must be remembered that legislatures are ultimate guardians of the liberties and welfare of the people in quite as great a degree as the courts," he went to the very essence of our constitutional system and the democratic conception of our society. He did not mean that for only some phases of civil government this Court was not to supplant legislatures and sit in judgment upon the right or wrong of a challenged measure. He was stating the comprehensive judicial duty and role of this Court in our constitutional scheme whenever legislation is sought to be nullified on any ground, namely, that responsibility for legislation lies with legislatures, answerable as they are directly to the people, and this Court's only and very narrow function is to determine whether within the broad grant of authority vested in legislatures they have exercised a judgment for which reasonable justification can be offered.

The framers of the federal Constitution might have chosen to assign an active share in the process of legislation to this Court. . . . But the framers of the Constitution denied such legislative powers to the federal judiciary. They chose instead to insulate the judiciary from the legislative function. They did not grant to this Court supervision over legislation.

The reason why from the beginning even the narrow judicial authority to nullify legislation has been viewed with a jealous eye is that it serves to prevent the full play of the democratic process. The fact that it may be an undemocratic aspect of our scheme of government does not call for its rejection or its disuse. But it is the best of reasons, as this Court has frequently recognized, for the greatest caution in its use.

The precise scope of the question before us defines the limits of the constitutional power that is in issue. The State of West Virginia requires all pupils to share in the salute to the flag as part of school training in citizenship. The present action is one to enjoin the enforcement of this requirement by those in school attendance. We have not before us any attempt by the State to punish disobedient children or visit penal consequences on their parents. All that is in question is the right of the state to compel participation in this exercise by those who choose to attend the public schools.

We are not reviewing merely the action of a local school board. The flag salute requirement in this case comes before us with the full authority of the State of West Virginia. We are in fact passing judgment on "the power of the State as a whole." Practically we are passing upon the political power of each of the forty-eight states. Moreover, since the First Amendment has been read into the Fourteenth, our problem is precisely the same as it would be if we had before us an Act of Congress for the District of Columbia. To suggest that we are here concerned with the heedless action of some village tyrants is to distort the augustness of the constitutional issue and the reach of the consequences of our decision. . . .

We are told that a flag salute is a doubtful substitute for adequate understanding of our institutions. The states that require such a school exercise do not have to justify it as the only means for promoting good citizenship in children, but merely as one of diverse means for accomplishing a worthy end. We may deem it a foolish measure, but the point is that this Court is not the organ of government to resolve doubts as to whether it will fulfill its purpose. Only if there be no doubt that any reasonable mind could entertain can we deny to the states the right to resolve doubts their way and not ours.

That which to the majority may seem essential for the welfare of the state may offend the consciences of a minority. But, so long as no inroads are made upon the actual exercise of religion by the minority, to deny the political power of the majority to enact laws concerned with civil matters, simply because they may offend the consciences of a minority, really means that the consciences of a minority are more sacred and more enshrined in the Constitution than the consciences of a majority.

We are told that symbolism is a dramatic but primitive way of communicating ideas. Symbolism is inescapable. Even the most sophisticated live by symbols. But it is not for this Court to make psychological judgments as to the effectiveness of a particular symbol in inculcating concededly indispensable feelings, particularly if the state happens to see fit to utilize the symbol that represents our heritage and our hopes. And surely only flippancy could be responsible for the suggestion that constitutional validity of a requirement to salute our flag implies equal validity of a requirement to salute a dictator. The significance of a symbol lies in what it represents. To reject the swastika does not imply rejection of the Cross. And so it bears repetition to say that it mocks reason and denies our whole history to find in the allowance of a requirement to salute our flag on fitting occasions the seeds of sanction for obeisance to a leader. To deny the power to employ educational symbols is to say that the state's educational system may not stimulate the imagination because this may lead to unwise stimulation. . . .

The flag salute exercise has no kinship whatever to the oath tests so odious in history. For the oath test was one of the instruments for suppressing heretical beliefs. Saluting the flag suppresses no belief nor curbs it. Children and their parents may believe what they please, avow their belief and practice it. It is not even remotely suggested that the requirement for saluting the flag involves the slightest restriction against the fullest opportunity on the part both of the children and of their parents to disavow as publicly as they choose to do so the meaning that others attach to the gesture of salute. All channels of affirmative free expression are open to both children and parents. Had we before us any act of the state putting the slightest curbs upon such free expression, I should not lag behind any member of this Court in striking down such an invasion of the right to freedom of thought and freedom of speech protected by the Constitution.

I am fortified in my view of this case by the history of the flag salute controversy in this Court. Five times has the precise question now before us been adjudicated. Four times the Court unanimously found that the requirement of such a school exercise was not beyond the powers of the states. Indeed in the first three cases to come before the Court the constitutional claim now sustained was deemed so clearly unmeritorious that this Court dismissed the appeals for want of a substantial federal question. . . .

What may be even more significant than this uniform recognition of state authority is the fact that every Justice—thirteen in all—who has hitherto participated in judging this matter has at one or more times found no constitutional infirmity in what is now condemned. Only the two Justices sitting for the first time on this matter have not heretofore found this legislation inoffensive to the "liberty" guaranteed by the Constitution. And among the Justices who sustained this measure were outstanding judicial leaders in the zealous enforcement of constitutional safeguards of civil liberties—men like Chief Justice HUGHES, Justice BRANDEIS, and Justice CARDOZO, to mention only those no longer on the Court.

One's conception of the Constitution cannot be severed from one's conception of a judge's function in applying it. The Court has no reason for existence if it merely reflects the pressures of the day. Our system is built on the faith that men set apart for this special function, freed from the influences of immediacy and form the deflections of worldly ambition, will become able to take a view of longer range than the period of responsibility entrusted to Congress and legislatures. We are dealing with matters as to which legislators and voters have conflicting views. Are we as judges to impose our strong convictions on where wisdom lies? That which three years ago had seemed to five successive

Courts to lie within permissible areas of legislation is now outlawed by the deciding shift of opinion of two Justices. What reason is there to believe that they or their successors may not have another view a few years hence? Is that which was deemed to be of so fundamental a nature as to be written into the Constitution to endure for all times to be the sport of shifting winds of doctrine? Of course, judicial opinions, even as to questions of constitutionality, are not immutable. As has been true in the past, the Court will from time to time reverse its position. But I believe that never before these Jehovah's Witnesses cases (except for minor deviations subsequently retraced) has this Court overruled decisions so as to restrict the powers of democratic government. Always heretofore, it has withdrawn narrow views of legislative authority so as to authorize what formerly it had denied.

In view of this history it must be plain that what thirteen Justices found to be within the constitutional authority of a state, legislators can not be deemed unreasonable in enacting. Therefore, in denying to the states what heretofore has received such impressive judicial sanction, some other tests of unconstitutionality must surely be guiding the Court than the absence of a rational justification for the legislation. But I know of no other test which this Court is authorized to apply in nullifying legislation.

In the past this Court has from time to time set its views of policy against that embodied in legislation by finding laws in conflict with what was called the "spirit of the Constitution." Such undefined destructive power was not conferred on this Court by the Constitution. Before a duly enacted law can be judicially nullified, it must be forbidden by some explicit restriction upon political authority in the Constitution. Equally inadmissible is the claim to strike down legislation because to us as individuals it seems opposed to the "plan and purpose" of the Constitution. That is too tempting a basis for finding in one's personal views the purposes of the Founders.

The uncontrollable power wielded by this Court brings it very close to the most sensitive areas of public affairs. As appeal from legislation to adjudication becomes more frequent, and its consequences more far-reaching, judicial self-restraint becomes more and not less important, lest we unwarrantably enter social and political domains wholly outside our concern. I think I appreciate fully the objections to the law before us. But to deny that it presents a question upon which men might reasonably differ appears to me to be intolerance. And since men may so reasonably differ, I deem it beyond my constitutional power to assert my view of the wisdom of this law against the view of the State of West Virginia.

Jefferson's opposition to judicial review has not been accepted by history, but it still serves as an admonition against confusion between judicial and political functions. As a rule of judicial self-restraint, it is still as valid as Lincoln's admonition. For those who pass laws not only are under duty to pass laws. They are also under duty to observe the Constitution. And even though legislation relates to civil liberties, our duty of deference to those who have the responsibility for making the laws is no less relevant or less exacting. And this is so especially when we consider the accidental contingencies by which one man may determine constitutionality and thereby confine the political power of the Congress of the United States and the legislatures of forty-eight states. The attitude of judicial humility which these considerations enjoin is not an abdication of the judicial function. It is a due observance of its limits. Moreover, it is to be borne in mind that in a question like this we are not passing on the proper distribution of political power as between the states and the central government. We are not discharging the basic function of this Court as the mediator of powers within the federal system. To strike down a law like this is to deny a power to all government.

Of course patriotism cannot be enforced by the flag salute. But neither can the liberal spirit be enforced by judicial invalidation of illiberal legislation. Our constant preoccupation with the constitutionality of legislation rather than with its wisdom tends to preoccupation of the American mind with a false value. The tendency of focusing attention on constitutionality is to make constitutionality synonymous with wisdom, to regard a law as all right if it is constitutional. Such an attitude is a great enemy of liberalism. Particularly in legislation affecting freedom of thought and freedom of speech much which should offend a free-spirited society is constitutional. Reliance for the most precious interests of civilization, therefore, must be found outside of their vindication in courts of law. Only a persistent positive translation of the faith of a free society into the convictions and habits and actions of a community is the ultimate reliance against unabated temptations to fetter the human spirit.

Wooley v. Maynard

430 U.S. 705, 97 S.Ct. 1428 (1977)

In 1974, George Maynard was cited in violation of New Hampshire's law requiring noncommercial vehicles to bear license plates embossed with the state motto, Live Free or Die. Maynard, a Jehovah's Witness, considered the motto repugnate to his moral, religious, and political beliefs and snipped the words *or Die* off of the plate. Before a judge, he pled not guilty and explained his religious objections to the motto. The judge, nonetheless found him guilty and imposed a $25 fine, which he also suspended "during good behavior." Once again, though, Maynard was cited for violating the law and in 1975 was fined $50 and sentenced to six months in jail. The judge suspended the jail sentence, but when Maynard refused to pay the fine as a matter of conscience the judge sentenced him to fifteen days in jail.

Maynard sought in federal district court an injunction against the enforcement of the penalties for violating New Hampshire's law on the grounds that it was unconstitutional. The court agreed and enjoined the state "from arresting and prosecuting [Maynard] at any time in the future for covering over that portion of [the] license plates that contains the motto 'Live Free or Die.'" The state's attorney general appealed to the Supreme Court.

Chief Justice BURGER delivers the opinion of the Court.

The issue on appeal is whether the State of New Hampshire may constitutionally enforce criminal sanctions against persons who cover the motto "Live Free or Die" on passenger vehicle license plates because that motto is repugnant to their moral and religious beliefs. . . .

We begin with the proposition that the right of freedom of thought protected by First Amendment against state action includes both the right to speak freely and the right to refrain from speaking at all. See *West Virginia State Board of Education v. Barnette* [319 U.S. 624 (1943)].

Here, as in *Barnette*, we are faced with a state measure which forces an individual, as part of his daily life—indeed constantly while his automobile is in public view—to be an instrument for fostering public adherence to an ideological point of view he finds unacceptable. In doing so, the State "invades the sphere of intellect and spirit which it is the purpose of the First Amendment to our Constitution to reserve from all official control."

New Hampshire's statute in effect requires that appellees use their private property as a "mobile billboard" for the State's ideological message—or suffer a penalty, as Maynard already has. As a condition to driving an automobile—a virtual necessity for most Americans—the Maynards must display "Live Free or Die" to hundreds of people each day. The fact that most individuals agree with the thrust of New Hampshire's motto is not the test; most Americans also find the flag salute acceptable. The First Amendment protects the right of individuals to hold a point of view different from the majority and to refuse to foster, in the way New Hampshire commands, an idea they find morally objectionable.

Identifying the Maynards' interests as implicating First Amendment protections does not end our inquiry however. We must also determine whether the State's countervailing interest is sufficiently compelling to justify requiring appellees to display the state motto on their license plates. . . .

The State first points out that only passenger vehicles, but not commercial, trailer, or other vehicles are required to display the state motto. Thus, the argument proceeds, officers of the law are more easily able to determine whether passenger vehicles are carrying the proper plates. However the record here reveals that New Hampshire passenger license plates normally consist of a specific configuration of letters and numbers, which makes them readily distinguishable from other types of plates, even without reference to state motto. Even were we to credit the State's reasons and "even though the governmental purpose be legitimate and substantial, that purpose cannot be pursued by means that broadly stifle fundamental personal liberties when the end can be more narrowly achieved. The breadth of legislative abridgment must be viewed in the light of less drastic means for achieving the same basic purpose.". . .

The State's second claimed interest is not ideologically neutral. The State is seeking to communicate to others an official view as to proper "appreciation of history, state pride, [and] individualism." Of course, the State may legitimately pursue such interests in any number of ways. However, where the State's interest is to disseminate an ideology, no matter how acceptable to some, such interest cannot outweigh an individual's First Amendment right to avoid becoming the courier for such message.

We conclude that the State of New Hampshire may not require appellees to display the state motto upon their vehicle license plates, and accordingly, we affirm the judgment of the District Court.

Justice WHITE, with whom Justice BLACKMUN and Justice REHNQUIST join, dissented in part.

Justice REHNQUIST, with whom Justice BLACKMUN joins, dissenting.

I not only agree with the Court's implicit recognition that there is no protected "symbolic speech" in this case, but I think that that conclusion goes far to undermine the Court's ultimate holding that there is an element of protected expression here. The State has not forced appellees to "say" anything; and it has not forced them to communicate ideas with nonverbal actions reasonably likened to "speech," such as wearing a lapel button promoting a political candidate or waving a flag as a symbolic gesture. The State has simply required that *all* noncommercial automobiles bear license tags with the state motto, "Live Free or Die." Appellees have not been forced to affirm or reject that motto; they are simply required by the State, under its police power, to carry a state auto license tag for identification and registration purposes. . . .

The Court cites *Barnette* for the proposition that there is a constitutional right, in some cases, to refrain from speaking." What the Court does not demonstrate is that there is any "speech" or "speaking" in the context of this case. . . .

For First Amendment principles to be implicated, the State must place the citizen in the position of either appearing to, or actually, "asserting as true" the message. This was the focus of *Barnette,* and clearly distinguishes this case from that one.

[T]here is nothing in state law which precludes appellees from displaying their disagreement with the state motto as long as the methods used do not obscure the license plates. Thus appellees could place on their bumper a conspicuous bumper sticker explaining in no uncertain terms that they do not profess the motto "Live Free or Die" and that they violently disagree with the connotations of that motto. Since any implication that they affirm the motto can be so easily displaced, I cannot agree that the state statutory system for motor vehicle identification and tourist promotion may be invalidated under the fiction that appellees are unconstitutionally forced to affirm, or profess belief in, the state motto.

The logic of the Court's opinion leads to startling, and I believe totally unacceptable, results. For example, the mottos "In God We Trust" and "E pluribus unum" appear on the coin and currency of the United States. I cannot imagine that the statutes, see 18 U.S.C. §§ 331 and 333, proscribing defacement of U. S. currency impinge upon the First Amendment rights of an atheist. The fact that an atheist carries and uses U. S. currency does not, in any meaningful sense, convey any affirmation of belief on his part in the motto "In God We Trust." Similarly, there is no affirmation of belief involved with the display of state license tags upon the private automobiles involved here.

Tinker v. Des Moines Independent Community School District

393 U.S. 503, 89 S.Ct. 733 (1969)

In December 1965, a group of adults and students in Des Moines, Iowa, held a meeting and decided to publicize their objections to the war in Vietnam by wearing black arm bands during the holiday season. The principals of the Des Moines schools became aware of the plan and promptly adopted a policy forbidding the wearing of arm bands in school and suspending any student who refused to comply.

John Tinker, a fifteen-year-old high-school student, and his sister, Mary Beth, a thirteen-year-old junior-high-school student, wore black arm bands to school and were immediately sent home and suspended until they agreed to no longer wear the arm bands. They and their parents asked a federal district court for an injunction restraining school officials from enforcing the policy against wearing black arm bands. The Court, however, upheld the school's authority. On appeal to the Court of Appeals for the Eighth Circuit, the judges were evenly divided and accordingly upheld the lower court's ruling without issuing an opinion. The Tinkers, thereupon, appealed to the Supreme Court, which granted *certiorari.*

Justice FORTAS delivers the opinion of the Court.

[T]he wearing of an armband for the purpose of expressing certain views is the type of symbolic act that is within the Free Speech Clause of the First Amendment. . . . It [is] closely akin to "pure speech" which, have repeatedly held, is entitled to comprehensive protection under the First Amendment.

First Amendment rights, applied in light of the special characteristics of the school environment, are available to teachers and students. It can hardly be argued that either students or teachers shed their constitutional rights to freedom of speech or expression at the schoolhouse gate. This has been the unmistakable holding of this Court for almost 50 years. In *Meyer v. Nebraska,* 262 U.S. 390 (1923), and *Bartels v. Iowa,* 262 U.S. 404 (1923), this Court, in opinions by Justice McREYNOLDS, held that the Due Process Clause of the Fourteenth Amendment prevents States from forbidding the teaching of a foreign language to young students. Statutes to this effect, the Court held, unconstitutionally interfere with the liberty of teacher, student, and parent. . . .

The problem posed by the present case does not relate to regulation of the length of skirts or the type of clothing, to hair style, or deportment. It does not concern aggressive, disruptive action or even group demonstrations. Our problem involves direct, primary First Amendment rights akin to "pure speech."

The school officials banned and sought to punish petitioners for a silent, passive expression of opinion, unaccompanied by any disorder or disturbance on the part of petitioners. There is here no evidence whatever of petitioners' interference, actual or nascent, with the schools' work or of collision with the rights of other students to be secure and to be let alone. Accordingly, this case does not concern speech or action that intrudes upon the work of the schools or the rights of other students. . . .

The District Court concluded that the action of the school authorities was reasonable because it was based upon their fear of a disturbance from the wearing of the armbands. But, in our system, undifferentiated fear or apprehension of disturbance is not enough to overcome the right to freedom of expression. . . .

[T]he school authorities did not purport to prohibit the wearing of all symbols of political or controversial significance. The record shows that students in some of the schools wore buttons relating to national political campaigns, and some even wore the Iron Cross, traditionally a symbol of Nazism. The order prohibiting the wearing of armbands did not extend to these. Instead, a particular symbol—black armbands worn to exhibit opposition to this Nation's involvement in Vietnam—was singled out for prohibition. Clearly, the prohibition of expression of one particular opinion, at least without evidence that it is necessary to avoid material and substantial interference with schoolwork or discipline, is not constitutionally permissible. . . .

If a regulation were adopted by school officials forbidding discussion of the Vietnam conflict, or the expression by any student of opposition to it anywhere on school property except as part of a prescribed classroom exercise, it would be obvious that the regulation would violate the constitutional rights of students, at least if it could not be justified by a showing that the students' activities would materially and substantially disrupt the work and discipline of the school. . . . In the circumstances of the present case, the prohibition of the silent, passive "witness of the armbands," as one of the children called it, is no less offensive to the constitution's guarantees. . . .

We reverse and remand for further proceedings consistent with this opinion.

Justice STEWART concurred.

Justice WHITE concurred.

Justice BLACK dissenting.

Even a casual reading of the record shows that this armband did divert students' minds from the regular lessons, and that talk, comments, etc., made John Tinker "self-conscious" in attending school with his armband. While the absence of obscene remarks or boisterous and loud disorder perhaps justifies the Court's statement that the few armband students did not actually "disrupt" the classwork, I think the record overwhelmingly shows that the armbands did exactly what the elected school officials and principals foresaw they would, that is, took the students' minds off their classwork and diverted them to thoughts about the highly emotional subject of the Vietnam war. And I repeat that if the time has come when pupils of state-supported schools, kindergartens, grammar schools, or high schools, can defy and flout orders of school officials to keep their minds on their own schoolwork, it is the beginning of a new revolutionary era of permissiveness in this country fostered by the judiciary.

Justice HARLAN dissenting.

I would, in cases like this, cast upon those complaining the burden of showing that a particular school measure was motivated by other than legitimate school concerns—for example, a desire to prohibit the expression of an unpopular point of view, while permitting expression of the dominant opinion.

Finding nothing in this record which impugns the good faith of respondents in promulgating the armband regulation, I would affirm the judgment below.

Texas v. Johnson
109 S.Ct. 2533 (1989)

During the 1984 Republican National Convention, Gregory Johnson participated in a political demonstration in Dallas, Texas, to protest the policies of the Reagan administration. After a march through the streets, Johnson burned the American flag while protesters chanted. No one was physically injured or threatened with injury. Johnson was arrested, tried, and convicted of flag desecration in violation of a Texas statute, and a state appeals court affirmed. However, the Texas Court of Criminal Appeals reversed, holding that Johnson's flag burning was expressive conduct protected by the First Amendment. The state appealed that decision to the Supreme Court.

Justice BRENNAN delivers the opinion of the Court.

Johnson was convicted of flag desecration for burning the flag rather than for uttering insulting words. This fact somewhat complicates our consideration of his conviction under the First Amendment. We must first determine whether Johnson's burning of the flag constituted expressive conduct, permitting him to invoke the First Amendment in challenging his conviction. If his conduct was expressive, we next decide whether the State's regulation is related to the suppression of free expression. See, *e.g., United States v. O'Brien,* 391 U.S. 367 (1968). If the State's regulation is not related to expression, then the less stringent standard we announced in *United States v. O'Brien* for regulations of noncommunicative conduct controls. If it is, then we are outside of *O'Brien*'s test, and we must ask whether this interest justifies Johnson's conviction under a more demanding standard. A third possibility is that the State's asserted interest is simply not implicated on these facts, and in that event the interest drops out of the picture. . . .

The First Amendment literally forbids the abridgement only of "speech," but we have long recognized that its protection does not end at the spoken or written word. While we have rejected "the view that an apparently limitless variety of conduct can be labeled 'speech' whenever the person engaging in the conduct intends thereby to express an idea," *United States v. O'Brien,* we have acknowledged that conduct may be "sufficiently imbued with elements of communication to fall within the scope of the First and Fourteenth Amendments."

In deciding whether particular conduct possesses sufficient communicative elements to bring the First Amendment into play, we have asked whether "[a]n intent to convey a particularized message was present, and [whether] the likelihood was great that the message would be understood by those who viewed it." Hence, we have recognized the expressive nature of students' wearing of black armbands to protest American military involvement in Vietnam, *Tinker v. Des Moines Independent Community School Dist.,* 393 U.S. 503 (1969); of a sit-in by blacks in a "whites only" area to protest segregation, *Brown v. Louisiana,* 383 U.S. 131 (1966); of the wearing of American military uniforms in a dramatic presentation criticizing American involvement in Vietnam, *Schacht v. United States,* 398 U.S. 58 [1970], and of picketing about a wide variety of causes, see, *e.g., Food Employees v. Logan Valley Plaza, Inc.,* 391 U.S. 308 (1968); *United States v. Grace,* 461 U.S. 171 (1983).

Especially pertinent to this case are our decisions recognizing the communicative nature of conduct relating to flags. Attaching a peace sign to the flag, *Spence [v. Washington,* 418 U.S. 405 (1974)], saluting the flag, [*West Virginia State Board of Education v. Barnette,* 319 U.S. 624 (1943)], and displaying a red flag, *Stromberg v. California,* 283 U.S. 359 (1931), we have held, all may find shelter under the First Amendment. See also *Smith v. Grogen,* 415 U.S. 566 (1974) (WHITE, J., concurring in judgment) (treating flag "contemptuously" by wearing pants with small flag sewn into their seat is expressive conduct). That we have had little difficulty identifying an expressive element in conduct relating to flags should not be surprising. The very purpose of a national flag is to serve as a symbol of our country; it is, one might say, "the one visible manifestation of two hundred years of nationhood." Thus, we have observed:

"[T]he flag salute is a form of utterance. Symbolism is a primitive but effective way of communicating ideas. The use of an emblem or flag to symbolize some system, idea, institution, or personality, is a short cut from mind to mind. Causes and nations, political parties, lodges and ecclesiastical groups seek to knit the loyalty of their followings to a flag or banner, a color or design." *Barnett.* . . .

We have not automatically concluded, however, that any action taken with respect to our flag is expressive. Instead, in characterizing such action for First Amendment purposes, we have considered the context in which it occurred. . . .

The State of Texas conceded for purposes of its oral argument in this case that Johnson's conduct was expressive conduct. . . . Johnson burned an American flag as part—indeed, as the culmination—of a political demonstration that coincided with the convening of the Republican Party and its renomination of Ronald Reagan for President. The expressive, overtly political nature of this conduct was both intentional and overwhelmingly apparent. At his trial, Johnson explained his reasons for burning the flag as follows: "The American Flag was burned as Ronald Reagan was being renominated as President. And a more powerful statement of symbolic speech, whether you agree with it or not, couldn't have been made at that time. It's quite a just position [juxtaposition]. We had new patriotism and no patriotism." In these circumstances, Johnson's burning of the flag was conduct "sufficiently imbued with elements of communication," to implicate the First Amendment.

The Government generally has a freer hand in restricting expressive conduct than it has in restricting the written or spoken word. . . . It may not, however, proscribe particular conduct *because* it has expressive elements. . . . It is, in short, not simply the verbal or nonverbal nature of the expression, but the governmental interest at stake, that helps to determine whether a restriction on that expression is valid.

Thus, although we have recognized that where " 'speech' and 'nonspeech' elements are combined in the same course of conduct, a sufficiently important governmental interest in regulating the nonspeech element can justify incidental limitations on First Amendment freedoms," *O'Brien,* we have limited the applicability of *O'Brien*'s relatively lenient standard to those cases in which "the governmental interest is unrelated to the suppression of free expression." . . .

In order to decide whether *O'Brien*'s test applies here, therefore, we must decide whether Texas has asserted an interest in support of Johnson's conviction that is unrelated to the suppression of expression. If we find that an interest asserted by the State is simply not implicated on the facts before us, we need not ask whether *O'Brien*'s test applies. The State offers two separate interests to justify this conviction: preventing breaches of the peace, and preserving the flag as a symbol of nationhood and national unity. We hold that the first interest is not implicated on this record and that the second is related to the suppression of expression.

Texas claims that its interest in preventing breaches of the peace justifies Johnson's conviction for flag desecration. However, no disturbance of the peace actually occurred or threatened to occur because of Johnson's burning of the flag. Although the State stresses the disruptive behavior of the protestors during their march toward City Hall, it admits that "no actual breach of the peace occurred at the time of the flagburning or in response to the flagburning." . . .

The State also asserts an interest in preserving the flag as a symbol of nationhood and national unity. In *Spence,* we acknowledged that the Government's interest in preserving the flag's special symbolic value "is directly related to expression in the context of activity" such as affixing a peace symbol to a flag. We are equally persuaded that this interest is related to expression in the case of Johnson's burning of the flag. The State, apparently, is concerned that such conduct will lead people to believe either that the flag does not stand for nationhood and national unity, but instead reflects other, less positive concepts, or that the concepts reflected in the flag do not in fact exist, that is, we do not enjoy unity as a Nation. These concerns blossom only when a person's treatment of the flag communicates some message, and thus are related "to the suppression of free expression" within the meaning of *O'Brien.* We are thus outside of *O'Brien*'s test altogether.

It remains to consider whether the State's interest in preserving the flag as a symbol of nationhood and national unity justifies Johnson's conviction. . . .

Whether Johnson's treatment of the flag violated Texas law thus depended on the likely communicative impact of his expressive conduct. Our decision in *Boos v. Barry,* [108 S.Ct. 1157 (1988)], tells us that this restriction on Johnson's expression is content-based. In *Boos,* we considered the constitutionality of a law prohibiting "the display of any sign within 500 feet of a foreign embassy if that sign tends to bring that foreign government into 'public odium' or 'public disrepute.'" Rejecting the argument that the law was content-neutral because it was justified by "our international law obligation to shield diplomats from speech that offends their dignity," we held that "[t]he emotive impact of speech on its audience is not a 'secondary effect' " unrelated to the content of the expression itself.

According to the principles announced in *Boos*, Johnson's political expression was restricted because of the content of the message he conveyed. We must therefore subject the State's asserted interest in preserving the special symbolic character of the flag to "the most exacting scrutiny." *Boos v. Barry*. . . .

The State's argument is not that it has an interest simply in maintaining the flag as a symbol of *something*, no matter what it symbolizes; indeed, if that were the State's position, it would be difficult to see how that interest is endangered by highly symbolic conduct such as Johnson's. Rather, the State's claim is that it has an interest in preserving the flag as a symbol of *nationhood* and *national unity*, a symbol with a determinate range of meanings. According to Texas, if one physically treats the flag in a way that would tend to cast doubt on either the idea that nationhood and national unity are the flag's referents or that national unity actually exists, the message conveyed thereby is a harmful one and therefore may be prohibited.

If there is a bedrock principle underlying the First Amendment, it is that the Government may not prohibit the expression of an idea simply because society finds the idea itself offensive or disagreeable. . . .

We have not recognized an exception to this principle even where our flag has been involved. In *Street v. New York*, 394 U.S. 576 (1969), we held that a State may not criminally punish a person for uttering words critical of the flag. Rejecting the argument that the conviction could be sustained on the ground that Street had "failed to show the respect for our national symbol which may properly be demanded of every citizen," we concluded that "the constitutionally guaranteed 'freedom to be intellectually . . . diverse or even contrary,' and the 'right to differ as to things that touch the heart of the existing order,' encompass the freedom to express publicly one's opinions about our flag, including those opinions which are defiant or contemptuous." Nor may the Government, we have held, compel conduct that would evince respect for the flag. "To sustain the compulsory flag salute we are required to say that a Bill of Rights which guards the individual's right to speak his own mind, left it open to public authorities to compel him to utter what is not in his mind." . . .

In short, nothing in our precedents suggests that a State may foster its own view of the flag by prohibiting expressive conduct relating to it. To bring its argument outside our precedents, Texas attempts to convince us that even if its interest in preserving the flag's symbolic role does not allow it to prohibit words or some expressive conduct critical of the flag, it does permit it to forbid the outright destruction of the flag. The State's argument cannot depend here on the distinction between written or spoken words and nonverbal conduct. That distinction, we have shown, is of no moment where the nonverbal conduct is expressive, as it is here, and where the regulation of that conduct is related to expression, as it is here. . . .

There is, moreover, no indication—either in the text of the Constitution or in our cases interpreting it—that a separate juridical category exists for the American flag alone. Indeed, we would not be surprised to learn that the persons who framed our Constitution and wrote the Amendment that we now construe were not known for their reverence for the Union Jack. The First Amendment does not guarantee that other concepts virtually sacred to our Nation as a whole—such as the principle that discrimination on the basis of race is odious and destructive—will go unquestioned in the marketplace of ideas. See *Brandenburg v. Ohio*, 395 U.S. 444 (1969). We decline, therefore, to create for the flag an exception to the joust of principles protected by the First Amendment.

It is not the State's ends, but its means, to which we object. It cannot be gainsaid that there is a special place reserved for the flag in this Nation, and thus we do not doubt that the Government has a legitimate interest in making efforts to "preserv[e] the national flag as an unalloyed symbol of our country." . . . To say that the Government has an interest in encouraging proper treatment of the flag, however, is not to say that it may criminally punish a person for burning a flag as a means of political protest. . . .

The way to preserve the flag's special role is not to punish those who feel differently about these matters. It is to persuade them that they are wrong. . . .

Johnson was convicted for engaging in expressive conduct. The State's interest in preventing breaches of the peace does not support his conviction because Johnson's conduct did not threaten to disturb the peace. Nor does the State's interest in preserving the flag as a symbol of nationhood and national unity justify his criminal conviction for engaging in political expression. The judgment of the Texas Court of Criminal Appeals is therefore
Affirmed.

Justice KENNEDY concurring.

I write not to qualify the words Justice BRENNAN chooses so well, for he says with power all that is necessary to explain our ruling. I join his opinion without reservation, but with a keen sense that this case, like others before us from time to time, exacts its personal toll. This prompts me to add to our pages these few remarks. . . .

The hard fact is that sometimes we must make decisions we do not like. We make them because they are right, right in the sense that the law and the Constitution, as we see them, compel the result. And so great is our commitment to the process that, except in the rare case, we do not pause to express distaste for the result, perhaps for fear of undermining a valued principle that dictates the decision. This is one of those rare cases.

Our colleagues in dissent advance powerful arguments why respondent may be convicted for his expression, reminding us that among those who will be dismayed by our holding will be some who have had the singular honor of carrying the flag in battle. And I agree that the flag holds a lonely place of honor in an age when absolutes are distrusted and simple truths are burdened by unneeded apologetics.

With all respect to those views, I do not believe the Constitution gives us the right to rule as the dissenting members of the Court urge, however painful this judgment is to announce. Though symbols often are what we ourselves make of them, the flag is constant in expressing beliefs Americans share, beliefs in law and peace and that freedom which sustains the human spirit. The case here today forces recognition of the costs to which those beliefs commit us. It is poignant but fundamental that the flag protects those who hold it in contempt.

For all the record shows, this respondent was not a philosopher and perhaps did not even possess the ability to comprehend how repellent his statements must be to the Republic itself. But whether or not he could appreciate the enormity of the offense he gave, the fact remains that his acts were speech, in both the technical and the fundamental meaning of the Constitution. So I agree with the Court that he must go free.

Chief Justice REHNQUIST, with whom Justice WHITE and Justice O'CONNOR join, dissenting.

For more than 200 years, the American flag has occupied a unique position as the symbol of our Nation, a uniqueness that justifies a governmental prohibition against flag burning in the way respondent Johnson did here. . . .

No other American symbol has been as universally honored as the flag. In 1931, Congress declared "The Star Spangled Banner" to be our national anthem. In 1949, Congress declared June 14th to be Flag Day. In 1987, John Philip Sousa's "The Stars and Stripes Forever" was designated as the national march. Congress has also established "The Pledge of Allegiance to the Flag" and the manner of its deliverance. The flag has appeared as the principal symbol on approximately 33 United States postal stamps and in the design of at least 43 more, more times than any other symbol.

Both Congress and the States have enacted numerous laws regulating misuse of the American flag. Until 1967, Congress left the regulation of misuse of the flag up to the States. Now, however, Title 18 U.S.C. § 700(a), provides that:

> "Whoever knowingly casts contempt upon any flag of the United States by publicly mutilating, defacing, defiling, burning, or trampling upon it shall be fined not more than $1,000 or imprisoned for not more than one year, or both."

Congress has also prescribed detailed rules for the design of the flag the time and occasion of flag's display, the position and manner of its display, respect for the flag, and conduct during hoisting, lowering and passing of the flag. With the exception of Alaska and Wyoming, all of the States now have statutes prohibiting the burning of the flag. . . .

The American flag, then, throughout more than 200 years of our history, has come to be the visible symbol embodying our Nation. It does not represent the views of any particular political party, and it does not represent any particular political philosophy. The flag is not simply another "idea" or "point of view" competing for recognition in the marketplace of ideas. Millions and millions of Americans regard it with an almost mystical reverence regardless of what sort of social, political, or philosophical beliefs they may have. I cannot agree that the First Amendment invalidates the Act of Congress, and the laws of 48 of the 50 States, which make criminal the public burning of the flag. . . .

Here it may equally well be said that the public burning of the American flag by Johnson was no essential part of any exposition of ideas, and at the same time it had a tendency to incite a breach of the peace. Johnson was free to make any verbal denunciation of the flag that he wished; indeed, he was free to burn the flag in private. He could publicly burn other symbols of the Government or effigies of political leaders. He did lead a march through the streets of Dallas, and conducted a rally in front of the Dallas City Hall. He engaged in a "die-in" to protest nuclear weapons. He shouted out various slogans during the march, including: "Reagan, Mondale which will it be? Either one means World War III"; "Ronald Reagan, killer of the hour, Perfect example of U.S. power"; and "red, white and blue, we spit on you, you stand for plunder, you will go under." For none of these acts was he arrested or prosecuted; it was only when he proceeded to burn publicly an American flag stolen from its rightful owner that he violated the Texas statute. . . .

The result of the Texas statute is obviously to deny one in Johnson's frame of mind one of many means of "symbolic speech." Far from being a case of "one picture being worth a thousand words," flag burning is the equivalent of an inarticulate grunt or roar that, it seems fair to say, is most likely to be indulged in not to express any particular idea, but to antagonize others. . . .

Uncritical extension of constitutional protection to the burning of the flag risks the frustration of the very purpose for which organized governments are instituted. The Court decides that the American flag is just another symbol, about which not only must opinions pro and con be tolerated, but for which the most minimal public respect may not be enjoined. The government may conscript men into the Armed Forces where they must fight and perhaps die for the flag, but the government may not prohibit the public burning of the banner under which they fight. I would uphold the Texas statute as applied in this case.

Justice STEVENS dissenting.

The Court is . . . quite wrong in blandly asserting that respondent "was prosecuted for his expression of dissatisfaction with the policies of this country, expression situated at the core of our First Amendment values." Respondent was prosecuted because of the method he chose to express his dissatisfaction with those policies. Had he chosen to spray paint—or perhaps convey with a motion picture projector—his message of dissatisfaction on the facade of the Lincoln Memorial, there would be no question about the power of the Government to prohibit his means of expression. The prohibition would be supported by the legitimate interest in preserving the quality of an important national asset. Though the asset at stake in this case is intangible, given its unique value, the same interest supports a prohibition on the desecration of the American flag.

(2) Speech-Plus-Conduct

Speech-plus-conduct includes activities such as peaceful picketing, boycotts, and demonstrations. Individuals engaged in these activities may receive some First Amendment protection, but it depends on the circumstances and they do not enjoy the same freedom as those "who communicate ideas by pure speech."[1] Moreover, individuals remain subject to laws making it illegal to trespass onto private property without the owner's permission, for example, and laws forbidding the "breach of the peace," disorderly conduct, blocking traffic, resisting arrest, and inciting to riot.

The Court extended First Amendment protection to speech-plus-conduct initially by developing the "public forum" doctrine in recognition of the importance of discussion of public affairs in public streets, parks, and facilities. The concept of a public forum was introduced into constitutional law by Justice Roberts in *Hague v. Committee for Industrial Organization (CIO)*, 307 U.S.

496 (1937). There the CIO was denied permission to use public halls for a rally in Jersey City, New Jersey, and its members were arrested and removed from the city for publicly discussing and distributing leaflets on the labor movement. When striking down the city's ordinance prohibiting assemblies "in or upon the public streets, highways, public parks or public buildings" without a permit from the director of public safety, Justice Roberts observed,

Wherever the title of streets and parks may rest, they have immemorially been held in trust for the use of the public and, time out of mind, have been used for purposes of assembly, communicating thoughts between citizens, and discussing public questions. Such use of the streets and public places has, from ancient times, been a part of the privileges, immunities, rights and liberties of citizens. The privilege of a citizen of the United States to use the streets and parks for communication of views on national questions may be regulated in the interest of all; it is not absolute, but relative, and must be exercised in consonance with peace and good order; but is must not, in the guise of regulation, be abridged or denied.

Subsequently, the concept of a public forum was expanded to include municipal auditoriums, sidewalks, shopping centers, criminal trials, and the public areas surrounding schools, courthouses, embassies, and state capitol buildings.

Access to a public forum, however, is conditional. States and localities may impose reasonable "time, place, and manner" restrictions governing the use of public streets, parks, and other public facilities. They may also require permits for parades, marches, and demonstrations, so long as those restrictions are evenly applied and not overly broad so as to allow local officials to censor particular groups. In *Cox v. New Hampshire*, 312 U.S. 569 (1941), for example, the Court unanimously upheld the convictions of a group of Jehovah's Witnesses who marched single file along a downtown street, carrying placards, without first obtaining a special permit for "parades or processions."[2] Moreover, in *Ward v. Rock Against Racism*, 109 S.Ct. 2746 (1989), the Rehnquist Court indicated that it was prepared to give states and localities greater leeway in imposing time, place, and manner restrictions. By a vote of six to three, New York's ordinance requiring concerts in Central Park to use a city-owned sound system and engineer to operate the system was upheld. And the majority ruled that time, place, and manner restrictions do not have to meet the least restrictive alternative test that the Court applies in other areas of regulation imposing on First Amendment freedoms. Subsequently, *United States v. Kokinda*, 110 S.Ct. 3115 (1990), held that post offices may ban all solicitations on their property. Four members of the Court—Chief Jus-

THE DEVELOPMENT OF LAW
Rulings Extending the Concept of a Public Forum

Case	Ruling
Hague v. CIO, 307 U.S. 496 (1937)	Public streets and meeting halls.
Edwards v. South Carolina, 371 U.S. 229 (1963)	Steps of state capitol building.
Cox v. Louisiana, 379 U.S. 536 (1965)	Streets surrounding state capitol.
Cox v. Louisiana, 379 U.S. 559 (1965)	Streets and sidewalk near courthouse.
Police Department of City of Chicago v. Mosley, 408 U.S. 92 (1972)	Sidewalks and streets in front of school.
Chief of the Capitol Police v. Jeanette Rankin Brigade, 409 U.S. 972 (1972)	Peaceful protests in Lafayette Park.
Southern Promotions v. Conrad, 420 U.S. 546 (1975)	Municipal auditorium.
Richmond Newspapers, Inc. v. Virginia, 448 U.S. 358 (1980)	Criminal trials.
Widmar v. Vincent, 454 U.S. 263 (1981)	State University facilities that have been established as an open forum cannot be denied to religious groups.
United States v. Grace, 461 U.S. 171 (1982)	Steps of the Supreme Court of the United States.
Board of Airport Commissioners of Los Angeles v. Jews for Jesus, Inc., 482 U.S. 569 (1987)	Struck down a "First Amendment free zone," which banned all First Amendment expression, solicitations, and canvassing in central airport terminal.
Boos v. Barry, 485 U.S. 312 (1988)	Struck down statute prohibiting protests within 500 feet of an embassy.

tice Rehnquist and Justices O'Connor, White, and Scalia—also held that a sidewalk on postal property was not a public forum, and thus solicitations could be banned there as well. Justice Kennedy, casting the crucial fifth vote, however, concluded that the Court need not address the public forum issue, because the post office's ban on solicitations was a reasonable time, place and manner restriction. By contrast, dissenting Justices Brennan, Marshall, Blackmun, and Stevens contended that the public side-

DEVELOPMENT OF LAW
Places That Have Been Held Not to Be Public Forums

Case	Ruling
Lehman v. City of Shaker Heights, 418 U.S. 298 (1974)	Bus placards
Adderly v. Florida, 385 U.S. 385 U.S. 39 (1966)	Area surrounding jails
Flower v. United States, 407 U.S. 197 (1972)	Army bases
Greer v. Spock, 424 U.S. 828 (1976)	Military bases
United States v. Kokinda, 110 S.Ct. 3115 (1990)	Sidewalks on property of U.S. post offices (plurality holding)

walks outside of post offices constituted public forums entitled to First Amendment protection.

In addition to time, place, and manner restrictions and required permits, courts may issue injunctions against or limiting demonstrations, marches, and parades. The Court in *Walker v. City of Birmingham* (1967) (see page 611), arising from Martin Luther King's defiance of a court order against a march in Birmingham, Alabama, upheld the power of courts to enjoin particular marches and to find those who fail to comply with their orders in contempt of court.

It bears emphasizing that the concept of public forum and time, place, and manner restrictions apply only to public streets and other public places not otherwise restricted to the public. Generally, individuals have no First Amendment rights to intrude on private property and may be prosecuted for trespass or nuisance.[3] However, in *Amalgamated Food Employees Union v. Logan Valley Plaza,* 391 U.S. 308 (1968), the Court (six to three) upheld the right of a labor union to picket outside a store in a privately owned shopping center on the grounds that the Logan Valley Plaza was the only shopping center in the community and, hence, was functionally equivalent for First Amendment purposes to a downtown business district and the only forum available for the union to publicize its labor dispute. But after Nixon's four appointees joined the Court, the justices five to four (with Justices Brennan, Douglas, Marshall, and Stewart dissenting) held that a privately owned shopping center could prohibit the distribution of handbills protesting the draft and the

Vietnam War. In *Lloyd Corporation v. Tanner,* 407 U.S. 551 (1972), Justice Powell, writing for the majority, thought that there were "adequate alternative avenues of communication" available. Then in *Hudgens v. National Labor Relations Board,* 424 U.S. 507 (1976), involving another labor picketing dispute, the justices (voting six to two) rejected the *Logan Valley* ruling and Justice Stewart's opinion for the Court contented that the First Amendment guarantee for freedom of expression was inapplicable to shopping centers. But, finally, in *PruneYard Shopping Center v. Robins* (1980) (see page 617), the Court unanimously held that California could under its own state constitution permit the distribution of pamphlets and petitions in shopping malls and confer greater freedom of expression than the Court does when interpreting and applying the First Amendment.

NOTES

1. *Cox v. Louisiana,* 379 U.S. 536 (1965).
2. See also *Niemotko v. Maryland,* 340 U.S. 268 (1951); *Poulos v. New Hampshire,* 345 U.S. 395 (1951); *Kunz v. New York,* 290 U.S. 36 (1951); and *Cameron v. Johnson,* 381 U.S. 741 (1965).
3. But see *Gregory v. Chicago,* 394 U.S. 111 (1969) (upholding the picketing of black activists on the sidewalk outside of the home of Chicago Mayor Richard Daley).

Walker v. City of Birmingham
388 U.S. 307, 87 S.Ct. 1824 (1967)

In the early 1960s, there remained bitter opposition to the Supreme Court's school desegregation ruling in *Brown v. Board of Education,* 347 U.S. 483 (1954) (see Chapter 12), particularly in states like Alabama. In Birmingham, schools, restaurants, hotels, and movie theaters remained segregated. To publicize the segregation and to pressure city businesses, civil rights organizations decided to hold marches and sit-ins during the week of Easter Sunday, in April 1963. The leaders of these groups included the Reverend Martin Luther King, Jr., Reverend Wyatt T. Walker, and Reverend Ralph Abernathy of the Southern Christian Leadership Conference (SCLC), and Reverend Fred L. Shuttlesworth, the leader of the Alabama Christian Movement for Human Rights (ACMHR) and pastor of the Bethel Baptist Church in Birmingham.

On April 3, 1963, two representatives of these civil rights groups went to the Birmingham City Hall to apply for a permit to picket and parade, which under the city's ordinance had to be approved by the entire city commission. They were told, however, by one of the commissioners, "Bull" Connor, that a permit would not be granted. Two days later, Shuttlesworth sent a telegram to him requesting a permit, and Connor responded with another, telling Shuttlesworth to apply to the entire commission. But given the city's history of segregation and of denial of permits, Shuttlesworth made no further attempt to obtain the necessary permit.

On April 6, Shuttlesworth lead a protest march in downtown Birmingham and sit-ins were held at segregated lunch counters in the city. These activities continued for three days. On April 10, King, Walker, Abernathy, and others from SCLC arrived in Birmingham to participate in the Easter-weekend demonstrations. But on that day, city attorneys asked a state judge, William Jenkins, Jr., for a temporary restraining order against the ACMHR and SCLC. Judge Jenkins issued an *ex parte* injunction, that is, an injunction based on hearing only the city's attorneys and giving lawyers for the civil rights groups no opportunity to present their side. Under the injunction, the ACMHC and the SCLC were to halt their activities, were denied permission to conduct their Easter weekend marches, and informed that if they proceeded with their plans they would be held in contempt of court.

After receiving the restraining order, King, Walker, Abernathy, and Shuttlesworth announced that they would defy the court order and claimed that the injunction was based on an unconstitutional ordinance that violated their First Amendment rights. On Good Friday, April 12, King and Abernathy led about fifty followers out of the Sixteenth Street Baptist Church and within blocks had gathered several hundred additional supporters. But before marching very far, police moved in and arrested King and Abernathy, who were immediately jailed.

Anticipating the arrests, Reverend Walker did not participate in the march. He tried to get the Kennedy administration and the Department of Justice to intervene, but failed. On Easter Sunday, Walker and others led another march; they too were arrested. The following day, their attorneys filed a motion to dissolve the injunction on several grounds, including that it was a denial of First Amendment freedoms, that the demonstrations were peaceful protests and not parades under the meaning of the city ordinance, that the ordinance was applied in an arbitrary and discriminatory way, and that the case should be removed to federal courts because the prosecutions aimed at denying the civil rights leaders' First Amendment freedoms.

Two weeks after the Easter weekend marches and arrests, Judge Jenkins upheld the city's ordinance and found the civil rights leaders in contempt of court. Attorneys for King, Walker, and the others appealed. The Alabama Supreme Court granted an appeal in August 1963, but did not hand down its ruling until December 9, 1965. Then the state supreme court upheld the actions of the lower court. Another appeal was promptly made to the Supreme Court, which granted review. The justices split five to four, with Justice Stewart writing the opinion for the majority and Chief Justice Warren, joined by Justice Fortas, and Justices Douglas and Brennan writing separate dissenting opinions.

Justice STEWART delivers the opinion of the Court.

In the present case . . . we are asked to hold that this rule of law, upon which the Alabama courts relied, was constitutionally impermissible. We are asked to say that the Constitution compelled Alabama to allow the petitioners to violate this injunction, to organize and engage in these mass street parades and demonstrations, without any previous effort on their part to have the injunction dissolved or modified, or any attempt to secure a parade permit in accordance with its terms. . . . [W]e cannot accept the petitioners' contentions in the circumstances of this case.

Without question the state court that issued the injunction had, as a court of equity, jurisdiction over the petitioners and over the subject matter of the controversy. And this is not a case where the injunction was transparently invalid or had only a frivolous pretense to validity. We have consistently recognized the strong interest of state and local governments in regulating the use of their streets and other public places. . . .

When protest takes the form of mass demonstrations, parades, or picketing on public streets and sidewalks, the free passage of traffic and the prevention of public disorder and violence become important objects of legitimate state concern. As the Court stated, in *Cox v. State of Louisiana,* [379 U.S. 559 (1965)], "We emphatically reject the notion . . . that the First and Fourteenth Amendments afford the same kind of freedom to those who would communicate ideas by conduct such as patrolling, marching, and picketing on streets and highways, as these amendments afford to those who communicate ideas by pure speech." . . .

The generality of the language contained in the Birmingham

parade ordinance upon which the injunction was based would unquestionably raise substantial constitutional issues concerning some of its provisions. . . . The petitioners, however, did not even attempt to apply to the Alabama courts for an authoritative construction of the ordinance. The breadth and vagueness of the injunction itself would also unquestionably be subject to substantial constitutional question. But the way to raise that question was to apply to the Alabama courts to have the injunction modified or dissolved. The injunction in all events clearly prohibited mass parading without a permit, and the evidence shows that the petitioners fully understood that prohibition when they violated it.

The petitioners also claim that they were free to disobey the injunction because the parade ordinance on which it was based had been administered in the past in an arbitrary and discriminatory fashion. In support of this claim they sought to introduce evidence that, a few days before the injunction issued, requests for permits to picket had been made to a member of the city commission. One request had been rudely rebuffed, and this same official had later made clear that he was without power to grant the permit alone, since the issuance of such permits was the responsibility of the entire city commission. Assuming the truth of this proffered evidence, it does not follow that the parade ordinance was void on its face. The petitioners, moreover, did not apply for a permit either to the commission itself or to any commissioner after the injunction issued. Had they done so, and had the permit been refused, it is clear that their claim of arbitrary or discriminatory administration of the ordinance would have been considered by the state circuit court upon a motion to dissolve the injunction. . . .

The rule of law that Alabama followed in this case reflects a belief that in the fair administration of justice no man can be judge in his own case, however exalted his station, however righteous his motives, and irrespective of his race, color, politics, or religion. This Court cannot hold that the petitioners were constitutionally free to ignore all the procedures of the law and carry their battle to the streets. One may sympathize with the petitioners' impatient commitment to their cause. But respect for judicial process is a small price to pay for the civilizing hand of law, which alone can give abiding meaning to constitutional freedom.

Chief Justice WARREN, with whom Justice BRENNAN and Justice FORTAS join, dissenting.

The salient facts can be stated very briefly. Petitioners are Negro ministers who sought to express their concern about racial discrimination in Birmingham, Alabama, by holding peaceful protest demonstrations in that city on Good Friday and Easter Sunday 1963. For obvious reasons, it was important for the significance of the demonstrations that they be held on those particular dates. A representative of petitioners' organization went to the City Hall and asked "to see the person or persons in charge to issue permits, permits for parading, picketing, and demonstrating." She was directed to Public Safety Commissioner Connor, who denied her request for a permit in terms that left no doubt that petitioners were not going to be issued a permit under any circumstances. "He said, 'No you will not get a permit in Birmingham, Alabama to picket. I will picket you over to the City Jail,' and he repeated that twice." A second, telegraphic request was also summarily denied, in a telegram signed by "Eugene 'Bull' Connor," with the added information that permits could be issued only by the full City Commission, a three-man body consisting of Commissioner Connor and two others. According to petitioner's offer of proof, the truth of which is assumed for purposes of this case, parade permits had uniformly been issued for all other groups by the city clerk on the request of the traffic bureau of the police department, which was under Commissioner Connor's direction. The requirement that the approval of the full Commission be obtained was applied only to this one group.

Understandably convinced that the City of Birmingham was not going to authorize their demonstrations under any circumstances, petitioners proceeded with their plans despite Commissioner Connor's orders. On Wednesday, April 10, at 9 in the evening, the city filed in a state circuit court a bill of complaint seeking an *ex parte* injunction. The complaint recited that petitioners were engaging in a series of demonstrations as "part of a massive effort . . . to forcibly integrate all business establishments, churches, and other institutions" in the city, with the result that the police department was strained in its resources and the safety, peace, and tranquility were threatened. . . . Faced with these recitals, the Circuit Court issued the injunction in the form requested, and in effect ordered petitioners and all other persons having notice of the order to refrain for an unlimited time from carrying on any demonstrations without a permit. A permit, of course, was clearly unobtainable: the city would not have sought this injunction if it had any intention of issuing one.

Petitioners were served with copies of the injunction at various times on Thursday and on Good Friday. Unable to believe that such a blatant and broadly drawn prior restraint on their First Amendment rights could be valid, they announced their intention to defy it and went ahead with the planned peaceful demonstrations on Easter weekend. On the following Monday, when they promptly filed a motion to dissolve the injunction, the court found them in contempt, holding that they had waived all their First Amendment rights by disobeying the court order.

These facts lend no support to the court's charges that petitioners were presuming to act as judges in their own case, or that they had a disregard for the judicial process. They did not flee the jurisdiction or refuse to appear in the Alabama courts. Having violated the injunction, they promptly submitted themselves to the courts to test the constitutionality of the injunction and the ordinance it parroted. . . .

The Court concedes that "[t]he generality of the language contained in the Birmingham parade ordinance upon which the injunction was based would unquestionably raise substantial constitutional issues concerning some of its provisions." That concession is well-founded but minimal. I believe it is patently unconstitutional on its face. Our decisions have consistently held that picketing and parading are means of expression protected by the First Amendment, and that the right to picket or parade may not be subjected to the unfettered discretion of local officials. . . . Although a city may regulate the manner of use of its streets and sidewalks in the interest of keeping them open for the movement of traffic, it may not allow local officials unbridled discretion to decide who shall be allowed to parade or picket and who shall not. . . .

I do not believe that giving this Court's seal of approval to such a gross misuse of the judicial process is likely to lead to greater respect for the law any more than it is likely to lead to greater protection for First Amendment freedoms. The *ex parte* temporary injunction has a long and odious history in this country, and its susceptibility to misuse is all too apparent from the facts of the case. As a weapon against strikes, it proved so effective in the hands of judges friendly to employers that Congress was forced to take the drastic step of removing from federal district courts the jurisdiction to issue injunctions in labor disputes. The labor injunction fell into disrepute largely because it was abused in precisely the same way that the injunctive power was abused in this case. Judges who were not sympathetic to the union cause commonly issued, without notice or hearing, broad restraining orders addressed to large numbers of persons and forbidding them to engage in acts that were either legally permissible or, if illegal, that could better have been left to the regular course of criminal prosecution. The injunctions might later be dissolved, but in the meantime strikes would be crippled because the occasion on which concerted activity might have been effective had passed. Such injunctions so long discredited as weapons against concerted labor activities, have now been given new life by this Court as weapons against the exercise of First Amendment freedoms. Respect for the courts and for judicial process was not increased by the history of the labor injunction.

Justices DOUGLAS and BRENNAN dissented in separate opinions.

PruneYard Shopping Center v. Robins
447 U.S. 74, 100 S.Ct. 2035 (1980)

PruneYard Shopping Center is a twenty-one-acre, privately owned shopping complex in Campbell, California. While open to the public, the center had a policy of not allowing publicly expressive activities, such as circulating petitions, not related to its commercial purposes. On a Saturday afternoon, Michael Robins and several other high-school students set up a card table in the central courtyard and asked passersby to sign petitions opposing a United Nations resolution against Zionism that were to be sent to the president and Congress. A security guard informed them of PruneYard's policy against noncommercial solicitation and suggested they move to a public sidewalk outside of the shopping center. They did, but later filed a lawsuit in the California Superior Court for Santa Clara County, seeking to enjoin PruneYard from denying them access to the center for the purpose of circulating their petitions. The superior court denied they had enforceable free speech claims under the First Amendment and the California Constitution. On appeal to the California State Supreme Court, however, that decision was reversed. The California Supreme Court held that the state's constitution protected "speech and petitioning, reasonably exercised, in shopping centers even when the centers are privately owned." Attorneys for PruneYard Shopping Center appealed that ruling to the Supreme Court.

Justice REHNQUIST delivers the opinion of the Court.

Appellant PruneYard is a privately owned shopping center in the city of Campbell, Cal. It covers approximately 21 acres— five devoted to parking and 16 occupied by walkways, plazas, sidewalks, and buildings that contain more than 65 specialty shops, 10 restaurants, and a movie theater. The PruneYard is open to the public for the purpose of encouraging the patronizing of its commercial establishments. It has a policy not to permit any visitor or tenant to engage in any publicly expressive activity, including the circulation of petitions, that is not directly related to its commercial purposes. This policy has been strictly enforced in a nondiscriminatory fashion. The PruneYard is owned by appellant Fred Sahadi.

Appellees are high school students who sought to solicit support for their opposition to a United Nations resolution against "Zionism." On a Saturday afternoon they set up a card table in a corner of PruneYard's central courtyard. They distributed pamphlets and asked passersby to sign petitions, which were to be sent to the President and Members of Congress. Their activity was peaceful and orderly and so far as the record indicates was not objected to by PruneYard's patrons.

Soon after appellees had begun soliciting signatures, a security guard informed them that they would have to leave because their activity violated PruneYard regulations. The guard suggested that they move to the public sidewalk at the PruneYard's perimeter. Appellees immediately left the premises and later filed this lawsuit in the California Superior Court of Santa Clara County. They sought to enjoin appellants from denying them access to the PruneYard for the purpose of circulating their petitions. . . .

Appellants first contend that *Lloyd v. Tanner,* 407 U.S. 551 (1972), prevents the State from requiring a private shopping center owner to provide access to persons exercising their state constitutional rights of free speech and petition when adequate alternative avenues of communication are available. *Lloyd* dealt with the question whether under the Federal Constitution a privately owned shopping center may prohibit the distribution of handbills on its property when the handbilling is unrelated to the shopping center's operations. The shopping center had adopted a strict policy against the distribution of handbills within the building complex and its malls, and it made no exceptions to this rule. Respondents in *Lloyd* argued that because the shopping center was open to the public, the First Amendment prevents the private owner from enforcing the handbilling restriction on shopping center premises. In rejecting this claim we substantially repudiated the rationale of *Logan Valley,* which was later overruled in *Hudgens v. NLRB,* 424 U.S. 507 (1975). We stated that property does not "lose its private character merely because the public is generally invited to use it for designated purposes," and that "[t]he essentially private character of a store and its privately owned abutting property does not change by virtue of being large or clustered with other stores in a modern shopping center."

Our reasoning in *Lloyd,* however, does not . . . limit the authority of the State to exercise its police power or its sovereign right to adopt in its own Constitution individual liberties more expansive than those conferred by the Federal Constitution. In *Lloyd, supra,* there was no state constitutional or statutory provision that had been construed to create rights to the use of private property by strangers, comparable to those found to exist by the California Supreme Court here. It is, of course, well-established that a State in the exercise of its police power may adopt reasonable restrictions on private property so long as the restrictions do not amount to a taking without just compensation or contravene any other federal constitutional provision. *Lloyd* held that when a shopping center owner opens his private property to the public for the purpose of shopping, the First Amendment to the United States Constitution does not thereby create individual rights in expression beyond those already existing under applicable law. . . .

Appellants finally contend that a private property owner has a First Amendment right not to be forced by the State to use his property as a forum for the speech of others. They state that in *Wooley v. Maynard*, [430 U.S. 705] (1977), this Court concluded that a State may not constitutionally require an individual to participate in the dissemination of an ideological message by displaying it on his private property in a manner and for the express purpose that it be observed and read by the public. This rationale applies here, they argue, because the message of *Wooley* is that the State may not force an individual to display any message at all.

Wooley, however, was a case in which the government itself prescribed the message, required it to be displayed openly on appellee's personal property that was used "as part of his daily life," and refused to permit him to take any measures to cover up the motto even though the Court found that the display of the motto served no important state interest. Here, by contrast, there are a number of distinguishing factors. Most important, the shopping center by choice of its owner is not limited to the personal use of appellants. It is instead a business establishment that is open to the public to come and go as they please. The views expressed by members of the public in passing out pamphlets or seeking signatures for a petition thus will not likely be identified with those of the owner. Second, no specific message is dictated by the State to be displayed on appellants' property. There consequently is no danger of governmental discrimination for or against a particular message. Finally, as far as appears here appellants can expressly disavow any connection with the message by simply posting signs in the area where the speakers or handbillers stand. Such signs, for example, could disclaim any sponsorship of the message and could explain that the persons are communicating their own messages by virtue of state law. . . .

We conclude that neither appellants' federally recognized property rights nor their First Amendment rights have been infringed by the California Supreme Court's decision recognizing a right of appellees to exercise state protected rights of expression and petition on appellants' property. The judgment of the Supreme Court of California is therefore

Affirmed.

Justices BLACKMUN, MARSHALL, WHITE, and POWELL concurred in separate opinions.

I. FREEDOM OF ASSOCIATION

The First Amendment's provision for "the right of the people to peaceably assemble, and to petition the Government for a redress of grievances" provides the textual basis for the Court's recognition of a right of association and associational privacy. But the Court also recognized that the freedom of association is implicit in the very structure of the First Amendment's guarantees for a "system of freedom of expression" and the Constitution's framework for the operation of free government. In *Sweezy v. New Hampshire*, 354 U.S. 234 (1957), the Court thus observed that "Our form of government is built on the premise that every citizen shall have the right to engage in political expression and association. This right was enshrined in the First Amendment of the Bill of Rights." More than a century before, Alexis de Tocqueville found that in "no country in the world has the principle of association been more successfully used or more unsparingly applied to a multitude of different objects, than in America," when proclaiming, "The most natural privilege of a man next to the right of acting for himself, is that of combining his exertions with those of his fellow creatures and of acting in common with them. The right of association therefore appears to be as almost inalienable in its nature as the right of personal liberty. No legislator can attack it without impairing the foundations of society."[1]

The Court formally proclaimed a First Amendment right of association and associational privacy in *National Association for the Advancement of Colored People v. Alabama* (1958) (see page 628), when unanimously reversing a contempt citation for the NAACP's refusal to turn over lists of members to Alabama's state attorney general. The Court in the 1950s and 1960s, however, remained divided over the scope of freedom of association, especially when confronted with First Amendment challenges to congressional investigations (see Vol. 1, Ch. 5) and state and federal prosecutions of members of the Communist party and other "subversive" organizations (see section A, in this chapter). The year after *NAACP v. Alabama,* for example, the justices split five to four (with Chief Justice Warren and Justices Black, Brennan, and Douglas in dissent) in *Uphaus v. Wyman*, 260 U.S. 72 (1959), holding that New Hampshire could compel the production of membership lists of "Communist front" organizations. But the next year in *Bates v. City of Little Rock*, 364 U.S. 479 (1960), and *Sheldon v. Tucker*, 364 U.S. 516 (1960), the Court reaffirmed that compelled disclosure of membership lists denies individuals' freedom of association and associational privacy. *Sheldon* struck down as overly broad an Arkansas statute requiring teachers to file affidavits listing all organizations to which they belonged in the preceding five years. There Stewart pointed out that "to compel a teacher to disclose his every associational tie is to impair that teacher's right of free association, a right closely allied to freedom of speech, and a right which, like free speech, lies at the foundation of a free society." Still, the justices, divided five to four as in *Uphaus,* upheld the provisions of the Internal Security Act of 1950, making it unlawful to be a member of the Communist party and requiring members of subversive organizations to register with the Subversive Activities Control Board, in *Communist Party v. Subversive Activities Control Board (SACB),* 367 U.S. 1 (1961), and *Scales v. United States,* 367 U.S. 203 (1961).[2]

The Warren Court's rulings in the 1950s and early 1960s extended First Amendment protection to groups and organizations formed or associated for lawful purposes, but not to those, such as the Communist party, which were deemed to have subversive purposes. In *NAACP v. Alabama,* the Court thus distinguished an earlier ruling, *Bryant v. Zimmerman,* 278 U.S. 63 (1928), upholding a New York anti–Klu Klux Klan statute requiring oathbound organizations to submit membership lists on the basis of the Klan's illegal activities. This was the basis for the Court's denial of First Amendment claims whenever associations were found or deemed to have unlawful purposes. As the Court explained, in *DeJonge v. Oregon,* 299 U.S. 353 (1937), "The right of peaceable assembly is a right cognate to those of free speech and free press and is equally fundamental," but it did not extend to associations that "incite[d] violence and crime," which could also be prosecuted under laws punishing criminal conspiracies, among other illegal activities.

The Court's dichotomy between nonsubversive and subversive organizations was problematic because organizations may have both legal and illegal goals, and thus individual members might be punished for knowing but guiltless behavior; their only crime being guilt by association. In addition, states could thwart the activities of organizations, such as the NAACP, by claiming they were subversive or infiltrated by other subversive organizations.

The balance on the Warren Court, though, shifted in 1962 when Justice Goldberg, a prominent union lawyer and a successful labor negotiator, was named to the bench. He sided with Chief Justice Warren and Justices Black, Brennan, and Douglas in forming a solid majority for extending greater First Amendment protection, which held even after Goldberg's resignation in 1965 with President Johnson's appointments of Justices Fortas (in 1965) and Marshall (in 1967). *Gibson v. Florida Legislative Investigation Committee,* 372 U.S. 539 (1963) (see Vol. 1, Ch. 5), signaled that the Court would no longer presume the validity of governmental inquiries, but require that the government establish an "immediate, substantial, and subordinating state interest necessary to sustain its right of inquiry into the membership lists of a nonsubversive organization." Along with that ruling, in *NAACP v. Button*, 371 U.S. 415 (1963), the Court (with Justices Clark, Harlan, Stewart, and White in partial dissent) held that the NAACP's litigation activities aimed at forcing desegregation were protected under the First Amendment. In Justice Brennan's words, litigation is a "form of political expression" and "for such a group association for litigation may be the most effective form of political association." Subsequently, the Court held that the Subversive Activities Control Board (SACB) could not revoke the passports of individuals who registered, as required under the Internal Security Act of 1950, as members of the Communist party.[3] And the SACB's ordering all Communists to register with the federal government was overturned in *American Committee for Protection of Foreign Born v. SACB*, 380 U.S. 503 (1965). Finally, in *United States v. Robel*, 389 U.S. 258 (1967), over the dissent of Justices Harlan and White, a section of the Internal Security Act making it unlawful for a member of a Communist-action organization to work in a defense facility was held to violate the First Amendment. The statute, in the Court's view, swept too broadly and "indiscriminately across all types of associations with Communist-action groups, without regard to the quality or degree of membership. . . . The statute quite literally establishes guilt by association alone, without any need to establish that an individual's association poses the threat feared by the Government in proscribing it."

The scope of First Amendment protection for freedom of association and expression was also expanded in cases challenging the constitutionality of loyalty oaths and the firing of public employees for their political beliefs, associations, and activities. However, over First Amendment objections the Court approved restrictions on political activities imposed on federal career civil servants under the Hatch Act or Federal Lobbying Act, forbidding active participating in political campaigns. The law was upheld in *United States v. Harris*, 347 U.S. 612 (1954), and again in *United States Civil Service Commission v. National Association of Letter Carriers*, 413 U.S. 548 (1973). In the words of Justice White, who authored the majority's opinion in the latter six-to-three ruling, "It is in the best interest of the country, indeed essential, that federal service should depend upon meritorious performance rather than political service, and that the political influence of federal employees on others and on the electorial process should be limited." In *Lyng v. International Union, United Automobile, Aerospace and Agricultural Workers of America*, 485 U.S. 360

(1988), the Court upheld over the First Amendment objections of union a 1981 amendment to the Food Stamp Act, which makes households ineligible for food stamps if a member of the household is on a strike.

CONSTITUTIONAL HISTORY

Loyalty Oaths and the First Amendment

Loyalty oaths have been required since the colonial period; indeed, the first item printed on the first printing press in the colonies in 1639 was a loyalty oath. But as professor Sanford Levinson points out in *Constitutional Faiths:*[*]

> The controversy about loyalty oaths . . . is as old as their use. Roger Williams is only the most famous early protestant against the Massachusetts Bay Colony oath; since then, the conflict between the proponents and opponents of oath-taking has never ceased. . . . Loyalty oaths have returned to the forefront of American political consciousness whenever the United States has been (or has been perceived as being) at war. Thus the great clash of 1861–1865 provoked both the Union and the Confederacy to guarantee the loyalty of their citizens by requiring oaths. In the modern period, the "Cold War" has generated demand for proofs of loyalty. . . . Those who regard themselves as "liberal" in their political views, however, have criticized loyalty oaths. Many would argue that a liberal state has no business inquiring into the political views held by its members. As members of the polity, our obligation is not to affirm or otherwise hold certain beliefs, but rather only to behave in conformity with legal requirements.

In *West Virginia State Board of Education v. Barnette* (1943) (see page 582), the Court struck down West Virginia's law compelling schoolchildren to recite the pledge of allegiance—a quintessential American loyalty oath. Yet in *Garner v. Board of Public Works*, 341 U.S. 716 (1951), the Court upheld a law requiring public employees to swear that they were not members of the Communist party.

The Court gradually imposed restrictions on states' requiring and use of loyalty oaths, however. In *Wieman v. Updegraff*, 344 U.S. 183 (1952), for instance, the Court held that membership in the Communist party alone could not be the basis for excluding people from public service. *Konigsberg v. State Bar of California*, 353 U.S. 252 (1957), held that states could not deny an attorney admission to the bar because he refused to answer questions about being a member of subversive organizations and *Schware v. Board of Bar Examiners of the State of New York*, 353 U.S. 232 (1957), held that a person could not be precluded from taking a state bar exam due to past association with the Communist party. Soo too, *Baird v. State Bar of Arizona*, 401 U.S. 1 (1971), held that the refusal to process Ms. Baird's application to practice law because she refused to answer questions about whether she had ever been a member of the Communist party violated her First Amendment freedoms. New York's requirement that attorneys list all organizations to which they belonged since the age of sixteen as a condition for admission into the state bar was struck down in *Application of Stolar,* 401 U.S. 23 (1971).

The Warren Court struck down loyalty oaths for teachers in *Baggett v. Bullitt,* 377 U.S. 360 (1964), and *Elfrand v. Russell,* 384 U.S. 11 (1966). In *United States v. Brown,* 381 U.S. 437 (1965), the Court overturned a provision of the Taft-Hartley Act, or Labor Management Relations Act of 1947, making it a crime for a member of the Communist party to work for a labor union. [The Vinson Court in *American Communications Association v. Douds,* 339 U.S. 382 (1950), had upheld a non-Communist oath required for labor union officers, but the oath was repealed in 1959.] *Whitehill v. Elkins,* 389 U.S. 54 (1967), invalidated Maryland's requiring all state employees to take an oath swearing that they were not subversive persons. And a loyalty oath for candidates of political parties that was required before they could have their names placed on election ballots was struck down in *Communist Party of Indiana v. Whitcomb,* 414 U.S. 441 (1974).

In *Law Students v. Wadmond,* 401 U.S. 154 (1971), however, a bare majority of the Burger Court (with Justices Black, Brennan, Douglas, and Marshall in dissent), upheld New York's requiring applicants to the state bar to take an oath to uphold the Constitution. A year later, in *Cole v. Richardson,* 405 U.S. 676 (1972), Chief Justice Burger upheld Massachusetts's loyalty oath and the dismissal of a research sociologist from a state hospital for refusing to take the following oath: "I do solemnly swear (or affirm) that I will uphold and defend the Constitution of the United States of America and the Constitution of the Commonwealth of Massachusetts and that I will oppose the overthrow of the government of the United States or of this Commonwealth by force, violence or by any illegal or unconstitutional method." Over the objections of dissenting Justices Brennan, Douglas, and Marshall that the last part of the oath was too sweeping, Chief Justice Burger found the oath to impose no obligation for "specific, positive action" and to merely require that state employees "live by the constitutional processes of our system." He underscored, however, that

> neither federal nor state government may condition employment on taking oaths that impinge on rights guaranteed by the First and Fourteenth Amendments respectively, as for example those relating to political beliefs. . . . Nor may employment be conditioned on an oath that one has not engaged, or will not engage, in protected speech activities such as the following: criticizing institutions of government; discussing political doctrine that approves the overthrow of certain forms of government; and supporting candidates for political office. . . . Employment may not be conditioned on an oath denying past, or abjuring future, associational activities within constitutional protection; such protected activities include membership in organizations having illegal purposes unless one knows of the purpose and shares a specific intent to promote the illegal purpose.

Source: For further discussion of loyality oaths, see Stanford Levinson, *Constitutional Faith* (Princeton, NJ: Princeton University Press, 1988).

In another highly controversial ruling in *Elrod v. Burns,* 427 U.S. 347 (1976), the justices (voting five to three and with Stevens not participating), struck down the practice of patronage dismissals as an unconstitutional restriction on city employees' First Amendment freedoms. The controversy and struggle within the Court over systems of political patronage and dismissal of public employees continued in *Brant v. Finkel,* 445 U.S. 507 (1980). In that case, the justices six to three (with Justices Stewart, Powell, and Rehnquist in dissent) held that the First Amendment protects district attorneys from being discharged for expressing their political views. After Stewart retired and was replaced by O'Connor, however, the Court held (five to four, with Justices Brennan, Blackmun, Marshall, and Stevens now in dissent) that the firing of state attorneys general for political reasons does not violate the First Amendment.[4] But then Justice Brennan marshaled a bare majority, in *Rutan v. Republican Party of Illinois,* 110 S.Ct. 2729 (1990), for eliminating political patronage in the hiring and firing of most public employees (see, Vol. 1, Ch. 8).

The protection accorded freedom of association extends to a broad range of groups, associations and organizations, including public interest groups,[5] unions,[6] political parties,[7] and married couples.[8] But the right of association and associational privacy does not extend to individuals' claims to anonymity. In *Laird v. Tatum,* 408 U.S. 1 (1972), the Burger Court, over the sharp dissents of Justices Douglas, Brennan, Marshall, and Stewart, upheld the army's surveillance of political protesters at rallies, demonstrations, and marches against America's involvement in the Vietnam War.

Nor does the First Amendment right of association present a barrier to state and federal laws prohibiting invidious discrimination in privately owned businesses serving the public or private associations and clubs. The freedom of association is basically the freedom to discriminate—the freedom to choose with whom one associates and in what context and for what purpose. But the Court has held that not all private associations and discriminations receive First Amendment protection; those associations discriminating against racial minorities and women may not find a haven in the First Amendment right of association.

While the Warren Court broadened the First Amendment to include a right of association and associational privacy in cases such as *NAACP v. Alabama,* it was reluctant to tackle the competing First Amendment claims of those who protested segregation with sit-ins, and those who discriminated against blacks in their private businesses and associations. Over the objections of dissenting Justices Black and Douglas, the Court upheld a lower court's ordering the integration of the Wisconsin state bar association in *Lathrop v. Donahue*, 367 U.S. 820 (1961). But when it came to cases challenging the convictions for trespass of blacks who demonstrated with sit-ins at racially segregated lunch counters, and raising the claim of owners of segregated restaurants that they had a right to decide who to serve, the Court split three ways. In *Bell v. Maryland*, 378 U.S. 226 (1964), Justice Brennan's opinion for the Court simply declined to confront the issue when it remanded the case back to the Maryland Supreme Court. Justices Douglas and Goldberg, along with Chief Justice Warren, however, were prepared to hold that individuals have no First Amendment right to racially discriminate in their accommodations open to the public. They were unable to forge a majority, though, because Justices Clark and Stewart were unwilling to go that far and joined Brennan instead. Notably, Goldberg's concurring opinion distinguished between restaurants open to the public and private places, such as individuals' homes and private clubs. In the latter, he did not doubt that individuals could associate and discriminate racially, as he explained, because the First Amendment guarantees the "right of every person to close his home or club to any person or to choose his social intimates and business partners solely on the basis of personal prejudice including race." Dissenting Justices Black, Harlan, and White agreed that individuals could associate and racially discriminate in their private affairs, but they did not think that either the Fourteenth Amendment's equal protection clause forbade private discrimination in public accommodations or that the First Amendment protected the protesters of segregated lunch counters. In Black's words:

The right to freedom of expression is a right to express views—not a right to force other people to supply a platform or a pulpit. It is argued that this supposed constitutional right to invade other people's property would not mean that a man's home, his private club, or his church could be forcibly entered or used against his will—only his store or place of business which he has himself "opened to the public" by selling goods or services for money. . . . But the whole quarrel . . . [here is] that instead of being open to all, the restaurant refused service to Negroes.

Times change and the Warren Court was at a great turning point in the history of constitutional politics. In 1964, Congress passed the Civil Rights Act, or Public Accommodations Act, banning racial discrimination or segregation in public accommodations. The Court upheld that legislation in *Heart of Atlanta Motel v. United States*, 379 U.S. 241 (1964) (see Vol. 1, Ch. 6), and avoided becoming further entangled with the remaining issues of discrimination in private clubs and associations. Exempted from the Civil Rights Act are boarding houses renting less than five rooms, private clubs and other enterprises not open to the general public.

As times change, so does the Court. With states and localities pushing to eliminate discrimination based on race and gender in the 1970s and 1980s, the Burger and Rehnquist Courts finally confronted the issue of whether freedom of association extended to private clubs discriminating racially or against women. In *Roberts v. United States Jaycees* (1984) (see page 631), the First Amendment freedom of association argument of the Jaycees was rejected by the Court in upholding a Minnesota human rights law, compelling the Jaycees to accept women as regular members. On the basis of the analysis in *United States Jaycees*, the Rehnquist Court subsequently upheld state laws barring all-male clubs from discriminating against women, in *Board of Directors of Rotary International v. Rotary Club of Duarte*, 481 U.S. 537 (1987), and *New York State Club Association, Inc. v. City of New York*, 487 U.S. 1 (1988). In *City of Dallas v. Stanglin*, 490 U.S. 1591 (1989), Chief Justice Rehnquist further ruled that an ordinance limiting certain dance halls to only fourteen through eighteen year olds did not deny adults' freedom of association under the First Amendment.

NOTES

1. Alexis de Tocqueville, *Democracy in America*, Vol. 2, ed. Phillips Bradley (New York: Vintage Books, 1954), 196.

2. In *Camp v. Board of Public Education*, 368 U.S. 278 (1961), the Court also upheld a state regulation requiring an affidavit for public employees that they are not members of a subversive organization.

3. *Aptheker v. United States*, 378 U.S. 500 (1964).

4. *Connick v. Myers*, 461 U.S. 138 (1983).

5. See *NAACP v. Button*, 371 U.S. 415 (1963).

6. In *International Association of Machinists v. Street*, 367 U.S. 740 (1961), the Court upheld closed union shops. See also *Brotherhood of Railway Trainmen v. Virginia State Bar*, 377 U.S. 1 (1964). In *Jones v. North Carolina Prisoners' Labor Union, Inc.*, 433 U.S. 119 (1977), however, the Court upheld restrictions on a prison inmates' "labor union" mailings for membership and solicitations. In *Minnesota State Board for Community Colleges v. Knight*, 465 U.S. 271 (1984), the Court held that a state's requiring public employees to engage in official exchanges of views only through their professional representatives did not violate the First Amendment.

7. In *Cousins v. Wigoda*, 419 U.S. 477 (1975), the Court upheld the national political party's power to specify how delegates from state political party will be selected. In *Democratic Party of the United States v. Wisconsin*, 442 U.S. 107 (1981), Wisconsin's rule on binding primaries

was found to violate the First Amendment. In *Brown v. Socialist Workers 74 Campaign Committee*, 459 U.S. 87 (1982), the Court held that disclosure of membership lists of the Socialist Workers party violated the First Amendment. However, the Court upheld the disclosure provisions of the Federal Election Campaign Act in *Buckley v. Valeo*, 424 U.S. 1 (1976), which is reprinted in part in Volume 1, Chapter 8.

8. See *Griswold v. Connecticut*, 381 U.S. 479 (1965) (see Chapters 2 and 11).

SELECTED BIBLIOGRAPHY

Abernathy, Glen. *The Right of Assembly and Association*, 2nd ed. Columbia: University of South Carolina, 1981.
Fellman, David. *The Constitutional Right of Association* Chicago: University of Chicago Press, 1963.
Kalven, Harry, Jr. *The Negro & The First Amendment*. Chicago: University of Chicago Press, 1965.
Levinson, Sanford. *Constitutional Faith*, Princeton, NJ: Princeton University Press, 1988, Chapt. 3.

National Association for the Advancement of Colored People v. Alabama
357 U.S. 449, 78 S.Ct. 1163 (1958)

The National Association for the Advancement of Colored People (NAACP) encountered bitter opposition in the South for bringing litigation challenging racial discrimination. Hostility mounted following its victory in the landmark school desegregation ruling in *Brown v. Board of Education*, 347 U.S. 483 (1954) (see Chapter 12). As the NAACP sought to force compliance with *Brown*, southern hostility led to efforts by the states to prevent the NAACP from bringing more litigation. In 1956, Alabama's state attorney general sought to enjoin the NAACP from conducting business in the state under a law requiring out-of-state corporations to register and satisfy certain reporting requirements before doing business in the state. The NAACP was incorporated in New York and considered itself exempt from Alabama's law requiring, among other things, filing with the state certain records and membership lists, including the names and addresses of all members residing in the state. While filing the registration forms, the NAACP refused to give up its membership lists. For that it was found in contempt and fined $100,000.

The state supreme court declined to review an appeal and the NAACP appealed to the Supreme Court.

Justice HARLAN delivers the opinion of the Court.

We review from the standpoint of its validity under the Federal Constitution a judgment of civil contempt entered against petitioner, the National Association for the Advancement of Colored People, in the courts of Alabama. The question presented is whether Alabama, consistently with the Due Process Clause of the Fourteenth Amendment, can compel petitioner to reveal to the State's Attorney General the names and addresses of all its Alabama members and agents, without regard to their positions or functions in the Association. The judgment of contempt was based upon petitioner's refusal to comply fully with a court order requiring in part the production of membership lists. . . .

Alabama has a statute similar to those of many other States which requires a foreign corporation, except as exempted, to qualify before doing business by filing its corporate charter with the Secretary of State and designating a place of business and an agent to receive service of process. . . . [The NAACP] has never complied with the qualification statute, from which it considered itself exempt.

In 1956 the Attorney General of Alabama brought an equity suit in the State Circuit Court, Montgomery County, to enjoin the Association from conducting further activities within, and to oust it from, the State. . . .

[T]he State moved for the production of a large number of the Association's records and papers, including bank statements, leases, deeds, and records containing the names and addresses of all Alabama "members" and "agents" of the Association. It alleged that all such documents were necessary for adequate preparation for the hearing, in view of petitioner's denial of the conduct of intrastate business within the meaning of the qualification statute. Over petitioner's objections, the court ordered the production of a substantial part of the requested records, including the membership lists. . . .

Thereafter petitioner . . . produced substantially all the data called for by the production order except its membership lists, as to which it contended that Alabama could not constitutionally compel disclosure, and moved to modify or vacate the contempt judgment, or stay its execution pending appellate review. This motion was denied. While a similar stay application, which was later denied, was pending before the Supreme Court of Alabama, the Circuit Court made a further order adjudging petitioner in continuing contempt and increasing the fine already imposed to $100,000. . . .

It is beyond debate that freedom to engage in association for the advancement of beliefs and ideas is an inseparable aspect of the "liberty" assured by the Due Process Clause of the Fourteenth Amendment, which embraces freedom of speech. . . .

The fact that Alabama, so far as is relevant to the validity of the contempt judgment presently under review, has taken no direct action, to restrict the right of petitioner's members to associate freely, does not end inquiry into the effect of the production order. In the domain of these indispensable liberties; whether of speech, press, or association, the decisions of this Court recognize that abridgement of such rights, even though unintended, may inevitably follow from varied forms of governmental action. . . .

It is hardly a novel perception that compelled disclosure of affiliation with groups engaged in advocacy may constitute as effective a restraint on freedom of association as the forms of governmental action in the cases above were thought likely to produce upon the particular constitutional rights there involved. This Court has recognized the vital relationship between freedom to associate and privacy in one's associations. . . . Inviolability of privacy in group association may in many circumstances be indispensable to preservation of freedom of association, particularly where a group espouses dissident beliefs.

We think that the production order, in the respects here drawn in question, must be regarded as entailing the likelihood of a substantial restraint upon the exercise by petitioner's members of their right to freedom of association. Petitioner has made an uncontroverted showing that on past occasions revelation of the identity of its rank-and-file members has exposed these members to economic reprisal, loss of employment, threat of physical coercion, and other manifestations of public hostility. Under these circumstances, we think it apparent that compelled disclosure of petitioner's Alabama membership is likely to affect adversely the ability of petitioner and its members to pursue their collective effort to foster beliefs which they admittedly have the right to advocate, in that it may induce members to withdraw from the Association and dissuade others from joining it because of fear of exposure of their beliefs shown through their associations and of the consequences of this exposure.

It is not sufficient to answer, as the State does here, that whatever repressive effect compulsory disclosure of names of petitioner's members may have upon participation by Alabama citizens in petitioner's activities follows not from *state* action but from *private* community pressures. The crucial factor is the interplay of governmental and private action, for it is only after the initial exertion of state power represented by the production order that private action takes hold.

We turn to the final question whether Alabama has demonstrated an interest in obtaining the disclosures it seeks from petitioner which is sufficient to justify the deterrent effect which we have concluded these disclosures may well have on the free exercise by petitioner's members of their constitutionally protected right of association. Such a ". . . subordinating interest of the State must be compelling," *Sweezy v. New Hampshire*, 354 U.S. 234 [1957] (concurring opinion). . . .

Whether there was "justification" in this instance turns solely on the substantiality of Alabama's interest in obtaining the membership lists. . . . The exclusive purpose was to determine whether petitioner was conducting intrastate business in violation of the Alabama foreign corporation registration statute, and the membership lists were expected to help resolve this question. . . . Without intimating the slightest view upon the merits of these issues, we are unable to perceive that the disclosure of the names of petitioner's rank-and-file members has a substantial bearing. As matters stand in the state court, petitioner (1) has admitted its presence and conduct of activities in Alabama since 1918; (2) has offered to comply in all respects with the state qualification statute, although preserving its contention that the statute does not apply to it; and (3) has apparently complied satisfactorily with the production order, except for the membership lists, by furnishing the Attorney General with varied business records, its charter and statement of purposes, the names of all of its directors and officers, and with the total number of its Alabama members and the amount of their dues. . . .

We hold that the immunity from state scrutiny of membership lists which the Association claims on behalf of its members is here so related to the right of the members to pursue their lawful private interests privately and to associate freely with others in so doing as to come within the protection of the Fourteenth Amendment. And we conclude that Alabama has fallen short of showing a controlling justification for the deterrent effect on the free enjoyment of the right to associate which disclosure of membership lists is likely to have. Accordingly, the judgment of civil contempt and the $100,000 fine which resulted from petitioner's refusal to comply with the production order in this respect must fall.

Roberts v. United States Jaycees
468 U.S. 609, 104 S.Ct. 3244 (1984)

The United States Jaycees is a nonprofit organization devoted to promoting the growth and development of young men's civic organizations. According to its bylaws, regular membership was limited to men between the ages of eighteen and thirty-five, while women and older men could be associate members. The latter could not vote or hold local or national office, however. Two local chapters in Minnesota had been violating the bylaws for several years by admitting women as regular members. After imposing a number of sanctions, including denying their members eligibility for state and national offices, the United States Jaycees revoked charters of these two chapters. That prompted members of the two chapters to file a discrimination claim with the Minnesota Department of Human Rights, alleging that the exclusion of women from full membership violated the Minnesota Human Rights Act, which makes it "an unfair discriminatory practice . . . [t]o deny any person the full and equal enjoyment of the goods, services, facilities, privileges, advantages, and accommodations of a place of public accommodation because of race, color, creed, religion, disability, national origin or sex." Before a hearing took place, however, the Jaycees brought a lawsuit against Kathryn Roberts, the acting commissioner of the state's Department of Human Rights, to prevent enforcement of the law. The Jaycees claimed that requiring it to accept women as regular members would violate its male members' First Amendment rights of free speech and association. A federal district court ruled against the Jaycees, but the Court of Appeals for the Eighth Circuit found the application of the state's law to the Jaycees would produce a "direct and substantial" interference with its members' First Amendment freedoms. Roberts and the state of Minnesota appealed that decision to the Supreme Court.

Justice BRENNAN delivers the opinion of the Court.

This case requires us to address a conflict between a State's efforts to eliminate gender-based discrimination against its citizens and the constitutional freedom of association asserted by members of a private organization. . . .

The Court has long recognized that, because the Bill of Rights is designed to secure individual liberty, it must afford the formation and preservation of certain kinds of highly personal relationships a substantial measure of sanctuary from unjustified interference by the State. Without precisely identifying every consideration that may underlie this type of constitutional protection, we have noted that certain kinds of personal bonds have played a crticial role in the culture and traditions of the Nation by cultivating and transmitting shared ideals and beliefs; they thereby foster diversity and act as critical buffers between the individual and the power of the State. Moreover, the constitutional shelter afforded such relationships reflects the realization that individuals draw much of their emotional enrichment from close ties with others. . . .

The personal affiliations that exemplify these considerations, and that therefore suggest some relevant limitations on the relationships that might be entitled to this sort of constitutional protection, are those that attend the creation and sustenance of a family—marriage, childbirth, the raising and education of children, and cohabitation with one's relatives. . . . Conversely, an association lacking these qualities—such as a large business enterprise—seems remote from the concerns giving rise to this constitutional protection. Accordingly, the Constitution undoubtedly imposes constraints on the State's power to control the selection of one's spouse that would not apply to regulations affecting the choice of one's fellow employees. . . .

Between these poles, of course, lies a broad range of human relationships that may make greater or lesser claims to constitutional protection from particular incursions by the State. Determining the limits of state authority over an individual's freedom to enter into a particular association therefore unavoidably entails a careful assessment of where that relationship's objective characteristics locate it on a spectrum from the most intimate to the most attenuated of personal attachments. We need not mark the potentially significant points on this terrain with any precision. We note only that factors that may be relevant include size, purpose, policies, selectivity, congeniality, and other characteristics that in a particular case may be pertinent. In this case, however, several features of the Jaycees clearly place the organization outside of the category of relationships worthy of this kind of constitutional protection. . . .

The undisputed facts reveal that the local chapters of the Jaycees are large and basically unselective groups. At the time of the state administrative hearing, the Minneapolis chapter had approximately 430 members, while the St. Paul chapter had about 400. . . .

In short, the local chapters of the Jaycees are neither small nor selective. Moreover, much of the activity central to the formation and maintenance of the association involves the participation of strangers to that relationship. Accordingly, we conclude that the Jaycees chapters lack the distinctive characteristics that might afford constitutional protection to the decision of its members to exclude women. . . .

[W]e have long understood as implicit in the right to engage in activities protected by the First Amendment a corresponding right to associate with others in pursuit of a wide variety of political, social, economic, educational, religious, and cultural ends. . . .

The right to associate for expressive purposes is not, however, absolute. Infringements on that right may be justified by regulations adopted to serve compelling state interests, unrelated to the suppression of ideas, that cannot be achieved through means significantly less restrictive of associational freedoms. . . . We are persuaded that Minnesota's compelling interest in eradicating discrimination against its female citizens justifies the impact that application of the statute to the Jaycees may have on the male members' associational freedoms.

On its face, the Minnesota Act does not aim at the suppression of speech, does not distinguish between prohibited and permitted activity on the basis of viewpoint, and does not license enforcement authorities to administer the statute on the basis of such constitutionally impermissible criteria. Nor does the Jaycees contend that the Act has been applied in this case for the purpose of hampering the organization's ability to express its views. Instead, as the Minnesota Supreme Court explained, the Act reflects the State's strong historical commitment to eliminating discrimination and assuring its citizens equal access to publicly available goods and services. That goal, which is unrelated to the suppression of expression, plainly serves compelling state interests of the highest order. . . .

In applying the Act to the Jaycees, the State has advanced those interests through the least restrictive means of achieving its ends. Indeed, the Jaycees has failed to demonstrate that the Act imposes any serious burdens on the male members' freedom of expressive association. . . .

There is . . . no basis in the record for concluding that admission of women as full voting members will impede the organization's ability to engage in these protected activities or to disseminate its preferred views. The Act requires no change in the Jaycees' creed of promoting the interests of young men, and it imposes no restrictions on the organization's ability to exclude individuals with ideologies or philosophies different from those of its existing members. . . . Moreover, the Jaycees already invites women to share the group's views and philosophy and to participate in much of its training and community activities. Accordingly, any claim that admission of women as full voting members will impair a symbolic message conveyed by the very fact that women are not permitted to vote is attenuated at best. . . .

In the absence of a showing far more substantial than that attempted by the Jaycees, we decline to indulge in the sexual stereotyping that underlies appellee's contention that, by allowing women to vote, application of the Minnesota Act will change the content or impact of the organization's speech. . . .

The judgment of the Court of Appeals is Reversed.

Justice REHNQUIST concurred.

The CHIEF JUSTICE and Justice BLACKMUN did not participate in the decision of this case.

Justice O'CONNOR concurred in a separate opinion.

6

FREEDOM FROM AND OF RELIGION

RELIGIOUS FREEDOM IS guaranteed in the two opening clauses of the First Amendment: "Congress shall make no law respecting an establishment of religion, or prohibiting the free exercise thereof." Together, the clauses guarantee freedom from and of religion by pointing in opposite directions. The establishment clause points toward a principle of the separation of government from religion, neither should involve itself with the other. The free exercise clause suggests a principle of voluntarism—freedom from coercion in choosing a religion or no religion.

Religious freedom has never been absolute, however. The First Amendment, as the Court observed in *Cantwell v. Connecticut*, 310 U.S. 296 (1940), "embraces two concepts—freedom to believe and freedom to act. The first is absolute but, in the nature of things, the second cannot be. Conduct remains subject to regulation of society." Drawing on the distinction between belief and action, the Court thus wrote into constitutional law a third principle of religious freedom that runs back to Thomas Jefferson, who in his *Bill for Establishing Religious Freedom* for the state of Virginia in 1779, observed that "the acts of the body," unlike "the operations of the mind, are subject to the coercion of the laws."[1]

Nor does the text and historical record of the First Amendment provide simple interpretative solutions for the continuing controversies in constitutional politics over religious freedom. What is "an establishment of religion," for example, and what is a "law respecting" the establishment of religion? What is and who defines *religion*? Many of the contemporary disputes over the separation of government and religion, moreover, could not have been foreseen during the founding period; there was no controversy over school prayer because there was no system of public education.

The traditions and aspirations of religious freedom from the colonial through the revolutionary period and to the time the First Amendment was adopted and ratified in 1791 were complex and occasionally conflicting. Although populated by many escaping religious persecution in England or on the European Continent, colonial settlements remained religious enclaves, discriminating against those of other faiths. In Massachusetts, the established Congregational Church taxed and harassed Quakers, Baptists, and others. In Virginia and four other southern colonies, the (Anglican) Church of England was established.

As the colonies developed and their leaders moved toward the Declaration of Independence, religious freedom grew and began to take on new meaning. With that conceptual change came a rejection of the European understanding of established church-states. England, Scotland, and Germany had established churches, while the Roman Catholic Church was established in Italy, Spain, and elsewhere. But in 1774 when the British Parliament passed a statute establishing both Anglicanism and Catholicism in Canada, the Continential Congress protested with "astonishment, that a British Parliament should ever consent to establish in that country a religion that has deluged [England] in blood, and dispersed bigotry, persecution, murder and rebellion through every part of the world."[2]

By the 1770s, the original thirteen colonies, always predominantly Protestant, were on their way to a new form of establishmentism, unlike the European single state-church denomination. Christianity or Protestantism, in contrast with Judaism, Islam, and Hinduism (as well as, for some colonists, Catholicism), was established in the northern colonies, but allowed for multiple churches and denominations. Maryland's "declaration of rights" in 1776, for instance, recognized the religious freedom of "persons professing the Christian religion." In 1778, South Carolina's constitution proclaimed that "the Christian Protestant religion shall be deemed . . . the established religion of this state." Notably, four colonies (Rhode Island, Pennsylvania, Delaware, and New Jersey) never established a state religion.[3]

Religious freedom found expression in Article VI of the Constitution, providing that "no religious Test shall ever be required as a Qualification to any Office or public Trust under the United

States." But that was not enough to silence critics pressing for the addition of a bill of rights. When defending the Constitution during Virginia's ratifying convention on June 12, 1788, Madison sought to reassure those fearing government would deny religious freedom:

If there were a majority of one sect, a bill of rights would be a poor protection for liberty. Happily for the states, they enjoy the utmost freedom of religion. This freedom arises from that multiplicity of sects, which pervades America, and which is the best and only security for religious liberty in any society. For where there is such a variety of sects, there cannot be a majority of any one sect to oppress and persecute the rest. . . . A particular state might concur in one religious project. But the United States abound in such a variety of sects, that it is a strong security against religious persecution, and it is sufficient to authorize a conclusion, that no one sect will ever be able to outnumber or depress the rest.[4]

Madison failed to dissuade those seeking further protection for religious freedom. While ratifying the Constitution, the Virginia convention proposed the addition of a bill of rights, including the following:

That religion or the duty which we owe to our Creator, and the manner of discharging it can be directed only by reason and conviction, not by force or violence, and therefore all men have an equal, natural and unalienable right to the free exercise of religion according to the dictates of conscience, and that no particular religious sect or society ought to be favored or established by Law in preference to others.[5]

Defenders of religious freedom, however, were not of one mind. Some maintained that disestablishment of church and state was necessary to safeguard religion from the corrosive influence of politics. When celebrating the purity of evangelical faith in 1644, Roger Williams proclaimed that God commanded that "the most Paganish, Jewish, Turkish, or Antichristian consciences and worships, be granted to all men in all Nations and Countries." And he invoked the metaphor of a "wall of separation" in defense of the integrity of religion.

First, the faithful labors of many witnesses of Jesus Christ, extant to the world, abundantly proving that the church of the Jews under the Old Testament in the antitype were both separate from the world; and that when they have opened a gap in the hedge or *wall of separation* between the garden of the church and the wilderness of the world, God hath ever broke down the wall itself, removed the candlestick, and made His garden a wilderness, as at this day. And that therefore if He will ever please to restore His garden and paradise again, it must of necessity be walled in peculiarly unto Himself from the world; and that all that shall be saved out of the world are to be transplanted out of the wilderness of the world, and added unto His church or garden.[6]

More than 150 years later, President Jefferson again relied on the metaphor of a wall of separation in his famous letter to the Danbury Baptist Association in 1802:

Believing with you that religion is a matter which lies solely between man and his God, that he owes account to none other for his faith or his worship, that the legislative powers of government reach actions only, and not opinions, I contemplate with sovereign reverence that act of the whole American people which declared that their legislature should "make no law respecting an establishment of religion, or prohibiting the free exercise thereof," thus building a wall of separation between Church and State.[7]

Unlike those who shared Roger Williams's view, Jefferson was more concerned about insulating government from the influences of religion and religious fervor. In his home state of Virginia, Jefferson had fought for religious freedom—freedom not just for Protestants or Christians. As he reflected about the opposition in 1779 to his "Bill for Establishing Religious Freedom":

Where the preamble declares, that coercion is a departure from the plan of the holy author of our religion, an amendment was proposed, by inserting the word "Jesus Christ," that it should read, "a departure from the plan of Jesus Christ, the holy author of our religion;" the insertion was rejected by a great majority, in proof that they meant to comprehend, within the mantle of its protection, the Jew and the Gentile, the Christian and Mohometan, the Hindoo, and Infidel of every denomination.[8]

James Madison agreed that a wall of separation would help preserve the integrity of government, but he also thought that it might benefit religion as well. Madison, along with Jefferson opposed proposals to establish religious taxes in Virginia. In his famous "Memorial and Remonstrance against Religious Assessments" in 1785, he persuasively argued against government support of religion. Governmental assistance to religious establishments, Madison maintained, tended to divide society into factions and produce "pride and indolence in the clergy; ignorance and servility in the laity; in both, superstition, bigotry and persecution." Nor did Madison think government depended on the support of religion. "That is not a just government," he wrote in 1792, in which "a man's religious rights are violated by penalties, or fettered by tests, or taxes by a hierarchy."[9]

But Madison proved unsuccessful in persuading the First Congress that the states as well as the federal government should be barred from passing laws respecting the establishment of religion and religious freedom. On June 8, 1789, in the House of Representatives, Madison introduced a series of proposed amendments to the Constitution, among them: "The civil rights of none shall be abridged on account of religious belief or worship, nor shall any national religion be established, nor shall the full and equal rights of conscience be in any manner, or on any pretext, infringed." And another: "No State shall violate the equal rights of conscience, or the freedom of the press, or the trial by jury in criminal cases."[10]

Without debate, Madison's proposals were referred to a special committee, of which he was a member. Within a week, the committee reported back to the full House. Madison's proposals remained intact, except for some editing: the words "civil rights" and "national" were deleted. The House devoted a single day to considering the amendment. As a result of a motion by Fisher Ames, and further stylistic changes, the revised amendment read: "Congress shall make no law establishing religion, or prohibiting the free exercise thereof, nor shall the rights of conscience be infringed."

The House's proposed amendments were debated in secret by the Senate in September. The *Senate Journal,* however, records three unsuccessful motions to change the amendment on September 3. All would have narrowed the amendment to ban establishments preferring "one religious sect or society," or "any particular denomination of religion in preference to another." But six weeks later, the Senate voted to amend the House's version to read: "Congress shall make no law establishing articles of faith or a mode of worship, or prohibiting the free exercise of religion." This change narrowed the religion clauses to barring Congress only from endorsing a single denomination or national religion. Under it, Congress could provide nondiscriminatory government aid to all religions (something Baptists bitterly opposed).

The Senate's changes provoked opposition in the House. A joint conference committee, chaired by Madison, was created to resolve the differences between the House and Senate versions of the proposed amendments. Finally, on September 24, the House agreed to accept the Senate's version of other amendments on the condition that the amendment on religion be changed to its present form: "Congress shall make no laws respecting an establishment of religion, or prohibiting the free exercise thereof." The Senate agreed; Congress adopted the religion clauses.

Madison's efforts to guarantee "the full and equal rights of conscience" and to forbid the states from violating "the equal rights of conscience" nevertheless failed. States continued vestiges of establishment and restrictions on religious freedom. Massachusetts, for one, denied Jews the right to hold public office until 1828 and did not remove its final vestiges of establishment until 1833.

Not until *Cantwell v. Connecticut*, 310 U.S. 296 (1940), did the Hughes Court hold the free exercise clause applicable to the states. In Justice Roberts's words, "The Fourteenth Amendment has rendered the legislatures of the states as incompetent as Congress to enact" laws denying the free exercise of religion. Seven years later, the Vinson Court made the establishment clause applicable to the states in *Everson v. Board of Education of Ewing Township* (1947) (see page 655), in which Justice Black, for a bare majority, wrote the high-wall theory of the separation of government from religion into constitutional law, but upheld the reimbursement of the costs of transporting children to private religious schools.

Since *Cantwell* and *Everson*, controversy has infused and surrounded the Court's interpretation of the religion clauses. But before turning to the Court's rulings and rival interpretations of the religion clauses, it may be helpful to consider two widely different approaches to religious freedom that have animated constitutional politics: nonpreferentialism and the high-wall theory of the separation of government and religion.

President Ronald Reagan's attorney general, Edwin Meese III, took the nonpreferentialism position in 1985 when he advocated

the First Amendment forbade the establishment of a particular religion or a particular church. It also precluded the federal government from favoring one church, or one church group over another. That's what the First Amendment did, but it did not go further. It did not, for example, preclude federal aid to religious groups so long as that assistance furthered a public purpose and so long as it did not discriminate in favor of one religious group against another.[11]

Chief Justices Burger and Rehnquist, along with other justices, championed this view, as well as political scientist Walter Berns. "There was no dispute with respect to the principles on which the Constitution was built," Berns claims, when observing that "stated in its most radical form, [the Framers] all agreed that our institutions do *not* presuppose a providential Supreme Being." But, he adds, "whereas our institutions do not presuppose a Supreme Being, their preservation does." And on that basis Berns reasons that "[l]iberal democracy must preserve what it cannot itself generate, and it must do this without jeopardizing the private character of religion." Thus *Everson*, from Berns's perspective, wrongly launched "an interpretation under which the First Amendment forbids precisely what many a man in the First Congress went to such pains to protect—namely, public support of religion, albeit on a nondiscriminatory basis." While criticizing the Court for too broadly interpreting the establishment clause, he criticizes the Court for narrowly interpretating the free exercise clause so as to allow individuals to define *religion* for themselves and obtain exemptions from certain laws and government regulations. As Berns puts it:

A private person may think He has (and the Constitution protects his right to think He has), but he may not act on the basis of this opinion, not when the law commands otherwise. His belief, however, profound, has in the eyes of the Constitution the status of a mere opinion. His belief that God forbids him to kill another human being occupies the same status as another person's belief that he must worship a golden calf, or still another's belief that she must immolate herself on her dead husband's funeral pyre. Constitutionally, these are mere opinions, and the law may require the one to bear arms and forbid the second to hoard gold and the third to commit suttee.. . . . The First Amendment requires Congress to tolerate religious opinions—all of them—but it is a matter for Congress to decide whether various acts ("acts of the body") shall be permitted.[12]

By contrast, Justice Black's opinion in *Everson* resurrected Madison and Jefferson's high-wall theory of separation of government and religion. Historian Leonard Levy supports this interpretation when attacking the nonpreferentialist's approach to the religion clauses:

The fundamental defect of the nonpreferential interpretation is that it results in the unhistorical contention that the First Amendment augmented a nonexistent congressional power to legislate in the field of religion [since Article I does not give Congress any legislative powers over religion].. . . . Preferring 'religion over irreligion' is a red herring; the question of such a preference was not an issue. The government possessed no power to aid irreligion or religion.. . . .

Nonpreferentialism, unfortunately, is but a pose for those who think that religion needs to be patronized and promoted by government. When they speak of nonpreferential aid, they speak euphemistically as if they are not partisan. In fact they really are preferentialists.. . . . Nonpreferentialists prefer government sponsorship and subsidy of religion rather than allow it to compete on its merits against irreligion and indifference. They prefer government nurture of religion because they mistakenly dread government neutrality as too risky, and so they condemn it as hostility. They prefer what they call, again euphemistically, accommodation.[13]

Conflicts in constitutional politics over religious freedom, however, involve not only deciding between and applying the nonprefentialist or accommodationist approach versus the high-wall theory of separation of government and religion. In the contemporary administrative state, laws and exemptions from laws may be challenged for violating either the establishment clause or the free exercise clause. There is an essential tension between these two guarantees. Exemption from the draft for conscientious (religious) objection to killing and war, for instance, may be defended by claiming the free exercise clause, but attacked under the establishment clause for aiding religion. Scholarships, grants, tax credits, or reimbursements have, likewise, been viewed as infringing on, alternatively, one or the other religion clauses. In *Witters v. Washington Department of Services for the Blind*, 474 U.S. 481 (1986), for example, the Court confronted a controversy over the denial of aid for vocational rehabilitation, available under state law, to Larry Witters by the Washington State Commission for the Blind. Witters's application for financial aid was denied because he wanted to pursue a Bible studies degree at a private Christian college. The Commission's denial of financial aid might have been viewed as infringing on Witter's free exercise of religion, but the Washington State Supreme Court ruled that giving assistance to Witters would have the primary effect of advancing religion and so violated the establishment clause. On appeal, the Supreme Court reversed that decision and held that such assistance does not violate the establishment clause. It is such disputes over the boundaries between government and religion in constitutional politics that this chapter examines.

NOTES

1. Thomas Jefferson, in *The Writings of Thomas Jefferson*, Vol. 2, ed. Paul Ford (New York: Putnam's Sons, 1892–1899), 237–239.

2. "Continental Congress to the People of Great Britain, October 21, 1774," in *The Founders' Constitution*, Vol. 5, ed. Philip Kurland and Ralph Lerner (Chicago: University of Chicago Press, 1987), 61.

3. See Leonard Levy, *The Establishment Clause: Religion and the First Amendment* (New York: Macmillian, 1986), 61.

4. James Madison, in *The Founders' Constitution*, Vol. 5, ed. Kurland and Lerner, 88.

5. "Virginia Ratifying Convention," in *The Founders' Constitution*, Vol. 5, ed. Kurland and Lerner, 89.

6. Quoted in Leonard Levy, *The Establishment Clause* (New York: Oxford), 184.

7. Thomas Jefferson, "Letter to Danbury Baptist Association, January 1, 1802," in *The Founders' Constitution*, Vol. 5, ed. Kurland and Lerner, 96.

8. Thomas Jefferson, in *The Founders' Constitution*, Vol. 5, ed. Kurland and Lerner, 85.

9. James Madison, *The Papers of James Madison*, Vol. 14, ed. Robert Rutland (Chicago: University of Chicago Press, 1983), 266–267.

10. Joseph Gales and W. W. Seaton, *The Debates and Proceedings in the Congress of the United States* Vol. 1 (Washington, DC: Gales and Seaton, 1834–1856), 451–452.

11. Edwin Meese III, "Address before the Christian Legal Society," given in San Diego, CA, Sept. 29, 1985.

12. Walter Berns, *The First Amendment and the Future of American Democracy* (New York: Basic Books, 1976), 10, 12, 34, 60, and 48–49. For similar positions, see Edward S. Corwin, "The Supreme Court as a National School Board," 14 *Law and Contemporary Problems* 3 (1949); and Michael Malbin, *Religion and Politics: The Intentions of the Authors of the First Amendment* (Washington, DC: American Enterprise Institute, 1978).

13. Levy, *The Establishment Clause*, 93–94 and 118. See also Jesse Choper, "The Establishment Clause and Aid to Parochial Schools," 56 *California Law Review* 260 (1968); and J. Choper, "Religion in the Public Schools: A Proposed Constitutional Standard," 47 *University of Minnesota Law Review* 329 (1963).

SELECTED BIBLIOGRAPHY

Berns, Walter. *The First Amendment and the Future of American Democracy.* New York: Basic Books, 1976, Chapt. 2.

Howe, Mark DeWolfe. *The Garden and the Wilderness: Religion and Government in American Constitutional History.* Chicago: University of Chicago Press, 1965.

Tussman, Joseph. *The Supreme Court on Church and State.* New York: Oxford University Press, 1962.

Sorauf, Frank. *The Wall of Separation: The Constitutional Politics of Church and State.* Princeton, NJ: Princeton University Press, 1976.

Pfeffer, Leo. *Church, State and Freedom.* Boston: Beacon Press, 1967.

Stokes, Anson, and Pfeffer, Leo. *Church and State in the United States.* New York: Harper & Row, 1965.

A. THE (DIS)ESTABLISHMENT OF RELIGION

In the constitutional politics of interpreting and applying the establishment clause, the Court has been divided over three rival interpretative principles and tests for the separation of government from religion: (1) "strict separation" requires state neutrality and a secular purpose for legislation, but may permit some benefits or indirect support for religion; (2) "strict neutrality" requires not merely a secular purpose for legislation but bars all laws that either aid or hinder religion; and, alternatively, (3) an "accommodationist" approach, while maintaining that laws must have a secular purpose, allows for governmental accommodation of religion in ways that further religious freedom without endorsing a particular religion.

Strict separation of government and religion holds "that government can do nothing which involves governmental support of religion or which is favorable to the cultivation of religious interests."[1] In *Everson v. Board of Education of Ewing Township* (1947) (see page 655), the Vinson Court embraced this theory and wrote Jefferson's metaphor of a wall of separation into constitutional law. However, the justices split five to four because the majority decided to construe New Jersey's program of reimbursing parents for the cost of busing children to private schools, including parochial schools, as a "subsidy to parents not churches." Justice Black's opinion for the majority suggested that strict separation need not preclude a state's "benevolent neutrality" toward religion.[2] So too, in *Corporation of Presiding Bishops v. Amos*, 483 U.S. 327 (1987), the Rehnquist Court ruled that the establishment clause was not violated by allowing nonprofit (Morman) industries from hiring only religiously faithful employees.

The four dissenters in *Everson* agreed that the establishment clause embodies a high-wall principle of separation, but viewed the majority's holding as a breach of the wall. In their view, strict neutrality was required; that is, religion "may not be used as a basis for classification for purposes of governmental action, whether that action be the conferring of rights or privileges or the imposition of duties or obligations."[3]

A year after *Everson*, the Court struck down a "released-time program," allowing public-school children to attend religious instruction on campus grounds, in *McCollum v. Board of Education*, 333 U.S. 203 (1948). The religious instructors were not paid by the city, but the use of the classrooms in public schools was held to violate the establishment clause. In a second case, involving students going off campus for religious instruction, however, the Court upheld the released-time program on the grounds that the religious instruction did not occur on school property, and did not involve the expenditure of public funds and there was no evidence that the students were being compelled to attend the off-campus classes on religion. In *Zorach v. Clauson*, 343 U.S. 306 (1952), dissenting Justices Black, Jackson, and Frankfurter contended that even this released-time program breached the high wall of separation between government and religion.

The Vinson Court thus agreed that the establishment clause requires state neutrality and that governmental programs must have a secular purpose, but disagreed over whether religion might indirectly benefit or receive assistance from government.

As the Court's composition changed, the Warren Court moved constitutional law in the direction of a high wall of separation, and then the Burger and Rehnquist Courts swung back toward allowing governmental accommodation of religion. Since *Everson*, though, the justices have remained split on the tests for determining whether public-school facilities may be used for religious purposes and in what other ways government may accommodate religion. In *School District of Grand Rapids v. Ball*, 473 U.S. 373 (1985), for example, a bare majority (with Chief Justice Burger and Justices O'Connor, Rehnquist, and White dissenting) held that shared time and community education programs, providing religious classes to nonpublic-school students, had "the primary or principal effect of advancing religion."[4] However, in *Widmar v. Vincent*, 454 U.S. 263 (1981), the Court struck down a Missouri statute prohibiting the use of university buildings and grounds "for purposes of religious worship," which had been used to deny a student religious group access to the facilities of a state university. There, with only Justice White dissenting, the Court distinguished earlier holdings and observed that "University students are . . . less impressionable than younger students and should be able to appreciate that the university's policy is one of neutrality towards religion." The Court's holding in *Widmar* that an equal access policy at the level of universities did not violate the establishment clause encouraged members of Congress to extend that principle to primary and secondary schools. Congress did so with the passage of the Equal Access Act of 1984, which bars public schools from discriminating against meetings on school grounds of student activity groups on the basis of "religious, political, philosophical or other content of the speech at such meetings." When the constitutionality of that legislation was challenged in *Board of Education of the Westside Community Schools v. Mergens*, 110 S.Ct. 2356 (1990), the Rehnquist Court upheld the law, with only Justice Stevens dissenting. In that case, the school board had prohibited a Christian Bible club from meeting on school grounds. The board contended that if the religious club was allowed to meet it would have to have a faculty sponsor, which in turn would violate the establishment clause. But, writing for the Court, Justice O'Connor held that the school board had violated the provisions of the Equal Access Act and that those provisions did not violate the establishment clause. In her view, the act neither had a primary effect of advancing religion nor excessively entangle government and religion, even though the student religious meetings would be held on school grounds and under the school's aegis.

The Warren Court generated a continuing storm of controversy when holding that public-school systems may not require children to recite either nondenominational prayers or the Lord's Prayer, in *Engel v. Vitale* (1962) (see page 663) and *Abington School District v. Schempp* (1963) (see page 669). In *Schempp*, the Court drew on its earlier rationale, in *McGowan v. State of Maryland*, 366 U.S. 420 (1961), for upholding blue laws, or Sunday closing laws, and formulated a two-part test for laws under the establishment clause: whether laws have "a secular legislative purpose and a primary effect that neither advances nor inhibits religion."

By the end of the Warren Court era, the wall of separation appeared firmly entrenched in constitutional law. In charting the boundaries between religion and government, the Warren Court had pushed constitutional law in the direction of strict neutrality when applying *Shempp's* secular purpose–secular effect test, much as the dissenters in *Everson* had urged. In Chief Justice Warren's last term, the Court unanimously agreed to strike down Arkansas's law forbidding the teaching of evolution in public schools in *Epperson v. Arkansas*, 393 U.S. 97 (1968).

CONSTITUTIONAL HISTORY

Sunday Closing Laws, the Sabbath, and the Establishment Clause

In *McGowan v. State of Maryland*, 366 U.S. 420 (1961), Chief Justice Earl Warren upheld Maryland's law requiring all businesses to be closed on Sundays. In his opinion, Chief Justice Warren observed,

Sunday Closing Laws go far back into American history, having been brought to the colonies with a background of English legislation dating to the thirteenth century. . . .

But, despite the strongly religious origin of these laws, beginning before the eighteenth century, nonreligious arguments for Sunday closing began to be heard more distinctly and the statutes began to lose some of their totally religious flavor. . . .

Secular justifications have been advanced for making Sunday a day of rest, a day when people may recover from the labors of the week just passed and may physically and mentally prepare for the week's work to come. . . .

[T]he "Establishment" Clause does not ban federal or state regulation of conduct whose reason or effect merely happens to coincide or harmonize with the tenets of some or all religions. In many instances, the Congress or state legislatures conclude that the general welfare of society, wholly apart from any religious considerations, demands such regulation. Thus, for temporal purposes, murder is illegal. And the fact that this agrees with the dictates of the Judeo-Christian religions while it may disagree with others does not invalidate the regulation. So too with the questions of adultery and polygamy. . . .

It is true that if the State's interest were simply to provide for its citizens a periodic respite from work, a regulation demanding that everyone rest one day in seven, leaving the choice of the day to the individual, would suffice.

However, the State's purpose is not merely to provide a one-day-in-seven work stoppage. In addition to this, the State seeks to set one day apart from all others as a day of rest, repose, recreation and tranquility—a day which all members of the family and community have the opportunity to spend and enjoy together, a day on which there exists relative quiet and disassociation from the everyday intensity of commercial activities, a day on which people may visit friends and relatives who are not available during working days. . . .

Finally, we should make clear that . . . [w]e do not hold that Sunday legislation may not be a violation of the "Establishment" Clause if it can be demonstrated that its purpose—evidenced either on the face of the legislation, in conjunction with its legislative history, or in its operative effect—is to use the State's coercive power to aid religion.

Also in *McGowan*, Justice Douglas dissented with a sharply worded opinion, in which he countered that

[t]he question is not whether one day out of seven can be imposed by a State as a day of rest. The question is not whether Sunday can by force of custom and habit be retained as a day of rest. The question is whether a State can impose criminal sanctions on those who, unlike the Christian majority that makes up our society, worship on a different day or do not share the religious scruples of the majority.

If the "free exercise" of religion were subject to reasonable regulations, as it is under some constitutions, or if all laws "respecting the establishment of religion" were not proscribed, I could understand how rational men, representing a predominantly Christian civilization, might think these Sunday laws did not unreasonably interfere with anyone's free exercise of religion and took no step toward a burdensome establishment of any religion. . . .

But those who fashioned the First Amendment decided that if and when God is to be served, His service will not be motivated by coercive measures of government. . . .

It seems to me plain that by these laws the States compel one, under sanction of law, to refrain from work or recreation on Sunday because of the majority's religious views about that day. The State by law makes Sunday a symbol of respect or adherence. Refraining from work or recreation in deference to the majority's religious feelings about Sunday is within every person's choice.

The Warren Court also rejected the First Amendment objections to Sunday closing laws raised by Orthodox Jews, for whom Saturday is the Sabbath, in *Braunfeld v. Brown*, 366 U.S. 599 (1961). Another pertinent case is *Two-Guys from Harrison Allentown v. McGinley*, 366 U.S. 582 (1961).

In addition to holding Sunday closing laws violate neither the establishment clause nor the free exercise clause, the Burger Court (with only Justice Rehnquist dissenting) later struck down a Connecticut statute giving Sabbath observers an absolute right not to work on their Sabbath as running afoul of the establishment clause, in *Estate of Thorton v. Caldor*, 472 U.S. 703 (1985).

The direction of constitutional law, however, began to shift when Chief Justice Burger was appointed and came to the Court in 1969. As the composition of the bench further changed with the appointees of Republican Presidents Nixon and Reagan, the balance on the Court moved toward greater accommodation of government support of religion. Burger took an activist role in redirecting the interpretation and application of the establishment clause. He signaled his disagreement with the Warren Court's strict interpretation in *Walz v. Tax Commission of City of New York,* 397 U.S. 664 (1971). There the Court rejected a challenge to New York's tax exemption for "real or personal property used exclusively for religious, educational or charitable purposes." And Burger found occasion to interpret *Everson* to uphold governmental benevolent neutrality, as well as to advance his accommodationist interpretation of the religion clauses. "[T]here is room for play in the joints productive of a benevolent neutrality which will permit religious exercise to exist without sponsorship and without interference," Burger claimed, when explaining that

[i]n attempting to articulate the scope of the two Religion Clauses, the Court's opinions reflect the limitations inherent in formulating general principles on a case-by-case basis. The considerable internal inconsistency in the opinions of the Court derives from what, in retrospect, may have been too sweeping utterances on aspects of these clauses that seemed clear in relation to the particular cases but have limited meaning as general principles. . . .

The course of constitutional neutrality in this area cannot be an absolutely straight line; rigidity could well defeat the basic purpose of these provisions, which is to insure that no religion be sponsored or favored, none commanded, and none inhibited. The general principle deducible from the First Amendment and all that has been said by the Court is this: that we will not tolerate either governmentally established religion or governmental interference with religion.

Burger, however, went a step further by suggesting that government support of religion was permissible so long as there was "no excessive governmental entanglement with religion":

We must also be sure that the end result—the effect—is not an excessive government entanglement with religion. The test is inescapably one of degree. Either course, taxation of churches or exemptions, occasions some degree of involvement with religion. . . . [The question is] whether it is a continuing one calling for official and continuing surveillance leading to an impermissible degree of entanglement.

When introducing the idea of "excessive governmental entanglement with religion" in *Walz,* Burger failed to mention the Warren Court's *Schempp* test. But, the following year in *Lemon v. Kurtzman* (1971) (see page 675), which involves reimbursement for private religious schools of the cost of teachers' salaries and instructional materials in secular subjects, he turned *Schempp's* two-prong test (whether a statute has a secular purpose and its primary effect neither advances nor inhibits religion) into a three-prong test by adding that a "statute must not foster 'an excessive government entanglement with religion.'"

The *Lemon* test allowed the Burger Court to move in the direc-

---

THE DEVELOPMENT OF LAW

Major Rulings Upholding Governmental Aid or Support of Religion over Establishment Clause Objections

Case	Vote	Kind of Aid/Support for Religion Upheld
Everson v. Board of Education of Ewing Township, New Jersey, 330 U.S. 1 (1947)	5:4	Bus fare reimbursement for parents of children attending private religious schools.
Zorach v. Clauson, 343 U.S. 306 (1952)	6:3	Released-time program for religious instruction in class held off campus.
Walz v. Tax Commission of the City of New York, 397 U.S. 664 (1970)	7:1	Tax exemption for property used solely for religious purposes as permissible benevolent neutrality.
Tilton v. Richardson, 403 U.S. 672 (1971)	5:4	Most of a $240 million federal funding program for the construction of academic buildings on private sectarian and secular colleges; not enough entanglement of church and state to violate establishment clause.
Hunt v. McNair, 413 U.S. 734 (1973)	6:3	South Carolina's state bond issue for construction of academic buildings for nonreligious purposes by private religious schools.
Meek v. Pittenger, 413 U.S. 349 (1973)	6:3	Loan of secular textbooks from public schools to private and parochial schools.
Roemer v. Maryland Public Works Board, 426 U.S. 736 (1976)	5:4	General-purpose funds for nonsectarian purposes to colleges and universities with religious affiliations.

Case	Vote	Activity/Assistance Held Unconstitutional
Wolman v. Walter, 433 U.S. 229 (1977)	8:1	Diagnostic and therapeutic testing services provided to private primary and secondary schools affiliated with particular religions.
Committee for Public Education and Religious Liberty v. Regan, 444 U.S. 646 (1980)	5:4	Reimbursement for certain expenses for record keeping and testing incurred by private schools due to state regulations.
Mueller v. Allen, 463 U.S. 388 (1983)	5:4	Annual tax deduction of $700 for parents of children in elementary and secondary schools run by religious organizations; a neutral accommodation.
Marsh v. Chambers, 463 U.S. 783 (1983)	5:4	State practice of a chaplain opening sessions of legislature.
Lynch v. Donnelly, 465 U.S. 688 (1984)	5:4	City-sponsored display of crèche as part of Christmas display in park; accommodation and crèche viewed as a secular symbol.
Bowen v. Kendrick, 487 U.S. 589 (1988)	5:4	Authorization of federal funds for public and private organizations under Adolescent Family Life Act for premarital counseling services by organizations affiliated with established churches.
Board of Education of the Westside Community Schools v. Mergens, 110 S.Ct. 2356 (1990)	8:1	Upheld the Equal Access Act of 1984, which bars public schools from discriminating against meetings on school grounds of student activity groups on the basis of "religious, political, philosophical or other content of the speech at such meetings."

tion of permitting governmental accommodation of religion. But the *Lemon* test requires the Court to sharply distinguish between the level of educational institution (primary and secondary schools versus institutions of higher education) and the particular kinds of assistance, services, and benefits extended by the government. At the same time, the line of separation between government and religion became less clear, turning on the degree of entanglement, and thus the particular facts of and kind of entanglement presented in each case. Reliance on *Lemon* also meant that whether governmental support of religion survives establishment clause objections depends on the policy goals of the majority on the Court. In a companion ruling handed down with *Lemon*, for example, the justices voted five to four in upholding a federal program providing construction grants to colleges and universities. The majority had no problem with these grants going to religiously affiliated schools and, in contrast to *Lemon*, held the program survived *Lemon's* three-prong test as follows: (1) The buildings to be constructed had a secular purpose and were to be used only for nonreligious purposes. (2) Unlike the primary and secondary schools in *Lemon*, in the view of the majority, church-related colleges are not "permeated" with religion and students are "less impressionable and less susceptible to church indoctrination." Finally, (3) the grants were on a one-time basis and, hence, did not give rise to excessive government entanglement with religion.[5]

The difficulties in and disagreements about applying *Lemon* further divided the Court over whether *Lemon* should be abandoned in favor of another accommodationist approach or in favor of returning to a strict interpretation of the wall of separation between government and religion. In *Wolman v. Walter*, 433 U.S. 229 (1977), for example, when upholding certain diagnostic and therapeutic testing services to be provided to primary and secondary schools affiliated with particular religions in Ohio, the justices could not agree on the application of *Lemon's* tests, and Blackmun's opinion for the Court simply failed to mention it. Only Burger, Powell, and Stewart continued (although not always wholeheartedly) to support *Lemon*. Rehnquist, O'Connor, White, and Scalia, although inclined toward an accommodationist approach to the establishment clause, have criticized the *Lemon* tests. Brennan, Marshall, and Stevens, while relying on *Lemon* in some of their opinions for the Court, have also suggested abandoning *Lemon* to return to a strict separation of government from religion. Dissenting in *Committee for Public Education and Religious Liberty v. Regan*, 444 U.S. 646 (1980), Stevens observed that

the entire enterprise of trying to justify various types of subsidies to nonpublic schools should be abandoned. Rather than continuing with the susyphean task of trying to patch together the "blurred, indistinct, and variable barrier" described in *Lemon v. Kurtzman*, . . . I would resurrect the "high and impregnable" wall between church and state constructed by the Framers of the First Amendment. See *Everson v. Board of Education.*

As a result of the Court's failure to agree on an interpretative approach and test for applying the establishment clause, the justices sometimes invoke *Lemon's* three-prong test[6] and at other times pay little or no attention to it.[7] *Stone v. Graham* (1980) (see page 684) is illustrative. There in a *per curiam* opinion for a bare majority, the *Lemon* tests were recited verbatim, but the Court struck Kentucky's law requiring the posting of the Ten Commandments in school classrooms simply because it lacked a secular purpose.

Stone v. Graham also underscores the importance of whether the justices construe the legislative purpose of a law to be secular or religious. In *Schempp*, when rejecting the school board's arguments that its Bible-reading program aimed at promoting civil values and teaching literature, the Court countered that "the place of the Bible as an instrument of religion cannot be gainsaid." In *Stone*, the majority held that posting the Ten Commandments "serves no . . . educational function."

The continuing struggle within the Court is registered in four recent important rulings. Splitting five to four in *Lynch v. Donnelly*, 465 U.S. 668 (1984), the Court upheld the Pawtucket, Rhode Island, display of the crèche during the Christmas holiday season. Notably, Burger's opinion for the majority interpreted the crèche to be a secular, not a religious, symbol and found no excessive government entanglement with religion, prompting Brennan to issue a sharply worded dissent, which Marshall, Blackmun, and Stevens joined.

The following year, the justices divided six to three in *Wallace v. Jaffree* (1985) (see page 686) in striking down Alabama's law requiring a moment of silence in public schools for mediation or voluntary prayer. Along with Stevens's opinion for the Court, relying on *Lemon*, compare O'Connor's concurring opinion and Burger's dissenting opinion, both criticizing reliance on and application of *Lemon*. The dissenting opinion of Rehnquist is also notable in attacking not only *Lemon* but the Court's understanding of the establishment clause since *Everson.*

In *Edwards v. Aguillard* (1987) (see page 702), Justice Brennan forged a seven to two ruling overturning Louisiana's law requiring the teaching of creationism. Compare his opinion with the lengthy dissenting opinion of Justice Scalia, which Chief Justice Rehnquist joined.

Finally, in *County of Allegheny v. American Civil Liberties Union Greater Pittsburgh Chapter* (1989) (see page 713) the Rehnquist

Court reconsidered under what circumstances local governments may display the crèche and menorah. There, again, splitting five to four the justices held that the display of a crèche inside a city building violated the establishment clause, and limited *Lynch v. Donnelly*, as well as rejected Chief Justice Burger's analysis there. At the same time, the Court upheld the display of the menorah next to a Christmas tree outside a city/county office building. In both *Lynch* and *County of Allegheny*, Justice O'Connor cast the crucial vote in determining the outcome and the Court's line drawing between religion and government.

THE DEVELOPMENT OF LAW

Major Rulings Striking Down Laws and Policies for Violating the Establishment Clause

Case	Vote	Activity/Assistance Held Unconstitutional
McCollum v. Board of Education, 333 U.S. 203 (1948)	8:1	Released-time program for religious instruction held on school grounds.
Engel v. Vitale, 370 U.S. 421 (1962)	6:1	A twenty two-word nondenominational prayer written for students in public school.
Abington School District v. Schempp and Murray v. Curlett, 374 U.S. 203	8:1	Reading of Lord's Prayer and Bible verses in public schools.
Epperson v. Arkansas, 393 U.S. 97 (1968)	9:0	Arkansas's "monkey law," forbidding the teaching of evolutionary theory.
Lemon v. Kurtzman, 403 U.S. 602 (1971)	8:0	Direct aid to parochial schools, including use of public funds to pay salaries of parochial teachers.
Essex v. Wolman, 409 U.S. 808 (1972)	8:1	Annual tuition rebate of $90 per child attending religion-affiliated schools.
Levitt v. Commission for Public Education and Religious Liberty, 413 U.S. 472 (1973); *Committee for Public Education and Religious Liberty v. Nyquist,* 413 U.S. 756 (1973); *Sloan v. Lemon,* 413 U.S. 825 (1973)	8:1 6:3	Financial aid for parochial schools, including tuition reimbursement, tax exemptions, and special counseling services and loan of educational equipment.

Case	Vote	Activity/Assistance Held Unconstitutional
Meek v. Pittenger, 421 U.S. 349 (1975)	6:3	Counseling, testing, remedial classes, equipment, and other auxiliary services given to schools affiliated with religious organizations.
Wolman v. Walter, 433 U.S. 229 (1977)	5:4	Financial aid for field trips and class paraphernalia provided to private schools affiliated with religious organizations.
New York v. Cathedral Academy, 434 U.S. 125 (1977)	6:3	Direct reimbursement to parochial schools for record keeping and testing services.
Stone v. Graham, 449 U.S. 39 (1980)	5:4	Kentucky law requiring the posting of the Ten Commandments in classrooms.
Widmar v. Vincent, 454 U.S. 263 (1981)	8:1	Missouri's prohibition of the use of state university buildings for "religious worship."
Larkin v. Grendel's Den, 454 U.S. 1140 (1982)	5:4	Law giving churches veto over issuance of liquor licenses.
Wallace v. Jaffree, 472 U.S. 38 (1985)	6:3	Alabama law authorizing a one-minute of silence in public schools for meditation or voluntary prayer.
Aguilar v. Felton, 473 U.S. 402 (1985)	5:4	Instructional services given and provided on grounds of parochial schools.
Edwards v. Aguillard, 482 U.S. 578 (1987)	7:2	Louisiana law requiring the teaching of creationism to balance the teaching of evolution.
Texas Monthy, Inc. v. Bullock, 489 U.S. 1 (1989)	6:3	Texas law giving tax exemption to religious periodicals.

NOTES

1. Paul Kauper, *Religion and the Constitution* (Baton Rouge: Louisiana State University Press, 1964), 59. The principle of state neutrality is also illustrated in *Presbyterian Church in United States v. Mary Elizabeth Blue Hull Memorial Presbyterian Church,* 393 U.S. 440 (1969), holding that the First Amendment bars civil courts from awarding church property based on ecclesiastical doctrine. The Supreme Court also held that courts have no jurisdiction over disputes arising from defrocking of bishops and over the allocation of church property in *Serbian Eastern*

Orthodox Diocese for the United States and Canada v. Milivojevich, 426 U.S. 696 (1976).

2. In *Luetkemeyer v. Kaulfman,* 419 U.S. 880 (1974), the Court summarily affirmed a lower court ruling that the free exercise clause was not violated by Missouri's providing free bus transportation for public-school children, but not to those attending parochial schools. In dissent, Justice White maintained as well that there was no violation of the establishment clause, in view of *Everson.* Notably, in *Bradfield v. Roberts,* 175 U.S. 291 (1899), the federal funding for the care of indigent patients in a Catholic hospital was upheld, and in *Quick Bear v. Laupp,* 210 U.S. 50 (1908) the Court allowed the disbursement of funds, appropriated for the Sioux Indians, to parochial schools as tuition payments.

3. Philip Kurland, "Of Church and State and the Supreme Court," 29 *University of Chicago Law Review* 5 (1961).

4. In another case, *Bender v. Williamsport Area School District,* 475 U.S. 534, 106 S.Ct. 1326 (1986), a bare majority denied standing to a parent and school board member to challenge the school district's decision not to permit a student prayer club to hold meetings during regularly scheduled activities period. But the four dissenters (Chief Justice Burger and Justices Rehnquist, Powell, and White) contended that the club's meeting on school grounds did not violate the establishment clause.

5. *Tilton v. Richardson,* 403 U.S. 672 (1971).

6. See, for example, *Stone v. Graham,* 449 U.S. 39 (1980); *Committee for Public Education and Religious Liberty v. Regan,* 444 U.S. 646 (1980); *Larkin v. Grendel's Den, Inc.,* 459 U.S. 116 (1982); *Aguilar v. Felton,* 473 U.S. 402 (1985); and *Texas Monthly, Inc. v. Bullock,* 489 U.S. 1 (1989).

7. See, for example, *Larson v. Valente,* 456 U.S. 228 (1982); and *Marsh v. Chambers,* 463 U.S. 783 (1983).

SELECTED BIBLIOGRAPHY

Kauper, Paul. *Religion and the Constitution.* Baton Rouge: Louisiana State University Press, 1964.

Levy, Leonard. *The Establishment Clause: Religion and the First Amendment.* New York: Macmillan, 1986.

Oaks, Dallin, ed. *The Wall between Church and State.* Chicago: University of Chicago Press, 1963.

Everson v. Board of Education of Ewing Township
330 U.S. 1, 67 S.Ct. 504 (1947)

Arch Everson filed a suit challenging the constitutionality of an authorization for reimbursement of parents with children in private schools for the cost of busing their children to schools. The Board of Education of Ewing Township had adopted the plan under a New Jersey statute permitting local school districts to make their own rules for the transportation of children to and from schools. Most of the private schools in the area were Catholic parochial schools. A state court struck down the program, the New Jersey Court of Errors and Appeals reversed, holding that neither the state law nor the school board's resolution violated the state or federal Constitution. Everson then turned to the Supreme Court, which granted review.

Justice BLACK delivers the opinion of the Court.

The New Jersey statute is challenged as a "law respecting an establishment of religion.". . . These words of the First Amendment reflected in the minds of early Americans a vivid mental picture of conditions and practices which they fervently wished to stamp out in order to preserve liberty for themselves and for their posterity. Doubtless their goal has not been entirely reached; but so far has the Nation moved toward it that the expression "law respecting an establishment of religion," probably does not so vividly remind present-day Americans of the evils, fears, and political problems that caused that expression to be written into our Bill of Rights. Whether this New Jersey law is one respecting the "establishment of religion" requires an understanding of the meaning of that language, particularly with respect to the imposition of taxes. Once again, therefore, it is not inappropriate briefly to review the background and environment of the period in which that constitutional language was fashioned and adopted.

A large proportion of the early settlers of this country came here from Europe to escape the bondage of laws which compelled them to support and attend government favored churches. The centuries immediately before and contemporaneous with the colonization of America had been filled with turmoil, civil strife, and persecutions, generated in large part by established sects determined to maintain their absolute political and religious supremacy. With the power of government supporting them, at various times and places, Catholics had persecuted Protestants, Protestants had persecuted Catholics, Protestant sects had persecuted other Protestant sects, Catholics of one shade of belief had persecuted Catholics of another shade of belief, and all of these had from time to time persecuted Jews. In efforts to force loyalty to whatever religious group happened to be on top and in league with the government of a particular time and place, men and women had been fined, cast in jail, cruelly tortured, and killed. . . .

These practices of the old world were transplanted to and began to thrive in the soil of the new America. The very characters granted by the English Crown to the individuals and companies designated to make the laws which would control the destinies of the colonials authorized these individuals and companies to erect religious establishments which all, whether believers or non-believers, would be required to support and attend. An exercise of this authority was accompanied by a repetition of many of the old world practices and persecutions. Catholics found themselves hounded and proscribed because of their faith; Quakers who followed their conscience went to jail; Baptists were peculiarly obnoxious to certain dominant Protestant sects; men and women of varied faiths who happened to be in a minority in a particular locality were persecuted because they steadfastly persisted in worshipping God only as their own consciences dictated. And all of these dissenters were compelled to pay tithes and taxes to support government-sponsored churches whose ministers preached inflammatory sermons designed to strengthen and consolidate the established faith by generating a burning hatred against dissenters.

These practices became so commonplace as to shock the freedom-loving colonials into a feeling of abhorrence. The imposition of taxes to pay ministers' salaries and to build and maintain churches and church property aroused their indignation. It was these feelings which found expression in the First Amendment. No one locality and no one group throughout the Colonies can rightly be given entire credit for having aroused the sentiment that culminated in adoption of the Bill of Rights' provisions embracing religious liberty. But Virginia, where the established church had achieved a dominant influence in political affairs and where many excesses attracted wide public attention, provided a great stimulus and able leadership for the movement. The people there, as elsewhere, reached the conviction that individual religious liberty could be achieved best under a government which was stripped of all power to tax, to support, or otherwise to assist any or all religions, or to interfere with the beliefs of any religious individual or group.

The movement toward this end reached its dramatic climax in Virginia in 1785–86 when the Virginia legislative body was about to renew Virginia's tax levy for the support of the established church. Thomas Jefferson and James Madison led the fight against this tax. Madison wrote his great Memorial and Remonstrance against the law. In it, he eloquently argued that a true religion did not need the support of law; that no person, either believer or non-believer, should be taxed to support a religious institution of any kind; that the best interest of a society required that the minds of men always be wholly free; and that cruel persecutions were the inevitable result of government-established religions. Madison's Remonstrance received strong support throughout Virginia, and the Assembly postponed consideration of the proposed tax measure until its next session. When the proposal came up for consideration at that session, it not only died in committee, but the Assembly enacted the famous "Virginia Bill for Religious Liberty" originally written by Thomas Jefferson. The preamble to that Bill stated among other things that

"Almighty God hath created the mind free; that all attempts to influence it by temporal punishments, or burthens, or by civil incapacitations, tend only to beget habits of hypocrisy and meanness, and are a departure from the plan of the Holy author of our religion who being Lord both of body and mind, yet chose not to propagate it by coercions on either; . . . that to compel a man to furnish contributions of money for the propagation of opinions which he disbelieves, is sinful and tyrannical; that even the forcing him to support this or that teacher of his own religious persuasion, is depriving him of the comfortable liberty of giving his contributions to the particular pastor, whose morals he would make his pattern. . . ."

And the statute itself enacted

"That no man shall be compelled to frequent or support any religious worship, place, or ministry whatsoever, nor shall be enforced, restrained, molested, or burthened, in his body or goods, nor shall otherwise suffer on account of his religious opinions or belief. . . ."

This Court has previously recognized that the provisions of the First Amendment, in the drafting and adoption of which Madison and Jefferson played such leading roles, had the same objective and were intended to provide the same protection against governmental intrusion on religious liberty as the Virginia statute.

Prior to the adoption of the Fourteenth Amendment, the First Amendment did not apply as a restraint against the states. Most of them did soon provide similar constitutional protections for religious liberty. But some states persisted for about half a century in imposing restraints upon the free exercise of religion and in discriminating against particular religious groups. In recent years, so far as the provision against the establishment of a religion is concerned, the question has most frequently arisen in connection with proposed state aid to church schools and efforts to carry on religious teachings in the public schools in accordance with the tenets of a particular sect. Some churches have either sought or accepted state financial support for their schools. Here again the efforts to obtain state aid or acceptance of it have not been limited to any one particular faith. The state courts, in the main, have remained faithful to the language of their own constitutional provisions designed to protect religious freedom and to separate religious and governments. Their decisions, however, show the difficulty in drawing the line between tax legislation which provides funds for the welfare of the general public and that which is designed to support institutions which teach religion.

The meaning and scope of the First Amendment, preventing establishment of religion or prohibiting the free exercise thereof, in the light of its history and the evils it was designed forever to suppress, have been several times elaborated by the decisions of this Court prior to the application of the First Amendment to the states by the Fourteenth. The broad meaning given the Amendment by these earlier cases has been accepted by this Court in its decisions concerning an individual's religious freedom rendered since the Fourteenth Amendment was interpreted to make the prohibitions of the First applicable to state action abridging religious freedom. There is every reason to give the same application and broad interpretation to the "establishment of religion" clause. . . .

The "establishment of religion" clause of the First Amendment means at least this: Neither a state nor the Federal Government can set up a church. Neither can pass laws which aid one religion, aid all religions, or prefer one religion over another. Neither can force nor influence a person to go to or to remain away from church against his will or force him to profess a belief or disbelief in any religion. No person can be punished for entertaining or professing religious beliefs or disbeliefs, for church attendance or non-attendance. No tax in any amount, large or small, can be levied to support any religious activities or institutions, whatever they may be called, or whatever form they may adopt to teach or practice religion. Neither a state nor the Federal Government can, openly or secretly, participate in the affairs of any religious organizations or groups and vice versa. In the words of Jefferson, the clause against establishment of religion by law was intended to erect "a wall of separation between Church and State."

We must consider the New Jersey statute in accordance with the foregoing limitations imposed by the First Amendment. But we must not strike that state statute down if it is within the state's constitutional power even though it approaches the verge of that power. New Jersey cannot consistently with the "establishment of religion" clause of the First Amendment contribute tax-raised funds to the support of an institution which teaches the tenets and faith of any church. On the other hand, other language of the amendment commands that New Jersey cannot hamper its citizens in the free exercise of their own religion. Consequently, it cannot exclude individual Catholics, Lutherans, Mohammedans, Baptists, Jews, Methodists, Non-believers, Presbyterians, or the members of any other faith, *because of their faith, or lack of it,* from receiving the benefits of public welfare legislation. While we do not mean to intimate that a state could not provide transportation only to children attending public schools, we must be careful, in protecting the citizens of New Jersey against state-established churches, to be sure that we do not inadvertently prohibit New Jersey from extending its general State law benefits to all its citizens without regard to their religious belief.

Measured by these standards, we cannot say that the First Amendment prohibits New Jersey from spending tax-raised funds to pay the bus fares of parochial school pupils as a part of a general program under which it pays the fares of pupils attending public and other schools. It is undoubtedly true that children are helped to get to church schools. There is even a possibility that some of the children might not be sent to the church schools if the parents were compelled to pay their children's bus fares out of their own pockets when transportation to a public school would have been paid for by the State. The same possibility exists where the state requires a local transit company to provide reduced fares to school children including those attending parochial schools, or where a municipally owned transportation system undertakes to carry all school children free of charge. Moreover, state-paid policemen, detailed to protect children going to and from church schools from the very real hazards of traffic, would serve much the same purpose and accomplish much the same result as state provisions intended to guarantee free transportation of a kind which the state deems to be best for the school children's welfare. And parents might refuse to risk their children to the serious danger of traffic accidents going to and from parochial schools, the approaches to which were not protected by policemen. Similarly, parents might be reluctant to permit their children to attend schools which the state had cut off from such general government services as ordinary police and fire protection, connections for sewage disposal, public highways and sidewalks. Of course, cutting off church schools from these services, so separate and so indisputably marked off from the religious function, would make it far more difficult for the schools to operate. But such is obviously not the purpose of the First Amendment. That Amendment requires the state to be a neutral in its relations with groups of religious believers and non-believers; it does not require the state to be their adversary. State power is no more to be used so as to handicap religions, than it is to favor them. . . .

The First Amendment has erected a wall between church and state. That wall must be kept high and impregnable. We could not approve the slightest breach. New Jersey has not breached it here.

Affirmed.

Justice JACKSON dissented in a separate opinion.

Justice RUTLEDGE, with whom Justice FRANKFURTER, Justice JACKSON, and Justice BURTON join, dissenting.

The Amendment's purpose was not to strike merely at the official establishment of a single sect, creed or religion, outlawing only a formal relation such as had prevailed in England and some of the colonies. Necessarily it was to uproot all such relationships. But the object was broader than separating church and state in this narrow sense. It was to create a complete and permanent separation of the spheres of religious activity and civil authority by comprehensively forbidding every form of public aid or support for religion. In proof the Amendment's wording and history unite with this Court's consistent utterances whenever attention has been fixed directly upon the question.

"Religion" appears only once in the Amendment. But the word governs two prohibitions and governs them alike. It does not have two meanings, one narrow to forbid "an establishment" and another, much broader, for securing "the free exercise thereof." "Thereof" brings down "religion" with its entire and exact content, no more and no less, from the first into the second guaranty, so that Congress and now the states are as broadly restricted concerning the one as they are regarding the other. . . .

Compulsory attendance upon religious exercises went out early in the process of separating church and state, together with forced observance of religious forms and ceremonies. Test oaths and religious qualification for office followed later. These things none devoted to our great tradition of religious liberty would think of bringing back. Hence today, apart from efforts to inject religious training or exercises and sectarian issues into the public schools, the only serious surviving threat to maintaining that complete and permanent separation of religion and civil power which the First Amendment commands is through use of the taxing power to support religion, religious establishments, or establishments having a religious foundation whatever their form or special religious function.

Does New Jersey's action furnish support for religion by use of the taxing power? Certainly it does, if the test remains undiluted as Jefferson and Madison made it, that money taken by taxation from one is not to be used or given to support another's religious training or belief, or indeed one's own. Today as then the furnishing of "contributions of money for the propagation of opinions which he disbelieves" is the forbidden exaction; and the prohibition is absolute for whatever measure brings that consequence and whatever mount may be sought or given to that end.

The funds used here were raised by taxation. The Court does not dispute nor could it that their use does in fact give aid and encouragement to religious instruction. It only concludes that this aid is not "support" in law. But Madison and Jefferson were concerned with aid and support in fact not as a legal conclusion "entangled in precedents." Remonstrance. Here parents pay money to send their children to parochial schools and funds raised by taxation are used to reimburse them. This not only helps the children to get to school and the parents to send them. It aids them in a substantial way to get the very thing which they are sent to the particular school to secure, namely, religious training and teaching. . . .

To say that New Jersey's appropriation and her use of the power of taxation for raising the funds appropriated are not for public purposes but are for private ends, is to say that they are for the support of religion and religious teaching. Conversely, to say that they are for public purposes is to say that they are not for religious ones.

This is precisely for the reason that education which includes religious training and teaching, and its support, have been made matters of private right and function not public, by the very terms of the First Amendment. That is the effect not only in its guaranty of religion's free exercise, but also in the prohibition of establishments. . . .

The reasons underlying the Amendment's policy have not vanished with time or diminished in force. Now as when it was adopted the price of religious freedom is double. It is that the church and religion shall live both within and upon that freedom. There cannot be freedom of religion, safeguarded by the state, and intervention by the church or its agencies in the state's domain or dependency on its largess. Madison's Remonstrance. The great condition of religious liberty is that it be maintained free from sustenance, as also from other interferences, by the state. For when it comes to rest upon that secular foundation it vanishes with the resting. Public money devoted to payment of religious costs, educational or other, brings the quest for more. It brings too the struggle of sect against sect for the larger share or for any. Here one by numbers alone will benefit most, there another. That is precisely the history of societies which have had an established religion and dissident groups. It is the very thing Jefferson and Madison experienced and sought to guard against, whether in its blunt or in its more screened forms. . . .

No one conscious of religious values can be unsympathetic toward the burden which our constitutional separation puts on parents who desire religious instruction mixed with secular for their children. They pay taxes for others' children's education, at the same time the added cost of instruction for their own. Nor can one happily see benefits denied to children which others receive, because in conscience they or their parents for them desire a different kind of training others do not demand.

But if those feelings should prevail, there would be an end to our historic constitutional policy and command. No more unjust or discriminatory in fact is it to deny attendants at religious schools the cost of their transportation than it is to deny them tuitions, sustenance for their teachers, or any other educational expense which others receive at public cost. Hardship in fact there is which none can blink. But, for assuring to those who undergo it the greater, the most comprehensive freedom, it is one written by design and firm intent into our basic law. . . .

That policy necessarily entails hardship upon persons who forego the right to educational advantages the state can supply in order to secure others it is precluded from giving. Indeed this may hamper the parent and the child forced by conscience to that choice. But it does not make the state unneutral to withhold what the Constitution forbids it to give. On the contrary it is only by observing the prohibition rigidly that the state can maintain its neutrality and avoid partisanship in the dissensions inevitable when sect opposes sect over demands for public moneys to further religious education, teaching or training in any form or degree, directly or indirectly. . . .

Now as in Madison's day it is one of principle, to keep separate the separate spheres as the First Amendment drew them; to prevent the first experiment upon our liberties; and to keep the question from becoming entangled in corrosive precedents. We should not be less strict to keep strong and untarnished the one side of the shield of religious freedom than we have been of the other.

The judgment should be reversed.

Engel v. Vitale
370 U.S. 421, 82 S.Ct. 1261 (1962)

Steven Engel and several other parents of school-age children sued the principal and the Board of Education of Union Free School District No. 9, in New Hyde Park, New York, for requiring students to recite at the beginning of each school day a nondenominational prayer. The prayer, written by the State Board of Regents, was as follows: "Almighty God, we acknowledge our dependence upon Thee, and we beg Thy blessings upon us, our parents, our teachers and our country." An order upholding the power of New York to adopt and require children to recite this prayer was issued by a state court and affirmed by the New York Court of Appeals. Engel made a final appeal to the Supreme Court.

Justice BLACK delivers the opinion of the Court.

We think that by using its public school system to encourage recitation of the Regents' prayer, the State of New York has adopted a practice wholly inconsistent with the Establishment Clause. There can, of course, be no doubt that New York's program of daily classroom invocation of God's blessings as prescribed in the Regents' prayer is a religious activity. . . .

The petitioners contend among other things that the state laws requiring or permitting use of the Regents' prayer must be struck down as a violation of the Establishment Clause because that prayer was composed by governmental officials as a part of a governmental program to further religious beliefs. For this reason, petitioners argue, the State's use of the Regents' prayer in its public school system breaches the constitutional wall of separation between Church and State. We agree with that contention since we think that the constitutional prohibition against laws respecting an establishment of religion must at least mean that in this country it is no part of the business of government to compose official prayers for any group of the American people to recite as a part of a religious program carried on by government.

It is a matter of history that this very practice of establishing governmentally composed prayers for religious services was one of the reasons which caused many of our early colonists to leave England and seek religious freedom in America. The Book of Common Prayer, which was created under governmental direction and which was approved by Acts of Parliament in 1548 and 1549, set out in minute detail the accepted form and content of prayer and other religious ceremonies to be used in the established, tax-supported Church of England. . . .

[G]roups, lacking the necessary political power to influence the Government on the matter, decided to leave England and its established church and seek freedom in America from England's governmentally ordained and supported religion.

It is an unfortunate fact of history that when some of the very groups which had most strenuously opposed the established Church of England found themselves sufficiently in control of colonial governments in this country to write their own prayers into law, they passed laws making their own religion the official religion of their respective colonies. Indeed, as late as the time of the Revolutionary War, there were established churches in at least eight of the thirteen former colonies and established religions in at least four of the other five. But the successful Revolution against English political domination was shortly followed by intense opposition to the practice of establishing religion by law. This opposition crystallized rapidly into an effective political force in Virginia where the minority religious groups such as Presbyterians, Lutherans, Quakers and Baptists had gained such strength that the adherents to the established Episcopal Church were actually a minority themselves. In 1785–1786, those opposed to the established Church, led by James Madison and Thomas Jefferson, who, though themselves not members of any of these dissenting religious groups, opposed all religious establishments by law on grounds of principle, obtained the enactment of the famous "Virginia Bill for Religious Liberty" by which all religious groups were placed on an equal footing so far as the State was concerned. Similar though less far-reaching legislation was being considered and passed in other States.

By the time of the adoption of the Constitution, our history shows that there was a widespread awareness among many Americans of the dangers of a union of Church and State. These people knew, some of them from bitter personal experience, that one of the greatest dangers to the freedom of the individual to worship in his own way lay in the Government's placing its official stamp of approval upon one particular kind of prayer or one particular form of religious services. They knew the anguish, hardship and bitter strife that could come when zealous religious groups struggled with one another to obtain the Government's stamp of approval from each King, Queen, or Protector that came to temporary power. The Constitution was intended to avert a part of this danger by leaving the government of this country in the hands of the people rather than in the hands of any monarch. But this safeguard was not enough. Our Founders were no more willing to let the content of their prayers and their privilege of praying whenever they pleased be influenced by the ballot box than they were to let these vital matters of personal conscience depend upon the succession of monarchs. The First Amendment was added to the Constitution to stand as a guarantee that neither the power nor the prestige of the Federal Government would be used to control, support or influence the kinds of prayer the American people can say—that the people's religions must not be subjected to the pressures of government for change each time a new political administration is elected to office. Under that Amendment's prohibition against governmental establishment of religion, as reinforced by the provisions of the Fourteenth Amendment, government in this country, be it state or federal, is without power to prescribe by law any particular form of prayer which is to be used as an official prayer in carrying on any program of governmentally sponsored religious activity.

There can be no doubt that New York's state prayer program officially establishes the religious beliefs embodied in the Regents' prayer. The respondents' argument to the contrary, which is largely based upon the contention that the Regents' prayer is "non-denominational" and the fact that the program, as modified and approved by state courts, does not require all pupils to recite the prayer but permits those who wish to do so to remain silent or be excused from the room, ignores the essential nature of the program's constitutional defects. Neither the fact that the prayer may be denominationally neutral nor the fact that its observance on the part of the students is voluntary can serve to free it from the limitations of the Establishment Clause, as it might from the Free Exercise Clause, of the First Amendment, both of which are operative against the States by virtue of the Fourteenth Amendment. Although these two clauses may in certain instances overlap, they forbid two quite different kinds of governmental encroachment upon religious freedom. The Establishment Clause, unlike the Free Exercise Clause, does not depend upon any showing of direct governmental compulsion and is violated by the enactment of laws which establish an official religion whether those laws operate directly to coerce nonobserving individuals or not. This is not to say, of course, that laws officially prescribing a particular form of religious worship do not involve coercion of such individuals. When the power, prestige and financial support of government is placed behind a particular religious belief, the indirect coercive pressure upon religious minorities to conform to the prevailing officially approved religion is plain. But the purposes underlying the Establishment Clause go much further than that. Its first and most immediate purpose rested on the belief that a union of government and religion tends to destroy government and to degrade religion. The history of governmentally established religion, both in England and in this country, showed that whenever government had allied itself with one particular form of religion, the inevitable result had been that it had incurred the hatred, disrespect and even contempt of those who held contrary beliefs. That same history showed that many people had lost their respect for any religion that had relied upon the support of government to spread its faith. The Establishment Clause thus stands as an expression of principle on the part of the Founders of our Constitution that religion is too personal, too sacred, too holy, to permit its "unhallowed perversion" by a civil magistrate. Another purpose of the Establishment Clause rested upon an awareness of the historical fact that governmentally established religions and religious persecutions go hand in hand. . . . The New York laws officially prescribing the Regents' prayer are inconsistent both with the purposes of the Establishment Clause and with the Establishment Clause itself.

It has been argued that to apply the Constitution in such a way as to prohibit state laws respecting an establishment of religious services in public schools is to indicate a hostility toward religion or toward prayer. Nothing, of course, could be more wrong. . . . It is neither sacrilegious nor antireligious to say that each separate government in this country should stay out of the business of writing or sanctioning official prayers and leave that purely religious function to the people themselves and to those the people choose to look to for religious guidance. . . .

To those who may subscribe to the view that because the Regents' official prayer is so brief and general there can be no danger to religious freedom in its governmental establishment, however, it may be appropriate to say in the words of James Madison, the author of the First Amendment:

"[I]t is proper to take alarm at the first experiment on our liberties. . . . Who does not see that the same authority which can establish Christianity, in exclusion of all other Religions, may establish with the same ease any particular sect of Christians, in exclusion of all other Sects? That the same authority which can force a citizen to contribute three pence only of his property for the support of any one establishment, may force him to conform to any other establishment in all cases whatsoever?"

The judgment of the Court of Appeals of New York is reversed and the cause remanded for further proceedings not inconsistent with this opinion.

Reversed and remanded.

Justice FRANKFURTER did not participate in the decision of this case.

Justice WHITE did not participate in the consideration or decision of this case.

Justice DOUGLAS concurring.

As I read this regulation, a child is free to stand or not stand, to recite or not recite, without fear of reprisal or even comment by the teacher or any other school official.

In short, the only one who need utter the prayer is the teacher; and no teacher is complaining of it. Students can stand mute or even leave the classroom, if they desire. . . .

The question presented by this case is therefore an extremely narrow one. It is whether New York oversteps the bounds when it finances a religious exercise.

What New York does on the opening of its public schools is what we do when we open court. Our Crier has from the beginning announced the convening of the Court and then added "God save the United States and this Honorable Court." That utterance is a supplication, a prayer in which we, the judges, are free to join, but which we need not recite any more than the students need recite the New York prayer.

What New York does on the opening of its public schools is what each House of Congress does at the opening of each day's business. . . .

In New York the teacher who leads in prayer is on the public payroll; and the time she takes seems minuscule as compared with the salaries appropriated by state legislatures and Congress for chaplains to conduct prayers in the legislative halls. Only a bare fraction of the teacher's time is given to reciting this short 22-word prayer, about the same amount of time that our Crier spends announcing the opening of our sessions and offering a prayer for this Court. Yet for me the principle is the same, no matter how briefly the prayer is said, for in each of the instances given the person praying is a public official on the public payroll, performing a religious exercise in a governmental institution. It is said that the element of coercion is inherent in the giving of this prayer. If that is true here, it is also true of the prayer with which this Court is convened, and of those that open the Congress. Few adults, let alone children, would leave our courtroom or the Senate or the House while those prayers are being given. Every such audience is in a sense a "captive" audience.

At the same time I cannot say that to authorize this prayer is to establish a religion in the strictly historic meaning of those words. A religion is not established in the usual sense merely by letting those who choose to do so say the prayer that the public school teacher leads. Yet once government finances a religious exercise it inserts a divisive influence into our communities. . . .

By reason of the First Amendment government is commanded "to have no interest in theology or ritual" for on those matters "government must be neutral." The First Amendment leaves the Government in a position not of hostility to religion but of neutrality. The philosophy is that the atheist or agnostic—the non-believer—is entitled to go his own way. The philosophy is that if government interferes in matters spiritual, it will be a divisive force. The First Amendment teaches that a government neutral in the field of religion better serves all religious interests. . . .

I therefore join the Court in reversing the judgment below.

Justice STEWART dissenting.

The Court today decides that in permitting this brief non-denominational prayer the school board has violated the Constitution of the United States. I think this decision is wrong. . . .

With all respect, I think the Court has misapplied a great constitutional principle. I cannot see how an "official religion" is established by letting those who want to say a prayer say it. On the contrary, I think that to deny the wish of these school children to join in reciting this prayer is to deny them the opportunity of sharing in the spiritual heritage of our nation. . . .

At the opening of each day's Session of this Court we stand, while one of our officials invokes the protection of God. Since the days of John Marshall our Crier has said, "God save the United States and this Honorable Court." Both the Senate and the House of Representatives open their daily Sessions with prayer. . . .

Countless similar examples could be listed, but there is no need to belabor the obvious. It was all summed up by this Court just ten years ago in a single sentence: "We are a religious people whose institutions presuppose a Supreme Being." *Zorach v. Clauson,* 343 U.S. 306 [1952].

I do not believe that this Court, or the Congress, or the President has by the actions and practices I have mentioned established an "official religion" in violation of the Constitution. And I do not believe the State of New York has done so in this case.

Abington School District v. Schempp and *Murray v. Curlett,*
374 U.S. 203, 83 S.Ct. 1560 (1963)

The Supreme Court granted and consolidated these two cases. Each involved disputes arising from state laws requiring schools to begin each with readings from the Bible. Edward Schempp challenged Pennsylvania's law declaring that "At least ten verses from the Holy Bible shall be read, without comment, at the opening of each public school day. Any child shall be excused from such Bible reading, or attending such Bible reading, upon written request of his parent or guardian." A three-judge federal district court struck down the state's law as a violation of the First Amendment and the school board appealed directly to the Supreme Court. The companion case was brought by Madalyn Murray and her son, both professed atheists. They challenged the constitutionality of a rule of the school board of Baltimore, Maryland, requiring students to recite the Lord's Prayer at the opening of each school day. A state court and the Maryland Court of Appeals had upheld the school board.

Justice CLARK delivers the opinion of the Court.

The wholesome "neutrality" of which this Court's cases speak . . . stems from a recognition of the teachings of history that powerful sects or groups might bring about a fusion of governmental and religious functions or a concert or dependency of one upon the other to the end that official support of the State or Federal Government would be placed behind the tenets of one or of all orthodoxies. This the Establishment Clause prohibits. And a further reason for neutrality is found in the Free Exercise Clause, which recognizes the value of religious training, teaching and observance and, more particularly, the right of every person to freely choose his own course with reference thereto, free of any compulsion from the state. This the Free Exercise Clause guarantees. Thus . . . the two clauses may overlap. . . . [T]he Establishment Clause has been directly considered by this Court eight times in the past score of years and, with only one Justice dissenting on the point, it has consistently held that the clause withdrew all legislative power respecting religious belief or the expression thereof. The test may be stated as follows: what are the purpose and the primary effect of the enactment? If either is the advancement or inhibition of religion then the enactment exceeds the scope of legislative power as circumscribed by the Constitution. That is to say that to withstand the strictures of the Establishment Clause there must be a secular legislative purpose and a primary effect that neither advances nor inhibits religion. The Free Exercise Clause, likewise considered many times here, withdraws from legislative power, state and federal, the exertion of any restraint on the free exercise of religion. Its purpose is to secure religious liberty in the individual by prohibiting any invasions thereof by civil authority. Hence it is necessary in a free exercise case for one to show the coercive effect of the enactment as it operates against him in the practice of his religion. The distinction between the two clauses is apparent—a violation of the Free Exercise Clause is predicated on coercion while the Establishment Clause violation need not be so attended.

Applying the Establishment Clause principles to the cases at bar we find that the States are requiring the selection and reading at the opening of the school day of verses from the Holy Bible and the recitation of the Lord's Prayer by the students in unison. These exercises are prescribed as part of the curricular activities of students who are required by law to attend school. They are held in the school buildings under the supervision and with the participation of teachers employed in those schools. . . . The trial court in [*Schempp*] has found that such an opening exercise is a religious ceremony and was intended by the State to be so. We agree with the trial court's finding as to the religious character of the exercises. Given that finding, the exercises and the law requiring them are in violation of the Establishment Clause.

There is no such specific finding as to the religious character of the exercises in [*Murray*] and the State contends (as does the State in [*Schempp*]) that the program is an effort to extend its benefits to all public school children without regard to their religious belief. Included within its secular purposes, it says, are the promotion of moral values, the contradiction to the materialistic trends of our times, the perpetuation of our institutions and the teaching of literature. The case came up on demurrer, of course, to a petition which alleged that the uniform practice under the rule had been to read from the King James version of the Bible and that the exercise was sectarian. The short answer, therefore, is that the religious character of the exercise was admitted by the State. But even if its purpose is not strictly religious, it is sought to be accomplished through readings, without comment, from the Bible. Surely the place of the Bible as an instrument of religion cannot be gainsaid, and the State's recognition of the pervading religious character of the ceremony is evident from the rule's specific permission of the alternative use of the Catholic Douay version as well as the recent amendment permitting nonattendance at the exercises. None of these factors is consistent with the contention that the Bible is here used either as an instrument for nonreligious moral inspiration or as a reference for the teaching of secular subjects.

The conclusion follows that in both cases the laws require religious exercises and such exercises are being conducted in direct violation of the rights of the appellees and petitioners. Nor are these required exercises mitigated by the fact that individual students may absent themselves upon parental request, for that fact furnishes no defense to a claim of unconstitutionality under the Establishment Clause. . . . Further, it is no defense to urge that the religious practices here may be relatively minor encroachments on the First Amendment. The breach of neutrality that is today a trickling stream may all too soon become a raging torrent and, in the words of Madison, "it is proper to take alarm at the first experiment on our liberties.". . .

It is insisted that unless these religious exercises are permitted a "religion of secularism" is established in the schools. We agree of course that the State may not establish a "religion of secularism" in the sense of affirmatively opposing or showing hostility to religion, thus "preferring those who believe in no religion over those who do believe." We do not agree, however, that this decision in any sense has that effect. In addition, it might well be said that one's education is not complete without a study of comparative religion or the history of religion and its relationship to the advancement of civilization. It certainly may be said that the Bible is worthy of study for its literary and historic qualities. Nothing we have said here indicates that such study of the Bible or of religion, when presented objectively as part of a secular program of education, may not be effected consistently with the First Amendment. But the exercises here do not fall into those categories. They are religious exercises, required by the States in violation of the command of the First Amendment that the Government maintain strict neutrality, neither aiding nor opposing religion.

Finally, we cannot accept that the concept of neutrality, which does not permit a State to require a religious exercise even with the consent of the majority of those affected, collides with the majority's right to free exercise of religion. While the Free Exercise Clause clearly prohibits the use of state action to deny the rights of free exercise to *anyone,* it has never meant that a majority could use the machinery of the State to practice its beliefs. Such a contention was effectively answered by Justice JACKSON for the Court in *West Virginia Board of Education v. Barnette*, 319 U.S. 624 (1943). . . .

The place of religion in our society is an exalted one, achieved through a long tradition of reliance on the home, the church and the inviolable citadel of the individual heart and mind. We have come to recognize through bitter experience that it is not within the power of government to invade that citadel, whether its purpose or effect be to aid or oppose, to advance or retard. In the relationship between man and religion, the State is firmly committed to a position of neutrality. Though the application of that rule requires interpretation of a delicate sort, the rule itself is clearly and concisely stated in the words of the First Amendment.

Justice DOUGLAS concurring.

I join the opinion of the Court and add a few words in explanation. . . .

In these cases we have no coercive religious exercise aimed at making the students conform. The prayers announced are not compulsory, though some may think they have that indirect effect because the nonconformist student may be induced to participate for fear of being called an "oddball." But that coercion, if it be present, has not been shown: so the vices of the present regimes are different.

These regimes violate the Establishment Clause in two different ways. In each case the State is conducting a religious exercise; and, as the Court holds, that cannot be done without violating the "neutrality" required of the State by the balance of power between individual, church and state that has been struck by the First Amendment. But the Establishment Clause is not limited to precluding the State itself from conducting religious exercises. It also forbids the State to employ its facilities or funds in a way that gives any church, or all churches, greater strength in our society than it would have by relying on its members alone. Thus, the present regimes must fall under that clause for the additional reason that public funds, though small in amount, are being used to promote a religious exercise. Through the mechanism of the State, all of the people are being required to finance a religious exercise that only some of the people want and that violates the sensibilities of others.

The most effective way to establish any institution is to finance it; and this truth is reflected in the appeals by church groups for public funds to finance their religious schools. Financing a church either in its strictly religious activities or in its other activities is equally unconstitutional, as I understand the Establishment Clause. Budgets for one activity may be technically separable from budgets for others. But the institution is an inseparable whole, a living organism, which is strengthened in proselytizing when it is strengthened in any department by contributions from other than its own members.

Justice BRENNAN concurring.

[T]he history which our prior decisions have summoned to aid interpretation of the Establishment Clause permits little doubt that its prohibition was designed comprehensively to prevent those official involvements of religion which would tend to foster or discourage religious worship or belief.

But an awareness of history and an appreciation of the aims of the Founding Fathers do not always resolve concrete problems. The specific question before us has, for example, aroused vigorous dispute whether the architects of the First Amendment—James Madison and Thomas Jefferson particularly—understood the prohibition against any "law respecting an establishment of religion" to reach devotional exercises in the public schools. . . .

A too literal quest for the advice of the Founding Fathers upon the issues of these cases seems to me futile and misdirected for several reasons: First, on our precise problem the historical record is at best ambiguous, and statements can readily be found to support either side of the proposition. The ambiguity of history is understandable if we recall the nature of the problems uppermost in the thinking of the statesmen who fashioned the religious guarantees; they were concerned with far more flagrant intrusions of government into the realm of religion than any that our century has witnessed. While it is clear to me that the Framers meant the Establishment Clause to prohibit more than the creation of an established federal church such as existed in England, I have no doubt that, in their preoccupation with the imminent question of established churches, they gave no distinct consideration to the particular question whether the clause also forbade devotional exercises in public institutions.

Second, the structure of American education has greatly changed since the First Amendment was adopted. In the context of our modern emphasis upon public education available to all citizens, any views of the eighteenth century as to whether the exercises at bar are an "establishment" offer little aid to decision. Education, as the Framers knew it, was in the main confined to private schools more often than not under strictly sectarian supervision. Only gradually did control of education pass largely to public officials. It would, therefore, hardly be significant if the fact was that the nearly universal devotional exercises in the schools of the young Republic did not provoke criticism; even today religious ceremonies in church-supported private schools are constitutionally unobjectionable.

Third, our religious composition makes us a vastly more diverse people than were our forefathers. They knew differences chiefly among Protestant sects. Today the Nation is far more heterogeneous religiously, including as it does substantial minorities not only of Catholics and Jews but as well of those who worship according to no version of the Bible and those who worship no God at all. In the face of such profound changes, practices which may have been objectionable to no one in the time of Jefferson and Madison may today be highly offensive to many persons, the deeply devout and the nonbelievers alike.

Whatever Jefferson or Madison would have thought of Bible reading or the recital of the Lord's Prayer in what few public schools existed in their day, our use of the history of their time must limit itself to broad purposes, not specific practices. By such a standard, I am persuaded, as is the Court, that the devotional exercises carried on in the Baltimore and Abington schools offend the First Amendment because they sufficiently threaten in our day those substantive evils the fear of which called forth the Establishment Clause of the First Amendment. . . .

Fourth, the American experiment in free public education available to all children has been guided in large measure by the dramatic evolution of the religious diversity among the population which our public schools serve. The interaction of these two important forces in our national life has placed in bold relief certain positive values in the consistent application to public institutions generally, and public schools particularly, of the constitutional decree against official involvements of religion which might produce the evils the Framers meant the Establishment Clause to forestall. The public schools are supported entirely, in most communities, by public funds—funds exacted not only from parents, nor alone from those who hold particular religious views, nor indeed from those who subscribe to any creed at all. It is implicit in the history and character of American public education that the public schools serve a uniquely *public* function: the training of American citizens in an atmosphere free of parochial, divisive, or separatist influences of any sort—an atmosphere in which children may assimilate a heritage common to all American groups and religions. . . .

Attendance at the public schools has never been compulsory; parents remain morally and constitutionally free to choose the academic environment in which they wish their children to be educated. The relationship of the Establishment Clause of the First Amendment to the public school system is preeminently that of reserving such a choice to the individual parent, rather than vesting it in the majority of voters of each State or school district. The choice which is thus preserved is between a public secular education with its uniquely democratic values, and some form of private or sectarian education, which offers values of its own. In my judgment the First Amendment forbids the State to inhibit that freedom of choice by diminishing the attractiveness of either alternative—either by restricting the liberty of the private schools to inculcate whatever values they wish, or by jeopardizing the freedom of the public schools from private or sectarian pressures. The choice between these very different forms of education is one—very much like the choice of whether or not to worship, which our Constitution leaves to the individual parent. It is no proper function of the state or local government to influence or restrict that election.

Justice GOLDBERG, with whom Justice HARLAN joined, concurred.

Justice STEWART dissented.

Lemon v. Kurtzman, Earley v. DiCenso, and *Robinson v. DiCenso,*
403 U.S. 602, 91 S.Ct. 2105 (1971)

These three cases brought controversies over laws in Pennsylvania and Rhode Island that provided for direct and indirect financial support of private primary and secondary schools, some of which were run by religious organizations. The cases were consolidated for oral argument and decision. Chief Justice Burger discusses the programs of each state at the outset of his opinion for the Court.

Chief Justice BURGER delivers the opinion of the Court.

Pennsylvania has adopted a statutory program that provides financial support to nonpublic elementary and secondary schools by way of reimbursement for the cost of teachers' salaries, textbooks, and instructional materials in specified secular subjects. Rhode Island has adopted a statute under which the State pays directly to teachers in nonpublic elementary schools a supplement of 15% of their annual salary. Under each statute state aid has been given to church-related educational institutions. We hold that both statutes are unconstitutional.

I

The Rhode Island Statute The Rhode Island Salary Supplement Act was enacted in 1969. It rests on the legislative finding that the quality of education available in nonpublic elementary schools has been jeopardized by the rapidly rising salaries needed to attract competent and dedicated teachers. The Act authorizes state officials to supplement the salaries of teachers of secular subjects in nonpublic elementary schools by paying directly to a teacher an amount not in excess of 15% of his current annual salary. As supplemented, however, a nonpublic school teacher's salary cannot exceed the maximum paid to teachers in the State's public schools, and the recipient must be certified by the state board of education in substantially the same manner as public school teachers.

In order to be eligible for the Rhode Island salary supplement, the recipient must teach in a nonpublic school at which the average per-pupil expenditure on secular education is less than the average in the State's public schools during a specified period. Appellant State Commissioner of Education also requires eligible schools to submit financial data. If this information indicates a per-pupil expenditure in excess of the statutory limitation, the records of the school in question must be examined in order to assess how much of the expenditure is attributable to secular education and how much to religious activity.

The Act also requires that teachers eligible for salary supplements must teach only those subjects that are offered in the State's public schools. They must use "only teaching materials which are used in the public schools." Finally, any teacher applying for a salary supplement must first agree in writing "not to teach a course in religion for so long as or during such time as he or she receives any salary supplements" under the Act. . . .

A three-judge federal court found that Rhode Island's nonpublic elementary schools accommodated approximately 25% of the State's pupils. About 95% of these pupils attended schools affiliated with the Roman Catholic church. To date some 250 teachers have applied for benefits under the Act. All of them are employed by Roman Catholic schools. . . .

The District Court concluded that the Act violated the Establishment Clause, holding that it fostered "excessive entanglement" between government and religion. In addition two judges thought that the Act had the impermissible effect of giving "significant aid to a religious enterprise." We affirm.

The Pennsylvania Statute Pennsylvania has adopted a program that has some but not all of the features of the Rhode Island program. The Pennsylvania Nonpublic Elementary and Secondary Education Act was passed in 1968 in response to a crisis that the Pennsylvania Legislature found existed in the State's nonpublic schools due to rapidly rising costs. . . .

The statute authorizes appellee state Superintendent of Public Instruction to "purchase" specified "secular educational services" from nonpublic schools. Under the "contracts" authorized by the statute, the State directly reimburses nonpublic schools solely for their actual expenditures for teachers' salaries, textbooks, and instructional materials. A school seeking reimbursement must maintain prescribed accounting procedures that identify the "separate" cost of the "secular educational service." These accounts are subject to state audit. . . .

There are several significant statutory restrictions on state aid. Reimbursement is limited to courses "presented in the curricula of the public schools." It is further limited "solely" to courses in the following "secular" subjects: mathematics, modern foreign languages, physical science, and physical education. Textbooks and instructional materials included in the program must be approved by the state Superintendent of Public Instruction. Finally, the statute prohibits reimbursement for any course that contains "any subject matter expressing religious teaching, or the morals or forms of worship of any sect.". . .

It appears that some $5 million has been expended annually under the Act. The State has now entered into contracts with some 1,181 nonpublic elementary and secondary schools with a student population of some 535,215 pupils—more than 20% of the total number of students in the State. More than 96% of these pupils attend church-related schools, and most of these schools are affiliated with the Roman Catholic church. . . .

A three-judge federal court . . . held that the Act violated neither the Establishment nor the Free Exercise Clause. . . . We reverse. . . .

II

The language of the Religion Clauses of the First Amendment is at best opaque, particularly when compared with other portions of the Amendment. Its authors did not simply prohibit the establishment of a state church or a state religion, an area history shows they regarded as very important and fraught with great dangers. Instead they commanded that there should be "no law *respecting* an establishment of religion." A law may be one "respecting" the forbidden objective while falling short of its total realization. A law "respecting" the proscribed result, that is, the establishment of religion, is not always easily identifiable as one violative of the Clause. A given law might not *establish* a state religion but nevertheless be one "respecting" that end in the sense of being a step that could lead to such establishment and hence offend the First Amendment. . . .

Every analysis in this area must begin with consideration of the cumulative criteria developed by the Court over many years. Three such tests may be learned from our cases. First, the statute must have a secular legislative purpose; second, its principal or primary effect must be one that neither advances or inhibits religion; finally, the statute must not foster "an excessive government Entanglement with religion.". . .

Inquiry into the legislative purposes of the Pennsylvania and Rhode Island statutes affords no basis for a conclusion that the legislative intent was to advance religion. On the contrary, the statutes themselves clearly state that they are intended to enhance the quality of the secular education in all schools covered by the compulsory attendance laws. There is no reason to believe the legislatures meant anything else. . . .

The legislatures of Rhode Island and Pennsylvania have concluded that secular and religious education are identifiable and separable. In the abstract we have no quarrel with this conclusion.

The two legislatures, however, have also recognized that church-related elementary and secondary schools have a significant religious mission and that a substantial portion of their activities is religiously oriented. They have therefore sought to create statutory restrictions designed to guarantee the separation between secular and religious educational functions and to ensure that State financial aid supports only the former. All these provisions are precautions taken in candid recognition that these programs approached, even if they did not intrude upon, the forbidden areas under the Religion Clauses. We need not decide whether these legislative precautions restrict the principal or primary effect of the programs to the point where they do not offend the Religion Clauses, for we conclude that the cumulative impact of the entire relationship arising under the statutes in each State involves excessive entanglement between government and religion.

III

In *Walz v. Tax Commission,* [397 U.S. 664 (1970)], the Court upheld state tax exemptions for real property owned by religious organizations and used for religious worship. That holding, however, tended to confine rather than enlarge the area of permissible state involvement with religious institutions by calling for close scrutiny of the degree of entanglement involved in the relationship. The objective is to prevent, as far as possible, the intrusion of either into the precincts of the other.

Our prior holdings do not call for total separation between church and state; total separation is not possible in an absolute sense. Some relationship between government and religious organizations is inevitable. . . . Fire inspections, building and zoning regulations, and state requirements under compulsory school-attendance laws are examples of necessary and permissible contacts. . . . Judicial caveats against entanglement must recognize that the line of separation, far from being a "wall," is a blurred, indistinct, and variable barrier depending on all the circumstances of a particular relationship.

This is not to suggest, however, that we are to engage in a legalistic minuet in which precise rules and forms must govern. A true minuet is a matter of pure form and style, the observance of which is itself the substantive end. Here we examine the form of the relationship for the light that it casts on the substance.

In order to determine whether the government entanglement with religion is excessive, we must examine the character and purposes of the institutions that are benefited, the nature of the aid that the State provides, and the resulting relationship between the government and the religious authority. . . . Here we find that both statutes foster an impermissible degree of entanglement.

(a) *Rhode Island program* The church schools involved in the program are located close to parish churches. . . . The school buildings contain identifying religious symbols such as crosses on the exterior and crucifixes, and religious paintings and statutes either in the classrooms or hallways. Although only approximately 30 minutes a day are devoted to direct religious instruction, there are religiously oriented extracurricular activities. Approximately two-thirds of the teachers in these schools are nuns of various religious orders. Their dedicated efforts provide an atmosphere in which religious instruction and religious vocations are natural and proper parts of life in such schools. . . .

This process of inculcating religious doctrine is, of course, enhanced by the impressionable age of the pupils, in primary schools particularly. In short, parochial schools involve substantial religious activity and purpose.

The substantial religious character of these church-related schools gives rise to entangling church-state relationships of the kind the Religion Clauses sought to avoid. . . .

The dangers and corresponding entanglements are enhanced by the particular form of aid that the Rhode Island Act provides. Our decisions from *Everson* to *Allen* have permitted the States to provide church-related schools with secular, neutral, or nonideological services, facilities, or materials. Bus transportation, school lunches, public health services, and secular textbooks supplied in common to all students were not thought to offend the Establishment Clause. . . .

In [*Board of Education v. Allen,* 392 U.S. 236 (1968)] the Court refused to make assumptions, on a meager record, about the religious content of the textbooks that the State would be asked to provide. We cannot, however, refuse here to recognize that teachers have a substantially different ideological character from books. In terms of potential for involving some aspect of faith or morals in secular subjects, a textbook's content is ascertainable, but a teacher's handling of a subject is not. We cannot ignore the danger that a teacher under religious control and discipline poses to the separation of the religious from the purely secular aspects of precollege education. The conflict of functions inheres in the situation.

In our view the record shows these dangers are present to a substantial degree. . . .

The schools are governed by the standards set forth in a "Handbook of School Regulations," which has the force of synodal law in the diocese. It emphasizes the role and importance of the teacher in parochial schools: "The prime factor for the success or the failure of the school is the spirit and personality, as well as the professional competency, of the teacher. . . ." The Handbook also states that: "Religious formation is not confined to formal courses; nor is it restricted to a single subject area.". . .

Several teachers testified, however, that they did not inject religion into their secular classes. . . . But what has been recounted suggests the potential if not actual hazards of this form of state aid. The teacher is employed by a religious organization, subject to the direction and discipline of religious authorities, and works in a system dedicated to rearing children in a particular faith. These controls are not lessened by the fact that most of the lay teachers are of the Catholic faith. Inevitably some of a teacher's responsibilities hover on the border between secular and religious orientation.

We need not and do not assume that teachers in parochial schools will be guilty of bad faith or any conscious design to evade the limitations imposed by the statute and the First Amendment. We simply recognize that a dedicated religious person, teaching in a school affiliated with his or her faith and operated to inculcate its tenets, will inevitably experience great difficulty in remaining religiously neutral. Doctrines and faith are not inculcated or advanced by neutrals. With the best of intentions such a teacher would find it hard to make a total separation between secular teaching and religious doctrine. What would appear to some to be essential to good citizenship might well for others border on or constitute instruction in religion. Further difficulties are inherent in the combination of religious discipline and the possibility of disagreement between teacher and religious authorities over the meaning of the statutory restrictions. . . .

The Rhode Island Legislature has not, and could not, provide state aid on the basis of a mere assumption that secular teachers under religious discipline can avoid conflicts. The State must be certain, given the Religion Clauses, that subsidized teachers do not inculcate religion—indeed the State here has undertaken to do so. To ensure that no trespass occurs, the State has therefore carefully conditioned its aid with pervasive restrictions. . . .

A comprehensive, discriminating, and continuing state surveillance will inevitably be required to ensure that these restrictions are obeyed and the First Amendment otherwise respected. Unlike a book, a teacher cannot be inspected once so as to determine the extent and intent of his or her personal beliefs and subjective acceptance of the limitations imposed by the First Amendment. These prophylactic contacts will involve excessive and enduring entanglement between state and church.

There is another area of entanglement in the Rhode Island program that gives concern. The statute excludes teachers employed by nonpublic schools whose average per-pupil expenditures on secular education equal or exceed the comparable figures for public schools. In the event that the total expenditures of an otherwise eligible school exceed this norm, the program requires the government to examine the school's records in order to determine how much of the total expenditures is attributable to secular education and how much to religious activity. This kind of state inspection and evaluation of the religious content of a religious organization is fraught with the sort of entanglement that the Constitution forbids. It is a relationship pregnant with dangers of excessive government direction of church schools and hence of churches. . . .

(b) *Pennsylvania program* As we noted earlier, the very restrictions and surveillance necessary to ensure that teachers play a strictly nonideological role give rise to entanglements between church and state. The Pennsylvania statute, like that of Rhode Island, fosters this kind of relationship. . . .

The Pennsylvania statute, moreover, has the further defect of providing state financial aid directly to the church-related schools. This factor distinguishes both *Everson* and *Allen,* for in both those cases the Court was careful to point out that state aid was provided to the student and his parents—not to the church-related school. . . . The history of government grants of a continuing cash subsidy indicates that such programs have almost always been accompanied by varying measures of control and surveillance. The government cash grants before us now provide no basis for predicting that comprehensive measures of surveillance and controls will not follow. . . .

IV

A broader base of entanglement of yet a different character is presented by the devisive political potential of these state programs. In a community where such a large number of pupils are served by church-related schools, it can be assumed that state assistance will entail considerable political activity. Partisans of parochial schools, understandably concerned with rising costs and sincerely dedicated to both the religious and secular educational missions of their schools, will inevitably champion this cause and promote political action to achieve their goals. Those who oppose state aid, whether for constitutional, religious, or fiscal reasons, will inevitably respond and employ all of the usual political campaign techniques to prevail. Candidates will be forced to declare and voters to choose. . . .

Ordinarily political debate and division, however vigorous or even partisan, are normal and healthy manifestations of our democratic system of government, but political division along religious lines was one of the principal evils against which the First Amendment was intended to protect. The potential divisiveness of such conflict is a threat to the normal political process. It conflicts with our whole history and tradition to permit questions of the Religion Clauses to assume such importance in our legislatures and in our elections that they could divert attention from the myriad issues and problems that confront every level of government. The highways of church and state relationships are not likely to be one-way streets, and the Constitution's authors sought to protect religious worship from the pervasive power of government. The history of many countries attests to the hazards of religion's intruding into the political arena or of political power intruding into the legitimate and free exercise of religious belief. . . .

The potential for political divisiveness related to religious belief and practice is aggravated in these two statutory programs by the need for continuing annual appropriations and the likelihood of larger and larger demands as costs and populations grow. The Rhode Island District Court found that the parochial school system's "monumental and deepening financial crisis" would "inescapably" require larger annual appropriations subsidizing greater percentages of the salaries of lay teachers. Although no facts have been developed in this respect in the Pennsylvania case, it appears that such pressures for expanding aid have already required the state legislature to include a portion of the state revenues from cigarette taxes in the program.

We have no long history of state aid to church-related educational institutions comparable to 200 years of tax exemption for churches. Indeed, the state programs before us today represent something of an innovation. We have already noted that modern governmental programs have self-perpetuating and self-expanding propensities. These internal pressures are only enhanced when the schemes involve institutions whose legitimate needs are growing and whose interests have substantial political support. Nor can we fail to see that in constitutional adjudication some steps, which when taken were thought to approach "the verge," have become the platform for yet further steps. A certain momentum develops in constitutional theory and it can be a "downhill thrust" easily set in motion but difficult to retard or stop. Development by momentum is not invariably bad; indeed, it is the way the common law has grown, but it is a force to be recognized and reckoned with. The dangers are increased by the difficulty of perceiving in advance exactly where the "verge" of the precipice lies. As well as constituting an independent evil against which the Religion Clauses were intended to protect, involvement or entanglement between government and religion serves as a warning signal. . . .

The merit and benefits of these schools . . . are not the issue before us in these cases. The sole question is whether state aid to these schools can be squared with the dictates of the Religion Clauses. Under our system the choice has been made that government is to be entirely excluded from the area of religious instruction and churches excluded from the affairs of government. The Constitution decrees that religion must be a private matter for the individual, the family, and the institutions of private choice, and that while some involvement and entanglement are inevitable, lines must be drawn.

Justice MARSHALL did not participate in the consideration or decision of *Lemon.*

Justice DOUGLAS, whom Justice BLACK joins, concurring.

We said in unequivocal words in *Everson v. Board of Education,* 330 U.S. 1 [1947], "No tax in any amount, large or small, can be levied to support any religious activities or institutions, whatever they may be called, or whatever form they may adopt to teach or practice religion." We reiterated the same idea in *Zorach v. Clauson,* [343 U.S. 306 (1952)]; and in *McGowan v. Maryland,* [366 U.S. 420 (1961)]; and in *Torcaso v. Watkins,* [367 U.S. 488 (1961)]. We repeated the same idea in *McCollum v. Board of Education,* and added that a State's tax-supported public schools could not be used "for the dissemination of religious doctrines" nor could a State provide the church "pupils for their religious classes through use of the state's compulsory public school machinery.". . . .

Yet in spite of this long and consistent history there are those who have the courage to announce that a State may nonetheless finance the *secular* part of a sectarian school's educational program. That, however, makes a grave constitutional decision turn merely on cost accounting and bookkeeping entries. A history class, a literature class, or a science class in a parochial school is not a separate institute; it is part of the organic whole which the State subsidizes. The funds are used in these cases to pay or help pay the salaries of teachers in parochial schools; and the presence of teachers is critical to the essential purpose of the parochial school, *viz.*, to advance the religious endeavors of the particular church. It matters not that the teacher receiving taxpayers' money only teaches religion a fraction of the time. Nor does it matter that he or she teaches no religion. The school is an organism living on one budget. What the taxpayers give for salaries of those who teach only the humanities or science without any trace of proseletyzing enables the school to use all of its own funds for religious training. . . .

In my view the taxpayers' forced contribution to the parochial schools in the present cases violates the First Amendment.

Stone v. Graham
449 U.S. 41, 101 S.Ct. 192 (1980)

Sydell Stone and several other parents sought an injunction preventing James Graham, superintendent of public schools in Kentucky, from enforcing a state law requiring the posting of a copy of the Ten Commandments on the wall of each public classroom in that state. A lower court upheld the constitutionality of the statute and on appeal the Kentucky Supreme Court affirmed. Stone then made an appeal to the Supreme Court.

PER CURIAM.

We reverse. . . .

We conclude that Kentucky's statute requiring the posting of the Ten Commandments in public schoolrooms had no secular legislative purpose, and is therefore unconstitutional.

The Commonwealth insists that the statute in question serves a secular legislative purpose, observing that the legislature required the following notation in small print at the bottom of each display of the Ten Commandments: "The secular application of the Ten Commandments is clearly seen in its adoption as the fundamental legal code of Western Civilization and the Common Law of the United States." 1978 Ky. Acts, ch. 436, § 1 (effective June 17, 1978), Ky.Rev.Stat. § 158.178 (1980).

The trial court found the "avowed" purpose of the statute to be secular, even as it labeled the statutory declaration "self-serving." Under this Court's rulings, however, such an "avowed" secular purpose is not sufficient to avoid conflict with the First Amendment. In *Abington School District v. Schempp,* 374 U.S. 203 (1963), this Court held unconstitutional the daily reading of Bible verses and the Lord's Prayer in the public schools, despite the school district's assertion of such secular purposes as "the promotion of moral values, the contradiction to the materialistic trends of our times, the perpetuation of our institutions and the teaching of literature."

The pre-eminent purpose for posting the Ten Commandments

on schoolroom walls is plainly religious in nature. The Ten Commandments are undeniably a sacred text in the Jewish and Christian faiths, and no legislative recitation of a supposed secular purpose can blind us to that fact. The Commandments do not confine themselves to arguably secular matters, such as honoring one's parents, killing or murder, adultery, stealing, false witness, and covetousness. See Exodus 20: 12–17; Deuteronomy 5: 16–21. Rather, the first part of the Commandments concerns the religious duties of believers: worshipping the Lord God alone, avoiding idolatry, not using the Lord's name in vain, and observing the Sabbath Day. See Exodus 20: 1–11; Deuteronomy 5: 6–15.

This is not a case in which the Ten Commandments are integrated into the school curriculum, where the Bible may constitutionally be used in an appropriate study of history, civilization, ethics, comparative religion, or the like. . . .

It does not matter that the posted copies of the Ten Commandments are financed by voluntary private contributions, for the mere posting of the copies under the auspices of the legislature provides the "official support of the State Government" that the Establishment Clause prohibits. Nor is it significant that the Bible verses involved in this case are merely posted on the wall, rather than read aloud as in *Schempp* and *Engel*, for "it is no defense to urge that the religious practices here may be relatively minor encroachments on the First Amendment." *Abington School District v. Schempp.* We conclude that Ky.Rev.Stat. § 158.178 (1980) violates the first part of the *Lemon v. Kurtzman*, [403 U.S. 602 (1971)], test, and thus the Establishment Clause of the Constitution.

Chief Justice BURGER and Justices BLACKMUN and Justice STEWART dissented, noting that they thought the Court should have heard oral arguments on the case, rather than summarily deciding and reversing the courts of Kentucky.

Justice REHNQUIST dissenting.

With no support beyond its own *ipse dixit*, the Court concludes that the Kentucky statute involved in this case "has *no* secular legislative purpose," (emphasis supplied), and that "[t]he pre-eminent purpose for posting the Ten Commandments on schoolroom walls is plainly religious in nature." This even though, as the trial court found, "[t]he General Assembly thought the statute had a secular legislative purpose and specifically said so." The Court's summary rejection of a secular purpose articulated by the legislature and confirmed by the state court is without precedent in Establishment Clause jurisprudence. This Court regularly looks to legislative articulations of a statute's purpose in Establishment Clause cases and accords such pronouncements the deference they are due. . . . The fact that the asserted secular purpose may overlap with what some may see as a religious objective does not render it unconstitutional. As this Court stated in *McGowan v. Maryland*, [366 U.S. 420] (1961), in upholding the validity of Sunday closing laws, "the present purpose and effect of most of [these laws] is to provide a uniform day of rest for all citizens; the fact that this day is Sunday, a day of particular significance for the dominant Christian sects, does not bar the state from achieving its secular goals.". . .

The Court rejects the secular purpose articulated by the State because the Decalogue is "undeniably a sacred text." It is equally undeniable, however, as the elected representatives of Kentucky determined, that the Ten Commandments have had a significant impact on the development of secular legal codes of the Western World. . . .

The Establishment Clause does not require that the public sector be insulated from all things which may have a religious significance or origin. . . .

I therefore dissent from what I cannot refrain from describing as a cavalier summary reversal, without benefit of oral argument or briefs on the merits, of the highest court of Kentucky.

Wallace v. Jaffree
472 U.S. 38, 105 S.Ct. 2479 (1985)

The pertinent facts in this controversy, involving a challenge to Georgia's law requiring that each school day begin with a moment of silent prayer or meditation, are stated by Justice Stevens in his opinion for the Court. (Excerpts from the lower court's opinion are reprinted in Chapter 2.)

Justice STEVENS delivers the opinion of the Court.

Appellee Ishmael Jaffree is a resident of Mobile County, Alabama. On May 28, 1982, he filed a complaint on behalf of three of his minor children; two of them were second-grade students and the third was then in kindergarten. The complaint named members of the Mobile County School Board, various school officials, and the minor plaintiffs' three teachers as defendants. The complaint alleged that the appellees brought the action "seeking principally a declaratory judgment and an injunction restraining the Defendants and each of them from maintaining or allowing the maintenance of regular religious prayer services or other forms of religious observances in the Mobile County Public Schools in violation of the First Amendment as made applicable to states by the Fourteenth Amendment to the United States Constitution." The complaint further alleged that two of the children had been subjected to various acts of religious indoctrination "from the beginning of the school year in September, 1981"; that the defendant teachers had "on a daily basis" led their classes in saying certain prayers in unison; that the minor children were exposed to ostracism from their peer group class members if they did not participate; and that Ishmael Jaffree had repeatedly but unsuccessfully requested that the devotional services be stopped. . . .

The District Court found that during that academic year each of the minor plaintiffs' teachers had led classes in prayer activities, even after being informed of appellees' objections to these activities.

In its lengthy conclusions of law, the District Court reviewed a number of opinions of this Court interpreting the Establishment Clause of the First Amendment, and then embarked on a fresh examination of the question whether the First Amendment imposes any barrier to the establishment of an official religion by the State of Alabama. After reviewing at length what it perceived to be newly discovered historical evidence, the District Court concluded that "the establishment clause of the first amendment to the United States Constitution does not prohibit the state from establishing a religion." In a separate opinion, the District Court dismissed appellees' challenge to the three Alabama statutes because of a failure to state any claim for which relief could be granted. The court's dismissal of this challenge was also based on its conclusion that the Establishment Clause did not bar the States from establishing a religion.

The Court of Appeals . . . not surprisingly, reversed. . . .

Our unanimous affirmance of the Court of Appeals' judgment . . . makes it unnecessary to comment at length on the District Court's remarkable conclusion that the Federal Constitution imposes no obstacle to Alabama's establishment of a state religion. Before analyzing the precise issue that is presented to us, it is nevertheless appropriate to recall how firmly embedded in our constitutional jurisprudence is the proposition that the several States have no greater power to restrain the individual freedoms protected by the First Amendment than does the Congress of the United States. . . .

When the Court has been called upon to construe the breadth of the Establishment Clause, it has examined the criteria developed over a period of years. Thus, in *Lemon v. Kurtzman*, 403 U.S. 602 (1972), we wrote:

"Every analysis in this area must begin with consideration of the cumulative criteria developed by the Court over many years. Three such tests may be gleaned from our cases. First, the statute must have a secular legislative purpose; second, its principal or primary effect must be one that neither advances nor inhibits religion . . . finally, the statute must not foster 'an excessive government entanglement with religion.' ". . . It is the first of these three criteria that is most plainly implicated by this case. As the District Court correctly recognized, no consideration of the second or third criteria is necessary if a statute does not have a clearly secular purpose. For even though a statute that is motivated in part by a religious purpose may satisfy the first criterion, see, *e.g., Abington School Dist. v. Schempp,* . . . the First Amendment requires that a statute must be invalidated if it is entirely motivated by a purpose to advance religion."

In applying the purpose test, it is appropriate to ask "whether government's actual purpose is to endorse or disapprove of religion." In this case, the answer to that question is dispositive. For the record not only provides us with an unambiguous affirmative answer, but it also reveals that the enactment of [the Alabama law] was not motivated by any clearly secular purpose—indeed, the statute had *no* secular purpose.

The sponsor of the bill that became [law], Senator Donald Holmes, inserted into the legislative record—apparently without dissent—a statement indicating that the legislation was an "effort to return voluntary prayer" to the public schools. Later Senator Holmes confirmed this purpose before the District Court. In response to the question whether he had any purpose for the legislation other than returning voluntary prayer to public schools, he stated, "No, I did not have no other purpose in mind." The State did not present evidence of *any* secular purpose. . . .

We must, therefore, conclude that the Alabama Legislature intended to change existing law and that it was motivated by the same purpose that the Governor's Answer to the Second Amended Complaint expressly admitted; that the statement inserted in the legislative history revealed; and that Senator Holmes' testimony frankly described. The Legislature enacted [the statute authorizing teachers to lead students in a moment of "silent meditation or voluntary prayer"] despite the existence of [an earlier law permitting teachers to begin each school day with a period of silence "for meditation"] for the sole purpose of expressing the State's endorsement of prayer activities for one minute at the beginning of each school day. The addition of "or voluntary prayer" indicates that the State intended to characterize prayer as a favored practice. Such an endorsement is not consistent with the established principle that the Government must pursue a course of complete neutrality toward religion.

The importance of that principle does not permit us to treat this as an inconsequential case involving nothing more than a few words of symbolic speech on behalf of the political majority. For whenever the State itself speaks on a religious subject, one of the questions that we must ask is "whether the Government intends to convey a message of endorsement or disapproval of religion." The well-supported concurrent findings of the District Court and the Court of Appeals—that [the Alabama statute] was intended to convey a message of State-approval of prayer activities in the public schools—make it unnecessary, and indeed inappropriate, to evaluate the practical significance of the addition of the words "or voluntary prayer" to the statute. Keeping in mind, as we must, "both the fundamental place held by the Establishment Clause in our constitutional scheme and the myriad, subtle ways in which Establishment Clause values can be eroded," we conclude that [the statute] lates the First Amendment.

The judgment of the Court of Appeals is affirmed.

Justice POWELL concurring.

My concurrence is prompted by Alabama's persistence in attempting to institute state-sponsored prayer in the public schools by enacting three successive statutes. I agree fully with Justice O'CONNOR's assertion that some moment-of-silence statutes may be constitutional, a suggestion set forth in the Court's opinion as well.

Justice O'CONNOR concurring.

I write separately to identify the peculiar features of the Alabama law that render it invalid, and to explain why moment of silence laws in other States do not necessarily manifest the same infirmity. . . .

It once appeared that the Court had developed a workable standard by which to identify impermissible government establishments of religion. See *Lemon v. Kurtzman* (1971). Under the now familiar *Lemon* test, statutes must have both a secular legislative purpose and a principal or primary effect that neither advances nor inhibits religion, and in addition they must not foster excessive government entanglement with religion. Despite its initial promise, the *Lemon* test has proven problematic: The required inquiry into "entanglement" has been modified and questioned, see *Mueller v. Allen,* 463 U.S. 388 (1983), and in one case we have upheld state action against an Establishment Clause challenge without applying the *Lemon* test at all. *Marsh v. Chambers,* 463 U.S. 783 (1983). . . .

I am not ready to abandon all aspects of the *Lemon* test. I do believe, however, that the standards announced in *Lemon* should be reexamined and refined in order to make them more useful in achieving the underlying purpose of the First Amendment. We must strive to do more than erect a constitutional "signpost," to be followed or ignored in a particular case as our predilections may dictate. Instead, our goal should be "to frame a principle for constitutional adjudication that is not only grounded in the history and language of the first amendment, but one that is also capable of consistent application to the relevant problems.". . .

[R]eligious liberty protected by the Establishment Clause is infringed when the government makes adherence to religion relevant to a person's standing in the political community. Direct government action endorsing religion or a particular religious practice is invalid under this approach because it "sends a message to nonadherents that they are outsiders, not full members of the political community, and an accompanying message to adherents that they are insiders, favored members of the political community." Under this view, *Lemon's* inquiry as to the purpose and effect of a statute requires courts examine whether government's purpose is to endorse religion and whether the statute actually conveys a message of endorsement.

The endorsement test is useful because of the analytic content it gives to the *Lemon*-mandated inquiry into legislative purpose and effect. In this country, church and state must necessarily operate within the same community. Because of this co-existence, it is inevitable that the secular interests of Government and the religious interests of various sects and their adherents will frequently intersect, conflict, and combine. A statute that ostensibly promotes a secular interest often has an incidental or even a primary effect of helping or hindering a sectarian belief. Chaos would ensue if every such statute were invalid under the Establishment Clause. For example, the State could not criminalize murder for fear that it would thereby promote the Biblical command against killing. The task for the Court is to sort out those statutes and government practices whose purpose and effect go against the grain of religious liberty protected by the First Amendment.

The endorsement test does not preclude government from acknowledging religion or from taking religion into account in making law and policy. It does preclude government from conveying or attempting to convey a message that religion or a particular religious belief is favored or preferred. Such an endorsement infringes the religious liberty of the nonadherent, for "[w]hen the power, prestige and financial support of government is placed behind a particular religious belief, the indirect coercive pressure upon religious minorities to conform to the prevailing officially approved religion is plain." *Engel v. Vitale,* [370 U.S. 421 (1962)]. At issue today is whether state moment of silence statues in general, and Alabama's moment of silence statute in particular, embody an impermissible endorsement of prayer in public schools.

Twenty-five states permit or require public school teachers to have students observe a moment of silence in their classrooms. A few statutes provide that the moment of silence is for the purpose of meditation alone. The typical statute, however, calls for a moment of silence at the beginning of the school day during which students may meditate, pray, or reflect on the activities of the day. . . .

Relying on this Court's decisions disapproving vocal prayer and Bible reading in the public schools, see *Abington School District v. Schempp,* [374 U.S. 203 (1963)]; [and] *Engel v. Vitale,* the courts that have struck down the moment of silence statutes generally conclude that their purpose and effect is to encourage prayer in public schools.

The *Engel* and *Abington* decisions are not dispositive on the constitutionality of moment of silence laws. In those cases, public school teachers and students led their classes in devotional exercises. . . . The Court reviewed the purpose and effect of the statutes, concluded that they required religious exercises, and therefore found them to violate the Establishment Clause. Under all of these statutes, a student who did not share the religious beliefs expressed in the course of the exercise was left with the choice of participating, thereby compromising the nonadherent's beliefs, or withdrawing, thereby calling attention to his or her non-conformity. The decisions acknowledged the coercion implicit under the statutory schemes, but they expressly turned only on the fact that the government was sponsoring a manifestly religious exercise.

A state sponsored moment of silence in the public schools is different from state sponsored vocal prayer or Bible reading. First, a moment of silence is not inherently religious. Silence, unlike prayer or Bible reading, need not be associated with a religious exercise. Second, a pupil who participates in a moment of silence need not compromise his or her beliefs. During a moment of silence, a student who objects to prayer is left to his or her own thoughts, and is not compelled to listen to the prayers or thoughts of others. For these simple reasons, a moment of silence statute does not stand or fall under the Establishment Clause according to how the Court regards vocal prayer or Bible reading. . . . It is difficult to discern a serious threat to religious liberty from a room of silent, thoughtful schoolchildren.

By mandating a moment of silence, a State does not necessarily endorse any activity that might occur during the period. Even if a statute specifies that a student may choose to pray silently during a quiet moment, the State has not thereby encouraged prayer over other specified alternatives. Nonetheless, it is also possible that a moment of silence statute, either as drafted or as actually implemented, could effectively favor the child who prays over the child who does not. For example, the message of endorsement would seem inescapable if the teacher exhorts children to use the designated time to pray. Similarly, the face of the statute or its legislative history may clearly establish that it seeks to encourage or promote voluntary prayer over other alternatives, rather than merely provide a quiet moment that may be dedicated to prayer by those so inclined. The crucial question is whether the State has conveyed or attempted to convey the message that children should use the moment of silence for prayer. This question cannot be answered in the abstract, but instead requires courts to examine the history, language, and administration of a particular statute to determine whether it operates as an endorsement of religion. . . .

Before reviewing Alabama's moment of silence law to determine whether it endorses prayer, some general observations on the proper scope of the inquiry are in order. First, the inquiry into the purpose of the legislature in enacting a moment of silence law should be deferential and limited. In determining whether the government intends a moment of silence statute to convey a message of endorsement or disapproval of religion, a court has no license to psychoanalyze the legislators. If a legislature expresses a plausible secular purpose for a moment of silence statute in either the text or the legislative history, or if the statute disclaims an intent to encourage prayer over alternatives during a moment of silence, then courts should generally defer to that stated intent. . . . The relevant issue is whether an objective observer, acquainted with the text, legislative history, and implementation of the statute, would perceive it as a state endorsement of prayer in public schools. . . .

A moment of silence law that is clearly drafted and implemented so as to permit prayer, meditation, and reflection within the prescribed period, without endorsing one alternative over the others, should pass this test.

The analysis above suggests that moment of silence laws in many States should pass Establishment Clause scrutiny because they do not favor the child who chooses to pray during a moment of silence over the child who chooses to meditate or reflect. [The Alabama statute] does not stand on the same footing. However deferentially one examines its text and legislative history, however objectively one views the message attempted to be conveyed to the public, the conclusion is unavoidable that the purpose of the statute is to endorse prayer in public schools. I accordingly agree . . . that the Alabama statute has a purpose which is in violation of the Establishment Clause, and cannot be upheld. . . .

In his dissenting opinion, Justice REHNQUIST suggests that a long line of this Court's decisions are inconsistent with the intent of the drafters of the Bill of Rights. He urges the Court to correct the historical inaccuracies in its past decisions by embracing a far more restricted interpretation of the Establishment

Clause, an interpretation that presumably would permit vocal group prayer in public schools. . . .

Justice REHNQUIST does not assert, however, that the drafters of the First Amendment expressed a preference for prayer in public schools, or that the practice of prayer in public schools enjoyed uninterrupted government endorsement from the time of enactment of the Bill of Rights to the present era. The simple truth is that free public education was virtually non-existent in the late eighteenth century. Since there then existed few government-run schools, it is unlikely that the persons who drafted the First Amendment, or the state legislators who ratified it, anticipated the problems of interaction of church and state in the public schools. Even at the time of adoption of the Fourteenth Amendment, education in Southern States was still primarily in private hands, and the movement toward free public schools supported by general taxation had not taken hold.

This uncertainty as to the intent of the Framers of the Bill of Rights does not mean we should ignore history for guidance on the role of religion in public education. The Court has not done so. When the intent of the Framers is unclear, I believe we must employ both history and reason in our analysis. The primary issue raised by Justice REHNQUIST's dissent is whether the historical fact that our Presidents have long called for public prayers of Thanks should be dispositive on the constitutionality of prayer in public schools. I think not. At the very least, Presidential proclamations are distinguishable from school prayer in that they are received in a non-coercive setting and are primarily directed at adults, who presumably are not readily susceptible to unwilling religious indoctrination. This Court's decisions have recognized a distinction when government sponsored religious exercises are directed at impressionable children who are required to attend school, for then government endorsement is much more likely to result in coerced religious beliefs. Although history provides a touchstone for constitutional problems, the Establishment Clause concern for religious liberty is dispositive here.

Chief Justice BURGER dissenting.

Some who trouble to read the opinions in this case will find it ironic—perhaps even bizarre—that on the very day we heard arguments in this case, the Court's session opened with an invocation for Divine protection. Across the park a few hundred yards away, the House of Representatives and the Senate regularly open each session with a prayer. These legislative prayers are not just one minute in duration, but are extended, thoughtful invocations and prayers for Divine guidance. They are given, as they have been since 1789, by clergy appointed as official Chaplains and paid from the Treasury of the United States. Congress has also provided chapels in the Capitol, at public expense, where Members and others may pause for prayer, meditation—or a moment of silence.

Inevitably some wag is bound to say that the Court's holding today reflects a belief that the historic practice of the Congress and this Court is justified because members of the Judiciary and Congress are more in need of Divine guidance than are schoolchildren. Still others will say that all this controversy is "much ado about nothing," since no power on earth—including this Court and Congress—can stop any teacher from opening the school day with a moment of silence for pupils to meditate, to plan their day—or to pray if they voluntarily elect to do so.

I make several points about today's curious holding.

(a) It makes no sense to say that Alabama has "endorsed prayer" by merely enacting a new statute "to specify expressly that voluntary prayer is *one* of the authorized activities during a moment of silence" (O'CONNOR, J., concurring in the judgment) (emphasis added). To suggest that a moment-of-silence statute that includes the word "prayer" unconstitutionally endorses religion, while one that simply provides for a moment of silence does not, manifests not neutrality but hostility toward religion.

(b) The inexplicable aspect of the foregoing opinions; however, is what they advance as support for the holding concerning the purpose of the Alabama legislature. Rather than determining legislative purpose from the face of the statute as a whole, the opinions rely on three factors in concluding that the Alabama legislature had a "wholly religious" purpose for enacting the statute under review: (i) statements of the statute's sponsor, (ii) admissions in Governor James' Answer to the Second Amended Complaint, and (iii) the difference between [the present statute] and its predecessor statute.

Curiously, the opinions do not mention that *all* of the sponsor's statements relied upon—including the statement "inserted" into the Senate Journal—were made *after* the legislature had passed the statute; indeed, the testimony that the Court finds critical was given well over a year after the statute was enacted. . . . [T]here is not a shred of evidence that the legislature as a whole shared the sponsor's motive or that a majority in either house was even aware of the sponsor's view of the bill when it was passed. The sole relevance of the sponsor's statements, therefore, is that they reflect the personal, subjective motives of a single legislator. No case in the 195-year history of this Court supports the disconcerting idea that postenactment statements by individual legislators are relevant in determining the constitutionality of legislation. . . .

(c) The Court's extended treatment of the "test" of *Lemon* suggests a naive preoccupation with an easy, bright-line approach for addressing constitutional issues. We have repeatedly cautioned that *Lemon* did not establish a rigid caliper capable of resolving every Establishment Clause issue, but that it sought only to provide "signposts.". . .

(d) The notion that the Alabama statute is a step toward creating an established church borders on, if it does not trespass into the ridiculous. The statute does not remotely threaten religious liberty; it affirmatively furthers the values of religious freedom and tolerance that the Establishment Clause was designed to protect.

The Court today has ignored the wise admonition of Justice GOLDBERG that "the measure of constitutional adjudication is the ability and willingness to distinguish between real threat and mere shadow." *School District v. Schempp* (1963) (concurring opinion). The innocuous statute that the Court strikes down does not even rise to the level of "mere shadow." Justice O'CONNOR paradoxically acknowledges, "It is difficult to discern a serious threat to religious liberty from a room of silent, thoughtful schoolchildren." I would add to that, "even if they choose to pray."

Justice WHITE dissenting.

As I read the filed opinions, a majority of the Court would approve statutes that provided for a moment of silence but did not mention prayer. But if a student asked whether he could pray during that moment, it is difficult to believe that the teacher could not answer in the affirmative. If that is the case, I would not invalidate a statute that at the outset provided the legislative answer to the question "May I pray?" This is so even if the Alabama statute is infirm, which I do not believe it is, because of its peculiar legislative history.

I appreciate Justice REHNQUIST's explication of the history of the religion clauses of the First Amendment. Against that history, it would be quite understandable if we undertook to reassess our cases dealing with these clauses, particularly those dealing with the Establishment Clause. Of course, I have been out of step with many of the Court's decisions dealing with this subject matter, and it is thus not surprising that I would support a basic reconsideration of our precedents.

Justice REHNQUIST dissenting.

Thirty-eight years ago this Court, in *Everson v. Board of Education* [330 U.S. 1] (1947) summarized its exegesis of Establishment Clause doctrine thus:

"In the words of Jefferson, the clause against establishment of religion by law was intended to erect 'a wall of separation between church and State.' *Reynolds v. United States,* [98 U.S. 145 (1879).]"

This language from *Reynolds,* a case involving the Free Exercise Clause of the First Amendment rather than the Establishment Clause, quoted from Thomas Jefferson's letter to the Danbury Baptist Association the phrase "I contemplate with sovereign reverence that act of the whole American people which declared that their legislature should 'make no law respecting an establishment of religion, or prohibiting the free exercise thereof,' thus building a wall of separation between church and State."

It is impossible to build sound constitutional doctrine upon a mistaken understanding of constitutional history, but unfortunately the Establishment Clause has been expressly freighted with Jefferson's misleading metaphor for nearly forty years. Thomas Jefferson was of course in France at the time the constitutional amendments known as the Bill of Rights were passed by Congress and ratified by the states. His letter to the Danbury Baptist Association was a short note of courtesy, written fourteen years after the amendments were passed by Congress. He would seem to any detached observer as a less than ideal source of contemporary history as to the meaning of the Religion Clauses of the First Amendment.

Jefferson's fellow Virginian James Madison, with whom he was joined in the battle for the enactment of the Virginia Statute of Religious Liberty of 1786, did play as large a part as anyone in the drafting of the Bill of Rights. He had two advantages over Jefferson in this regard: he was present in the United States, and he was a leading member of the First Congress. But when we turn to the record of the proceedings in the First Congress leading up to the adoption of the Establishment Clause of the Constitution, including Madison's significant contributions thereto, we see a far different picture of its purpose than the highly simplified "wall of separation between church and State.". . .

On the basis of the record of these proceedings in the House of Representatives, James Madison was undoubtedly the most important architect among the members of the House of the amendments which became the Bill of Rights, but it was James Madison speaking as an advocate of sensible legislative compromise, not as an advocate of incorporating the Virginia Statute of Religious Liberty into the United States Constitution. During the ratification debate in the Virginia Convention, Madison had actually opposed the idea of any Bill of Rights. His sponsorship of the amendments in the House was obviously not that of a zealous believer in the necessity of the Religion Clauses, but of one who felt it might do some good, could do no harm, and would satisfy those who had ratified the Constitution on the condition that Congress propose a Bill of Rights. His original language "nor shall any national religion be established" obviously does not conform to the "wall of separation" between church and State idea which latter day commentators have ascribed to him. His explanation on the floor of the meaning of his language—"that Congress should not establish a religion, and enforce the legal observation of it by law" is of the same ilk. When he replied to Huntington in the debate over the proposal which came from the Select Committee of the House, he urged that the language "no religion shall be established by law" should be amended by inserting the word "national" in front of the word "religion."

It seems indisputable from these glimpses of Madison's thinking, as reflected by actions on the floor of the House in 1789, that he saw the amendment as designed to prohibit the establishment of a national religion, and perhaps to prevent discrimination among sects. He did not see it as requiring neutrality on the part of government between religion and irreligion. Thus the Court's opinion in *Everson*—while correct in bracketing Madison and Jefferson together in their exertions in their home state leading to the enactment of the Virginia Statute of Religious Liberty—is totally incorrect in suggesting that Madison carried these views onto the floor of the United States House of Representatives when he proposed the language which would ultimately become the Bill of Rights.

The repetition of this error in the Court's opinion in [*McCollum v. Board of Education* (1948) and *Engel v. Vitale* (1962)] does not make it any sounder historically. Finally, in *Abington School Board District v. Schempp* [1963], the Court made the truly remarkable statement that "the views of Madison and Jefferson, preceded by Roger Williams came to be incorporated not only in the Federal Constitution but likewise in those of most of our States" (footnote omitted). On the basis of what evidence we have, this statement is demonstrably incorrect as a matter of history. And its repetition in varying forms in succeeding opinions of the Court can give it no more authority than it possesses as a matter of fact; *stare decisis* may bind courts as to matters of law, but it cannot bind them as to matters of history. . . .

None of the other Members of Congress who spoke during the August 15th debate expressed the slightest indication that they thought the language before them from the Select Committee, or the evil to be aimed at, would require that the Government be absolutely neutral as between religion and irreligion. The evil to be aimed at, so far as those who spoke were concerned, appears to have been the establishment of a national church, and perhaps the preference of one religious sect over another, but it was definitely not concern about whether the Government might aid all religions evenhandedly. . . .

The actions of the First Congress, which re-enacted the Northwest Ordinance for the governance of the Northwest Territory in 1789, confirm the view that Congress did not mean that the Government should be neutral between religion and irreligion. The House of Representatives took up the Northwest Ordinance on the same day as Madison introduced his proposed amendments which became the Bill of Rights; while at that time the Federal Government was of course not bound by draft amendments to the Constitution which had not yet been proposed by Congress, say nothing of ratified by the States, it seems highly unlikely that the House of Representatives would simultaneously consider proposed amendments to the Constitution and enact an important piece of territorial legislation which conflicted with the intent of those proposals. The Northwest Ordinance, 1 Stat. 50, reenacted the Northwest Ordinance of 1787 and provided that "[r]eligion, morality, and knowledge, being necessary to good government and the happiness of mankind, schools and the means of education shall forever be encouraged.". . .

As the United States moved from the 18th into the 19th century, Congress appropriated time and again public moneys in support of sectarian Indian education carried on by religious organizations. Typical of these was Jefferson's treaty with the Kaskaskia Indians, which provided annual cash support for the Tribe's Roman Catholic priest and church. It was not until 1897, when aid to sectarian education for Indians had reached $500,000 annually, that Congress decided thereafter to cease appropriating money for education in sectarian schools. . . . This history shows the fallacy of the notion found in *Everson* that "no tax in any amount" may be levied for religious activities in any form. . . .

It would seem from this evidence that the Establishment Clause of the First Amendment had acquired a well-accepted meaning: it forbade establishment of a national religion, and forbade preference among religious sects or denominations. Indeed, the first American dictionary defined the word "establishment" as "the act of establishing, founding, ratifying or ordainin(g,") such as in "[t]he episcopal form of religion, so called, in England." The Establishment Clause did not require government neutrality between religion and irreligion nor did it prohibit the federal government from providing non-discriminatory aid to religion. There is simply no historical foundation for the proposition that the Framers intended to build the "wall of separation" that was constitutionalized in *Everson*.

Notwithstanding the absence of an historical basis for this theory of rigid separation, the wall idea might well have served as a useful albeit misguided analytical concept, had it led this Court to unified and principled results in Establishment Clause cases. The opposite, unfortunately, has been true; in the 38 years since

Everson our Establishment Clause cases have been neither principaled nor unified. Our recent opinions, many of them hopelessly divided pluralities, have with embarassing candor conceded that the "wall of separation" is merely a "blurred, indistinct, and variable barrier," which "is not wholly accurate" and can only be "dimly perceived.". . .

Whether due to its lack of historical support or its practical workability, the *Everson* "wall" has proven all but useless as a guide to sound constitutional adjudication. . . .

But the greatest injury of the "wall" notion is its mischievous diversion of judges from the actual intentions of the drafters of the Bill of Rights. The "crucible of litigation," is well adapted to adjudicating factual disputes on the basis of testimony presented in court, but no amount of repetition of historical errors in judicial opinions can make the errors true. The "wall of separation between church and State" is a metaphor based on bad history, a metaphor which has proved useless as a guide to judging. It should be frankly and explicitly abandoned.

The Court has more recently attempted to add some mortar to *Everson's* wall through the three-part test of *Lemon,* which served at first to offer a more useful test for purposes of the Establishment Clause than did the "wall" metaphor. Generally stated, the *Lemon* test proscribes state action that has a sectarian purpose or effect, or causes an impermissible governmental entanglement with religion. . . .

Lemon cited *Board of Education v. Allen,* [392 U.S. 236] (1968), as the source of the "purpose" and "effect" prongs of the three-part test. The *Allen* opinion explains, however, how it inherited the purpose and effect elements from *Schempp* and *Everson,* both of which contain the historical errors described above. Thus the purpose and effect prongs have the same historical deficiencies as the wall concept itself: they are in no way based on either the language or intent of the drafters.

The secular purpose prong has proven mercurial in application because it has never been fully defined, and we have never fully stated how the test is to operate. If the purpose prong is intended to void those aids to sectarian institutions accompanied by a stated legislative purpose to aid religion, the prong will condemn nothing so long as the legislature utters a secular purpose and says nothing about aiding religion. Thus the constitutionality of a statute may depend upon what the legislators put into the legislative history and, more importantly, what they leave out. The purpose prong means little if it only requires the legislature to express any secular purpose and omit all sectarian references, because legislators might do just that. Faced with a valid legislative secular purpose, we could not properly ignore that purpose without a factual basis for doing so.

However, if the purpose prong is aimed to void all statutes enacted with the intent to aid sectarian institutions, whether stated or not, then most statutes providing any aid, such as textbooks or bus rides for sectarian school children, will fail because one of the purposes behind every statute, whether stated or not, is to aid the target of its largesse. In other words, if the purpose prong requires an absence of *any* intent to aid sectarian institutions, whether or not expressed, few state laws in this area could pass the test, and we would be required to void some state aids to religion which we have already upheld.

The entanglement prong of the *Lemon* test came from *Walz v. Tax Commission.* . . . We have not always followed *Walz's* reflective inquiry into entanglement, however. One of the difficulties with the entanglement prong is that, when divorced from the logic of *Walz,* it creates an "insoluable paradox" in school aid cases: we have required aid to parochial schools to be closely watched lest it be put to sectarian use, yet this close supervision itself will create an entanglement. . . .

The entanglement test . . . also ignores the myriad state administrative regulations properly placed upon sectarian institutions such as curriculum, attendance, and certification requirements for sectarian schools, or fire and safety regulations for churches. Avoiding entanglement between church and State may be an important consideration in a case like *Walz,* but if the entanglement prong were applied to all state and church relations in the automatic manner in which it has been applied to school aid cases, the State could hardly require anything of church-related institutions as a condition for receipt of financial assistance.

These difficulties arise because the *Lemon* test has no more grounding in the history of the First Amendment than does the wall theory upon which it rests. The three-part test represents a determined effort to craft a workable rule from an historically faulty doctrine; but the rule can only be as sound as the doctrine it attempts to service. The three-part test has simply not provided adequate standards for deciding. Establishment Clause cases, as this Court has slowly come to realize. Even worse, the *Lemon* test has caused this Court to fracture into unworkable plurality opinions, depending upon how each of the three factors applies to a certain state action. The reults from our school services cases show the difficulty we have encountered in making the *Lemon* test yield principled results.

For example, a State may lend to parochial school children geography textbooks that contain maps of the United States, but the State may not lend maps of the United States for use in geography class. A State may lend textbooks on American colonial history, but it may not lend a film on George Washington, or a film projector to show it in history class. A State may lend classroom workbooks, but may not lend workbooks in which the parochial school children write, thus rendering them nonreusable. A State may pay for bus transportation to religious schools but may not pay for bus transportation from the parochial school to the public zoo or natural history museum for a field trip. A State may pay for diagnostic services conducted in the parochial school but therapeutic services must be given in a different building; speech and hearing "services" conducted by the State inside the sectarian school are forbidden, but the State may conduct speech and hearing diagnostic testing inside the sectarian school. . . . A State may give cash to a parochial school to pay for the administration of State-written tests and state-ordered reporting services, but it may not provide funds for teacher-prepared tests on secular subjects. Religious instruction may not be given in public school, but the public school may release students during the day for religion classes elsewhere, and may enforce attendance at those classes with its truancy laws.

These results violate the historically sound principle "that the Establishment Clause does not forbid governments . . . to [provide] general welfare under which benefits are distributed to private individuals, even though many of those individuals may elect to use those benefits in ways that 'aid' religious instruction or worship."

The true meaning of the Establishment Clause can only be seen in its history. As drafters of our Bill of Rights, the Framers inscribed the principles that control today. Any deviation from their intentions frustrates the permanence of that Charter and will only lead to the type of unprincipled decisionmaking that has plagued our Establishment Clause cases since *Everson*.

The Framers intended the Establishment Clause to prohibit the designation of any church as a "national" one. The Clause was also designed to stop the Federal Government from asserting a preference for one religious denomination or sect over others. Given the "incorporation" of the Establishment Clause as against the States via the Fourteenth Amendment in *Everson*, States are prohibited as well from establishing a religion or discriminating between sects. As its history abundantly shows, however, nothing in the Establishment Clause requires government to be strictly neutral between religion and irreligion, nor does that Clause prohibit Congress or the States from pursuing legitimate secular ends through nondiscriminatory sectarian means. . . .

The State surely has a secular interest in regulating the manner in which public schools are conducted. Nothing in the Establishment Clause of the First Amendment, properly understood, prohibits any such generalized "endorsement" of prayer. I would therefore reverse the judgment of the Court of Appeals in *Wallace v. Jaffree*.

Edwards v. Aguillard
482 U.S. 578, 107 S.Ct. 2573 (1987)

In 1982, the Louisiana legislature passed the "Balanced Treatment for Creation-Science and Evolution-Science in Public School Instruction" Act. The law did not require the teaching of either creationism or evolutionary theory, but only required that both must be taught if either was part of a school's curriculum. Don Aguillard and parents of children attending Louisiana public schools, teachers, and some religious leaders challenged the constitutionality of the law in federal district court. That court found the law to violate the establishment clause of the First Amendment and a court of appeals affirmed. The state appealed those rulings to the Supreme Court.

Justice BRENNAN delivers the opinion of the Court.

The question for decision is whether Louisiana's "Balanced Treatment for Creation-Science and Evolution-Science in Public School Instruction" Act (Creationism Act), is facially invalid as violative of the Establishment Clause of the First Amendment.

The Creationism Act forbids the teaching of the theory of evolution in public schools unless accompanied by instruction in "creation science." No school is required to teach evolution or creation science. If either is taught, however, the other must also be taught. . . .

Appellees attacked the Act as facially invalid because it violated the Establishment Clause and made a motion for summary judgment. The District Court . . . held that there can be no valid secular reason for prohibiting the teaching of evolution, a theory historically opposed by some religious denominations. The court further concluded that "the teaching of 'creation-science' and 'creationism,' as contemplated by the statute, involves teaching 'tailored to the principles' of a particular religious sect or group of sects." The District Court therefore held that the Creationism Act violated the Establishment Clause either because it prohibited the teaching of evolution or because it required the teaching of creation science with the purpose of advancing a particular religious doctrine.

The Court of Appeals affirmed. [And we now affirmed the lower court's ruling.] . . .

[I]n employing the three-pronged *Lemon* test, we must do so mindful of the particular concerns that arise in the context of public elementary and secondary schools. We now turn to the evaluation of the Act under the *Lemon* test.

Lemon's first prong focuses on the purpose that animated adoption of the Act. "The purpose prong of the *Lemon* test asks whether government's actual purpose is to endorse or disapprove of religion." A governmental intention to promote religion is clear when the State enacts a law to serve a religious purpose. This intention may be evidenced by promotion of religion in general, *Wallace v. Jaffree*, [472 U.S. 38 (1985)], or by advancement of a particular religious belief, e.g., *Stone v. Graham*, [449 U.S. 41 (1980)], (invalidating requirement to post Ten Commandments, which are "undeniably a sacred text in the Jewish and Christian faiths"), *Epperson v. Arkansas*, [393 U.S. 97 (1968)] (holding that banning the teaching of evolution in public schools violates the First Amendment since "teaching and learning" must not "be tailored to the principles or prohibitions of any religious sect or dogma"). If the law was enacted for the purpose of endorsing religion, "no consideration of the second or third criteria [of *Lemon*] is necessary." In this case, the petitioners have identified no clear secular purpose for the Louisiana Act.

True, the Act's stated purpose is to protect academic freedom. This phrase might, in common parlance, be understood as referring to enhancing the freedom of teachers to teach what they will. The Court of Appeals, however, correctly concluded that the Act was not designed to further that goal. . . .

It is clear from the legislative history that the purpose of the legislative sponsor, Senator Bill Keith, was to narrow the science curriculum. During the legislative hearings, Senator Keith stated: "My preference would be that neither [creationism nor evolution] be taught." Such a ban on teaching does not promote—indeed, it undermines—the provision of a comprehensive scientific education.

It is equally clear that requiring schools to teach creation science with evolution does not advance academic freedom. The Act does not grant teachers a flexibility that they did not already possess to supplant the present science curriculum with the presentation of theories, besides evolution, about the origin of life. . . .

Furthermore, the goal of basic "fairness" is hardly furthered by the Act's discriminatory preference for the teaching of creation science and against the teaching of evolution. While requiring that curriculum guides be developed for creation science, the Act says nothing of comparable guides for evolution. Similarly, research services are supplied for creation science but not for evolution. Only "creation scientists" can serve on the panel that supplies the resource services. The Act forbids school boards to discriminate against anyone who "chooses to be a creation-scientist" or to teach "creationism," but fails to protect those who choose to teach evolution or any other non-creation science theory, or who refuse to teach creation science.

If the Louisiana legislature's purpose was solely to maximize the comprehensiveness and effectiveness of science instruction, it would have encouraged the teaching of all scientific theories about the origins of humankind. But under the Act's requirements, teachers who were once free to teach any and all facets of this subject are now unable to do so. Moreover, the Act fails even to ensure that creation science will be taught, but instead requires the teaching of this theory only when the theory of evolution is taught. Thus we agree with the Court of Appeals' conclusion that the Act does not serve to protect academic freedom, but has the distinctly different purpose of discrediting "evolution by counterbalancing its teaching at every turn with the teaching of creation science. . . ."

In this case, the purpose of the Creationism Act was to restructure the science curriculum to conform with a particular religious viewpoint. Out of many possible science subjects taught in the public schools, the legislature chose to affect the teaching of the one scientific theory that historically has been opposed by certain religious sects. As in *Epperson,* the legislature passed the Act to give preference to those religious groups which have as one of their tenets the creation of humankind by a divine creator. The "overriding fact" that confronted the Court in *Epperson* was "that Arkansas' law selects from the body of knowledge a particular segment which it proscribes for the sole reason that it is deemed to conflict with . . . a particular interpretation of the Book of Genesis by a particular religious group." Similarly, the Creationism Act is designed *either* to promote the theory of creation science which embodies a particular religious tenet by requiring that creation science be taught whenever evolution is taught *or* to prohibit the teaching of a scientific theory disfavored by certain religious sects by forbidding the teaching of evolution when creation science is not also taught. The Establishment Clause, however, "forbids *alike* the preference of a religious doctrine *or* the prohibition of theory which is deemed antagonistic to a particular dogma." (emphasis added). Because the primary purpose of the Creationism Act is to advance a particular religious belief, the Act endorses religion in violation of the First Amendment.

We do not imply that a legislature could never require that scientific critiques of prevailing scientific theories be taught. Indeed, the Court acknowledged in *Stone* [*v. Graham*] that its decision forbidding the posting of the Ten Commandments did not mean that no use could ever be made of the Ten Commandments, or that the Ten Commandments played an exclusively religious role in the history of Western Civilization. In a similar way, teaching a variety of scientific theories about the origins of humankind to schoolchildren might be validly done with the clear secular intent of enhancing the effectiveness of science instruction. But because the primary purpose of the Creationism Act is to endorse a particular religious doctrine, the Act furthers religion in violation of the Establishment Clause.

Justice POWELL, with whom Justice O'CONNOR joins, concurring.

When, as here, "both courts below are unable to discern an arguably valid secular purpose, this Court normally should hesitate to find one." My examination of the language and the legislative history of the Balanced Treatment Act confirms that the intent of the Louisiana legislature was to promote a particular religious belief. The legislative history of the Arkansas statute prohibiting the teaching of evolution examined in *Epperson v. Arkansas*, 393 U.S. 97 (1968), was strikingly similar to the legislative history of the Balanced Treatment Act. In *Epperson*, the Court found:

> "It is clear that fundamentalist sectarian conviction was and is the law's reason for existence. Its antecedent, Tennessee's 'monkey law,' candidly stated its purpose: to make it unlawful 'to teach any theory that denies the story of the Divine Creation of man as taught in the Bible, and to teach instead that man has descended from a lower order of animals.' Perhaps the sensational publicity attendant upon the *Scopes* trial induced Arkansas to adopt less explicit language. It eliminated Tennessee's reference to 'the story of the Divine creation of man' as taught in the Bible, but there is no doubt that the motivation for the law was the same: to suppress the teaching of a theory which, it was thought, 'denied' the divine creation of man."

Here, it is clear that religious belief is the Balanced Treatment Act's "reason for existence." The tenets of creation-science parallel the Genesis story of creation, and this is a religious belief. . . .

[T]he statements of purpose of the sources of creation-science in the United States make clear that their purpose is to promote a religious belief. I find no persuasive evidence in the legislative history that the legislature's purpose was any different. The fact that the Louisiana legislature purported to add information to the school curriculum rather than detract from it as in *Epperson* does not affect my analysis. Both legislatures acted with the unconstitutional purpose of structuring the public school curriculum to make it compatible with a particular religious belief: the "divine creation of man.". . .

Even though I find Louisiana's Balanced Treatment Act unconstitutional, I adhere to the view "that the States and locally elected school boards should have the responsibility for determining the educational policy of the public schools." A decision respecting the subject matter to be taught in public schools does not violate the Establishment Clause simply because the material to be taught " 'happens to coincide or harmonize with the tenets of some or all religions.' ". . . In the context of a challenge under the Establishment Clause, interference with the decisions of these authorities is warranted only when the purpose for their decisions is clearly religious. . . .

As a matter of history, school children can and should properly be informed of all aspects of this Nation's religious heritage. I would see no constitutional problem if school children were taught the nature of the Founding Father's religious beliefs and how these beliefs affected the attitudes of the times and the structure of our government. Courses in comparative religion of course are customary and constitutionally appropriate. In fact, since religion permeates our history, a familiarity with the nature of religious beliefs is necessary to understand many historical as well as contemporary events. In addition, it is worth noting that the Establishment Clause does not prohibit *per se* the educational use of religious documents in public school education. Although this Court has recognized that the Bible is "an instrument of religion," it also has made clear that the Bible "may constitutionally be used in an appropriate study of history, civilization, ethics, comparative religion, or the like." The book is, in fact, "the world's all-time best seller" with undoubted literary and historic value apart from its religious content. The Establishment Clause is properly understood to prohibit the use of the Bible and other religious documents in public school education only when the purpose of the use is to advance a particular religious belief.

Justice WHITE concurred.

Justice SCALIA, with whom the CHIEF JUSTICE joins, dissenting.

Even if I agreed with the questionable premise that legislation can be invalidated under the Establishment Clause on the basis of its motivation alone, without regard to its effects, I would still find no justification for today's decision. The Louisiana legislators who passed the "Balanced Treatment for Creation-Science and Evolution-Science Act," each of whom had sworn to support the Constitution, were well aware of the potential Establishment Clause problems and considered that aspect of the legislation with great care. After seven hearings and several months of study, resulting in substantial revision of the original proposal, they approved the Act overwhelmingly and specifically articulated the secular purpose they meant it to serve. Although the record contains abundant evidence of the sincerity of that purpose (the only issue pertinent to this case), the Court today holds, essentially on the basis of "its visceral knowledge regarding what *must* have motivated the legislators" (emphasis added), that the members of the Louisiana Legislature knowingly violated their oaths and then lied about it. I dissent. . . .

It is clear, first of all, that regardless of what "legislative purpose" may mean in other contexts, for the purpose of the *Lemon* test it means the "actual" motives of those responsible for the challenged action. . . . Thus, if those legislators who supported the Balanced Treatment Act *in fact* acted with a "sincere" secular purpose, the Act survives the first component of the *Lemon* test, regardless of whether that purpose is likely to be achieved by the provisions they enacted.

Our cases have also confirmed that when the *Lemon* Court referred to "a secular . . . purpose," . . . it meant *"a* secular purpose.". . . In all three cases in which we struck down laws under the Establishment Clause for lack of a secular purpose, we found that the legislature's sole motive was to promote religion. See *Wallace v. Jaffree, Stone v. Graham, Epperson v. Arkansas.* Thus, the majority's invalidation of the Balanced Treatment Act is defensible only if the record indicates that the Louisiana Legislature had *no* secular purpose.

It is important to stress that the purpose forbidden by *Lemon* is the purpose to "advance religion.". . . Our cases in no way imply that the Establishment Clause forbids legislators merely to act upon their religious convictions. We surely would not strike down a law providing money to feed the hungry or shelter the homeless if it could be demonstrated that, but for the religious beliefs of the legislators, the funds would not have been approved. Also, political activism by the religiously motivated is part of our heritage. Notwithstanding the majority's implication to the contrary, we do not presume that the sole purpose of a law is to advance religion merely because it was supported strongly by organized religions or by adherents of particular faiths. To do so would deprive religious men and women of their right to participate in the political process. Today's religious activism may give us the Balanced Treatment Act, but yesterday's resulted in the abolition of slavery, and tomorrow's may bring relief for famine victims.

Similarly, we will not presume that a law's purpose is to advance religion merely because it " 'happens to coincide or harmonize with the tenets of some or all religions,' " or, because it benefits religion, even substantially. We have, for example, turned back Establishment Clause challenges to restrictions on abortion funding, *Harris v. McRae,* [448 U.S. 297 (1980)], and to Sunday closing laws, *McGowan v. Maryland,* [366 U.S. 420 (1961)], despite the fact that both "agre[e] with the dictates of [some] Judaeo-Christian religions." Thus, the fact that creation science coincides with the beliefs of certain religions, a fact upon which the majority relies heavily, does not itself justify invalidation of the Act.

Finally, our cases indicate that even certain kinds of governmental actions undertaken with the specific intention of improving the position of religion do not "advance religion" as that term is used in *Lemon*. Rather, we have said that in at least two circumstances government *must* act to advance religion, and that in a third it *may* do so.

First, . . . a State which discovers that its employees are inhibiting religion must take steps to prevent them from doing so, even though its purpose would clearly be to advance religion. *Cf. Walz v. Tax Comm'n of New York City*, [397 U.S. 664 (1970)]. Thus, if the Louisiana Legislature sincerely believed that the State's science teachers were being hostile to religion, our cases indicate that it could act to eliminate that hostility without running afoul of *Lemon's* purpose test.

Second, we have held that intentional governmental advancement of religion is sometimes required by the Free Exercise Clause. For example, we held that in some circumstances States must accommodate the beliefs of religious citizens by exempting them from generally applicable regulations. We have not yet come close to reconciling *Lemon* and our Free Exercise cases, and typically we do not really try. . . . It is clear, however, that members of the Louisiana Legislature were not impermissibly motivated for purpose of the *Lemon* test if they believed that approval of the Balanced Treatment Act was *required* by the Free Exercise Clause. . . .

It is possible, then, that even if the sole motive of those voting for the Balanced Treatment Act was to advance religion, and its passage was not actually required, or even believed to be required, by either the Free Exercise or Establishment Clauses, the Act would nonetheless survive scrutiny under *Lemon's* purpose test. . . .

I think it would be extraordinary to invalidate the Balanced Treatment Act for lack of a valid secular purpose. Striking down a law approved by the democratically elected representatives of the people is no minor matter. . . . Even if the legislative history were silent or ambiguous about the existence of a secular purpose—and here it is not—the statute should survive *Lemon's* purpose test. But even more validation than mere legislative history is present here. The Louisiana Legislature explicitly set forth its secular purpose ("protecting academic freedom") in the very text of the Act. . . .

The Court seeks to evade the force of this expression of purpose by stubbornly misinterpreting it, and then finding that the provisions of the Act do not advance that misinterpreted purpose, thereby showing it to be a sham. The Court first surmises that "academic freedom" means "enhancing the freedom of teachers to teach what they will"—even though "academic freedom" in that sense has little scope in the structured elementary and secondary curriculums with which the Act is concerned. Alternatively, the Court suggests that it might mean "maximiz[ing] the comprehensiveness and effectiveness of science instruction"—though that is an exceeding strange interpretation of the words, and one that is refuted on the very face of the statute. Had the Court devoted to this central question of the meaning of the legislatively expressed purpose, a small fraction of the research into legislative history that produced its quotations of religiously motivated statements by individual legislators, it would have discerned quite readily what "academic freedom" meant: *students' freedom from indoctrination.* The legislature wanted to ensure that students would be free to decide for themselves how life began, based upon a fair and balanced presentation of the scientific evidence— that is, to protect "the right of each [student] voluntarily to determine what to believe (and what not to believe) free of any coercive pressures from the State." The legislature did not care *whether* the topic of origins was taught; it simply wished to ensure that *when* the topic was taught, students would receive " 'all of the evidence.' ". . .

The Act's reference to "creation" is not convincing evidence of religious purpose. The Act defines creation science as *"scientific evidenc[e]."*. . .

We have no basis on the record to conclude that creation science need be anything other than a collection of scientific data supporting the theory that life abruptly appeared on earth. Creation science, its proponents insist, no more must explain *whence* life came than evolution must explain whence came the inanimate materials from which it says life evolved. But even if that were not so, to posit a past creator is not to posit the eternal and personal God who is the object of religious veneration. Indeed, it is not even to posit the *"unmoved* mover" hypothesized by Aristotle and other notably nonfundamentalist philosophers. . . .

It is undoubtedly true that what prompted the Legislature to direct its attention to the misrepresentation of evolution in the schools (rather than the inaccurate presentation of other topics) was its awareness of the tension between evolution and the religious beliefs of many children. But even appellees concede that a valid secular purpose is not rendered impermissible simply because its pursuit is prompted by concern for religious sensitivities. If a history teacher falsely told her students that the bones of Jesus Christ had been discovered, or a physics teacher that the Shroud of Turin had been conclusively established to be inexplicable on the basis of natural causes, I cannot believe (despite the majority's implication to the contrary, that legislators or school board members would be constitutionally prohibited from taking corrective action, simply because that action was prompted by concern for the religious beliefs of the misinstructed students.

In sum, even if one concedes, for the sake of argument, that a majority of the Louisiana Legislature voted for the Balanced Treatment Act partly in order to foster (rather than merely eliminate discrimination against) Christian fundamentalist beliefs, our cases establish that that alone would not suffice to invalidate the Act, so long as there was a genuine secular purpose as well. We have, moreover, no adequate basis for disbelieving the secular purpose set forth in the Act itself, or for concluding that it is a sham enacted to conceal the legislators' violation of their oaths of office. I am astonished by the Court's unprecedented readiness to reach such a conclusion, which I can only attribute to an intellectual predisposition created by the facts and the legend of *Scopes v. State,* 154 Tenn. 105, 289 S.W. 363 (1927)—an instinctive reaction that any governmentally imposed requirements bearing upon the teaching of evolution must be a manifestation of Christian fundamentalist repression. In this case, however, it seems to me the Court's position is the repressive one. The people of Louisiana, including those who are Christian fundamentalists, are quite entitled, as a secular matter, to have whatever scientific evidence there may be against evolution presented in their schools, just as Mr. Scopes was entitled to present whatever scientific evidence there was for it. Perhaps what the Louisiana Legislature has done is unconstitutional because there *is* no such evidence, and the scheme they have established will amount to no more than a presentation of the Book of Genesis. But we cannot say that on the evidence before us in this summary judgment context, which includes ample uncontradicted testimony that "creation science" is a body of scientific knowledge rather than revealed belief. *Infinitely less* can we say (or should we say) that the scientific evidence for evolution is so conclusive that no one could be gullible enough to believe that there is any real scientific evidence to the contrary, so that the legislation's stated purpose must be a lie. Yet that illiberal judgment, that *Scopes*-in-reverse, is ultimately the basis on which the Court's facile rejection of the Louisiana Legislature's purpose must rest. . . .

Because I believe that the Balanced Treatment Act had a secular purpose, which is all the first component of the *Lemon* test requires, I would reverse the judgment of the Court of Appeals and remand for further consideration.

I have to this point assumed the validity of the *Lemon* "purpose" test. In fact, however, I think the pessimistic evaluation that the CHIEF JUSTICE made of the totality of *Lemon* is particularly applicable to the "purpose" prong: it is "a constitutional theory [that] has no basis in the history of the amendment it seeks to interpret, is difficult to apply and yields unprincipled results." *Wallace v. Jaffree* (REHNQUIST, J., dissenting).

Our cases interpreting and applying the purpose test have made such a maze of the Establishment Clause that even the most conscientious governmental officials can only guess what motives will be held unconstitutional. We have said essentially the following: Government may not act with the purpose of advancing religion, except when forced to do so by the Free Exercise Clause (which is now and then); or when eliminating existing governmental hostility to religion (which exists sometimes); or even when merely accommodating governmentally uninhibited religious practices, except that at some point (it is unclear where) intentional accommodation results in the fostering of religion, which is of course unconstitutional. . . .

But the difficulty of knowing what vitiating purpose one is looking for is as nothing compared with the difficulty of knowing how or where to find it. For while it is possible to discern the objective "purpose" of a statute (*i.e.*, the public good at which its provisions appear to be directed), or even the formal motivation for a statute where that is explicitly set forth (as it was, to no avail, here), discerning the subjective motivation of those enacting the statute is, to be honest, almost always an impossible task. The number of possible motivations, to begin with, is not binary, or indeed even finite. In the present case, for example, a particular legislator need not have voted for the Act either because he wanted to foster religion or because he wanted to improve education. He may have thought the bill would provide jobs for his district, or may have wanted to make amends with a faction of his party he had alienated on another vote, or he may have been a close friend of the bill's sponsor, or he may have been repaying a favor he owed the Majority Leader, or he may have hoped the Governor would appreciate his vote and make a fundraising appearance for him, or he may have been pressured to vote for a bill he disliked by a wealthy contributor or by a flood of constituent mail, or he may have been seeking favorable publicity, or he may have been reluctant to hurt the feelings of a loyal staff member who worked on the bill, or he may have been settling an old score with a legislator who opposed the bill, or he may have been mad at his wife who opposed the bill, or he may have been intoxicated and utterly *un*motivated when the vote was called, or he may have accidentally voted "yes" instead of "no," or, of course, he may have had (and very likely did have) a combination of some of the above and many other motivations. To look for *the sole purpose* of even a single legislator is probably to look for something that does not exist.

Putting that problem aside, however, where ought we to look for the individual legislator's purpose? We cannot of course assume that every member present (if, as is unlikely, we know who or even how many they were) agreed with the motivation expressed in a particular legislator's pre-enactment floor or committee statement. Quite obviously, "[w]hat motivates one legislator to make a speech about a statute is not necessarily what motivates scores of others to enact it." Can we assume, then, that they all agree with the motivation expressed in the staff-prepared committee reports they might have read—even though we are unwilling to assume that they agreed with the motivation expressed in the

very statute that they voted for? Should we consider post-enactment floor statements? Or post-enactment testimony from legislators, obtained expressly for the lawsuit? Should we consider media
reports on the realities of the legislative bargaining? All of these
sources, of course, are eminently manipulable. Legislative histories
can be contrived and sanitized, favorable media coverage orchestrated, and post-enactment recollections conveniently distorted.
Perhaps most valuable of all would be more objective indications—
for example, evidence regarding the individual legislators' religious affiliations. And if that, why not evidence regarding the
fervor or tepidity of their beliefs?

Having achieved, through these simple means, an assessment
of what individual legislators intended, we must still confront
the question (yet to be addressed in any of our cases) how *many*
of them must have the invalidating intent. If a state senate approves a bill by vote of 26 to 25, and only one of the 26 intended
solely to advance religion, is the law unconstitutional? What if
13 of the 26 had that intent? What if 3 of the 26 had the impermissible intent, but 3 of the 25 voting against the bill were motivated
by religious hostility or were simply attempting to "balance" the
votes of their impermissibly motivated colleagues? Or is it possible
that the intent of the bill's sponsor is alone enough to invalidate
it—on a theory, perhaps, that even though everyone else's intent
was pure, what they produced was the fruit of a forbidden tree?

Because there are no good answers to these questions, this
Court has recognized from Chief Justice MARSHALL to Chief
Justice WARREN that determining the subjective intent of legislators is a perilous enterprise. It is perilous, I might note, not just
for the judges who will very likely reach the wrong result, but
also for the legislators who find that they must assess the validity
of proposed legislation—and risk the condemnation of having
voted for an unconstitutional measure—not on the basis of what
the legislation contains, nor even on the basis of what they themselves intend, but on the basis of what *others* have in mind.

Given the many hazards involved in assessing the subjective
intent of governmental decisionmakers, the first prong of *Lemon*
is defensible, I think, only if the text of the Establishment Clause
demands it. That is surely not the case. The Clause states that
"Congress shall make no law respecting an establishment of religion.". . . It is, in short, far from an inevitable reading of the
Establishment Clause that it forbids all governmental action intended to advance religion; and if not inevitable, any reading
with such untoward consequences must be wrong.

In the past we have attempted to justify our embarrassing Establishment Clause jurisprudence on the ground that it "sacrifices
clarity and predictability for flexibility.". . . I think it time that
we sacrifice some "flexibility" for "clarity and predictability." Abandoning *Lemon*'s purpose test—a test which exacerbates the tension

between the Free Exercise and Establishment Clauses, has no basis in the language or history of the amendment, and, as today's decision shows, has wonderfully flexible consequences—would be a good place to start.

County of Allegheny v. American Civil Liberties Union Greater Pittsburgh Chapter

109 S.Ct. 3086 (1989)

Justice Harry Blackmun discusses the facts in his opinion announcing the decision of the Court, as do various other justices in their concurring and dissenting opinions.

Justice BLACKMUN delivers the opinion of the Court, in which Justice O'CONNOR and Justice STEVENS join in part, and in which Justice STEVENS joins in part.

This litigation concerns the constitutionality of two recurring holiday displays located on public property in downtown Pittsburgh. The first is a crèche placed on the Grand Staircase of the Allegheny County Courthouse. The second is a Chanukah menorah placed just outside the City-County Building, next to a Christmas tree and a sign saluting liberty. The Court of Appeals for the Third Circuit ruled that each display violates the Establishment Clause of the First Amendment because each has the impermissible effect of endorsing religion. We agree that the crèche display has that unconstitutional effect but reverse the Court of Appeals' judgment regarding the menorah display.

I

A

Since 1981, the county has permitted the Holy Name Society, a Roman Catholic group, to display a crèche in the County Courthouse during the Christmas holiday season. Christmas, we note perhaps needlessly, is the holiday when Christians celebrate the birth of Jesus of Nazareth, whom they believe to be the Messiah. Western churches have celebrated Christmas Day on December 25 since the fourth century. As observed in this Nation, Christmas has a secular as well as a religious dimension.

The crèche in the County Courthouse, like other crèches, is a visual representation of the scene in the manger in Bethlehem shortly after the birth of Jesus, as described in the Gospels of Luke and Matthew. The crèche includes figures of the infant

Jesus, Mary, Joseph, farm animals, shepherds, and wise men, all placed in or before a wooden representation of a manger, which has at its crest an angel bearing a banner that proclaims "Gloria in Excelsis Deo!"

During the 1986–1987 holiday season, the crèche was on display on the Grand Staircase from November 26 to January 9. It had a wooden fence on three sides and bore a plaque stating: "This Display Donated by the Holy Name Society." Sometime during the week of December 2, the county placed red and white poinsettia plants around the fence. The county also placed a small evergreen tree, decorated with a red bow, behind each of the two endposts of the fence. These trees stood alongside the manger backdrop, and were slightly shorter than it was. The angel thus was at the apex of the crèche display. Altogether, the crèche, the fence, the poinsettias, and the trees occupied a substantial amount of space on the Grand Staircase. No figures of Santa Claus or other decorations appeared on the Grand Staircase. . . .

B

The City-County Building is separate and a block removed from the County Courthouse and, as the name implies, is jointly owned by the city of Pittsburgh and Allegheny County. . . .

For a number of years, the city has had a large Christmas tree under the middle arch outside the Grant Street entrance. Following this practice, city employees on November 17, 1986, erected a 45-foot tree under the middle arch and decorated it with lights and ornaments. . . .

At least since 1982, the city has expanded its Grant Street holiday display to include a symbolic representation of Chanukah, an 8-day Jewish holiday that begins on the 25th day of the Jewish lunar month of Kislev. The 25th of Kislev usually occurs in December and thus Chanukah is the annual Jewish holiday that falls closest to Christmas Day each year. In 1986, Chanukah began at sundown on December 26. . . .

Chanukah, like Christmas, is a cultural event as well as a religious holiday. Indeed, the Chanukah story always has had a political or national as well as a religious dimension: it tells of national heroism in addition to divine intervention. Also, Chanukah, like Christmas, is a winter holiday; according to some historians, it was associated in ancient times with the winter solstice. Just as some Americans celebrate Christmas without regard to its religious significance, some nonreligious American Jews celebrate Chanukah as an expression of ethnic identity, and "as a cultural or national event, rather than as a specifically religious event.". . .

II

This litigation began on December 10, 1986, when respondents, the Greater Pittsburgh Chapter of the American Civil Liberties

Union and seven local residents, filed suit against the county and the city, seeking permanently to enjoin the county from displaying the crèche in the County Courthouse and the city from displaying the menorah in front of the City-County Building. Respondents claim that the displays of the crèche and the menorah each violate the Establishment Clause of the First Amendment, made applicable to state governments by the Fourteenth Amendment. See *Wallace v. Jaffree,* 472 U.S. 38 (1985). . . .

On May 8, 1987, the District Court denied respondent's request for a permanent injunction. Relying on *Lynch v. Donnelly,* [465 U.S. 668 (1984)], the court stated that "the crèche was but part of the holiday decoration of the stairwell and a foreground for the highschool choirs which entertained each day at noon." Regarding the menorah, the court concluded that "it was but an insignificant part of another holiday display." The court also found that "the displays had a secular purpose" and "did not create an excessive entanglement of government with religion.". . .

Respondents appealed, and a divided panel of the Court of Appeals reversed. . . .

III

A

In the course of adjudicating specific cases, this Court has come to understand the Establishment Clause to mean that government may not promote or affiliate itself with any religious doctrine or organization, may not discriminate among persons on the basis of their religious beliefs and practices, may not delegate a governmental power to a religious institution, and may not involve itself too deeply in such an institution's affairs. Although "the myriad, subtle ways in which Establishment Clause values can be eroded," *Lynch v. Donnelly* (O'CONNOR, J., concurring), are not susceptible to a single verbal formulation, this Court has attempted to encapsulate the essential precepts of the Establishment Clause. . . .

Under the *Lemon* analysis, a statute or practice which touches upon religion, if it is to be permissible under the Establishment Clause, must have a secular purpose; it must neither advance nor inhibit religion in its principal or primary effect; and it must not foster an excessive entanglement with religion. This trilogy of tests has been applied regularly in the Court's later Establishment Clause cases.

Our subsequent decisions further have refined the definition of governmental action that unconstitutionally advances religion. In recent years, we have paid particularly close attention to whether the challenged governmental practice either has the purpose or effect of "endorsing" religion, a concern that has long had a place in our Establishment Clause jurisprudence. . . .

Of course, the word "endorsement" is not self-defining. Rather, it derives its meaning from other words that this Court has found useful over the years in interpreting the Establishment Clause. . . .

Whether the key word is "endorsement," "favoritism," or "promotion," the essential principle remains the same. The Establishment Clause, at the very least, prohibits government from appearing to take a position on questions of religious belief or from "making adherence to a religion relevant in any way to a person's standing in the political community." *Lynch v. Donnelly.* . . .

We have had occasion in the past to apply Establishment Clause principles to the government's display of objects with religious significance. In *Stone v. Graham,* 449 U.S. 39 (1980), we held that the display of a copy of the Ten Commandments on the walls of public classrooms violates the Establishment Clause. Closer to the facts of this litigation is *Lynch v. Donnelly* in which we considered whether the city of Pawtucket, R.I., had violated the Establishment Clause by including a crèche in its annual Christmas display, located in a private park within the downtown shopping district. By a 5–4 decision in that difficult case, the Court upheld inclusion of the crèche in the Pawtucket display, holding that the inclusion of the crèche did not have the impermissible effect of advancing or promoting religion.

The rationale of the majority opinion in *Lynch* is none too clear: the opinion contains two strands, neither of which provides guidance for decision in subsequent cases. First, the opinion states that the inclusion of the crèche in the display was "no more an advancement or endorsement of religion" than other "endorsements" this Court has approved in the past—but the opinion offers no discernible measure for distinguishing between permissible and impermissible endorsements. Second, the opinion observes that any benefit the government's display of the crèche gave to religion was no more than "indirect, remote, and incidental"—without saying how or why.

Although Justice O'CONNOR joined the majority opinion in *Lynch,* she wrote a concurrence that differs in significant respects from the majority opinion. The main difference is that the concurrence provides a sound analytical framework for evaluating governmental use of religious symbols.

First and foremost, the concurrence squarely rejects any notion that this Court will tolerate some government endorsement of religion. Rather, the concurrence recognizes any endorsement of religion as "invalid," because it "sends a message to nonadherents that they are outsiders, not full members of the political community, and an accompanying message to adherents that they are insiders, favored members of the political community."

Second, the concurrence articulates a method for determining whether the government's use of an object with religious meaning has the effect of endorsing religion. The effect of the display depends upon the message that the government's practice communicates: the question is "what viewers may fairly understand to be the purpose of the display." That inquiry, of necessity, turns upon the context in which the contested object appears: "a typical museum setting, though not neutralizing the religious content of a religious painting, negates any message of endorsement of that content." The concurrence thus emphasizes that the constitutionality of the crèche in that case depended upon its "particular physicalsetting," and further observes: "Every government practice must be judged in its unique circumstances to determine whether it [endorses] religion."

The concurrence applied this mode of analysis to the Pawtucket crèche, seen in the context of that city's holiday celebration as a whole. In addition to the crèche, the city's display contained: a Santa Claus House with a live Santa distributing candy; reindeer pulling Santa's sleigh; a live 40-foot Christmas tree strung with lights; statues of carolers in old-fashioned dress; candy-striped poles; a "talking" wishing well; a large banner proclaiming "SEASONS GREETINGS"; a miniature "village" with several houses and a church; and various "cut-out" figures, including those of a clown, a dancing elephant, a robot, and a teddy bear. The concurrence concluded that both because the crèche is "a traditional symbol" of Christmas, a holiday with strong secular elements, and because the crèche was "displayed along with purely secular symbols," the crèche's setting "changes what viewers may fairly understand to be the purpose of the display" and "negates any message of endorsement" of "the Christian beliefs represented by the crèche.". . .

The four *Lynch* dissenters agreed with the concurrence that the controlling question was "whether Pawtucket ha[d] run afoul of the Establishment Clause by endorsing religion through its display of the crèche." (BRENNAN, J., dissenting). The dissenters also agreed with the general proposition that the context in which the government uses a religious symbol is relevant for determining the answer to that question. They simply reached a different answer: the dissenters concluded that the other elements of the Pawtucket display did not negate the endorsement of Christian faith caused by the presence of the crèche. They viewed the inclusion of the crèche in the city's overall display as placing "the government's imprimatur of approval on the particular religious beliefs exemplified by the crèche." Thus, they stated: "The effect on minority religious groups, as well as on those who may reject all religion, is to convey the message that their views are not similarly worthy of public recognition nor entitled to public support."

Thus, despite divergence at the bottom line, the five Justices in concurrence and dissent in *Lynch* agreed upon the relevant constitutional principles: the government's use of religious symbolism is unconstitutional if it has the effect of endorsing religious beliefs, and the effect of the government's use of religious symbolism depends upon its context. These general principles are sound, and have been adopted by the Court in subsequent cases. . . .

IV

We turn first to the county's crèche display. There is no doubt, of course, that the crèche itself is capable of communicating a religious message. . . .

Under the Court's holding in *Lynch*, the effect of a crèche display turns on its setting. Here, unlike in *Lynch*, nothing in the context of the display detracts from the crèche's religious message. The *Lynch* display comprised a series of figures and objects, each group of which had its own focal point. Santa's house and his reindeer were objects of attention separate from the crèche, and had their specific visual story to tell. Similarly, whatever a "talking" wishing well may be, it obviously was a center of attention separate from the crèche. Here, in contrast, the crèche stands alone: it is the single element of the display on the Grand Staircase. . . .

Nor does the fact that the crèche was the setting for the county's annual Christmas carole-program diminish its religious meaning. . . .

Furthermore, the crèche sits on the Grand Staircase, the "main" and "most beautiful part" of the building that is the seat of county government. No viewer could reasonably think that it occupies this location without the support and approval of the government. Thus, by permitting the "display of the crèche in this particular physical setting," the county sends an unmistakable message that it supports and promotes the Christian praise to God that is the crèche's religious message.

The fact that the crèche bears a sign disclosing its ownership by a Roman Catholic organization does not alter this conclusion. On the contrary, the sign simply demonstrates that the government is endorsing the religious message of that organization, rather than communicating a message of its own. But the Establishment Clause does not limit only the religious content of the government's own communications. It also prohibits the government's support and promotion of religious communications by religious organizations. . . . Indeed, the very concept of "endorsement" conveys the sense of promoting someone else's message. Thus, by prohibiting government endorsement of religion, the Establishment Clause prohibits precisely what occurred here: the government's lending its support to the communication of a religious organization's religious message. . . .

In sum, *Lynch* teaches that government may celebrate Christmas in some manner and form, but not in a way that endorses Christian doctrine. Here, Allegheny County has transgressed this line. It has chosen to celebrate Christmas in a way that has the effect of endorsing a patently Christian message: Glory to God for the birth of Jesus Christ. Under *Lynch,* and the rest of our cases, nothing more is required to demonstrate a violation of the Establishment Clause. The display of the crèche in this context, therefore, must be permanently enjoined.

V

Justice KENNEDY and the three Justices who join him would find the display of the crèche consistent with the Establishment Clause. He argues that this conclusion necessarily follows from the Court's decision in *Marsh v. Chambers,* 463 U.S. 783 (1983), which sustained the constitutionality of legislative prayer. He also asserts that the crèche, even in this setting, poses "no realistic risk" of "represent[ing] an effort to proselytize," having repudiated the Court's endorsement inquiry in favor of a "proselytization" approach. The Court's analysis of the crèche, he contends, "reflects an unjustified hostility toward religion.". . .

Justice KENNEDY's reading of *Marsh* would gut the core of the Establishment Clause, as this Court understands it. The history of this Nation, it is perhaps sad to say, contains numerous examples of official acts that endorsed Christianity specifically. Some of these examples date back to the Founding of the Republic, but this heritage of official discrimination against non-Christians has no place in the jurisprudence of the Establishment Clause. Whatever else the Establishment Clause may mean (and we have held it to mean no official preference even for religion over nonreligion), it certainly means at the very least that government may not demonstrate a preference for one particular sect or creed (including a preference for Christianity over other religions). . . .

C

Although Justice KENNEDY repeatedly accuses the Court of harboring a "latent hostility" or "callous indifference" toward religion, nothing could be further from the truth, and the accusations could be said to be as offensive as they are absurd. Justice KENNEDY apparently has misperceived a respect for religious pluralism, a respect commanded by the Constitution, as hostility or indifference to religion. No misperception could be more antithetical to the values embodied in the Establishment Clause.

Justice KENNEDY's accusations are shot from a weapon triggered by the following proposition: if government may celebrate the secular aspects of Christmas, then it must be allowed to celebrate the religious aspects as well becuase, otherwise, the government would be discriminating against citizens who celebrate Christmas as a religious, and not just a secular, holiday. This proposition, however, is flawed at its foundation. The government does not discriminate against any citizen on the basis of the citizen's religious faith if the government is secular in its functions and operations. On the contrary, the Constitution mandates that the government remain secular, rather than affiliating itself with religious beliefs or institutions, precisely in order to avoid discriminating among citizens on the basis of their religious faiths.

A secular state, it must be remembered, is not the same as an atheistic or antireligious state. A secular state establishes neither atheism nor religion as its official creed. Justice KENNEDY thus has it exactly backwards when he says that enforcing the Constitution's requirement that government remain secular is a prescription of orthodoxy. It follows directly from the Constitution's proscription against government affiliation with religious beliefs or institutions that there is no orthodoxy on religious matters in the secular state. Although Justice KENNEDY accuses the Court of "an Orwellian rewriting of history," perhaps it is Justice KENNEDY himself who has slipped into a form of Orwellian newspeak when he equates the constitutional command of secular government with a prescribed orthodoxy.

To be sure, in a pluralistic society there may be some would-be theocrats, who wish that their religion were an established creed, and some of them perhaps may be even audacious enough to claim that the lack of established religion discriminates against their preferences. But this claim gets no relief, for it contradicts the fundamental premise of the Establishment Clause itself. The antidiscrimination principle inherent in the Establishment Clause necessarily means that would-be discriminators on the basis of religion cannot prevail.

For this reason, the claim that prohibiting government from celebrating Christmas as a religious holiday discriminates against Christians in favor of nonadherents must fail. Celebrating Christmas as a religious, as opposed to a secular, holiday, necessarily entails professing, proclaiming, or believing that Jesus of Nazareth, born in a manger in Bethlehem, is the Christ, the Messiah. If the government celebrates Christmas as a religious holiday (for example, by issuing an official proclamation saying: "We rejoice in the glory of Christ's birth!"), it means that the government really is declaring Jesus to be the Messiah, a specifically Christian belief. In contrast, confining the government's own celebration of Christmas to the holiday's secular aspects does *not* favor the religious beliefs of non-Christians over those of Christians. Rather, it simply permits the government to acknowledge the holiday without expressing an allegiance to Christian beliefs, an allegiance that would truly favor Christians over non-Christians. To be sure, some Christians may wish to see the government proclaim its allegiance to Christianity in a religious celebration of Christmas, but the Constitution does not permit the gratification of that desire, which would contradict the " 'logic of secular liberty' " it is the purpose of the Establishment Clause to protect. . . .

VI

The display of the Chanukah menorah in front of the City-County Building may well present a closer constitutional question. The menorah, one must recognize, is a religious symbol: it serves to commemorate the miracle of the oil as described in the Talmud. But the menorah's message is not exclusively religious. The menorah is the primary visual symbol for a holiday that, like Christmas, has both religious and secular dimensions.

Moreover, the menorah here stands next to a Christmas tree and a sign saluting liberty. While no challenge has been made here to the display of the tree and the sign, their presence is obviously relevant in determining the effect of the menorah's display. The necessary result of placing a menorah next to a Christmas tree is to create an "overall holiday setting" that represents both Christmas and Chanukah—two holidays, not one.

The mere fact that Pittsburgh displays symbols of both Christmas and Chanukah does not end the constitutional inquiry. If the city celebrates both Christmas and Chanukah as religious holidays, then it violates the Establishment Clause. The simultaneous endorsement of Judaism and Christianity is no less constitutionally infirm than the endorsement of Christianity alone.

Conversely, if the city celebrates both Christmas and Chanukah as secular holidays, then its conduct is beyond the reach of the Establishment Clause. Because government may celebrate Christmas as a secular holiday, it follows that government may also acknowledge Chanukah as a secular holiday. Simply put, it would be a form of discrimination against Jews to allow Pittsburgh to celebrate Christmas as a cultural tradition while simultaneously disallowing the city's acknowledgment of Chanukah as a contemporaneous cultural tradition.

Accordingly, the relevant question for Establishment Clause purposes is whether the combined display of the tree, the sign, and the menorah has the effect of endorsing both Christian and Jewish faiths, or rather simply recognizes that both Christmas and Chanukah are part of the same winter-holiday season, which has attained a secular status in our society. Of the two interpretations of this particular display, the latter seems far more plausible and is also in line with *Lynch.*

The Christmas tree, unlike the menorah, is not itself a religious symbol. Although Christmas trees once carried religious connotations, today they typify the secular celebration of Christmas. . . .

The tree, moreover, is clearly the predominant element in the city's display. The 45-foot tree occupies the central position beneath the middle archway in front of the Grant Street entrance to the City-County Building; the 18-foot menorah is positioned to one side. Given this configuration, it is much more sensible to interpret the meaning of the menorah in light of the tree, rather than *vice versa*. In the shadow of the tree, the menorah is readily understood as simply a recognition that Christmas is not the only traditional way of observing the winter-holiday season. In these circumstances, then, the combination of the tree and the menorah communicates, not a simultaneous endorsement of both Christian and Jewish faith, but instead, a secular celebration of Christmas coupled with an acknowledgment of Chanukah as a contemporaneous alternative tradition. . . .

The Mayor's sign further diminishes the possibility that the tree and the menorah will be interpreted as a dual endorsement of Christianity and Judaism. The sign states that during the holiday season the city salutes liberty. Moreover, the sign draws upon the theme of light, common to both Chanukah and Christmas as winter festivals, and links that theme with this Nation's legacy of freedom, which allows an American to celebrate the holiday season in whatever way he wishes, religiously or otherwise. . . .

Given all these considerations, it is not "sufficiently likely" that residents of Pittsburgh will perceive the combined display of the tree, the sign, and the menorah as an "endorsement" or "disapproval . . . of their individual religious choices.". . .

The conclusion here that, in this particular context, the menorah's display does not have an effect of endorsing religious faith does not foreclose the possibility that the display of the menorah might violate either the "purpose" or "entanglement" prong of the *Lemon* analysis. These issues were not addressed by the Court of Appeals and may be considered by that court on remand.

VII

Lynch v. Donnelly confirms, and in no way repudiates, the long-standing constitutional principle that government may not engage in a practice that has the effect of promoting or endorsing religious beliefs. The display of the crèche in the County Courthouse has this unconstitutional effect. The display of the menorah in front of the City-County Building, however, does not have this effect, given its "particular physical setting."

The judgment of the Court of Appeals is affirmed in part and reversed in part, and the cases are remanded for further proceedings.

It is so ordered.

Justice O'CONNOR, with whom Justice BRENNAN and Justice STEVENS join, concurring in part.

I

I joined the majority opinion in *Lynch* because, as I read that opinion, it was consistent with the analysis set forth in my separate concurrence, which stressed that "[e]very government practice must be judged in its *unique circumstances* to determine whether it constitutes an endorsement or disapproval of religion." Indeed, by referring repeatedly to "inclusion of the crèche" in the larger holiday display, the *Lynch* majority recognized that the crèche had to be viewed in light of the total display of which it was a part. Moreover, I joined the Court's discussion in Part II of *Lynch* concerning government acknowledgments of religion in American life because, in my view, acknowledgments such as the legislative prayers upheld in *Marsh v. Chambers,* 463 U.S. 783 (1983), and the printing of "In God We Trust" on our coins serve the secular purposes of "solemnizing public occasions, expressing confidence in the future and encouraging the recognition of what is worthy of appreciation in society." Because they serve such secular purposes and because of their "history and ubiquity," such government acknowledgments of religion are not understood as conveying an endorsement of particular religious beliefs. At the same time, it is clear that "[g]overnment practices that purport to celebrate or acknowledge events with religious significance must be subjected to careful judicial scrutiny.". . .

For the reasons stated in Part IV of the Court's opinion in this case, I agree that the crèche displayed on the Grand Staircase of the Allegheny County Courthouse, the seat of county government, conveys a message to nonadherents of Christianity that they are not full members of the political community, and a corresponding message to Christians that they are favored members of the political community. In contrast to the crèche in *Lynch,* which was displayed in a private park in the city's commercial district as part of a broader display of traditional secular symbols of the holiday season, this crèche stands alone in the County Courthouse. The display of religious symbols in public areas of core government buildings runs a special risk of "mak[ing] religion relevant, in reality or public perception, to status in the political community.". . .

The Court correctly concludes that placement of the central religious symbol of the Christmas holiday season at the Allegheny County Courthouse has the unconstitutional effect of conveying a government endorsement of Christianity.

II

In his separate opinion, Justice KENNEDY asserts that the endorsement test "is flawed in its fundamentals and unworkable in practice." In my view, neither criticism is persuasive. As a theoretical matter, the endorsement test captures the essential command of the Establishment Clause, namely, that government must not make a person's religious beliefs relevant to their standing in the political community by conveying a message "that religion or a particular religious belief is favored or preferred.". . .

We live in a pluralistic society. Our citizens come from diverse religious traditions or adhere to no particular religious beliefs at all. If government is to be neutral in matters of religion, rather than showing either favoritism or disapproval towards citizens based on their personal religious choices, government cannot endorse the religious practices and beliefs of some citizens without sending a clear message to nonadherents that they are outsiders or less than full members of the political community.

An Establishment Clause standard that prohibits only "coercive" practices or overt efforts at government proselytization, but fails to take account of the numerous more subtle ways that government can show favoritism to particular beliefs or convey a message of disapproval to others, would not, in my view, adequately protect the religious liberty or respect the religious diversity of the members of our pluralistic political community. Thus, this Court has never relied on coercion alone as the touchstone of Establishment Clause analysis. . . .

Justice KENNEDY submits that the endorsement test is inconsistent with our precedents and traditions because, in his words, if it were "applied without artificial exceptions for historical practice," it would invalidate many traditional practices recognizing the role of religion in our society. This criticism shortchanges both the endorsement test itself and my explanation of the reason why certain longstanding government acknowledgments of religion do not, under that test, convey a message of endorsement. Practices such as legislative prayers or opening Court sessions with "God save the United States and this honorable Court," serve the secular purposes of "solemnizing public occasions," and "expressing confidence in the future.". . .

These examples of ceremonial deism do not survive Establishment Clause scrutiny simply by virtue of their historical longevity alone. Historical acceptance of a practice does not in itself validate that practice under the Establishment Clause if the practice violates the values protected by that Clause, just as historical acceptance of racial or gender based discrimination does not immunize such practices from scrutiny under the 14th Amendment. As we recognized in *Walz v. Tax Comm'n of New York City*, 397 U.S. 664 (1970), "no one acquires a vested or protected right in violation of the Constitution by long use, even when that span of time covers our entire national existence and indeed predates it."

Under the endorsement test, the "history and ubiquity" of a practice is relevant not because it creates an "artificial exception" from that test. On the contrary, the "history and ubiquity" of a practice is relevant because it provides part of the context in which a reasonable observer evaluates whether a challenged governmental practice conveys a message of endorsement of religion. It is the combination of the longstanding existence of practices such as opening legislative sessions with legislative prayers or opening Court sessions with "God save the United States and this honorable Court," as well as their nonsectarian nature, that lead me to the conclusion that those particular practices, despite their religious roots, do not convey a message of endorsement of particular religious beliefs. . . .

Contrary to Justice KENNEDY's assertions, neither the endorsement test nor its application in this case reflect "an unjustified hostility toward religion." Instead, the endorsement standard recognizes that the religious liberty so precious to the citizens who make up our diverse country is protected, not impeded, when government avoids endorsing religion or favoring particular beliefs over others. Clearly, the government can *acknowledge* the role of religion in our society in numerous ways that do not amount to an endorsement. . . . Moreover, the government can *accommodate* religion by lifting government-imposed burdens on religion. See *Wallace v. Jaffree* (opinion concurring in judgment). Indeed, the Free Exercise Clause may mandate that it do so in particular cases. . . .

III

For reasons which differ somewhat from those set forth in Part VI of Justice BLACKMUN's opinion, I also conclude that the city of Pittsburgh's combined holiday display of a Chanukah menorah, a Christmas tree, and a sign saluting liberty does not have the effect of conveying an endorsement of religion. I agree with Justice BLACKMUN that the Christmas tree, whatever its origins, is not regarded today as a religious symbol. Although Justice BLACKMUN's opinion acknowledges that a Christmas tree alone conveys no endorsement of Christian beliefs, it formulates the question posed by Pittsburgh's combined display of the tree and the menorah as whether the display "has the effect of endorsing *both* Christian and Jewish faiths, or rather simply recognizes that both Christmas and Chanukah are part of the same winter-holiday season, which has attained a secular status in our society.". . .

That formulation of the question disregards the fact that the Christmas tree is a predominantly secular symbol and, more significantly, obscures the religious nature of the menorah and the holiday of Chanukah. The opinion is correct to recognize that the religious holiday of Chanukah has historical and cultural as well as religious dimensions, and that there may be certain "secular aspects" to the holiday. But that is not to conclude, however, as Justice BLACKMUN seems to do, that Chanukah has become a "secular holiday" in our society. The Easter holiday celebrated by Christians may be accompanied by certain "secular aspects" such as Easter bunnies and Easter egg hunts; but it is nevertheless a religious holiday. Similarly, Chanukah is a religious holiday with strong historical components particularly important to the Jewish people. Moreover, the menorah is the central religious symbol and ritual object of that religious holiday. Under Justice BLACKMUN's view, however, the menorah "has been relegated to the role of a neutral harbinger of the holiday season," almost devoid of any religious significance. In my view, the relevant question for Establishment Clause purposes is whether the city of Pittsburgh's display of the menorah, the religious symbol of a religious holiday, next to a Christmas tree and a sign saluting liberty sends a message of government endorsement of Judaism or whether it sends a message of pluralism and freedom to choose one's own beliefs.

In characterizing the message conveyed by this display as either a "double endorsement" or a secular acknowledgment of the winter holiday season, the opinion states that "[i]t is distinctly implausible to view the combined display of the tree, the sign, and the menorah as endorsing Jewish faith alone." That statement, however, seems to suggest that it would be implausible for the city to endorse a faith adhered to by a minority of the citizenry. Regardless of the plausibility of a putative governmental purpose, the more important inquiry here is whether the governmental display of a minority faith's religious symbol could ever reasonably be understood to convey a message of endorsement of that faith. A menorah standing alone at city hall may well send such a message to nonadherents, just as in this case the crèche standing alone at the Allegheny County Courthouse sends a message of governmental endorsement of Christianity, whatever the county's purpose in authorizing the display may have been. Thus, the question here is whether Pittsburgh's holiday display conveys a message of endorsement of Judaism, when the menorah is the only religious symbol in the combined display and when the opinion acknowledges that the tree cannot reasonably be understood to convey an endorsement of Christianity. One need not characterize Chanukah as a "secular holiday" or strain to argue that the menorah has a "secular dimension," in order to conclude that the city of Pittsburgh's combined display does not convey a message of endorsement of Judaism or of religion in general.

In setting up its holiday display, which included the lighted tree and the menorah, the city of Pittsburgh stressed the theme of liberty and pluralism by accompanying the exhibit with a sign bearing the following message: "During this holiday season, the City of Pittsburgh salutes liberty. Let these festive lights remind us that we are the keepers of the flame of liberty and our legacy of freedom." This sign indicates that the city intended to convey its own distinctive message of pluralism and freedom. By accompanying its display of a Christmas tree—a secular symbol of the Christmas holiday season—with a salute to liberty, and by adding a religious symbol from a Jewish holiday also celebrated at roughly the same time of year, I conclude that the city did not endorse Judaism or religion in general, but rather conveyed a message of pluralism and freedom of belief during the holiday season. . . .

In my view, Justice BLACKMUN's new rule, that an inference of endorsement arises every time government uses a symbol with religious meaning if a "more secular alternative" is available, is too blunt an instrument for Establishment Clause analysis, which depends on sensitivity to the context and circumstances presented by each case. Indeed, the opinion appears to recognize the importance of this contextual sensitivity by creating an exception to its new rule in the very case announcing it: the opinion acknowledges that "a purely secular symbol" of Chanukah is available, namely, a dreidel or four-sided top, but rejects the use of such a symbol because it "might be interpreted by some as mocking the celebration of Chanukah." This recognition that the more *religious* alternative may, depending on the circumstances, convey a message that is least likely to implicate Establishment Clause concerns is an excellent example of the need to focus on the specific practice in question in its particular physical setting and context in determining whether government has conveyed or attempted to convey a message that religion or a particular religious belief is favored or preferred.

In sum, I conclude that the city of Pittsburgh's combined holiday display had neither the purpose nor the effect of endorsing religion, but that Allegheny County's crèche display had such an effect. Accordingly, I join Parts I, II, III-A, IV, V, and VII of the Court's opinion and concur in the judgment.

Justice BRENNAN, with whom Justice MARSHALL and Justice STEVENS join, concurring in part and dissenting in part.

According to the Court, the crèche display sends a message endorsing Christianity because the crèche itself bears a religious meaning, because an angel in the display carries a banner declaring "Glory to God in the highest!," and because the floral decorations surrounding the crèche highlighted it rather than secularized it. The display of a Christmas tree and Chanukah menorah, in contrast, is said to show no endorsement of a particular faith or faiths, or of religion in general, because the Christmas tree is a secular symbol which brings out the secular elements of the menorah. And, Justice BLACKMUN concludes, even though the menorah has religious aspects, its display reveals no endorsement of religion because no other symbol could have been used to represent the secular aspects of the holiday of Chanukah without mocking its celebration. Rather than endorsing religion, therefore, the display merely demonstrates that "Christmas is not the only traditional way of observing the winter-holiday season," and confirms our "cultural diversity."

Thus, the decision as to the menorah rests on three premises:

the Christmas tree is a secular symbol; Chanukah is a holiday with secular dimensions, symbolized by the menorah; and the government may promote pluralism by sponsoring or condoning displays having strong religious associations on its property. None of these is sound.

I

The first step toward Justice BLACKMUN's conclusion is the claim that, despite its religious origins, the Christmas tree is a secular symbol. . . .

Thus, while acknowledging the religious origins of the Christmas tree, Justices BLACKMUN and O'CONNOR dismiss their significance. In my view, this attempt to take the "Christmas" out of the Christmas tree is unconvincing. That the tree may, without controversy, be deemed a secular symbol if found alone, does not mean that it will be so seen when combined with other symbols or objects. . . . [T]he "pluralism" to which Justice O'CON-NOR refers is *religious* pluralism, and the "freedom of belief" she emphasizes is freedom of *religious* belief. The display of the tree and the menorah will symbolize such pluralism and freedom only if more than one religion is represented; if only Judaism is represented, the scene is about Judaism, not about pluralism. Thus, the pluralistic message Justice O'CONNOR stresses *depends on* the tree's possessing some religious significance.

In asserting that the Christmas tree, regardless of its surroundings, is a purely secular symbol, Justices BLACKMUN and O'CONNOR ignore the precept they otherwise so enthusiastically embrace: that context is all-important in determining the message conveyed by particular objects. . . .

Positioned as it was, the Christmas tree's religious significance was bound to come to the fore. Situated next to the menorah—which, Justice BLACKMUN acknowledges, is "a symbol with religious meaning," and indeed, is "the central religious symbol and ritual object of" Chanukah (O'CONNOR, J.)—the Christmas tree's religious dimension could not be overlooked by observers of the display. Even though the tree alone may be deemed predominantly secular, it can hardly be so characterized when placed next to such a forthrightly religious symbol. Consider a poster featuring a star of David, a statue of Buddha, a Christmas tree, a mosque, and a drawing of Krishna. There can be no doubt that, when found in such company, the tree serves as an unabashedly religious symbol.

Justice BLACKMUN believes that it is the tree that changes the message of the menorah, rather than the menorah that alters our view of the tree. After the abrupt dismissal of the suggestion that the flora surrounding the crèche might have diluted the religious character of the display at City Hall, his quick conclusion that the Christmas tree had a secularizing effect on the menorah is surprising. The distinguishing characteristic, it appears, is the size of the tree. The tree, we are told, is much taller—2½ times taller, in fact—than the menorah, and is located directly under one of the building's archways, whereas the menorah "is positioned to one side . . . [i]n the shadow of the tree.". . .

As a factual matter, it seems to me that the sight of an 18-foot menorah would be far more eye-catching than that of a rather conventionally sized Christmas tree. It also seems to me likely that the symbol with the more singular message will predominate over one lacking such a clear meaning. . . .

I would not, however, presume to say that my interpretation of the tree's significance is the "correct" one, or the one shared by most visitors to the City-County Building. I do not know how we can decide whether it was the tree that stripped the religious connotations from the menorah, or the menorah that laid bare the religious origins of the tree. Both are reasonable interpretations of the scene the city presented, and thus both, I think, should satisfy Justice BLACKMUN's requirement that the display "be judged according to the standard of a 'reasonable observer.' " I shudder to think that the only "reasonable observer" is one who shares the particular views on perspective, spacing, and accent expressed in Justice BLACKMUN's opinion, thus making analysis under the Establishment Clause look more like an exam in Art 101 than an inquiry into constitutional law.

II

The second premise on which today's decision rests is the notion that Chanukah is a partly secular holiday, for which the menorah can serve as a secular symbol. It is no surprise and no anomaly that Chanukah has historical and societal roots that range beyond the purely religious. I would venture that most, if not all, major religious holidays have beginnings and enjoy histories studded with figures, events, and practices that are not strictly religious. It does not seem to me that the mere fact that Chanukah shares this kind of background makes it a secular holiday in any meaningful sense. The menorah is indisputably a religious symbol, used ritually in a celebration that has deep religious significance. That, in my view, is all that need be said. Whatever secular practices the holiday of Chanukah has taken on in its contemporary observance are beside the point. . . .

I cannot, in short, accept the effort to transform an emblem of religious faith into the innocuous "symbol for a holiday that . . . has both religious and secular dimensions."

III

Justice BLACKMUN, in his acceptance of the city's message of "diversity," and, even more so, Justice O'CONNOR, in her approval of the "message of pluralism and freedom to choose one's own beliefs," appear to believe that, where seasonal displays are concerned, more is better. Whereas a display might be constitutionally problematic if it showcased the holiday of just one religion, those problems vaporize as soon as more than one religion is included. I know of no principle under the Establishment Clause, however, that permits us to conclude that governmental promotion of religion is acceptable so long as one religion is not favored. We have, on the contrary, interpreted that Clause to require neutrality, not just among religions, but between religion and nonreligion. . . .

The uncritical acceptance of a message of religious pluralism also ignores the extent to which even that message may offend. Many religious faiths are hostile to each other, and indeed, refuse even to participate in ecumenical services designed to demonstrate the very pluralism Justices BLACKMUN and O'CONNOR extol. To lump the ritual objects and holidays of religions together without regard to their attitudes toward such inclusiveness, or to decide which religions should be excluded because of the possibility of offense, is not a benign or beneficent celebration of pluralism: it is instead an interference in religious matters precluded by the Establishment Clause.

Justice STEVENS, with whom Justice BRENNAN and Justice MARSHALL join, concurring in part and dissenting in part.

In my opinion the Establishment Clause should be construed to create a strong presumption against the display of religious symbols on public property. There is always a risk that such symbols will offend nonmembers of the faith being advertised as well as adherents who consider the particular advertisement disrespectful. Some devout Christians believe that the crèche should be placed only in reverential settings, such as a church or perhaps a private home; they do not countenance its use as an aid to commercialization of Christ's birthday. In this very case, members of the Jewish faith firmly opposed the use to which the menorah was put by the particular sect that sponsored the display at Pittsburgh's City-County Building. . . .

Application of a strong presumption against the public use of religious symbols scarcely will "require a relentless extirpation of all contact between government and religion" (KENNEDY, J., concurring in judgment in part and dissenting in part), for it will prohibit a display only when its message, evaluated in the context in which it is presented, is nonsecular. For example, a carving of Moses holding the Ten Commandments, if that is the only adornment on a courtroom wall, conveys an equivocal message, perhaps of respect for Judaism, for religion in general, or for law. The addition of carvings depicting Confucius and

Mohammed may honor religion, or particular religions, to an extent that the First Amendment does not tolerate any more than it does "the permanent erection of a large Latin cross on the roof of city hall.". . .

Thus I find wholly unpersuasive Justice KENNEDY's attempts to belittle the importance of the obvious differences between the display of the crèche in this case and that in *Lynch v. Donnelly* (1984). Even if I had not dissented from the Court's conclusion that the crèche in *Lynch* was constitutional, I would conclude that Allegheny County's unambiguous exposition of a sacred symbol inside its courthouse promoted Christianity to a degree that violated the Establishment Clause. Accordingly, I concur in the Court's judgment regarding the crèche for substantially the same reasons discussed in Justice BRENNAN's dissent, which I join, as well as Part IV of Justice BLACKMUN's opinion and Part I of Justice O'CONNOR's opinion.

I cannot agree with the Court's conclusion that the display at Pittsburgh's City-County Building was constitutional. Standing alone in front of a governmental headquarters, a lighted, 45-foot evergreen tree might convey holiday greetings linked too tenuously to Christianity to have constitutional moment. Juxtaposition of this tree with an 18-foot menorah does not make the latter secular, as Justice BLACKMUN contends. Rather, the presence of the Chanukah menorah, unquestionably a religious symbol, gives religious significance to the Christmas tree. The overall display thus manifests governmental approval of the Jewish and Christian religions.

Justice KENNEDY, with whom the CHIEF JUSTICE, Justice WHITE, and Justice SCALIA join, concurring in the judgment in part and dissenting in part.

The majority holds that the County of Allegheny violated the Establishment Clause by displaying a crèche in the county courthouse, because the "principal or primary effect" of the display is to advance religion within the meaning of *Lemon v. Kurtzman,* 403 U.S. 602 (1971). This view of the Establishment Clause reflects an unjustified hostility toward religion, a hostility inconsistent with our history and our precedents, and I dissent from this holding. The crèche display is constitutional, and, for the same reasons, the display of a menorah by the city of Pittsburgh is permissible as well. On this latter point, I concur in the result, but not the reasoning, of Part VI of Justice BLACKMUN's opinion. . . .

Rather than requiring government to avoid any action that acknowledges or aids religion, the Establishment Clause permits government some latitude in recognizing and accommodating the central role religion plays in our society. *Lynch v. Donnelly,* [and] *Walz v. Tax Comm'n.* Any approach less sensitive to our heritage would border on latent hostility toward religion, as it would require government in all its multifaceted roles to acknowledge only the secular, to the exclusion and so to the detriment of the religious. A categorical approach would install federal courts as jealous guardians of an absolute "wall of separation," sending a clear message of disapproval. In this century, as the modern administrative state expands to touch the lives of its citizens in such diverse ways and redirects their financial choices through programs of its own, it is difficult to maintain the fiction that requiring government to avoid all assistance to religion can in fairness be viewed as serving the goal of neutrality. . . .

The ability of the organized community to recognize and accommodate religion in a society with a pervasive public sector requires diligent observance of the border between accommodation and establishment. Our cases disclose two limiting principles: government may not coerce anyone to support or participate in any religion or its exercise; and it may not, in the guise of avoiding hostility or callous indifference, give direct benefits to religion in such a degree that it in fact "establishes a [state] religion or religious faith, or tends to do so." *Lynch v. Donnelly.* These two principles, while distinct, are not unrelated, for it would be difficult indeed to establish a religion without some measure of more or less subtle coercion, be it in the form of taxation to supply the substantial benefits that would sustain a state-established faith, direct compulsion to observance, or governmental exhortation to religiosity that amounts in fact to proselytizing. . . .

If government is to participate in its citizens' celebration of a holiday that contains both a secular and a religious component, enforced recognition of only the secular aspect would signify the callous indifference toward religious faith that our cases and traditions do not require; for by commemorating the holiday only as it is celebrated by nonadherents, the government would be refusing to acknowledge the plain fact, and the historical reality, that many of its citizens celebrate its religious aspects as well. Judicial invalidation of government's attempts to recognize the religious underpinnings of the holiday would signal not neutrality but a pervasive intent to insulate government from all things religious. The Religion Clauses do not require government to acknowledge these holidays or their religious component; but our strong tradition of government accommodation and acknowledgment permits government to do so. . . .

There is no suggestion here that the government's power to coerce has been used to further the interests of Christianity or Judaism in any way. No one was compelled to observe or participate in any religious ceremony or activity. Neither the city nor the county contributed significant amounts of tax money to serve the cause of one religious faith. The crèche and the menorah are purely passive symbols of religious holidays. Passersby who disagree with the message conveyed by these displays are free to ignore them, or even to turn their backs, just as they are free to do when they disagree with any other form of government speech.

There is no realistic risk that the crèche or the menorah represent an effort to proselytize or are otherwise the first step down the road to an establishment of religion. *Lynch* is dispositive of this claim with respect to the crèche, and I find no reason for reaching a different result with respect to the menorah. Both are the traditional symbols of religious holidays that over time have acquired a secular component. . . .

Respondents say that the religious displays involved here are distinguishable from the crèche in *Lynch* because they are located on government property and are not surrounded by the candy canes, reindeer, and other holiday paraphernalia that were a part of the display in *Lynch*. Nothing in Chief Justice BURGER's opinion for the Court in *Lynch* provides support for these purported distinctions. After describing the facts, the *Lynch* opinion makes no mention of either of these factors. It concentrates instead on the significance of the crèche as part of the entire holiday season. Indeed, it is clear that the Court did not view the secular aspects of the display as somehow subduing the religious message conveyed by the crèche, for the majority expressly rejected the dissenters' suggestion that it sought " 'to explain away the clear religious import of the crèche' " or had "equated the crèche with a Santa's house or reindeer." Crucial to the Court's conclusion was not the number, prominence, or type of secular items contained in the holiday display but the simple fact that, when displayed by government during the Christmas season, a crèche presents no realistic danger of moving government down the forbidden road toward an establishment of religion. Whether the crèche be surrounded by poinsettias, talking wishing wells, or carolers, the conclusion remains the same, for the relevant context is not the items in the display itself but the season as a whole.

The fact that the crèche and menorah are both located on government property, even at the very seat of government, is likewise inconsequential. . . .

Our cases do not suggest, moreover, that the use of public property necessarily converts otherwise permissible government conduct into an Establishment Clause violation. To the contrary, in some circumstances the First Amendment may *require* that government property be available for use by religious groups, see *Widmar v. Vincent*, 454 U.S. 263 (1981); *Fowler v. Rhode Island*, 345 U.S. 67 (1953); *Niemotko v. Maryland*, 340 U.S. 268 (1951), and even where not required, such use has long been permitted. The prayer approved in *Marsh v. Chambers*, [463 U.S. 783 (1983)], for example, was conducted in the legislative chamber of the State of Nebraska, surely the single place most likely to be thought the center of state authority.

Nor can I comprehend why it should be that placement of a government-owned crèche on private land is lawful while placement of a privately owned crèche on public land is not. If anything, I should have thought government ownership of a religious symbol presented the more difficult question under the Establishment Clause, but as *Lynch* resolved that question to sustain the government action, the sponsorship here ought to be all the easier to sustain. In short, nothing about the religious displays here distinguishes them in any meaningful way from the crèche we permitted in *Lynch.*

If *Lynch* is still good law—and until today it was—the judgment below cannot stand. I accept and indeed approve both the holding and the reasoning of Chief Justice BURGER's opinion in *Lynch,* and so I must dissent from the judgment that the crèche display is unconstitutional. On the same reasoning, I agree that the menorah display is constitutional.

The majority invalidates display of the crèche, not because it disagrees with the interpretation of *Lynch* applied above, but because it chooses to discard the reasoning of the *Lynch* majority opinion in favor of Justice O'CONNOR's concurring opinion in that case. . . . As a general rule, the principle of *stare decisis* directs us to adhere not only to the holdings of our prior cases, but also to their explications of the governing rules of law. Since the majority does not state its intent to overrule *Lynch,* I find its refusal to apply the reasoning of that decision quite confusing.

Even if *Lynch* did not control, I would not commit this Court to the test applied by the majority today. The notion that cases arising under the Establishment Clause should be decided by an inquiry into whether a " 'reasonable observer' " may " 'fairly understand' " government action to " 'sen[d] a message to nonadherents that they are outsiders, not full members of the political community,' " is a recent, and in my view most unwelcome, addition to our tangled Establishment Clause jurisprudence. Although a scattering of our cases have used "endorsement" as another word for "preference" or "imprimatur," the endorsement test applied by the majority had its genesis in Justice O'CONNOR's concurring opinion in *Lynch.*

For the reasons expressed below, I submit that the endorsement test is flawed in its fundamentals and unworkable in practice. The uncritical adoption of this standard is every bit as troubling as the bizarre result it produces in the case before us. . . .

If the endorsement test, applied without artificial exceptions for historical practice, reached results consistent with history, my objections to it would have less force. But, as I understand that test, the touchstone of an Establishment Clause violation is whether nonadherents would be made to feel like "outsiders" by government recognition or accommodation of religion. Few of our traditional practices recognizing the part religion plays in our society can withstand scrutiny under a faithful application of this formula. . . .

If the intent of the Establishment Clause is to protect individuals from mere feelings of exclusion, then legislative prayer cannot escape invalidation. It has been argued that "[these] government acknowledgments of religion serve, in the only ways reasonably possible in our culture, the legitimate secular purposes of solemnizing public occasions, expressing confidence in the future, and encouraging the recognition of what is worthy of appreciation in society." *Lynch* (O'CONNOR, J., concurring). I fail to see why prayer is the only way to convey these messages; appeals to patriotism, moments of silence, and any number of other approaches would be as effective, were the only purposes at issue the ones described by the *Lynch* concurrence. Nor is it clear to me why "encouraging the recognition of what is worthy of appreciation in society" can be characterized as a purely secular purpose, if it can be achieved only through religious prayer. No doubt prayer is "worthy of appreciation," but that is most assuredly not because it is secular. Even accepting the secular-solemnization explanation at face value, moreover, it seems incredible to suggest that the average observer of legislative prayer who either believes in no religion or whose faith rejects the concept of God would not receive the clear message that his faith is out of step with the political norm. Either the endorsement test must invalidate scores of traditional practices recognizing the place religion holds in our culture, or it must be twisted and stretched to avoid inconsistency with practices we know to have been permitted in the past, while condemning similar practices with no greater endorsement effect simply by reason of their lack of historical antecedent. Neither result is acceptable. . . .

The result the Court reaches in this case is perhaps the clearest illustration of the unwisdom of the endorsement test. Although Justice O'CONNOR disavows Justice BLACKMUN's suggestion that the minority or majority status of a religion is relevant to the question whether government recognition constitutes a forbidden endorsement, the very nature of the endorsement test, with its emphasis on the feelings of the objective observer, easily lends itself to this type of inquiry. If there be such a person as the "reasonable observer," I am quite certain that he or she will take away a salient message from our holding in this case: the Supreme Court of the United States has concluded that the First Amendment creates classes of religions based on the relative numbers of their adherents. Those religions enjoying the largest following must be consigned to the status of least-favored faiths so as to avoid any possible risk of offending members of minority religions.

I would be the first to admit that many questions arising under the Establishment Clause do not admit of easy answers, but whatever the Clause requires, it is not the result reached by the Court today.

The approach adopted by the majority contradicts important values embodied in the Clause. Obsessive, implacable resistance to all but the most carefully scripted and secularized forms of accommodation requires this Court to act as a censor, issuing national decrees as to what is orthodox and what is not. What is orthodox, in this context, means what is secular; the only Christmas the State can acknowledge is one in which references to religion have been held to a minimum. The Court thus lends its assistance to an Orwellian rewriting of history as many understand it. I can conceive of no judicial function more antithetical to the First Amendment.

A further contradiction arises from the majority's approach, for the Court also assumes the difficult and inappropriate task of saying what every religious symbol means. Before studying this case, I had not known the full history of the menorah, and I suspect the same was true of my colleagues. More important, this history was, and is, likely unknown to the vast majority of people of all faiths who saw the symbol displayed in Pittsburgh. Even if the majority is quite right about the history of the menorah, it hardly follows that this same history informed the observers' view of the symbol and the reason for its presence. This Court is ill-equipped to sit as a national theology board, and I question both the wisdom and the constitutionality of its doing so. Indeed, were I required to choose between the approach taken by the majority and a strict separationist view, I would have to respect the consistency of the latter.

The case before us is admittedly a troubling one. It must be conceded that, however neutral the purpose of the city and county, the eager proselytizer may seek to use these symbols for his own ends. The urge to use them to teach or to taunt is always present. It is also true that some devout adherents of Judaism or Christianity may be as offended by the holiday display as are nonbelievers, if not more so. To place these religious symbols in a common hallway or sidewalk, where they may be ignored or even insulted, must be distasteful to many who cherish their meaning.

For these reasons, I might have voted against installation of these particular displays were I a local legislative official. But we have no jurisdiction over matters of taste within the realm of constitutionally permissible discretion. Our role is enforcement of a written Constitution. In my view, the principles of the Establishment Clause and our Nation's historic traditions of diversity and pluralism allow communities to make reasonable judgments respecting the accommodation or acknowledgment of holidays with both cultural and religious aspects. No constitutional violation occurs when they do so by displaying a symbol of the holiday's religious origins.

I dissent.

B. FREE EXERCISE OF RELIGION

The free exercise clause embodies the principle of freedom from governmental coercion in choosing a religion or no religion. That guarantee is not absolute, however. Individuals may be prosecuted for certain religious practices (handling poisonous snakes or taking illegal drugs) and compelled to comply with regulations and laws (such as Sunday closing laws) that contravene their religious beliefs. Still, the Court has interpreted the free exercise clause to require state neutrality with regard to religion. A law may not discriminate on the basis of religion nor have a religious purpose. On this basis, in *Toracso v. Watkins,* 367 U.S. 488 (1961), the Court struck down Maryland's law requiring as a condition of holding public office that individuals take an oath declaring their "belief in the existence of God." In *McDaniel v. Paty,* 435 U.S. 618 (1978), a Tennessee statute forbidding ministers and priests from serving as delegates to state constitutional conventions was overturned. Over free exercise objections, the Court has also upheld laws that have a secular purpose but which forbid Mormans from practicing polygamy,[1] required smallpox vaccinations,[2] the closing of businesses on Sundays,[3] and prohibited the distribution of handbills and solicitations on fairgrounds.[4]

State neutrality and rigid enforcement of the secular regulation principle, however, has been criticized for being too harsh, taking little or no account of the impact on individuals' religious lives of coercive laws. As an alternative, or exception to strict state neutrality, the Court invented the "least drastic means test," when striking down a South Carolina law denying unemployment compensation to a Seventh Day Adventist who refused to work on the Sabbath, in *Sherbert v. Verner* (1963) (see page 745). On this test, the Court considers whether states might achieve their objectives through other, less drastic means.

In *Wisconsin v. Yoder* (1972) (see page 752), Chief Justice Burger advanced his accommodationist approach in carving out an exception for the Amish from compulsory school attendance beyond the eighth grade. When accommodating free exercise claims the Court basically balances those claims against competing governmental interests, taking into consideration the nature of the regulation, the centrality of a religious belief, and the equality in treatment of religion. In *Cruz v. Beto,* 405 U.S. 319 (1972), for instance, the Court ruled that where Catholic, Protestant, and Jewish prison inmates were allowed to hold religious services, the state could not deny the same right of free exercise to Buddhists. By contrast, in *O'Lone v. Shabazz*, 482 U.S. 342 (1987), a bare majority of the Rehnquist Court held that Islamic prisoners could be denied the right to attend services in jail for security reasons.

The Court also held that governmental interests may simply outweigh free exercise claims, despite their coercive effect on religious beliefs and practices. In *Goldman v. Weinberger*, 475 U.S. 503 (1986), the justices (six to three) upheld the air force's prohibition of wearing yarmulkes by Orthodox Jewish officers. The following year, however, Congress passed a law permitting members of the military to wear religious apparel indoors, while on duty, so long as it does not interfere with their military duties and is "neat and conservative." In *Lyng v. Northwest Indian Cemetery Protective Association*, 485 U.S. 439 (1988), the Court upheld the forest service's permitting road constructions and timber harvests in areas of the national forest that were traditionally used for religious purposes by Indian tribes.

When confronted with free exercise claims, the Court may not be able to avoid the issue of what is religion? And who should define *religious beliefs*—the government, the Court, or the individual? When upholding a congressional statute banning and punishing polygamy, which Mormans practiced as a religious belief, in *Reynolds v. United States*, 98 U.S. 145 (1879), Chief Justice Waite observed, "The word 'religion' is not defined in the Constitution. We must go elsewhere, therefore, to ascertain its meaning, and no where more appropriately, we think, than to the history of the times in the midst of which the provision was adopted." After surveying the founding period, Waite found no religious support for the practice of polygamy (the Morman church was not established until the late nineteenth century) and found support for the statute, which had the secular purpose of enforcing the standards of "civilized society," in Jefferson's "Bill for Establishing Religious Freedom," allowing government to "interfere when [religious] principles break out into overt acts against peace and good order." But dissenting in *Everson*, Justice Rutledge cautioned against the Court's trying to define religion for free exercise purposes, while refusing to do so under the establishment clause:

"Religion" appears only once in the [First] Amendment. But the word governs two prohibitions and governs them alike. It does not have two meanings, one narrow to forbid "an establishment" and another, much broader, for securing "the free exercise thereof." "Thereof" brings down "religion" with its entire and exact content, no more and no less, from the first into the second guaranty, so that Congress and now the states are broadly restricted concerning the one as they are regarding the other.

The Court, once again, confronted the problem in *United States v. Ballard*, 322 U.S. 78 (1944), involving the prosecution of the leaders of the "I Am" religion for mail fraud. Guy Ballard, the founder of the religion, claimed to be the messenger of a Master Saint Germain and to have powers to cure diseases. Ballard's widow and son were charged with making claims about curing diseases that they knew were false. But the Court held that at their trial the jury could not be allowed to determine the truth or falsity of the Ballards' claims; it could determine only whether the Ballards sincerely believed their claims, or instead were deceitful and guilty of misrepresentations. "Men may believe what they cannot prove," Justice Douglas wrote, adding, "They may not be put to the proof of their religious doctrines or beliefs. . . . The First Amendment does not select any one group or any one type of religion for preferred treatment." The majority did not go far enough for dissenting Justice Jackson, who argued:

In the first place, as a matter of either practice or philosophy I do not see how we can separate an issue as to what is believed from considerations as to what is believable. . . . In the second place, any inquiry into intellectual honesty in religion raises profound psychological problems. . . . And then I do not know what degree of skepticism or disbelief in a religious representation amounts to actionable fraud.

In a dissenting opinion, Chief Justice Stone found it hard "to say that freedom of thought and worship includes freedom to procure money by making knowingly false statements about one's religious experiences," and explained that

if it were shown that a defendant in this case had asserted as a part of the alleged fraudulent scheme, that he had physically shaken hands with St. Germain in San Francisco on a day named, or that, as the indictment here alleges, by the exertion of his spiritual power he "had in fact cured . . . hundreds of persons afflicted with diseases and ailments:, I should not doubt that it would be open to the Government to submit to the jury proof that he had never been in San Francisco and that no such cures had ever been effected.

Stone and Jackson agreed that the Ballards could have been prosecuted for misrepresenting "that funds are being used to build a church when in fact they are being used for personal purposes." (In 1987–1988, televangelicalists Jim and Tammy Bakker were indicted and prosecuted for tax evasion and misappropriation of monies given by their disciples to their television ministry.)

While the government may prosecute religious leaders and their followers for crimes such as tax evasion, fraud, misrepresentations, and child abuse, the Court has suggested that it may be futile for the government to try to define religion for free exercise purposes.[5] At least the Court gave an expansive reading to religion in the conscientious objector cases arising from a federal statute allowing exemptions from military service for an individual "who, by reason of religious training or belief, is conscientiously opposed to participation in war in any form." *Religious training and belief* was defined by Congress as "an individual's belief in relation to a Supreme Being involving duties superior to those arising from any human relation, but . . . not any essentially political, sociological, or philosophical views or a merely personal moral code." When hearing an appeal of three men, who did not subscribe to a traditional religion but claimed not to be "irreligious or aetheists," in *United States v. Seeger*, 380 U.S. 163 (1965), the Court unanimously held that they were entitled to conscientious exemption because the test of one's religious belief "in a relation to a Supreme Being" is "whether a given belief that is sincere and meaningful occupies a place in the life of its possessor parallel to that filled by the orthodox belief in God of one who clearly qualifies for the exemption. Where such beliefs have parallel positions in the lives of their respective holders we cannot say that one is "in relation to a Supreme Being" and the other is not." Congress responded to *Seeger* by deleting the language "in a relation to a Supreme Being." But the Court went even farther in *Welsh v. United States*, 398 U.S. 333 (1970), holding that an individual who denied that his beliefs opposing war were religious was, nonetheless, entitled to conscientious objector status because his ethical and moral beliefs were parallel to and just as strong as religious convictions.

Finally, the Court applied *Sherbert's* balancing test in several cases to prohibit the denial of unemployment compensation to individuals who lost their jobs because of their religious beliefs. See, for example, *Thomas v. Review Board of Indiana* (1981) and *Hobbie v. Unemployment Appeals Commission of Florida* (1987), in the table on page 741. However, in *Employment Division, Department of Human Resources of Oregon v. Smith* (1990) (see page 757), Justice Scalia rejected further application of *Sherbert's* balancing test and its requirement that states show a compelling interest in regulations to justify overriding free exercise claims. Relying on *Smith*, the Rehnquist Court reaffirmed its jurisprudential shift and unwillingness to make religious exceptions for individuals from general regulations, when vacating a state supreme court decision exempting the Amish from highway safety laws in *Minnesota v. Hershberger*, 110 S.Ct. 1918 (1990).

THE DEVELOPMENT OF LAW
Major Rulings Denying Free Exercise Claims

Case	Vote	Ruling
Reynolds v. United States, 90 U.S. 145 (1879)	9:0	Upheld a congressional statute banning polygamy over the religious objections of Mormons.
Hamilton v. Regents of the University of California, 293 U.S. 245 (1934)	9:0	Upheld compulsory courses in military science over the religious objections of religious students.
Minersville v. Gobitis, 310 U.S. 586 (1940)	8:1	Upheld compulsory flag salute over the objections of Jehovah's Witnesses.
Prince v. Massachusetts, 321 U.S. 158 (1944)	8:1	Upheld statute forbidding minors from selling newspapers on streets over the objections of Jehovah's Witnesses.
McGowan v. Maryland, 366 U.S. 420 (1961); *Braunfeld v. Brown*, 366 U.S. 599 (1961)	6:3 7:2	Upheld Sunday closing laws over the objections of Orthodox Jews who recognize Saturday as the Sabbath.
Garber v. Kansas, 389 U.S. 51 (1967)	6:3	Rejected Amish claim of a right to refuse to send children to public schools.
Gillette v. United States and *Negre v. Larsen*, 401 U.S. 437 (1971)	8:1	Denied conscientious objection status to those opposing *certain* wars and "unjust" wars.
Heffron v. International Society for Krishna Consciousness, 452 U.S. 640 (1981)	5:4	Upheld law banning sales and solicitations at fairground by a religious group.
United States v. Lee, 455 U.S. 252 (1982)	8:0	Amish employers must pay social security taxes, even though Congress exempted self-employed Amish from paying the taxes.
Bob Jones University and Goldsboro Christian School v. United States, 461 U.S. 574 (1983)	8:1	Upheld IRS's withdrawing of tax-exempt status for educational institutions that discriminate racially.
Tony and Susan Alamo Foundation v. Secretary of Labor, 471 U.S. 290 (1985)	9:0	Religious organizations must comply with federal minimum wage laws.
Goldman v. Weinberger, 475 U.S. 503 (1986)	5:4	Orthodox Jewish rabbi and air force captain may not wear

Case	Vote	Ruling
		yarmulke contrary to military dress code.
Bowen v. Roy, 476 U.S. 693 (1986)	8:1	Government may use social security numbers despite religious objections.
O'Lone v. Shabazz, 482 U.S. 342 (1987)	5:4	For security reasons, Islamic prisoners may be denied right to attend religious services.
Lyng v. Northwest Indian Cemetery Protective Association, 485 U.S. 439 (1988)	5:3	With Scalia not participating, Court held that the forest service may permit road construction and timber harvesting in areas of national parks traditionally used for religious purposes by Indian tribes.
Hernandez v. Commissioner of Internal Revenue, 109 S.Ct. 2136 (1989)	5:2	Upheld IRS decision that fixed donations to Church of Scientology by members are not tax-deductable contributions.
Swaggart v. Board of Equalization of California, 110 S.Ct. 688 (1990)	9:0	Upheld California's 6 percent sales tax as applied to sales of religious materials sold by Jimmy Swaggart Ministries at "evangelistic crusades" in the state and through mail-order sales to state residents.
Employment Division, Department of Human Resources of Oregon v. Smith, 110 S.Ct. 1595 (1990)	6:3	Held that the free exercise clause does not prohibit the application of Oregon's drug laws to the ceremonial use of peyote by members of the Native American Church and that members of the church could be denied unemployment compensation after they were fired from their jobs as drug-rehabilitation counselors because of their ceremonial use of peyote.
Minnesota v. Hershberger, 110 S.Ct. 1918 (1990)	7:2	Vacated a decision of the Minnesota Supreme Court that exempted the Amish from complying with highway safety laws.

THE DEVELOPMENT OF LAW
Major Rulings Upholding Free Exercise Claims

Case	Vote	Ruling
Cantwell v. Connecticut, 310 U.S. 296 (1940)	9:0	Struck down permit requirement for soliciting funds on public streets challenged by Jehovah's Witnesses.
Murdock v. Commonwealth of Pennsylvania, 319 U.S. 105 (1943)	5:4	Struck down license tax on canvassing and soliciting as applied to Jehovah's Witnesses.
Martin v. Struthers, 319 U.S. 141 (1943)	5:4	Overturned ordinance forbidding door-to-door solicitations as applied to Jehovah's Witnesses.
Douglas v. City of Jeanette, 319 U.S. 157 (1943)	9:0	After citizens' complaints, police may not stop Jehovah's Wintesses from proselytizing on Sundays.
West Virginia State Board of Education v. Barnette, 319 U.S. 624 (1943)	6:3	Overturned compulsory flag salute statute.
Jamison v. Texas, 318 U.S. 413 (1943)	8:0	Overturned statute barring handbill distributions as related to religious activities.
United States v. Ballard, 322 U.S. 78 (1944)	5:4	The truth of religious beliefs may not be judged by jury at trials.
Girouard v. United States, 328 U.S. 61 (1946)	5:3	Naturalization may not be denied to conscientious objectors.
Marsh v. Alabama, 326 U.S. 501 (1946)	5:3	Distribution of religious literature cannot be banned in private company town.
Niemotko v. Maryland, 340 U.S. 268 (1951)	9:0	Use of public parks may not be denied to Jehovah's Witnesses.
Torcaso v. Watkins, 367 U.S. 488 (1961)	9:0	Struck down required oath declaring belief in God for public office.
Sherbert v. Verner, 374 U.S. 398 (1963)	7:2	Overturned denial of unemployment compensation to Seventh Day Adventist who was fired for refusing to work on Sabbath.
United States v. Seeger, 380 U.S. 380 (1965)	9:0	Broadly interpreted religious training and belief in according conscientious objector status.

Case	Vote	Ruling
Wisconsin v. Yoder, 406 U.S. 205 (1972)	6:1	Amish are exempt from sending children to school beyond the eighth grade.
Wooley v. Maynard, 430 U.S. 705 (1977)	7:2	Upheld claim of Jehovah's Witnesses that they could not be compelled to bear license plates with the motto Live Free or Die.
McDaniel v. Paty, 435 U.S. 618 (1978)	8:0	Religious leaders may not be disqualified from serving as delegates to state constitutional conventions.
Thomas v. Review Board of Indiana Employment Security Division, 450 U.S. 707 (1981)	8:1	State may not deny unemployment compensation to individual who terminated employment because of religious objection to working in the production of armaments.
Hobbie v. Unemployment Appeals Commission of Florida, 480 U.S. 136 (1987)	8:1	Applied *Sherbert* in holding that denial of unemployment compensation benefits must withstand strict scrutiny and that it is immaterial that claimant had a religious conversion during course of employment. Chief Justice Rehnquist dissented.
Frazee v. Illinois Department of Employment Security, 489 U.S. 829 (1989)	9:0	Held denial of unemployment compensation to worker who refused to work on Sabbath, even though refusal was not based on a religious sect's doctrines, violated the free exercise clause.

NOTES

1. *Reynolds v. United States*, 98 U.S. 145 (1890).
2. *Jacobson v. Massachusetts*, 197 U.S. 11 (1905).
3. See, for example, *Braunfeld v. Brown*, 366 U.S. 599 (1961).
4. *Heffron v. International Society for Krishna Consciousness*, 455 U.S. 252 (1981).

5. See Note, "Toward a Constitutional Definition of Religion," 91 *Harvard Law Review* 1056 (1978); and Jesse Choper, "Defining 'Religion' in the First Amendment," 1982 *University of Illinois Law Review* 579.

SELECTED BIBLIOGRAPHY

Choper, Jesse. "The Religion Clauses of the First Amendment: Reconciling the Conflict." 41 *University of Pittsburgh Law Review* 673 (1980).
Manwaring, David. *Render unto Ceaser: The Flag Salute Controversy.* Chicago: University of Chicago Press, 1962.
Pfeffer, Leo. *God, Ceaser and the Constitution.* Boston: Beacon Press, 1975.

Sherbert v. Verner

374 U.S. 398, 83 S.Ct. 1790 (1963)

Justice Brennan discusses the facts in this case, involving a claim that the denial of unemployment benefits to an individual who refused to work on her Sabbath violated the free exercise clause, in his opinion announcing the decision of the Court.

Justice BRENNAN delivers the opinion of the Court.

Appellant, a member of the Seventh-day Adventist Church was discharged by her South Carolina employer because she would not work on Saturday, the Sabbath Day of her faith. When she was unable to obtain other employment because from conscientious scruples she would not take Saturday work, she filed a claim for unemployment compensation benefits under the South Carolina Unemployment Compensation Act. . . .

The appellee Employment Security Commission, in administrative proceedings under the statute, found that appellant's restriction upon her availability for Saturday work brought her within the provision disqualifying for benefits insured workers who fail, without good cause, to accept "suitable work when offered . . . by the employment office or the employer. . . ." The Commission's finding was sustained by the Court of Common Pleas for Spartanburg County. That court's judgment was in turn affirmed by the South Carolina Supreme Court, which rejected appellant's contention that, as applied to her, the disqualifying provisions of the South Carolina statute abridged her right to the free exercise of her religion secured under the Free Exercise Clause of the

First Amendment through the Fourteenth Amendment. . . . We reverse the judgment of the South Carolina Supreme Court and remand for further proceedings not inconsistent with this opinion.

I

. . . Plainly enough, appellant's conscientious objection to Saturday work constitutes no conduct prompted by religious principles of a kind within the reach of state legislation. If, therefore, the decision of the South Carolina Supreme Court is to withstand appellant's constitutional challenge, it must be either because her disqualification as a beneficiary represents no infringement by the State of her constitutional rights of free exercise, or because any incidental burden on the free exercise of appellant's religion may be justified by a "compelling state interest in the regulation of a subject within the State's constitutional power to regulate. . . ." *NAACP v. Button*, 371 U.S. 415 [(1963)].

II

We turn first to the question whether the disqualification for benefits imposes any burden on the free exercise of appellant's religion. We think it is clear that it does. In a sense the consequences of such a disqualification to religious principles and practices may be only an indirect result of welfare legislation within the State's general competence to enact; it is true that no criminal sanctions directly compel appellant to work a six-day week. But this is only the beginning, not the end, of our inquiry. For "[i]f the purpose or effect of a law is to impede the observance of one or all religions or is to discriminate invidiously between religions, that law is constitutionally invalid even though the burden may be characterized as being only indirect." Braunfeld v. Brown. Here not only is it apparent that appellant's declared ineligibility for benefits derives solely from the practice of her religion, but the pressure upon her to forego that practice is unmistakable. The ruling forces her to choose between following the precepts of her religion and forfeiting benefits, on the one hand, and abandoning one of the precepts of her religion in order to accept work, on the other hand. Governmental imposition of such a choice puts the same kind of burden upon the free exercise of religion as would a fine imposed against appellant for her Saturday worship.

Nor may the South Carolina court's construction of the statute be saved from constitutional infirmity on the ground that unemployment compensation benefits are not appellant's "right" but merely a "privilege." It is too late in the day to doubt that the liberties of religion and expression may be infringed by the denial of or placing of conditions upon a benefit or privilege. . . .

III

We must next consider whether some compelling state interest enforced in the eligibility provisions of the South Carolina statute justifies the substantial infringement of appellant's First Amendment right. It is basic that no showing merely of a rational relationship to some colorable state interest would suffice; in this highly sensitive constitutional area, "[o]nly the gravest abuses, endangering paramount interests, give occasion for permissible limitation," *Thomas v. Collins*, 323 U.S. 516 [1945]. No such abuse or danger has been advanced in the present case. The appellees suggest no more than a possibility that the filing of fraudulent claims by unscrupulous claimants feigning religious objections to Saturday work might not only dilute the unemployment compensation fund but also hinder the scheduling by employers of necessary Saturday work. But that possibility is not apposite here because no such objection appears to have been made before the South Carolina Supreme Court, and we are unwilling to assess the importance of an asserted state interest without the views of the state court. Nor, if the contention had been made below, would the record appear to sustain it. . . . For even if the possibility of spurious claims did threaten to dilute the fund and disrupt the scheduling of work, it would plainly be incumbent upon the appellees to demonstrate that no alternative forms of regulation would combat such abuses without infringing First Amendment rights.

In these respects, then, the state interest asserted in the present case is wholly dissimilar to the interests which were found to justify the less direct burden upon religious practices in *Braunfeld v. Brown*, [366 U.S. 599 (1961)]. The Court recognized that the Sunday closing law which that decision sustained undoubtedly served "to make the practice of [the Orthodox Jewish merchants'] religious beliefs more expensive." But the statute was nevertheless saved by a countervailing factor which finds no equivalent in the instant case—a strong state interest in providing one uniform day of rest for all workers. That secular objective could be achieved, the Court found, only by declaring Sunday to be that day of rest. Requiring exemptions for Sabbatarians, while theoretically possible, appeared to present an administrative problem of such magnitude, or to afford the exempted class so great a competitive advantage, that such a requirement would have rendered the entire statutory scheme unworkable. In the present case no such justifications underlie the determination of the state court that appellant's religion makes her ineligible to receive benefits.

IV

In holding as we do, plainly we are not fostering the "establishment" of the Seventh-day Adventist religion in South Carolina, for the extension of unemployment benefits to Sabbatarians in common with Sunday worshippers reflects nothing more than the governmental obligation of neutrality in the face of religious differences, and does not represent that involvement of religious with secular institutions which it is the object of the Establishment Clause to forestall. See School District of *Abington Township v. Schempp*, 374 U.S. 203 [1963]. Nor does the recognition of the appellant's right to unemployment benefits under the state statute serve to abridge any other person's religious liberties. Nor do we, by our decision today, declare the existence of a constitutional right to unemployment benefits on the part of all persons whose religious convictions are the cause of their unemployment. This is not a case in which an employee's religious convictions serve to make him a nonproductive member of society. See note 2, supra. Finally, nothing we say today constrains the States to adopt any particular form or scheme of unemployment compensation. Our holding today is only that South Carolina may not constitutionally apply the eligibility provisions so as to constrain a worker to abandon his religious convictions respecting the day of rest.

Justice DOUGLAS concurring.

This case is resolvable not in terms of what an individual can demand of government, but solely in terms of what government may not do to an individual in violation of his religious scruples. The fact that government cannot exact from me a surrender of one iota of my religious scruples does not, of course, mean that I can demand of government a sum of money, the better to exercise them. For the Free Exercise Clause is written in terms of what the government cannot do to the individual, not in terms of what the individual can exact from the government.

Those considerations, however, are not relevant here. If appellant is otherwise qualified for unemployment benefits, payments will be made to her not as a Seventh-day Adventist, but as an unemployed worker. Conceivably these payments will indirectly benefit her church, but no more so than does the salary of any public employee. Thus, this case does not involve the problems of direct or indirect state assistance to a religious organization— matters relevant to the Establishment Clause, not in issue here.

Justice STEWART concurring.

Although fully agreeing with the result which the Court reaches in this case, I cannot join the Court's opinion. This case presents a double-barreled dilemma, which in all candor I think the Court's opinion has not succeeded in papering over. The dilemma ought to be resolved. . . .

I am convinced that no liberty is more essential to the continued vitality of the free society which our Constitution guarantees than is the religious liberty protected by the Free Exercise Clause explicit in the First Amendment and imbedded in the Fourteenth. And I regret that on occasion, and specifically in *Braunfeld v. Brown,* the Court has shown what has seemed to me a distressing insensitivity to the appropriate demands of this constitutional guarantee. By contrast I think that the Court's approach to the Establishment Clause has on occasion, and specifically in *Engel, Schempp* and *Murray,* been not only insensitive, but positively wooden, and that the Court has accorded to the Establishment Clause a meaning which neither the words, the history, nor the intention of the authors of that specific constitutional provision even remotely suggests.

But my views as to the correctness of the Court's decisions in these cases are beside the point here. The point is that the decisions are on the books. And the result is that there are many situations where legitimate claims under the Free Exercise Clause will run into head-on collision with the Court's insensitive and sterile construction of the Establishment Clause. The controversy now before us is clearly such a case.

Because the appellant refuses to accept available jobs which would require her to work on Saturdays, South Carolina has declined to pay unemployment compensation benefits to her. Her refusal to work on Saturdays is based on the tenets of her religious faith. The Court says that South Carolina cannot under these circumstances declare her to be not "available for work" within the meaning of its statute because to do so would violate her constitutional right to the free exercise of her religion.

Yet what this Court has said about the Establishment Clause must inevitably lead to a diametrically opposite result. . . .

To require South Carolina to so administer its laws as to pay public money to the appellant under the circumstances of this case is thus clearly to require the State to violate the Establishment Clause as construed by this Court. This poses no problem for me, because I think the Court's mechanistic concept of the Establishment Clause is historically unsound and constitutionally wrong. . . . And I think that the guarantee of religious liberty embodied in the Free Exercise Clause affirmatively requires government to create an atmosphere of hospitality and accommodation to individual belief or disbelief. In short, I think our Constitution commands the positive protection by government of religious freedom—not only for a minority, however small—not only for the majority, however large—but for each of us.

South Carolina would deny unemployment benefits to a mother unavailable for work on Saturdays because she was unable to get a babysitter. Thus, we do not have before us a situation where a State provides unemployment compensation generally, and singles out for disqualification only those persons who are unavailable for work on religious grounds. This is not, in short, a scheme which operates so as to discriminate against religion as such. But the Court nevertheless holds that the State must prefer a religious over a secular ground for being unavailable for work—that state financial support of the appellant's religion is constitutionally required to carry out "the governmental obligation of neutrality in the face of religious differences. . . ."

Yet in cases decided under the Establishment Clause the Court has decreed otherwise. It has decreed that government must blind itself to the differing religious beliefs and traditions of the people. With all respect, I think it is the Court's duty to face up to the dilemma posed by the conflict between the Free Exercise Clause of the Constitution and the Establishment Clause as interpreted by the Court. . . .

My second difference with the Court's opinion is that I cannot agree that today's decision can stand consistently with *Braunfeld v. Brown*. The Court says that there was a "less direct burden upon religious practices" in that case than in this. With all respect, I think the Court is mistaken, simply as a matter of fact. . . .

We deal here not with a criminal statute, but with the particularized administration of South Carolina's Unemployment Compensation Act. Even upon the unlikely assumption that the appellant could not find suitable non-Saturday employment, the appellant at the worst would be denied a maximum of 22 weeks of compensation payments. I agree with the Court that the possibility of that denial is enough to infringe upon the appellant's constitutional right to the free exercise of her religion. But it is clear to me that in order to reach this conclusion the court must explicitly reject the reasoning of *Braunfeld v. Brown*. I think the *Braunfeld* case was wrongly decided and should be overruled, and accordingly I concur in the result reached by the Court in the case before us.

Justice HARLAN with whom Justice WHITE joins, dissenting.

In the present case all that the state court has done is to apply . . . accepted principles. Since virtually all of the mills in the Spartanburg area were operating on a six-day week, the appellant was "unavailable for work," and thus ineligible for benefits, when personal considerations prevented her from accepting employment on a full-time basis in the industry and locality in which she had worked. The fact that these personal considerations sprang from her religious convictions was wholly without relevance to the state court's application of the law. Thus in no proper sense can it be said that the State discriminated against the appellant on the basis of her religious beliefs or that she was denied benefits *because* she was a Seventh-day Adventist. She was denied benefits just as any other claimant would be denied benefits who was not "available for work" for personal reasons.

With this background, this Court's decision comes into clearer focus. What the Court is holding is that if the State chooses to condition unemployment compensation on the applicant's availability for work, it is constitutionally compelled to *carve out an exception*—and to provide benefits—for those whose unavailability is due to their religious convictions. Such a holding has particular significance in two respects.

First. Despite the Court's protestations to the contrary, the decision necessarily overrules *Braunfeld v. Brown.* which held that it did not offend the "Free Exercise" Clause of the Constitution for a State to forbid a Sabbatarian to do business on Sunday. The secular purpose of the statute before us today is even clearer than that involved in *Braunfeld.* And just as in *Braunfeld*—where exceptions to the Sunday closing laws for Sabbatarians would have been inconsistent with the purpose to achieve a uniform day of rest and would have required case-by-case inquiry into religious beliefs—so here, an exception to the rules of eligibility based on religious convictions would necessitate judicial examination of those convictions and would be at odds with the limited purpose of the statute to smooth out the economy during periods of industrial instability. Finally, the indirect financial burden of the present law is far less than that involved in Braunfeld. . . .

Second. The implications of the present decision are far more troublesome than its apparently narrow dimensions would indicate at first glance. The meaning of today's holding, as already noted, is that the State must furnish unemployment benefits to one who is unavailable for work if the unavailability stems from the exercise of religious convictions. The State, in other words, must *single out* for financial assistance those whose behavior is religiously motivated, even though it denies such assistance to others whose identical behavior (in this case, inability to work no Saturdays) is not religiously motivated.

It has been suggested that such singling out of religious conduct for special treatment may violate the constitutional limitations on state action. My own view, however, is that at least under the circumstances of this case it would be a permissible accommodation of religion for the State, if it *chose* to do so, to create an exception to its eligibility requirements for persons like the appellant. The constitutional obligation of "neutrality," see *School District of Abington Township v. Schempp,* is not so narrow a channel that the slightest deviation from an absolutely straight course leads to condemnation. . . .

The State violates its obligation of neutrality when, for example, it mandates a daily religious exercise in its public schools, with all the attendant pressures on the school children that such an exercise entails. See *Engel v. Vitale,* 370 U.S. 421 [1962]. *School*

District of Abington Township v. Schempp, supra. But there is, I believe, enough flexibility in the Constitution to permit a legislative judgment accommodating an unemployment compensation law to the exercise of religious beliefs such as appellant's.

For very much the same reasons, however, I cannot subscribe to the conclusion that the State is constitutionally *compelled* to carve out an exception to its general rule of eligibility in the present case. Those situations in which the Constitution may require special treatment on account of religion are, in my view, few and far between, and this view is amply supported by the course of constitutional litigation in this area.

Wisconsin v. Yoder
406 U.S. 208, 92 S.Ct. 1527 (1972)

Jonas Yoder and Wallace Miller, members of the Old Order Amish religion, and Adin Yutzy, a member of the Conservative Amish Mennonite Church, were charged, tried, and convicted of violating the compulsory school-attendance law in Green County Court, Wisconsin, and fined $5 each. Under Wisconsin's compulsory school-attendance law, children were required to attend public or private school until reaching the age of sixteen. Yoder, Miller, and Yutzy, however, refused to send their children, ages fourteen and fifteen, to public school after they completed the eighth grade. And when defending their actions, they claimed the compulsory-attendance law violated their free exercise of religion under the First and Fourteenth Amendments. A state appeals court affirmed their convictions, but the Wisconsin Supreme Court reversed and found that the application of the law denied the Amish's First Amendment rights. The state of Wisconsin appealed to the Supreme Court.

Chief Justice BURGER delivers the opinion of the Court.

Amish objection to formal education beyond the eighth grade is firmly grounded in these central religious concepts. They object to the high school, and higher education generally, because the values they teach are in marked variance with Amish values and the Amish way of life; they view secondary school education as an impermissible exposure of their children to a "worldly" influence in conflict with their beliefs. The high school tends to emphasize intellectual and scientific accomplishments, self-distinction, competitiveness, worldly success, and social life with other students. Amish society emphasizes informal learning-through-doing; a life of "goodness," rather than a life of intellect; wisdom, rather than technical knowledge, community welfare, rather than competition; and separation from, rather than integration with, contemporary worldly society.

Formal high school education beyond the eighth grade is contrary to Amish beliefs, not only because it places Amish children in an environment hostile to Amish beliefs with increasing emphasis on competition in class work and sports and with pressure to conform to the styles, manners, and ways of the peer group, but also because it takes them away from their community, physically and emotionally, during the crucial and formative adolescent period of life. During this period, the children must acquire Amish attitudes favoring manual work and self-reliance and the specific skills needed to perform the adult role of an Amish farmer or housewife. They must learn to enjoy physical labor. Once a child has learned basic reading, writing, and elementary mathematics, these traits, skills, and attitudes admittedly fall within the category of those best learned through example and "doing" rather than in a classroom. And, at this time in life, the Amish child must also grow in his faith and his relationship to the Amish community if he is to be prepared to accept the heavy obligations imposed by adult baptism. . . .

The Amish do not object to elementary education through the first eight grades as a general proposition because they agree that their children must have basic skills in the "three R's" in order to read the Bible, to be good farmers and citizens, and to be able to deal with non-Amish people when necessary in the course of daily affairs. They view such a basic education as acceptable because it does not significantly expose their children to worldly values or interfere with their development in the Amish community during the crucial adolescent period. While Amish accept compulsory elementary education generally, wherever possible they have established their own elementary schools in many respects like the small local schools of the past. In the Amish belief higher learning tends to develop values they reject as influences that alienate man from God. . . .

There is no doubt as to the power of a State, having a high responsibility for education of its citizens, to impose reasonable regulations for the control and duration of basic education. . . .

[A] State's interest in universal education, however highly we rank it, is not totally free from a balancing process when it impinges on fundamental rights and interests, such as those specifically protected by the Free Exercise Clause of the First Amendment, and the traditional interest of parents with respect to the religious upbringing of their children. . . .

It follows that in order for Wisconsin to compel school attendance beyond the eighth grade against a claim that such attendance interferes with the practice of a legitimate religious belief, it must appear either that the State does not deny the free exercise of religious belief by its requirement, or that there is a state interest of sufficient magnitude to override the interest claiming protection under the Free Exercise Clause. . . .

The essence of all that has been said and written on the subject is that only those interests of the highest order and those not otherwise served can overbalance legitimate claims to the free exercise of religion. We can accept it as settled, therefore, that, however strong the State's interest in universal compulsory education, it is by no means absolute to the exclusion or subordination of all other interests. . . .

We come then to the quality of the claims of the respondents concerning the alleged encroachment of Wisconsin's compulsory school-attendance statute on their rights and the rights of their children to the free exercise of the religious beliefs they and their forbears have adhered to for almost three centuries. In evaluating those claims we must be careful to determine whether the Amish religious faith and their mode of life are, as they claim, inseparable and interdependent. A way of life, however virtuous and admirable, may not be interposed as a barrier to reasonable state regulation of education if it is based on purely secular considerations; to have the protection of the Religion Clauses, the claims must be rooted in religious belief. Although a determination of what is a "religious" belief or practice entitled to constitutional protection may present a most delicate question, the very concept of ordered liberty precludes allowing every person to make his own standards on matters of conduct in which society as a whole has important interests. Thus, if the Amish asserted their claims because of their subjective evaluation and rejection of the contemporary secular values accepted by the majority, much as Thoreau rejected the social values of his time and isolated himself at Walden Pond, their claims would not rest on a religious basis. Thoreau's choice was philosophical and personal rather than religious, and such belief does not rise to the demands of the Religion Clauses.

Giving no weight to such secular considerations, however, we see that the record in this case abundantly supports the claim that the traditional way of life of the Amish is not merely a matter of personal preference, but one of deep religious conviction, shared by an organized group, and intimately related to daily living. . . .

[The] unchallenged testimony of acknowledged experts in education and religious history, almost 300 years of consistent practice, and strong evidence of a sustained faith pervading and regulating respondents' entire mode of life support the claim that enforcement of the State's requirement of compulsory formal education after the eighth grade would gravely endanger if not destroy the free exercise of respondents' religious beliefs. . . .

We turn, then, to the State's broader contention that its interest in its system of compulsory education is so compelling that even the established religious practices of the Amish must give way. Where fundamental claims of religious freedom are at stake, however, we cannot accept such a sweeping claim; despite its admitted validity in the generality of cases, we must searchingly examine the interests that the State seeks to promote by its requirement for compulsory education to age 16, and the impediment to those objectives that would flow from recognizing the claimed Amish exemption. . . .

The State advances two primary arguments in support of its system of compulsory education. It notes, as Thomas Jefferson pointed out early in our history, that some degree of education is necessary to prepare citizens to participate effectively and intelligently in our open political system if we are to preserve freedom and independence. Further, education prepares individuals to be self-reliant and self-sufficient participants in society. We accept these propositions.

However, the evidence adduced by the Amish in this case is persuasively to the effect that an additional one or two years of formal high school for Amish children in place of their long-established program of informal vocational education would do little to serve those interests. Respondents' experts testified at trial, without challenge, that the value of all education must be assessed in terms of its capacity to prepare the child for life. It is one thing to say that compulsory education for a year or two beyond the eighth grade may be necessary when its goal is the preparation of the child for life in modern society as the majority live, but it is quite another if the goal of education be viewed as the preparation of the child for life in the separated agrarian community that is the keystone of the Amish faith. . . .

Contrary to the suggestion of the dissenting opinion of Justice DOUGLAS, our holding today in no degree depends on the assertion of the religious interest of the child as contrasted with that of the parents. It is the parents who are subject to prosecution here for failing to cause their children to attend school, and it is their right of free exercise, not that of their children, that must determine Wisconsin's power to impose criminal penalties on the parent. The dissent argues that a child who expresses a desire to attend public high school in conflict with the wishes of his parents should not *be* prevented from doing so. There is no reason for the Court to consider that point since it is not an issue in the case. The children are not parties to this litigation. The State has at no point tried this case on the theory that respondents were preventing their children from attending school against their expressed desires, and indeed the record is to the contrary. . . .

Our holding in no way determines the proper resolution of possible competing interests of parents, children, and the State in an appropriate state court proceeding in which the power of the State is asserted on the theory that Amish parents are preventing their minor children from attending high school despite their expressed desires to the contrary. Recognition of the claim of the State in such a proceeding would, of course, call into question traditional concepts of parental control over the religious upbringing and education of their minor children recognized in this Court's past decisions. It is clear that such an intrusion by a State into family decisions in the area of religious training would give rise to grave questions of religious freedom. . . . On this record we neither reach nor decide those issues. . . .

For the reasons stated we hold, with the Supreme Court of Wisconsin, that the First and Fourteenth Amendments prevent the State from compelling respondents to cause their children to attend formal high school to age 16.

Justice POWELL and Justice REHNQUIST did not participate in the consideration or decision of this case.

Justice STEWART, with whom Justice BRENNAN joins, concurring.

Decision in cases such as this and the administration of an exemption for Old Order Amish from the State's compulsory school-attendance laws will inevitably involve the kind of close and perhaps repeated scrutiny of religious practices, as is exemplified in today's opinion, which the Court has heretofore been anxious to avoid. But such entanglement does not create a forbidden establishment of religion where it is essential to implement free exercise values threatened by an otherwise neutral program instituted to foster some permissible, nonreligious state objective. I join the Court because the sincerity of the Amish religious policy here is uncontested, because the potentially adverse impact of the state requirement is great, and because the State's valid interest in education has already been largely satisfied by the eight years the children have already spent in school.

Justice DOUGLAS dissenting in part.

Religion is an individual experience. It is not necessary, nor even appropriate, for every Amish child to express his views on the subject in a prosecution of a single adult. Crucial, however, are the views of the child whose parent is the subject of the suit. Frieda Yoder has in fact testified that her own religious views are opposed to high-school education. I therefore join the judgment of the Court as to respondent Jonas Yoder. But Frieda Yoder's views may not be those of Vernon Yutzy or Barbara Miller. I must dissent, therefore, as to respondents Adin Yutzy and Wallace Miller as their motion to dismiss also raised the question of their children's religious liberty. . . .

On this important and vital matter of education, I think the children should be entitled to be heard. While the parents, absent dissent, normally speak for the entire family, the education of the child is a matter on which the child will often have decided views. He may want to be a pianist or an astronaut or an ocean geographer. To do so he will have to break from the Amish tradition.

It is the future of the student, not the future of the parents, that is imperilled in today's decision. If a parent keeps his child out of school beyond the grade school, then the child will be forever barred from entry into the new and amazing world of diversity that we have today. The child may decide that that is the preferred course, or he may rebel. It is the student's judgment, not his parent's, that is essential if we are to give full meaning to what we have said about the Bill of Rights and of the right of students to be masters of their own destiny. If he is harnessed to the Amish way of life by those in authority over him and if his education in truncated, his entire life may be stunted and deformed. The child, therefore, should be given an opportunity to be heard before the State gives the exemption which we honor today.

Employment Division, Department of Human Resource of Oregon v. Smith

110 S.Ct. 1595 (1990)

Two native Americans, Alfred Smith and Galen Black, were fired from their jobs with a private drug rehabilitation organization because they took peyote (an intoxicating drug produced from mescal cacti). Both were members of the Native American Church and ingested peyote for sacramental purposes in religious ceremonies. When they later applied for unemployment compensation, Oregon's Employment Division denied them benefits on the grounds that their discharge was for work-related "misconduct." A state appellate court reversed that decision, holding that the denial of benefits violated Smith's and Black's rights under the First Amendment free exercise clause. The state then appealed to the Oregon Supreme Court, which affirmed the lower court. It did so, however, on construing the purpose of the misconduct provision, under which Smith was denied benefits, to be one of preserving the financial integrity of the state's compensation fund and not that of enforcing the state's criminal laws against drug usage. Citing *Sherbert v. Verner* (1963) (see page 745), the Oregon Supreme Court concluded that Smith was entitled to unemployment benefits because the state's interest in the compensation fund did not outweigh the burden imposed on Smith's religious beliefs and practices.

In 1987, Oregon appealed the ruling of its state's supreme court to the U.S. Supreme Court, contending that its criminal laws against peyote consumption were relevant to balancing the state's interests in denying benefits and Smith's First Amendment claims. In *Employment Division, Department of Human Resources of Oregon v. Smith*, 485 U.S. 660 (1988) (*Smith I*), a majority of the Court agreed, when vacating the decision and remanding the case back to the Oregon Supreme Court. But when doing so, the Court noted that the state supreme court had not decided whether the sacramental use of peyote was in fact proscribed under state law. Until the state court ruled on that issue, the Supreme Court declined to address the question of "whether the practice is protected by the Federal Constitution." On remand, the Oregon Supreme Court held that its state laws made no exception for the sacramental use of peyote, but interpreted the First Amendment to protect such usage and reaffirmed its previous ruling that Smith was entitled to unemployment benefits. The state, again, appealed to the U.S. Supreme Court, which granted *certiorari.*

Writing for the Court, Justice Scalia reversed and rejected the state supreme court's application of *Sherbert*'s balancing test. Chief Justice Rehnquist and Justices Stevens, Kennedy, and White joined his opinion. In a separate opinion, Justice O'Connor concurred in the result yet rejected Justice Scalia's reasoning and abandonment of *Sherbert*'s analysis. Justices Brennan and Marshall concurred in her reasoning, but disagreed with her conclusion that Smith was not entitled to benefits. Thus they also joined Justice Blackmun's dissenting opinion.

Justice SCALIA delivered the opinion of the Court.

This case requires us to decide whether the Free Exercise Clause of the First Amendment permits the State of Oregon to include religiously inspired peyote use within the reach of its general criminal prohibition on use of that drug, and thus permits the State to deny unemployment benefits to persons dismissed from their jobs because of such religiously inspired use. . . .

II

Respondents' claim for relief rests on our decisions in *Sherbert v. Verner*, [374 U.S. 398 (1963)]; *Thomas v. Review Board, Indiana Employment Security Div.*, [450 U.S. 707 (1981)]; and *Hobbie v. Unemployment Appeals Comm'n of Florida*, 480 U.S. 136 (1987), in which we held that a State could not condition the availability of unemployment insurance on an individual's willingness to forego conduct required by his religion. As we observed in *Smith I*, however, the conduct at issue in those cases was not prohibited by law. We held that distinction to be critical, for "if Oregon does prohibit the religious use of peyote, and if that prohibition is consistent with the Federal Constitution, there is no federal right to engage in that conduct in Oregon," and "the State is free to withhold unemployment compensation from respondents for engaging in work-related misconduct, despite its religious motivation." Now that the Oregon Supreme Court has confirmed that Oregon does prohibit the religious use of peyote, we proceed to consider whether that prohibition is permissible under the Free Exercise Clause. . . .

The free exercise of religion means, first and foremost, the right to believe and profess whatever religious doctrine one desires. Thus, the First Amendment obviously excludes all "governmental regulation of religious *beliefs* as such." *Sherbert v. Verner, supra.* . . .

But the "exercise of religion" often involves not only belief and profession but the performance of (or abstention from) physical acts: assembling with others for a worship service, participating in sacramental use of bread and wine, proselytizing, abstaining from certain foods or certain modes of transportation. It would be true, we think (though no case of ours has involved the point), that a state would be "prohibiting the free exercise [of religion]" if it sought to ban such acts or abstentions only when they are engaged in for religious reasons, or only because of the religious belief that they display. It would doubtless be unconstitutional, for example, to ban the casting of "statues that are to be used for worship purposes," or to prohibit bowing down before a golden calf.

Respondents in the present case, however, seek to carry the meaning of "prohibiting the free exercise [of religion]" one large step further. They contend that their religious motivation for using peyote places them beyond the reach of a criminal law that is not specifically directed at their religious practice, and that is concededly constitutional as applied to those who use the drug for other reasons. They assert, in other words, that "prohibiting the free exercise [of religion]" includes requiring any individual to observe a generally applicable law that requires (or forbids) the performance of an act that his religious belief forbids (or requires). As a textual matter, we do not think the words must be given that meaning. It is no more necessary to regard the collection of a general tax, for example, as "prohibiting the free exercise [of religion]" by those citizens who believe support of organized government to be sinful, than it is to regard the same tax as "abridging the freedom . . . of the press" of those publishing companies that must pay the tax as a condition of staying in business. It is a permissible reading of the text, in the one case as in the other, to say that if prohibiting the exercise of religion (or burdening the activity of printing) is not the object of the tax but merely the incidental effect of a generally applicable and otherwise valid provision, the First Amendment has not been offended. . . .

Our decisions reveal that the latter reading is the correct one. We have never held that an individual's religious beliefs excuse him from compliance with an otherwise valid law prohibiting conduct that the State is free to regulate. [Cited *Minersville School District Bd. of Ed. v. Gobitis*, 310 U.S. 586 (1940), *Reynolds v. United States*, 98 U.S. 145 (1879), *Prince v. Massachusetts*, 321 U.S. 158 (1944), *Braunfeld v. Brown*, 366 U.S. 599 (1961), and *Gillette v. United States*, 410 U.S. 437 (1971).] . . .

The only decisions in which we have held that the First Amendment bars application of a neutral, generally applicable law to religiously motivated action have involved not the Free Exercise Clause alone, but the Free Exercise Clause in conjunction with other constitutional protections, such as freedom of speech and of the press, see *Cantwell v. Connecticut*, [310 U.S. 296 (1940)], (invalidating a licensing system for religious and charitable solicitations under which the administrator had discretion to deny a license to any cause he deemed nonreligious); *Murdock v. Pennsylvania*, 319 U.S. 105 (1943) (invalidating a flat tax on solicitation as applied to the dissemination of religious ideas); *Follett v. McCormick*, 321 U.S. 573 (1944) (same), or the right of parents, acknowledged in *Pierce v. Society of Sisters*, 268 U.S. 510 (1925), to direct the education of their children, see *Wisconsin v. Yoder*, 406 U.S. 208 (1972) (invalidating compulsory school-attendance laws as applied to Amish parents who refused on religious grounds to send their children to school). Some of our cases prohibiting compelled expression, decided exclusively upon free speech grounds, have also involved freedom of religion, cf. *Wooley v. Maynard*, 430 U.S. 705 (1977) (invalidating compelled display of a license plate slogan that offended individual religious beliefs); *West Virginia Board of Education v. Barnette*, 319 U.S. 624 (1943) (invalidating compulsory flag salute statute challenged by religious objectors). . . .

The present case does not present such a hybrid situation, but a free exercise claim unconnected with any communicative activity or parental right. Respondents urge us to hold, quite simply, that when otherwise prohibitable conduct is accompanied by religious convictions, not only the convictions but the conduct itself must be free from governmental regulation. . . .

Respondents argue that even though exemption from generally applicable criminal laws need not automatically be extended to religiously motivated actors, at least the claim for a religious exemption must be evaluated under the balancing test set forth in *Sherbert v. Verner* (1963). Under the *Sherbert* test, governmental actions that substantially burden a religious practice must be justified by a compelling governmental interest. . . . Applying that test we have, on three occasions, invalidated state unemployment compensation rules that conditioned the availability of benefits upon an applicant's willingness to work under conditions forbidden by his religion. See *Sherbert v. Verner, supra; Thomas v. Review Board, Indiana Employment Div.* (1981); *Hobbie v. Unemployment Appeals Comm'n of Florida* (1987). We have never invalidated any governmental action on the basis of the *Sherbert* test except the denial of unemployment compensation. . . .

Even if we were inclined to breathe into *Sherbert* some life beyond the unemployment compensation field, we would not apply it to require exemptions from a generally applicable criminal law. . . .

We conclude today that the sounder approach, and the approach in accord with the vast majority of our precedents, is to hold the test inapplicable to such challenges. The government's ability to enforce generally applicable prohibitions of socially harmful conduct, like its ability to carry out other aspects of public policy, "cannot depend on measuring the effects of a governmental action on a religious objector's spiritual development." *Lyng* [*v. Northwest Indian Cemetery Association*, 485 U.S. 439 (1988)]. To make an individual's obligation to obey such a law contingent upon the law's coincidence with his religious beliefs, except where the State's interest is "compelling"—permitting him, by virtue of his beliefs, "to become a law unto himself," *Reynolds v. United States*—contradicts both constitutional tradition and common sense.

The "compelling government interest" requirement seems benign, because it is familiar from other fields. But using it as the standard that must be met before the government may accord different treatment on the basis of race, see, *e.g., Palmore v. Sidoti,* 466 U.S. 429 (1984), or before the government may regulate the content of speech, see, *e.g., Sable Communications of California v. FCC,* 109 S.Ct. 2829 (1989), is not remotely comparable to using it for the purpose asserted here. What it produces in those other fields—equality of treatment, and an unrestricted flow of contending speech—are constitutional norms; what it would produce here—a private right to ignore generally applicable laws— is a constitutional anomaly.

Nor is it possible to limit the impact of respondents' proposal by requiring a "compelling state interest" only when the conduct prohibited is "central" to the individual's religion. It is no more appropriate for judges to determine the "centrality" of religious beliefs before applying a "compelling interest" test in the free exercise field, than it would be for them to determine the "importance" of ideas before applying the "compelling interest" test in the free speech field. What principle of law or logic can be brought to bear to contradict a believer's assertion that a particular act is "central" to his personal faith? . . .

If the "compelling interest" test is to be applied at all, then, it must be applied across the board, to all actions thought to be religiously commanded. Moreover, if "compelling interest" really means what it says (and watering it down here would subvert its rigor in the other fields where it is applied), many laws will not meet the test. Any society adopting such a system would be courting anarchy, but that danger increases in direct proportion to the society's diversity of religious beliefs, and its determination to coerce or suppress none of them. . . .

Values that are protected against government interference through enshrinement in the Bill of Rights are not thereby banished from the political process. Just as a society that believes in the negative protection accorded to the press by the First Amendment is likely to enact laws that affirmatively foster the dissemination of the printed word, so also a society that believes in the negative protection accorded to religious belief can be expected to be solicitous of that value in its legislation as well. It is therefore not surprising that a number of States have made an exception to their drug laws for sacramental peyote use. But to say that a nondiscriminatory religious-practice exemption is permitted, or even that it is desirable, is not to say that it is constitutionally required, and that the appropriate occasions for its creation can be discerned by the courts. It may fairly be said that leaving accommodation to the political process will place at a relative disadvantage those religious practices that are not widely engaged in; but that unavoidable consequence of democratic government must be preferred to a system in which each conscience is a law unto itself or in which judges weigh the social importance of all laws against the centrality of all religious beliefs. . . .

Because respondents' ingestion of peyote was prohibited under Oregon law, and because that prohibition is constitutional, Oregon may, consistent with the Free Exercise Clause, deny respondents unemployment compensation when their dismissal results from use of the drug. The decision of the Oregon Supreme Court is accordingly reversed.

It is so ordered.

Justice O'CONNOR, with whom Justice BRENNAN, Justice MARSHALL, and Justice BLACKMUN join in parts I and II, concurring.

Although I agree with the result the Court reaches in this case, I cannot join its opinion. In my view, today's holding dramatically departs from well-settled First Amendment jurisprudence, appears unnecessary to resolve the question presented, and is incompatible with our Nation's fundamental commitment to individual religious liberty. . . .

II

The Court today extracts from our long history of free exercise precedents the single categorical rule that "if prohibiting the exercise of religion . . . is . . . merely the incidental effect of a generally applicable and otherwise valid provision, the First Amendment has not been offended." Indeed, the Court holds that where the law is a generally applicable criminal prohibition, our usual free exercise jurisprudence does not even apply. To reach this sweeping result, however, the Court must not only give a strained reading of the First Amendment but must also disregard our consistent application of free exercise doctrine to cases involving generally applicable regulations that burden religious conduct. . . .

The Court today . . . interprets the Clause to permit the government to prohibit, without justification, conduct mandated by an individual's religious beliefs, so long as that prohibition is generally applicable. But a law that prohibits certain conduct—conduct that happens to be an act of worship for someone—manifestly does prohibit that person's free exercise of his religion. A person who is barred from engaging in religiously motivated conduct is barred from freely exercising his religion. Moreover, that person is barred from freely exercising his religion regardless of whether the law prohibits the conduct only when engaged in for religious reasons, only by members of that religion, or by all persons. It is difficult to deny that a law that prohibits religiously motivated conduct, even if the law is generally applicable, does not at least implicate First Amendment concerns.

The Court responds that generally applicable laws are "one large step" removed from laws aimed at specific religious practices. The First Amendment, however, does not distinguish between laws that are generally applicable and laws that target particular religious practices. Indeed, few States would be so naive as to enact a law directly prohibiting or burdening a religious practice as such. Our free exercise cases have all concerned generally applicable laws that had the effect of significantly burdening a religious practice. If the First Amendment is to have any vitality, it ought not be construed to cover only the extreme and hypothetical situation in which a State directly targets a religious practice. . . .

To say that a person's right to free exercise has been burdened, of course, does not mean that he has an absolute right to engage in the conduct. Under our established First Amendment jurisprudence, we have recognized that the freedom to act, unlike the freedom to believe, cannot be absolute. Instead, we have respected both the First Amendment's express textual mandate and the governmental interest in regulation of conduct by requiring the Government to justify any substantial burden on religiously motivated conduct by a compelling state interest and by means narrowly tailored to achieve that interest. . . .

The compelling interest test effectuates the First Amendment's command that religious liberty is an independent liberty, that it occupies a preferred position, and that the Court will not permit encroachments upon this liberty, whether direct or indirect, unless required by clear and compelling governmental interests "of the highest order," [*Wisconsin v.*] *Yoder* [406 U.S. 208 (1972)]. . . .

In my view, however, the essence of a free exercise claim is relief from a burden imposed by government on religious practices or beliefs, whether the burden is imposed directly through laws that prohibit or compel specific religious practices, or indirectly through laws that, in effect, make abandonment of one's own religion or conformity to the religious beliefs of others the price of an equal place in the civil community. . . .

Indeed, we have never distinguished between cases in which a State conditions receipt of a benefit on conduct prohibited by religious beliefs and cases in which a State affirmatively prohibits such conduct. The *Sherbert* compelling interest test applies in both kinds of cases. . . .

Finally, the Court today suggests that the disfavoring of minority religions is an "unavoidable consequence" under our system of government and that accommodation of such religions must be left to the political process. In my view, however, the First Amendment was enacted precisely to protect the rights of those whose religious practices are not shared by the majority and may be viewed with hostility. The history of our free exercise doctrine amply demonstrates the harsh impact majoritarian rule has had on unpopular or emerging religious groups such as the Jehovah's Witnesses and the Amish. . . .

III

The Court's holding today not only misreads settled First Amendment precedent; it appears to be unnecessary to this case. I would reach the same result applying our established free exercise jurisprudence. . . .

[T]he critical question in this case is whether exempting respondents from the State's general criminal prohibition "will unduly interfere with fulfillment of the governmental interest." Although the question is close, I would conclude that uniform application of Oregon's criminal prohibition is "essential to accomplish," its overriding interest in preventing the physical harm caused by the use of a Schedule I controlled substance. Oregon's criminal prohibition represents that State's judgment that the possession and use of controlled substances, even by only one person, is inherently harmful and dangerous. Because the health effects caused by the use of controlled substances exist regardless of the motivation of the user, the use of such substances, even for religious purposes, violates the very purpose of the laws that prohibit them. . . .

For these reasons, I believe that granting a selective exemption in this case would seriously impair Oregon's compelling interest in prohibiting possession of peyote by its citizens. Under such circumstances, the Free Exercise Clause does not require the State to accommodate respondents' religiously motivated conduct. . . .

I would therefore adhere to our established free exercise jurisprudence and hold that the State in this case has a compelling interest in regulating peyote use by its citizens and that accommodating respondents' religiously motivated conduct "will unduly interfere with fulfillment of the governmental interest." Accordingly, I concur in the judgment of the Court.

Justice BLACKMUN, with whom Justice BRENNAN and Justice MARSHALL join, dissenting.

This Court over the years painstakingly has developed a consistent and exacting standard to test the constitutionality of a state statute that burdens the free exercise of religion. Such a statute may stand only if the law in general, and the State's refusal to allow a religious exemption in particular, are justified by a compelling interest that cannot be served by less restrictive means.

Until today, I thought this was a settled and inviolate principle of this Court's First Amendment jurisprudence. The majority, however, perfunctorily dismisses it as a "constitutional anomaly." As carefully detailed in Justice O'CONNOR's concurring opinion . . . the majority is able to arrive at this view only by mischaracterizing this Court's precedents. The Court discards leading free exercise cases such as *Cantwell v. Connecticut* (1940), and *Wisconsin v. Yoder* (1972), as "hybrid.". . . The Court views traditional free exercise analysis as somehow inapplicable to criminal prohibitions (as opposed to conditions on the receipt of benefits), and to state laws of general applicability (as opposed, presumably, to laws that expressly single out religious practices). The Court cites cases in which, due to various exceptional circumstances, we found strict scrutiny inapposite, to hint that the Court has repudiated that standard altogether. In short, it effectuates a wholesale overturning of settled law concerning the Religion Clauses of our Constitution. One hopes that the Court is aware of the consequences, and that its result is not a product of overreaction to the serious problems the country's drug crisis has generated.

This distorted view of our precedents leads the majority to

conclude that strict scrutiny of a state law burdening the free exercise of religion is a "luxury" that a well-ordered society cannot afford, and that the repression of minority religions is an "unavoidable consequence of democratic government." I do not believe the Founders thought their dearly bought freedom from religious persecution a "luxury," but an essential element of liberty—and they could not have thought religious intolerance "unavoidable," for they drafted the Religion Clauses precisely in order to avoid that intolerance.

For these reasons, I agree with Justice O'CONNOR's analysis of the applicable free exercise doctrine, and I join parts I and II of her opinion. As she points out, "the critical question in this case is whether exempting respondents from the State's general criminal prohibition: 'will unduly interfere with fulfillment of the governmental interest.'" I do disagree, however, with her specific answer to that question.

The State's interest in enforcing its prohibition, in order to be sufficiently compelling to outweigh a free exercise claim, cannot be merely abstract or symbolic. The State cannot plausibly assert that unbending application of a criminal prohibition is essential to fulfill any compelling interest, if it does not, in fact, attempt to enforce that prohibition. In this case, the State actually has not evinced any concrete interest in enforcing its drug laws against religious users of peyote. Oregon has never sought to prosecute respondents, and does not claim that it has made significant enforcement efforts against other religious users of peyote. The State's asserted interest thus amounts only to the symbolic preservation of an unenforced prohibition. . . .

The State proclaims an interest in protecting the health and safety of its citizens from the dangers of unlawful drugs. It offers, however, no evidence that the religious use of peyote has ever harmed anyone. . . .

The fact that peyote is classified as a Schedule I controlled substance does not, by itself, show that any and all uses of peyote, in any circumstance, are inherently harmful and dangerous. The Federal Government, which created the classifications of unlawful drugs from which Oregon's drug laws are derived, apparently does not find peyote so dangerous as to preclude an exemption for religious use. . . .

The carefully circumscribed ritual context in which respondents used peyote is far removed from the irresponsible and unrestricted recreational use of unlawful drugs. The Native American Church's internal restrictions on, and supervision of, its members' use of peyote substantially obviate the State's health and safety concerns. . . .

Moreover, just as in *Yoder,* the values and interests of those seeking a religious exemption in this case are congruent, to a great degree, with those the State seeks to promote through its drug laws. . . . Not only does the Church's doctrine forbid nonreligious use of peyote; it also generally advocates self-reliance, familial responsibility, and abstinence from alcohol. . . . Far from promoting the lawless and irresponsible use of drugs, Native American Church members' spiritual code exemplifies values that Oregon's drug laws are presumably intended to foster. . . .

Finally, although I agree with Justice O'CONNOR that courts should refrain from delving into questions of whether, as a matter of religious doctrine, a particular practice is "central" to the religion, I do not think this means that the courts must turn a blind eye to the severe impact of a State's restrictions on the adherents of a minority religion. . . .

If Oregon can constitutionally prosecute them for this act of worship, they, like the Amish, may be "forced to migrate to some other and more tolerant region." *Yoder.* This potentially devastating impact must be viewed in light of the federal policy—reached in reaction to many years of religious persecution and intolerance—of protecting the religious freedom of Native Americans. See, American Indian Religious Freedom Act, 92 Stat. 469 (1978). . . .

The American Indian Religious Freedom Act, in itself, may not create rights enforceable against government action restricting religious freedom, but this Court must scrupulously apply its free exercise analysis to the religious claims of Native Americans, however unorthodox they may be. Otherwise, both the First Amendment and the stated policy of Congress will offer to Native Americans merely an unfulfilled and hollow promise.

For these reasons, I conclude that Oregon's interest in enforcing its drug laws against religious use of peyote is not sufficiently compelling to outweigh respondents' right to the free exercise of their religion. Since the State could not constitutionally enforce its criminal prohibition against respondents, the interests underlying the State's drug laws cannot justify its denial of unemployment benefits. Absent such justification, the State's regulatory interest in denying benefits for religiously motivated "misconduct," is indistinguishable from the state interests this Court has rejected in *Frazee, Hobbie, Thomas,* and *Sherbert.* The State of Oregon cannot, consistently with the Free Exercise Clause, deny respondents unemployment benefits.

I dissent.

7

THE FOURTH AMENDMENT GUARANTEE AGAINST UNREASONABLE SEARCHES AND SEIZURES

T HE FOURTH AMENDMENT guarantees individuals the freedom from unreasonable searches and seizures in providing that "[t]he right of the people to be secure in their persons, houses, papers, and effects, against unreasonable searches and seizures, shall not be violated, and no Warrants shall issue, but upon probable cause, supported by Oath or affirmation, and particularly describing the place to be searched, and the persons or things to be seized." Although the most detailed guarantee in the Bill of Rights, its key elements are not self-explanatory. The Supreme Court, moreover, has often been divided over whether the unreasonable searches and seizures clause is an independent standard, or whether it stands in conjunction with the second, warrant clause, allowing searches and seizures on (1) the issuance of a warrant by a judge or magistrate, (2) based on police showing "probable cause" for an arrest or for a search and seizure, and (3) "particularly describing the place to be searched," and the specific "persons or things to be seized."

The central purpose of the amendment was to deny the government the power to make general searches. The English Parliament permitted "writs of assistance" or general searches in granting police, and even innkeepers in port towns, the authority to search and seize luggage for illegally imported monies and other goods. General warrants were also used against political and religious dissidents. In 1662, Parliament codified writs of assistance, allowing royalist judges to authorize police and customs inspectors to make general searches of all houses for contraband and other illegal items.

By the 1760s, there was strong resistance in the colonies to writs of assistance and general searches. In a famous Massachusetts case, *Paxton's Case,* Quincy's *Mass. Rpts.* 51 (1761), when unsuccessfully arguing that writs of assistance were contrary to the Magna Carta of 1215 (the first great English charter expressing the ideas of the supremacy of law and that there are fundamental rights that the state may not deny), James Otis invoked the principle that "[a] man's house is his castle; and while he is quiet, he is well guarded as a prince in castle."[1] That view was even more eloquently expressed by William Pitt, the Elder, who explained, "The Poorest man may in his cottage bid defiance to all the force of the Crown. It may be frail—its roof may shake—the wind may blow through it—the storm may enter—the rain may enter—but the King of England cannot enter—all his force dares not cross the threshold of the ruined tenement."[2]

The outcry of colonists against the Crown's use of general searches led to states sharply limiting searches and seizures in their constitutions. General warrants were denounced as "grievous and oppressive" in Virginia's Declaration of Rights in 1776. Later at that state's convention on ratifying the Constitution, Patrick Henry pressed for the adoption of a bill of rights and argued that

[t]he officer of Congress may come upon you now, fortified with all the terrors of paramount federal authority. Excisemen may come in multitudes; for the limitations of their numbers no man knows. They may, unless the general government be restrained by a bill of rights, or some similar restrictions, go into your cellars and rooms, and search, ransack, and measure, everything you eat, drink, and wear. They ought to be restrained within proper bounds.

Subsequently, in the First Congress, James Madison introduced the initial proposal for limiting searches and seizures by the government. It read, "The right of the people to be secured in their persons, houses, papers, and effects, shall not be violated by warrants issuing without probable cause, supported by an oath or affirmation, and not particularly describing the place to be searched or the persons or things to be seized."[3] At Elbridge Gerry's suggestion, the word *secured* was changed to *secure* and the clause "against unreasonable searches and seizures" was inserted; another stylistic change rendered "by warrants issuing" to "and no warrants shall issue." No further changes were made, and after the adoption and ratification of the Bill of Rights, Madison's revised proposal became the Fourth Amendment.

Despite the aim of foreclosing the possibility of general searches, the strictures of the amendment have an open texture and inescapable ambiguity. What constitutes, for example, "probable cause" for issuing a warrant? Is a warrantless search or seizure automatically "unreasonable" if not supported by probable cause? Does every arrest or search require prior judicial approval? How is the right against unreasonable searches and seizures to be enforced? Must illegally obtained evidence by police be excluded from use at trial? And does the amendment only restrict the police—what about other law-enforcement and administrative officials? These and other questions arise in interpreting the Fourth Amendment and led the Supreme Court to develop a complex set of sometimes cross-cutting and confusing rulings. Together, those rulings enforcing the key elements of the amendment and allowing for exceptions to the warrant requirement define the boundaries between reasonable and unreasonable searches and seizures.

NOTES

1. See Jacob W. Landynski, *Search and Seizure and the Supreme Court* (Baltimore, MD: Johns Hopkins University Press, 1966); Nelson B. Lasson, *The History and Development of the Fourth Amendment to the United States Constitution* (Baltimore, MD: Johns Hopkins University Press, 1937); and David H. Flaherty, *Privacy in Colonial New England* (Charlottesville: University Press of Virginia, 1972).

2. Quoted in *Frank v. Maryland*, 359 U.S. 360, 378 (1959), by Justice Douglas in a dissenting opinion.

3. Quoted in Jonathan Elliot, ed., *The Debates in the Several Conventions on the Adoption of the Federal Constitution* Vol. 3 (New York: Burt Franklin Reprints, 1974), 448–449.

SELECTED BIBLIOGRAPHY

LaFave, Wayne, *Search and Seizure: A Treatise on the Fourth Amendment.* Mineola, NY: Foundation Press, 1978.

Landynski, Jacob W. *Search and Seizure and the Supreme Court.* Baltimore, MD: Johns Hopkins University Press, 1966.

Lasson, Nelson B. *The History and Development of the Fourth Amendment to the United States Constitution.* Baltimore, MD: Johns Hopkins University Press, 1937.

Levy, Leonard W. *Against the Law: The Nixon Court and Criminal Justice.* New York: Harper & Row, 1974.

A. REQUIREMENTS FOR A WARRANT AND REASONABLE SEARCHES AND SEIZURES

As a general rule (subject to the exceptions discussed in section B, in this chapter), police must obtain a search warrant from a "neutral and detached magistrate." The Court made this requirement applicable to the states in *Wolf v. Colorado*, 338 U.S. 25 (1949). In *Coolidge v. New Hampshire*, 403 U.S. 443 (1971), the Court underscored the importance of judicial approval of warrants, when holding invalid a warrant issued by an attorney general;[1] and *Connelly v. Georgia*, 429 U.S. 245 (1977), declined to permit a justice of the peace to issue warrants, where his salary was paid in part by warrant fees.

When obtaining warrants police must demonstrate probable cause that a person has committed a crime to obtain an arrest warrant and show probable cause to believe that contraband or the instrumentalities of crime will be found in a particular place when seeking a search warrant. Although the Fourth Amendment does not specify the basis for warrantless searches and seizures by police, they too must be based on probable cause.[2] Regardless of whether police seek an arrest or a search warrant, they must supply the same quantum of evidence when establishing probable cause.[3] Probable cause for making an arrest turns on "whether at that moment [of arrest] the facts and circumstances within [the officers'] knowledge and of which they [have] reasonably trustworthy information [are] sufficient to warrant a prudent man in believing that the [suspect] had committed or was committing an offense."[4] And the test is objective in the sense that a judge (or "reasonable" person) would agree that enough evidence exists to support a police officer's determination; in other words, the subjective judgment of an officer alone does not support a finding of probable cause.

In determining whether probable cause has been reasonably established, judges consider the *specificity* of what is to be searched and the *particularity* of what is to be seized. Because police often rely on informants, the Court also demands that police show that their information is *reliable,* not vague, and sufficient for judges to draw their own conclusions about.[5] Hearsay evidence may be used,[6] yet police must attest to the reliability of informants, although they need not demonstrate their credulity.[7]

The Warren Court established a two-prong test for determining probable cause when holding that police failed to establish that in an affidavit for a warrant that simply claimed "reliable information from a credible person" indicated "narcotics and narcotics paraphernalia" were kept at certain location. In that case, *Aguilar v. Texas*, 378 U.S. 108 (1964), the Court held that police must explain (1) how it is that an informant knows what he claims to know and (2) why they believe the information to be accurate and reliable. The more conservative Burger and Rehnquist Courts, however, abandoned that test. *Illinois v. Gates*, 462 U.S. 213 (1983), held that the *Aguillar* factors—showing the basis and veracity of informers' tips—were "relevant considerations" but no longer independent requirements. "[A] deficiency in one may be compensated for," Rehnquist held, "by a strong showing as to the other." In *Gates*, and *Massachusetts v. Upton*, 466 U.S. 727 (1984), the Court ruled that judges may determine whether "the totality of the circumstances" presented by police justify a finding of probable cause.[8]

Although search warrants authorize police to search only particular locations and to seize specific items, police had long been allowed to conduct searches when making arrests, without or without arrest warrants. Until the Warren Court era, moreover, police were permitted to undertake rather sweeping searches when armed with only an arrest warrant. *Harris v. United States*, 331 U.S. 145 (1947), for instance, allowed the search of a four-room apartment based only on an arrest warrant for the occupant. And *United States v. Rabinowitz*, 339 U.S. 56 (1950), permitted police to search a one-room office in the home of a stamp dealer who was arrested for selling fraudulent stamps. The Warren Court, however, signaled a change in *Chapman v. United States*, 365 U.S. 610 (1961), when disapproving of a warrantless search of a rented house, which police entered through an unlocked window with the owner's (but not the renter's) consent. There, Justice Charles Whittaker observed that

[n]o reason is offered for not obtaining a search warrant except the inconvenience of the officers and some slight delay necessary to prepare papers and present the evidence to a magistrate. These are never very convincing reasons and, in these circumstances, certainly are not enough to by-pass the constitutional requirement. No suspect was fleeing or likely to take flight. The search was of a permanent premises, not of a movable vehicle. No evidence or contraband was threatened with removal or destruction.

Harris and *Rabinowitz* were finally expressly overruled in *Chimel v. California* (1969) (see page 776).

Chimel's ruling that police, armed with only an arrest warrant or when they have probable cause to make an arrest, are constrained in searching only what is in "plain view" and in "the immediate area" surrounding an arrestee have been repeatedly reaffirmed. But the Court's rulings usually turn on the particular circumstances of each case.[9] Compare, for example, the circumstances and rulings in *Washington v. Chrisman* (1982) (see page 780) and *Arizona v. Hicks* (1987) (see page 784).

As *Arizona v. Hicks* indicates, the Burger and Rehnquist Courts, although occasionally sharply split, continue to draw a line limiting the scope of warrantless searches made in connection with arrests. In *Yabarra v. Illinois*, 444 U.S. 85 (1979), the Court also held that a warrant authorizing police to search a small tavern and the bartender for narcotics did not justify a pat-down search of patrons of the bar. Voting six to three in *Payton v. New York*, 445 U.S. 573 (1980), the justices struck down a state statute authorizing police to enter private residences without a warrant to make routine felony arrests. In *Steagald v. United States*, 451 U.S. 204 (1981), the Court held that police needed a search warrant to enter the home of a third party when attempting to arrest a person for which they had a valid arrest warrant. And in *Welsh v. Wisconsin*, 466 U.S. 470 (1984), the Court rejected a warrantless nighttime entry into a house by police to arrest an individual for driving under the influence of alcohol. In a brief *per curiam* opinion in *Smith v. Ohio*, 110 S.Ct. 1288 (1990), the Rehnquist Court reaffirmed that a warrantless search of a man on the street, which then gave rise to probable cause for his arrest, was no justification for the search incident to that arrest. But in *Horton v. California*, 110 S.Ct. 2301 (1990), the Court ruled that a warrantless search and seizure was permissible under the plain view doctrine, because the defendant's criminal conduct was immediately apparent to police officers. Justices Brennan and Marshall dissented.

With Justices Brennan, Blackmun, and Marshall dissenting, the Rehnquist Court approved of a search based on a valid warrant for the search of a third-floor apartment but where police searched the wrong apartment on the floor due to their mistaken belief that there was only one apartment on the floor.[10]

In *Maryland v. Buie*, 110 S.Ct. 1093 (1990), the Rehnquist Court gave police authority to make "protective sweeps" of the premises when arresting a person in his home, if they reasonably believe (although do not have probable cause to believe) that the area may harbor another individual who poses a danger to them. Here, police had arrest warrants for Jerome Buie and a suspected accomplice in the robbery of a Godfather's Pizza restaurant by two men, one of whom wore a red running suit. They had a secretary call his home to see if he was there before they arrived. When the police arrived at Buie's house, they quickly entered and fanned out through the first and second floors.

Failing to find Buie, the police shouted down to the basement and ordered anyone there to come out. Buie soon appeared. And an officer then went down into the basement to see if "there was someone else" there, whereupon he discovered a red running suit. At his trial, Buie's attorney argued that the running suit had been seized pursuant to an illegal search and should be excluded as evidence. The trial court and state appellate court disagreed. On appeal to the Supreme Court, writing for the majority, Justice White upheld such protective searches, observing

[t]hat Buie had an expectation of privacy in those remaining areas of his house . . . does not mean such rooms were immune from entry. . . . In the instant case, there is an analogous interest of the officers in taking steps to assure themselves that the house in which a suspect is being or has just been arrested is not harboring other persons who are dangerous and who could unexpectedly launch an attack. The risk of danger in the context of an arrest in the home is as great as, if not greater than, it is in an on-the-street or roadside investigatory encounter. . . .

To reach our conclusion today, . . . we need not disagree with the Court's statement in *Chimel* that "the invasion of privacy that results from a top-to-bottom search of a man's house [cannot be characterized] as "minor," . . . The type of search we authorize today is far removed from the "top-to-bottom" search involved in *Chimel;* moreover, it is decidedly not "automati[c]" but may be conducted only when justified by a reasonable, articulable suspicion that the house is harboring a person posing a danger to those on the arrest scene.

But dissenting Justice Brennan, joined by Justice Marshall, countered that the Court had extended the holding in *Terry v. Ohio* (1968) (see page 794) "into the home, dispensing with the Fourth Amendment's general requirements of a warrant and probable cause and carving a 'reasonable suspicion' exception for protective sweeps in private dwellings." Justice Brennan pointed out that,

[i]n *Terry,* the Court held that a police officer may briefly detain a suspect based on a reasonable suspicion of criminal activity and may conduct a limited "frisk" of the suspect for concealed weapons in order to protect herself from personal danger. The Court deemed such a frisk "reasonable" under the Fourth Amendment in light of the special 'need for law enforcement officers to protect themselves and other prospective victims of violence' during investigative detentions.

Brennan also conceded "that officers executing an arrest warrant within a private dwelling have an interest in protecting themselves." But he maintained that the majority offers no support for its assumption that the danger of ambush during planned home arrests approaches the danger of unavoidable "on-the-beat" confrontations in "the myriad daily situations in which policemen and citizens confront each other on the street." In any event, the Court's implicit judgment that a protective sweep constitutes a "minimally intrusive" search akin to that involved in *Terry* markedly undervalues the nature and scope of the privacy interests involved.

The obligation of police to obtain a search warrant (if circumstances permit and when a search is not incident to an arrest) holds. But the more conservative Burger and Rehnquist Courts have tended to be less tough on law-enforcement interests. The Warren Court held in *Jones v. United States*, 382 U.S. 36 (1960), for instance, that the search of a house of a man arrested two blocks away was not permissible as a search incident to arrest. In *Hill v. California*, 40 U.S. 797 (1974), the Burger Court held that the arrest of the wrong man permitted a search of the immediate area surrounding him as a search incident to his arrest. In *G. M. Leasing Corporation v. United States*, 429 U.S. 338 (1977), the warrantless search of the office of a corporation was allowed, but not that of the company's cars parked in its lot. In *Mincey v. Arizona*, 437 U.S. 385 (1978), the Court disallowed a warrantless search of the murder scene in an accused's apartment four days after his arrest. But in *United States v. Edwards*, 415 U.S. 800 (1974), a bare majority of the Court allowed the warrantless search of an accused's bodily clothing ten hours after his arrest and substitute clothing was given to him. The Court also permits warrantless searches of individuals arrested and taken into custody,[11] as well as delayed searches of automobiles that are impounded after the driver's arrest.[12]

NOTES

1. However, *Shadwick v. City of Tampa*, 407 U.S. 345 (1972), permitted the delegation of responsibility for issuing warrants to municipal county clerks.

2. See *Wong Sun v. United States*, 371 U.S. 471 (1963).

3. See *Spinelli v. United States*, 393 U.S. 410 (1969), and *Draper v. United States*, 358 U.S. 307 (1959).

4. *Beck v. Ohio*, 362 U.S. 309 (1960).

5. *Jones v. United States*, 362 U.S. 309 (1960).

6. See *McGray v. Illinois*, 386 U.S. 300 (1967).

7. See *United States v. Harris*, 403 U.S. 513 (1971), and *Adams v. Williams*, 407 U.S. 143 (1972).

8. At the same time, the Court holds that, notwithstanding its totality of circumstances approach to determining probable cause, the balance between individual rights and law-enforcement interests that is struck in determining probable cause is not drawn on a case-by-case basis, see *Dunaway v. New York,* 442 U.S. 200 (1979).

9. See *Ker v. California,* 374 U.S. 23 (1963) (upholding an arrest for possession of marijuana based on police seeing the plants in a kitchen window); *Vale v. Louisiana,* 399 U.S. 30 (1970) (overturning a warrantless search of a house of man arrested on its entry steps); and *Lo-Ji Sales v. New York,* 442 U.S. 319 (1979) (reaffirming that the Fourth Amendment forbids open-ended searches of a retail store).

10. *Maryland v. Garrison,* 480 U.S. 79 (1987).

11. *Gustafson v. Florida,* 414 U.S. 260 (1973) (allowing full-body search of man arrested for traffic violation and taken into custody). In *United States v. Montoya DeHernandez,* 473 U.S. 531 (1985), the Court held that it was not unreasonable to detain a suspected smuggler for sixteen hours.

12. See *Chambers v. Maroney,* 399 U.S. 42 (1970) (upholding search of a car taken to the police station by police who had probable cause to stop the car and believed it contained stolen guns and money); and *South Dakota v. Opperman,* 428 U.S. 543 (1976) (upheld a routine inventory search of a locked car that was impounded).

Chimel v. California
395 U.S. 752, 89 S.Ct. 2034 (1969)

Late one afternoon in September 1965, three police officers arrived at Ted Chimel's home in Santa Ann, California. They had a warrant to arrest him for burglary of a coin shop. Chimel was not at home but his wife allowed the police to wait in the house until he returned from work. When he arrived, police handed him the arrest warrant and asked whether they could look around his house. Chimel objected but was told that "on the basis of a lawful arrest" the police could conduct a search. The police searched the entire three-bedroom house, including the attic, the garage, and a small workshop. They seized numerous coins, medals, and tokens, which were later used as evidence against Chimel at trial. Following his conviction, Chimel unsuccessfully appealed to a state appellate court and the California Supreme Court, contending that the police had unlawfully searched his house. Failing in those efforts, Chimel appealed to the Supreme Court, which granted review.

Justice STEWART delivers the opinion of the Court.

This case raises basic questions concerning the permissible scope under the Fourth Amendment of a search incident to a lawful arrest. . . .

In 1950, [the Court handed down] *United States v. Rabinowitz,* 339 U.S. 56 [1950], the decision upon which California primarily relies in the case now before us. In *Rabinowitz,* federal authorities had been informed that the defendant was dealing in stamps bearing forged overprints. On the basis of that information they secured a warrant for his arrest, which they executed at his one-room business office. At the time of the arrest, the officers "searched the desk, safe, and file cabinets in the office for about an hour and a half," and seized 573 stamps with forged overprints. The stamps were admitted into evidence at the defendant's trial, and this Court affirmed his conviction, rejecting the contention that the warrantless search had been unlawful. The Court held that the search in its entirety fell within the principle giving law enforcement authorities "[t]he right 'to search the place where the arrest is made in order to find and seize things connected with the crime. . . .'" The test, said the Court, "is not whether it is reasonable to procure a search warrant, but whether the search was reasonable.". . .

Rabinowitz has come to stand for the proposition, *inter alia,* that a warrantless search "incident to a lawful arrest" may generally extend to the area that is considered to be in the "possession" or under the "control" of the person arrested. And it was on the basis of that proposition that the California courts upheld the search of the petitioner's entire house in this case. That doctrine, however, at least in the broad sense in which it was applied by the California courts in this case, can withstand neither historical nor rational analysis.

Even limited to its own facts, the *Rabinowitz* decision was, as we have seen, hardly founded on an unimpeachable line of authority. [Justice STEWART, after reviewing cases following *Rabinowitz,* concluded that the Fourth] Amendment was in large part a reaction to the general warrants and warrantless searches that had so alienated the colonists and had helped speed the movement for independence. In the scheme of the Amendment, therefore, the requirement that "no Warrants shall issue, but upon probable cause," plays a crucial part. . . .

A similar analysis underlies the "search incident to arrest" principle, and marks its proper extent. When an arrest is made, it is reasonable for the arresting officer to search the person arrested in order to remove any weapons that the latter might seek to use in order to resist arrest or effect his escape. Otherwise, the officer's safety might well be endangered, and the arrest itself frustrated. In addition, it is entirely reasonable for the arresting officer to search for and seize any evidence on the arrestee's person in order to prevent its concealment or destruction. And the area into which an arrestee might reach in order to grab a weapon or evidentiary items must, of course, be governed by a like rule. A gun on a table or in a drawer in front of one who is arrested can be as dangerous to the arresting officer as one concealed in the clothing of the person arrested. There is ample justification, therefore, for a search of the arrestee's person and the area "within his immediate control"—construing that phrase to mean the area from within which he might gain possession of a weapon or destructible evidence.

There is no comparable justification, however, for routinely searching any room other than that in which an arrest occurs—or, for that matter, for searching through all the desk drawers or other closed or concealed areas in that room itself. Such searches, in the absence of well-recognized exceptions, may be made only under the authority of a search warrant. The "adherence to judicial processes" mandated by the Fourth Amendment requires no less. . . .

It is argued in the present case that it is "reasonable" to search a man's house when he is arrested in it. But that argument is founded on little more than a subjective view regarding the acceptability of certain sorts of police conduct, and not on considerations relevant to Fourth Amendment interests. Under such an unconfined analysis, Fourth Amendment protection in this area would approach the evaporation point. It is not easy to explain why, for instance, it is less subjectively "reasonable" to search a man's house when he is arrested on his front lawn—or just down the street—than it is when he happens to be in the house at the time of arrest. . . .

The petitioner correctly points out that one result of decisions such as *Rabinowitz* and *Harris* [v. *United States,* 331 U.S. 14 (1947)], is to give law enforcement officials the opportunity to engage in searches not justified by probable cause, by the simple expedient of arranging to arrest suspects at home rather than elsewhere. We do not suggest that the petitioner is necessarily correct in his assertion that such a strategy was utilized here, but the fact remains that had he been arrested earlier in the day, at his place of employment rather than at home, no search of his house could have been made without a search warrant. In any event, even apart from the possibility of such police tactics, the general point so forcefully made by Judge Learned Hand in *United States v. Kirschenblatt,* 2 Cir., 16 F.2d 202 [1926], remains:

"After arresting a man in his house, to rummage at will among his papers in search of whatever will convict him, appears to us to be indistinguishable from what might be done under a general warrant; indeed, the warrant would give more protection, for presumably it must be issued by a magistrate. True, by hypothesis the power would not exist, if the supposed offender were not found on the premises; but it is small consolation to know that one's papers are safe only so long as one is not at home.". . .

Application of sound Fourth Amendment principles to the facts of this case produces a clear result. The search here went far beyond the petitioner's person and the area from within which he might have obtained either a weapon or something that could have been used as evidence against him. There was no constitutional justification, in the absence of a search warrant, for extending the search beyond that area. The scope of the search was, therefore, "unreasonable" under the Fourth and Fourteenth Amendments and the petitioner's conviction cannot stand. Reversed.

Justice HARLAN concurring.

I join the Court's opinion with these remarks concerning a factor to which the Court has not alluded.

The only thing that has given me pause in voting to overrule *Harris* and *Rabinowitz* is that as a result of *Mapp v. Ohio,* [367 U.S. 643] (1961), and *Ker v. California,* [372 U.S. 23] (1963), every change in Fourth Amendment law must now be obeyed by state officials facing widely different problems of local law enforcement. We simply do not know the extent to which cities and towns across the Nation are prepared to administer the greatly expanded warrant system which will be required by today's decision; nor can we say with assurance that in each and every local situation, the warrant requirement plays an essential role in the protection of those fundamental liberties protected against state infringement by the Fourteenth Amendment. . . .

This federal-state factor has not been an easy one for me to resolve, but in the last analysis I cannot in good conscience vote to perpetuate bad Fourth Amendment law.

Justice WHITE, with whom Justice BLACK joins, dissenting.

Few areas of the law have been as subject to shifting constitutional standards over the last 50 years as that of the search "incident to an arrest." There has been a remarkable instability in this whole area, which has seen at least four major shifts in emphasis. Today's opinion makes an untimely fifth. In my view, the Court should not now abandon the old rule. . . .

[T]he Court must decide whether a given search is reasonable. The Amendment does not proscribe "warrantless searches" but instead it proscribes "unreasonable searches" and this Court has never held nor does the majority today assert that warrantless searches are necessarily unreasonable.

Applying this reasonableness test to the area of searches incident to arrests, one thing is clear at the outset. Search of an arrested man and of the items within his immediate reach must in almost every case be reasonable. There is always a danger that the suspect will try to escape, seizing concealed weapons with which to overpower and injure the arresting officers, and there is a danger that he may destroy evidence vital to the prosecution. Circumstances in which these justifications would not apply are sufficiently rare that inquiry is not made into searches of this scope, which have been considered reasonable throughout.

The justifications which make such a search reasonable obviously do not apply to the search of areas to which the accused does not have ready physical access. This is not enough, however, to prove such searches unconstitutional. The Court has always held, and does not today deny, that when there is probable cause to search and it is "impracticable" for one reason or another to get a search warrant, then a warrantless search may be reasonable. . . .

This case provides a good illustration of my point that it is unreasonable to require police to leave the scene of an arrest in order to obtain a search warrant when they already have probable cause to search and there is a clear danger that the items for which they may reasonably search will be removed before they return with a warrant. Petitioner was arrested in his home after an arrest whose validity will be explored below, but which I will now assume was valid. There was doubtless probable cause not only to arrest petitioner, but also to search his house. He had obliquely admitted, both to a neighbor and to the owner of the burglarized store, that he had committed the burglary. In light of this, and the fact that the neighbor had seen other admittedly stolen property in petitioner's house, there was surely probable cause on which a warrant could have issued to search the house for the stolen coins. Moreover, had the police simply arrested petitioner, taken him off to the station house, and later returned with a warrant, it seems very likely that petitioner's wife, who in view of petitioner's generally garrulous nature must have known of the robbery, would have removed the coins. For the police to search the house while the evidence they had probable cause to search out and seize was still there cannot be considered unreasonable.

Washington v. Chrisman
455 U.S. 1, 102 S.Ct. 812 (1982)

Chief Justice Warren Burger reviews the facts in this case, involving a police search of a student dormatory room, in his announcement of the decision of the Court.

Chief Justice BURGER delivers the opinion of the Court.

We granted certiorari to consider whether a police officer may, consistent with the Fourth Amendment, accompany an arrested person into his residence and seize contraband discovered there in plain view.

On the evening of January 21, 1978, Officer Daugherty of the Washington State University police department observed Carl Overdahl, a student at the University, leave a student dormitory carrying a half-gallon bottle of gin. Because Washington law forbids possession of alcoholic beverages by persons under 21, and Overdahl appeared to be under age, the officer stopped him and asked for identification. Overdahl said that his identification was in his dormitory room and asked if the officer would wait while he went to retrieve it. The officer answered that under the circumstances he would have to accompany Overdahl, to which Overdahl replied "O.K."

Overdahl's room was approximately 11 by 17 feet and located on the 11th floor of the dormitory. Respondent Chrisman, Overdahl's roommate, was in the room when the officer and Overdahl entered. The officer remained in the open doorway, leaning against the doorjamb while watching Chrisman and Overdahl. He observed that Chrisman, who was in the process of placing a small box in the room's medicine cabinet, became nervous at the sight of an officer.

Within 30 to 45 seconds after Overdahl entered the room, the officer noticed seeds and a small pipe lying on a desk 8 to 10 feet from where he was standing. From his training and experience, the officer believed the seeds were marihuana and the pipe was of a type used to smoke marihuana. He entered the room and examined the pipe and seeds, confirming that the seeds were marihuana and observing that the pipe smelled of marihuana. . . .

Respondent was charged with one count of possessing more than 40 grams of marihuana and one count of possessing LSD, both felonies under Wash.Rev.Code § 69.–50.401(c). A pretrial motion to suppress the evidence seized in the room was denied; respondent was convicted of both counts. On appeal, the Washington Court of Appeals affirmed the convictions upholding the validity of the search. . . .

The Supreme Court of Washington reversed. . . .

We granted certiorari . . . and reverse.

The "plain view" exception to the Fourth Amendment warrant requirement permits a law enforcement officer to seize what clearly is incriminating evidence or contraband when it is discovered in a place where the officer has a right to be. *Coolidge v. New Hampshire,* 403 U.S. 443 (1971); *Harris v. United States,* 390 U.S. 234 (1968). Here, the officer had placed Overdahl under lawful arrest, and therefore was authorized to accompany him to his room for the purpose of obtaining identification. The officer had a right to remain literally at Overdahl's elbow at all times; nothing in the Fourth Amendment is to the contrary. . . .

We hold . . . that it is not "unreasonable" under the Fourth Amendment for a police officer, as a matter of routine, to monitor the movements of an arrested person, as his judgment dictates, following the arrest. The officer's need to ensure his own safety—as well as the integrity of the arrest—is compelling. Such surveillance is not an impermissible invasion of the privacy or personal liberty of an individual who has been arrested. . . .

Respondent nevertheless contends that the officer lacked authority to *seize* the contraband, even though in plain view, because he was "outside" the room at the time he made his observations. . . .

We reject this contention. Respondent's argument, if accepted, would have the perverse effect of penalizing the officer for exercising more restraint than was required under the circumstances. Moreover, it ignores the fundamental premise that the Fourth Amendment protects only against unreasonable intrusions into an individual's privacy. . . .

The "intrusion" in this case occurred when the officer, quite properly, followed Overdahl into a private area to a point from which he had unimpeded view of and access to the area's contents and its occupants. His right to custodial control did not evaporate with his choice to hesitate briefly in the doorway rather than at some other vantage point inside the room. It cannot be gainsaid that the officer would have had unrestricted access to the room at the first indication that he was in danger, or that evidence might be destroyed—or even upon reassessment of the wisdom of permitting a distance between himself and Overdahl.

This is a classic instance of incriminating evidence found in plain view when a police officer, for unrelated but entirely legitimate reasons, obtains lawful access to an individual's area of privacy. The Fourth Amendment does not prohibit seizure of evidence of criminal conduct found in these circumstances.

Justice WHITE, with whom Justice BRENNAN and Justice MARSHALL join, dissenting.

The record in this case is clear . . . that Daugherty did not leave the doorway and enter the room in order to protect himself or maintain control over respondent. Daugherty's uncontradicted testimony was that he entered the room solely to confirm his suspicion that the seeds and the seashell he had observed from the doorway were marijuana seeds and a seashell pipe that had been used to smoke marijuana. Daugherty made no claim that he entered the room as a necessary incident to the permission given Overdahl to secure his identification. Rather, he claimed that the entry was justified because of what was in plain view on the desk inside the room.

The plain view doctrine, however, does not authorize an officer to enter a dwelling without a warrant to seize contraband merely because the contraband is visible from outside the dwelling. This is settled law. As the Court said in *Coolidge v. New Hampshire* [403, U.S. 443] (1971):

> "[P]lain view *alone* is never enough to justify the warrantless seizure of evidence. This is simply a corollary of the familiar principle discussed above, that no amount of probable cause can justify a warrantless search or seizure absent 'exigent circumstances.' Incontrovertible testimony of the senses that an incriminating object is on premises belonging to a criminal suspect may establish the fullest possible measure of probable cause. But even where the object is contraband, this Court has repeatedly stated and enforced the basic rule that the police may not enter and make a warrantless seizure. . . .

Coolidge emphasized that the plain view doctrine applies only after a lawful search is in progress or the officer was otherwise legally present at the place of the seizure. The initial intrusion must be justified by a warrant, by an exception to the warrant requirement, or by other circumstances authorizing his presence.

If a police officer passing by an open door of a home sees incriminating evidence within the house, his observation may provide probable cause for the issuance of a search warrant. Yet the officer may not enter the home without a warrant unless an exception to the warrant requirement applies. This rule is fully supported by *Coolidge v. New Hampshire, supra,* and the cases cited in the Court's opinion in that case. Any contrary rule would severely undercut the protection afforded by the Fourth Amendment, for it is the physical entry of the home that is the chief evil against which the Amendment is directed. . . .

I perceive no justification for what is in effect a per se rule that an officer in Daugherty's circumstances could always enter the room and stay at the arrestee's elbow. This would be true only if there were no limits to the conditions which the officer could attach when he permits his charge to return to his room. I doubt, for example, that he could insist that he be permitted to search desks, closets, drawers or cabinets. Likewise, he should not be permitted to invade living quarters any more than is necessary to maintain control and protect himself. Bright-line rules are indeed useful and sometimes necessary, but the Court should move with some care where the home or living quarters are involved.

Arizona v. Hicks

480 U.S. 321, 107 S.Ct. 1149 (1987)

Justice Antonin Scalia presents the pertinent facts in his opinion for the Court in this case, involving a police search and the application of the plain view doctrine.

Justice SCALIA delivers the opinion of the Court.

In *Coolidge v. New Hampshire*, 403 U.S. 43 (1971), we said that in certain circumstances a warrantless seizure by police of an item that comes within plain view during their lawful search of a private area may be reasonable under the Fourth Amendment. . . . We granted certiorari . . . in the present case to decide whether this "plain view" doctrine may be invoked when the police have less than probable cause to believe that the item in question is evidence of a crime or is contraband.

I

On April 18, 1984, a bullet was fired through the floor of respondent's apartment, striking and injuring a man in the apartment below. Police officers arrived and entered respondent's apartment to search for the shooter, for other victims, and for weapons. They found and seized three weapons, including a sawed-off rifle, and in the course of their search also discovered a stocking-cap mask.

One of the policemen, Officer Nelson, noticed two sets of expensive stereo components, which seemed out of place in the squalid and otherwise ill-appointed four-room apartment. Suspecting that they were stolen, he read and recorded their serial numbers—moving some of the components, including a Bang and Olufsen turntable, in order to do so—which he then reported by phone to his headquarters. On being advised that the turntable had been taken in an armed robbery, he seized it immediately. It was later determined that some of the other serial numbers matched those on other stereo equipment taken in the same armed robbery, and a warrant was obtained and executed to seize that equipment as well. Respondent was subsequently indicted for the robbery.

The state trial court granted respondent's motion to suppress the evidence that had been seized. The Court of Appeals of Arizona affirmed. It was conceded that the initial entry and search, although warrantless, were justified by the exigent circumstance of the shooting. The Court of Appeals viewed the obtaining of the serial numbers, however, as an additional search, unrelated to that exigency. . . . Both courts—the trial court explicitly and the Court of Appeals by necessary implication—rejected the State's contention that Officer Nelson's actions were justified under the "plain view" doctrine of *Coolidge v. New Hampshire, supra.* The Arizona Supreme Court denied review, and the State filed this petition.

II

Officer Nelson's moving of the equipment . . . constitute[d] a "search" separate and apart from the search for the shooter, victims, and weapons that was the lawful objective of his entry into the apartment. Merely inspecting those parts of the turntable that came into view during the latter search would not have constituted an independent search, because it would have produced no additional invasion of respondent's privacy interest. But taking action, unrelated to the objectives of the authorized intrusion, which exposed to view concealed portions of the apartment or its contents, did produce a new invasion of respondent's privacy unjustified by the exigent circumstance that validated the entry. . . . It matters not that the search uncovered nothing of any great personal value to the respondent—serial numbers rather than (what might conceivably have been hidden behind or under the equipment) letters or photographs. A search is a search, even if it happens to disclose nothing but the bottom of a turntable.

III

The remaining question is whether the search was "reasonable" under the Fourth Amendment.

On this aspect of the case we reject, at the outset, the apparent position of the Arizona Court of Appeals that because the officers' action directed to the stereo equipment was unrelated to the justification for their entry into respondent's apartment, it was *ipso facto* unreasonable. That lack of relationship *always* exists with regard to action validated under the "plain view" doctrine; where action is taken for the purpose justifying the entry, invocation of the doctrine is superfluous. . . .

We turn, then, to application of the doctrine to the facts of this case. "It is well established that under certain circumstances the police may *seize* evidence in plain view without a warrant," *Coolidge.* Those circumstances include situations "[w]here the initial intrusion that brings the police within plain view of such [evidence] is supported . . . by one of the recognized exceptions to the warrant requirement," such as the exigent-circumstances intrusion here. It would be absurd to say that an object could lawfully be seized and taken from the premises, but could not be moved for closer examination. It is clear, therefore, that the search here was valid if the "plain view" doctrine would have sustained a seizure of the equipment.

There is no doubt it would have done so if Officer Nelson

had probable cause to believe that the equipment was stolen. The State has conceded, however, that he had only a "reasonable suspicion," by which it means something less than probable cause. . . .

We now hold that probable cause is required. To say otherwise would be to cut the "plain view" doctrine loose from its theoretical and practical moorings. The theory of that doctrine consists of extending to nonpublic places such as the home, where searches and seizures without a warrant are presumptively unreasonable, the police's longstanding authority to make warrantless seizures in public places of such objects as weapons and contraband. And the practical justification for that extension is the desirability of sparing police, whose viewing of the object in the course of a lawful search is as legitimate as it would have been in a public place, the inconvenience and the risk—to themselves or to preservation of the evidence—of going to obtain a warrant. . . . Dispensing with the need for a warrant is worlds apart from permitting a lesser standard of *cause* for the seizure than a warrant would require, *i.e.*, the standard of probable cause. No reason is apparent why an object should routinely be seizable on lesser grounds, during an unrelated search and seizure, than would have been needed to obtain a warrant for that same object if it had been known to be on the premises.

We do not say, of course, that a seizure can never be justified on less than probable cause. We have held that it can—where, for example, the seizure is minimally intrusive and operational necessities render it the only practicable means of detecting certain types of crime. See, *e.g., United States v. Cortez,* 449 U.S. 411 (1981) (investigative detention of vehicle suspected to be transporting illegal aliens); *United States v. Place,* 462 U.S. 696 [1983] (seizure of suspected drug dealer's luggage at airport to permit exposure to specially trained dog). No special operational necessities are relied on here, however—but rather the mere fact that the items in question came lawfully within the officer's plain view. That alone cannot supplant the requirement of probable cause. . . .

Justice O'CONNOR's dissent suggests that we uphold the action here on the ground that it was a "cursory inspection" rather than a "full-blown search," and could therefore be justified by reasonable suspicion instead of probable cause. As already noted, a truly cursory inspection—one that involves merely looking at what is already exposed to view, without disturbing it—is not a "search" for Fourth Amendment purposes, and therefore does not even require reasonable suspicion. We are unwilling to send police and judges into a new thicket of Fourth Amendment law, to seek a creature of uncertain description that is neither a plain-view inspection nor yet a "full-blown search." Nothing in the prior opinions of this Court supports such a distinction. . . .

For the reasons stated, the judgment of the Court of Appeals of Arizona is

Affirmed.

Justice WHITE concurred in a separate opinion.

Justice POWELL, with whom the CHIEF JUSTICE and Justice O'CONNOR join, dissenting.

The Court holds that there was an unlawful search of the turntable. It agrees that the "mere recording of the serial numbers did not constitute a seizure." Thus, if the computer had identified as stolen property a component with a visible serial number, the evidence would have been admissible. But the Court further holds that "Officer Nelson's moving of the equipment . . . did constitute a 'search.'. . ." It perceives a constitutional distinction between reading a serial number on an object and moving or picking up an identical object to see its serial number. . . . With all respect, this distinction between "looking" at a suspicious object in plain view and "moving" it even a few inches trivializes the Fourth Amendment. The Court's new rule will cause uncertainty, and could deter conscientious police officers from lawfully obtaining evidence necessary to convict guilty persons. Apart from the importance of rationality in the interpretation of the Fourth Amendment, today's decision may handicap law enforcement without enhancing privacy interests. Accordingly, I dissent.

Justice O'CONNOR, with whom the CHIEF JUSTICE and Justice POWELL join, dissenting.

The Court today gives the right answer to the wrong question. The Court asks whether the police must have probable cause before either seizing an object in plain view or conducting a full-blown search of that object, and concludes that they must. I agree. In my view, however, this case presents a different question: whether police must have probable cause before conducting a cursory inspection of an item in plain view. Because I conclude that such an inspection is reasonable if the police are aware of facts or circumstances that justify a reasonable suspicion that the item is evidence of a crime, I would reverse the judgment of the Arizona Court of Appeals, and therefore dissent. . . .

When a police officer makes a cursory inspection of a suspicious item in plain view in order to determine whether it is indeed evidence of a crime, there is no "exploratory rummaging." Only those items that the police officer "reasonably suspects" as evidence of a crime may be inspected, and perhaps more importantly, the scope of such an inspection is quite limited. In short, if police officers have a reasonable, articulable suspicion that an object they come across during the course of a lawful search is evidence of crime, in my view they may make a cursory examination of the object to verify their suspicion. If the officers wish to go beyond such a cursory examination of the object, however, they must have probable cause.

B. EXCEPTIONS TO THE WARRANT REQUIREMENT

There are a number of exceptions to the Fourth Amendment's command that police obtain a warrant prior to conducting a search. Besides conducting searches incident to an arrest and after taking a person into custody (as discussed in section A, of this chapter), police may undertake *consent searches*—searches of persons and their property after being given their consent. While it seems obvious that individuals may waive their rights, whose and what kind of consent is necessary for a police search has proven problematic.

The Court maintains that police may not conduct a warrantless search of an apartment or hotel room without the occupant's consent and despite having the owner's permission.[1] However, with Justices Brennan, Marshall, and Stevens in dissent, *Illinois v. Rodriguez*, 110 S.Ct. 2793 (1990), held that incriminating evidence may be used at trial even though it was seized during a warrantless entry into a home by police officers who were let in by a person they mistakenly thought was authorized to consent to a search. "What we hold today does not suggest that law enforcement officers may always accept a person's invitation to enter," wrote Justice Scalia, when holding that "consent to enter must be judged against an objective standard: would the facts available to the officer . . . warrant a man of reasonable caution in the belief that the consenting party had authority over the premises?"

Traditionally, consent searches were justified on the theory that individuals could waive their Fourth Amendment rights. But in *Scheckloth v. Bustamonte*, 412 U.S. 218 (1973), the Burger Court appeared to dismiss that theory in holding that the underlying issue is whether consent may be reasonably deemed to be "voluntary" based on the circumstances surrounding a particular search. There the Court ruled that when a suspect is not in custody but police make a consent search, the state must show only that the consent was voluntarily given, even though the suspect had no knowledge that he could refuse to agree to the search. Dissenting Justice Brennan protested that

The Court holds today that an individual can effectively waive this right even though he is totally ignorant of the fact that, in the absence of his consent, such invasions of his privacy would be constitutionally prohibited. It wholly escapes me how our citizens can meaningfully be said to have waived something as precious as a constitutional guarantee without ever being aware of its existence. In my view, the Court's conclusion is supported neither by "linguistics," nor by "epistemology," nor, indeed, by "common sense."

The next year, *United States v. Matlock*, 415 U.S. 164 (1974), held that police could search a bedroom inhabited by two persons so long as they obtained the consent of one of the two. When distinguishing earlier rulings denying consent searches based on a landlord's consent, Justice White explained that "it is reasonable to recognize that any of the co-inhabitants has the right to permit the inspection in his own right common area to be searched." In *Illinois v. Batchelder*, 463 U.S. 1112 (1983), the Court also upheld implied consent laws, requiring drivers to submit to breathalyzer tests or have their licenses automatically revoked.

Another exception is the so-called *open fields doctrine*—allowing police to search and seize illegal items that are in open public view—announced in *Hester v. United States*, 265 U.S. 57 (1924). On this doctrine, the Court upheld a warrantless search of land on which marijuana was growing in *Oliver v. United States*, 466 U.S. 170 (1984). Two years later, the justices split five to four when rejecting an individual's claim of Fourth Amendment–protected privacy interests against the aerial observation by police from helicopters flying over his fenced-in backyard in which he grew marijuana. Along with that ruling in *California v. Ciraolo* (1986) (see page 883), the justices rejected the Fourth Amendment arguments of Dow Chemical Company, who objected to the Environmental Protection Agency's aerial photography of its site when inspecting for pollution violations in *Dow Chemical Company v. United States*, 476 U.S. 227 (1986). In *United States v. Dunn*, 480 U.S. 294 (1987), the Rehnquist Court further extended the open fields doctrine when permitting a search of a barn in an open field at night by police armed with a flashlight but no warrant. And in *Florida v. Riley*, 488 U.S. 445 (1988), by a five-to-four vote the Court again rejected Fourth Amendment privacy claims when holding that police do not need a search warrant for searches of private property by helicopters flying 400 feet above ground.

More controversial is the exception the Warren Court carved out in *Terry v. Ohio* (1968) (see page 794), allowing police without either a warrant or probable cause to *stop and frisk* individuals who look suspicious. There the Court explicitly balanced Fourth

Amendment interests against those of law enforcement. Notice, though, Chief Justice Warren approved of such searches only to the extent that they were "limited to outer clothing . . . in an attempt to discover weapons which might be used to assault [a police officer]." A companion ruling, *Sibron v. New York*, 392 U.S. 40 (1968), underscored *Terry's* limited holding in refusing to permit the search of a drug suspect who police had no reason to believe was armed or dangerous; as Chief Justice Warren emphasized, "the police officer is not entitled to seize and search every person whom he sees on the street."

The *Terry* exception has been enlarged by the Burger and Rehnquist Courts to allow greater leeway for police to stop and search suspicious individuals. In *Adams v. Williams*, 407 U.S. 590 (1972), the Court permitted the stopping and frisking of an individual by an officer, who had no personal knowledge of him and merely relied on a tip that he was carrying narcotics and had a gun. The officer went to a vehicle in which the man was sitting and, as the man rolled down the door window, the officer reached in and grabbed the man's loaded gun. *United States v. Sokolow* (1989) (see page 801) underscores that the police no longer need have probable cause to stop and frisk suspicious individuals. When upholding law enforcement officers' investigative stop of a suspected drug courier at an airport, Chief Justice Rehnquist ruled that there need be only a "reasonable suspicion" for stopping a suspect—something more than a "hunch" and considerably less than probable cause.

In addition, in a broad holding in *United States v. Verdugo-Urquidez*, 110 S.Ct. 1056 (1990), Chief Justice Rehnquist announced that the Fourth Amendment does not forbid warrantless searches and seizures by government agents of the property in foreign countries of aliens who have been arrested and are jailed in the United States. He reasoned that, unlike the Fifth Amendment, which applies to criminal trials, the Fourth Amendment does not apply to aliens or their property outside of the United States. He did so by construing the Fourth Amendment right "of the people to be secure in their persons, houses, papers, and effects" to carve out for constitutional protection only those persons who are part of the national community and to exclude those who are aliens outside of U.S. territory. While joining in the decision, Justice Kennedy rejected the chief justice's reading of the phrase *the people* as a limitation on the application of the Fourth Amendment. For Justice Kennedy, it was enough that "[t]he absence of local judges or magistrates available to issue warrants, the differing and perhaps unascertainable conceptions of reasonableness and privacy that prevail abroad, and the need to cooperate with foreign officials all indicate that the Fourth

Amendment's warrant requirement should not apply in Mexico as it does in this country." Dissenting Justice Brennan, joined by Justice Marshall, however, objected that the

[r]espondent is entitled to the protections of the Fourth Amendment because our Government, by investigating him and attempting to hold him accountable under United States criminal laws, has treated him as a member of our community for purposes of enforcing our laws. He has become, quite literally, one of the governed. Fundamental fairness and the ideals underlying our Bill of Rights compel the conclusion that when we impose "societal obligations," such as the obligation to comply with our criminal laws, on foreign nationals, we in turn are obliged to respect certain correlative rights, among them the Fourth Amendment.

By concluding that respondent is not one of "the people" protected by the Fourth Amendment, the majority disregards basic notions of mutuality. If we expect aliens to obey our laws, aliens should be able to expect that we will obey our Constitution when we investigate, prosecute, and punish them.

In a separate opinion, Justice Blackmun dissented as well.

Still another exception pertains to when police conduct a search within the context of *hot pursuit* and other *exigent circumstances* to prevent the destruction of evidence. *United States v. Santana* (1976) (see page 807) indicates how fine a line the Court sometimes draws in permitting the warrantless entry into private homes and in distinguishing prior rulings allowing for warrantless arrests in exigent situations[3] and where police are in hot pursuit chasing an automobile.[4] Along with *Santana* the Court held, in *United States v. Watson*, 423 U.S. 411 (1976), that an arrest may be made in public places without a warrant, even if police have time to obtain one. But subsequently the Court limited *Santana* and *Watson* in ruling that, except where there are truly exigent circumstances, police must obtain a warrant before entering private premises to make an arrest.[5]

Finally, the Court once maintained, but no longer does, that police could not seize, with or without a warrant, *mere evidence*—clothing, private papers, and the like—but only illegal items, such as weapons, contraband, etc. In *Gould v. United States*, 255 U.S. 298 (1921), the Court ruled that unlawfully seized papers could be suppressed at trial on the grounds that the Fourth Amendment permitted the government only to seize that property over which it could also assert a property interest at common law, as with the seizure of stolen goods. The Court reasoned that

search warrants may not be used as a means of gaining access to a man's house or office and papers solely for the purpose of making search to secure evidence to be used against him in a criminal or penal proceeding, but that they may be resorted to only when a primary right to such search and seizure may be found in the interest which the public or the complainant may have in the property to be seized, or in the right to the possession of it, or when a valid exercise of the police power renders possession of the property by the accused unlawful and provides that it may be taken.

The mere evidence rule was an "attempt by the Supreme Court to strike a Fourth Amendment balance between the government's interest in gathering evidence of criminal activity and the individual's reasonable expectations of privacy."[6] Applications of the rule, however, led to inconsistent, sometimes illogical, results,[7] and eventually to the Court's reconsideration of the rule.[8] The mere evidence rule was finally abandoned in *Warden v. Hayden*, 387 U.S. 294 (1967), in which the Court explained that

[t]he premise that property interest control the right of the Government to search and seize has been discredited. Searches and seizures may be "unreasonable" within the Fourth Amendment even though the Government asserts a superior property interest at common law. We have recognized that the principal object of the Fourth Amendment is the protection of privacy rather than property, and have increasingly discarded fictional and procedural barriers rested on property concepts.

Ironically, the Court's abandonment of the mere evidence rule resulted in less Fourth Amendment protection for individuals' privacy interests in their private papers. The Court subsequently held that the Fourth Amendment does not bar the government from obtaining through a subpoena *duces tecum* (an order requiring the production of papers and documents) individuals' private papers held by their accountants, attorneys and banks.[9]

NOTES

1. *Chapman v. United States*, 365 U.S. 610 (1961) (landlord's consent for search of tenant's room was not enough); *Stoner v. California*, 376 U.S. 483 (1964) (striking down a search of a hotel room without the consent of the occupant, although the hotel clerk gave permission for the search).

2. In *United States v. Mendenhall*, 446 U.S. 544 (1980), the Court also upheld the stopping and search of a woman at an airport based on her fitting a "drug courier profile." A bare majority found that her agreeing to accompany agents to their office was voluntary and thus she had not been "seized" for the purposes of the Fourth Amendment. However, in *Florida v. Royer*, 460 U.S. 492 (1983), the Court rejected the arrest of person based on a drug courier profile as unreason-

able, observing "that a person has been 'seized' within the meaning of the Fourth Amendment only if, in view of all the circumstances surrounding the incident, a reasonable person would have believed that he was not free to leave."

3. See *Warden v. Hayden*, 387 U.S. 294 (1967).

4. See *Johnson v. United States*, 333 U.S. 10 (1948).

5. *Payton v. New York*, 445 U.S. 573 (1980).

6. Note, "Papers, Privacy and the Fourth and Fifth Amendments: A Constitutional Analysis," 69 *Northwestern University Law Review* 633 (1974).

7. Compare *Marron v. United States*, 275 U.S. 192 (1927), with *United States v. Lefkowitz*, 285 U.s. 452 (1932).

8. See *Jones v. United States*, 362 U.S. 257 (1960).

9. See *Couch v. United States*, 409 U.S. 322 (1973); *United States v. Miller*, 425 U.S. 564 (1976); *California Bankers Association v. Shultz*, 416 U.S. 21 (1974); and David M. O'Brien, "Reasonable Expectations of Privacy: Principles and Policies of Fourth Amendment-Protected Privacy," 13 *New England Law Review* 662 (1978). See also *Zurcher v. Stanford Daily*, in Chapter 5.

INSIDE THE COURT

Memorandum from Justice William J. Brennan to Chief Justice Earl Warren on *Terry v. Ohio*

March 14, 1968

RE: *The "Stop and Frisk" Cases*

Dear Chief:

I have heard from Bill [Douglas] and Abe [Fortas] something of their comments upon your opinions, and other suggestions for changes. I've read also, of course, the views stated by Hugo [Black], John [Harlan] and Byron [White] in their circulations. All of this has prompted me to do some extended and hard thinking which I hope I may share with you.

I'm attaching a rather extensive suggested revision of your *Terry* opinion with explanatory notes outlining my reasons, and also a rather extensively foot-noted memorandum stating my reasons for the conviction I've reached (contrary to my previous view) that we should not handle this question as a matter of "probable cause" and the Warrant Clause, but as a matter of the Reasonableness Clause. I hope you won't think me presumptuous to submit my thoughts in this form. I do it only because I think it's the best way for me to state them. . . .

I've become acutely concerned that the mere fact of our affirmance in *Terry* will be taken by police all over the country as our license to them to carry on, indeed widely expand, present "aggressive surveillance" techniques which the press tells us are being deliberately employed in Miami, Chicago, Detroit and other ghetto cities. This is happening, of course, in response to the "crime in the streets" alarums [sic] being sounded in this election year in the Congress, the White House and every Governor's office. Much of what I suggest be omitted from your opinion strikes me as susceptible to being read as sounding the same note. This seems to me to be particularly unfortunate since our affirmance surely does this: from here on out, it becomes entirely unnecessary for the police to establish "probable cause to *arrest*" to support weapons charges; an officer can move against anyone he *suspects* has a weapon and get a conviction if he "frisks" him and finds one. In this lies the terrible risk that police will conjure up "suspicious circumstances," and courts will credit their versions. It will not take much of this to aggravate the already white heat resentment of ghetto Negroes against the police—and the Court will become the scapegoat.

The alternative would of course mean a reversal of this conviction—a holding that there is no constitutional authority to frisk for weapons unless the officer has probable cause to *arrest* for the crime of carrying a weapon. I recognize that police will frisk anyway and try to make a case that the frisk was incident to an arrest for public drunkenness, vagrancy, loitering, breach of the peace, et. etc.—but at times I think these abuses would be more tolerable than those I apprehend may follow our legitimating of frisks on the basis of suspicious circumstances.

This states frankly my worries. But if we are to affirm *Terry,* I think the tone of our opinion may be even more important than what we say. If I have exceeded the proprieties, I hope you will forgive me—I am truly worried.

Sincerely,
Bill [Brennan]

Source: Papers of Chief Justice Earl Warren, Manuscripts Room, Library of Congress, Washington, D.C.

Terry v. Ohio
392 U.S. 1, 88 S.Ct. 1868 (1968)

Chief Justice Earl Warren discusses the facts in this case, upholding a police officer's stopping and frisking of individuals who he had a reasonable suspicion might be contemplating a robbery, at the outset of his opinion for the Court.

Chief Justice WARREN delivered the opinion of the Court.

This case presents serious questions concerning the role of the Fourth Amendment in the confrontation on the street between the citizen and the policeman investigating suspicious circumstances.

Petitioner Terry was convicted of carrying a concealed weapon and sentenced to the statutorily prescribed term of one to three years in the penitentiary. Following the denial of a pretrial motion to suppress, the prosecution introduced in evidence two revolvers and a number of bullets seized from Terry and a codefendant, Richard Chilton, by Cleveland Police Detective Martin McFadden. At the hearing on the motion to suppress this evidence, Officer McFadden testified that while he was patrolling in plain clothes in downtown Cleveland at approximately 2:30 in the afternoon of October 31, 1963, his attention was attracted by two men, Chilton and Terry, standing on the corner of Huron Road and Euclid Avenue. He had never seen the two men before, and he was unable to say precisely what first drew his eye to them. However, he testified that he had been a policeman for 39 years and a detective for 35 and that he had been assigned to patrol this vicinity of downtown Cleveland for shoplifters and pickpockets for 30 years. He explained that he had developed routine habits of observation over the years and that he would "stand and watch people or walk and watch people at many intervals of the day." He added: "Now, in this case when I looked over they didn't look right to me at the time."

His interest aroused, Officer McFadden took up a post of observation in the entrance to a store 300 to 400 feet away from two men. . . . He saw one of the men leave the other one and walk southwest on Huron Road, past some stores. The man paused for a moment and looked in a store window, then walked on a short distance, turned around and walked back toward the corner, pausing once again to look in the same store window. He rejoined his companion at the corner, and the two conferred briefly. Then the second man went through the same series of motions, strolling down Huron Road, looking in the same window, walking on a short distance, turning back, peering in the store window again, and returning to confer with the first man at the corner. The two men repeated this ritual alternately between five and six times apiece—in all, roughly a dozen trips. At one point, while the two were standing together on the corner, a third man approached them and engaged them briefly in conversation. This man then left the two others and walked west on Euclid Avenue. Chilton and Terry resumed their measured pacing, peering and conferring. After this had gone on for 10 to 12 minutes, the two men walked off together, heading west on Euclid Avenue, following the path taken earlier by the third man.

By this time Officer McFadden had become thoroughly suspicious. He . . . suspected the two men of "casing a job, a stickup," and . . . he considered it his duty as a police officer to investigate further. . . . Thus, Officer McFadden followed Chilton and Terry and saw them stop in front of Zucker's store to talk to the same man who had conferred with them earlier on the street corner. Deciding that the situation was ripe for direct action, Officer McFadden approached the three men, identified himself as a police officer and asked for their names. At this point his knowledge was confined to what he had observed. . . . When the men "mumbled something" in response to his inquiries, Officer McFadden grabbed petitioner Terry, spun him around so that they were facing the other two, with Terry between McFadden and the others, and patted down the outside of his clothing. In the left breast pocket of Terry's overcoat Officer McFadden felt a pistol. He reached inside the overcoat pocket, but was unable to remove the gun. At this point, keeping Terry between himself and the others, the officer ordered all three men to enter Zucker's store. As they went in, he removed Terry's overcoat completely, removed a .38-caliber revolver from the pocket and ordered all three men to face the wall with their hands raised. Officer McFadden proceeded to pat down the outer clothing of Chilton and the third man, Katz. He discovered another revolver in the outer pocket of Chilton's overcoat, but no weapons were found on Katz. The officer testified that he only patted the men down to see whether they had weapons, and that he did not put his hands beneath the outer garments of either Terry or Chilton until he felt their guns. . . .

On the motion to suppress the guns the prosecution took the position that they had been seized following a search incident to a lawful arrest. The trial court rejected this theory, stating that it "would be stretching the facts beyond reasonable comprehension" to find that Officer McFadden had had probable cause to arrest the men before he patted them down for weapons. However, the court denied the defendants' motion on the ground that Officer McFadden, on the basis of his experience, "had reasonable cause to believe . . . that the defendants were conducting themselves suspiciously, and some interrogation should be made of their action." Purely for his own protection, the court held, the officer had the right to pat down the outer clothing of these men, who he had reasonable cause to believe might be armed. . . . We granted certiorari to determine whether the admission of the revolvers in evidence violated petitioner's rights under the Fourth Amendment, made applicable to the States by the Fourteenth. We affirm the conviction.

[Here, t]he question is whether in all the circumstances of this on-the-street encounter, [the individual's] right to personal security was violated by an unreasonable search and seizure. . . .

Our first task is to establish at what point in this encounter the Fourth Amendment becomes relevant. That is, we must decide whether and when Officer McFadden "seized" Terry and whether and when he conducted a "search.". . . . It is quite plain that the Fourth Amendment governs "seizures" of the person which do not eventuate in a trip to the station house and prosecution for crime—"arrests" in traditional terminology. It must be recognized that whenever a police officer accosts an individual and restrains his freedom to walk away, he has "seized" that person. And it is nothing less than sheer torture of the English language to suggest that a careful exploration of the outer surfaces of a person's clothing all over his or her body in an attempt to find weapons is not a "search." Moreover, it is simply fantastic to urge that such a procedure performed in public by a policeman while the citizen stands helpless, perhaps facing a wall with his hands raised, is a "petty indignity." It is a serious intrusion upon the sanctity of the person, which may inflict great indignity and arouse strong resentment, and it is not to be undertaken lightly.

The danger in the logic which proceeds upon distinctions between a "stop" and an "arrest," or "seizure" of the person, and between a "frisk" and a "search" is twofold. It seeks to isolate from constitutional scrutiny the initial stages of the contact between the policeman and the citizen. And by suggesting a rigid all-or-nothing model of justification and regulation under the Amendment, it obscures the utility of limitations upon the scope, as well as the initiation, of police action as a means of constitutional regulation. . . .

The distinctions of classical "stop-and-frisk" theory thus serve to divert attention from the central inquiry under the Fourth Amendment—the reasonableness in all the circumstances of the particular governmental invasion of a citizen's personal security. "Search" and "seizure" are not talismans. We therefore reject the notions that the Fourth Amendment does not come into play at all as a limitation upon police conduct if the officers stop short of something called a "technical arrest" or a "full-blown search.". . .

The crux of this case . . . is not the propriety of Officer McFadden's taking steps to investigate petitioner's suspicious behavior, but rather, whether there was justification for McFadden's invasion of Terry's personal security by searching him for weapons in the course of that investigation. We are now concerned with more than the governmental interest in investigating crime; in addition, there is the more immediate interest of the police officer in taking steps to assure himself that the person with whom he is dealing is not armed with a weapon that could unexpectedly and fatally be used against him. Certainly it would be unreasonable to require that police officers take unnecessary risks in the performance of their duties. American criminals have a long tradition of armed violence, and every year in this country many law enforcement officers are killed in the line of duty, and thousands more are wounded. Virtually all of these deaths and a substantial portion of the injuries are inflicted with guns and knives.

In view of these facts, we cannot blind ourselves to the need for law enforcement officers to protect themselves and other prospective victims of violence in situations where they may lack probable cause for an arrest. When an officer is justified in believing that the individual whose suspicious behavior he is investigating at close range is armed and presently dangerous to the officer or to others, it would appear to be clearly unreasonable to deny the officer the power to take necessary measures to determine whether the person is in fact carrying a weapon and to neutralize the threat of physical harm. . . .

We conclude that the revolver seized from Terry was properly admitted in evidence against him. At the time he seized petitioner and searched him for weapons, Officer McFadden had reasonable grounds to believe that petitioner was armed and dangerous, and it was necessary for the protection of himself and others to take swift measures to discover the true facts and neutralize the threat of harm if it materialized. The policeman carefully restricted his search to what was appropriate to the discovery of the particular items which he sought. Each case of this sort will, of course, have to be decided on its own facts. We merely hold today that where a police officer observes unusual conduct which leads him reasonably to conclude in light of his experience that criminal activity may be afoot and that the persons with whom he is dealing may be armed and presently dangerous, where in the course of investigating this behavior he identifies himself as a policeman and makes reasonable inquiries, and where nothing in the initial stages of the encounter serves to dispel his reasonable fear for his own or others' safety, he is entitled for the protection of himself and others in the area to conduct a carefully limited search of the outer clothing of such persons in an attempt to discover weapons which might be used to assault him.

Such a search is a reasonable search under the Fourth Amendment, and any weapons seized may properly be introduced in evidence against the person from whom they were taken.

Affirmed.

Justice BLACK concurred.

Justice HARLAN concurring.

While I unreservedly agree with the Court's ultimate holding in this case, I am constrained to fill in a few gaps, as I see them, in its opinion. I do this because what is said by this Court today will serve as initial guidelines for law enforcement authorities and courts throughout the land as this important new field of law develops.

A police officer's right to make an on-the-street "stop" and an accompanying "frisk" for weapons is of course bounded by the protections afforded by the Fourth and Fourteenth Amendments. The Court holds, and I agree, that while the right does not depend upon possession by the officer of a valid warrant, nor upon the existence of probable cause, such activities must be reasonable under the circumstances as the officer credibly relates them in court. Since the question in this and most cases is whether evidence produced by a frisk is admissible, the problem is to determine what makes a frisk reasonable. . . .

The state courts held . . . that when an officer is lawfully confronting a possibly hostile person in the line of duty he has a right, springing only from the necessity of the situation and not from any broader right to disarm, to frisk for his own protection. This holding, with which I agree and with which I think the Court agrees, offers the only satisfactory basis I can think of for affirming this conviction. The holding has, however, two logical corollaries that I do not think the Court has fully expressed.

In the first place, if the frisk is justified in order to protect the officer during an encounter with a citizen, the officer must first have constitutional grounds to insist on an encounter, to make a *forcible* stop. Any person, including a policeman, is at liberty to avoid a person he considers dangerous. If and when a policeman has a right instead to disarm such a person for his own protection, he must first have a right not to avoid him but to be in his presence. That right must be more than the liberty (again, possessed by every citizen) to address questions to other persons, for ordinarily the person addressed has an equal right to ignore his interrogator and walk away; he certainly need not submit to a frisk for the questioner's protection. I would make it perfectly clear that the right to frisk in this case depends upon the reasonableness of a forcible stop to investigate a suspected crime.

Where such a stop is reasonable, however, the right to frisk must be immediate and automatic if the reason for the stop is, as here, an articulable suspicion of a crime of violence. Just as a full search incident to a lawful arrest requires no additional justification, a limited frisk incident to a lawful stop must often be rapid and routine. There is no reason why an officer, rightfully but forcibly confronting a person suspected of a serious crime, should have to ask one question and take the risk that the answer might be a bullet. . . .

Officer McFadden's right to interrupt Terry's freedom of movement and invade his privacy arose only because circumstances warranted forcing an encounter with Terry in an effort to prevent or investigate a crime. Once that forced encounter was justified, however, the officer's right to take suitable measures for his own safely followed automatically.

Justice WHITE concurring.

I think an additional word is in order concerning the matter of interrogation during an investigative stop. There is nothing in the Constitution which prevents a policeman from addressing questions to anyone on the streets. Absent special circumstances, the person approached may not be detained or frisked but may refuse to cooperate and go on his way. However, given the proper circumstances, such as those in this case, it seems to me the person may be briefly detained against his will while pertinent questions are directed to him. Of course, the person stopped is not obliged to answer, answers may not be compelled, and refusal to answer furnishes no basis for an arrest, although it may alert the officer to the need for continued observation. In my view, it is temporary detention, warranted by the circumstances, which chiefly justifies the protective frisk for weapons. Perhaps the frisk itself, where proper, will have beneficial results whether questions are asked or not. If weapons are found, an arrest will follow. If none are found, the frisk may nevertheless serve preventive ends because of its unmistakable message that suspicion has been aroused. But if the investigative stop is sustainable at all, constitutional rights are not necessarily violated if pertinent questions are asked and the person is restrained briefly in the process.

Justice DOUGLAS, dissenting.

I agree that petitioner was "seized" within the meaning of the Fourth Amendment. I also agree that frisking petitioner and his companions for guns was a "search." But it is a mystery how that "search" and that "seizure" can be constitutional by Fourth Amendment standards, unless there was "probable cause" to believe that (1) a crime had been committed or (2) a crime was in the process of being committed or (3) a crime was about to be committed.

The opinion of the Court disclaims the existence of "probable cause." If loitering were in issue and that was the offense charged, there would be "probable cause" shown. But the crime here is carrying concealed weapons; and there is no basis for concluding that the officer had "probable cause" for believing that that crime was being committed. Had a warrant been sought, a magistrate would, therefore, have been unauthorized to issue one, for he can act only if there is a showing of "probable cause." We hold today that the police have greater authority to make a "seizure" and conduct a "search" than a judge has to authorize such action.

We have said precisely the opposite over and over again. . . .

The infringement on personal liberty of any "seizure" of a person can only be "reasonable" under the Fourth Amendment if we require the police to possess "probable cause" before they seize him. Only that line draws a meaningful distinction between an officer's mere inkling and the presence of facts within the officer's personal knowledge which would convince a reasonable man that the person seized has committed, is committing, or is about to commit a particular crime. . . .

To give the police greater power than a magistrate is to take a long step down the totalitarian path. Perhaps such a step is desirable to cope with modern forms of lawlessness. But if it is taken, it should be the deliberate choice of the people through a constitutional amendment.

United States v. Sokolow

490 U.S. 1, 109 S.Ct. 1581 (1989)

Chief Justice William H. Rehnquist reviews the circumstances giving rise to this case, involving a warrantless search and seizure of Andrew Sokolow at the Honolulu, Hawaii, airport by drug enforcement agents, in his opinion for the Court.

Chief Justice REHNQUIST delivers the opinion of the Court.

Respondent Andrew Sokolow was stopped by Drug Enforcement Administration (DEA) agents upon his arrival at Honolulu International Airport. The agents found 1,063 grams of cocaine in his carry-on luggage. When respondent was stopped, the agents knew, *inter alia,* that (1) he paid $2,100 for two airplane tickets from a roll of $20 bills; (2) he traveled under a name that did not match the name under which his telephone number was listed; (3) his original destination was Miami, a source city for illicit drugs; (4) he stayed in Miami for only 48 hours, even though a round-trip flight from Honolulu to Miami takes 20 hours; (5) he appeared nervous during his trip; and (6) he checked none of his luggage. A divided panel of the United States Court of Appeals for the Ninth Circuit held that the DEA agents did not have a reasonable suspicion to stop respondent, as required by the Fourth Amendment. We take the contrary view.

This case involves a typical attempt to smuggle drugs through one of the Nation's airports. On a Sunday in July 1984, respondent went to the United Airlines ticket counter at Honolulu Airport, where he purchased two round-trip tickets for a flight to Miami leaving later that day. The tickets were purchased in the names of "Andrew Kray" and "Janet Norian," and had open return dates. Respondent paid $2,100 for the tickets from a large roll of $20 bills, which appeared to contain a total of $4,000. He also gave the ticket agent his home telephone number. The ticket agent noticed that respondent seemed nervous; he was about 25 years old; he was dressed in a black jumpsuit and wore gold jewelry; and he was accompanied by a woman, who turned out to be Janet Norian. Neither respondent nor his companion checked any of their four pieces of luggage.

After the couple left for their flight, the ticket agent informed Officer John McCarthy of the Honolulu Police Department of respondent's cash purchase of tickets to Miami. Officer McCarthy determined that the telephone number respondent gave to the ticket agent was subscribed to a "Karl Herman," who resided at 348-A Royal Hawaiian Avenue in Honolulu. Unbeknownst to McCarthy (and later to the DEA agents), respondent was Herman's roommate. The ticket agent identified respondent's voice on the answering machine at Herman's number. Officer McCarthy was unable to find any listing under the name "Andrew Kray" in Hawaii. McCarthy subsequently learned that return reservations from Miami to Honolulu had been made in the names of Kray and Norian, with their arrival scheduled for July 25, three days after respondent and his companion had left. He also learned that Kray and Norian were scheduled to make stopovers in Denver and Los Angeles.

On July 25, during the stopover in Los Angeles, DEA agents identified respondent. He "appeared to be very nervous and was looking all around the waiting area.". . . Later that day, at 6:30 P.M., respondent and Norian arrived in Honolulu. As before, they had not checked their luggage. Respondent was still wearing a black jumpsuit and gold jewelry. The couple proceeded directly to the street and tried to hail a cab, where Agent Richard Kempshall and three other DEA agents approached them. Kempshall displayed his credentials, grabbed respondent by the arm and moved him back onto the sidewalk. Kempshall asked respondent for his airline ticket and identification; respondent said that he had neither. He told the agents that his name was "Sokolow," but that he was traveling under his mother's maiden name, "Kray."

Respondent and Norian were escorted to the DEA office at the airport. There, the couple's luggage was examined by "Donker," a narcotics detector dog, which alerted to respondent's brown shoulder bag. The agents arrested respondent. He was advised of his constitutional rights and declined to make any statements. The agents obtained a warrant to search the shoulder bag. They found no illicit drugs, but the bag did contain several suspicious documents indicating respondent's involvement in drug trafficking. The agents had Donker reexamine the remaining luggage, and this time the dog alerted to a medium sized Louis Vuitton bag. By now, it was 9:30 P.M., too late for the agents to obtain a second warrant. They allowed respondent to leave for the night, but kept his luggage. The next morning, after a second dog confirmed Donker's alert, the agents obtained a warrant and found 1,063 grams of cocaine inside the bag.

Respondent was indicted for possession with the intent to distribute cocaine in violation of 21 U.S.C. § 841(a)(1). The United States District Court for Hawaii denied his motion to suppress the cocaine and other evidence seized from his luggage, finding that the DEA agents had a reasonable suspicion that he was involved in drug trafficking when they stopped him at the airport. Respondent then entered a conditional plea of guilty to the offense charged.

The United States Court of Appeals for the Ninth Circuit reversed respondent's conviction by a divided vote, holding that the DEA agents did not have a reasonable suspicion to justify the stop. . . .

The Court of Appeals held that the DEA agents seized respondent when they grabbed him by the arm and moved him back onto the sidewalk. The Government does not challenge that conclusion, and we assume—without deciding—that a stop occurred here. Our decision, then, turns on whether the agents had a reasonable suspicion that respondent was engaged in wrongdoing when they encountered him on the sidewalk. In *Terry v. Ohio,* [392 U.S. 1] (1968), we held that the police can stop and briefly detain a person for investigative purposes if the officer has a reasonable suspicion supported by articulable facts that criminal activity "may be afoot," even if the officer lacks probable cause.

The officer, of course, must be able to articulate something more than an "inchoate and unparticularized suspicion or 'hunch'." The Fourth Amendment requires "some minimal level of objective justification" for making the stop. *INS v. Delgado,* 466 U.S. 210, 217, 104 S.Ct. 1758, (1984). That level of suspicion is considerably less than proof of wrongdoing by a preponderance of the evidence. We have held that probable cause means "a fair probability that contraband or evidence of a crime will be found," *Illinois v. Gates,* 462 U.S. 213 (1983), and the level of suspicion required for a *Terry* stop is obviously less demanding than that for probable cause. See *United States v. Montoya de Hernandez,* 473 U.S. 531 (1985).

The concept of reasonable suspicion like probable cause is not readily or even usefully, reduced to a neat set of legal rules." *Gates, supra.* We think the Court of Appeals' effort to refine and elaborate the requirements of "reasonable suspicion" in this case create unnecessary difficulty in dealing with one of the relatively simple concepts embodied in the Fourth Amendment. In evaluating the validity of a stop such as this, we must consider "the totality of the circumstances—the whole picture." *United States v. Cortez*, 449 U.S. 411 [1981]. As we said in *Cortez:*

"The process does not deal with hard certainties, but with probabilities. Long before the law of probabilities was articulated as such, practical people formulated certain common-sense conclusions about human behavior; jurors as fact-finders are permitted to do the same—and so are law enforcement officers.". . .

We hold that the agents had a reasonable basis to suspect that respondent was transporting illegal drugs on these facts. The judgment of the Court of Appeals is therefore reversed and the case remanded for further proceedings consistent with our decision.

It is so ordered.

Justice MARSHALL, with whom Justice BRENNAN joins, dissenting.

Because the strongest advocates of Fourth Amendment rights are frequently criminals, it is easy to forget that our interpretations of such rights apply to the innocent and the guilty alike. *Illinois v. Gates*, 462 U.S. 213 (1983) (BRENNAN, J., dissenting). In the present case, the chain of events set in motion when respondent Andrew Sokolow was stopped by Drug Enforcement Administration (DEA) agents at Honolulu International Airport led to the discovery of cocaine and, ultimately, to Sokolow's conviction for drug trafficking. But in sustaining this conviction on the ground that the agents reasonably suspected Sokolow of ongoing criminal activity, the Court diminishes the rights of *all* citizens to "to be secure in their persons," U.S. Const., Amdt. IV, as they traverse the Nation's airports. Finding this result constitutionally impermissible, I dissent.

The Fourth Amendment cabins government's authority to intrude on personal privacy and security by requiring that searches and seizures usually be supported by a showing of probable cause. The reasonable-suspicion standard is a derivation of the probable cause command, applicable only to those brief detentions which fall short of being full-scale searches and seizures and which are necessitated by law-enforcement exigencies such as the need to stop ongoing crimes, to prevent imminent crimes, and to protect law-enforcement officers in highly charged situations. *Terry v. Ohio* (1968). By requiring reasonable suspicion as a prerequisite to such seizures, the Fourth Amendment protects innocent persons from being subjected to "overbearing or harassing" police conduct carried out solely on the basis of imprecise stereotypes of what criminals look like, or on the basis of irrelevant personal characteristics such as race. . . .

To deter such egregious police behavior, we have held that a suspicion is not reasonable unless officers have based it on "specific and articulable facts." [See *Terry* and] see also *United States v. Brignoni-Ponce,* 422 U.S. 873 (1975). It is not enough to suspect that an individual has committed crimes in the past, harbors unconsummated criminal designs, or has the propensity to commit crimes. On the contrary, before detaining an individual, law enforcement officers must reasonably suspect that he is engaged in, or poised to commit, a criminal act *at that moment.*

The rationale for permitting brief, warrantless seizures is, after all, that it is impractical to demand strict compliance with the Fourth Amendment's ordinary probable-cause requirement in the face of ongoing or imminent criminal activity demanding "swift action predicated upon the on-the-spot observations of the officer on the beat." *Terry, supra.* Observations raising suspicions of past criminality demand no such immediate action, but instead should appropriately trigger routine police investigation, which may ultimately generate sufficient information to blossom into probable cause.

Evaluated against this standard, the facts about Andrew Sokolow known to the DEA agents at the time they stopped him fall short of reasonably indicating that he was engaged at the time in criminal activity. It is highly significant that the DEA agents stopped Sokolow because he matched one of the DEA's "profiles" of a paradigmatic drug courier. In my view, a law enforcement officer's mechanistic application of a formula of personal and behavioral traits in deciding whom to detain can only dull the officer's ability and determination to make sensitive and fact-specific inferences "in light of his experience," *Terry,* particularly in ambiguous or borderline cases. Reflexive reliance on a profile of drug courier characteristics runs a far greater risk than does ordinary, case-by-case police work, of subjecting innocent individuals to unwarranted police harassment and detention. . . .

That the factors comprising the drug courier profile relied on in this case are especially dubious indices of ongoing criminal activity is underscored by *Reid v. Georgia,* 448 U.S. 438 (1980), a strikingly similar case. There, four facts, encoded in a drug courier profile, were alleged in support of the DEA's detention of a suspect at the Atlanta Airport. First, Reid had arrived from Fort Lauderdale, Florida, a source city for cocaine. Second, he arrived in the early morning, when law enforcement activity is diminished. Third, he and his companion appeared to have no luggage other than their shoulder bags. And fourth, he and his companion appeared to be trying to conceal the fact that they were traveling together. . . .

This collection of facts, we held, was inadequate to support a finding of reasonable suspicion. All but the last of these facts, we observed, "describe a very large category of presumably innocent travelers, who would be subject to virtually random seizures were the Court to conclude that as little foundation as there was in this case could justify a seizure." The sole fact that suggested criminal activity was that Reid "preceded another person and occasionally looked backward at him as they proceeded through the concourse." This observation did not of itself provide a reasonable basis for suspecting wrongdoing, for inferring criminal activity from such evidence reflected no more than an " 'inchoate and unparticularized suspicion or "hunch." ' ". . . quoting *Terry*.

The facts known to the DEA agents at the time they detained the traveler in this case are scarcely more suggestive of ongoing criminal activity than those in *Reid*. Unlike traveler Reid, who sought to conceal the fact that he was traveling with a companion, and who even attempted to run away after being approached by a DEA agent, traveler Sokolow gave no indications of evasive activity. On the contrary, the sole behavioral detail about Sokolow noted by the DEA agents was that he was nervous. With news accounts proliferating of plane crashes, near-collisions, and air terrorism, there are manifold and good reasons for being agitated while awaiting a flight, reasons that have nothing to do with one's involvement in a criminal endeavor. . . .

Finally, that Sokolow paid for his tickets in cash indicates no imminent or ongoing criminal activity. The majority "feel[s] confident" that "[m]ost business travelers . . . purchase airline tickets by credit card or check." Why the majority confines its focus only to "business travelers" I do not know, but I would not so lightly infer ongoing crime from the use of legal tender. Making major cash purchases, while surely less common today, may simply reflect the traveler's aversion to, or inability to obtain, plastic money. Conceivably, a person who spends large amounts of cash may be trying to launder his proceeds from *past* criminal enterprises by converting them into goods and services. But, as I have noted, investigating completed episodes of crime goes beyond the appropriately limited purview of the brief, *Terry*-style seizure. Moreover, it is unreasonable to suggest that, had Sokolow left the airport, he would have been gone forever and thus immune from subsequent investigation. Sokolow, after all, had given the airline his phone number, and the DEA, having ascertained that it was indeed Sokolow's voice on the answering machine at that number, could have learned from that information where Sokolow resided.

The fact is that, unlike the taking of patently evasive action, *Florida v. Rodriguez,* 469 U.S. 1 (1984), the use of an alias, *Florida v. Royer,* 460 U.S. 491 (1983), the casing of a store, *Terry,* or the provision of a reliable report from an informant that wrongdoing is imminent, *Illinois v. Gates,* nothing about the characteristics shown by airport traveler Sokolow reasonably suggests that criminal activity is afoot. The majority's hasty conclusion to the contrary serves only to indicate its willingness, when drug crimes or anti-drug policies are at issue, to give short shrift to constitutional rights.

United States v. Santana

427 U.S. 38, 96 S.Ct. 2406 (1976)

The facts in this case are given by Justice William Rehnquist in his opinion announcing the ruling of the Court, upholding the warrantless search and seizure of Ms. Santana in her home based on the fact police were in hot pursuit of her and had probable cause to suspect her of dealing drugs.

Justice REHNQUIST delivered the opinion of the Court.

Michael Gilletti, an undercover officer with the Philadelphia Narcotics Squad arranged a heroin "buy" with one Patricia McCafferty (from whom he had purchased narcotics before). McCafferty told him it would cost $115 "and we will go down to Mom Santana's for the dope."

Gilletti notified his superiors of the impending transaction, recorded the serial numbers of $110 [*sic*] in marked bills, and went to meet McCafferty at a prearranged location. She got in his car and directed him to drive to 2311 North Fifth Street, which, as she had previously informed him, was respondent Santana's residence.

McCafferty took the money and went inside the house, stopping briefly to speak to respondent Alejandro who was sitting on the front steps. She came out shortly afterwards and got into the car. Gilletti asked for the heroin; she thereupon extracted from her bra several glassine envelopes containing a brownish-white powder and gave them to him.

Gilletti then stopped the car, displayed his badge, and placed McCafferty under arrest. He told her that the police were going back to 2311 North Fifth Street and that he wanted to know where the money was. She said, "Mom has the money." At this point Sergeant Pruitt and other officers came up to the car. Gilletti showed them the envelope and said "Mom Santana has the money." Gilletti then took McCafferty to the police station.

Pruitt and the others then drove approximately two blocks back to 2311 North Fifth Street. They saw Santana standing in the doorway of the house with a brown paper bag in her hand. They pulled up to within 15 feet of Santana and got out of their van, shouting "police," and displaying their identification. As the officers approached, Santana retreated into the vestibule of her house.

The officers followed through the open door, catching her in the vestibule. As she tried to pull away, the bag tilted and "two bundles of glazed paper packets with a white powder" fell to the floor. Respondent Alejandro tried to make off with the dropped envelopes but was forcibly restrained. When Santana was told to empty her pockets she produced $135, $70 of which could be identified as Gilletti's marked money. The white powder in the bag was later determined to be heroin. . . .

In *United States v. Watson*, 423 U.S. 411 (1976), we held that the warrantless arrest of an individual in a public place upon probable cause did not violate the Fourth Amendment. Thus the first question we must decide is whether, when the police first sought to arrest Santana, she was in a public place.

While it may be true that under the common law of property the threshold of one's dwelling is "private," as is the yard surrounding the house, it is nonetheless clear that under the cases interpreting the Fourth Amendment Santana was in a "public" place. She was not in an area where she had any expectation of privacy. . . . She was not merely visible to the public but was as exposed to public view, speech, hearing, and touch as if she had been standing completely outside her house. Thus, when the police, who concededly had probable cause to do so, sought to arrest her, they merely intended to perform a function which we have approved in *Watson.*

The only remaining question is whether her act of retreating into her house could thwart an otherwise proper arrest. We hold that it could not. In *Warden v. Hayden*, 387 U.S. 294 (1967), we recognized the right of police, who had probable cause to believe that an armed robber had entered a house a few minutes before, to make a warrantless entry to arrest the robber and to search for weapons. This case, involving a true "hot pursuit," is clearly governed by *Warden;* the need to act quickly here is even greater than in that case while the intrusion is much less. The District Court was correct in concluding that "hot pursuit" means some sort of a chase, but it need not be an extended hue and cry "in and about [the] public streets." The fact that the pursuit here ended almost as soon as it began did not render it any the less a "hot pursuit" sufficient to justify the warrantless entry into Santana's house. Once Santana saw the police, there was likewise a realistic expectation that any delay would result in destruction of evidence. Once she had been arrested the search, incident to that arrest, which produced the drugs and money was clearly justified. . . .

We thus conclude that a suspect may not defeat an arrest which has been set in motion in a public place, and is therefore proper under *Watson,* by the expedient of escaping to a private place. The judgment of the Court of Appeals is

Reversed.

Justice WHITE concurred.

Justice STEVENS, with whom Justice STEWART joins, concurring.

When Officer Gilletti placed McCafferty under arrest, the police had sufficient information to obtain a warrant for the arrest of Santana in her home. It is therefore important to note that their failure to obtain a warrant at that juncture was both (a) a justifiable police decision, and (b) even if not justifiable, harmless.

Justice MARSHALL, with whom Justice BRENNAN joins, dissenting.

[I]f I correctly read the Court's citation to the "open fields" doctrine . . . the Court holds that the police may enter upon private property to make warrantless arrests of persons who are in plain view and outdoors; and the Court applies that doctrine today to persons who are arguably within their homes but who are "as exposed" to the public as if they were outside. But . . . if plain view were the touchstone, Santana would have been just as liable to warrantless arrest as she retreated several feet inside her open door as she was when standing in the doorway.

The Court's doctrine, then, appears *sui generis,* useful only in arresting persons who are "as exposed to public view, speech, hearing, and touch," as though in the unprotected outdoors. Narrow though it may be, however, the Court's approach does not depend on whether exigency justifies an arrest on private property, and thus I cannot join it.

Justice STEVENs focuses on what I believe to be the right question in this case—whether there were exigent circumstances—and reaches an affirmative answer because he finds a "significant risk that the marked money would no longer be in Santana's possession if the police waited until a warrant could be obtained." I agree that there were exigent circumstances in this case. . . .

I do not believe, however, that these exigent circumstances automatically validate Santana's arrest. The exigency that justified the entry and arrest was solely a product of police conduct. Had Officer Gilletti driven McCafferty to a more remote location before arresting her, it appears that no exigency would have been created by the arrest; in such an event a warrant would have been necessary, in my view, before Santana could have been arrested. It is not apparent on this record why Officer Gilletti arrested McCafferty so close to Santana's home when the arresting officers were clearly aware that such a nearby arrest would necessitate the prompt arrest of Santana. While a police decision that the time is right to arrest a suspect should properly be given great deference, the power to arrest is an awesome one and is subject to abuse. An arrest may permit a search of premises incident to the arrest, a search that otherwise could be carried out only upon probable cause and pursuant to a search warrant. Likewise, an arrest in circumstances such as those presented here may create exigency that may justify a search or another arrest. When an arrest is so timed that it is no more than an attempt to circumvent the warrant requirement, I would hold the subsequent arrest or search unlawful.

C. THE SPECIAL PROBLEMS OF AUTOMOBILES IN A MOBILE SOCIETY

Automobiles pose special Fourth Amendment problems. This is because of their mobility and the possibility of criminal suspects escaping and destroying evidence. The Court's rulings have made automobile searches and seizures not just another exception to the warrant requirement, but a "whole new ball game" as to what is an unreasonable search and seizure.

The leading case distinguishing automobiles from "houses, papers, and effects" for Fourth Amendment purposes is *Carroll v. United States,* 267 U.S. 132 (1925). There Chief Justice William Howard Taft observed that

The guaranty of freedom from unreasonable searches and seizures by the Fourth Amendment has been construed, practically since the beginning of government, as recognizing a necessary difference between a search of a store, dwelling house, or other structure in respect of which a proper official warrant readily may be obtained and a search of a ship, motor boat, wagon, or automobile for contraband goods, where it is not practicable to secure a warrant, because the vehicle can be quickly moved out of the locality or jurisdiction in which the warrant must be sought.

But in finding warrantless searches and seizures of automobiles permissible, Taft added,

It would be intolerable and unreasonable if [police] were authorized to stop every automobile on the chance of finding [illegal goods], and thus subject all persons lawfully using the highways to the inconvenience and indignity of such a search. Travelers may be so stopped in crossing an international boundary because of national self-protection reasonably requiring one entering the country to identify himself as entitled to come in, and his belongings as effects which may be lawfully brought in. But those lawfully within the country, entitled to use the public highways, have a right to free passage without interruption or search unless there is known to a competent official, authorized to search, probable cause for believing that their vehicles are carrying contraband or illegal merchandise.

Subsequently, in *Chambers v. Maroney,* 399 U.S. (1970), the Court reaffirmed that warrantless searches of automobiles and their contents are permissible under the Fourth Amendment on the rationale given in *Carroll.*

Following the *Carroll-Chambers* doctrine, controversy revolved around how far police could go in stopping and searching vehicles and their occupants. In *United States v. Robinson* (1968) (see page 815), the Court held that police, without a warrant but based on probable cause, could conduct a rather extensive search of a driver arrested for a traffic offense. A companion case, *Gustafson v. Florida,* 414 U.S. 260 (1973), upheld the full-body search of a driver who was arrested and taken into custody. In *Pennsylvania v. Mimms,* 434 U.S. 106 (1977), the justices (six to three) also upheld an officer's frisking a driver who, after stopping a car with an expired license plate, asked the driver to step out of his car and produce his driver's license. At that point, the officer noticed that the driver had a large "bulge" in his sports jacket and patted him down.

In *Delaware v. Prouse* (1978) (see page 821), the Court drew a line at police making routine stops of vehicles for the purpose of checking drivers' licenses and car registrations, holding that police must have probable cause or a reasonable suspicion to believe that a vehicle or its occupants have violated some law. However, in *Alabama v. White,* 110 S.Ct. 2412 (1990), the Rehnquist Court held that police may stop and question individuals traveling in their automobiles based on anonymous tips and if they obtain some corroboration that establishes a reasonable suspicion of the occupants' criminal activity. Justices Stevens, Marshall, and Brennan dissented from that ruling, as they also did in *Michigan State Police v. Sitz,* 110 S.Ct. 2481 (1990). In *Sitz,* the Court ruled that highway sobriety checkpoints were permissible, even though police had no reasonable suspicion to believe that drivers were intoxicated. Unlike *Prouse,* Chief Justice Rehnquist emphasized that this case did not involve random highway stops and statistical evidence showed that about 1.5 percent of the drivers stopped were arrested for alcohol impairment. "The balance of the state's interest in preventing drunken driving," he concluded, "and the degree of intrusion upon individual motorists who are briefly stopped weighs in favor of the state program."

THE DEVELOPMENT OF LAW
Automobiles and Border Patrol Searches

Due to an increasing number of illegal aliens coming from Mexico and Central and South America, the U.S. Border Patrol became more aggressive in stopping and searching automobiles. The Court in turn faced a rash of cases challenging the constitutionality of these searches.

Case	Vote	Ruling
Almeida-Sanchez v. United States, 413 U.S. 266 (1973)	5:4	Warrantless search of cars, without probable cause by roving border patrol agents twenty miles north of the border violated the Fourth Amendment.
United States v. Brignoni-Ponce, 422 U.S. 873 (1975)	9:0	Except at the border, roving border patrol agents may stop cars only if they have reasonable suspicion and specific and articulable facts indicating that a vehicle contains illegal aliens; Mexican ancestry of occupants alone is not grounds for reasonable suspicion.
United States v. Ortiz, 422 U.S. 891 (1975)	9:0	Fourth Amendment forbids border patrol searches at fixed check-points distantly removed from the border and requires probable cause for searches.
United States v. Martinez-Fuerte, 428 U.S. 543 (1976)	7:2	Vehicles may be stopped at a fixed checkpoint for brief questioning of occupants and vehicles may be directed selectively to a secondary inspection point, even when the basis for doing so is the "apparent Mexican ancestry" of occupants of the vehicle.

Once police stop a vehicle, they may search the area in plain view around the driver, and if they have a reasonable suspicion of finding illegal items or make a protective search to discover weapons, they may search the entire interior of the vehicle.[1] In *New York v. Class*, 475 U.S. 106 (1986), for example, voting 5 to 4 the justices upheld a search of a car based on an officer's spotting a gun under the front seat, when looking through the front window to see the vehicle identification number on the dashboard. The Court underscored how far police may go in

California v. Carney, 471 U.S. 386 (1985), upholding a warrantless search of the entire interior of a mobile home that was parked in a public parking lot, where police had probable cause to believe that the occupant was selling marijuana. Warrantless searches of the exterior of vehicles[2] and inventory searches of impounded automobiles are also permissible.[3]

A series of cases presented the Court with another line-drawing problem as to how far police may go in searching containers found in a vehicle. Initially, in *United States v. Chadwick,* 433 U.S. 1 (1977), the Court held that a locked footlocker that had been loaded into the trunk of an automobile could not be searched without a warrant. On Joseph Chadwick's arrival by train in Boston from San Diego, he was arrested at a waiting vehicle by federal agents, who had been alerted that he was a possible drug trafficker. They arrested Chadwick and seized the automobile and the footlocker, which they had probable cause to believe contained narcotics. At a federal building an hour and half after the arrest, the agents opened the footlocker without Chadwick's consent or a search warrant. The Court disallowed that search, observing that "[b]y placing personal effects inside a double-locked footlocker, [Chadwick] manifested an expectation that the contents would remain free from public examination. No less than one who locks the doors of his home against intruders, one who safeguards his personal possessions in this manner is due the protection of the Fourth Amendment Warrant Clause."

Two years later, *Arkansas v. Sanders,* 442 U.S. 753 (1979), again addressed the issue of whether luggage could be searched without a warrant along with the rest of a vehicle. There, Little Rock, Arkansas, police had a tip that Lonnie Sanders would arrive at the airport carrying a green suitcase, holding marijuana. After he arrived, police watched him retrieve the suitcase from the baggage claim area and place it in the trunk of a taxi. The officers followed the taxi a short distance and then stopped it. Without Sanders's permission, they opened the suitcase containing marijuana. The issue in *Sanders,* as Justice Powell observed, was "whether the warrantless search of [Sanders's] suitcase falls on the *Chadwick* or the *Chambers-Carroll* side of the Fourth Amendment line." When holding that *Chadwick* was controlling there, Justice Powell explained that

[t]he only question . . . is whether the police, rather than immediately searching the suitcase without a warrant, should have taken it, along with [Sanders], to the police station and there obtained a warrant for the search. A lawful search of luggage generally may be performed only pursuant to a warrant. In *Chadwick* we declined an invitation to extend the *Carroll* exception to all searches of luggage, noting that

neither of the two polices supporting warrantless searches of automobiles applies to luggage. Here, as in *Chadwick*, the officers had seized the luggage and had it exclusively within their control at the time of the search. Consequently, "there was not the slightest danger that [the luggage] or its contents could have been removed before a valid search warrant could be obtained." [Quoting *Chadwick*.] And, as we observed in that case, luggage is a common repository for one's personal effects, and therefore is inevitably associated with the expectation of privacy. . . .

In sum, we hold that the warrant requirement of the Fourth Amendment applies to personal luggage taken from an automobile to the same degree it applies to such luggage in other locations. Thus, insofar as the police are entitled to search such luggage without a warrant, their actions must be justified under some exception to the warrant requirement other than that applicable to automobiles stopped on the highway. Where—as in the present case—the police, without endangering themselves or risking loss of the evidence, lawfully have detained one suspected of criminal activity and secured his suitcase, they should delay the search thereof until after judicial approval has been obtained. In this way, the constitutional right of suspects to prior judicial review of searches will be fully protected.

Justices Blackmun and Rehnquist dissented, contending that the Court had undercut the *Carroll-Chambers* doctrine and invited litigation over all kinds of articles that might be found in vehicles—"the briefcase, the wallet, the package, the paper bag, and every other kind of container."

Subsequently, in *Robbins v. California*, 453 U.S. 420 (1981), the Court held that an opaque container in the trunk of a car could not be searched without a warrant, even though police had probable cause to search the vehicle and the container. In this case, police had stopped a station wagon that was being driven erratically and when the driver opened the door of the vehicle they smelled marijuana. A search of the passenger compartment yielded some marijuana. After arresting Jeffrey Robbins, the police then opened the tailgate of the station wagon and searched a recessed luggage compartment, where they found two green garbage bags containing marijuana.

But in *United States v. Ross* (1982) (see page 826) the Court overturned *Robbins*. Notice that Justice Stevens in his opinion for the Court maintained that *Chadwick* and *Sanders* remained valid, and compare the views of the dissenters. Since *Ross*, the Court has held that police may stop and detain suspects and during their detention use a narcotics-detection dog to sniff their luggage for narcotics.[4] In *United States v. Johns*, 469 U.S. 478 (1985), the Court construed *Ross* to permit a warrantless search of packages that police took from a vehicle and had probable cause to believe contained contraband. And *Colorado v. Bertine*,

479 U.S. 367 (1987), upheld a police search of a backpack lying in the front seat of an automobile, whose driver was arrested for drunk driving.[5] However, in *Florida v. Wells,* 110 S.Ct. 1632 (1990), the Rehnquist Court unanimously held that in the absence of a police department policy on the opening of closed containers found in impounded automobiles during routine inventory searches, police may not open suitcases and other closed containers. In Chief Justice Rehnquist's words, "Our view that standardized criteria or established routine must regulate the opening of containers found during inventory searches is based on the principle that an inventory search must not be a ruse for a general rummaging in order to discover incriminating evidence."

NOTES

1. *New York v. Belton,* 453 U.S. 454 (1981); and *Michigan v. Long,* 463 U.S. 1032 (1983).
2. *Cardwell v. Lewis,* 417 U.S. 583 (1964) (with probable cause, warrantless inspection of exterior of care is permissible). *Harris v. United States,* 390 U.S. 234 (1968) upheld the use of an automobile registration card found in plain view in an impounded car. See *Texas v. Brown,* 460 U.S. 730 (1983).
3. In *Preston v. United States,* 376 U.S. 364 (1964), however, the Warren Court held that a search of car, after the driver's arrest and the car was taken to a garage, was too remote to be search incident to an arrest. But *Chambers v. Maroney,* 399 U.S. 42 (1970), upheld the search of a car in a police station, and *South Dakota v. Opperman,* 428 U.S. 543 (1976), upheld routine inventory searches of locked cars impounded by police.
4. *United States v. Place,* 462 U.S. 696 (1983).
5. Also in *United States v. Jacobsen,* 466 U.S. 109 (1984), the Court found no Fourth Amendment violation where employees of private freight company opened a damaged package to note its contents and found white powder wrapped in plastic bags, and notified federal agents who seized and tested the powder.

United States v. Robinson
414 U.S. 218, 94 S.Ct. 467 (1973)

Justice William Rehnquist discusses the facts in his opinion for the Court in this case that involves a search incident to the arrest of the driver of an automobile.

Justice REHNQUIST delivered the opinion of the Court.

Respondent Robinson was convicted in United States District Court for the District of Columbia of the possession and facilitation of concealment of heroin in violation of 26 U.S.C. § 4704(a) (1964 ed.), and 21 U.S.C. § 174 (1964 ed.). He was sentenced to concurrent terms of imprisonment for these offenses. On his appeal to the Court of Appeals for the District of Columbia Circuit, that court first remanded the case to the District Court for an evidentiary hearing concerning the scope of the search of respondent's person which had occurred at the time of his arrest. The District Court made findings of fact and conclusions of law adverse to respondent, and he again appealed. This time the Court of Appeals en banc reversed the judgment of conviction, holding that the heroin introduced in evidence against respondent had been obtained as a result of a search which violated the Fourth Amendment to the United States Constitution. . . .

[A]t approximately 11 P.M., Officer Richard Jenks, a 15-year veteran of the District of Columbia Metropolitan Police Department, observed the respondent driving a 1965 Cadillac near the intersection of 8th and C Streets, N.E., in the District of Columbia. Jenks, as a result of previous investigation following a check of respondent's operator's permit four days earlier, determined there was reason to believe that respondent was operating a motor vehicle after the revocation of his operator's permit. . . .

Jenks signaled respondent to stop the automobile, which respondent did, and all three of the occupants emerged from the car. At that point Jenks informed respondent that he was under arrest for "operating after revocation and obtaining a permit by misrepresentation." It was assumed by the Court of Appeals, and is conceded by the respondent here, that Jenks had probable cause to arrest respondent, and that he effected a full-custody arrest.

In accordance with procedures prescribed in police department instructions, Jenks then began to search respondent. He explained at a subsequent hearing that he was "face-to-face" with the respondent, and "placed [his] hands on [the respondent], my right-hand to his left breast like this (demonstrating) and proceeded to pat him down thus [with the right hand]." During this patdown, Jenks felt an object in the left breast pocket of the heavy coat respondent was wearing, but testified that he "couldn't tell what it was" and also that he "couldn't actually tell the size of it." Jenks then reached into the pocket and pulled out the object, which turned out to be a "crumpled up cigarette package." Jenks testified that at this point he still did not know what was in the package:

> "As I felt the package I could feel objects in the package but I couldn't tell what they were. . . . I knew they weren't cigarettes."

The officer then opened the cigarette pack and found 14 gelatin capsules of white powder which he thought to be, and which later analysis proved to be, heroin. Jenks then continued his search of respondent to completion, feeling around his waist and trouser legs, and examining the remaining pockets. The heroin seized from the respondent was admitted into evidence at the trial which resulted in his conviction in the District Court. . . .

We conclude that the search conducted by Jenks in this case did not offend the limits imposed by the Fourth Amendment, and we therefore reverse the judgment of the Court of Appeals.

It is well settled that a search incident to a lawful arrest is a traditional exception to the warrant requirement of the Fourth Amendment. This general exception has historically been formulated into two distinct propositions. The first is that a search may be made of the *person* of the arrestee by virtue of the lawful arrest. The second is that a search may be made of the area within the control of the arrestee. . . .

In its decision of this case, the Court of Appeals decided that even after a police officer lawfully places a suspect under arrest for the purpose of taking him into custody, he may not ordinarily proceed to fully search the prisoner. He must, instead, conduct a limited frisk of the outer clothing and remove such weapons that he may, as a result of that limited frisk, reasonably believe and ascertain that the suspect has in his possession. While recognizing that *Terry v. Ohio,* [392 U.S. 1 (1968)], dealt with a permissible "frisk" incident to an investigative stop based on less than probable cause to arrest, the Court of Appeals felt that the principles of that case should be carried over to this probable-cause arrest for driving while one's license is revoked. Since there would be no further evidence of such a crime to be obtained in a search of the arrestee, the court held that only a search for weapons could be justified.

Terry v. Ohio, supra, did not involve an arrest for probable cause, and it made quite clear that the "protective frisk" for weapons which it approved might be conducted without probable cause. This Court's opinion explicitly recognized that there is a "distinction in purpose, character, and extent between a search incident to an arrest and a limited search for weapons.". . . *Terry,* therefore, affords no basis to carry over to a probable-cause arrest the limitations this Court placed on a stop-and-frisk search permissible without probable cause. . . .

Virtually all of the statements of this Court affirming the existence of an unqualified authority to search incident to a lawful arrest are dicta. We would not, therefore, be foreclosed by principles of *stare decisis* from further examination into history and practice in order to see whether the sort of qualifications imposed by the Court of Appeals in this case were in fact intended by the Framers of the Fourth Amendment or recognized in cases decided prior to *Weeks* [*v. United States*, 232 U.S. 383 (1914)]. Unfortunately such authorities as exist are sparse. Such common-law treatises as Blackstone's Commentaries and Holmes' Common Law are simply silent on the subject. . . .

While these earlier authorities are sketchy, they tend to support the broad statement of the authority to search incident to arrest found in the successive decisions of this Court, rather than the restrictive one which was applied by the Court of Appeals in this case. . . .

It is scarcely open to doubt that the danger to an officer is far greater in the case of the extended exposure which follows the taking of a suspect into custody and transporting him to the police station than in the case of the relatively fleeting contact resulting from the typical *Terry*-type stop. This is an adequate basis for treating all custodial arrests alike for purposes of search justification.

The search of respondent's person conducted by Officer Jenks in this case and the seizure from him of the heroin, were permissible under established Fourth Amendment law. While thorough, the search partook of none of the extreme or patently abusive characteristics which were held to violate the Due Process Clause of the Fourteenth Amendment in *Rochin v. California*, 342 U.S. 165 (1952). Since it is the fact of custodial arrest which gives rise to the authority to search, it is of no moment that Jenks did not indicate any subjective fear of the respondent or that he did not himself suspect that respondent was armed. Having in the course of a lawful search come upon the crumpled package of cigarettes, he was entitled to inspect it; and when his inspection revealed the heroin capsules, he was entitled to seize them as "fruits, instrumentalities, or contraband" probative of criminal conduct.

Justice MARSHALL, with whom Justice DOUGLAS and Justice BRENNAN join, dissenting.

Certain fundamental principles have characterized this Court's Fourth Amendment jurisprudence over the years. Perhaps the most basic of these was expressed by Justice BUTLER, speaking for a unanimous Court in *Go-Bart Co. v. United States*, 282 U.S. 344 (1931): "There is no formula for the determination of reasonableness. Each case is to be decided on its own facts and circumstances." . . . As we recently held: "The constitutional validity of a warrantless search is preeminently the sort of question which can only be decided in the concrete factual context of the individual case." *Sibron v. New York*, 392 U.S. 40 (1968). And the intensive, at times painstaking, case-by-case analysis characteristic of our Fourth Amendment decisions bespeaks our "jealous regard for maintaining the integrity of individual rights." *Mapp v. Ohio*, 367 U.S. 643 [1961].

In the present case, however, the majority turns its back on these principles, holding that "the fact of the lawful arrest" always establishes the authority to conduct a full search of the arrestee's person, regardless of whether in a particular case "there was present one of the reasons supporting the authority for a search of the person incident to a lawful arrest." The majority's approach represents a clear and marked departure from our long tradition of case-by-case adjudication of the reasonableness of searches and seizures under the Fourth Amendment. I continue to believe that "[t]he scheme of the Fourth Amendment becomes meaningful only when it is assured that at some point the conduct of those charged with enforcing the laws can be subjected to the more detached, neutral scrutiny of a judge who must evaluate the reasonableness of a particular search or seizure in light of the particular circumstances." *Terry v. Ohio*, 392 U.S. 1 (1968). Because I find the majority's reasoning to be at odds with these fundamental principles, I must respectfully dissent. . . .

No question is raised here concerning the lawfulness of the patdown of respondent's coat pocket. . . .

With respect to the removal of the unknown object from the coat pocket, the first issue presented is whether that aspect of the search can be sustained as part of the limited frisk for weapons. The weapons search approved by the Court of Appeals was modeled upon the narrowly drawn protective search for weapons authorized in *Terry,* which consists "of a limited patting of the outer clothing of the suspect for concealed objects which might be used as instruments of assault.". . .

In the present case, however, Officer Jenks had no reason to believe and did not in fact believe that the object in respondent's coat pocket was a weapon. He admitted later that the object did not feel like a gun. . . .

Since the removal of the object from the pocket cannot be justified as part of a limited *Terry* weapons frisk, the question arises whether it is reasonable for a police officer, when effecting an in-custody arrest of a traffic offender, to make a fuller search of the person than is permitted pursuant to *Terry.*

The underlying rationale of a search incident to arrest of a traffic offender initially suggests as reasonable a search whose scope is similar to the protective weapons frisk permitted in *Terry.* A search incident to arrest, as the majority indicates, has two basic functions: the removal of weapons the arrestee might use to resist arrest or effect an escape, and the seizure of evidence or fruits of the crime for which the arrest is made, so as to prevent their concealment or destruction. . . .

The Government does not now contend that the search of respondent's pocket can be justified by any need to find and seize evidence in order to prevent its concealment or destruction, for, as the Court of Appeals found, there is no evidence or fruits of the offense with which respondent was charged. The only rationale for a search in this case, then, is the removal of weapons which the arrestee might use to harm the officer and attempt an escape. This rationale, of course, is identical to the rationale of the search permitted in *Terry*. . . . Since the underlying rationale of a *Terry* search and the search of a traffic violator are identical, the Court of Appeals held that the scope of the searches must be the same. And in view of its conclusion that the removal of the object from respondent's coat pocket exceeded the scope of a lawful *Terry* frisk, a conclusion not disputed by the Government or challenged by the majority here, the plurality of the Court of Appeals held that the removal of the package exceeded the scope of a lawful search incident to arrest of a traffic violator.

The problem with this approach, however, is that it ignores several significant differences between the context in which a search incident to arrest for a traffic violation is made, and the situation presented in *Terry*. Some of these differences would appear to suggest permitting a more thorough search in this case than was permitted in *Terry;* other differences suggest a narrower, more limited right to search than was there recognized.

The most obvious difference between the two contexts relates to whether the officer has cause to believe that the individual he is dealing with possesses weapons which might be used against him. *Terry* did not permit an officer to conduct a weapons frisk of anyone he lawfully stopped on the street, but rather, only where "he has reason to believe that he is dealing with an armed and dangerous individual. . . ."

Nor was there any particular reason in this case to believe that respondent was dangerous. He had not attempted to evade arrest, but had quickly complied with the police both in bringing his car to a stop after being signaled to do so and in producing the documents Officer Jenks requested. In fact, Jenks admitted that he searched respondent face to face rather than in spread-eagle fashion because he had no reason to believe respondent would be violent. . . .

The majority opinion [also] fails to recognize that the search conducted by Officer Jenks did not merely involve a search of respondent's person. It also included a separate search of effects found on his person. And even were we to assume, *arguendo*, that it was reasonable for Jenks to remove the object he felt in respondent's pocket, clearly there was no justification consistent with the Fourth Amendment which would authorize his opening the package and looking inside. . . .

The Government argues that it is difficult to see what constitutionally protected "expectation of privacy" a prisoner has in the interior of a cigarette pack. One wonders if the result in this case would have been the same were respondent a businessman who was lawfully taken into custody for driving without a license and whose wallet was taken from him by the police. Would it be reasonable for the police officer, because of the possibility that a razor blade was hidden somewhere in the wallet, to open it, remove all the contents, and examine each item carefully? Or suppose a lawyer lawfully arrested for a traffic offense is found to have a sealed envelope on his person. Would it be permissible for the arresting officer to tear open the envelope in order to make sure that it did not contain a clandestine weapon—perhaps a pin or a razor blade? . . .

I, for one, cannot characterize any of these intrusions into the privacy of an individual's papers and effects as being negligible incidents to the more serious intrusion into the individual's privacy stemming from the arrest itself. Nor can any principled distinction be drawn between the hypothetical searches I have posed and the search of the cigarette package in this case. The only reasoned distinction is between warrantless searches which serve legitimate protective and evidentiary functions and those that do not.

Delaware v. Prouse
440 U.S. 648, 99 S.Ct. 1391 (1979)

William Prouse's car was stopped by a patrolman. As the officer walked toward the car, he smelled marijuana and subsequently seized marijuana that he saw in plain view on the floor of the car. Later, at a hearing on motion to suppress the evidence against Prouse, the officer testified that he had not observed any traffic violation or other suspicious activity, but was not busy and decided to make a routine stop to check the driver's license and vehicle registration. The trial judge suppressed the evidence for being obtained in violation of the Fourth Amendment, and the Delaware Supreme Court affirmed. The state then appealed to the Supreme Court, which granted *certiorari*.

Justice WHITE delivered the opinion of the Court.

The question is whether it is an unreasonable seizure under the Fourth and Fourteenth Amendments to stop an automobile, being driven on a public highway, for the purpose of checking the driving license of the operator and the registration of the car, where there is neither probable cause to believe nor reasonable suspicion that the car is being driven contrary to the laws governing the operation of motor vehicles or that either the car or any of its occupants is subject to seizure or detention in connection with the violation of any other applicable law. . . .

The Fourth and Fourteenth Amendments are implicated in this case because stopping an automobile and detaining its occupants constitute a "seizure" within the meaning of those Amendments, even though the purpose of the stop is limited and the resulting detention quite brief. . . . The essential purpose of the proscriptions in the Fourth Amendment is to impose a standard of "reasonableness" upon the exercise of discretion by government officials, including law enforcement agents, in order " 'to safeguard the privacy and security of individuals against arbitrary invasions. . . .' " *Marshall v. Barlow's, Inc.,* 436 U.S. 307 (1978), quoting *Camara v. Municipal Court,* 387 U.S. 523 (1967). Thus, the permissibility of a particular law enforcement practice is judged by balancing its intrusion on the individual's Fourth Amendment interests against its promotion of legitimate governmental interests. Implemented in this manner, the reasonableness standard usually requires, at a minimum, that the facts upon which an intrusion is based be capable of measurement against "an objective standard," whether this be probable cause or a less stringent test. In those situations in which the balance of interests precludes insistence upon "some quantum of individualized suspicion," other safeguards are generally relied upon to assure that the individual's reasonable expectation of privacy is not "subject to the discretion of the official in the field," *Camara v. Municipal Court.* . . .

In this case, however, the State of Delaware urges that patrol officers be subject to no constraints in deciding which automobiles shall be stopped for a license and registration check because the State's interest in discretionary spot checks as a means of ensuring the safety of its roadways outweighs the resulting intrusion on the privacy and security of the persons detained.

We have only recently considered the legality of investigative stops of automobiles where the officers making the stop have neither probable cause to believe nor reasonable suspicion that either the automobile or its occupants are subject to seizure under the applicable criminal laws. . . .

Although not dispositive, [earlier] decisions undoubtedly provide guidance in balancing the public interest against the individual's Fourth Amendment interests implicated by the practice of spot checks such as occurred in this case. We cannot agree that stopping or detaining a vehicle on an ordinary city street is less intrusive than a roving-patrol stop on a major highway and that it bears greater resemblance to a permissible stop and secondary detention at a checkpoint near the border. In this regard, we note that [*United States v.*] *Brignoni-Ponce,* [422 U.S. 873 (1975)], was not limited to roving-patrol stops on limited-access roads, but applied to any roving-patrol stop by Border Patrol agents on any type of roadway on less than reasonable suspicion. We cannot assume that the physical and psychological intrusion visited upon the occupants of a vehicle by a random stop to check documents is of any less moment than that occasioned by a stop by border agents on roving patrol. Both of these stops generally entail law enforcement officers signaling a moving automobile to pull over to the side of the roadway, by means of a possibly unsettling show of authority. Both interfere with freedom of movement, are inconvenient, and consume time. Both may create substantial anxiety. For Fourth Amendment purposes, we also see insufficient resemblance between sporadic and random stops of individual vehicles making their way through city traffic and those stops occasioned by roadblocks where all vehicles are brought to a halt or to a near halt, and all are subjected to a show of the police power of the community. "At traffic checkpoints the motorist can see that other vehicles are being stopped, he can see visible signs of the officers' authority, and he is much less likely to be frightened or annoyed by the intrusion.". . .

The question remains, however, whether in the service of these important ends the discretionary spot check is a sufficiently productive mechanism to justify the intrusion upon Fourth Amendment interests which such stops entail. On the record before us, that question must be answered in the negative. Given the alternative mechanisms available, both those in use and those that might be adopted, we are unconvinced that the incremental contribution to highway safety of the random spot check justifies the practice under the Fourth Amendment.

The foremost method of enforcing traffic and vehicle safety regulations, it must be recalled, is acting upon observed violations. Vehicle stops for traffic violations occur countless times each day; and on these occasions, licenses and registration papers are subject to inspection and drivers without them will be ascertained. Furthermore, drivers without licenses are presumably the less safe drivers whose propensities may well exhibit themselves. Absent some empirical data to the contrary, it must be assumed that finding an unlicensed driver among those who commit traffic violations is a much more likely event than finding an unlicensed driver by choosing randomly from the entire universe of drivers. If this were not so, licensing of drivers would hardly be an effective means of promoting roadway safety. It seems common sense that the percentage of all drivers on the road who are driving without a license is very small and that the number of licensed drivers who will be stopped in order to find one unlicensed operator will be large indeed. The contribution to highway safety made by discretionary stops selected from among drivers generally will therefore be marginal at best. Furthermore, and again absent something more than mere assertion to the contrary, we find it difficult to believe that the unlicensed driver would not be deterred by the possibility of being involved in a traffic violation or having some other experience calling for proof of his entitlement to drive but that he would be deterred by the possibility that he would be one of those chosen for a spot check. In terms of actually discovering unlicensed drivers or deterring them from driving, the spot check does not appear sufficiently productive to qualify as a reasonable law enforcement practice under the Fourth Amendment.

Much the same can be said about the safety aspects of automobiles as distinguished from drivers. Many violations of minimum vehicle-safety requirements are observable, and something can be done about them by the observing officer, directly and immediately. Furthermore, in Delaware, as elsewhere, vehicles must carry and display current license plates, which themselves evidence that the vehicle is properly registered; and, under Delaware law, to qualify for annual registration a vehicle must pass the annual safety inspection and be properly insured. It does not appear, therefore, that a stop of a Delaware-registered vehicle is necessary in order to ascertain compliance with the State's registration requirements; and, because there is nothing to show that a significant percentage of automobiles from other States do not also require license plates indicating current registration, there is no basis for concluding that stopping even out-of-state cars for document checks substantially promotes the State's interest.

The marginal contribution to roadway safety possibly resulting from a system of spot checks cannot justify subjecting every occupant of every vehicle on the roads to a seizure—limited in magnitude compared to other intrusions but nonetheless constitutionally cognizable—at the unbridled discretion of law enforcement officials. To insist neither upon an appropriate factual basis for suspicion directed at a particular automobile nor upon some other substantial and objective standard or rule to govern the exercise of discretion "would invite intrusions upon constitutionally guaranteed rights based on nothing more substantial than inarticulate hunches . . ." *Terry v. Ohio.* By hypothesis, stopping apparently safe drivers is necessary only because the danger presented by some drivers is not observable at the time of the stop. When there is not probable cause to believe that a driver is violating any one of the multitude of applicable traffic and equipment regulations—or other articulable basis amounting to reasonable suspicion that the driver is unlicensed or his vehicle unregistered— we cannot conceive of any legitimate basis upon which a patrolman could decide that stopping a particular driver for a spot check would be more productive than stopping any other driver. This kind of standardless and unconstrained discretion is the evil the Court has discerned when in previous cases it has insisted that the discretion of the official in the field be circumscribed, at least to some extent. . . .

An individual operating or traveling in an automobile does not lose all reasonable expectation of privacy simply because the automobile and its use are subject to government regulation. Automobile travel is a basic, pervasive, and often necessary mode of transportation to and from one's home, workplace, and leisure activities. Many people spend more hours each day traveling in cars than walking on the streets. Undoubtedly, many find a greater sense of security and privacy in traveling in an automobile than they do in exposing themselves by pedestrian or other modes of travel. Were the individual subject to unfettered governmental intrusion every time he entered an automobile, the security guaranteed by the Fourth Amendment would be seriously circumscribed. . . .

Accordingly, we hold that except in those situations in which there is at least articulable and reasonable suspicion that a motorist is unlicensed or that an automobile is not registered, or that either the vehicle or an occupant is otherwise subject to seizure for violation of law, stopping an automobile and detaining the driver in order to check his driver's license and the registration of the automobile are unreasonable under the Fourth Amendment. This holding does not preclude the State of Delaware or other States from developing methods for spot checks that involve less intrusion or that do not involve the unconstrained exercise of discretion. Questioning of all oncoming traffic at roadblock-type stops is one possible alternative. We hold only that persons in automobiles on public roadways may not for that reason alone have their travel and privacy interfered with at the unbridled discretion of police officers. The judgment below is affirmed.

Justice BLACKMUN, with whom Justice POWELL joins, concurring.

The Court, carefully protects from the reach of its decision other less intrusive spot checks "that do not involve the unconstrained exercise of discretion." The roadblock stop for all traffic is given as an example. I necessarily assume that the Court's reservation also includes other not purely random stops (such as every 10th car to pass a given point) that equate with, but are less intrusive than, a 100% roadblock stop. And I would not regard the present case as a precedent that throws any constitutional shadow upon the necessarily somewhat individualized and perhaps largely random examinations by game wardens in the performance of their duties. In a situation of that type, it seems to me, the Court's balancing process, and the value factors under consideration, would be quite different.

Justice REHNQUIST dissenting.

As the Court correctly points out, people are not shorn of their Fourth Amendment protection when they step from their homes onto the public sidewalks or from the sidewalks into their automobiles. But a random license check of a motorist operating a vehicle on highways owned and maintained by the State is quite different from a random stop designed to uncover violations of laws that have nothing to do with motor vehicles. No one questions that the State may require the licensing of those who drive on its highways and the registration of vehicles which are driven on those highways. If it may insist on these requirements, it obviously may take steps necessary to enforce compliance. The reasonableness of the enforcement measure chosen by the State is tested by weighing its intrusion on the motorists' Fourth Amendment interests against its promotion of the State's legitimate interests. . . .

Noting that "finding an unlicensed driver among those who commit traffic violations is a much more likely event than finding an unlicensed driver by choosing randomly from the entire universe of drivers," the Court concludes that the contribution to highway safety made by random stops would be marginal at best. The State's primary interest, however, is in traffic safety, not in apprehending unlicensed motorists for the sake of apprehending unlicensed motorists. The whole point of enforcing motor vehicle safety regulations is to remove from the road the unlicensed driver before he demonstrates why he is unlicensed. The Court would apparently prefer that the State check licenses and vehicle registrations as the wreckage is being towed away.

Nor is the Court impressed with the deterrence rationale, finding it inconceivable that an unlicensed driver who is not deterred by the prospect of being involved in a traffic violation or other incident requiring him to produce a license would be deterred by the possibility of being subjected to a spot check. The Court arrives at its conclusion without the benefit of a shred of empirical data in this record suggesting that a system of random spot checks would fail to deter violators. In the absence of such evidence, the State's determination that random stops would serve a deterrence function should stand.

United States v. Ross
456 U.S. 798, 102 S.Ct. 2157 (1982)

In his opinion for the Court, Justice John Paul Stevens recounts the facts in this case arising from a warrantless search of an automobile by police who had probable cause to believe that it contained drugs.

Justice STEVENS delivered the opinion of the Court.

In *Carroll v. United States*, [267 U.S. 132 (1925)], the Court held that a warrantless search of an automobile stopped by police officers who had probable cause to believe the vehicle contained contraband was not unreasonable within the meaning of the Fourth Amendment. The Court in *Carroll* did not explicitly address the scope of the search that is permissible. In this case, we consider the extent to which police officers—who have legitimately stopped an automobile and who have probable cause to believe that contraband is concealed somewhere within it—may conduct a probing search of compartments and containers within the vehicle whose contents are not in plain view. We hold that they may conduct a search of the vehicle that is as thorough as a magistrate could authorize in a warrant "particularly describing the place to be searched."

I

In the evening of November 27, 1978, an informant who had previously proved to be reliable telephoned Detective Marcum of the District of Columbia Police Department and told him that an individual known as "Bandit" was selling narcotics kept in the trunk of a car parked at 439 Ridge Street. The informant stated that he had just observed "Bandit" complete a sale and that "Bandit" had told him that additional narcotics were in the trunk. The informant gave Marcum a detailed description of "Bandit" and stated that the car was a "purplish maroon" Chevrolet Malibu with District of Columbia license plates.

Accompanied by Detective Cassidy and Sergeant Gonzales, Marcum immediately drove to the area and found a maroon Malibu parked in front of 439 Ridge Street. A license check disclosed that the car was registered to Albert Ross; a computer check on Ross revealed that he fit the informant's description and used the alias "Bandit." In two passes through the neighborhood the officers did not observe anyone matching the informant's description. To avoid alerting persons on the street, they left the area.

The officers returned five minutes later and observed the maroon Malibu turning off Ridge Street onto Fourth Street. They pulled alongside the Malibu, noticed that the driver matched the informant's description, and stopped the car. Marcum and Cassidy told the driver—later identified as Albert Ross, the respondent in this action—to get out of the vehicle. While they searched Ross, Sergeant Gonzales discovered a bullet on the car's front seat. He searched the interior of the car and found a pistol in the glove compartment. Ross then was arrested and handcuffed. Detective Cassidy took Ross' keys and opened the trunk, where he found a closed brown paper bag. He opened the bag and discovered a number of glassine bags containing a white powder. Cassidy replaced the bag, closed the trunk, and drove the car to headquarters.

At the police station Cassidy thoroughly searched the car. In addition to the "lunch-type" brown paper bag, Cassidy found in the trunk a zippered red leather pouch. He unzipped the pouch and discovered $3,200 in cash. The police laboratory later determined that the powder in the paper bag was heroin. No warrant was obtained.

Ross was charged with possession of heroin with intent to distribute, in violation of 21 U.S.C. § 841(a). Prior to trial, he moved to suppress the heroin found in the paper bag and the currency found in the leather pouch. After an evidentiary hearing, the District Court denied the motion to suppress. The heroin and currency were introduced in evidence at trial and Ross was convicted.

A three-judge panel of the Court of Appeals reversed the conviction. . . .

The entire Court of Appeals then voted to rehear the case en banc. A majority of the court rejected the panel's conclusion that a distinction of constitutional significance existed between the two containers found in respondent's trunk; it held that the police should not have opened either container without first obtaining a warrant.

II

We begin with a review of the decision in *Carroll* itself. . . .

[T]he exception to the warrant requirement established in *Carroll*—the scope of which we consider in this case—applies only to searches of vehicles that are supported by probable cause. In this class of cases, a search is not unreasonable if based on facts that would justify the issuance of a warrant, even though a warrant has not actually been obtained.

III

The rationale justifying a warrantless search of an automobile that is believed to be transporting contraband arguably applies with equal force to any movable container that is believed to be carrying an illicit substance. That argument, however, was squarely rejected in *United States v. Chadwick* [433 U.S. 1 (1977)]. . . .

The Court in *Chadwick* specifically rejected the argument that the warrantless search was "reasonable" because a footlocker has some of the mobile characteristics that support warrantless searches of automobiles. The Court recognized that "a person's expectations of privacy in personal luggage are substantially greater than in an automobile," and noted that the practical problems associated with the temporary detention of a piece of luggage during the period of time necessary to obtain a warrant are significantly less than those associated with the detention of an automobile. In ruling that the warrantless search of the footlocker was unjustified, the Court reaffirmed the general principle that closed packages and containers may not be searched without a warrant. In sum, the Court in *Chadwick* declined to extend the rationale of the "automobile exception" to permit a warrantless search of any movable container found in a public place.

The facts in *Arkansas v. Sanders*, 442 U.S. 753 [1979], were similar to those in *Chadwick*. . . .

The Court in *Sanders* did not, however, rest its decision solely on the authority of *Chadwick*. In rejecting the State's argument that the warrantless search of the suitcase was justified on the ground that it had been taken from an automobile lawfully stopped on the street, the Court broadly suggested that a warrantless search of a container found in an automobile could never be sustained as part of a warrantless search of the automobile itself. The Court did not suggest that it mattered whether probable cause existed to search the entire vehicle. It is clear, however, that in neither *Chadwick* nor *Sanders* did the police have probable cause to search the vehicle or anything within it except the footlocker in the former case and the green suitcase in the latter.

Robbins v. California, 453 U.S. 420 [1981], however, was a case in which suspicion was not directed at a specific container. In that case the Court for the first time was forced to consider whether police officers who are entitled to conduct a warrantless search of an automobile stopped on a public roadway may open a container found within the vehicle. . . .

Writing for a plurality, Justice STEWART rejected the argument that the outward appearance of the packages precluded Robbins from having a reasonable expectation of privacy in their contents. He also squarely rejected the argument that there is a constitutional distinction between searches of luggage and searches of "less worthy" containers. Justice STEWART reasoned that all containers are equally protected by the Fourth Amendment unless their contents are in plain view. The plurality concluded that the warrantless search was impermissible because *Chadwick* and *Sanders* had established that "a closed piece of luggage found in a lawfully searched car is constitutionally protected to the same extent as are closed pieces of luggage found anywhere else.". . .

Unlike *Chadwick* and *Sanders*, in this case police officers had probable cause to search respondent's entire vehicle. Unlike *Robbins*, in this case the parties have squarely addressed the question whether, in the course of a legitimate warrantless search of an automobile, police are entitled to open containers found within the vehicle. We now address that question. Its answer is determined by the scope of the search that is authorized by the exception to the warrant requirement set forth in *Carroll*.

IV

. . . As we have stated, the decision in *Carroll* was based on the Court's appraisal of practical considerations viewed in the perspective of history. It is therefore significant that the practical consequences of the *Carroll* decision would be largely nullified if the permissible scope of a warrantless search of an automobile did not include containers and packages found inside the vehicle. Contraband goods rarely are strewn across the trunk or floor of a car; since by their very nature such goods must be withheld from public view, they rarely can be placed in an automobile unless they are enclosed within some form of container. The Court in *Carroll* held that "contraband goods *concealed* and illegally transported in an automobile or other vehicle may be searched for without a warrant." (emphasis added). As we noted in *Henry v. United States*, 361 U.S. 98 [1959], the decision in *Carroll* "merely relaxed the requirements for a warrant on grounds of practicability." It neither broadened nor limited the scope of a lawful search based on probable cause.

A lawful search of fixed premises generally extends to the entire area in which the object of the search may be found and is not limited by the possibility that separate acts of entry or opening may be required to complete the search. Thus, a warrant that authorizes an officer to search a home for illegal weapons also provides authority to open closets, chests, drawers, and containers in which the weapon might be found. A warrant to open a footlocker to search for marihuana would also authorize the opening of packages found inside. A warrant to search a vehicle would support a search of every part of the vehicle that might contain the object of the search. When a legitimate search is under way, and when its purpose and its limits have been precisely defined, nice distinctions between closets, drawers, and containers, in the case of a home, or between glove compartments, upholstered seats, trunks, and wrapped packages, in the case of a vehicle, must give way to the interest in the prompt and efficient completion of the task at hand.

This rule applies equally to all containers, as indeed we believe it must. One point on which the Court was in virtually unanimous agreement in *Robbins* was that a constitutional distinction between "worthy" and "unworthy" containers would be improper. Even though such a distinction perhaps could evolve in a series of cases in which paper bags, locked trunks, lunch buckets, and orange crates were placed on one side of the line or the other, the central purpose of the Fourth Amendment forecloses such a distinction. For just as the most frail cottage in the kingdom is absolutely entitled to the same guarantees of privacy as the most majestic mansion, so also may a traveler who carries a toothbrush and a few articles of clothing in a paper bag or knotted scarf claim an equal right to conceal his possessions from official inspection as the sophisticated executive with the locked attaché case. . . .

In the same manner, an individual's expectation of privacy in a vehicle and its contents may not survive if probable cause is given to believe that the vehicle is transporting contraband. Certainly the privacy interests in a car's trunk or glove compartment may be no less than those in a movable container. An individual undoubtedly has a significant interest that the upholstery of his automobile will not be ripped or a hidden compartment within it opened. These interests must yield to the authority of a search, however, which—in light of *Carroll*—does not itself require the prior approval of a magistrate. The scope of a warrantless search based on probable cause is no narrower—and no broader—than the scope of a search authorized by a warrant supported by probable cause. Only the prior approval of the magistrate is waived; the search otherwise is as the magistrate could authorize.

The scope of a warrantless search of an automobile thus is not defined by the nature of the container in which the contraband is secreted. Rather, it is defined by the object of the search and the places in which there is probable cause to believe that it may be found. Just as probable cause to believe that a stolen lawnmower may be found in a garage will not support a warrant to search an upstairs bedroom, probable cause to believe that undocumented aliens are being transported in a van will not justify a warrantless search of a suitcase. Probable cause to believe that a container placed in the trunk of a taxi contains contraband or evidence does not justify a search of the entire cab. . . .

The judgment of the Court of Appeals is reversed. The case is remanded for further proceedings consistent with this opinion.

It is so ordered.

Justice BLACKMUN concurred.

Justice WHITE dissented.

Justice MARSHALL, with whom Justice BRENNAN joins, dissenting.

The majority today not only repeals all realistic limits on warrantless automobile searches, it repeals the Fourth Amendment warrant requirement itself. By equating a police officer's estimation of probable cause with a magistrate's, the Court utterly disregards the value of a neutral and detached magistrate. For as we recently, and unanimously, reaffirmed:

> "The warrant traditionally has represented an independent assurance that a search and arrest will not proceed without probable cause to believe that a crime has been committed and that the person or place named in the warrant is involved in the crime. Thus, an issuing magistrate must meet two tests. He must be neutral and detached, and he must be capable of determining whether probable cause exists for the requested arrest or search. This Court long has insisted that inferences of probable cause be drawn by 'a neutral and detached magistrate instead of being judged by the officer engaged in the often competitive enterprise of ferreting out crime.'" *Shadwick v. City of Tampa,* 407 U.S. 345 (1972), quoting *Johnson v. United States,* 333 U.S. 10 (1948).

A police officer on the beat hardly satisfies these standards. In adopting today's new rule, the majority opinion shows contempt for these Fourth Amendment values, ignores this Court's precedents, is internally inconsistent, and produces anomalous and unjust consequences. I therefore dissent. . . .

The majority's rule is flatly inconsistent with these established Fourth Amendment principles concerning the scope of the automobile exception and the importance of the warrant requirement. Historically, the automobile exception has been limited to those situations where its application is compelled by the justifications described above. Today, the majority makes no attempt to base its decision on these justifications. This failure is not surprising, since the traditional rationales for the automobile exception plainly do not support extending it to the search of a container found inside a vehicle.

The practical mobility problem—deciding what to do with both the car and the occupants if an immediate search is not conducted—is simply not present in the case of movable containers, which can easily be seized and brought to the magistrate. The lesser-expectation-of-privacy rationale also has little force. A container, as opposed to the car itself, does not reflect diminished privacy interests. Moreover, the practical corollary that this Court has recognized—that depriving occupants of the use of a car may be a greater intrusion than an immediate search—is of doubtful relevance here, since the owner of a container will rarely suffer significant inconvenience by being deprived of its use while a warrant is being obtained.

The majority's rule masks the startling assumption that a policeman's determination of probable cause is the functional equivalent of the determination of a neutral and detached magistrate. This assumption ignores a major premise of the warrant requirement—the importance of having a neutral and detached magistrate determine whether probable cause exists. The majority's explanation that the scope of the warrantless automobile search will be "limited" to what a magistrate could authorize is thus inconsistent with our cases, which firmly establish that an on-the-spot determination of probable cause is *never* the same as a decision by a neutral and detached magistrate. . . .

The majority's argument that its decision is supported by our decisions in *Carroll* and *Chambers* is misplaced. The Court in *Carroll* upheld a warrantless search of an automobile for contraband on the basis of the impracticability of securing a warrant in cases involving the transportation of contraband goods. The Court did not, however, suggest that obtaining a warrant for the search of an automobile is always impracticable. . . .

[T]he Court's argument that allowing warrantless searches of certain integral compartments of the car in *Carroll* and *Chambers*, while protecting movable containers within the car, would be "illogical" and "absurd," ignores the reason why this Court has allowed warrantless searches of automobile compartments. Surely an integral compartment within a car is just as mobile, and presents the same practical problems of safekeeping, as the car itself. This cannot be said of movable containers located within the car. The fact that there may be a high expectation of privacy in both containers and compartments is irrelevant, since the privacy rationale is not, and cannot be, the justification for the warrantless search of compartments.

The Court's second argument, which focuses on the practical advantages to police of the *Carroll* doctrine, fares no better. The practical considerations which concerned the *Carroll* Court involved the difficulty of immobilizing a vehicle while a warrant must be obtained. The Court had no occasion to address whether *containers* present the same practical difficulties as the car itself or integral compartments of the car. They do not. *Carroll* hardly suggested, as the Court implies, that a warrantless search is justified simply because it assists police in obtaining more evidence. . . .

Finally, the majority's new rule is theoretically unsound and will create anomalous and unwarranted results. These consequences are readily apparent from the Court's attempt to reconcile its new rule with the holdings of *Chadwick* and *Sanders*. The Court suggests that probable cause to search only a container does not justify a warrantless search of an automobile in which it is placed, absent reason to believe that the contents could be secreted elsewhere in the vehicle. This, the majority asserts, is an indication that the new rule is carefully limited to its justification, and is not inconsistent with *Chadwick* and *Sanders*. But why is such a container more private, less difficult for police to seize and store, or in any other relevant respect more properly subject to the warrant requirement, than a container that police discover in a probable-cause search of an entire automobile? This rule plainly has peculiar and unworkable consequences: the Government "must show that the investigating officer knew enough but not too much, that he had sufficient knowledge to establish probable cause but insufficient knowledge to know exactly where the contraband was located.". . .

The Court today ignores the clear distinction that *Chadwick* established between movable containers and automobiles. It also rejects all of the relevant reasoning of *Sanders* and offers a substitute rationale that appears inconsistent with the result. *Sanders* is therefore effectively overruled. And the Court unambiguously overrules "the disposition" of *Robbins*, though it gingerly avoids stating that it is overruling the case itself.

The only convincing explanation I discern for the majority's broad rule is expediency: it assists police in conducting automobile searches, ensuring that the private containers into which criminal suspects often place goods will no longer be a Fourth Amendment shield. . . .

This case will have profound implications for the privacy of citizens traveling in automobiles, as the Court well understands.

"For countless vehicles are stopped on highways and public streets every day and our cases demonstrate that it is not uncommon for police officers to have probable cause to believe that contraband may be found in a stopped vehicle." A closed paper bag, a toolbox, a knapsack, a suitcase, and an attaché case can alike be searched without the protection of the judgment of a neutral magistrate, based only on the rarely disturbed decision of a police officer that he has probable cause to search for contraband in the vehicle. The Court derives satisfaction from the fact that its rule does not exalt the rights of the wealthy over the rights of the poor. A rule so broad that all citizens lose vital Fourth Amendment protection is no cause for celebration.

I dissent.

D. OTHER GOVERNMENTAL SEARCHES IN THE ADMINISTRATIVE STATE

The Supreme Court permits a lower standard than probable cause for the issuance of warrants for administrative searches—searches by public officials other than police, such as housing inspectors. The Court also allows for some types of warrantless administrative searches, depending on the kind of the search and the manner in which it is conducted. Whether an administrative warrant is required turns on the Court's balancing of individuals' privacy interests against competing governmental interests in conducting various types of searches—housing inspections, for example, welfare visitations, or inspections for violation of health, safety and environmental regulations.

Initially, in *Frank v. Maryland,* 359 U.S. 360 (1959), the Court held that administrative searches were outside the purview of the Fourth Amendment, when permitting warrantless housing inspections conducted at reasonable times and aimed at enforcing health regulations. Justice Felix Frankfurter held that only searches aimed at obtaining evidence of criminal activity required prior judicial approval. But dissenting Chief Justice Warren and Justices Black, Douglas, and Brennan complained that the majority's distinction between criminal and civil searches diluted Fourth Amendment–protected privacy interests. The amendment, in Justice Douglas's words,

> was designed to protect the citizen against uncontrolled invasion of his privacy. It does not make the home a place of refuge from the law. It only requires the sanction of the judiciary rather than the executive before that privacy may be invaded. History shows that all officers tend to be officious; and health inspectors, making out a case for criminal prosecution of the citizen are no exception. . . . One invasion of privacy by an official of the government can be as oppressive as another. . . . It would seem that the public interest in protecting privacy is equally as great in one case as another.

Frank's dissenters continued objecting to the formalistic dichotomy between criminal and civil searches, but they could not win a majority over to their side until the Court's composition changed. Finally, they were joined by Justices Byron White and Abe Fortas, who had replaced on the bench two members of the *Frank* majority. In two companion 1967 cases—*Camara v. Municipal Court,* 387 U.S. 523 (1967), and *See v. City of Seattle,* 387 U.S. 541 (1967)—the Court held that a search warrant was required when a owner denies permission for entry and search of his premises by housing and safety inspectors.

Writing for the Court in *Camera,* Justice White ruled, on the one hand, that the Fourth Amendment bars prosecution of a person for refusing to permit administrative officials to conduct warrantless inspections and, on the other hand, that administrative warrants may be issued on showing less than probable cause, as required in criminal cases. The standard for issuing administrative warrants, he explained,

> will vary with the municipal program being enforced, may be based upon the passage of time, the nature of the building (e.g., a multifamily apartment house), or the condition of the entire area, but they will not necessarily depend upon specific knowledge of the conditions of the particular dwelling. It has been suggested that to so vary the probable cause test from the standard applied in criminal cases would be to

authorize a "synthetic search warrant" and thereby to lessen the overall protections of the Fourth Amendment. . . . But we do not agree. The warrant procedure is designed to guarantee that a decision to search private property is justified by a reasonable governmental interest. But reasonableness is still the ultimate standard. If a valid public interest justifies the intrusion contemplated, there is probable cause to issue a suitably restricted search warrant.

Probable cause remains required for search warrants aimed at uncovering evidence of criminal activity, but administrative searches may be based "balancing the need to search against the invasions which the search entails."

Whether an administrative warrant is required depends on the government's interests and the type and manner of the search, as well as the competing interests in personal privacy. In *Marshall v. Barlow's Inc.*, 436 U.S. 307 (1978), for example, the Court struck down a provision in the Occupational Safety and Health Act, authorizing warrantless inspections of workplaces for safety violations. When holding that the businessman's right of privacy included the right to have a magistrate determine the reasonableness of a search according to an "administrative plan containing neutral criteria," Justice White emphasized that, "[i]f the government intrudes on a person's property, the privacy interest suffers whether the government's motivation is to investigate violations of criminal laws or breaches of other statutory or regulatory standards."

Warrantless searches of mines and heavily regulated commercial business are permissible, however. In *New York v. Burger*, 482 U.S. 691 (1987), the Court upheld the warrantless search of an automobile junkyard. There Justice Blackmun explained that

[t]he Court long has recognized that the Fourth Amendment's prohibition on unreasonable searches and seizures is applicable to commercial premises, as well as to private homes. *See v. City of Seattle* (1967). An owner or operator of a business thus has an expectation of privacy in commercial property, which society is prepared to consider to be reasonable, see *Katz v. United States*, 389 U.S. 347 (1967) (Harlan, J., concurring). . . . An expectation of privacy in commercial premises, however, is different from, and indeed less than, a similar expectation in an individual's home. . . . Because the owner or operator of commercial premises in a "closely regulated" industry has a reduced expectation of privacy, the warrant and probable-cause requirements, which fulfill the traditional Fourth Amendment standard of reasonableness for a government search . . . have lessened application in this context. Rather, we conclude that, as in other situations of "special need," see *New Jersey v. T.L.O.*, 469 U.S. 325 (1985) [holding that a high school principal may search the belongings of students], where the privacy interests of the owner are weakened and the government interests in regulating particular businesses are concomitantly heightened, a war-

THE DEVELOPMENT OF LAW

Searches by Government Officials in the Administrative State

Case	Vote	Ruling
Frank v. Maryland, 359 U.S. 360 (1959)	5:4	Warrant requirement does not apply to housing and health inspections, if conducted at reasonable times.
Abel v. United States, 362 U.S. 217 (1960)	5:4	Immigration officers may seize allegedly forged birth certificates without warrant.
Ohio ex. rel. Eaton v. Price, 364 U.S. 263 (1960)	4:4	Affirmed by an equally divided Court a lower court ruling upholding an ordinance authorizing housing inspectors to enter homes without warrants.
Camera v. Municipal Court, 387 U.S. 523 (1967); and *See v. City of Seattle*, 387 U.S. 541 (1967)	6:3	Search warrant required for housing and safety inspections.
Colonnade Catering Corporation v. United States, 397 U.S. 72 (1970)	6:3	Inspection for liquor license by IRS agents did not justify breaking and entering locked storeroom.
Wyman v. James, 400 U.S. 309 (1971)	6:3	Social workers may make warrantless searches of welfare recipients' homes.
United States v. Biswell, 406 U.S. 311 (1972)	8:1	Upheld warrantless search of gun dealer's locked storeroom during business hours under Gun Control Act of 1968.
Air Pollution Variance Board of State of Colorado v. Western Alflfa Corporation, 416 U.S. 861 (1974)	9:0	Upheld health inspector's entry of outdoor premises without consent of owner to observe smoke plumes.
California Bankers Association v. Shultz, 416 U.S. 21 (1974)	6:3	Upheld the recording keeping and mandatory reporting of depositors' financial transactions under the Bank Secrecy Act.
United States v. Bisceglia, 420 U.S. 141 (1975)	7:2	The IRS has the power to issue "John Doe" summons to banks to identify depositors who filed fraudulent tax returns.
United States v. Miller, 425 U.S. 435 (1976)	7:2	Held depositors have no Fourth Amendment–protected interests in bank deposits.

Case	Vote	Ruling
United States v. Ramsey, 431 U.S. 606 (1977)	6:3	Customs officials may open mail without a warrant in search for narcotics.
Marshall v. Barlow's, Inc., 436 U.S. 307 (1978)	5:3	Struck down section of the Occupational Safety and Health Act authorizing agents to make warrantless inspections for safety violations.
Michigan v. Tyler, 436 U.S. 499 (1978)	6:3	Firefighters need no warrant to enter premises to fight a fire, but thereafter must obtain a warrant when investigating cause of fire.
Donovan v. Dewey, 452 U.S. 594 (1981)	8:1	Upheld warrantless inspection of mines.
Michigan v. Clifford, 464 U.S. 387 (1984)	5:4	Administrative warrant required for a postfire search; criminal warrant necessary if the object of search is evidence of criminal activity.
Hudson v. Palmer, 468 U.S. 517 (1984)	6:3	Prison inmates have no reasonable expectation of privacy in prison cells from searches by guards.
New Jersey v. T.L.O., 469 U.S. 325 (1985)	6:3	Upheld principal's search of students' purse.
United States v. Jones, 469 U.S. 478 (1985); and *United States v. Sharpe,* 470 U.S. 675 (1985)	7:2 7:2	U.S. customs officials may search a trunk with probable cause but no warrant; and a drug enforcement agent may delay a passenger at the airport without a warrant.
O'Connor v. Ortega, 480 U.S. 709 (1987)	5:4	State hospital supervisor's warrantless search of employee's office for work-related items upheld.
New York v. Burger, 482 U.S. 691 (1987)	6:3	Warrantless administrative search of "heavily regulated" commercial premises—here, a junkyard—permissible.
Griffin v. Wisconsin, 868 U.S. 483 (1987).	5:4	Upheld warrantless search of probationer's home on "reasonable grounds," rather than probable cause, for search.
National Treasury Employees Union v. Von Raab, 489 U.S. 656 (1989)	5:4	Upheld U.S. Custom Services drug-testing program for employees.
Skinner v. Railway Labor Executives' Association, 489 U.S. 602 (1989)	6:3	Mandatory drug and alcohol testing for employees involved in accidents upheld.

rantless inspection of commercial premises may well be reasonable within the meaning of the Fourth Amendment.

Blackmun proceeded to hold that warrantless administrative searches would "be deemed to be reasonable only so long as three criteria are met":

First, there must be a "substantial" government interest that informs the regulatory scheme pursuant to which the inspection is made. . . . Second, the warrantless inspections must be "necessary to further [the] regulatory scheme." . . . Finally, "the statute's inspection program, in terms of the certainty and regularity of its application, [must] provid[e] a constitutionally adequate substitute for a warrant." . . . In other words, the regulatory scheme must perform the two basic functions of a warrant: it must advise the owner of the commercial premises that the search is being made pursuant to the law and has a properly limited scope, and it must limit the discretion of the inspecting officers.

The Court has also been sharply split on according Fourth Amendment protection for the privacy interests of public employees. In *O'Connor v. Ortega* (1987) (see page 839), the justices voted five to four to uphold a state hospital supervisor's warrantless search of an employee's office for work-related items.

Even more controversial for the Court and the country is the issue of drug and alcohol testing of public employees. In *National Treasury Employees Union v. Von Raab* (1989) (see page 848), the Rehnquist Court split five to four when upholding the U.S. Custom Service's drug-testing program for employees. In *Skinner v. Railway Labor Executives' Association* (1989) (see page 857), the justices divided six to three over allowing mandatory drug and alcohol tests for railroad workers involved in serious accidents.

O'Connor v. Ortega
480 U.S. 709, 107 S.Ct. 1492 (1987)

The facts in this case, involving a supervisor's search of a public employee's office, are discussed in Justice Sandra O'Connor's opinion for the Court.

Justice O'CONNOR, with whom the CHIEF JUSTICE and Justice WHITE and Justice POWELL join, delivers the opinion of the Court.

This suit under 42 U.S.C. § 1983 presents two issues concerning the Fourth Amendment rights of public employees. First, we must determine whether the respondent, a public employee, had a reasonable expectation of privacy in his office, desk, and file cabinets at his place of work. Second, we must address the appropriate Fourth Amendment standard for a search conducted by a public employer in areas in which a public employee is found to have a reasonable expectation of privacy.

I

In July 1981, Hospital officials, including Dr. Dennis O'Connor, the Executive Director of the Hospital, became concerned about possible improprieties in Dr. Ortega's management of the residency program. In particular, the Hospital officials were concerned with Dr. Ortega's acquisition of an Apple II computer for use in the residency program. . . . Additionally, the Hospital officials were concerned with charges that Dr. Ortega had sexually harassed two female Hospital employees, and had taken inappropriate disciplinary action against a resident. . . .

Dr. O'Connor selected several Hospital personnel to conduct the investigation, including an accountant, a physician, and a Hospital security officer. . . .

The resulting search of Dr. Ortega's office was quite thorough. The investigators entered the office a number of times and seized several items from Dr. Ortega's desk and file cabinets, including a Valentine's card, a photograph, and a book of poetry all sent to Dr. Ortega by a former resident physician. These items were later used in a proceeding before a hearing officer of the California State Personnel Board to impeach the credibility of the former resident, who testified on Dr. Ortega's behalf. The investigators also seized billing documentation of one of Dr. Ortega's private patients under the California Medicaid program. The investigators did not otherwise separate Dr. Ortega's property from state property because, as one investigator testified, "[t]rying to sort State from nonState, it was too much to do, so I gave it up and boxed it up." Thus, no formal inventory of the property in the office was ever made. . . .

The District Court . . . concluded that the search was proper because there was a need to secure state property in the office. The Court of Appeals for the Ninth Circuit affirmed in part and reversed in part, concluding that Dr. Ortega had a reasonable expectation of privacy in his office. . . . The Court of Appeals also concluded—albeit without explanation—that the search violated the Fourth Amendment. . . .

We granted certiorari, and now reverse and remand.

II

Our cases establish that Dr. Ortega's Fourth Amendment rights are implicated only if the conduct of the Hospital officials at issue in this case infringed "an expectation of privacy that society is prepared to consider reasonable." We have no talisman that determines in all cases those privacy expectations that society is prepared to accept as reasonable. Instead, "the Court has given weight to such factors as the intention of the Framers of the Fourth Amendment, the uses to which the individual has put a location, and our societal understanding that certain areas deserve the most scrupulous protection from government invasion.". . .

Because the reasonableness of an expectation of privacy, as well as the appropriate standard for a search, is understood to differ according to context, it is essential first to delineate the boundaries of the workplace context. The workplace includes those areas and items that are related to work and are generally within the employer's control. At a hospital, for example, the hallways, cafeteria, offices, desks, and file cabinets, among other areas, are all part of the workplace. These areas remain part of the workplace context even if the employee has placed personal items in them, such as a photograph placed in a desk or a letter posted on an employee bulletin board.

Not everything that passes through the confines of the business address can be considered part of the workplace context, however. An employee may bring closed luggage to the office prior to leaving on a trip, or a handbag or briefcase each workday. While whatever expectation of privacy the employee has in the existence and the outward appearance of the luggage is affected by its presence in the workplace, the employee's expectation of privacy in the *contents* of the luggage is not affected in the same way. The appropriate standard for a workplace search does not necessarily apply to a piece of closed personal luggage, a handbag or a briefcase that happens to be within the employer's business address. . . .

Given the societal expectations of privacy in one's place of work . . . we reject the contention made by the Solicitor General and petitioners that public employees can never have a reasonable expectation of privacy in their place of work. Individuals do not lose Fourth Amendment rights merely because they work for the government instead of a private employer. The operational realities of the workplace, however, may make *some* employees' expectations of privacy unreasonable when an intrusion is by a supervisor rather than a law enforcement official. Public employees' expectations of privacy in their offices, desks, and file cabinets, like similar expectations of employees in the private sector, may be reduced by virtue of actual office practices and procedures, or by legitimate regulation. . . . The employee's expectation of privacy must be assessed in the context of the employment relation. An office is seldom a private enclave free from entry by supervisors, other employees and business and personal invitees. Instead, in many cases offices are continually entered by fellow employees and other visitors during the workday for conferences, consultations, and other work-related visits. Simply put, it is the nature of government offices that others—such as fellow employees, supervisors, consensual visitors, and the general public—may have frequent access to an individual's office. . . . Given the great variety of work environments in the public sector, the question of whether an employee has a reasonable expectation of privacy must be addressed on a case-by-case basis. . . .

[W]e recognize that the undisputed evidence suggests that Dr. Ortega had a reasonable expectation of privacy in his desk and file cabinets. The undisputed evidence discloses that Dr. Ortega did not share his desk or file cabinets with any other employees. Dr. Ortega had occupied the office for 17 years and he kept materials in his office, which included personal correspondence, medical files, and correspondence from private patients unconnected to the Hospital, personal financial records, teaching aids and notes, and personal gifts and mementos. The files on physicians in residency training were kept outside Dr. Ortega's office. Indeed, the only items found by the investigators were apparently personal items because, with the exception of the items seized for use in the administrative hearings, all the papers and effects found in the office were simply placed in boxes and made available to Dr. Ortega. . . .

III

Having determined that Dr. Ortega had a reasonable expectation of privacy in his office, the Court of Appeals simply concluded without discussion that the "search . . . was not a reasonable search under the fourth amendment." But . . . "[t]o hold that the Fourth Amendment applies to searches conducted by [public employers] is only to begin the inquiry into the standards governing such searches. . . . [W]hat is reasonable depends on the context within which a search takes place." *New Jersey v. T.L.O.*, [469 U.S. 325 (1985)]. Thus, we must determine the appropriate standard of reasonableness applicable to the search. A determination of the standard of reasonableness applicable to a particular class of searches requires "balanc[ing] the nature and quality of the intrusion on the individual's Fourth Amendment interests against the importance of the governmental interests alleged to justify the intrusion." In the case of searches conducted by a public employer, we must balance the invasion of the employee's legitimate expectations of privacy against the government's need for supervision, control and the efficient operation of the workplace. . . .

In our view, requiring an employer to obtain a warrant whenever the employer wished to enter an employee's office, desk, or file cabinets for a work-related purpose would seriously disrupt the routine conduct of business and would be unduly burdensome. . . .

In contrast to other circumstances in which we have required warrants, supervisors in offices such as at the Hospital are hardly in the business of investigating the violation of criminal laws. Rather, work-related searches are merely incident to the primary business of the agency. Under these circumstances, the imposition of a warrant requirement would conflict with "the common-sense realization that government offices could not function if every employment decision became a constitutional matter.". . .

Whether probable cause is an inappropriate standard for public employer searches of their employees' offices presents a more difficult issue. For the most part, we have required that a search be based upon probable cause, but as we noted in *New Jersey v. T.L.O.,* "[t]he fundamental command of the Fourth Amendment is that searches and seizures be reasonable, and although 'both the concept of probable cause and the requirement of a warrant bear on the reasonableness of a search . . . in certain limited circumstances neither is required.' ". . .

Thus, "[w]here a careful balancing of governmental and private interests suggests that the public interest is best served by a Fourth Amendment standard of reasonableness that stops short of probable cause, we have not hesitated to adopt such a standard." We have concluded, for example, that the appropriate standard for administrative searches is not probable cause in its traditional meaning. Instead, an administrative warrant can be obtained if there is a showing that reasonable legislative or administrative standards for conducting an inspection are satisfied. . . .

Because the parties in this case have alleged that the search was either a noninvestigatory work-related intrusion or an investigatory search for evidence of suspected work-related employee misfeasance, we undertake to determine the appropriate Fourth Amendment standard of reasonableness *only* for these two types of employer intrusions and leave for another day inquiry into other circumstances.

The governmental interest justifying work-related intrusions by public employers is the efficient and proper operation of the workplace. . . . To ensure the efficient and proper operation of the agency, therefore, public employers must be given wide latitude to enter employee offices for work-related, noninvestigatory reasons.

We come to a similar conclusion for searches conducted pursuant to an investigation of work-related employee misconduct. Even when employers conduct an investigation, they have an interest substantially different from "the normal need for law enforcement.". . .

Public employers have an interest in ensuring that their agencies operate in an effective and efficient manner, and the work of these agencies inevitably suffers from the inefficiency, incompetence, mismanagement or other work-related misfeasance of its employees. Indeed, in many cases, public employees are entrusted with tremendous responsibility, and the consequences of their misconduct or incompetence to both the agency and the public interest can be severe. In contrast to law enforcement officials, therefore, public employers are not enforcers of the criminal law; instead, public employers have a direct and overriding interest in ensuring that the work of the agency is conducted in a proper and efficient manner. In our view, therefore, a probable cause requirement for searches of the type at issue here would impose intolerable burdens on public employers. The delay in correcting the employee misconduct caused by the need for probable cause rather than reasonable suspicion will be translated into tangible and often irreparable damage to the agency's work, and ultimately to the public interest. . . .

In sum, we conclude that the "special needs, beyond the normal need for law enforcement make the . . . probable-cause requirement impracticable," for legitimate work-related, noninvestigatory intrusions as well as investigations of work-related misconduct. A standard of reasonableness will neither unduly burden the efforts of government employers to ensure the efficient and proper operation of the workplace, nor authorize arbitrary intrusions upon the privacy of public employees. We hold, therefore, that public employer intrusions on the constitutionally protected privacy interests of government employees for noninvestigatory, work-related purposes, as well as for investigations of work-related misconduct, should be judged by the standard of reasonableness under all the circumstances. Under this reasonableness standard, both the inception and the scope of the intrusion must be reasonable. . . .

A search to secure state property is valid as long as the petitioners had a reasonable belief that there was government property in Dr. Ortega's office which needed to be secured, and the scope of the intrusion was itself reasonable in light of this justification. Indeed, the petitioners have put forward evidence that they had such a reasonable belief; at the time of the search, petitioners knew that Dr. Ortega had removed the computer from the Hospital. The removal of the computer—together with the allegations of mismanagement of the residency program and sexual harassment—may have made the search reasonable at its inception under the standard we have put forth in this case. As with the District Court order, therefore, the Court of Appeals conclusion that summary judgment was appropriate cannot stand.

Justice SCALIA concurring.

Although I share the judgment that this case must be reversed and remanded, I disagree with the reason for the reversal given by the plurality opinion, and with the standard it prescribes for the Fourth Amendment inquiry.

To address the latter point first: The plurality opinion instructs the lower courts that existence of Fourth Amendment protection for a public employee's business office is to be assessed "on a case-by-case basis," in light of whether the office is "so open to fellow employees or the public that no expectation of privacy is reasonable." No clue is provided as to how open "so open" must be; much less is it suggested how police officers are to gather the facts necessary for this refined inquiry. Even if I did not disagree with the plurality as to what result the proper legal standard should produce in the case before us, I would object to the formulation of a standard so devoid of content that it produces rather than eliminates uncertainty in this field.

Whatever the plurality's standard means, however, it must be wrong if it leads to the conclusion on the present facts that if Hospital officials had extensive "work-related reasons to enter Dr. Ortega's office" no Fourth Amendment protection existed. It is privacy that is protected by the Fourth Amendment, not solitude. A man enjoys Fourth Amendment protection in his home, for example, even though his wife and children have the run of the place—and indeed, even though his landlord has the right to conduct unannounced inspections at any time. Similarly, in my view, one's personal office is constitutionally protected against warrantless intrusions by the police, even though employer and co-workers are not excluded. . . . Just as the secretary working for a corporation in an office frequently entered by the corporation's other employees is protected against unreasonable searches of that office by the government, so also is the government secretary working in an office frequently entered by other government employees. There is no reason why this determination that a legitimate expectation of privacy exists should be affected by the fact that the government, rather than a private entity, is the employer. Constitutional protection against *unreasonable* searches by the government does not disappear merely because the government has the right to make reasonable intrusions in its capacity as employer.

I cannot agree, moreover, with the plurality's view that the reasonableness of the expectation of privacy (and thus the existence of Fourth Amendment protection) changes "when an intrusion is by a supervisor rather than a law enforcement official." The identity of the searcher (police vs. employer) is relevant not to whether Fourth Amendment protections apply, but only to whether the search of a protected area is reasonable. Pursuant to traditional analysis the former question must be answered on a more "global" basis. Where, for example, a fireman enters a private dwelling in response to an alarm, we do not ask whether the occupant has a reasonable expectation of privacy (and hence

Fourth Amendment protection) vis-a-vis firemen, but rather whether—given the fact that the Fourth Amendment covers private dwellings—intrusion for the purpose of extinguishing a fire is reasonable. Cf. *Michigan v. Tyler,* 436 U.S. 499 (1978). A similar analysis is appropriate here.

I would hold, therefore, that the offices of government employees, and a *fortiori* the drawers and files within those offices, are covered by Fourth Amendment protections as a general matter. (The qualifier is necessary to cover such unusual situations as that in which the office is subject to unrestricted public access, so that it is "expose[d] to the public" and therefore "not a subject of Fourth Amendment protection." *Katz v. United States,* 389 U.S. 347 (1967)). Since it is unquestioned that the office here was assigned to Dr. Ortega, and since no special circumstances are suggested that would call for an exception to the ordinary rule, I would agree with the District Court and the Court of Appeals that Fourth Amendment protections applied.

The case turns, therefore, on whether the Fourth Amendment was violated—*i.e.,* whether the governmental intrusion was reasonable. It is here that the government's status as employer, and the employment-related character of the search, become relevant. While as a general rule warrantless searches are *per se* unreasonable, we have recognized exceptions when "special needs, beyond the normal need for law enforcement, make the warrant and probable cause requirement impracticable. . . ." *New Jersey v. T.L.O.* Such "special needs" are present in the context of government employment. The government, like any other employer, needs frequent and convenient access to its desks, offices, and file cabinets for work-related purposes. I would hold that government searches to retrieve work-related materials or to investigate violations of workplace rules—searches of the sort that are regarded as reasonable and normal in the private-employer context—do not violate the Fourth Amendment.

Justice BLACKMUN, with whom Justice BRENNAN, Justice MARSHALL, and Justice STEVENS join, dissenting.

The facts of this case are simple and straightforward. Dr. Ortega had an expectation of privacy in his office, desk, and file cabinets, which were the target of a search by petitioners that can be characterized only as investigatory in nature. Because there was no "special need," see *New Jersey v. T.L.O.* (1985) (opinion concurring in the judgment), to dispense with the warrant and probable-cause requirements of the Fourth Amendment, I would evaluate the search by applying this traditional standard. Under that standard, this search clearly violated Dr. Ortega's Fourth Amendment rights. . . .

[T]he plurality observes that an appropriate standard of reasonableness to be applied to a public employer's search of the employee's workplace is arrived at from "balancing" the privacy interests of the employee against the public employer's interests justifying the intrusion. Under traditional Fourth Amendment jurisprudence, however, courts abandon the warrant and probable-cause requirements, which constitute the standard of reasonableness for a government search that the Framers established, "[o]nly in those exceptional circumstances in which special needs, beyond the normal need for law enforcement, make the warrant and probable-cause requirement impracticable . . ." *New Jersey v. T.L.O.* (opinion concurring in judgment). . . .

[Here, t]here was no special practical need that might have justified dispensing with the warrant and probable cause requirements. Without sacrificing their ultimate goal of maintaining an effective institution devoted to training and healing, to which the disciplining of Hospital employees contributed, petitioners could have taken any evidence of Dr. Ortega's alleged improprieties to a magistrate in order to obtain a warrant.

Furthermore, this seems to be exactly the kind of situation where a neutral magistrate's involvement would have been helpful in curtailing the infringement upon Dr. Ortega's privacy. . . .

Even were I to accept the proposition that this case presents a situation of "special need" calling for an exception to the warrant and probable-cause standard, I believe that the plurality's balancing of the public employer's and the employee's respective interests to arrive at a different standard is seriously flawed. . . . First, sweeping with a broad brush, the plurality announces a rule that dispenses with the warrant requirement in every public employer's search of an employee's office, desk, or file cabinets because it "would seriously disrupt the routine conduct of business and would be unduly burdensome." The plurality reasons that a government agency could not conduct its work in an efficient manner if an employer needed a warrant for every routine entry into an employee's office in search of a file or correspondence, or for every investigation of suspected employee misconduct. In addition, it argues that the warrant requirement, if imposed on an employer who would be unfamiliar with this procedure, would prove "unwieldy.". . .

The danger in formulating a standard on the basis of "assumed" facts becomes very clear at this stage of the plurality's opinion. Whenever the Court has arrived at a standard of reasonableness other than the warrant and probable cause requirements, it has first found, through analysis of a factual situation, that there is a nexus between this other standard, the employee's privacy interests, and the government purposes to be served by the search. Put another way, the Court adopts a new standard only when it is satisfied that there is no alternative in the particular circumstances. In *Terry v. Ohio* (1968), the Court concluded that, as a practical matter, brief on-the-spot stops of individuals by police officers need not be subject to a warrant. Still concerned, however, with the import of the warrant requirement, which provides the "neutral scrutiny of a judge," the Court weighed in detail the law enforcement and the suspect's interests in the circumstances of the protective search. The resulting standard constituted the equivalent of the warrant: judging the officer's behavior from a reasonable or objective standard. . . .

A careful balancing with respect to the warrant requirement is absent from the plurality's opinion, an absence that is inevitable in light of the gulf between the plurality's analysis and any concrete factual setting. It is certainly correct that a public employer cannot be expected to obtain a warrant for every routine entry into an employee's workplace. This situation, however, should not justify dispensing with a warrant in all searches by the employer. The warrant requirement is perfectly suited for many work-related searches, including the instant one. . . .

By ignoring the specific facts of this case, and by announcing in the abstract a standard as to the reasonableness of an employer's workplace searches, the plurality undermines not only the Fourth Amendment rights of public employees but also any further analysis of the constitutionality of public employer searches.

I respectfully dissent.

National Treasury Employees Union v. Von Raab
489 U.S. 656, 109 S.Ct. 1384 (1989)

Justice Anthony Kennedy discusses the facts in this case, arising from a challenge to the U.S. Customs Service's mandatory drug-testing program, at the outset of his opinion for the Court.

Justice KENNEDY delivers the opinion of the Court.

We granted certiorari to decide whether it violates the Fourth Amendment for the United States Customs Service to require a urinalysis test from employees who seek transfer or promotion to certain positions.

I
A

The United States Customs Service, a bureau of the Department of the Treasury, is the federal agency responsible for processing persons, carriers, cargo, and mail into the United States, collecting revenue from imports, and enforcing customs and related laws.

See Customs USA, Fiscal Year 1985, p. 4. An important responsibility of the Service is the interdiction and seizure of contraband, including illegal drugs. . . . In the routine discharge of their duties, many Customs employees have direct contact with those who traffic in drugs for profit. Drug import operations, often directed by sophisticated criminal syndicates, *United States v. Mendenhall,* 446 U.S. 544 (1980) (POWELL, J., concurring), may be effected by violence or its threat. As a necessary response, many Customs operatives carry and use firearms in connection with their official duties. . . .

In December 1985, respondent, the Commissioner of Customs, established a Drug Screening Task Force to explore the possibility of implementing a drug screening program within the Service. After extensive research and consultation with experts in the field, the Task Force concluded "that drug screening through urinalysis is technologically reliable, valid and accurate." Citing this conclusion, the Commissioner announced his intention to require drug tests of employees who applied for, or occupied, certain positions within the Service. . . .

In May 1986, the Commissioner announced implementation of the drug-testing program. Drug tests were made a condition of placement or employment for positions that meet one or more of three criteria. The first is direct involvement in drug interdiction or enforcement of related laws, an activity the Commissioner deemed fraught with obvious dangers to the mission of the agency and the lives of customs agents. The second criterion is a requirement that the incumbent carry firearms, as the Commissioner concluded that "[p]ublic safety demands that employees who carry deadly arms and are prepared to make instant life or death decisions be drug free." The third criterion is a requirement for the incumbent to handle "classified" material, which the Commissioner determined might fall into the hands of smugglers if accessible to employees who, by reason of their own illegal drug use, are susceptible to bribery or blackmail. . . .

After an employee qualifies for a position covered by the Customs testing program, the Service advises him by letter that his final selection is contingent upon successful completion of drug screening. An independent contractor contacts the employee to fix the time and place for collecting the sample. On reporting for the test, the employee must produce photographic identification and remove any outer garments, such as a coat or a jacket, and personal belongings. The employee may produce the sample behind a partition, or in the privacy of a bathroom stall if he so chooses. To ensure against adulteration of the specimen, or substitution of a sample from another person, a monitor of the same sex as the employee remains close at hand to listen for the normal sounds of urination. Dye is added to the toilet water to prevent the employee from using the water to adulterate the sample. . . .

The laboratory tests the sample for the presence of marijuana, cocaine, opiates, amphetamines, and phencyclidine. Two tests are used. An initial screening test uses the enzyme-multiplied-immunoassay technique (EMIT). Any specimen that is identified as positive on this initial test must then be confirmed using gas chromatography/mass spectrometry (GC/MS). Confirmed positive results are reported to a "Medical Review Officer," "[a] licensed physician . . . who has knowledge of substance abuse disorders and has appropriate medical training to interpret and evaluate the individual's positive test result together with his or her medical history and any other relevant biomedical information." HHS Reg. § 1.2, 53 Fed.Reg. 11980 (1988); HHS Reg. § 2.4(g), *id.*, at 11983. After verifying the positive result, the Medical Review Officer transmits it to the agency.

Customs employees who test positive for drugs and who can offer no satisfactory explanation are subject to dismissal from the Service. Test results may not, however, be turned over to any other agency, including criminal prosecutors, without the employee's written consent.

B

Petitioners, a union of federal employees and a union official, commenced this suit in the United States District Court for the Eastern District of Louisiana on behalf of current Customs Service employees who seek covered positions. Petitioners alleged that the Custom Service drug-testing program violated the Fourth Amendment. The District Court agreed. 649 F.Supp. 380 (1986). . . . The court enjoined the drug testing program, and ordered the Customs Service not to require drug tests of any applicants for covered positions.

A divided panel of the United States Court of Appeals for the Fifth Circuit vacated the injunction. 816 F.2d 170 (1987). The court agreed with petitioners that the drug screening program, by requiring an employee to produce a urine sample for chemical testing, effects a search within the meaning of the Fourth Amendment. . . . [But] the court further found that the Government has a strong interest in detecting drug use among employees who meet the criteria of the Customs program. It reasoned that drug use by covered employees casts substantial doubt on their ability to discharge their duties honestly and vigorously, undermining public confidence in the integrity of the Service and concomitantly impairing the Service's efforts to enforce the drug laws. . . .

We now affirm so much of the judgment of the court of appeals as upheld the testing of employees directly involved in drug interdiction or required to carry firearms. We vacate the judgment to the extent it upheld the testing of applicants for positions

requiring the incumbent to handle classified materials, and remand for further proceedings.

II

. . . We have recognized before that requiring the Government
to procure a warrant for every work-related intrusion "would
conflict with 'the common-sense realization that government offices could not function if every employment decision became a
constitutional matter.'" *O'Connor v. Ortega,* [480 U.S. 709
(1987)]; *New Jersey v. T.L.O.,* [469 U.S. 325 (1985)] (noting that
"[t]he warrant requirement . . . is unsuited to the school environment: requiring a teacher to obtain a warrant before searching
a child suspected of an infraction of school rules (or of the criminal
law) would unduly interfere with the maintenance of the swift
and informal disciplinary procedures needed in the schools").
Even if Customs Service employees are more likely to be familiar
with the procedures required to obtain a warrant than most other
Government workers, requiring a warrant in this context would
serve only to divert valuable agency resources from the Service's
primary mission. The Customs Service has been entrusted with
pressing responsibilities, and its mission would be compromised
if it were required to seek search warrants in connection with
routine, yet sensitive, employment decisions.

Furthermore, a warrant would provide little or nothing in the
way of additional protection of personal privacy. A warrant serves
primarily to advise the citizen that an intrusion is authorized by
law and limited in its permissible scope and to interpose a neutral
magistrate between the citizen and the law enforcement officer
"engaged in the often competitive enterprise of ferreting out
crime." *Johnson v. United States,* 333 U.S. 10 (1948). But in the
present context, "the circumstances justifying toxicological testing
and the permissible limits of such intrusions are defined narrowly
and specifically . . . and doubtless are well known to covered
employees." Under the Customs program, every employee who
seeks a transfer to a covered position knows that he must take a
drug test, and is likewise aware of the procedures the Service
must follow in administering the test. A covered employee is
simply not subject "to the discretion of the official in the field."
Camara v. Municipal Court, 387 U.S. 523 (1967). The process becomes automatic when the employee elects to apply for, and
thereafter pursue, a covered position. Because the Service does
not make a discretionary determination to search based on a
judgment that certain conditions are present, there are simply
"no special facts for a neutral magistrate to evaluate.". . .

Even where it is reasonable to dispense with the warrant requirement in the particular circumstances, a search ordinarily must
be based on probable cause. Our cases teach, however, that the
probable-cause standard "'is peculiarly related to criminal investi-

gations.' " In particular, the traditional probable-cause standard may be unhelpful in analyzing the reasonableness of routine administrative functions especially where the Government seeks to *prevent* the development of hazardous conditions or to detect violations that rarely generate articulable grounds for searching any particular place or person. . . . Our precedents have settled that, in certain limited circumstances, the Government's need to discover such latent or hidden conditions, or to prevent their development, is sufficiently compelling to justify the intrusion on privacy entailed by conducting such searches without any measure of individualized suspicion. We think the Government's need to conduct the suspicionless searches required by the Customs program outweighs the privacy interests of employees engaged directly in drug interdiction, and of those who otherwise are required to carry firearms.

The Customs Service is our Nation's first line of defense against one of the greatest problems affecting the health and welfare of our population. . . .

It is readily apparent that the Government has a compelling interest in ensuring that front-line interdiction personnel are physically fit, and have unimpeachable integrity and judgment. Indeed, the Government's interest here is at least as important as its interest in searching travelers entering the country. We have long held that travelers seeking to enter the country may be stopped and required to submit to a routine search without probable cause, or even founded suspicion, "because of national self protection reasonably requiring one entering the country to identify himself as entitled to come in, and his belongings as effects which may be lawfully brought in." *Carroll v. United States,* 267 U.S. 132 (1925). This national interest in self protection could be irreparably damaged if those charged with safeguarding it were, because of their own drug use, unsympathetic to their mission of interdicting narcotics. A drug user's indifference to the Service's basic mission or, even worse, his active complicity with the malefactors, can facilitate importation of sizable drug shipments or block apprehension of dangerous criminals. The public interest demands effective measures to bar drug users from positions directly involving the interdiction of illegal drugs. . . .

Against these valid public interests we must weigh the interference with individual liberty that results from requiring these classes of employees to undergo a urine test. The interference with individual privacy that results from the collection of a urine sample for subsequent chemical analysis could be substantial in some circumstances. We have recognized, however, that the "operational realities of the workplace" may render entirely reasonable certain work-related intrusions by supervisors and co-workers that might be viewed as unreasonable in other contexts. See *O'Connor v. Ortega.* While these operational realities will rarely affect an employee's expectations of privacy with respect to searches of his person, or of personal effects that the employee may bring to the workplace, is plain that certain forms of public employment may diminish privacy expectations even with respect to such personal searches. . . .

We think Customs employees who are directly involved in the interdiction of illegal drugs or who are required to carry firearms in the line of duty likewise have a diminished expectation of privacy in respect to the intrusions occasioned by a urine test. Unlike most private citizens or government employees in general, employees involved in drug interdiction reasonably should expect effective inquiry into their fitness and probity. Much the same is true of employees who are required to carry firearms. Because successful performance of their duties depends uniquely on their judgment and dexterity, these employees cannot reasonably expect to keep from the Service personal information that bears directly on their fitness. . . . While reasonable tests designed to elicit this information doubtless infringe some privacy expectations, we do not believe these expectations outweigh the Government's compelling interests in safety and in the integrity of our borders. . . .

In sum, we believe the Government has demonstrated that its compelling interests in safeguarding our borders and the public safety outweigh the privacy expectations of employees who seek to be promoted to positions that directly involve the interdiction of illegal drugs or that require the incumbent to carry a firearm. We hold that the testing of these employees is reasonable under the Fourth Amendment.

We are unable, on the present record, to assess the reasonableness of the Government's testing program insofar as it covers employees who are required "to handle classified material.". . . We readily agree that the Government has a compelling interest in protecting truly sensitive information from those who, "under compulsion of circumstances or for other reasons, . . . might compromise [such] information." *Department of the Navy v. Egan*, 484 U.S. 518 (1988). . . .

We also agree that employees who seek promotions to positions where they would handle sensitive information can be required to submit to a urine test under the Service's screening program, especially if the positions covered under this category require background investigations, medical examinations, or other intrusions that may be expected to diminish their expectations of privacy in respect of a urinalysis test. . . .

It is not clear, however, whether the category defined by the Service's testing directive encompasses only those Customs employees likely to gain access to sensitive information. Employees who are tested under the Service's scheme include those holding such diverse positions as "Accountant," "Accounting Technician,"

"Animal Caretaker," "Attorney (All)," "Baggage Clerk," "Co-op Student (All)," "Electric Equipment Repairer," "Mail Clerk/Assistant," and "Messenger." We assume these positions were selected for coverage under the Service's testing program by reason of the incumbent's access to "classified" information, as it is not clear that they would fall under either of the two categories we have already considered. Yet it is not evident that those occupying these positions are likely to gain access to sensitive information, and this apparent discrepancy raises in our minds the question whether the Service has defined this category of employees more broadly than necessary to meet the purposes of the Commissioner's directive.

We cannot resolve this ambiguity on the basis of the record before us, and we think it is appropriate to remand the case to the court of appeals for such proceedings as may be necessary to clarify the scope of this category of employees subject to testing. Upon remand the court of appeals should examine the criteria used by the Service in determining what materials are classified and in deciding whom to test under this rubric. In assessing the reasonableness of requiring tests of these employees, the court should also consider pertinent information bearing upon the employees' privacy expectations, as well as the supervision to which these employees are already subject.

III

Where the Government requires its employees to produce urine samples to be analyzed for evidence of illegal drug use, the collection and subsequent chemical analysis of such samples are searches that must meet the reasonableness requirement of the Fourth Amendment. Because the testing program adopted by the Customs Service is not designed to serve the ordinary needs of law enforcement, we have balanced the public interest in the Service's testing program against the privacy concerns implicated by the tests, without reference to our usual presumption in favor of the procedures specified in the Warrant Clause, to assess whether the tests required by Customs are reasonable.

We hold that the suspicionless testing of employees who apply for promotion to positions directly involving the interdiction of illegal drugs, or to positions which require the incumbent to carry a firearm, is reasonable. The Government's compelling interests in preventing the promotion of drug users to positions where they might endanger the integrity of our Nation's borders or the life of the citizenry outweigh the privacy interests of those who seek promotion to these positions, who enjoy a diminished expectation of privacy by virtue of the special, and obvious, physical and ethical demands of those positions. We do not decide whether testing those who apply for promotion to positions where they would handle "classified" information is reasonable because we find the record inadequate for this purpose.

The judgment of the Court of Appeals for the Fifth Circuit is affirmed in part and vacated in part, and the case is remanded for further proceedings consistent with this opinion.

It is so ordered.

Justice MARSHALL, with whom Justice BRENNAN joins, dissenting.

For the reasons stated in my dissenting opinion in *Skinner v. Railway Labor Executives Association*, [489 U.S. 602 (1989)]. I also dissent from the Court's decision in this case. Here, as in *Skinner*, the Court's abandonment of the Fourth Amendment's express requirement that searches of the person rest on probable cause is unprincipled and unjustifiable. But even if I believed that balancing analysis was appropriate under the Fourth Amendment, I would still dissent from today's judgment, for the reasons stated by Justice SCALIA in his dissenting opinion.

Justice SCALIA, with whom Justice STEVENS joins, dissenting.

The issue in this case is not whether Customs Service employees can constitutionally be denied promotion, or even dismissed, for a single instance of unlawful drug use, at home or at work. They assuredly can. The issue here is what steps can constitutionally be taken to *detect* such drug use. . . .

Until today this Court had upheld a bodily search separate from arrest and without individualized suspicion of wrongdoing only with respect to prison inmates, relying upon the uniquely dangerous nature of that environment. See *Bell v. Wolfish*, 441 U.S. 520 (1979). Today, in *Skinner*, we allow a less intrusive bodily search of railroad employees involved in train accidents. I joined the Court's opinion there because the demonstrated frequency of drug and alcohol use by the targeted class of employees, and the demonstrated connection between such use and grave harm, rendered the search a reasonable means of protecting society. I decline to join the Court's opinion in the present case because neither frequency of use nor connection to harm is demonstrated or even likely. In my view the Customs Service rules are a kind of immolation of privacy and human dignity in symbolic opposition to drug use.

The Fourth Amendment protects the "right of the people to be secure in their persons, houses, papers, and effects, against unreasonable searches and seizures." While there are some absolutes in Fourth Amendment law, as soon as those have been left behind and the question comes down to whether a particular search has been "reasonable," the answer depends largely upon the social necessity that prompts the search. . . .

The Court's opinion in the present case, however, will be searched in vain for real evidence of a real problem that will be solved by urine testing of Customs Service employees. Instead, there are assurances that "[t]he Customs Service is our Nation's first line of defense against one of the greatest problems affecting the health and welfare of our population," that "[m]any of the Service's employees are often exposed to [drug smugglers] and to the controlled substances they seek to smuggle into the country," that "Customs officers have been the targets of bribery by drug smugglers on numerous occasions, and several have been removed from the Service for accepting bribes and other integrity violations.". . .

What is absent in the Government's justifications—notably absent, revealingly absent, and as far as I am concerned dispositively absent—is the recitation of *even a single instance* in which any of the speculated horribles actually occurred: an instance, that is, in which the cause of bribe-taking, or of poor aim, or of unsympathetic law enforcement, or of compromise of classified information, was drug use. . . .

The Court's response to this lack of evidence is that "[t]here is little reason to believe that American workplaces are immune from [the] pervasive social problem" of drug abuse. Perhaps such a generalization would suffice if the workplace at issue could produce such catastrophic social harm that no risk whatever is tolerable—the secured areas of a nuclear power plant, for example. But if such a generalization suffices to justify demeaning bodily searches, without particularized suspicion, to guard against the bribing or blackmailing of a law enforcement agent, or the careless use of a firearm, then the Fourth Amendment has become frail protection indeed. . . .

Today's decision would be wrong, but at least of more limited effect, if its approval of drug testing were confined to that category of employees assigned specifically to drug interdiction duties. Relatively few public employees fit that description. But in extending approval of drug testing to that category consisting of employees who carry firearms, the Court exposes vast numbers of public employees to this needless indignity. . . .

There is only one apparent basis that sets the testing at issue here apart from all these other situations—but it is not a basis upon which the Court is willing to rely. I do not believe for a minute that the driving force behind these drug-testing rules was any of the feeble justifications put forward by counsel here and accepted by the Court. The only plausible explanation, in my view, is what the Commissioner himself offered in the concluding sentence of his memorandum to Customs Service employees announcing the program: "Implementation of the drug screening program would set an important example in our country's struggle with this most serious threat to our national health and security." Or as respondent's brief to this Court asserted: "if a law enforcement agency and its employees do not take the law seriously, neither will the public on which the agency's effectiveness depends." What better way to show that the Government is serious about its "war on drugs" than to subject its employees on the front line of that war to this invasion of their privacy and affront to their dignity? To be sure, there is only a slight chance that it will prevent some serious public harm resulting from Service employee drug use, but it will show to the world that the Service is "clean," and—most important of all—will demonstrate the determination of the Government to eliminate this scourge of our society! I think it obvious that this justification is unacceptable; that the impairment of individual liberties cannot be the means of making a point; that symbolism, even symbolism for so worthy a cause as the abolition of unlawful drugs, cannot validate an otherwise unreasonable search.

Skinner v. Railway Labor Executives' Association
489 U.S. 602, 109 S.Ct. 1402 (1989)

Justice Anthony Kennedy discusses the facts in his opinion for the Court, upholding mandatory blood and urine tests of railroad employees who are involved in train accidents.

Justice KENNEDY delivers the opinion of the Court.

The Federal Railroad Safety Act of 1970 authorizes the Secretary of Transportation to "prescribe, as necessary, appropriate rules, regulations, orders, and standards for all areas of railroad safety." 84 Stat. 971, 45 U.S.C. § 431(a). Finding that alcohol and drug abuse by railroad employees poses a serious threat to safety, the Federal Railroad Administration (FRA) has promulgated regulations that mandate blood and urine tests of employees who are involved in certain train accidents. The FRA also has adopted regulations that do not require, but do authorize, railroads to administer breath and urine tests to employees who violate certain safety rules. The question presented by this case is whether these regulations violate the Fourth Amendment.

The problem of alcohol use on American railroads is as old as the industry itself, and efforts to deter it by carrier rules began at least a century ago. . . .

In July 1983, the FRA expressed concern that these industry efforts were not adequate to curb alcohol and drug abuse by railroad employees. The Agency pointed to evidence indicating that on-the-job intoxication was a significant problem in the railroad industry. The Agency also found, after a review of accident investigation reports, that from 1972 to 1983 "the nation's railroads experienced at least 21 significant train accidents involving alcohol or drug use as a probable cause or contributing factor," and that these accidents "resulted in 25 fatalities, 61 non-fatal injuries, and property damage estimated at $19 million (approximately $27 million in 1982 dollars)." 48 Fed.Reg. 30726 (1983). The FRA further identified "an additional 17 fatalities to operating employees working on or around rail rolling stock that involved alcohol or drugs as a contributing factor.". . .

[The] FRA, in 1985, promulgated regulations addressing the problem of alcohol and drugs on the railroads. The final regulations apply to employees assigned to perform service subject to the Hours of Service Act of 1907, ch. 2939, 34 Stat. 1415, 45 U.S.C. § 61 et seq. The regulations prohibit covered employees from using or possessing alcohol or any controlled substance. 49 CFR § 219.101(a)(1) (1987). The regulations further prohibit those employees from reporting for covered service while under the influence or impaired by alcohol, or while having a blood alcohol concentration of .04 or more, or while under the influence of or impaired by any controlled substance. § 219.101(a)(2). The regulations do not restrict, however, a railroad's authority to impose an absolute prohibition on the presence of alcohol or any drug in the body fluids of persons in its employ. . . . Toxicological testing is required following a "major train accident," which is defined as any train accident that involves (i) a fatality, (ii) the release of hazardous material accompanied by an evacuation or a reportable injury, or (iii) damage to railroad property of $500,000. The railroad has the further duty of collecting blood and urine samples for testing after an "impact accident," which is defined as a collision that results in a reportable injury, or in damage to railroad property of $50,000 or more. § 219.201(a)(2). Finally, the railroad is also obligated to test after "[a]ny train incident that involves a fatality to any on-duty railroad employee." § 219.201(a)(3).

After occurrence of an event which activates its duty to test, the railroad must transport all crew members and other covered employees directly involved in the accident or incident to an independent medical facility, where both blood and urine samples must be obtained from each employee. After the samples have been collected, the railroad is required to ship them by prepaid air freight to the FRA laboratory for analysis. There, the samples are analyzed using "state-of-the-art equipment and techniques" to detect and measure alcohol and drugs. The FRA proposes to place primary reliance on analysis of blood samples, as blood is "the only available body fluid . . . that can provide a clear indication not only of the presence of alcohol and drugs but also their current impairment effects." Urine samples are also necessary, however, because drug traces remain in the urine longer than in blood, and in some cases it will not be possible to transport employees to a medical facility before the time it takes for certain drugs to be eliminated from the bloodstream. In those instances, a "positive urine test, taken with specific information on the pattern of elimination for the particular drug and other information on the behavior of the employee and the circumstances of the accident, may be crucial to the determination of" the cause of an accident. . . .

The regulations require that the FRA notify employees of the results of the tests and afford them an opportunity to respond in writing before preparation of any final investigative report. Employees who refuse to provide required blood or urine samples may not perform covered service for nine months, but they are entitled to a hearing concerning their refusal to take the test. . . .

Subpart D further provides that whenever the results of either breath or urine tests are intended for use in a disciplinary proceeding, the employee must be given the opportunity to provide a blood sample for analysis at an independent medical facility. § 219.303(c). If an employee declines to give a blood sample, the railroad may presume impairment, absent persuasive evidence to the contrary, from a positive showing of controlled substance residues in the urine. The railroad must, however, provide detailed notice of this presumption to its employees, and advise them of their right to provide a contemporaneous blood sample. . . .

We granted the Government's petition for a writ of certiorari, to consider whether the regulations invalidated by the Court of Appeals violate the Fourth Amendment. We now reverse. . . .

Although the Fourth Amendment does not apply to a search or seizure, even an arbitrary one, effected by a private party on his own initiative, the Amendment protects against such intrusions if the private party acted as an instrument or agent of the Government. . . .

The fact that the Government has not compelled a private party to perform a search does not, by itself, establish that the search is a private one. Here, specific features of the regulations combine to convince us that the Government did more than adopt a passive position toward the underlying private conduct. . . .

[W]e are unwilling to accept petitioners' submission that tests conducted by private railroads in reliance on Subpart D will be primarily the result of private initiative. The Government has removed all legal barriers to the testing authorized by Subpart D and indeed has made plain not only its strong preference for testing, but also its desire to share the fruits of such intrusions. In addition, it has mandated that the railroads not bargain away the authority to perform tests granted by Subpart D. These are clear indices of the Government's encouragement, endorsement, and participation, and suffice to implicate the Fourth Amendment. . . .

We have long recognized that a "compelled intrusio[n] into the body for blood to be analyzed for alcohol content" must be deemed a Fourth Amendment search. See *Schmerber v. California,* 384 U.S. 757 (1966). In light of our society's concern for the security of one's person, see, *e.g., Terry v. Ohio,* 392 U.S. 1 (1968), it is obvious that this physical intrusion, penetrating beneath the skin, infringes an expectation of privacy that society is prepared to recognize as reasonable. The ensuing chemical analysis of the sample to obtain physiological data is a further invasion of the tested employee's privacy interests. Much the same is true of the breath-testing procedures required under Subpart D of the regulations. Subjecting a person to a breathalyzer test, which generally requires the production of alveolar or "deep lung" breath for chemical analysis, implicates similar concerns about bodily integrity and, like the blood-alcohol test we considered in *Schmerber,* should also be deemed a search. . . .

Unlike the blood-testing procedure at issue in *Schmerber,* the procedures prescribed by the FRA regulations for collecting and testing urine samples do not entail a surgical intrusion into the body. It is not disputed, however, that chemical analysis of urine, like that of blood, can reveal a host of private medical facts about an employee, including whether she is epileptic, pregnant, or diabetic. Nor can it be disputed that the process of collecting the sample to be tested, which may in some cases involve visual or aural monitoring of the act of urination, itself implicates privacy interests. . . .

In view of our conclusion that the collection and subsequent analysis of the requisite biological samples must be deemed Fourth Amendment searches, we need not characterize the employer's antecedent interference with the employee's freedom of movement as an independent Fourth Amendment seizure. . . .

In most criminal cases, we strike this balance in favor of the procedures described by the Warrant Clause of the Fourth Amendment. . . . We have recognized exceptions to this rule, however, "when 'special needs, beyond the normal need for law enforcement, make the warrant and probable-cause requirement impracticable.' ". . . When faced with such special needs, we have not hesitated to balance the governmental and privacy interests to assess the practicality of the warrant and probable cause requirements in the particular context. . . .

The Government's interest in regulating the conduct of railroad employees to ensure safety, like its supervision of probationers or regulated industries, or its operation of a government office, school, or prison, "likewise presents 'special needs' beyond normal law enforcement that may justify departures from the usual warrant and probable-cause requirements.". . .

The FRA has prescribed toxicological tests, not to assist in the prosecution of employees but rather "to prevent accidents and casualties in railroad operations that result from impairment of employees by alcohol or drugs." 49 CFR § 219.1(a) (1987). This governmental interest in ensuring the safety of the traveling public and of the employees themselves plainly justifies prohibiting covered employees from using alcohol or drugs on duty, or while subject to being called for duty. This interest also "require[s] and justif[ies] the exercise of supervision to assure that the restrictions are in fact observed." The question that remains, then, is whether the Government's need to monitor compliance with these restrictions justifies the privacy intrusions at issue absent a warrant or individualized suspicion. . . .

[I]mposing a warrant requirement in the present context would add little to the assurances of certainty and regularity already afforded by the regulations, while significantly hindering, and in many cases frustrating, the objectives of the Government's testing program. We do not believe that a warrant is essential to render the intrusions here at issue reasonable under the Fourth Amendment.

Our cases indicate that even a search that may be performed without a warrant must be based, as a general matter, on probable cause to believe that the person to be searched has violated the law. When the balance of interests precludes insistence on a showing of probable cause, we have usually required "some quantum of individualized suspicion" before concluding that a search is reasonable. We made it clear, however, that a showing of individualized suspicion is not a constitutional floor, below which a search must be presumed unreasonable. In limited circumstances, where the privacy interests implicated by the search are minimal, and where an important governmental interest furthered by the intrusion would be placed in jeopardy by a requirement of individualized suspicion, a search may be reasonable despite the absence of such suspicion. We believe this is true of the intrusions in question here. . . .

Like breath tests, urine tests are not invasive of the body and, under the regulations, may not be used as an occasion for inquiring into private facts unrelated to alcohol or drug use. We recognize, however, that the procedures for collecting the necessary samples, which require employees to perform an excretory function traditionally shielded by great privacy, raise concerns not implicated by blood or breath tests. While we would not characterize these additional privacy concerns as minimal in most contexts, we note that the regulations endeavor to reduce the intrusiveness of the collection process. The regulations do not require that samples be furnished under the direct observation of a monitor, despite the desirability of such a procedure to ensure the integrity of the sample. The sample is also collected in a medical environment, by personnel unrelated to the railroad employer, and is thus not unlike similar procedures encountered often in the context of a regular physical examination.

More importantly, the expectations of privacy of covered employees are diminished by reason of their participation in an industry that is regulated pervasively to ensure safety, a goal dependent, in substantial part, on the health and fitness of covered employees. . . .

We conclude that the compelling government interests served by the FRA's regulations would be significantly hindered if railroads were required to point to specific facts giving rise to a reasonable suspicion of impairment before testing a given employee. In view of our conclusion that, on the present record, the toxicological testing contemplated by the regulations is not an undue infringement on the justifiable expectations of privacy of covered employees, the Government's compelling interests outweigh privacy concerns.

Justice STEVENS concurred in a separate opinion.

Justice MARSHALL, with whom Justice BRENNAN joins, dissenting.

The issue in this case is not whether declaring a war on illegal drugs is good public policy. The importance of ridding our society of such drugs is, by now, apparent to all. Rather, the issue here is whether the Government's deployment in that war of a particularly draconian weapon—the compulsory collection and chemical testing of railroad workers' blood and urine—comports with the Fourth Amendment. Precisely because the need for action against the drug scourge is manifest, the need for vigilance against unconstitutional excess is great. History teaches that grave threats to liberty often come in times of urgency, when constitutional rights seem too extravagant to endure.

The Court today takes its longest step yet toward reading the probable-cause requirement out of the Fourth Amendment. For the fourth time in as many years, a majority holds that a "special nee[d], beyond the normal need for law enforcement," makes the "requirement" of probable cause "impracticable.". . .

In the four years since this Court, in [New Jersey v.] T.L.O., [469 U.S. 325 (1985)], first began recognizing "special needs" exceptions to the Fourth Amendment, the clarity of Fourth

Amendment doctrine has been badly distorted, as the Court has eclipsed the probable-cause requirement in a patchwork quilt of settings: public school principals' searches of students' belongings, *T.L.O.;* public employers' searches of employees' desks, *O'Connor [v. Ortega,* 480 U.S. 709 (1987)] and probation officers' searches of probationers' homes, *Griffin [v. Wisconsin,* 483 U.S. 868 (1987)]. Tellingly, each time the Court has found that "special needs" counseled ignoring the literal requirements of the Fourth Amendment for such full-scale searches in favor of a formless and unguided "reasonableness" balancing inquiry, it has concluded that the search in question satisfied that test. I have joined dissenting opinions in each of these cases, protesting the "jettison-[ing of] . . . the only standard that finds support in the text of the Fourth Amendment" and predicting that the majority's "Rohrschach-like 'balancing test' " portended "a dangerous weakening of the purpose of the Fourth Amendment to protect the privacy and security of our citizens." *T.L.O.* . . .

In widening the "special needs" exception to probable cause to authorize searches of the human body unsupported by *any* evidence of wrongdoing, the majority today completes the process begun in *T.L.O.* of eliminating altogether the probable-cause requirement for civil searches—those undertaken for reasons "beyond the normal need for law enforcement." In its place, the majority substitutes a manipulable balancing inquiry under which, upon the mere assertion of a "special need," even the deepest dignitary and privacy interests become vulnerable to governmental incursion. By its terms, however, the Fourth Amendment—unlike the Fifth and Sixth—does not confine its protections to either criminal or civil actions. Instead, it protects generally "[t]he right of the people to be secure."

The fact is that the malleable "special needs" balancing approach can be justified only on the basis of the policy results it allows the majority to reach. The majority's concern with the railroad safety problems caused by drug and alcohol abuse is laudable; its cavalier disregard for the text of the Constitution is not. There is no drug exception to the Constitution, any more than there is a communism exception or an exception for other real or imagined sources of domestic unrest. *Coolidge v. New Hampshire,* 403 U.S. 443 (1971). Because abandoning the explicit protections of the Fourth Amendment seriously imperils "the right to be let alone—the most comprehensive of rights and the right most valued by civilized men," *Olmstead v. United States,* 277 U.S. 438 (1928) (BRANDEIS, J., dissenting), I reject the majority's "special needs" rationale as unprincipled and dangerous. . . .

It is no answer to suggest, as does the majority, that railroad workers have relinquished the protection afforded them by this Fourth Amendment requirement, either by "participat[ing] in an industry that is regulated pervasively to ensure safety" or by undergoing periodic fitness tests pursuant to state law or to collective-bargaining agreements. . . .

Our decisions in the regulatory search area refute the suggestion that the heavy regulation of the railroad industry eclipses workers' rights under the Fourth Amendment to insist upon a showing of probable cause when their bodily fluids are being extracted. This line of cases has exclusively involved searches of employer *property,* with respect to which "[c]ertain industries have such a history of government oversight that no reasonable expectation of privacy could exist for a *proprietor* over the *stock* of such an enterprise." *Marshall v. Barlow's, Inc.,* 436 U.S. 307 [1978]. Never have we intimated that regulatory searches reduce employees' rights of privacy in their *persons.* . . .

The majority's suggestion that railroad workers' privacy is only minimally invaded by the collection and testing of their bodily fluids because they undergo periodic fitness tests, is equally baseless. As an initial matter, even if participation in these fitness tests did render "minimal" an employee's "interest in bodily security," such minimally intrusive searches of the person require, under our precedents, a justificatory showing of individualized suspicion. More fundamentally, railroad employees are *not* routinely required to submit to blood or urine tests to gain or to maintain employment, and railroad employers do not ordinarily have access to employees' blood or urine, and certainly not for the purpose of ascertaining drug or alcohol usage. That railroad employees sometimes undergo tests of eyesight, hearing, skill, intelligence, and agility hardly prepares them for Government demands to submit to the extraction of blood, to excrete under supervision, or to have these bodily fluids tested for the physiological and psychological secrets they may contain. Surely employees who release basic information about their financial and personal history so that employers may ascertain their "ethical fitness" do not, by so doing, relinquish their expectations of privacy with respect to their personal letters and diaries, revealing though these papers may be of their character.

I recognize that invalidating the fullscale searches involved in the FRA's testing regime for failure to comport with the Fourth Amendment's command of probable cause may hinder the Government's attempts to make rail transit as safe as humanly possible. But constitutional rights have their consequences, and one is that efforts to maximize the public welfare, no matter how well-intentioned, must always be pursued within constitutional boundaries. Were the police freed from the constraints of the Fourth Amendment for just one day to seek out evidence of criminal wrongdoing, the resulting convictions and incarcerations would probably prevent thousands of fatalities. Our refusal to tolerate this spectre reflects our shared belief that even beneficent governmental power—whether exercised to save money, save lives, or make the trains run on time—must always yield to "a resolute loyalty to constitutional safeguards." *Almeida-Sanchez v. United States*, 413 U.S. 266 (1973). The Constitution demands no less loyalty here. . . .

The majority's trivialization of the intrusions on worker privacy posed by the FRA's testing program is matched at the other extreme by its blind acceptance of the Government's assertion that testing will "dete[r] employees engaged in safety-sensitive tasks from using controlled substances or alcohol," and "help railroads obtain invaluable information about the causes of major accident[s]." With respect, first, to deterrence, it is simply implausible that testing employees *after* major accidents occur, 49 CFR § 219.201(a)(1) (1987), will appreciably discourage them from using drugs or alcohol. As Justice STEVENS observes in his concurring opinion:

> "Most people—and I would think most railroad employees as well—do not go to work with the expectation that they may be involved in a major accident, particularly one causing such catastrophic results as loss of life or the release of hazardous material requiring an evacuation. Moreover, even if they are conscious of the possibilities that such an accident might occur and that alcohol or drug use might be a contributing factor, if the risk of serious personal injury does not deter their use of these substances, it seems highly unlikely that the additional threat of loss of employment would have any effect on their behavior."

Under the majority's deterrence rationale, people who skip school or work to spend a sunny day at the zoo will not taunt the lions because their truancy or absenteeism might be discovered in the event they are mauled. It is, of course, the fear of the accident, not the fear of a postaccident revelation, that deters. The majority's credulous acceptance of the FRA's deterrence rationale is made all the more suspect by the agency's failure to introduce, in an otherwise ample administrative record, *any* studies explaining or supporting its theory of accident deterrence.

The poverty of the majority's deterrence rationale leaves the Government's interest in diagnosing the causes of major accidents as the sole remaining justification for the FRA's testing program. I do not denigrate this interest, but it seems a slender thread from which to hang such an intrusive program, particularly given that the knowledge that one or more workers were impaired at the time of an accident falls far short of proving that substance abuse caused or exacerbated that accident. Some corroborative evidence is needed: witness or coworker accounts of a worker's misfeasance, or at least indications that the cause of the accident was within a worker's area of responsibility. Such particularized facts are, of course, the very essence of the individualized suspicion requirement which the respondent railroad workers urge, and which the Court of Appeals found to "pos[e] no insuperable burden on the government.". . .

In his first dissenting opinion as a Member of this Court, Oliver Wendell Holmes observed:

> "Great cases, like hard cases, make bad law. For great cases are called great, not by reason of their real importance in shaping the law of the future, but because of some accident of immediate overwhelming interest which appeals to the feelings and distorts the judgment. These immediate interests exercise a kind of hydraulic pressure which makes what previously was clear seem doubtful, and before which even well settled principles of law will bend." *Northern Securities Co. v. United States,* 193 U.S. 197 (1904).

A majority of this Court, swept away by society's obsession with stopping the scourge of illegal drugs, today succumbs to the popular pressures described by Justice HOLMES. In upholding the FRA's plan for blood and urine testing, the majority bends time-honored and textually-based principles of the Fourth Amendment—principles the Framers of the Bill of Rights designed to ensure that the Government has a strong and individualized justification when it seeks to invade an individual's privacy. I believe the Framers would be appalled by the vision of mass governmental intrusions upon the integrity of the human body that the majority allows to become reality. The immediate victims of the majority's constitutional timorousness will be those railroad workers whose bodily fluids the Government may now forcibly collect and analyze. But ultimately, today's decision will reduce the privacy all citizens may enjoy, for, as Justice Holmes understood, principles of law, once bent, do not snap back easily. I dissent.

E. WIRETAPPING, BUGGING, AND POLICE SURVEILLANCE

Advances in science and technology often generate controversies that the Framers never envisioned and that challenge established constitutional doctrine. The telephone and radio were such a technological change, for with them came the possibility of eavesdropping on private conversations at great distances. Governmental intrusions by means of wiretapping and other electronic monitoring devices eventually led to a new interpretative approach to the Fourth Amendment.

Fourth Amendment protection for personal privacy was initially discussed in *Boyd v. United States,* 116 U.S. 616 (1886).

When declaring unconstitutional a statute allowing the government to order individuals to produce private papers and invoices as mere evidence of illegally imported goods, the Court laid the basis for a liberal construction of the Fourth Amendment. In *Boyd*, the Court observed that "constitutional provisions for the security of person and property should be liberally construed. A close and literal construction deprives them of half their efficacy, and leads to gradual depreciation of the right." In his opinion for the Court, Justice Joseph Bradley reasoned that individuals have an "indefeasible" right of private property in the common law and under the Fourth Amendment, which renders "unreasonable" any governmental search or seizure of private papers and other property as mere evidence of criminal activities. In an often-quoted passage, he explained that

[t]he principles laid down in *Entrick v. Carrington* [19 Howard State Records 1029 (K.B. 1765), holding general warrants to be illegal] affect the very essence of constitutional liberty and security. They reach farther than the concrete form of the case then before the court, with its adventitious circumstances; they apply to all invasions on the part of the government and its employees of the sanctity of a man's home and the privacies of life. It is not the breaking of his doors, and the rummaging of his drawers, that constitutes the essence of the offence; but it is the invasion of his indefeasible right of personal security, personal liberty and private property, where that right has never been forfeited by his conviction of some public offense,—it is the invasion of this sacred right which underlies and constitutes the essence of Lord Camden's judgment. Breaking into a house and opening boxes and drawers are circumstances of aggravation; but any forcible and compulsory extortion of a man's own testimony or of his private papers to be used as evidence to convict him of crime or to forfeit his goods, is within the condemation of that judgment. In this regard, the Fourth and Fifth Amendments run almost into each other.

Boyd stood as a watershed ruling for not only laying the basis for a liberal construction of Fourth Amendment–protected privacy, but in defining constitutionally protected privacy interests in terms of common law property rights. As a result, the scope of Fourth Amendment protection extended beyond "persons, houses, papers, and effects" to include other "constitutionally protected areas"—business offices,[1] stores,[2] hotel rooms,[3] apartments,[4] automobiles,[5] and taxicabs.[6]

The Court's analysis in *Boyd* and other cases of constitutionally protected areas greatly expanded protection for privacy interests and did so on an objective standard: Individuals' privacy interests were protected against unreasonable searches and seizures in those areas where they had proprietary interests as well. But by linking privacy interests to common law property rights, the Court created an obstacle for dealing with Fourth Amendment challenges to governmental intrusions by means of wiretaps and electronic surveillance. Traditionally, common law recognized no "search" unless there was an actual physical trespass on private property and no "seizure" unless tangible items were taken. Wiretapping, of course, involves neither a physical trespass nor the taking of tangible property.

When first confronted with the issue of wiretapping in *Olmstead v. United States* (1928) (see page 874), the justices split five to four on holding that because the interception of telephone conversations occurs without entry into private premises there is no "search" of a constitutionally protected area, and further that conversations are not things that can be "seized" under the Fourth Amendment. But compare Chief Justice Taft's strict construction and application of the underlying property principles of the Fourth Amendment with the interpretations offered in the dissenting opinions of Justices Pierce Butler and Louis Brandeis. Attempting to combine a strict construction with a liberal application of common law principles, Butler finds proprietary interests in the wire violated by the tap. By contrast, Brandeis advances both a liberal construction and application of the Fourth Amendment in contending that constitutionally protected privacy interests should not be confined to traditional categories of searches involving physical trespass and seizures of tangible materials.

Olmstead stood for almost forty years. For a time, the Court evaded ruling again on the constitutionality of wiretaps by treating the issue as a matter of interpreting the Federal Communications Act of 1934, which prohibited the interception and divulgence of telephone and telegraph communications.[7] In 1942, however, the Court extended *Olmstead*'s trespass theory to the use of detectaphones—devices placed against a wall that detects sounds on the other side. In *Goldman v. United States*, 316 U.S. 129 (1942), federal agents without a warrant entered a suspect's office and planted a dictaphone with wires leading to an office next door, but the next day the dictaphone broke and the agents used a detectaphone instead. The Court held that evidence obtained by the use of detectaphone was admissible because no physical trespass was involved; whereas, evidence gathered from the dictaphone would have been inadmissible.

Although still relying on *Olmstead-Goldman*'s trespass theory in 1961, the Court rejected *Olmstead*'s holding that conversations per se have no Fourth Amendment protection because they are not tangible objects that may be seized. In *Silverman v. United States*, 365 U.S. 505 (1961), federal agents without a warrant drove a "spike mike" into a wall to overhear conversations. They made contact with a heating duct serving the house and, thereby, were able to monitor conversations throughout the house. The mike's penetration of the duct, the Court held, constituted "an actual intrusion of a constitutionally protected area." The Court remained unwilling, though, to overturn *Olmstead.* Writing for the majority, Justice Potter Stewart claimed to "find no occasion to re-examine *Goldman* here, but we decline to go beyond it, by even a fraction of an inch." Concurring Justice Douglas urged abandonment of *Olmstead's* trespass theory of Fourth Amendment protection:

The depth of the penetration of the electronic device—even the degree of its remoteness from the inside of the house—is not the measure of the injury. . . . Our concern should not be with the trivialities of the local law of trespass, as the opinion of the Court indicates. But neither should the command of the Fourth Amendment be limited by nice distinctions turning on the kind of electronic equipment employed. Rather the sole concern should be with whether the privacy of the home is invaded.

Finally, in the landmark ruling *Katz v. United States* (1967) (see page 878), *Olmstead's* trespass theory was overturned. In holding that police must first obtain a warrant before undertaking a wiretap, even of a public telephone, Justice Stewart advanced a new standard for triggering the guarantees of the Fourth Amendment: whether individuals have "reasonable expectations of privacy." Notice that this standard is more subjective than that in *Boyd* and *Olmstead,* which made proprietary rights the basis for defining "constitutionally protected areas" under the Fourth Amendment. For that reason, concurring Justice John Harlan endeavored to clarify and qualify the majority's holding by proposing a two-prong test—"first that a person have exhibited an actual (subjective) expectation of privacy and, second, that the expectation be one that society is prepared to recognize as 'reasonable.' "

Katz's theory of "reasonable expectations of privacy" and Harlan's two-prong test for applying that standard made the reasonableness of searches context dependent. As the Court in *Terry v. Ohio* (1968) (see page 794) observed, "wherever an individual may habor a reasonable 'expectation of privacy,'. . . he is entitled to be free from unreasonable governmental intrusion" but "the specific content and incidents of this right [of privacy] must be shaped by the context in which it is asserted." As a result, the Court faces the task of deciding whether an expectation of privacy is "reasonable" and one "society is prepared to recognize as 'reasonable.' " While the Warren Court tended to expand Fourth Amendment protection along these lines, the more conservative

THE DEVELOPMENT OF LAW
Other Important Rulings on Governmental Wiretapping and Electronic Surveillance

Case	Vote	Ruling
United States v. United States District Court, 407 U.S. 297 (1972)	8:0	Rejects claim of the Nixon administration that there was a national security exception to the requirement that judges approve warrants for wiretaps upon the request of the attorney general, as required by the Omnibus Crime Control and Safe Streets Act (OCCSS Act) of 1968.
United States v. Kahn, 415 U.S. 143 (1974)	6:3	Upheld use of wiretapped evidence, obtained pursuant to a wiretap as authorized by the OCCSS Act, against the wife of a man who was the subject of a warrant for wiretapping.
United States v. Giordano, 416 U.S. 505 (1974)	5:4	Authority for issuing wiretaps under the OCCSS Act cannot be delegated from the attorney general to the assistant attorney general.
United States v. Donovan, 429 U.S. 413 (1977)	6:3	Under the OCCSS Act, police must identify all persons for whom they have probable cause to obtain wiretap warrant, but failure to do so did not trigger suppression of evidence under the statute.
United States v. New York Telephone Company, 434 U.S. 159 (1977)	5:4	OCCSS Act does not cover "pen registers"—devices that record the numbers dialed from a phone.
Scott v. United States, 436 U.S. 128 (1978)	7:2	Upheld wiretapping of all phone calls under a warrant issued pursuant to OCCSS Act.
Dalia v. United States, 441 U.S. 238 (1979)	6:3	No need to obtain separate warrant to make a covert entry to plant an authorized wiretap.
Smith v. Maryland, 442 U.S. 735 (1979)	6:3	Upheld use of pen registers.
United States v. Kaio, 468 U.S. 705 (1984)	6:3	Planting of beepers does not require authorization of search warrant.

Burger and Rehnquist Courts have cut back by narrowing construing "reasonable expectations of privacy" under the Fourth Amendment. In cases like *Santana* (see page 807), warrantless arrests and searches were upheld, despite individuals' being in their homes or areas in which they have proprietary interests, because the Court found no "reasonable expectation of privacy."[8] So too, the Court contracted the scope of Fourth Amendment protection by denying that individuals have reasonable expectations of privacy against warrantless searches of private papers held by their attorneys[9] and bank records.[10] "*Katz* has not eliminated property considerations—ownership, possession, occupancy—but has changed their role from legal touchstones for the Fourth Amendment to standards by which expectations of privacy are evaluated."[11]

California v. Ciraolo (1986) (see page 883) illustrates the Court's analysis in holding that people have no reasonable expectation of privacy against warrantless police surveillance by helicopters. In other rulings, the Court has denied that individuals have Fourth Amendment protected expectations of privacy against police placing beepers on packages being transported[12] and against warrantless searches of their garbage left in containers for collection.[13]

Along with *Katz*, in *Berger v. State of New York*, 388 U.S. 41 (1967), the Court decided the question left unanswered by *Silverman*'s holding that conversations receive Fourth Amendment protection; namely, what constitutes a reasonable search and seizure by electronic eavesdropping. When striking down New York's eavesdropping statute and acknowledging that "eavesdropping involves an intrusion on privacy that is broad in scope," the Court established specific constitutional requirements: police may be authorized by a judge to eavesdrop only on (1) showing probable cause, (2) describing with specificity the object to be seized, (3) giving notice to the subject of the search, and (4) authorization must be for a limited time only, and (5) require that police return to the magistrate the specific items seized.

As to government informants and secret agents, the Court maintains that individuals simply assume the risk that they are dealing with undercover police and that their conversations are being recorded.[14] In *United States v. White*, 401 U.S. 745 (1971), for example, the Court adhered to its *assumption of risk rule* when upholding a conviction based on evidence obtained by an informer who carried an electronic transmitter. Justice White, for the majority, found no constitutionally significant difference between electronically equipped and nonequipped informers, explaining that

[o]ur problem is not what the privacy expectations of particular defendants in particular situations may be or the extent to which they may in fact have relied on the discretion of their companions. Very probably, individual defendants neither know nor suspect that their colleagues have gone or will go to the police or are carrying recorders or transmitters. Otherwise, conversation would cease and our problem with these encounters would be nonexistent or far different from those now before us. Our problem, in terms of the principles announced in *Katz*, is what expectations of privacy are constitutionally "justifiable"—what expectations the Fourth Amendment will protect in the absence of a warrant. So far, the law permits the frustration of actual expectations of privacy by permitting authorities to use the testimony of those associates who for one reason or another have determined to turn to the police, as well as by authorizing the use of informants. . . . If the law gives no protection to the wrongdoer whose trusted accomplice is or becomes a police agent, neither should it protect him when that same agent has recorded or transmitted the conversations which are later offered in evidence to prove the State's case.

But dissenting Justice Harlan countered that the majority "ignored the differences occasioned by third-party monitoring and recording which insures full and accurate disclosure of all that is said," and warned that

[i]t is too easy to forget—and, hence, too often forgotten—that the issue here is whether to interpose a search warrant procedure between law enforcement agencies engaging in electronic eavesdropping and the public generally. By casting its "risk analysis" solely in terms of the expectations and risks that "wrongdoers" or "one contemplating illegal activities" ought to bear, the plurality opinion, I think, misses the mark entirely. . . . Interposition of a warrant requirement is designed not to shield "wrongdoers," but to secure a measure of privacy and a sense of personal security throughout our society.

Justices Marshall and Douglas agreed. In the latter's words:

The issue in this case is clouded and concealed by the very discussion of it in legalistic terms. What the ancients knew as "eavesdropping," we now call "electronic surveillance"; but to equate the two is to treat man's first gun powder on the same level as the nuclear bomb. Electronic surveillance is the greatest leveler of human privacy ever known. How most forms of it can be held "reasonable" within the meaning of the Fourth Amendment is a mystery. To be sure, the Constitution and Bill of Rights are not to be read as covering only the technology known in the 18th century. Otherwise its concept of "commerce" would be hopeless when it comes to the management of modern affairs. At the same time the concepts of privacy which the Founders enshrined in the Fourth Amendment vanish completely when we slavishly allow an all-powerful government, proclaiming law and order, efficiency, and other benign purposes, to penetrate all the walls and doors which men need to shield them from the pressures of a turbulent life around them and give them the health and strength to carry on.

NOTES

1. *Silverthorne Lumber Co. v. United States*, 251 U.S. 385 (1920).
2. *Amos v. United States*, 255 U.S. 313 (1921).
3. *Stoner v. California*, 376 U.S. 483 (1964); *United States v. Jeffers*, 342 U.S. 48 (1951); and *Lustig v. United States*, 338 U.S. 74 (1949).
4. *Jones v. United States*, 362 U.S. 257 (1960).
5. *Henry v. United States*, 361 U.S. 98 (1959).
6. *Rios v. United States*, 364 U.S. 253 (1960).
7. *Nardone v. United States*, 302 U.S. 379 (1937). However, in *Schwartz v. Texas*, 344 U.S. 199 (1952), the Court held, assuming that Congress had not preempted the area of wiretap legislation, that wiretapped evidence could be "divulged" in state courts if obtained by state agents. Five years later the Court nevertheless extended the act to exclude illegally state-gathered wiretap evidence in federal courts. *Benanti v. United States*, 355 U.S. 96 (1957). Finally, in *Lee v. Florida*, 392 U.S. 378 (1968), the Court overturned *Schwartz* when holding that the Act prohibited the admission of state-gathered evidence even in state courts.
8. See *Rakas v. Illinois*, 439 U.S. 128 (1978), holding that passengers in an automobile have no valid Fourth Amendment valims or legitimate expectations of privacy against searches of automobiles or seizures of evidence therein. See also *Brown v. United States*, 411 U.S. 223 (1973).
9. See *United States v. Miller*, 425 U.S. 435 (1976).
10. *California Bankers Association v. Shultz*, 416 U.S. 21 (1974).
11. Comment, "Government Access to Bank Records," 83 *Yale Law Journal* 1461 (1974).
12. *United States v. Knotts*, 460 U.S. 276 (1983).
13. *California v. Greenwood*, 108 S.Ct. 1625 (1988).
14. See *On Lee v. United States*, 343 U.S. 747 (1952); *Hoffa v. United States*, 385 U.S. 293 (1966); *Lewis v. United States*, 385 U.S. 206 (1966); and *Osborn v. United States*, 385 U.S. 323 (1966).

INSIDE THE COURT

Letter from Chief Justice Taft on *Olmstead v. United States*, Holmes, Prohibition, and the Supreme Court

On June 12, 1928, Chief Justice William Howard Taft sent his brother, Horace Taft, the following letter:

> I am interested in what you say as to the comment on our decision and opinion in the wiretapping case. Holmes has written the nastiest opinion in dissent and Brandeis is fuller of eloquence and idealism. Someone sent me an editorial from The World [a newspaper], I think it is. The truth is that Holmes wrote it the other way till Brandeis got after him and induced him to change on the ground that a state law in Washington forbids wiretapping. Holmes in his opinion really admits that the Fourth Amendment does not cover wiretapping. If it does not, then the law is all against his conclusion on which he rests his case, but he is a law unto himself if Brandeis says yes. It has an element of humor for me that the public seemed to be affected by the fact that it is against the bootleggers and assumes that it was that which

carried the day. Of course that had nothing to do with the conclusion. The telephone might just as well have been used to carry on a conspiracy to rob, to murder, to commit treason. The truth is we have to face the problems presented by new inventions. Many of them are most useful to the criminals in their war against society and are at once availed of, and these idealist gentlemen urge a conclusion which facilitates the crime by their use and furnishes immunity from conviction by seeking to bring its use by government officers within the obstruction of the Bill of Rights and the Fourth Amendment. I have a very violent attack on me this morning from Mississippi by someone who only signs Alexander Hamilton and Patrick Henry. I fear he is a bootlegger. I have some supporting letters, but on the whole I look most for condemnation. Holmes says the misdemeanor of the State of Washington is a crime but he does not realise or consider that the admissibility of evidence in the federal courts is determined not by a statute but by the common law. More than this, a large majority of the state supreme courts refuse to follow the *Weeks* case [proclaiming the exclusionary rule, prohibiting the use of illegally obtained evidence in federal courts] decided by our Court as to the inadmissibility of evidence secured in violation of the Fourth Amendment. Chief Judge Cardozo speaking for the Court of Appeals of New York writes an opinion showing that 31 state supreme courts are against it and only 14 for it. They have had in New York a case decided by their Appellate Division following the same principle in which the evidence of the policemen who listened in by wiretapping was held to be admissible although the law of New York forbids wiretapping as a misdemeanor. Of course one does not like to be held up as one who favors the worst morals, but we have to put up with such attacks in our efforts to follow the old time common law recognized by all authorities, English and American, that if evidence is pertinent it is admissible however obtained. Cardozo argues that this view is the proper one in defense of society. We have hard enough time to convict without presenting immunity to worst advanced and progressive criminals. I shall continue to be worried by attacks from all the academic lawyers who write college law journals, but I suppose it is not a basis for impeachment. We pointed out that Congress can change the rule if it sees fit. It will be of interest to see whether Congress will do it. Here it may be that the Prohibitionists in Congress will oppose such legislation not because of their sensitiveness to the scope of the Fourth Amendment but just because they are in favor of convicting bootleggers. Indeed most of the opposing views are due and will be due to that issue solely.

In 1934, Congress passed the Federal Communications Act, prohibiting the interception and divulgence of telephone and telegraph communications.

Source: Oliver Wendell Holmes Papers, Manuscripts Room, Harvard Law School.

Olmstead v. United States
277 U.S. 438, 48 S.Ct. 564 (1928)

Roy Olmstead was indicted and convicted in federal district court of illegally importing and selling liquor in violation of the National Prohibition Act. At his trial, prosecutors introduced incriminating evidence obtained by wiretaps on telephone lines between his home and office. Olmstead challenged the constitutionality of using this evidence on the grounds that it was obtained in violation of the Fourth Amendment guarantee against unreasonable searches and seizures and the Fifth Amendment guarantee against being compelled to testify against oneself. But an appellate court affirmed his conviction, and Olmstead appealed to the Supreme Court.

Chief Justice TAFT delivers the opinion of the Court.

There is no room in the present case for applying the Fifth Amendment, unless the Fourth Amendment was first violated. There was no evidence of compulsion to induce the defendants to talk over their many telephones. They were continually and voluntarily transacting business without knowledge of the interception. Our consideration must be confined to the Fourth Amendment. . . .

The well-known historical purpose of the Fourth Amendment, directed against general warrants and writs of assistance, was to prevent the use of governmental force to search a man's house, his person, his papers, and his effects, and to prevent their seizure against his will. . . .

The amendment itself shows that the search is to be of material things—the person, the house, his papers, or his effects. The description of the warrant necessary to make the proceeding lawful is that it must specify the place to be searched and the person or *things* to be seized. . . .

The amendment does not forbid what was done here. There was no searching. There was no seizure. The evidence was secured by the use of the sense of hearing and that only. There was no entry of the houses or offices of the defendants. . . .

The language of the amendment cannot be extended and expanded to include telephone wires, reaching to the whole world from the defendant's house or office. The intervening wires are not part of his house or office, any more than are the highways along which they are stretched. . . .

Congress may, of course, protect the secrecy of telephone messages by making them, when intercepted, inadmissible in evidence in federal criminal trials, by direct legislation, and thus depart from the common law of evidence. But the courts may not adopt such a policy by attributing an enlarged and unusual meaning to the Fourth Amendment. The reasonable view is that one who installs in his house a telephone instrument with connecting wires intends to project his voice to those quite outside, and that the wires beyond his house, and messages while passing over them, are not within the protection of the Fourth Amendment. Here those who intercepted the projected voices were not in the house of either party to the conversation. . . .

We think, therefore, that the wire tapping here disclosed did not amount to a search or seizure within the meaning of the Fourth Amendment.

Justice BRANDEIS dissenting.

The government makes no attempt to defend the methods employed by its officers. Indeed, it concedes that, if wire tapping can be deemed a search and seizure within the Fourth Amendment, such wire tapping as was practiced in the case at bar was an unreasonable search and seizure, and that the evidence thus obtained was inadmissible. But it relies on the language of the amendment, and it claims that the protection given thereby cannot properly be held to include a telephone conversation. . . .

When the Fourth and Fifth Amendments were adopted, "the form that evil had theretofore taken" had been necessarily simple. Force and violence were then the only means known to man by which a government could directly effect self-incrimination. It could compel the individual to testify—a compulsion effected, if need be, by torture. It could secure possession of his papers and other articles incident to his private life—a seizure effected, if need be, by breaking and entry. Protection against such invasion of "the sanctities of a man's home and the privacies of life" was provided in the Fourth and Fifth Amendments by specific language. *Boyd v. United States,* 116 U.S. 616 [1886]. But "time works changes, brings into existence new conditions and purposes." Subtler and more far-reaching means of invading privacy have become available to the government. Discovery and invention have made it possible for the government, by means far more effective than stretching upon the rack, to obtain disclosure in court of what is whispered in the closet.

Moreover, "in the application of a Constitution, our contemplation cannot be only of what has been, but of what may be." The progress of science in furnishing the government with means of espionage is not likely to stop with wire tapping. Ways may some day be developed by which the government, without removing papers from secret drawers, can reproduce them in court, and by which it will be enabled to expose to a jury the most intimate occurrences of the home. Advances in the psychic and related sciences may bring means of exploring unexpressed beliefs, thoughts and emotions. . . . Can it be that the Constitution affords no protection against such invasions of individual security? . . .

Time and again this court, in giving effect to the principle underlying the Fourth Amendment, has refused to place an unduly literal construction upon it. . . .

The protection guaranteed by the amendments is much broader

in scope. The makers of our Constitution undertook to secure conditions favorable to the pursuit of happiness. They recognized the significance of man's spiritual nature, of his feelings and of his intellect. They knew that only a part of the pain, pleasure and satisfactions of life are to be found in material things. They sought to protect Americans in their beliefs, their thoughts, their emotions and their sensations. They conferred, as against the government, the right to be let alone—the most comprehensive of rights and the right most valued by civilized men. To protect, that right, every unjustifiable intrusion by the government upon the privacy of the individual, whatever the means employed, must be deemed a violation of the Fourth Amendment. And the use, as evidence in a criminal proceeding, of facts ascertained by such intrusion must be deemed a violation of the Fifth.

Applying to the Fourth and Fifth Amendments the established rule of construction, the defendants' objections to the evidence obtained by wire tapping must, in my opinion, be sustained. It is, of course, immaterial where the physical connection with the telephone wires leading into the defendants' premises was made. And it is also immaterial that the intrusion was in aid of law enforcement. Experience should teach us to be most on our guard to protect liberty when the government's purposes are beneficient. Men born to freedom are naturally alert to repel invasion of their liberty by evil-minded rulers. The greatest dangers to liberty lurk in insidious encroachment by men of zeal, well-meaning but without understanding. . . .

Decency, security, and liberty alike demand that government officials shall be subjected to the same rules of conduct that are commands to the citizen. In a government of laws, existence of the government will be imperiled if it fails to observe the law scrupulously. Our government is the potent, the omnipresent teacher. For good or for ill, it teaches the whole people by its example. Crime is contagious. If the government becomes a law-breaker, it breeds contempt for law; it invites every man to become a law unto himself; it invites anarchy. To declare that in the administration of the criminal law the end justifies the means— to declare that the government may commit crimes in order to secure the conviction of a private criminal—would bring terrible retribution. Against that pernicious doctrine this court should resolutely set its face.

Justice HOLMES and Justice STONE dissented.

Justice BUTLER, dissenting.

The single question for consideration is this: May the government, consistently with that clause, have its officers whenever they see fit, tap wires, listen to, take down, and report the private messages and conversations transmitted by telephones? . . .

Telephones are used generally for transmission of messages concerning official, social, business and personal affairs including communications that are private and privileged—those between physician and patient, lawyer and client, parent and child, husband and wife. The contracts between telephone companies and users contemplate the private use of the facilities employed in the service. The communications belong to the parties between whom they pass. During their transmission the exclusive use of the wire belongs to the persons served by it. Wire tapping involves interference with the wire while being used. Tapping the wires and listening in by the officers literally constituted a search for evidence. As the communications passed, they were heard and taken down. . . .

This court has always construed the Constitution in the light of the principles upon which it was founded. The direct operation or literal meaning of the words used do not measure the purpose or scope of its provisions. Under the principles established and applied by this court, the Fourth Amendment safeguards against all evils that are like and equivalent to those embraced within the ordinary meaning of its words. . . .

When the facts in these cases are truly estimated, a fair application of that principle decides the constitutional question in favor of the petitioners. With great deference, I think they should be given a new trial.

Katz v. United States
389 U.S. 347, 88 S.Ct. 507 (1967)

Charles Katz was convicted in federal district court of violating federal law for placing bets and wagers from a public telephone booth in Los Angeles to bookies in Boston and Miami. Federal Bureau of Investigation agents had recorded his conversations with an electronic listening device placed outside the booth, and those recorded conversations were used against him at trial. After a federal appellate court rejected an appeal of his conviction, Katz appealed to the Supreme Court.

Justice STEWART delivers the opinion of the Court.

The petitioner was convicted in the District Court for the Southern District of California under an eight-count indictment charging him with transmitting wagering information by telephone from Los Angeles to Miami and Boston in violation of a federal statute. At trial the Government was permitted, over the petitioner's objection, to introduce evidence of the petitioner's end of telephone conversations, overheard by FBI agents who had attached an electronic listening and recording device to the outside of the public telephone booth from which he had placed his calls. In affirming his conviction, the Court of Appeals rejected the contention that the recordings had been obtained in violation of the Fourth Amendment. . . .

We granted certiorari in order to consider the constitutional questions thus presented.

The petitioner has phrased those questions as follows:

"A. Whether a public telephone booth is a constitutionally protected area so that evidence obtained by attaching an electronic listening recording device to the top of such a booth is obtained in violation of the right to privacy of the user of the booth.

"B. Whether physical penetration of a constitutionally protected area is necessary before a search and seizure can be said to be violative of the Fourth Amendment to the United States Constitution."

We decline to adopt this formulation of the issues. In the first place the correct solution of Fourth Amendment problems is not necessarily promoted by incantation of the phrase "constitutionally protected area." Secondly, the Fourth Amendment cannot be translated into a general constitutional "right to privacy." That Amendment protects individual privacy against certain kinds of governmental intrusion, but its protections go further, and often have nothing to do with privacy at all. Other provisions of the Constitution protect personal privacy from other forms of governmental invasion. But the protection of a person's *general* right to privacy—his right to be let alone by other people—is, like the protection of his property and of his very life, left largely to the law of the individual States.

Because of the misleading way the issues have been formulated, the parties have attached great significance to the characterization of the telephone booth from which the petitioner placed his calls. The petitioner has strenuously argued that the booth was a "constitutionally protected area." The Government has maintained with equal vigor that it was not. But this effort to decide whether or not a given "area," viewed in the abstract, is "constitutionally protected" deflects attention from the problem presented by this case. For the Fourth Amendment protects people, not places. What a person knowingly exposes to the public, even in his own home or office, is not a subject of Fourth Amendment protection. But what he seeks to preserve as private, even in an area accessible to the public, may be constitutionally protected. . . .

The Government stresses the fact that the telephone booth from which the petitioner made his calls was constructed partly of glass, so that he was as visible after he entered it as he would have been if he had remained outside. But what he sought to exclude when he entered the booth was not the intruding eye— it was the uninvited ear. He did not shed his right to do so simply because he made his calls from a place where he might be seen. . . . One who occupies it, shuts the door behind him, and pays the toll that permits him to place a call is surely entitled to assume that the words he utters into the mouthpiece will not be broadcast to the world. To read the Constitution more narrowly is to ignore the vital role that the public telephone has come to play in private communication. . . .

We conclude that the underpinnings of *Olmstead* and *Goldman* have been so eroded by our subsequent decisions that the "trespass" doctrine there enunciated can no longer be regarded as controlling. The Government's activities in electronically listening to and recording the petitioner's words violated the privacy upon which he justifiably relied while using the telephone booth and thus constituted a "search and seizure" within the meaning of the Fourth Amendment. The fact that the electronic device employed to achieve that end did not happen to penetrate the wall of the booth can have no constitutional significance.

The question remaining for decision, then, is whether the search and seizure conducted in this case complied with constitutional standards. In that regard, the Government's position is that its agents acted in an entirely defensible manner: They did not begin their electronic surveillance until investigation of the petitioner's activities had established a strong probability that he was using the telephone in question to transmit gambling information to persons in other States, in violation of federal law. Moreover, the surveillance was limited, both in scope and in duration, to the specific purpose of establishing the contents of the petitioner's unlawful telephonic communications. The agents confined their surveillance to the brief periods during which he used the telephone booth, and they took great care to overhear only the conversations of the petitioner himself. . . .

It is apparent that the agents in this case acted with restraint. Yet the inescapable fact is that this restraint was imposed by the agents themselves, not by a judicial officer. They were not required, before commencing the search to present their estimate of probable cause for detached scrutiny by a neutral magistrate. They were not compelled during the conduct of the search itself, to observe precise limits established in advance by a specific court order. Nor were they directed, after the search had been completed, to notify the authorizing magistrate in detail of all that had been seized. In the absence of such safeguards, this Court has never sustained a search upon the sole ground that officers reasonably expected to find evidence of a particular crime and voluntarily confined their activities to the least intrusive means consistent with that end. . . .

Wherever a man may be, he is entitled to know that he will remain free from unreasonable searches and seizures. The government agents here ignored "the procedure of antecedent justification . . . that is central to the Fourth Amendment," a procedure that we hold to be a constitutional precondition of the kind of electronic surveillance involved in this case. Because the surveillance here failed to meet that condition, and because it led to the petitioner's conviction, the judgment must be reversed.

Justice MARSHALL did not participate in the consideration or decision of this case.

Justice DOUGLAS, with whom Justice BRENNAN joined, concurred in a separate opinion.

Justice WHITE concurred in a separate opinion.

Justice HARLAN concurring.

I join the opinion of the Court, which I read to hold only (a) that an enclosed telephone booth is an area where, like a home, *Weeks v. United States*, 232 U.S. 383 (1914), and unlike a field, *Hester v. United States*, 265 U.S. 57 (1924), a person has a constitutionally protected reasonable expectation of privacy; (b) that electronic as well as physical intrusion into a place that is in this sense private may constitute a violation of the Fourth Amendment; and (c) that the invasion of a constitutionally protected area by federal authorities is, as the Court has long held, presumptively unreasonable in the absence of a search warrant.

As the Court's opinion states, "the Fourth Amendment protects people, not places." The question, however, is what protection it affords to those people. Generally, as here, the answer to that question requires reference to a "place." My understanding of the rule that has emerged from prior decisions is that there is a twofold requirement, first that a person have exhibited an actual (subjective) expectation of privacy and, second, that the expectation be one that society is prepared to recognize as "reasonable." Thus a man's home is, for most purposes, a place where he expects privacy, but objects, activities, or statements that he exposes to the "plain view" of outsiders are not "protected" because no intention to keep them to himself has been exhibited. On the other hand, conversations in the open would not be protected against being overheard, for the expectation of privacy under the circumstances would be unreasonable.

Justice BLACK dissenting.

My basic objection is twofold: (1) I do not believe that the words of the Amendment will bear the meaning given them by today's decision, and (2) I do not believe that it is the proper role of this Court to rewrite the Amendment in order "to bring it into harmony with the times" and thus reach a result that many people believe to be desirable. . . .

The Fourth Amendment says that

> "The right of the people to be secure in their persons, houses, papers, and effects, against unreasonable searches and seizures, shall not be violated, and no Warrants shall issue, but upon probable cause, supported by Oath or affirmation, and particularly describing the place to be searched, and the persons or things to be seized."

The first clause protects "persons, houses, papers, and effects, against unreasonable searches and seizures. . . ." These words connote the idea of tangible things with size, form, and weight, things capable of being searched, seized, or both. The second clause of the Amendment still further establishes its Framers' purpose to limit its protection to tangible things by providing that no warrants shall issue but those "particularly describing the place to be searched, and the persons or things to be seized." A conversation overheard by eavesdropping, whether by plain snooping or wiretapping, is not tangible and, under the normally accepted meanings of the words, can neither be searched nor seized. . . .

Tapping telephone wires, of course, was an unknown possibility at the time the Fourth Amendment was adopted. But eavesdropping (and wiretapping is nothing more than eavesdropping by telephone) was. . . . There can be no doubt that the Framers were aware of this practice, and if they had desired to outlaw or restrict the use of evidence obtained by eavesdropping, I believe that they would have used the appropriate language to do so in the Fourth Amendment. They certainly would not have left such a task to the ingenuity of language-stretching judges.

Since I see no way in which the word of the Fourth Amendment can be construed to apply to eavesdropping, that closes the matter for me. In interpreting the Bill of Rights, I willingly go as far as a liberal construction of the language takes me, but I simply cannot in good conscience give a meaning to words which they have never before been thought to have and which they certainly do not have in common ordinary usage. I will not distort the words of the Amendment in order to "keep the Constitution up to date" or "to bring it into harmony with the times." It was never meant that this Court have such power, which in affect would make us a continuously functioning constitutional convention.

California v. Ciraolo
476 U.S. 207, 106 S.Ct. 1809 (1986).

Chief Justice Warren Burger discusses the facts of this case, involving a warrantless search for marijuana plants by police helicopter, at the outset of his opinion for the Court.

Chief Justice BURGER delivers the opinion of the Court.

We granted certiorari to determine whether the Fourth Amendment is violated by aerial observation without a warrant from an altitude of 1,000 feet of a fenced-in backyard within the curtilage of a home.

I

On September 2, 1982, Santa Clara Police received an anonymous telephone tip that marijuana was growing in respondent's backyard. Police were unable to observe the contents of respondent's yard from ground level because of a 6-foot outer fence and a 10-foot inner fence completely enclosing the yard. Later that day, Officer Shutz, who was assigned to investigate, secured a private plane and flew over respondent's house at an altitude of 1,000 feet, within navigable airspace; he was accompanied by Officer Rodriguez. Both officers were trained in marijuana identification. From the overflight, the officers readily identified marijuana plants 8 feet to 10 feet in height growing in a 15-by-25 foot plot in respondent's yard; they photographed the area with a standard 35mm camera.

On September 8, 1982, Officer Shutz obtained a search warrant on the basis of an affidavit describing the anonymous tip and their observations; a photograph depicting respondent's house, the backyard, and neighboring homes was attached to the affidavit as an exhibit. The warrant was executed the next day and 73 plants were seized; it is not disputed that these were marijuana.

After the trial court denied respondent's motion to suppress the evidence of the search, respondent pleaded guilty to a charge of cultivation of marijuana. The California Court of Appeal reversed, however, on the ground that the warrantless aerial *observation* of respondent's yard which led to the issuance of the warrant violated the Fourth Amendment. That court held first that respondent's backyard marijuana garden was within the "curtilage" of his home, under *Oliver v. United States*, 466 U.S. 170 (1984). The court emphasized that the height and existence of the two fences constituted "objective criteria from which we may conclude he manifested a reasonable expectation of privacy by any standard.". . .

II

The touchstone of Fourth Amendment analysis is whether a person has a "constitutionally protected reasonable expectation of privacy." *Katz v. United States*, 389 U.S. 347 (1967) (HARLAN, J., concurring). *Katz* posits a two-part inquiry: first, has the individual manifested a subjective expectation of privacy in the object of the challenged search? Second, is society willing to recognize that expectation as reasonable?

Clearly—and understandably—respondent has met the test of manifesting his own subjective intent and desire to maintain privacy as to his unlawful agricultural pursuits. . . . It can reasonably be assumed that the 10-foot fence was placed to conceal the marijuana crop from at least street level views. . . .

Yet a 10-foot fence might not shield these plants from the eyes of a citizen or a policeman perched on the top of a truck or a 2-level bus. Whether respondent therefore manifested a subjective expectation of privacy from *all* observations of his backyard, or whether instead he manifested merely a hope that no one would observe his unlawful gardening pursuits, is not entirely clear in these circumstances. . . .

We turn, therefore, to the second inquiry under *Katz*, *i.e.*, whether that expectation is reasonable. In pursuing this inquiry, we must keep in mind that "[t]he test of legitimacy is not whether the individual chooses to conceal assertedly 'private' activity," but instead "whether the government's intrusion infringes upon the personal and societal values protected by the Fourth Amendment.". . .

Respondent argues that because his yard was in the curtilage of his home, no governmental aerial observation is permissible under the Fourth Amendment without a warrant. . . . The protection afforded the curtilage is essentially a protection of families and personal privacy in an area intimately linked to the home, both physically and psychologically, where privacy expectations are most heightened. The claimed area here was immediately adjacent to a suburban home, surrounded by high double fences. This close nexus to the home would appear to encompass this small area within the curtilage. . . .

That the area is within the curtilage does not itself bar all police observation. The Fourth Amendment protection of the home has never been extended to require law enforcement officers to shield their eyes when passing by a home on public thorough-fares. Nor does the mere fact that an individual has taken measures to restrict some views of his activities preclude an officer's observations from a public vantage point where he has a right to be and which renders the activities clearly visible. . . .

The observations by Officers Shutz and Rodriquez in this case took place within public navigable airspace in a physically nonintrusive manner; from this point they were able to observe plants readily discernable to the naked eye as marijuana. That the observation from aircraft was directed at identifying the plants and the officers were trained to recognize marijuana is irrelevant. Such observation is precisely what a judicial officer needs to provide a basis for a warrant. Any member of the public flying in this airspace who glanced down could have seen everything that these officers observed. On this record, we readily conclude that respondent's expectation that his garden was protected from such observation is unreasonable and is not an expectation that society is prepared to honor.

Justice POWELL, with whom Justice BRENNAN, Justice MAR-SHALL, and Justice BLACKMUN join, dissenting.

Concurring in *Katz v. United States*, 389 U.S. 347 (1967), Justice HARLAN warned that any decision to construe the Fourth Amendment as proscribing only physical intrusions by police onto private property "is, in the present day, bad physics as well as bad law, for reasonable expectations of privacy may be defeated by electronic as well as physical invasion." Because the Court today ignores that warning in an opinion that departs significantly from the standard developed in *Katz* for deciding when a Fourth Amendment violation has occurred, I dissent. . . .

The Fourth Amendment protects "[t]he right of the people to be secure in their persons, houses, papers, and effects, against unreasonable searches and seizures." While the familiar history of the Amendment need not be recounted here, we should remember that it reflects a choice that our society should be one in which citizens "dwell in reasonable security and freedom from surveillance.". . . Since that choice was made by the Framers of the Constitution, our cases construing the Fourth Amendment have relied in part on the common law for instruction on "what sorts of searches the Framers . . . regarded as reasonable." But we have repeatedly refused to freeze " 'into constitutional law those enforcement practices that existed at the time of the Fourth Amendment's passage.' " Rather, we have construed the Amendment " 'in light of contemporary norms and conditions,' " in order to prevent "any stealthy encroachments" on our citizens' right to be free of arbitrary official intrusion, *Boyd v. United States*,

116 U.S. 616 (1886). Since the landmark decision in *Katz v. United States,* the Court has fulfilled its duty to protect Fourth Amendment rights by asking if police surveillance has intruded on an individual's reasonable expectation of privacy. . . .

Our decisions following the teaching of *Katz* illustrate that this inquiry "normally embraces two discrete questions." "The first is whether the individual, by his conduct, has 'exhibited an actual (subjective) expectation of privacy.' " The second is whether that subjective expectation "is 'one that society is prepared to recognize as "reasonable." ' ". . .

While the Court today purports to reaffirm this analytical framework, its conclusory rejection of respondent's expectation of privacy in the yard of his residence as one that "is unreasonable," represents a turning away from the principles that have guided our Fourth Amendment inquiry. . . .

The Court begins its analysis of the Fourth Amendment issue posed here by deciding that respondent had an expectation of privacy in his backyard. I agree with that conclusion because of the close proximity of the yard to the house, the nature of some of the activities respondent conducted there, and because he had taken steps to shield those activities from the view of passersby. The Court then implicitly acknowledges that society is prepared to recognize his expectation as reasonable with respect to ground-level surveillance, holding that the yard was within the curtilage, an area in which privacy interests have been afforded the "most heightened" protection. . . . Since Officer Shutz could not see into this private family area from the street, the Court certainly would agree that he would have conducted an unreasonable search had he climbed over the fence, or used a ladder to peer into the yard without first securing a warrant.

The Court concludes, nevertheless, that Shutz could use an airplane—a product of modern technology—to intrude visually into respondent's yard. The Court argues that respondent had no reasonable expectation of privacy from aerial observation. It notes that Shutz was "within public navigable airspace," when he looked into and photographed respondent's yard. It then relies on the fact that the surveillance was not accompanied by a physical invasion of the curtilage. Reliance on the *manner* of surveillance is directly contrary to the standard of *Katz,* which identifies a constitutionally protected privacy right by focusing on the interests of the individual and of a free society. Since *Katz,* we have consistently held that the presence or absence of physical trespass by police is constitutionally irrelevant to the question whether society is prepared to recognize an asserted privacy interest as reasonable. . . .

The Court's holding, therefore, must rest solely on the fact that members of the public fly in planes and may look down at homes as they fly over them. The Court does not explain why it finds this fact to be significant. One may assume that the Court believes that citizens bear the risk that air travelers will observe activities occurring within backyards that are open to the sun and air. This risk, the Court appears to hold, nullifies expectations of privacy in those yards even as to purposeful police surveillance from the air. . . .

This line of reasoning is flawed. First, the actual risk to privacy from commercial or pleasure aircraft is virtually nonexistent. . . . The risk that a passenger on such a plane might observe private activities, and might connect those activities with particular people, is simply too trivial to protect against. It is no accident that, as a matter of common experience, many people build fences around their residential areas, but few build roofs over their backyards. Therefore, contrary to the Court's suggestion, people do not " 'knowingly expos[e]' " their residential yards " 'to the public' " merely by failing to build barriers that prevent aerial surveillance. . . .

The only possible basis for this holding is a judgment that the risk to privacy posed by the remote possibility that a private airplane passenger will notice outdoor activities is equivalent to the risk of official aerial surveillance. But the Court fails to acknowledge the qualitative difference between police surveillance and other uses made of the air space. Members of the public use the air space for travel, business, or pleasure, not for the purpose of observing activities taking place within residential yards. Here, police conducted an overflight at low altitude solely for the purpose of discovering evidence of crime within a private enclave into which they were constitutionally forbidden to intrude at ground level without a warrant. It is not easy to believe that our society is prepared to force individuals to bear the risk of this type of warrantless police intrusion into their residential areas. . . .

[T]his Court recognized long ago that the essence of a Fourth Amendment violation is "not the breaking of [a person's] doors, and the rummaging of his drawers," but rather is "the invasion of his indefeasible right of personal security, personal liberty and private property." Rapidly advancing technology now permits police to conduct surveillance in the home itself, an area where privacy interests are most cherished in our society, without any physical trespass. While the rule in *Katz* was designed to prevent silent and unseen invasions of Fourth Amendment privacy rights in a variety of settings, we have consistently afforded heightened protection to a person's right to be left alone in the privacy of his house. The Court fails to enforce that right or to give any weight to the longstanding presumption that warrantless intrusions into the home are unreasonable. I dissent.

F. THE EXCLUSIONARY RULE

If police do not honor the commands of the Fourth Amendment and make an unreasonable search and seizure, what is to be done? In England and some other countries, illegally obtained evidence may be used against a defendant and are not grounds for appealing a conviction. But he or she has the right to sue for civil damages, or call for criminal proceedings against the officers who violated the law.[1] In *Weeks v. United States*, 232 U.S. 383 (1914), however, the Court adopted the exclusionary rule—prohibiting the admission of illegally seized evidence at trial.

The basis for and application of the exclusionary rule has been a source of continuing controversy. Some justices and scholars defend the rule as a *constitutional principle* essential to the rights guaranteed by the Fourth Amendment.[2] But this rationale has been criticized for "making the tail of the exclusionary rule wag the dog of the Fourth Amendment."[3] Others claim that the rule is simply an *evidentiary rule* that should be limited or eliminated based on considerations of public policy. One policy argument for the exclusionary rule is that it preserves *judicial integrity;* the judiciary's prestige would be damaged if judges were complacent about allowing the use of illegally obtained evidence by prosecutors in convicting defendants for breaking the law.[4] Critics of the constitutional status of the exclusionary rule more often argue that the rule is defensible only if it succeeds in promoting a policy of deterring police from illegal searches and seizures.[5] The *deterrence rationale,* in turn, has generated debate over whether the exclusionary rule indeed deters police, whether it has a direct or indirect effect on police misconduct, and how significant empirical studies are and should be for determining the fate of the exclusionary rule.[6]

Writing for the majority in *Weeks v. United States,* Justice William Day refused to distinguish between the seizure and introduction at trial of illegally obtained evidence, but was ambiguous about whether the exclusionary rule was a constitutional requirement or simply an evidentiary rule that could be expanded or contracted depending on public policy considerations. To allow the use of illegally seized evidence, Day observed, "would be to affirm by judicial decision a manifest neglect if not an open defiance of the prohibitions . . . of the Constitution." And he suggested that the exclusionary rule was essential to the personal rights secured by the Fourth Amendment, observing that without it claims against unreasonable "invasions of the home and privacy of the citizens" would have little practical feasibility; "[i]f letters and private documents can thus be seized and held and used in evidence against a citizen accused of an offense, the protection of the Fourth Amendment declaring his right to be secure against such searches and seizures is of no value, and, so far as those thus placed are concerned, might as well be stricken from the Constitution." Yet Day also noted that the exclusionary rule expressed the Court's disapproval of illegal police conduct and recognition of the need to preserve the integrity of the judicial system. In his words, "The tendency of those who execute the criminal laws of the country to obtain conviction by means of unlawful seizures and enforced confessions . . . should find no sanction in the judgments of the courts . . . charged at all times with the support of the Constitution." As a result of Day's ambiguous opinion, it was debatable whether the exclusionary rule expressed a constitutional principle or simply registered a policy aimed at enhancing judicial integrity and deterring police misconduct.

The status of the exclusionary rule remained problematic thirty-five years later when the Court made the Fourth Amendment but not the exclusionary rule applicable to the states under the Fourteenth Amendment. (For further discussion of federal-state relations and the Court's nationalization of the Bill of Rights, see Chapter 4, in this volume, and Vol. 1, Ch. 7.) In *Wolf v. Colorado*, 338 U.S. 25 (1949), Justice Felix Frankfurter observed that "[t]he security of one's privacy against arbitrary intrusion by the police—which is at the core the Fourth Amendment—is basic to a free society. It is therefore implicit in "the concept of ordered liberty" and as such enforceable against the states through the Due Process Clause." But he held the exclusionary rule to be a nonconstitutional remedy and took a dim view of Justice Day's rationale for the rule, terming it a mere "judicial implication" without foundation in the Fourth Amendment. Likewise, Justice Hugo Black reiterated that the "federal exclusionary rule is not a command of the Fourth Amendment but is a judicially created rule of evidence which Congress might negate."

Wolf's dissenters (Justices Douglas, Murphy, and Rutledge) had quite a different interpretation. They contended that the Fourth Amendment's guarantee of a right of privacy required the exclusion of illegally obtained evidence and that the exclusionary rule was the only means of giving "content to the commands of the Fourth Amendment."

As a consequence of *Wolf*'s holding that the Fourth Amendment but not the exclusionary rule applied to the states, the Court had to decide on a case-by-case basis whether illegal searches and seizures by state police violated the due process clause of the Fourteenth Amendment.[7] In addition, because the exclusionary rule only applied if federal agents were guilty of unlawful searches and seizures, state police who illegally obtained evidence could turn it over on a "silver platter" to federal prosecutors for use in federal courts. The Warren Court finally abandoned what became known as "the silver platter doctrine" in *Elkins v. United States*, 364 U.S. 206 (1960).

In *Elkins*, a bare majority agreed with *Wolf*'s dissenters on the application of the exclusionary rule, but not its underlying rationale. The distinction drawn in *Wolf* between the Fourth Amendment's requirements imposed on the federal government and those of the due process clause of the Fourteenth Amendment imposed on the states was finally eliminated. And the Court held that evidence illegally seized by state police could no longer be turned over to federal agents and used in federal courts. But the majority declined to make the exclusionary rule fully applicable to the states and accepted *Wolf*'s reasoning that "[t]he rule is calculated to prevent, not repair. Its purpose is to deter— to compel respect for the constitutional guaranty in the only effectively available way—by removing the incentive to disregard it."

Two years after *Elkins*, the Warren Court nevertheless held in a landmark ruling in *Mapp v. Ohio* (1961) (see page 895) that the exclusionary rule limits the states as well as the federal government. Notice that Justice Tom Clark's opinion for the majority rationalized the exclusionary rule in terms of constitutional principles, including the right of privacy, as well as the policies of preserving judicial integrity and deterring police misconduct. However, in *Linkletter v. Walker* (see Chapter 2), the Court identified deterrence as the principal rationale for the exclusionary rule, when denying retroactivity to its holding in *Mapp*. There, Justice Clark observed that "[w]e cannot say that this purpose [deterrence] would be advanced by making the rule retrospective. . . . Nor would it add harmony to the delicate state-federal relationship of which we have spoken as part and parcel of the purpose of *Mapp*. Finally, the ruptured privacy of the victim's homes and effects cannot be restored. Reparation comes too late."

Subsequent rulings of Burger and Rehnquist Courts have not only focused on deterrence as the rationale for the rule but on that basis criticized the rule and limited its scope. In *United States v. Calandra*, 414 U.S. 338 (1974), for example, the Court held that the exclusionary rule did not apply to questions asked of a grand jury witness that were based on evidence obtained by an illegal search and seizure of his papers. By divorcing the exclusionary rule from its rationale as a safeguard for Fourth Amendment rights, the rule's role in safeguarding privacy interests diminished. As Justice Powell viewed it in his opinion for the Court: "[T]he rule is a judicially created remedy designed to safeguard Fourth Amendment rights generally through its deterrent effect, rather than a personal constitutional right of the party aggrieved."

The Burger and Rehnquist Courts have cut back on the application of the exclusionary rule in a number of other ways as well. In *United States v. Janis,* 428 U.S. 433 (1976), the Court held that illegally obtained evidence may be used in civil trials; there, in a suit to recover unpaid federal income taxes. And in a sweeping ruling in *Stone v. Powell,* 428 U.S. 465 (1976), the Court ruled that state prisoners may no longer petition for a writ of habeas corpus in federal district courts to review their convictions, when they already have had the opportunity on direct appeal to argue that their Fourth Amendment rights were violated. Writing for the majority, Justice Powell held that the costs of overturning convictions in cases where illegally obtained evidence was used at trial simply outweighed the whatever benefits the exclusionary rule has in deterring police misconduct. And he stressed that the exclusionary rule

deflects the truthfinding process and often frees the guilty. The disparity in particular cases between the error committed by the police and the windfall afforded a guilty defendant by application of the rule is contrary to the idea of proportionality that is essential to the concept of justice. Thus, although the rule is thought to deter unlawful police activity in part through the nurturing of respect for Fourth Amendment values, if applied indiscriminately it may well have the opposite effect of generating disrespect for the law and administration of justice. These long-recognized costs of the rule persist when a criminal conviction is sought to be overturned on collateral review on the ground that a search-and-seizure claim was erroneously rejected by two or more tiers of state courts.

But dissenting Justice Brennan countered,

To sanction disrespect and disregard for the Constitution in the name of protecting society from lawbreakers is to make the government itself lawless and to subvert those values upon which our ultimate freedom and liberty depend. . . . Enforcement of *federal* constitutional rights that redress constitutional violations directed against the "guilty" is a particular function of *federal* habeas review, lest judges trying the "morally unworthy" be tempted not to execute the supreme law of the land. State judges popularly elected may have difficulty resisting popular pressures not experienced by federal judges given lifetime tenure designed to immunize them from such influences, and the federal habeas statutes reflect the Congressional judgment that such detached review is a salutary safeguard against *any* detention of an individual "in violation of the Constitution or laws of the United States."

Although the Burger and Rehnquist Courts have not expressly overturned *Mapp* or abandoned the exclusionary rule, they have been willing to carve out exceptions to the application of the rule. One long-standing exception to the exclusionary rule, however, permits prosecutors to introduce at trial illegally obtained evidence for the purpose of discrediting the defendant's *own* testimony.[8] In *United States v. Havens*, 446 U.S. 620 (1980), the Burger Court expanded this exception to allow prosecutors to use illegally obtained evidence to impeach the testimony during cross-examination of an accomplice called to testify for the defendant. But Justice Brennan commanded a bare majority of the Court in *James v. Illinois*, 110 S.Ct. 648 (1990), barring further expansion of this exception to the exclusionary rule. In this case, Justice Brennan held that the prosecution may not introduce illegally obtained evidence to impeach the testimony of *any* witness called by a defendant. Chief Justice Rehnquist and Justices Kennedy, O'Connor, and Scalia dissented.

In *Nix v. Williams* (1984) (see page 903), the Burger Court upheld an "inevitable discovery" exception to the exclusionary rule. In a companion ruling, *Segura v. United States*, 468 U.S. 796 (1984), the justices split five to four on holding that the exclusionary rule does not prohibit the use of illegally obtained evidence that police would have later found as a result of other independent sources. In still two more 1984 rulings, *United States v. Leon* and *Massachusetts v. Sheppard* (see page 909), the Court legitimated a "good faith" exception to the exclusionary rule. Subsequently, in *Illinois v. Krull*, 480 U.S. 340 (1987), in the view of four dissenters (Justices Brennan, Marshall, Stevens, and O'Connor), the Rehnquist Court extended the good faith exception by holding that the Fourth Amendment does not require the exclusion at trial of evidence found by police acting under a statute authorizing warrantless searches, but that was later struck down as unconstitutional.

NOTES

1. See J. David Hirschel, "What Can We Learn from the English Approach to the Problem of Illegally Obtained Evidence?" 67 *Judicature*

9 (Apr. 1984). In his dissenting opinion in *Bivens v. Six-Unknown Named Agents*, 403 U.S. 388 (1971), Chief Justice Burger urged that the exclusionary rule be abandoned and that in its place a system of tort remedies be established, permitting defendants to sue police for unlawful searches and seizures while allowing illegally obtained evidence to be used.

2. See Thomas S. Schrock and Robert C. Welsh, "Up from Calandra: The Exclusionary Rule as a Constitutional Requirement," 59 *Minnesota Law Review* 251 (1974); and Yale Kamisar, "Does (Did) (Should) the Exclusionary Rule Rest on a 'Principled Basis' Rather Than an 'Empirical Proposition'?" 16 *Creighton Law Review* 565 (1983); and Yale Kamisar, " 'Comparative Reprehensibility' and the Fourth Amendment Exclusionary Rule," 86 *Michigan Law Review* 1 (1987).

3. Anthony Amsterdam, "Perspectives on the Fourth Amendment," 58 *Minnesota Law Review* 369 (1974).

4. See Henry Henderson, "Justice in the Eighties: The Exclusionary Rule and the Principle of Judicial Integrity," 65 *Judicature* 354 (1982).

5. See Dallin Oaks, "Studying the Exclusionary Rule in Search and Seizure," 37 *University of Chicago Law Review* 665 (1970); Stephen Schlesinger, *Exclusionary Injustice: The Problem of Illegally Obtained Evidence* (New York: Dekker, 1977); and Malcolm Wilkey, *Enforcing the Fourth Amendment by Alternatives to the Exclusionary Rule* (Washington, DC: National Legal Center for the Public Interest, 1982).

6. See Stephen Schlesinger, "The Exclusionary Rule: Have Proponents Proven That It Is a Deterrent to Police?" 62 *Judicature* 404 (1979); Bradley Canon, "The Exclusionary Rule: Have Critics Proven That It Doesn't Deter Police?" 62 *Judicature* 398 (1979); Note, "The Exclusionary Rule and Deterrence: An Empirical Study of Chicago Narcotics Officers," 54 *University of Chicago Law Review* 1016 (1987); Note, "On the Limitations of Empirical Evaluations of the Exclusionary Rule," 69 *Northwestern University Law Review* 740 (1974).

7. See *Rochin v. California* (1952), in Chapter 4.

8. See *Walder v. United States*, 347 U.S. 62 (1954).

SELECTED BIBLIOGRAPHY

Amsterdam, Anthony. *Perspectives on the Fourth Amendment*. St. Paul: Minnesota Law Review Foundation, 1974.

Griswold, Erwin. *Search and Seizure*. Lincoln: University of Nebraska, 1975.

Schlesinger, Stephen. *Exclusionary Injustice*. New York: Dekker, 1977.

Wilkey, Malcolm. *Enforcing the Fourth Amendment by Alternatives to the Exclusionary Rule*. Washington, D.C.: National Legal Center for the Public Interest, 1982.

INSIDE THE COURT
Letter from Justice Stewart to Justice Clark
on *Mapp v. Ohio*

Supreme Court of the United States
Washington 25, D. C.

CHAMBERS OF
JUSTICE POTTER STEWART

May 1, 1961

No. 236 - Mapp v. Ohio

Dear Tom,

As I am sure you anticipated, your proposed opinion in this case came as quite a surprise. In all honesty, I seriously question the wisdom of using this case as a vehicle to overrule an important doctrine so recently established and so consistently adhered to. Without getting into the merits, I point out only that the idea of overruling <u>Wolf</u> was urged in the brief and oral argument only by amicus curiae and was not even discussed at the Conference, where we all agreed, as I recollect it, that the judgment should be reversed on First Amendment grounds. If <u>Wolf</u> is to be reconsidered, I myself would much prefer to <u>do</u> so only in a case that required it, and only after argument of the case by competent counsel and a full Conference discussion.

Sincerely yours,

P.S.

[handwritten margin notes:]
C/v of Wolf urged only in amicus - not discussed at Conference - Rev on 1st amend - grounds

If Wolf to be reconsidered shoud be only when required + after argument by competent counsel + full conference dis - cussion -

Mr. Justice Clark

Source: Justice Tom C. Clark Papers, Manuscripts Room, School of Law, University of Texas at Austin.

Mapp v. Ohio
367 U.S. 643, 81 S.Ct. 1684 (1961)

Justice Tom Clark discusses the facts in his opinion for the Court, which made the Fourth Amendment exclusionary rule applicable in state as well as federal courts.

Justice CLARK delivers the opinion of the Court.

Appellant stands convicted of knowingly having had in her possession and under her control certain lewd and lascivious books, pictures, and photographs in violation of § 2905.34 of Ohio's Revised Code. . . .

On May 23, 1957, three Cleveland police officers arrived at appellant's residence in that city pursuant to information that "a person [was] hiding out in the home, who was wanted for questioning in connection with a recent bombing, and that there was a large amount of policy paraphernalia being hidden in the home." Miss Mapp and her daughter by a former marriage lived on the top floor of the two-family dwelling. Upon their arrival at that house, the officers knocked on the door and demanded entrance but appellant, after telephoning her attorney, refused to admit them without a search warrant. They advised their headquarters of the situation and undertook a surveillance of the house.

The officers again sought entrance some three hours later when four or more additional officers arrived on the scene. When Miss Mapp did not come to the door immediately, at least one of the several doors to the house was forcibly opened and the policemen gained admittance. Meanwhile Miss Mapp's attorney arrived, but the officers, having secured their own entry, and continuing in their defiance of the law, would permit him neither to see Miss Mapp nor to enter the house. It appears that Miss Mapp was halfway down the stairs from the upper floor to the front door when the officers, in this highhanded manner, broke into the hall. She demanded to see the search warrant. A paper, claimed to be a warrant, was held up by one of the officers. She grabbed the "warrant" and placed it in her bosom. A struggle ensued in which the officers recovered the piece of paper and as a result of which they handcuffed appellant because she had been "belligerent" in resisting their official rescue of the "warrant" from her person. Running roughshod over appellant, a policeman "grabbed" her, "twisted [her] hand," and she "yelled [and] pleaded with him" because "it was hurting." Appellant, in handcuffs, was then forcibly taken upstairs to her bedroom where the officers searched a dresser, a chest of drawers, a closet and some suitcases.

They also looked into a photo album and through personal papers belonging to the appellant. The search spread to the rest of the second floor including the child's bedroom, the living room, the kitchen and a dinette. The basement of the building and a trunk found therein were also searched. The obscene materials for possession of which she was ultimately convicted were discovered in the course of that widespread search. . . .

The State says that even if the search were made without authority, or otherwise unreasonably, it is not prevented from using the unconstitutionally seized evidence at trial, citing *Wolf v. People of State of Colorado,* [338 U.S. 25], 1949, in which this Court did indeed hold "that in a prosecution in a State court for a State crime the Fourteenth Amendment does not forbid the admission of evidence obtained by an unreasonable search and seizure.". . .

[I]t is urged once again that we review that holding.

I

Seventy-five years ago, in *Boyd v. United States,* [116 U.S. 616], 1886 considering the Fourth and Fifth Amendments as running "almost into each other" on the facts before it, this Court held that the doctrines of those Amendments

"apply to all invasions on the part of the government and its employees of the sanctity of a man's home and the privacies of life. It is not the breaking of his doors, and the rummaging of his drawers, that constitutes the essence of the offence; but it is the invasion of his indefeasible right of personal security, personal liberty and private property. . . . Breaking into a house and opening boxes and drawers are circumstances of aggravation; but any forcible and compulsory extortion of a man's own testimony or of his private papers to be used as evidence to convict him of crime or to forfeit his goods, is within the condemnation . . . [of those Amendments]."

The Court noted that

"constitutional provisions for the security of person and property should be liberally construed. . . . It is the duty of courts to be watchful for the constitutional rights of the citizen, and against any stealthy encroachments thereon.". . .

In this jealous regard for maintaining the integrity of individual rights, the Court gave life to Madison's prediction that "independent tribunals of justice . . . will be naturally led to resist every encroachment upon rights expressly stipulated for in the Constitution by the declaration of rights." I Annals of Cong. 439 (1789). . . .

Less than 30 years after *Boyd,* this Court, in *Weeks v. United States,* [232 U.S. 383], 1914, stated that "the 4th Amendment, . . . put the courts of the United States and Federal officials, in the exercise of their power and authority, under limitations and restraints [and] . . . forever secure[d] the people, their persons, houses, papers, and effects, against all unreasonable searches and seizures under the guise of law . . . and the duty of giving to it force and effect is obligatory upon all entrusted under our Federal system with the enforcement of the laws.". . .

[T]he Court in that case clearly stated that use of the seized evidence involved "a denial of the constitutional rights of the accused." Thus, in the year 1914, in the *Weeks* case, this Court "for the first time" held that "in a federal prosecution the Fourth Amendment barred the use of evidence secured through an illegal search and seizure." This Court has ever since required of federal law officers a strict adherence to that command which this Court has held to be a clear, specific, and constitutionally required—even if judicially implied—deterrent safeguard without insistence upon which the Fourth Amendment would have been reduced to "a form of words.". . .

II

In 1949, 35 years after *Weeks* was announced, this Court, in *Wolf v. People of State of Colorado*, again for the first time, discussed the effect of the Fourth Amendment upon the States through the operation of the Due Process Clause of the Fourteenth Amendment. It said:

"[W]e have no hesitation in saying that were a State affirmatively to sanction such police incursion into privacy it would run counter to the guaranty of the Fourteenth Amendment."

Nevertheless, after declaring that the "security of one's privacy against arbitrary intrusion by the police" is "implicit in 'the concept of ordered liberty' and as such enforceable against the States through the Due Process Clause," cf. *Palko v. State of Connecticut*, [302 U.S. 319], 1937, and announcing that it "stoutly adhere[d]" to the *Weeks* decision, the Court decided that the *Weeks* exclusionary rule would not then be imposed upon the States as "an essential ingredient of the right." The Court's reasons for not considering essential to the right to privacy, as a curb imposed upon the States by the Due Process Clause, that which decades before had been posited as part and parcel of the Fourth Amendment's limitation upon federal encroachment of individual privacy, were bottomed on factual considerations.

While they are not basically relevant to a decision that the exclusionary rule is an essential ingredient of the Fourth Amendment as the right it embodies is vouchsafed against the States by the Due Process Clause, we will consider the current validity of the factual grounds upon which *Wolf* was based.

The Court in *Wolf* first stated that "[t]he contrariety of views of the States" on the adoption of the exclusionary rule of *Weeks* was "particularly impressive," and, in this connection, that it could not "brush aside the experience of States which deem the incidence of such conduct by the police too slight to call for a deterrent remedy . . . by overriding the [States'] relevant rules of evidence." While in 1949, prior to the *Wolf* case, almost two-thirds of the States were opposed to the use of the exclusionary rule, now, despite the *Wolf* case, more than half of those since passing upon it, by their own legislative or judicial decision, have wholly or partly adopted or adhered to the *Weeks* rule. . . . Significantly, among those now following the rule is California, which, according to its highest court, was "compelled to reach that conclusion because other remedies have completely failed to secure compliance with the constitutional provisions. . . ." In connection with this California case, we note that the second basis elaborated in *Wolf* in support of its failure to enforce the exclusionary doctrine against the States was that "other means of protection" have been afforded "the right to privacy." The experience of California that such other remedies have been worthless and futile is buttressed by the experience of other States. . . .

[Notably,] the force of [the] reasoning [in Wolf] has been largely vitiated by later decisions of this Court. These include the recent discarding of the "silver platter" doctrine which allowed federal judicial use of evidence seized in violation of the Constitution by state agents, *Elkins v. United States,* [364 U.S. 206 (1960)], the relaxation of the formerly strict requirements as to standing to challenge the use of evidence thus seized, so that now the procedure of exclusion, "ultimately referable to constitutional safeguards," is available to anyone even "legitimately on [the] premises" unlawfully searched, *Jones v. United States,* [362 U.S. 257], 1960; and finally, the formulation of a method to prevent state use of evidence unconstitutionally seized by federal agents, *Rea v. United States,* [350 U.S. 214], 1956. . . .

It, therefore, plainly appears that the factual considerations supporting the failure of the *Wolf* Court to include the *Weeks* exclusionary rule when it recognized the enforceability of the right to privacy against the States in 1949, while not basically relevant to the constitutional consideration, could not, in any analysis, now be deemed controlling.

III

Today we once again examine *Wolf*'s constitutional documentation of the right to privacy free from unreasonable state intrusion, and, after its dozen years on our books, are led by it to close the only courtroom door remaining open to evidence secured by official lawlessness in flagrant abuse of that basic right, reserved to all persons as a specific guarantee against that very same unlawful conduct. We hold that all evidence obtained by searches and seizures in violation of the Constitution is, by that same authority, inadmissible in a state court.

IV

Since the Fourth Amendment's right of privacy has been declared enforceable against the States through the Due Process Clause of the Fourteenth, it is enforceable against them by the same sanction of exclusion as is used against the Federal Government. Were it otherwise, then just as without the *Weeks* rule the assurance against unreasonable federal searches and seizures would be "a form of words," valueless and undeserving of mention in a perpetual charter of inestimable human liberties, so too, without that rule the freedom from state invasions of privacy would be so ephemeral and so neatly severed from its conceptual nexus with the freedom from all brutish means of coercing evidence as not to merit this Court's high regard as a freedom "implicit in 'the concept of ordered liberty.' " At the time that the Court held in *Wolf* that the Amendment was applicable to the States through the Due Process Clause, the cases of this Court, as we have seen, have steadfastly held that as to federal officers the Fourth Amendment included the exclusion of the evidence seized in violation of its provisions. Even *Wolf* "stoutly adhered" to that proposition. The right to privacy, when conceded operatively enforceable against the States, was not susceptible of destruction by avulsion of the sanction upon which its protection and enjoyment had always been deemed dependent under the *Boyd, Weeks* and *Silverthorne* [*Lumber Co. v. United States,* 251 U.S. 385 (1920)], cases. Therefore, in extending the substantive protections of due process to all constitutionally unreasonable searches—state or federal—it was logically and constitutionally necessary that the exclusion doctrine—an essential part of the right to privacy— be also insisted upon as an essential ingredient of the right newly recognized by the *Wolf* case. In short, the admission of the new constitutional right by *Wolf* could not consistently tolerate denial of its most important constitutional privilege, namely, the exclusion of the evidence which an accused had been forced to give by reason of the unlawful seizure. To hold otherwise is to grant the right but in reality to withhold its privilege and enjoyment. Only last year the Court itself recognized that the purpose of the exclusionary rule "is to deter—to compel respect for the constitutional guarantee in the only effectively available way—by removing the incentive to disregard it in *Elkins v. United States. . . .*

Indeed, we are aware of no restraint, similar to that rejected today conditioning the enforcement of any other basic constitutional right. The right to privacy, no less important than any other right carefully and particularly reserved to the people, would stand in marked contrast to all other rights declared as "basic to a free society." *Wolf v. People of State of Colorado*. This Court has not hesitated to enforce as strictly against the States as it does against the Federal Government the rights of free speech and of a free press, the rights to notice and to a fair, public trial, including, as it does, the right not to be convicted by use of a coerced confession, however logically relevant it be, and without regard to its reliability. And nothing could be more certain than that when a coerced confession is involved, "the relevant rules of evidence" are overridden without regard to "the incidence of such conduct by the police," slight or frequent. Why should not the same rule apply to what is tantamount to coerced testimony by way of unconstitutional seizure of goods, papers, effects, documents, etc.? . . .

V

Moreover, our holding that the exclusionary rule is an essential part of both the Fourth and Fourteenth Amendments is not only the logical dictate of prior cases, but it also makes very good sense. There is no war between the Constitution and common sense. Presently, a federal prosecutor may make no use of evidence illegally seized, but a State's attorney across the street may, although he supposedly is operating under the enforceable prohibitions of the same Amendment. Thus the State, by admitting evidence unlawfully seized, serves to encourage disobedience to the Federal Constitution which it is bound to uphold. . . .

In non-exclusionary States, federal officers, being human, were by it invited to and did, as our cases indicate, step across the street to the State's attorney with their unconstitutionally seized evidence. Prosecution on the basis of that evidence was then had in a state court in utter disregard of the enforceable Fourth Amendment. If the fruits of an unconstitutional search had been inadmissible in both state and federal courts, this inducement to evasion would have been sooner eliminated. . . .

There are those who say, as did Justice (then Judge) CARDOZO, that under our constitutional exclusionary doctrine "[t]he criminal is to go free because the constable has blundered." *People v. Defore,* [242 N.Y. 13 (1926)]. In some cases this will undoubtedly be the result. But, as was said in *Elkins,* "there is another consideration—the imperative of judicial integrity." The criminal goes free, if he must, but it is the law that sets him free. Nothing can destroy a government more quickly than its failure to observe its own laws, or worse, its disregard of the character of its own existence. . . .

The ignoble shortcut to conviction left open to the State tends to destroy the entire system of constitutional restraints on which the liberties of the people rest. Having once recognized that the right to privacy embodied in the Fourth Amendment is enforceable against the States, and that the right to be secure against rude invasions of privacy by state officers is, therefore, constitutional in origin, we can no longer permit that right to remain an empty promise. Because it is enforceable in the same manner and to like effect as other basic rights secured by the Due Process Clause, we can no longer permit it to be revocable at the whim of any police officer who, in the name of law enforcement itself, chooses to suspend its enjoyment. Our decision, founded on reason and truth, gives to the individual no more than that which the Constitution guarantees him, to the police officer no less than that to which honest law enforcement is entitled, and, to the courts, that judicial integrity so necessary in the true administration of justice.

The judgment of the Supreme Court of Ohio is reversed and the cause remanded for further proceedings not inconsistent with this opinion.

Reversed and remanded.

Justice BLACK concurring.

I am still not persuaded that the Fourth Amendment, standing alone, would be enough to bar the introduction into evidence against an accused of papers and effects seized from him in violation of its commands. For the Fourth Amendment does not itself contain any provision expressly precluding the use of such evidence, and I am extremely doubtful that such a provision could properly be inferred from nothing more than the basic command against unreasonable searches and seizures. Reflection on the problem, however, in the light of cases coming before the Court since Wolf, has led me to conclude that when the Fourth Amendment's ban against unreasonable searches and seizures is considered together with the Fifth Amendment's ban against compelled self-incrimination, a constitutional basis emerges which not only justifies but actually requires the exclusionary rule.

Justice DOUGLAS concurred in a separate opinion.

Justice STEWART, memorandum.

I express no view as to the merits of the constitutional issue which the Court today decides. I would, however, reverse the judgment in this case, because I am persuaded that the provision of § 2905.34 of the Ohio Revised Code, upon which the petitioner's conviction was based, is, in the words of Justice HARLAN, not "consistent with the rights of free thought and expression assured against state action by the Fourteenth Amendment."

Justice HARLAN, with whom Justice FRANKFURTER and Justice WHITTAKER join, dissenting.

From the Court's statement of the case one would gather that the central, if not controlling, issue on this appeal is whether illegally state-seized evidence is Constitutionally admissible in a state prosecution, an issue which would of course face us with the need for re-examining *Wolf.* However, such is not the situation. For, although that question was indeed raised here and below among appellant's subordinate points, the new and pivotal issue brought to the Court by this appeal is whether § 2905.34 of the Ohio Revised Code making criminal the *mere* knowing possession or control of obscene material, and under which appellant has been convicted, is consistent with the rights of free thought and expression assured against state action by the Fourteenth Amendment. That was the principal issue which was decided by the Ohio Supreme Court, which was tendered by appellant's Jurisdictional Statement, and which was briefed and argued in this Court.

In this posture of things, I think it fair to say that five members of this Court have simply "reached out" to overrule *Wolf.* With all respect for the views of the majority, and recognizing that *stare decisis* carries different weight in Constitutional adjudication than it does in nonconstitutional decision, I can perceive no justification for regarding this case as an appropriate occasion for re-examining *Wolf.* . . .

I would not impose upon the States this federal exclusionary remedy. The reasons given by the majority for now suddenly turning its back on *Wolf* seem to me notably unconvincing.

First, it is said that "the factual grounds upon which *Wolf* was based" have since changed, in that more States now follow the Weeks exclusionary rule than was so at the time Wolf was decided. While that is true, a recent survey indicates that at present one-half of the States still adhere to the common-law non-exclusionary rule, and one, Maryland, retains the rule as to felonies. But in any case surely all this is beside the point, as the majority itself indeed seems to recognize. Our concern here, as it was in Wolf, is not with the desirability of that rule but only with the question whether the States are Constitutionally free to follow it or not as they may themselves determine, and the relevance of the disparity of views among the States on this point lies simply in the fact that the judgment involved is a debatable one. Moreover, the very fact on which the majority relies, instead of lending support to what is now being done, points away from the need of replacing voluntary state action with federal compulsion.

The preservation of a proper balance between state and federal responsibility in the administration of criminal justice demands patience on the part of those who might like to see things move faster among the States in this respect. Problems of criminal law enforcement vary widely from State to State. . . . For us the question remains, as it has always been, one of state power, not one of passing judgment on the wisdom of one state course or another. In my view this Court should continue to forbear from fettering the States with an adamant rule which may embarrass them in coping with their own peculiar problems in criminal law enforcement. . . .

In conclusion, it should be noted that the majority opinion in this case is in fact an opinion only for the *judgment* overruling *Wolf*, and not for the basic rationale by which four members of the majority have reached that result. For my Brother BLACK is unwilling to subscribe to their view that the Weeks exclusionary rule derives from the Fourth Amendment itself, but joins the majority opinion on the premise that its end result can be achieved by bringing the Fifth Amendment to the aid of the Fourth. . . .*

On that score I need only say that whatever the validity of the "Fourth-Fifth Amendment" correlation which the *Boyd* case found, we have only very recently again reiterated the long-established doctrine of this Court that the Fifth Amendment privilege against self-incrimination is not applicable to the States. . . .

I regret that I find so unwise in principle and so inexpedient in policy a decision motivated by the high purpose of increasing respect for Constitutional rights. But in the last analysis I think this Court can increase respect for the Constitution only if it rigidly respects the limitations which the Constitution places upon it, and respects as well the principles inherent in its own processes. In the present case I think we exceed both, and that our voice becomes only a voice of power, not of reason.

Nix v. Williams

467 U.S. 431, 104 S.Ct. 2501 (1984)

Chief Justice Warren Burger discusses the facts in his opinion for the Court, upholding an inevitable discovery exception to the application of the exclusionary rule.

Chief Justice BURGER delivers the opinion of the Court.

We granted certiorari to consider whether, at respondent Williams' second murder trial in state court, evidence pertaining to the discovery and condition of the victim's body was properly

---

* My Brother STEWART concurs in the Court's judgment on grounds which have nothing to do with *Wolf*.

admitted on the ground that it would ultimately or inevitably have been discovered even if no violation of any constitutional or statutory provision had taken place.

I

A. On December 24, 1968, 10-year-old Pamela Powers disappeared from a YMCA building in Des Moines, Iowa, where she had accompanied her parents to watch an athletic contest. Shortly after she disappeared, Williams was seen leaving the YMCA carrying a large bundle wrapped in a blanket; a 14-year-old boy who had helped Williams open his car door reported that he had seen "two legs in it and they were skinny and white."

Williams' car was found the next day 160 miles east of Des Moines in Davenport, Iowa. Later several items of clothing belonging to the child, some of Williams' clothing, and an army blanket like the one used to wrap the bundle that Williams carried out of the YMCA were found at a rest stop on Interstate 80 near Grinnell, between Des Moines and Davenport. A warrant was issued for Williams' arrest.

Police surmised that Williams had left Pamela Powers or her body somewhere between Des Moines and the Grinnell rest stop where some of the young girl's clothing had been found. On December 26, the Iowa Bureau of Criminal Investigation initiated a large-scale search. . . .

Meanwhile, Williams surrendered to local police in Davenport, where he was promptly arraigned. Williams contacted a Des Moines attorney who arranged for an attorney in Davenport to meet Williams at the Davenport police station. Des Moines police informed counsel they would pick Williams up in Davenport and return him to Des Moines without questioning him. Two Des Moines detectives then drove to Davenport, took Williams into custody, and proceeded to drive him back to Des Moines.

During the return trip, one of the policemen, Detective Leaming, began a conversation with Williams, saying:

"I want to give you something to think about while we're traveling down the road. . . . They are predicting several inches of snow for tonight, and I feel that you yourself are the only person that knows where this little girl's body is . . . and if you get a snow on top of it you yourself may be unable to find it. And since we will be going right past the area [where the body is] on the way into Des Moines, I feel that we could stop and locate the body, that the parents of this little girl should be entitled to a Christian burial for the little girl who was snatched away from them on Christmas [E]ve and murdered. . . . [A]fter a snow storm [we may not be] able to find it at all."

Leaming told Williams he knew the body was in the area of Mitchellville—a town they would be passing on the way to Des Moines. He concluded the conversation by saying "I do not want you to answer me. . . . Just think about it. . . ."

Later, as the police car approached Grinnell, Williams asked Leaming whether the police had found the young girl's shoes. After Leaming replied that he was unsure, Williams directed the police to a point near a service station where he said he had left the shoes; they were not found. As they continued to drive to Des Moines, Williams asked whether the blanket had been found and then directed the officers to a rest area in Grinnell where he said he had disposed of the blanket; they did not find the blanket. At this point Leaming and his party were joined by the officers in charge of the search. As they approached Mitchellville, Williams, without any further conversation, agreed to direct the officers to the child's body.

The officers directing the search had called off the search at 3 P.M., when they left the Grinnell Police Department to join Leaming at the rest area. At that time, one search team near the Jasper County-Polk County line was only two and one-half miles from where Williams soon guided Leaming and his party to the body. The child's body was found next to a culvert in a ditch beside a gravel road in Polk County, about two miles south of Interstate 80, and essentially within the area to be searched.

B. First Trial: In February 1969 Williams was indicted for first-degree murder. Before trial in the Iowa court, his counsel moved to suppress evidence of the body and all related evidence including the condition of the body as shown by the autopsy. The ground for the motion was that such evidence was the "fruit" or product of Williams' statements made during the automobile ride from Davenport to Des Moines and prompted by Leaming's statements. The motion to suppress was denied.

The jury found Williams guilty of first-degree murder; the judgment of conviction was affirmed by the Iowa Supreme Court. Williams then sought release on habeas corpus in the United States District Court for the Southern District of Iowa. That court concluded that the evidence in question had been wrongly admitted at Williams' trial, a divided panel of the Court of Appeals for the Eighth Circuit agreed. . . .

We granted certiorari, and a divided Court affirmed, holding that Detective Leaming had obtained incriminating statements from Williams by what was viewed as interrogation in violation of his right to counsel. *Brewer v. Williams*, 430 U.S. 387 (1977). This Court's opinion noted, however, that although Williams' incriminating statements could not be introduced into evidence at a second trial, evidence of the body's location and condition "might well be admissible on the theory that the body would have been discovered in any event, even had incriminating statements not been elicited from Williams."

C. *Second Trial:* At Williams' second trial in 1977 in the Iowa court, the prosecution did not offer Williams' statements into evidence, nor did it seek to show that Williams had directed the police to the child's body. However, evidence of the condition of her body as it was found, articles and photographs of her clothing, and the results of post mortem medical and chemical tests on the body were admitted. The trial court concluded that the State had proved by a preponderance of the evidence that, if the search had not been suspended and Williams had not led the police to the victim, her body would have been discovered *"within a short time"* in essentially the same condition as it was actually found. . . .

On appeal, the Supreme Court of Iowa again affirmed. That court held that there was in fact a "hypothetical independent source" exception to the exclusionary rule:

"After the defendant has shown unlawful conduct on the part of the police, the State has the burden to show by a preponderance of the evidence that (1) the police did not act in bad faith for the purpose of hastening discovery of the evidence in question, and (2) that the evidence in question would have been discovered by lawful means.". . .

In 1980 Williams renewed his attack on the state-court conviction by seeking a writ of habeas corpus in the United States District Court for the Southern District of Iowa. The District Court conducted its own independent review of the evidence and concluded, as had the state courts, that the body would inevitably have been found by the searchers in essentially the same condition it was in when Williams led police to its discovery. The District Court denied Williams' petition. . . .

The Court of Appeals for the Eighth Circuit reversed. . . .

We granted the State's petition for certiorari, and we reverse.

II

A The Iowa Supreme Court correctly stated that the "vast majority" of all courts, both state and federal, recognize an inevitable discovery exception to the exclusionary rule. We are now urged to adopt and apply the so-called ultimate or inevitable discovery exception to the exclusionary rule. . . .

Williams contends that evidence of the body's location and condition is "fruit of the poisonous tree," *i.e.*, the "fruit" or product of Detective Leaming's plea to help the child's parents give her "a Christian burial," which this Court had already held equated to interrogation. He contends that admitting the challenged evidence violated the Sixth Amendment whether it would have been inevitably discovered or not. Williams also contends that, if the inevitable discovery doctrine is constitutionally permissible, it must include a threshold showing of police good faith.

B The doctrine requiring courts to suppress evidence as the tainted "fruit" of unlawful governmental conduct had its genesis in *Silverthorne Lumber Co. v. United States,* 251 U.S. 385 (1920); there, the Court held that the exclusionary rule applies not only to the illegally obtained evidence itself, but also to other incriminating evidence derived from the primary evidence. . . .

The core rationale consistently advanced by this Court for extending the exclusionary rule to evidence that is the fruit of unlawful police conduct has been that this admittedly drastic and socially costly course is needed to deter police from violations of constitutional and statutory protections. This Court has accepted the argument that the way to ensure such protections is to exclude evidence seized as a result of such violations notwithstanding the high social cost of letting persons obviously guilty go unpunished for their crimes. On this rationale, the prosecution is not to be put in a better position than it would have been in if no illegality had transpired.

By contrast, the derivative evidence analysis ensures that the prosecution is not put in a *worse* position simply because of some earlier police error or misconduct. The independent source doctrine allows admission of evidence that has been discovered by means wholly independent of any constitutional violation. That doctrine, although closely related to the inevitable discovery doctrine, does not apply here; Williams' statements to Leaming indeed led police to the child's body, but that is not the whole story. The independent source doctrine teaches us that the interest of society in deterring unlawful police conduct and the public interest in having juries receive all probative evidence of a crime are properly balanced by putting the police in the same, not a *worse,* position that they would have been in if no police error or misconduct had occurred. When the challenged evidence has an independent source, exclusion of such evidence would put the police in a worse position than they would have been in absent any error or violation. There is a functional similarity between these two doctrines in that exclusion of evidence that would inevitably have been discovered would also put the government in a worse position, because the police would have obtained that evidence if no misconduct had taken place. Thus, while the independent source exception would not justify admission of evidence in this case, its rationale is wholly consistent with and justifies our adoption of the ultimate or inevitable discovery exception to the exclusionary rule. . . .

The requirement that the prosecution must prove the absence of bad faith, imposed here by the Court of Appeals, would place courts in the position of withholding from juries relevant and undoubted truth that would have been available to police absent any unlawful police activity. Of course, that view would put the police in a *worse* position than they would have been in if no unlawful conduct had transpired. And, of equal importance, it wholly fails to take into account the enormous societal cost of excluding truth in the search for truth in the administration of justice. Nothing in this Court's prior holdings supports any such formalistic, pointless, and punitive approach. . . .

Exclusion of physical evidence that would inevitably have been discovered adds nothing to either the integrity or fairness of a criminal trial. The Sixth Amendment right to counsel protects against unfairness by preserving the adversary process in which the reliability of proffered evidence may be tested in cross-examination. Here, however, Detective Leaming's conduct did nothing to impugn the reliability of the evidence in question—the body of the child and its condition as it was found, articles of clothing found on the body, and the autopsy. No one would seriously contend that the presence of counsel in the police car when Leaming appealed to Williams' decent human instincts would have had any bearing on the reliability of the body as evidence. Suppression, in these circumstances, would do nothing whatever to promote the integrity of the trial process, but would inflict a wholly unacceptable burden on the administration of criminal justice. . . .

C On this record it is clear that the search parties were approaching the actual location of the body, and we are satisfied, along with three courts earlier, that the volunteer search teams would have resumed the search had Williams not earlier led the police to the body and the body inevitably would have been found. The evidence asserted by Williams as newly discovered, *i.e.,* certain photographs of the body and deposition testimony of Agent Ruxlow made in connection with the federal habeas proceeding, does not demonstrate that the material facts were inadequately developed in the suppression hearing in state court or that Williams was denied a full, fair, and adequate opportunity to present all relevant facts at the suppression hearing.

The judgment of the Court of Appeals is reversed, and the case is remanded for further proceedings consistent with this opinion.

It is so ordered.

Justice WHITE concurring.

I join fully in the opinion of the Court. I write separately only to point out that many of Justice STEVENS' remarks are beside the point when it is recalled that *Brewer v. Williams,* 430 U.S. 387 (1977), was a 5–4 decision and that four Members of the Court, including myself, were of the view that Detective Leaming had done nothing wrong at all, let alone anything unconstitutional. . . . That five Justices later thought he was mistaken does not call for making him out to be a villain or for a lecture on deliberate police misconduct and its resulting costs to society.

Justice STEVENS concurred.

Justice BRENNAN, with whom Justice MARSHALL joins, dissenting.

I agree that in these circumstances the "inevitable discovery" exception to the exclusionary rule is consistent with the requirements of the Constitution.

In its zealous efforts to emasculate the exclusionary rule, however, the Court loses sight of the crucial difference between the "inevitable discovery" doctrine and the "independent source" exception from which it is derived. When properly applied, the "independent source" exception allows the prosecution to use evidence only if it was, in fact, obtained by fully lawful means. It therefore does no violence to the constitutional protections that the exclusionary rule is meant to enforce. The "inevitable discovery" exception is likewise compatible with the Constitution, though it differs in one key respect from its next of kin: specifically, the evidence sought to be introduced at trial has not actually been obtained from an independent source, but rather would have been discovered as a matter of course if independent investigations were allowed to proceed.

In my view, this distinction should require that the government satisfy a heightened burden of proof before it is allowed to use such evidence. The inevitable discovery exception necessarily implicates a hypothetical finding that differs in kind from the factual finding that precedes application of the independent source rule. To ensure that this hypothetical finding is narrowly confined to circumstances that are functionally equivalent to an independent source, and to protect fully the fundamental rights served by the exclusionary rule, I would require clear and convincing evidence before concluding that the government had met its burden of proof on this issue.

United States v. Leon
468 U.S. 902, 104 S.Ct. 3405 (1984)

and

Massachusetts v. Sheppard
468 U.S. 981, 104 S.Ct. 3424 (1984)

In August 1981, a confidential informant told a police officer in Burbank, California, that two persons he knew as "Armando" and "Patsy" were selling cocaine and methaqualone at their home. The informant gave the police their address but also claimed that they generally kept only small quantities of drugs there, and stored the rest at another location. On the basis of this information, police initiated an extensive investigation focusing on the residence of Armando Sanchez, who had previously been arrested for possessing marijuana, and Patsy Stewart, who had no prior criminal record. Later, two other residences were also staked out.

In the course of the investigation, officers observed a car belonging to Richardo Del Castillo, who had previously been arrested for possessing fifty pounds of marijuana, arrive at Sanchez's house. The driver entered the house and left shortly thereafter carrying a small paper bag. A check of Del Castillo's probation records led police to Alberto Leon. Leon had been arrested in 1980 on drug charges, and one of his companions informed police that Leon was heavily involved with importing drugs into the country. Police in Burbank also learned from police in Glendale, California, that Leon was living in a house on South Sunset Canyon in Burbank.

One day during their surveillance of Sanchez and Stewart, police observed them board separate flights for Miami, Florida, and later return to Los Angeles together. At the airport, Sanchez and Stewart were stopped and agreed to a search of their luggage. A small amount of marijuana was discovered, but they were allowed to leave the airport.

Based on these and other observations, officer Cyril Rombach applied for a warrant to search the residences of Sanchez, Stewart, and Leon for a long list of items related to drug trafficking. A warrant was issued in September 1981 by a judge and the ensuing search produced a large quantity of drugs. All three were indicted by a grand jury and charged with conspiracy to possess and distribute cocaine and other drugs.

Leon and the others filed motions to suppress the evidence seized pursuant to the warrant. A district court judge granted part of their motions to suppress on concluding that the police had failed to establish probable cause in their application for a warrant. In response to a request from the government, the court made clear that Officer Rombach had acted in good faith, but rejected the government's argument that the Fourth Amendment exclusionary rule should not apply where evidence is seized by police who reasonably and in good faith rely on a search warrant.

Subsequently, a divided panel of the Court of Appeals for the Ninth Circuit affirmed, finding that Officer Rombach's affidavit failed to meet the two-prong test for establishing probable cause as required in *Aguilar v. Texas,* 378 U.S. 108 (1964), and *Spinelli v. United States,* 393 U.S. 410 (1969).[*]

The Reagan administration appealed the appellate court's decision and asked the Supreme Court to decide "[w]hether the Fourth Amendment exclusionary rule should be modified so as not to bar the admission of evidence seized in reasonable, good-faith reliance on a search warrant that is subsequently held to be defective."

The Court granted certiorari in this case, along with another, *Massachusetts v. Sheppard,* and upheld the good-faith exception to the exclusionary rule. In the *Massachusetts* case, police relied in good faith on a warrant usually issued for searches for controlled substances, instead of an arrest warrant, when making an arrest. A judge signed the wrong warrant after finding that police had established probable cause in their application, even though they used the wrong application form because their office had run out of (and on Sunday they could not obtain) the proper warrant forms.

Justice Byron White wrote the opinion for the majority in both cases. Only his opinion in *United States v. Leon* appears here. Justice William Brennan's opinion, dissenting in both cases, follows. In a separate opinion Justice John Paul Stevens, dissented in *United States v. Leon* and concurred in *Massachusetts v. Sheppard.*

Justice WHITE delivers the opinion of the Court.

This case presents the question whether the Fourth Amendment exclusionary rule should be modified so as not to bar the use in the prosecution's case in chief of evidence obtained by officers acting in reasonable reliance on a search warrant issued by a detached and neutral magistrate but ultimately found to be unsupported by probable cause. To resolve this question, we must consider once again the tension between the sometimes competing goals of, on the one hand, deterring official misconduct and removing inducements to unreasonable invasions of privacy and, on the other, establishing procedures under which criminal defendants are "acquitted or convicted on the basis of all the evidence which exposes the truth.". . .

The Fourth Amendment contains no provision expressly precluding the use of evidence obtained in violation of its commands, and an examination of its origin and purposes makes clear that the use of fruits of a past unlawful search or seizure "work[s] no new Fourth Amendment wrong." *United States v. Calandra,*

---

[*] But that test and those rulings were later overturned in *Illinois v. Gates,* 462 U.S. 213 (1983), as discussed in section A, of this chapter.

414 U.S. 338 (1974). The wrong condemned by the Amendment is "fully accomplished" by the unlawful search or seizure itself, and the exclusionary rule is neither intended nor able to "cure the invasion of the defendant's rights which he has already suffered." *Stone v. Powell,* [428 U.S. 465 (1976)] (WHITE, J., dissenting). The rule thus operates as "a judicially created remedy designed to safeguard Fourth Amendment rights generally through its deterrent effect, rather than a personal constitutional right of the party aggrieved." *United States v. Calandra. . . .*

The substantial social costs exacted by the exclusionary rule for the vindication of Fourth Amendment rights have long been a source of concern. "Our cases have consistently recognized that unbending application of the exclusionary sanction to enforce ideals of governmental rectitude would impede unacceptably the truth-finding functions of judge and jury." *United States v. Payner,* 447 U.S. 727 (1980). An objectionable collateral consequence of this interference with the criminal justice system's truth-finding function is that some guilty defendants may go free or receive reduced sentences as a result of favorable plea bargains. Particularly when law enforcement officers have acted in objective good faith or their transgressions have been minor, the magnitude of the benefit conferred on such guilty defendants offends basic concepts of the criminal justice system. Indiscriminate application of the exclusionary rule, therefore, may well "generat[e] disrespect for the law and administration of justice." Accordingly, "[a]s with any remedial device, the application of the rule has been restricted to those areas where its remedial objectives are thought most efficaciously served.". . .

Close attention to those remedial objectives has characterized our recent decisions concerning the scope of the Fourth Amendment exclusionary rule. The Court has, to be sure, not seriously questioned, "in the absence of a more efficacious sanction, the continued application of the rule to suppress evidence from the [prosecution's] case where a Fourth Amendment violation has been substantial and deliberate. . . ." *Franks v. Delaware,* 438 U.S. 154 (1978); *Stone v. Powell, supra.* Nevertheless, the balancing approach that has evolved in various contexts—including criminal trials—"forcefully suggest[s] that the exclusionary rule be more generally modified to permit the introduction of evidence obtained in the reasonable good-faith belief that a search or seizure was in accord with the Fourth Amendment." *Illinois v. Gates,* 462 U.S., at 255 . . . (WHITE, J., concurring in judgment). . . .

As yet, we have not recognized any form of good-faith exception to the Fourth Amendment exclusionary rule. But the balancing approach that has evolved during the years of experience with the rule provides strong support for the modification currently urged upon us. As we discuss below, our evaluation of the costs and benefits of suppressing reliable physical evidence seized by officers reasonably relying on a warrant issued by a detached and neutral magistrate leads to the conclusion that such evidence should be admissible in the prosecution's case in chief.

Because a search warrant "provides the detached scrutiny of a neutral magistrate, which is a more reliable safeguard against improper searches than the hurried judgment of a law enforcement officer 'engaged in the often competitive enterprise of ferreting out crime,' " *United States v. Chadwick,* 433 U.S. 1 (1977) (quoting *Johnson v. United States,* 333 U.S. 10 (1948)), we have expressed a strong preference for warrants and declared that "in a doubtful or marginal case a search under a warrant may be sustainable where without one it would fall." *United States v. Ventresca,* 380 U.S. 102 (1965). Reasonable minds frequently may differ on the question whether a particular affidavit establishes probable cause, and we have thus concluded that the preference for warrants is most appropriately effectuated by according "great deference" to a magistrate's determination.

Deference to the magistrate, however, is not boundless. It is clear, first, that the deference accorded to a magistrate's finding of probable cause does not preclude inquiry into the knowing or reckless falsity of the affidavit on which that determination was based. Second, the courts must also insist that the magistrate purport to "perform his 'neutral and detached' function and not serve merely as a rubber stamp for the police." A magistrate failing to "manifest that neutrality and detachment demanded of a judicial officer when presented with a warrant application" and who acts instead as "an adjunct law enforcement officer" cannot provide valid authorization for an otherwise unconstitutional search.

Third, reviewing courts will not defer to a warrant based on an affidavit that does not "provide the magistrate with a substantial basis for determining the existence of probable cause." *Illinois v. Gates.* "Sufficient information must be presented to the magistrate to allow that official to determine probable cause; his action cannot be a mere ratification of the bare conclusions of others." Even if the warrant application was supported by more than a "bare bones" affidavit, a reviewing court may properly conclude that, notwithstanding the deference that magistrates deserve, the warrant was invalid because the magistrate's probable-cause determination reflected an improper analysis of the totality of the circumstances, or because the form of the warrant was improper in some respect.

Only in the first of these three situations, however, has the Court set forth a rationale for suppressing evidence obtained pursuant to a search warrant; in the other areas, it has simply excluded such evidence without considering whether Fourth Amendment interests will be advanced. To the extent that proponents of exclusion rely on its behavioral effects on judges and magistrates in these areas, their reliance is misplaced. First, the exclusionary rule is designed to deter police misconduct rather than to punish the errors of judges and magistrates. Second, there exists no evidence suggesting that judges and magistrates are inclined to ignore or subvert the Fourth Amendment or that lawlessness among these actors requires application of the extreme sanction of exclusion.

Third, and most important, we discern no basis, and are offered none, for believing that exclusion of evidence seized pursuant to a warrant will have a significant deterrent effect on the issuing judge or magistrate. Many of the factors that indicate that the exclusionary rule cannot provide an effective "special" or "general" deterrent for individual offending law enforcement officers apply as well to judges or magistrates. And, to the extent that the rule is thought to operate as a "systemic" deterrent on a wider audience, it clearly can have no such effect on individuals empowered to issue search warrants. Judges and magistrates are not adjuncts to the law enforcement team; as neutral judicial officers, they have no stake in the outcome of particular criminal prosecutions. The threat of exclusion thus cannot be expected significantly to deter them. Imposition of the exclusionary sanction is not necessary meaningfully to inform judicial officers of their errors, and we cannot conclude that admitting evidence obtained pursuant to a warrant while at the same time declaring that the warrant was somehow defective will in any way reduce judicial officers' professional incentives to comply with the Fourth Amendment, encourage them to repeat their mistakes, or lead to the granting of all colorable warrant requests.

If exclusion of evidence obtained pursuant to a subsequently invalidated warrant is to have any deterrent effect, therefore, it must alter the behavior of individual law enforcement officers or the policies of their departments. One could argue that applying the exclusionary rule in cases where the police failed to demonstrate probable cause in the warrant application deters future inadequate presentations or "magistrate shopping" and thus promotes the ends of the Fourth Amendment. Suppressing evidence obtained pursuant to a technically defective warrant supported by probable cause also might encourage officers to scrutinize more closely the form of the warrant and to point out suspected judicial errors. We find such arguments speculative and conclude that suppression of evidence obtained pursuant to a warrant should be ordered only on a case-by-case basis and only in those unusual cases in which exclusion will further the purposes of the exclusionary rule.

We have frequently questioned whether the exclusionary rule can have any deterrent effect when the offending officers acted in the objectively reasonable belief that their conduct did not violate the Fourth Amendment. "No empirical researcher, proponent or opponent of the rule, has yet been able to establish with any assurance whether the rule has a deterrent effect. . . ." *United States v. Janis,* [428 U.S. 433 (1976)]. But even assuming that the rule effectively deters some police misconduct and provides incentives for the law enforcement profession as a whole to conduct itself in accord with the Fourth Amendment, it cannot be expected, and should not be applied, to deter objectively reasonable law enforcement activity. . . .

In short, where the officer's conduct is objectively reasonable, "excluding the evidence will not further the ends of the exclusionary rule in any appreciable way; for it is painfully apparent that . . . the officer is acting as a reasonable officer would and should act in similar circumstances. Excluding the evidence can in no way affect his future conduct unless it is to make him less willing to do his duty." *Stone v. Powell,* (WHITE, J., dissenting).

This is particularly true, we believe, when an officer acting with objective good faith has obtained a search warrant from a judge or magistrate and acted within its scope. In most such cases, there is no police illegality and thus nothing to deter. It is the magistrate's responsibility to determine whether the officer's allegations establish probable cause and, if so, to issue a warrant comporting in form with the requirements of the Fourth Amendment. In the ordinary case, an officer cannot be expected to question the magistrate's probable-cause determination or his judgment that the form of the warrant is technically sufficient. Penalizing the officer for the magistrate's error, rather than his own, cannot logically contribute to the deterrence of Fourth Amendment violations.

We conclude that the marginal or nonexistent benefits produced by suppressing evidence obtained in objectively reasonable reliance on a subsequently invalidated search warrant cannot justify the substantial costs of exclusion. We do not suggest, however, that exclusion is always inappropriate in cases where an officer has obtained a warrant and abided by its terms. . . . [T]he officer's reliance on the magistrate's probable-cause determination and on the technical sufficiency of the warrant he issues must be objectively reasonable, and it is clear that in some circumstances the officer will have no reasonable grounds for believing that the warrant was properly issued.

Suppression therefore remains an appropriate remedy if the magistrate or judge in issuing a warrant was misled by information in an affidavit that the affiant knew was false or would have known was false except for his reckless disregard of the truth. . . . The exception we recognize today will also not apply in cases where the issuing magistrate wholly abandoned his judicial role in the manner condemned in *Lo-Ji Sales, Inc. v. New York,* 442 U.S. 319 (1979); in such circumstances, no reasonably well trained officer should rely on the warrant. Nor would an officer manifest objective good faith in relying on a warrant based on an affidavit "so lacking in indicia of probable cause as to render official belief in its existence entirely unreasonable." Finally, depending on the circumstances of the particular case, a warrant may be so facially deficient—*i.e.*, in failing to particularize the place to be searched or the things to be seized—that the executing officers cannot reasonably presume it to be valid. . . .

In so limiting the suppression remedy, we leave untouched the probable-cause standard and the various requirements for a valid warrant. Other objections to the modification of the Fourth Amendment exclusionary rule we consider to be insubstantial. The good-faith exception for searches conducted pursuant to warrants is not intended to signal our unwillingness strictly to enforce the requirements of the Fourth Amendment, and we do not believe that it will have this effect. As we have already suggested, the good-faith exception, turning as it does on objective reasonableness, should not be difficult to apply in practice. . . .

When the principles we have enunciated today are applied to the facts of this case, it is apparent that the judgment of the Court of Appeals cannot stand. The Court of Appeals applied the prevailing legal standards to Officer Rombach's warrant application and concluded that the application could not support the magistrate's probable-cause determination. In so doing, the court clearly informed the magistrate that he had erred in issuing the challenged warrant. This aspect of the court's judgment is not under attack in this proceeding.

Having determined that the warrant should not have issued, the Court of Appeals understandably declined to adopt a modification of the Fourth Amendment exclusionary rule that this Court had not previously sanctioned. Although the modification finds strong support in our previous cases, the Court of Appeals' commendable self-restraint is not to be criticized. We have now re-examined the purposes of the exclusionary rule and the propriety of its application in cases where officers have relied on a subsequently invalidated search warrant. Our conclusion is that the rule's purposes will only rarely be served by applying it in such circumstances.

In the absence of an allegation that the magistrate abandoned his detached and neutral role, suppression is appropriate only if the officers were dishonest or reckless in preparing their affidavit or could not have harbored an objectively reasonable belief in the existence of probable cause. Only respondent Leon has contended that no reasonably well trained police officer could have believed that there existed probable cause to search his house; significantly, the other respondents advance no comparable argument. Officer Rombach's application for a warrant clearly was supported by much more than a "bare bones" affidavit. The affidavit related the results of an extensive investigation and, as the opinions of the divided panel of the Court of Appeals make clear, provided evidence sufficient to create disagreement among thoughtful and competent judges as to the existence of probable cause. Under these circumstances, the officers' reliance on the magistrate's determination of probable cause was objectively reasonable, and application of the extreme sanction of exclusion is inappropriate.

Accordingly, the judgment of the Court of Appeals is Reversed.

Justice BLACKMUN concurring.

As the Court's opinion in this case makes clear, the Court has narrowed the scope of the exclusionary rule because of an empirical judgment that the rule has little appreciable effect in cases where officers act in objectively reasonable reliance on search warrants. Because I share the view that the exclusionary rule is not a constitutionally compelled corollary of the Fourth Amendment itself, I see no way to avoid making an empirical judgment of this sort, and I am satisfied that the Court has made the correct one on the information before it. Like all courts, we face institutional limitations on our ability to gather information about "legislative facts," and the exclusionary rule itself has exacerbated the shortage of hard data concerning the behavior of police officers in the absence of such a rule. Nonetheless, we cannot escape the responsibility to decide the question before us, however imperfect our information may be, and I am prepared to join the Court on the information now at hand.

What must be stressed, however, is that any empirical judgment about the effect of the exclusionary rule in a particular class of cases necessarily is a provisional one. By their very nature, the assumptions on which we proceed today cannot be cast in stone. To the contrary, they now will be tested in the real world of state and federal law enforcement, and this Court will attend to the results. If it should emerge from experience that, contrary to our expectations, the good-faith exception to the exclusionary rule results in a material change in police compliance with the Fourth Amendment, we shall have to reconsider what we have undertaken here. The logic of a decision that rests on untested predictions about police conduct demands no less.

If a single principle may be drawn from this Court's exclusionary rule decisions, from *Weeks* through *Mapp v. Ohio,* 367 U.S. 643 (1961), to the decisions handed down today, it is that the scope of the exclusionary rule is subject to change in light of changing judicial understanding about the effects of the rule outside the confines of the courtroom. It is incumbent on the Nation's law enforcement officers, who must continue to observe the Fourth Amendment in the wake of today's decisions, to recognize the double-edged nature of that principle.

Justice BRENNAN, with whom Justice MARSHALL joins, dissenting.

Ten years ago in *United States v. Calandra*, 414 U.S. 338 (1974), I expressed the fear that the Court's decision "may signal that a majority of my colleagues have positioned themselves to reopen the door [to evidence secured by official lawlessness] still further and abandon altogether the exclusionary rule in search-and-seizure cases." Since then, in case after case, I have witnessed the Court's gradual but determined strangulation of the rule. It now appears that the Court's victory over the Fourth Amendment is complete. That today's decisions represent the *pièce de résistance* of the Court's past efforts cannot be doubted, for today the Court sanctions the use in the prosecution's case in chief of illegally obtained evidence against the individual whose rights have been violated—a result that had previously been thought to be foreclosed.

The Court seeks to justify this result on the ground that the "costs" of adhering to the exclusionary rule in cases like those before us exceed the "benefits." But the language of deterrence and of cost/benefit analysis, if used indiscriminately, can have a narcotic effect. It creates an illusion of technical precision and ineluctability. It suggests that not only constitutional principle but also empirical data support the majority's result. When the Court's analysis is examined carefully, however, it is clear that we have not been treated to an honest assessment of the merits of the exclusionary rule, but have instead been drawn into a curious world where the "costs" of excluding illegally obtained evidence loom to exaggerated heights and where the "benefits" of such exclusion are made to disappear with a mere wave of the hand.

The majority ignores the fundamental constitutional importance of what is at stake here. While the machinery of law enforcement and indeed the nature of crime itself have changed dramatically since the Fourth Amendment became part of the Nation's fundamental law in 1791, what the Framers understood then remains true today—that the task of combating crime and convicting the guilty will in every era seem of such critical and pressing concern that we may be lured by the temptations of expediency into forsaking our commitment to protecting individual liberty and privacy. It was for that very reason that the Framers of the Bill of Rights insisted that law enforcement efforts be permanently and unambiguously restricted in order to preserve personal freedoms. In the constitutional scheme they ordained, the sometimes unpopular task of ensuring that the government's enforcement efforts remain within the strict boundaries fixed by the Fourth Amendment was entrusted to the courts. . . .

A proper understanding of the broad purposes sought to be served by the Fourth Amendment demonstrates that the principles embodied in the exclusionary rule rest upon a far firmer constitutional foundation than the shifting sands of the Court's deterrence rationale. But even if I were to accept the Court's chosen method of analyzing the question posed by these cases, I would still conclude that the Court's decision cannot be justified. . . .

At bottom, the Court's decision turns on the proposition that the exclusionary rule is merely a " 'judicially created remedy designed to safeguard Fourth Amendment rights generally through its deterrent effect, rather than a personal constitutional right. . . .

The essence of this view, as expressed initially in the *Calandra* opinion and as reiterated today, is that the sole "purpose of the Fourth Amendment is to prevent unreasonable governmental intrusions into the privacy of one's person, house, papers, or effects. The wrong condemned is the unjustified governmental invasion of these areas of an individual's life. That wrong . . . is *fully accomplished* by the original search without probable cause." (emphasis added). This reading of the Amendment implies that its proscriptions are directed solely at those government agents who may actually invade an individual's constitutionally protected privacy. The courts are not subject to any direct constitutional duty to exclude illegally obtained evidence, because the question of the admissibility of such evidence is not addressed by the Amendment. This view of the scope of the Amendment relegates the judiciary to the periphery. Because the only constitutionally cognizable injury has already been "fully accomplished" by the police by the time a case comes before the courts, the Constitution is not itself violated if the judge decides to admit the tainted evidence. Indeed, the most the judge *can* do is wring his hands and hope that perhaps by excluding such evidence he can deter future transgressions by the police.

Such a reading appears plausible, because, as critics of the exclusionary rule never tire of repeating, the Fourth Amendment makes no express provision for the exclusion of evidence secured in violation of its commands. A short answer to this claim, of course, is that many of the Constitution's most vital imperatives are stated in general terms and the task of giving meaning to these precepts is therefore left to subsequent judicial decisionmaking in the context of concrete cases. . . .

A more direct answer may be supplied by recognizing that the Amendment, like other provisions of the Bill of Rights, restrains the power of the government as a whole; it does not specify only a particular agency and exempt all others. The judiciary is responsible, no less than the executive, for ensuring that constitutional rights are respected.

When that fact is kept in mind, the role of the courts and their possible involvement in the concerns of the Fourth Amendment comes into sharper focus. Because seizures are executed principally to secure evidence, and because such evidence generally has utility in our legal system only in the context of a trial supervised by a judge, it is apparent that the admission of illegally obtained evidence implicates the same constitutional concerns as the initial seizure of that evidence. Indeed, by admitting unlawfully seized evidence, the judiciary becomes a part of what is in fact a single governmental action prohibited by the terms of the Amendment. Once that connection between the evidence-gathering role of the police and the evidence-admitting function of the courts is acknowledged, the plausibility of the Court's interpretation becomes more suspect. Certainly nothing in the language or history of the Fourth Amendment suggests that a recognition of this evidentiary link between the police and the courts was meant to be foreclosed. It is difficult to give any meaning at all to the limitations imposed by the Amendment if they are read to proscribe only certain conduct by the police but to allow other agents of the same government to take advantage of evidence secured by the police in violation of its requirements. The Amendment therefore must be read to condemn not only the initial unconstitutional invasion of privacy—which is done, after all, for the purpose of securing evidence—but also the subsequent use of any evidence so obtained.

The Court evades this principle by drawing an artificial line between the constitutional rights and responsibilities that are engaged by actions of the police and those that are engaged when a defendant appears before the courts. According to the Court, the substantive protections of the Fourth Amendment are wholly exhausted at the moment when police unlawfully invade an individual's privacy and thus no substantive force remains to those protections at the time of trial when the government seeks to use evidence obtained by the police.

I submit that such a crabbed reading of the Fourth Amendment casts aside the teaching of those Justices who first formulated the exclusionary rule, and rests ultimately on an impoverished understanding of judicial responsibility in our constitutional scheme. For my part, "[t]he right of the people to be secure in their persons, houses, papers, and effects, against unreasonable searches and seizures" comprises a personal right to exclude all evidence secured by means of unreasonable searches and seizures. The right to be free from the initial invasion of privacy and the right of exclusion are coordinate components of the central embracing right to be free from unreasonable searches and seizures.

Such a conception of the rights secured by the Fourth Amendment was unquestionably the original basis of what has come to be called the exclusionary rule when it was first formulated in *Weeks v. United States,* 232 U.S. 383 (1914). . . . As the Court in *Weeks* clearly recognized, the obligations cast upon government by the Fourth Amendment are not confined merely to the police. In the words of Justice HOLMES: "If the search and seizure are unlawful as invading personal rights secured by the Constitution those rights would be infringed yet further if the evidence were allowed to be used." *Dodge v. United States,* 272 U.S. 530 (1926).

That conception of the rule, in my view, is more faithful to the meaning and purpose of the Fourth Amendment and to the judiciary's role as the guardian of the people's constitutional liberties. In contrast to the present Court's restrictive reading, the Court in *Weeks* recognized that, if the Amendment is to have any meaning, police and the courts cannot be regarded as constitutional strangers to each other; because the evidence-gathering role of the police is directly linked to the evidence-admitting function of the courts, an individual's Fourth Amendment rights may be undermined as completely by one as by the other.

From the foregoing, it is clear why the question whether the exclusion of evidence would deter future police misconduct was never considered a relevant concern in the early cases from *Weeks* to *Olmstead.* In those formative decisions, the Court plainly understood that the exclusion of illegally obtained evidence was compelled not by judicially fashioned remedial purposes, but rather by a direct constitutional command. A new phase in the history of the rule, however, opened with the Court's decision in *Wolf v. Colorado,* 338 U.S. 25 (1949). Although that decision held that the security of one's person and privacy protected by the Fourth Amendment was "implicit in 'the concept of ordered liberty' and as such enforceable against the States through the Due Process Clause" of the Fourteenth Amendment, the Court went on, in what can only be regarded as a *tour de force* of constitutional obfuscation, to say that the "ways of enforcing such a basic right raise questions of a different order." Notwithstanding the force of the *Weeks* doctrine that the Fourth Amendment required exclusion, a state court was free to admit illegally seized evidence, according to the Court in *Wolf,* so long as the State had devised some other "effective" means of vindicating a defendant's Fourth Amendment rights. . . .

Twelve years later, in *Mapp v. Ohio,* 367 U.S. 643 (1961), however, the Court restored the original understanding of the *Weeks* case by overruling the holding of *Wolf* and repudiating its rationale. Although in the course of reaching this conclusion the Court in *Mapp* responded at certain points to the question, first raised in *Wolf,* of whether the exclusionary rule was an "effective" remedy

compared to alternative means of enforcing the right it nevertheless expressly held that "all evidence obtained by searches and
seizures in violation of the Constitution is, *by that same authority,*
inadmissible in a state court." (emphasis added). In the Court's
view, the exclusionary rule was not one among a range of options
to be selected at the discretion of judges; it was "an essential
part of both the Fourth and Fourteenth Amendments." Rejection
of the *Wolf* approach was constitutionally required, the Court
explained, because "the admission of the new constitutional right
by *Wolf* could not consistently tolerate denial of its most important
constitutional privilege, namely, the exclusion of the evidence
which an accused had been forced to give by reason of the unlawful
seizure. To hold otherwise is to grant the right but in reality to
withhold its privilege and enjoyment." Indeed, no other explanation suffices to account for the Court's holding in *Mapp,* since
the only possible predicate for the Court's conclusion that the
States were bound by the Fourteenth Amendment to honor the
Weeks doctrine is that the exclusionary rule was "part and parcel
of the Fourth Amendment's limitation upon [governmental] en-
croachmant of individual privacy.". . .

Despite this clear pronouncement, however, the Court since
Calandra has gradually pressed the deterrence rationale for the
rule back to center stage. The various arguments advanced by
the Court in this campaign have only strengthened my conviction
that the deterrence theory is both misguided and unworkable.
First, the Court has frequently bewailed the "cost" of excluding
reliable evidence. In large part, this criticism rests upon a refusal
to acknowledge the function of the Fourth Amendment itself.
If nothing else, the Amendment plainly operates to disable the
government from gathering information and securing evidence
in certain ways. In practical terms, of course, this restriction of
official power means that some incriminating evidence inevitably
will go undetected if the government obeys these constitutional
restraints. It is the loss of that evidence that is the "price" our
society pays for enjoying the freedom and privacy safeguarded
by the Fourth Amendment. Thus, some criminals will go free
not, in Justice (then Judge) CARDOZO's misleading epigram,
"because the constable has blundered," *People v. Defore,* 242 N.Y.
13 (1926), but rather because official compliance with Fourth
Amendment requirements makes it more difficult to catch criminals. Understood in this way, the Amendment directly contemplates that some reliable and incriminating evidence will be lost
to the government; therefore, it is not the exclusionary rule, but
the Amendment itself that has imposed this cost.

In addition, the Court's decisions over the past decade have
made plain that the entire enterprise of attempting to assess the
benefits and costs of the exclusionary rule in various contexts is
a virtually impossible task for the judiciary to perform honestly

or accurately. Although the Court's language in those cases suggests that some specific empirical basis may support its analyses, the reality is that the Court's opinions represent inherently unstable compounds of intuition, hunches, and occasional pieces of partial and often inconclusive data. . . . To the extent empirical data are available regarding the general costs and benefits of the exclusionary rule, such data have shown, on the one hand, as the Court acknowledges today, that the costs are not as substantial as critics have asserted in the past, and, on the other hand, that while the exclusionary rule may well have certain deterrent effects, it is extremely difficult to determine with any degree of precision whether the incidence of unlawful conduct by police is now lower than it was prior to *Mapp.* . . .

By remaining within its redoubt of empiricism and by basing the rule solely on the deterrence rationale, the Court has robbed the rule of legitimacy. A doctrine that is explained as if it were an empirical proposition but for which there is only limited empirical support is both inherently unstable and an easy mark for critics. The extent of this Court's fidelity to Fourth Amendment requirements, however, should not turn on such statistical uncertainties. . . . Rather than seeking to give effect to the liberties secured by the Fourth Amendment through guesswork about deterrence, the Court should restore to its proper place the principle framed 70 years ago in *Weeks* that an individual whose privacy has been invaded in violation of the Fourth Amendment has a right grounded in that Amendment to prevent the government from subsequently making use of any evidence so obtained. . . .

Even if I were to accept the Court's general approach to the exclusionary rule, I could not agree with today's result. There is no question that in the hands of the present Court the deterrence rationale has proved to be a powerful tool for confining the scope of the rule. In *Calandra,* for example, the Court concluded that the "speculative and undoubtedly minimal advance in the deterrence of police misconduct," was insufficient to outweigh the "expense of substantially impeding the role of the grand jury." In *Stone v. Powell,* the Court found that "the additional contribution, if any, of the consideration of search-and-seizure claims of state prisoners on collateral review is small in relation to the costs." In *United States v. Janis,* 428 U.S. 433 (1976), the Court concluded that "exclusion from federal civil proceedings of evidence unlawfully seized by a state criminal enforcement officer has not been shown to have a sufficient likelihood of deterring the conduct of the state police so that it outweighs the societal costs imposed by the exclusion.". . . And in an opinion handed down today, the Court finds that the "balance between costs and benefits comes out against applying the exclusionary rule in civil deportation hearings held by the [Immigration and Naturalization Service]." *INS v. Lopez-Mendoza,* 468 U.S. 1032 [1984].

Thus, in this bit of judicial stagecraft, while the sets sometimes change, the actors always have the same lines. Given this well-rehearsed pattern, one might have predicted with some assurance how the present case would unfold. First there is the ritual incantation of the "substantial social costs" exacted by the exclusionary rule, followed by the virtually foreordained conclusion that, given the marginal benefits, application of the rule in the circumstances of these cases is not warranted. Upon analysis, however, such a result cannot be justified even on the Court's own terms.

At the outset, the Court suggests that society has been asked to pay a high price—in terms either of setting guilty persons free or of impeding the proper functioning of trials—as a result of excluding relevant physical evidence in cases where the police, in conducting searches and seizing evidence, have made only an "objectively reasonable" mistake concerning the constitutionality of their actions. . . . But what evidence is there to support such a claim?

Significantly, the Court points to none, and, indeed, as the Court acknowledges . . . recent studies have demonstrated that the "costs" of the exclusionary rule—calculated in terms of dropped prosecutions and lost convictions—are quite low. Contrary to the claims of the rule's critics that exclusion leads to "the release of countless guilty criminals," *Bivens v. Six Unknown Federal Narcotics Agents*, 403 U.S. 388 (1971) (BURGER, C.J., dissenting), these studies have demonstrated that federal and state prosecutors very rarely drop cases because of potential search and seizure problems. For example, a 1979 study prepared at the request of Congress by the General Accounting Office reported that only 0.4% of all cases actually declined for prosecution by federal prosecutors were declined primarily because of illegal search problems. . . .

Of course, these data describe only the costs attributable to the exclusion of evidence in all cases; the costs due to the exclusion of evidence in the narrower category of cases where police have made objectively reasonable mistakes must necessarily be even smaller. The Court, however, ignores this distinction and mistakenly weighs the aggregated costs of exclusion in *all* cases, irrespective of the circumstances that led to exclusion, against the potential benefits associated with only those cases in which evidence is excluded because police reasonably but mistakenly believe that their conduct does not violate the Fourth Amendment. When such faulty scales are used, it is little wonder that the balance tips in favor of restricting the application of the rule.

What then supports the Court's insistence that this evidence be admitted? Apparently, the Court's only answer is that even though the costs of exclusion are not very substantial, the potential deterrent effect in these circumstances is so marginal that exclusion cannot be justified. The key to the Court's conclusion in this respect is its belief that the prospective deterrent effect of the exclusionary rule operates only in those situations in which police officers, when deciding whether to go forward with some particular search, have reason to know that their planned conduct will violate the requirements of the Fourth Amendment. If these officers in fact understand (or reasonably should understand because the law is well settled) that their proposed conduct will offend the Fourth Amendment and that, consequently, any evidence they seize will be suppressed in court, they will refrain from conducting the planned search. In those circumstances, the incentive system created by the exclusionary rule will have the hoped-for deterrent effect. But in situations where police officers reasonably (but mistakenly) believe that their planned conduct satisfies Fourth Amendment requirements—presumably either (a) because they are acting on the basis of an apparently valid warrant, or (b) because their conduct is only later determined to be invalid as a result of a subsequent change in the law or the resolution of an unsettled question of law—then such officers will have no reason to refrain from conducting the search and the exclusionary rule will have no effect.

At first blush, there is some logic to this position. Undoubtedly, in the situation hypothesized by the Court, the existence of the exclusionary rule cannot be expected to have any deterrent effect on the particular officers at the moment they are deciding whether to go forward with the search. Indeed, the subsequent exclusion of any evidence seized under such circumstances appears somehow "unfair" to the particular officers involved. As the Court suggests, these officers have acted in what they thought was an appropriate and constitutionally authorized manner, but then the fruit of their efforts is nullified by the application of the exclusionary rule.

The flaw in the Court's argument, however, is that its logic captures only one comparatively minor element of the generally acknowledged deterrent purposes of the exclusionary rule. To be sure, the rule operates to some extent to deter future misconduct by individual officers who have had evidence suppressed in their own cases. But what the Court overlooks is that the deterrence rationale for the rule is not designed to be, nor should it be thought of as, a form of "punishment" of individual police officers for their failures to obey the restraints imposed by the Fourth Amendment. Instead, the chief deterrent function of the rule is its tendency to promote institutional compliance with Fourth Amendment requirements on the part of law enforcement agencies generally. Thus, as the Court has previously recognized, "over the long term, [the] demonstration [provided by the exclusionary rule] that our society attaches serious consequences to violation of constitutional rights is thought to encourage those who formulate law enforcement policies, and the officers who implement them, to incorporate Fourth Amendment ideals into their value system." *Stone v. Powell.* It is only through such an institutionwide mechanism that information concerning Fourth Amendment standards can be effectively communicated to rank-and-file officers.

If the overall educational effect of the exclusionary rule is considered, application of the rule to even those situations in which individual police officers have acted on the basis of a reasonable but mistaken belief that their conduct was authorized can still be expected to have a considerable long-term deterrent effect. If evidence is consistently excluded in these circumstances, police departments will surely be prompted to instruct their officers to devote greater care and attention to providing sufficient information to establish probable cause when applying for a warrant, and to review with some attention the form of the warrant that they have been issued, rather than automatically assuming that whatever document the magistrate has signed will necessarily comport with Fourth Amendment requirements.

After today's decisions, however, that institutional incentive will be lost. Indeed, the Court's "reasonable mistake" exception to the exclusionary rule will tend to put a premium on police ignorance of the law. Armed with the assurance provided by today's decisions that evidence will always be admissible whenever an officer has "reasonably" relied upon a warrant, police departments will be encouraged to train officers that if a warrant has simply been signed, it is reasonable, without more, to rely on it. Since in close cases there will no longer be any incentive to err on the side of constitutional behavior, police would have every reason to adopt a "let's-wait-until-it's-decided" approach in situations in which there is a question about a warrant's validity or the basis for its issuance.

Although the Court brushes these concerns aside, a host of grave consequences can be expected to result from its decision to carve this new exception out of the exclusionary rule. A chief consequence of today's decisions will be to convey a clear and unambiguous message to magistrates that their decisions to issue warrants are now insulated from subsequent judicial review. Creation of this new exception for good-faith reliance upon a warrant implicitly tells magistrates that they need not take much care in reviewing warrant applications, since their mistakes will from now on have virtually no consequence: If their decision to issue a warrant was correct, the evidence will be admitted; if their decision was incorrect but the police relied in good faith on the warrant, the evidence will also be admitted. Inevitably, the care and attention devoted to such an inconsequential chore will dwindle. Although the Court is correct to note that magistrates do not share the same stake in the outcome of a criminal case as the police, they nevertheless need to appreciate that their role is of some moment in order to continue performing the important task of carefully reviewing warrant applications. Today's decisions effectively remove that incentive.

Justice STEVENS concurred in *Massachusetts v. Sheppard* and dissented in *United States v. Leon* in a separate opinion.

8

THE FIFTH
AMENDMENT
GUARANTEE AGAINST
SELF-ACCUSATION

T HE FIFTH AMENDMENT's provision that "[n]o person . . .
shall be compelled in any criminal case to be a witness
against himself" gave constitutional effect to an old common
law maxim: "No man is bound to betray [accuse] himself."[1] That
maxim can be traced to Englishman John Lambert, an obdurate
heretic, who in 1537, while chained to a stake, protested the
inquisitorial practices of ecclesiastical courts. Not until the middle
of the seventeenth century, however, was the principle that no
man is bound to accuse himself firmly embedded in English
common law. Yet by the close of that century the principle had
become part of the legal systems in the colonies. Six of the
original thirteen states included the guarantee in their state constitutions or bills of rights, and in the remaining it was recognized
by their courts.

Although the common law maxim no man is bound to accuse
himself provided the historical basis for the Fifth Amendment,
the drafters of the Bill of Rights were apparently unsure of its
precise scope. Initially, George Mason, as author of the Virginia
Declaration of Rights, urged the constitutionality of this rule
of evidence as part of accepted accusatorial criminal procedure:

That in all capital or criminal prosecutions a man hath a right to demand
the cause and nature of his accusation, to be confronted with the accusers
and witnesses, to call for evidence in favor, and to a speedy trial by

an impartial jury of twelve men of his vicinage, without whose unanimous consent he cannot be found guilty; *nor can he be compelled to give evidence against himself;* that no man be deprived of his liberty, except by the law of the land or the judgment of his peers.[2]

Mason's formulation, however, fell short of the common law protection for witnesses as well as the accused.

By comparison, James Madison's draft of the proposed amendment embraced the broad scope of the traditional common law maxim: "No person shall be subject, except in cases of impeachment, to more than one punishment or trial for the same offense; *nor shall be compelled to be a witness against himself;* nor be deprived of life, liberty, or property, without due process of law; nor be obliged to relinquish his property, where it may be necessary for public use, without just compensation."

Madison's proposal broadly applied to civil and criminal proceedings as well as to all stages of the legal process, including both legislative and judicial inquiries. Indeed, because Madison collapsed the maxim "No man is bound to accuse himself" with another—"No man should be a witness in his own case"—his formulation would have applied "to any testimony that fell short of making one vulnerable, but that nevertheless exposed him to public disgrace or obloquy, or other injury to name of reputation," and would extended protection to third-party witnesses in civil and criminal proceedings.[3]

In the House committee assigned to finalize the Bill of the Rights, John Lawrence suggested that the clause constituted "a general declaration in some degree contrary to laws passed" and should be "confined to criminal cases." The clause was amended without discussion and adopted unanimously.[4] Inclusion of the phrase "in any criminal case" limited the scope of the guarantee, ostensibly precluding invocation of the right during police interrogations and by parties and witnesses in civil and equity suits as well as in nonjudicial proceedings, such as grand jury and legislative investigations.

But the Supreme Court has interpreted the guarantee to be "as broad as the mischief against which it seeks to guard."[5] The scope of the amendment extends beyond criminal trials to grand jury proceedings;[6] to legislative investigations;[7] and, in some circumstances, to witnesses in civil and criminal cases where truthful assertions might result in forfeiture, penalty, or criminal prosecution.[8] The Warren Court's landmark ruling in *Miranda v. Arizona* (1966) (see page 945) "expanded the right beyond all precedent, yet not beyond its historical spirit and purpose"[9] in extending the guarantee to police interrogations. As a consequence, the Fifth Amendment's guarantee applies from the time police begin "to focus on a particular suspect" through "custodial interrogation"[10] to the trial itself as well as to other quasi-judicial and nonjudicial proceedings.[11] In addition, individuals may not be disbarred or lose their jobs simply because they plead their Fifth Amendment right to remain silent.[12]

Although, historically, rejecting a strict construction of the amendment, the Court has imposed two crucial restrictions by loosely construing the guarantee to confer "a privilege against self-incrimination." First, the inference that the amendment grants only a *privilege* rather than a *right* has great jurisprudential significance. Privileges differ from rights: whereas privileges are granted (and revocable) by the government, rights do not derive from the government and limit the exercise of governmental power. As the prominent historian Leonard W. Levy observes, "to speak of the 'privilege' against self-incrimination, degrades it, inadvertently, in comparison to other constitutional rights."[13] Second, the amendment literally does not protect merely self-incrimination. As Levy points out:

> [T]o speak of a right against self-incrimination stunts the wide right not to give evidence against oneself. . . . The "right against self-incrimination" is a shorthand gloss of modern origin that implies a restriction not in the constitutional clause. The right not to be witness against oneself imports a principle of wider reach, applicable at least in criminal cases, to the self-production of any adverse evidence, including evidence that made one the herald of his own infamy, thereby publicly disgracing him. The clause extended, in otherwords, to all the injurious as well as incriminating consequences of disclosures.[14]

In sum, the shorthand version of the guarantee as a privilege against self-incrimination unnecessarily limits the scope of the Fifth Amendment.

The primary effect of the Fifth Amendment remains that in criminal trials the accused cannot be compelled to take the witness stand. It is also improper for judges to comment on a defendant's refusal to testify.[15] Witnesses must explicitly claim the right to remain silent, otherwise they are considered to have tacitly waived it.[16] Judges ultimately decide whether a claim to exercise the right is valid.[17] Even in criminal cases, the accused may refuse to answer only questions tantamount to admissions of guilt but not when self-incrimination is "of an imaginary and unsubstantial character, having reference to some extraordinary and barely possible contingency, so improbable that no reasonable man would suffer it to influence his conduct."[18]

The scope of the Fifth Amendment, however, depends on the Supreme Court's construction of the purposes and policies behind the amendment, which in turn depends on the politics of the Court and its composition. *Murphy v. Waterfront Commission,*

CONSTITUTIONAL HISTORY

The Accusatorial and Inquisitorial Systems Compared in Medieval Period

Common Law Safeguards: Accusatorial System	Civil and Canon Law: Inquisitorial System
Grand jury screens charges and issues detailed indictment	No provision for specification and revelation of charges
Substantially public proceedings	Proceedings shrouded in secrecy
Confrontation of accused and accusors in court with sworn testimony before a jury	Nonconfrontational—no revelation of names of witnesses against accused
Presumption of innocence: prosecution must prove its case	Presumption of guilt of the accused
Accused could not give sworn testimony, even if he wanted to testify	Forced to submit self-incriminating oath
Accused tried by public evidence	Accused tried by secret interrogations
Judge presides over trial—an oral combat before jury of peers of the accused	Judge functions as official prosecutor
Conviction based on jury verdict	Judges decide guilt or innocence
Torture regarded as illegal	Torture routinely used
No double jeopardy	Suspects could be indefinitely retried

---

387 U.S. 52 (1964), concisely elucidated the "complex of values" underlying the right against self-accusation:

It reflects many of our fundamental values and most noble aspirations: our unwillingness to subject those suspected of crime to the cruel trilemma of self-accusation, perjury, or contempt; our preference for an accusatorial rather than an inquisitorial system of criminal justice; our fear that self-incrimination will be elicited by inhumane treatment and abuses; our sense of fair play which dictates a "fair state-individual balance by requiring the government . . . in its contest with the individual to shoulder the entire load," . . . our respect for the inviolability of the human personality and of the right of each individual "to a private enclave where he may lead a private life," . . . our distrust of self-deprecatory statements; and our realization that the privilege while "a shelter to the guilty," has often [been] "a protection to the innocent."

From this complex of values, three basic rationales stand out: the guarantee's role in (1) maintaining a responsible accusatorial system, (2) preventing cruel and inhumane treatment of suspects, and (3) offering protection for personal privacy. Each implies a different interpretative approach toward the amendment. Together, they define the jurisprudential basis for the struggle within the Court over defining the scope of the Fifth Amendment.

The "fox hunter's reason" was how Jeremy Bentham, an eighteenth-century English philosopher and legal reformer, characterized the basis for the privilege against self-incrimination. Just as in a fox hunt certain rules govern the ways by which fox hunters may capture the fox, so too evidentiary rules define an acceptable process for prosecuting suspects of criminal activity in an accusatorial system. Both the rules of fox hunting and of the criminal justice system are predicated on the notion of fairness—fair treatment of the fox and criminal suspect. In Bentham words, "[I]t consists in introducing upon the carpet of legal procedure the ideal of *fairness*, in the sense in which the word is used by sportsmen. The fox is to have a fair chance for his life: he must have (so close is the analogy) what is called *law:* leave to run a certain length of way, for the express purpose of giving him a chance for escape.[19]

How does the Fifth Amendment's guarantee serve the ideal of justice as fair treatment in accusatory systems? Justice Abe Fortas explained that

[t]o maintain a "fair state-individual balance," to require the government "to shoulder the entire load," . . . to respect the inviolability of the human personality, our accusatory system of criminal justice demands that the government seeking to punish an individual produce the evidence by its own independent labors, rather than by cruel, simple expedient of compelling it from his own mouth. . . . The principle that a man is not obliged to furnish the state with ammunition to use against him is basic to this conception. Equals, meeting in battle, owe no such duty to one another, regardless of the obligations that they may be under prior to battle. A sovereign state has the right to defend itself, and within the limits of accepted procedure, to punish infractions of the rules that govern its relationships with its sovereign individual to surrender or impair his right of self-defense.[20]

On this interpretation, the Fifth Amendment has instrumental value in securing a "fair fight" and a "fair state-individual balance"; the right against compelled self-incrimination is not an end in itself. But if the amendment only has instrumental value, then its scope is limited to those contexts in which individuals face the threat of prosecution. And the government is forbidden from only exerting "genuine compulsion" in securing a suspect's self-incriminating statements. Where disclosures are not incriminating (merely embarrassing) or when incriminating testimony is given in exchange for a grant of immunity, the amendment offers no protection. This was the view taken in *United States v. Washington*, 431 U.S. 181 (1977): "Absent some officially coerced self-accusation the Fifth Amendment privilege is not violated by even the most damning admissions. . . . The constitutional guarantee is only that the witness be not *compelled* to give self-incriminating testimony. The test is whether, considering the totality of the circumstances, the free will of the witness was overborne."

A rival interpretation is grounded in what Bentham termed "an old woman's reason"; namely, the belief that it is cruel and inhumane to force a person to partake in his own undoing. From this perspective, the Fifth Amendment embodies an end in itself—respect for the moral dignity of the individual—and confers a right to remain silent. "The essence of [the old woman's] reason," as Bentham put it, "is contained in the word *hard:* 'tis hard upon a man to be obliged to criminate himself.' " And Bentham viewed dimly "this plea of tenderness, this double-distilled and treble-refined sentimentality," claiming that it only served the guilty: "Hard it is upon a man, it must be confessed, to be obliged to do anything that he does not like. That he should not much like to do what is meant by his [in]criminating himself, is natural enough; for what it leads to, is, his being punished. What is not less hard is in a man's being punished, that, and no more, is there in his thus being made to incriminate himself."

History, however, shows that respect for human dignity played an important role in the development of a right against self-accusation. In the late sixteenth century, Puritan leaders attacked the *ex officio* oath on the grounds that "[m]uch more is it equall that a mans owne private faults should remayne private to God and himselfe till the Lord discover them. And in regard of this righte consider howe the Lord ordained wittnesses where by the magistrate should seeke into the offences of his subjects and not by oathe rifle the secrets of theare hearts."[21] Colonial common law also offered protection "against physical compulsion and against the moral compulsion that an oath to a revengeful God commands of a pious soul."[22] It is to this history and interpretation that Justice Douglas appealed when dissenting, in *Ullmann v. United States*, 350 U.S. 422 (1956), from the Court's upholding the constitutionality of grants of immunity:

The guarantee against self-incrimination contained in the Fifth Amendment is not only a protection against conviction and prosecution but a safeguard of conscience and human dignity and freedom of expression as well. . . . [T]he Framers put it well beyond the power of Congress to *compel* anyone to confess his crimes. The evil to be guarded against was partly self-accusation under legal compulsion. But that was only a part of the evil. The conscience and dignity of man were also involved.

Notwithstanding the moral appeal of the old woman's rationale, critics charge that it "confronts the clear fact that the rule against self-incrimination is psychologically and morally unacceptable as a general governing principle in human relations."[23] Court of Appeals Judge Henry J. Friendly, for one, argued that "[n]o parent would teach such a doctrine to his children; the lesson parents preach is that a misdeed, even a serious one, will generally be forgiven; a failure to make a clean breast of it will not be. Every day people are being asked to explain their conduct to parents, employers, and teachers."[24] However, there is a vast difference between the state compelling a person to incriminate himself and a person's revelations to his or her lover, parents, friends, or employer, as well as between the kinds of sanctions that may result from those self-revelations.

Finally, "the hermit's rationale" draws attention to the amendment's protection for personal privacy. This view of the amendment was often advanced during the Warren Court era.[25] In particular, in *Warden v. Hayden,* 387 U.S. 294 (1967), Justice Douglas observed that "[p]rivacy involves the choice of the individual to disclose or to reveal what he believes, what he thinks, what he possesses. . . . That dual aspect of privacy means that the individual should have the freedom to select for himself the time and circumstances when he will share his secrets with others and decide the extent of that sharing. This is his prerogative, not the State's."

The hermit's rationale invited sharp criticism, however. Law professor Bernard Meltzer countered that "[t]here is no coherent notion of privacy that explains the privilege; rather it is the privilege that produces a degree of privacy by insulating the suspect or defendant" from compelled self-incrimination.[26] Judge Friendly charged that

[f]ar from being a moral doctrine, the privacy justification is about as immoral as one could imagine. To be sure, there may be offenses, for example, fornication and adultery, where the individual's right to be left alone may transcend the state's interest. . . . [But] can it be seriously argued that when a murder or rape or kidnapping has been committed, a citizen is morally justified in withholding his aid simply because he does not want to be bothered and prefers to remain in a "private enclave" from which the state has cause to believe he departed in order to do violence to another?[27]

Friendly, though, may simply take the privacy rationale too far, for as political scientist Robert Gerstein points out, "The right of privacy cannot be understood as embodying the rule that 'privacy may be never violated.' The alternative is to look at the right of privacy not as an absolute rule but as a principle which would establish privacy as a value of great significance, not to be interfered with lightly by governmental authority." Also, "[t]he case for allowing the privilege [may be] strongest when all these purposes"—the fox hunter's, the old woman's and the hermit's rationales—are "served by its application."[28]

The importance of these competing rationales is underscored by Justice John Harlan's observation, dissenting in *Garrity v. New Jersey*, 385 U.S. 493 (1967): "The Constitution contains no formulae within which we can calculate the areas . . . to which the privilege should extend, and the Court has therefore been obliged to fashion for itself standards for the application of the privilege." Consider how these competing rationales enter into the Court's rulings on coerced confessions and police interrogations, grants of immunity, and its distinction between "real" and "testimonial" evidence, as well as on claims to Fifth Amendment protection for required records and private papers, in the following sections of this chapter.

NOTES

1. See Leonard Levy, *The Origins of the Fifth Amendment* (New York: Oxford University Press, 1968).

2. "Virginia Declaration of Rights," in *The Federal and State Constitutions, Colonial Charters, and Other Organic Laws,* ed. F. Thorpe (New York: Harper & Brothers, 1898). Emphasis added.

3. Levy, *The Origins of the Fifth Amendment,* 243–244.

4. "Amendments reported by the House Select Committee, July 28, 1789," in *Documentary History of the Constitution of the United States,* Vol. 5, 186.

5. *Counselman v. Hitchcock,* 142 U.S. 547 (1892).

6. See *Lefkowitz v. Cunningham,* 429 U.S. 893 (1970); *California v. Byers,* 402 U.S. 424 (1971); *United States v. Kordel,* 397 U.S. 1 (1970); and *Marbury v. Madison,* 5 U.S. 137 (1803).

7. See *Watkins v. United States,* 354 U.S. 178 (1957); and *Bart v. United States,* 349 U.S. 219 (1955).

8. *McCarthy v. Arndstein,* 266 U.S. 34 (1924);

9. Levy, *The Origins of the Fifth Amendment,* 38.

10. *Escobedo v. Illinois,* 378 U.S. 478 (1964).

11. See *Miranda v. Arizona,* (page 945) (police interrogations); *Emspack v. United States,* 349 U.S. 190 (1955), and *Quinn v. United States,* 349 U.S. 155 (1955) (legislative investigations); *McCarthy v. Arndstein,* 266 U.S. 34 (1924) (civil proceedings); *ICC v. Brimson,* 154 U.S.

447 (1894) (administrative investigations); *Counselman v. Hitchcock*, 142 U.S. 547 (1892) (grand jury proceedings).

12. See *Regan v. New York*, 349 U.S. 105 (1954); *Slochower v. Board of Education*, 350 U.S. 551 (1956); *Spavack v. Klein*, 385 U.S. 511 (1967); *Gardson v. Broderick*, 392 U.S. 273 (1968); *Uniform Sanitation Men's Association v. Commissioner of Sanitation of the City of New York*, 392 U.S. 280 (1968); *Lefkowitz v. Turley*, 414 U.S. 70 (1973); and *Lefkowitz v. Cunningham*, 431 U.S. 801 (1977).

13. Leonard Levy, "The Right Against Self-Incrimination," 29 *Journal of Politics* 3 (1969).

14. Levy, *The Origins of the Fifth Amendment*, 425–427.

15. See *Griffin v. California*, 380 U.S. 609 (1965). But also see *United States v. Young*, 470 U.S. 1 (1985) (a five-to-four ruling upholding a prosecutor's statements that the defendant was guilty and urging the jury to do its job).

16. *California v. Byers*, 402 U.S. 424 (1971); *Rogers v. United States*, 340 U.S. 367 (1951); and *United States v. Monia*, 317 U.S. 434 (1943).

17. *Mackey v. United States*, 401 U.S. 667 (1971); *Hoffman v. United States*, 341 U.S. 479 (1955); and *Mason v. United States*, 244 U.S. 362 (1917).

18. *Emspack v. United States*, 349 U.S. 190 (1955).

19. Jeremy Bentham, *A Rationale of Judicial Evidence* (1827), 238–239. The discussion in this section draws on David M. O'Brien, "The Fifth Amendment: Fox Hunters, Old Women, Hermits, and the Burger Court," 54 *Notre Dame Lawyer* 26 (1978).

20. Abe Fortas, "The Fifth Amendment: Nemo Tenetur Prodere Seipsum," 25 *Cleveland Bar Association Journal* 95 (1954).

21. Quoted in Levy, *The Origins of the Fifth Amendment*, 177.

22. R. Carter Pittman, "The Colonial and Constitutional History of the Privilege against Self-Incrimination," 21 *Virginia Law Review* 783 (1935).

23. David Louisell, "Criminal Discovery and Self-Incrimination," 53 *California Law Review* 95 (1965). See also Sidney Hook, *Common Sense and the Fifth Amendment* (New York: Criterion, 1959).

24. Henry J. Friendly, "The Fifth Amendment Tomorrow: The Case for Constitutional Change," 37 *Cincinnati Law Review* 673 (1968).

25. See *Miranda v. Arizona*, (page 945), *Tehan v. Shott*, 382 U.S. 406, 416 (1966); *Murphy v. Waterfront Commission*, 387 U.S. 52, 55 (1964); *Feldman v. United States*, 322 U.S. 487, 489–490 (1964); and *Boyd v. United States*, 116 U.S. 616, 630 (1886). See also Michael Dann, "The Fifth Amendment Privilege against Self-Incrimination: Extorting Physical Evidence from a Suspect," 43 *California Law Review* 597 (1970); Charles Fried, "Privacy," 77 *Yale Law Journal* 475 (1968); and Robert McKay, "Self-Incrimination and the New Privacy," in *The Supreme Court Review* ed. Philip Kurland (Chicago: University of Chicago Press, 1967), 209.

26. Bernard Meltzer, "Required Records, the McCarran Act, and the Privilege against Self-Incrimination," 13 *University of Chicago Law Review* 687 (1950).

27. Friendly, "The Fifth Amendment Tomorrow," 689.

28. Robert Gerstein, "Privacy and Self-Incrimination," 80 *Ethics* 87 (1970).

SELECTED BIBLIOGRAPHY

Baker, Liva. *Miranda: Crime, Law and Politics*. New York: Atheneum, 1983.

Hook, Sidney. *Common Sense and the Fifth Amendment*. New York: Criterion, 1959.

Kamisar, Yale. *Police Interrogation and Confessions: Essays in Law and Policy*. Ann Arbor: University of Michigan Press, 1980.

Levy, Leonard W. *Origins of the Fifth Amendment*. New York: Oxford University Press, 1968.

Packer, Herbert L. *The Limits of the Criminal Sanction*. Stanford, CA: Stanford University Press, 1968.

A. COERCED CONFESSIONS AND POLICE INTERROGATIONS

The issues that arise with police interrogations and coerced confessions were long avoided by the Court until the Fifth Amendment was applied to the states in *Malloy v. Hogan*, 378 U.S. 1 (1964). However, in the 1930s and 1940s the Court confronted police practices and the rights of the accused under the due process clause of the Fourteenth Amendment. In *Brown v. Mississippi*, 297 U.S. 278 (1936), for example, police physically tortured a suspect and Chief Justice Charles Evans Hughes responded with a unanimous opinion warning that "the freedom of constitutional government . . . is limited by the requirement of due process of law. Because a State may dispense with a jury trial, it does not follow that it may substitute trial by ordeal. The rack and torture chamber may not be substituted for the witness stand." Subsequently, *Ashcraft v. Tennessee*, 322 U.S. 143 (1944), held that the use of some confessions violates the due process clause because they are the result of "inherently coercive" police interrogations; here, Ashcraft's confession came after thirty-six hours of continuous police questioning under electrical lights. On a case-by-case basis in the 1950s, the Court found a number of police interrogations so psychologically coercive as to run afoul of the due process clause.[1] And in *Mallory v. United States*, 354 U.S. 449 (1957), the Court held that a confession was improper where the defendant had not been properly arraigned first.

A problem with the Court's looking at the "totality of the circumstances" in each case to determine whether a confession was coerced and for a violation of a suspect's Fifth Amendment rights (and the Sixth Amendment right to counsel) was that it provided little guidance for police and lower courts. In the 1940s and 1950s police in many areas of the country were still not required to be high-school graduates and the quality of state court judges was much lower than today. Still, the Court remained reluctant to establish a "bright line" ruling on how far police could go when interrogating suspects. In *Crooker v. California*, 357 U.S. 433 (1958), for instance, the justices split five to four in holding that the denial of the presence of an attorney during police questioning did not violate the rights of an accused man who had a college degree and some law-school training. Yet in the following year the Court unanimously held that the presence of counsel was required when the defendant confessed during a three o'clock-in-the-morning interrogation by police in *Spano v. New York*, 360 U.S. 315 (1959).

A solid majority on the Warren Court (after the appointment of Justice Arthur Goldberg in 1962) finally came together in establishing a bright line rule for police interrogations.[2] In *Massiah v. United States*, 377 U.S. 201 (1964), the Court held that a defendant's Fifth and Sixth Amendment rights were violated by a prosecutor's use as evidence of his incriminating statements made to a codefendant after being indicted and which were overheard by police on a radio with the codefendant's permission. Splitting five to four in *Escobedo v. Illinois*, 378 U.S. 478 (1964), the Court went even further. For a bare majority, Justice Goldberg held that no "meaningful distinction" could be drawn between police interrogations before and after a suspect's formal indictment. Individuals have the right to the presence of an attorney at the time they become suspects and the focus of police investigations. In Justice Goldberg's words:

We hold, therefore, that where, as here, the investigation is no longer a general inquiry into an unsolved crime but has begun to focus on a particular suspect, the suspect has been taken into police custody, the police carry out a process of interrogations that lends itself to eliciting incriminating statements, the suspect has requested and been denied an opportunity to consult with his lawyer, and the police have not effectively warned him of his absolute constitutional right to remain silent, the accused has been denied "the assistance of counsel" in violation of the Sixth Amendment of the Constitution . . . [and] no statement elicited by the police during the interrogation may be used against him at a criminal trial.

Escobedo laid the basis for the five-to-four ruling in *Miranda v. Arizona* (1966) (see page 945) in which Chief Justice Earl

Warren set down a code of conduct for police interrogations, requiring police to inform suspects of their rights to remain silent and to have an attorney present during police questioning. As a result, the totality of circumstances standard was replaced by *Miranda*'s bright line rule.

The year after *Miranda,* the Court carried its protection for the rights of the accused even further when holding that the requirements of the due process clause apply to juvenile courts.[3] Historically, juveniles were treated differently from adults on the theory that the state is not an adversary but rather represents parental authority (*parens patriae*) in bringing civil (not criminal) proceedings against them.[4] *In re Gault* (1967) (see page 958) extended to juvenile courts the rights of notification of charges, timely hearings, representation by counsel, and the right to confront accusers, as well as the Fifth Amendment's right to remain silent.

In re Gault spearheaded a number of other rulings ensuring juveniles of the rights of the accused. Subsequently, the Court ruled that the same standard of proof for guilt must apply in juvenile courts as in other criminal proceedings[5] and that the prohibition against double jeopardy also applies.[6] But *Fare v. Michael C.,* 442 U.S. 707 (1979), held that whether a juvenile's confession may be used as evidence in court, where he asked to see his probation officer rather than an attorney, depends on the total of circumstances. *Schall v. Martin,* 467 U.S. 253 (1984), upheld the pretrial detention of juveniles deemed by a judge to be a "serious risk."

Miranda ignited a long-running political controversy. Congress responded in the Crime Control and Safe Streets Act of 1968 by providing that in federal courts confessions are admissible based on the totality of circumstances rule (not *Miranda,* which still applies in state courts). Although *Miranda* has not been overturned, the Burger and Rehnquist Courts have sharply cut back on its application. The Court has not abandoned *Miranda*'s premise that "interrogation of persons suspected or accused of crime contains inherently compelling pressures which work to undermine the individual's will to resist and to compel him to speak where he would not otherwise do so freely." But as the Court has become more conservative (with the addition of appointees of Presidents Richard Nixon and Ronald Reagan), the justices have reevaluated the necessity of full *Miranda* warnings in every circumstance and distinguished *Miranda* requirements as mere "prophylactic rules" from the Fifth Amendment's guarantee, thereby limiting the contexts and circumstances in which police must honor *Miranda.*

Because the Court construes *Miranda* to be a procedural (not a constitutional) ruling, it allows prosecutorial use of incriminating statements made without the benefit of full *Miranda* warnings and without a "knowing and intelligent" waiver of a defendant's Fifth Amendment rights.[7] *Harris v. New York,* 401 U.S. 222 (1971), for example, held that statements, otherwise inadmissible against the defendant because of the failure to satisfy *Miranda,* may be used to impeach the defendant's testimony at trial. In *Oregon v. Hass,* 420 U.S. 714 (1975), *Harris* was extended to permit the defendant's impeachment by use of statements obtained while he was in police custody and after he requested an attorney but before the lawyer arrived. And *Michigan v. Tucker,* 417 U.S. 433 (1975), held that the Fifth Amendment was not violated by the prosecution's use of testimony of a witness discovered as the result of the defendant's statements to police given in the absence of *Miranda* warnings. Again, in *Michigan v. Mosley,* 423 U.S. 96 (1975), the Court sustained a police interrogation, after a two-hour interval, of a suspect who had earlier claimed his right to remain silent.

Although not overruling *Miranda,* the Court has significantly limited its application by distinguishing the circumstances in which it applies on a case-by-case basis. In doing so, the Court has redefined the nature of personal compulsion that triggers the Fifth Amendment's protection and returned to the pre–*Miranda* standard of "considering the totality of circumstances, [whether] the free will of the witness is overbore."[8] Three recent cases—*Rhode Island v. Innis* (1980) (see page 969), *Colorado v. Connelly* (1986) (see page 974), and *Duckworth v. Eagan* (1989) (see page 978)—illustrate the Court's current analysis.

Still, even though the Burger and Rehnquist Courts have recognized exceptions to *Miranda*'s application (see the cases listed and discussed in the box on p. 965), a majority of the Court remains committed to upholding *Miranda.* In a six-to-two ruling with Justice David Souter not participating and Chief Justice Rehnquist and Justice Scalia in dissent) in *Minnick v. Mississippi,* 111 S. Ct. 486 (1990), the Court reinforced *Miranda*'s protections by reaffirming that once an accused person in police custody requests an attorney, police may not initiate further questioning until an attorney is available and present during the questioning. In an earlier decision, *Edwards v. Arizona,* 451 U.S. 477 (1981), the Burger Court held that under *Miranda* once an accused asks for an attorney he may not be subjected to another round of questioning "until counsel has been made available to him." But subsequently the Mississippi State Supreme Court narrowly interpreted *Edwards* to permit the use at trial of incriminating statements obtained during a police interrogation from Robert Minnick in the absence of his lawyer. The Rehnquist Court, however, overturned that ruling in *Minnick v. Mississippi.*

Robert Minnick was the prime suspect in a 1986 burglary and murder, and Mississippi police obtained a warrant for his arrest. Four months later Minnick was arrested by police and held in jail in California until authorities from Mississippi arrived. After his arrest, during a weekend in jail Minnick requested and was permitted to talk several times with a lawyer. But when a county sheriff from Mississippi arrived on Monday, jail officials ordered him to answer the sheriff's questions and, in the absence of his attorney, Minnick made incriminating statements that Mississippi courts allowed to be used as evidence against him. The state supreme court rejected Minnick's appeal of his murder conviction on the grounds that *Miranda* and *Edwards* only require police to permit a suspect to consult with an attorney at least once and, after that, police may undertake further interrogations even in the absence of the suspect's attorney. Minnick appealed that ruling and interpretation of *Miranda* and *Edwards* to the Supreme Court.

Writing for the majority in *Minnick v. Mississippi,* Justice Anthony Kennedy explained that

> To protect the privilege against self-incrimination guaranteed by the Fifth Amendment, we have held that police must terminate interrogation of an accused in custody if the accused requests the assistance of counsel. *Miranda v. Arizona,* 384 U.S. 436 (1966). We reinforced the protections of *Miranda* in *Edwards v. Arizona,* 451 U.S. 477 (1981), which held that once the accused requests counsel, officials may not reinitiate questioning "until counsel has been made available" to him. The issue in the case before us is whether *Edward's* protection ceases once the suspect has consulted with an attorney. . . .

> *Edwards* is "designed to prevent police from badgering a defendant into waiving his previously asserted *Miranda* rights." *Michigan v. Harvey,* 110 S. Ct. 1176 (1990). The rule ensures that any statement made in subsequent interrogation is not the result of coercive pressures. *Edwards* conserves judicial resources which would otherwise be expended in making difficult determinations of voluntariness, and implements the protections of *Miranda* in practical and straightforward terms.

> The merit of the *Edwards* decision lies in the clarity of its command and the certainty of its application. . . .

> The Mississippi Supreme Court relied on our statement in *Edwards* that an accused who invokes his right to counsel "is not subject to further interrogation by the authorities until counsel has been made available to him. . . ." We do not interpret this language to mean, as the Mississippi court thought, that the protection of *Edwards* terminates once counsel has consulted with the suspect. In context, the requirement that counsel be "made available" to the accused refers to more than an opportunity to consult with an attorney outside the interrogation room. . . .

> We consider our ruling to be an appropriate and necessary application of the *Edwards* rule. A single consultation with an attorney does not

remove the suspect from persistent attempts by officials to persuade him to waive his rights, or from the coercive pressures that accompany custody and that may increase as custody is prolonged. . . . We decline to remove protection from police-initiated questioning based on isolated consultations with counsel who is absent when the interrogation resumes.

The exception to *Edwards* here proposed is inconsistent with *Edward's* purpose to protect the suspect's right to have counsel present at custodial interrogation. It is inconsistent as well with *Miranda*.

In a sharply worded dissenting opinion, which Chief Justice Rehnquist joined, Justice Antonin Scalia countered that

The Court today establishes an irrebuttable presumption that a criminal suspect, after invoking his *Miranda* right to counsel, can *never* validly waive that right during any police-initiated encounter, even after the suspect has been provided multiple *Miranda* warnings and has actually consulted his attorney. This holding builds on foundations already established in *Edwards v. Arizona,* but "the rule of *Edwards* is our rule, not a constitutional command; and it is our obligation to justify its expansion." *Arizona v. Roberson,* 108 S. Ct. 2093 (1988) (Kennedy, J., dis. op.) Because I see no justification for applying *Edward's* irrebuttable presumption when a criminal suspect has actually consulted with his attorney, I respectfully dissent. . . .

The confession must be suppressed, not because it was "compelled," nor even because it was obtained from an individual who could realistically be assumed to be unaware of his rights, but simply because this Court sees fit to prescribe as a "systemic assurance" that a person in custody who has once asked for counsel cannot thereafter be approached by the police unless counsel is present. Of course the Constitution's proscription of compelled testimony does not remotely authorize this incursion upon state practices. . . .

One should not underestimate the extent to which the Court's expansion of *Edwards* constricts law enforcement. Today's ruling, that the invocation of a right to counsel permanently prevents a police-initiated waiver, makes it largely impossible for the police to urge a prisoner who has initially declined to confess to change his mind—or, indeed, even to ask whether he has changed his mind. . . .

Today's extension of the *Edwards* prohibition is the latest stage of prophylaxis built on prophylaxis, producing a veritable fairyland castle of imagined constitutional restrictions upon law enforcement.

NOTES

1. See *Leyra v. Denno,* 347 U.S. 556 (1954); *Fikes v. Alabama,* 352 U.S. 191 (1957); and *Payne v. Arizona,* 356 U.S. 560 (1958).

2. See *Haynes v. Washington,* 373 U.S. 503 (1963) (holding that a written confession was involuntary because the accused had been held incomunicato); and *Jackson v. Denno,* 378 U.S. 368 (1964).

3. In *Gallegos v. Colorado*, 370 U.S. 49 (1962), the Court held that the due process clause was violated by a confession of a fourteen-year-old boy held by police for five days before his parents were sent for.

4. Relying on the theory of *parens patriae* in according juveniles less protection under the Bill of Rights than adults, the Court in *Ingraham v. Wright*, 430 U.S. 651 (177), upheld corporal punishment in public schools. The Court also upheld laws permitting parents to admit their minor children to mental hospitals without a hearing. *O'Connor v. Donaldson*, 422 U.S. 563 (1975), held that adults may not be committed to a mental institution under the due process clause without a hearing on their commitment at which time they may contest their institutionalization. But see *Secretary of Public Welfare v. Institutionalized Juveniles*, 422 U.S. 640 (1979); and *Parham v. J.R.*, 422 U.S. 584 (1979).

5. *In re Winship*, 397 U.S. 358 (1970).

6. *Breed v. Jones*, 421 U.S. 519 (1975).

7. See *Harris v. New York*, 401 U.S. 222 (1971); *Michigan v. Tucker*, 417 U.S. 433 (1974); *Michigan v. Mosley*, 423 U.S. 96 (1975); *Oregon v. Hass*, 420 U.S. 714 (1975); *Doyle v. New York*, 426 U.S. 610 (1976); *Oregon v. Mathiason*, 429 U.S. 492 (1977); and *United States v. Wong*, 431 U.S. 174 (1977).

8. *United States v. Wong*, 431 U.S. 174 (1977).

INSIDE THE COURT
Chief Justice Earl Warren, *Miranda v. Arizona*, and the Attack on the Court

The Warren Court was sharply criticized for "being soft on criminals" because of its rulings on the rights of the accused. During the 1968 presidential election, Richard Nixon made law and order a campaign issue, promising if elected to appoint strict constructionists to the Court who would overturn the controversial rulings of the Warren Court. Warren and Nixon knew each other from the 1950s when Warren was the popular governor of California and Nixon was a young Republican congressman from that state. Fearing that Nixon would win the election, Warren offered to retire in 1968 so Democratic President Lyndon Johnson could appoint his successor. But LBJ's nomination of Justice Abe Fortas to be chief justice met opposition in the Senate, and Fortas was forced to withdraw from consideration. Warren stayed on the Court until after the election, and then President Nixon nominated Warren E. Burger to become chief justice in 1969.

Years later in his memoirs, Chief Justice Warren reflected on the campaign against the Court and *Miranda*, observing that the

attack centered on the case of *Miranda v. Arizona*. . . . [But there] was really nothing new in this except to require police and prosecutors to advise the poor, the ignorant, and the unwary of a basic constitutional right in a manner which had been followed by the Federal Bureau of Investigation procedures for many years. It was of no assistance to hardened underworld types because they already know what their rights are and demand them. And so it is with all sophisticated criminals and affluent prisoners who had ready access to their lawyers. However, because so many people who are arrested are poor and illiterate, short-cut methods and often cruelties are perpetrated to obtain convictions.*

Before going to the Court in 1953, Warren had worked his way up in politics by serving as California's attorney general. And he had a keen understanding of law-enforcement practices that influenced the drafting of his opinion in *Miranda*. When working on *Miranda*, Warren specifically recalled a controversy involving a law professor's seminar for Minneapolis-area police and Minnesota's state attorney general (and later senator and vice-president) Walter Mondale. At the seminar, police were told how to adhere to the Court's decisions and still maintain past interrogation practices. "For instance, you're supposed to arraign a prisoner before a magistrate without unreasonable delay," the law professor advised. "But if the magistrate goes hunting for the weekend on a Friday afternoon at 3:00 P.M., you can arrange to arrest your suspect at 3:30. That way you've got the whole weekend." Mondale took the law professor to task at a news conference, responding, "Some persons claim the Supreme Court has gone too far. Others claim to know how constitutional protections may be avoided by tricky indirection. Both viewpoints are wrong—this [seminar] was called to assist us in better fulfilling our sworn duty to uphold the Constitution. It was not called to second guess the Supreme Court." Warren, though, knew full well that not all state attorneys general and police would support the Court's rulings. He, therefore, strove to outline in *Miranda* a code for police procedures governing the interrogation of criminal suspects that police could not easily evade.

After Warren circulated his draft of *Miranda* to the other justices, his trusted ally on the Court, William Brennan, responded with a twenty-one page list of suggested revisions. At the outset, Brennan emphasized the importance of careful drafting in *Miranda*. "[T]his will be one of the most important opinions of our time," Brennan explained when making "one major suggestion": It goes to the basic trust of the approach to be taken. In your very first sentence you state that the root problem is 'the *role* society must *assume*, consistent with the federal Constitution, in prosecuting individuals for crime.' I would suggest that the root issue is 'the *restraints* society must *observe*, consistent with the federal Constitution, in prosecuting individuals for crime.'" Warren made that and numerous other changes before handing down the opinion for Court in *Miranda v. Arizona*.

Sources: Materials in the Earl Warren Papers and William J. Brennan, Jr., Papers, Manuscripts Room, Library of Congress.

---

* Earl Warren, *The Memoirs of Chief Justice Earl Warren* (New York: Doubleday, 1977), 316–317.

Miranda v. Arizona
384 U.S. 436, 86 S.Ct. 1602 (1966)

On March 3, 1963, an eighteen-year-old girl was kidnapped and raped on the outskirts of Phoenix, Arizona. Ten days later, police arrested Ernesto A. Miranda, a twenty-three-year-old indigent with a ninth-grade education. (A doctor who later examined Miranda diagnosed him as schizophrenic, although "alert and oriented as to time, place, and person," and competent to stand trial.) At the police station, the rape victim identified Miranda standing in a police lineup as her attacker. Two officers subsequently took Miranda to a separate room and interrogated him. At first denying his guilt, Miranda eventually confessed later and wrote out and signed a brief statement admitting and describing the crime. Following Miranda's trial and conviction, his attorneys appealed on the grounds that Miranda's confession had been coerced and that police had violated his Fifth Amendment rights. The Supreme Court granted review, along with three other cases raising the issue of the admissibility into evidence of confessions obtained during police interrogations.

Chief Justice WARREN delivers the opinion of the Court.

The cases before us raise questions which go to the roots of our concepts of American criminal jurisprudence: the restraints society must observe consistent with the Federal Constitution in prosecuting individuals for crime. More specifically, we deal with the admissibility of statements obtained from an individual who is subjected to custodial police interrogation and the necessity for procedures which assure that the individual is accorded his privilege under the Fifth Amendment to the Constitution not to be compelled to incriminate himself.

We dealt with certain phases of this problem recently in *Escobedo v. State of Illinois,* 378 U.S. 478 (1964). There, as in the four cases before us, law enforcement officials took the defendant into custody and interrogated him in a police station for the purpose of obtaining a confession. The police did not effectively advise him of his right to remain silent or of his right to consult with his attorney. Rather, they confronted him with an alleged accomplice who accused him of having perpetrated a murder. When the defendant denied the accusation and said "I didn't shoot Manuel, you did it," they handcuffed him and took him to an interrogation room. There, while handcuffed and standing, he was questioned for four hours until he confessed. During this interrogation, the police denied his request to speak to his attorney, and they prevented his retained attorney, who had come to the police station, from consulting with him. At his trial, the State, over his objection, introduced the confession against him. We held that the statements thus made were constitutionally inadmissible. . . .

We granted certiorari in these cases in order further to explore some facets of the problems, thus exposed, of applying the privilege against self-incrimination to in-custody interrogation, and to give concrete constitutional guidelines for law enforcement agencies and courts to follow.

We start here, as we did in *Escobedo*, with the premise that our holding is not an innovation in our jurisprudence, but is an application of principles long recognized and applied in other settings. We have undertaken a thorough re-examination of the *Escobedo* decision and the principles it announced, and we reaffirm it. That case was but an explication of basic rights that are enshrined in our Constitution—that "No person . . . shall be compelled in any criminal case to be a witness against himself," and that "the accused shall . . . have the Assistance of Counsel"— rights which were put in jeopardy in that case through official overbearing. . . .

Our holding will be spelled out with some specificity in the pages which follow but briefly stated it is this: the prosecution may not use statements, whether exculpatory or inculpatory, stemming from custodial interrogation of the defendant unless it demonstrates the use of procedural safeguards effective to secure the privilege against self-incrimination. By custodial interrogation, we mean questioning initiated by law enforcement officers after a person has been taken into custody or otherwise deprived of his freedom of action in any significant way. As for the procedural safeguards to be employed, unless other fully effective means are devised to inform accused persons of their right of silence and to assure a continuous opportunity to exercise it, the following measures are required. Prior to any questioning, the person must be warned that he has a right to remain silent, that any statement he does make may be used as evidence against him, and that he has a right to the presence of an attorney, either retained or appointed. The defendant may waive effectuation of these rights, provided the waiver is made voluntarily, knowingly and intelligently. If, however, he indicates in any manner and at any stage of the process that he wishes to consult with an attorney before speaking there can be no questioning. Likewise, if the individual is alone and indicates in any manner that he does not wish to be interrogated, the police may not question him. The mere fact that he may have answered some questions or volunteered some statements on his own does not deprive him of the right to refrain from answering any further inquiries until he has consulted with an attorney and thereafter consents to be questioned.

The constitutional issue we decide in each of these cases is the admissibility of statements obtained from a defendant questioned while in custody or otherwise deprived of his freedom of action in any significant way. In each, the defendant was questioned by police officers, detectives, or a prosecuting attorney in a room in which he was cut off from the outside world. In none of these cases was the defendant given a full and effective warning of his rights at the outset of the interrogation process. In all the cases, the questioning elicited oral admissions, and in three of them, signed statements as well which were admitted at their trials. They all thus share salient features—incommunicado interrogation of individuals in a police-dominated atmosphere, resulting in self-incriminating statements without full warnings of constitutional rights.

An understanding of the nature and setting of this in-custody interrogation is essential to our decisions today. The difficulty in depicting what transpires at such interrogations stems from the fact that in this country they have largely taken place incommunicado. From extensive factual studies undertaken in the early 1930's, including the famous Wickersham Report to Congress by a Presidential Commission, it is clear that police violence and the "third degree" flourished at that time. In a series of cases decided by this Court long after these studies, the police resorted to physical brutality—beatings, hanging, whipping—and to sustained and protracted questioning incommunicado in order to extort confessions. The Commission on Civil Rights in 1961 found much evidence to indicate that "some policemen still resort to physical force to obtain confessions.". . .

Unless a proper limitation upon custodial interrogation is achieved—such as these decisions will advance—there can be no assurance that practices of this nature will be eradicated in the foreseeable future. . . .

[W]e stress that the modern practice of in-custody interrogation is psychologically rather than physically oriented. As we have stated before, "Since *Chambers v. State of Florida,* 309 U.S. 227, [(1940)], this Court has recognized that coercion can be mental, as well as physical, and that the blood of the accused is not the only hallmark of an unconstitutional inquisition." *Blackburn v. State of Alabama,* 361 U.S. 199 (1960). Interrogation still takes place in privacy. Privacy results in secrecy and this in turn results in a gap in our knowledge as to what in fact goes on in the interrogation rooms. A valuable source of information about present police practices, however, may be found in various police manuals and texts which document procedures employed with success in the past, and which recommend various other effective tactics. These texts are used by law enforcement agencies themselves as guides. . . .

[T]he setting prescribed by the manuals and observed in practice

[is] clear. In essence, it is this: To be alone with the subject is essential to prevent distraction and to deprive him of any outside support. The aura of confidence in his guilt undermines his will to resist. He merely confirms the preconceived story the police seek to have him describe. Patience and persistence, at times relentless questioning, are employed. To obtain a confession, the interrogator must "patiently maneuver himself or his quarry into a position from which the desired objective may be attained." When normal procedures fail to produce the needed result, the police may resort to deceptive stratagems such as giving false legal advice. It is important to keep the subject off balance, for example, by trading on his insecurity about himself or his surroundings. The police then persuade, trick, or cajole him out of exercising his constitutional rights.

Even without employing brutality, the "third degree" or the specific stratagems described above, the very fact of custodial interrogation exacts a heavy toll on individual liberty and trades on the weakness of individuals. . . .

The potentiality for compulsion is forcefully apparent, for example, in *Miranda,* where the indigent Mexican defendant was a seriously disturbed individual with pronounced sexual fantasies. . . . To be sure, the records do not evince overt physical coercion or patent psychological ploys. The fact remains that in none of these cases did the officers undertake to afford appropriate safeguards at the outset of the interrogation to insure that the statements were truly the product of free choice.

It is obvious that such an interrogation environment is created for no purpose other than to subjugate the individual to the will of his examiner. This atmosphere carries its own badge of intimidation. To be sure, this is not physical intimidation, but it is equally destructive of human dignity. The current practice of incommunicado interrogation is at odds with one of our Nation's most cherished principles—that the individual may not be compelled to incriminate himself. Unless adequate protective devices are employed to dispel the compulsion inherent in custodial surroundings, no statement obtained from the defendant can truly be the product of his free choice. . . .

[T]he constitutional foundation underlying the privilege is the respect a government—state or federal—must accord to the dignity and integrity of its citizens. To maintain a "fair state-individual balance," to require the government "to shoulder the entire load," to respect the inviolability of the human personality, our accusatory system of criminal justice demands that the government seeking to punish an individual produce the evidence against him by its own independent labors, rather than by the cruel, simple expedient of compelling it from his own mouth. In sum, the privilege is fulfilled only when the person is guaranteed the right "to remain silent unless he chooses to speak in the unfettered exercise of his own will.". . .

The question in these cases is whether the privilege is fully applicable during a period of custodial interrogation. . . . We are satisfied that all the principles embodied in the privilege apply to informal compulsion exerted by law-enforcement officers during in-custody questioning. An individual swept from familiar surroundings into police custody, surrounded by antagonistic forces, and subjected to the techniques of persuasion described above cannot be otherwise than under compulsion to speak. As a practical matter, the compulsion to speak in the isolated setting of the police station may well be greater than in courts or other official investigations, where there are often impartial observers to guard against intimidation or trickery. . . .

Today, then, there can be no doubt that the Fifth Amendment privilege is available outside of criminal court proceedings and serves to protect persons in all settings in which their freedom of action is curtailed in any significant way from being compelled to incriminate themselves. We have concluded that without proper safeguards the process of in-custody interrogation of persons suspected or accused of crime contains inherently compelling pressures which work to undermine the individual's will to resist and to compel him to speak where he would not otherwise do so freely. In order to combat these pressures and to permit a full opportunity to exercise the privilege against self-incrimination, the accused must be adequately and effectively apprised of his rights and the exercise of those rights must be fully honored.

It is impossible for us to foresee the potential alternatives for protecting the privilege which might be devised by Congress or the States in the exercise of their creative rule-making capacities. Therefore we cannot say that the Constitution necessarily requires adherence to any particular solution for the inherent compulsions of the interrogation process as it is presently conducted. Our decision in no way creates a constitutional straitjacket which will handicap sound efforts at reform, nor is it intended to have this effect. We encourage Congress and the States to continue their laudable search for increasingly effective ways of protecting the rights of the individual while promoting efficient enforcement of our criminal laws. However, unless we are shown other procedures which are at least as effective in apprising accused persons of their right of silence and in assuring a continuous opportunity to exercise it, the following safeguards must be observed.

At the outset, if a person in custody is to be subjected to interrogation, he must first be informed in clear and unequivocal terms that he has the right to remain silent. For those unaware of the privilege, the warning is needed simply to make them aware of it—the threshold requirement for an intelligent decision as to its exercise. More important, such a warning is an absolute prerequisite in overcoming the inherent pressures of the interrogation atmosphere. It is not just the subnormal or woefully ignorant who succumb to an interrogator's imprecations, whether implied or expressly stated, that the interrogation will continue until a confession is obtained or that silence in the face of accusation is itself damning and will bode ill when presented to a jury. Further, the warning will show the individual that his interrogators are prepared to recognize his privilege should he choose to exercise it. . . .

The warning of the right to remain silent must be accompanied by the explanation that anything said can and will be used against the individual in court. This warning is needed in order to make him aware not only of the privilege, but also of the consequences of forgoing it. It is only through an awareness of these consequences that there can be any assurance of real understanding and intelligent exercise of the privilege. . . .

[T]he right to have counsel present at the interrogation is indispensable to the protection of the Fifth Amendment privilege under the system we delineate today. Our aim is to assure that the individual's right to choose between silence and speech remains unfettered throughout the interrogation process. . . . Thus, the need for counsel to protect the Fifth Amendment privilege comprehends not merely a right to consult with counsel prior to questioning, but also to have counsel present during any questioning if the defendant so desires. . . .

If an individual indicates that he wishes the assistance of counsel before any interrogation occurs, the authorities cannot rationally ignore or deny his request on the basis that the individual does not have or cannot afford a retained attorney. The financial ability of the individual has no relationship to the scope of the rights involved here. The privilege against self-incrimination secured by the Constitution applies to all individuals. . . . The cases before us as well as the vast majority of confession cases with which we have dealt in the past involve those unable to retain counsel. While authorities are not required to relieve the accused of his poverty, they have the obligation not to take advantage of indigence in the administration of justice. . . .

In order fully to apprise a person interrogated of the extent of his rights under this system then, it is necessary to warn him not only that he has the right to consult with an attorney, but also that if he is indigent a lawyer will be appointed to represent him. Without this additional warning, the admonition of the right to consult with counsel would often be understood as meaning only that he can consult with a lawyer if he has one or has the funds to obtain one. The warning of a right to counsel would be hollow if not couched in terms that would convey to the indigent—the person most often subjected to interrogation—the knowledge that he too has a right to have counsel present. . . .

Once warnings have been given, the subsequent procedure is clear. If the individual indicates in any manner, at any time prior to or during questioning, that he wishes to remain silent, the interrogation must cease. At this point he has shown that he intends to exercise his Fifth Amendment privilege; any statement taken after the person invokes his privilege cannot be other than the product of compulsion, subtle or otherwise. Without the right to cut off questioning, the setting of in-custody interrogation operates on the individual to overcome free choice in producing a statement after the privilege has been once invoked. If the individual states that he wants an attorney, the interrogation must cease until an attorney is present. At that time, the individual must have an opportunity to confer with the attorney and to have him present during any subsequent questioning. If the individual cannot obtain an attorney and he indicates that he wants one before speaking to police, they must respect his decision to remain silent. . . .

The principles announced today deal with the protection which must be given to the privilege against self-incrimination when the individual is first subjected to police interrogation while in custody at the station or otherwise deprived of his freedom of action in any significant way. It is at this point that our adversary system of criminal proceedings commences, distinguishing itself at the outset from the inquisitorial system recognized in some countries. Under the system of warnings we delineate today or under any other system which may be devised and found effective, the safeguards to be erected about the privilege must come into play at this point.

Our decision is not intended to hamper the traditional function of police officers in investigating crime. When an individual is in custody on probable cause, the police may, of course, seek out evidence in the field to be used at trial against him. Such investigation may include inquiry of persons not under restraint. General on-the-scene questioning as to facts surrounding a crime or other general questioning of citizens in the fact-finding process is not affected by our holding. It is an act of responsible citizenship for individuals to give whatever information they may have to aid in law enforcement. In such situations the compelling atmosphere inherent in the process of in-custody interrogation is not necessarily present.

In dealing with statements obtained through interrogation, we do not purport to find all confessions inadmissible. Confessions remain a proper element in law enforcement. Any statement given freely and voluntarily without any compelling influences is, of course, admissible in evidence. The fundamental import of the privilege while an individual is in custody is not whether he is allowed to talk to the police without the benefit of warnings and counsel, but whether he can be interrogated. There is no requirement that police stop a person who enters a police station and states that he wishes to confess to a crime, or a person who calls the police to offer a confession or any other statement he desires to make. Volunteered statements of any kind are not barred by the Fifth Amendment and their admissibility is not affected by our holding today.

To summarize, we hold that when an individual is taken into custody or otherwise deprived of his freedom by the authorities in any significant way and is subjected to questioning, the privilege against self-incrimination is jeopardized. Procedural safeguards must be employed to protect the privilege and unless other fully effective means are adopted to notify the person of his right of silence and to assure that the exercise of the right will be scrupulously honored, the following measures are required. He must be warned prior to any questioning that he has the right to remain silent, that anything he says can be used against him in a court of law, that he has the right to the presence of an attorney, and that if he cannot afford an attorney one will be appointed for him prior to any questioning if he so desires. Opportunity to exercise these rights must be afforded to him throughout the interrogation. After such warnings have been given, and such opportunity afforded him, the individual may knowingly and intelligently waive these rights and agree to answer questions or make a statement. But unless and until such warnings and waiver are demonstrated by the prosecution at trial, no evidence obtained as a result of interrogation can be used against him. . . .

In announcing these principles, we are not unmindful of the burdens which law enforcement officials must bear, often under trying circumstances. We also fully recognize the obligation of all citizens to aid in enforcing the criminal laws. This Court, while protecting individual rights, has always given ample latitude to law enforcement agencies in the legitimate exercise of their duties. The limits we have placed on the interrogation process should not constitute an undue interference with a proper system of law enforcement. . . .

Over the years the Federal Bureau of Investigation has compiled an exemplary record of effective law enforcement while advising any suspect or arrested person, at the outset of an interview, that he is not required to make a statement, that any statement may be used against him in court, that the individual may obtain the services of an attorney of his own choice and, more recently, that he has a right to free counsel if he is unable to pay. A letter received from the Solicitor General in response to a question from the Bench makes it clear that the present pattern of warnings and respect for the rights of the individual followed as a practice by the FBI is consistent with the procedure which we delineate today. . . .

Because of the nature of the problem and because of its recurrent significance in numerous cases, we have to this point discussed the relationship of the Fifth Amendment privilege to police interrogation without specific concentration on the facts of the cases before us. We turn now to these facts to consider the application to these cases of the constitutional principles discussed above. In each instance, we have concluded that statements were obtained from the defendant under circumstances that did not meet constitutional standards for protection of the privilege.

Justice CLARK concurring and dissenting in part.

I am unable to join the majority because its opinion goes too far on too little, while my dissenting brethren do not go quite far enough. Nor can I join in the Court's criticism of the present practices of police and investigatory agencies as to custodial interrogation. The materials it refers to as "police manuals" are, as I read them, merely writings in this field by professors and some police officers. Not one is shown by the record here to be the official manual of any police department, much less in universal use in crime detection. Moreover the examples of police brutality mentioned by the Court are rare exceptions to the thousands of cases that appear every year in the law reports. The police agencies—all the way from municipal and state forces to the federal bureaus—are responsible for law enforcement and public safety in this country. I am proud of their efforts, which in my view are not fairly characterized by the Court's opinion. . . .

The rule prior to today—as Justice GOLDBERG, the author of the Court's opinion in *Escobedo,* stated it in *Haynes v. Washington,* [373 U.S. 503 (1963)]—depended upon "a totality of circumstances evidencing an involuntary . . . admission of guilt.". . .

I would continue to follow that rule. Under the "totality of circumstances" rule of which my Brother GOLDBERG spoke in *Haynes,* I would consider in each case whether the police officer prior to custodial interrogation added the warning that the suspect might have counsel present at the interrogation and, further, that a court would appoint one at his request if he was too poor to employ counsel. In the absence of warnings, the burden would be on the State to prove that counsel was knowingly and intelligently waived or that in the totality of the circumstances, including the failure to give the necessary warnings, the confession was clearly voluntary.

Rather than employing the arbitrary Fifth Amendment rule which the Court lays down I would follow the more pliable dictates of the Due Process Clauses of the Fifth and Fourteenth Amendments which we are accustomed to administering and which we know from our cases are effective instruments in protecting persons in police custody. In this way we would not be acting in the dark nor in one full sweep changing the traditional rules of custodial interrogation which this Court has for so long recognized as a justifiable and proper tool in balancing individual rights against the rights of society.

Justice HARLAN, with whom Justice STEWART and Justice WHITE join, dissenting.

Without at all subscribing to the generally black picture of police conduct painted by the Court, I think it must be frankly recognized at the outset that police questioning allowable under due process precedents may inherently entail some pressure on the suspect and may seek advantage in his ignorance or weaknesses. The atmosphere and questioning techniques, proper and fair though they be, can in themselves exert a tug on the suspect to confess, and in this light "[t]o speak of any confessions of crime made after arrest as being 'voluntary' or 'uncoerced' is somewhat inaccurate, although traditional. A confession is wholly and incontestably voluntary only if a guilty person gives himself up to the law and becomes his own accuser." *Ashcraft v. State of Tennessee,* 322 U.S. 143 [(1944)] (JACKSON, J., dissenting). Until today, the role of the Constitution has been only to sift out *undue* pressure, not to assure spontaneous confessions. . . .

What the Court largely ignores is that its rules impair, if they will not eventually serve wholly to frustrate, an instrument of law enforcement that has long and quite reasonably been thought worth the price paid for it. There can be little doubt that the Court's new code would markedly decrease the number of confessions. To warn the suspect that he may remain silent and remind him that his confession may be used in court are minor obstructions. To require also an express waiver by the suspect and an end to questioning whenever he demurs must heavily handicap questioning. And to suggest or provide counsel for the suspect simply invites the end of the interrogation. . . .

In conclusion: Nothing in the letter or the spirit of the Constitution or in the precedents squares with the heavy-handed and one-sided action that is so precipitously taken by the Court in the name of fulfilling its constitutional responsibilities.

Justice WHITE, with whom Justice HARLAN and Justice STEWART join, dissenting.

I.

The proposition that the privilege against self-incrimination forbids in-custody interrogation without the warnings specified in the majority opinion and without a clear waiver of counsel has no significant support in the history of the privilege or in the language of the Fifth Amendment. As for the English authorities and the common-law history, the privilege, firmly established in the second half of the seventeenth century, was never applied except to prohibit compelled judicial interrogations. The rule excluding coerced confessions matured about 100 years later, "[b]ut there is nothing in the reports to suggest that the theory has its roots in the privilege against self-incrimination. . . ."

That the Court's holding today is neither compelled nor even strongly suggested by the language of the Fifth Amendment, is at odds with American and English legal history, and involves a departure from a long line of precedent does not prove either that the Court has exceeded its powers or that the Court is wrong or unwise in its present reinterpretation of the Fifth Amendment. It does, however, underscore the obvious—that the Court has not discovered or found the law in making today's decision, nor has it derived it from some irrefutable sources; what it has done is to make new law and new public policy in much the same way that it has in the course of interpreting other great clauses of the Constitution. This is what the Court historically has done. Indeed, it is what it must do and will continue to do until and unless there is some fundamental change in the constitutional distribution of governmental powers.

But if the Court is here and now to announce new and fundamental policy to govern certain aspects of our affairs, it is wholly legitimate to examine the mode of this or any other constitutional decision in this Court and to inquire into the advisability of its end product in terms of the long-range interest of the country. At the very least, the Court's text and reasoning should withstand analysis and be a fair exposition of the constitutional provision which its opinion interprets. Decisions like these cannot rest alone on syllogism, metaphysics or some ill-defined notions of natural justice, although each will perhaps play its part. In proceeding to such constructions as it now announces, the Court should also duly consider all the factors and interests bearing upon the cases, at least insofar as the relevant materials are available; and if the necessary considerations are not treated in the record or obtainable from some other reliable source, the Court should not proceed to formulate fundamental policies based on speculation alone.

First, we may inquire what are the textual and factual bases of this new fundamental rule. To reach the result announced on the grounds it does, the Court must stay within the confines of the Fifth Amendment, which forbids self-incrimination only if *compelled*. Hence the core of the Court's opinion is that because of the "compulsion inherent in custodial surroundings, no statement obtained from [a] defendant [in custody] can truly be the product of his free choice," absent the use of adequate protective devices as described by the Court. However, the Court does not point to any sudden inrush of new knowledge requiring the rejection of 70 years' experience. . . . Rather than asserting new knowledge, the Court concedes that it cannot truly know what occurs during custodial questioning, because of the innate secrecy of such proceedings. It extrapolates a picture of what it conceives to be the norm from police investigatorial manuals, published in 1959 and 1962 or earlier, without any attempt to allow for adjustments in police practices that may have occurred in the wake of more recent decisions of state appellate tribunals or this Court. . . . Insofar as appears from the Court's opinion, it has not examined a single transcript of any police interrogation, let alone the interrogation that took place in any one of these cases which it decides today. Judged by any of the standards for empirical investigation utilized in the social sciences the factual basis for the Court's premise is patently inadequate. . . .

[Moreover,] it has never been suggested, until today, that such questioning was so coercive and accused persons so lacking in hardihood that the very first response to the very first question following the commencement of custody must be conclusively presumed to be the product of an overborne will. . . .

[E]ven if one assumed that there was an adequate factual basis for the conclusion that all confessions obtained during in-custody interrogation are the product of compulsion, the rule propounded by the Court will still be irrational, for, apparently, it is only if the accused is also warned of his right to counsel and waives both that right and the right against self-incrimination that the inherent compulsiveness of interrogation disappears. But if the defendant may not answer without a warning a question such as "Where were you last night?" without having his answer be a compelled one, how can the Court ever accept his negative answer to the question of whether he wants to consult his retained counsel or counsel whom the court will appoint? And why if counsel is present and the accused nevertheless confesses, or counsel tells the accused to tell the truth, and that is what the accused does, is the situation any less coercive insofar as the accused is concerned? The Court apparently realizes its dilemma of foreclosing questioning without the necessary warnings but at the same time permitting the accused, sitting in the same chair in front of the same policemen, to waive his right to consult an attorney. It expects, however, that the accused will not often waive the right; and if it is claimed that he has, the State faces a severe, if not impossible burden of proof.

All of this makes very little sense in terms of the compulsion which the Fifth Amendment proscribes. That amendment deals with compelling the accused himself. It is his free will that is involved. Confessions and incriminating admissions, as such, are not forbidden evidence; only those which are compelled are banned. I doubt that the Court observes these distinctions today.

By considering any answers to any interrogation to be compelled regardless of the content and course of examination and by escalating the requirements to prove waiver, the Court not only prevents the use of compelled confessions but for all practical purposes forbids interrogation except in the presence of counsel. . . .

Criticism of the Court's opinion, however, cannot stop with a demonstration that the factual and textual bases for the rule it proponds are, at best, less than compelling. Equally relevant is an assessment of the rule's consequences measured against community values. The Court's duty to assess the consequences of its action is not satisfied by the utterance of the truth that a value of our system of criminal justice is "to respect the inviolability of the human personality" and to require government to produce the evidence against the accused by its own independent labors. More than the human dignity of the accused is involved; the human personality of others in the society must also be preserved. . . .

The rule announced today . . . is a deliberate calculus to prevent interrogations, to reduce the incidence of confessions and pleas of guilty and to increase the number of trials. . . .

In some unknown number of cases the Court's rule will return a killer, a rapist or other criminal to the streets and to the environment which produced him, to repeat his crime whenever it pleases him. As a consequence, there will not be a gain, but a loss, in human dignity. The real concern is not the unfortunate consequences of this new decision on the criminal law as an abstract, disembodied series of authoritative proscriptions, but the impact on those who rely on the public authority for protection and who without it can only engage in violent self-help with guns, knives and the help of their neighbors similarly inclined. . . .

Much of the trouble with the Court's new rule is that it will operate indiscriminately in all criminal cases, regardless of the severity of the crime or the circumstances involved. It applies to every defendant, whether the professional criminal or one committing a crime of momentary passion who is not part and parcel of organized crime. It will slow down the investigation and the apprehension of confederates in those cases where time is of the essence, such as kidnapping; those involving national security; and some of those involving organized crime. . . .

At the same time, the Court's *per se* approach may not be justified on the ground that it provides a "bright line" permitting the authorities to judge in advance whether interrogation may safely be pursued without jeopardizing the admissibility of any information obtained as a consequence. Nor can it be claimed that judicial time and effort, assuming that is a relevant consideration, will be conserved because of the ease of application of the new rule. Today's decision leaves open such questions as whether the accused was in custody, whether his statements were spontaneous or the product of interrogation, whether the accused has effectively waived his rights, and whether nontestimonial evidence introduced at trial is the fruit of statements made during a prohibited interrogation, all of which are certain to prove productive of uncertainty during investigation and litigation during prosecution. For all these reasons, if further restrictions on police interrogation are desirable at this time, a more flexible approach makes much more sense than the Court's constitutional straitjacket.

An early "impeach Earl Warren" sign in 1960. The sign was constructed by those who thought the Warren Court had gone too far in protecting the rights of the accused. *Paul Conklin.*

In re Gault
387 U.S. 1, 87 S.Ct. 1428 (1967)

Police arrested Gerald Gault, a fifteen year old, after a neighbor, Mrs. Cook, complained that he had made lewd remarks to her over the telephone. Gault's parents were neither notified by the police nor given a copy of the affidavit they filed for a court hearing. Gault was not advised of his rights to remain silent and to have the assistance of counsel. Moreover, Mrs. Cook was never called as a witness and no record was made of the court proceedings. Gault was found to be a juvenile delinquent and sentenced to a state industrial school for a maximum of six years (until he reached the age of twenty-one). Because under Arizona law there was no appeal in juvenile cases, the Gaults filed a petition for a writ of *habeas corpus* in state court. They challenged the constitutionality of Arizona's Juvenile Code for failing to afford juveniles numerous procedural guarantees that applied to adult criminal trials under the Fourteenth Amendment. A state superior court dismissed the writ and the Arizona Supreme Court affirmed. The Gaults then appealed to the Supreme Court, which granted *certiorari*.

Justice FORTAS delivers the opinion of the Court.

[A]ppellants. . . urge that we hold the Juvenile Code of Arizona invalid on its face or as applied in this case because, contrary to the Due Process Clause of the Fourteenth Amendment, the juvenile is taken from the custody of his parents and committed to a state institution pursuant to proceedings in which the Juvenile Court has virtually unlimited discretion, and in which the following basic rights are denied:

1. Notice of the charges;
2. Right to counsel;
3. Right to confrontation and cross-examination;
4. Privilege against self-incrimination;
5. Right to a transcript of the proceedings; and
6. Right to appellate review. . . .

From the inception of the juvenile court system, wide differences have been tolerated—indeed insisted upon—between the procedural rights accorded to adults and those of juveniles. In practically all jurisdictions, there are rights granted to adults which are withheld from juveniles. In addition to the specific problems involved in the present case, for example, it has been held that the juvenile is not entitled to bail, to indictment by grand jury, to a public trial or to trial by jury. It is frequent practice that rules governing the arrest and interrogation of adults by the police are not observed in the case of juveniles.

The history and theory underlying this development are well-known, but a recapitulation is necessary for purposes of this opinion. The Juvenile Court movement began in this country at the end of the last century. From the juvenile court statute adopted in Illinois in 1899, the system has spread to every State in the Union, the District of Columbia, and Puerto Rico. . . .

The early reformers were appalled by adult procedures and penalties, and by the fact that children could be given long prison sentences and mixed in jails with hardened criminals. They were profoundly convinced that society's duty to the child could not be confined by the concept of justice alone. They believed that society's role was not to ascertain whether the child was "guilty" or "innocent," but "What is he, how has he become what he is, and what had best be done in his interest and in the interest of the state to save him from a downward career." The child—essentially good, as they saw it—was to be made "to feel that he is the object of [the state's] care and solicitude," not that he was under arrest or on trial. The rules of criminal procedure were therefore altogether inapplicable. The apparent rigidities, technicalities, and harshness which they observed in both substantive and procedural criminal law were therefore to be discarded. The idea of crime and punishment was to be abandoned. The child was to be "treated" and "rehabilitated" and the procedures, from apprehension through institutionalization, were to be "clinical" rather than punitive.

These results were to be achieved, without coming to conceptual and constitutional grief, by insisting that the proceedings were not adversary, but that the state was proceeding as *parens patriae.* The Latin phrase proved to be a great help to those who sought to rationalize the exclusion of juveniles from the constitutional scheme; but its meaning is murky and its historic credentials are of dubious relevance. The phrase was taken from chancery practice, where, however, it was used to describe the power of the state to act *in loco parentis* for the purpose of protecting the property interests and the person of the child. But there is no trace of the doctrine in the history of criminal jurisprudence. At common law, children under seven were considered incapable of possessing criminal intent. Beyond that age, they were subjected to arrest, trial, and in theory to punishment like adult offenders. In these old days, the state was not deemed to have authority to accord them fewer procedural rights than adults.

The right of the state, as *parens patriae,* to deny to the child procedural rights available to his elders was elaborated by the assertion that a child, unlike an adult, has a right "not to liberty but to custody." He can be made to attorn to his parents, to go to school, etc. If his parents default in effectively performing their custodial functions—that is, if the child is "delinquent"— the state may intervene. In doing so, it does not deprive the child of any rights, because he has none. It merely provides the "custody" to which the child is entitled. On this basis, proceedings involving juveniles were described as "civil" not "criminal" and therefore not subject to the requirements which restrict the state when it seeks to deprive a person of his liberty.

Accordingly, the highest motives and most enlightened impulses led to a peculiar system for juveniles, unknown to our law in any comparable context. The constitutional and theoretical basis for this peculiar system is—to say the least—debatable. . . . In 1937, Dean Pound wrote: "The powers of the Star Chamber were a trifle in comparison with those of our juvenile courts. . . ." The absence of substantive standards has not necessarily meant that children receive careful, compassionate, individualized treatment. The absence of procedural rules based upon constitutional principle has not always produced fair, efficient, and effective procedures. . . .

Failure to observe the fundamental requirements of due process has resulted in instances, which might have been avoided, of unfairness to individuals and inadequate or inaccurate findings of fact and unfortunate prescriptions of remedy. Due process of law is the primary and indispensable foundation of individual freedom. It is the basic and essential term in the social compact which defines the rights of the individual and delimits the powers which the state may exercise. . . .

It is claimed that juveniles obtain benefits from the special procedures applicable to them which more than offset the disadvantages of denial of the substance of normal due process. As we shall discuss, the observance of due process standards, intelligently and not ruthlessly administered, will not compel the States to abandon or displace any of the substantive benefits of the juvenile process. But it is important, we think, that the claimed benefits of the juvenile process should be candidly appraised. Neither sentiment nor folklore should cause us to shut our eyes, for example, to such startling findings as that reported in an exceptionally reliable study of repeaters or recidivism conducted by the Stanford Research Institute for the President's Commission on Crime in the District of Columbia. This Commission's Report states:

> "In fiscal 1966 approximately 66 percent of the 16- and 17-year-old juveniles referred to the court by the Youth Aid Division had been before the court previously. In 1965, 56 percent of those in the Receiving Home were repeaters. The SRI study revealed that 61 percent of the sample Juvenile Court referrals in 1965 had been previously referred at least once and that 42 percent had been referred at least twice before."

Certainly, these figures and the high crime rates among juveniles to which we have referred could not lead us to conclude that the absence of constitutional protections reduces crime, or that the juvenile system, functioning free of constitutional inhibitions as it has largely done, is effective to reduce crime or rehabilitate offenders. We do not mean by this to denigrate the juvenile court process or to suggest that there are not aspects of the juvenile system relating to offenders which are valuable. But the features of the juvenile system which its proponents have asserted are of unique benefit will not be impaired by constitutional domestication. . . .

Further, it is urged that the juvenile benefits from informal proceedings in the court. The early conception of the Juvenile Court proceeding was one in which a fatherly judge touched the heart and conscience of the erring youth by talking over his problems, by paternal advice and admonition, and in which, in extreme situations, benevolent and wise institutions of the State provided guidance and help "to save him from a downward career." Then, as now, goodwill and compassion were admirably prevalent. But recent studies have, with surprising unanimity, entered sharp dissent as to the validity of this gentle conception. They suggest that the appearance as well as the actuality of fairness, impartiality and orderliness—in short, the essentials of due process—may be a more impressive and more therapeutic attitude so far as the juvenile is concerned. . . .

Ultimately, however, we confront the reality of that portion of the Juvenile Court process with which we deal in this case. A boy is charged with misconduct. The boy is committed to an institution where he may be restrained of liberty for years. It is of no constitutional consequence—and of limited practical meaning—that the institution to which he is committed is called an Industrial School. The fact of the matter is that, however euphemistic the title, a "receiving home" or an "industrial school" for juveniles is an institution of confinement in which the child is incarcerated for a greater or lesser time. His world becomes "a building with whitewashed walls, regimented routine and institutional hours. . . ." Instead of mother and father and sisters and brothers and friends and classmates, his world is peopled by guards, custodians, state employees, and "delinquents" confined with him for anything from waywardness to rape and homicide.

In view of this, it would be extraordinary if our Constitution did not require the procedural regularity and the exercise of care implied in the phrase "due process." Under our Constitution, the condition of being a boy does not justify a kangaroo court. The traditional ideas of Juvenile Court procedure, indeed, contemplated that time would be available and care would be used to establish precisely what the juvenile did and why he did it—was it a prank of adolescence or a brutal act threatening serious consequences to himself or society unless corrected? Under traditional notions, one would assume that in a case like that of Gerald Gault, where the juvenile appears to have a home, a working mother and father, and an older brother, the Juvenile Judge would have made a careful inquiry and judgment as to the possibility that the boy could be disciplined and dealt with at home, despite his previous transgressions. Indeed, so far as appears in the record before us, except for some conversation with Gerald about his school work and his "wanting to go to. . . Grand Canyon with his father," the points to which the judge directed his attention were little different from those that would be involved in determining any charge of violation of a penal statute. The essential difference between Gerald's case and a normal criminal case is that safeguards available to adults were discarded in Gerald's case. The summary procedure as well as the long commitment was possible because Gerald was 15 years of age instead of over 18. . . .

[Justice FORTAS concluded by holding that in juvenile proceedings: (1) due process requires adequate and timely notice of the charges against an individual, (2) there is a right to counsel, (3) the privilege against self-incrimination is applicable, and (4) "absent a valid confession, a determination of delinquency and an order to a state institution cannot be sustained in the absence of sworn testimony subjected to the opportunity for cross-examination." Justice FORTAS did not rule on whether juveniles have a right to a transcript of their proceedings or on their right to appellate review.]

Justice BLACK, concurring.

Where a person, infant or adult, can be seized by the State, charged, and convicted for violating a state criminal law, and then ordered by the State to be confined for six years, I think the Constitution requires that he be tried in accordance with the guarantees of all the provisions of the Bill of Rights made applicable to the States by the Fourteenth Amendment. Undoubtedly this would be true of an adult defendant, and it would be a plain denial of equal protection of the laws—an invidious discrimination—to hold that others subject to heavier punishments could, because they are children, be denied these same constitutional safeguards. I consequently agree with the Court that the Arizona law as applied here denied to the parents and their son the right of notice, right to counsel, right against self-incrimination, and right to confront the witnesses against young Gault. Appellants are entitled to these rights, not because "fairness, impartiality and orderliness—in short, the essentials of due process"—require them and not because they are "the procedural rules which have been fashioned from the generality of due process," but because they are specifically and unequivocally granted by provisions of the Fifth and Sixth Amendments which the Fourteenth Amendment makes applicable to the States.

Justice WHITE concurred.

Justice HARLAN concurring in part and dissenting in part.

The proper issue here is . . . not whether the State may constitutionally treat juvenile offenders through a system of specialized courts, but whether the proceedings in Arizona's juvenile courts include procedural guarantees which satisfy the requirements of the Fourteenth Amendment. Among the first premises of our constitutional system is the obligation to conduct any proceeding in which an individual may be deprived of liberty or property in a fashion consistent with the "traditions and conscience of our people.". . .

I . . . suggest three criteria by which the procedural requirements of due process should be measured here: first, no more restrictions should be imposed than are imperative to assure the proceedings' fundamental fairness; second, the restrictions which are imposed should be those which preserve, so far as possible, the essential elements of the State's purpose; and finally, restrictions should be chosen which will later permit the orderly selection of any additional protections which may ultimately prove necessary. In this way, the Court may guarantee the fundamental fairness of the proceeding, and yet permit the State to continue development of an effective response to the problems of juvenile crime.

Measured by these criteria, only three procedural requirements should, in my opinion, now be deemed required of state juvenile courts by the Due Process Clause of the Fourteenth Amendment: first, timely notice must be provided to parents and children of the nature and terms of any juvenile court proceeding in which a determination affecting their rights or interests may be made; second, unequivocal and timely notice must be given that counsel may appear in any such proceeding in behalf of the child and its parents, and that in cases in which the child may be confined in an institution, counsel may, in circumstances of indigency, be appointed for them; and third, the court must maintain a written record, or its equivalent, adequate to permit effective review on appeal or in collateral proceedings. These requirements would guarantee to juveniles the tools with which their rights could be fully vindicated, and yet permit the States to pursue without unnecessary hindrance the purposes which they believe imperative in this field. Further, their imposition now would later permit more intelligent assessment of the necessity under the Fourteenth Amendment of additional requirements, by creating suitable records from which the character and deficiencies of juvenile proceedings could be accurately judged. . . .

Finally, I turn to assess the validity of this juvenile court proceeding under the criteria discussed in this opinion. Measured by them, the judgment below must, in my opinion, fall. Gerald Gault and his parents were not provided adequate notice of the terms and purposes of the proceedings in which he was adjudged delinquent; they were not advised of their rights to be represented by counsel; and no record in any form was maintained of the proceedings. It follows, for the reasons given in this opinion, that Gerald Gault was deprived of his liberty without due process of law, and I therefore concur in the judgment of the Court.

Justice STEWART dissenting.

The Court today uses an obscure Arizona case as a vehicle to impose upon thousands of juvenile courts throughout the Nation restrictions that the Constitution made applicable to adversary criminal trials. I believe the Court's decision is wholly unsound as a matter of constitutional law, and sadly unwise as a matter of judicial policy.

Juvenile proceedings are not criminal trials. They are not civil trials. They are simply not adversary proceedings. Whether treating with a delinquent child, a neglected child, a defective child, or a dependent child, a juvenile proceeding's whole purpose and mission is the very opposite of the mission and purpose of a prosecution in a criminal court. The object of the one is correction of a condition. The object of the other is conviction and punishment for a criminal act. . . .

I possess neither the specialized experience nor the expert knowledge to predict with any certainty where may lie the brightest hope for progress in dealing with the serious problems of juvenile delinquency. But I am certain that the answer does not lie in the Court's opinion in this case, which serves to convert a juvenile proceeding into a criminal prosecution.

The inflexible restrictions that the Constitution so wisely made applicable to adversary criminal trials have no inevitable place in the proceedings of those public social agencies known as juvenile or family courts. And to impose the Court's long catalog of requirements upon juvenile proceedings in every area of the country is to invite a long step backwards into the nineteenth century.

THE DEVELOPMENT OF LAW

Burger and Rehnquist Court Rulings on Coerced Confessions and Limiting Miranda

Case	Vote	Ruling
Parker v. North Carolina, 397 U.S. 790 (1970)	6:3	Defendant's guilty plea was voluntary where, after an allegedly coerceive interrogation, it was given one month later and he testified at trial that it was voluntary.
North Carolina v. Alford, 400 U.S. 25 (1970)	6:3	A guilty plea, made on advice of counsel, was not compelled merely because the plea was a way of avoiding the death penalty.
Harris v. New York, 401 U.S. 222 (1971)	5:4	Incriminating statements without being given *Miranda* warnings

Case	Vote	Ruling
		may be used to impeach accused's testimony at trial.
Lego v. Twomey, 404 U.S. 477 (1972)	4:3	Preponderance of evidence is the standard for proving that a confession is voluntary.
Milton v. Wainwright, 407 U.S. 605 (1972)	5:4	Held that it was a harmless error to introduce at trial a confession obtained by a fellow prisoner (and undercover police officer) in a jail cell after the defendant had been indicted.
Michigan v. Tucker, 417 U.S. 433 (1974)	8:1	Upheld the use of a witness at trial who was discovered as a result of questioning of defendant who had not received *Miranda* warnings.
Oregon v. Hass, 420 U.S. 714 (1975)	6:2	Upheld use of incriminating statements made by defendant in police car after being given *Miranda* warnings and requesting the presence of counsel, but where defendant was told that counsel could not be telephoned until they reached police station.
Michigan v. Mosley, 423 U.S. 96 (1975)	7:2	Once *Miranda* warnings are given and accused indicates desire to remain silent, any police questioning must be in presence of an attorney. But, here, questioning stopped and was resumed two hours later, and the incriminating statements that were thereby elicited could be used at trial.
Beckwith v. United States, 425 U.S. 341 (1976)	8:1	Statements made to an Internal Revenue Service agent during a noncustodial interview without *Miranda* warnings could be used at trial.
United States v. Mandjano, 426 U.S. 564 (1976)	9:0	*Miranda* does require the suppression of false statements at trial which were made to a grand jury, even though defendent had not been given *Miranda* warnings or told that he was a suspect.
Oregon v. Mathiason, 429 U.S. 711 (1977)	6:3	*Miranda* is not violated where a person on parole voluntarily goes to police station at officer's request, agrees to a thirty-minute interview, and is allowed to leave but

Case	Vote	Ruling
		is later arrested based on incriminating statements made in the interview.
United States v. Washington, 431 U.S. 181 (1977); and *United States v. Wong*, 431 U.S. 174 (1977)	7:2	Held that prosecutors may use at trial incriminating statements made by a witness before a grand jury even though the witness was not told that he was in danger of being indicted; as a result, perjured testimony before grand jury may be used at trial even though defendant had not received an effective warning of his rights.
North Carolina v. Butler, 441 U.S. 369 (1979)	6:3	Held that it is not necessary for a suspect to expressly waive rights during a custodial interrogation.
Rhode Island v. Innis, 446 U.S. 291 (1980)	6:3	*Miranda* comes into operation at time of "interrogation."
California v. Prysock, 453 U.S. 355 (1981)	6:3	Precise language of *Miranda* warning is not necessary when informing suspects of their rights.
Oregon v. Bradshaw, 462 U.S. 1039 (1983)	5:4	Held that the initiation of a conversation with the police by a defendant amounts to a waiver of *Miranda* rights.
California v. Beheler, 463 U.S. 1121 (1983)	6:3	*Miranda* is not required when the suspect voluntarily goes to the police station for questioning and is allowed to leave and later is arrested.
Minnesota v. Murphy, 465 U.S. 420 (1984)	6:3	Probation officer who obtained incriminating information from parole was not obliged to give *Miranda* warnings.
Oregon v. Elstad, 470 U.S. 298 (1985)	6:3	Upheld the use of an initial culpatory statement, made in violation of *Miranda*, because it was voluntarily given by the defendant in his home.
Moran v. Burbine, 475 U.S. 412 (1986)	6:3	Defendant's *Miranda* rights were not violated by police questioning in the absence of an attorney, when they failed to inform the defendant that an attorney had been retained by his sister for him and was trying to reach him.
Michigan v. Jackson, 475 U.S. 625 (1986)	6:3	Held that once a defendant has been charged and requests an attorney any subsequent waiver of Sixth

Case	Vote	Ruling
		Amendment rights is presumed invalid if incriminating statements are made pursuant to a police-initiated conversation.
Allen v. Illinois, 478 U.S. 364 (1986)	5:4	Fifth Amendment does not apply to incriminating statements made in proceedings to commit a person said to be sexually dangerous to a psychiatric prison.
Colorado v. Connelly, 479 U.S. 157 (1986)	7:2	Fifth Amendment not violated by the confession of a mentally ill man who told police that the "voice of God" told him to confess to a murder.
Arizona v. Mauro, 481 U.S. 520 (1987)	5:4	*Miranda* not violated when defendant was informed of rights, requested an attorney, and was allowed to have a telephone conversation with his wife, which the police recorded and later introduced as evidence against the defendant.
Pennsylvania v. Burder, 488 U.S. 9 (1988)	7:2	Held that ordinary traffic stops are not custodial stops for the purposes of *Miranda,* and police do not have to read drivers their *Miranda* rights.
Duckworth v. Eagan, 109 S.Ct. 2875 (1989)	5:4	When advising suspects of their rights, the police may depart from the actual wording of the rights set down in *Miranda.*
Michigan v. Harvey, 110 S.Ct. 1176 (1990)	5:4	Held that, notwithstanding the ruling in *Michigan v. Jackson* (1986), prosecutors may use for impeachment purposes incriminating statements made by a defendant after requesting an attorney and during a police-initiated conversation.
New York v. Harris, 110 S.Ct. 1640 (1990)	5:4	Held that the exclusionary rule does not bar prosecutors from using a defendant's incriminating statements made after a warrantless and nonconsensual entry into his home.
Illinois v. Perkins, 110 S.Ct. 2394 (1990)	8:1	The Court held that a defendant, who was jailed but not yet arraigned, had no right to be informed by a police undercover

Case	Vote	Ruling
		agent posing as a fellow inmate of his *Miranda* rights before seeking to elicit his incriminating statements; Justice Marshall dissented.

Rhode Island v. Innis

446 U.S. 291, 100 S.Ct. 1682 (1980)

Justice Potter Stewart discusses the facts, involving the issue of what is a police interrogation and when is a confession compelled by police in violation of *Miranda*, in his opinion for the Court.

Justice STEWART delivers the opinion of the Court.

On the night of January 12, 1975, John Mulvaney, a Providence, R.I., taxicab driver, disappeared after being dispatched to pick up a customer. His body was discovered four days later buried in a shallow grave in Coventry, R.I. He had died from a shotgun blast aimed at the back of his head.

On January 17, 1975, shortly after midnight, the Providence police received a telephone call from Gerald Aubin, also a taxicab driver, who reported that he had just been robbed by a man wielding a sawed-off shotgun. Aubin further reported that he had dropped off his assailant near Rhode Island College in a section of Providence known as Mount Pleasant. While at the Providence police station waiting to give a statement, Aubin noticed a picture of his assailant on a bulletin board. Aubin so informed one of the police officers present. The officer prepared a photo array, and again Aubin identified a picture of the same person. That person was the respondent. Shortly thereafter, the Providence police began a search of the Mount Pleasant area.

At approximately 4:30 A.M. on the same date, Patrolman Lovell, while cruising the streets of Mount Pleasant in a patrol car, spotted the respondent standing in the street facing him. When Patrolman Lovell stopped his car, the respondent walked towards it. Patrolman Lovell then arrested the respondent, who was unarmed, and advised him of his so-called *Miranda* rights. While the two men waited in the patrol car for other police officers to arrive, Patrolman Lovell did not converse with the respondent other than to respond to the latter's request for a cigarette.

Within minutes, Sergeant Sears arrived at the scene of the arrest, and he also gave the respondent the *Miranda* warnings. Immediately thereafter, Captain Leyden and other police officers arrived. Captain Leyden advised the respondent of his *Miranda* rights. The respondent stated that he understood those rights and wanted to speak with a lawyer. Captain Leyden then directed that the respondent be placed in a "caged wagon," a four-door police car with a wire screen mesh between the front and rear seats, and be driven to the central police station. . . .

While en route to the central station, Patrolman Gleckman initiated a conversation with Patrolman McKenna concerning the missing shotgun. . . . Patrolman McKenna apparently shared his fellow officer's concern. . . . While Patrolman Williams said nothing, he overheard the conversation between the two officers:

"A. He [Gleckman] said it would be too bad if the little— I believe he said a girl—would pick up the gun, maybe kill herself."

The respondent then interrupted the conversation, stating that the officers should turn the car around so he could show them where the gun was located. At this point, Patrolman McKenna radioed back to Captain Leyden that they were returning to the scene of the arrest and that the respondent would inform them of the location of the gun. At the time the respondent indicated that the officers should turn back, they had traveled no more than a mile, a trip encompassing only a few minutes.

The police vehicle then returned to the scene of the arrest where a search for the shotgun was in progress. There, Captain Leyden again advised the respondent of his *Miranda* rights. The respondent replied that he understood those rights but that he "wanted to get the gun out of the way because of the kids in the area in the school." The respondent then led the police to a nearby field, where he pointed out the shotgun under some rocks by the side of the road. . . .

It was the view of the state appellate court that, even though the police officers may have been genuinely concerned about the public safety and even though the respondent had not been addressed personally by the police officers, the respondent nonetheless had been subjected to "subtle coercion" that was the equivalent of "interrogation" within the meaning of the *Miranda* opinion. . . .

We granted certiorari to address for the first time the meaning of "interrogation" under *Miranda v. Arizona.* . . .

In the present case, the parties are in agreement that the respondent was fully informed of his *Miranda* rights and that he invoked his *Miranda* right to counsel when he told Captain Leyden that he wished to consult with a lawyer. It is also uncontested that the respondent was "in custody" while being transported to the police station.

The issue, therefore, is whether the respondent was "interrogated" by the police officers in violation of the respondent's undisputed right under *Miranda* to remain silent until he had consulted with a lawyer. In resolving this issue, we first define the term "interrogation" under *Miranda* before turning to a consideration of the facts of this case.

The starting point for defining "interrogation" in this context is, of course, the Court's *Miranda* opinion. There the Court observed that "[b]y custodial interrogation, we mean *questioning* initiated by law enforcement officers after a person has been taken into custody or otherwise deprived of his freedom of action in any significant way." (emphasis added). This passage and other references throughout the opinion to "questioning" might suggest that the *Miranda* rules were to apply only to those police interrogation practices that involve express questioning of a defendant while in custody.

We do not, however, construe the *Miranda* opinion so narrowly. The concern of the Court in *Miranda* was that the "interrogation environment" created by the interplay of interrogation and custody would "subjugate the individual to the will of his examiner" and thereby undermine the privilege against compulsory self-incrimination. The police practices that evoked this concern included several that did not involve express questioning. For example, one of the practices discussed in *Miranda* was the use of line-ups in which a coached witness would pick the defendant as the perpetrator. . . .

This is not to say, however, that all statements obtained by the police after a person has been taken into custody are to be considered the product of interrogation. As the Court in *Miranda* noted:

> "Confessions remain a proper element in law enforcement. Any statement given freely and voluntarily without any compelling influences is, of course, admissible in evidence. *The fundamental import of the privilege while an individual is in custody is not whether he is allowed to talk to the police without the benefit of warnings and counsel, but whether he can be interrogated.* . . . Volunteered statements of any kind are not barred by the Fifth Amendment and their admissibility is not affected by our holding today." (emphasis added).

It is clear therefore that the special procedural safeguards outlined in *Miranda* are required not where a suspect is simply taken into custody, but rather where a suspect in custody is subjected to interrogation. "Interrogation," as conceptualized in the *Miranda* opinion, must reflect a measure of compulsion above and beyond that inherent in custody itself.

We conclude that the *Miranda* safeguards come into play whenever a person in custody is subjected to either express questioning or its functional equivalent. That is to say, the term "interrogation" under *Miranda* refers not only to express questioning, but also to any words or actions on the part of the police (other than those normally attendant to arrest and custody) that the police should know are reasonably likely to elicit an incriminating response from the suspect. . . .

Turning to the facts of the present case, we conclude that the respondent was not "interrogated" within the meaning of *Miranda*. It is undisputed that the first prong of the definition of "interrogation" was not satisfied, for the conversation between Patrolmen Gleckman and McKenna included no express questioning of the respondent. Rather, that conversation was, at least in form, nothing more than a dialogue between the two officers to which no response from the respondent was invited.

Moreover, it cannot be fairly concluded that the respondent was subjected to the "functional equivalent" of questioning. It cannot be said, in short, that Patrolmen Gleckman and McKenna should have known that their conversation was reasonably likely to elicit an incriminating response from the respondent. There is nothing in the record to suggest that the officers were aware that the respondent was peculiarly susceptible to an appeal to his conscience concerning the safety of handicapped children. Nor is there anything in the record to suggest that the police knew that the respondent was unusually disoriented or upset at the time of his arrest.

The case thus boils down to whether, in the context of a brief conversation, the officers should have known that the respondent would suddenly be moved to make a self-incriminating response. Given the fact that the entire conversation appears to have consisted of no more than a few off hand remarks, we cannot say that the officers should have known that it was reasonably likely that Innis would so respond. . . .

For the reasons stated, the judgment of the Supreme Court of Rhode Island is vacated, and the case is remanded to that court for further proceedings not inconsistent with this opinion.

It is so ordered.

Justice WHITE concurred.

Chief Justice BURGER concurred.

Justice MARSHALL, with whom Justice BRENNAN joins, dissenting.

I am substantially in agreement with the Court's definition of "interrogation" within the meaning of *Miranda v. Arizona.* . . . In my view, the *Miranda* safeguards apply whenever police conduct is intended or likely to produce a response from a suspect in custody. As I read the Court's opinion, its definition of "interrogation" for *Miranda* purposes is equivalent, for practical purposes, to my formulation, since it contemplates that "where a police practice is designed to elicit an incriminating response from the accused, it is unlikely that the practice will not also be one which the police should have known was reasonably likely to have that effect." Thus, the Court requires an objective inquiry into the likely effect of police conduct on a typical individual, taking into account any special susceptibility of the suspect to certain kinds of pressure of which the police know or have reason to know.

I am utterly at a loss, however, to understand how this objective standard as applied to the facts before us can rationally lead to the conclusion that there was no interrogation. . . .

The Court attempts to characterize Gleckman's statements as "no more than a few off hand remarks" which could not reasonably have been expected to elicit a response. If the statements had been addressed to respondent, it would be impossible to draw such a conclusion. The simple message of the "talking back and forth" between Gleckman and McKenna was that they had to find the shotgun to avert a child's death.

One can scarcely imagine a stronger appeal to the conscience of a suspect—*any* suspect—than the assertion that if the weapon is not found an innocent person will be hurt or killed. And not just any innocent person, but an innocent child—a little girl—a helpless, handicapped little girl on her way to school. The notion that such an appeal could not be expected to have any effect unless the suspect were known to have some special interest in handicapped children verges on the ludicrous. As a matter of fact, the appeal to a suspect to confess for the sake of others, to "display some evidence of decency and honor," is a classic interrogation technique. . . . This is not a case where police officers speaking among themselves are accidentally overheard by a suspect. These officers were "talking back and forth" in close quarters with the handcuffed suspect, traveling past the very place where they believed the weapon was located. They knew petitioner would hear and attend to their conversation, and they are chargeable with knowledge of and responsibility for the pressures to speak which they created.

I firmly believe that this case is simply an aberration, and that in future cases the Court will apply the standard adopted today in accordance with its plain meaning.

Justice STEVENS dissented in a separate opinion.

Colorado v. Connelly
479 U.S. 157, 107 S.Ct. 515 (1986)

Chief Justice William Rehnquist discusses the facts in his opinion for the Court, upholding the admissibility as evidence of an incriminating confession made by a mentally ill man, Francis Connelly.

Chief Justice REHNQUIST delivers the opinion of the Court.

In this case, the Supreme Court of Colorado held that the United States Constitution requires a court to suppress a confession when the mental state of the defendant, at the time he made the confession, interfered with his "rational intellect" and his "free will." . . . We conclude that the admissibility of this kind of statement is governed by state rules of evidence, rather than by our previous decisions regarding coerced confessions and *Miranda* waivers. We therefore reverse.

On August 18, 1983, Officer Patrick Anderson of the Denver Police Department was in uniform, working in an off-duty capacity in downtown Denver. Respondent Francis Connelly approached Officer Anderson and, without any prompting, stated that he had murdered someone and wanted to talk about it. Anderson immediately advised respondent that he had the right to remain silent, that anything he said could be used against him in court, and that he had the right to an attorney prior to any police questioning. Respondent stated that he understood these rights, but he still wanted to talk about the murder. . . .

At a [subsequent] preliminary hearing, respondent moved to suppress all of his statements. Doctor Jeffrey Metzner, a psychiatrist employed by the state hospital, testified that respondent was suffering from chronic schizophrenia and was in a psychotic state at least as of August 17, 1983, the day before he confessed. Metzner's interviews with respondent revealed that respondent was following the "voice of God." This voice instructed respondent to withdraw money from the bank, to buy an airplane ticket, and to fly from Boston to Denver. When respondent arrived from Boston, God's voice became stronger and told respondent either to confess to the killing or to commit suicide. Reluctantly following the command of the voices, respondent approached Officer Anderson and confessed. . . .

On the basis of this evidence the Colorado trial court decided that respondent's statements must be suppressed because they were "involuntary." . . .

The Colorado Supreme Court affirmed. . . .

The difficulty with the approach of the Supreme Court of Colorado is that it fails to recognize the essential link between coercive activity of the State, on the one hand, and a resulting confession by a defendant, on the other. The flaw in respondent's constitutional argument is that it would expand our previous line of "voluntariness" cases into a far-ranging requirement that courts must divine a defendant's motivation for speaking or acting as he did even though there be no claim that governmental conduct coerced his decision.

The most outrageous behavior by a private party seeking to secure evidence against a defendant does not make that evidence inadmissible under the Due Process Clause. . . . Moreover, suppressing respondent's statements would serve absolutely no purpose in enforcing constitutional guarantees. The purpose of excluding evidence seized in violation of the Constitution is to substantially deter future violations of the Constitution. Only if we were to establish a brand new constitutional right—the right of a criminal defendant to confess to his crime only when totally rational and properly motivated—could respondent's present claim be sustained. . . .

Respondent would now have us require sweeping inquiries into the state of mind of a criminal defendant who has confessed, inquiries quite divorced from any coercion brought to bear on the defendant by the State. We think the Constitution rightly leaves this sort of inquiry to be resolved by state laws governing the admission of evidence and erects no standard of its own in this area. . . .

We hold that coercive police activity is a necessary predicate to the finding that a confession is not "voluntary" within the meaning of the Due Process Clause of the Fourteenth Amendment. We also conclude that the taking of respondent's statements, and their admission into evidence, constitute no violation of that Clause. . . .

We also think that the Supreme Court of Colorado was mistaken in . . . importing into this area of constitutional law notions of "free will" that have no place there. There is obviously no reason to require more in the way of a "voluntariness" inquiry in the *Miranda* waiver context than in the Fourteenth Amendment confession context. The sole concern of the Fifth Amendment, on which *Miranda* was based, is governmental coercion. . . . The voluntariness of a waiver of this privilege has always depended on the absence of police overreaching, not on "free choice" in any broader sense of the word. . . .

Respondent urges this Court to adopt his "free will" rationale, and to find an attempted waiver invalid whenever the defendant feels compelled to waive his rights by reason of any compulsion, even if the compulsion does not flow from the police. But such a treatment of the waiver issue would "cut this Court's holding in [*Miranda*] completely loose from its own explicitly stated rationale." *Miranda* protects defendants against government coercion leading them to surrender rights protected by the Fifth Amendment; it goes no further than that. Respondent's perception of coercion flowing from the "voice of God," however important or significant such a perception may be in other disciplines, is a matter to which the United States Constitution does not speak.

Justice BLACKMUN, concurred in part.

Justice STEVENS concurring in part and dissenting in part.

I agree . . . that . . . the United States Constitution does not require suppression of [precustodial] statements, but in reaching that conclusion, unlike the Court, I am perfectly willing to accept the state trial court's finding that the statements were involuntary. . . .

When the officer whom respondent approached elected to handcuff him and to take him into custody, the police assumed a fundamentally different relationship with him. Prior to that moment, the police had no duty to give respondent *Miranda* warnings and had every right to continue their exploratory conversation with him. Once the custodial relationship was established, however, the questioning assumed a presumptively coercive character. In my opinion the questioning could not thereafter go forward in the absence of a valid waiver of respondent's constitutional rights unless he was provided with counsel. Since it is undisputed that respondent was not then competent to stand trial, I would also conclude that he was not competent to waive his constitutional right to remain silent. . . .

Accordingly, I concur in the judgment insofar as it applies to respondent's precustodial statements but respectfully dissent from the Court's disposition of the question that was not presented by the certiorari petition.

Justice BRENNAN, with whom Justice MARSHALL joins, dissenting.

Because I believe that the use of a mentally ill person's involuntary confession is antithetical to the notion of fundamental fairness embodied in the Due Process Clause, I dissent. . . .

Today's decision restricts the application of the term "involuntary" to those confessions obtained by police coercion. Confessions by mentally ill individuals or by persons coerced by parties other than police officers are now considered "voluntary." The Court's failure to recognize all forms of involuntariness or coercion as antithetical to due process reflects a refusal to acknowledge free will as a value of constitutional consequence. But due process derives much of its meaning from a conception of fundamental fairness that emphasizes the right to make vital choices voluntarily. . . .

Since the Court redefines voluntary confessions to include confessions by mentally ill individuals, the reliability of these confessions becomes a central concern. A concern for reliability is inherent in our criminal justice system, which relies upon accusatorial rather than inquisitorial practices. While an inquisitorial system prefers obtaining confessions from criminal defendants, an accusatorial system must place its faith in determinations of "guilt by evidence independently and freely secured.". . .

Because the admission of a confession so strongly tips the balance against the defendant in the adversarial process, we must be especially careful about a confession's reliability. We have to date not required a finding of reliability for involuntary confessions only because *all* such confessions have been excluded upon a finding of involuntariness, regardless of reliability. See, *Jackson v. Denno*, 378 U.S. 368 (1964). The Court's adoption today of a restrictive definition of an "involuntary" confession will require heightened scrutiny of a confession's reliability.

The instant case starkly highlights the danger of admitting a confession by a person with a severe mental illness. The trial court made no findings concerning the reliability of Mr. Connelly's involuntary confession, since it believed that the confession was excludable on the basis of involuntariness. However, the overwhelming evidence in the record points to the unreliability of Mr. Connelly's delusional mind. . . .

Moreover, the record is barren of any corroboration of the mentally ill defendant's confession. No physical evidence links the defendant to the alleged crime. Police did not identify the alleged victim's body as the woman named by the defendant. Mr. Connelly identified the alleged scene of the crime, but it has not been verified that the unidentified body was found there or that a crime actually occurred there. There is not a shred of competent evidence in this record linking the defendant to the charged homicide. There is only Mr. Connelly's confession.

Minimum standards of due process should require that the trial court find substantial indicia of reliability, on the basis of evidence extrinsic to the confession itself, before admitting the confession of a mentally ill person into evidence. I would require the trial court to make such a finding on remand. To hold otherwise allows the State to imprison and possibly to execute a mentally ill defendant based solely upon an inherently unreliable confession. . . .

Duckworth v. Eagan
109 S.Ct. 2875 (1989)

When first questioned by police about the stabbing of a woman, Gary Eagan made an exculpatory statement after being read and signing a waiver form that provided that if he could not afford a lawyer, one would be appointed for him "if and when you go to court." But a day later when being questioned again and after signing a different waiver form, Eagan confessed to the stabbing and led officers to a site where they recovered pertinent physical evidence. Over Eagan's attorney's objections, his two statements were admitted into evidence during trial. Following his conviction, Eagan unsuccessfully appealed to the Indiana Supreme Court and then applied for a writ of *habeas corpus* in federal district court. Eagan claimed, among other things, that his confession was inadmissible because the first waiver form did not comply with the requirements of *Miranda v. Arizona* (see page 945). The court denied his petition, holding that the record showed adherence to *Miranda*. But the Court of Appeals for the Seventh Circuit reversed on the grounds that the police informing Eagan that counsel would be appointed "if and when you go to court" was constitutionally defective, since it failed to make a clear and unequivocal warning that Eagan had a right to an appointed attorney before interrogation and because the police warning linked the right to counsel to a future event. The state appealed that ruling to the Supreme Court, which granted review.

Chief Justice REHNQUIST delivers the opinion of the Court.

[C]ertiorari . . . [was granted] to resolve a conflict among the lower courts as to whether informing a suspect that an attorney would be appointed for him "if and when you go to court" renders *Miranda* warnings inadequate. We agree with the majority of the lower courts that it does not.

In *Miranda v. Arizona*, 384 U.S. 436 (1966), the Court established certain procedural safeguards that require police to advise criminal suspects of their rights under the Fifth and Fourteenth Amendments before commencing custodial interrogation. In now-familiar words, the Court said that the suspect must be told that "he has the right to remain silent, that anything he says can be used against him in a court of law, that he has the right to the presence of an attorney, and that if he cannot afford an attorney one will be appointed for him prior to any questioning if he so desires." The Court in *Miranda* "presumed that interrogation in certain custodial circumstances is inherently coercive and . . . that statements made under those circumstances are inadmissible unless the suspect is specifically warned of his *Miranda* rights and freely decides to forgo those rights." *New York v. Quarles*, 467 U.S. 649 (1984). . . .

We have never insisted that *Miranda* warnings be given in the exact form described in that decision. In *Miranda* itself, the Court said that "[t]he warnings required and the waiver necessary in accordance with our opinion today are, *in the absence of a fully effective equivalent*, prerequisites to the admissibility of any statement made by a defendant.". . .

Miranda has not been limited to stationhouse questioning, see *Rhode Island v. Innis*, [446 U.S. 291 (1980)] (police car), and the officer in the field may not always have access to printed *Miranda* warnings, or he may inadvertently depart from routine practice, particularly if a suspect requests an elaboration of the warnings. The prophylactic *Miranda* warnings are "not themselves rights protected by the Constitution but [are] instead measures to insure that the right against compulsory self-incrimination [is] protected." *Michigan v. Tucker*, 417 U.S. 433 (1974). Reviewing courts therefore need not examine *Miranda* warnings as if construing a will or defining the terms of an easement. The inquiry is simply whether the warnings reasonably "conve[y] to [a suspect] his rights as required by *Miranda*." [*California v.*] *Prysock*, [453 U.S. 355 (1981)] . . .

We think the initial warnings given to respondent touched all of the bases required by *Miranda*. The police told respondent that he had the right to remain silent, that anything he said could be used against him in court, that he had the right to speak to an attorney before and during questioning, that he had "this right to the advice and presence of a lawyer even if [he could] not afford to hire one," and that he had the "right to stop answering at any time until [he] talked to a lawyer." . . . [T]he police also added that they could not provide respondent with a lawyer, but that one would be appointed "if and when you go to court." The Court of Appeals thought this "if and when you go to court" language suggested that "only those accused who can afford an attorney have the right to have one present before answering any questions," and "implie[d] that if the accused does not 'go to court,' *i.e.*[,] the government does not file charges, the accused is not entitled to [counsel] at all.". . .

In our view, the Court of Appeals misapprehended the effect of the inclusion of "if and when you go to court" language in *Miranda* warnings. First, this instruction accurately described the procedure for the appointment of counsel in Indiana. . . . We think it must be relatively commonplace for a suspect, after receiving *Miranda* warnings, to ask *when* he will obtain counsel. The "if and when you go to court" advice simply anticipates that question. Second, *Miranda* does not require that attorneys be producible on call, but only that the suspect be informed, as here, that he has the right to an attorney before and during questioning, and that an attorney would be appointed for him if he could not afford one. The Court in *Miranda* emphasized that it was not suggesting that "each police station must have a 'station house lawyer' present at all times to advise prisoners." If the police cannot provide appointed counsel, *Miranda* requires only that the police not question a suspect unless he waives his right to counsel. Here, respondent did just that.

The judgment of the Court of Appeals is accordingly reversed, and the case is remanded for further proceedings not inconsistent with our decision.

It is so ordered.

Justice O'CONNOR, with whom Justice SCALIA joins, concurring.

I concur in the CHIEF JUSTICE's opinion for the Court. I write separately to address an alternative ground for decision in this case which was raised, but not relied upon by the District Court. In my view, the rationale of our decision in *Stone v. Powell*, 428 U.S. 465 (1976), dictates that the suppression remedy be unavailable to respondent on federal habeas.

Justice MARSHALL, with whom Justice BRENNAN joins, and with whom Justice BLACKMUN and Justice STEVENS join as to Part I, dissenting.

I

The majority holds today that a police warning advising a suspect that he is entitled to an appointed lawyer only "if and when he goes to court" satisfies the requirements of *Miranda v. Arizona*, 384 U.S. 436 (1966). The majority reaches this result by seriously mischaracterizing that decision. Under *Miranda*, a police warning must *"clearly infor[m]"* a suspect taken into custody "that if he cannot afford an attorney one will be appointed for him *prior to any questioning* if he so desires." A warning qualified by an "if and when you go to court" caveat does nothing of the kind; instead, it leads the suspect to believe that a lawyer will not be provided until some indeterminate time in the future *after questioning*. I refuse to acquiesce in the continuing debasement of this historic precedent, and therefore dissent. I also write to express my disagreement with Justice O'CONNOR's uninvited suggestion that the rationale of *Stone v. Powell*, 428 U.S. 465 (1976), should be extended to bar federal habeas review of *Miranda* claims.

In concluding that the first warning given to respondent Eagan satisfies the dictates of *Miranda,* the majority makes a mockery of that decision. Eagan was initially advised that he had the right to the presence of counsel before and during questioning. But in the very next breath, the police informed Eagan that, if he could not afford a lawyer, one would be appointed to represent him only "if and when" he went to court. As the Court of Appeals found, Eagan could easily have concluded from the "if and when" caveat that only "those accused who can afford an attorney have the right to have one present before answering any questions; those who are not so fortunate must wait." Eagan was, after all, never told that questioning would be *delayed* until a lawyer was appointed "if and when" Eagan did, in fact, go to court. Thus, the "if and when" caveat may well have had the effect of negating the initial promise that counsel could be present. At best, a suspect like Eagan "would not know . . . whether or not he had a right to the services of a lawyer."

In lawyer-like fashion, the CHIEF JUSTICE parses the initial warnings given Eagan and finds that the most plausible interpretation is that Eagan would not be questioned until a lawyer was appointed when he later appeared in court. What goes wholly overlooked in the CHIEF JUSTICE's analysis is that the recipients of police warnings are often frightened suspects unlettered in the law, not lawyers or judges or others schooled in interpreting legal or semantic nuance. Such suspects can hardly be expected to interpret, in as facile a manner as the CHIEF JUSTICE, "the pretzel-like warnings here—intertwining, contradictory, and ambiguous as they are." The majority thus refuses to recognize that "[t]he warning of a right to counsel would be hollow if not couched in terms that would convey to the indigent—the person most often subjected to interrogation—the knowledge that he too has the right to have counsel present." *Miranda.* . . .

Even if the typical suspect could draw the inference the majority does—that questioning will not commence until a lawyer is provided at a later court appearance—a warning qualified by an "if and when" caveat still fails to give a suspect any indication of *when* he will be taken to court. Upon hearing the warnings given in this case, a suspect would likely conclude that no lawyer would be provided until trial. In common parlance, "going to court" is synonymous with "going to trial." Furthermore, the negative implication of the caveat is that, if the suspect is never taken to court, he "is not entitled to an attorney at all." An unwitting suspect harboring uncertainty on this score is precisely the sort of person who may feel compelled to talk "voluntarily" to the police, without the presence of counsel, in an effort to extricate himself from his predicament. . . .

Miranda, it is true, does not require the police to have a "station house lawyer" ready at all times to counsel suspects taken into custody. But if a suspect does not understand that a lawyer will be made available within a reasonable period of time after he has been taken into custody and advised of his rights, the suspect may decide to talk to the police *for that reason alone.* The threat of an indefinite deferral of interrogation, in a system like Indiana's, thus constitutes an effective means by which the police can pressure a suspect to speak without the presence of counsel. . . .

The majority's misreading of *Miranda*—stating that police warnings need only "touc[h] all of the bases required by *Miranda,*" that *Miranda* warnings need only be "reasonably conve[yed]" to a suspect (citation omitted), and that *Miranda* warnings are to be measured not point by point but "in their totality" —is exacerbated by its interpretation of *California v. Prysock,* 453 U.S. 355 (1981) (*per curiam*), a decision that squarely supports Eagan's claim in this case. The juvenile suspect in *Prysock* was initially told that he had the right to have a lawyer present before and during questioning. He then was told that that he had the right to have his parents present as well. At this point the suspect was informed that a lawyer would be appointed to represent him at no cost if he could not afford one. The California Court of Appeal ruled these warnings insufficient because the suspect was not expressly told of his right to an appointed attorney before and during questioning. This Court reversed, finding that "nothing in the warnings given respondent suggested any limitation on the right to the presence of appointed counsel.". . .

In reaching this result, the *Prysock* Court pointedly distinguished a series of lower court decisions that had found inadequate warnings in which "the reference to the right to appointed counsel was linked with some future point in time.". . .

It poses no great burden on law enforcement officers to eradicate the confusion stemming from the "if and when" caveat. Deleting the sentence containing the offending language is all that needs to be done. Purged of this language, the warning tells the suspect in a straightforward fashion that he has the right to the presence of a lawyer before and during questioning, and that a lawyer will be appointed if he cannot afford one. The suspect is given no reason to believe that the appointment of an attorney may come after interrogation. . . .

II

Not content with disemboweling *Miranda* directly, Justice O'CONNOR seeks to do so indirectly as well, urging that federal courts be barred from considering *Miranda* claims on habeas corpus review. In *Stone v. Powell,* 428 U.S. 465 (1976), the Court held that a state prisoner may not seek federal habeas corpus relief on the ground that evidence was obtained in violation of his Fourth Amendment rights if the state courts had provided a full and fair opportunity for litigation of that claim. I joined Justice BRENNAN's dissenting opinion in that case, in which he warned that the majority's rationale "portends substantial evisceration of federal habeas corpus jurisdiction." . . . Today, however, Justice O'CONNOR seeks to extend *Stone* beyond the Fourth Amendment even though this issue was not raised by petitioner Duckworth below or in his petition for certiorari. Her concurring opinion evinces such a palpable distaste for collateral review of state court judgments that it can only be viewed as a harbinger of future assaults on federal habeas corpus.

Stone was wrong when it was decided and it is wrong today. I have read and reread the federal habeas corpus statute, but I am unable to find any statement to the effect that certain federal claims are unworthy of collateral protection, or that certain federal claims are more worthy of collateral protection than others. Congress did not delineate "second class" claims when it created federal habeas jurisdiction. On the contrary, Congress deemed *all* federal claims worthy of collateral protection when it extended the writ to any person "in custody pursuant to the judgment of a State Court . . . in violation of the Constitution or laws or treaties of the United States." At a time when plain language is supposed to count for something, Justice O'CONNOR's suggestion that the Court carve out an exception that has no rooting in the text of the habeas statute is difficult to justify.

Under Article III of the Constitution, Congress—not this Court—determines the scope of jurisdiction of the inferior federal courts. Congress is undoubtedly aware that federal habeas review of state criminal convictions might disserve interests of comity and finality and might make the enforcement of state criminal laws more difficult. Congress has determined, however, that the individual's interest in vindicating his federal rights in a federal forum outweighs these concerns. Federal courts, not state courts, thus have the "last say."

It is not only disapprobation for federal habeas review that pervades Justice O'CONNOR's concurring opinion, but also a profound distaste for *Miranda*. How else to explain the remarkable statement that "*no* significant federal values are at stake" when *Miranda* claims are raised in federal habeas corpus proceedings? But irrespective of one's view of the merits of *Miranda*, the critical point is that *Miranda* is *still good law.* . . .

Justice O'CONNOR'S extension of *Stone* overlooks another difference between claims based on the exclusionary rule and claims based on *Miranda*. According to the *Stone* majority, the primary justification for the exclusionary rule is the deterrence of police misconduct. By contrast, the rights secured by *Miranda* go to the heart of our accusatorial system—"a system in which the State must establish guilt by evidence independently and freely secured and may not by coercion prove its charge against an accused out of his own mouth." *Rogers v. Richmond*, 365 U.S. 534 (1961). Justice O'CONNOR recognizes as much, acknowledging that the privilege against self-incrimination reflects the longstanding belief that "the extraction of proof of guilt from the criminal defendant himself . . . is often an adjunct to tyranny and may lead to the conviction of innocent persons." Unlike the exclusionary rule, which purportedly exists solely for deterrence purposes, the *Miranda* requirements thus serve to protect "a criminal suspect's exercise of [a] privilege which is one of the distinctive components of our criminal law.". . .

Justice O'CONNOR attempts to elide this distinction by advocating that only "nonconstitutional" *Miranda* claims be barred on federal habeas. By this she presumably means those claims that are based on so called "*voluntary*" statements." *Oregon v. Elstad,* 470 U.S. 298 (1985) (emphasis in original). I have never accepted the proposition that there is any such a thing as a "nonconstitutional" *Miranda* claim based on "voluntary" statements. The explicit premise of *Miranda* is that, unless a suspect taken into custody is properly advised of his rights, "no statement obtained from the [suspect] can truly be the product of his free choice" as a matter of federal constitutional law.

In any event, I vehemently oppose the suggestion that it is for the Court to decide, based on our own vague notions of comity, finality, and the intrinsic value of particular constitutional rights, which claims are worthy of collateral federal review and which are not. Congress already engaged in that balancing process when it created habeas review and extended the federal courts' jurisdiction to all claims based on a violation of federal law. The federal courts have been reviewing *Miranda* claims on federal habeas for 23 years and Congress has never even remotely indicated that they have been remiss in doing so. To the extent Justice O'CONNOR is unhappy with *Miranda*, she should address that decision head-on. But an endrun through the habeas statute is judicial activism at its worst.

B. GRANTS OF IMMUNITY

Grants of immunity—immunizing a person from prosecution in exchange for incriminating testimony—have been upheld since *Brown v. United States,* 161 U.S. 591 (1896). There the Court ruled that the primary function of the Fifth Amendment is "to secure the witness against prosecution which might be aided directly or indirectly by his disclosure." Consequently, individuals may be forced to forego their Fifth Amendment rights when offered immunity, even though their testimony opens them to infamy and disgrace.[1] Refusing to testify after being granted immunity constitutes contempt of court for which a person may be punished.

Traditionally, individuals received complete immunity, barring prosecution for crimes related to their testimony. In *Ullmann v. United States, 3*50 U.S. 422 (1952), the Court upheld the Federal Immunity Act of 1954 and subsequently held that grants of immunity are as broad as the privilege against self-incrimination that individuals forfeit. The Court also held, in *Murphy v. Waterfront Commission*, 378 U.S. 52 (1964), that defendants granted immunity by states may not later be prosecuted under federal law on the basis of their incriminating testimony.

Congress, however, cut back on the scope of immunity grants in the Omnibus Crime Control and Safe Streets Act of 1968 by providing for only "use" or "testimonial" immunity. Transactional immunity accords full immunity from prosecution for an offense about which an individual testifies. By contrast, use immunity does not foreclose the possibility of prosecution based on other independently obtained evidence. Use or testimonial immunity was upheld in *Kastigar v. United States* (1972) (see page 985).

NOTE

1. See *Ullmann v. United States*, 350 U.S. 422 (1956); and *United States v. Wilson*, 421 U.S. 309 (1975).

Kastigar v. United States
406 U.S. 441, 92 S.Ct. 1653 (1972)

Charles Kastigar was subpoenaed to appear before a federal grand jury. Because he was anticipated to invoke his Fifth Amendment right to remain silent, federal prosecutors secured from a federal district court a court order directing him to answer questions under a grant of immunity. Kastigar, however, opposed the order, contending that the scope of the immunity was not coextensive with the scope of his Fifth Amendment right. The district court rejected his contention and ordered Kastigar to appear and to answer the grand jury's questions. Kastigar appeared but refused to answer certain questions, again, claiming the Fifth Amendment. As a result, he was found in contempt of court and arrested. Kastigar appealed to the Court of Appeals for the Ninth Circuit, which affirmed the lower court, and then appealed to the Supreme Court.

Justice POWELL delivers the opinion of the Court.

This case presents the question whether the United States Government may compel testimony from an unwilling witness, who invokes the Fifth Amendment privilege against compulsory self-incrimination, by conferring on the witness immunity from use of the compelled testimony in subsequent criminal proceedings, as well as immunity from use of evidence derived from the testimony. . . .

[T]he power to compel testimony is not absolute. There are a number of exemptions from the testimonial duty, the most important of which is the Fifth Amendment privilege against compulsory self-incrimination. The privilege reflects a complex of our fundamental values and aspirations, and marks an important advance in the development of our liberty. It can be asserted in any proceeding, civil or criminal, administrative or judicial, investigatory or adjudicatory; and it protects against any disclosures which the witness reasonably believes could be used in a criminal prosecution or could lead to other evidence that might be so used. This Court has been zealous to safeguard the values which underlie the privilege.

Immunity statutes, which have historical roots deep in Anglo-American jurisprudence, are not incompatible with these values. Rather, they seek a rational accommodation between the imperatives of the privilege and the legitimate demands of government to compel citizens to testify. The existence of these statutes reflects the importance of testimony, and the fact that many offenses are of such a character that the only persons capable of giving useful testimony are those implicated in the crime. Indeed, their origins were in the context of such offenses, and their primary use has been to investigate such offenses. . . .

Petitioners contend, first, that the Fifth Amendment's privilege against compulsory self-incrimination, which is that "[n]o person . . . shall be compelled in any criminal case to be a witness against himself," deprives Congress of power to enact laws that compel self-incrimination, even if complete immunity from prosecution is granted prior to the compulsion of the incriminatory testimony. They ask us to reconsider and overrule *Brown v. Walker*, 161 U.S. 591 (1896), and *Ullmann v. United States*, [350 U.S. 422 (1952)], decisions that uphold the constitutionality of immunity statutes.

We find no merit to this contention and reaffirm the decisions in *Brown* and *Ullmann*.

Petitioners' second contention is that the scope of immunity provided by the federal witness immunity statute, 18 U.S.C. § 6002, is not coextensive with the scope of the Fifth Amendment privilege against compulsory self-incrimination, and therefore is not sufficient to supplant the privilege and compel testimony over a claim of the privilege. The statute provides that when a witness is compelled by district court order to testify over a claim of the privilege:

"the witness may not refuse to comply with the order on the basis of his privilege against self-incrimination; but no testimony or other information compelled under the order (or any information directly or indirectly derived from such testimony or other information) may be used against the witness in any criminal case, except a prosecution for perjury, giving a false statement, or otherwise failing to comply with the order.". . .

Petitioners draw a distinction between statutes that provide transactional immunity and those that provide, as does the statute before us, immunity from use and derivative use. They contend that a statute must at a minimum grant full transactional immunity in order to be coextensive with the scope of the privilege. . . .

The statute's explicit proscription of the use in any criminal case of "testimony or other information compelled under the order (or any information directly or indirectly derived from such testimony or other information)" is consonant with Fifth Amendment standards. We hold that such immunity from use and derivative use is coextensive with the scope of the privilege against self-incrimination, and therefore is sufficient to compel testimony over a claim of the privilege. While a grant of immunity must afford protection commensurate with that afforded by the privilege, it need not be broader. Transactional immunity, which accords full immunity from prosecution for the offense to which the compelled testimony relates, affords the witness considerably broader protection than does the Fifth Amendment privilege. The privilege has never been construed to mean that one who invokes it cannot subsequently be prosecuted. Its sole concern is to afford protection against being "forced to give testimony leading to the infliction of penalties affixed to . . . criminal acts.'". . .

There can be no justification in reason or policy for holding that the Constitution requires an amnesty grant where, acting pursuant to statute and accompanying safeguards, testimony is compelled in exchange for immunity from use and derivative use when no such amnesty is required where the government, acting without colorable right, coerces a defendant into incriminating himself.

We conclude that the immunity provided by 18 U.S.C. § 6002 leaves the witness and the prosecutorial authorities in substantially the same position as if the witness had claimed the Fifth Amendment privilege. The immunity therefore is coextensive with the privilege and suffices to supplant it. The judgment of the Court of Appeals for the Ninth Circuit accordingly is
Affirmed.

Justice BRENNAN and Justice REHNQUIST did not participate in the consideration or decision of this case.

Justice DOUGLAS dissenting.

When we allow the prosecution to offer only "use" immunity
we allow it to grant far less than it has taken away. For while
the precise testimony that is compelled may not be used, leads
from that testimony may be pursued and used to convict the
witness. My view is that the framers put it beyond the power of
Congress to *compel* anyone to confess his crimes. The Self-Incrimination Clause creates, as I have said before, "the federally protected right of silence," making it unconstitutional to use a law
"to pry open one's lips and make him a witness against himself."
Ullmann v. United States.

Justice MARSHALL dissented.

C. REAL VERSUS TESTIMONIAL EVIDENCE

The Supreme Court has limited the scope of the Fifth Amendment by drawing a distinction between "real" and "testimonial"
evidence. No protection is afforded real or physical evidence,
such as blood, handwriting, or voice samples. Only testimonial
evidence (oral testimony) receives protection. As the Court observed, the amendment "prohibits compelling a person to *speak*
and incriminate himself but it does not prohibit compelled revelation of *written* thoughts."[1]

The distinction between real and testimonial evidence derives
from a 1910 ruling that a suspect may be compelled to cooperate
with police by putting on a blouse to determine whether it fits.
In *Holt v. United States*, 218 U.S. 245 (1910), the Court explained
that "the prohibition of compelling a man to be a witness against
himself is a prohibition of physical or moral compulsion to *extort
communications* from him, not an exclusion of his body as evidence
when it may be material." The distinction was not further elaborated until *Schmerber v. State of California* (1966) (see page 990),
upholding the taking of blood samples from a driver at the
time of his arrest following an automobile accident. Since *Schmerber*, handwriting samples, voice samples, and scrappings from
under a suspect's fingernails, among other physical evidence
have been held not to violate the Fifth Amendment.

Rulings on Real Versus Testimonial Evidence[a]

Case	Vote	Ruling
Breithaupt v. Abram, 352 U.S. 432 (1957)	6:3	Upheld police taking of blood sample of a driver involved in an automobile accident.
Schmerber v. California, 384 U.S. 757 (1966)	5:4	Upheld taking of blood sample in a hospital of a driver who appeared intoxicated.
United States v. Wade, 388 U.S. 218 (1967)	5:4	Held that compelling suspect to voice the words of a bank robber in a postindictment lineup was permissible.
Gilbert v. California, 388 U.S. 263 (1967)	5:4	Upheld taking of handwritting sample from suspect in absence of counsel.
United States v. Dionisio, 410 U.S. 1 (1973)	6:3	Upheld use of voice samples presented to grand jury.
Cupp v. Murphy, 412 U.S. 291 (1973)	9:0	Upheld police taking a sample of scrapping from fingernails of individual who was not under arrest and had voluntarily gone to police station house.
Estelle v. Williams, 425 U.S. 501 (1976)	7:2	Accused cannot be compelled to stand trial dressed in prison clothes; but, here, the failure to raise an objection negated any compulsion that would have violated the Fifth Amendment.
Wyrick v. Fields, 459 U.S. 42 (1982)	8:1	A defendant who agrees, on advice of counsel, to submit to polygraph test may be subsequently questioned about results.
Pennsylvania v. Muniz, 110 S.Ct. 2638 (1990)	8:1	Upheld the admissibility at trial of videotapes of suspects answering questions of police at the time of their booking. Writing for the majority, Justice Brennan said that the videotapes, showing slurred speech and other signs of intoxication, were physical—not testimonial—evidence and, therefore, not covered by the Fifth Amendment's privilege against self-incrimination; Justice Marshall dissented.

[a] See also the drug testing cases in Chapter 7.

NOTE

1. See *Fisher v. United States,* 425 U.S. 391 (1976).

Schmerber v. State of California
384 U.S. 757, 86 S.Ct. 1826 (1966)

Justice William J. Brennan discusses the facts in his opinion for the Court upholding, over Fifth Amendment objections, the taking of blood samples of a driver involved in an automobile accident to determine whether he was intoxicated at the time of the accident.

Justice BRENNAN delivers the opinion of the Court.

Petitioner was convicted in Los Angeles Municipal Court of the criminal offense of driving an automobile while under the influence of intoxicating liquor. He had been arrested at a hospital while receiving treatment for injuries suffered in an accident involving the automobile that he had apparently been driving. At the direction of a police officer, a blood sample was then withdrawn from petitioner's body by a physician at the hospital. The chemical analysis of this sample revealed a percent by weight of alcohol in his blood at the time of the offense which indicated intoxication, and the report of this analysis was admitted in evidence at the trial. Petitioner objected to receipt of this evidence of the analysis on the ground that the blood had been withdrawn despite his refusal, on the advice of his counsel, to consent to the test. He contended that in that circumstance the withdrawal of the blood and the admission of the analysis in evidence denied him due process of law under the Fourteenth Amendment, as well as specific guarantees of the Bill of Rights secured against the States by that Amendment: his privilege against self-incrimination under the Fifth Amendment; his right to counsel under the Sixth Amendment; and his right not to be subjected to unreasonable searches and seizures in violation of the Fourth Amendment. The Appellate Department of the California Superior Court rejected these contentions and affirmed the conviction. . . .

THE DUE PROCESS CLAUSE CLAIM

Breithaupt [*v. Abram,* 352 U.S. 432 (1957)] was also a case in which police officers caused blood to be withdrawn from the driver of an automobile involved in an accident, and in which there was ample justification for the officer's conclusion that the driver was under the influence of alcohol. There, as here, the extraction was made by a physician in a simple, medically acceptable manner in a hospital environment.

There, however, the driver was unconscious at the time the blood was withdrawn and hence had no opportunity to object to the procedure. We affirmed the conviction there resulting from the use of the test in evidence, holding that under such circumstances the withdrawal did not offend "that 'sense of justice' of which we spoke in *Rochin v.* [*People of*] *California*, [342 U.S. 165 (1952)]. *Breithaupt* thus requires the rejection of petitioner's due process argument, and nothing in the circumstances of this case or in supervening events persuades us that this aspect of *Breithaupt* should be overruled.

THE PRIVILEGE AGAINST SELF-INCRIMINATION CLAIM

Breithaupt summarily rejected an argument that the withdrawal of blood and the admission of the analysis report involved in that state case violated the Fifth Amendment privilege of any person not to "be compelled in any criminal case to be a witness against himself," citing *Twining v. State of New Jersey*, 211 U.S. 78 [(1908)]. But that case, holding that the protections of the Fourteenth Amendment do not embrace this Fifth Amendment privilege, has been succeeded by *Malloy v. Hogan*, 378 U.S. 1 [(1964)]. We there held that "[t]he Fourteenth Amendment secures against state invasion the same privilege that the Fifth Amendment guarantees against federal infringement—the right of a person to remain silent unless he chooses to speak in the unfettered exercise of his own will, and to suffer no penalty . . . for such silence." We therefore must now decide whether the withdrawal of the blood and admission in evidence of the analysis involved in this case violated petitioner's privilege. We hold that the privilege protects an accused only from being compelled to testify against himself, or otherwise provide the State with evidence of a testimonial or communicative nature, and that the withdrawal of blood and use of the analysis in question in this case did not involve compulsion to these ends.

It could not be denied that in requiring petitioner to submit to the withdrawal and chemical analysis of his blood the State compelled him to submit to an attempt to discover evidence that might be used to prosecute him for a criminal offense. He submitted only after the police officer rejected his objection and directed the physician to proceed. The officer's direction to the physician to administer the test over petitioner's objection constituted compulsion for the purposes of the privilege. The critical question, then, is whether petitioner was thus compelled "to be a witness against himself.". . .

It is clear that the protection of the privilege reaches an accused's communications, whatever form they might take, and the compulsion of responses which are also communications, for example, compliance with a subpoena to produce one's papers. *Boyd v. United States*, 116 U.S. 616 [(1886)]. On the other hand, both federal and state courts have usually held that it offers no protection against compulsion to submit to fingerprinting, photographing, or measurements, to write or speak for identification, to appear in court, to stand, to assume a stance, to walk, or to make a particular gesture. The distinction which has emerged, often expressed in different ways, is that the privilege is a bar against compelling "communications" or "testimony," but that compulsion which makes a suspect or accused the source of "real or physical evidence" does not violate it. . . .

In the present case, [n]ot . . . even a shadow of testimonial compulsion upon or enforced communication by the accused was involved either in the extraction or in the chemical analysis. Petitioner's testimonial capacities were in no way implicated; indeed, his participation, except as a donor, was irrelevant to the results of the test, which depend on chemical analysis and on that alone. Since the blood test evidence, although an incriminating product of compulsion, was neither petitioner's testimony nor evidence relating to some communicative act or writing by the petitioner, it was not inadmissible on privilege grounds.

D. REQUIRED RECORDS, PRIVATE PAPERS, AND CUSTODIAL POSSESSION

Another limitation on the Fifth Amendment is the "required records" doctrine—that is, records required to be kept to provide information for regulatory agencies receive no Fifth Amendment protection. *Shapiro v. United States*, 335 U.S. 1 (1948), held that required records have "public aspects" that foreclose protection for personal information also contained therein. Twenty years later, in *Grosso v. United States*, 390 U.S. 62 (1968), the Court clarified the doctrine:

The premises of the doctrine, as it is described in *Shapiro*, are evidently these: first, the purpose of the United States's inquiry must be essentially regulatory; second, information is to be obtained by requiring the preservation of records of a kind which the regulated party has customarily kept; and third, the records themselves must have issued "public aspects" which render them analogous to public documents.

Income tax returns are required records and the Fifth Amendment is no defense against prosecution for failing to file tax returns.[1] The problem posed by illegal-income earners and the reporting requirements in filing tax returns, however, continued to be presented to the Court. In *United States v. Murdock*, 284 U.S. 141 (1931), a taxpayer filed a return claiming certain deductions but refused on Fifth Amendment grounds to answer questions concerning them, for which he was prosecuted for willful failure to supply necessary information. Although the taxpayer's Fifth Amendment claim was invalid, the Court held that a good faith claim of the amendment bars conviction for willfully failing to answer the IRS's questions. But in *Marchetti v. United States*, 390 U.S. 39 (1968), the Court struck down an IRS regulation requiring gamblers to register and to submit monthly information concerning their wagering activities. It did so on the grounds that the information was not customarily kept, the reports had no public records aspects, and the requirements were directed at a "select group inherently suspect of criminal activities."

INSIDE THE COURT

Marchetti v. United States and *Grosso v. United States*

Marchetti v. United States, 390 U.S. 39 (1968), and *Grosso v. United States*, 390 U.S. 62 (1968), raised the issue of whether requiring gamblers to register with the Internal Revenue Service and pay an occupational tax on their gambling earnings violates the Fifth Amendment privilege against self-incrimination. By registering with the IRS, a gambler becomes open to state and federal prosecution for engaging in organized and illegal gambling and thus incriminates himself.

Justice John Harlan was assigned to draft an opinion for the Court. But his first draft met with opposition from Justices Brennan and Douglas. Initially, Brennan sought accommodation:

I think your conclusion is fully supported without that part of your Part III. . . . I expect, however, that you'd rather not omit that portion. Could you stop at Part III at page 10, and make a new section IV beginning with the [next] full paragraph. . . . If so, I could file a concurrance stating that I join the judgment of reversal for the reasons expressed in Parts I, II, IV and V of your opinion.

Douglas, however, immediately circulated a concurrance for *Marchetti* and a dissenting opinion for *Grosso*. Although Brennan preferred these drafts, he thought it wiser to try to mediate the growing dispute within the majority. "Is there anything about Parts I, II, IV and V which you can't join?" Brennan wrote Douglas, emphasizing that "it might be helpful on this prickly problem if we could join as much as possible of what John has written." Justice Hugo Black (the senior associate who assigned the opinion because Chief Justice Warren found no Fifth Amendment violation in requiring gamblers to register) agreed. But Black told Harlan: "With my constitutional beliefs I could not possibly agree with any part of subdivision III of your opinion except the next to the last sentence in the last paragraph."

After thinking it over for two days, Harlan offered a compromise: "Because of the fact that you, Bill Douglas and Bill Brennan feel so strongly that Part III of my opinion in this case contains implications that were never intended on my part—namely that the taxing power may in some circumstances override the protections afforded by the Fifth Amendment privilege—I have decided to delete that section of my opinion, and am recirculating accordingly." With his revised draft of *Marchetti*, Harlan was able to hang on to a bare majority, but found himself completely alone on his *Grosso* draft.

Discouraged by the growing dissension, Harlan wrote to Black:

> I am faced with the unusual experience of having to withdraw from the opinion which I prepared for the Court in this case under your assignment. I intend to propose at next Thursday's Conference that this case, and also No. 181, *Grosso v. United States*, be set for reargument next Term, as suggested by Brother White in his separate opinion, dissenting in *Marchetti*, and concurring in the judgment in *Grosso*.

Harlan's proposal was accepted and the case was reargued the next term. Tempers cooled, and Harlan further modified his approach; this eventually enabled him to command a solid majority on both opinions. In the end, only Chief Justice Warren dissented from the ruling striking down laws requiring gamblers to register as a violation of the Fifth Amendment.

Source: Memoranda in the William J. Brennan, Jr., Papers, Manuscripts Room, Library of Congress; and John M. Harlan Papers, in the Seeley G. Mudd Library, Princeton University.

A series of rulings on claims to Fifth Amendment protection for private papers firmly established that "a party is privileged from producing . . . evidence, but not from its production."[2] Individuals may claim Fifth Amendment privacy interests and, for example, quash an administrative subpoena directing them to produce papers or documents in which they have privacy interests. But they have no Fifth Amendment protection against the government subpoenaing their papers held by a bank, accountant or attorney.

In *Couch v. United States*, 409 U.S. 322 (1973), for instance, Mrs. Couch was denied any reasonable expectation of privacy under the Fifth Amendment to intervene with an IRS summons of her accountant to turnover her business records. There the Court stressed that "no Fourth or Fifth Amendment claim can prevail where . . . there exists no legitimate expectation of privacy and no semblance of governmental compulsion against the person of the accused. . . . The criterion for Fifth Amendment immunity remains not the ownership of property, but the 'physical or moral compulsion exerted.' "

Two dissenters in *Couch* took quite a different view of the Fifth Amendment's protection for privacy. Justice Douglas urged that a "Fifth Amendment claim [is] valid *even in absence of personal compulsion* so long as [the] accused has a reasonable expectation of privacy in [the] articles subpoenaed." And dissenting Justice Marshall protested that "[t]he Fourth and Fifth Amendments do not speak to totally unrelated concerns. . . . Both involve aspects of a person's right to develop for himself a sphere of personal privacy. Where the amendments 'run almost into each other,' I would prohibit the Government from entering." According to Marshall, protection for private papers should turn on several factors: the nature of the documents (e.g., compare diaries and letters of extortion); what recipients of personal information do with it (e.g., compare attorneys' uses and trustees in a bankruptcy); the purposes of voluntarily relinquishing personal papers to another (e.g., compare attorneys or accountants' use in preparation of individuals' tax returns with copies of documents for use in blackmailing); and the steps that individuals take to ensure the privacy of their papers (e.g., compare placing papers in a safe-deposit box with filing them in a business office).

A majority of the Court, however, rejected such a broad interpretation of the Fifth Amendment. Three years after *Couch*, *Fisher v. United States*, 425 U.S. 391 (1976), held that individuals have no valid Fifth Amendment claims against their attorneys turning over documents related to their tax returns to the IRS, because that does "not 'compel' the taxpayer to do anything— and certainly [does] not compel him to be a 'witness against himself.'" Writing for the Court, Justice White underscored the rejection of privacy arguments for the privilege:

The Framers addressed the subject of personal privacy directly in the Fourth Amendment. They struck a balance so that when the State's reason to believe incriminating evidence will be found becomes sufficiently great, the invasion of privacy becomes justified and a warrant to search and seize will issue. They did not seek in still another Amendment—the Fifth—to achieve a general protection of privacy but to deal with the more specific issue of compelled self-incrimination. We cannot cut the Fifth Amendment completely loose from the morrings of its language, and make it serve as a general protection of privacy—a word not mentioned in its text and a concept directly addressed in the Fourth Amendment.

In *Baltimore City Department of Social Services v. Bouknight,* 110 S.Ct. 900 (1990), the Rehnquist Court further extended the *Schmerber* line of cases and those dealing with the production of required records and private papers. There, the Court held that a mother could not invoke the Fifth Amendment when resisting a juvenile court order to produce a child who was in her custody. Maurice Bouknight was an abused child who was taken for a time by social workers from his mother, Jacqueline Bouknight. After a subsequent hearing in juvenile court, the child was returned to her custody on certain conditions, including that she attend a parental training program, and under a protective supervision order. Eight months later after determining that Mrs. Bouknight was violating the conditions for custody of her child and that the child might be dead, social workers filed petitions to remove the child and to force Mrs. Bouknight to produce her child in court. Mrs. Bouknight in turn claimed that her Fifth Amendment guarantee against self-incrimination barred the juvenile court from compelling her to produce her child in court.

Writing for the majority in *Bouknight*, Chief Justice Rehnquist conceded that the order to produce the child compelled Mrs. Bouknight to make testimonial assertions, but that here, in a civil proceeding, she could not rely on the Fifth Amendment. The guarantee against self-incrimination was inapplicable because (1) Mrs. Bouknight had assumed custodial duties related to the child's production, analogous to those assumed with the production of required records; and (2) the production was part of a noncriminal proceeding. As Chief Justice Rehnquist put it, "In assuming the obligation attending [child] custody, Bouknight 'had accepted the incident obligation to permit inspection.' "

In dissent, Justice Marshall, joined by Justice Brennan rejected the majority's reasoning and reliance on earlier cases. On the one hand, Marshall argued that Mrs. Bouknight's custodial obligations were misanalogized to those of custodians of corporate entities. Bouknight was "not acting as a custodian in the traditional sense of that word because she is not acting *on behalf of the State*." On the other hand, prior cases upholding diminished Fifth Amendment protection for the production of required records and private papers dealt with purely civil regulatory systems and regulations aimed at the general public. But, here, Marshall contended that the civil proceeding against Mrs. Bouknight "*inevitably* intersects with criminal sanctions" for child abuse and "unambiguously indicates that Bouknight's Fifth Amendment privilege must be respected to protect her from the serious risk of self-incrimination."

THE DEVELOPMENT OF LAW
Rulings on Required Records and Private Papers

Case	Vote	Ruling
United States v. Sullivan, 274 U.S. 259 (1927)	9:0	Rejected Fifth Amendment objection to filing federal income tax return.
Shapiro v. United States, 335 U.S. 1 (1948)	5:4	Records required to be kept under the regulatory powers of Congress acquire a "public aspect" and have no Fifth Amendment protection.
Marchetti v. United States, 390 U.S. 39 (1968) and *Grosso v. United States,* 390 U.S. 62 (1968)	8:1	Internal Revenue Service requirement that individuals register as gamblers violates Fifth Amendment since gambling is illegal.
Haynes v. United States, 390 U.S. 6 (1968)	8:1	Fifth Amendment not violated by requirement that gun owners register their guns.
Leary v. United States, 395 U.S. 6 (1969)	9:0	No Fifth Amendment protection against registering and tax on importation of marijuana.
Minor v. United States, 396 U.S. 87 (1969)	7:2	Narcotic seller's rights were not violated by requirement to register and pay sales tax.
United States v. U.S. Coin and Currency, 401 U.S. 715 (1971)	5:4	Upheld *Marchetti;* Fifth Amendment bars IRS from requiring gamblers to register with federal government.
California v. Byers, 402 U.S. 424 (1971)	5:4	Upheld "hit-and-run" statute, requiring drivers who hit a parked car to stop and leave name and driver license number.
Bellis v. United States, 417 U.S. 85 (1974)	8:1	Fifth Amendment applies to only personal production of private papers—papers held by third parties (accountants, lawyers, etc.) are not protected.
California Bankers Association v. Shultz, 416 U.S. 21 (1974)	6:3	Upheld the Bank Secrecy Act, giving the IRS access to individuals' bank records.
Garner v. United States, 424 U.S. 648 (1976)	9:0	Held that an individual who could have but failed to raise a Fifth Amendment objection on a tax return was foreclosed from subsequently invoking the amendment.

Case	Vote	Ruling
Braswell v. United States, 487 U.S. 99 (1988)	5:4	The president (and sole shareholder) of a corporation cannot claim the Fifth Amendment in refusing to turnover corporate documents.
Doe v. United States, 487 U.S. 201 (1988)	8:1	Contents of foreign bank accounts are not protected by the Fifth Amendment.

NOTES

1. *United States v. Sullivan,* 274 U.S. 259 (1927).
2. *Johnson v. United States,* 228 U.S. 457 (1919).

9

THE RIGHTS TO COUNSEL AND OTHER PROCEDURAL GUARANTEES

ALONG WITH the Fourth Amendment and the Fifth Amendment's right against self-accusation and the due process clause, a number of other guarantees of the Fifth, Sixth, Seventh, and Eighth Amendments protect the rights of the accused. The Fifth Amendment provides for indictment by a grand jury and forbids holding defendants in double jeopardy. The Sixth Amendment guarantees an accused the assistance of counsel, the rights to be informed of charges and to confront accusers, as well as a right to a speedy and public trial by an impartial jury in all criminal cases. The Seventh Amendment guarantees a jury trial in civil cases where the controversy exceeds $20. The Eighth Amendment prohibits the imposition of excessive bail and fines, besides banning cruel and unusual punishments (see Chapter 10).

A. THE RIGHT TO COUNSEL

The Sixth Amendment guarantees the accused "the assistance of counsel for his defense." Literally, the guarantee confers a right of which one may avail himself but which the government is not obliged to ensure in all criminal cases. The year after the adoption and before the ratification of the Bill of Rights, Congress further indicated that the assistance of counsel was not mandatory in all criminal cases. The Federal Crimes Act of 1790 imposed a statutory duty on courts to assign counsel to represent defendants only in capital cases. In noncapital cases, the accused had a right to hire counsel but, if too poor to afford one, the government was not obligated to appoint one for his defense.

In *Johnson v. Zerbst*, 304 U.S. 458 (1938), the Hughes Court fundamentally changed the right to counsel in federal courts. There, in an appeal from a conviction for counterfeiting, the Court noted that the "right to be heard would be, in many cases, of little avail if it did not comprehend the right to be heard by counsel" and ruled that "the Sixth Amendment withholds from federal courts, in all criminal proceedings, the power and authority to deprive an accused of his life or liberty unless he has or waives the assistance of counsel."

The Court remained reluctant to impose the right to counsel on state courts, however. In its first confrontation with that issue in the famous *Scottsboro* case—*Powell v. Alabama* (1932) (see page 1004)—the Hughes Court declined to apply the Sixth Amendment to state criminal courts. The Court did hold that under the circumstances of the case the due process clause of the Fifth Amendment required the trial court "to make an effective appointment of counsel." In this case, the "Scottsboro boys," as the several young black defendants were known, were accused of the capital offense of raping a white girl. They were tried before an all-white jury, without the assistance of counsel, in a small southern town, Scottsboro, Alabama.

In the 1940s and 1950s, the Stone and Vinson Courts continued to defer to the states, but ruled on a case-by-case basis that some defendants had to be retried and given the assistance of counsel. In *Betts v. Brady*, 316 U.S. 455 (1942), the Stone Court interpreted *Powell* to require the appointment of counsel only in "special circumstances" and in capital cases. There, Betts, an indigent white man, was indicted for robbery and requested but was denied counsel. Conceding that a layman might encounter difficulties with courtroom procedures when defending himself, Justice Owen Roberts nonetheless held that Betts was "of ordinary intelligence and ability to take care of his own interests on the trial of [a] narrow issue." Three dissenters, Justices Black, Douglas, and Murphy, protested the refusal to extend the right to counsel to all indigents. "[A]ny other practice seems to me to defeat the promise of our democratic society to provide equal justice under the law," charged Justice Black. "A practice cannot be reconciled with 'common and fundamental ideas of fairness and right,' which subjects innocent men to increased dangers of conviction merely because of their poverty."

THE DEVELOPMENT OF LAW

Rulings Extending the Right to Counsel Throughout the Criminal Justice System

Stage of Criminal Justice System	Case
Quasi arrest	*Orozco v. Texas,* 394 U.S. 324 (1969)
Arrest	*Miranda v. Arizona,* 384 U.S. 436 (1966)
Preindictment preliminary hearing	*Coleman v. Alabama,* 399 U.S. 1 (1970)
Preindictment confession	*Escobedo v. Illinois,* 378 U.S. 478 (1964)
Postindictment	*Massiah v. United States,* 377 U.S. 201 (1964)
Preliminary hearings	*White v. Maryland,* 373 U.S. 59 (1963)
Arraignment	*Hamilton v. Alabama,* 368 U.S. 52 (1961)
Lineups	*United States v. Wade,* 388 U.S. 218 (1967); and *Gilbert v. California,* 388 U.S. 263 (1967)
Trials	*Gideon v. Wainwright,* 372 U.S. 335 (1963), as modified by *Argersinger v. Hamlin,* 407 U.S. 25 (1972), and *Scott v. Illinois,* 440 U.S. 367 (1979)
Appeals	*Douglas v. California,* 372 U.S. 535 (1963)
Probation hearings	*Mempa v. Rhay,* 389 U.S. 128 (1967)
Revocation of probation or parole	*Gagnon v. Scarpelli,* 411 U.S. 778 (1973)

Although adhering to the special circumstances rule and upholding several convictions obtained without the defendant's assistance of counsel,[1] the Vinson Court held that counsel was required in capital cases;[2] when the conduct of a trial judge was questionable;[3] where defendants were young, ignorant, or otherwise handicapped;[4] and in legally complex cases.[5]

Finally, in *Gideon v. Wainwright* (1963) (see page 1008), the Warren Court overturned *Betts* and extended the right to counsel to the accused in all states in all criminal cases. *Argersinger v. Hamlin* (1972) (see page 1012) then applied the right to counsel to all offenses involving the possibility of imprisonment, regardless whether they were petty, misdeamenor, or felony offenses. As a result of a series of rulings, the right to counsel now extends to virtually every stage of the criminal justice system: from when police make a quasi-arrest or arrest, to preindictment preliminary hearings and confessions before and after indictment, as well as to preliminary hearings, arraignment proceedings, police line-ups, the trial, and subsequent proceedings on sentencing, appeals, and probation hearings. In addition, *Faretta v. California,* 422 U.S. 806 (1975), held that a defendant may waive the right to counsel and represent themselves, if the trial judge finds them competent to do so.[6]

In the 1970s and 1980s, the Burger and Rehnquist Courts qualified the application of the right to counsel in a number of areas. Besides the exceptions for the presence of counsel during police questioning and interrogation (see Chapter 8), counsel is not required during hearings on the competency of witnesses

The Scottsboro boys with their attorney Samuel S. Leibowitz. The Scottsboro boys were initially tried before an all-white jury, without the assistance of counsel in a small town, Scottsboro, Alabama, for allegedly raping a white girl. They were sentenced to death, but their convictions were appealed and led to the Supreme Court's important ruling in *Powell v. Alabama* (1932). *Brown Brothers.*

testifying against the defendant,[7] nor need counsel be present at postgrand jury indictment lineups[8] or at photo-identification hearings.[9] *Scott v. Illinois*, 440 U.S. 367 (1979), limited *Argersinger* to require court-appointed attorneys only in cases where defendants are in fact sentenced to jail terms.[10] The right to counsel on appeal was limited in *Ross v. Moffitt*, 417 U.S. 600 (1974), holding that the assistance of counsel applies only to the first appeal and not to further discretionary appeals. *Pennsylvania v. Finley*, 107 S.Ct. 1990 (1987), further ruled that defendants have no right to court-appointed attorneys in postconviction proceedings or to insist that a court-appointed lawyer follow certain procedures when withdrawing from their appeals because the lawyer deems further appeals "frivolous."[11] Finally, there is no right to counsel at disciplinary hearings in prison[12] and proceedings on revoking parole.[13]

NOTES

1. See *Canizio v. New York*, 327 U.S. 82 (1946); and *Bute v. Illinois*, 333 U.S. 640 (1945).

2. *Tomkins v. Missouri*, 323 U.S. 485 (1945).

3. *Townsend v. Burke*, 334 U.S. 736 (1948); and *White v. Ragen*, 324 U.S. 760 (1945).

4. *De Meerleer v. Michigan*, 329 U.S. 663 (1947); *Marino v. Ragen*, 332 U.S. 561 (1947); *Moore v. Michigan*, 355 U.S. 155 (1957); *Massey v. Moorer*, 348 U.S. 105 (1954); *Hudson v. North Carolina*, 363 U.S. 697 (1960); and *Culombe v. Connecticut*, 367 U.S. 568 (1961).

5. *Cash v. Culver*, 358 U.S. 633 (1959).

6. *McKasle v. Wiggins*, 465 U.S. 168 (1984), however, held that the defendant's right to counsel in his own defense was not violated by the unsolicited participation of a standby counsel.

7. *Kentucky v. Stincer*, 482 U.S. 730 (1987), holding that the Sixth Amendment was not violated by denial of attendance of counsel during competency hearings for two minor victims whom the defendant was accused of sodomizing.

8. *Kirby v. Illinois*, 405 U.S. 951 (1972).

9. *United States v. Ash*, 413 U.S. 300 (1973). *Moore v. Illinois*, 434 U.S. 220 (1977), however, held that counsel must be present during a one-on-one corporeal identification of the defendant.

10. Notably, in *Herring v. New York*, 422 U.S. 853 (1975), the Court held that judges may not deny the right to counsel in nonjury trials.

11. In *Anders v. California*, 386 U.S. 738 (1967), the Court held that a court-appointed attorney who seeks to withdraw from a case because he deems further appeals frivolous must file a brief explaining the meritlessness of an appeal as well as anything that might be arguable on appeal, and a court must then determine that there are no nonfrivolous

issues. *Penson v. Ohio,* 488 U.S. 75 (1988), reaffirmed that a defendant's attorney after making a first appeal must file an *Anders* brief showing that further appeals are friviolous and justifying the attorney's request to withdraw.

12. *Baxter v. Palmigiano,* 425 U.S. 308 (1976).
13. *Gagnon v. Scarpelli,* 411 U.S. 778 (1973).

SELECTED BIBLIOGRAPHY

Graham, Fred. *The Self-Inflicted Wound.* New York: Macmillan, 1970.
Heller, F. *The Sixth Amendment to the Constitution of the United States.* Lawrence: University of Kansas, 1951.
Lewis, Anthony. *Gideon's Trumpet.* New York: Random House, 1964.
Norris, C. and Washington, S. *The Last of the Scottsboro Boys.* New York: Putnam, 1979.

Powell v. Alabama
287 U.S. 45, 53 S.Ct. 55 (1932)

In Scottsboro, Alabama, Ozie Powell and six other black youths were arrested, charged, and tried before an all-white jury for raping two white girls traveling on a train. Each was tried separately without the assistance of counsel, and on conviction they were sentenced to death. Their trials and convictions received wide publicity, and lawyers affiliated with the International Labor Defense, a Communist-front organization in New York, volunteered to represent them on appeal. After the Alabama Supreme Court affirmed their convictions, an appeal was made to the Supreme Court, which granted review. Justice George Sutherland's opinion for the majority discusses some additional facts in the case.

Justice SUTHERLAND delivers the opinion of the Court.

Before the train reached Scottsboro, Ala., a sheriff's posse seized the defendants and two other negroes. Both girls and the negroes then were taken to Scottsboro, the county seat. Word of their coming and of the alleged assault had preceded them, and they were met at Scottsboro by a large crowd. It does not sufficiently appear that the defendants were seriously threatened with, or that they were actually in danger of, mob violence; but it does appear that the attitude of the community was one of great hostility. The sheriff thought it necessary to call for the militia to assist in safeguarding the prisoners. Chief Justice ANDERSON pointed out in his opinion that every step taken from the arrest and arraignment to the sentence was accompanied by the military. Soldiers took the defendants to Gadsden for safe-keeping, brought them back to Scottsboro for arraignment, returned them to Gadsden for safe-keeping while awaiting trial, escorted them to Scottsboro for trial a few days later, and guarded the courthouse and grounds at every stage of the proceedings. It is perfectly apparent that the proceedings, from beginning to end, took place in an atmosphere of tense, hostile, and excited public sentiment. During the entire time, the defendants were closely confined or were under military guard. The record does not disclose their ages, except that one of them was nineteen; but the record clearly indicates that most, if not all, of them were truthful, and they are constantly referred to as "the boys." They were ignorant and illiterate. All of them were residents of other states, where alone members of their families or friends resided. . . .

[W]e confine ourselves . . . to the inquiry whether the defendants were in substance denied the right of counsel, and if so, whether such denial infringes the due process clause of the Fourteenth Amendment.

First. The record shows that immediately upon the return of the indictment defendants were arraigned and pleaded not guilty. Apparently they were not asked whether they had, or were able to employ, counsel, or wished to have counsel appointed; or whether they had friends or relatives who might assist in that regard if communicated with. That it would not have been an idle ceremony to have given the defendants reasonable opportunity to communicate with their families and endeavor to obtain counsel is demonstrated by the fact that very soon after conviction, able counsel appeared in their behalf. . . .

It is hardly necessary to say that the right to counsel being conceded, a defendant should be afforded a fair opportunity to secure counsel of his own choice. Not only was that not done here, but such designation of counsel as was attempted was either so definite or so close upon the trial as to amount to a denial of effective and substantial aid in that regard. . . .

[U]ntil the very morning of the trial no lawyer had been named or definitely designated to represent the defendants. Prior to that time, the trial judge had "appointed all the members of the bar" for the limited "purpose of arraigning the defendants." Whether they would represent the defendants thereafter, if no counsel appeared in their behalf, was a matter of speculation only, or, as the judge indicated, of mere anticipation on the part of the court. Such a designation, even if made for all purposes, would, in our opinion, have fallen far short of meeting, in any proper sense, a requirement for the appointment of counsel.

How many lawyers were members of the bar does not appear; but, in the very nature of things, whether many or few, they would not, thus collectively named, have been given that clear appreciation of responsibility or impressed with that individual sense of duty which should and naturally would accompany the appointment of a selected member of the bar, specifically named and assigned.

That this action of the trial judge in respect of appointment of counsel was little more than an expansive gesture, imposing no substantial or definite obligation upon any one. . . . [D]uring perhaps the most critical period of the proceedings against these defendants, that is to say, from the time of their arraignment until the beginning of their trial, when consultation, thorough-going investigation and preparation were vitally important, the defendants did not have the aid of counsel in any real sense, although they were as much entitled to such aid during that period as at the trial itself. . . .

The defendants, young, ignorant, illiterate, surrounded by hostile sentiment, haled back and forth under guard of soldiers, charged with an atrocious crime regarded with especial horror in the community where they were to be tried, were thus put in peril of their lives within a few moments after counsel for the first time charged with any degree of responsibility began to represent them. . . .

Under the circumstances disclosed, we hold that defendants were not accorded the right of counsel in any substantial sense. To decide otherwise, would simply be to ignore actualities. . . .

Second. The Constitution of Alabama provides that in all criminal prosecutions the accused shall enjoy the right to have the assistance of counsel; and a state statute requires the court in a capital case, where the defendant is unable to employ counsel, to appoint counsel for him. The state Supreme Court held that these provisions had not been infringed, and with that holding we are powerless to interfere. The question, however, which it is our duty, and within our power, to decide, is whether the denial of the assistance of counsel contravenes the due process clause of the Fourteenth Amendment to the Federal Constitution. . . .

In the light of the facts outlined in the forepart of this opinion—the ignorance and illiteracy of the defendants, their youth, the circumstances of public hostility, the imprisonment and the close surveillance of the defendants by the military forces, the fact that their friends and families were all in other states and communication with them necessarily difficult, and above all that they stood in deadly peril of their lives—we think the failure of the trial court to give them reasonable time and opportunity to secure counsel was a clear denial of due process.

But passing that, and assuming their inability, even if opportunity had been given, to employ counsel, as the trial court evidently did assume, we are of opinion that, under the circumstances just stated, the necessity of counsel was so vital and imperative that the failure of the trial court to make an effective appointment of counsel was likewise a denial of due process within the meaning of the Fourteenth Amendment. Whether this would be so in other criminal prosecutions, or under other circumstances, we need not determine. All that it is necessary now to decide, as we do decide, is that in a capital case, where the defendant is unable to employ counsel, and is incapable adequately of making his own defense because of ignorance, feeble-mindedness, illiteracy, or the like, it is the duty of the court, whether requested or not, to assign counsel for him as a necessary requisite of due process of law; and that duty is not discharged by an assignment at such a time or under such circumstances as to preclude the giving of effective aid in the preparation and trial of the case. To hold otherwise would be to ignore the fundamental postulate, already adverted to, "that there are certain immutable principles of justice which inhere in the very idea of free government which no member of the Union may disregard."

Justice BUTLER and Justice MCREYNOLD dissented.

Gideon v. Wainwright
372 U.S. 335, 83 S.Ct. 792 (1963)

Clarence Earl Gideon, a fifty-one-year-old rambler who was in and out of jails for most of his life, was convicted of breaking and entering into the Bay Harbor Poolroom in Panama City, Florida. At his trial, he claimed he was too poor to afford an attorney, and requested that one be provided. The judge refused, and Gideon was convicted and sentenced. But Gideon persisted. While serving a five-year sentence for petty larceny in the Florida State Prison, he mailed a petition, printed on lined paper obtained from a prison guard, to the Supreme Court.

Gideon did not know that he was asking the Court to reverse itself. In *Betts v. Brady* (1942) the Court had held that only in special circumstances, like those in the *Scottsboro* case, was counsel required. Justice Hugo Black, along with Justices Douglas and Murphy, had dissented in *Betts*. Only three members of the Court that decided *Betts*, however, remained when Gideon's petition was granted: two of the dissenters—Black and Douglas—and Felix Frankfurter, who was eighty years old, ill, and in his last year on the bench. They had been joined by Tom Clark and President Eisenhower's appointees—Warren, Harlan, Brennan, Whittaker, and Stewart. By the time *Gideon* was handed down, Frankfurter and Whittaker had retired. They had been replaced by President Kennedy's appointees—Arthur Goldberg and Byron White.

DIVISION OF CORRECTIONS
CORRESPONDENCE REGULATIONS

MAIL WILL NOT BE DELIVERED WHICH DOES NOT CONFORM WITH THESE RULES

No. 1 -- Only 2 letters each week, not to exceed 2 sheets letter-size 8 1/2 x 11" and written on one side only, and if ruled paper, do not write between lines. Your complete name must be signed at the close of your letter. Clippings, stamps, letters from other people, stationery or cash must not be enclosed in your letters.

No. 2 -- All letters must be addressed in the complete prison name of the inmate. Cell number, where applicable, and prison number must be placed in lower left corner of envelope, with your complete name and address in the upper left corner.

No. 3 -- Do not send any packages without a Package Permit. Unauthorized packages will be destroyed.

No. 4 -- Letters must be written in English only.

No. 5 -- Books, magazines, pamphlets, and newspapers of reputable character will be delivered only if mailed direct from the publisher.

No. 6 -- Money must be sent in the form of Postal Money Orders only, in the inmate's complete prison name and prison number.

INSTITUTION _____ CELL NUMBER _____

NAME _____ NUMBER _____

In The Supreme Court of The United States
— — — Washington D.C.
Clarence Earl Gideon
          Petitioner | Petition for a writ
          vs. | of Certiorari Directed
H.G. Cochran, Jr, as | To The Supreme Court
Director, Divisions | State of Florida.
of corrections State | No. 890 Misc.
of Florida. | OCT. TERM 1961

U.S. Supreme Court

To: The Honorable Earl Warren, Chief
Justice of the United States
      Comes now The petitioner, Clarence
Earl Gideon, a citizen of The United States
of America, in proper person, and appearing
as his own counsel. Who petitions This
Honorable Court for a Writ of Certiorari
directed to The Supreme Court of The State
of Florida. To review the order and Judgement of the court below denying The
petitioner a writ of Habeus Corpus.
      Petitioner submits That The Supreme
Court of The United States has The authority
and jurisdiction to review The final Judgement of The Supreme Court of The State
of Florida The highest court of The State
Under sec. 344(B) Title 28 U.S.C.A. and
Because The "Due process clause" of The

Clarence Gideon's petition, which led to the Warren Court's landmark ruling on the right to counsel. *Collection of the Supreme Court of the United States.*

Gideon fit the agenda of the Warren Court. In fact, Chief Justice Warren had told his law clerks to look for a case that would enable the Court to overrule *Betts*'s special circumstance rule for when the assistance of counsel was required for defendants in criminal cases. After granting Gideon's case, Warren asked prominent Washington, D.C., lawyer (and later Supreme Court justice) Abe Fortas to act as counsel for Gideon on his appeal. Because of Justice Black's long-standing interest in overturning *Betts*, Warren assigned him to write the opinion announcing the Court's decision.

Justice BLACK delivers the opinion of the Court.

Since 1942, when *Betts v. Brady*, 316 U.S. 455, was decided by a divided Court, the problem of a defendant's federal constitutional right to counsel in a state court has been a continuing source of controversy and litigation in both state and federal courts. To give this problem another review here, we granted certiorari. Since Gideon was proceeding *in forma pauperis*, we appointed counsel to represent him and requested both sides to discuss in their briefs and oral arguments the following: "Should this Court's holding in *Betts v. Brady*, be reconsidered?"

The facts upon which Betts claimed that he had been unconstitutionally denied the right to have counsel appointed to assist him are strikingly like the facts upon which Gideon here bases his federal constitutional claim. . . . Treating due process as "a concept less rigid and more fluid than those envisaged in other specific and particular provisions of the Bill of Rights," the Court held that refusal to appoint counsel under the particular facts and circumstances in the *Betts* case was not so "offensive to the common and fundamental ideas of fairness" as to amount to a denial of due process. Since the facts and circumstances of the two cases are so nearly indistinguishable, we think the *Betts v. Brady* holding if left standing would require us to reject Gideon's claim that the Constitution guarantees him the assistance of counsel. Upon full reconsideration we conclude that *Betts v. Brady* should be overruled. . . .

We accept *Betts v. Brady*'s assumption, based as it was on our prior cases, that a provision of the Bill of Rights which is "fundamental and essential to a fair trial" is made obligatory upon the States by the Fourteenth Amendment. We think the Court in Betts was wrong, however, in concluding that the Sixth Amendment's guarantee of counsel is not one of these fundamental rights. Ten years before *Betts v. Brady*, this Court, after full consideration of all the historical data examined in *Betts*, had unequivocally declared that "the right to the aid of counsel is of this fundamental character." *Powell v. Alabama*. . . . While the Court at the close of its *Powell* opinion did by its language, as this Court frequently does, limit its holding to the particular facts and circumstances of that case, its conclusions about the fundamental nature of the right to counsel are unmistakable.

In light of these and many other prior decisions of this Court, it is not surprising that the *Betts* Court, when faced with the contention that "one charged with crime, who is unable to obtain counsel, must be furnished counsel by the state," conceded that "[e]xpressions in the opinions of this court lend color to the argument. . . ." The fact is that in deciding as it did—that "appointment of counsel is not a fundamental right, essential to a fair trial"—the Court in *Betts v. Brady* made an abrupt break with its own well-considered precedents. In returning to these old precedents, sounder we believe than the new, we but restore constitutional principles established to achieve a fair system of justice. Not only these precedents but also reason and reflection require us to recognize that in our adversary system of criminal justice, any person haled into court, who is too poor to hire a lawyer, cannot be assured a fair trial unless counsel is provided for him. This seems to us to be an obvious truth. Governments, both state and federal, quite properly spend vast sums of money to establish machinery to try defendants accused of crime. Lawyers to prosecute are everywhere deemed essential to protect the public's interest in an orderly society. Similarly, there are few defendants charged with crime, few indeed, who fail to hire the best lawyers they can get to prepare and present their defenses. That government hires lawyers to prosecute and defendants who have the money hire lawyers to defend are the strongest indications of the widespread belief that lawyers in criminal courts are necessities, not luxuries. The right of one charged with crime to counsel may not be deemed fundamental and essential to fair trials in some countries, but it is in ours. From the very beginning, our state and national constitutions and laws have laid great emphasis on procedural and substantive safeguards designed to assure fair trials before impartial tribunals in which every defendant stands equal before the law. This noble ideal cannot be realized if the poor man charged with crime has to face his accusers without a lawyer to assist him. . . . The Court in *Betts v. Brady* departed from the sound wisdom upon which the Court's holding in *Powell v. Alabama* rested. Florida, supported by two other States, has asked that *Betts v. Brady* be left intact. Twenty-two States, as friends of the Court, argue that Betts was "an anachronism when handed down" and that it should now be overruled. We agree.

Justice DOUGLAS concurred in a separate opinion.

Justice CLARK concurring.

The Court's decision today . . . does no more than erase a distinction which has no basis in logic and an increasingly eroded basis in authority. . . .

I [also think] that the Constitution makes no distinction between capital and noncapital cases. The Fourteenth Amendment requires due process of law for the deprival of "liberty" just as for deprival of "life," and there cannot constitutionally be a difference in the quality of the process based merely upon a supposed difference in the sanction involved. How can the Fourteenth Amendment tolerate a procedure which it condemns in capital cases on the ground that deprival of liberty may be less onerous than deprival of life—a value judgment not universally accepted—or that only the latter deprival is irrevocable? I can find no acceptable rationalization for such a result, and I therefore concur in the judgment of the Court.

Justice HARLAN concurring.

I agree that *Betts v. Brady* should be overruled, but consider it entitled to a more respectful burial than has been accorded, at least on the part of those of us who were not on the Court when that case was decided.

I cannot subscribe to the view that *Betts v. Brady* represented "an abrupt break with its own well-considered precedents." . . . In 1932, in *Powell v. Alabama* . . . a capital case, this Court declared that under the particular facts there presented—"the ignorance and illiteracy of the defendants, their youth, the circumstances of public hostility . . . and above all that they stood in deadly peril of their lives"—the state court had a duty to assign counsel for the trial as a necessary requisite of due process of law. It is evident that these limiting facts were not added to the opinion as an afterthought; they were repeatedly emphasized and were clearly regarded as important to the result.

Thus when this Court, a decade later, decided *Betts v. Brady,* it did no more than to admit of the possible existence of special circumstances in noncapital as well as capital trials, while at the same time insisting that such circumstances be shown in order to establish a denial of due process. The right to appointed counsel had been recognized as being considerably broader in federal prosecutions, but to have imposed these requirements on the States would indeed have been "an abrupt break" with the almost immediate past. The declaration that the right to appointed counsel in state prosecutions, as established in *Powell v. Alabama,* was not limited to capital cases was in truth not a departure from, but an extension of, existing precedent. . . .

The special circumstances rule has been formally abandoned in capital cases, and the time has now come when it should be similarly abandoned in noncapital cases, at least as to offenses which, as the one involved here, carry the possibility of a substantial prison sentence. (Whether the rule should extend to *all* criminal cases need not now be decided.) This indeed does no more than to make explicit something that has long since been foreshadowed in our decisions.

Argersinger v. Hamlin
407 U.S. 25, 92 S.Ct. 2006 (1972)

In his opinion for the Court, Justice William O'Douglas discusses the pertinent facts involving the appeal of an individual's conviction for carrying a concealed weapon, a crime that was punishable by imprisonment for up to six months.

Justice DOUGLAS delivers the opinion of the Court.

Petitioner, an indigent, was charged in Florida with carrying a concealed weapon, an offense punishable by imprisonment up to six months, a $1,000 fine, or both. The trial was to a judge, and petitioner was unrepresented by counsel. He was sentenced to serve 90 days in jail, and brought this habeas corpus action in the Florida Supreme Court, alleging that, being deprived of his right to counsel, he was unable as an indigent layman properly to raise and present to the trial court good and sufficient defenses to the charge for which he stands convicted. The Florida Supreme Court by a four-to-three decision, in ruling on the right to counsel, followed the line we marked out in *Duncan v. Louisiana,* 391 U.S. 145 [(1968)], as respects the right to trial by jury and held that the right to court-appointed counsel extends only to trials "for non-petty offenses punishable by more than six months imprisonment.". . .

We reverse. . . .

Both *Powell* [*v. Alabama,* 287 U.S. 45 (1932)] and *Gideon* [*v. Wainwright,* 372 U.S. 335 (1963)] involved felonies. But their rationale has relevance to any criminal trial, where an accused is deprived of his liberty. *Powell* and *Gideon* suggest that there are certain fundamental rights applicable to all such criminal prosecutions. . . .

The requirement of counsel may well be necessary for a fair trial even in a petty-offense prosecution. We are by no means convinced that legal and constitutional questions involved in a case that actually leads to imprisonment even for a brief period are any less complex than when a person can be sent off for six months or more. . . .

The trial of vagrancy cases is illustrative. While only brief sentences of imprisonment may be imposed, the cases often bristle with thorny constitutional questions. . . .

In addition, the volume of misdemeanor cases, far greater in number than felony prosecutions, may create an obsession for speedy dispositions, regardless of the fairness of the result. . . .

That picture is seen in almost every report. "The misdemeanor trial is characterized by insufficient and frequently irresponsible preparation on the part of the defense, the prosecution, and the court. Everything is rush, rush.". . .

There is evidence of the prejudice which results to misdemeanor defendants from this "assembly-line justice." One study concluded that "[m]isdemeanants represented by attorneys are five times as likely to emerge from police court with all charges dismissed as are defendants who face similar charges without counsel." American Civil Liberties Union, Legal Counsel for Misdemeanants, Preliminary Report 1 (1970). . . .

We hold, therefore, that absent a knowing and intelligent waiver, no person may be imprisoned for any offense, whether classified as petty, misdemeanor, or felony, unless he was represented by counsel at his trial.

Chief Justice BURGER concurred in a separate opinion.

Justice BRENNAN with whom Justice DOUGLAS and Justice STEWART joined, concurred.

Justice POWELL, with whom Justice REHNQUIST joins, concurring.

There is a middle course, between the extremes of Florida's six-month rule and the Court's rule, which comports with the requirements of the Fourteenth Amendment. I would adhere to the principle of due process that requires fundamental fairness in criminal trials, a principle which I believe encompasses the right to counsel in petty cases whenever the assistance of counsel is necessary to assure a fair trial.

I am in accord with the Court that an indigent accused's need for the assistance of counsel does not mysteriously evaporate when he is charged with an offense punishable by six months or less. In *Powell v. Alabama* and *Gideon*, both of which involved felony prosecutions, this Court noted that few laymen can present adequately their own cases, much less identify and argue relevant legal questions. Many petty offenses will also present complex legal and factual issues that may not be fairly tried if the defendant is not assisted by counsel. Even in relatively simple cases, some defendants, because of ignorance or some other handicap, will be incapable of defending themselves. The consequences of a misdemeanor conviction, whether they be a brief period served under the sometimes deplorable conditions found in local jails or the effect of a criminal record on employability, are frequently of sufficient magnitude not to be casually dismissed by the label "petty."

Serious consequences also may result from convictions not punishable by imprisonment. Stigma may attach to a drunken-driving conviction or a hit-and-run escapade. Losing one's driver's license is more serious for some individuals than a brief stay in jail. . . .

This is not to say that due process requires the appointment of counsel in all petty cases, or that assessment of the possible consequences of conviction is the sole test for the need for assistance of counsel. The flat six-month rule of the Florida court and the equally inflexible rule of the majority opinion apply to *all* cases within their defined areas regardless of circumstances. It is precisely because of this mechanistic application that I find these alternatives unsatisfactory. Due process, perhaps the most fundamental concept in our law, embodies principles of fairness rather than immutable line drawing as to every aspect of a criminal trial. While counsel is often essential to a fair trial, this is by no means a universal fact. Some petty offense cases are complex; others are exceedingly simple. As a justification for furnishing counsel to indigents accused of felonies, this Court noted, "That government hires lawyers to prosecute and defendants who have the money hire lawyers to defend are the strongest indications of the widespread belief that lawyers in criminal courts are necessities, not luxuries." Yet government often does not hire lawyers to prosecute petty offenses; instead the arresting police officer presents the case. Nor does every defendant who can afford to do so hire lawyers to defend petty charges. Where the possibility of a jail sentence is remote and the probable fine seems small, or where the evidence of guilt is overwhelming, the costs of assistance of counsel may exceed the benefits. It is anomalous that the Court's opinion today will extend the right of appointed counsel to indigent defendants in cases where the right to counsel would rarely be exercised by nonindigent defendants.

Indeed, one of the effects of this ruling will be to favor defendants classified as indigents over those not so classified, yet who are in low-income groups where engaging counsel in a minor petty-offense case would be a luxury the family could not afford. The line between indigency and assumed capacity to pay for counsel is necessarily somewhat arbitrary, drawn differently from State to State and often resulting in serious inequities to accused persons. The Court's new rule will accent the disadvantage of being barely self-sufficient economically. . . .

The rule adopted today does not go all the way. It is limited to petty-offense cases in which the sentence is some imprisonment. The thrust of the Court's position indicates, however, that when the decision must be made, the rule will be extended to all petty-offense cases except perhaps the most minor traffic violations. . . .

Thus, although the new rule is extended today only to the imprisonment category of cases, the Court's opinion foreshadows the adoption of a broad prophylactic rule applicable to all petty offenses. No one can foresee the consequences of such a drastic enlargement of the constitutional right to free counsel. That even today's decision could have a seriously adverse impact upon the day-to-day functioning of the criminal justice system. We should be slow to fashion a new constitutional rule with consequences of such unknown dimensions, especially since it is supported neither by history nor precedent. . . .

I would hold that the right to counsel in petty-offense cases is not absolute but is one to be determined by the trial courts exercising a judicial discretion on a case-by-case basis. The determination should be made before the accused formally pleads; many petty cases are resolved by guilty pleas in which the assistance of counsel may be required. If the trial court should conclude that the assistance of counsel is not required in any case, it should state its reasons so that the issue could be preserved for review. The trial court would then become obligated to scrutinize carefully the subsequent proceedings for the protection of the defendant. If an unrepresented defendant sought to enter a plea of guilty, the Court should examine the case against him to insure that there is admissible evidence tending to support the elements of the offense. If a case went to trial without defense counsel, the court should intervene, when necessary, to insure that the defendant adequately brings out the facts in his favor and to prevent legal issues from being overlooked. Formal trial rules should not be applied strictly against unrepresented defendants. Finally, appellate courts should carefully scrutinize all decisions not to appoint counsel and the proceedings which follow.

It is impossible, as well as unwise, to create a precise and detailed set of guidelines for judges to follow in determining whether the appointment of counsel is necessary to assure a fair trial. Certainly three general factors should be weighed. First, the court should consider the complexity of the offense charged. . . .

Second, the court should consider the probable sentence that will follow if a conviction is obtained. The more serious the likely consequences, the greater is the probability that a lawyer should be appointed. . . .

Third, the court should consider the individual factors peculiar to each case. These, of course, would be the most difficult to anticipate. One relevant factor would be the competency of the individual defendant to present his own case. The attitude of the community toward a particular defendant or particular incident would be another consideration. But there might be other reasons why a defendant would have a peculiar need for a lawyer which would compel the appointment of counsel in a case where the court would normally think this unnecessary. Obviously, the sensitivity and diligence of individual judges would be crucial to the operation of a rule of fundamental fairness requiring the consideration of the varying factors in each case.

B. PLEA BARGAINING AND THE RIGHT TO EFFECTIVE COUNSEL

Plea bargaining is the practice of prosecutors and defense attorneys agreeing to terms on which the defendant agrees to plead guilty to a lesser charge than the one originally charged in exchange for a reduced sentence. Over 90 percent of all guilty pleas are the result of this practice. The advantage for the government is that it cuts the time and costs of attorneys, trials, and other resources of the criminal justice system. While the defendant receives a reduced sentence, he foregoes several constitutional rights, including, among others, the Fifth Amendment right against self-accusation and the Sixth Amendment rights to a public trial and to confront one's accusers as well as the presumption of innocence.

Brady v. United States, 397 U.S. 742 (1970), upheld the constitutionality of plea bargaining as having a "mutuality of advantage." The state, observed Justice White in his opinion for the Court, conserves "scarce judicial and prosecutorial resources" and achieves "more promptly imposed punishment;" while for the defendant, "his exposure is reduced, the correctional process can begin immediately, and the practical burdens of a trial are eliminated."

Critics of plea bargaining, though, question the constitutionality of defendants foregoing their constitutional rights and whether they are compelled to do so. The five-to-four ruling in *Bordenkircher v. Hayes* (1978) (see page 1020) illustrates the issue and how it has divided the Court.

Another issue arising with plea bargaining (and more generally with court-appointed attorneys) is whether defendants have a right to *effective* counsel. In *McMann v. Richardson,* 397 U.S. 759 (1970), three defendants claimed that their confessions were

THE DEVELOPMENT OF LAW
Other Rulings on Plea Bargaining

Case	Vote	Ruling
Moore v. State of Michigan, 355 U.S. 155 (1957)	5:4	Counsel required to advise a defendant, who was seventeen years old and had a seventh-grade education, on a plea of guilty to a murder charge.
McCarthy v. United States, 394 U.S. 459 (1969)	9:0	Held that guilty pleas must be personally presented to a judge and the latter must assess their voluntariness.
McMann v. Richardson, 397 U.S. 759 (1970)	6:3	A defendant who enters a guilty plea is not compelled under the Fifth Amendment merely because the plea was a way of avoiding the death penalty.
North Carolina v. Alford, 400 U.S. 25 (1970)	6:3	A guilty plea prevents a defendant from subsequently making a *habeas corpus* claim that his confession was coerced.
Santobello v. New York, 404 U.S. 257 (1971)	6:3	Once a state agrees to a plea bargain it must be honored; here, the state reneged on a bargain struck due to a change in prosecutors.
Henderson v. Morgan, 426 U.S. 637 (1976)	7:2	A guilty plea is involuntary where a man of low mental ability is not told that homicide is manslaughter rather than murder.
Cobitt v. New Jersey, 439 U.S. 212 (1978)	6:3	If a defendant agrees to a plea bargain that results in a sentence of less than lifetime imprisonment, the Fifth and Sixth Amendment are not violated.
Rummell v. Estelle, 445 U.S. 263 (1980)	5:4	The Eighth Amendment ban on cruel and unusual punishment was not violated when a prosecutor threatened a defendant, who insisted on his right to a jury trial, that if he did not agree to a plea bargain he would be indicted and tried under the state's criminal recidivist statute for having committed three prior felonies, and the defendant was sentenced to lifetime imprisonment.

Case	Vote	Ruling
Ricketts v. Adamson, 483 U.S 1 (1987)	5:4	Held that the Fifth Amendment guarantee against double jeopardy was not violated by the prosecution of a defendant on the original charge of murder because he breached a plea-bargain agreement to testify against codefendants.
Alabama v. Smith, 109 S.Ct. 2201 (1989)	8:1	Held there is no presumption a judge imposes a harsher sentence on a criminal defendant who is convicted after a trial, and after backing out of a plea-bargain agreement that had called for a lighter sentence.

coerced and their court-appointed attorney had incompetently represented them. But the Court held that their attorney was "reasonably competent" and they must assume the risk of "ordinary error" by their attorneys. *Henderson v. Morgan*, 426 U.S. 637 (1976), however, set aside a conviction because the defendant pled guilty to second-degree murder without being informed of the consequences. The Court, nonetheless, remains reluctant to find attorneys incompetent, even when they have little or no time to confer with their clients[1] and when they misinform their clients on plea bargaining.[2]

The right to counsel includes a right to effective counsel, as Justice Stevens explained in *United States v. Cronic*, 466 U.S. 640 (1984), because competent counsel is essential to the accusatory system and "the reliability of the trial process."[3] Accordingly, public defenders do not enjoy absolute immunity from being sued for incompetent representation.[4] The test for determining when the right to effective counsel has been denied was set forth by Justice O'Connor in *Strickland v. Washington*, 466 U.S. 668 (1984):

A convicted defendant's claim that counsel's assistance was so defective as to require reversal of a conviction or death sentence has two components. First, the defendant must show that counsel's performance was deficient. This requires showing that counsel made errors so serious that counsel was not functioning as the "counsel" guaranteed the defendant by the Sixth Amendment. Second, the defendant must show that the deficient performance prejudiced the defense. This requires showing that counsel's errors were so serious as to deprive the defendant of a fair trial, a trial whose result is reliable. Unless a defendant makes both showings, it cannot be said that the conviction or death sentence resulted from a breakdown in the adversary process that renders the result unreliable. . . .

More specific guidelines are not appropriate. The Sixth Amendment refers simply to "counsel," not specifying particular requirements of effective assistance. It relies instead on the legal profession's maintenance of standards sufficient to justify the law's presumption that counsel will fulfill the role in the adversary process that the Amendment envisions. . . . The proper measure of attorney performance remains simply reasonableness under prevailing professional norms.

Representation of a criminal defendant entails certain basic duties. Counsel's function is to assist the defendant, and hence counsel owes the client a duty of loyalty, a duty to avoid conflict of interest. . . . From counsel's function as assistant to the defendant derive the overarching duty to advocate the defendant's cause and the more particular duties to consult with the defendant on important decisions and to keep the defendant informed of important developments in the course of the prosecution. Counsel also has a duty to bring to bear such skill and knowledge as will render the trial a reliable adversial testing process.

These basic duties neither exhaustively define the obligations of counsel nor form a checklist for judicial evaluation of attorney performance. . . . No particular set of detailed rules for counsel's conduct can satisfactorily take account of the variety of circumstances faced by defense counsel or the range of legitimate decisions regarding how best to represent a criminal defendant. Any such set of rules would interfere with the constitutionally protected independence of counsel and restrict the wide latitude counsel must have in making tactical decisions. . . . Indeed, the existence of detailed guidelines for representation could distract from the overriding mission of vigorous advocacy of the defendant's cause. Moreover, the purpose of the effective counsel guarantee of the Sixth Amendment is not to improve the quality of legal representation, although that is a goal of considerable importance to the legal system. The purpose is simply to ensure that criminal defendants receive a fair trial.

O'Connor concluded by emphasizing the Court's deference to counsel in cases challenging their competence and effectiveness:

Judicial scrutiny of counsel's performance must be highly deferential. It is all too tempting for a defendant to second-guess counsel's assistance after conviction or adverse sentence, and it is all too easy for a court, examining counsel's defense after it has proved unsuccessful, to conclude that a particular act or omission of counsel was unreasonable. . . . A fair assessment of attorney performance requires that every effort be made to eliminate the distorting effects of hindsight, to reconstruct the circumstances of counsel's challenged conduct, and to evaluate the conduct from counsel's perspective at the time. Because of the difficulties inherent in making the evaluation, a court must indulge a strong presumption that counsel's conduct falls within the wide range of reasonable professional assistance; that is, the defendant must overcome the presumption that, under the circumstances, the challenged action "might be considered sound trial strategy." . . . There are countless ways to provide effective assistance in any given case. Even the best criminal defense attorneys would not defend a particular client in the same way.

Subsequently, the Court held that defendants have a right to effective counsel on their first appeal, *Evitts v. Lucey*, 469 U.S. 830 (1985). But when defendants tell their attorneys that they are going to lie on the witness stand, attorneys may withdraw from their cases without denying the right to effective counsel.[5] In *Mallard v. U.S. District Court*, 490 U.S. 296 (1989), the Court also held that a judge may not compel a lawyer to serve as a defendant's court-appointed counsel.

NOTES

1. See *Morris v. Slappy*, 461 U.S. 1 (1983); and *Chambers v. Maroney*, 399 U.S. 42 (1970).
2. See *North Carolina v. Alford*, 400 U.S. 25 (1970); and *Tollett v. Henderson*, 411 U.S. 258 (1976).
3. See also *Entsminger v. Iowa*, 386 U.S. 748 (1967), holding that defendant was denied the right to effective counsel when the court-appointed attorney failed to file the entire record on appeal.
4. *Ferri v. Ackerman*, 444 U.S. 193 (1979).
5. *Nix v. Whiteside*, 475 U.S. 157 (1986).

SELECTED BIBLIOGRAPHY

Heumann, M. *Plea Bargaining: The Experiences of Prosecutors, Judges, and Defense Attorneys*. Chicago: University of Chicago Press, 1978.
McDonald, William F., and Cramer, James A. eds. *Plea-Bargaining*. Lexington, MA: Lexington Books, 1980.
Nardulli, Peter, Eisenstein, James, and Flemming, Roy. *The Tenor of Justice: Criminal Courts and the Guilty Plea Process*. Urbana: University of Illinois Press, 1988.
Packer, Herbert. *The Limits of the Criminal Sanction*. Stanford, CA: Stanford University Press, 1968.

Bordenkircher v. Hayes
434 U.S. 357, 98 S.Ct. 663 (1978)

Justice Potter Stewart discusses the facts in his opinion for the Court, upholding a prosecutor's threat to indictment and conviction of Paul Hayes under Kentucky's Habitual Criminal Act because Mr. Hayes refused to agree to a plea bargain and insisted on a trial when he was charged with forging a check in the amount of $88.30. Three justices dissented from the Court's ruling.

Justice STEWART delivers the opinion of the Court.

The question in this case is whether the Due Process Clause of the Fourteenth Amendment is violated when a state prosecutor carries out a threat made during plea negotiations to reindict the accused on more serious charges if he does not plead guilty to the offense with which he was originally charged.

The respondent, Paul Lewis Hayes, was indicted by a Fayette County, Ky., grand jury on a charge of uttering a forged instrument in the amount of $88.30, an offense then punishable by a term of two to 10 years in prison. Ky.Rev.Stat. § 434.130 (repealed 1974). After arraignment, Hayes, his retained counsel, and the Commonwealth's attorney met in the presence of the clerk of the court to discuss a possible plea agreement. During these conferences the prosecutor offered to recommend a sentence of five years in prison if Hayes would plead guilty to the indictment. He also said that if Hayes did not plead guilty and "save the court the inconvenience and necessity of a trial," he would return to the grand jury to seek an indictment under the Kentucky Habitual Criminal Act, then Ky.Rev.Stat. § 431.190 (repealed 1975), which would subject Hayes to a mandatory sentence of life imprisonment by reason of his two prior felony convictions. Hayes chose not to plead guilty, and the prosecutor did obtain an indictment charging him under the Habitual Criminal Act. . . .

A jury found Hayes guilty on the principal charge of uttering a forged instrument and, in a separate proceeding, further found that he had twice before been convicted of felonies. As required by the habitual offender statute, he was sentenced to a life term in the penitentiary. . . .

It may be helpful to clarify at the outset the nature of the issue in this case. While the prosecutor did not actually obtain the recidivist indictment until after the plea conferences had ended, his intention to do so was clearly put forth at the outset of the plea negotiations. Hayes was thus fully informed of the true terms of the offer when he made his decision to plead not guilty. This is not a situation, therefore, where the prosecutor without notice brought an additional and more serious charge after plea negotiations relating only to the original indictment had ended with the defendant's insistence on pleading not guilty. As a practical matter, in short, this case would be no different if the grand jury had indicted Hayes as a recidivist from the outset, and the prosecutor had offered to drop that charge as part of the plea bargain.

The Court of Appeals nonetheless drew a distinction between "concessions relating to prosecution under an existing indictment," and threats to bring more severe charges not contained in the original indictment—a line it thought necessary in order to establish a prophylactic rule to guard against the evil of prosecutorial vindictiveness. . . .

We have recently had occasion to observe that "[w]hatever might be the situation in an ideal world, the fact is that the guilty plea and the often concomitant plea bargain are important components of this country's criminal justice system. Properly administered, they can benefit all concerned." *Blackledge v. Allison*, 431 U.S. 63 [(1977)]. The open acknowledgment of this previously clandestine practice has led this Court to recognize the importance of counsel during plea negotiations, *Brady v. United States*, 397 U.S. 742 [(1970)]. The need for a public record indicating that a plea was knowingly and voluntarily made, *Boykin v. Alabama*, 395 U.S. 238 [(1969)]. And the requirement that a prosecutor's plea bargaining promise must be kept, *Santobello v. New York*, 404 U.S. 257 [(1971)]. . . .

Plea bargaining flows from "the mutuality of advantage" to defendants and prosecutors, each with his own reasons for wanting to avoid trial. *Brady v. United States*. Defendants advised by competent counsel and protected by other procedural safeguards are presumptively capable of intelligent choice in response to prosecutorial persuasion, and unlikely to be driven to false self-condemnation. Indeed, acceptance of the basic legitimacy of plea bargaining necessarily implies rejection of any notion that a guilty plea is involuntary in a constitutional sense simply because it is the end result of the bargaining process. By hypothesis, the plea may have been induced by promises of a recommendation of a lenient sentence or a reduction of charges, and thus by fear of the possibility of a greater penalty upon conviction after a trial. . . .

While confronting a defendant with the risk of more severe punishment clearly may have a "discouraging effect on the defendant's assertion of his trial rights, the imposition of these difficult choices [is] an inevitable"—and permissible—"attribute of any legitimate system which tolerates and encourages the negotiation of pleas." It follows that, by tolerating and encouraging the negotiation of pleas, this Court has necessarily accepted as constitutionally legitimate the simple reality that the prosecutor's interest at the bargaining table is to persuade the defendant to forego his right to plead not guilty.

It is not disputed here that Hayes was properly chargeable under the recidivist statute, since he had in fact been convicted of two previous felonies. In our system, so long as the prosecutor has probable cause to believe that the accused committed an offense defined by statute, the decision whether or not to prosecute, and what charge to file or bring before a grand jury, generally rests entirely in his discretion. . . .

There is no doubt that the breadth of discretion that our country's legal system vests in prosecuting attorneys carries with it the potential for both individual and institutional abuse. And broad though that discretion may be, there are undoubtedly constitutional limits upon its exercise. We hold only that the course of conduct engaged in by the prosecutor in this case, which no more than openly presented the defendant with the unpleasant alternatives of foregoing trial or facing charges on which he was plainly subject to prosecution, did not violate the Due Process Clause of the Fourteenth Amendment.

Accordingly, the judgment of the Court of Appeals is Reversed.

Justice BLACKMUN, with whom Justice BRENNAN and Justice MARSHALL join, dissenting.

Prosecutorial vindictiveness, it seems to me, in the present narrow context, is the fact against which the Due Process Clause ought to protect. I perceive little difference between vindictiveness after what the Court describes, as the exercise of a "legal right to attack his original conviction," and vindictiveness in the "give-and-take negotiation common in plea bargaining." Prosecutorial vindictiveness in any context is still prosecutorial vindictiveness. The Due Process Clause should protect an accused against it, however it asserts itself.

Justice POWELL dissenting.

Although I agree with much of the Court's opinion, I am not satisfied that the result in this case is just or that the conduct of the plea bargaining met the requirements of due process.

Respondent was charged with the uttering of a single forged check in the amount of $88.30. Under Kentucky law, this offense was punishable by a prison term of from two to 10 years, apparently without regard to the amount of the forgery. During the course of plea bargaining, the prosecutor offered respondent a sentence of five years in consideration of a guilty plea. I observe, at this point, that five years in prison for the offense charged hardly could be characterized as a generous offer. Apparently respondent viewed the offer in this light and declined to accept it; he protested that he was innocent and insisted on going to trial. . . .

The prosecutor's initial assessment of respondent's case led him to forego an indictment under the habitual criminal statute.

The circumstances of respondent's prior convictions are relevant to this assessment and to my view of the case. Respondent was 17 years old when he committed his first offense. He was charged with rape but pled guilty to the lesser included offense of "detaining a female." One of the other participants in the incident was sentenced to life imprisonment. Respondent was sent not to prison but to a reformatory where he served five years. Respondent's second offense was robbery. This time he was found guilty by a jury and was sentenced to five years in prison, but he was placed on probation and served no time. Although respondent's prior convictions brought him within the terms of the Habitual Criminal Act, the offenses themselves did not result in imprisonment; yet the addition of a conviction on a charge involving $88.30 subjected respondent to a mandatory sentence of imprisonment for life. Persons convicted of rape and murder often are not punished so severely. . . .

It seems to me that the question to be asked under the circumstances is whether the prosecutor reasonably might have charged respondent under the Habitual Criminal Act in the first place. The deference that courts properly accord the exercise of a prosecutor's discretion perhaps would foreclose judicial criticism if the prosecutor originally had sought an indictment under that act, as unreasonable as it would have seemed. But here the prosecutor evidently made a reasonable, responsible judgment not to subject an individual to a mandatory life sentence when his only new offense had societal implications as limited as those accompanying the uttering of a single $88 forged check and when the circumstances of his prior convictions confirmed the inappropriateness of applying the habitual criminal statute. I think it may be inferred that the prosecutor himself deemed it unreasonable and not in the public interest to put this defendant in jeopardy of a sentence of life imprisonment. . . .

In most cases a court could not know why the harsher indictment was sought, and an inquiry into the prosecutor's motive would neither be indicated nor likely to be fruitful. In those cases, I would agree with the majority that the situation would not differ materially from one in which the higher charge was brought at the outset.

But this is not such a case. Here, any inquiry into the prosecutor's purpose is made unnecessary by his candid acknowledgement that he threatened to procure and in fact procured the habitual criminal indictment because of respondent's insistence on exercising his constitutional rights. . . .

The plea-bargaining process, as recognized by this Court, is essential to the functioning of the criminal-justice system. It normally affords genuine benefits to defendants as well as to society. And if the system is to work effectively, prosecutors must be accorded the widest discretion, within constitutional limits, in conducting bargaining. This is especially true when a defendant is represented by counsel and presumably is fully advised of his rights. Only in the most exceptional case should a court conclude that the scales of the bargaining are so unevenly balanced as to arouse suspicion. In this case, the prosecutor's actions denied respondent due process because their admitted purpose was to discourage and then to penalize with unique severity his exercise of constitutional rights. Implementation of a strategy calculated solely to deter the exercise of constitutional rights is not a constitutionally permissible exercise of discretion. I would affirm the opinion of the Court of Appeals on the facts of this case.

C. INDICTMENT BY A GRAND JURY

Embedded in the colonies as part of the English common law was the right to a jury trial. But, in the 1760s and 1770s, colonists deeply resented royalist judges and were hostile to the legal profession that defended the system. The institution of indictment by a grand jury grew out of colonial hostility toward royalist courts. Prosecuting officers had to make a prima facie case to a body of laymen that an individual violated criminal law, and if the grand jury was persuaded it would vote for an indictment on the charges presented. The original thirteen states, however, varied in the power given to juries. As Alexander Hamilton noted in *The Federalist,* No. 83, "no general rule could have been fixed by the Convention which would have corresponded with the circumstances of all the States."

The Fifth Amendment provides that "no person shall be held to answer for a capital [crime, which carries the death penalty] or otherwise infamous crime, unless on a presentment or indictment of a Grand Jury." This guarantee applies to only the national government because the Court has never reversed *Hurtado v. California,* 110 U.S. 516 (1884) (see Chapter 4), which ruled that the guarantee for an indictment by a grand jury does not apply to the states under the Fourteenth Amendment's due process clause. A grand jury consists of twelve to twenty-three laymen—typically selected by lot from voting rolls or chosen by local officials. The district attorney meets with the grand jury in secret sessions and has the power to inquire into any alleged offense as directed by the district attorney or as charged by a judge.

SELECTED BIBLIOGRAPHY

Frankel. Marvin, and Naftails, Gary. *The Grand Jury on Trial.* New York: Hill & Wang, 1975.

Scigliano, Robert. *The Michigan One-Man Grand Jury.* East Lansing: Michigan State University, 1957.

Younger, R. D. *The People's Panel: The Grand Jury in the United States, 1634–1941.* Providence: Brown University, 1963.

Hurtado v. California
110 U.S. 516, 4 S.Ct. 111 (1884)

The pertinent sections of this case are reprinted in Chapter 4 (see page 289).

D. THE RIGHT TO AN IMPARTIAL JURY TRIAL

The jury is a fact-finding institution that determines the guilt or innocence of defendants. Because juries are composed of laymen or "peers" drawn from the community of the accused, juries also represent the democratic subculture within the judicial system. Juries, as Justice White observed in *Duncan v. Louisiana,* 391 U.S. 145 (1968) (see Chapter 3): "prevent oppression by the Government . . . [and] safeguard against the corrupt or overzealous prosecutor and against the compliant, biased, or eccentric judge."

The Sixth Amendment (and Article III, Section 2 of the Constitution) provides that the accused "shall enjoy the right" to a jury trial in criminal cases. The Seventh Amendment guarantees a jury trial in civil cases "where the value in controversy shall exceed twenty dollars." *Granfianciera v. Nordberg,* 109 S.Ct. 2728 (1989), extended the Seventh Amendment right to a jury trial to defendants charged with bankruptcy fraud. The right to jury trials may be waived but "the consent of the government counsel and the sanction of the court must be had, in addition to the express and intelligent consent of the defendant."[1]

In federal courts, the right to a jury trial is limited to those cases subject to the Fifth Amendment's provision for a grand jury indictment. Consequently, jury trials are not required for some petty crimes.[2] Nor may jury trials be had on charges of being in contempt of court,[3] on petitions for the writ of *habeas corpus,* and in certain other civil and administrative proceedings, such as those for disbarment and deportation. Neither does the Sixth Amendment's guarantee apply to courts-martial.[4]

Duncan v. Louisiana made applicable to the states the right to a jury trial in all nonpetty cases. Nonpetty cases were defined in *Baldwin v. New York*, 399 U.S. 66 (1970), as those carrying a potential sentence of six months or more imprisonment. The requirement that a jury be "impartial" has given rise to numerous questions. In addition to the fair trial/free press controversy (discussed in Chapter 5), the composition and method of selecting of juries has often been contested. In the "second *Scottsboro* case," *Norris v. Alabama*, 294 U.S. 587 (1935), the Hughes Court held that the due process and equal protection clauses of the Fourteenth Amendment do not permit the exclusion of blacks from juries.[5] But in *Fay v. New York*, 322 U.S. 261 (1947), the Vinson Court ruled that the Sixth Amendment does not require proportional representation of a community, when upholding "blue ribbon" juries selected from "the upper economic and social stratum" and excluding manual workers.

The basic protection against racial, economic, and gender bias is the principle that juries must reflect a "cross-section of the community." In *Smith v. Texas*, 311 U.S. 128 (1940), the Court observed that "it is part of the established tradition in the use of juries as instruments of public justice that the jury be a body truly representative of the community." When holding that women could not be excluded as potential jurors in *Taylor v. Louisiana*, 419 U.S. 522 (1975), the fair cross-section requirement was reaffirmed "as fundamental to the jury trial guaranteed by the Sixth Amendment." Accordingly, the Court has struck down various methods for selecting jurors because they worked toward "the total exclusion" of blacks and women,[6] but also maintained that there is no right to include the presence of blacks or women on juries.[7] The principle of a fair cross-section of the community in jury selection is also included in the Federal Jury Selection and Service Act of 1974, barring the exclusion of potential jurors on account of race, color, religion, gender, national origin, and economic status.[8]

Defense attorneys may use their preemptory changes to exclude potential jurors who they believe might harbor racial prejudice. During *voir dire* examination of potential jurors, when the victim and the defendant are members of different racial groups, defense attorneys may also ask potential jurors questions about whether they have any racial bias.[9] Specifically, *Turner v. Murray*, 476 U.S. 28 (1986), held that, where a black man was sentenced to death for murdering a white jeweler, the defendant had a right to have prospective jurors informed of the victim's race and questioned about racial bias. *Batson v. Kentucky* (1986) (see page 1030) held that the Fourteenth Amendment forbids prosecutors from challenging potential jurors solely on the basis of race to secure an all-white jury. However, in *Holland v. Illinois*, 110 S.Ct. 803 (1990), writing for a bare majority, Justice Scalia held that a prosecutor's use of preemptory challenges so as to exclude all black potential jurors from a jury did not deny a white defendant's right to an impartial jury trial under the Sixth Amendment.

The issue of juror bias has posed special problems in jury selection for capital cases. Historically, potential jurors having constitutional objections to the death penalty were excluded from capital cases. But *Witherspoon v. Illinois,* 391 U.S. 510 (1968), held that jurors opposed to the death penalty were impermissibly excluded; otherwise, in Justice Potter Stewart's words, every jury would be a "hanging jury." *Maxwell v. Bishop,* 398 U.S. 262 (1970), ruled that the death penalty may not be imposed when prospective jurors are removed due to their opposition to capital punishment. But the Burger and Rehnquist Courts have reconsidered the issue. In *Darden v. Wainwright,* 477 U.S. 168 (1986), the justices held five to four that potential jurors who have religious objections to the death penalty may be excluded, and *A. L. Lockhart V. McCree* (1986) (see page 1036) held that "death qualified" juries are permissible.[10]

Traditionally, a common law jury was composed of twelve persons and *Thompson v. Utah,* 170 U.S. 343 (1898), held that the Sixth Amendment jury "constituted, as it was at common law, of twelve persons, neither more nor less." *Duncan v. Louisiana* implicitly posed the issue of whether states had to adher to twelve-member juries as well, or whether they were still free to experiment with jury size. In 1967, Florida enacted a law providing for six-member juries in all criminal cases, except for capital crimes. That law was immediately challenged and upheld in *Williams v. Florida* (1970) (see page 1045). In federal district courts, six-member juries had been used in *civil* cases, even before *Williams.* This was so despite the fact that the Seventh Amendment specifically refers to the common law jury in providing for jury trials in civil cases. A bare majority of the Court in *Colegrove v. Battin,* 413 U.S. 149 (1973), nevertheless, upheld six-member juries in civil cases. Writing for the majority, Justice Brennan deemed the common law jury to be not frozen into the Constitution. Justices Douglas, Marshall, Stewart, and Powell dissented from, what Marshall termed, the majority's upholding of a "six-man mutation . . . a different institution which functions differently, produces different results, and was wholly unknown to the Framers of the Seventh Amendment."

Once the Court abandoned the history and principle of twelve-member juries, it faced the question of where to draw a line on jury size. *Ballew v. Georgia,* 635 U.S. 223 (1978), finally drew the line at six when rejecting Georgia's use of five-member juries in criminal cases.

A related controversy arose with *Johnson v. Louisiana,* 406 U.S. 356 (1972), and *Apodaca v. Oregon,* 406 U.S. 404 (1972), holding that nonunanimous jury verdicts in criminal cases did not violate the Fourteenth Amendment's due process and equal protection clauses. In *Johnson,* a bare majority approved Louisiana's law permitting convictions based on a vote of nine out of twelve jurors. *Apodaca* upheld an Oregon statute under which two defendants were found guilty by jury votes of eleven to one and ten to two. In both, Justice White dismissed the history of unanimous verdicts and applied his *Williams's* analysis of the function of juries in concluding that nonunanimous and unanimous juries were "functionally equivalent." His opinion was so sweeping in rejecting the history of unanimity, dating back to 1367 and an accepted part of federal jury trials, that Justice Powell, although joining the majority, was moved to point out in a concurring opinion that unanimity in federal courts was "mandated by history."[11]

Together, *Williams v. Florida, Johnson,* and *Apodaca,* presented the issue of where the Court would draw the line on the permissibility of nonunanimous verdicts rendered by juries composed of less than twelve members. That issue was met in *Burch v. Louisiana* (1979) (see page 1048), holding that unanimous verdicts are required in six-member juries.

NOTES

1. *Patton v. United States,* 281 U.S. 276 (1980). See also *Singer v. United States,* 380 U.S. 24 (1965).
2. See *Cheff v. Schnackenberg,* 384 U.S. 373 (1966).
3. But see also *United States v. Barnett,* 376 U.S. 681 (1964); and *Cheff v. Schnackenberg,* 384 U.S. 373 (1966).
4. See *Ex parte Milligan,* 4 Wall. 2 (1866) (see Vol. 1, Ch. 3).
5. *Hernandez v. Texas,* 347 U.S. 475 (1954), extended the ruling in *Norris* to prohibit states from excluding Hispanics from juries. *Eubanks v. Louisiana,* 356 U.S. 584 (1958) overturned the conviction of a black man by an all-white jury.
6. See *Turner v. Fouche,* 396 U.S. 346 (1970); *Avery v. Georgia,* 345 U.S. 559 (1952); *Whitus v. Georgia* U.S. (1967); and *Turner v. Fouche,* 396 U.S. 346 (1970).
7. See *Swain v. Alabama,* 380 U.S. 202 (1965); *Carter v. Jury Commission of Greene County,* 396 U.S. 320 (1970).
8. See *Test v. United States,* 420 U.S. 28 (1975), allowing a defendant to inspect jury lists to determine whether a disproportionate number of people with Hispanic surnames have been excluded.

9. See *Ham v. South Carolina,* 409 U.S. 524 (1973); *Ristanino v. Ross,* 424 U.S. 589 (1976); and *Rosales-Lopez v. United States,* 451 U.S. 182 (1981).

10. See also *Wainwright v. Witt,* 469 U.S. 412 (1985). *Buchanan v. Kentucky,* 107 S.Ct. 2906 (1987), further upheld the use of death-qualified juries in a joint trial where a death sentence was sought for only one of the codefendants.

11. *Dicta* in *Maxwell v. Dow,* 176 U.S. 581 (1900), and *Jordon v. Massachusetts,* 255 U.S. 167 (1912), suggested that unanimous verdicts were not required in state courts. But both preceded *Duncan v. Louisiana's* extension of the jury requirement to the states.

SELECTED BIBLIOGRAPHY

Hastie, Reid, Penrod, Steven, and Pennington, Nancy. *Inside the Jury.* Cambridge, MA: Harvard University Press, 1983.

Jacob, Herbert. *Law and Politics in the United States.* Boston: Little, Brown, 1986.

Kalven, Harry. and Zeizel, Hans. *The American Jury.* Chicago: University of Chicago Press, 1966.

Simon, Rita. *The Jury: Its Role in American Society.* Lexington, MA: Lexington Books, 1980.

O'Brien, David M. "The Seduction of the Judiciary: Social Science and the Courts." 64 *Judicature* 8 (1980).

Sperlick, Peter. "Trial by Jury: It May Have a Future." In *The Supreme Court Review: 1978* edited by Philip Kurland and Gerhard Casper. Chicago: University of Chicago Press, 1979, 191.

Zeisel, Hans. "The Verdict of Five Out of Six Civil Jurors," 1982 *American Bar Foundation Research Journal,* 1982, 141.

Duncan v. Louisiana
391 U.S. 145, 88 S.Ct. 1444 (1968).

This case was reprinted in part in Chapter 4, page 319.

Batson v. Kentucky
476 U.S. 79, 106 S.Ct. 1712 (1986)

James Kirkland Batson, a black man, was tried for second-degree burglary and receiving stolen goods. Before his trial, the judge conducted *voir dire* examination of the jury venire and excused certain potential jurors. The prosecutor then used his peremptory challenges to strike all four black persons in the venire to secure an all-white jury. Batson's attorney moved to dismiss the jury for violating his client's Sixth and Fourteenth Amendments' guarantees of a jury drawn from a cross-section of the community. The trial judge denied the motion and Batson was tried and convicted. The Kentucky Supreme Court affirmed and Batson's attorney made a further appeal to the Supreme Court of the United States.

Justice POWELL delivers the opinion of the Court.

In *Swain v. Alabama,* [380 U.S. 202 (1965)], this Court recognized that a "State's purposeful or deliberate denial to Negroes on account of race of participation as jurors in the administration of justice violates the Equal Protection Clause." This principle has been "consistently and repeatedly" reaffirmed in numerous decisions of this Court both preceding and following *Swain.* We reaffirm the principle today.

More than a century ago, the Court decided that the State denies a black defendant equal protection of the laws when it puts him on trial before a jury from which members of his race have been purposefully excluded. *Strauder v. West Virginia* . . . 100 U.S. 303 (1880). . . .

In holding that racial discrimination in jury selection offends the Equal Protection Clause, the Court in *Strauder* recognized, however, that a defendant has no right to a "petit jury composed in whole or in part of persons of his own race." "The number of our races and nationalities stands in the way of evolution of such a conception" of the demand of equal protection. *Akins v. Texas,* 325 U.S. 398 (1945). But the defendant does have the right to be tried by a jury whose members are selected pursuant to nondiscriminatory criteria. The Equal Protection Clause guarantees the defendant that the State will not exclude members of his race from the jury venire on account of race, *Strauder,* or on the false assumption that members of his race as a group are not qualified to serve as jurors. . . .

The harm from discriminatory jury selection extends beyond that inflicted on the defendant and the excluded juror to touch the entire community. Selection procedures that purposefully exclude black persons from juries undermine public confidence in the fairness of our system of justice. . . .

In *Strauder,* the Court invalidated a state statute that provided that only white men could serve as jurors. We can be confident that no state now has such a law. The Constitution requires, however, that we look beyond the face of the statute defining juror qualifications and also consider challenged selection practices to afford "protection against action of the State through its administrative officers in effecting the prohibited discrimination.". . .

Accordingly, the component of the jury selection process at issue here, the State's privilege to strike individual jurors through peremptory challenges, is subject to the commands of the Equal Protection Clause. Although a prosecutor ordinarily is entitled to exercise permitted peremptory challenges "for any reason at all, as long as that reason is related to his view concerning the outcome" of the case to be tried, the Equal Protection Clause forbids the prosecutor to challenge potential jurors solely on account of their race or on the assumption that black jurors as a group will be unable impartially to consider the State's case against a black defendant.

The principles announced in *Strauder* never have been questioned in any subsequent decision of this Court. Rather, the Court has been called upon repeatedly to review the application of those principles to particular facts." A recurring question in these cases, as in any case alleging a violation of the Equal Protection Clause, was whether the defendant had met his burden of proving purposeful discrimination on the part of the State. . . .

The showing necessary to establish a prima facie case of purposeful discrimination in selection of the venire may be discerned in this Court's decisions. The defendant initially must show that he is a member of a racial group capable of being singled out for differential treatment. In combination with that evidence, a defendant may then make a prima facie case by proving that in the particular jurisdiction members of his race have not been summoned for jury service over an extended period of time. Proof of systematic exclusion from the venire raises an inference of purposeful discrimination because the "result bespeaks discrimination."

Since the ultimate issue is whether the State has discriminated in selecting the defendant's venire, however, the defendant may establish a prima facie case "in other ways than by evidence of long-continued unexplained absence" of members of his race "from many panels." In cases involving the venire, this Court has found a prima facie case on proof that members of the defendant's race were substantially underrepresented on the venire from which his jury was drawn and that the venire was selected under a practice providing "the opportunity for discrimination." This combination of factors raises the necessary inference of purposeful discrimination because the Court has declined to attribute to chance the absence of black citizens on a particular jury array where the selection mechanism is subject to abuse. When circumstances suggest the need, the trial court must undertake a "factual inquiry" that "takes into account all possible explanatory factors" in the particular case. . . .

While we recognize, of course, that the peremptory challenge occupies an important position in our trial procedures, we do not agree that our decision today will undermine the contribution the challenge generally makes to the administration of justice. The reality of practice, amply reflected in many state and federal court opinions, shows that the challenge may be, and unfortunately at times has been, used to discriminate against black jurors. By requiring trial courts to be sensitive to the racially discriminatory use of peremptory challenges, our decision enforces the mandate of equal protection and furthers the ends of justice. In view of the heterogeneous population of our nation, public respect for our criminal justice system and the rule of law will be strengthened if we ensure that no citizen is disqualified from jury service because of his race.

Justice WHITE concurred.

Justice STEVENS, with whom Justice BRENNAN joined, concurred.

Justice O'Connor concurred.

Chief Justice BURGER, with whom Justice REHNQUIST joins, dissenting.

Today the Court sets aside the peremptory challenge, a procedure which has been part of the common law for many centuries and part of our jury system for nearly 200 years. It does so on the basis of a constitutional argument that was rejected, without a single dissent, in *Swain v. Alabama* 380 U.S. 202 (1965). . . .

The Court's opinion, in addition to ignoring the teachings of history, also contrasts with *Swain* in its failure to even discuss the rationale of the peremptory challenge. *Swain* observed:

> "The function of the challenge is not only to eliminate extremes of partiality on both sides, but to assure the parties that the jurors before whom they try the case will decide on the basis of the evidence placed for them, and not otherwise. In this way the peremptory satisfies the rule that "to perform its high function in the best way, justice must satisfy the appearance of justice.'"

Permitting unexplained peremptories has long been regarded as a means to strengthen our jury system in other ways as well. One commentator has recognized:

"The peremptory, made without giving any reason, avoids trafficking in the core of truth in most common stereotypes. . . . Common human experience, common sense, psychosociological studies, and public opinion polls tell us that it is likely that certain classes of people statistically have predispositions that would make them inappropriate jurors for particular kinds of cases. But to allow this knowledge to be expressed in the evaluative terms necessary for challenges for cause would undercut our desire for a society in which all people are judged as individuals and in which each is held reasonable and open to compromise. . . . [For example,] [a]lthough experience reveals that black males as a class can be biased against young alienated blacks who have not tried to join the middle class, to enunciate this in the concrete expression required of a challenge for cause is societally divisive. Instead we have evolved in the peremptory challenge a system that allows the covert expression of what we dare not say but know is true more often than not." Babcock, Voir Dire. Preserving "Its Wonderful Power," 27 Stan.L.Rev. 545, 553–554 (1975).

For reasons such as these, this Court concluded in *Swain* that "the [peremptory] challenge is 'one of the most important of the rights' " in our justice system. *Swain.* . . .

Instead of even considering the history or function of the peremptory challenge, the bulk of the Court's opinion is spent recounting the well-established principle that intentional exclusion of racial groups from jury venires is a violation of the Equal Protection Clause. I too reaffirm that principle, which has been a part of our constitutional tradition since at least *Strauder v. West Virginia.* But if today's decision is nothing more than mere "application" of the "principles announced in *Strauder,*" as the Court maintains, some will consider it curious that the application went unrecognized for over a century. The Court in *Swain* had no difficulty in unanimously concluding that cases such as *Strauder* did not require inquiry into the basis for a peremptory, challenge. . . .

A moment's reflection quickly reveals the vast differences between the racial exclusions involved in *Strauder* and the allegations before us today:

"Exclusion from the venire summons process implies that the government (usually the legislative or judicial branch) . . . has made the general determination that those excluded are unfit to try *any* case. Exercise of the peremptory challenge, by contrast, represents the discrete decision, made by one of two or more opposed *litigants* in the trial phase of our adversary system of justice, that the challenged venireperson will likely be more unfavorable to that litigant in that *particular case* than others on the same venire.

"Thus, excluding a particular cognizable group from all venire pools is stigmatizing and discriminatory in several inter-related ways that the peremptory challenge is not. The former singles out the excluded group, while individuals of all groups are equally subject to peremptory challenge on any basis, including their group affiliation. Further, venire-pool exclusion bespeaks *a priori* across-the-board total unfitness, while peremptory-strike exclusion merely suggests potential partiality in a particular isolated case. Exclusion from venires focuses on the inherent attributes of the excluded group and infers its *inferiority*, but the peremptory does not. To suggest that a particular race is unfit to judge in any case necessarily is racially insulting. To suggest that each race may have its own special concerns, or even may tend to favor its own, is not." *United States v. Leslie*, 783 F.2d 541, 554 (CA5 1986) (en banc). . . .

Unwilling to rest solely on jury venire cases such as *Strauder*, the Court also invokes general equal protection principles in support of its holding. But peremptory challenges are often lodged, of necessity, for reasons "normally thought irrelevant to legal proceedings or official action, namely, the race, religion, nationality, occupation or affiliations of people summoned for jury duty." *Swain.* Moreover, in making peremptory challenges, both the prosecutor and defense attorney necessarily act on only limited information or hunch. The process can not be indicted on the sole basis that such decisions are made on the basis of "assumption" or "intuitive judgment." As a result, undulterated equal protection analysis is simply inapplicable to peremptory challenge exercised in any particular case.

Justice REHNQUIST, with whom the CHIEF JUSTICE joins, dissenting.

I cannot subscribe to the Court's unprecedented use of the Equal Protection Clause to restrict the historic scope of the peremptory challenge, which has been described as "a necessary part of trial by jury." . . . In my view, there is simply nothing "unequal" about the State using its peremptory challenges to strike blacks from the jury in cases involving black defendants, so long as such challenges are also used to exclude whites in cases involving white defendants, Hispanics in cases involving Hispanic defendants, Asians in cases involving Asian defendants, and so on. This case specific use of peremptory challenges by the State does not single out blacks, or members of any other race for that matter, for discriminatory treatment. Such use of peremptories is at best based upon seat-of-the-pants instincts, which are undoubtedly crudely stereotypical and may in many cases be hopelessly mistaken. But as long as they are applied across the board to jurors of all races and nationalities, I do not see—and the Court most certainly has not explained—how their use violates the Equal Protection Clause. . . .

The use of group affiliations, such as age, race, or occupation, as a "proxy" for potential juror partiality, based on the assumption or belief that members of one group are more likely to favor defendants who belong to the same group, has long been accepted as a legitimate basis for the State's exercise of peremptory challenges. Indeed, given the need for reasonable limitations on the time devoted to *voir dire*, the use of such "proxies" by both the State and the defendants may be extremely useful in eliminating from the jury persons who might be biased in one way or another. . . . I would therefore affirm the judgment of the court below.

A. L. Lockhart v. McCree
476 U.S. 162, 106 S.Ct. 1758 (1986)

A. L. Lockhart, the director of the Arkansas Department of Correction, appealed the Court of Appeals for the Eighth Circuit's affirmance of a federal district court's ruling. The district court had held that Ardia McCree's Sixth and Fourteenth Amendments' rights were violated in a capital case by a state trial judge's removal, over McCree's objections, of prospective jurors who stated that they would not under any circumstance vote to impose the death penalty. The Supreme Court granted review.

Justice REHNQUIST delivers the opinion of the Court.

In this case we address the question left open by our decision nearly 18 years ago in *Witherspoon v. Illinois*, 391 U.S. 510 (1968): Does the Constitution prohibit the removal for cause, prior to the guilt phase of a bifurcated capital trial, of prospective jurors whose opposition to the death penalty is so strong that it would prevent or substantially impair the performance of their duties as jurors at the sentencing phase of the trial? We hold that it does not. . . .

Before turning to the legal issues in the case, we are constrained to point out what we believe to be several serious flaws in the evidence upon which the courts below reached the conclusion that "death qualification" produces "conviction-prone" juries. McCree introduced into evidence some fifteen social science studies in support of his constitutional claims, but only six of the studies even purported to measure the potential effects on the guilt-innocence determination of the removal from the jury of "*Witherspoon* excludables.". . .

Of the six studies introduced by McCree that at least purported to deal with the central issue in this case, namely, the potential effects on the determination of guilt or innocence of excluding "*Witherspoon* excludables" from the jury, three were also before this Court when it decided *Witherspoon, supra*. There, this Court reviewed the studies and concluded:

> "The data adduced by the petitioner . . . are too tentative and fragmentary to establish that jurors not opposed to the death penalty tend to favor the prosecution in the determination of guilt. We simply cannot conclude, either on the basis of the record now before us or as a matter of judicial notice, that the exclusion of jurors opposed to capital punishment results in an unrepresentative jury on the issue of guilt or substantially increases the risk of conviction. In light of the presently available information, we are not prepared to announce a *per se* constitutional rule requiring the reversal of every conviction returned by a jury selected as this one was.". . .

It goes almost without saying that if these studies were "too tentative and fragmentary" to make out a claim of constitutional error in 1968, the same studies, unchanged but for having aged some eighteen years, are still insufficient to make out such a claim in this case.

Nor do the three post-*Witherspoon* studies introduced by McCree on the "death qualification" issue provide substantial support for the "*per se* constitutional rule" McCree asks this Court to adopt. All three of the "new" studies were based on the responses of individuals randomly selected from some segment of the population, but who were not actual jurors sworn under oath to apply the law to the facts of an actual case involving the fate of an actual capital defendant. We have serious doubts about the value of these studies in predicting the behavior of actual jurors.

Finally, and most importantly, only one of the six "death qualification" studies introduced by McCree even attempted to identify and account for the presence of so-called "nullifiers," or individuals who, because of their deep-seated opposition to the death penalty, would be unable to decide a capital defendant's guilt or innocence fairly and impartially. McCree concedes, as he must, that "nullifiers" may properly be excluded from the guilt-phase jury, and studies that fail to take into account the presence of such "nullifiers" thus are fatally flawed. Surely a "*per se* constitutional rule" as far-reaching as the one McCree proposes should not be based on the results of the lone study that avoids this fundamental flaw.

Having identified some of the more serious problems with

McCree's studies, however, we will assume for purposes of this opinion that the studies are both methodologically valid and adequate to establish that "death qualification" in fact produces juries somewhat more "conviction-prone" than "non-death-qualified" juries. We hold, nonetheless, that the Constitution does not prohibit the States from "death qualifying" juries in capital cases. . . .

The Eighth Circuit ruled that "death qualification" violated McCree's right under the Sixth Amendment. . . to a jury selected from a representative cross-section of the community. But we do not believe that the fair cross-section requirement, can, or should, be applied as broadly as that Court attempted to apply it. . . .

Even if we were willing to extend the fair cross-section requirement to petit juries, we would still reject the Eighth Circuit's conclusion that "death qualification" violates that requirement. The essence of a "fair cross-section" claim is the systematic exclusion of "a 'distinctive' group in the community.". . .

We have never attempted to precisely define the term "distinctive group," and we do not undertake to do so today. But we think it obvious that the concept of "distinctiveness" must be linked to the purposes of the fair cross-section requirement. In *Taylor* [*v. Louisiana*, 419 U.S. 522 (1975)] we identified those purposes as (1) "guard[ing] against the exercise of arbitrary power" and ensuring that the "commonsense judgment of the community" will act as "a hedge against the overzealous or mistaken prosecutor," (2) preserving "public confidence in the fairness of the criminal justice system," and (3) implementing our belief that "sharing in the administration of justice is a phase of civic responsibility.". . .

Our prior jury-representativeness cases, whether based on the fair cross-section component of the Sixth Amendment or the Equal Protection Clause of the Fourteenth Amendment, have involved such groups as blacks, see *Peters v. Kiff*, 407 U.S. 493 (1972) (plurality opinion) (equal protection), women, see *Taylor*, *supra* (same), and Mexican-Americans, see *Castaneda v. Partida*, 430 U.S. 482 (1977) (equal protection). The wholesale exclusion of these large groups from jury service clearly contravened all three of the aforementioned purposes of the fair cross-section requirement. Because these groups were excluded for reasons completely unrelated to the ability of members of the group to serve as jurors in a particular case, the exclusion raised at least the possibility that the composition of juries would be arbitrarily skewed in such a way as to deny criminal defendants the benefit of the common-sense judgment of the community. In addition, the exclusion from jury service of large groups of individuals not on the basis of their inability to serve as jurors, but on the basis of some immutable characteristic such as race, gender, or ethnic background, undeniably gave rise to an "appearance of unfairness." Finally, such exclusion improperly deprived members of these often historically disadvantaged groups of their right as citizens to serve on juries in criminal cases.

The group of "*Witherspoon* excludables" involved in the case at bar differs significantly from the groups we have previously recognized as "distinctive." "Death qualification," unlike the wholesale exclusion of blacks, women, or Mexican-Americans from jury service, is carefully designed to serve the State's concededly legitimate interest in obtaining a single jury that can properly and impartially apply the law to the facts of the case at both the guilt and sentencing phases of a capital trial. There is very little danger, therefore, and McCree does not even argue, that "death qualification" was instituted as a means for the State to arbitrarily skew the composition of capital-case juries.

Furthermore, unlike blacks, women, and Mexican-Americans, "*Witherspoon* excludables" are singled out for exclusion in capital cases on the basis of an attribute that is within the individual's control. It is important to remember that not all who oppose the death penalty are subject to removal for cause in capital cases; those who firmly believe that the death penalty is unjust may nevertheless serve as jurors in capital cases so long as they state clearly that they are willing to temporarily set aside their own beliefs in deference to the rule of law. Because the group of "*Witherspoon* excludables" includes only those who cannot and will not conscientiously obey the law with respect to one of the issues in a capital case, "death qualification" hardly can be said to create an "appearance of unfairness."

Finally, the removal for cause of "*Witherspoon* excludables" in capital cases does not prevent them from serving as jurors in other criminal cases, and thus leads to no substantial deprivation of their basic rights of citizenship. They are treated no differently than any juror who expresses the view that he would be unable to follow the law in a particular case. . . .

McCree argues, however, that this Court's decisions in *Witherspoon*, and *Adams v. Texas*, 448 U.S. 38 (1980), stand for the proposition that a State violates the Constitution whenever it "slants" the jury by excluding a group of individuals more likely than the population at large to favor the criminal defendant. We think McCree overlooks two fundamental differences between *Witherspoon* and *Adams* and the instant case, and therefore misconceives the import and scope of those two decisions.

First, the Court in *Witherspoon* viewed the Illinois system as having been deliberately slanted for the purpose of making the imposition of the death penalty more likely. The Court said:

"But when it swept from the jury all who expressed conscientious or religious scruples against capital punishment and all who opposed it in principle, the State crossed the line of neutrality. In its quest for a jury capable of imposing the death penalty, the State produced a jury uncommonly willing to condemn a man to die.

It is, of course, settled that a State may not entrust the determination of whether a man is innocent or guilty to a tribunal 'organized to convict.' . . . It requires but a short step from that principle to hold, as we do today, that a State may not entrust the determination of whether a man should live or die to a tribunal organized to return a verdict of death.". . .

Here, on the other hand, the removal for cause of "*Witherspoon* excludables" serves the State's entirely proper interest in obtaining a single jury that could impartially decide all of the issues in McCree's case. Arkansas by legislative enactment and judicial decision provides for the use of a unitary jury in capital cases. . . . We have upheld against constitutional attack the Georgia capital sentencing plan which provided that the same jury must sit in both phases of a bifurcated capital murder trial . . . and since then have observed that we are "unwilling to say that there is any one right way for a State to set up its capital sentencing scheme." *Spaziano v. Florida,* 468 U.S. 447 [(1984)]. . . .

Unlike the Illinois system criticized by the Court in *Witherspoon* the Arkansas system excludes from the jury only those who may properly be excluded from the penalty phase of the deliberations under *Witherspoon.* That State's reasons for adhering to its preference for a single jury to decide both the guilt and penalty phases of a capital trial are sufficient to negate the inference which the Court drew in *Witherspoon* concerning the lack of any neutral justification for the Illinois rule on jury challenges.

Second, and more importantly . . . *Witherspoon* . . . dealt with the special context of capital sentencing, where the range of jury discretion necessarily gave rise to far greater concern over the possible effects of an "imbalanced" jury. As we emphasized in *Witherspoon:*

"[I]n Illinois, as in other States, the jury is given broad discretion to decide whether or not death *is* 'the proper penalty' in a given case, and a juror's general views about capital punishment play an inevitable role in any such decision.

". . . Guided by neither rule nor standard, 'free to select or reject as it [sees] fit,' a jury that must choose between life imprisonment and capital punishment can do little more—and must do nothing less—than express the conscience of the community on the ultimate question of life or death.". . .

Because capital sentencing under the Illinois statute involved such an exercise of essentially unfettered discretion, we held that the State violated the Constitution when it "crossed the line of neutrality" and "produced a jury uncommonly willing to condemn a man to die.". . .

In the case at bar, by contrast, we deal not with capital sentencing, but with the jury's more traditional role of finding the facts and determining the guilt or innocence of a criminal defendant, where jury discretion is more channeled. . . .

In our view, it is simply not possible to define jury impartiality, for constitutional purposes, by reference to some hypothetical mix of individual viewpoints. Prospective jurors come from many different backgrounds, and have many different attitudes and predispositions. But the Constitution presupposes that a jury selected from a fair cross-section of the community is impartial, regardless of the mix of individual viewpoints actually represented on the jury, so long as the jurors can conscientiously and properly carry out their sworn duty to apply the law to the facts of the particular case. We hold that McCree's jury satisfied both aspects of this constitutional standard.

Justice BLACKMUN concurred.

Justice MARSHALL, with whom Justice BRENNAN and Justice STEVENS join, dissenting.

Respondent contends here that the "death-qualified" jury that convicted him, from which the State, as authorized by *Witherspoon,* had excluded all venirepersons unwilling to consider imposing the death penalty, was in effect "organized to return a verdict" of guilty. In support of this claim; he has presented overwhelming evidence that death-qualified juries are substantially more likely to convict or to convict on more serious charges than juries on which unalterable opponents of capital punishment are permitted to serve. Respondent does not challenge the application of *Witherspoon* to the jury in the sentencing stage of bifurcated capital cases. Neither does he demand that individuals unable to assess culpability impartially ("nullifiers") be permitted to sit on capital juries. All he asks is the chance to have his guilt or innocence determined by a jury like those that sit in non-capital cases—one whose composition has not been tilted in favor of the prosecution by the exclusion of a group of prospective jurors uncommonly aware of an accused's constitutional rights but quite capable of determining his culpability without favor or bias. . . .

In the wake of *Witherspoon,* a number of researchers set out to supplement the data that the Court had found inadequate in that case. The results of these studies were exhaustively analyzed by the District Court in this case, and can be only briefly summarized here. The data strongly suggest that death qualification excludes a significantly large subset—at least 11% to 17%—of potential jurors who could be impartial during the guilt phase of trial. Among the members of this excludable class are a disproportionate number of blacks and women.

The perspectives on the criminal justice system of jurors who survive death qualification are systematically different from those of the excluded jurors. Death-qualified jurors are, for example, more likely to believe that a defendant's failure to testify is indicative of his guilt, more hostile to the insanity defense, more mistrustful of defense attorneys, and less concerned about the danger of erroneous convictions. This pro-prosecution bias is reflected in the greater readiness of death-qualified jurors to convict or to convict on more serious charges. And, finally, the very process of death qualification—which focuses attention on the death penalty before the trial has even begun—has been found to predispose the jurors that survive it to believe that the defendant is guilty. . . .

The evidence thus confirms, and is itself corroborated by, the more intuitive judgments of scholars and of so many of the participants in capital trials—judges, defense attorneys, and prosecutors.

Respondent's case would of course be even stronger were he able to produce data showing the prejudicial effects of death qualification upon actual trials. Yet until a State permits two separate juries to deliberate on the same capital case and return simultaneous verdicts, defendants claiming prejudice from death qualification should not be denied recourse to the only available means of proving their case, recreations of the *voir dire* and trial processes. . . .

The chief strength of respondent's evidence lies in the essential unanimity of the results obtained by researchers using diverse subjects and varied methodologies. Even the Court's haphazard jabs cannot obscure the power of the array. Where studies have identified and corrected apparent flaws in prior investigations, the results of the subsequent work have only corroborated the conclusions drawn in the earlier efforts. Thus, for example, some studies might be faulted for failing to distinguish within the class of *Witherspoon*-excludables, between nullifiers (whom respondent concedes may be excluded from the guilt phase) and those who could assess guilt impartially. Yet their results are entirely consistent with those obtained after nullifiers had indeed been excluded. And despite the failure of certain studies to "allow for group deliberations," the value of their results is underscored by the discovery that initial verdict preferences, made prior to group deliberations, are a fair predictor of how a juror will vote when faced with opposition in the jury room.

The evidence adduced by respondent is quite different from the "tentative and fragmentary" presentation that failed to move this Court in *Witherspoon*. Moreover, in contrast to *Witherspoon*, the record in this case shows respondent's case to have been "subjected to the traditional testing mechanisms of the adversary process," *Ballew v. Georgia*, 435 U.S. 223 (1978) (POWELL, J., concurring in judgment). At trial, respondent presented three expert witnesses and one lay witness in his case in chief, and two additional lay witnesses in his rebuttal. Testimony by these witnesses permitted the District Court, and allows this Court, better to understand the methodologies used here and their limitations. Further testing of respondent's empirical case came at the hands of the State's own expert witnesses. Yet even after considering the evidence adduced by the State, the Court of Appeals properly noted: "there are no studies which contradict the studies submitted [by respondent]; in other words, all of the documented studies support the district court's findings.". . .

Faced with the near unanimity of authority supporting respondent's claim that death qualification gives the prosecution a particular advantage in the guilt phase of capital trials, the majority here makes but a weak effort to contest that proposition. Instead, it merely assumes for the purposes of this opinion "that 'death-qualification' in fact produces juries somewhat more 'conviction-prone' than 'non-death-qualified' juries," and then holds that this result does not offend the Constitution. This disregard for the clear import of the evidence tragically misconstrues the settled constitutional principles that guarantee a defendant the right to a fair trial and an impartial jury whose composition is not biased toward the prosecution. . . .

One need not rely on the analysis and assumptions of . . . *Witherspoon* to demonstrate that the exclusion of opponents of capital punishment capable of impartially determining culpability infringes a capital defendant's constitutional right to a fair and impartial jury. For the same conclusion is compelled by the analysis that in *Ballew v. Georgia,* 435 U.S. 223 (1978) led a majority of this Court to hold that a criminal conviction rendered by a five-person jury violates the Sixth and Fourteenth Amendments.

Faced with an effort by Georgia to reduce the size of the jury in a criminal case beyond the six-member jury approved by this Court in *Williams v. Florida,* 399 U.S. 78 (1970), this Court articulated several facets of the inquiry whether the reduction impermissibly "inhibit[ed] the functioning of the jury as an institution to a significant degree." First, the Court noted that "recent empirical data" had suggested that a five-member jury was "less likely to foster effective group deliberation" and that such a decline in effectiveness would likely lead "to inaccurate fact-finding and incorrect application of the common sense of the community to the facts." The Court advanced several explanations for this phenomenon:

> "As juries decrease in size, . . . they are less likely to have members who remember each of the important pieces of evidence or argument. Furthermore, the smaller the group, the less likely it is to overcome the biases of its members to obtain an accurate result. When individual and group decisionmaking were compared, it was seen that groups performed better be-

cause prejudices of individuals were frequently counterbalanced, and objectivity resulted.". . . .

The Court also cited empirical evidence suggesting "that the verdicts of jury deliberation in criminal cases will vary as juries become smaller, and that the variance amounts to an imbalance to the detriment of one side, the defense." Lastly, the Court observed that further reductions in jury size would also foretell problems "for the representation of minority groups in the community."

Each of the concerns that led this Court in *Ballew* to find that a misdemeanor defendant had been deprived of his constitutional right to a fair trial by jury is implicated by the process of death qualification, which threatens a defendant's interests to an even greater extent in cases where the stakes are substantially higher. When compared to the juries that sit in all other criminal trials, the death-qualified juries of capital cases are likely to be deficient in the quality of their deliberations, the accuracy of their results, the degree to which they are prone to favor the prosecution, and the extent to which they adequately represent minority groups in the community.

The data considered here, as well as plain common sense, leave little doubt that death qualification upsets the "counterbalancing of various biases" among jurors that *Ballew* identified as being so critical to the effective functioning of juries. . . .

Death qualification also implicates the *Ballew* Court's concern for adequate representation of minority groups. Because opposition to capital punishment is significantly more prevalent among blacks than among whites, the evidence suggests that death qualification will disproportionately affect the representation of blacks on capital juries. Though perhaps this effect may not be sufficient to constitute a violation of the Sixth Amendment's fair cross-section principle, see *Duren v. Missouri*, 439 U.S. 357 579 (1979), it is similar in magnitude to the reduction in minority representation that the *Ballew* Court found to be of "constitutional significance" to a defendant's right to a fair jury trial.

The principle of "impartiality" invoked in *Witherspoon* is thus not the only basis for assessing whether the exclusion of jurors unwilling to consider the death penalty but able impartially to determine guilt infringes a capital defendant's constitutional interest in a fair trial. By identifying the critical concerns that are subsumed in that interest, the *Ballew* Court pointed to an alternative approach to the issue, drawing on the very sort of empirical data that respondent has presented here. And viewed in light of the concerns articulated in *Ballew,* the evidence is sufficient to establish that death qualification constitutes a substantial threat to a defendant's Sixth and Fourteenth Amendment right to a fair jury trial—a threat constitutionally acceptable only if justified by a sufficient state interest. . . .

On occasion, this Court has declared what I believe should be obvious—that when a State seeks to convict a defendant of the most serious and severely punished offenses in its criminal code, any procedure that "diminish[es] the reliability of the guilt determination" must be struck down. *Beck v. Alabama,* [447 U.S. 625 (1980)]. But in spite of such declarations, I cannot help thinking that respondent here would have stood a far better chance of prevailing on his constitutional claims had he not been challenging a procedure peculiar to the administration of the death penalty. For in no other context would a majority of this Court refuse to find any constitutional violation in a state practice that systematically operates to render juries more likely to convict, and to convict on the more serious charges. I dissent.

Williams v. Florida

399 U.S. 78, 90 S.Ct. 1893 (1970)

Johnny Williams was tried by a six-member jury and convicted for robbery in Dade County, Florida. His attorneys appealed the conviction but a state appellate court affirmed. They made an appeal to the Supreme Court, which granted *certiorari.*

Justice WHITE delivers the opinion of the Court.

In *Duncan v. Louisiana,* 391 U.S. 79 (1968), we held that the Fourteenth Amendment guarantees a right to trial by jury in all criminal cases that—were they to be tried in a federal court—would come within the Sixth Amendment's guarantee. Petitioner's trial for robbery . . . clearly falls within the scope of that holding. The question in this case then is whether the constitutional guarantee of a trial by "jury" necessarily requires trial by exactly 12 persons, rather than some lesser number—in this case six. We hold that the 12-man panel is not a necessary ingredient of "trial by jury," and that respondent's refusal to impanel more than the six members provided for by Florida law did not violate petitioner's Sixth Amendment rights as applied to the States through the Fourteenth.

We had occasion in *Duncan v. Louisiana,* to review briefly the oft-told history of the development of trial by jury in criminal cases. That history revealed a long tradition attaching great importance to the concept of relying on a body of one's peers to determine guilt or innocence as a safeguard against arbitrary law enforcement. That same history, however, affords little insight into the considerations that gradually led the size of that body to be generally fixed at 12. . . . [W]hile sometime in the 14th century the size of the jury at common law came to be fixed generally at 12, that particular feature of the jury system appears to have been a historical accident, unrelated to the great purposes which gave rise to the jury in the first place. The question before us is whether this accidental feature of the jury has been immutably codified into our Constitution. . . .

While "the intent of the Framers" is often an elusive quarry, the relevant constitutional history casts considerable doubt on the easy assumption in our past decisions that if a given feature existed in a jury at common law in 1789, then it was necessarily preserved in the Constitution. Provisions for jury trial were first placed in the Constitution in Article III's provision that "[t]he Trial of all Crimes . . . shall be by Jury; and such Trial shall be held in the State where the said Crimes shall have been committed." The "very scanty history [of this provision] in the records of the Constitutional Convention" sheds little light either way on the intended correlation between Article III's "jury" and the features of the jury at common law. . . .

We do not pretend to be able to divine precisely what the word "jury" imported to the Framers, the First Congress, or the States in 1789. It may well be that the usual expectation was that the jury would consist of 12, and that hence, the most likely conclusion to be drawn is simply that little thought was actually given to the specific question we face today. But there is absolutely no indication in "the intent of the Framers" of an explicit decision to equate the constitutional and common-law characteristics of the jury. Nothing in this history suggests, then, that we do violence to the letter of the Constitution by turning to other than purely historical considerations to determine which features of the jury system, as it existed at common law, were preserved in the Constitution. The relevant inquiry, as we see it, must be the function that the particular feature performs and its relation to the purposes of the jury trial. Measured by this standard, the 12-man requirement cannot be regarded as an indispensable component of the Sixth Amendment.

The purpose of the jury trial, as we noted in *Duncan,* is to prevent oppression by the Government. . . . Given this purpose, the essential feature of a jury obviously lies in the interposition between the accused and his accuser of the commonsense judgment of a group of laymen, and in the community participation and shared responsibility that results from that group's determination of guilt or innocence. The performance of this role is not a function of the particular number of the body that makes up the jury. To be sure, the number should probably be large enough to promote group deliberation, free from outside attempts at intimidation, and to provide a fair possibility for obtaining a representative cross-section of the community. But we find little reason to think that these goals are in any meaningful sense less likely to be achieved when the jury numbers six, than when it numbers 12—particularly if the requirement of unanimity is retained. And, certainly the reliability of the jury as a factfinder hardly seems likely to be a function of its size. . . .

We conclude, in short, as we began: the fact that the jury at common law was composed of precisely 12 is a historical accident, unnecessary to effect the purposes of the jury system and wholly without significance "except to mystics." *Duncan v. Louisiana* (HARLAN, J., dissenting). To read the Sixth Amendment as forever codifying a feature so incidental to the real purpose of the Amendment is to ascribe a blind formalism to the Framers which would require considerably more evidence than we have been able to discover in the history and language of the Constitution or in the reasoning of our past decisions. . . . Legislatures may well have their own views about the relative value of the larger and smaller juries, and may conclude that, wholly apart from the jury's primary function, it is desirable to spread the collective responsibility for the determination of guilt among the larger group. In capital cases, for example, it appears that no State provides for less than 12 jurors—a fact that suggests implicit recognition of the value of the larger body as a means of legitimating society's decision to impose the death penalty. Our holding does no more than leave these considerations to Congress and the States, unrestrained by an interpretation of the Sixth Amendment that would forever dictate the precise number that can constitute a jury. Consistent with this holding, we conclude that petitioner's Sixth Amendment rights, as applied to the States through the Fourteenth Amendment, were not violated by Florida's decision to provide a six-man rather than a 12-man jury. . . .

Justice BLACKMUN did not participate in the consideration or decision of this case.

Chief Justice BURGER concurred.

Justice BLACK, with whom Justice DOUGLAS joins, concurring in part and dissenting in part.

The Court today holds that a State can, consistently with the Sixth Amendment to the United States Constitution, try a defendant in a criminal case with a jury of six members. I agree with that decison for substantially the same reasons given by the Court. My Brother HARLAN, however, charges that the Court's decision on this point is evidence that the "incorporation doctrine," through which the specific provisions of the Bill of Rights are made fully applicable to the States under the same standards applied in federal courts will somehow result in a "dilution" of the protections required by those provisions. He asserts that this Court's desire to relieve the States from the rigorous requirements of the Bill of Rights is bound to cause re-examination and modification of prior decisions interpreting those provisions as applied in federal courts in order simultaneously to apply the provisions equally to the State and Federal Governments and to avoid undue restrictions on the States. . . . [But, to]day's decision is in no way attributable to any desire to dilute the Sixth Amendment in order more easily to apply it to the States, but follows solely as a necessary consequence of our duty to reexamine prior decisions to reach the correct constitutional meaning in each case. The broad implications in early cases indicating that only a body of 12 members could satisfy the Sixth Amendment requirement arose in situations where the issue was not squarely presented and were based, in my opinion, on an improper interpretation of that amendment. Had the question presented here arisen in a federal court before our decision in *Duncan v. Louisiana*, this Court would still, in my view, have reached the result announced today. In my opinion the danger of diluting the Bill of Rights protections lies not in the "incorporation doctrine," but in the "shock the conscience" test on which my Brother HARLAN would rely instead—a test which depends, not on the language of the Constitution, but solely on the views of a majority of the Court as to what is "fair" and "decent."

Justice MARSHALL dissenting in part.

I adhere to the decision of the Court in *Thompson v. Utah*, 170 U.S. 343 (1898), that the jury guaranteed by the Sixth Amendment consists "of twelve persons, neither more nor less." As I see it, the Court has not made out a convincing case that the Sixth Amendment should be read differently than it was in *Thompson* even if the matter were now before us *de novo*—much less that an unbroken line of precedent going back over 70 years should be overruled.

Burch v. Louisiana
441 U.S. 130, 99 S.Ct. 1623 (1979)

Daniel Burch was tried for exhibiting two obscene motion pictures. The six-member jury found him guilty by a five-to-one vote. He was sentenced to two consecutive seven-month prison terms, which were suspended, and fined $1,000. Burch's attorney appealed the constitutionality of nonunanimous six-member jury verdicts. The Louisiana Supreme Court affirmed and Burch's attorney appealed to the Supreme Court.

Justice REHNQUIST delivers the opinion of the Court.

[W]e believe that conviction by a nonunanimous six-member jury in a state criminal trial for a nonpetty offense deprives an accused of his constitutional right to trial by jury.

Only in relatively recent years has this Court had to consider the practices of the several States relating to jury size and unanimity. . . .

The Court in *Duncan* [*v. Louisiana,* 391 U.S. 145 (1968)], held that because trial by jury in "serious" criminal cases is "fundamental to the American scheme of justice" and essential to due process of law, the Fourteenth Amendment guarantees a state criminal defendant the right to a jury trial in any case, which, if tried in a federal court, would require a jury under the Sixth Amendment. . . .

Two Terms later in *Williams v. Florida,* 399 U.S. 78 (1970), the Court held that this constitutional guarantee of trial by jury did not require a State to provide an accused with a jury of 12 members and that Florida did not violate the jury trial rights of criminal defendants charged with nonpetty offenses by affording them jury panels comprised of only six persons. . . .

[I]n *Apodaca v. Oregon* 106 U.S. 404 (1972), we upheld a state statute providing that only 10 members of a 12-person jury need concur to render a verdict in certain noncapital cases. In terms of the role of the jury as a safeguard against oppression, the plurality opinion perceived no difference between those juries required to act unanimously and those permitted to act by votes of 10 to two. . . . Nor was unanimity viewed by the plurality as contributing materially to the exercise of the jury's commonsense judgment or as a necessary precondition to effective application of the requirement that jury panels represent a fair cross-section of the community. . . .

[I]n *Ballew v. Georgia,* 135 U.S. 223 (1978), we held that conviction by a unanimous five-person jury in a trial for a nonpetty offense deprives an accused of his right to trial by jury. While readily admitting that the line between six members and five was not altogether easy to justify, at least five Members of the Court believed that reducing a jury to five persons in nonpetty cases raised sufficiently substantial doubts as to the fairness of the proceeding and proper functioning of the jury to warrant drawing the line at six. . . .

[T]his case lies at the intersection of our decisions concerning jury size and unanimity. As in *Ballew,* we do not pretend the ability to discern *a priori* a bright line below which the number of jurors participating in the trial or in the verdict would not permit the jury to function in the manner required by our prior cases. But having already departed from the strictly historical requirements of jury trial, it is inevitable that lines must be drawn somewhere if the substance of the jury trial right is to be preserved. . . . [M]uch the same reasons that led us in *Ballew* to decide that use of a five-member jury threatened the fairness of the proceeding and the proper role of the jury, lead us to conclude now that conviction for a nonpetty offense by only five members of a six-person jury presents a similar threat to preservation of the substance of the jury trial guarantee and justifies our requiring verdicts rendered by six-person juries to be unanimous. We are buttressed in this view by the current jury practices of the several States. It appears that of those States that utilize six-member juries in trials of nonpetty offenses, only two, including Louisiana, also allow nonunanimous verdicts. We think that this near uniform judgment of the Nation provides a useful guide in delimiting the line between those jury practices that are constitutionally permissible and those that are not. . . .

[O]n this record, any benefits that might accrue by allowing five members of a six-person jury to render a verdict, as compared with requiring unanimity of a six-member jury, are speculative, at best. More importantly, we think that when a State has reduced the size of its juries to the minimum number of jurors permitted by the Constitution, the additional authorization of nonunanimous verdicts by such juries sufficiently threatens the constitutional principles that led to the establishment of the size threshold that any countervailing interest of the State should yield.

Justice STEVENS concurred in a separate opinion.

Justice BRENNAN, with whom Justice STEWART and Justice MARSHALL joined, concurred in part and dissented in part in a separate opinion.

E. A SPEEDY AND PUBLIC TRIAL

A "speedy and public trial" is also a guarantee of the Sixth Amendment,[1] which was made applicable to the states in *Klopfer v. North Carolina*, 386 U.S. 213 (1967). But what is a *speedy* trial? In *Dickey v. Florida*, 398 U.S. 30 (1970), the Court found that a defendant was denied the right to a speedy trial where his trial took place eight years after an alleged offense, and he was available in the state for prosecution during that time. *Barker v.*

Wingo, 407 U.S. 514 (1972), however, held that a five-year delay between arrest and trial did not violate the Sixth Amendment. Congress responded with the federal Speedy Trial Act of 1974, requiring persons arrested to be charged within thirty days, arraigned ten days later, and a trial held within two months of arraignment. Charges may be dismissed, if a defendant moves for dismissal after the speedy-trial period has elapsed and no trial has commenced.[2]

NOTES

1. Also relevant are the cases and discussion of the public trial concept in Chapter 5.
2. See *Dillingham v. United States,* 423 U.S. 64 (1975); and *United States v. MacDonald,* 456 U.S. 1 (1982).

SELECTED BIBLIOGRAPHY

Eisenstein, James, and Jacob, Herbert. *Felony Justice.* Boston: Little, Brown, 1977.
Misner, R. *Speedy Trial: Federal and State Practices.* Charlottesville, VA: Michie, 1983.
Silberman, Charles. *Criminal Violence/Criminal Justice.* New York: Random House, 1978.

F. THE RIGHTS TO BE INFORMED OF CHARGES AND TO CONFRONT ACCUSERS

The accused has a right "to be informed of the nature and cause of the accusation against" him under the Sixth Amendment. This provision aims at ensuring defendants the opportunity to prepare adequate defenses. More often though defense attorneys challenge the constitutionality of criminal statutes for being "void for vagueness" under the due process clause. This principle—that a statute must specifically define and give notice of the kind of activity proscribed—was well-stated in *Connally v. General Construction Co.,* 269 U.S. 385 (1926):

That the terms of a penal statute . . . must be sufficiently explicit to inform those who are subject to it what conduct on their part will render them liable to its penalties, is a well-recognized requirement, consonant alike with ordinary notions of fair play and the settled rules of law. And a statute which either forbids or requires the doing of an act in terms so vague that men of common intelligence must necessarily guess at its meaning and differ as to its application, violates the first essential of due process of law.

The accused also has under the Sixth Amendment the right "to be confronted with the witnesses against him." This provision was made applicable to the states in *Pointer v. Texas*, 380 U.S. 400 (1965), where a transcript of a witness's testimony made at a preliminary hearing was introduced at trial because the witness had left the state. The accused also has the right to compel witnesses to appear in his favor in federal and state courts.[1] *Lee v. Illinois*, 476 U.S. 530 (1986), held five to four that the use of a codefendant's confession as evidence of a defendant's guilt violated the confrontation clause and was preumptively unreliable because the confession was given after being told that the defendant had implicated her in criminal activity. In *Olden v. Kentucky*, 488 U.S. 227 (1988), the Court held that a trial judge's refusal to permit a black defendant in a kidnapping, rape, and sodomy trial to cross-examine the white victim regarding her cohabitation with a black boyfriend violated the defendant's Sixth Amendment right to a confrontation of witnesses.

In two bitterly divided five-to-four decisions in 1990 involving the right of defendants to confront accusers cases involving alleged child abuse, Justice O'Connor held the balance.

Writing for a bare majority in *Maryland v. Craig*, 110 S.Ct. 3157 (1990), Justice O'Connor held that individuals charged with child abuse have no constitutional right to confront, at least once, their young accusers. In that case, O'Connor upheld the state's allowing four children to testify out of the presence of the defendant over a one-way, closed-circuit television. In her words, "A state's interest in the physical and psychological well-being of child-abuse victims may be sufficiently important to outweigh, at least in some cases, a defendant's right to face his or her accusers in court." But Justice Scalia countered in a dissenting opinion, joined by Justices Brennan, Marshall, and Stevens, that "[t]o say that a defendant loses his right to confront a witness when that would cause the witness not to testify is rather like saying that the defendant loses his right to counsel when counsel would save him."

In the second case, however, the four dissenters from *Craig* joined Justice O'Connor for another bare majority ruling in *Idaho v. Wright*, 110 S.Ct. 3139 (1990). In that case, Justice O'Connor rejected as hearsay evidence the testimony of a doctor, who had interviewed a two-and-a-half-year-old child about alleged sexual abuse. Although O'Connor refused to establish a bright line rule for when such testimony, in the absence of the victim's own testimony, could be introduced, she emphasized that such hearsay evidence must be so trustworthy as to render a cross-examination of the victim of marginal utility. Justice Kennedy dissented in an opinion that was joined by Chief Justice Rehnquist and Justices White and Blackmun.

NOTES

1. See *Washington v. Texas*, 388 U.S. 14 (1967). See also *Smith v. Illinois*, 390 U.S. 129 (1968); and *Barber v. Page*, 390 U.S. 719 (1968).

SELECTED BIBLIOGRAPHY

Goldstein, Abraham. *The Passive Judiciary: Prosecutorial Discretion and the Guilty Plea*. Baton Rouge: Louisiana State University Press, 1981.

Loftus, E. F. *Eyewitness Testimony*. Cambridge, MA: Harvard University Press, 1975.

Nagel, Stuart. *The Rights of the Accused*. Beverly Hills, CA: Sage Publications, 1972.

Walker, Samuel. *Sense and Nonsense about Crime*. Pacific Grove, CA: Brooks/Cole, 2d. ed. 1989.

G. THE GUARANTEE AGAINST DOUBLE JEOPARDY

The Fifth Amendment provides that defendants may not be twice held "in jeopardy of life or limb" for the same offense. The purpose of this guarantee, Justice Hugo Black explained in *Green v. United States*, 355 U.S. 184 (1957), is that "the State with all its resources and power should not be allowed to make repeated attempts to convict an individual for an alleged offense, thereby subjecting him to embarrassment, expense and ordeal and compelling him to live in a continuing state of anxiety and insecurity, as well as enhancing the possibility that even though innocent he may be found guilty."

The double jeopardy clause, however, was not deemed to be "fundamental" to the "concept of ordered liberty" so as to apply to the states in *Palko v. Connecticut* (1937) (see Chapter 4). Twenty years later a bare majority still clung to that view, but Chief Justice Earl Warren and Justices Brennan, Black, and Douglas dissented in *Bartkers v. Illinois*, 359 U.S. 721 (1959), as they often did until the Court's composition changed with the retirement of Justice Frankfurter in 1962. Then a solid majority of the Warren Court made the states bound by the double jeopardy clause in *Benton v. Maryland,* 395 U.S. 784 (1969). *Crist v. Bretz,* 437 U.S. 28 (1978) further held that states must observe the federal rule that the jeopardy clause is triggered once a jury is empaneled, and thus the defendant may not be retried for the same offense.

Like some other guarantees, the double jeopardy clause is not self-explanatory; much depends on how *jeopardy* is interpreted in the context of a legal proceeding and how the *same offense* is viewed. Defendants who have been acquitted or convicted and then retried by the same court, of course, have been placed in double jeopardy. *Waller v. Florida,* 397 U.S. 387 (1970), also held that defendants may not be retried for a different crime based on the same evidence. If a jury fails to reach a verdict and is dismissed, a second trial is permissible as a continuation of the first trial.[1] But the government may not appeal an acquital, even if egregious errors lead to the acquital.[2] The government may, though, retry a defendant who wins a motion for mistrial,[3] except when a mistrial is declared by a judge on his own, due to improper procedures.[4] An accused may waive the right against being held in double jeopardy when requesting a new trial or appealing a guilty verdict, but if the conviction is set aside on appeal a retrial for the same offense is permissible.[5]

Whether defendants are tried for the same offense depends on whether the trial takes place in the same jurisdiction and based on the same evidence. If two charges grow out of the same evidence, retrial on separate charges other than that litigated at the first trial is permissible.[6] *United States v. Halper,* 109 S.Ct. 1892 (1989), unanimously held that civil fines may not be place on top of criminal penalties for the same offense. In addition, in *Ashe v. Swenson,* 397 U.S. 505 (1978), the Court interpreted the double jeopardy clause to include the doctrine of "collateral estoppel"—that is, "when an issue of ultimate fact has once been determined by a valid and final judgment, that issue cannot again be litigated between the same parties in any future lawsuit."

The test for whether the double jeopardy clause is violated remains whether the same evidence is introduced in both trials.[7] Under *Blockburger v. United States,* 284 U.S. 299 (1932), successive prosecutions of criminal conduct under different statutes is forbidden, if they include identical statutory elements or lesser included offenses. In *Grady v. Corbin,* 110 S.Ct. 2084 (1990), a bare majority of the Court held that the double jeopardy clause bars a subsequent prosecution under a different statute when the government must show that the defendant's conduct constituted an offense for which the defendant had already been prosecuted for under another statute. Thomas Corbin, while driving intoxicated, ran his car into two others, killing one of the passengers. In a trial court, he pleaded guilty to traffic tickets charging him with driving while intoxicated and failing to keep on the right side of the road. Subsequently, a grand jury indicted him for reckless manslaughter. Writing for the majority, Justice Brennan held that the subsequent prosecution was barred because the state admitted that it would seek to establish Corbin's guilt by proving that he was driving in an intoxicated state and failed to stay on the right side of the road, two crimes for which he had previously pleaded guilty. However, Justice Brennan noted that Corbin could be prosecuted if the state relied on other evidence, such as he was driving too fast, to establish reckless manslaughter. Chief Justice Rehnquist and Justices O'Connor, Kennedy, and Scalia dissented. Moreover, in *Dowling v. United States*, 110 S.Ct. 668 (1990), the Rehnquist Court held that prosecutors may introduce at trial evidence relating to crimes for which the defendant in a prior trial had been acquitted. Only dissenting Justices Brennan, Marshall, and Stevens thought that the use of evidence from the first trial in a defendant's second trial violated the double jeopardy clause, because it effectively forced the defendant to counter charges for which he had already been acquitted.

The double jeopardy clause does not bar defendants from receiving a more severe sentence on retrial.[8] Nor does it forbid both federal and state governments from prosecuting the same offense.[9] *Poland v. Arizona*, 476 U.S. 147 (1986), construed the double jeopardy clause not to bar defendants from being retried and given capital punishment after they appealed their first conviction for first-degree murder and where an appellate court had reversed and ordered their retrial because of evidentiary problems even though it found that sufficient evidence had been presented for imposing a death sentence. But the Rehnquist Court split five to four in *Quinn v. Millsap*, 109 S.Ct. 2324 (1989). There, a defendant was sentenced to prison for two crimes— fifteen years for attempted robbery and life imprisonment for felony murder—stemming from the same offense. By the time a state court held invalid the multiple sentences for the same offense, the robbery sentence had been commuted and the time served credited to the life sentence. But a federal court of appeals threw out the life sentence on appeal. Writing for a bare majority, Justice Kennedy reversed, observing that "[n]either the Double Jeopardy Clause nor any other constitutional provision exists to provide unjustified windfalls." Siding with Justices Brennan,

Marshall, and Stevens, in dissent, Justice Scalia countered that "[a] technical rule with equitable exceptions is no rule at all. Three strikes is out. The state broke the rules here, and must abide by the result."

NOTES

1. *United States v. Perez,* 9 Wheat. 579 (1824).

2. *Sanabria v. United States,* 437 U.S. 54 (1978); and *Oregon v. Washington,* 434 U.S. 497 (1978).

3. See *United States v. Dinitz,* 424 U.S. 600 (1971); and *Oregon v. Kennedy,* 456 U.S. 667 (1987).

4. Compare *United States v. Jorn,* 400 U.S. 470 (1971) with *Illinois v. Somerville,* 410 U.S. 458 (1973).

5. See *United States v. Ball,* 163 U.S. 662 (1896) and compare *Burks v. United States,* 437 U.S. 1 (1978); *Hudson v. Louisiana,* 450 U.S. 40 (1981); and *Tibbs v. Florida,* 457 U.S. 31 (1982).

6. See *Morgan v. Devine,* 237 U.S. 632 (1915); and *United States v. Ewell,* 383 U.S. 116 (1966).

7. See *Hoag v. New York,* 356 U.S. 464 (1958); *Ashe v. Swenson,* 397 U.S. 436 (1978); and *United States v. Halper,* 109 S.Ct. 1892 (1989). *Lockhart v. Nelson,* 109 S.Ct. 285 (1988) held that the double jeopardy clause does not bar retrial after an appellate court has determined that evidence at the first trial was erroneously admitted.

8. See *United States v. DiFrancesco,* 449 U.S. 117 (1980); and *Chaffin v. Stynchcombem,* 412 U.S. 17 (1973). But compare *North Carolina v. Pierce,* 395 U.S. 711 (1964); and *Bullington v. Missouri,* 451 U.S. 430 (1981).

9. See *United States v. Lanza,* 260 U.S. 377 (1922); *Abbate v. United States,* 359 U.S. 187 (1959); *Bartkus v. Illinois,* 359 U.S. 121 (1959). The Court, however, has overturned the prosecution by local and state governments in the same jurisdiction of a defendant based on the same evidence. See *Waller v. Florida,* 397 U.S. 387 (1970); and *Missouri v. Hunter,* 459 U.S. 359 (1983).

SELECTED BIBLIOGRAPHY

Friedland, M. *Double Jeopardy.* New York: Oxford University Press, 1969.

Miller, L. *Double Jeopardy and the Federal System.* Chicago: University of Chicago Press, 1969.

Sigler, Jay. *Double Jeopardy: The Development of a Legal and Social Policy.* Ithica, NY: Cornell University Press, 1969.

H. THE GUARANTEE AGAINST EXCESSIVE BAIL AND FINES

The Eighth Amendment's provisions that "excessive bail shall not be required, nor excessive fines imposed" gave constitutional effect to rights dating back to the English Bill of Rights in 1689. Bail is a pledge of money or property by an accused that ostensibly guarantees his appearance at trial; it enables the accused to remain free while awaiting trial. The provision both limits Congress and federal courts in setting bail. Under the Bail Reform Act of 1966, those accused of noncapital federal offenses may be released on their own recognizance or on an unsecured bond, unless a judge deems that release would "not reasonably assure" their appearance in court.

Because of the concern over the number of crimes committed by repeat offenders while on bail and the battle against importers of drugs and narcotics, Congress passed the Bail Reform Act of 1984. It authorizes the pretrial detention of defendants who are deemed to pose a threat to the community. By a vote of six to three in *United States v. Salerno*, 481 U.S. 739 (1987), the Court upheld pretrial detention as "regulatory, not penal." Chief Justice Rehnquist's opinion for the Court explained,

The Bail Reform Act . . . narrowly focuses on a particular acute problem in which the government's interests are overwhelming. The Act operates only on individuals who have been arrested for a specific category of extremely serious offenses. Congress specifically found that these individuals are far more likely to be responsible for dangerous acts in the community after arrest. . . . While the government's general interest in preventing is compelling, even this interest is heightened when the government musters convincing proof that the arrestee, already indicted or held to answer for a serious crime, presents a demonstrable danger to the community. Under these narrow circumstances, society's interest in crime prevention is at its greatest.

On the other side of the scale, of course, is the individual's strong interest in liberty. We do not minimize the importance and fundamental nature of this right. But, as our cases hold, this right may, in circumstances where the government's interest is sufficiently weighty, be subordinated to the greater needs of society.

Two years later, in *Caplin & Drysdale v. United States* and *United States v. Monsanto*, 109 S.Ct. 2646 (1989), the Rehnquist Court held five to four that the Department of Justice may seize the money and property illegally acquired by criminal defendants who are facing trial even if they claim that those assests would be used to pay the costs of their defense at trial. In Justice White's words for the majority: "A defendant has no Sixth Amendment right to spend another person's money for services

Clarence Gideon in 1964. This photograph was taken two years after the landmark ruling by the Supreme Court, holding that all defendants accused of serious crimes have a right to representation by counsel. *Flip Schulke/© 1964 Time Warner Inc.*

rendered by an attorney, even if those funds are the only way that the defendant will be able to retain the attorney of his choice." In *Browning-Ferris v. Kelco,* 109 S.Ct. 2909 (1989), arising from a nuclear power company's challenge of the constitutionality of a huge punitive damage award, the Court ruled that the Eighth Amendment does not apply to civil suits in which the government has no participation.

I. INDIGENTS AND THE CRIMINAL JUSTICE SYSTEM

Beginning in the 1950s, the Warren Court held in a number of cases that the Fourteenth Amendment due process and equal protection clauses require states to provide indigents with certain resources for their defense at trial and on appeal. *Griffin v. Illinois,* 351 U.S. 12 (1956), is the leading case in which the Court struck down a statute granting free trial transcripts to indigents only for review of constitutional questions and where the defendant was given a death sentence. There, the Court held that the right of indigents to meaningful appellate review was denied unless they were furnished trial transcripts in any appeals. *Gideon v. Wainwright* (1963) (see page 1008), of course, extended the right to counsel to indigents at trial. However, after President Nixon's last two appointees—Justices Powell and Rehnquist—the Court became less sympathetic to claims of indigents. The Burger and Rehnquist Court have upheld constraints on indigents' access to the judicial system in several, although not all, rulings. Some of the major rulings on the rights of indigents are summarized in the following table.

THE DEVELOPMENT OF LAW

Other Rulings on Indigents and the Judicial System

Case	Vote	Ruling
Burns v. Ohio, 360 U.S. 252 (1959)	7:2	Indigents have the right to file an appeal.
Lane v. Brown, 372 U.S. 477 (1963)	9:0	Right to have trial transcript on appeal.
Hardy v. United States, 375 U.S. 277 (1964)	8:1	Court-appointed attorney is entitled to trial transcript.
Long v. District Court of Iowa, 385 U.S. 143 (1966)	9:0	Transcripts must be provided for *habeas corpus* proceedings on appeal.
Roberts v. LaVallee, 389 U.S. 40 (1967)	8:1	Indigents have a right to transcripts even after exhaustion of state appeals.
Gardner v. California, 393 U.S. 367 (1969)	6:3	Right to free trial transcript for preparation of *habeas corpus* petition.
Williams v. Oklahoma City, 395 U.S. 458 (1969)	9:0	States that permit appeals for any conviction may not deny right of appeal to indigents.

Case	Vote	Ruling
Williams v. Illinois, 399 U.S. 235 (1970)	9:0	Fourteenth Amendment forbids states from converting fines into prison sentences.
Mayer v. City of Chicago, 404 U.S. 189 (1971)	9:0	Struck down Illinois's law providing trial transcripts only in felony cases as constituting an "unreasonable distinction"; required transcripts in felony and nonfelony cases.
Tate v. Short, 401 U.S. 395 (1971)	9:0	An indigent convicted of traffic offenses may not be committed to a municipal prison farm because of inability to pay fine.
Boddie v. Connecticut, 401 U.S. 371 (1971)	8:1	Struck down filing fee required to have access to divorce court.
Schilb v. Kuebel, 404 U.S. 357 (1971)	6:3	States may require an accused to pay 10 percent of a bail bond or $25, whichever is greater, to secure a pretrial release from jail.
United States v. Kras, 409 U.S. 434 (1973)	5:4	Upheld a $50 filing fee for access to bankruptcy court.
Ortwein v. Schwab, 410 U.S. 656 (1973)	5:4	Upheld Oregon's $25 filing fee for those seeking an appeal of an adverse welfare benefits decision.
Fuller v. Oregon, 417 U.S. 40 (1974)	7:2	Upheld a probationary system requiring reimbursement of the state for fees and the expenses of attorneys.
Ross v. Moffitt, 417 U.S. 600 (1974)	6:3	Held that after the first appeal as of right, indigents have no right to a court-appointed attorney on further appeals to a state's highest court or to the United States Supreme Court.
Bounds v. Smith, 430 U.S. 817 (1977)	6:3	Prisons must provide adequate law libraries for prisoners who want to make a "meaningful appeal."
Ake v. Oklahoma, 470 U.S. 68 (1985)	8:1	If sanity is an issue at a defendant's trial, the state must provide a psychiatrist.
Pennsylvania v. Finley, 107 S.Ct. 1990 (1987)	5:4	There is no constitutional right to a court-appointed attorney in postconviction proceedings.
Murray v. Giarratano, 481 U.S. 551 (1989)	5:4	States are not required to furnish lawyers for indigents on death row who have lost initial rounds of appeals.

SELECTED BIBLIOGRAPHY

Casper, Jonathan. *American Criminal Justice: The Defendant's Perspective.* Englewood Cliffs, NJ: Prentice-Hall, 1972.

Lawrence, Susan. *The Poor in Court.* Princeton, NJ: Princeton University Press, 1990.

Lefstein, Norman. *Criminal Defense Services for the Poor.* Chicago: American Bar Association, 1982.

Legal Services Corporation. *Characteristics of Field Programs Supported by the Legal Services Corporation, Start of 1983—A Fact Book.* Washington, DC: Legal Services Corporation, 1983.

Weisbrod, Burton, Handler, Joel, and Komesar, Neil. *Public Interest Law.* Berkeley: University of California Press, 1978.

10

CRUEL AND UNUSUAL PUNISHMENT

THE EIGHTH AMENDMENT's ban on "cruel and unusual punishments" is another guarantee of the Bill of Rights rooted in the history of English common law. In 1583, the Archbishop of Canterbury turned the High Commission into an Ecclesiastical Court for punishing heretics and critics of the Crown. Torture was used to extract confessions and death was imposed for a large number of crimes. Opposition gradually mounted and led to the English Bill of Rights of 1689. Among those rights, the ban on "cruel and unusual punishments" registered not only opposition to the practices of the High Commission but also the imposition of punishments unauthorized by statute and disproportionate to the offense. The phrasing of English guarantee against "cruel and unusual punishments" reappeared in the United States in Virginia's Declaration of Rights in 1776. It was later incorporated verbatim in the Eighth Amendment.

Prior to the 1960s, the Supreme Court had little occasion to interpret the guarantee against "cruel and unusual punishments." But in the 1960s there was an organized legal attack on the constitutionality of capital punishment orchestrated by the American Civil Liberties Union and the National Association for the Advancement of Colored People (NAACP) Legal Defense Fund, among other organizations. In response to these pressures and litigation in the 1970s the Court began erecting barriers to the imposition of the death sentence. But that in turn made capital punishment a major political issue and invited the mobilization of forces pushing for a renewal of executions. With changes in the composition of the high bench in the 1970s and 1980s, the Court again responded and shifted direction.

Certain themes in the Court's initial interpretation of the guarantee against cruel and unusual punishments, however, laid the basis for its eventual application of the amendment in the area of capital punishment.[1] First, the Court indicated that the amendment does not ban unusual punishments but rather those that are barbaric in their cruelty. The Court's initial encounters with Eighth Amendment claims involved whether novel methods of execution ran afoul of the amendment. *Wilkerson v. Utah,* 99 U.S. 130 (1878), unanimously upheld public execution by musketry, and *In re Kemmler,* 136 U.S. 436 (1890), upheld electrocution, which though unusual at the time was more "humane" than hanging and other forms of execution. As Justice Stephen Field, in *O'Neil v. Vermont,* 144 U.S. 323 (1892), summarized:

That designation [cruel and unusual punishments], it is true, is usually applied to punishments which inflict torture, such as the rack, the thumbscrew, the iron boot, the stretching of limbs and the like, which are attended with acute pain and suffering. . . . The inhibition is directed, not only against punishments of the character mentioned, but against all punishments which by their excessive length or severity are greatly disproportionate to the offenses charged. The whole inhibition is against that which is excessive.

Second, the Court indicated that the intentions of those who carry out executions may not be controlling in applying the amendment. In the case of Willy Francis, a mechanical failure of the electric chair frustrated the state's first attempt to put him to death. And Francis appealed to the Court, contending that a second trip to the electric chair constituted cruel and unusual punishment. The justices by a vote of five to four rejected his claim, finding the unsuccessful execution an "unforseeable accident" but not intentional cruelty. *Louisiana ex rel. Francis v. Resweber,* 329 U.S. 459 (1947).

Finally, the Court indicated that punishments that are grossly disproportionate to the offense might violate the Eighth Amendment. The first ruling overturning a punishment under the amendment involved a Coast Guard officer, stationed in the Philippine Islands, who was convicted of falsifying public documents and sentenced to twelve years of incarceration, chained, and put under perpetual surveillance, as well as stripped of all civil liberties.[2] *Trop v. Dulles,* 356 U.S. 86 (1958) held that the loss of citizenship as a result of a courts-martial for wartime desertion constituted cruel and unusual punishment. In controversial although often-cited *dicta,* Chief Justice Warren added that "[t]he amendment must draw its meaning from evolving standards of decency that mark the progress of a maturing society."

NOTES

1. This discussion draws on Daniel Polsby, "The Death of Capital Punishment? *Furman v. Georgia,*" in *The Supreme Court: 1972* ed. Philip Kurland (Chicago: University of Chicago Press, 1973), 1.
2. *Weems v. United States,* 217 U.S. 349 (1910).

SELECTIVE BIBLIOGRAPHY

Bedau, Hugo, ed., *The Death Penalty in America,* 3rd ed. New York: Oxford University Press, 1982.

Berger, Raoul. *Death Penalties: The Supreme Court's Obstacle Course.* Cambridge: Harvard University Press, 1982.

Berns, Walter. *For Capital Punishment.* New York: Basic Books, 1979.

Black, Jr., Charles. *Capital Punishment: The Inevitability of Caprice and Mistake.* New York: Norton, 1974.

Bowers, William J. et al., *Legal Homicide: Death as Punishment in America, 1864–1982.* Boston: Northeastern University Press, 1984.

Prettyman, Barrett, Jr. *Death and the Supreme Court.* New York: Harcourt, Brace & World, 1961.

White, Welsh. *The Death Penalty in the Eighties.* Ann Arbor: University of Michigan Press, 1988.

A. NONCAPITAL PUNISHMENT

Robinson v. California (1962) (see page 1065) struck down a statute making narcotics addiction per se a criminal offense, with at least a mandatory ninety-day jail sentence. Besides finding the punishment disproportionate, the Warren Court indicated that the amendment might have broader application outside of the area of capital punishment. However, a bare majority of the Court refused to extend *Robinson* when upholding a conviction for public drunkenness of an ex-alcoholic and finding that alcoholism not to be a "disease," in *Powell v. Texas,* 392 U.S. 514 (1968). The Burger and Rehnquist Courts subsequently held that the conditions of prison isolation cells and prison officials' indifference to the illness of inmates may violate the Eighth Amendment,[1] but also refused to apply the amendment to corporal punishment in public schools,[2] and to the shooting without warning of a prisoner during the quelling of a prison riot.[3] In addition, the Court has been reluctant to strike down noncapital punishments as disproportionate to the crime. *Hutto v. Davis,* 454 U.S. 370 (1982), for instance, upheld a sentence of forty years' imprisonment for the possession and distribution of nine ounces of marijuana. By a vote of five to four in *Rummel v. Estelle* (1980) (see page 1068), Texas's habitual criminal offenders act was upheld as applied to a man convicted of three thefts totaling $289. The following year, however, Justice Blackmun, who cast the crucial fifth vote in *Rummel,* joined *Rummel's* four dissenters in *Solem v. Helm,* 463 U.S. 277 (1983), striking down as cruel and unusual punishment a life sentence imposed on a defendant convicted for writing a $100 bad check and who had six prior nonviolent offenses. See also *Bowers v. Hardwick* (see Chapter 11) in which Justice Powell indicates in his concurring opinion that prison sentences for violating sodomy laws might "create a serious Eighth Amendment issue."

NOTES

1. *Hutto v. Finney,* 437 U.S. 679 (1978); and *Estelle v. Gamble,* 429 U.S. 97 (1976).
2. *Ingraham v. Wright,* 430 U.S. 651 (1977).
3. *Whitley v. Albers,* 475 U.S. 312 (1986).

Robinson v. California
370 U.S. 660, 82 S.Ct. 1417 (1962)

Lawrence Robinson, a drug addict, was convicted under a state law making it a criminal offense to be addicted to narcotics and requiring on conviction at least ninety days' imprisonment in the county jail. On appeal, a state appellate court affirmed his conviction, and Robinson's attorney appealed to the Supreme Court, arguing that the punishment imposed violated the Eighth Amendment.

Justice STEWART delivers the opinion of the Court.

A California statute makes it a criminal offense for a person to "be addicted to the use of narcotics." This appeal draws into question the constitutionality of that provision of the state law, as construed by the California courts in the present case. . . .

This statute . . . is not one which punishes a person for the use of narcotics, for their purchase, sale or possession, or for antisocial or disorderly behavior resulting from their administration. It is not a law which even purports to provide or require medical treatment. Rather, we deal with a statute which makes the "status" of narcotic addiction a criminal offense, for which the offender may be prosecuted "at any time before he reforms." California has said that a person can be continuously guilty of this offense, whether or not he has ever used or possessed any narcotics within the State, and whether or not he has been guilty of any antisocial behavior there.

It is unlikely that any State at this moment in history would attempt to make it a criminal offense for a person to be mentally ill, or a leper, or to be afflicted with a venereal disease. A State might determine that the general health and welfare require that the victims of these and other human afflictions be dealt with by compulsory treatment, involving quarantine, confinement, or sequestration. But, in the light of contemporary human knowledge, a law which made a criminal offense of such a disease would doubtless be universally thought to be an infliction of cruel and unusual punishment in violation of the Eighth and Fourteenth Amendments.

We cannot but consider the statute before us as of the same category. In this Court counsel for the State recognized that narcotic addiction is an illness. Indeed, it is apparently an illness which may be contracted innocently or involuntarily. We hold that a state law which imprisons a person thus afflicted as a criminal, even though he has never touched any narcotic drug within the State or been guilty of any irregular behavior there, inflicts a cruel and unusual punishment in violation of the Fourteenth Amendment. To be sure, imprisonment for ninety days is not, in the abstract, a punishment which is either cruel or unusual. But the question cannot be considered in the abstract. Even one day in prison would be a cruel and unusual punishment for the "crime" of having a common cold.

We are not unmindful that the vicious evils of the narcotics traffic have occasioned the grave concern of government. There are, as we have said, countless fronts on which those evils may be legitimately attacked. We deal in this case only with an individual provision of a particularized local law as it has so far been interpreted by the California courts.

Reversed.

Justice FRANKFURTER did not participate in the consideration or decision of this case.

Justice DOUGLAS concurring.

While I join the Court's opinion, I wish to make more explicit the reasons why I think it is "cruel and unusual" punishment in the sense of the Eighth Amendment to treat as a criminal a person who is a drug addict. . . .

The question presented in the earlier cases concerned the degree of severity with which a particular offense was punished or the element of cruelty present. A punishment out of all proportion to the offense may bring it within the ban against "cruel and unusual punishment." So may the cruelty of the method of punishment, as, for example, disemboweling a person alive. See *Wilkerson v. Utah,* 99 U.S. 130 [1878]. But the principle that would deny power to exact capital punishment for a petty crime would also deny power to punish a person by fine or imprisonment for being sick.

The Eighth Amendment expresses the revulsion of civilized man against barbarous acts—the "cry of horror" against man's inhumanity to his fellow man. . . .

By the time of Coke, enlightenment was coming as respects the insane. Coke said that the execution of a madman "should be a miserable spectacle, both against law, and of extreme inhumanity and cruelty, and can be no example to others." 6 Coke's Third Inst. (4th ed. 1797), p. 6. Blackstone endorsed this view of Coke. . . .

We should show the same discernment respecting drug addiction. The addict is a sick person. He may, of course, be confined for treatment or for the protection of society. Cruel and unusual punishment results not from confinement, but from convicting the addict of a crime. The purpose of § 11721 is not to cure, but to penalize. Were the purpose to cure, there would be no need for a mandatory jail term of not less than 90 days. Contrary to my Brother CLARK, I think the means must stand constitutional scrutiny, as well as the end to be achieved. A prosecution for addiction, with its resulting stigma and irreparable damage to the good name of the accused, cannot be justified as a means of protecting society, where a civil commitment would do as well.

Justice HARLAN concurred.

Justice CLARK dissented.

Justice WHITE dissenting.

I deem this application of "cruel and unusual punishment" so novel that I suspect the Court was hard put to find a way to ascribe to the Framers of the Constitution the result reached today rather than to its own notions of ordered liberty. If this case involved economic regulation, the present Court's allergy to substantive due process would surely save the statute and prevent the Court from imposing its own philosophical predilections upon state legislatures or Congress. I fail to see why the Court deems it more appropriate to write into the Constitution its own abstract notions of how best to handle the narcotics problem, for it obviously cannot match either the States or Congress in expert understanding.

I respectfully dissent.

Rummel v. Estelle

445 U.S. 263, 100 S.Ct. 1133 (1980).

In his opinion announcing the decision of the Court, Justice William Rehnquist discusses the facts in this case challenging William Rummel's conviction and lifetime sentence under Texas's criminal recidivism law.

Justice REHNQUIST delivers the opinion of the Court.

Petitioner William James Rummel is presently serving a life sentence imposed by the State of Texas in 1973 under its "recidivist statute," formerly Art. 63 of its Penal Code, which provided that "Whoever shall have been three times convicted of a felony less than capital shall on such third conviction be imprisoned for life in the penitentiary."

[Rummel maintains] . . . that life imprisonment was "grossly disproportionate" to the three felonies that formed the predicate for his sentence and that therefore the sentence violated the ban on cruel and unusual punishments of the Eighth and Fourteenth Amendments. The District Court and the United States Court of Appeals for the Fifth Circuit rejected Rummel's claim, finding no unconstitutional disproportionality. We granted certiorari and now affirm.

In 1964 the State of Texas charged Rummel with fraudulent use of a credit card to obtain $80 worth of goods or services. Because the amount in question was greater than $50, the charged offense was a felony punishable by a minimum of two years and a maximum of 10 years in the Texas Department of Corrections. . . .

In 1969 the State of Texas charged Rummel with passing a forged check in the amount of $28.36, a crime punishable by imprisonment in a penitentiary for not less than two nor more than five years. . . .

In 1973 Rummel was charged with obtaining $120.75 by false pretenses. Because the amount obtained was greater than $50, the charged offense was designated "felony theft," which, by itself, was punishable by confinement in a penitentiary for not less than two nor more than 10 years. The prosecution chose, however, to proceed against Rummel under Texas' recidivist statute, and cited in the indictment his 1964 and 1969 convictions as requiring imposition of a life sentence if Rummel were convicted of the charged offense. A jury convicted Rummel of felony theft and also found as true the allegation that he had been convicted of two prior felonies. As a result . . . the trial court imposed upon Rummel the life sentence. . . .

This Court has on occasion stated that the Eighth Amendment prohibits imposition of a sentence that is grossly disproportionate to the severity of the crime. . . . In recent years this proposition has appeared most frequently in opinions dealing with the death penalty. See, *e.g., Coker v. Georgia,* 433 U.S. 584, (1977) (plurality opinion); *Gregg v. Georgia,* 428 U.S. 153 (1976) (plurality opinion); *Furman v. Georgia,* 408 U.S. 238 (1972) (POWELL, J., dissenting). Rummel cites these latter opinions dealing with capital punishment as compelling the conclusion that his sentence is disproportionate to his offenses. But as Justice STEWART noted in *Furman:*

> "The penalty of death differs from all other forms of criminal punishment, not in degree but in kind. It is unique in its total irrevocability. It is unique in its rejection of rehabilitation of the convict as a basic purpose of criminal justice. And it is unique, finally, in its absolute renunciation of all that is embodied in our concept of humanity.". . .

This theme, the unique nature of the death penalty for purposes of Eighth-Amendment analysis, has been repeated time and time again in our opinions. . . . Because a sentence of death differs in kind from any sentence of imprisonment, no matter how long, our decisions applying the prohibition of cruel and unusual punishments to capital cases are of limited assistance in deciding the constitutionality of the punishment meted out to Rummel. . . .

In an attempt to provide us with objective criteria against which we might measure the proportionality of his life sentence, Rummel points to certain characteristics of his offenses that allegedly render them "petty." He cites, for example, the absence of violence in his crimes. But the presence or absence of violence does not always affect the strength of society's interest in deterring a particular crime or in punishing a particular criminal. A high official in a large corporation can commit undeniably serious crimes in the area of antitrust, bribery, or clear air or water standards without coming close to engaging in any "violent" or short-term "life-threatening" behavior. Additionally, Rummel cites the "small" amount of money taken in each of his crimes. But to recognize that the State of Texas could have imprisoned Rummel for life if he had stolen $5,000, $50,000, or $500,000, rather than the $120.75 that a jury convicted him of stealing, is virtually to concede that the lines to be drawn are indeed "subjective," and therefore properly within the province of legislatures, not courts. Moreover, if Rummel had attempted to defraud his victim of $50,000, but had failed, no money whatsoever would have changed hands; yet Rummel would be no less blameworthy, only less skillful, than if he had succeeded.

In this case, however, we need not decide whether Texas could impose a life sentence upon Rummel merely for obtaining $120.75 by false pretenses. Had Rummel only committed that crime, under the law enacted by the Texas Legislature he could have been imprisoned for no more than 10 years. In fact, at the time that he obtained the $120.75 by false pretenses, he already had committed and had been imprisoned for two other felonies, crimes that Texas and other States felt were serious enough to warrant significant terms of imprisonment even in the absence of prior offenses. Thus the interest of the State of Texas here is not simply that of making criminal the unlawful acquisition of another person's property; it is in addition the interest, expressed in all recidivist statutes, in dealing in a harsher manner with those who by repeated criminal acts have shown that they are simply incapable of conforming to the norms of society as established by its criminal law. . . .

The purpose of a recidivist statute such as that involved here is not to simplify the task of prosecutors, judges, or juries. Its primary goals are to deter repeat offenders and, at some point in the life of one who repeatedly commits criminal offenses serious enough to be punished as felonies, to segregate that person from the rest of society for an extended period of time. This segregation and its duration are based not merely on that person's most recent offense but also on the propensities he has demonstrated over a period of time during which he has been convicted of and sentenced for other crimes. Like the line dividing felony theft from petty larceny, the point at which a recidivist will be deemed to have demonstrated the necessary propensities and the amount of time that the recidivist will be isolated from society are matters largely within the discretion of the punishing jurisdiction.

We therefore hold that the mandatory life sentence imposed upon this petitioner does not constitute cruel and unusual punishment under the Eighth and Fourteenth Amendments. The judgment of the Court of Appeals will be

Affirmed.

Justice STEWART concurred.

Justice POWELL, with whom Justice BRENNAN, Justice MAR-
SHALL, and Justice STEVENS join, dissenting.

I dissent because I believe that (i) the penalty for a noncapital
offense may be unconstitutionally disproportionate, (ii) the possibility of parole should not be considered in assessing the nature
of the punishment, (iii) a mandatory life sentence is grossly disproportionate as applied to petitioner, and (iv) the conclusion that
this petitioner has suffered a violation of his Eighth Amendment
rights is compatible with principles of judicial restraint and federalism. . . .

The scope of the Cruel and Unusual Punishments Clause extends not only to barbarous methods of punishment, but also to
punishments that are grossly disproportionate. Disproportionality
analysis measures the relationship between the nature and number
of offenses committed and the severity of the punishment inflicted
upon the offender. The inquiry focuses on whether, a person
deserves such punishment, not simply on whether punishment
would serve a utilitarian goal. A statute that levied a mandatory
life sentence for overtime parking might well deter vehicular
lawlessness, but it would offend our felt sense of justice. The
Court concedes today that the principle of disproportionality plays
a role in the review of sentences imposing the death penalty,
but suggests that the principle may be less applicable when a
noncapital sense is challenged. Such a limitation finds no support
in the history of Eighth Amendment jurisprudence.

The principle of disproportionality is rooted deeply in English
constitutional law. . . .

In *Weems v. United States,* 217 U.S. 349 (1910), a public official
convicted for falsifying a public record claimed that he suffered
cruel and unusual punishment when he was sentenced to serve
15 years imprisonment in hard labor with chains. . . . This Court
agreed that the punishment was cruel and unusual. . . .

Robinson v. California, [370 U.S. 660 (1962)], held that imprisonment for the crime of being a drug addict was cruel and unusual. . . .

In *Coker v. Georgia,* 433 U.S. 584 (1977), this Court held that
rape of an adult woman may not be punished by the death penalty.
The plurality opinion of Justice WHITE stated that a punishment
is unconstitutionally excessive "if it (1) makes no measurable contribution to acceptable goals of punishment and hence is nothing
more than the purposeless and needless imposition of pain and
suffering; or (2) is grossly out of proportion to the severity of
the crime." . . . The plurality concluded that the death penalty
was a grossly disproportionate punishment for the crime of
rape. . . .

In sum, a few basic principles emerge from the history of the Eighth Amendment. Both barbarous forms of punishment and grossly excessive punishments are cruel and unusual. A sentence may be excessive if it serves no acceptable social purpose, or is grossly disproportionate to the seriousness of the crime. The principle of disproportionality has been acknowledged to apply to both capital and noncapital sentences. . . .

The Eighth Amendment commands this Court to enforce the constitutional limitation of the Cruel and Unusual Punishments Clause. In discharging this responsibility, we should minimize the risk of constitutionalizing the personal predilictions of federal judges by relying upon certain objective factors. Among these are (i) the nature of the offense, see *Coker v. Georgia* (POWELL, J., concurring and dissenting); (ii) the sentence imposed for commission of the same crime in other jurisdictions, see *Coker v. Georgia, Gregg v. Georgia, Weems v. United States,* cf. *Trop v. Dulles,* [356 U.S. 86 (1958)]; and (iii) the sentence imposed upon other criminals in the same jurisdiction, *Weems v. United States.* . . .

Each of the crimes that underlies the petitioner's conviction as an habitual offender involves the use of fraud to obtain small sums of money ranging from $28.36 to $120.75. In total, the three crimes involved slightly more than $230. None of the crimes involved injury to one's person, threat of injury to one's person, violence, the threat of violence, or the use of a weapon. Nor does the commission of any such crimes ordinarily involve a threat of violent action against another person or his property. It is difficult to imagine felonies that pose less danger to the peace and good order of a civilized society than the three crimes committed by the petitioner. Indeed, the state legislature's recodification of its criminal law supports this conclusion. Since the petitioner was convicted as an habitual offender, the State has reclassified his third offense, theft by false pretext, as a misdemeanor. Texas Penal Code § 31.03(d)(3) (Vernon 1974) as amended (1979 Supp.). . . .

More than three-quarters of American jurisdictions have never adopted an habitual offender statute that would commit the petitioner to mandatory life imprisonment. The jurisdictions that currently employ habitual offender statutes either (i) require the commission of more than three offenses, (ii) require the commission of at least one violent crime, (iii) limit a mandatory penalty to less than life, or (iv) grant discretion to the sentencing authority. In none of the jurisdictions could the petitioner have received a mandatory life sentence merely upon the showing that he committed three nonviolent property-related offenses. . . .

Finally, it is necessary to examine the punishment that Texas provides for other criminals. First and second offenders who commit more serious crimes than the petitioner may receive markedly less severe sentences. The only first-time offender subject to a mandatory life sentence is a person convicted of capital murder. A person who commits a first-degree felony, including murder, aggravated kidnapping or aggravated rape, may be imprisoned from 5–99 years. Persons who commit a second-degree felony, including voluntary manslaughter, rape, or robbery, may be punished with a sentence of between two and 20 years. A person who commits a second felony is punished as if he had committed a felony of the next higher degree. Thus, a person who rapes twice may receive a five-year sentence. He also may, but need not, receive a sentence functionally equivalent to life imprisonment. . . .

Examination of the objective factors traditionally employed by the Court to assess the proportionality of a sentence demonstrates that petitioner suffers a cruel and unusual punishment. Petitioner has been sentenced to the penultimate criminal penalty because he committed three offenses defrauding others of about $230. The nature of the crimes does not suggest that petitioner ever engaged in conduct that threatened another's person, involved a trespass or endangered in any way the peace of society. A comparison of the sentence petitioner received with the sentences provided by habitual offender statutes of other American jurisdictions demonstrates that only two other States authorize the same punishment. A comparison of petitioner to other criminal sentenced in Texas shows that he has been punished for three property-related offenses with a harsher sentence than that given first-time offenders or two-time offenders convicted of far more serious offenses. The Texas system assumes that all three-time offenders deserve the same punishment whether they commit three murders or cash three fraudulent checks. . . .

My view, informed by examination of the "objective indicia that reflect the public attitude toward a given sanction," is that this punishment violates the principle of proportionality contained within the Cruel and Unusual Punishments Clause. . . .

I recognize that the difference between the petitioner's grossly disproportionate sentence and other prisoners' constitutionality valid sentences is not separated by the clear distinction that separates capital from noncapital punishment. "But the fact that a line has to be drawn somewhere does not justify its being drawn anywhere." *Pearce v. Commissioner,* 315 U.S. 543 (1942) (FRANKFURTER, J., dissenting). The Court has, in my view, chosen the easiest line rather than the best.

It is also true that this Court has not heretofore invalidated a mandatory life sentence under the Eighth Amendment. Yet our precedents establish that the duty to review the disproportionality of sentences extends to noncapital cases. The reach of the Eighth Amendment cannot be restricted only to those claims previously adjudicated under the Cruel and Unusual Punishments Clause. . . .

We are construing a living Constitution. The sentence imposed upon, the petitioner would be viewed as grossly unjust by virtually every layman and lawyer. In my view, objective criteria clearly establish that a mandatory life sentence for defrauding persons of about $230 crosses any rationally drawn line separating punishment that lawfully may be imposed from that which is proscribed by the Eighth Amendment. I would reverse the decision of the Court of Appeals.

B. CAPITAL PUNISHMENT

Social forces and litigation aimed at persuading the Court to declare capital punishment unconstitutional under the Eighth Amendment and the Fourteenth Amendment's equal protection clause finally reached the justices in the early 1970s. There had been a steady decline in the number of executions since the 1930s, when more than 165 convicts were annually put to death. Between 1960 and 1971, there were less than 52 executions per year, and that number dropped to less than 10 after 1967 when most states adopted a moritorium on carrying out death sentences. The moritorium and growing controversy over capital punishment was largely due to the pressures of the NAACP Legal Defense Fund, the American Civil Liberties Union (ACLU), and the American Bar Association (ABA). These groups pointed out the fact that black convicts disproportionately received death sentences, especially when convicted for rape. Variations among state laws and the absence of standards for imposing capital punishment raised the issue of whether executions violated the Fourteenth Amendment equal protection clause as well as whether they constituted cruel and unusual punishment under the Eighth Amendment.

The controversy over capital punishment proved divisive for the Court. Initially, in *McGautha v. California* and *Crampton v. Ohio*, 502 U.S. 183 (1971), the justices split six to three when holding that states need not specify in their statutes the factors that juries must consider when imposing death sentences. The Court also indicated that bifurcated trials—that is, a two-stage trial in which juries first determine a defendant's guilt and at a second decide on a sentence—are preferable to single trials in which juries simultaneously convict and sentence, but held that they were not constitutionally required. In Justice John Harlan's words: "To identify before the fact those characteristics of criminal homicides and their perpetrators which call for the death penalty, and to express those characteristics in language which can be fairly understood and applied by the sentencing authority, appear to be tasks which are beyond present human ability."

Despite the rulings in *McGautha* and *Crampton* just the year before, the imposition of capital punishment in one murder and two rape cases was held to violate the Eighth and Fourteenth Amendments in *Furman v. Georgia* (1972) (see page 1082) and two companion cases. The justices were sharply divided, however. The opinion announcing the Court's decision was a brief *per curiam* opinion followed by 231 pages of separate opinions filed by all nine justices, five concurring and four dissenting. Notice in the excerpts reprinted here that even those justices in the majority could not agree on the basis for the Court's ruling. Justices Douglas, Stewart, and White take an analytical approach, interpreting the Eighth Amendment in light of the commands of the Fourteenth Amendment's due process and equal protection clauses. Only Justices Brennan and Marshall address the normative question in maintaining that capital punishment is unconstitutional due to its severity, finality, excessiveness, and denial of human dignity. By contrast, the four dissenters question the role of the Court in overturning capital punishment laws and contend that it should defer to the states on the matter. Rehnquist's dissenting opinion, though, also takes up the normative question and justifies capital punishment on a theory of society's retribution.

Furman immediately escalated the controversy over capital punishment. Thirty-five states enacted new legislation specifying the factors that juries must consider when issuing death sentences. Georgia, Florida, Texas, and twenty-two other states adopted laws requiring juries to consider specific *aggravating factors* (justifying the imposition of capital punishment) and *mitigating factors* (justifying the imposition of an alternative sentence to the death penalty). Louisiana, North Carolina, Oklahoma, and seven other states mandated capital punishment for particular crimes.

By 1976 there were over 600 people on death row under the post-*Furman* laws and the Court faced numerous challenges to their constitutionality. In a batch of rulings handed down in 1976, the Court squarely ruled that capital punishment is not unconstitutional. In the leading case, *Gregg v. Georgia*, 428 U.S. 153 (1976), with only Brennan and Marshall dissenting, the Court upheld Georgia's statute specifying the aggravating and mitigating circumstances for imposing the death penalty and providing for bifurcated trials.

Woodson v. North Carolina, 428 U.S. 280 (1976), and *Roberts v. Louisiana*, 428 U.S. 325 (1976), however, on a five to four vote struck down laws requiring mandatory death sentences for certain crimes. There, a plurality of justices (Stewart, Powell, and Stevens) were joined by Brennan and Marshall (who continued to maintain their position that capital punishment is unconstitutional per se). Stewart's plurality opinion struck down mandatory death sentences for four reasons: (1) there was evidence that juries often fail to convict under mandatory death sentence statutes, (2) these laws provide no standards for guiding juries in their sentencing and fail to allow them to show mercy, (3) the laws also fail to provide for the "particularized consideration" of the accused and the circumstances of the crime, and (4) because capital punishment is different from every other form of punishment (in its finality), its imposition requires individualized sentencing.

The Court's insistence on individualized sentencing was further underscored in *Lockett v. Ohio* (1978) (see page 1100), holding that states may not limit the kinds of mitigating factors that juries may consider when deciding whether or not to impose the death penalty.

While the Court continued to confront numerous procedural challenges to the execution of death sentences, the 1976 rulings made clear that there was not a majority on the Court for striking down capital punishment per se. In what was widely regarded as the last major broadside attack on the wholesale imposition of the death penalty in *McCleskey v. Kemp* (1987) (see page 1107), the justices split five to four in holding that statistics, showing that blacks who murder whites receive the death penalty more often than whites who kill blacks, did not prove racial bias in the imposition of capital punishment.

One particularly controversial practice in the imposition of capital punishment was prosecutorial use during sentencing of so-called victim-impact statements (describing the victim and the impact of his or her murder on relatives). By a five-to-four vote, *Booth v. Maryland* (1987) (see page 1122) disapproved of the use of victim-impact statements. Justice Powell, the author of the Court's opinion, cast the deciding vote. When he retired at the end of the 1987 term, there was speculation that his replacement, Justice Anthony Kennedy, would tip the balance on the Court toward reconsidering and upholding victim-impact statements. But Justice White, who dissented in *Booth*, switched sides in *South Carolina v. Gathers*, 109 S.Ct. 2207 (1989), joining a bare majority for again disallowing the use of victim-impact statements.

Two other recurrent issues are the execution of minors and mentally retarded persons. A bare majority vacated the death sentence of a sixteen year old in *Eddings v. Oklahoma*, 455 U.S. 104 (1982). Then, six to three in *Thompson v. Oklahoma*, 487

CONSTITUTIONAL HISTORY

Capital Punishment in the States

Thirty-seven states have laws imposing capital punishment. Of those, Connecticut, New Hampshire, New Mexico, South Dakota, and Vermont have statutes but no death sentences have been imposed. The states that do not permit executions are Alaska, Hawaii, Iowa, Kansas, Maine, Massachusetts, Michigan, Minnesota, New York, North Dakota, Rhode Island, Wisconsin, and West Virginia.

State	Method	Minimum Age for Execution[ra]	Death Row Inmates as of 1987		
			White	Non-white	Total
Alabama	Electrocution	14	26	55	81
Arizona	Gas chamber	—	48	16	64
Arkansas	Injection	14	20	13	33
California	Gas chamber	18	83	112	195
Colorado	Gas chamber	18	1	1	2
Delaware	Injection	—	1	5	6
Florida	Electrocution	—	152	107	259
Georgia	Electrocution	17	57	52	109
Idaho	Injection or firing squad	14	13	1	14
Illinois	Injection	18	32	71	103
Indiana	Electrocution	10	21	19	40
Kentucky	Electrocution	14	22	8	30
Louisiana	Electrocution	15	25	24	49
Maryland	Gas chamber	—	4	14	18
Mississippi	Gas chamber or injection	13	20	25	45
Missouri	Gas chamber	14	26	21	47
Montana	Hanging or gas chamber	12	4	1	5
Nebraska	Electrocution	18	10	4	14
Nevada	Injection	16	23	16	39
New Jersey	Injection	18	11	14	25
North Carolina	Gas chamber or injection	14	23	42	65
Ohio	Electrocution	18	37	40	77
Oklahoma	Injection	—	50	18	68
Oregon	Injection	18	1	1	2
Pennsylvania	Electrocution	14	36	51	87
South Carolina	Electrocution	—	24	22	46

State	Method	Minimum Age for Execution[ra]	Death Row Inmates as of 1987		
			White	Non-white	Total
Tennessee	Electrocution	18	37	19	56
Texas	Injection	17	108	134	242
Utah	Firing squad or injection	14	3	4	7
Virginia	Electrocution	15	17	18	35
Washington	Electrocution	15	1	1	2
Wyoming	Injection	—	—	3	3
Totals:			936	932	1,868

[a] Note that nine states set no minimum age for executions. Of these, Arizona, Florida, Maryland, South Carolina, Washington, and Wyoming provide for age as a mitigating factor.

INSIDE THE COURT

Justice Arthur Goldberg's Role in the Controversy over Capital Punishment and Opinion in *Rudolph v. Alabama*

At the end of his first term on the Court (1962–1963), Justice Arthur Goldberg circulated to the other members of the Warren Court an unpublished twenty-page "Memorandum to the Conference from Mr. Justice Goldberg." In it he pointed out that a number of cases on the Court's docket involved capital punishment, but not one challenged its constitutionality per se. The "petitioners' failure to urge [the unconstitutionality of the death penalty] should not preclude this Court from considering this matter," observed Goldberg at the outset, pointing out that

> [t]his Court has never explicitly considered whether, and under what circumstances, the Eighth and Fourteenth Amendments to the United States Constitution proscribes the imposition of the death penalty. The Court has, of course, implicitly decided (in every case affirming a capital conviction) that the death penalty is constitutional. But in light of the worldwide trend toward abolition, I think this Court should now request argument and explicitly consider this constantly recurring issue.

Citing various studies on the imposition of capital punishment in the states and in other countries, Goldberg tried to persuade his brethren to adopt his position on capital punishment: "I am convinced that whatever may be said of times past, 'the evolving standards of decency that mark the progress of [our] maturing society' now condemn as barbaric and inhuman the deliberate institutionalized taking of human life by the state." But, except for Justice Brennan, no other member of the Warren Court yet wanted to confront the issue of capital punishment, nor strike it down as unconstitutional.

Failing to persuade other justices to reach out and tackle the constitutionality of capital punishment, Goldberg filed the following dissent from the denial of *certiorari* in *Rudolph v. Alabama*, 375 U.S. 889 (1963), a case appealing a death sentence imposed on a convicted rapist. This opinion is generally credited with sending a signal to lawyers around the country to challenge the constitutionality of capital punishment in their appeals and thereby force the Court's hand. Goldberg left the Court in 1965 but his position became championed by Justice Brennan in *Furman v. Georgia* (1972) (see page 1082) and in his subsequent opinions on capital punishment.

SUPREME COURT OF THE UNITED STATES

No. 308, Misc.—October Term, 1963.

Frank Lee Rudolph, Petitioner, *v.* State of Alabama.	On Petition for Writ of Certiorari and Affidavit In Forma Pauperis to the Supreme Court of Alabama.

[October 21, 1963.]

Mr. Justice Goldberg, with whom Mr. Justice Douglas and Mr. Justice Brennan join, dissenting.

I would grant certiorari in this case and in *Snider v. Cunningham*, 169, Misc., to consider whether the Eighth and Fourteenth Amendments to the United States Constitution permit the imposition of the death penalty on a convicted rapist who has neither taken nor endangered human life.

The following questions, *inter alia*, seem relevant and worthy of argument and consideration:

(1) In light of the trend both in this country and throughout the world against punishing rape by death,[1]

---

[1] The United Nations recently conducted a survey on the laws, regulations and practices relating to capital punishment throughout the world. In addition to the United States, 65 countries and territories responded. All but five—Nationalist China, Northern Rhodesia, Nyasaland, Republic of South Africa, and the United States—reported that their laws no longer permit the imposition of the death penalty for rape.

The following of the United States reported that their laws no longer permit the imposition of the death penalty for rape: Alaska, Arizona, California, Colorado, Connecticut, Delaware, Hawaii, Idaho, Illinois, Indiana, Iowa, Kansas, Maine, Massachusetts, Michigan, Minnesota, Montana, Nebraska, New Hampshire, New Jersey, New Mexico, New York, North Dakota, Ohio, Oregon, Pennsylvania, South Dakota, Tennessee, Utah, Vermont, Washington, Wisconsin and Wyoming. The laws of the remaining States permit the imposi-

RUDOLPH *v.* ALABAMA.

does the imposition of the death penalty by those States which retain it for rape violate "evolving standards of decency that mark the progress of [our] maturing society," [2] or "standards of decency more or less universally accepted?" [3]

(2) Is the taking of human life to protect a value other than human life consistent with the constitutional proscription against "punishments which by their exces-

---

tion of the death penalty for rape, but some States do not, in fact, impose it. United Nations, Capital Punishment (prepared by Mr. Marc Ancel, Justice of the French Supreme Court) (N. Y. 1962) 38, 71–75.

[2] *Trop* v. *Dulles*, 356 U. S. 86, 101 (opinion of WARREN, C. J., joined by Justices BLACK, DOUGLAS, and Whittaker).

[3] *Francis* v. *Resweber*, 329 U. S. 495, 469 (Frankfurter, J., concurring). See *Weems* v. *United States*, 217 U. S. 349, 373:

"Legislation, both statutory and constitutional, is enacted, it is true, from an experience of evils, but its general language should not, therefore, be necessarily confined to the form that evil had theretofore taken. Time works changes, brings into existence new conditions and purpose. Therefore, a principle to be vital must be capable of wider application than the mischief which gave it birth. This is peculiarly true of constitutions. They are not ephemeral enactments, designed to meeting passing occasions. They are, to use the words of Chief Justice Marshall, 'designed to approach immortality as nearly as human institutions can approach it.' The future is their care and provision for events of good and bad tendencies of which no prophecy can be made. In the application of a constitution, therefore, our contemplation cannot be only of what has been but of what may be. Under any other rule a constitution would indeed be as easy of application as it would be deficient in efficacy and power. Its general principles would have little value and be converted by precedent into impotent and lifeless formulas. Rights declared in words might be lost in reality."

Also see *Ex parte Wilson*, 114 U. S. 417, 427–428:

"What punishments may be considered as infamous may be affected by the changes of opinions from one age to another. In former times, being put in the stocks was not considered as necessarily infamous . . . . But at the present day [it] might be thought an infamous punishment."

RUDOLPH v. ALABAMA.

sive . . . severity are greatly disproportioned to the offenses charged?" [4]

(3) Can the permissible aims of punishment (*e. g.*, deterrence, isolation, rehabilitation) [5] be achieved as effectively by punishing rape less severely than by death (*e. g.*, by life imprisonment); [6] if so, does the imposition of the death penalty for rape constitute "unnecessary cruelty?" [7]

---

[4] *Weems* v. *United States*, 217 U. S. 349, 371. Cf. *Lambert* v. *California*, 355 U. S. 225, 231 (dissenting opinion of Frankfurter, J.).

[5] See, *e. g.*, *Williams* v. *New York*, 337 U. S. 241; *Trop* v. *Dulles*, 356 U. S. 86, 111 (concurring opinion of BRENNAN, J.); *Blyew* v. *United States*, 13 Wall. 581, 600.

[6] The United Nations Report on Capital Punishment noted: "In Canada, rape ceased to be punishable with death in 1954: it is reported that there were 37 convictions for rape in 1950, 44 in 1953 and only 27 in 1954, the year of abolition; from 1957 to 1959 a steady decrease in convictions was noted (from 56 to 44), while in the same period the population of Canada increased by 27 per cent." United Nations, Capital Punishment, *supra*, note 1, at 54–55.

Such statistics must of course be regarded with caution. See, *e. g.*, Royall Commission Report on Capital Punishment (1953) 24; Hart, Murder and Its Punishment, 12 N. W. L. Rev. 433, 457 (1957); Allen, Review, 10 Stan. L. Rev. 595, 600 (1958). In Canada, for example, the death sentence was rarely imposed for rape even prior to its formal abolition in 1954. In 1961 there was a slight increase in the number of convictions for rape. See United Nations, Capital Punishment, *supra*, note 1, at 55.

[7] *Weems* v. *United States*, 217 U. S. 349, 370. See *Robinson* v. *California*, 370 U. S. 660, 677 (concurring opinion of DOUGLAS, J.).

U.S. 815 (1988), the Court held that the Eighth Amendment forbids the execution of convicted murders who are fifteen years old or younger at the time of their crimes. But with Justice O'Connor casting the deciding vote in *Stanford v. Kentucky* (1989) (see page 1126), the Rehnquist Court held that the death penalty may be imposed on those who are sixteen years or older. The execution of mentally impaired convicts was first met in *Ford v. Wainwright*, 477 U.S. 399 (1986). There, the Eighth Amendment was held to bar the execution of convicts who are (or have gone while on death row) insane. However, in another five-to-four ruling in *Penry v. Lynaugh* (1989) (see page 1137) the execution of convicted murders who are mildly or moderately retarded was upheld.

Furman v. Georgia,

Jackson v. Georgia

and

Branch v. Texas
408 U.S. 238, 92 S.Ct. 2726 (1972)

William Furman was convicted and sentenced to death for murder. Lucious Jackson was sentenced to death after being convicted for rape. And Elmer Branch was sentenced to death on his conviction for rape. After unsuccessful appeals in the Georgia and Texas supreme courts, their attorneys appealed to the Supreme Court, which granted review and consolidated the cases for decision. The Court struck down Georgia's and Texas's laws for imposing capital punishment. Excerpts from the concurring and dissenting opinions are reprinted here.

Justice DOUGLAS, Justice BRENNAN, Justice STEWART, Justice WHITE, and Justice MARSHALL concurred in separate opinions.

The chief justice, Justice BLACKMUN, Justice POWELL, and Justice REHNQUIST dissented in separate opinions.

Justice DOUGLAS concurring.

That the requirements of due process ban cruel and unusual punishment is now settled. *Louisiana ex rel. Francis v. Resweber,* 329 U.S. 459 [1947] (BURTON, J., dissenting): *Robinson v. California,* 370 U.S. 660 [1962]. It is also settled that the proscription of cruel and unusual punishments forbids the judicial imposition of them as well as their imposition by the legislature. *Weems v. United States,* 217 U.S. 349 [1910].

It has been assumed in our decisions that punishment by death is not cruel, unless the manner of execution can be said to be inhuman and barbarous. *In re Kemmler,* 136 U.S. 436 [1890]. It is also said in our opinions that the proscription of cruel and unusual punishments "is not fastened to the obsolete, but may acquire meaning as public opinion becomes enlightened by a humane justice." *Weems v. United States, supra.* A like statement was made in *Trop v. Dulles,* 356 U.S. 86 [1958], that the Eighth Amendment "must draw its meaning from the evolving standards of decency that mark the progress of a maturing society.". . .

It would seem to be incontestable that the death penalty inflicted on one defendant is "unusual" if it discriminates against him by reason of his race, religion, wealth, social position, or class, or if it is imposed under a procedure that gives room for the play of such prejudices. . . .

The words "cruel and unusual" certainly include penalties that are barbaric. But the words, at least when read in light of the English proscription against selective and irregular use of penalties, suggest that it is "cruel and unusual" to apply the death penalty—or any other penalty—selectively to minorities whose numbers are few, who are outcasts of society, and who are unpopular, but whom society is willing to see suffer though it would not countenance general application of the same penalty across the board.". . .

In a Nation committed to equal protection of the laws there is no permissible "caste" aspect of law enforcement. Yet we know that the discretion of judges and juries in imposing the death penalty enables the penalty to be selectively applied, feeding prejudices against the accused if he is poor and despised, and lacking political clout, or if he is a member of a suspect or unpopular minority, and saving those who by social position may be in a more protected position. In ancient Hindu law a Brahman was exempt from capital punishment, and under that law, "[g]enerally, in the law books, punishment increased in severity as social status diminished." We have, I fear, taken in practice the same position, partially as a result of making the death penalty discretionary and partially as a result of the ability of the rich to purchase the services of the most respected and most resourceful legal talent in the Nation.

The high service rendered by the "cruel and unusual" punishment clause of the Eighth Amendment is to require legislatures to write penal laws that are evenhanded, nonselective, and nonarbitrary, and to require judges to see to it that general laws are not applied sparsely, selectively, and spottily to unpopular groups. . . .

Any law which is nondiscriminatory on its face may be applied in such a way as to violate the Equal Protection Clause of the Fourteenth Amendment. *Yick Wo v. Hopkins,* 118 U.S. 356 [1886]. Such conceivably might be the fate of a mandatory death penalty, where equal or lesser sentences were imposed on the elite, a harsher one on the minorities or members of the lower castes. Whether a mandatory death penalty would otherwise be constitutional is a question I do not reach.

I concur in the judgments of the Court.

Justice BRENNAN concurring.

Ours would indeed be a simple task were we required merely to measure a challenged punishment against those that history has long condemned. That narrow and unwarranted view of the Clause, however, was left behind with the 19th century. Our task today is more complex. We know "that the words of the [Clause] are not precise, and that their scope is not static." We know, therefore, that the Clause "must draw its meaning from the evolving standards of decency that mark the progress of a maturing society." That knowledge, of course, is but the beginning of the inquiry.

In *Trop v. Dulles,* it was said that "[t]he question is whether [a] penalty subjects the individual to a fate forbidden by the principle of civilized treatment guaranteed by the [Clause]." It was also said that a challenged punishment must be examined "in light of the basic prohibition against inhuman treatment" embodied in the Clause. It was said, finally, that:

> "The basic concept underlying the [Clause] is nothing less than the dignity of man. While the State has the power to punish, the [Clause] stands to assure that this power be exercised within the limits of civilized standards."

At bottom, then, the Cruel and Unusual Punishments Clause prohibits the infliction of uncivilized and inhuman punishments. The State, even as it punishes, must treat its members with respect for their intrinsic worth as human beings. A punishment is "cruel and unusual," therefore, if it does not comport with human dignity.

This formulation, of course, does not of itself yield principles for assessing the constitutional validity of particular punishments. Nevertheless, even though "[t]his Court has had little occasion to give precise content to the [Clause]," there are principles recognized in our cases and inherent in the Clause sufficient to permit a judicial determination whether a challenged punishment comports with human dignity.

The primary principle is that a punishment must not be so severe as to be degrading to the dignity of human beings. Pain, certainly, may be a factor in the judgment. The infliction of an extremely severe punishment will often entail physical suffering. See *Weems v. United States.* Yet the Framers also knew "that there could be exercises of cruelty by laws other than those which inflicted bodily pain or mutilation." Even though "[t]here may be involved no physical mistreatment, no primitive torture," *Trop v. Dulles, supra,* severe mental pain may be inherent in the infliction of a particular punishment. See *Weems v. United States, supra,* . . . That, indeed, was one of the conclusions underlying the holding of the plurality in *Trop v. Dulles* that the punishment of expatriation violates the Clause. And the physical and mental suffering inherent in the punishment of *cadena temporal,* was an obvious basis for the Court's decision in *Weems v. United States* that the punishment was "cruel and unusual."

More than the presence of pain, however, is comprehended in the judgment that the extreme severity of a punishment makes it degrading to the dignity of human beings. The barbaric punishments condemned by history, "punishments which inflict torture, such as the rack, the thumb-screw, the iron boot, the stretching of limbs, and the like," are, of course, "attended with acute pain and suffering." *O'Neil v. Vermont,* 144 U.S. 323 (1892) (FIELD, J., dissenting). When we consider why they have been condemned, however, we realize that the pain involved is not the only reason. The true significance of these punishments is that they treat members of the human race as nonhumans, as objects to be toyed with and discarded. They are thus inconsistent with the fundamental premise of the Clause that even the vilest criminal remains a human being possessed of common human dignity. . . .

In determining whether a punishment comports with human dignity, we are aided also by a second principle inherent in the Clause—that the State must not arbitrarily inflict a severe punishment. This principle derives from the notion that the State does not respect human dignity when, without reason, it inflicts upon some people a severe punishment that it does not inflict upon others. Indeed, the very words "cruel and unusual punishments" imply condemnation of the arbitrary infliction of severe punishments. And, as we now know, the English history of the Clause reveals a particular concern with the establishment of a safeguard against arbitrary punishments. . . .

A third principle inherent in the Clause is that a severe punishment must not be unacceptable to contemporary society. Rejection by society, of course, is a strong indication that a severe punishment does not comport with human dignity. In applying this principle, however, we must make certain that the judicial determination is as objective as possible. Thus, for example, *Weems v. United States,* and *Trop v. Dulles,* suggest that one factor that may be considered is the existence of the punishment in jurisdictions other than those before the Court. *Wilkerson v. Utah, supra,* suggests that another factor to be considered is the historic usage of the punishment. *Trop v. Dulles, supra,* combined present acceptance with past usage by observing that "the death penalty has been employed throughout our history, and, in a day when it is still widely accepted, it cannot be said to violate the constitutional concept of cruelty." In *Robinson v. California,* [370 U.S. 660 (1962)], which involved the infliction of punishment for narcotics addiction, the Court went a step further, concluding simply that "in the light of contemporary human knowledge, a law which made a criminal offense of such a disease would doubtless be universally thought to be an infliction of cruel and unusual punishment." . . .

The final principle inherent in the Clause is that a severe punishment must not be excessive. A punishment is excessive under this principle if it is unnecessary: The infliction of a severe punishment by the State cannot comport with human dignity when it is nothing more than the pointless infliction of suffering. If there is a significantly less severe punishment adequate to achieve the purposes for which the punishment is inflicted, cf. *Robinson v. California, supra,* (DOUGLAS, J., concurring); *Trop v. Dulles, supra,* (BRENNAN, J., concurring), the punishment inflicted is unnecessary and therefore excessive. . . .

Thus, although "the death penalty has been employed throughout our history." *Trop v. Dulles* . . . in fact the history of this punishment is one of successive restriction. What was once a common punishment has become, in the context of a continuing moral debate, increasingly rare. The evolution of this punishment evidences, not that it is an inevitable part of the American scene, but that it has proved progressively more troublesome to the national conscience. The result of this movement is our current system of administering the punishment, under which death sentences are rarely imposed and death is even more rarely inflicted. It is, of course, "We, the People" who are responsible for the rarity both of the imposition and the carrying out of this punishment. Juries, "express[ing] the conscience of the community on the ultimate question of life or death," *Witherspoon v. Illinois,* [391 U.S. 510 (1968)], have been able to bring themselves to vote for death in a mere 100 or so cases among the thousands tried each year where the punishment is available. Governors, elected by and acting for us, have regularly commuted a substantial number of those sentences. And it is our society that insists upon due process of law to the end that no person will be unjustly put to death, thus ensuring that many more of those sentences will not be carried out. In sum, we have made death a rare punishment today.

The progressive decline in, and the current rarity of, the infliction of death demonstrate that our society seriously questions the appropriateness of this punishment today. The States point out that many legislatures authorize death as the punishment for certain crimes and that substantial segments of the public, as reflected in opinion polls and referendum votes, continue to support it. Yet the availability of this punishment through statutory authorization, as well as the polls and referenda, which amount simply to approval of that authorization, simply underscores the extent to which our society has in fact rejected this punishment. When an unusually severe punishment is authorized for wide-scale application but not, because of society's refusal, inflicted save in a few instances, the inference is compelling that there is a deep-seated reluctance to inflict it. Indeed, the likelihood is great that the punishment is tolerated only because of its disuse. The objective indicator of society's view of an unusually severe punishment is what society does with it, and today society will inflict death upon only a small sample of the eligible criminals. Rejection could hardly be more complete without becoming absolute. At the very least, I must conclude that contemporary society views this punishment with substantial doubt. . . .

In sum, the punishment of death is inconsistent with all four principles: Death is an unusually severe and degrading punishment: there is a strong probability that it is inflicted arbitrarily; its rejection by contemporary society is virtually total; and there is no reason to believe that it serves any penal purpose more effectively than the less severe punishment of imprisonment. The function of these principles is to enable a court to determine whether a punishment comports with human dignity. Death, quite simply, does not.

Justice STEWART concurring.

The penalty of death differs from all other forms of criminal punishment, not in degree but in kind. It is unique in its total irrevocability. It is unique in its rejection of rehabilitation of the convict as a basic purpose of criminal justice. And it is unique, finally, in its absolute renunciation of all that is embodied in our concept of humanity.

For these and other reasons, at least two of my Brothers have concluded that the infliction of the death penalty is constitutionally impermissible in all circumstances under the Eight and Fourteenth Amendments. Their case is a strong one. But I find it unnecessary to reach the ultimate question they would decide. See *Ashwander v. Tennessee Valley Authority,* 297 U.S. 288 [1936] (BRANDEIS, J., concurring). . . .

Legislatures—state and federal—have sometimes specified that the penalty of death shall be the mandatory punishment for every person convicted of engaging in certain designated criminal conduct. . . .

These death sentences are cruel and unusual in the same way that being struck by lightning is cruel and unusual. For, of all the people convicted of rapes and murders in 1967 and 1968, many just as reprehensible as these, the petitioners are among a capriciously selected random handful upon whom the sentence of death has in fact been imposed. My concurring Brothers have demonstrated that, if any basis can be discerned for the selection of these few to be sentenced to die, it is the constitutionally impermissible basis of race. See *McLaughlin v. Florida,* 379 U.S. 184 [1964]. But racial discrimination has not been proved, and I put it to one side. I simply conclude that the Eighth and Fourteenth Amendments cannot tolerate the infliction of a sentence of death under legal systems that permit this unique penalty to be so wantonly and so freakishly imposed.

Justice WHITE concurring.

In joining the Court's judgments . . . I do not at all intimate that the death penalty is unconstitutional *per se* or that there is no system of capital punishment that would comport with the Eighth Amendment. That question, ably argued by several of my Brethren, is not presented by these cases and need not be decided. . . .

I need not restate the facts and figures that appear in the opinions of my Brethren. Nor can I "prove" my conclusion from these data. But, like my Brethren, I must arrive at judgment; and I can do no more than state a conclusion based on 10 years of almost daily exposure to the facts and circumstances of hundreds and hundreds of federal and state criminal cases involving crimes for which death is the authorized penalty. That conclusion . . . is that the death penalty is exacted with great infrequency even for the most atrocious crimes and that there is no meaningful basis for distinguishing the few cases in which it is imposed from the many cases in which it is not. The short of it is that the policy of vesting sentencing authority primarily in juries—a decision largely motivated by the desire to mitigate the harshness of the law and to bring community judgment to bear on the sentence as well as guilt or innocence—has so effectively achieved its aims that capital punishment within the confines of the statutes now before us has for all practical purposes run its course. . . .

In this respect, I add only that past and present legislative judgment with respect to the death penalty loses much of its force when viewed in light of the recurring practice of delegating sentencing authority to the jury and the fact that a jury, in its own discretion and without violating its trust or any statutory policy, may refuse to impose the death penalty no matter what the circumstances of the crime. Legislative "policy" is thus necessarily defined not by what is legislatively authorized but by what juries and judges do in exercising the discretion so regularly conferred upon them. In my judgment what was done in these cases violated the Eighth Amendment.

I concur in the judgments of the Court.

Justice MARSHALL concurring.

In order to assess whether or not death is an excessive or unnecessary penalty, it is necessary to consider the reasons why a legislature might select it as punishment for one or more offenses, and examine whether less severe penalties would satisfy the legitimate legislative wants as well as capital punishment. If they would, then the death penalty is unnecessary cruelty, and, therefore, unconstitutional.

There are six purposes conceivably served by capital punishment: retribution, deterrence, prevention of repetitive criminal acts, encouragement of guilty pleas and confessions, eugenics, and economy. . . .

[After examining and rejecting each rationale for capital punishment, Justice MARSHALL concluded:] [E]ven if capital punishment is not excessive, it nonetheless violates the Eighth Amendment because it is morally unacceptable to the people of the United States at this time in their history.

In judging whether or not a given penalty is morally acceptable, most courts have said that the punishment is valid unless "it shocks the conscience and sense of justice of the people."

Judge Frank once noted the problems inherent in the use of such a measuring stick:

> "[The court,] before it reduces a sentence as 'cruel and unusual,' must have reasonably good assurances that the sentence offends the 'common conscience.' And, in any context, such a standard—the community's attitude—is usually an unknowable. It resembles a slithery shadow, since one can seldom learn, at all accurately, what the community, or a majority, actually feels. Even a carefully-taken 'public opinion poll' would be inconclusive in a case like this."

While a public opinion poll obviously is of some assistance in indicating public acceptance or rejection of a specific penalty, its utility cannot be very great. This is because whether or not a punishment is cruel and unusual depends, not on whether its mere mention "shocks the conscience and sense of justice of the people," but on whether people who were fully informed as to the purposes of the penalty and its liabilities would find the penalty shocking, unjust, and unacceptable.

In other words, the question with which we must deal is not whether a substantial proportion of American citizens would today, if polled, opine that capital punishment is barbarously cruel, but whether they would find it to be so in the light of all information presently available.

This is not to suggest that with respect to this test of unconstitutionality people are required to act rationally; they are not. With respect to this judgment, a violation of the Eighth Amendment is totally dependent on the predictable subjective, emotional reactions of informed citizens.

It has often been noted that American citizens know almost nothing about capital punishment. Some of the conclusions arrived at in the preceding section and the supporting evidence would be critical to an informed judgment on the morality of the death penalty: *e.g.*, that the death penalty is no more effective a deterrent than life imprisonment, that convicted murderers are rarely executed, but are usually sentenced to a term in prison; that convicted murderers usually are model prisoners, and that they almost always become lawabiding citizens upon their release from prison; that the costs of executing a capital offender exceed the costs of imprisoning him for life; that while in prison, a convict under sentence of death performs none of the useful functions that life prisoners perform; that no attempt is made in the sentencing process to ferret out likely recidivists for execution; and that the death penalty may actually stimulate criminal activity.

This information would almost surely convince the average citizen that the death penalty was unwise, but a problem arises as to whether it would convince him that the penalty was morally reprehensible. This problem arises from the fact that the public's desire for retribution, even though this is a goal that the legislature cannot constitutionally pursue as its sole justification for capital punishment, might influence the citizenry's view of the morality of capital punishment. The solution to the problem lies in the fact that no one has ever seriously advanced retribution as a legitimate goal of our society. Defenses of capital punishment are always mounted on deterrent or other similar theories. This should not be surprising. It is the people of this country who have urged in the past that prisons rehabilitate as well as isolate offenders, and it is the people who have injected a sense of purpose into our penology. I cannot believe that at this stage in our history, the American people would ever knowingly support purposeless vengeance. Thus, I believe that the great mass of citizens would conclude on the basis of the material already considered that the death penalty is immoral and therefore unconstitutional.

But, if this information needs supplementing, I believe that the following facts would serve to convince even the most hesitant of citizens to condemn death as a sanction: capital punishment is imposed discriminatorily against certain identifiable classes of people; there is evidence that innocent people have been executed before their innocence can be proved; and the death penalty wreaks havoc with our entire criminal justice system. . . .

Assuming knowledge of all the facts presently available regarding capital punishment, the average citizen would, in my opinion, find it shocking to his conscience and sense of justice. For this reason alone capital punishment cannot stand.

Chief Justice BURGER, with whom Justice BLACKMUN, Justice POWELL, and Justice REHNQUIST join, dissenting.

If we were possessed of legislative power, I would either join with Justice BRENNAN and Justice MARSHALL or, at the very least, restrict the use of capital punishment to a small category of the most heinous crimes. Our constitutional inquiry, however, must be divorced from personal feelings as to the morality and efficacy of the death penalty, and be confined to the meaning and applicability of the uncertain language of the Eighth Amendment. There is no novelty in being called upon to interpret a constitutional provision that is less than self-defining, but, of all our fundamental guarantees, the ban on "cruel and unusual punishments" is one of the most difficult to translate into judicially manageable terms. The widely divergent views of the Amendment expressed in today's opinions reveal the haze that surrounds this constitutional command. Yet it is essential to our role as a court that we not seize upon the enigmatic character of the guarantee as an invitation to enact our personal predilections into law.

Although the Eighth Amendment literally reads as prohibiting only those punishments that are both "cruel" and "unusual," history compels the conclusion that the Constitution prohibits all punishments of extreme and barbarous cruelty, regardless of how frequently or infrequently imposed. . . .

I view these cases as turning on the single question whether capital punishment is "cruel" in the constitutional sense. The term "unusual" cannot be read as limiting the ban on "cruel" punishments or as somehow expanding the meaning of the term "cruel." For this reason I am unpersuaded by the facile argument that since capital punishment has always been cruel in the everyday sense of the word, and has become unusual due to decreased use, it is, therefore, now "cruel and unusual." . . .

Today the Court has not ruled that capital punishment is *per se* violative of the Eighth Amendment: nor has it ruled that the punishment is barred for any particular class or classes of crimes. The substantially similar concurring opinions of Justice STEWART and Justice WHITE, which are necessary to support the judgment setting aside petitioners' sentences, stop short of reaching the ultimate question. . . .

The critical factor in the concurring opinions of both Justice STEWART and Justice WHITE is the infrequency with which the penalty is imposed. This factor is taken not as evidence of society's abhorrence of capital punishment—the inference that petitioners would have the Court draw—but as the earmark of a deteriorated system of sentencing. It is concluded that petitioners' sentences must be set aside, not because the punishment is impermissibly cruel, but because juries and judges have failed to exercise their sentencing discretion in acceptable fashion. . . .

While I would not undertake to make a definitive statement as to the parameters of the Court's ruling, it is clear that if state legislatures and the Congress wish to maintain the availability of capital punishment, significant statutory changes will have to be made. Since the two pivotal concurring opinions turn on the assumption that the punishment of death is now meted out in a random and unpredictable manner, legislative bodies may seek to bring their laws into compliance with the Court's ruling by providing standards for juries and judges to follow in determining the sentence in capital cases or by more narrowly defining the crimes for which the penalty is to be imposed. If such standards can be devised or the crimes more meticulously defined, the result cannot be detrimental. . . .

Since there is no majority of the Court on the ultimate issue presented in these cases, the future of capital punishment in this country has been left in an uncertain limbo. Rather than providing a final and unambiguous answer on the basic constitutional question, the collective impact of the majority's ruling is to demand an undetermined measure of change from the various state legislatures and the Congress. While I cannot endorse the process of decisionmaking that has yielded today's result and the restraints that that result imposes on legislative action, I am not altogether displeased that legislative bodies have been given the opportunity, and indeed unavoidable responsibility, to make a thorough re-evaluation of the entire subject of capital punishment. If today's opinions demonstrate nothing else, they starkly show that this is an area where legislatures can act far more effectively than courts.

The legislatures are free to eliminate capital punishment for specific crimes or to carve out limited exceptions to a general abolition of the penalty, without adherence to the conceptual strictures of the Eighth Amendment. The legislatures can and should make an assessment of the deterrent influence of capital punishment, both generally and as affecting the commission of specific types of crimes. If legislatures come to doubt the efficacy of capital punishment, they can abolish it, either completely or on a selective basis. If new evidence persuades them that they

have acted unwisely, they can reverse their field and reinstate
the penalty to the extent it is thought warranted. An Eighth
Amendment ruling by judges cannot be made with such flexibility
or discriminating precision.

Justice BLACKMUN dissenting.

I join the respective opinions of the CHIEF JUSTICE, Justice
POWELL, and Justice REHNQUIST, and add only the following,
somewhat personal, comments.

Cases such as these provide for me an excruciating agony of
the spirit. I yield to no one in the depth of my distaste, antipathy,
and, indeed, abhorrence, for the death penalty, with all its aspects
of physical distress and fear and of moral judgment exercised
by finite minds. That distaste is buttressed by a belief that capital
punishment serves no useful purpose that can be demonstrated.
For me, it violates childhood's training and life's experiences,
and is not compatible with the philosophical convictions I have
been able to develop. It is antagonistic to any sense of "reverence
for life." Were I a legislator, I would vote against the death penalty
for the policy reasons argued by counsel for the respective petitioners and expressed and adopted in the several opinions filed by
the Justices who vote to reverse these judgments. . . .

To reverse the judgments in these cases is, of course, the easy
choice. It is easier to strike the balance in favor of life and against
death. It is comforting to relax in the thoughts—perhaps the
rationalizations—that this is the compassionate decision for a maturing society; that this is the moral and the "right" thing to
do; that thereby we convince ourselves that we are moving down
the road toward human decency; that we value life even though
that life has taken another or others or has grievously scarred
another or others and their families; and that we are less barbaric
than we were in 1879, or in 1890, or in 1910, or in 1947, or in
1958, or in 1963, or a year ago, in 1971, when *Wilkerson, Kemmler,
Weems, Francis, Trop, Rudolph,* and *McGautha* were respectively
decided.

This, for me, is good argument, and it makes some sense. But
it is good argument and it makes sense only in a legislative and
executive way and not as a judicial expedient. As I have said
above, were I a legislator, I would do all I could to sponsor and
to vote for legislation abolishing the death penalty. And were I
the chief executive of a sovereign State, I would be sorely tempted
to exercise executive clemency as Governor Rockefeller of Arkansas did recently just before he departed from office. There—on
the Legislative Branch of the State or Federal Government, and
secondarily, on the Executive Branch—is where the authority
and responsibility for this kind of action lies. The authority should

not be taken over by the judiciary in the modern guise of an Eighth Amendment issue.

I do not sit on these cases, however, as a legislator, responsive, at least in part, to the will of constituents. Our task here, as must so frequently be emphasized and re-emphasized, is to pass upon the constitutionality of legislation that has been enacted and that is challenged. This is the sole task for judges. We should not allow our personal preferences as to the wisdom of legislative and congressional action, or our distaste for such action, to guide our judicial decision in cases such as these. The temptations to cross that policy line are very great. In fact, as today's decision reveals, they are almost irresistible.

Justice POWELL, with whom the CHIEF JUSTICE, Justice BLACKMUN, and Justice REHNQUIST join, dissenting.

With deference and respect for the views of the Justices who differ, it seems to me that all these studies—both in this country and elsewhere—suggest that, as a matter of policy and precedent, this is a classic case for the exercise of our oft-announced allegiance to judicial restraint. I know of no case in which greater gravity and delicacy have attached to the duty that this Court is called on to perform whenever legislation—state or federal—is challenged on constitutional grounds. It seems to me that the sweeping judicial action undertaken today reflects a basic lack of faith and confidence in the democratic process. Many may regret, as I do, the failure of some legislative bodies to address the capital punishment issue with greater frankness or effectiveness. Many might decry their failure either to abolish the penalty entirely or selectively, or to establish standards for its enforcement. But impatience with the slowness, and even the unresponsiveness, of legislatures is no justification for judicial intrusion upon their historic powers. Rarely has there been a more appropriate opportunity for this Court to heed the philosophy of Justice OLIVER WENDELL HOLMES. As Justice FRANKFURTER reminded the Court in *Trop* [*v. Dulles* (1958)]:

> "[T]he whole of [Justice HOLMES'] work during his thirty years of service on this Court should be a constant reminder that the power to invalidate legislation must not be exercised as if, either in constitutional theory or in the art of government. It stood as the sole bulwark against unwisdom or excesses of the moment.". . .

Justice REHNQUIST, with whom the CHIEF JUSTICE, Justice BLACKMUN, and Justice POWELL join, dissenting.

Whatever its precise rationale, today's holding necessarily brings into sharp relief the fundamental question of the role of judicial review in a democratic society. How can government by the elected representatives of the people co-exist with the power of the federal judiciary, whose members are constitutionally insulated from responsiveness to the popular will, to declare invalid laws duly enacted by the popular branches of government?

The answer, of course, is found in Hamilton's Federalist Paper No. 78 and in Chief Justice MARSHALL's classic opinion in *Marbury v. Madison,* 1 Cranch 137, (1803). An oft-told story since then, it bears summarization once more. Sovereignty resides ultimately in the people as a whole and, by adopting through their States a written Constitution for the Nation and subsequently adding amendments to that instrument, they have both granted certain powers to the National Government, and denied other powers to the National and the State Governments. Courts are exercising no more than the judicial function conferred upon them by Art. III of the Constitution when they assess, in a case before them, whether or not a particular legislative enactment is within the authority granted by the Constitution to the enacting body, and whether it runs afoul of some limitation placed by the Constitution on the authority of that body. For the theory is that the people themselves have spoken in the Constitution, and therefore its commands are superior to the commands of the legislature, which is merely an agent of the people.

The Founding Fathers thus wisely sought to have the best of both worlds, the undeniable benefits of both democratic self-government and individual rights protected against possible excesses of that form of government.

The courts in cases properly before them have been entrusted under the Constitution with the last word, short of constitutional amendment, as to whether a law passed by the legislature conforms to the Constitution. But just because courts in general, and this Court in particular, do have the last word, the admonition of Justice STONE dissenting in *United States v. Butler,* [297 U.S. 1 (1936)], must be constantly borne in mind:

> "[W]hile unconstitutional exercise of power by the executive and legislative branches of the government is subject to judicial restraint, the only check upon our own exercise of power is our own sense of self-restraint." . . .

The very nature of judicial review, as pointed out by Justice STONE in his dissent in the *Butler* case, makes the courts the least subject to Madisonian check in the event that they shall, for the best of motives, expand judicial authority beyond the limits contemplated by the Framers. It is for this reason that judicial self-restraint is surely an implied, if not an expressed, condition of the grant of authority of judicial review. The Court's holding in these cases has been reached, I believe, in complete disregard of that implied condition.

THE DEVELOPMENT OF LAW
Post-*Furman* Rulings on Capital Punishment

Case	Vote	Ruling
Gregg v. Georgia, 428 U.S. 153 (1976) *Jurek v. Texas*, 428 U.S. 262 (1976) *Profflitt v. Florida*, 428 U.S. 242 (1976)	7:2	Capital punishment not per se unconstitutional, but statutes must specify the aggravating factors (for which juries may impose death sentences) and the mitigating factors (which juries must consider in deciding whether or not to impose a death sentence); bifurcated trials were upheld.
Woodson v. North Carolina, 428 U.S. 280 (1976), and *Roberts v. Louisiana*, 428 U.S. 325 (1976)	5:4 6:3	Mandatory death sentences for certain crimes held impermissible.
Gilmore v. Utah, 419 U.S. 1012 (1976)	6:3	Terminated stay of execution for a convict who waived all constitutional rights and demanded to be executed.
Roberts v. Louisiana, 431 U.S. 633 (1977)	6:3	Held unconstitutional mandatory death sentences for the crime of killing a police officer where juries are not permitted to consider mitigating circumstances.
Coker v. Georgia, 433 U.S. 584 (1977)	6:3	Held that capital punishment is disproportionate for the crime of rape.
Lockett v. Ohio, 438 U.S. 586 (1978), and *Bell v. Ohio*, 438 U.S. 637 (1978)	6:3 7:2	Held that states may not limit the mitigating factors juries consider in imposing the death sentence; must allow for individualized sentencing.
Beck v. Alabama, 447 U.S. 625 (1980)	7:2	Upheld the imposition of death sentence after a jury verdict, when the jury was not permitted to consider the possibility of finding a verdict of guilty to a lesser offense.

Case	Vote	Ruling
Eddings v. Oklahoma, 455 U.S. 104 (1982)	5:4	Vacated death sentence for a sixteen year old who plead guilty.
Enmund v. Florida, 458 U.S. 782 (1982)	5:4	Held that the Eighth Amendment forbids the imposition of capital punishment on those who aid and abet, but do not commit, a felony in which a murder is also committed.
Barefoot v. Estelle, 463 U.S. 880 (1983)	6:3	Held that federal courts may use special, speeded-up procedures for handling appeals by death row inmates.
California v. Ramos, 463 U.S. 992 (1984)	5:4	Upheld state laws requiring juries to be told by a judge that the governor has the authority to commute life sentences and open up the possibility of parole.
Pulley v. Harris, 465 U.S. 37 (1984)	7:2	Held that the Eighth Amendment does not require state appellate courts to review for proportionality the imposition of capital punishment.
Ford v. Wainwright, 477 U.S. 399 (1986)	6:3	Held that Eighth Amendment bars execution of convict who is (or has gone) insane while on death row.
Tison v. Arizona, 481 U.S. 137 (1987)	7:2	Held permissible the execution of convict who participated in a felony that resulted in a death and whose mental state is described as "reckless indifference" to matters of life and death.
McCleskey v. Kemp, 481 U.S. 279 (1987)	5:4	Held that studies showing that blacks who murder whites receive the death penalty more often than whites who murder blacks does not show that decision makers are racially biased and

Case	Vote	Ruling
		hence imposition of capital punishment is not unconstitutional.
Booth v. Maryland, 482 U.S. 496 (1987)	5:4	States may not allow prosecutors to use victim-impact statements (describing the victim and the impact of murder on victim's family) at sentencing phase of capital murder trials.
Sumner v. Shuman, 483 U.S. 66 (1987)	6:3	Struck down statute imposing mandatory death sentences for prison inmates convicted of murder while serving life sentences.
Thompson v. Oklahoma, 487 U.S. 815 (1988)	5:3	Eighth Amendment forbids the execution of convicted murderers who were fifteen years old or younger at the time of their crimes.
Maynard v. Cartwright, 487 U.S. 356 (1988)	9:0	Struck down Oklahoma law allowing juries to impose death penalty for persons convicted of "especially heinous, atrocious, or cruel" murder; the law failed to guide jury's discretion.
South Carolina v. Gathers, 109 S.Ct. 2207 (1989)	5:4	Victim-impact statements are impermissible.
Hildwin v. Florida, 109 S.Ct. 2055 (1989)	7:2	States do not have to require juries to specify the aggravating factors for which they impose the death penalty.
Penry v. Lynaugh, 109 S.Ct. 2934 (1989)	5:4	Upheld the imposition of capital punishment of convicted murderers who are mildly or moderately retarded.
Stanford v. Kentucky, 109 S.Ct. 2969 (1989); and *Wilkins v. Missouri,* 109 S.Ct. 2969 (1989)	5:4	The death penalty may be imposed on convicted murderers who were sixteen or older at the time of their crimes.

Case	Vote	Ruling
Blystone v. Pennsylvania, 110 S.Ct. 1078 (1990)	5:4	Upheld Pennsylvania's law *mandating* the death penalty for certain crimes, when a jury finds no mitigating circumstances and at least one aggravating circumstance for the imposition of a capital punishment sentence.
Boyde v. California, 110 S.Ct. 1191 (1990)	5:4	Held that the Eighth Amendment was not violated by a state's requiring that juries be instructed that they "shall impose" the death penalty if they conclude that aggravating circumstances outweigh the mitigating circumstances for the imposition of a death sentence.
McKoy v. North Carolina, 110 S.Ct. 1227 (1990)	6:3	Struck down a state statute allowing juries to weigh only those mitigating factors that were unanimously agreed to by a jury for impermissibly limiting juries' consideration of mitigating factors bearing on its decision to impose the death penalty.
Lewis v. Jeffers, 110 S.Ct. 3092 (1990)	5:4	Held that federal appellate courts, when finding whether an aggravating circumstance justifies the imposition of the death penalty, should determine whether "any rational trier of fact could have found" the elements of aggravating circumstances rather than engaging in a case-by-case comparison with other murders in a state; Justices Brennan, Marshall, Blackmun, and Stevens dissented.

Case	Vote	Ruling
Walton v. Arizona, 110 S.Ct. 3047 (1990)	5:4	Upheld Arizona's law permitting judges, rather than juries, to determine whether the punishment for first-degree murder should be death or life in prison; Justices Brennan, Marshall, Blackmun, and Stevens dissented.

Lockett v. Ohio
438 U.S. 586, 98 S.Ct. 2954 (1978)

Chief Justice Warren Burger discusses the facts in his opinion for the Court, striking down that portion of Ohio's capital punishment law that restricted the mitigating factors to be considered when imposing the death penalty. In separate opinions Justices Blackmun and Marshall concurred, and Justice Rehnquist filed an opinion concurring in part and dissenting in part.

We granted certiorari in this case to consider, among other questions, whether Ohio violated the Eighth and Fourteenth Amendments by sentencing Sandra Lockett to death pursuant to a statute that narrowly limits the sentencer's discretion to consider the circumstances of the crime and the record and character of the offender as mitigating factors.

I

Lockett was charged with aggravated murder with the aggravating specifications (1) that the murder was "committed for the purpose of escaping detection, apprehension, trial, or punishment" for aggravated robbery, and (2) that the murder was "committed . . . while committing, attempting to commit, or fleeing immediately after committing or attempting to commit aggravated robbery." That offense was punishable by death in Ohio. . . .

Lockett became acquainted with Parker and Nathan Earl Dew while she and a friend, Joanne Baxter, were in New Jersey. Parker and Dew then accompanied Lockett, Baxter, and Lockett's brother back to Akron, Ohio, Lockett's home town. After they arrived in Akron, Parker and Dew needed money for the trip back to New Jersey. Dew suggested that he pawn his ring. Lockett overheard his suggestion, but felt that the ring was too beautiful to pawn, and suggested instead that they could get some money by robbing a grocery store and a furniture store in the area. . . .

The next day Parker, Dew, Lockett, and her brother gathered at Baxter's apartment. Lockett's brother asked if they were "still going to do it," and everyone, including Lockett, agreed to proceed. The four then drove by the pawnshop several times and parked the car. Lockett's brother and Dew entered the shop. Parker then left the car and told Lockett to start it again in two minutes. The robbery proceeded according to plan until the pawnbroker grabbed the gun when Parker announced the "stickup." The gun went off with Parker's finger on the trigger firing a fatal shot into the pawnbroker.

Parker went back to the car where Lockett waited with the engine running. While driving away from the pawnshop, Parker told Lockett what had happened. She took the gun from the pawnshop and put it into her purse. Lockett and Parker drove to Lockett's aunt's house and called a taxicab. Shortly thereafter, while riding away in a taxicab, they were stopped by the police. . . .

[At the conclusion of her trial, the judge] instructed the jury that, before it could find Lockett guilty, it had to find that she purposely had killed the pawnbroker while committing or attempting to commit aggravated robbery. The jury was further charged that one who

> "purposely aids, helps, associates himself or herself with another for the purpose of committing a crime is regarded as if he or she were the principal offender and is just as guilty as if the person performed every act constituting the offense.". . .

The jury found Lockett guilty as charged.

Once a verdict of aggravated murder with specifications had been returned, the Ohio death penalty statute required the trial judge to impose a death sentence unless, after "considering the nature and circumstances of the offense" and Lockett's "history, character, and condition," he found by a preponderance of the evidence that (1) the victim had induced or facilitated the offense, (2) it was unlikely that Lockett would have committed the offense but for the fact that she "was under duress, coercion, or strong provocation," or (3) the offense was "primarily the product of [Lockett's] psychosis or mental deficiency.". . .

In accord with the Ohio statute, the trial judge requested a presentence report as well as psychiatric and psychological reports. The reports contained detailed information about Lockett's intelligence, character, and background. The psychiatric and psychological reports described her as a 21-year-old with low average or average intelligence, and not suffering from a mental deficiency. . . .

After considering the reports and hearing argument on the penalty issue, the trial judge concluded that the offense had not been primarily the product of psychosis or mental deficiency. Without specifically addressing the other two statutory mitigating factors, the judge said that he had "no alternative, whether [he] like[d] the law or not" but to impose the death penalty. He then sentenced Lockett to death. . . .

Prior to *Furman v. Georgia*, 408 U.S. 238 (1972), every State that authorized capital punishment had abandoned mandatory death penalties, and instead permitted the jury unguided and unrestrained discretion regarding the imposition of the death penalty in a particular capital case. Mandatory death penalties had proved unsatisfactory, as the plurality noted in *Woodson v. North Carolina*, 428 U.S. 280 (1976), in part because juries, "with some regularity, disregarded their oaths and refused to convict defendants where a death sentence was the automatic consequence of a guilty verdict."

This Court had never intimated prior to *Furman* that discretion in sentencing offended the Constitution. See *Pennsylvania ex rel. Sullivan v. Ashe*, 302 U.S. 51 (1937); *Williams v. New York*, 337 U.S. 241 (1949); *Williams v. Oklahoma*, 358 U.S. 576 (1959). As recently as *McGautha v. California*, 402 U.S. 183 (1971), the Court had specifically rejected the contention that discretion in imposing the death penalty violated the fundamental standards of fairness embodied in Fourteenth Amendment due process . . . and had asserted that States were entitled to assume that "jurors confronted with the truly awesome responsibility of decreeing death for a fellow human [would] act with due regard for the consequences of their decision.". . .

The constitutional status of discretionary sentencing in capital cases changed abruptly, however, as a result of the separate opinions supporting the judgment in *Furman*. The question in *Furman* was whether "the imposition and carrying out of the death penalty [in the cases before the Court] constitute[d] cruel and unusual punishment in violation of the Eighth and Fourteenth Amendments." Two Justices concluded that the Eighth Amendment prohibited the death penalty altogether and on that ground voted to reverse the judgments sustaining the death penalties. *Id.* (BRENNAN, J., concurring); *id.*, (MARSHALL, J., concurring). Three Justices were unwilling to hold the death penalty *per se* unconstitutional under the Eighth and Fourteenth Amendments, but voted to reverse the judgments on other grounds. In separate opinions, the three concluded that discretionary sentencing, unguided by legislatively defined standards, violated the Eighth Amendment because it was "pregnant with discrimination," *id.* (DOUGLAS, J., concurring), because it permitted the death penalty to be "wantonly" and "freakishly" imposed, *id.*, (STEWART, J., concurring), and because it imposed the death penalty with "great infrequency" and afforded "no meaningful basis for distinguishing the few cases in which it [was] imposed from the many cases in which it [was] not," *id.* (WHITE, J., concurring). Thus, what had been approved under the Due Process Clause of the Fourteenth Amendment in *McGautha* became impermissible under the Eighth and Fourteenth Amendments by virtue of the judgment in *Furman.* See, *Gregg v. Georgia,* 428 U.S. 153 (1976) (opinion of STEWART, POWELL, and STEVENS, JJ.).

Predictably, the variety of opinions supporting the judgment in *Furman* engendered confusion as to what was required in order to impose the death penalty in accord with the Eighth Amendment. Some States responded to what was thought to be the command of *Furman* by adopting mandatory death penalties for a limited category of specific crimes thus eliminating all discretion from the sentencing process in capital cases. Other States attempted to continue the practice of individually assessing the culpability of each individual defendant convicted of a capital offense and, at the same time, to comply with *Furman,* by providing standards to guide the sentencing decision.

Four years after *Furman,* we considered Eighth Amendment issues posed by five of the post-*Furman* death penalty statutes. Four Justices took the position that all five statutes complied with the Constitution; two Justices took the position that none of them complied. Hence, the disposition of each case varied according to the votes of three Justices who delivered a joint opinion in each of the five cases upholding the constitutionality of the statutes of Georgia, Florida, and Texas, and holding those of North Carolina and Louisiana unconstitutional.

The joint opinion reasoned that, to comply with *Furman,* sentencing procedures should not create "a substantial risk that the [death penalty will] be inflicted in an arbitrary and capricious manner." *Gregg v. Georgia, supra.* In the view of the three Justices, however, *Furman* did not require that all sentencing discretion be eliminated, but only that it be "directed and limited," so that the death penalty would be imposed in a more consistent and rational manner and so that there would be a "meaningful basis for distinguishing the . . . cases in which it is imposed from . . . the many cases in which it is not." The plurality concluded, in the course of invalidating North Carolina's mandatory death penalty statute, that the sentencing process must permit consideration of the "character and record of the individual offender and the circumstances of the particular offense as a constitutionally indispensable part of the process of inflicting the penalty of death." *Woodson v. North Carolina.* In order to ensure the reliability, under Eighth Amendment standards, of the determination that "death is the appropriate punishment in a specific case.". . .

In the last decade, many of the States have been obliged to revise their death penalty statutes in response to the various opinions supporting the judgments in *Furman* and *Gregg* and its companion cases. The signals from this Court have not, however, always been easy to decipher. The States now deserve the clearest guidance that the Court can provide; we have an obligation to reconcile previously differing views in order to provide that guidance.

With that obligation in mind we turn to Lockett's attack on the Ohio statute. . . .

We begin by recognizing that the concept of individualized sentencing in criminal cases generally, although not constitutionally required, has long been accepted in this country. . . .

Although legislatures remain free to decide how much discretion in sentencing should be reposed in the judge or jury in noncapital cases, the plurality opinion in *Woodson*, after reviewing the historical repudiation of mandatory sentencing in capital cases concluded that

> "in capital cases the fundamental respect for humanity underlying the Eighth Amendment . . . requires consideration of the character and record of the individual offender and the circumstances of the particular offense as a constitutionally indispensable part of the process of inflicting the penalty of death."

That declaration rested "on the predicate that the penalty of death is qualitatively different" from any other sentence. We are satisfied that this qualitative difference between death and other penalties calls for a greater degree of reliability when the death sentence is imposed. The mandatory death penalty statute in *Woodson* was held invalid because it permitted *no* consideration of "relevant facets of the character and record of the individual offender or the circumstances of the particular offense." The plurality did not attempt to indicate, however, which facets of an offender or his offense it deemed "relevant" in capital sentencing or what degree of consideration of "relevant facets" it would require.

We are now faced with those questions and we conclude that the Eighth and Fourteenth Amendments require that the sentencer, in all but the rarest kind of capital case, not be precluded from considering, *as a mitigating factor,* any aspect of a defendant's character or record and any of the circumstances of the offense that the defendant proffers as a basis for a sentence less than death. We recognize that, in noncapital cases, the established practice of individualized sentences rests not on constitutional commands, but on public policy enacted into statutes. The considerations that account for the wide acceptance of individualization of sentences in noncapital cases surely cannot be thought less important in capital cases. Given that the imposition of death by public authority is so profoundly different from all other penalties, we cannot avoid the conclusion that an individualized decision is essential in capital cases. The need for treating each defendant in a capital case with that degree of respect due the uniqueness of the individual is far more important than in noncapital cases. A variety of flexible techniques—probation, parole, work furloughs, to name a few—and various postconviction remedies may be available to modify an initial sentence of confinement in noncapital cases. The nonavailability of corrective or modifying mechanisms with respect to an executed capital sentence underscores the need for individualized consideration as a constitutional requirement in imposing the death sentence.

There is no perfect procedure for deciding in which cases governmental authority should be used to impose death. But a statute that prevents the sentencer in all capital cases from giving independent mitigating weight to aspects of the defendant's character and record and to circumstances of the offense proffered in mitigation creates the risk that the death penalty will be imposed in spite of factors which may call for a less severe penalty. When the choice is between life and death, that risk is unacceptable and incompatible with the commands of the Eighth and Fourteenth Amendments.

II

The Ohio death penalty statute does not permit the type of individualized consideration of mitigating factors we now hold to be required by the Eighth and Fourteenth Amendments in capital cases. . . .

[Under the statute now before us, once] a defendant is found guilty of aggravated murder with at least one of seven specified aggravating circumstances, the death penalty must be imposed unless, considering "the nature and, circumstances of the offense and the history, character, and condition of the offender," the sentencing judge determines that at least one of the following mitigating circumstances is established by a preponderance of the evidence:

"(1) The victim of the offense induced or facilitated it.

"(2) It is unlikely that the offense would have been committed, but for the fact that the offender was under duress, coercion, or strong provocation.

"(3) The offense was primarily the product of the offender's psychosis or mental deficiency, though such condition is insufficient to establish the defense of insanity." Ohio Rev.Code Ann. § 2929.04(B) (1975). . . .

We see, therefore, that once it is determined that the victim did not induce or facilitate the offense, that the defendant did not act under duress or coercion, and that the offense was not primarily the product of the defendant's mental deficiency, the Ohio statute mandates the sentence of death. The absence of direct proof that the defendant intended to cause the death of the victim is relevant for mitigating purposes only if it is determined that it sheds some light on one of the three statutory mitigating factors. Similarly, consideration of a defendant's comparatively minor role in the offense, or age, would generally not be permitted, as such, to affect the sentencing decision.

The limited range of mitigating circumstances which may be considered by the sentencer under the Ohio statute is incompatible with the Eighth and Fourteenth Amendments. To meet constitutional requirements, a death penalty statute must not preclude consideration of relevant mitigating factors.

Accordingly, the judgment under review is reversed to the extent that it sustains the imposition of the death penalty; the case is remanded for further proceedings.

Justice BRENNAN did not participate in the consideration or decision of this case.

Justice BLACKMUN concurred in part in a separate opinion.

Justice MARSHALL concurred.

Justice REHNQUIST concurring in part and dissenting in part.

The CHIEF JUSTICE states: "We do not write on a 'clean slate.'" But it can scarcely be maintained that today's decision is the logical application of a coherent doctrine first espoused by the opinions leading to the Court's judgment in *Furman*, and later elaborated in the *Woodson* series of cases decided two Terms ago. Indeed, it cannot even be responsibly maintained that it is a principled application of the plurality and lead opinions in the *Woodson* series of cases, without regard to *Furman*. The opinion strives manfully to appear as a logical exegesis of those opinions, but I believe that it fails in the effort. We are now told, in effect, that in order to impose a death sentence the judge or jury must receive in evidence whatever the defense attorney wishes them to hear. I do not think The CHIEF JUSTICE's effort to trace this quite novel constitutional principle back to the plurality and lead opinions in the *Woodson* cases succeeds.

It seems to me indisputably clear from today's opinion that while we may not be writing on a clean slate, the Court is scarcely faithful to what has been written before. Rather, it makes a third distinct effort to address the same question, an effort which derives little support from any of the various opinions in *Furman* or from the prevailing opinions in the *Woodson* cases. As a practical matter, I doubt that today's opinion will make a great deal of difference in the manner in which trials in capital cases are conducted, since I would suspect that it has been the practice of most trial judges to permit a defendant to offer virtually any sort of evidence in his own defense as he wished. But as my Brother WHITE points out in his dissent, the theme of today's opinion; far from supporting those views expressed in *Furman* which did appear to be carried over to the *Woodson* cases, tends to undercut those views. If a defendant as a matter of constitutional law is to be permitted to offer as evidence in the sentencing hearing any fact, however bizarre, which he wishes, even though the most sympathetically disposed trial judge could conceive of no basis upon which the jury might take it into account in imposing a sentence, the new constitutional doctrine will not eliminate arbitrariness or freakishness in the imposition of sentences, but will codify and institutionalize it. By encouraging defendants in capital cases, and presumably sentencing judges and juries, to take into consideration anything under the sun as a "mitigating circumstance," it will not guide sentencing discretion but will totally unleash it. . . .

I continue to view *McGautha* as a correct exposition of the limits of our authority to revise state criminal procedures in capital cases under the Eighth and Fourteenth Amendments. Sandra Lockett was fairly tried, and was found guilty of aggravated murder. I do not think Ohio was required to receive any sort of mitigating evidence which an accused or his lawyer wishes to offer, and therefore I disagree with [that part] of the plurality's opinion [which holds contrariwise].

McCleskey v. Kemp,
481 U.S. 279, 107 S.Ct. 1756 (1987).

Justice Lewis F. Powell discusses the facts in his opinion announcing the decision of a majority of the Court. The Court rejected the argument that statistical studies—showing that black defendants who murder white victims are more likely to receive the death penalty than white defendants charged with murdering white or black victims—establish the basis for declaring the death sentence imposed on Warren McCleskey, a black man, unconstitutional under the Eighth and Fourteenth Amendments. In separate opinions Justice Brennan, joined by Justice Marshall, Justice Blackmun, and Justice Stevens dissented.

Justice POWELL delivers the opinion of the Court.

This case presents the question whether a complex statistical study that indicates a risk that racial considerations enter into capital sentencing determinations proves that petitioner McCleskey's capital sentence is unconstitutional under the Eighth or Fourteenth Amendment.

I

McCleskey, a black man, was convicted of two counts of armed robbery and one count of murder. . . .

On appeal, the Supreme Court of Georgia affirmed the convictions and sentences. . . .

McCleskey next filed a petition for a writ of habeas corpus in the federal District Court for the Northern District of Georgia. His petition raised 18 claims, one of which was that the Georgia capital sentencing process is administered in a racially discriminatory manner in violation of the Eighth and Fourteenth Amendments to the United States Constitution. In support of his claim, McCleskey proffered a statistical study performed by Professors David C. Baldus, George Woodworth, and Charles Pulaski (the Baldus study) that purports to show a disparity in the imposition of the death sentence in Georgia based on the race of the murder victim and, to a lesser extent, the race of the defendant. The Baldus study is actually two sophisticated statistical studies that examine over 2,000 murder cases that occurred in Georgia during the 1970s. The raw numbers collected by Professor Baldus indicate that defendants charged with killing white persons received the death penalty in 11% of the cases, but defendants charged with killing blacks received the death penalty in only 1% of the cases. The raw numbers also indicate a reverse racial disparity according to the race of the defendant: 4% of the black defendants received the death penalty, as opposed to 7% of the white defendants.

Baldus also divided the cases according to the combination of the race of the defendant and the race of the victim. He found that the death penalty was assessed in 22% of the cases involving black defendants and white victims; 8% of the cases involving white defendants and white victims; 1% of the cases involving black defendants and black victims; and 3% of the cases involving white defendants and black victims. Similarly, Baldus found that prosecutors sought the death penalty in 70% of the cases involving black defendants and white victims; 32% of the cases involving white defendants and white victims: 15% of the cases involving black defendants and black victims; and 19% of the cases involving white defendants and black victims.

Baldus subjected his data to an extensive analysis, taking account of 230 variables that could have explained the disparities on nonracial grounds. One of his models concludes that, even after taking account of 39 nonracial variables, defendants charged with killing white victims were 4.3 times as likely to receive a death sentence as defendants charged with killing blacks. According to this model, black defendants were 1.1 times as likely to receive a death sentence as other defendants. Thus, the Baldus study indicates that black defendants, such as McCleskey, who kill white victims have the greatest likelihood of receiving the death penalty. . . .

McCleskey's first claim is that the Georgia capital punishment statute violates the Equal Protection Clause of the Fourteenth Amendment. He argues that race has infected the administration of Georgia's statute in two ways: persons who murder whites are more likely to be sentenced to death than persons who murder blacks, and black murderers are more likely to be sentenced to death than white murderers. As a black defendant who killed a white victim, McCleskey claims that the Baldus study demonstrates that he was discriminated against because of his race and because of the race of his victim. . . .

We agree with the Court of Appeals, and every other court that has considered such a challenge, that this claim must fail.

Our analysis begins with the basic principle that a defendant who alleges an equal protection violation has the burden of proving "the existence of purposeful discrimination." A corollary to this principle is that a criminal defendant must prove that the purposeful discrimination "had a discriminatory effect" on him. Thus, to prevail under the Equal Protection Clause, McCleskey must prove that the decisionmakers in *his* case acted with discriminatory purpose. He offers no evidence specific to his own case that would support an inference that racial considerations played a part in his sentence. Instead, he relies solely on the Baldus study. . . .

The Court has accepted statistics as proof of intent to discriminate in certain limited contexts. First, this Court has accepted statistical disparities as proof of an equal protection violation in the selection of the jury venire in a particular district. Although statistical proof normally must present a "stark" pattern to be accepted as the sole proof of discriminatory intent under the Constitution, *Arlington Heights v. Metropolitan Housing Dev. Corp.*, 429 U.S. 252 (1977), "[b]ecause of the nature of the jury-selection task, we have permitted a finding of constitutional violation even when the statistical pattern does not approach [such] extremes.". . . Second, this Court has accepted statistics in the form of multiple regression analysis to prove statutory violations under Title VII. *Bazemore v. Friday*, [478 U.S. 385 (1986)] (opinion of BRENNAN. J., concurring in part).

But the nature of the capital sentencing decision, and the relationship of the statistics to that decision, are fundamentally different from the corresponding elements in the venire-selection or Title VII cases. Most importantly, each particular decision to impose the death penalty is made by a petit jury selected from a properly constituted venire. Each jury is unique in its composition, and the Constitution requires that its decision rest on consideration of innumerable factors that vary according to the characteristics of the individual defendant and the facts of the particular capital offense. Thus, the application of an inference drawn from the general statistics to a specific decision in a trial and sentencing simply is not comparable to the application of an inference drawn from general statistics to a specific venire-selection or Title VII case. In those cases, the statistics relate to fewer entities, and fewer variables are relevant to the challenged decisions. . . .

Finally, McCleskey's statistical proffer must be viewed in the context of his challenge. McCleskey challenges decisions at the heart of the State's criminal justice system. . . .

Implementation of these laws necessarily requires discretionary judgments. Because discretion is essential to the criminal justice process, we would demand exceptionally clear proof before we would infer that the discretion has been abused. The unique nature of the decisions at issue in this case also counsel against adopting such an inference from the disparities indicated by the Baldus study. Accordingly, we hold that the Baldus study is clearly insufficient to support an inference that any of the decisionmakers in McCleskey's case acted with discriminatory purpose.

McCleskey also suggests that the Baldus study proves that the State as a whole has acted with a discriminatory purpose. He appears to argue that the State has violated the Equal Protection Clause by adopting the capital punishment statute and allowing it to remain in force despite its allegedly discriminatory application. But " [d]iscriminatory purpose' . . . implies more than intent as volition or intent as awareness of consequences. It implies that the decisionmaker, in this case a state legislature, selected or reaffirmed a particular course of action at least in part 'because of,' not merely 'in spite of,' its adverse effects upon an identifiable group.". . .

For this claim to prevail, McCleskey would have to prove that the Georgia Legislature enacted or maintained the death penalty statute *because of* an anticipated racially discriminatory effect. In *Gregg v. Georgia,* 428 U.S. 153 (1976), this Court found that the Georgia capital sentencing system could operate in a fair and neutral manner. There was no evidence then, and there is none now, that the Georgia Legislature enacted the capital punishment statute to further a racially discriminatory purpose. . . .

McCleskey also argues that the Baldus study demonstrates that the Georgia capital sentencing system violates the Eighth Amendment. . . .

Two principal decisions guide our resolution of McCleskey's Eighth Amendment claim. In *Furman v. Georgia,* 408 U.S. 238 (1972), the Court concluded that the death penalty was so irrationally imposed that any particular death sentence could be presumed excessive. Under the statutes at issue in *Furman,* there was no basis for determining in any particular case whether the penalty was proportionate to the crime: "the death penalty [was] exacted with great infrequency even for the most atrocious crimes and . . . there [was] no meaningful basis for distinguishing the few cases in which it [was] imposed from the many cases in which it [was] not.". . .

In *Gregg,* the Court specifically addressed the question left open in *Furman*—whether the punishment of death for murder is "under all circumstances, 'cruel and unusual' in violation of the Eighth and Fourteenth Amendments of the Constitution." We noted that the imposition of the death penalty for the crime of murder "has a long history of acceptance both in the United States and in England." During the 4-year period between *Furman* and *Gregg,* at least 35 states had reenacted the death penalty, and Congress had authorized the penalty for aircraft piracy. The "actions of juries" were "fully compatible with the legislative judgments." We noted that any punishment might be unconstitutionally severe if inflicted without penological justification, but concluded:

> "Considerations of federalism, as well as respect for the ability of a legislature to evaluate, in terms of its particular State, the moral consensus concerning the death penalty and its social utility as a sanction, require us to conclude, in the absence of more convincing evidence, that the infliction of death as a punishment for murder is not without justification and thus is not unconstitutionally severe.". . .

The second question before the Court in *Gregg* was the constitutionality of the particular procedures embodied in the Georgia capital punishment statute. We explained the fundamental principle of *Furman,* that "where discretion is afforded a sentencing body on a matter so grave as the determination of whether a human life should be taken or spared, that discretion must be suitably directed and limited so as to minimize the risk of wholly arbitrary and capricious action." Numerous features of the then new Georgia statute met the concerns articulated in *Furman.* The Georgia system bifurcates guilt and sentencing proceedings so that the jury can receive all relevant information for sentencing without the risk that evidence irrelevant to the defendant's guilt will influence the jury's consideration of that issue. The statute narrows the class of murders subject to the death penalty to cases in which the jury finds at least one statutory aggravating circumstance beyond a reasonable doubt. Conversely, it allows the defendant to introduce any relevant mitigating evidence that might influence the jury not to impose a death sentence. The procedures also require a particularized inquiry into " 'the circumstances of the offense together with the character and propensities of the offender.'" Thus, "while some jury discretion still exists, 'the discretion to be exercised is controlled by clear and objective standards so as to produce non-discriminatory application.'" Moreover, the Georgia system adds "an important additional safeguard against arbitrariness and caprice" in a provision for automatic appeal of a death sentence to the State Supreme Court. The statute requires that court to review each sentence to determine whether it was imposed under the influence of passion or prejudice, whether the evidence supports the jury's finding of a statutory aggravating circumstance, and whether the sentence is disproportionate to sentences imposed in generally similar murder cases. To aid the court's review, the trial judge answers a questionnaire about the trial, including detailed questions as to "the quality of the defendant's representation [and] whether race played a role in the trial.". . .

In the cases decided after *Gregg,* the Court has imposed a number of requirements on the capital sentencing process to ensure that capital sentencing decisions rest on the individualized inquiry contemplated in *Gregg.* . . .

In contrast to the carefully defined standards that must narrow a sentencer's discretion to *impose* the death sentence, the Constitution limits a State's ability to narrow a sentencer's discretion to consider relevant evidence that might cause it to *decline to impose* the death sentence. . . .

Although our constitutional inquiry has centered on the procedures by which a death sentence is imposed, we have not stopped at the face of a statute, but have probed the application of statutes to particular cases. For example, in *Godfrey v. Georgia,* 446 U.S. 420 (1980), the Court invalidated a Georgia Supreme Court interpretation of the statutory aggravating circumstance that the murder be "outrageously or wantonly vile, horrible or inhuman in that it involved torture, depravity of mind, or an aggravated battery to the victim.". . . Although that court had articulated an adequate limiting definition of this phrase, we concluded that its interpretation in *Godfrey* was so broad that it may have vitiated the role of the aggravating circumstance in guiding the sentencing jury's discretion.

Finally, where the objective indicia of community values have demonstrated a consensus that the death penalty is disproportionate as applied to a certain class of cases, we have established substantive limitations on its application. In *Coker v. Georgia,* 433 U.S. 584 (1977), the Court held that a State may not constitutionally sentence an individual to death for the rape of an adult woman. . . .

In sum, our decisions since *Furman* have identified a constitutionally permissible range of discretion in imposing the death penalty. First, there is a required threshold below which the death penalty cannot be imposed. In this context, the State must establish rational criteria that narrow the decisionmaker's judgment as to whether the circumstances of a particular defendant's case meet the threshold. Moreover, a societal consensus that the death penalty is disproportionate to a particular offense prevents a State from imposing the death penalty for that offense. Second, States cannot limit the sentencer's consideration of any relevant circumstance that could cause it to decline to impose the penalty. In this respect, the State cannot channel the sentencer's discretion, but must allow it to consider any relevant information offered by the defendant.

In light of our precedents under the Eighth Amendment, McCleskey cannot argue successfully that his sentence is "disproportionate to the crime in the traditional sense." See *Pulley v. Harris,* 465 U.S. 37 (1984). He does not deny that he committed a murder in the course of a planned robbery, a crime for which this Court has determined that the death penalty constitutionally may be imposed. *Gregg v. Georgia.* . . . His disproportionality claim "is of a different sort." *Pulley v. Harris.* McCleskey argues that the sentence in his case is disproportionate to the sentences in other murder cases.

On the one hand, he cannot base a constitutional claim on an argument that his case differs from other cases in which defendants *did* receive the death penalty. On automatic appeal, the Georgia Supreme Court found that McCleskey's death sentence was not disproportionate to other death sentences imposed in the State. . . .

On the other hand, absent a showing that the Georgia capital punishment system operates in an arbitrary and capricious manner, McCleskey cannot prove a constitutional violation by demonstrating that other defendants who may be similarly situated did *not* receive the death penalty. In *Gregg,* the Court confronted the argument that "the opportunities for discretionary action that are inherent in the processing of any murder case under Georgia law," specifically the opportunities for discretionary leniency, rendered the capital sentences imposed arbitrary and capricious. We rejected this contention. . . .

Because McCleskey's sentence was imposed under Georgia sentencing procedures that focus discretion "on the particularized nature of the crime and the particularized characteristics of the individual defendant," we lawfully may presume that McCleskey's death sentence was not "wantonly and freakishly" imposed and thus that the sentence is not disproportionate within any recognized meaning under the Eighth Amendment.

Although our decision in *Gregg* as to the facial validity of the Georgia capital punishment statute appears to foreclose McCleskey's disproportionality argument, he further contends that the Georgia capital punishment system is arbitrary and capricious in *application,* and therefore his sentence is excessive, because racial considerations may influence capital sentencing decisions in Georgia. We now address this claim.

To evaluate McCleskey's challenge, we must examine exactly what the Baldus study may show. Even Professor Baldus does not contend that his statistics *prove* that race enters into any capital sentencing decisions or that race was a factor in McCleskey's particular case. Statistics at most may show only a likelihood that a particular factor entered into some decisions. There is, of course, some risk of racial prejudice influencing a jury's decision in a criminal case. There are similar risks that other kinds of prejudice will influence other criminal trials. . . .

McCleskey asks us to accept the likelihood allegedly shown by the Baldus study as the constitutional measure of an unacceptable risk of racial prejudice influencing capital sentencing decisions. This we decline to do. . . .

At most, the Baldus study indicates a discrepancy that appears to correlate with race. Apparent disparities in sentencing are an inevitable part of our criminal justice system. The discrepancy indicated by the Baldus study is "a far cry from the major systemic defects identified in *Furman*." As this Court has recognized, any mode for determining guilt or punishment "has its weaknesses and the potential for misuse.". . . Despite these imperfections, our consistent rule has been that constitutional guarantees are met when "the mode [for determining guilt or punishment] itself has been surrounded with safeguards to make it as fair as possible." Where the discretion that is fundamental to our criminal process is involved, we decline to assume that what is unexplained is invidious. In light of the safeguards designed to minimize racial bias in the process, the fundamental value of jury trial in our criminal justice system, and the benefits that discretion provides to criminal defendants, we hold that the Baldus study does not demonstrate a constitutionally significant risk of racial bias affecting the Georgia capital-sentencing process.

Two additional concerns inform our decision in this case. First, McCleskey's claim, taken to its logical conclusion, throws into serious question the principles that underlie our entire criminal justice system. The Eighth Amendment is not limited in application to capital punishment, but applies to all penalties. Thus, if we accepted McCleskey's claim that racial bias has impermissibly tainted the capital sentencing decision, we could soon be faced with similar claims as to other types of penalty. Moreover, the claim that his sentence rests on the irrelevant factor of race easily could be extended to apply to claims based on unexplained discrepancies that correlate to membership in other minority groups, and even to gender. . . . Also, there is no logical reason that such a claim need be limited to racial or sexual bias. If arbitrary and capricious punishment is the touchstone under the Eighth Amendment, such a claim could—at least in theory—be based upon any arbitrary variable, such as the defendant's facial characteristics, or the physical attractiveness of the defendant or the victim, that some statistical study indicates may be influential in jury decisionmaking. As these examples illustrate, there is no limiting principle to the type of challenge brought by McCleskey. . . .

Second, McCleskey's arguments are best presented to the legislative bodies. It is not the responsibility—or indeed even the right—of this Court to determine the appropriate punishment for particular crimes. It is the legislatures, the elected representatives of the people, that are "constituted to respond to the will and consequently the moral values of the people." Legislatures also are better qualified to weigh and "evaluate the results of statistical studies in terms of their own local conditions and with a flexibility of approach that is not available to the courts." Capital punishment is now the law in more than two thirds of our States. It is the ultimate duty of courts to determine on a case-by-case basis whether these laws are applied consistently with the Constitution. Despite McCleskey's wide ranging arguments that basically challenge the validity of capital punishment in our multi-racial society, the only question before us is whether in his case, the law of Georgia was properly applied. We agree with the District Court and the Court of Appeals for the Eleventh Circuit that this was carefully and correctly done in this case.

Justice BRENNAN, with whom Justice MARSHALL joins, and with whom Justice BLACKMUN and Justice STEVENS join in part, dissenting.

I

Adhering to my view that the death penalty is in all circumstances cruel and unusual punishment forbidden by the Eighth and Fourteenth Amendments, I would vacate the decision below insofar as it left undisturbed the death sentence imposed in this case. . . .

II

At some point in this case, Warren McCleskey doubtless asked his lawyer whether a jury was likely to sentence him to die. A candid reply to this question would have been disturbing. First, counsel would have to tell McCleskey that few of the details of the crime or of McCleskey's past criminal conduct were more important than the fact that his victim was white. Furthermore, counsel would feel bound to tell McCleskey that defendants charged with killing white victims in Georgia are 4.3 times as likely to be sentenced to death as defendants charged with killing blacks. Petitioner's Exhibit DB 82. In addition, frankness would compel the disclosure that it was more likely than not that the race of McCleskey's victim would determine whether he received a death sentence: 6 of every 11 defendants convicted of killing a white person would not have received the death penalty if their victims had been black, while, among defendants with aggravating and mitigating factors comparable to McCleskey, 20 of every 34 would not have been sentenced to die if their victims had been black. Finally, the assessment would not be complete without the information that cases involving black defendants and white victims are more likely to result in a death sentence than cases featuring any other racial combination of defendant and victim. The story could be told in a variety of ways, but McCleskey could not fail to grasp its essential narrative line: there was a significant chance that race would play a prominent role in determining if he lived or died.

The Court today holds that Warren McCleskey's sentence was constitutionally imposed. It finds no fault in a system in which lawyers must tell their clients that race casts a large shadow on the capital sentencing process. The Court arrives at this conclusion by stating that the Baldus Study cannot *"prove* that race enters into any capital sentencing decisions or that race was a factor in McCleskey's particular case." Since, according to Professor Baldus, we cannot say "to a moral certainty" that race influenced a decision, we can identify only "a likelihood that a particular factor entered into some decisions," and "a discrepancy that appears to correlate with race. This "likelihood" and "discrepancy," holds the Court, is insufficient to establish a constitutional violation. The Court reaches this conclusion by placing four factors on the scales opposite McCleskey's evidence: the desire to encourage sentencing discretion, the existence of "statutory safeguards" in the Georgia scheme, the fear of encouraging wide spread challenges to other sentencing decisions, and the limits of the judicial role. The Court's evaluation of the significance of petitioner's evidence is fundamentally at odds with our consistent concern for rationality in capital sentencing, and the considerations that the majority invokes to discount that evidence cannot justify ignoring its force.

III

[O]ur inquiry under the Eighth Amendment has not been directed to the validity of the individual sentences before us. In *Godfrey,* for instance, the Court struck down the petitioner's sentence because the vagueness of the statutory definition of heinous crimes created a *risk* that prejudice or other impermissible influences *might have infected* the sentencing decision. In vacating the sentence, we did not ask whether it was likely that Godfrey's own sentence reflected the operation of irrational considerations. Nor did we demand a demonstration that such considerations had actually entered into other sentencing decisions involving heinous crimes. . . .

Defendants challenging their death sentences thus never have had to prove that impermissible considerations have actually infected sentencing decisions. We have required instead that they establish that the system under which they were sentenced posed a significant risk of such an occurrence. McCleskey's claim does differ, however, in one respect from these earlier cases: it is the first to base a challenge not on speculation about how a system *might* operate, but on empirical documentation of how it *does* operate.

The Court assumes the statistical validity of the Baldus study and acknowledges that McCleskey has demonstrated a risk that racial prejudice plays a role in capital sentencing in Georgia Nonetheless, it finds the probability of prejudice insufficient to create constitutional concern. Close analysis of the Baldus study, however, in light of both statistical principles and human experience, reveals that the risk that race influenced McCleskey's sentence is intolerable by any imaginable standard.

The Baldus study indicates that, after taking into account some 230 nonracial factors that might legitimately influence a sentencer, the jury *more likely than not* would have spared McCleskey's life had his victim been black. The study distinguishes between those cases in which (1) the jury exercises virtually no discretion because the strength or weakness of aggravating factors usually suggests that only one outcome is appropriate; and (2) cases reflecting an "intermediate" level of aggravation, in which the jury has considerable discretion in choosing a sentence. McCleskey's case falls into the intermediate range. In such cases, death is imposed in 34% of white-victim crimes and 14% of black-victim crimes, a difference of 139% in the rate of imposition of the death penalty. In other words, just under 59%—almost 6 in 10—defendants comparable to McCleskey would not have received the death penalty if their victims had been black.

Furthermore, even examination of the sentencing system as a whole, factoring in those cases in which the jury exercises little discretion, indicates the influence of race on capital sentencing. For the Georgia system as a whole, race accounts for a six percentage point difference in the rate at which capital punishment is imposed. Since death is imposed in 11% of all white-victim cases, the rate in comparably aggravated black-victim cases is 5%. The rate of capital sentencing in a white-victim case is thus 120% greater than the rate in a black-victim case. Put another way, over half—55%—of defendants in white-victim crimes in Georgia would not have been sentenced to die if their victims had been black. Of the more than 200 variables potentially relevant to a sentencing decision, race of the victim is a powerful explanation for variation in death sentence rates—as powerful as nonracial aggravating factors such as a prior murder conviction or acting as the principal planner of the homicide.

These adjusted figures are only the most conservative indication of the risk that race will influence the death sentences of defendants in Georgia. Data unadjusted for the mitigating or aggravating effect of other factors show an even more pronounced disparity by race. The capital sentencing rate for all white-victim cases was almost *11 times* greater than the rate for black-victim cases. Supp. Exh. 47. Furthermore, blacks who kill whites are sentenced to death at nearly *22 times* the rate of blacks who kill blacks, and more than *7 times* the rate of whites who kill blacks. *Ibid.* In addition, prosecutors seek the death penalty for 70% of black defendants with white victims, but for only 15% of black defendants with black victims, and only 19% of white defendants with black victims. Since our decision upholding the Georgia capital-sentencing system in *Gregg*, the State has executed 7 persons. All of the 7 were convicted of killing whites, and 6 of the 7 executed were black. Such execution figures are especially striking in light of the fact that, during the period encompassed by the Baldus study, only 9.2% of Georgia homicides involved black defendants and white victims, while 60.7% involved black victims.

McCleskey's statistics have particular force because most of them are the product of sophisticated multiple-regression analysis. Such analysis is designed precisely to identify patterns in the aggregate, even though we may not be able to reconstitute with certainty any individual decision that goes to make up that pattern. Multiple-regression analysis is particularly well-suited to identify the influence of impermissible considerations in sentencing, since it is able to control for permissible factors that may explain an apparent arbitrary pattern. While the decision-making process of a body such as a jury may be complex, the Baldus study provides a massive compilation of the details that are most relevant to that decision. . . .

The statistical evidence in this case thus relentlessly documents the risk that McCleskey's sentence was influenced by racial considerations. This evidence shows that there is a better than even chance in Georgia that race will influence the decision to impose the death penalty: a majority of defendants in white-victim crimes would not have been sentenced to die if their victims had been black. In determining whether this risk is acceptable, our judgment must be shaped by the awareness that "[t]he risk of racial prejudice infecting a capital sentencing proceeding is especially serious in light of the complete finality of the death sentence.". . .

Evaluation of McCleskey's evidence cannot rest solely on the numbers themselves. We must also ask whether the conclusion suggested by those numbers is consonant with our understanding of history and human experience. Georgia's legacy of a race-conscious criminal justice system, as well as this Court's own recognition of the persistent danger that racial attitudes may affect criminal proceedings, indicate that McCleskey's claim is not a fanciful product of mere statistical artifice.

For many years, Georgia operated openly and formally precisely the type of dual system the evidence shows is still effectively in place. The criminal law expressly differentiated between crimes committed by and against blacks and whites, distinctions whose lineage traced back to the time of slavery. During the colonial period, black slaves who killed whites in Georgia, regardless of whether in self-defense or in defense of another, were automatically executed. . . .

By the time of the Civil War, a dual system of crime and punishment was well established in Georgia. The state criminal code contained separate sections for "Slaves and Free Persons of Color," and for all other persons. . . .

Formal dual criminal laws may no longer be in effect, and intentional discrimination may no longer be prominent. Nonetheless, "subtle, less consciously held racial attitudes" continue to be of concern, and the Georgia system gives such attitudes considerable room to operate. The conclusions drawn from McCleskey's statistical evidence are therefore consistent with the lessons of social experience.

The majority thus misreads our Eighth Amendment jurisprudence in concluding that McCleskey has not demonstrated a degree of risk sufficient to raise constitutional concern. The determination of the significance of his evidence is at its core an exercise in human moral judgment, not a mechanical statistical analysis. It must first and foremost be informed by awareness of the fact that death is irrevocable, and that as a result "the qualitative difference of death from all other punishments requires a greater degree of scrutiny of the capital sentencing determination." For this reason, we have demanded a uniquely high degree of rationality in imposing the death penalty. A capital-sentencing system in which race more likely than not plays a role does not meet this standard. It is true that every nuance of decision cannot be statistically captured, nor can any individual judgment be plumbed with absolute certainty. Yet the fact that we must always act without the illumination of complete knowledge cannot induce paralysis when we confront what is literally an issue of life and death. Sentencing data, history, and experience all counsel that Georgia has provided insufficient assurance of the heightened rationality we have required in order to take a human life. . . .

Warren McCleskey's evidence confronts us with the subtle and persistent influence of the past. His message is a disturbing one to a society that has formally repudiated racism, and a frustrating one to a Nation accustomed to regarding its destiny as the product of its own will. Nonetheless, we ignore him at our peril, for we remain imprisoned by the past as long as we deny its influence in the present.

It is tempting to pretend that minorities on death row share a fate in no way connected to our own, that our treatment of them sounds no echoes beyond the chambers in which they die. Such an illusion is ultimately corrosive, for the reverberations of injustice are not so easily confined. "The destinies of the two races in this country are indissolubly linked together," and the way in which we choose those who will die reveals the depth of moral commitment among the living.

The Court's decision today will not change what attorneys in Georgia tell other Warren McCleskeys about their chances of execution. Nothing will soften the harsh message they must convey, nor alter the prospect that race undoubtedly will continue to be a topic of discussion. McCleskey's evidence will not have obtained judicial acceptance, but that will not affect what is said on death row. However many criticisms of today's decision may be rendered, these painful conversations will serve as the most eloquent dissents of all.

Justice BLACKMUN, with whom Justice MARSHALL and Justice STEVENS join and with whom Justice BRENNAN joins in part, dissenting.

The Court today seems to give a new meaning to our recognition that death is different. Rather than requiring "a correspondingly greater degree of scrutiny of the capital sentencing determination," *California v. Ramos*, 463 U.S. 992 (1983), the Court relies on the very fact that this is a case involving capital punishment to apply a *lesser* standard of scrutiny under the Equal Protection Clause. The Court concludes that "legitimate" explanations outweigh McCleskey's claim that his death sentence reflected a constitutionally impermissible risk of racial discrimination. The Court explains that McCleskey's evidence is too weak to require rebuttal "because a legitimate and unchallenged explanation for the decision is apparent from the record: McCleskey committed an act for which the United States Constitution and Georgia laws permit imposition of the death penalty." The Court states that it will not infer a discriminatory purpose on the part of the state legislature because "there were legitimate reasons for the Georgia Legislature to adopt and maintain capital punishment."

The Court's assertion that the fact of McCleskey's conviction undermines his constitutional claim is inconsistent with a long and unbroken line of this Court's case law. The Court on numerous occasions during the past century has recognized that an otherwise legitimate basis for a conviction does not outweigh an equal protection violation. In cases where racial discrimination in the administration of the criminal-justice system is established, it has held that setting aside the conviction is the appropriate remedy. . . .

Under *Batson v. Kentucky*, [476 U.S. 79 (1986)], and the framework established in *Castaneda v. Partida*, [430 U.S. 482 (1977)], McCleskey must meet a three-factor standard. First, he must establish that he is a member of a group "that is a recognizable, distinct class, singled out for different treatment." Second, he must make a showing of a substantial degree of differential treatment. Third, he must establish that the allegedly discriminatory procedure is susceptible to abuse or is not racially neutral. . . .

There can be no dispute that McCleskey has made the requisite showing under the first prong of the standard. The Baldus study demonstrates that black persons are a distinct group that are singled out for different treatment in the Georgia capital-sentencing system. . . .

With respect to the second prong, McCleskey must prove that there is a substantial likelihood that his death sentence is due to racial factors. The Court of Appeals assumed the validity of the Baldus study and found that it "showed that systemic and substantial disparities existed in the penalties imposed upon homicide defendants in Georgia based on the race of the homicide victim, that the disparities existed at a less substantial rate in death sentencing based on race of defendants, and that the factors of race of the victim and defendant were at work in Fulton County." The question remaining therefore is at what point does that disparity become constitutionally unacceptable. . . .

McCleskey demonstrated the degree to which his death sentence was affected by racial factors by introducing multiple-regression analyses that explain how much of the statistical distribution of the cases analyzed is attributable to the racial factors. . . .

In sum, McCleskey has demonstrated a clear pattern of differential treatment regarding to race that is "unexplainable on grounds other than race."

Justice STEVENS, with whom Justice BLACKMUN joins, dissenting.

In this case it is claimed—and the claim is supported by elaborate studies which the Court properly assumes to be valid—that the jury's sentencing process was likely distorted by racial prejudice. The studies demonstrate a strong probability that McCleskey's sentencing jury, which expressed "the community's outrage—its sense that an individual has lost his moral entitlement to live,"— was influenced by the fact that McCleskey is black and his victim was white, and that this same outrage would not have been generated if he had killed a member of his own race. This sort of disparity is constitutionally intolerable. It flagrantly violates the Court's prior "insistence that capital punishment be imposed fairly, and with reasonable consistency, or not at all."

The Court's decision appears to be based on a fear that the acceptance of McCleskey's claim would sound the death knell for capital punishment in Georgia. If society were indeed forced to choose between a racially discriminatory death penalty (one that provides heightened protection against murder "for whites only") and no death penalty at all, the choice mandated by the Constitution would be plain. But the Court's fear is unfounded. One of the lessons of the Baldus study is that there exist certain categories of extremely serious crimes for which prosecutors consistently seek, and juries consistently impose, the death penalty without regard to the race of the victim or the race of the offender. If Georgia were to narrow the class of death-eligible defendants to those categories, the danger of arbitrary and discriminatory imposition of the death penalty would be significantly decreased, if not eradicated. As Justice BRENNAN has demonstrated in his dissenting opinion, such a restructuring of the sentencing scheme is surely not too high a price to pay.

Booth v. Maryland
482 U.S. 66, 107 S.Ct. 2529 (1987)

Justice Lewis F. Powell discusses the facts in his opinion for the Court, rejecting prosecutors' use at the sentencing stage of a capital murder trial of victim-impact statements—which describe the emotional impact and opinions of the relatives of a murder victim about the crime—for violating the Eighth Amendment. In two separate opinions Justices White and Scalia, joined by Chief Justice Rehnquist and Justice O'Connor, dissented.

Justice POWELL delivers the opinion of the Court.

The question presented is whether the Constitution prohibits a jury from considering a "victim impact statement" during the sentencing phase of a capital murder trial.

In 1983, Irvin Bronstein, 78, and his wife Rose, 75, were robbed and murdered in their West Baltimore home. The murderers, John Booth and Willie Reid, entered the victims' home for the apparent purpose of stealing money to buy heroin. Booth, a neighbor of the Bronsteins, knew that the elderly couple could identify him. The victims were bound and gagged, and then stabbed repeatedly in the chest with a kitchen knife. The bodies were discovered two days later by the Bronsteins' son.

A jury found Booth guilty of two counts of first-degree murder, two counts of robbery, and conspiracy to commit robbery. The prosecution requested the death penalty, and Booth elected to have his sentence determined by the jury instead of the judge. . . . Under a Maryland statute, the presentence report in all felony cases also must include a victim impact statement (VIS), describing the effect of the crime on the victim and his family. . . .

The VIS in Booth's case was based on interviews with the Bronsteins' son, daughter, son-in-law, and granddaughter. Many of their comments emphasized the victims' outstanding personal qualities, and noted how deeply the Bronsteins would be missed. Other parts of the VIS described the emotional and personal problems the family members have faced as a result of the crimes. . . .

The VIS in this case provided the jury with two types of information. First, it described the personal characteristics of the victims and the emotional impact of the crimes on the family. Second, it set forth the family members' opinions and characterizations of the crimes and the defendant. For the reasons stated below, we find that this information is irrelevant to a capital sentencing decision, and that its admission creates a constitutionally unacceptable risk that the jury may impose the death penalty an arbitrary and capricious manner. . . .

While the full range of foreseeable consequences of a defendant's actions may be relevant in other criminal and civil contexts, we cannot agree that it is relevant in the unique circumstance of a capital sentencing hearing. In such a case, it is the function of the sentencing jury to "express the conscience of the community on the ultimate question of life or death." When carrying out this task the jury is required to focus on the defendant as a "uniquely individual human bein[g]." The focus of a VIS, however, is not on the defendant, but on the character and reputation of the victim and the effect on his family. These factors may be wholly unrelated to the blameworthiness of a particular defendant. As our cases have shown, the defendant often will not know the victim, and therefore will have no knowledge about the existence or characteristics of the victim's family. Moreover, defendants rarely select their victims based on whether the murder will have an effect on anyone other than the person murdered. Allowing the jury to rely on a VIS therefore could result in imposing the death sentence because of factors about which the defendant was unaware, and that were irrelevant to the decision to kill. This evidence thus could divert the jury's attention away from the defendant's background and record, and the circumstances of the crime. . . .

Nor is there any justification for permitting such a decision to turn on the perception that the victim was a sterling member of the community rather than someone of questionable character. This type of information does not provide a "principled way to distinguish [cases] in which the death penalty was imposed, from the many cases in which it was not."

We also note that it would be difficult—if not impossible—to provide a fair opportunity to rebut such evidence without shifting the focus of the sentencing hearing away from the defendant. . . .

We thus reject the contention that the presence or absence of emotional distress of the victim's family, or the victim's personal characteristics, are proper sentencing considerations in a capital case.

The second type of information presented to the jury in the VIS was the family members' opinions and characterizations of the crimes. . . .

One can understand the grief and anger of the family caused by the brutal murders in this case, and there is no doubt that jurors generally are aware of these feelings. But the formal presentation of this information by the State can serve no other purpose than to inflame the jury and divert it from deciding the case on the relevant evidence concerning the crime and the defendant. . . . The admission of these emotionally-charged opinions as to what conclusions the jury should draw from the evidence clearly is inconsistent with the reasoned decisionmaking we require in capital cases.

We conclude that the introduction of a VIS at the sentencing phase of a capital murder trial violates the Eighth Amendment, and therefore the Maryland statute is invalid to the extent it requires consideration of this information.

Justice WHITE, with whom the CHIEF JUSTICE, Justice O'CONNOR and Justice SCALIA join, dissenting.

The Court's judgment is based on the premises that the harm that a murderer causes a victim's family does not in general reflect on his blameworthiness, and that only evidence going to blameworthiness is relevant to the capital sentencing decision. Many if not most jurors, however, will look less favorably on a capital defendant when they appreciate the full extent of the harm he caused, including the harm to the victim's family. There is nothing aberrant in a juror's inclination to hold a murderer accountable not only for his internal disposition in committing the crime but also for the full extent of the harm he caused; many if not most persons would also agree, for example, that someone who drove his car recklessly through a stoplight and unintentionally killed a pedestrian merits significantly more punishment than someone who drove his car recklessly through the same stoplight at a time when no pedestrian was there to be hit. I am confident that the Court would not overturn a sentence for reckless homicide by automobile merely because the punishment exceeded the maximum sentence for reckless driving; and I would hope that the Court would not overturn the sentence in such a case if a judge mentioned, as relevant to his sentencing decision, the fact that the victim was a mother or father. But if punishment can be enhanced in noncapital cases on the basis of the harm caused, irrespective of the offender's specific intention to cause such harm, I fail to see why the same approach is unconstitutional in death cases. If anything, I would think that victim impact statements are particularly appropriate evidence in capital sentencing hearings: the State has a legitimate interest in counteracting the mitigating evidence which the defendant is entitled to put in, see, *e.g., Eddings v. Oklahoma*, 455 U.S. 104 (1982), by reminding the sentencer that just as the murderer should be considered as an individual, so too the victim is an individual whose death represents a unique loss to society and in particular to his family. . . .

The Court's reliance on the alleged arbitrariness that can result from the differing ability of victims' families to articulate their sense of loss is a makeweight consideration: No two prosecutors have exactly the same ability to present their arguments to the jury; no two witnesses have exactly the same ability to communicate the facts; but there is no requirement in capital cases that the evidence and argument be reduced to the lowest common denominator.

The supposed problems arising from a defendant's rebuttal of victim impact statements are speculative and unconnected to the facts of this case. No doubt a capital defendant must be allowed to introduce relevant evidence in rebuttal to a victim impact statement, but Maryland has in no wise limited the right of defendants in this regard. Petitioner introduced no such rebuttal evidence, probably because he considered, wisely, that it was not in his best interest to do so. At bottom, the Court's view seems to be that it is somehow unfair to confront a defendant with an account of the loss his deliberate act has caused the victim's family and society. I do not share that view, but even if I did I would be unwilling to impose it on States that see matters differently.

Justice SCALIA, with whom the CHIEF JUSTICE, Justice WHITE, and Justice O'CONNOR join, dissenting.

The Court's opinion does not explain why a defendant's *eligibility* for the death sentence can (*and always does*) turn upon considerations not relevant to his moral guilt. If a bank robber aims his gun at a guard, pulls the trigger, and kills his target, he may be put to death. If the gun unexpectedly misfires, he may not. His moral guilt in both cases is identical, but his responsibility in the former is greater. . . .

In sum, the principle upon which the Court's opinion rests—that the imposition of capital punishment is to be determined solely on the basis of moral guilt—does not exist, neither in the text of the Constitution, nor in the historic practices of our society, nor even in the opinions of this Court.

Recent years have seen an outpouring of popular concern for what has come to be known as "victims' rights"—a phrase that describes what its proponents feel is the failure of courts of justice to take into account in their sentencing decisions not only the factors mitigating the defendant's moral guilt, but also the amount of harm he has caused to innocent members of society. Many citizens have found one-sided and hence unjust the criminal trial in which a parade of witnesses comes forth to testify to the pressures beyond normal human experience that drove the defendant to commit his crime, with no one to lay before the sentencing authority the full reality of human suffering the defendant has produced—which (and *not* moral guilt alone) is one of the reasons society deems his act worthy of the prescribed penalty. Perhaps these sentiments do not sufficiently temper justice with mercy, but that is a question to be decided through the democratic processes of a free people, and not by the decrees of this Court. There is nothing in the Constitution that dictates the answer, no more in the field of capital punishment than elsewhere.

To require, as we have, that all mitigating factors which render capital punishment a harsh penalty in the particular case be placed before the sentencing authority, while simultaneously requiring, as we do today, that evidence of much of the human suffering the defendant has inflicted be suppressed, is in effect to prescribe a debate on the appropriateness of the capital penalty with one side muted. If that penalty is constitutional, as we have repeatedly said it is, it seems to me not remotely unconstitutional to permit both the pros and the cons in the particular case to be heard.

Stanford v. Kentucky,

and

Wilkins v. Missouri
109 S.Ct. 2969 (1989)

Kevin Stanford was seventeen and four months old at the time he was convicted of murder, sodomy, robbery, and receiving stolen property, and was sentenced to death. Heath Wilkins was sixteen years and six months old when he was convicted of murder in Missouri. Both appealed their convictions and sentences and after each was affirmed, respectively, by the Kentucky and Missouri state supreme courts, they appealed to the Supreme Court. Their cases were granted and consolidated for oral argument and decision. Justice Scalia announced the decision of the Court, Justice O'Connor concurred in a separate opinion, and Justices Marshall, Blackmun, and Stevens joined Justice Brennan's dissenting opinion.

Justice SCALIA, with whom the CHIEF JUSTICE, Justice WHITE, and Justice KENNEDY join in part, delivers the opinion of the Court.

These two consolidated cases require us to decide whether the imposition of capital punishment on an individual for a crime committed at 16 or 17 years of age constitutes cruel and unusual punishment under the Eighth Amendment. . . .

II

The thrust of both Wilkins' and Stanford's arguments is that imposition of the death penalty on those who were juveniles when they committed their crimes falls within the Eighth Amendment's prohibition against "cruel and unusual punishments." Wilkins would have us define juveniles as individuals 16 years of age and under; Stanford would draw the line at 17.

Neither petitioner asserts that his sentence constitutes one of "those modes or acts of punishment that had been considered cruel and unusual at the time that the Bill of Rights was adopted." *Ford v. Wainwright*, 477 U.S. 399 (1986). Nor could they support such a contention. . . .

Thus petitioners are left to argue that their punishment is contrary to the "evolving standards of decency that mark the progress of a maturing society," *Trop v. Dulles*, 356 U.S. 86 (1958) (plurality opinion). They are correct in asserting that this Court has "not confined the prohibition embodied in the Eighth Amendment to 'barbarous' methods that were generally outlawed in the 18th century," but instead has interpreted the Amendment "in a flexible and dynamic manner." *Gregg v. Georgia,* 428 U.S. 153 (1976). In determining what standards have "evolved," however, we have looked not to our own conceptions of decency, but to those of modern American society as a whole. . . . This approach is dictated both by the language of the Amendment—which proscribes only those punishments that are both "cruel and *unusual*"—and by the "deference we owe to the decisions of the state legislatures under our federal system," *Gregg v. Georgia.* . . .

III

Of the 37 States whose laws permit capital punishment, 15 decline to impose it upon 16-year-old offenders and 12 decline to impose it on 17-year-old offenders. This does not establish the degree of national consensus this Court has previously thought sufficient to label a particular punishment cruel and unusual. In invalidating the death penalty for rape of an adult woman, we stressed that Georgia was the *sole* jurisdiction that authorized such a punishment. See *Coker v. Georgia,* [433 U.S. 584 (1977)]. In striking down capital punishment for participation in a robbery in which an accomplice takes a life, we emphasized that only eight jurisdictions authorized similar punishment. *Enmund v. Florida,* [458 U.S. 782 (1982)]. In finding that the Eighth Amendment precludes execution of the insane and thus requires an adequate hearing on the issue of sanity, we relied upon (in addition to the common-law rule) the fact that "no State in the Union" permitted such punishment. *Ford v. Wainwright.* And in striking down a life sentence without parole under a recidivist statute, we stressed that "[i]t appears that [petitioner] was treated more severely than he would have been in any other State." *Solem v. Helm,* 463 U.S. 277 (1983).

Since a majority of the States that permit capital punishment authorize it for crimes committed at age 16 or above, petitioners' cases are more analogous to *Tison v. Arizona,* 481 U.S. 137 (1987) than *Coker, Enmund, Ford,* and *Solem.* In *Tison,* which upheld Arizona's imposition of the death penalty for major participation in a felony with reckless indifference to human life, we noted that only 11 of those jurisdictions imposing capital punishment rejected its use in such circumstances. As we noted earlier, here the number is 15 for offenders under 17, and 12 for offenders under 18. We think the same conclusion as in *Tison* is required in this case.

Petitioners make much of the recently enacted federal statute providing capital punishment for certain drug-related offenses, but limiting that punishment to offenders 18 and over. The Anti-Drug Abuse Act of 1988. That reliance is entirely misplaced. To begin with, the statute in question does not embody a judgment by the Federal Legislature that *no* murder is heinous enough to warrant the execution of such a youthful offender, but merely that the narrow class of offense it defines is not. The congressional judgment on the broader question, if apparent at all, is to be found in the law that permits 16- and 17-year-olds (after appropriate findings) to be tried and punished as adults for *all* federal offenses, including those bearing a capital penalty that is not limited to 18-year-olds. Moreover, even if it were true that no federal statute permitted the execution of persons under 18, that would not remotely establish—in the face of a substantial number of state statutes to the contrary—a national consensus that such punishment is inhumane, any more than the absence of a federal lottery establishes a national consensus that lotteries are socially harmful. To be sure, the absence of a federal death penalty for 16- or 17-year-olds (if it existed) might be evidence that there is no national consensus *in favor* of such punishment. It is not the burden of Kentucky and Missouri, however, to establish a national consensus approving what their citizens have voted to do; rather, it is the "heavy burden" of petitioners to establish a national consensus *against* it. As far as the primary and most reliable indication of consensus is concerned—the pattern of enacted laws—petitioners have failed to carry that burden.

IV

[A] Wilkins and Stanford argue, however, that even if the laws themselves do not establish a settled consensus, the application of the laws does. That contemporary society views capital punishment of 16- and 17-year-old offenders as inappropriate is demonstrated, they say, by the reluctance of juries to impose, and prosecutors to seek, such sentences. Petitioners are quite correct that a far smaller number of offenders under 18 than over 18 have been sentenced to death in this country. From 1982 through 1988, for example, out of 2,106 total death sentences, only 15 were imposed on individuals who were 16 or under when they committed their crimes, and only 30 on individuals who were 17 at the time of the crime. And it appears that actual executions for crimes committed under age 18 accounted for only about two percent of the total number of executions that occurred between 1642 and 1986. . . . These statistics, however, carry little significance. Given the undisputed fact that a far smaller percentage of capital crimes is committed by persons under 18 than over 18, the discrepancy in treatment is much less than might seem. Granted, however, that a substaintial discrepancy exists, that does not establish the requisite proposition that the death sentence for offenders under 18 is categorically unacceptable to prosecutors and juries. To the contrary, it is not only possible but overwhelmingly probable that the very considerations which induce petitioners and their supporters to believe that death should *never* be imposed on offenders under 18 cause prosecutors and juries to believe that it should *rarely* be imposed.

[B] This last point suggests why there is also no relevance to the laws cited by petitioners and their *amici* which set 18 or more as the legal age for engaging in various activities, ranging from driving to drinking alcoholic beverages to voting. It is, to begin with, absurd to think that one must be mature enough to drive carefully, to drink responsibly, or to vote intelligently, in order to be mature enough to understand that murdering another human being is profoundly wrong, and to conform one's conduct to that most minimal of all civilized standards. . . .

What displays society's views on this latter point are not the ages set forth in the generalized system of driving, drinking, and voting laws cited by petitioners and their *amici,* but the ages at which the States permit their particularized capital punishment systems to be applied.

V

Having failed to establish a consensus against capital punishment for 16- and 17-year-old offenders through state and federal statutes and the behavior of prosecutors and juries, petitioners seek to demonstrate it through other indicia, including public opinion polls, the views of interest groups and the positions adopted by various professional associations. We decline the invitation to rest constitutional law upon such uncertain foundations. A revised national consensus so broad, so clear and so enduring as to justify a permanent prohibition upon all units of democratic government must appear in the operative acts (laws and the application of laws) that the people have approved.

We also reject petitioners' argument that we should invalidate capital punishment of 16- and 17-year-old offenders on the ground that it fails to serve the legitimate goals of penology. According to petitioners, it fails to deter because juveniles, possessing less developed cognitive skills than adults, are less likely to fear death; and it fails to exact just retribution because juveniles, being less mature and responsible, are also less morally blameworthy. In support of these claims, petitioners and their supporting *amici* marshall an array of socioscientific evidence concerning the psychological and emotional development of 16- and 17-year-olds.

If such evidence could conclusively establish the entire lack of deterrent effect and moral responsibility, resort to the Cruel and Unusual Punishments Clause would be unnecessary; the Equal Protection Clause of the Fourteenth Amendment would invalidate these laws for lack of rational basis. But as the adjective "socioscientific" suggests (and insofar as evaluation of moral responsibility is concerned perhaps the adjective "ethicoscientific" would be more apt), it is not demonstrable that no 16-year-old is "adequately responsible" or significantly deterred. It is rational, even if mistaken, to think the contrary. The battle must be fought, then, on the field of the Eighth Amendment; and in that struggle socioscientific, ethicoscientific, or even purely scientific evidence is not an available weapon. The punishment is either "cruel *and* unusual" (*i.e.,* society has set its face against it) or it is not. The audience for these arguments, in other words, is not this Court but the citizenry of the United States. It is they, not we, who must be persuaded. For as we stated earlier, our job is to *identify* the "evolving standards of decency"; to determine, not what they *should* be, but what they *are.* We have no power under the Eighth Amendment to substitute our belief in the scientific evidence for the society's apparent skepticism. In short, we emphatically reject petitioner's suggestion that the issues in this case permit us to apply our "own informed judgment," regarding the desirability of permitting the death penalty for crimes by 16- and 17-year-olds. . . .

We discern neither a historical nor a modern societal consensus forbidding the imposition of capital punishment on any person who murders at 16 or 17 years of age. Accordingly, we conclude that such punishment does not offend the Eighth Amendment's prohibition against cruel and unusual punishment.

The judgments of the Supreme Court of Kentucky and the Supreme Court of Missouri are therefore

Affirmed.

Justice O'CONNOR, concurring in part.

Last Term, in *Thompson v. Oklahoma*, [108 S.Ct. 2687] (1988) (concurring in judgment), I expressed the view that a criminal defendant who would have been tried as a juvenile under state law, but for the granting of a petition waiving juvenile court jurisdiction, may only be executed for a capital offense if the State's capital punishment statute specifies a minimum age at which the commission of a capital crime can lead to an offender's execution and the defendant had reached that minimum age at the time the crime was committed. As a threshold matter, I indicated that such specificity is not necessary to avoid constitutional problems if it is clear that no national consensus forbids the imposition of capital punishment for crimes committed at such an age. Applying this two-part standard in *Thompson*, I concluded that Oklahoma's imposition of a death sentence on an individual who was 15 years old at the time he committed a capital offense should be set aside. Applying the same standard today, I conclude that the death sentences for capital murder imposed by Missouri and Kentucky on petitioners Wilkins and Stanford respectively should not be set aside because it is sufficiently clear that no national consensus forbids the imposition of capital punishment on 16 or 17-year-old capital murderers. . . .

I am unable, however, to join the remainder of the plurality's opinion for reasons I stated in *Thompson*. Part V of the plurality's opinion "emphatically reject[s]," the suggestion that, beyond an assessment of the specific enactments of American legislatures, there remains a constitutional obligation imposed upon this Court to judge whether the " 'nexus between the punishment imposed and the defendant's blameworthiness' " is proportional. *Thompson*, quoting *Enmund v. Florida*, 458 U.S. 782 (1982) (dissenting opinion). Part IV-B of the plurality's opinion specifically rejects as irrelevant to Eighth Amendment considerations state statutes that distinguish juveniles from adults for a variety of other purposes. In my view, this Court does have a constitutional obligation to conduct proportionality analysis.

Justice BRENNAN, with whom Justice MARSHALL, Justice BLACKMUN, and Justice STEVENS join, dissenting.

I believe that to take the life of a person as punishment for a crime committed when below the age of 18 is cruel and unusual and hence is prohibited by the Eighth Amendment.

The method by which this Court assesses a claim that a punishment is unconstitutional because it is cruel and unusual is established by our precedents, and it bears little resemblance to the method four Members of the Court apply in this case. To be sure, we *begin* the task of deciding whether a punishment is unconstitutional by reviewing legislative enactments and the work of sentencing juries relating to the punishment in question, to determine whether our Nation has set its face against a punishment to an extent that it can be concluded that the punishment offends our "evolving standards of decency." *Trop v. Dulles* (1958) (plurality opinion). The Court undertakes such an analysis in this case. But Justice SCALIA, in his separate opinion on this point, would treat the Eighth Amendment inquiry as *complete* with this investigation. . . . In my view, that inquiry must in this case go beyond age-based statutory classifications relating to matters other than capital punishment, and must also encompass what Justice SCALIA calls, with evident but misplaced disdain, "ethicoscientific" evidence. Only then can we be in a position to judge, as our cases require, whether a punishment is unconstitutionally excessive, either because it is disproportionate given the culpability of the offender, or because it serves no legitimate penal goal. . . .

The Court's discussion of state laws concerning capital sentencing, gives a distorted view of the evidence of contemporary standards that these legislative determinations provide. Currently, 12 of the States whose statutes permit capital punishment specifically mandate that offenders under age 18 not be sentenced to death. When one adds to these 12 States the 15 (including the District of Columbia) in which capital punishment is not authorized at all, it appears that the governments in fully 27 of the States have concluded that no one under 18 should face the death penalty. A further 3 States explicitly refuse to authorize sentences of death for those who committed their offense when under 17, making a total of 30 States that would not tolerate the execution of petitioner Wilkins. Congress' most recent enactment of a death penalty statute also excludes those under 18.

In 18 States that have a death penalty, no minimum age for capital sentences is set in the death penalty statute. The notion that these States have consciously authorized the execution of juveniles derives from the congruence in those jurisdictions of laws permitting state courts to hand down death sentences, on the one hand, and, on the other, statutes permitting the transfer of offenders under 18 from the juvenile to state court systems for trial in certain circumstances. I would not assume, however, in considering how the States stand on the moral issue that underlies the constitutional question with which we are presented, that a legislature that has never specifically considered the issue has made a conscious moral choice to permit the execution of juveniles. On a matter of such moment that most States have expressed an explicit and contrary judgment, the decisions of legislatures that are only implicit, and that lack the "earmarks of careful consideration that we have required for other kinds of decisions leading to the death penalty," must count for little. I do not suggest, of course, that laws of these States cut *against* the constitutionality of the juvenile death penalty—only that accuracy demands that the baseline for our deliberations should be that 27 States refuse to authorize a sentence of death in the circumstances of petitioner Stanford's case, and 30 would not permit Wilkins' execution; that 18 States have not squarely faced the question; and that only the few remaining jurisdictions have explicitly set an age below 18 at which a person may be sentenced to death.

The application of these laws is another indicator the Court agrees to be relevant. The fact that juries have on occasion sentenced a minor to death shows, the Court says, that the death penalty for adolescents is not categorically unacceptable to juries. This, of course, is true; but it is not a conclusion that takes Eighth Amendment analysis very far. Just as we have never insisted that a punishment have been rejected unanimously by the States before we may judge it cruel and unusual, so we have never adopted the extraordinary view that a punishment is beyond Eighth Amendment challenge if it is sometimes handed down by a jury. . . .

Both in absolute and in relative terms, imposition of the death penalty on adolescents is distinctly unusual. Adolescent offenders make up only a small proportion of the current death row population: 30 out of a total of 2,186 inmates, or 1.37 percent. NAACP Legal Defense and Educational Fund, Inc. (LDF), Death Row, U.S.A. (Mar. 1, 1989). Eleven minors were sentenced to die in 1982; 9 in 1983; 6 in 1984; 5 in 1985; 7 in 1986; and 2 in 1987. Forty-one, or 2.3 percent, of the 1,813 death sentences imposed between January 1, 1982, and June 30, 1988, were for juvenile crimes. And juvenile offenders are significantly less likely to receive the death penalty than adults. During the same period, there were 97,086 arrests of adults for homicide, and 1,772 adult death sentences, or 1.8 percent; and 8,911 arrests of minors for homicide, compared to 41 juvenile death sentences, or 0.5 percent.

The Court speculates that this very small number of capital sentences imposed on adolescents indicates that juries have considered the youth of the offender when determining sentence, and have reserved the punishment for rare cases in which it is nevertheless appropriate. The State of Georgia made a very similar and equally conjectural argument in *Coker*—that "as a practical matter juries simply reserve the extreme sanction for extreme cases of rape, and that recent experience . . . does not prove that jurors consider the death penalty to be a disproportionate punishment for every conceivable instance of rape." This Court, however, summarily rejected this claim, noting simply that in the vast majority of cases, Georgia juries had not imposed the death sentence for rape. It is certainly true that in the vast majority of cases, juries have not sentenced juveniles to death, and it seems to me perfectly proper to conclude that a sentence so rarely imposed is "unusual."

Further indicators of contemporary standards of decency that should inform our consideration of the Eighth Amendment question are the opinions of respected organizations. . . . Where organizations with expertise in a relevant area have given careful consideration to the question of a punishment's appropriateness, there is no reason why that judgment should not be entitled to attention as an indicator of contemporary standards. There is no dearth of opinion from such groups that the state-sanctioned killing of minors is unjustified. A number, indeed, have filed briefs *amicus curiae* in these cases, in support of petitioners. The American Bar Association has adopted a resolution opposing the imposition of capital punishment upon any person for an offense committed while under age 18, as has the National Council of Juvenile and Family Court Judges. The American Law Institute's Model Penal Code similarly includes a lower age limit of 18 for the death sentence. And the National Commission on Reform of the Federal Criminal Laws also recommended that 18 be the minimum age.

Our cases recognize that objective indicators of contemporary standards of decency in the form of legislation in other countries is also of relevance to Eighth Amendment analysis. . . .

Many countries, of course—over 50, including nearly all in Western Europe—have formally abolished the death penalty, or have limited its use to exceptional crimes such as treason. Twenty-seven others do not in practice impose the penalty. Of the nations that retain capital punishment, a majority—65—prohibit the execution of juveniles. Sixty-one countries retain capital punishment and have no statutory provision exempting juveniles, though some of these nations are ratifiers of international treaties that do prohibit the execution of juveniles. Since 1979, Amnesty International has recorded only eight executions of offenders under 18 throughout the world, three of these in the United States. The other five executions were carried out in Pakistan, Bangladesh, Rwanda, and Barbados. In addition to national laws, three leading human rights treaties ratified or signed by the United States explicitly prohibit juvenile death penalties. Within the world community, the imposition of the death penalty for juvenile crimes appears to be overwhelmingly disapproved.

Together, the rejection of the death penalty for juveniles by a majority of the States, the rarity of the sentence for juveniles, both as an absolute and a comparative matter, the decisions of respected organizations in relevant fields that this punishment is unacceptable, and its rejection generally throughout the world, provide to my mind a strong grounding for the view that it is not constitutionally tolerable that certain States persist in authorizing the execution of adolescent offenders. It is unnecessary, however, to rest a view that the Eighth Amendment prohibits the execution of minors solely upon a judgment as to the meaning to be attached to the evidence of contemporary values outlined above, for the execution of juveniles fails to satisfy two well-established and independent Eighth Amendment requirements—that a punishment not be disproportionate, and that it make a contribution to acceptable goals of punishment.

Justice SCALIA forthrightly states in his separate opinion that Eighth Amendment analysis is at an end once legislation and jury verdicts relating to the punishment in question are analyzed as indicators of contemporary values. A majority of the Court rejected this revisionist view as recently as last Term, see *Thompson* [*v. Oklahoma* (1988)], and does so again in this case and in *Penry v. Lynaugh*. We need not and should not treat this narrow range of factors as determinative of our decision whether a punishment violates the Constitution because it is excessive. . . .

Justice SCALIA's approach would largely return the task of defining the contours of Eighth Amendment protection to political majorities. But

> "[t]he very purpose of a Bill of Rights was to withdraw certain subjects from the vicissitudes of political controversy, to place them beyond the reach of majorities and officials and to establish them as legal principles to be applied by the courts. One's right to life, liberty, and property, to free speech, a free press, freedom of worship and assembly, and other fundamental rights may not be submitted to vote; they depend on the outcome of no elections." *West Virginia Board of Education v. Barnette,* 319 U.S. 624 (1943). . . .

There can be no doubt at this point in our constitutional history that the Eighth Amendment forbids punishment that is wholly disproportionate to the blameworthiness of the offender. . . .

Proportionality analysis requires that we compare "the gravity of the offense," understood to include not only the injury caused, but also the defendant's culpability, with "the harshness of the penalty." In my view, juveniles so generally lack the degree of responsibility for their crimes that is a predicate for the constitutional imposition of the death penalty that the Eighth Amendment forbids that they receive that punishment.

Legislative determinations distinguishing juveniles from adults abound. These age-based classifications reveal much about how our society regards juveniles as a class, and about societal beliefs regarding adolescent levels of responsibility. . . .

To be sure, the development of cognitive and reasoning abilities and of empathy, the acquisition of experience upon which these abilities operate and upon which the capacity to make sound value judgments depends, and in general the process of maturation into a self-directed individual fully responsible for his or her actions, occur by degrees. But the factors discussed above indicate that 18 is the dividing line that society has generally drawn, the point at which it is thought reasonable to assume that persons have an ability to make and a duty to bear responsibility for their judgments. Insofar as age 18 is a necessarily arbitrary social choice as a point at which to acknowledge a person's maturity and responsibility, given the different developmental rates of individuals, it is in fact "a conservative estimate of the dividing line between adolescence and adulthood. Many of the psychological and emotional changes that an adolescent experiences in maturing do not actually occur until the early 20s.". . .

I believe that the Eighth Amendment requires that a person who lacks that full degree of responsibility for his or her actions associated with adulthood not be sentenced to death. Hence it is constitutionally inadequate that a juvenile offender's level of responsibility be taken into account only along with a host of other factors that the court or jury may decide outweigh that want of responsibility.

Immaturity that constitutionally should operate as a bar to a disproportionate death sentence does *not* guarantee that a minor will not be transferred for trial to the adult court system. Rather, the most important considerations in the decision to transfer a juvenile offender are the seriousness of the offense, the extent of prior delinquency, and the response to prior treatment within the juvenile justice system. . . . Psychological, intellectual and other personal characteristics of juvenile offenders receive little attention at the transfer stage, and cannot account for differences between those transferred and those who remain in the juvenile court system. Nor is an adolescent's lack of full culpability isolated at the sentencing stage as a factor that determinatively bars a death sentence. A jury is free to weigh a juvenile offender's youth and lack of full responsibility against the heinousness of the crime and other aggravating factors—and, finding the aggravating factors weightier, to sentence even the most immature of 16- or

17-year olds to be killed. By no stretch of the imagination, then, are the transfer and sentencing decisions designed to isolate those juvenile offenders who are exceptionally mature and responsible, and who thus stand out from their peers as a class.

It is thus unsurprising that individualized consideration at transfer and sentencing has not in fact ensured that juvenile offenders lacking an adult's culpability are not sentenced to die. Quite the contrary. Adolescents on death row appear typically to have a battery of psychological, emotional, and other problems going to their likely capacity for judgment and level of blameworthiness. . . .

Juveniles very generally lack that degree of blameworthiness that is, in my view, a constitutional prerequisite for the imposition of capital punishment under our precedents concerning the Eighth Amendment proportionality principle. The individualized consideration of an offender's youth and culpability at the transfer stage and at sentencing has not operated to ensure that the only offenders under 18 singled out for the ultimate penalty are exceptional individuals whose level of responsibility is more developed than that of their peers. In that circumstance, I believe that the same categorical assumption that juveniles as a class are insufficiently mature to be regarded as fully responsible that we make in so many other areas is appropriately made in determining whether minors may be subjected to the death penalty. . . . I would hold that the Eighth Amendment prohibits the execution of any person for a crime committed below the age of 18.

Penry v. Lynaugh
109 S.Ct. 2934 (1989)

Johnny Penry was charged with capital murder in a Texas state court. He was found competent to stand trial, though a psychologist testified that Penry was mildly to moderately retarded and had the mental age of a six and a half year old. At the guilt-innocence phase of the trial, his attorney raised an insanity defense and presented psychiatric testimony that Penry suffered from a combination of organic brain damage and moderate retardation, which resulted in poor impulse control and an inability to learn from experience. Evidence also indicated that he had been abused as a child. The prosecution introduced evidence that Penry was legally sane, but had an antisocial personality. The jury rejected Penry's insanity defense, and found him guilty of capital murder. Subsequently, at the sentencing stage of the trial, the jury was instructed by the judge to consider all the evidence introduced at the trial when answering the following "special issues" and deciding whether to impose a death sentence: (1) whether Penry's conduct was committed deliberately and with the reasonable expectation that death would result, (2) whether there was a probability that Penry would be a continuing threat to society, and (3) whether the killing was unreasonable in response to any provocation by the victim. When giving the jury these instructions, the trial court also rejected Penry's attorney's request that the judge define the terms in the "special issues" and authorize a grant of mercy based on the existence of mitigating circumstances. The jury answered yes to each of the special issues and, as required under Texas's law, the court sentenced Penry to death.

Penry's attorney unsuccessfully sought *habeas corpus* relief in federal district court and then appealed to the Court of Appeals for the Fifth Circuit, which affirmed the lower court. A final appeal was made to the Supreme Court, which granted *certiorari*.

Justice O'CONNOR delivers the opinion of the Court.

We granted certiorari to resolve two questions. First, was Penry sentenced to death in violation of the Eighth Amendment because the jury was not adequately instructed to take into consideration all of his mitigating evidence and because the terms in the Texas special issues were not defined in such a way that the jury could consider and give effect to his mitigating evidence in answering them? Second, is it cruel and unusual punishment under the Eighth Amendment to execute a mentally retarded person with Penry's reasoning ability? . . .

III

Underlying *Lockett* [*v. Ohio*, 438 U.S. 586 (1978)] and *Eddings* [*v. Oklahoma*, 455 U.S. 104 (1982)], is the principle that punishment should be directly related to the personal culpability of the criminal defendant. If the sentencer is to make an individualized assessment of the appropriateness of the death penalty, "evidence about the defendant's background and character is relevant because of the belief, long held by this society, that defendants who commit criminal acts that are attributable to a disadvantaged background, or to emotional and mental problems, may be less culpable than defendants who have no such excuse." *California v. Brown*, 479 U.S. 538 (1987). Moreover, *Eddings* makes clear that it is not enough simply to allow the defendant to present mitigating evidence to the sentencer. The sentencer must also be able to consider and give effect to that evidence in imposing sentence. *Hitchcock v. Dugger*, 481 U.S. 393 (1987). Only then can we be sure that the sentencer has treated the defendant as a "uniquely individual human bein[g]" and has made a reliable determination that death is the appropriate sentence. *Woodson* [*v. North Carolina*, 428 U.S. 280 (1976)]. "Thus, the sentence imposed at the penalty stage should reflect a reasoned *moral* response to the defendant's background, character, and crime." *California v. Brown.* . . .

Although Penry offered mitigating evidence of his mental retardation and abused childhood as the basis for a sentence of life imprisonment rather than death, the jury that sentenced him was only able to express its views on the appropriate sentence by answering three questions: Did Penry act deliberately when he murdered Pamela Carpenter? Is there a probability that he will be dangerous in the future? Did he act unreasonably in response to provocation? The jury was never instructed that it could consider the evidence offered by Penry as *mitigating* evidence and that it could give mitigating effect to that evidence in imposing sentence.

Like the petitioner in *Franklin v. Lynaugh*, [487 U.S. 164 (1988)], Penry contends that in the absence of his requested jury instructions, the Texas death penalty statute was applied in an unconstitutional manner by precluding the jury from acting upon the particular mitigating evidence he introduced. . . .

In *Franklin*, however, the five concurring and dissenting Justices stressed that "the right to have the sentencer consider and weigh relevant mitigating evidence would be meaningless unless the sentencer was also permitted to give effect to its consideration" in imposing sentence. . . .

Penry argues that his mitigating evidence of mental retardation and childhood abuse has relevance to his moral culpability beyond the scope of the special issues, and that the jury was unable to express its "reasoned moral response" to that evidence in determining whether death was the appropriate punishment. We agree. Thus, we reject the State's contrary argument that the jury was able to consider and give effect to all of Penry's mitigating evidence in answering the special issues without any jury instructions on mitigating evidence.

The first special issue asks whether the defendant acted "deliberately and with the reasonable expectation that the death of the deceased . . . would result." Neither the Texas Legislature nor the Texas Court of Criminal Appeals have defined the term "deliberately," and the jury was not instructed on the term, so we do not know precisely what meaning the jury gave to it. Assuming, however, that the jurors in this case understood "deliberately" to mean something more than that Penry was guilty of "intentionally" committing murder, those jurors may still have been unable to give effect to Penry's mitigating evidence in answering the first special issue. . . .

Penry's mental retardation was relevant to the question whether he was capable of acting "deliberately," but it also "had relevance to [his] moral culpability beyond the scope of the special verdict questio[n]." Personal culpability is not solely a function of a defendant's capacity to act "deliberately." A rational juror at the penalty phase of the trial could have concluded, in light of Penry's confession, that he deliberately killed Pamela Carpenter to escape detection. Because Penry was mentally retarded, however, and thus less able than a normal adult to control his impulses or to evaluate the consequences of his conduct, and because of his history of childhood abuse, that same juror could also conclude that Penry was less morally "culpable than defendants who have no such excuse," but who acted "deliberately" as that term is commonly understood. . . .

In the absence of jury instructions defining "deliberately" in a way that would clearly direct the jury to consider fully Penry's mitigating evidence as it bears on his personal culpability, we cannot be sure that the jury was able to give effect to the mitigating evidence of Penry's mental retardation and history of abuse in answering the first special issue. Without such a special instruction, a juror who believed that Penry's retardation and background diminished his moral culpability and made imposition of the death penalty unwarranted would be unable to give effect to that conclusion if the juror also believed that Penry committed the crime "deliberately." Thus, we cannot be sure that the jury's answer to the first special issue reflected a "reasoned moral response" to Penry's mitigating evidence. . . .

"In contrast to the carefully defined standards that must narrow a sentencer's discretion to *impose* the death sentence, the Constitution limits a State's ability to narrow a sentencer's discretion to consider relevant evidence that might cause it to *decline to impose* the death sentence." *McCleskey v. Kemp,* 481 U.S. 279 (1987). Indeed, it is precisely because the punishment should be directly related to the personal culpability of the defendant that the jury must be allowed to consider and give effect to mitigating evidence relevant to a defendant's character or record or the circumstances of the offense. Rather than creating the risk of an unguided emotional response, full consideration of evidence that mitigates against the death penalty is essential if the jury is to give a " 'reasoned *moral* response to the defendant's background, character, and crime.' " In order to ensure "reliability in the determination that death is the appropriate punishment in a specific case," the jury must be able to consider and give effect to any mitigating evidence relevant to a defendant's background, character, or the circumstances of the crime.

In this case, in the absence of instructions informing the jury that it could consider and give effect to the mitigating evidence of Penry's mental retardation and abused background by declining to impose the death penalty, we conclude that the jury was not provided with a vehicle for expressing its "reasoned moral response" to that evidence in rendering its sentencing decision. Our reasoning in *Lockett* and *Eddings* thus compels a remand for resentencing so that we do not "risk that the death penalty will be imposed in spite of factors which may call for a less severe penalty.". . .

IV

Penry's second claim is that it would be cruel and unusual punishment, prohibited by the Eighth Amendment, to execute a mentally retarded person like himself with the reasoning capacity of a 7 year old. He argues that because of their mental disabilities, mentally retarded people do not possess the level of moral culpability to justify imposing the death sentence. He also argues that there is an emerging national consensus against executing the mentally retarded. The State responds that there is insufficient evidence of a national consensus against executing the retarded, and that existing procedural safeguards adequately protect the interests of mentally retarded persons such as Penry. . . .

[B] The Eighth Amendment categorically prohibits the infliction of cruel and unusual punishments. At a minimum, the Eighth Amendment prohibits punishment considered cruel and unusual at the time the Bill of Rights was adopted. *Ford v. Wainwright* [477 U.S. 399 (1986)]. The prohibitions of the Eighth Amendment are not limited, however, to those practices condemned by the common law in 1789. . . . The prohibition against cruel and unusual punishments also recognizes the "evolving standards of decency that mark the progress of a maturing society." *Trop v. Dulles,* [356 U.S. 86 (1958)]. In discerning those "evolving standards," we have looked to objective evidence of how our society views a particular punishment today. See *Coker v. Georgia,* [433 U.S. 584 (1977)]. The clearest and most reliable objective evidence of contemporary values is the legislation enacted by the country's legislatures. We have also looked to data concerning the actions of sentencing juries. . . .

It was well settled at common law that "idiots," together with "lunatics," were not subject to punishment for criminal acts committed under those incapacities. . . .

There was no one definition of idiocy at common law, but the term "idiot" was generally used to describe persons who had a total lack of reason or understanding, or an inability to distinguish between good and evil. . . .

The common law prohibition against punishing "idiots" and "lunatics" for criminal acts was the precursor of the insanity defense, which today generally includes "mental defect" as well as "mental disease" as part of the legal definition of insanity. . . .

The common law prohibition against punishing "idiots" generally applied, however, to persons of such severe disability that they lacked the reasoning capacity to form criminal intent or to understand the difference between good and evil. In the 19th and early 20th centuries, the term "idiot" was used to describe the most retarded of persons, corresponding to what is called "profound" and "severe" retardation today. . . .

The common law prohibition against punishing "idiots" for their crimes suggests that it may indeed be "cruel and unusual" punishment to execute persons who are profoundly or severely retarded and wholly lacking the capacity to appreciate the wrongfulness of their actions. Because of the protections afforded by the insanity defense today, such a person is not likely to be convicted or face the prospect of punishment. Moreover, under *Ford v. Wainwright,* 477 U.S. 399 (1986), someone who is "unaware of the punishment they are about to suffer and why they are to suffer it" cannot be executed. . . .

Such a case is not before us today. Penry was found competent to stand trial. In other words, he was found to have the ability to consult with his lawyer with a reasonable degree of rational understanding, and was found to have a rational as well as factual understanding of the proceedings against him. In addition, the jury rejected his insanity defense, which reflected their conclusion that Penry knew that his conduct was wrong and was capable of conforming his conduct to the requirements of the law.

Penry argues, however, that there is objective evidence today of an emerging national consensus against execution of the mentally retarded, reflecting the "evolving standards of decency that mark the progress of a maturing society.". . .

Only one State, however, explicitly bans execution of retarded persons who have been found guilty of a capital offense. . . .

In our view, the single state statute prohibiting execution of the mentally retarded, even when added to the 14 States that have rejected capital punishment completely, does not provide sufficient evidence at present of a national consensus.

Penry does not offer any evidence of the general behavior of juries with respect to sentencing mentally retarded defendants, nor of decisions of prosecutors. He points instead to several public opinion surveys that indicate strong public opposition to execution of the retarded. For example, a poll taken in Texas found that 86% of those polled supported the death penalty, but 73% opposed its application to the mentally retarded. . . . The public sentiment expressed in these and other polls and resolutions may ultimately find expression in legislation, which is an objective indicator of contemporary values upon which we can rely. But at present, there is insufficient evidence of a national consensus against executing mentally retarded people convicted of capital offenses for us to conclude that it is categorically prohibited by the Eighth Amendment. . . .

In sum, mental retardation is a factor that may well lessen a defendant's culpability for a capital offense. But we cannot conclude today that the Eighth Amendment precludes the execution of any mentally retarded person of Penry's ability convicted of a capital offense simply by virtue of their mental retardation alone. So long as sentencers can consider and give effect to mitigating evidence of mental retardation in imposing sentence, an individualized determination of whether "death is the appropriate punishment" can be made in each particular case. While a national consensus against execution of the mentally retarded may someday emerge reflecting the "evolving standards of decency that mark the progress of a maturing society," there is insufficient evidence of such a consensus today.

Accordingly, the judgment below is affirmed in part and reversed in part, and the case is remanded for further proceedings consistent with this opinion.

It is so ordered.

Justice BRENNAN, with whom Justice MARSHALL joins, concurring in part and dissenting in part.

I agree that the jury instructions given at sentencing in this case deprived petitioner of his constitutional right to have a jury consider all mitigating evidence that he presented before sentencing him to die. I would also hold, however, that the Eighth Amendment prohibits the execution of offenders who are mentally retarded and who thus lack the full degree of responsibility for their crimes that is a predicate for the constitutional imposition of the death penalty. . . .

Lack of culpability as a result of mental retardation is simply not isolated at the sentencing stage as a factor that determinatively bars a death sentence; for individualized consideration at sentencing is not designed to ensure that mentally retarded offenders are not sentenced to death if they are not culpable to the degree necessary to render execution a proportionate response to their crimes. When Johnny Penry is resentenced, absent a change in Texas law there will be nothing to prevent the jury, acting lawfully, from sentencing him to death once again—even though it finds his culpability significantly reduced by reason of mental retardation. I fail to see how that result is constitutional, in the face of the acknowledged Eighth Amendment requirement of proportionality.

There is a second ground upon which I would conclude that the execution of mentally retarded offenders violates the Eighth Amendment: killing mentally retarded offenders does not measurably further the penal goals of either retribution or deterrence. . . .

Furthermore, killing mentally retarded offenders does not measurably contribute to the goal of deterrence. It is highly unlikely that the exclusion of the mentally retarded from the class of those eligible to be sentenced to death will lessen any deterrent effect the death penalty may have for nonretarded potential offenders, for they, of course, will under present law remain at risk of execution. And the very factors that make it disproportionate and unjust to execute the mentally retarded also make the death penalty of the most minimal deterrent effect so far as retarded potential offenders are concerned. . . .

Because I believe that the Eighth Amendment to the United States Constitution stands in the way of a State killing a mentally retarded person for a crime for which, as a result of her disability, she is not fully culpable, I would reverse the judgment of the Court of Appeals in its entirety.

Justice STEVENS, with whom Justice BLACKMUN joined, concurred in part and dissented in part.

Justice SCALIA, with whom the CHIEF JUSTICE, Justice WHITE, and Justice KENNEDY join, concurring in part and dissenting in part.

I disagree with the holding in Part II-B of the Court's opinion that petitioner's contention, that his sentencing was unconstitutional because the Texas jury was not permitted fully to consider and give effect to the mitigating evidence of his mental retardation and background of abuse, does not seek the application of a "new rule" and is therefore not barred by *Teague* [*v. Lane,* 489 U.S. 288 (1989)]. I also disagree with the disposition of the merits of this contention, in Part III of the Court's opinion. . . .

[O]ur law regarding capital sentencing has sought to strike a balance between complete discretion, which produces "wholly arbitrary and capricious action," *Gregg* [*v. Georgia,* 428 U.S. 153 (1976)], and no discretion at all, which prevents the individuating characteristics of the defendant and of the crime to be taken into account, *Woodson.* . . . That is why, in *Jurek* [*v. North Carolina,* 428 U.S. 280 (1976)], we did not regard the Texas Special Issues as inherently bad, but to the contrary thought them a desirable means of "focus[ing] the jury's objective consideration of the particularized circumstances," or, as the plurality put it in *Franklin,* [*v. Texas,* 428 U.S. 262 (1976)], "channel[ing] jury discretion . . . to achieve a more rational and equitable administration of the death penalty." In providing for juries to consider all mitigating circumstances insofar as they bear upon (1) deliberateness, (2) future dangerousness, and (3) provocation, it seems to me Texas had adopted a rational scheme that meets the two concerns of our Eighth Amendment jurisprudence. The Court today demands that it be replaced, however, with a scheme that simply dumps before the jury all sympathetic factors bearing upon the defendant's background and character, and the circumstances of the offense, so that the jury may decide without further guidance whether he "lacked the moral culpability to be sentenced to death," "did not deserve to be sentenced to death," or "was not sufficiently culpable to deserve the death penalty." The Court seeks to dignify this by calling it a process that calls for a "reasoned moral response,"—but reason has nothing to do with it, the Court having eliminated the structure that required reason. It is an unguided, emotional "moral response" that the Court demands be allowed— an outpouring of personal reaction to all the circumstances of a defendant's life and personality, an unfocused sympathy. Not only have we never before said the Constitution requires this, but the line of cases following *Gregg* sought to eliminate precisely the unpredictability it produces. . . .

The Court cannot seriously believe that rationality and predictability can be achieved, and capriciousness avoided, by " 'narrow-[ing] a sentencer's discretion to *impose* the death sentence,' " but expanding his discretion " 'to *decline to impose* the death sentence.' " The decision whether to impose the death penalty is a unitary one; unguided discretion not to impose is unguided discretion to impose as well. In holding that the jury had to be free to deem Penry's mental retardation and sad childhood relevant for whatever purpose it wished, the Court has come full circle, not only permitting but requiring what *Furman* once condemned. "Freakishly" and "wantonly," *Furman*, have been rebaptized "reasoned moral response." I do not think the Constitution forbids what the Court imposes here, but I am certain it does not require it.

I respectfully dissent.

11

THE RIGHT OF PRIVACY

A RIGHT of privacy is not specifically provided for in the Constitution or the Bill of Rights. Yet both embody the principle of limited government and hence the idea that individuals in some degree enjoy a "right to be let alone." As Justice Louis Brandeis, dissenting from the Court's initial denial of Fourth Amendment protection against wiretaps in *Olmstead v. United States* (1928) (see Chapter 7), observed:

The makers of our Constitution undertook to secure conditions favorable to the pursuit of happiness. They recognized the significance of man's spiritual nature, of his feelings and of his intellect. They knew that only part of the pain, pleasure, and satisfactions of life are to be found in material things. They sought to protect Americans in their beliefs, their thoughts, their emotions and their sensations. They conferred as against the Government, the right to be let alone—the most comprehensive of rights and the right most valued by civilized man.

Neither common law nor constitutional law, however, recognized a right of privacy until the late nineteenth century. In his treatise *The Law of Torts* (1888), Judge Thomas Cooley planted the seed for the development of a right of privacy by noting for the first time a right to be let alone. Two years later, writing in the *Harvard Law Review,* Samuel Warren and Louis Brandeis cultivated the idea by arguing that common law protection for property rights was evolving toward a "recognition of man's spiritual nature."[1] Their analysis of privacy as the right to be let alone sparked the development of a right of privacy in tort law (law dealing with private injuries, such as the public revelations of embarrassing personal facts and the appropriation for commercial purposes of an individual's name or likeness). Between 1890 and 1941, state courts in twelve states recognized a right of privacy; the number increased to eighteen by 1956 and then to more than thirty-one states by 1960.[2]

The Supreme Court initially acknowledged protection for privacy interests under the Fourth and Fifth Amendments in *Boyd v. United States*, 116 U.S. 616 (1886) (see Chapter 7), when holding that those amendments apply "to all invasions on the part of the government and its employees of the sanctity of a man's home and the privacies of life. It is not the breaking of his doors, and the rummaging of his drawers, that constitutes the essence of the offense, but it is the invasion of his indefeasible right of personal security, personal liberty and private property." Subsequently, the Court incorporated an analysis of individuals' "reasonable expectations of privacy" into Fourth Amendment jurisprudence. *Katz v. United States*, 389 U.S. 347 (1967) (see Chapter 7), and *Terry v. Ohio*, 392 U.S. 1 (1968) (see Chapter 7), for example, reaffirmed that "wherever an individual may harbor a reasonable 'expectation of privacy,' . . . he is entitled to be free from unreasonable governmental intrusion," when explaining that "the specific content and incidents of this right [of privacy] must be shaped by the context in which it is asserted."

In a series of other rulings, the Court also acknowledged protection for privacy interests under the Fifth Amendment (see Chapter 8). In addition, by the 1960s the Court had also affirmed First Amendment protection for privacy interests. As early as 1920, Justice Brandeis, dissenting from the Court's upholding of a law forbidding the teaching and advocacy of pacifism in *Gilbert v. Minnesota*, 254 U.S. 352 (1920), contended that the amendment protects "the privacy and freedom of the home. Father and mother may follow the promptings of religious belief, of conscience or of conviction, and teach son or daughter the doctrine of pacifism." When holding that individuals may possess obscenity in their homes in *Stanley v. Georgia* (1969) (see Chapter 5), the Court reaffirmed that individuals have First Amendment–protected privacy interests in their homes.[3] The Court as well formally acknowledged a First Amendment right of associational privacy in *National Association for the Advancement of Colored People v. Alabama* (1958) (see Chapter 5), and extended its protection to a broad range of religious, economic, political and social activities and associations.

Still, the Warren Court's declaration of a constitutional right of privacy in *Griswold v. Connecticut* (1965) (see page 308) provoked a continuing controversy in constitutional politics. The right of privacy, according to Justice William Douglas, may be found in the penumbras, or shadows, of the First, Third, Fourth, Fifth, and Ninth Amendments and applied to the states under the Fourteenth Amendment due process clause. Dissenting justices Hugo Black and Potter Stewart countered that *Griswold*'s majority was turning "sumersaults with history" and becoming a "super-legislature" by creating a right of privacy out-of-whole-constitutional cloth. Notice, however, that at the outset of his opinion in *Griswold* that Justice Douglas disclaims undertaking the kind of substantive due process analysis associated with the discredited *Lochner* era. During that era the Court created and enforced a "liberty of contract" and ultimately precipitated the 1937 constitutional crisis over its invalidation of New Deal and progressive economic legislation (see Chapter 3). Still, Black and Stewart, and a good number of Court watchers, remained unpersuaded.

No less controversial, as Justices Black and Stewart suggest, is the reliance of Justice Douglas and concurring Justice Arthur Goldberg on the Ninth Amendment. That amendment provides that "[t]he enumeration in the Constitution of certain rights shall not be construed to deny or disparage others retained by the people." Despite the criticism of Justices Black and Stewart, though, neither Douglas nor Goldberg contends that the Ninth Amendment provides an independent basis for the Court's articulation of unenumerated rights. Instead, they maintain that the amendment only provides a *rule of construction* for ensuring the "requisite latitude" of guarantees of the Bill of Rights. As Justice Douglas later explained, "The Ninth Amendment obviously does not create federally enforceable rights. . . . But a catalogue of these rights customary, traditional, and time-honored rights, amenities, privileges and immunities. . . . Many of them in my view come within the meaning of the term 'liberty' as used in the Fourteenth Amendment."[4] When defending this interpretation of the Ninth Amendment, justices and commentators frequently turn to the correspondence between James Madison and Thomas Jefferson over the adoption of the Bill of Rights. Both initially feared "that a positive declaration of some of the most essential rights could not be obtained in the requisite latitude" but eventually agreed that a bill of rights would put "into the hands of the judiciary" a "legal check" on the exercise of governmental power (see Chapter 4.) When proposing amendments to the Constitution in the first Congress, Madison thus argued:

It has been objected also against a bill of rights, that, by enumerating particular exceptions to the grant of power, it would disparage those rights which were not placed in that enumeration; and it might follow by implication, that those rights which were not singled out, were intended to be assigned into the hands of the General Government, and were consequently insecure. This is one of the most plausible arguments I have ever heard urged against the admission of a bill of rights into this system; but, I conceive, that it may be guarded against. I have attempted it, as gentlemen may see by turning to the [proposed amendment that eventually became the Ninth Amendment].[5]

Still, critics counter that there is a difference in kind, rather than simply degree, between the Court's recognition of protection for personal privacy as part of the "requisite latitude," for example, given the Fourth Amendment and the creation of a broad constitutional right of privacy.[6]

The debate sparked by the Warren Court's ruling on the right of privacy in *Griswold* erupted into a major political controversy with the Burger Court's 1973 ruling in *Roe v. Wade*, (1973) (see page 1164) striking down a Texas law that sharply limited the availability of abortions. The Burger and Rehnquist Courts limited the application of the right of privacy to areas primarily involving reproductive freedom. While the Rehnquist Court (as indicated in the next section) has been more willing to uphold state laws restricting access to abortions, there has been no indication that the Court would overturn *Griswold*. Both the Burger and Rehnquist Courts, though, have refused to extend the right of privacy to protect other areas of personal autonomy. As a result, a broader range of privacy interests are protected under the specific guarantees of the First, Fourth, and Fifth Amendments than the Court has acknowledged in its application of the right of privacy.

NOTES

1. S. Warren and L. Brandeis, "The Right of Privacy," 4 *Harvard Law Review* 193 (1890).

2. See William Prosser, "Privacy," 48 *California Law Review* 383 (1960).

3. See also *Cohen v. California* (1971) and *Federal Communications v. Pacific Foundation* (1978), both in Chapter 5.

4. *Doe v. Bolton*, 410 U.S. 179 (1973).

5. James Madison, House of Representatives, in *The Debates and Proceedings in the Congress of the United States*, Vol. 1 (Washington, DC: Gales and Seaton, 1834), 455. See also Bennett Patterson, *The Forgotten Ninth Amendment* (Indianapolis: Bobbs-Merrill, 1955).

6. See, for example, Robert Bork, *The Tempting of America* (New York: Free Press, 1990), 99.

SELECTED BIBLIOGRAPHY

Barnett, Randy, ed. *The Rights Retained By The People: The History and Meaning of the Ninth Amendment.* Fairfax, VA: George Mason University Press, 1989.

Flaherty, David. *Privacy in Colonial New England.* Charlottesville: University of Press of Virginia, 1972.

Miller, Arthur R. *The Assault on Privacy.* Ann Arbor: University of Michigan Press, 1971.

O'Brien, David M. *Privacy, Law, and Public Policy.* New York: Praeger, 1979.

Pember, Don. *Privacy and the Press.* Seattle: University of Washington Press, 1972.

Westin, Alan F. *Privacy and Freedom.* New York: Atheneum, 1970.

A. PRIVACY AND REPRODUCTIVE FREEDOM

The Supreme Court initially acknowledged protection under the Fourteenth Amendment due process clause for personal privacy and freedom from governmental intrusions into the area of marriage, reproduction, and child-rearing in the 1920s, during the height of the *Lochner* era (see Chapter 3). In *Meyer v. Nebraska*, 262 U.S. 390 (1923), the Court struck down a state law, passed shortly after World War I and amid opposition to peace negotiations with Germany, forbidding the teaching of German and modern languages other than English in private and public schools. There, Justice James McReynolds observed,

With doubt, [the Fourteenth Amendment guarantee that "No state . . . shall deprive any person of life, liberty or property without due process of law"] denotes not merely freedom from bodily restraint but also the right of the individual to contract, to engage in any of the common occupations of life, to acquire useful knowledge, to marry, establish a home and bring up children, to worship God according to the dictates of his own conscience, and generally to enjoy these privileges long recognized at common law as essential to the orderly pursuit of happiness by free men.

Two years later, *Pierce v. Society of Sisters,* 268 U.S. 510 (1925), overturned an Oregon law requiring primary and secondary school children to attend public rather than private schools on the grounds that it interfered "with the liberty of parents and guardians to direct the upbringing and education of children under their control."

The first major ruling extending protection to reproductive freedom, however, came in *Skinner v. Oklahoma*, 316 U.S. 535 (1942). Indeed, in *Buck v. Bell*, 274 U.S. 200 (1927), the Court upheld a Virginia law, passed in response to the eugenics movement, requiring the sterilization of persons confined to state mental health institutions (see Chapter 3). But in *Skinner* the Court unanimously overturned a state law providing for the sterilization of "habitual criminals." Jack Skinner had been convicted of stealing chickens in 1926, of robbery in 1929, and again in 1934. In 1936, the state attorney general instituted proceedings against Skinner under Oklahoma's 1935 Habitual Criminal Sterilization Act, which authorized the sterilization of individuals who had been convicted two or more times of certain "felonies involving moral turpitude." Skinner challenged the constitutionality of Oklahoma's law as a violation of the Fourteenth Amendment due process and equal protection clauses. When striking down the law for running afoul of the equal protection clause because it permitted the sterilization of those convicted of crimes such as embezzlement but not those convicted of larceny, Justice William Douglas explained,

We are dealing here with legislation which involves one of the basic civil rights of man. Marriage and procreation are fundamental to the very existence and survival of the race. The power to sterilize, if exercised, may have subtle, far-reaching and devastating effects. In evil or reckless hands it can cause races or types which are inimical to the dominant group to wither and disappear. There is no redemption for the individual whom the law touches. Any experiment which the State conducts is to his irreparable injury. He is forever deprived of a basic liberty.

Later, *Loving v. Virginia*, 388 U.S. 1 (1967), struck down a state miscegenation law. And, when holding that states may not deny parents, who failed to meet child-support obligations, the Court "reaffirm[ed] the fundamental character of the right to marry" in *Zablocki v. Redhail*, 434 U.S. 374 (1978).

Beginning in the 1940s, individuals began attacking the constitutionality of laws prohibiting the use of contraceptives, but the Court refused to hear their appeals. (See Inside the Court: Standing and the Connecticut Birth Control Cases on page 109). Finally, in *Griswold v. Connecticut* (1965) (see page 308) the Court struck down Connecticut's statute as a denial of the right of privacy of married couples. Seven years later, over the dissent of Chief Justice Warren Burger, *Eisenstadt v. Baird*, 405 U.S. 438 (1972) overturned a Massachusetts law forbidding the use of contraceptives by unmarried individuals. In his opinion for the Court, Justice William J. Brennan observed that

[w]hatever the rights of the individual to access to contraceptives may be, the rights must be the same for the unmarried and the married alike. If under *Griswold* the distribution of contraceptives to married persons cannot be prohibited, a ban on distribution to unmarried persons would be equally impermissible. It is true that in *Griswold* the right of privacy in question inhered in the marital relationship. Yet the marital couple is not an independent entity with a mind and heart of its own, but an association of two individuals each with a separate intellectual and emotional makeup. If the right of privacy means anything, it is the right of the *individual*, married or single, to be free from unwarranted governmental intrusion into matters so fundamentally affecting a person as the decision whether to bear or beget a child.

A year before *Eisenstadt*, a bare majority of the Burger Court upheld the District of Columbia's law allowing abortions not only to save a woman's life but also to maintain her physical and psychological well-being. But in *United States v. Vuitch*, 402 U.S. 62 (1971), the Court declined to rule on whether a woman's right of privacy included her decision to terminate or carry an unwanted pregnancy to term. Yet the Court could not escape deciding that question. Just one month after deciding *Vuitch*, the Court granted review to abortion cases, *Roe v. Wade* (1973) (see page 1164) and *Doe v. Bolton*, 410 U.S. 179 (1973). A movement to liberalize abortion laws had grown throughout the turbulent 1960s with demands for women's rights. The legal reforms pushed by women's pro-choice advocates were in some respects little more than a return to the legal status of abortions a century earlier. Until the mid-nineteenth century, most states permitted abortions, except after quickening—the first movement of the fetus—and then an abortion was usually considered only a minor offense. After the Civil War, antiabortionists persuaded states to toughen their laws, and by 1910 every state, except Kentucky, had made abortion a felony. But by the late 1960s, fourteen states had liberalized laws to permit abortions when the woman's health was in danger, when there was a likelihood of fetal abnormality, and when the woman was a victim of rape or incest. Four states—Alaska, Hawaii, New York, and Washington—had gone so far as to repeal all criminal penalities for abortions performed in early pregnancy.

When handing down *Roe v. Wade* the Court elevated the issue of abortion to the national political agenda and sparked a larger political struggle in the country. States could no longer categorically proscribe abortions or make them unnecessarily difficult to obtain. The promotion of maternal care and the preservation of the life of a fetus were not sufficiently "compelling state interests" to justify restrictive abortion laws. During roughly the first trimester (three months) of a pregnancy, the decision on abortion is that of a woman and her doctor. During the second, the Court ruled, states may regulate abortions, but only in ways reasonably related to its interest in safeguarding the health of women. In the third trimester, states' interests in preserving the life of the unborn become compelling, and they may limit, even ban, abortions, except when necessary to save a woman's life. *Roe* was thus controversial in not only extending the right of privacy in this area, but in Justice Harry Blackmun's trimester approach to balancing the interests of women seeking abortions and those of the states.

In the years after *Roe*, thirty-four states passed new abortion laws. Some were in conformity with the Court's ruling—requiring, for example, that abortions be performed by licensed physicians—but others sought to limit the impact of *Roe*. States tried to restrict the availability of abortions in several ways: by requiring the informed consent of a husband or that of parents for a minor's abortion, by forbiding the advertising of abortion clinics, and by withholding state funds for abortions not medically necessary. In addition, ten states passed laws or resolutions pledging to ban or severely restrict abortions, and fifteen others left their pre-*Roe* laws on the books, in anticipation of *Roe*'s being eventually overturned.

Initially, the Burger Court basically stood its ground, striking down most state and local attempts to limit the impact of *Roe*. However, in three 1977 decisions the Court (dividing six to three) upheld some state restrictions on the availability of abortions. In *Beal v. Doe*, 432 U.S. 438 (1977), and *Maher v. Roe* (1977) (see page 1180), a majority of the Court approved restrictions on the public funding of nontherapeutic abortions. In *Poelker v. Doe*, 432 U.S. 59 (1977), the Court upheld a city's policy of refusing nontherapeutic abortions in public hospitals. As the Court's composition further changed in the 1980s, pressure mounted with speculation that *Roe* might be further restricted, if not reversed.

Opposition came not only from the states, but also from Congress and the president. Congress failed to pass a constitutional amendment overturning *Roe*, but succeeded in limiting the reach of the Court's ruling in a number of ways. In the decade and a half following *Roe*, Congress enacted over 30 laws restricting the availability of abortions. Among these statutes, Congress barred the use of funds for programs in which abortion is included as a method of family planning; barred government officials from ordering recipients of federal funds to perform abortions; barred lawyers working in federally funded legal aid programs from giving assistance to those seeking "nontherapeutic" abortions; provided that employees are not required to pay health insurance benefits for abortions, except to save a woman's life; prohibited the use of federal employee health benefits to pay for abortions, except when a woman's life is imperiled; prohibited the use of foreign aid funds for abortions; and prohibited federal prisons from paying for pregnant inmates' abortions. In *Harris v. McRae*, 448 U.S. 297 (1980), the Court split five to four when upholding the so-called Hyde Amendment (named after its sponsor, Republican Representative Henry Hyde of Illinois), which forbids under the Medicaid program federal funding of nontherapeutic abortions. Again, voting five to four in *Bowen v. Kendrick*, 487 U.S. 589 (1988), the Court upheld the Adolescent Family Life Act, which prohibits federal funding of organizations involved with abortions, while allowing the funding of religious groups advocating self-discipline as a form of birth control.

By the 1980s, abortion was an issue in presidential politics as well. The 1980, 1984 and 1988 Republican platforms, endorsed by President Reagan, supported a constitutional amendment "to restore protection of the right to life for unborn children." During the 1988 presidential election, Reagan's successor, Vice-President George Bush, called for the criminalization of abortion and penalties for doctors who perform them. It was, though, during Reagan's era that forces opposed to *Roe* gathered momentum and received legitimacy from the president.

The strategy of the Reagan administration was twofold: appoint to the federal bench only those opposed to abortion and initiate litigation that might undercut and ultimately lead to overturning *Roe*. But even after the retirements of Justices William O. Douglas and Potter Stewart—and the appointments of John Paul Stevens in 1975 and Sandra Day O'Connor in 1981—the Court continued to reaffirm its basic ruling in *Roe*. In *City of Akron v. Akron Center for Reproductive Health*, 462 U.S. 416 (1983), for example, the Court struck down several restrictions imposed on women seeking abortions, including requirements that they sign informed consent forms and wait at least twenty-four hours afterward before having an abortion, along with requiring doctors to perform abortions after the first trimester in a hospital and dispose of fetal remains "in a humane and sanitary way."

In *City of Akron*, Reagan's solicitor general, Rex Lee, asked the justices to reconsider *Roe* but stopped short of urging its reversal. Still, only Justice O'Connor, joined by Justices Rehnquist and White (who had dissented in *Roe*), appeared sympathetic in her dissenting opinion suggesting a willingness to reconsider, if not overturn, *Roe*. Justice Lewis F. Powell, however, countered that the majority would not yield to pressure from within or from outside the Court. *Roe* "was considered with special care" and "joined by the Chief Justice and six other Justices," Powell emphasized, adding that "the Court repeatedly and consistently has accepted and applied the basic principle that a woman has a fundamental right to make the highly personal choice whether or not to terminate her pregnancy." Justice Powell, then, stressed that,

[this and other cases] come to us after we held in *Roe v. Wade* . . . that the right of privacy, grounded in the concept of personal liberty guaranteed by the Constitution, encompasses a woman's right to decide whether to terminate her pregnancy. Legislative responses to the Court's decision have required us on several occasions, and again today, to define the limits of a State's authority to regulate the performance of abortions. And arguments continue to be made, in these cases as well, that we erred in interpreting the Constitution. Nonetheless, the doctrine of *stare decisis*, while perhaps never entirely persuasive on a constitutional question, is a doctrine that demands respect in a society governed by the rule of law. We respect it today, and reaffirm *Roe v. Wade*.

But in her dissenting opinion in *City of Akron*, Justice O'Connor strongly attacked the majority's opinion and the constitutional theory and trimester-approach of *Roe*, explaining that,

[t]he trimester or "three-stage" approach adopted by the Court in *Roe*, and, in a modified form, employed by the Court to analyze the state regulations in these cases, cannot be supported as a legitimate or useful framework for accommodating the woman's right and the State's interests. The decision of the Court today graphically illustrates why the trimester approach is a completely unworkable method of accommodating the conflicting personal rights and compelling state interests that are involved in the abortion context.

As the Court indicates today, the State's compelling interest in maternal health changes as medical technology changes, and any health regulation must not "depart from accepted medical practice.". . . In applying this standard, the Court holds that "the safety of second-trimester abortions has increased dramatically" since 1973, when *Roe* was decided. . . . Although a regulation such as one requiring that all second-trimester abortions be performed in hospitals "had strong support" in 1973 "as a reasonable health regulation,". . . this regulation can no longer stand because, according to the Court's diligent research into medical and scientific literature, the dilation and evacuation procedure (D & E), used in 1973 only for first-trimester abortions, "is now widely and successfully used for second trimester abortions." Further, the medical literature relied on by the Court indicates that the D & E procedure may be performed in an appropriate non-hospital setting for "at least . . . the early weeks of the second trimester. . . ." The Court then chooses the period of 16 weeks of gestation as that point at which D

& E procedures may be performed safely in a non-hospital setting, and thereby invalidates the Akron hospitalization regulation.

It is not difficult to see that despite the Court's purported adherence to the trimester approach adopted in *Roe,* the lines drawn in that decision have now been "blurred" because of what the Court accepts as technological advancements in the safety of abortion procedure. . . .

Just as improvement in medical technology inevitably will move *forward* the point at which the State may regulate for reasons of maternal health, different technological improvements will move *backwards* the point of viability at which the State may proscribe abortions except when necessary to preserve the life and health of the mother. . . .

The *Roe* framework, then, is clearly on a collision course with itself. As the medical risks of various abortion procedures decrease, the point at which the State may regulate for reasons of maternal health is moved further forward to actual childbirth. As medical science becomes better able to provide for the separate existence of the fetus, the point of viability is moved further back toward conception. . . . The *Roe* framework is inherently tied to the state of medical technology that exists whenever particular litigation ensues. Although legislatures are better suited to make necessary factual judgments in this area, the Court's framework forces legislatures, as a matter of constitutional law, to speculate about what constitutes "accepted medical practice" at any given time. Without the necessary expertise or ability, courts must then pretend to act as science review boards and examine those legislative judgments. . . .

The fallacy inherent in the *Roe* framework is apparent: just because the State has a compelling interest in ensuring maternal safety once an abortion may be more dangerous in childbirth, it simply does not follow that the State has *no* interest before that point that justifies state regulation to ensure that first-trimester abortions are performed as safely as possible.

The state interest in potential human life is likewise extant throughout pregnancy. In *Roe,* the Court held that although the State had an important and legitimate interest in protecting potential life, that interest could not become compelling until the point at which the fetus was viable. The difficulty with this analysis is clear: *potential* life is no less potential in the first weeks of pregnancy than it is at viability or afterward. At any stage in pregnancy, there is the *potential* for human life. Although the Court refused to "resolve the difficult question of when life begins," . . . the Court chose the point of viability—when the fetus is *capable* of life independent of its mother—to permit the complete proscription of abortion. The choice of viability as the point at which the state interest in *potential* life becomes compelling is not less arbitrary than choosing any point before viability or any point afterward. Accordingly, I believe that the State's interest in protecting potential human life exists throughout the pregnancy. . . .

Justice O'Connor also proposed that the Court abandon *Roe*'s trimester-approach and adopt the test of whether state regulations place an "undue burden" on women seeking abortions:

"*Roe* did not declare an unqualified 'constitutional right to an abortion.' . . . Rather, the right protects the woman from unduly burdensome interference with her freedom to decide whether to terminate her pregnancy." *Maher* . . .

The requirement that state interference "infringe substantially" or "heavily burden" a right before heightened scrutiny is applied is not novel in our fundamental rights jurisprudence or restricted to the abortion context. . . . If the impact of the regulation does not rise to the level appropriate for our strict scrutiny, then our inquiry is limited to whether the state law bears "some rational relationship to legitimate state purposes.". . .

The "undue burden" required in the abortion cases represents the required threshold inquiry that must be conducted before this Court can require a State to justify its legislative actions under the exacting "compelling state interest" standard. . . .

The "unduly burdensome" standard is particularly appropriate in the abortion context because of the *nature* and *scope* of the right that is involved. The privacy right involved in the abortion context "cannot be said to be absolute." *Roe* . . . Rather, the *Roe* right is intended to protect against state action "drastically limiting the availability and safety of the desired service,". . . or against "official interference" and "coercive restraint" imposed on the abortion decision. . . . That a state regulation may "inhibit" abortions to some degree does not require that we find that the regulation is invalid. . . .

In two companion cases handed down along with *City of Akron*, the justices split five to four (with Justice Powell casting the crucial fifth vote) in upholding a Missouri law requiring pathology reports for all abortions, the presence of a second physician during abortions performed after viability, and the parental consent for minors seeking abortions. They also sustained the constitutionality of a Virginia statute mandating that second-trimester abortions be performed in licensed outpatient clinics in *Planned Parenthood Association of Kansas City Missouri v. Ashcroft*, 462 U.S. 476 (1983), and *Simopoulos v. Virginia*, 462 U.S. 506 (1983).

Three years after *City of Akron*, the Reagan administration renewed its attack on *Roe*. This time, Reagan's second solicitor general, Harvard Law School professor Charles Fried, dared to do what his predecessor refused: He questioned the Court's wisdom and argued that *Roe* be overturned. In support of Pennsylvania's Governor Richard Thornburgh's appeal of a circuit court ruling, striking down a state law limiting the availability of abortions, Fried filed an extraordinary *amicus curiae* ("friend of the court") brief. There, he boldly proclaimed "the textual, doctrinal and historical basis for *Roe v. Wade* is so far flawed and . . . a source of such instability in the law that this Court should reconsider that decision and on reconsideration abandon it."

But a majority of the Court was still in no mood to reconsider *Roe* and again rebuffed the Reagan administration when handing down *Thornburgh v. American College of Obstetricians*, 476 U.S. 747 (1986). A majority of the Court, moreover, appeared impatient with the administration's persistence in trying to undo *Roe*. When announcing the decision from the bench, Blackmun exclaimed, "We reaffirm *once again* the general principles of *Roe*." However, Chief Justice Burger broke with *Roe*'s supporters in *Thornburgh*, joining Justices O'Connor, Rehnquist, and White in dissent, and indicated that *Roe* should be "reexamined."

The five-to-four split in *Thornburgh* further escalated speculation about how another Reagan appointee might affect the Court and *Roe*. As the Court's composition changed in the 1980s support for *Roe* among the justices appeared to decline from seven to two, to six to three, and to five to four. Then within a week of the ruling on *Thornburgh*, Chief Justice Burger announced that he would step down from the Court. Reagan immediately responded by shrewdly elevating Justice Rehnquist, one of *Roe*'s sharpest critics, to the chief justiceship and naming Antonin Scalia to his seat on the bench.

As long as Justice Powell remained on the Court, he held the pivotal vote for upholding *Roe*. When he announced his retirement in June 1987, Reagan's nomination of Judge Robert H. Bork—one of *Roe*'s harshest critics—set off a political firestorm. After a bitter Senate battle, Judge Bork's nomination was rejected by the widest margin (fifty-eight to forty-two) of any Supreme Court nominee. Reagan's second nominee, Judge Douglas Ginsburg, was forced to withdraw from consideration, but his third nominee, Judge Anthony Kennedy, won easy Senate confirmation.

In the final days of the Reagan administration, the Court thus seemed poised to reconsider, and possibly overturn, *Roe*. Indeed, a few weeks before the Senate confirmed Justice Kennedy, the justices split four to four, thereby affirming by an equally divided Court a lower court's ruling, striking down a law requiring parental notification for teenagers seeking abortions. *Hartigan v. Zbaraz*, 484 U.S. 171 (1987). Subsequently, during the summer of 1988 assistant attorney general William Bradford Reynolds and others in Reagan's Department of Justice talked Missouri's attorney general William Webster into seizing an opportunity afforded by appealing another appellate court's invalidation of that state's restrictions on abortions. Webster's legal strategy was to defend Missouri's law as "nothing more than regulat[ing] abortions within the parameters allowed by

Roe v. Wade." But he was persuaded to repeat word for word in his brief filed before the Court the language Fried used in his *Thornburgh* brief demanding *Roe's* reversal. In *Webster v. Reproductive Health Services* (1989) (see page 1189) the Rehnquist Court was bitterly divided, yet clearly indicated that there was a majority inclined to cut back sharply, if not completely to overturn, *Roe* and to return the battle over abortion to the states. The following term, in 1990 the Court upheld two state laws prohibiting teenage girls from obtaining abortions without first notifying their parents (see the following table).

SELECTED BIBLIOGRAPHY

Butler, J. D., and Walbert, David, eds. *Abortion, Medicine, and the Law.* New York: Facts on File, 1986.

Faux, Marian. *Roe v. Wade.* New York: Macmillian, 1988.

Guttmacher, Alan, ed. *The Case for Legalized Abortion Now.* Berkeley, CA: Diablo, 1967.

Mohr, James. *Abortion in America.* New York: Oxford University Press, 1978.

Noonam, John. *The Morality of Abortion.* Cambridge, MA: Harvard University Press, 1970.

Rubin, Eva. *Abortion, Politics, and the Courts.* Westport, CT: Greenwood, 1982.

Tribe, Laurence. *Abortion: The Clash of Absolutes.* New York: W.W. Norton, 1990.

Justice William O. Douglas. Justice Douglas was the author of the Court's controversial ruling in *Griswold v. Connecticut* (1965), proclaiming a constitutional right of privacy. *Photo Division, CBS Television*

Griswold v. Connecticut
381 U.S. 479 (1965)

See Chapter 4, where *Griswold v. Connecticut* is reprinted in part. See also Inside the Court: Standing and the Connecticut Birth Control Cases (on page 109) and Inside the Court: The Theory and Drafting of Justice Douglas's Opinion in *Griswold v. Connecticut* (on page 308).

INSIDE THE COURT
The Oral Argument and Decision-Making Process in *Roe v. Wade*

On December 13, 1971, the Court heard oral arguments in the case. Sarah Weddington began her argument by pointing out that women like Jane Roe, who were poor and for whom abortions were not necessary to saving their lives, had no real choice. They faced unwanted childbirth or attempting medically unsafe self-abortions that could result in their death. But Weddington's argument was diverted when Justice Byron White observed that "so far on the merits, you've told us about the important impact of the law, and you made a very eloquent policy argument against it." But he added, "we cannot here be involved simply with matters of policy, as you know." White wanted to know what was the constitutional basis for a woman's right to have an abortion and for the Court's overturning the Texas law. Appropriate arguments could be drawn from the Ninth Amendment's guarantee of rights retained by the people, Weddington responded, or the protection for rights of persons to life, liberty, and the pursuit of happiness under the Fourteenth Amendment. If *liberty* is meaningful, she concluded, "that liberty to these women would mean liberty from being forced to continue the unwanted pregnancy."

"It's an old joke, but when a man argues against two beautiful ladies like this, they are going to have the last word." There was no laughter in the courtroom, however, at that opening remark by Jay Floyd, the assistant attorney general of Texas who was before the Court to defend the abortion law. This controversy is not one for the courts, he argued, and arguments about freedom of choice are misleading. Floyd pressed the point:

> There are situations in which, of course as the Court knows, no remedy is provided. Now I think she makes her choice prior to the time she becomes pregnant. That is the time of the choice. It's like, more or less, the first three or four years of our life we don't remember anything. But, once a child is born, a woman no longer has a choice, and I think pregnancy then terminates that choice. That's when.

However, one of the justices impatiently shot back, "Maybe she makes her choice when she decides to live in Texas." Laughter almost drowned out Floyd's feeble reply, "There is no restriction on moving."

"What is Texas' interest? What is Texas' interest in the statute?" demanded Justice Marshall. The state has "recognized the humanness of the embryo, or the fetus," Floyd explained, and has "a compelling interest because of the protection of fetal life." Yet, interjected Justice Potter Stewart, "Texas does not attempt to punish a woman who herself performs an abortion on herself." "That is correct," Floyd continued,

> And the matter has been brought to my attention: Why not punish for murder, since you are destroying what you—or what has been said to be a human being? I don't know, except that I will say this. As medical science progresses, maybe the law will progress along with it. Maybe at one time it could be possible, I suppose, statutes could be passed. Whether or not that would be constitutional or not, I don't know.

But, Stewart countered, "we're dealing with the statute as it is. There's no state, is there, that equates abortion with murder? Or is there?" There was none, Floyd admitted and then hastened to emphasize that although courts had not recognized the unborn as having legal rights, states have a legitimate interest in protecting the unborn. As to a woman's choice on abortion, Floyd reiterated, "we feel that this choice is left up to the woman prior to the time she becomes pregnant. This is the time of choice."

When the justices later discussed *Roe* in private conference, Burger noted that the case had not been argued very well. He also thought because the case presented such a "sensitive issue," it should be set for reargument so that recently appointed Justices Lewis Powell and William Rehnquist could participate and a full Court reach a decision. As chief justice, he led the discussion observing that the Texas law was "certainly arcane," although not unconstitutional. He was inclined but not yet committed to the view that the law should fall for vagueness. Senior Associate Justice Douglas spoke next. He disagreed and had no doubt that the statute was unconstitutional. For Douglas, the Texas law was not merely vague but impinged on a woman's right of privacy. Brennan and Stewart agreed, as later did Marshall. White came out on the other side. He could not go along with the argument that women have a constitutional right of privacy, giving them a choice on abortion. A right of privacy is not specifically mentioned in the Constitution. Blackmun, then the newest member of the Court, spoke last: "Don't think there's an absolute right to do what you will with [your] body." But this statute was poorly drawn, Blackmun observed. It's too restrictive—it "doesn't go as far as it should and impinges too far on [Roe's] Ninth Amendment rights." Blackmun appeared in the middle, but inclined toward the position of Douglas, Brennan, Stewart, and Marshall.

After conference the chief justice, if he is in the majority, by tradition assigns a justice to write the opinion justifying the Court's decision. On the abortion cases Burger appeared to be in the minority, but he nonetheless gave the assignment to Blackmun. When Douglas complained, Burger responded that the issues were so complex and the conference discussion so diverse "that there were, literally, not enough columns to mark up an accurate reflection of the voting" in his docket book. He "therefore marked down no vote and said this was a case that would have to stand or fall on the writing, when it was done."

Assigned to write the Court's opinion in late December 1971, Blackmun did not circulate a first draft until May 18, 1972. Although striking down Texas's law, his draft opinion did so on Burger's view that the law was vague rather than on the majority's view that it violated a woman's constitutional right of privacy. Douglas and Brennan wanted to know why the opinion failed to address the core issue, "which would make reaching the vagueness issue unnecessary." Blackmun claimed that he was "flexible as to results." A freshman in his second year on the Court and assigned to write a very difficult opinion, Blackmun found himself in the middle of the cross-pressures of a growing dispute. Blackmun was himself psychologically and intellectually torn by the dispute. "Although it would prove costly to [him] personally, in the light of energy and hours expended," Blackmun concluded he would move for reargument. He explained that "on an issue so sensitive and so emotional as this one, the country deserves the conclusion of a nine-man, not a seven-man court, whatever the ultimate decision may be." Then Justices Powell and Rehnquist (who had not participated in the case) voted for a rehearing. That made a majority of five for carrying *Roe* over to the next term.

On October 11, 1972, the Court heard rearguments. For a second time Weddington stood before the high bench to ask that it rule that women have a right to choose to continue or terminate a pregnancy. But her arguments were repeatedly interrupted by questions from the bench about the rights of the unborn. Justice White put it bluntly, "would you lose your case if the fetus was a person?" That would require a balancing of interests, Weddington replied, but that was not at issue here, because it had not been asserted that a fetus has any constitutional rights. The issue was simply a conflict between the constitutional rights of women and the statutory interests of the state. The state would have to establish that the fetus is a "person" under the Fourteenth Amendment or some other part of the Constitution, before it would have a compelling interest in prohibiting abortions and require the Court to strike a balance with the constitutional rights of a woman.

"That's what's involved in this case? Weighing one life against another?" White again asserted toward the end of Weddington's oral argument time. No, she insisted in her concluding exchange with the justices:

Stewart: Well, if—if it were established that an unborn fetus is a person, with the protection of the Fourteenth Amendment, you would have almost an impossible case here, would you not?

Weddington: I would have a very difficult case.

Stewart: I'm sure you would. So, if you had the same kind of thing, you'd have to say that this would be the equivalent—after the child was born, if the mother thought it bothered her health any having the child around, she could have it killed. Isn't that correct.

Weddington: That's correct. That—

Burger: Could Texas constitutionally, in your view, declare that—by statute, that the fetus is a person, for all constitutional purposes, after the third month of gestation?

Weddington: I do not believe that the State legislature can determine the meaning of the Federal Constitution. It is up to this Court to make that determination.

Chief Justice Burger then called Robert C. Flowers, who had replaced Floyd and as assistant attorney general represented Texas before the Court. From the outset, Flowers faced a steady barrage of questions about whether a fetus is a "person" under the Constitution. He was driven to concede that no case had recognized the fetus as a person and that the Fourteenth Amendment extends protection only to those born or naturalized in the United States. At the prodding of White, he was forced to agree that the case would be lost if the fetus is not recognized as a person. Yet, Flowers continued to insist that the unborn are entitled to constitutional protection. In response to questions from Justices Marshall and Rehnquist, however, he could not supply any medical evidence that a fetus is a person at the time of inception. Finally, Flowers confessed that he knew of no way "that any court or any legislature or any doctor anywhere can say that here is the dividing line. Here is not a life; and here is a life, after conception."

Whether a fetus is a person, Flowers argued, is an issue that should be left to the state legislatures. But that argument underscored the Court's dilemma and aroused Stewart: "Well, if you're right that an unborn fetus is a person, then you can't leave it to the legislature to play fast and loose dealing with that person. In other words, if you're correct, in your basic submission that an unborn fetus is a person, then abortion laws such as that which New York has are grossly unconstitutional, isn't it?" Liberal abortion laws, Flowers urged, allow "the killing of people."

Weddington had a few minutes to give a final rebuttal, but most of her time was consumed by questions from the bench. "We are not here to advocate abortion." Weddington concluded, stressing that

> [w]e do not ask this Court to rule that abortion is good, or desirable in any particular situation. We are here to advocate that the decision as to whether or not a particular woman will continue to carry or will terminate a pregnancy is a decision that should be made by that individual; that, in fact, she has a constitutional right to make that decision for herself; and that the State has shown no interest in interfering with that decision.

About a month after the Court heard the rearguments, Blackmun had finished a new draft of his opinion for *Roe.* "It has been an interesting assignment," he observed when circulating the draft that eventually became the Court's final opinion. Justices Douglas, Brennan, Marshall, and Stewart immediately agreed to join. Shortly thereafter, Powell also signed on, commending Blackmun for his "exceptional scholarship." By mid-January Burger had also agreed, although he would add a short concurring opinion, saying that he did not support "abortion on demand." Justices Rehnquist and White were the only dissenters.

Source: Transcripts of oral arguments and materials in the Papers of Justice William J. Brennan, Jr., Library of Congress.

Roe v. Wade
410 U.S. 113, 93 S.Ct. 705 (1973)

In 1969, a high-school dropout, who was divorced and had a five-year-old daughter and little money, Norma McCorvey, unsuccessfully sought an abortion in Texas. Texas, like most other states at the time, prohibited abortions unless necessary to save a woman's life. McCorvey carried her pregnancy and gave up the child she bore for adoption. The lawyer who arranged for the adoption also introduced McCorvey to two recent graduates of the University of Texas Law School, Sarah Weddington and Linda Coffee. The three women decided to challenge the constitutionality of Texas's law and McCorvey became "Jane Roe" in a test case against Henry Wade, the criminal district attorney for Dallas County, Texas. Wade appealed to the Supreme Court the decision of a three-judge federal district court, striking down Texas's law. The Court granted review and heard oral arguments in 1971 and then carried the case over for rearguments in 1972. Justice Blackmun finally handed down the Court's opinion on January 23, 1973.

Justice BLACKMUN delivers the opinion of the Court.

This Texas federal appeal . . . present[s] constitutional challenges to state criminal abortion legislation. The Texas statutes under attack here are typical of those that have been in effect in many States for approximately a century. . . .

We forthwith acknowledge our awareness of the sensitive and emotional nature of the abortion controversy, of the vigorous opposing views, even among physicians, and of the deep and seemingly absolute convictions that the subject inspires. . . .

Our task, of course, is to resolve the issue by constitutional measurement, free of emotion and of predilection. We seek earnestly to do this, and, because we do, we have inquired into, and in this opinion place some emphasis upon, medical and medical-legal history and what that history reveals about man's attitudes toward the abortion procedure over the centuries. . . .

The Texas statutes that concern us here make it a crime to "procure an abortion," as therein defined, or to attempt one, except with respect to "an abortion procured or attempted by medical advice for the purpose of saving the life of the mother." Similar statutes are in existence in a majority of the States. . . .

The principal thrust of appellant's attack on the Texas statutes is that they improperly invade a right, said to be possessed by the pregnant woman, to choose to terminate her pregnancy. Appellant would discover this right in the concept of personal "liberty" embodied in the Fourteenth Amendment's Due Process Clause; or in personal, marital, familial, and sexual privacy said to be protected by the Bill of Rights or its penumbras, see Griswold v. Connecticut; or among those rights reserved to the people by the Ninth Amendment, *Griswold v. Connecticut,* [381 U.S. 479 (1965)] (GOLDBERG, J., concurring). Before addressing this claim, we feel it desirable briefly to survey, in several aspects, the history of abortion, for such insight as that history may afford us, and then to examine the state purposes and interests behind the criminal abortion laws.

It perhaps is not generally appreciated that the restrictive criminal abortion laws in effect in a majority of States to day are of relatively recent vintage. Those laws, generally proscribing abortion or its attempt at any time during pregnancy except when necessary to preserve the pregnant woman's life, are not of ancient or even of common-law origin. Instead, they derive from statutory changes effected, for the most part, in the latter half of the 19th century. . . .

[A]bortion was practiced in Greek times as well as in the Roman Era. . . . Greek and Roman Law afforded little protection to the unborn. . . .

It is undisputed that at common law, abortion performed *before* "quickening"—the first recognizable movement of the fetus *in utero,* appearing usually from the 16th to the 18th week of pregnancy—was not an indictable offense. . . . In this country, the law in effect in all but a few States until mid-19th century was the pre-existing English common law. Connecticut, the first State to enact abortion legislation, adopted in 1821 that part of Lord Ellenborough's Act that related to a woman "quick with child." The death penalty was not imposed. Abortion before quickening was made a crime in that State only in 1860. In 1828, New York enacted legislation that, in two respects, was to serve as a model for early anti-abortion statutes. First, while barring destruction of an unquickened fetus as well as a quick fetus, it made the former only a misdemeanor, but the latter second-degree manslaughter. Second, it incorporated a concept of therapeutic abortion by providing that an abortion was excused if it "shall have been necessary to preserve the life of such mother, or shall have been advised by two physicians to be necessary for such purpose." By 1840, when Texas had received the common law, only eight American States had statutes dealing with abortion. It was not until after the War Between the States that legislation began generally to replace the common law. Most of these initial statutes dealt severely with abortion after quickening but were lenient with it before quickening. . . .

Gradually, in the middle and late 19th century the quickening distinction disappeared from the statutory law of most States and the degree of the offense and the penalties were increased. By the end of the 1950's a large majority of the jurisdictions banned abortion, however and whenever performed, unless done to save or preserve the life of the mother. . . .

It is thus apparent that at common law, at the time of the adoption of our Constitution, and throughout the major portion of the 19th century, abortion was viewed with less disfavor than under most American statutes currently in effect. Phrasing it another way, a woman enjoyed a substantially broader right to terminate a pregnancy than she does in most States today. . . .

Three reasons have been advanced to explain historically the enactment of criminal abortion laws in the 19th century and to justify their continued existence.

It has been argued occasionally that these laws were the product of a Victorian social concern to discourage illicit sexual conduct. Texas, however, does not advance this justification in the present case. . . .

A second reason is concerned with abortion as a medical procedure. When most criminal abortion laws were first enacted, the procedure was a hazardous one for the woman. . . . Thus, it has been argued that a State's real concern in enacting a criminal abortion law was to protect the pregnant woman, that is, to restrain her from submitting to a procedure that placed her life in serious jeopardy.

Modern medical techniques have altered this situation. Appellants and various *amici* refer to medical data indicating that abortion in early pregnancy, that is, prior to the end of the first trimester, although not without its risk, is now relatively safe. Mortality rates for women undergoing early abortions, where the procedure is legal, appear to be as low as or lower than the rates for normal childbirth. Consequently, any interest of the State in protecting the woman from an inherently hazardous procedure, except when it would be equally dangerous for her to forgo it, has largely disappeared. Of course, important state interests in the areas of health and medical standards do remain. The State has a legitimate interest in seeing to it that abortion, like any other medical procedure, is performed under circumstances that insure maximum safety for the patient. This interest obviously extends at least to the performing physician and his staff, to the facilities involved, to the availability of after-care, and to adequate provision for any complication or emergency that might arise. The prevalence of high mortality rates at illegal "abortion mills" strengthens, rather than weakens, the State's interest in regulating the conditions under which abortions are performed. Moreover, the risk to the woman increases as her pregnancy continues. Thus, the State retains a definite interest in protecting the woman's own health and safety when an abortion is proposed at a late stage of pregnancy.

The third reason is the State's interest—some phrase it in terms of duty—in protecting prenatal life. Some of the argument for this justification rests on the theory that a new human life is present from the moment of conception. The State's interest and general obligation to protect life then extends, it is argued, to prenatal life. Only when the life of the pregnant mother herself is at stake, balanced against the life she carries within her, should the interest of the embryo or fetus not prevail. Logically, of course, a legitimate state interest in this area need not stand or fall on acceptance of the belief that life begins at conception or at some other point prior to live birth. In assessing the State's interest, recognition may be given to the less rigid claim that as long as at least *potential* life is involved, the State may assert interests beyond the protection of the pregnant woman alone. . . .

The Constitution does not explicitly mention any right of privacy. In a line of decisions, however, going back perhaps as far as *Union Pacific R. Co. v. Botsford,* 141 U.S. 250 (1891), the Court has recognized that a right of personal privacy, or a guarantee of certain areas or zones of privacy, does exist under the Constitution. In varying contexts, the Court or individual Justices have, indeed, found at least the roots of that right in the First Amendment, *Stanley v. Georgia,* 394 U.S. 557 (1969); in the Fourth and Fifth Amendments, *Terry v. Ohio,* 392 U.S. 1 (1968), *Katz v. United States,* 389 U.S. 347 (1967); *Boyd v. United States,* 116 U.S. 616 (1886), see *Olmstead v. United States,* 277 U.S. 438 (1928) (BRANDEIS, J., dissenting); in the penumbras of the Bill of Rights, *Griswold v. Connecticut;* in the Ninth Amendment, *id.* (GOLDBERG, J., concurring); or in the concept of liberty guaranteed by the first section of the Fourteenth Amendment, see *Meyer v. Nebraska,* 262 U.S. 390 (1923). These decisions make it clear that only personal rights that can be deemed "fundamental" or "implicit in the concept of ordered liberty," *Palko v. Connecticut,* [302 U.S. 319] (1937), are included in this guarantee of personal privacy. They also make it clear that the right has some extension to activities relating to marriage, *Loving v. Virginia,* 388 U.S. 1 (1967); procreation, *Skinner v. Oklahoma,* 316 U.S. 535 (1942); contraception, *Eisenstadt v. Baird,* [405 U.S. 438 (1972)]; family relationships, *Prince v. Massachusetts,* 321 U.S. 158 (1944); and child rearing and education, *Pierce v. Society of Sisters,* 268 U.S. 510 (1925). . . .

This right of privacy, whether it be founded in the Fourteenth Amendment's concept of personal liberty and restrictions upon state action, as we feel it is, or, as the District Court determined, in the Ninth Amendment's reservation of rights to the people, is broad enough to encompass a woman's decision whether or not to terminate her pregnancy. The detriment that the State would impose upon the pregnant woman by denying this choice altogether is apparent. Specific and direct harm medically diagnosable even in early pregnancy may be involved. Maternity, or additional offspring, may force upon the woman a distressful life and future. Psychological harm may be imminent. Mental and physical health may be taxed by child care. There is also the distress, for all concerned, associated with the unwanted child, and there is the problem of bringing a child into a family already unable, psychologically and otherwise, to care for it. In other cases, as in this one, the additional difficulties and continuing stigma of unwed motherhood may be involved. All these are factors the woman and her responsible physician necessarily will consider in consultation.

On the basis of elements such as these, appellant and some *amici* argue that the woman's right is absolute and that she is entitled to terminate her pregnancy at whatever time, in whatever way, and for whatever reason she alone chooses. With this we do not agree. . . . The Court's decisions recognizing a right of privacy also acknowledge that some state regulation in areas protected by that right is appropriate. As noted above, a State may properly assert important interests in safeguarding health, in maintaining medical standards, and in protecting potential life. . . .

We, therefore, conclude that the right of personal privacy includes the abortion decision, but that this right is not unqualified and must be considered against important state interests in regulation. . . .

Where certain "fundamental rights" are involved, the Court has held that regulation limiting these rights may be justified only by a "compelling state interest," and that legislative enactments must be narrowly drawn to express only the legitimate state interests at stake. . . .

The appellee and certain *amici* argue that the fetus is a "person" within the language and meaning of the Fourteenth Amendment. In support of this, they outline at length and in detail the well-known facts of fetal development. If this suggestion of personhood is established, the appellant's case, of course, collapses, for the fetus' right to life would then be guaranteed specifically by the Amendment. The appellant conceded as much on reargument. On the other hand, the appellee conceded on reargument that no case could be cited that holds that a fetus is a person within the meaning of the Fourteenth Amendment.

The Constitution does not define "person" in so many words. Section 1 of the Fourteenth Amendment contains three references to "person." The first, in defining "citizens," speaks of "persons born or naturalized in the United States." The word also appears both in the Due Process Clause and in the Equal Protection Clause. "Person" is used in other places in the Constitution: in the listing of qualifications for Representatives and Senators, Art. I, § 2, cl. 2, and § 3, cl. 3; in the Apportionment Clause, Art. I, § 2, cl. 3; in the Migration and Importation provision, Art. I, § 9, cl. 1; in the Emolument Clause, Art. I, § 9, cl. 8; in the Electors provisions, Art. II, § 1, cl. 2, and the superseded cl. 3; in the provision outlining qualifications for the office of President, Art. II, § 9, cl. 5; in the Extradition provisions, Art. IV, § 2, cl. 2, and the superseded Fugitive Slave Clause 3; and in the Fifth, Twelfth, and Twenty-second Amendments, as well as in §§ 2 and 3 of the Fourteenth Amendment. But in nearly all these instances, the use of the word is such that it has application only postnatally. None indicates, with any assurance, that it has any possible prenatal application.

All this, together with our observation, *supra,* that throughout the major portion of the 19th century prevailing legal abortion practices were far freer than they are today, persuades us that the word "person," as used in the Fourteenth Amendment, does not include the unborn. . . .

This conclusion, however, does not of itself fully answer the contentions raised by Texas, and we pass on to other considerations.

The pregnant woman cannot be isolated in her privacy. She carries an embryo and, later, a fetus, if one accepts the medical definitions of the developing young in the human uterus. The situation therefore is inherently different from marital intimacy, or bedroom possession of obscene material, or marriage, or procreation, or education, with which *Eisenstadt* and *Griswold, Stanley, Loving, Skinner* and *Pierce* and *Meyer* were respectively concerned. As we have intimated above, it is reasonable and appropriate for a State to decide that at some point in time another interest, that of health of the mother or that of potential human life, becomes significantly involved. The woman's privacy is no longer sole and any right of privacy she possesses must be measured accordingly.

Texas urges that, apart from the Fourteenth Amendment, life begins at conception and is present throughout pregnancy, and that, therefore, the State has a compelling interest in protecting that life from and after conception. We need not resolve the difficult question of when life begins. When those trained in the respective disciplines of medicine, philosophy, and theology are unable to arrive at any consensus, the judiciary, at this point in the development of man's knowledge, is not in a position to speculate as to the answer.

It should be sufficient to note briefly the wide divergence of thinking on this most sensitive and difficult question. There has always been strong support for the view that life does not begin until live birth. This was the belief of the Stoics. It appears to be the predominant, though not the unanimous, attitude of the Jewish faith. It may be taken to represent also the position of a large segment of the Protestant community, insofar as that can be ascertained; organized groups that have taken a formal position on the abortion issue have generally regarded abortion as a matter for the conscience of the individual and her family. As we have noted, the common law found greater significance in quickening. Physicians and their scientific colleagues have regarded that event with less interest and have tended to focus either upon conception, upon live birth, or upon the interim point at which the fetus becomes "viable," that is, potentially able to live outside the mother's womb, albeit with artificial aid. Viability is usually placed at about seven months (28 weeks) but may occur earlier, even at 24 weeks. The Aristotelian theory of "mediate animation," that held sway throughout the Middle Ages and the Renaissance in Europe, continued to be official Roman Catholic dogma until the 19th century, despite opposition to this "ensoulment" theory from those in the Church who would recognize the existence of life from the moment of conception. . . .

In areas other than criminal abortion, the law has been reluctant to endorse any theory that life, as we recognize it, begins before live birth or to accord legal rights to the unborn except in narrowly defined situations and except when the rights are contingent upon live birth. . . .

In view of all this, we do not agree that, by adopting one theory of life, Texas may override the rights of the pregnant woman that are at stake. We repeat, however, that the State does have an important and legitimate interest in preserving and protecting the health of the pregnant woman, whether she be a resident of the State or a nonresident who seeks medical consultation and treatment there, and that it has still *another* important and legitimate interest in protecting the potentiality of human life. These interests are separate and distinct. Each grows in substantiality as the woman approaches term and, at a point during pregnancy, each becomes "compelling."

With respect to the State's important and legitimate interest in the health of the mother, the "compelling" point, in the light of present medical knowledge, is at approximately the end of the first trimester. This is so because of the now-established medical fact that until the end of the first trimester mortality in abortion may be less than mortality in normal childbirth. It follows that, from and after this point, a State may regulate the abortion procedure to the extent that the regulation reasonably relates to the preservation and protection of maternal health. Examples of permissible state regulation in this area are requirements as to the qualifications of the person who is to perform the abortion; as to the licensure of that person; as to the facility in which the procedure is to be performed, that is, whether it must be a hospital or may be a clinic or some other place of less-than-hospital status; as to the licensing of the facility; and the like.

This means, on the other hand, that, for the period of pregnancy prior to this "compelling" point, the attending physician, in consultation with his patient, is free to determine, without regulation by the State, that, in his medical judgment, the patient's pregnancy should be terminated. If that decision is reached, the judgment may be effectuated by an abortion free of interference by the State.

With respect to the State's important and legitimate interest in potential life, the "compelling" point is at viability. This is so because the fetus then presumably has the capability of meaningful life outside the mother's womb. State regulation protective of fetal life after viability thus has both logical and biological justifications. If the State is interested in protecting fetal life after viability, it may go so far as to proscribe abortion during that period, except when it is necessary to preserve the life or health of the mother.

Measured against these standards, Art. 1196 of the Texas Penal Code . . . sweeps too broadly. The statute makes no distinction between abortions performed early in pregnancy and those performed later, and it limits to a single reason, "saving" the mother's life, the legal justification for the procedure. The statute, therefore, cannot survive the constitutional attack made upon it here. . . .

To summarize and to repeat:

1. A state criminal abortion statute of the current Texas type, that excepts from criminality only a *life-saving* procedure on behalf of the mother, without regard to pregnancy stage and without recognition of the other interests involved, is violative of the Due Process Clause of the Fourteenth Amendment.

(a) For the stage prior to approximately the end of the first trimester, the abortion decision and its effectuation must be left to the medical judgment of the pregnant woman's attending physician.

(b) For the stage subsequent to approximately the end of the first trimester, the State, in promoting its interest in the health of the mother, may, if it chooses, regulate the abortion procedure in ways that are reasonably related to maternal health.

(c) For the stage subsequent to viability, the State in promoting its interest in the potentiality of human life may, if it chooses, regulate, and even proscribe, abortion except where it is necessary, in appropriate medical judgment, for the preservation of the life or health of the mother. . . .

This holding, we feel, is consistent with the relative weights of the respective interests involved, with the lessons and examples of medical and legal history, with the lenity of the common law, and with the demands of the profound problems of the present day.

Justice STEWART concurring.

[I]t was clear to me then, and it is equally clear to me now, that the *Griswold* decision can be rationally understood only as a holding that the Connecticut statute substantively invaded the "liberty" that is protected by the Due Process Clause of the Fourteenth Amendment. As so understood, *Griswold* stands as one in a long line of . . . cases decided under the doctrine of substantive due process, and I now accept it as such. . . .

[T]he Court today is correct in holding that the right asserted by Jane Roe is embraced within the personal liberty protected by the Due Process Clause of the Fourteenth Amendment.

It is evident that the Texas abortion statute infringes that right directly. Indeed, it is difficult to imagine a more complete abridgment of a constitutional freedom than that worked by the inflexible criminal statute now in force in Texas. The question then becomes whether the state interests advanced to justify this abridgment can survive the "particularly careful scrutiny" that the Fourteenth Amendment here requires.

The asserted state interests are protection of the health and safety of the pregnant woman, and protection of the potential future human life within her. These are legitimate objectives, amply sufficient to permit a State to regulate abortions as it does other surgical procedures, and perhaps sufficient to permit a State to regulate abortions more stringently or even to prohibit them in the late stages of pregnancy. But such legislation is not before us, and I think the Court today has thoroughly demonstrated that these state interests cannot constitutionally support the broad abridgment of personal liberty worked by the existing Texas law.

Justice REHNQUIST dissenting.

I have difficulty in concluding, as the Court does, that the right of "privacy" is involved in this case. Texas, by the statute here challenged, bars the performance of a medical abortion by a licensed physician on a plaintiff such as Roe. A transaction resulting in an operation such as this is not "private" in the ordinary usage of that word. Nor is the "privacy" that the Court finds here even a distant relative of the freedom from searches and seizures protected by the Fourth Amendment to the Constitution, which the Court has referred to as embodying a right to privacy. . . .

If the Court means by the term "privacy" no more than that the claim of a person to be free from unwanted state regulation of consensual transactions may be a form of "liberty" protected by the Fourteenth Amendment, there is no doubt that similar claims have been upheld in our earlier decisions on the basis of that liberty. I agree with the statement of Justice STEWART in his concurring opinion that the "liberty," against deprivation of which without due process the Fourteenth Amendment protects, embraces more than the rights found in the Bill of Rights. But that liberty is not guaranteed absolutely against deprivation, only against deprivation without due process of law. The test traditionally applied in the area of social and economic legislation is whether or not a law such as that challenged has a rational relation to a valid state objective. *Williamson v. Lee Optical Co.*, 348 U.S. 483 (1955).

The Due Process Clause of the Fourteenth Amendment undoubtedly does place a limit, albeit a broad one, on legislative power to enact laws such as this. If the Texas statute were to prohibit an abortion even where the mother's life is in jeopardy, I have little doubt that such a statute would lack a rational relation to a valid state objective under the test stated in *Williamson, supra*. But the Court's sweeping invalidation of any restrictions on abortion during the first trimester is impossible to justify under that standard, and the conscious weighing of competing factors that the Court's opinion apparently substitutes for the established test is far more appropriate to a legislative judgment than to a judicial one. . . .

While the Court's opinion quotes from the dissent of Justice HOLMES in *Lochner v. New York*, 198 U.S. 45 (1905), the result it reaches is more closely attuned to the majority opinion of Justice PECKHAM in that case. As in *Lochner* and similar cases applying substantive due process standards to economic and social welfare legislation, the adoption of the compelling state interest standard will inevitably require this Court to examine the legislative policies and pass on the wisdom of these policies in the very process of deciding whether a particular state interest put forward may or may not be "compelling." The decision here to break pregnancy into three distinct terms and to outline the permissible restrictions the State may impose in each one, for example, partakes more of judicial legislation than it does of a determination of the intent of the drafters of the Fourteenth Amendment.

The fact that a majority of the States reflecting, after all the majority sentiment in those States, have had restrictions on abortions for at least a century is a strong indication, it seems to me, that the asserted right to an abortion is not "so rooted in the traditions and conscience of our people as to be ranked as fundamental.". . .

To reach its result, the Court necessarily has had to find within the Scope of the Fourteenth Amendment a right that was apparently completely unknown to the drafters of the Amendment. As early as 1821, the first state law dealing directly with abortion was enacted by the Connecticut Legislature. By the time of the adoption of the Fourteenth Amendment in 1868, there were at least 36 laws enacted by state or territorial legislatures limiting abortion. . . .

The only conclusion possible from this history is that the drafters did not intend to have the Fourteenth Amendment withdraw from the States the power to legislate with respect to this matter.

Chief Justice BURGER and Justice DOUGLAS concurred in separate opinions.

Justice WHITE dissented in a separate opinion.

THE DEVELOPMENT OF LAW
Other Post-*Roe* Rulings on Abortion

Case	Vote	Ruling
Doe v. Bolton, 410 U.S. 179 (1973)	7:2	A companion case decided along with *Roe v. Wade*, which extended *Roe*, in holding that states may not criminalize abortions, or make abortions unreasonably difficult to obtain; *Doe* struck down state requirements that abortions be performed in licensed hospitals; that abortions be approved beforehand by a hospital committee; and that two physicians concur in the abortion decision.
Bigelow v. Virginia, 421 U.S. 809 (1975)	7:2	Held that states may not proscribe newspaper advertisements for abortions and abortion-related services.
Planned Parenthood of Central Missouri v. Danforth, 428 U.S. 552 (1976)	5:4	Ruled that informed consent statutes, requiring doctors to obtain the written con-

Case	Vote	Ruling
		sent of a woman after informing her of the dangers of abortion and possible alternatives, were permissible if the requirements were related to maternal health and not overbearing; the requirements must also be narrowly drawn so as not to unduly interfere with the physican-patient relationship; and in addition, the Court upheld requiring doctors to provide information to states on each abortion performed, so long as the reporting-requirements related to maternal health remain confidential and are not overbearing. The Court, however, struck down fetal-protection statutes that pertain only to previable fetuses and require doctors to use available means to save the life of fetuses; finally, the Court held that "it is not the proper function of the legislature or the courts to place viability, which is essentially a medical concept, at a specific point in the gestation period. The time which viability is achieved may vary with each pregnancy, and the determination of whether a particular fetus is viable is, and must be, a matter for the judgment of the attending physician."
Bellotti v. Baird, 428 U.S. 132 (1976)	9:0	Overturned a law requiring parental consent for minors seeking abortions.

Case	Vote	Ruling
Carey v. Population Services International, 431 U.S. 678 (1977)	7:2	Held that prohibitions on sales and advertisements of contraceptives for minors is unconstitutional.
Beal v. Doe, 432 U.S. 438 (1977)	6:3	Held that nothing in the language or history of Title XIX of the Social Security Act required the funding of nontherapeutic abortions as a condition of a state's participating in the Medicaid program established under the act; the Court indicated that Title XIX left states free to include coverage for nontherapeutic abortions if they choose to do so, but also that they could refuse to fund unnecessary medical services.
Maher v. Roe, 432 U.S. 464 (1977)	6:3	Upheld Connecticut's refusal to reimburse Medicaid recipients for abortion expenses except where the attending physician certifies that an abortion is medically or psychiatrically necessary.
Poelker v. Doe, 432 U.S. 59 (1977)	6:3	Upheld the policy of the city of St. Louis, Missouri, to deny indigent pregnant women access to nontherapeutic abortions in *public* hospitals.
Colautti v. Franklin, 439 U.S. 379 (1979)	6:3	Struck down a fetal-protection statute that applied to viable fetuses and held that state statutes must precisely set forth the standards for determining viability; in addition, the Court noted that fetal-protection laws must specify whether a doctor's paramount duty is to the

Case	Vote	Ruling
		patient or whether the doctor must balance the possible danger to the patient against the increased odds of fetal survival.
Bellotti v. Baird, 443 U.S. 622 (1979)	9:0	Ruled that while states may require minors to obtain parental consent, they must provide an alternative judicial procedure for procuring authorization of a minor's abortion, if parental consent is denied or the minor does not want to seek it.
Harris v. McRae, 448 U.S. 297 (1980)	5:4	Upheld the Hyde Amendment to the Medicaid program that limited federal funding for nontherapeutic abortions; the Court also upheld the right of a state to fund only those medically necessary abortions for which it received federal reimbursement.
H. L. v. Matheson, 450 U.S. 398 (1981)	6:3	Upheld a Utah statute requiring physicians to notify parents, "if possible," prior to performing an abortion on their minor daughter (1) when the girl is living with and dependent on her parents, (2) when she is not emancipated by marriage or otherwise, and (3) when she has made no claim or showing as to her maturity or as to her relationship with her parents.
Akron v. Akron Center for Reproductive Health, 462 U.S. 416 (1983)	6:3	Struck down five sections of a city ordinance for unduly restricting a woman's right to obtain an abortion; the sections provided that (1)

Case	Vote	Ruling
		after the first trimester of a pregnancy, all abortions be performed in a hospital; (2) there be notification of consent by parents before abortions are performed on unmarried minors; (3) the attending physician make certain specified statements to a patient so that the patient's consent for an abortion would amount to "informed consent"; (4) there be a twenty-four-hour waiting period between the time a patient signs the consent form and when an abortion is performed; and (5) fetal remains be disposed of in a "humane and sanitary manner."
Planned Parenthood Association of Kansas City v. Ashcroft, 462 U.S. 476 (1983)	6:3 & 5:4	Invalidated Missouri's second-trimester hospitalization requirement, but a bare majority struck down the state's requirement that after twelve weeks of pregnancy, all abortions be performed in a hospital and (voting five to four) *upheld* three other sections of Missouri's law—they required (1) pathological reports for each abortion performed, (2) the presence of a second doctor during abortions performed after viability, and (3) parental consent or consent from a juvenile court for minors before obtaining an abortion.
Simopoulos v. Virginia, 462 U.S. 506 (1983)	8:1	Upheld Virginia's mandatory hospitalization requirement for abortions per-

Case	Vote	Ruling
		formed in the second trimester.
Thornburg v. American College of Obstetricians & Gynecologists, 476 U.S. 747 (1986)	5:4	Struck down a Pennsylvania law requiring (1) women to be advised of medical assistance and that the natural father is responsible for child support, (2) physicians to inform women of the detrimental effects and risks of abortion, (3) doctors to report all abortions to the state, (4) a higher degree of care in postviability abortions in an attempt to save the life of the fetus, and (5) the presence of a second physician during the performance of all abortions.
Bowen v. Kendrick, 487 U.S. 589 (1988)	5:4	Upheld the Adolescent Family Life Act, which prohibits federal funding of organizations involved with abortions, while permitting funding of religious groups advocating self-discipline as a form of birth control.
Hodgson v. Minnesota, 110 S.Ct. 2926 (1990)	5:4	With Justice O'Connor casting the crucial vote, a bare majority agreed that, without a judicial bypass option, the state's requirement that minors notify both parents before obtaining an abortion, was unconstitutional— on that issue, Justice O'Connor joined Justices Brennan, Blackmun, Marshall, and Stevens. But O'Connor also joined Chief Justice Rehnquist and Justices Scalia, Kennedy, and White in upholding the constitutionality of the par-

Case	Vote	Ruling
		ential notification law. In separate opinions, Justice Stevens contended that the law was unconstitutional even without the judicial bypass option, and Justice Kennedy claimed that the judicial bypass option was constitutionally unnecessary.
Ohio v. Akron Center for Reproductive Health, 110 S.Ct. 2972 (1990)	6:3	Writing for the Court, Justice Kennedy upheld Ohio's law requiring to notify at least one parent, while also providing a judicial bypass option, before obtaining an abortion.

Maher v. Roe

432 U.S. 464, 97 S.Ct. 2376 (1977)

Two indigent women, known as Susan Roe and Mary Poe, sued Edward Maher, the commissioner of Connecticut's Department of Social Services, and challenged the constitutionality of a state regulation prohibiting the funding of abortions that are not medically necessary. The state interpreted Title XIX of the Social Security Act, which establishes the Medicaid program under which participating states may provide federally funded medical assistance to needy persons, to forbid the funding of nontherapeutic abortions. Roe, an unmarried mother of three children, was unable to obtain an abortion because her doctor refused to certify that an abortion was medically necessary. Poe, a sixteen-year-old high-school junior, had an abortion but, because she failed to obtain a certificate of medical necessity, the Department of Social Services refused to reimburse the hospital for Poe's $244 hospital bill.

A federal district court rejected Connecticut's interpretation of Title XIX when holding that the Social Security Act not only allowed funding of nontherapeutic abortions but required it. On appeal, the Court of Appeals for the Second Circuit ruled that the Social Security Act permitted (but did not require) state funding of abortions and remanded the case back to the district court, which then overturned Connecticut's regulation forbidding the funding of nontherapeutic abortions.

Maher appealed that ruling to the Supreme Court which granted review. The Court handed down its decision along with *Beal v. Doe,* 432 U.S. 438 (1977), which held that the Social Security Act does not require states to pay for nontherapeutic abortions as a condition of their participating in the Medicaid program.

Justice POWELL delivers the opinion of the Court.

[W]e hold today that Title XIX of the Social Security Act does not require the funding of nontherapeutic abortions as a condition of participation in the joint federal-state medicaid program established by that statute. . . .

The Constitution imposes no obligation on the States to pay the pregnancy-related medical expenses of indigent women, or indeed to pay any of the medical expenses of indigents. But when a State decides to alleviate some of the hardships of poverty by providing medical care, the manner in which it dispenses benefits is subject to constitutional limitations. Appellees' claim is that Connecticut must accord equal treatment to both abortion and childbirth, and may not evidence a policy preference by funding only the medical expenses incident to childbirth. This challenge to the classifications established by the Connecticut regulation presents a question arising under the Equal Protection Clause of the Fourteenth Amendment. . . .

This case involves no discrimination against a suspect class. An indigent woman desiring an abortion does not come within the limited category of disadvantaged classes so recognized by our cases. Nor does the fact that the impact of the regulation falls upon those who cannot pay lead to a different conclusion. In a sense, every denial of welfare to an indigent creates a wealth classification as compared to nonindigents who are able to pay for the desired goods or services. But this Court has never held that financial need alone identifies a suspect class for purposes of equal protection analysis. . . . Accordingly, the central question in this case is whether the regulation "impinges upon a fundamental right explicitly or implicitly protected by the Constitution.". . .

At issue in *Roe* [*v. Wade,* 410 U.S. 113 (1973)], was the constitutionality of a Texas law making it a crime to procure or attempt to procure an abortion, except on medical advice for the purpose of saving the life of the mother. . . . [W]e concluded that the Fourteenth Amendment's concept of personal liberty affords constitutional protection against state interference with certain aspects of an individual's personal "privacy," including a woman's decision to terminate her pregnancy. . . .

The Texas law in *Roe* was a stark example of impermissible interference with the pregnant woman's decision to terminate her pregnancy. In subsequent cases, we have invalidated other types of restrictions, different in form but similar in effect, on the woman's freedom of choice. . . .

The Connecticut regulation before us is different in kind from the laws invalidated in our previous abortion decisions. The Connecticut regulation places no obstacles—absolute or otherwise—in the pregnant woman's path to an abortion. An indigent woman who desires an abortion suffers no disadvantage as a consequence of Connecticut's decision to fund childbirth; she continues as before to be dependent on private sources for the service she desires. The State may have made childbirth a more attractive alternative, thereby influencing the woman's decision, but it has imposed no restriction on access to abortions that was not already there. The indigency that may make it difficult—and in some cases, perhaps, impossible—for some women to have abortions is neither created nor in any way affected by the Connecticut regulation. We conclude that the Connecticut regulation does not impinge upon the fundamental right recognized in *Roe*.

Our conclusion signals no retreat from *Roe* or the cases applying it. There is a basic difference between direct state interference with a protected activity and state encouragement of an alternative activity consonant with legislative policy. Constitutional concerns are greatest when the State attempts to impose its will by force of law; the State's power to encourage actions deemed to be in the public interest is necessarily far broader.

The question remains whether Connecticut's regulation can be sustained under the less demanding test of rationality that applies in the absence of a suspect classification or the impingement of a fundamental right. This test requires that the distinction drawn between childbirth and nontherapeutic abortion by the regulation be "rationally related" to a "constitutionally permissible" purpose. We hold that the Connecticut funding scheme satisfies this standard.

Roe itself explicitly acknowledged the State's strong interest in protecting the potential life of the fetus. That interest exists throughout the pregnancy, "grow[ing] in substantiality as the woman approaches term." Because the pregnant woman carries a potential human being she "cannot be isolated in her privacy. . . . [Her] privacy is no longer sole and any right of privacy she possesses must be measured accordingly.". . . The State unquestionably has a "strong and legitimate interest in encouraging normal childbirth,". . . an interest honored over the centuries. Nor can there be any question that the Connecticut regulation rationally furthers that interest. The medical costs associated with childbirth are substantial, and have increased significantly in recent years. As recognized by the District Court in this case, such costs are significantly greater than those normally associated with elective abortions during the first trimester. The subsidizing of costs incident to childbirth is a rational means of encouraging childbirth.

We certainly are not unsympathetic to the plight of an indigent woman who desires an abortion, but "the Constitution does not provide judicial remedies for every social and economic ill."

Justice BRENNAN, with whom Justice MARSHALL and Justice BLACKMUN join, dissenting.

[A] distressing insensitivity to the plight of impoverished pregnant women is inherent in the Court's analysis. The stark reality for too many, not just "some," indigent pregnant women is that indigency makes access to competent licensed physicians not merely "difficult" but "impossible." As a practical matter, many indigent women will feel they have no choice but to carry their pregnancies to term because the State will pay for the associated medical services, even though they would have chosen to have abortions if the State had also provided funds for that procedure, or indeed if the State had provided funds for neither procedure. This disparity in funding by the State clearly operates to coerce indigent pregnant women to bear children they would not otherwise choose to have, and just as clearly, this coercion can only operate upon the poor, who are uniquely the victims of this form of financial pressure. . . .

The Court's premise is that only an equal protection claim is presented here. Claims of interference with enjoyment of fundamental rights have, however, occupied a rather protean position in our constitutional jurisprudence. Whether or not the Court's analysis may reasonably proceed under the Equal Protection Clause, the Court plainly errs in ignoring, as it does, the unanswerable argument of appellee, and holding of the District Court, that the regulation unconstitutionally impinges upon her claim of privacy derived from the Due Process Clause.

Roe v. Wade and cases following it hold that an area of privacy invulnerable to the State's intrusion surrounds the decision of a pregnant woman whether or not to carry her pregnancy to term. The Connecticut scheme clearly infringes upon that area of privacy by bringing financial pressures on indigent women that force them to bear children they would not otherwise have. That is an obvious impairment of the fundamental right established by *Roe*. . . .

Until today, I had not thought the nature of the fundamental right established in *Roe* was open to question, let alone susceptible to the interpretation advanced by the Court. The fact that the

Demonstration on the steps of the Supreme Court Building protesting rulings on abortion. *UPI/Bettmann Newsphotos.*

Connecticut scheme may not operate as an absolute bar preventing all indigent women from having abortions is not critical. What is critical is that the State has inhibited their fundamental right to make that choice free from state interference.

Nor does the manner in which Connecticut has burdened the right freely to choose to have an abortion save its Medicaid program. The Connecticut scheme cannot be distinguished from other grants and withholdings of financial benefits that we have held unconstitutionally burdened a fundamental right. *Sherbert v. Verner,* [374 U.S. 398 (1963)], struck down a South Carolina statute that denied unemployment compensation to a woman who for religious reasons could not work on Saturday, but that would have provided such compensation if her unemployment had stemmed from a number of other nonreligious causes. . . . *Sherbert* held that "the pressure upon her to forgo [her religious] practice [was] unmistakable," and therefore held the effect was the same as a fine imposed for Saturday worship. Here, though the burden is upon the right to privacy derived from the Due Process Clause and not upon freedom of religion under the Free Exercise Clause of the First Amendment, the governing principle is the same, for Connecticut grants and withholds financial benefits in a manner that discourages significantly the exercise of a fundamental constitutional right.

INSIDE THE COURT

The Oral Arguments in *Webster v. Reproductive Health Center*

Oral arguments in *Webster v. Reproductive Center* were heard on April 26, 1989 and proved illuminating. William Webster and Frank Sussman, representing the Reproductive Health Services, each had a half hour argue before the Court. In addition, the Rehnquist Court took the unusual step of granting ten minutes for the federal government to present its views. The solicitor general for the incoming administration of President George Bush had not yet been confirmed by the Senate, and Bush's attorney general, Richard Thornburgh, decided against arguing the case. Instead, former Solicitor General Charles Fried was brought back and once again had his day in Court.

Webster's strategy was to defend Missouri's law as technically within the parameters for state regulation set by *Roe* and to leave Fried to make the broadside attack. Webster told the Court, for example, that the law's preamble declaring that life begins at conception that that "unborn children have protectable interests in life, health, and well-being" was unenforceable and guaranteed no "substantive right." In response to questions from Justices Stevens and Kennedy about the state's requiring doctors to perform certain tests pertaining to the "gestational age, weight, and lung maturity of" the unborn, Webster claimed that were not mandatory and in any event, as with other provisions of Missouri's law, carried no penalty. As for the state's prohibiting the use of public funds and facilities for abortions, he pointed to precedents in which the Court had upheld similar restrictions.

Fried next took to the lectern and set about arguing that the Court should overturn *Roe*. "We are not asking the Court to unravel the fabric . . . of privacy rights which this Court has woven in cases like *Meyer* and *Pierce* and *Moore* and *Griswold*." Fried argued, "Rather, we are asking the Court to pull this one thread. And the reason is well stated in *Harris v. McRae*: Abortion is different." "Your position," asked Justice Kennedy, "then is that *Griswold* is correct and should be retained?" "Exactly," replied Fried, prompting a further exchange:

Justice Kennedy: Is that because there is a fundamental right involved in that case?

Mr. Fried: In *Griswold* there was a right which was well established in a whole fabric of quite concrete matters, quite concrete.
     It involved not an abstraction such as the right to control one's body, an abstraction such as the right to be let alone, it involved quite concrete intrusions into the details of marital intimacy. And that was emphasized by the Court and is a very important aspect of the Court's decision.

Justice Kennedy: Does the case stand for the proposition that there is a right to determine whether to procreate?

Mr. Fried: *Griswold* surely does not stand for that proposition. . . .

Justice Kennedy: What is the right involved in *Griswold*?

Mr. Fried: The right involved in *Griswold*, as the Court clearly stated, was the right not to have the state intrude into, in a very violent way, into the details, inquire into the details of marital intimacy. There was a great deal of talk about inquiry into the marital bedroom, and I think that is a very different story from what we have here.

Justice O'Connor: Do you say there is no fundamental right to decide whether to have a child or not? . . . Do you deny that the Constitution protects [the right to procreate]?

Mr. Fried: I would hesitate to formulate the right in such abstract terms, and I think the Court prior to *Roe* quite prudently also avoided such sweeping generalities. That was the wisdom of *Griswold*.

Justice O'Connor: Do you think that the state has the right to, if in a future century we had a serious overpopulation problem, has a right to require women to have abortions after so many children?

Mr. Fried: I surely do not. That would be quite a different matter.

Justice O'Connor: What do you rest that on?

Mr. Fried: Because unlike abortion, which involves the purposeful termination of future life, that would involve not preventing an operation by violently taking hands on, laying hands on a woman and submitting her to an operation and a whole constellation—

Justice O'Connor: And you would rest that on substantive due process protection?

Mr. Fried: Absolutely.

Justice Kennedy: How do you define the liberty interests of the woman in that connection?

Mr. Fried: The liberty interest against a seizure would be involved. That is how the Court analyzed the matter in *Griswold*. That is how Justice Harlan analyzed the matter in his dissent in *Poe v. Ullman*, which is, in some sense, the root of this area of law.

Justice Kennedy: How do you define the interest, the liberty interest, of a woman in an abortion case?

Mr. Fried: Well, I would think that there are liberty interests involved in terms perhaps of the contraceptive interest, but there is an interest at all points, however the interest of the woman is defined, at all points it is an interest which is matched by the state's interest in potential life.

Justice Kennedy: I understand it is matched, but I want to know how you define it.

Mr. Fried: I would define it in terms of the concrete impositions on the woman which so offended the Court in *Griswold* and which are not present in the *Roe* situation. Finally, I would like to make quite clear that in our view, if *Roe* were overruled, this Court would have to continue to police the far outer boundaries of abortion regulation under a due process rational basis test and that that test is muscular enough, as Chief Justice Rehnquist said in his dissent in *Roe*, to strike down any regulation which did not make adequate provision—

Justice Brennan: Mr. Fried, do I correctly read what your brief says . . . that *Griswold* is a Fourth Amendment case?

Mr. Fried: It is a case which draws on the Fourth Amendment. It is not itself a Fourth Amendment case, it is a Fourteenth Amendment case. But I would like to emphasize that the Court would have ample power under our submission to strike down any regulation which did not make proper provision for cases where the life of the mother was at risk. . . .
  We are not here today suggesting that the Court would, therefore, allow extreme and extravagant and bloodthirsty regulations and that it

would lack the power to strike those down if they were presented to it. But it is a mistake to think that alone, among government institutions—

Justice Stevens: Mr. Fried, is there a difference between the court's power in the case of an abortion that would be life threatening to the woman and an abortion that would merely cause her severe and prolonged disease? Is there a constitutional difference?

Mr. Fried: I think that is a matter of degree, and it is perfectly clear that severe health effects shade over into a threat to the life. I cannot promise the Court that our submission would dispense the Federal courts from considering matters like that, but I also very much doubt that the Court would be presented with many such situations.

What is necessary is for the Court to return to legislatures an opportunity in some substantial way to express their preference, which the Court says they may express, for normal childbirth over abortion, and *Roe* stands as a significant barrier to that.

Justice White: Does your submission suggest that a public hospital, in a state that permits abortion, could not allow abortions?

Mr. Fried: It is quite clear that a public hospital may, under this Court's decision in *Maher* and in *McRae*, may do as Missouri has here done and say that public funds cannot be expended.

Justice White: Suppose there is a state that permits abortions and they are done in public hospitals. Do you think that is a—you say that there is human life involved, that is destroyed in abortions? Is there some problem about the state permitting abortions?

Mr. Fried: Oh, no, I think there is not. As I have indicated, I think the Constitution takes no position on this point. There is a certain logic in some of the provisions which say that there should be, that there should be protection further back. But the country's experience and the Court's experience under the constitutionalization of that issue has been so regrettable that I could not in conscience recommend that it be constitutionalized in some other way at another point in the spectrum.

When concluding his arguments, Fried implored, "[I]f the Court does not in this case in its prudence decide to reconsider *Roe,* I would ask at least that it say nothing here that would further entrench this decision as a secure premise for reasoning in future cases."

In light of Fried's arguments, Susman two days earlier had prophetically, although unwittingly, hit on the idea of arguing not merely that *Griswold* and *Roe* were inextricably linked in the landscape of constitutional law but that contraception and abortion were not easily distinguishable in contemporary science and medicine; unlike condoms, modern birth control pills, and IUDs operate as abortifacients. "For better or worse," he argued "there no longer exists any bright line between the fundamental right that was established in *Griswold* and the fundamental right of abortion that was established in *Roe.* These two rights, because of advances in medicine and science, now overlap. They coalesce and merge and they are not distinct." Justice Scalia appeared unpersuaded and asked: "Excuse me, you find it hard to draw a line between those two but easy to draw a line between first, second, and third trimester." Susman's response was cut off by Scalia's continued questioning:

Justice Scalia: I don't see why a court that can draw that line can't separate abortion from birth control quite readily.

Mr. Susman: If I may suggest the reasons in response to your question, Justice Scalia. The most common forms of what we generically in common parlance call contraception today, IUD's, low-dose birth control pills, which are the safest type of birth control pills available, act as abortifacients. They are correctly labeled as both.

Under this statute, which defines fertilization as the point of beginning, those forms of contraception are also abortifacients. Science and medicine refers to them as both. We are not still dealing with the common barrier methods of *Griswold*. We are no longer just talking about condoms and diaphragms.

Things have changed. The bright line, if there ever was one, has now been extinguished. That's why I suggest to this Court that we need to deal with one right, the right to procreate. We are no longer taling about two rights.

Justice Kennedy: Do you agree that the state can forbid abortions save to preserve the life of the mother after the fetus is, say, eight months old?

Mr. Susman: If I understand the question, Justice Kennedy, I think the health risks of the woman always are supreme at any stage of pregnancy.

Justice Kennedy: Suppose the health rights of the mother are not involved? The life or health of the mother is not involved, can the state prohibit an abortion after the fetus is eight months old?

Mr. Susman: Yes. I am willing to recognize the compelling interest granted in *Roe* of the state in potential fetal life after the point of viability.

Justice Kennedy: But that is a line-drawing, isn't it?

Mr. Susman: Yes, it is. But that is a line that is more easily drawn. I think there are many cogent reasons for picking the point of viability, which is what we have today under *Roe*.

First of all, historically, both at common law and in early statutes, this was always the line chosen. Whether it was called quickening or viability, there is little difference time-wise.

Justice O'Connor: Well, there is a difference, is there not, in those two?

Mr. Susman: Technically, between those two definitions, Justice O'Connor, yes. Quickening had less of a medical significance. It was . . . when the woman could first detect movement.

Justice O'Connor: When the fetus was first felt by the mother?

Mr. Susman: A kick, yes, absolutely, approximately two or three weeks before what we would consider viability today. The second good reason, I think, for remaining with viability as our dividing line in this context, Justice Kennedy, is that it is one that the physician can determine on a case-by-case basis without periodic recourse to the courts.

Thirdly, it is the point that the physician can determine with or without the assistance of the woman. It is a medical judgment, I agree, and not a medical fact. One cannot pinpoint viability to a day or to an hour or to a second.

I would suggest again, as I indicated, that the line has now been erased. It is interesting also to note at the same time that the definition of conception or fertilization chosen by this statute does not even comport with the medical definition. The definition of conception promulgated, for example, by the American College of Obstetricians and Gynecologists, starts a week later than the definition that this section has chosen to use.

It is at all stages of procreation, whether before or after conception, that the standards of what constitute fundamental liberty are amply satisfied. Procreational interests are, indeed, implicit in the concept of ordered liberty, and neither liberty nor justice would exist without them.

It is truly a liberty whose exercise is deeply rooted in this nation's history and tradition. . . .

Thirty percent of pregnancies in this country today terminate in abortion. It is a high rate. It is a rate that sometimes astounds people, but it is a rate that has not changed one whit from the time the Constitution was enacted through the 1800's and through the 1900's. That has always been the rate.

It is significantly less than the worldwide rate. Worldwide, 40 percent of all pregnancies terminate in abortion. Abortion today is the most common surgical procedure in the United States with the possible exception of contraception.

It remains today, as it was in the days of *Roe*, 17 times safer than childbirth, 100 times safer than appendectomy, a safe procedure, minor surgery.

I suggest that there can be no ordered liberty for women without control over their education, their employment, their health, their childbearing and their personal aspirations. There does, in fact, exist a deeply rooted tradition that the government steer clear of decisions affecting the bedroom, childbearing and the doctor-patient relations as it pertains to these concerns.

After his thirty minutes were exhausted, Susman emerged (along with Webster) from the Court to tell reporters how pleased he was with the arguments in the case. More than two months passed before the Court announced its decision in *Webster* on the last day of the Court's term, Monday July 3, 1989.

Webster v. Reproductive Health Services

109 S.Ct. 3040 (1989)

Fifteen years after *Roe v. Wade* was handed down, the Court appeared poised to reconsider, and possibly to overturn, *Roe*. In those years, the composition of the high bench had dramatically changed. Justice William O. Douglas had been replaced by President Gerald R. Ford's appointee, John Paul Stevens, in 1975. President Ronald Reagan named Sandra Day O'Connor to fill Justice Potter Stewart's seat in 1981. Five years later, Reagan elevated Justice William H. Rehnquist to the chief justiceship, when Warren Burger retired, and appointed Justice Antonin Scalia. Then in June 1987 Justice Lewis Powell (who had come to cast the crucial vote for upholding *Roe*) retired and Reagan eventually won Senate confirmation for Justice Anthony Kennedy in February 1988.

During the summer of 1988 Assistant Attorney General William Bradford Reynolds and others in Reagan's Department of Justice talked Missouri's attorney general, William Webster, into seizing an opportunity afforded by appealing an appellate court's invalidation of that state restrictions on abortions. At issue in

Webster was the constitutionality of four provisions of Missouri's 1986 abortion law: (1) decreeing that life begins at conception and that "unborn children have protectable interest in life, health, and well-being," (2) requiring physicians, prior to performing an abortion on a woman believed to be twenty or more weeks pregnant, to test the fetus's "gestational age, weight, and lung maturity," (3) prohibiting public employees and facilities from being used to perform abortions not necessary to save a woman's life, and (4) making it unlawful to use public funds, employees, and facilities for the purpose of "encouraging or counseling" a woman to have an abortion except when her life is in danger. The Court granted review and on Monday, July 3, 1989, Chief Justice Rehnquist read aloud portions of his opinion upholding Missouri's regulations and revealed the bitter divisions among the justices. Only Justices Kennedy and White joined Rehnquist's opinion; Justices O'Connor and Scalia concurred in separate opinions. Justice Blackmun, the author of *Roe,* also took the unusual step of reading from the bench his dissenting opinion, which Justices Brennan and Marshall joined. Justice Stevens also read from his separate opinion.

Chief Justice REHNQUIST, with whom Justice WHITE and Justice KENNEDY join, delivers the opinion of the Court.

This appeal concerns the constitutionality of a Missouri statute regulating the performance of abortions. The United States Court of Appeals for the Eighth Circuit struck down several provisions of the statute on the ground that they violated this Court's decision in *Roe v. Wade,* 410 U.S. 113 (1973), and cases following it. We noted probable jurisdiction, and now reverse. . . .

II

Decision of this case requires us to address four sections of the Missouri Act: (a) the preamble; (b) the prohibition on the use of public facilities or employees to perform abortions; (c) the prohibition on public funding of abortion counseling; and (d) the requirement that physicians conduct viability tests prior to performing abortions. We address these *seriatim.*

[A] The Act's preamble . . . sets forth "findings" by the Missouri legislature that "[t]he life of each human being begins at conception," and that "[u]nborn children have protectable interests in life, health, and well-being." Mo. Rev. Stat. §§ 1.205.1(1), (2) (1986). The Act then mandates that state laws be interpreted to provide unborn children with "all the rights, privileges, and immunities available to other persons, citizens, and residents of this state," subject to the Constitution and this Court's precedents.

The State contends that the preamble itself is precatory and imposes no substantive restrictions on abortions, and that appellees therefore do not have standing to challenge it. Appellees, on the other hand, insist that the preamble is an operative part of the Act intended to guide the interpretation of other provisions of the Act. They maintain, for example, that the preamble's definition of life may prevent physicians in public hospitals from dispensing certain forms of contraceptives, such as the intrauterine device. . . .

In our view, the Court of Appeals misconceived the meaning of the *Akron* [*v. Akron Center for Reproductive Health,* 462 U.S. 416 (1983)] dictum, which was only that a State could not "justify" an abortion regulation otherwise invalid under *Roe* v. *Wade* on the ground that it embodied the State's view about when life begins. Certainly the preamble does not by its terms regulate abortion or any other aspect of appellees' medical practice. The Court has emphasized that *Roe v. Wade* "implies no limitation on the authority of a State to make a value judgment favoring childbirth over abortion." *Maher v. Roe,* 432 U.S. [464 (1977)]. The preamble can be read simply to express that sort of value judgment.

We think the extent to which the preamble's language might be used to interpret other state statutes or regulations is something that only the courts of Missouri can definitively decide. . . . We therefore need not pass on the constitutionality of the Act's preamble.

[*B*] Section 188.210 provides that "[i]t shall be unlawful for any public employee within the scope of his employment to perform or assist an abortion, not necessary to save the life of the mother," while § 188.215 makes it "unlawful for any public facility to be used for the purpose of performing or assisting an abortion not necessary to save the life of the mother." The Court of Appeals held that these provisions contravened this Court's abortion decisions. We take the contrary view.

As we said earlier this Term in *DeShaney v. Winnebago County Dept. of Social Services,* [489 U.S. 656] (1989) "our cases have recognized that the Due Process Clauses generally confer no affirmative right to governmental aid, even where such aid may be necessary to secure life, liberty, or property interests of which the government itself may not deprive the individual." In *Maher v. Roe,* the Court upheld a Connecticut welfare regulation under which Medicaid recipients received payments for medical services related to childbirth, but not for nontherapeutic abortions. Relying on *Maher,* the Court in *Poelker v. Doe,* 432 U.S. 519 (1977), held that the city of St. Louis committed "no constitutional violation . . . in electing, as a policy choice, to provide publicly financed hospital services for childbirth without providing corresponding services for nontherapeutic abortions."

More recently, in *Harris v. McRae,* 448 U.S. 297 (1980), the Court upheld "the most restrictive version of the Hyde Amendment," which withheld from States federal funds under the Medicaid program to reimburse the costs of abortions, " 'except where the life of the mother would be endangered if the fetus were carried to term.' " As in *Maher* and *Poelker,* the Court required only a showing that Congress' authorization of "reimbursement for medically necessary services generally, but not for certain medically necessary abortions" was rationally related to the legitimate governmental goal of encouraging childbirth. . . .

Just as Congress' refusal to fund abortions in *McRae* left "an indigent woman with at least the same range of choice in deciding whether to obtain a medically necessary abortion as she would have had if Congress had chosen to subsidize no health care costs at all," Missouri's refusal to allow public employees to perform abortions in public hospitals leaves a pregnant woman with the same choices as if the State had chosen not to operate any public hospitals at all. The challenged provisions only restrict a woman's ability to obtain an abortion to the extent that she chooses to use a physician affiliated with a public hospital. This circumstance is more easily remedied, and thus considerably less burdensome, than indigency, which "may make it difficult—and in some cases, perhaps, impossible—for some women to have abortions" without public funding. *Maher.* Having held that the State's refusal to fund abortions does not violate *Roe v. Wade,* it strains logic to reach a contrary result for the use of public facilities and employees. If the State may "make a value judgment favoring childbirth over abortion and . . . implement that judgment by the allocation of public funds," *Maher,* surely it may do so through the allocation of other public resources, such as hospitals and medical staff. . . .

Maher, Poelker, and *McRae* all support the view that the State need not commit any resources to facilitating abortions, even if it can turn a profit by doing so. In *Poelker,* the suit was filed by an indigent who could not afford to pay for an abortion, but the ban on the performance of nontherapeutic abortions in city-owned hospitals applied whether or not the pregnant woman could pay. The Court emphasized that the Mayor's decision to prohibit abortions in city hospitals was "subject to public debate and approval or disapproval at the polls," and that "the Constitution does not forbid a State or city, pursuant to democratic processes, from expressing a preference for normal childbirth as St. Louis has done." Thus we uphold the Act's restrictions on the use of public employees and facilities for the performance or assistance of nontherapeutic abortions. . . .

[D] Section 188.029 of the Missouri Act provides:

"Before a physician performs an abortion on a woman he has reason to believe is carrying an unborn child of twenty or more weeks gestational age, the physician shall first determine if the unborn child is viable by using and exercising that degree of care, skill, and proficiency commonly exercised by the ordinarily skillful, careful, and prudent physician engaged in similar practice under the same or similar conditions. In making this determination of viability, the physician shall perform or cause to be performed such medical examinations and tests as are necessary to make a finding of the gestational age, weight, and lung maturity of the unborn child and shall enter such findings and determination of viability in the medical record of the mother."

As with the preamble, the parties disagree over the meaning of this statutory provision. The State emphasizes the language of the first sentence, which speaks in terms of the physician's determination of viability being made by the standards of ordinary skill in the medical profession. Appellees stress the language of the second sentence, which prescribes such "tests as are necessary" to make a finding of gestational age, fetal weight, and lung maturity. . . .

We think the viability-testing provision makes sense only if the second sentence is read to require only those tests that are useful to making subsidiary findings as to viability. If we construe this provision to require a physician to perform those tests needed to make the three specified findings *in all circumstances,* including when the physician's reasonable professional judgment indicates that the tests would be irrelevant to determining viability or even dangerous to the mother and the fetus, the second sentence of § 188.029 would conflict with the first sentence's *requirement* that a physician apply his reasonable professional skill and judgment. It would also be incongruous to read this provision, especially the word "necessary," to require the performance of tests irrelevant to the expressed statutory purpose of determining viability. . . .

The viability-testing provision of the Missouri Act is concerned with promoting the State's interest in potential human life rather than in maternal health. Section 188.029 creates what is essentially a presumption of viability at 20 weeks, which the physician must rebut with tests indicating that the fetus is not viable prior to performing an abortion. It also directs the physician's determination as to viability by specifying consideration, if feasible, of gestational age, fetal weight, and lung capacity. The District Court found that "the medical evidence is uncontradicted that a 20-week fetus is *not* viable," and that "23½ to 24 weeks gestation is the earliest point in pregnancy where a reasonable possibility of viability exists." But it also found that there may be a 4-week error in estimating gestational age, which supports testing at 20 weeks.

In *Roe v. Wade,* the Court recognized that the State has "important and legitimate" interests in protecting maternal health and in the potentiality of human life. During the second trimester, the State "may, if it chooses, regulate the abortion procedure in ways that are reasonably related to maternal health." After viability, when the State's interest in potential human life was held to become compelling, the State "may, if it chooses, regulate, and even proscribe, abortion except where it is necessary, in appropriate medical judgment, for the preservation of the life or health of the mother.". . .

We think that the doubt cast upon the Missouri statute by these cases is not so much a flaw in the statute as it is a reflection of the fact that the rigid trimester analysis of the course of a pregnancy enunciated in *Roe* has resulted in subsequent cases like *Colautti* and *Akron* making constitutional law in this area a virtual Procrustean bed. Statutes specifying elements of informed consent to be provided abortion patients, for example, were invalidated if they were thought to "structur[e] . . . the dialogue between the woman and her physician." *Thornburgh v. American College of Obstetricians and Gynecologists,* 476 U.S. 747 (1986). As the dissenters in *Thornburgh* pointed out, such a statute would have been sustained under any traditional standard of judicial review (WHITE, J., dissenting), or for any other surgical procedure except abortion. (BURGER, C. J., dissenting).

Stare decisis is a cornerstone of our legal system, but it has less power in constitutional cases, where, save for constitutional amendments, this Court is the only body able to make needed changes. See *United States v. Scott,* 437 U.S. 82, 101 (1978). We have not refrained from reconsideration of a prior construction of the Constitution that has proved "unsound in principle and unworkable in practice." *Garcia v. San Antonio Metropolitan Transit Authority,* 469 U.S. 528, 546 (1985); see *Solorio v. United States,* 483 U.S. 435, 448–450 (1987); *Erie R. Co. v. Tompkins,* 304 U.S. 64, 74–78 (1938). We think the *Roe* trimester framework falls into that category.

In the first place, the rigid *Roe* framework is hardly consistent with the notion of a Constitution cast in general terms, as ours is, and usually speaking in general principles, as ours does. The key elements of the *Roe* framework—trimesters and viability—are not found in the text of the Constitution or in any place else one would expect to find a constitutional principle. Since the bounds of the inquiry are essentially indeterminate, the result has been a web of legal rules that have become increasingly intricate, resembling a code of regulations rather than a body of constitutional doctrine. As Justice WHITE has put it, the trimester framework has left this Court to serve as the country's "*ex officio* medical board with powers to approve or disapprove medical and operative practices and standards throughout the United

States." *Planned Parenthood of Central Missouri v. Danforth*, [428 U.S. 552 (1976)] (opinion concurring in part and dissenting in part).

In the second place, we do not see why the State's interest in protecting potential human life should come into existence only at the point of viability, and that there should therefore be a rigid line allowing state regulation after viability but prohibiting it before viability. The dissenters in *Thornburgh*, writing in the context of the *Roe* trimester analysis, would have recognized this fact by positing against the "fundamental right" recognized in *Roe* the State's "compelling interest" in protecting potential human life throughout pregnancy. "[T]he State's interest, if compelling after viability, is equally compelling before viability." *Thornburgh*, (WHITE, J., dissenting); see *id.* (O'CONNOR, J., dissenting) ("State has compelling interests in ensuring maternal health and in protecting potential human life, and these interests exist 'throughout pregnancy'") (citation omitted).

The tests that § 188.029 requires the physician to perform are designed to determine viability. The State here has chosen viability as the point at which its interest in potential human life must be safeguarded. See Mo. Rev. Stat. § 188.030 (1986) ("No abortion of a viable unborn child shall be performed unless necessary to preserve the life or health of the woman"). It is true that the tests in question increase the expense of abortion, and regulate the discretion of the physician in determining the viability of the fetus. Since the tests will undoubtedly show in many cases that the fetus is not viable, the tests will have been performed for what were in fact second-trimester abortions. But we are satisfied that the requirement of these tests permissibly furthers the State's interest in protecting potential human life, and we therefore believe § 188.029 to be constitutional.

The dissent takes us to task for our failure to join in a "great issues" debate as to whether the Constitution includes an "unenumerated" general right to privacy as recognized in cases such as *Griswold v. Connecticut*, 381 U.S. 479 (1965), and *Roe*. But *Griswold v. Connecticut*, unlike *Roe*, did not purport to adopt a whole framework, complete with detailed rules and distinctions, to govern the cases in which the asserted liberty interest would apply. As such, it was far different from the opinion, if not the holding, of *Roe* v. *Wade*, which sought to establish a constitutional framework for judging state regulation of abortion during the entire term of pregnancy. That framework sought to deal with areas of medical practice traditionally subject to state regulation, and it sought to balance once and for all by reference only to the calendar the claims of the State to protect the fetus as a form of human life against the claims of a woman to decide for herself whether or not to abort a fetus she was carrying. The experience of the Court in applying *Roe* v. *Wade* in later cases suggests to us that there is wisdom in not unnecessarily attempting to elaborate the abstract differences between a "fundamental right" to abortion, as the Court described it in *Akron,* a "limited fundamental constitutional right," which Justice BLACKMUN'S dissent today treats *Roe* as having established, or a liberty interest protected by the Due Process Clause, which we believe it to be. The Missouri testing requirement here is reasonably designed to ensure that abortions are not performed where the fetus is viable—an end which all concede is legitimate—and that is sufficient to sustain its constitutionality.

The dissent also accuses us of cowardice and illegitimacy in dealing with "the most politically divisive domestic legal issue of our time." There is no doubt that our holding today will allow some governmental regulation of abortion that would have been prohibited under the language of cases such as *Colautti v. Franklin,* 439 U.S. 379 (1979), and *Akron v. Akron Center for Reproductive Health, Inc., supra.* But the goal of constitutional adjudication is surely not to remove inexorably "politically divisive" issues from the ambit of the legislative process, whereby the people through their elected representatives deal with matters of concern to them. The goal of constitutional adjudication is to hold true the balance between that which the Constitution puts beyond the reach of the democratic process and that which it does not. We think we have done that today. The dissent's suggestion that legislative bodies, in a Nation where more than half of our population is women, will treat our decision today as an invitation to enact abortion regulation reminiscent of the dark ages not only misreads our views but does scant justice to those who serve in such bodies and the people who elect them.

III

Both appellants and the United States as *Amicus Curiae* have urged that we overrule our decision in *Roe v. Wade.* The facts of the present case, however, differ from those at issue in *Roe.* Here, Missouri has determined that viability is the point at which its interest in potential human life must be safeguarded. In *Roe,* on the other hand, the Texas statute criminalized the performance of *all* abortions, except when the mother's life was at stake. This case therefore affords us no occasion to revisit the holding of *Roe,* which was that the Texas statute unconstitutionally infringed the right to an abortion derived from the Due Process Clause, and we leave it undisturbed. To the extent indicated in our opinion, we would modify and narrow *Roe* and succeeding cases.

Because none of the challenged provisions of the Missouri Act properly before us conflict with the Constitution, the judgment of the Court of Appeals is
Reversed.

Justice O'CONNOR concurring in part.

I concur in Parts I, II–A, II–B, and II–C of the Court's opinion.

I

Nothing in the record before us or the opinions below indicates that subsections 1(1) and 1(2) of the preamble to Missouri's abortion regulation statute will affect a woman's decision to have an abortion. Justice STEVENS suggests that the preamble may also "interfere[ ] with contraceptive choices," because certain contraceptive devices act on a female ovum after it has been fertilized by a male sperm. The Missouri Act defines "conception" as "the fertilization of the ovum of a female by a sperm of a male,". . . and invests "unborn children" with "protectable interests in life, health, and well-being," from "the moment of conception. . . ." Justice STEVENS asserts that any possible interference with a woman's right to use such post-fertilization contraceptive devices would be unconstitutional under *Griswold v. Connecticut* and our subsequent contraception cases. Similarly, certain *amici* suggest that the Missouri Act's preamble may prohibit the developing technology of *in vitro* fertilization, a technique used to aid couples otherwise unable to bear children in which a number of ova are removed from the woman and fertilized by male sperm. . . .

It may be correct that the use of postfertilization contraceptive devices is constitutionally protected by *Griswold* and its progeny but, as with a woman's abortion decision, nothing in the record or the opinions below indicates that the preamble will affect a woman's decision to practice contraception. . . . Neither is there any indication of the possibility that the preamble might be applied to prohibit the performance of *in vitro* fertilization. I agree with the Court, therefore, that all of these intimations of unconstitutionality are simply too hypothetical to support the use of declaratory judgment procedures and injunctive remedies in this case.

Similarly, it seems to me to follow directly from our previous decisions concerning state or federal funding of abortions, that appellees' facial challenge to the constitutionality of Missouri's ban on the utilization of public facilities and the participation of public employees in the performance of abortions not necessary to save the life of the mother cannot succeed. Given Missouri's definition of "public facility" as "any public institution, public facility, public equipment, or any physical asset owned, leased, or controlled by this state or any agency or political subdivisions thereof," there may be conceivable applications of the ban on the use of public facilities that would be unconstitutional. Appellees and *amici* suggest that the State could try to enforce the ban against private hospitals using public water and sewage lines, or against private hospitals leasing state-owned equipment or state land. Whether some or all of these or other applications of

§ 188.215 would be constitutional need not be decided here. *Maher, Poelker,* and *McRae* stand for the proposition that some quite straightforward applications of the Missouri ban on the use of public facilities for performing abortions would be constitutional and that is enough to defeat appellees' assertion that the ban is facially unconstitutional. . . .

I also agree with the Court that, under the interpretation of § 188.205 urged by the State and adopted by the Court, there is no longer a case or controversy before us over the constitutionality of that provision. I would note, however, that this interpretation of § 188.205 is not binding on the Supreme Court of Missouri which has the final word on the meaning of that State's statutes. . . .

II

In its interpretation of Missouri's "determination of viability" provision, Mo. Rev. Stat. § 188.029 (1986), see *ante,* at 15–23, the plurality has proceeded in a manner unnecessary to deciding the question at hand. I agree with the plurality that it was plain error for the Court of Appeals to interpret the second sentence of Mo. Rev. Stat. § 188.029 as meaning that "doctors *must* perform tests to find gestational age, fetal weight and lung maturity." When read together with the first sentence of § 188.029—which requires a physician to "determine if the unborn child is viable by using and exercising that degree of care, skill, and proficiency commonly exercised by the ordinary skillful, careful, and prudent physician engaged in similar practice under the same or similar conditions"—it would be contradictory nonsense to read the second sentence as requiring a physician to perform viability examinations and tests in situations where it would be careless and imprudent to do so. The plurality is quite correct: "the viability-testing provision makes sense only if the second sentence is read to require only those tests that are useful to making subsidiary findings as to viability," and, I would add, only those examinations and tests that it would not be imprudent or careless to perform in the particular medical situation before the physician.

Unlike the plurality, I do not understand these viability testing requirements to conflict with any of the Court's past decisions concerning state regulation of abortion. Therefore, there is no necessity to accept the State's invitation to reexamine the constitutional validity of *Roe v. Wade,* 410 U.S. 113 (1973). Where there is no need to decide a constitutional question, it is a venerable principle of this Court's adjudicatory processes not to do so for "[t]he Court will not 'anticipate a question of constitutional law in advance of the necessity of deciding it.'" *Ashwander v. TVA,* 297 U.S. 288, 346 (1936) (BRANDEIS, J., concurring). Neither will it generally "formulate a rule of constitutional law broader than is required by the precise facts to which it is to be applied."

Quite simply, "[i]t is not the habit of the court to decide questions of a constitutional nature unless absolutely necessary to a decision of the case." *Burton v. United States,* 196 U.S. 283, 295 (1905). The Court today has accepted the State's every interpretation of its abortion statute and has upheld, under our existing precedents, every provision of that statute which is properly before us. Precisely for this reason reconsideration of *Roe* falls not into any "good-cause exception" to this "fundamental rule of judicial restraint. . . ." When the constitutional invalidity of a State's abortion statute actually turns on the constitutional validity of *Roe v. Wade,* there will be time enough to reexamine *Roe.* And to do so carefully.

In assessing § 188.029 it is especially important to recognize that appellees did not appeal the District Court's ruling that the first sentence of § 188.029 is constitutional. There is, accordingly, no dispute between the parties before us over the constitutionality of the "presumption of viability at 20 weeks," created by the first sentence of § 188.029. If anything might arguably conflict with the Court's previous decisions concerning the determination of viability, I would think it is the introduction of this presumption. The plurality refers to a passage from *Planned Parenthood of Central Missouri v. Danforth,* 428 U.S. 52, 64 (1976): "The time when viability is achieved may vary with each pregnancy, and the determination of whether a particular fetus is viable is, and must be, a matter for the judgment of the responsible attending physician." The 20-week presumption of viability in the first sentence of § 188.029, it could be argued (though, I would think, unsuccessfully), restricts "the judgment of the responsible attending physician," by imposing on that physician the burden of overcoming the presumption. This presumption may be a "superimpos[ition] [of] state regulation on the medical determination of whether a particular fetus is viable," but, if so, it is a restriction on the physician's judgment that is not before us. As the plurality properly interprets the second sentence of § 188.029, it does nothing more than delineate means by which the unchallenged 20-week presumption of viability may be overcome if those means are useful in doing so and can be prudently employed. . . .

I do not think the second sentence of § 188.029, as interpreted by the Court, imposes a degree of state regulation on the medical determination of viability that in any way conflicts with prior decisions of this Court. As the plurality recognizes, the requirement that, where not imprudent, physicians perform examinations and tests useful to making subsidiary findings to determine viability "promot[es] the State's interest in potential human life rather than in maternal health." No decision of this Court has held that the State may not directly promote its interest in potential life when viability is possible. Quite the contrary. In *Thornburgh v. American College of Obstetricians and Gynecologists,* the Court considered a constitutional challenge to a Pennsylvania statute requiring that a second physician be present during an abortion performed "when viability is possible." For guidance, the Court looked to the earlier decision in *Planned Parenthood Assn. of Kansas City, Missouri, Inc. v. Ashcroft*, upholding a Missouri statute requiring the presence of a second physician during an abortion performed after viability. The *Thornburgh* majority struck down the Pennsylvania statute merely because the statute had no exception for emergency situations and not because it found a constitutional difference between the State's promotion of its interest in potential life when viability is possible and when viability is certain. Despite the clear recognition by the *Thornburgh* majority that the Pennsylvania and Missouri statutes differed in this respect, there is no hint in the opinion of the *Thornburgh* Court that the State's interest in potential life differs depending whether it seeks to further that interest postviability or when viability is possible. Thus, all nine Members of the *Thornburgh* Court appear to have agreed that it is not constitutionally impermissible for the State to enact regulations designed to protect the State's interest in potential life when viability is possible. That is exactly what Missouri has done in § 188.029. . . .

Finally, and rather half-heartedly, the plurality suggests that the marginal increase in the cost of an abortion created by Missouri's viability testing provision may make § 188.029, even as interpreted, suspect under this Court's decision in *Akron* . . . striking down a second-trimester hospitalization requirement. . . . I dissented from the Court's opinion in *Akron* because it was my view that, even apart from *Roe*'s trimester framework which I continue to consider problematic, see *Thornburgh*, the *Akron* majority had distorted and misapplied its own standard for evaluating state regulation of abortion which the Court had applied with fair consistency in the past: that, previability, "a regulation imposed on a lawful abortion is not unconstitutional unless it unduly burdens the right to seek an abortion.". . .

It is clear to me that requiring the performance of examinations and tests useful to determining whether a fetus is viable, when viability is possible, and when it would not be medically imprudent to do so, does not impose an undue burden on a woman's abortion decision. On this ground alone I would reject the suggestion that § 188.029 as interpreted is unconstitutional. More to the point, however, just as I see no conflict between § 188.029 and *Colautti* or any decision of this Court concerning a State's ability to give effect to its interest in potential life, I see no conflict between § 188.029 and the Court's opinion in *Akron*. The second-trimester hospitalization requirement struck down in *Akron* imposed, in the majority's view, "a heavy, and unnecessary, burden," more than doubling the cost of "women's access to a relatively inexpensive, otherwise accessible, and safe abortion procedure."

By contrast, the cost of examinations and tests that could usefully and prudently be performed when a woman is 20–24 weeks pregnant to determine whether the fetus is viable would only marginally, if at all, increase the cost of an abortion. See Brief for American Association of Prolife Obstetricians and Gynecologists et al. as *Amici Curiae* 3 ("At twenty weeks gestation, an ultrasound examination to determine gestational age is standard medical practice. It is routinely provided by the plaintiff clinics. An ultrasound examination can effectively provide all three designated findings of sec. 188.029"); ("A finding of fetal weight can be obtained from the same ultrasound test used to determine gestational age"); ("There are a number of different methods in standard medical practice to determine fetal lung maturity at twenty or more weeks gestation. The most simple and most obvious is by inference. It is well known that fetal lungs do not mature until 33–34 weeks gestation. . . . If an assessment of the gestational age indicates that the child is less than thirty-three weeks, a general finding can be made that the fetal lungs are not mature. This finding can then be used by the physician in making his determination of viability under section 188.029"). . . .

Moreover, the examinations and tests required by § 188.029 are to be performed when viability is possible. This feature of § 188.029 distinguishes it from the second-trimester hospitalization requirement struck down by the *Akron* majority. As the Court recognized in *Thornburgh,* the State's compelling interest in potential life postviability renders its interest in determining the critical point of viability equally compelling. Under the Court's precedents, the same cannot be said for the *Akron* second-trimester hospitalization requirement. As I understand the Court's opinion in *Akron,* therefore, the plurality's suggestion today that *Akron* casts doubt on the validity of § 188.029, even as the Court has interpreted it, is without foundation and cannot provide a basis for reevaluating *Roe.*

Justice SCALIA concurring in part.

I join Parts I, II-A, II-B, and II-C of the opinion of the CHIEF JUSTICE. As to Part II-D, I share Justice BLACKMUN's view that it effectively would overrule *Roe v. Wade,* 410 U.S. 113 (1973). I think that should be done, but would do it more explicitly. Since today we contrive to avoid doing it, and indeed to avoid almost any decision of national import, I need not set forth my reasons, some of which have been well recited in dissents of my colleagues in other cases. . . .

The outcome of today's case will doubtless be heralded as a triumph of judicial statesmanship. It is not that, unless it is statesmanlike needlessly to prolong this Court's self-awarded sovereignty over a field where it has little proper business since the answers to most of the cruel questions posed are political and not juridical—a sovereignty which therefore quite properly, but to the great damage of the Court, makes it the object of the sort of organized public pressure that political institutions in a democracy ought to receive.

Justice O'CONNOR's assertion that a " 'fundamental rule of judicial restraint' " requires us to avoid reconsidering *Roe*, cannot be taken seriously. By finessing *Roe* we do not, as she suggests, adhere to the strict and venerable rule that we should avoid " 'decid[ing] questions of a constitutional nature.' " We have not disposed of this case on some statutory or procedural ground, but have decided, and could not avoid deciding, whether the Missouri statute meets the requirements of the United States Constitution. The only choice available is whether, in deciding that constitutional question, we should use *Roe v. Wade* as the benchmark, or something else. What is involved, therefore, is not the rule of avoiding constitutional issues where possible, but the quite separate principle that we will not " 'formulate a rule of constitutional law broader than is required by the precise facts to which it is to be applied.' " The latter is a sound general principle, but one often departed from when good reason exists. Just this Term, for example, in an opinion authored by Justice O'CONNOR, despite the fact that we had already held a racially based set-aside unconstitutional because unsupported by evidence of identified discrimination, which was all that was needed to decide the case, we went on to outline the criteria for properly tailoring race-based remedies in cases where such evidence is present. *Richmond v. J. A. Croson Co.,* [488 U.S. 469] (1989). . . .

The Court has often spoken more broadly than needed in precisely the fashion at issue here, announcing a new rule of constitutional law when it could have reached the identical result by applying the rule thereby displaced. . . . It would be wrong, in any decision, to ignore the reality that our policy not to "formulate a rule of constitutional law broader than is required by the precise facts" has a frequently applied good-cause exception. But it seems particularly perverse to convert the policy into an absolute in the present case, in order to place beyond reach the inexpressibly "broader-than-was-required-by-the-precise-facts" structure established by *Roe v. Wade.*

The real question, then, is whether there are valid reasons to go beyond the most stingy possible holding today. It seems to me there are not only valid but compelling ones. Ordinarily, speaking no more broadly than is absolutely required avoids throwing settled law into confusion; doing so today preserves a chaos that is evident to anyone who can read and count. Alone sufficient to justify a broad holding is the fact that our retaining control, through *Roe*, of what I believe to be, and many of our citizens recognize to be, a political issue, continuously distorts the public perception of the role of this Court. We can now look forward to at least another Term with carts full of mail from the public, and streets full of demonstrators, urging us—their unelected and life-tenured judges who have been awarded those extraordinary, undemocratic characteristics precisely in order that we might follow the law despite the popular will—to follow the popular will. Indeed, I expect we can look forward to even more of that than before, given our indecisive decision today. And if these reasons for taking the unexceptional course of reaching a broader holding are not enough, then consider the nature of the constitutional question we avoid: In most cases, we do no harm by not speaking more broadly than the decision requires. Anyone affected by the conduct that the avoided holding would have prohibited will be able to challenge it himself, and have his day in court to make the argument. Not so with respect to the harm that many States believed, pre-*Roe*, and many may continue to believe, is caused by largely unrestricted abortion. That will continue to occur if the States have the constitutional power to prohibit it, and would do so, but we skillfully avoid telling them so. Perhaps those abortions cannot constitutionally be proscribed. That is surely an arguable question, the question that reconsideration of *Roe v. Wade* entails. But what is not at all arguable, it seems to me, is that we should decide now and not insist that we be run into a corner before we grudgingly yield up our judgment. The only sound reason for the latter course is to prevent a change in the law—but to think that desirable begs the question to be decided.

It was an arguable question today whether § 188.029 of the Missouri law contravened this Court's understanding of *Roe v. Wade*, and I would have examined *Roe* rather than examining the contravention. Given the Court's newly contracted abstemiousness, what will it take, one must wonder, to permit us to reach that fundamental question? The result of our vote today is that we will not reconsider that prior opinion, even if most of the Justices think it is wrong, unless we have before us a statute that in fact contradicts it—and even then (under our newly discovered "no-broader-than-necessary" requirement) only minor problematical aspects of *Roe* will be reconsidered, unless one expects State legislatures to adopt provisions whose compliance with *Roe* cannot even be argued with a straight face. It thus appears that the mansion of constitutionalized abortion-law, constructed overnight in *Roe v. Wade*, must be disassembled door-jamb by door-jamb, and never entirely brought down, no matter how wrong it may be.

Of the four courses we might have chosen today—to reaffirm *Roe*, to overrule it explicitly, to overrule it *sub silentio*, or to avoid the question—the last is the least responsible. On the question of the constitutionality of § 188.029, I concur in the judgment of the Court and strongly dissent from the manner in which it has been reached.

Justice BLACKMUN, with whom Justice BRENNAN and Justice MARSHALL join, concurring in part and dissenting in part.

Today, *Roe v. Wade,* and the fundamental constitutional right of women to decide whether to terminate a pregnancy, survive but are not secure. Although the Court extricates itself from this case without making a single, even incremental, change in the law of abortion, the plurality and Justice SCALIA would overrule *Roe* (the first silently, the other explicitly) and would return to the States virtually unfettered authority to control the quintessentially intimate, personal, and life-directing decision whether to carry a fetus to term. Although today, no less than yesterday, the Constitution and the decisions of this Court prohibit a State from enacting laws that inhibit women from the meaningful exercise of that right, a plurality of this Court implicitly invites every state legislature to enact more and more restrictive abortion regulations in order to provoke more and more test cases, in the hope that sometime down the line the Court will return the law of procreative freedom to the severe limitations that generally prevailed in this country before January 22, 1973. Never in my memory has a plurality announced a judgment of this Court that so foments disregard for the law and for our standing decisions.

Nor in my memory has a plurality gone about its business in such a deceptive fashion. At every level of its review, from its effort to read the real meaning out of the Missouri statute, to its intended evisceration of precedents and its deafening silence about the constitutional protections that it would jettison, the plurality obscures the portent of its analysis. With feigned restraint, the plurality announces that its analysis leaves *Roe* "undisturbed," albeit "modif[ied] and narrow[ed]." But this disclaimer is totally meaningless. The plurality opinion is filled with winks, and nods, and knowing glances to those who would do away with *Roe* explicitly, but turns a stone face to anyone in search of what the plurality conceives as the scope of a woman's right under the Due Process Clause to terminate a pregnancy free from the coercive and brooding influence of the State. The simple truth is that *Roe* would not survive the plurality's analysis, and that the plurality provides no substitute for *Roe*'s protective umbrella.

I fear for the future. I fear for the liberty and equality of the millions of women who have lived and come of age in the 16 years since *Roe* was decided. I fear for the integrity of, and public esteem for, this Court.

I dissent.

I

The plurality parades through the four challenged sections of the Missouri statute *seriatim*. I shall not do this, but shall relegate most of my comments as to those sections to the margin. Although I disagree with the plurality's, consideration of §§ 1.205, 188.210, and 188.215, and am especially disturbed by its misapplication of our past decisions in upholding Missouri's ban on the performance of abortions at "public facilities," the plurality's discussion of these provisions is merely prologue to its consideration of the statute's viability-testing requirement, § 188.029—the only section of the Missouri statute that the plurality construes as implicating *Roe* itself. There, tucked away at the end of its opinion, the plurality suggests a radical reversal of the law of abortion; and there, primarily, I direct my attention.

In the plurality's view, the viability-testing provision imposes a burden on second-trimester abortions as a way of furthering the State's interest in protecting the potential life of the fetus. Since under the *Roe* framework, the State may not fully regulate abortion in the interest of potential life (as opposed to maternal health) until the third trimester, the plurality finds it necessary, in order to save the Missouri testing provision, to throw out *Roe*'s trimester framework. In flat contradiction to *Roe,* the plurality concludes that the State's interest in potential life is compelling before viability, and upholds the testing provision because it "permissibly furthers" that state interest.

[A] At the outset, I note that in its haste to limit abortion rights, the plurality compounds the errors of its analysis by needlessly reaching out to address constitutional questions that are not actually presented. The conflict between § 188.029 and *Roe*'s trimester framework, which purportedly drives the plurality to reconsider our past decisions, is a contrived conflict: the product of an aggressive misreading of the viability-testing requirement and a needlessly wooden application of the *Roe* framework.

The plurality's reading of § 188.029 (also joined by Justice O'CONNOR) is irreconcilable with the plain language of the statute and is in derogation of this Court's settled view that " 'district courts and courts of appeals are better schooled in and more able to interpret the laws of their respective States.' " Abruptly setting aside the construction of § 188.029 adopted by both the District Court and Court of Appeals as "plain error," the plurality reads the viability-testing provision as requiring only that before a physician may perform an abortion on a woman whom he believes to be carrying a fetus of 20 or more weeks gestational age, the doctor must determine whether the fetus is viable and, as part of that exercise, must, to the extent feasible and consistent with sound medical practice, conduct tests necessary to make findings of gestational age, weight, and lung maturity. But the plurality's reading of the provision, according to which the statute requires the physician to perform tests only in order to determine *viability*, ignores the statutory language explicitly directing that "the physician *shall* perform or cause to be performed such medical examinations and tests as are *necessary to make a finding of the gestational age, weight, and lung maturity* of the unborn child and *shall* enter such findings" in the mother's medical record. § 188.029 (emphasis added). The statute's plain language requires the physician to undertake whatever tests are necessary to determine gestational age, weight, and lung maturity, regardless of whether these tests are necessary to a finding of viability, and regardless of whether the tests subject the pregnant woman or the fetus to additional health risks or add substantially to the cost of an abortion.

Had the plurality read the statute as written, it would have had no cause to reconsider the *Roe* framework. As properly construed, the viability-testing provision does not pass constitutional muster under even a rational-basis standard, the least restrictive level of review applied by this Court. By mandating tests to determine fetal weight and lung maturity for every fetus thought to be more than 20 weeks gestational age, the statute requires physicians to undertake procedures, such as amniocentesis, that, in the situation presented, have no medical justification, impose significant additional health risks on both the pregnant woman and the fetus, and bear no rational relation to the State's interest in protecting fetal life. As written, § 188.029 is an arbitrary imposition of discomfort, risk, and expense, furthering no discernible interest except to make the procurement of an abortion as arduous and difficult as possible. Thus, were it not for the plurality's tortured effort to avoid the plain import of § 188.029, it could have struck down the testing provision as patently irrational irrespective of the *Roe* framework.

The plurality eschews this straightforward resolution, in the hope of precipitating a constitutional crisis. Far from avoiding constitutional difficulty, the plurality attempts to engineer a dramatic retrenchment in our jurisprudence by exaggerating the conflict between its untenable construction of § 188.029 and the *Roe* trimester framework.

No one contests that under the *Roe* framework the State, in order to promote its interest in potential human life, may regulate and even proscribe non-therapeutic abortions once the fetus becomes viable. *Roe.* If, as the plurality appears to hold, the testing provision simply requires a physician to use appropriate and medically sound tests to determine whether the fetus is actually viable when the estimated gestational age is greater than 20 weeks (and therefore within what the District Court found to be the margin of error for viability, then I see little or no conflict with *Roe.* Nothing in *Roe*, or any of its progeny, holds that a State may not effectuate its compelling interest in the potential life of a viable fetus by seeking to ensure that no viable fetus is mistakenly aborted because of the inherent lack of precision in estimates of gestational age. A requirement that a physician make a finding of viability, one way or the other, for every fetus that falls within the range of possible viability does no more than preserve the State's recognized authority. Although, as the plurality correctly points out, such a testing requirement would have the effect of imposing additional costs on second-trimester abortions where the tests indicated that the fetus was not viable, these costs would be merely incidental to, and a necessary accommodation of, the State's unquestioned right to prohibit non-therapeutic abortions after the point of viability. In short, the testing provision, as construed by the plurality is consistent with the *Roe* framework and could be upheld effortlessly under current doctrine.

How ironic it is, then, and disingenuous, that the plurality scolds the Court of Appeals for adopting a construction of the statute that fails to avoid constitutional difficulties. *Ante,* at 16. By distorting the statute, the plurality manages to avoid invalidating the testing provision on what should have been noncontroversial constitutional grounds; having done so, however, the plurality rushes headlong into a much deeper constitutional thicket, brushing past an obvious basis for upholding § 188.029 in search of a pretext for scuttling the trimester framework. Evidently, from the plurality's perspective, the real problem with the Court of Appeals' construction of § 188.029 is not that it raised a constitutional difficulty, but that it raised the wrong constitutional difficulty—one not implicating *Roe.* The plurality has remedied that, traditional canons of construction and judicial forbearance notwithstanding.

[B] Having set up the conflict between § 188.029 and the *Roe* trimester framework, the plurality summarily discards *Roe*'s analytic core as " 'unsound in principle and unworkable in practice.' " This is so, the plurality claims, because the key elements of the framework do not appear in the text of the Constitution, because the framework more closely resembles a regulatory code than a body of constitutional doctrine, and because under the framework the State's interest in potential human life is considered compelling only after viability, when, in fact, that interest is equally compelling throughout pregnancy. The plurality does not bother to explain these alleged flaws in *Roe.* Bald assertion masquerades as reasoning. The object, quite clearly, is not to persuade, but to prevail.

[1] The plurality opinion is far more remarkable for the arguments that it does not advance than for those that it does. The plurality does not even mention, much less join, the true jurisprudential debate underlying this case: whether the Constitution includes an "unenumerated" general right to privacy as recognized in many of our decisions, most notably *Griswold v. Connecticut,*

and *Roe*, and, more specifically, whether and to what extent such a right to privacy extends to matters of childbearing and family life, including abortion. See, *e.g., Eisenstadt v. Baird*, 405 U.S. 438 (1972) (contraception); *Loving v. Virginia*, 388 U.S. 1 (1967) (marriage); *Skinner v. Oklahoma ex re. Williamson*, 316 U.S. 535 (1942) (procreation); *Pierce v. Society of Sisters*, 268 U.S. 510 (1925) (childrearing). These are questions of unsurpassed significance in this Court's interpretation of the Constitution, and mark the battleground upon which this case was fought, by the parties, by the Solicitor General as *amicus* on behalf of petitioners, and by an unprecedented number of *amici*. On these grounds, abandoned by the plurality, the Court should decide this case.

But rather than arguing that the text of the Constitution makes no mention of the right to privacy, the plurality complains that the critical elements of the *Roe* framework—trimesters and viability—do not appear in the Constitution and are, therefore, somehow inconsistent with a Constitution cast in general terms. . . . Were this a true concern, we would have to abandon most of our constitutional jurisprudence. As the plurality well knows, or should know, the "critical elements" of countless constitutional doctrines nowhere appear in the Constitution's text. The Constitution makes no mention, for example, of the First Amendment's "actual malice" standard for proving certain libels, see *New York Times v. Sullivan*, [376 U.S. 254] (1964), or of the standard for determining when speech is obscene. See *Miller v. California*, [413 U.S. 15] (1973). Similarly, the Constitution makes no mention of the rational-basis test, or the specific verbal formulations of intermediate and strict scrutiny by which this Court evaluates claims under the Equal Protection Clause. The reason is simple. Like the *Roe* framework, these tests or standards are not, and do not purport to be, rights protected by the Constitution. Rather, they are judge-made methods for evaluating and measuring the strength and scope of constitutional rights or for balancing the constitutional rights of individuals against the competing interests of government.

With respect to the *Roe* framework, the general constitutional principle, indeed the fundamental constitutional right, for which it was developed is the right to privacy, a species of "liberty" protected by the Due Process Clause, which under our past decisions safeguards the right of women to exercise some control over their own role in procreation. As we recently reaffirmed in *Thornburgh v. American College of Obstetricians and Gynecologists* (1986), few decisions are "more basic to individual dignity and autonomy" or more appropriate to that "certain private sphere of individual liberty" that the Constitution reserves from the intrusive reach of government than the right to make the uniquely personal, intimate, and self-defining decision whether to end a pregnancy. It is this general principle, the " 'moral fact that a person belongs to himself and not others nor to society as a whole,'" that is found in the Constitution. The trimester framework simply defines and limits that right to privacy in the abortion context to accommodate, not destroy, a State's legitimate interest in protecting the health of pregnant women and in preserving potential human life. Fashioning such accommodations between individual rights and the legitimate interests of government, establishing benchmarks and standards with which to evaluate the competing claims of individuals and government, lies at the very heart of constitutional adjudication. To the extent that the trimester framework is useful in this enterprise, it is not only consistent with constitutional interpretation, but necessary to the wise and just exercise of this Court's paramount authority to define the scope of constitutional rights.

[2] The plurality next alleges that the result of the trimester framework has "been a web of legal rules that have become increasingly intricate, resembling a code of regulations rather than a body of constitutional doctrine." Again, if this were a true and genuine concern, we would have to abandon vast areas of our constitutional jurisprudence. The plurality complains that under the trimester framework the Court has distinguished between a city ordinance requiring that second-trimester abortions be performed in clinics and a state law requiring that these abortions be performed in hospitals, or between laws requiring that certain information be furnished to a woman by a physician or his assistant and those requiring that such information be furnished by the physician exclusively. Are these distinctions any finer, or more "regulatory," than the distinctions we have often drawn in our First Amendment jurisprudence, where, for example, we have held that a "release time" program permitting public-school students to leave school grounds during school hours to receive religious instruction does not violate the Establishment Clause, even though a release-time program permitting religious instruction on school grounds does violate the Clause? . . .

That numerous constitutional doctrines result in narrow differentiations between similar circumstances does not mean that this Court has abandoned adjudication in favor of regulation. Rather, these careful distinctions reflect the process of constitutional adjudication itself, which is often highly fact-specific, requiring such determinations as whether state laws are "unduly burdensome" or "reasonable" or bear a "rational" or "necessary" relation to asserted state interests. In a recent due process case, the CHIEF JUSTICE wrote for the Court: "[M]any branches of the law abound in nice distinctions that may be troublesome but have been thought nonetheless necessary: 'I do not think we need trouble ourselves with the thought that my view depends upon differences of degree. The whole law does so as soon as it is civilized.'" *Daniels v. Williams,* 474 U.S. 327, 334 (1986). . . .

These "differences of degree" fully account for our holdings in *Simopoulos* and *Akron*. Those decisions rest on this Court's reasoned and accurate judgment that hospitalization and doctor-counselling requirements unduly burdened the right of women to terminate a pregnancy and were not rationally related to the State's asserted interest in the health of pregnant women, while Virginia's *substantially less restrictive* regulations were not unduly burdensome and did rationally serve the State's interest. That the Court exercised its best judgment in evaluating these markedly different statutory schemes no more established the Court as an " 'ex officio medical board,' " than our decisions involving religion in the public schools establish the Court as a national school board, or our decisions concerning prison regulations establish the Court as a bureau of prisons. If, in delicate and complicated areas of constitutional law, our legal judgments "have become increasingly intricate," it is not, as the plurality contends, because we have overstepped our judicial role. Quite the opposite: the rules are intricate because we have remained conscientious in our duty to do justice carefully, especially when fundamental rights rise or fall with our decisions.

[3] Finally, the plurality asserts that the trimester framework cannot stand because the State's interest in potential life is compelling throughout pregnancy, not merely after viability. The opinion contains not one word of rationale for its view of the State's interest. This "it-is-so-because-we-say-so" jurisprudence constitutes nothing other than an attempted exercise of brute force; reason, much less persuasion, has no place. . . .

For my own part, I remain convinced, as six other Members of this Court 16 years ago were convinced, that the *Roe* framework, and the viability standard in particular, fairly, sensibly, and effectively functions to safeguard the constitutional liberties of pregnant women while recognizing and accommodating the State's interest in potential human life. The viability line reflects the biological facts and truths of fetal development; it marks that threshold moment prior to which a fetus cannot survive separate from the woman and cannot reasonably and objectively be regarded as a subject of rights or interests distinct from, or paramount to, those of the pregnant woman. At the same time, the viability standard takes account of the undeniable fact that as the fetus evolves into its postnatal form, and as it loses its dependence on the uterine environment, the State's interest in the fetus' potential human life, and in fostering a regard for human life in general, becomes compelling. As a practical matter, because viability follows "quickening"—the point at which a woman feels movement in her womb—and because viability occurs no earlier than 23 weeks gestational age, it establishes an easily applicable standard for regulating abortion while providing a pregnant woman ample time to exercise her fundamental right with her responsible physician to terminate her pregnancy. Although I have stated previously for a majority of this Court that "[c]onstitutional rights do not always have easily ascertainable boundaries," to seek and establish those boundaries remains the special responsibility of this Court. *Thornburgh.* In *Roe,* we discharged that responsibility as logic and science compelled. The plurality today advances not one reasonable argument as to why our judgment in that case was wrong and should be abandoned.

[C] Having contrived an opportunity to reconsider the *Roe* framework, and then having discarded that framework, the plurality finds the testing provision unobjectionable because it "permissibly furthers the State's interest in protecting potential human life." This newly minted standard is circular and totally meaningless. Whether a challenged abortion regulation "permissibly furthers" a legitimate state interest is the *question* that courts must answer in abortion cases, not the standard for courts to apply. In keeping with the rest of its opinion, the plurality makes no attempt to explain or to justify its new standard, either in the abstract or as applied in this case. Nor could it. The "permissibly furthers" standard has no independent meaning, and consists of nothing other than what a majority of this Court may believe at any given moment in any given case. The plurality's novel test appears to be nothing more than a dressed-up version of rational-basis review, this Court's most lenient level of scrutiny. One thing is clear, however: were the plurality's "permissibly furthers" standard adopted by the Court, for all practical purposes, *Roe* would be overruled.

The "permissibly furthers" standard completely disregards the irreducible minimum of *Roe:* the Court's recognition that a woman has a limited fundamental constitutional right to decide whether to terminate a pregnancy. That right receives no meaningful recognition in the plurality's written opinion. Since, in the plurality's view, the State's interest in potential life is compelling as of the moment of conception, and is therefore served only if abortion is abolished, every hindrance to a woman's ability to obtain an abortion must be "permissible." Indeed, the more severe the hindrance, the more effectively (and permissibly) the State's interest would be furthered. A tax on abortions or a criminal prohibition would both satisfy the plurality's standard. So, for that matter, would a requirement that a pregnant woman memorize and recite today's plurality opinion before seeking an abortion.

The plurality pretends that *Roe* survives, explaining that the facts of this case differ from those in *Roe:* here, Missouri has chosen to assert its interest in potential life only at the point of viability, whereas, in *Roe,* Texas had asserted that interest from the point of conception, criminalizing all abortions, except where the life of the mother was at stake. This, of course, is a distinction without a difference. The plurality repudiates every principle for which *Roe* stands; in good conscience, it cannot possibly believe that *Roe* lies "undisturbed" merely because this case does not call upon the Court to reconsider the Texas statute, or one like it. If the Constitution permits a State to enact any statute that reasonably furthers its interest in potential life, and if that interest arises as of conception, why would the Texas statute fail to pass muster? One suspects that the plurality agrees. It is impossible to read the plurality opinion and especially its final paragraph, without recognizing its implicit invitation to every State to enact more and more restrictive abortion laws, and to assert their interest in potential life as of the moment of conception. All these laws will satisfy the plurality's non-scrutiny, until sometime, a new regime of old dissenters and new appointees will declare what the plurality intends: that *Roe* is no longer good law.

[D] Thus, "not with a bang, but a whimper," the plurality discards a landmark case of the last generation, and casts into darkness the hopes and visions of every woman in this country who had come to believe that the Constitution guaranteed her the right to exercise some control over her unique ability to bear children. The plurality does so either oblivious or insensitive to the fact that millions of women, and their families, have ordered their lives around the right to reproductive choice, and that this right has become vital to the full participation of women in the economic and political walks of American life. The plurality would clear the way once again for government to force upon women the physical labor and specific and direct medical and psychological harms that may accompany carrying a fetus to term. The plurality would clear the way again for the State to conscript a woman's body and to force upon her a "distressful life and future.". . .

The result, as we know from experience, would be that every year hundreds of thousands of women, in desperation, would defy the law, and place their health and safety in the unclean and unsympathetic hands of back-alley abortionists, or they would attempt to perform abortions upon themselves, with disastrous results. Every year, many women, especially poor and minority women, would die or suffer debilitating physical trauma, all in the name of enforced morality or religious dictates or lack of compassion, as it may be.

Of the aspirations and settled understandings of American women, of the inevitable and brutal consequences of what it is doing, the tough-approach plurality utters not a word. This silence is callous. It is also profoundly destructive of this Court as an institution. To overturn a constitutional decision is a rare and grave undertaking. To overturn a constitutional decision that secured a fundamental personal liberty to millions of persons would be unprecedented in our 200 years of constitutional history. Although the doctrine of *stare decisis* applies with somewhat diminished force in constitutional cases generally, even in ordinary constitutional cases "any departure from *stare decisis* demands special justification.". . . This requirement of justification applies with unique force where, as here, the Court's abrogation of precedent would destroy people's firm belief, based on past decisions of this Court, that they possess an unabridgeable right to undertake certain conduct. . . .

[T]he plurality pretends that it leaves *Roe* standing, and refuses even to discuss the real issue underlying this case: whether the Constitution includes an unenumerated right to privacy that encompasses a woman's right to decide whether to terminate a pregnancy. To the extent that the plurality does criticize the *Roe* framework, these criticisms are pure *ipse dixit.*

This comes at a cost. The doctrine of *stare decisis* "permits society to presume that bedrock principles are founded in the law rather than in the proclivities of individuals, and thereby contributes to the integrity of our constitutional system of government, both in appearance and in fact." Today's decision involves the most politically divisive domestic legal issue of our time. By refusing to explain or to justify its proposed revolutionary revision in the law of abortion, and by refusing to abide not only by our precedents, but also by our canons for reconsidering those precedents, the plurality invites charges of cowardice and illegitimacy to our door. I cannot say that these would be undeserved.

II

For today, at least, the law of abortion stands undisturbed. For today, the women of this Nation still retain the liberty to control their destinies. But the signs are evident and very ominous, and a chill wind blows.

I dissent.

Justice STEVENS, concurring in part and dissenting in part.

I am persuaded that the absence of any secular purpose for the legislative declarations that life begins at conception and that conception occurs at fertilization makes the relevant portion of the preamble invalid under the Establishment Clause of the First Amendment to the Federal Constitution. This conclusion does not, and could not, rest on the fact that the statement happens to coincide with the tenets of certain religions, or on the fact that the legislators who voted to enact it may have been motivated by religious considerations. Rather, it rests on the fact that the preamble, an unequivocal endorsement of a religious tenet of some but by no means all Christian faiths, serves no identifiable secular purpose. That fact alone compels a conclusion that the statute violates the Establishment Clause. . . .

The preamble to the Missouri statute endorses the theological position that there is the same secular interest in preserving the life of a fetus during the first 40 or 80 days of pregnancy as there is after viability—indeed, after the time when the fetus has become a "person" with legal rights protected by the Constitution. To sustain that position as a matter of law, I believe Missouri has the burden of identifying the secular interests that differentiate the first 40 days of pregnancy from the period immediately before or after fertilization when, as *Griswold* and related cases establish, the Constitution allows the use of contraceptive procedures to prevent potential life from developing into full personhood. Focusing our attention on the first several weeks of pregnancy is especially appropriate because that is the period when the vast majority of abortions are actually performed.

As a secular matter, there is an obvious difference between the state interest in protecting the freshly fertilized egg and the state interest in protecting a 9-month-gestated, fully sentient fetus on the eve of birth. There can be no interest in protecting the newly fertilized egg from physical pain or mental anguish, because the capacity for such suffering does not yet exist; respecting a developed fetus, however, that interest is valid. In fact, if one prescinds the theological concept of ensoulment—or one accepts St. Thomas Aquinas' view that ensoulment does not occur for at least 40 days, a State has no greater secular interest in protecting the potential life of an embryo that is still "seed" than in protecting the potential life of a sperm or an unfertilized ovum.

There have been times in history when military and economic interests would have been served by an increase in population. No one argues today, however, that Missouri can assert a societal interest in increasing its population as its secular reason for fostering potential life. Indeed, our national policy, as reflected in legislation the Court upheld last Term, is to prevent the potential life that is produced by "pregnancy and childbirth among unmarried adolescents." *Bowen v. Kendrick* [487 U.S. 589 (1988)]. . . .

Bolstering my conclusion that the preamble violates the First Amendment is the fact that the intensely divisive character of much of the national debate over the abortion issue reflects the deeply held religious convictions of many participants in the debate. . . .

In my opinion the preamble to the Missouri statute is unconstitutional for two reasons. To the extent that it has substantive impact on the freedom to use contraceptive procedures, it is inconsistent with the central holding in *Griswold*. To the extent that it merely makes "legislative findings without operative effect," as the State argues, it violates the Establishment Clause of the First Amendment. Contrary to the theological "finding" of the Missouri Legislature, a woman's constitutionally protected liberty encompasses the right to act on her own belief that—to paraphrase St.

Thomas Aquinas—until a seed has acquired the powers of sensation and movement, the life of a human being has not yet begun.

B. PRIVACY AND PERSONAL AUTONOMY

Griswold v. Connecticut invited further litigation aimed at expanding the right of privacy to include a broad and diverse range of interests in personal autonomy. State and lower federal courts broadly construed the right of privacy, for example, to allow cancer patients to use Laetrile, a drug that had not yet been approved by the Food and Drug Administration;[1] and to outweigh state interests in requiring motorcyclists to wear helmets.[2]

The Burger and Rehnquist Courts, however, have largely rebuffed claims to broaden the scope of the right of privacy. In *Kelly v. Johnson*, 425 U.S. 238 (1976), for instance, the Court upheld a regulation limiting the length of policemen's hair.[3] In his opinion announcing the decision, Justice Rehnquist distinguished the " 'liberty' interest" claimed in *Kelly* from that in *Griswold* and *Roe* on the grounds that "those cases involved a substantial claim of infringement on the individual's freedom of choice with respect to certain basic matters of procreation, marriage, and family life." But dissenting Justice Thurgood Marshall, joined by Justice Brennan, protested:

I think it clear that the Fourteenth Amendment . . . protects against comprehensive regulation of what citizens may or may not wear. . . . An individual's personal appearance may reflect, sustain, and nourish his personality and may well be used as a means of expressing his attitude and lifestyle. In taking control over a citizen's personal appearance, the government forces him to sacrifice substantial elements of his integrity and indentity as well. To say that the liberty guarantee of the Fourteenth Amendment does not encompass matters of personal appearance would be fundamentally inconsistent with the values of privacy, self-identity, autonomy, and personal integrity that . . . the Constitution was designed to protect.

In *Moore v. City of East Cleveland*, 431 U.S. 494 (1977), though, a bare majority overturned a city ordinance limiting the occupancy of any dwelling to members of the same "family" and narrowly defined "family" to include only a "few categories of related individuals." Inex Moore, a grandmother, was convicted of violating the ordinance and sentenced to five days in jail and fined $25, because she lived with her two grandsons; one of whom came to live with her after his mother's death. When striking down the ordinance, Justice Powell explained,

When a city undertakes such intrusive regulation of the family . . . the usual judicial deference to the legislature is inappropriate. "This Court has long recognized that freedom of personal choice in matters of marriage and family life is one of the liberties protected by the Due Process Clause of the Fourteenth Amendment." [Citing *Meyer, Pierce, Skinner, Griswold,* and *Roe.*] . . . When government intrudes on choices concerning family living arrangements, this Court must examine carefully the importance of the governmental interests advanced and the extent to which they are served by the challenged regulation. When thus examined, this ordinance cannot survive. The city seeks to justify it as a means of preventing overcrowding, minimizing traffic and parking congestion, and avoiding an undue financial burden on the school system. Although these are legitimate goals, the ordinance serves them marginally, at best. . . .

Substantive due process has at times been a treacherous field for this Court. There *are* risks when the judicial branch gives enhanced protection to certain substantive liberties without the guidance of the more specific provisions of the Bill of Rights. As the history of the *Lochner* era demonstrates, there is reason for concern lest the only limits to such judicial intervention become the predilections of those who happen at the time to be Members of this Court. That history counsels caution and restraint. But it does not counsel abandonment. . . .

Our decisions establish that the Constitution protects the sanctity of the family precisely because the institution of the family is deeply rooted in this Nation's history and tradition. It is through the family that we inculcate and pass down many of our most cherished values, moral and cultural. . . . The tradition of uncles, aunts, cousins, and especially grandparents sharing a household along with parents has roots equally venerable and equally deserving of constitutional recognition. . . . The choice of relatives in this degree of kinship to live together may not lightly be denied by the State. . . . The Constitution prevents East Cleveland from standardizing its children—and its adults—by forcing all to live in certain narrowly defined family patterns.

But dissenting Justice Potter Stewart, joined by Justice Rehnquist, countered that,

[t]o suggest that the biological fact of common ancestry necessarily gives related persons constitutional rights of association superior to those of unrelated persons is to misunderstand the nature of the associational freedoms that the Constitution has been understood to protect. Freedom of association has been constitutionally recognized because it is often indispensable to effectuation of explicit First Amendment guarantees. . . .

In a case such as this one, where the challenged ordinance intrudes upon no substantively protected constitutional right, it is not the Court's business to decide whether its application in a particular case seems inequitable, or even absurd.

In separate opinions, Chief Justice Burger and Justice White also dissented. The latter, after strongly objecting to the majority's broad reading of the Due Process Clause and exercise of judicial review, concluded:

> The ordinance . . . denies appellant the opportunity to live with all her grandchildren in this particular suburb; she is free to do so in other parts of the Cleveland metropolitan area. If there is power to maintain the character of a single-family neighborhood, as there surely is, some limit must be placed on the reach of the "family." Had it been our task to legislate, we might have approached the problem in a different manner than did the drafters of this ordinance; but I have no trouble in concluding that the normal goals of zoning regulation are present here and that the ordinance serves these goals by limiting, in identifiable circumstances, the number of people who can occupy a single household. The ordinance does not violate the Due Process Clause.

Moore v. City of East Cleveland underscores the struggles within the Court and the majority's concern with limiting the application of the right of privacy to matters directly bearing on the "family—marriage; childbirth; the raising and education of children; and cohabitation with one's relatives."[4] Accordingly, the Court has also rejected claims of "informational privacy"—that is privacy interests in "avoiding disclosure of personal matters" in, for example, bank, tax, and medical records; and in "independence in making certain kinds of important decisions" that may be diminished due to developments in computer technology and telecommunications.

Whalen v. Roe (1976) (see page 1219) provides the Court's most comprehensive discussion of claims to informational privacy. There Justice Stevens upheld regulations requiring the reporting and maintaining of computerized records on individuals purchasing certain dangerous drugs. See also the treatment of privacy claims and the First Amendment in *Cox Broadcasting Co. v. Cohn* (1975) (in Chapter 5), *Federal Communications Commission v. Pacifica Foundation* (1978) (in Chapter 5), and Fourth Amendment–protected privacy interests (see Chapter 7), as well as Fifth Amendment–privacy claims with regard to private papers and required records (see Chapter 8). The problems of safeguarding interests in informational privacy remain largely matters for Congress and state legislatures. The Fair Credit Reporting Act of 1970 (regulating consumer reports), the Crime Control Act of 1973 (regulating access to individuals' criminal records), and the Family Educational Rights and Privacy Act of 1974 (regulating access to student educational records), for instance, safeguard specific kinds of interests in informational privacy. The Privacy Act of 1974 embodies the most comprehensive statutory scheme for safeguarding privacy interests by regulating the collection and utilization of personal information by federal agencies.[5]

Both *Moore* and *Whalen v. Roe* indicate the Court's reluctance to expand the right of privacy to provide broader protection for claims of sexual autonomy and personal lifestyle choices. In the 1970s and 1980s, though, the movement to recognize homosexual rights prompted new legislation and litigation in the courts. Twenty-three states repealed laws penalizing sexual activities between consenting adults and three state supreme courts (in Massachusetts, New York, and Pennsylvania) struck down laws punishing homosexual relations. Twenty-four states continue to outlaw homosexual activities: in nine states such activities are a misdemeanor and in fifteen others they are a felony, carrying penalties in excess of a year in imprisonment.

The Court avoided directly ruling on claims that the right of privacy includes sexual freedom between consenting adults in the privacy of their homes until *Bowers v. Hardwick* (1986) (see page 1224). Then the justices split five to four, with Justice Powell casting the controlling vote, for upholding Georgia's law making heterosexual and homosexual sodomy a crime.

The Rehnquist Court is unlikely in the near future to expand the scope of the right of privacy to include broader claims of sexual freedom. But the Court will certainly continue to confront claims of personal autonomy. In the 1989–1990 term, for example, the Court faced for the first time the claim that the right of privacy includes a "right to die." In *Cruzan by Cruzan v. Director, Missouri Department of Health* (1990) (see page 1233), the Court upheld the interests of the state of Missouri over the privacy claims of parents who sued to remove a feeding tube inserted in their daughter, Nancy Cruzan, who is brain injured and who doctors say will remain unconscious for the next thirty years unless the tube is removed and she is allowed to die. Writing for a bare majority, Chief Justice Rehnquist rejects further extension of the right of privacy into this vexing area of social policy. He ruled as well that the Constitution permits, but does not require, states to demand "clear and convincing" evidence that an incompetent patient would have wanted to discontinue life-support equipment. However, Chief Justice Rehnquist also construed the Fourteenth Amendment's due process clause to guarantee a liberty interest that protects the right of individuals to terminate unwanted medical treatment, if they are able to express or had clearly expressed (in a living will, for example) their desire to have medical treatment terminated in the event that they become incompetent. With the exception of Justice Scalia, all of the justices (including those in dissent) endorsed this interpretation of the Fourteenth Amendment's protection for individuals' liberty interests.

NOTES

1. *Rutherford v. United States,* 438 F.Supp. 1287 (W.D. Oka., 1977), reversed on other grounds, 442 U.S. 544 (1979).
2. *People v. Fries,* 42 Ill. 2d 446, 250 N.E. 2d 149 (1969).
3. See also *Paul v. Davis,* 424 U.S. 693 (1976), rejecting a claim of personal privacy and reputation when upholding the distribution by police of fliers, containing mug shot photos captioned "Active Shoplifters," to local merchants.
4. See *Roberts v. United States Jaycees,* 468 U.S. 609 (1984) in Chapter 5.
5. See United States Privacy Protection Study Commission, *Personal Privacy in an Information Society* (Washington, DC: Government Printing Office, 1977).

SELECTED BIBLIOGRAPHY

Fried, Charles. *An Anatomy of Values.* Cambridge, MA: Harvard University Press, 1970.
Irons, Peter. *The Courage of Their Convictions.* New York: Free Press, 1988, Ch. 16.
United States Privacy Protection Study Commission. *Personal Privacy in an Information Society.* Washington, DC: U.S. Government Printing Office, 1977.
Young, J. B., ed. *Privacy.* New York: Wiley, 1978.

Whalen v. Roe
429 U.S. 589, 97 S.Ct. 869 (1977)

Following the passage of the New York State Controlled Substances Act of 1972, several physicians and patients filed suit against Robert Whalen, the state's commission of health, and sought to enjoin his enforcement of portions of the law. Under that law, doctors were required to fill out prescription drug forms for certain potentially harmful drugs, retaining one copy, sending another copy to the dispensing pharmacy, and sending a third copy to the state department of health. The forms identified the doctor; the prescription; and the name, address, and age of the patient. The Department of Health in turn was required to code and computerize the records for investigators. The physicians and patients contended that the reporting and record-keeping requirements violated their constitutional right of privacy. A federal district court agreed and enjoined enforcement of provisions of the law. Whalen appealed that ruling to the Supreme Court, which granted review and reversed the lower court.

Justice STEVENS delivers the opinion of the Court.

The constitutional question presented is whether the State of New York may record, in a centralized computer file, the names and addresses of all persons who have obtained, pursuant to a doctor's prescription, certain drugs for which there is both a lawful and an unlawful market.

The District Court enjoined enforcement of the portions of the New York State Controlled Substances Act of 1972 which require such recording on the ground that they violate appellees' constitutionally protected rights of privacy. We noted probable jurisdiction of the appeal by the Commissioner of Health . . . and now reverse.

Many drugs have both legitimate and illegitimate uses. In response to a concern that such drugs were being diverted into unlawful channels, in 1970 the New York Legislature created a special commission to evaluate the State's drug-control laws. The commission found the existing laws deficient in several respects. There was no effective way to prevent the use of stolen or revised prescriptions, to prevent unscrupulous pharmacists from repeatedly refilling prescriptions, to prevent users from obtaining prescriptions from more than one doctor, or to prevent doctors from over-prescribing, either by authorizing an excessive amount in one prescription or by giving one patient multiple prescriptions. In drafting new legislation to correct such defects, the commission [created a reporting system]. . . .

Appellees contend that the statute invades a constitutionally protected "zone of privacy." The cases sometimes characterized as protecting "privacy" have in fact involved at least two different kinds of interests. One is the individual interest in avoiding disclosure of personal matters, and another is the interest in independence in making certain kinds of important decisions. Appellees argue that both of these interests are impaired by this statute. . . .

We are persuaded, however, that the New York program does not, on its face, pose a sufficiently grievous threat to either interest to establish a constitutional violation.

Public disclosure of patient information can come about in three ways. Health Department employees may violate the statute by failing, either deliberately or negligently, to maintain proper security. A patient or a doctor may be accused of a violation and the stored data may be offered in evidence in a judicial proceeding. Or, thirdly, a doctor, a pharmacist, or the patient may voluntarily reveal information on a prescription form.

The third possibility existed under the prior law and is entirely unrelated to the existence of the computerized data bank. Neither of the other two possibilities provides a proper ground for attacking the statute as invalid on its face. There is no support in the record, or in the experience of the two States that New York has emulated, for an assumption that the security provisions of the statute will be administered improperly. And the remote possibility that judicial supervision of the evidentiary use of particular items of stored information will provide inadequate protection against unwarranted disclosures is surely not a sufficient reason for invalidating the entire patient-identification program.

Even without public disclosure, it is, of course, true that private information must be disclosed to the authorized employees of the New York Department of Health. Such disclosures, however, are not significantly different from those that were required under the prior law. Nor are they meaningfully distinguishable from a host of other unpleasant invasions of privacy that are associated with many facets of health care. Unquestionably, some individuals' concern for their own privacy may lead them to avoid or to postpone needed medical attention. Nevertheless, disclosures of private medical information to doctors, to hospital personnel, to insurance companies, and to public health agencies are often an essential part of modern medical practice even when the disclosure may reflect unfavorably on the character of the patient. Requiring such disclosures to representatives of the State having responsibility for the health of the community, does not automatically amount to an impermissible invasion of privacy. . . .

We hold that neither the immediate nor the threatened impact of the patient-identification requirements in the New York State Controlled Substances Act . . . is sufficient to constitute an invasion of any right or liberty protected by the Fourteenth Amendment. . . .

A final word about issues we have not decided. We are not unaware of the threat to privacy implicit in the accumulation of vast amounts of personal information in computerized data banks or other massive government files. The collection of taxes, the distribution of welfare and social security benefits, the supervision of public health, the direction of our Armed Forces, and the enforcement of the criminal laws all require the orderly preservation of great quantities of information, much of which is personal in character and potentially embarrassing or harmful if disclosed. The right to collect and use such data for public purposes is typically accompanied by a concomitant statutory or regulatory duty to avoid unwarranted disclosures. Recognizing that in some circumstances that duty arguably has its roots in the Constitution, nevertheless New York's statutory scheme, and its implementing administrative procedures, evidence a proper concern with, and protection of, the individual's interest in privacy. We therefore need not, and do not, decide any question which might be presented by the unwarranted disclosure of accumulated private data—whether intentional or unintentional—or by a system that did not contain comparable security provisions. We simply hold that this record does not establish an invasion of any right or liberty protected by the Fourteenth Amendment.

Reversed.

Justice BRENNAN concurred in a separate opinion.

Justice STEWART concurring.

Griswold . . . held that a State cannot constitutionally prohibit

a married couple from using contraceptives in the privacy of their home. Although the broad language of the opinion includes a discussion of privacy, the constitutional protection there discovered also related to (1) marriage, . . . (2) privacy *in the home,* . . . and (3) the right to use contraceptives. . . . Whatever the *ratio decidendi* of *Griswold,* it does not recognize a general interest in freedom from disclosure of private information.

INSIDE THE COURT
The Right to Privacy and Sexual Freedom

When the Court heard oral arguments for *Bowers v. Hardwick,* Hardwick was represented by Harvard Law School professor Laurence Tribe. He knew that the Court would be sharply split when deciding the case and that Justice Lewis Powell would likely cast the deciding vote. Just a year earlier, in Justice Powell's absence, the justices split four to four in *Board of Education of Oklahoma City v. National Gay Task Force,* 470 U.S. 903 (1985), leaving intact a lower court ruling overturning an Oklahoma law providing for the dismissal of teachers who advocate homosexual relations. Tribe thus pitched his arguments for overturning Georgia's law at Justice Powell. "This case is about the limits of government power," he argued, reminding the justices they had held that individuals have constitutionally protected privacy interests in their homes. The question was whether states have a compelling interest in dictating, as Tribe put it, "how every adult, married or unmarried, in every bedroom in Georgia will behave in the closest and most intimate personal association with another adult." But Powell interrupted from the bench to ask whether that meant that states could not proscribe consensual sodomy in "a motel room or the back of an automobile or [public] toilet or wherever." Knowing that a decade earlier the Court had denied, in *Commonwealth's Attorney for the City of Richmond v. Doe,* 425 U.S. 901 (1976), an appeal of a man's conviction under Virginia's sodomy law for having homosexual relations in a public bathroom, Tribe was evasive. On Powell's persistence and chiding him for avoiding his "public toilet" question, Tribe finally conceded certain behavior in public places could be outlawed, but underscored that "there is something special about a home."

Justice Powell was tentatively persuaded by Tribe's arguments. At the justices' private conference two days later, Chief Justice Burger began discussion of the case and voted to uphold Georgia's law. Justice Brennan countered that such laws violate individuals' privacy rights in their homes and voted to overturn the law. Justice White followed by siding with Burger, while Justices Marshall and Blackmun agreed with Brennan. Powell spoke next. He was troubled by the facts in this case. Powell agreed that individuals enjoy a right of privacy in their homes. But he was torn by two facts pointing in opposite directions. Punishment for sodomy in Georgia carried twenty years' imprisonment, which seemed unfair. Still Powell was concerned about overturning the law because Hardwick had not actually been tried and convicted. He would tentatively vote to strike the law down, but much turned on how the Court's opinion was written. Justice Rehnquist followed, voting to uphold the law, as did Justice O'Connor. Justice Stevens then voted to strike down the law. Because there appeared five votes to affirm the lower court's invalidation of Georgia's law, after conference Justice Blackmun was assigned to write an opinion for the majority. Justice White would undertake to write an opinion for the dissenters, rejecting any extension of the right of privacy in this area.

Weeks passed before Justice Blackmun's draft circulated among the chambers. When it did, Justices Brennan, Marshall, and Stevens were still with him. But, Justice Powell found the draft disturbing; it was too sweeping in its language and use of precedents. Specifically, Blackmun cited and relied on Powell's opinion in *Moore v. City of East Cleveland,* 431 U.S. 494 (1977), striking down a zoning ordinance. Powell had upheld Moore's right of privacy in her home, but never dreamed that his opinion would become a basis for limiting states' power to regulate sodomy and sexual activities. He simply could not join Blackmun's opinion. Powell notified Chief Justice Burger that he was switching his vote and would write a separate opinion.

Justice White's draft thus became the opinion for the majority and Blackmun's that for the four dissenters. Justice Powell's concurring opinion returns to the fact that Hardwick was not tried and convicted, and stresses that if penalities for sodomy (such as the twenty-year sentence that Hardwick would have faced) were imposed, they might violate the Eighth Amendment's ban against cruel and unusual punishment.

Bowers v. Hardwick

478 U.S. 186, 106 S.Ct. 2841 (1986)

On a Saturday morning in Atlanta, Georgia, Michael Hardwick was arrested in his bedroom after a police officer discovered him in bed with another male. The officer was there to serve an arrest warrant for Hardwick's failure to appear in court on a charge of drinking in public. One of Hardwick's housemates had answered the door when he arrived and told the officer that Michael was not at home, but that he could look in his room. After Hardwick's arrest, the local prosecutor decided (as was his practice) not to seek an indictment under Georgia's law punishing heterosexual and homosexual sodomy. He dropped the sodomy charge against Hardwick. However, Hardwick had already joined forces with the American Civil Liberties Union in filing a lawsuit, challenging the constitutionality of the law. Federal district court Judge Robert Hall dismissed their suit, but the Eleventh Circuit Court of Appeals reversed in holding that the right of privacy protects individuals from punishment for their "consensual sexual behavior." That ruling was appealed by Georgia's attorney general, Michael Bowers, to the Supreme Court, which granted review.

Justice WHITE delivers the opinion of the Court.

In August 1982, respondent was charged with violating the Georgia statute criminalizing sodomy by committing that act with another adult male in the bedroom of respondent's home. After a preliminary hearing, the District Attorney decided not to present the matter to the grand jury unless further evidence developed.

Respondent then brought suit in the Federal District Court, challenging the constitutionality of the statute insofar as it criminalized consensual sodomy. He asserted that he was a practicing homosexual, that the Georgia sodomy statute, as administered by the defendants, placed him in imminent danger of arrest, and that the statute for several reasons violates the Federal Constitution.

This case does not require a judgment on whether laws against sodomy between consenting adults in general, or between homosexuals in particular, are wise or desirable. It raises no question about the right or propriety of state legislative decisions to repeal their laws that criminalize homosexual sodomy, or of state court decisions invalidating those laws on state constitutional grounds. The issue presented is whether the Federal Constitution confers a fundamental right upon homosexuals to engage in sodomy and hence invalidates the laws of the many States that still make such conduct illegal and have done so for a very long time. The case also calls for some judgment about the limits of the Court's role in carrying out its constitutional mandate.

We first register our disagreement with . . . respondent that the Court's prior cases have construed the Constitution to confer a right of privacy that extends to homosexual sodomy and for all intents and purposes have decided this case. The reach of this line of cases was sketched in *Carey v. Population Services International*, 431 U.S. 678 (1977). *Pierce v. Society of Sisters*, 268 U.S. 510 (1925), and *Meyer v. Nebraska*, 262 U.S. 390 (1923), were described as dealing with child rearing and education; *Prince v. Massachusetts*, 321 U.S. 158 (1944), with family relationships; *Skinner v. Oklahoma ex rel. Williamson*, 316 U.S. 535 (1942), with procreation; *Loving v. Virginia*, 388 U.S. 1 (1967), with marriage; *Griswold v. Connecticut*, 381 U.S. 479 (1965); and *Eisenstadt v. Baird*, 405 U.S. 438 (1972), with contraception; and *Roe v. Wade*, 410 U.S. 113 (1973), with abortion. The latter three cases were interpreted as construing the Due Process Clause of the Fourteenth Amendment to confer a fundamental individual right to decide whether or not to beget or bear a child. . . .

Accepting the decisions in these cases and the above description of them, we think it evident that none of the rights announced in those cases bears any resemblance to the claimed constitutional right of homosexuals to engage in acts of sodomy that is asserted in this case. No connection between family, marriage, or procreation on the one hand and homosexual activity on the other has been demonstrated, either by the Court of Appeals or by respondent. Moreover, any claim that these cases nevertheless stand for the proposition that any kind of private sexual conduct between consenting adults is constitutionally insulated from state proscription is unsupportable.

Precedent aside, however, respondent would have us announce . . . a fundamental right to engage in homosexual sodomy. This we are quite unwilling to do. It is true that despite the language of the Due Process Clauses of the Fifth and Fourteenth Amendments, which appears to focus only on the processes by which life, liberty, or property is taken, the cases are legion in which those Clauses have been interpreted to have substantive content, subsuming rights that to a great extent are immune from federal or state regulation or proscription. Among such cases are those recognizing rights that have little or no textual support in the constitutional language. *Meyer, Prince,* and *Pierce* fall in this category, as do the privacy cases from *Griswold* to *Carey*.

Striving to assure itself and the public that announcing rights not readily identifiable in the Constitution's text involves much more than the imposition of the Justices' own choice of values on the States and the Federal Government, the Court has sought to identify the nature of the rights qualifying for heightened judicial protection. In *Palko v. Connecticut*, 302 U.S. 319 (1937), it was said that this category includes those fundamental liberties that are "implicit in the concept of ordered liberty," such that "neither liberty nor justice would exist if [they] were sacrificed." A different description of fundamental liberties appeared in *Moore v. East Cleveland*, 431 U.S. 494 (1977) (opinion of POWELL, J.), where they are characterized as those liberties that are "deeply rooted in this Nation's history and tradition.". . .

It is obvious to us that neither of these formulations would extend a fundamental right to homosexuals to engage in acts of consensual sodomy. Proscriptions against that conduct have ancient roots. Sodomy was a criminal offense at common law and was forbidden by the laws of the original thirteen States when they ratified the Bill of Rights. In 1868, when the Fourteenth Amendment was ratified, all but 5 of the 37 States in the Union had criminal sodomy laws. In fact, until 1961, all 50 States outlawed sodomy, and today, 24 States and the District of Columbia continue to provide criminal penalties for sodomy performed in private and between consenting adults. Against this background, to claim that a right to engage in such conduct is "deeply rooted in this Nation's history and tradition" or "implicit in the concept of ordered liberty" is, at best, facetious.

Nor are we inclined to take a more expansive view of our authority to discover new fundamental rights imbedded in the Due Process Clause. The Court is most vulnerable and comes nearest to illegitimacy when it deals with judge-made constitutional law having little or no cognizable roots in the language or design of the Constitution. That this is so was painfully demonstrated by the face-off between the Executive and the Court in the 1930's, which resulted in the repudiation of much of the substantive gloss that the Court had placed on the Due Process Clause of the Fifth and Fourteenth Amendments. There should be, therefore, great resistance to expand the substantive reach of those Clauses, particularly if it requires redefining the category of rights deemed to be fundamental. Otherwise, the Judiciary necessarily takes to itself further authority to govern the country without express constitutional authority. The claimed right pressed on us today falls far short of overcoming this resistance. . . .

Accordingly, the judgment of the Court of Appeals is
Reversed.

Chief Justice BURGER concurring.

I join the Court's opinion, but I write separately to underscore my view that in constitutional terms there is no such thing as a fundamental right to commit homosexual sodomy. . . .

This is essentially not a question of personal "preferences" but rather of the legislative authority of the State. I find nothing in the Constitution depriving a State of the power to enact the statute challenged here.

Justice POWELL concurring.

I join the opinion of the Court. I agree with the Court that there is no fundamental right—*i.e.*, no substantive right under the Due Process Clause—such as that claimed by respondent, and found to exist by the Court of Appeals. This is not to suggest, however, that respondent may not be protected by the Eighth Amendment of the Constitution. The Georgia statute at issue in this case, Ga.Code Ann. § 16–6–2, authorizes a court to imprison a person for up to 20 years for a single private, consensual act of sodomy. In my view, a prison sentence for such conduct—certainly a sentence of long duration—would create a serious Eighth Amendment issue. Under the Georgia statute a single act of sodomy, even in the private setting of a home, is a felony comparable in terms of the possible sentence imposed to serious felonies such as aggravated battery, § 16–5–24, first degree arson, § 16–7–60 and robbery, § 16–8–40.

In this case, however, respondent has not been tried, much less convicted and sentenced. Moreover, respondent has not raised the Eighth Amendment issue below. For these reasons this constitutional argument is not before us.

Justice BLACKMUN, with whom Justice BRENNAN, Justice MARSHALL, and Justice STEVENS join, dissenting.

This case is no more about "a fundamental right to engage in homosexual sodomy," as the Court purports to declare, than *Stanley v. Georgia*, 394 U.S. 557 (1969), was about a fundamental right to watch obscene movies, or *Katz v. United States*, 389 U.S. 347 (1967), was about a fundamental right to place interstate bets from a telephone booth. Rather, this case is about "the most comprehensive of rights and the right most valued by civilized men," namely, "the right to be let alone." *Olmstead v. United States*, 277 U.S. 438 (1928) (BRANDEIS, J., dissenting).

The statute at issue, Ga.Code Ann. § 16–6–2, denies individuals the right to decide for themselves whether to engage in particular forms of private, consensual sexual activity. The Court concludes that § 16–6–2 is valid essentially because "the laws of . . . many States . . . still make such conduct illegal and have done so for a very long time." But the fact that the moral judgments expressed by statutes like § 16–6–2 may be "natural and familiar . . . ought not to conclude our judgment upon the question whether statutes embodying them conflict with the Constitution of the United States." *Roe v. Wade,* 410 U.S. 113 (1973), quoting *Lochner v. New York,* (198 U.S. 45 (1905) (HOLMES, J., dissenting). Like Justice HOLMES, I believe that "[i]t is revolting to have no better reason for a rule of law than that so it was laid down in the time of Henry IV. It is still more revolting if the grounds upon which it was laid down have vanished long since, and the rule simply persists from blind imitation of the past." Holmes, The Path of the Law, 10 Harv.L.Rev. 457, 469 (1897). I believe we must analyze respondent's claim in the light of the values that underlie the constitutional right to privacy. If that right means anything, it means that, before Georgia can prosecute its citizens for making choices about the most intimate aspects of their lives, it must do more than assert that the choice they have made is an "'abominable crime not fit to be named among Christians.'". . .

A fair reading of the statute and of the complaint clearly reveals that the majority has distorted the question this case presents.

First, the Court's almost obsessive focus on homosexual activity is particularly hard to justify in light of the broad language Georgia has used. Unlike the Court, the Georgia Legislature has not proceeded on the assumption that homosexuals are so different from other citizens that their lives may be controlled in a way that would not be tolerated if it limited the choices of those other citizens. Rather, Georgia has provided that "[a] person commits the offense of sodomy when he performs or submits to any sexual act involving the sex organs of one person and the mouth or anus of another." The sex or status of the persons who engage in the act is irrelevant as a matter of state law. In fact, to the extent I can discern a legislative purpose for Georgia's 1968 enactment of § 16–6–2, that purpose seems to have been to broaden the coverage of the law to reach heterosexual as well as homosexual activity. . . .

Second, I disagree with the Court's refusal to consider whether § 16–6–2 runs afoul of the Eighth or Ninth Amendments or the Equal Protection Clause of the Fourteenth Amendment. . . . Even if respondent did not advance claims based on the Eighth or Ninth Amendments, or on the Equal Protection Clause, his complaint should not be dismissed if any of those provisions could entitle him to relief. I need not reach either the Eighth Amendment or the Equal Protection Clause issues because I believe that Hardwick has stated a cognizable claim that § 16–6–2 interferes with constitutionally protected interests in privacy and freedom of intimate association. . . .

The Court concludes today that none of our prior cases dealing with various decisions that individuals are entitled to make free of governmental interference "bears any resemblance to the claimed constitutional right of homosexuals to engage in acts of sodomy that is asserted in this case." While it is true that these cases may be characterized by their connection to protection of the family, the Court's conclusion that they extend no further than this boundary ignores the warning in *Moore v. East-Cleveland*, 431 U.S. 494 (1977), against "clos[ing] our eyes to the basic reasons why certain rights associated with the family have been accorded shelter under the Fourteenth Amendment's Due Process Clause." We protect those rights not because they contribute, in some direct and material way, to the general public welfare, but because they form so central a part of an individual's life. "[T]he concept of privacy embodies the 'moral fact that a person belongs to himself and not others nor to society as a whole.' ". . .

Only the most willful blindness could obscure the fact that sexual intimacy is "a sensitive, key relationship of human existence, central to family life, community welfare, and the development of human personality," *Paris Adult Theatre I v. Slaton*, [413 U.S. 49 (1973)]. The fact that individuals define themselves in a significant way through their intimate sexual relationships with others suggests, in a Nation as diverse as ours, that there may be many "right" ways of conducting those relationships, and that much of the richness of a relationship will come from the freedom an individual has to *choose* the form and nature of these intensely personal bonds. . . .

In a variety of circumstances we have recognized that a necessary corollary of giving individuals freedom to choose how to conduct their lives is acceptance of the fact that different individuals will make different choices. For example, in holding that the clearly important state interest in public education should give way to a competing claim by the Amish to the effect that extended formal schooling threatened their way of life, the Court declared: "There can be no assumption that today's majority is 'right' and the Amish and others like them are 'wrong.' A way of life that is odd or even erratic but interferes with no rights or interests of others is not to be condemned because it is different." *Wisconsin v. Yoder*, [406 U.S. 215 (1972)]. The Court claims that its decision today merely refuses to recognize a fundamental right to engage in homosexual sodomy; what the Court really has refused to recognize is the fundamental interest all individuals have in controlling the nature of their intimate associations with others.

The behavior, for which Hardwick faces prosecution occurred in his own home, a place to which the Fourth Amendment attaches special significance. The Court's treatment of this aspect of the case is symptomatic of its overall refusal to consider the broad principles that have informed our treatment of privacy in specific cases. Just as the right to privacy is more than the mere aggregation of a number of entitlements to engage in specific behavior, so too, protecting the physical integrity of the home is more than merely a means of protecting specific activities that often take place there. . . .

The Court's failure to comprehend the magnitude of the liberty interests at stake in this case leads it to slight the question whether petitioner, on behalf of the State, has justified Georgia's infringement on these interests. I believe that neither of the two general justifications for § 16–6–2 that petitioner has advanced warrants dismissing respondent's challenge for failure to state a claim.

First, petitioner asserts that the acts made criminal by the statute may have serious adverse consequences for "the general public health and welfare," such as spreading communicable diseases or fostering other criminal activity. Inasmuch as this case was dismissed by the District Court on the pleadings, it is not surprising that the record before us is barren of any evidence to support petitioner's claim. In light of the state of the record, I see no justification for the Court's attempt to equate the private, consensual sexual activity at issue here with the "possession in the home of drugs, firearms, or stolen goods," to which *Stanley* refused to extend its protection. None of the behavior so mentioned in *Stanley* can properly be viewed as "[v]ictimless," drugs and weapons are inherently dangerous, and for property to be "stolen," someone must have been wrongfully deprived of it. Nothing in the record before the Court provides any justification for finding the activity forbidden by § 16–6–2 to be physically dangerous, either to the persons engaged in it or to others.

The core of petitioner's defense of § 16–6–2, however, is that respondent and others who engage in the conduct prohibited by § 16–6–2 interfere with Georgia's exercise of the " 'right of the Nation and of the States to maintain a decent society,' " *Paris Adult Theatre I v. Slaton.* Essentially, petitioner argues, and the Court agrees, that the fact that the acts described in § 16–6–2 "for hundreds of years, if not thousands, have been uniformly condemned as immoral" is a sufficient reason to permit a State to ban them today. . . .

I cannot agree that either the length of time a majority has held its convictions or the passions with which it defends them can withdraw legislation from this Court's scrutiny. . . . As Justice JACKSON wrote so eloquently for the Court in *West Virginia Board of Education v. Barnette,* [319 U.S. 624] (1943), "we apply the limitations of the Constitution with no fear that freedom to be intellectually and spiritually diverse or even contrary will disintegrate the social organization. . . . [F]reedom to differ is not limited to things that do not matter much. That would be a mere shadow of freedom. The test of its substance is the right to differ as to things that touch the heart of the existing order." It is precisely because the issue raised by this case touches the heart of what makes individuals what they are that we should be especially sensitive to the rights of those whose choices upset the majority.

The assertion that "traditional Judeo-Christian values proscribe" the conduct involved cannot provide an adequate justification for § 16–6–2. That certain, but by no means all, religious groups condemn the behavior at issue gives the State no license to impose their judgments on the entire citizenry. The legitimacy of secular legislation depends instead on whether the State can advance some justification for its law beyond its conformity to religious doctrine. . . .

Nor can § 16–6–2 be justified as a "morally neutral" exercise of Georgia's power to "protect the public environment," *Paris Adult Theatre I*. Certainly, some private behavior can affect the fabric of society as a whole. Reasonable people may differ about whether particular sexual acts are moral or immoral, but "we have ample evidence for believing that people will not abandon morality, will not think any better of murder, cruelty and dishonesty, merely because some private sexual practice which they abominate is not punished by the law." Petitioner and the Court fail to see the difference between laws that protect public sensibilities and those that enforce private morality. Statutes banning public sexual activity are entirely consistent with protecting the individual's liberty interest in decisions concerning sexual relations: the same recognition that those decisions are intensely private which justifies protecting them from governmental interference can justify protecting individuals from unwilling exposure to the sexual activities of others. But the mere fact that intimate behavior may be punished when it takes place in public cannot dictate how States can regulate intimate behavior that occurs in intimate places. . . .

This case involves no real interference with the rights of others, for the mere knowledge that other individuals do not adhere to one's value system cannot be a legally cognizable interest, let alone an interest that can justify invading the houses, hearts, and minds of citizens who choose to live their lives differently.

Justice STEVENS, with whom Justice BRENNAN and Justice MARSHALL join, dissenting.

Like the statute that is challenged in this case, the rationale of the Court's opinion applies equally to the prohibited conduct regardless of whether the parties who engage in it are married or unmarried, or are of the same or different sexes. Sodomy was condemned as an odious and sinful type of behavior during the formative period of the common law. That condemnation was equally damning for heterosexual and homosexual sodomy. Moreover, it provided no special exemption for married couples.

The license to cohabit and to produce legitimate offspring simply did not include any permission to engage in sexual conduct that was considered a "crime against nature.". . .

Our prior cases make two propositions abundantly clear. First, the fact that the governing majority in a State has traditionally viewed a particular practice as immoral is not a sufficient reason for upholding a law prohibiting the practice; neither history nor tradition could save a law prohibiting miscegenation from constitutional attack. Second, individual decisions by married persons, concerning the intimacies of their physical relationship, even when not intended to produce offspring, are a form of "liberty" protected by the Due Process Clause of the Fourteenth Amendment. . . .

In consideration of claims of this kind, the Court has emphasized the individual interest in privacy, but its decisions have actually been animated by an even more fundamental concern. As I wrote some years ago:

"These cases do not deal with the individual's interest in protection from unwarranted public attention, comment, or exploitation. They deal, rather, with the individual's right to make certain unusually important decisions that will affect his own, or his family's, destiny. . . ." [Quoting *Fitzgerald v. Porter Memorial Hospital*, 523 F.d 716 (CA7 1975)].

Society has every right to encourage its individual members to follow particular traditions in expressing affection for one another and in gratifying their personal desires. It, of course, may prohibit an individual from imposing his will on another to satisfy his own selfish interests. It also may prevent an individual from interfering with, or violating, a legally sanctioned and protected relationship, such as marriage. And it may explain the relative advantages and disadvantages of different forms of intimate expression. But when individual married couples are isolated from observation by others, the way in which they voluntarily choose to conduct their intimate relations is a matter for them—not the State—to decide. The essential "liberty" that animated the development of the law in cases like *Griswold, Eisenstadt,* and *Carey* surely embraces the right to engage in nonreproductive, sexual conduct that others may consider offensive or immoral.

Paradoxical as it may seem, our prior cases thus establish that a State may not prohibit sodomy within "the sacred precincts of marital bedrooms," *Griswold,* or, indeed, between unmarried heterosexual adults. *Eisenstadt.* In all events, it is perfectly clear that the State of Georgia may not totally prohibit the conduct proscribed by § 16–6–2 of the Georgia Criminal Code.

If the Georgia statute cannot be enforced as it is written—if the conduct it seeks to prohibit is a protected form of liberty for the vast majority of Georgia's citizens—the State must assume the burden of justifying a selective application of its law. Either the persons to whom Georgia seeks to apply its statute do not have the same interest in "liberty" that others have, or there must be a reason why the State may be permitted to apply a generally applicable law to certain persons that it does not apply to others.

The first possibility is plainly unacceptable. Although the meaning of the principle that "all men are created equal" is not always clear, it surely must mean that every free citizen has the same interest in "liberty" that the members of the majority share. From the standpoint of the individual, the homosexual and the heterosexual have the same interest in deciding how he will live his own life, and, more narrowly, how he will conduct himself in his personal and voluntary associations with his companions. State intrusion into the private conduct of either is equally burdensome.

The second possibility is similarly unacceptable. A policy of selective application must be supported by a neutral and legitimate interest—something more substantial than a habitual dislike for, or ignorance about, the disfavored group. Neither the State nor the Court has identified any such interest in this case. . . .

I respectfully dissent.

Cruzan by Cruzan v. Director, Missouri Department of Health
110 S.Ct. 2841 (1990).

Late in the night of January 11, 1983, Nancy Cruzan, at the age of twenty-five, was thrown from her car as it crashed off the road not far from her home in Catersville, Missouri. By the time police and paramedics arrived and restarted her heart and lungs, her brain had been deprived of oxygen for twelve to fourteen minutes. She never regained consciousness. In the hospital, Miss Cruzan's parents approved the surgical insertion of feeding tube into her body to keep her alive. Her doctors agreed that she would never regain consciousness and that her cerebral cortex was atrophying. Without removing the feeding tube, they also agreed, Miss Cruzan could persist in a vegetative state for another thirty years.

In early 1987, Miss Cruzan's parents decided to seek permission to have the feeding tubes removed. A year later, in 1988 a state trial judge granted the Cruzans permission, but the state appealed to the Missouri Supreme Court. By a vote of four to three, the state supreme court reversed. The majority cited the preamble to the state's 1986 abortion law, which the U.S. Supreme Court upheld in *Webster v. Reproductive Health Services* (1989) (see page 1189) and which proclaims the state's "unqualified" interest in preserving the "sanctity of human life." The majority also held that the Cruzans could not assert a constitutional right of privacy to make a decision "for an incompetent in the absence of the formalities required under Missouri's Living Will statutes" or without establishing "clear and convincing evidence" that Miss Cruzan would have wanted the feeding tubes removed.

The Cruzans appealed the Missouri Supreme Court's decision to the U.S. Supreme Court, which granted *certiorari*. The Bush administration and various antiabortion rights groups filed briefs supporting the state, while the American Civil Liberties Union and other groups supported the Cruzans. In the meantime, while defending the state's decision, Missouri's attorney general, William Webster, endeavored to render the case moot. He drafted a bill, approved by Cruzan's attorneys, that would have allowed the Cruzans to remove the feeding tube from their daughter. The bill would have permitted the removal of life-support systems from patients (1) who were in a "persistent oblivious state" for at least thirty-six months, (2) whose family agreed to the removal of life-support systems, and (3) for which three physicians concurred that there was no likelihood of recovery. In addition, the bill would have provided that a patient's wishes to have such systems discontinued needed to be shown only on a "preponderance of the evidence," rather than the more rigorous standard of "clear and convincing" proof. But the Missouri state legislature refused to enact the bill into law.

On June 25, 1990, the Supreme Court handed down its decision. Writing for a bare majority, Chief Justice Rehnquist upheld the state supreme court's ruling. Justices Scalia and O'Connor wrote separate concurring opinions, and Justices Brennan and Stevens, joined by Justices Blackmun and Marshall, dissented in separate opinions.

Chief Justice REHNQUIST delivers the opinion of the Court.

At common law, even the touching of one person by another without consent and without legal justification was a battery. Before the turn of the century, this Court observed that "[n]o right is held more sacred, or is more carefully guarded, by the common law, than the right of every individual to the possession and control of his own person, free from all restraint or interference of others, unless by clear and unquestionable authority of law." *Union Pacific R. Co. v. Botsford*, 141 U. S. 250, 251 (1891). . . .

The logical corollary of the doctrine of informed consent is that the patient generally possesses the right not to consent, that is, to refuse treatment. Until about 15 years ago and the seminal decision in *In re Quinlan*, 70 N. J. 10 [1976], cert. denied *sub nom., Garger v. New Jersey*, 429 U.S. 922 (1976), the number of right-to-refuse-treatment decisions were relatively few. Most of the earlier cases involved patients who refused medical treatment forbidden by their religious beliefs, thus implicating First Amendment rights as well as common law rights of self-determination. More recently, however, with the advance of medical technology capable of sustaining life well past the point where natural forces would have brought certain death in earlier times, cases involving the right to refuse life-sustaining treatment have burgeoned. . . .

[T]he common-law doctrine of informed consent is viewed as generally encompassing the right of a competent individual to refuse medical treatment. Beyond that, these decisions demonstrate both similarity and diversity in their approach to decision of what all agree is a perplexing question with unusually strong moral and ethical overtones. State courts have available to them for decision a number of sources—state constitutions, statutes, and common law—which are not available to us. In this Court, the question is simply and starkly whether the United States Constitution prohibits Missouri from choosing the rule of decision which it did. This is the first case in which we have been squarely presented with the issue of whether the United States Constitution grants what is in common parlance referred to as a "right to die." We follow the judicious counsel of our decision in *Twin City Bank v. Nebeker*, 167 U. S. 196, 202 (1897), where we said that in deciding "a question of such magnitude and importance . . . it is the [better] part of wisdom not to attempt, by any general statement, to cover every possible phase of the subject."

The Fourteenth Amendment provides that no State shall "deprive any person of life, liberty, or property, without due process of law." The principle that a competent person has a constitutionally protected liberty interest in refusing unwanted medical treatment may be inferred from our prior decisions. In *Jacobson v. Massachusetts*, 197 U. S. 11, 24–30 (1905), for instance, the Court balanced an individual's liberty interest in declining an unwanted smallpox vaccine against the State's interest in preventing disease. . . .

But determining that a person has a "liberty interest" under the Due Process Clause does not end the inquiry; "whether respondent's constitutional rights have been violated must be determined by balancing his liberty interests against the relevant state interests." *Youngberg v. Romeo*, 457 U. S. 307, 321 (1982). . . .

[F]or purposes of this case, we assume that the United States Constitution would grant a competent person a constitutionally protected right to refuse lifesaving hydration and nutrition.

Petitioners go on to assert that an incompetent person should possess the same right in this respect as is possessed by a competent person. . . .

The difficulty with petitioners' claim is that in a sense it begs the question: an incompetent person is not able to make an informed and voluntary choice to exercise a hypothetical right to refuse treatment or any other right. Such a "right" must be exercised for her, if at all, by some sort of surrogate. Here, Missouri has in effect recognized that under certain circumstances a surrogate may act for the patient in electing to have hydration and nutrition withdrawn in such a way as to cause death, but it has established a procedural safeguard to assure that the action of the surrogate conforms as best it may to the wishes expressed by the patient while competent. Missouri requires that evidence of the incompetent's wishes as to the withdrawal of treatment be proved by clear and convincing evidence. The question, then, is whether the United States Constitution forbids the establishment of this procedural requirement by the State. We hold that it does not.

Whether or not Missouri's clear and convincing evidence requirement comports with the United States Constitution depends in part on what interests the State may properly seek to protect in this situation. Missouri relies on its interest in the protection and preservation of human life, and there can be no gainsaying this interest. As a general matter, the States—indeed, all civilized nations—demonstrate their commitment to life by treating homicide as serious crime. Moreover, the majority of States in this country have laws imposing criminal penalties on one who assists another to commit suicide. We do not think a State is required to remain neutral in the face of an informed and voluntary decision by a physically-able adult to starve to death.

But in the context presented here, a State has more particular interests at stake. The choice between life and death is a deeply personal decision of obvious and overwhelming finality. We believe Missouri may legitimately seek to safeguard the personal element of this choice through the imposition of heightened evidentiary requirements. It cannot be disputed that the Due Process Clause protects an interest in life as well as an interest in refusing life-sustaining medical treatment. Not all incompetent patients will have loved ones available to serve as surrogate decisionmakers.

In our view, Missouri has permissibly sought to advance these interests through the adoption of a "clear and convincing" standard of proof to govern such proceedings. "The function of a standard of proof, as that concept is embodied in the Due Process Clause and in the realm of factfinding, is to 'instruct the factfinder concerning the degree of confidence our society thinks he should have in the correctness of factual conclusions for a particular type of adjudication.'" *Addington v. Texas,* 441 U. S. 418, 423

(1979) (quoting *In re Winship,* 397 U. S. 358, 370 (1970) (HAR-LAN, J., concurring)). . . .

We think it self-evident that the interests at stake in the instant proceedings are more substantial, both on an individual and societal level, than those involved in a run-of-the-mine civil dispute. But not only does the standard of proof reflect the importance of a particular adjudication, it also serves as "a societal judgment about how the risk of error should be distributed between the litigants." The more stringent the burden of proof a party must bear, the more that party bears the risk of an erroneous decision. We believe that Missouri may permissibly place an increased risk of an erroneous decision on those seeking to terminate an incompetent individual's life-sustaining treatment. An erroneous decision not to terminate results in a maintenance of the status quo; the possibility of subsequent developments such as advancements in medical science, the discovery of new, evidence regarding the patient's intent, changes in the law, or simply the unexpected death of the patient despite the administration of life-sustaining treatment, at least create the potential that a wrong decision will eventually be corrected or its impact mitigated. An erroneous decision to withdraw life-sustaining treatment, however, is not susceptible of correction. . . .

In sum, we conclude that a State may apply a clear and convincing evidence standard in proceedings where a guardian seeks to discontinue nutrition and hydration of a person diagnosed to be in a persistent vegetative state. We note that many courts which have adopted some sort of substituted judgment procedure in situations like this, whether they limit consideration of evidence to the prior expressed wishes of the incompetent individual, or whether they allow more general proof of what the individual's decision would have been, require a clear and convincing standard of proof for such evidence. . . .

No doubt is engendered by anything in this record but that Nancy Cruzan's mother and father are loving and caring parents. If the State were required by the United States Constitution to repose a right of "substituted judgment" with anyone, the Cruzans would surely qualify. But we do not think the Due Process Clause requires the State to repose judgment on these matters with anyone but the patient herself. Close family members may have a strong feeling—a feeling not at all ignoble or unworthy, but not entirely disinterested, either—that they do not wish to witness the continuation of the life of a loved one which they regard as hopeless, meaningless, and even degrading. But there is no automatic assurance that the view of close family members will necessarily be the same as the patient's would have been had she been confronted with the prospect of her situation while competent. All of the reasons previously discussed for allowing Missouri to require clear and convincing evidence of the patient's wishes lead us to conclude that the State may choose to defer only to those wishes, rather than confide the decision to close family members.

The judgment of the Supreme Court of Missouri is Affirmed.

Justice O'CONNOR concurring.

I agree that a protected liberty interest in refusing unwanted medical treatment may be inferred from our prior decisions, and that the refusal of artificially delivered food and water is encompassed within that liberty interest. I write separately to clarify why I believe this to be so.

As the Court notes, the liberty interest in refusing medical treatment flows from decisions involving the State's invasions into the body. Because our notions of liberty are inextricably entwined with our idea of physical freedom and self-determination, the Court has often deemed state incursions into the body repugnant to the interests protected by the Due Process Clause. . . .

Accordingly, the liberty guaranteed by the Due Process Clause must protect, if it protects anything, an individual's deeply personal decision to reject medical treatment, including the artificial delivery of food and water.

I also write separately to emphasize that the Court does not today decide the issue whether a State must also give effect to the decisions of a surrogate decisionmaker. In my view, such a duty may well be constitutionally required to protect the patient's liberty interest in refusing medical treatment. Few individuals provide explicit oral or written instructions regarding their intent to refuse medical treatment should they become incompetent. States which decline to consider any evidence other than such instructions may frequently fail to honor a patient's intent. Such failures might be avoided if the State considered an equally probative source of evidence: the patient's appointment of a proxy to make health care decisions on her behalf. Delegating the authority to make medical decisions to a family member or friend is becoming a common method of planning for the future. . . .

Today's decision, holding only that the Constitution permits a State to require clear and convincing evidence of Nancy Cruzan's desire to have artificial hydration and nutrition withdrawn, does not preclude a future determination that the Constitution requires the States to implement the decisions of a patient's duly appointed surrogate. Nor does it prevent States from developing other approaches for protecting an incompetent individual's liberty interest in refusing medical treatment. As is evident from the Court's survey of state court decisions, no national consensus has yet emerged on the best solution for this difficult and sensitive problem. Today we decide only that one State's practice does not violate the Constitution; the more challenging task of crafting appropriate procedures for safeguarding incompetents' liberty interests is entrusted to the "laboratory" of the States, *New State Ice Co. v. Liebmann,* 285 U. S. 262, 311 (1932) (BRANDEIS, J., dissenting), in the first instance.

Justice SCALIA concurring.

The various opinions in this case portray quite clearly the difficult, indeed agonizing, questions that are presented by the constantly increasing power of science to keep the human body alive for longer than any reasonable person would want to inhabit it. The States have begun to grapple with these problems through legislation. I am concerned, from the tenor of today's opinions, that we are poised to confuse that enterprise as successfully as we have confused the enterprise of legislating concerning abortion—requiring it to be conducted against a background of federal constitutional imperatives that are unknown because they are being newly crafted from Term to Term. That would be a great misfortune.

While I agree with the Court's analysis today, and therefore join in its opinion, I would have preferred that we announce, clearly and promptly, that the federal courts have no business in this field; that American law has always accorded the State the power to prevent, by force if necessary, suicide—including suicide by refusing to take appropriate measures necessary to preserve one's life; that the point at which life becomes "worthless," and the point at which the means necessary to preserve it become "extraordinary" or "inappropriate," are neither set forth in the Constitution nor known to the nine Justices of this Court any better than they are known to nine people picked at random from the Kansas City telephone directory; and hence, that even when it *is* demonstrated by clear and convincing evidence that a patient no longer wishes certain measures to be taken to preserve her life, it is up to the citizens of Missouri to decide, through their elected representatives, whether that wish will be honored. It is quite impossible (because the Constitution says nothing about the matter) that those citizens will decide upon a line less lawful than the one we would choose; and it is unlikely (because we know no more about "life-and-death" than they do) that they will decide upon a line less reasonable.

The text of the Due Process Clause does not protect individuals against deprivations of liberty *simpliciter.* It protects them against deprivations of liberty "without due process of law." To determine that such a deprivation would not occur if Nancy Cruzan were forced to take nourishment against her will, it is unnecessary to reopen the historically recurrent debate over whether "due process" includes substantive restrictions. . . . It is at least true that no "substantive due process" claim can be maintained unless the claimant demonstrates that the State has deprived him of a right historically and traditionally protected against State interference. *Michael H. v. Gerald D.*, [109 S.Ct. 2333] (1989) (plurality opinion); *Bowers v. Hardwick*, 478 U.S. 186 (1986). . . . That cannot possibly be established here. . . .

I assert only that the Constitution has nothing to say about [a "right to die"]. To raise up a constitutional right here we would have to create out of nothing (for it exists neither in text nor tradition) some constitutional principle whereby, although the State may insist that an individual come in out of the cold and eat food, it may not insist that he take medicine; and although it may pump his stomach empty of poison he has ingested, it may not fill his stomach with food he has failed to ingest. Are there, then, no reasonable and humane limits that ought not to be exceeded in requiring an individual to preserve his own life? There obviously are, but they are not set forth in the Due Process Clause. What assures us that those limits will not be exceeded is the same constitutional guarantee that is the source of most of our protection—what protects us, for example, from being assessed a tax of 100% of our income above the subsistence level, from being forbidden to drive cars, or from being required to send our children to school for 10 hours a day, none of which horribles is categorically prohibited by the Constitution. Our salvation is the Equal Protection Clause, which requires the democratic majority to accept for themselves and their loved ones what they impose on you and me. This Court need not, and has no authority to, inject itself into every field of human activity where irrationality and oppression may theoretically occur, and if it tries to do so it will destroy itself.

Justice BRENNAN, with whom Justice MARSHALL and Justice BLACKMUN join, dissenting.

Because I believe that Nancy Cruzan has a fundamental right to be free of unwanted artificial nutrition and hydration, which right is not outweighed by any interests of the State, and because I find that the improperly biased procedural obstacles imposed by the Missouri Supreme Court impermissibly burden that right, I respectfully dissent. Nancy Cruzan is entitled to choose to die with dignity. . . .

The question before this Court is a relatively narrow one: whether the Due Process Clause allows Missouri to require a now-incompetent patient in an irreversible persistent vegetative state to remain on life-support absent rigorously clear and convincing evidence that avoiding the treatment represents the patient's prior, express choice. . . .

The starting point for our legal analysis must be whether a competent person has a constitutional right to avoid unwanted medical care. Earlier this Term, this Court held that the Due Process Clause of the Fourteenth Amendment confers a significant liberty interest in avoiding unwanted medical treatment. *Washington v. Harper,* [110 S.Ct. 1028] (1990). Today, the Court concedes that our prior decisions "support the recognition of a general liberty interest in refusing medical treatment.". . .

But if a competent person has a liberty interest to be free of unwanted medical treatment, as both the majority and Justice O'CONNOR concede, it must be fundamental. "We are dealing here with [a decision] which involves one of the basic civil rights of man." *Skinner v. Oklahoma ex rel. Williamson,* 316 U. S. 535, 541 (1942) (invalidating a statute authorizing sterilization of certain felons).

The right to be free from medical attention without consent, to determine what shall be done with one's own body, *is* deeply rooted in this Nation's traditions, as the majority acknowledges. This right has long been "firmly entrenched in American tort law" and is securely grounded in the earliest common law. See also *Mills v. Rogers,* 457 U. S. 291 (1982) ("the right to refuse any medical treatment emerged from the doctrines of trespass and battery, which were applied to unauthorized touchings by a physician"). . . .

That there may be serious consequences involved in refusal of the medical treatment at issue here does not vitiate the right under our common law tradition of medical self-determination. . . .

The right to be free from unwanted medical attention is a right to evaluate the potential benefit of treatment and its possible consequences according to one's own values and to make a personal decision whether to subject oneself to the intrusion. For a patient like Nancy Cruzan, the sole benefit of medical treatment is being kept metabolically alive. Neither artificial nutrition nor any other form of medical treatment available today can cure or in any way ameliorate her condition. Irreversibly vegetative patients are devoid of thought, emotion and sensation; they are permanently and completely unconscious. . . .

There are also affirmative reasons why someone like Nancy might choose to forgo artificial nutrition and hydration under these circumstances. Dying is personal. And it is profound. For many, the thought of an ignoble end, steeped in decay, is abhorrent. A quiet, proud death, bodily integrity intact, is a matter of extreme consequence. . . .

Although the right to be free of unwanted medical intervention, like other constitutionally protected interests, may not be absolute, no State interest could outweigh the rights of an individual in Nancy Cruzan's position. Whatever a State's possible interests in mandating life-support treatment under other circumstances, there is no good to be obtained here by Missouri's insistence that Nancy Cruzan remain on life-support systems if it is indeed her wish not to do so. Missouri does not claim, nor could it, that society as a whole will be benefited by Nancy's receiving medical treatment. No third party's situation will be improved and no harm to others will be averted.

The only state interest asserted here is a general interest in the preservation of life. But the State has no legitimate general interest in someone's life, completely abstracted from the interest of the person living that life, that could outweigh the person's choice to avoid medical treatment. . . . Thus, the State's general interest in life must accede to Nancy Cruzan's particularized and intense interest in self-determination in her choice of medical treatment. There is simply nothing legitimately within the State's purview to be gained by superseding her decision.

Moreover, there may be considerable danger that Missouri's rule of decision would impair rather than serve any interest the State does have in sustaining life. Current medical practice recommends use of heroic measures if there is a scintilla of a chance that the patient will recover, on the assumption that the measures will be discontinued should the patient improve. When the President's Commission in 1982 approved the withdrawal of life support equipment from irreversibly vegetative patients, it explained that "[a]n even more troubling wrong occurs when a treatment that might save life or improve health is not started because the health care personnel are afraid that they will find it very difficult to stop the treatment if, as is fairly likely, it proves to be of little benefit and greatly burdens the patient.". . .

This is not to say that the State has no legitimate interests to assert here. As the majority recognizes, Missouri has a *parens patriae* interest in providing Nancy Cruzan, now incompetent, with as accurate as possible a determination of how she would exercise her rights under these circumstances. Second, if and when it is determined that Nancy Cruzan would want to continue treatment, the State may legitimately assert an interest in providing that treatment. But *until* Nancy's wishes have been determined, the only state interest that may be asserted is an interest in safeguarding the accuracy of that determination.

Accuracy, therefore, must be our touchstone. Missouri may constitutionally impose only those procedural requirements that serve to enhance the accuracy of a determination of Nancy Cruzan's wishes or are at least consistent with an accurate determination. The Missouri "safeguard" that the Court upholds today does not meet that standard. The determination needed in this context is whether the incompetent person would choose to live in a persistent vegetative state on life-support or to avoid this medical treatment. Missouri's rule of decision imposes a markedly asymmetrical evidentiary burden. Only evidence of specific statements of treatment choice made by the patient when competent is admissible to support a finding that the patient, now in a persistent vegetative state, would wish to avoid further medical treatment. Moreover, this evidence must be clear and convincing. No proof is required to support a finding that the incompetent person would wish to continue treatment. . . .

The majority offers several justifications for Missouri's heightened evidentiary standard. First, the majority explains that the State may constitutionally adopt this rule to govern determinations of an incompetent's wishes in order to advance the State's substantive interests, including its unqalified interest in the preservation of human life. Missouri's evidentiary standard, however, cannot rest on the State's own interest in a particular substantive result. To be sure, courts have long erected clear and convincing evidence standards to place the greater risk of erroneous decisions on those bringing disfavored claims.[16] In such cases, however, the choice to discourage, certain claims was a legitimate, constitutional policy choice. In contrast, Missouri has no such power to disfavor a choice by Nancy Cruzan to avoid medical treatment, because Missouri has no legitimate interest in providing Nancy with treatment until it is established that this represents her choice. Just as a State may not override Nancy's choice directly, it may not do so indirectly through the imposition of a procedural rule.

The majority claims that the allocation of the risk of error is justified because it is more important not to terminate life-support for someone who would wish it continued than to honor the wishes of someone who would not. An erroneous decision to terminate life-support is irrevocable, says the majority, while an erroneous decision not to terminate "results in a maintenance of the status quo." But, from the point of view of the patient, an erroneous decision in either direction is irrevocable. An erroneous decision to terminate artificial nutrition and hydration, to be sure, will lead to failure of that last remnant of physiological life, the brain stem, and result in complete brain death. An erroneous decision not to terminate life-support, however, robs a patient of the very qualities protected by the right to avoid unwanted medical treatment. His own degraded existence is perpetuated; his family's suffering is protracted; the memory he leaves behind becomes more and more distorted. . . .

Even more than its heightened evidentiary standard, the Missouri court's categorical exclusion of relevant evidence dispenses with any semblence of accurate factfinding. The court adverted to no evidence supporting its decision, but held that no clear and convincing, inherently reliable evidence had been presented to show that Nancy would want to avoid further treatment. In doing so, the court failed to consider statements Nancy had made to family members and a close friend. The court also failed to consider testimony from Nancy's mother and sister that they were certain that Nancy would want to discontinue to artificial nutrition and hydration, even after the court found that Nancy's family was loving and without malignant motive. The court also failed to consider the conclusions of the guardian ad litem, appointed by the trial court, that there was clear and convincing evidence that Nancy would want to discontinue medical treatment and that this was in her best interests. The court did not specifically define what kind of evidence it would consider clear and convincing, but its general discussion suggests that only a living will or equivalently formal directive from the patient when competent would meet this standard. . . .

Too few people execute living wills or equivalently formal directives for such an evidentiary rule to ensure adequately that the wishes of incompetent persons will be honored. While it might be a wise social policy to encourage people to furnish such instructions, no general conclusion about a patient's choice can be drawn from the absence of formalities. The probability of becoming irreversibly vegetative is so low that many people may not feel an urgency to marshal formal evidence of their preferences. Some may not wish to dwell on their own physical deterioration and mortality. Even someone with a resolute determination to avoid life-support under circumstances such as Nancy's would still need to know that such things as living wills exist and how to execute one. Often legal help would be necessary, especially given the majority's apparent willingness to permit States to insist that a person's wishes are not truly known unless the particular medical treatment is specified. . . .

I do not suggest that States must sit by helplessly if the choices of incompetent patients are in danger of being ignored. Even if the Court had ruled that Missouri's rule of decision is unconstitutional, as I believe it should have, States would nevertheless remain free to fashion procedural protections to safeguard the interests of incompetents under these circumstances. The Constitution provides merely a framework here: protections must be genuinely aimed at ensuring decisions commensurate with the will of the patient, and must be reliable as instruments to that end. Of the many States which have instituted such protections, Missouri is virtually the only one to have fashioned a rule that lessens the likelihood of accurate determinations. In contrast, nothing in the Constitution prevents States from reviewing the advisability of a family decision, by requiring a court proceeding or by appointing an impartial guardian ad litem. . . .

Finally, I cannot agree with the majority that where it is not possible to determine what choice an incompetent patient would make, a State's role as *parens patriae* permits the State automatically to make that choice itself. . . .

The majority justifies its position by arguing that, while close family members may have a strong feeling about the question, "there is no automatic assurance that the view of close family members will necessarily be the same as the patient's would have been had she been confronted with the prospect of her situation while competent." I cannot quarrel with this observation. But it leads only to another question: Is there any reason to suppose that a State is *more* likely to make the choice that the patient would have made than someone who knew the patient intimately? To ask this is to answer it. As the New Jersey Supreme Court observed: "Family members are best qualified to make substituted judgments for incompetent patients not only because of their peculiar grasp of the patient's approach to life, but also because of their special bonds with him or her. . . . It is . . . they who treat the patient as a person, rather than a symbol of a cause." *In re Jobes,* 108 N. J. 394, 416 (1987). The State, in contrast, is a stranger to the patient.

I respectfully dissent.

Justice STEVENS dissented in a separate opinion.

12

THE EQUAL PROTECTION OF THE LAWS

A GUARANTEE for "the equal protection of the laws" did not find its way into the Constitution until the ratification of the Fourteenth Amendment in 1868. Then, over a half century lapsed before the Supreme Court began enforcing it as a serious barrier to racial segregation and other kinds of nonracial discrimination as well. The Court, though, never narrowly interpreted the Fourteenth Amendment simply to require the evenhanded application of the laws. On such a view, states could deny blond-haired individuals public employment or benefits so long as they rigorously denied all blond-haired applicants. But such a narrow reading was rejected in *Yick Wo v. Hopkins*, 118 U.S. 356 (1886). When striking down San Francisco's "safety" ordinance, making it illegal to operate laundries in other than stone or brick buildings (and which was used to put Chinese laundries out of business), the Court observed that "[t]hough the law itself be fair on its face and impartial in appearance, yet, if it is applied and administered by public authority with an evil eye and an unjust hand, so as practically to make unjust and illegal discrimination between persons in similar circumstances, material to their rights, the denial of equal justice is . . . within the prohibition of the Constitution." At the same time, the equal protection clause has never been broadly construed to forbid all discrimination or inequities before the law.

This is so because all laws—all legislative classifications—discriminate and treat people differently.

The central problem for the Court lies in giving content and application to the principle of *legal equality*—equality before the law. Just as controversial as whether the Fourteenth Amendment aimed to ensure equal voting rights (see Vol. 1, Ch. 8), and whether it applied the guarantees of the Bill of Rights to the states (see Chapter 4), has been whether the amendment forbids racial segregation, as well as other kinds of nonracial discrimination. Justices, historians, and legal scholars, have long debated the legislative history of the Fourteenth Amendment. Some contend that the Thirty-ninth Congress, which drafted and adopted the amendment, aimed to give the federal government broad powers to ensure the rights of blacks and to advance the political ideal of equality.[1] Others marshal evidence that the amendment was not designed to forbid racial segregation;[2] indeed, it neither granted voting rights to blacks nor prohibited racial segregation.[3] Still others conclude that the historical record "is not entirely consistent"[4] and that the amendment is "so broad and general that [it] could be used to support almost anything."[5]

As with other controversies in constitutional politics, the debate over the equal protection clause reflects rival interpretations of politics and the politics of interpretation.[6] Moreover, as historian and Harvard law school professor William Nelson points out, whether the equal protection clause applies to claims of nonracial discrimination that come before the Court in this century is "a question that never occurred to the Reconstruction generation and hence cannot be answered by examining the records of its actual thought." Even issues that Congress extensively debated, such as voting rights for blacks and segregation, went unresolved and inconsistencies remained. As Nelson's underscores, "history can never tell us how the founding generation would have resolved inconsistencies that it did not, in fact, resolve."[7]

Once the Supreme Court turned to enforcing the equal protection clause in the twentieth century, it evolved standards for what legislative classifications are permissible and which discriminate in invidious, unconstitutional ways. Shortly after the Court's switch-in-time-that-saved-nine and abandonment of heightened review of economic legislation in 1937 (see Chapter 3), Justice Harlan F. Stone planted the seed for the modern Court's equal protection analysis. He did so in footnote four of *United States v. Carolene Products, Co.*, 304 U.S. 144 (1938), which upheld Congress's power to ban the shipment in interstate commerce of skim milk compounded with fat or other nonmilk products. In his opinion, Justice Stone reaffirmed that no longer would heightened scrutiny be given to legislation regulating economic activities; instead the Court would presume "that it rests upon some rational basis." But at that point he added the following three-paragraph footnote, pointing out that heightened scrutiny might be given to legislation affecting fundamental rights or which singles out racial and other "discrete and insular minorities":

There may be narrower scope for operation of the presumption of constitutionality when legislation appears on its face to be within a specific prohibition of the Constitution, such as those of the first ten amendments, which are deemed equally specific when held to be embraced within the Fourteenth. See *Stromberg v. California,* 283 U.S. 359 [1931]; *Lovell v. Griffin,* 303 U.S. 444 [*1938*].

It is unnecessary to consider now whether legislation which restricts those political processes which can ordinarily be expected to bring about repeal of undesirable legislation, is to be subjected to more exacting judicial scrutiny under the general prohibitions of the Fourteenth Amendment than are other types of legislation. On restrictions upon the right to vote, see *Nixon v. Herndon,* 273 U.S. 536 [1927]; *Nixon v. Condon,* 286 U.S. 73 [1932]; on restrictions upon the dissemination of information, see *Near v. Minnesota* 283 U.S. 697 [1931]; *Grosjean v. American Press Co.,* 297 U.S. 233 [1936]; *Lovell v. Griffin* [1938]; on interferences with political organizations, see *Stromberg v. California* [1931]; *Fiske v. Kansas* [1927]; *Whitney v. California,* 274 U.S. 357 [1927]; *Herndon v. Lowry* [1937]; and see Holmes, J., in *Gitlow v. New York,* 268 U.S. 652 [1925]; as to peaceable assembly, see *De Jonge v. Oregon,* 299 U.S. 353 [1937].

Nor need we inquire whether similar considerations enter into the review of statutes directed at particular religious, *Pierce v. Society of Sisters,* 268 U.S. 510 [1925], or national, *Meyer v. Nebraska,* 262 U.S. 390 [1923]; *Bartels v. Iowa,* 262 U.S. 404 [1923]; *Farrington v. Tokushige,* 273 U.S. 284 [1927], or racial minorities, *Nixon v. Herndon* [1927]; *Nixon v. Condon* [1932]; whether prejudices against discrete and insular minorities may be a special condition, which tends seriously to curtail the operation of those political processes ordinarily thought to be relied upon to protect minorities, and which may call for a correspondingly more searching judicial inquiry. . . .

The third paragraph of Justice Stone's footnote laid the basis for what evolved into a two- (and, later, a three-) tiered set of standards for judicial review under the equal protection clause.[8] By emphasizing the post-1937 Court's presumption of a rational basis for economic legislation, Justice Stone pointed the way toward heightened scrutiny (*strict scrutiny*) of legislation based on "suspect classifications," such as religion and race, or which impinged on "fundamental rights."

Justice Stone, though, used neither the phrase *fundamental rights* nor *strict scrutiny.* Four years later, in *Skinner v. Oklahoma,* 316 U.S. 535 (1942), Justice Douglas made the case for heightened judicial scrutiny of legislation affecting fundamental rights. Striking down a law requiring the forced sterilization of individuals convicted of two or more felonies involving moral turpitude, he observed that "[w]e are dealing here with legislation which involves one of the basic civil rights of man. Marriage and procreation are fundamental to the very existence and survival of the race." Ironically, the strict scrutiny test has its origins in an opinion by Justice Hugo Black, *upholding* the internment of Japanese-Americans during World War II. In *Korematsu v. United States*, 323 U.S. 214 (1944) (see Vol. 1, Ch. 3), Justice Black observed that "all legal restrictions which curtail the civil rights of a single racial group are immediately suspect. That is not to say that all such restrictions are unconstitutional. It is to say that courts must subject them to the most rigid scrutiny."

It remained for the Warren Court (1953–1969) to develop a two-tier approach to judicial review under the equal protection clause. When reviewing economic legislation, the Court gives *minimal scrutiny* and applies the *rational basis test*, asking simply whether legislation is reasonable and has a rational, conceivable basis. Under this test, legislation is invariably upheld. Indeed, only twice since 1937 have economic regulations been found irrational and unconstitutional under the Fourteenth Amendment. In *Morey v. Doud*, 354 U.S. 459 (1957), the Warren Court struck down Illinois's law exempting the American Express Company from licensing requirements for companies issuing money orders. In *Allegheny Pittsburgh Coal Co. v. County Commission*, 488 U.S. 336 (1989), the Rehnquist Court unanimously concluded that the equal protection clause was violated when a West Virginia county tax assessor valued real estate property "on the basis of its recent purchase price, but made only minor modifications in the assessments of land which had not been recently sold," resulting in the property of Allegheny Pittsburgh Coal Company to be "assessed at roughly 8 to 35 times more than comparable neighboring property." The county assessor's practice, in Chief Justice Rehnquist's words, was not "rationally related" to the state's law that property "be taxed at a rate uniform throughout the state according to its estimated market value."

By contrast, the strict scrutiny test applies to "suspect classifications," such as race, and legislation affecting fundamental rights. On this standard of review, legislation is sustained only if there is "a compelling state interest" in the legislative classification. *Korematsu* was the exception rather than the rule; when the Court applies this standard, legislation invariably falls.

The Warren Court's two-level analysis of equal protection claims proved as controversial as it was instrumental to forging an "egalitarian revolution" in constitutional law. Conservatives and strict constructionists criticized the Court for inventing new fundamental rights that they claimed lacked constitutional foundation.[9] Nor was the application of suspect classifications unproblematic. These classifications were "suspect" because they discriminated against individuals on the basis of immutable characteristics—characteristics, such as race, gender, age, and illegitimacy—which people do not choose and cannot readily, if at all, change (although, sex changes and notice of paternity are possible). By the end of the Warren Court era, the problem facing the justices was one of consistency in determining what classifications were suspect; notably, the Court was also split over whether gender, like race, was a suspect category. In addition, the Court was criticized for encouraging individuals to define their rights in terms of membership in groups and for inviting interest-group litigation. Finally, because legislation was invariably struck down under the strict scrutiny test and upheld under the rational basis test, the Warren Court's two-tier analysis was criticized for being too rigid, for being "strict in theory and fatal in fact."

By the 1970s and 1980s, the Court and the country were changing in response to the Warren Court's "egalitarian revolution." While litigation brought new claims of nonracial discrimination, the Court's composition also changed with the appointments of Republican Presidents Richard Nixon, Gerald Ford, and Ronald Reagan. As the high bench became more conservative, the Burger Court (1969–1986) and the Rehnquist Court (1986—) sought retrenchment, refusing to expand the list of fundamental rights, suspect classifications, and quasi-suspect categories like gender. Moreover, the Burger Court evolved a third, *intermediate* standard of judicial review: the "exacting scrutiny" or "strict rationality" test.[10] With this test, the Court looks for a "substantial relationship between the means and ends of legislation," and may or may not strike down legislation, for instance, discriminating on the basis of gender (see section D, in this chapter). In addition, the contemporary Court is resistant to attempts to heightened judicial review for new claims of quasi-suspect classifications. Indeed, the Rehnquist Court is inclined to evaluate claims of racial discrimination under the strict scrutiny test and all other equal protection claims under the rational basis test.

Illustrative of the Court's recent equal protection analysis is *City of Cleburne, Texas v. Cleburne Living Center*, 473 U.S. 432 (1985), involving a challenge to a Texas zoning law. The law required a special city permit, renewable each year, for the construction of "hospitals for the insane or feeble-minded, or alcoholic or drug addicts, or penal or correctional institutions." The

THE DEVELOPMENT OF LAW

The Supreme Court's Tests and Standards for Applying the Equal Protection Clause

Tiers of Analysis	Standard of Judicial Review	Legislative Classifications	Claims of Fundamental Rights
Upper Tier Applies to suspect classifications and fundamental rights	Strict Scrutiny Test: Is there a compelling state interest to a legislative classification?	Race See *Brown v. Board of Education of Topeka, Kansas* and *City of Richmond v. J. A. Croson* Alienage But see *Plyler v. Doe*	Right to vote See Vol. 1, Ch. 8 Right to interstate travel See *Shapiro v. Thompson*
Intermediate Tier Applies to quasi-suspect categories	Exacting Scrutiny or Strict Rationality Test: Is there a substantial relationship in fact between the means and ends of legislation?	Gender See *Craig v. Boren* Affirmative Action See *Regents of the University of California v. Bakke* Illegitimacy See table on page 1480 Alienage See *Plyler v. Doe*	
Lower Tier Applies to economic regulation and nonsuspect classifications	Minimal Scrutiny Rational Basis Test: Is there a rational basis, reasonable basis for legislation?	Indigency See *San Antonio Independent School District v. Rodriguez* Age Alienage Where an essential governmental function is implicated; see table on page 1484	Education, Housing, Welfare See *San Antonio Independent School District v. Rodriguez*

Cleburne Living Center wanted to operate a group home for thirteen mentally retarded men and women, but was denied a permit because the city concluded that the home should be classified as a "hospital for the feeble-minded." A federal district court upheld the city's decision. But an appellate court reversed, holding "that mental retardation is a 'quasi-suspect' classification and that the ordinance violated the Equal Protection Clause because it did not substantially further an important governmental purpose." On appeal to the Supreme Court, Justice White held that the lower court erred in finding mental retardation to be a quasi-suspect classification justifying heightened judicial review. Although finding "a lesser standard of scrutiny [to be] appropriate," he nevertheless concluded "that under that standard the ordinance is invalid as applied in this case," explaining that

> where individuals in the group affected by a law have distinguishing characteristics relevant to interests the state has the authority to implement, the courts have been very reluctant, as they should be in our federal system, and with respect for our separation of powers, to closely scrutinize legislative choices as to whether, how and to what extent those interests should be pursued. In such cases, the Equal Protection Clause requires only a rational means to serve a legitimate end.

The Court's analysis and evolving standards for judicial review under the equal protection clause are examined in this chapter in terms of the political struggles within the Court and the country over the historical quest for equality. The next section examines racial discrimination before and after the ratification of the Fourteenth Amendment and the role the Court played in the constitutional politics of racial segregation and desegregation. Section B turns to the Court's rulings on school desegregation. Section C takes up the controversy over affirmative action and reverse discrimination. Finally, section D considers nonracial classifications and challenges to discrimination based on gender, indigency, illegitimacy, alienage, and age.

NOTES

1. See Horace Flack, *The Adoption of the Fourteenth Amendment* (Baltimore, MD: Johns Hopkins University Press, 1908); Jacobus tenBroek, *The Antislavery Origins of the Fourteenth Amendment* (Berkeley: University of California Press, 1951); William Wiecek, *The Sources of Antislavery Constitutionalism in America* (Ithaca, NY: Cornell University Press, 1977);

and Howard Graham, *Everyman's Constitution: Historical Essays on the Fourteenth Amendment, the "Conspiracy Theory," and American Constitutionalism* (Madison: State Historical Society of Wisconsin, 1968).

2. See Alexander Bickel, "The Original Understanding and the Segregation Decision," 69 *Harvard Law Review* 1 (1955).

3. Raoul Berger, *Government by Judiciary: The Transformation of the Fourteenth Amendment* (Cambridge, MA: Harvard University Press, 1977).

4. See Earl Maltz, "The Fourteenth Amendment as Political Compromise—Section One in the Joint Committee on Reconstruction," 45 *Ohio State Law Journal* 933 (1984); and E. Matlz, "The Concept of Equal Protection of the Laws—A Historical Inquiry," 22 *San Diego Law Review* 499 (1985).

5. See Judith Baer, *Equality under the Constitution: Reclaiming the Fourteenth Amendment* (Ithaca, NY: Cornell University Press, 1983), 102–103.

6. See and compare William Brock, *An American Crisis: Congress and the Reconstruction* (New York: St. Martin's Press, 1963); Michael Les Benedict, *A Compromise of Principle: Congressional Republicans and Reconstruction* (New York: Norton, 1974).

7. William Nelson, *The Fourteenth Amendment* (Cambridge, MA: Harvard University Press, 1988).

8. The footnote was actually initially drafted by Justice Stone's law clerk, Louis Lusky, and revised after Chief Justice Hughes's made some suggestions. See Louis Lusky, *By What Right?* (Charlottesville, VA: Michie, 1975).

9. See, for example, the right to travel in *Shapiro v. Thompson* (on page 1457) and the right to privacy in *Griswold v. Connecticut* (in Chapter 4).

10. See Gerald Gunther, "In Search of Evolving Doctrine on a Changing Court: A Model for a New Equal Protection," 86 *Harvard Law Review* 1 (1972).

SELECTED BIBLIOGRAPHY

Baer, Judith. *Equality under the Constitution: Reclaiming the Fourteenth Amendment.* Ithaca, NY: Cornell University Press, 1983.

Bakin, T. M. "The Footnote," 83 *Northwestern University Law Review* 275 (1989).

Berger, Raoul. *Government by the Judiciary: The Transformation of the Fourteenth Amendment.* Cambridge, MA: Harvard University Press, 1977.

Karst, Kenneth. *Belonging to America: Equal Citizenship and the Constitution.* New Haven, CT: Yale University Press, 1989.

Nelson, William E. *The Fourteenth Amendment: From Political Principle to Judicial Doctrine.* Cambridge, MA: Harvard University Press, 1988.

Schwartz, Bernard, ed. *The Fourteenth Amendment.* New York: New York University Press, 1970.

A. RACIAL DISCRIMINATION AND STATE ACTION

"Our Constitution," in the words of Justice John Marshall Harlan dissenting alone in *Plessy v. Ferguson* (1896) (see page 1287), "is color-blind, and neither knows nor tolerates classes among citizens." However, the history of constitutional politics, both before and after the ratification of the Fourteenth Amendment, belies that noble aspiration and appeal to future generations. While the Declaration of Independence proclaimed that "all men are created equal," the Constitution was far from color-blind.

Opposition to slavery emerged during the Revolutionary War, particularly after slaves served as soldiers in the colonial battle for freedom from the English Crown. After winning independence, laws abolishing slavery were passed in six northern colonies (Pennsylvania, Massachusetts, Connecticut, Rhode Island, New York, and New Jersey). Still Thomas Jefferson and others won approval of the Northwest Ordinance of 1787, forbidding slavery in western territories north of the Ohio River, only after agreeing that fugitive slaves "may be lawfully reclaimed."

The Constitutional Convention compromised on the question of slavery, even though the words *slavery* and *slaves* never appear in the document. Article I, Section 2 provides that, for the purposes of taxation and representation in the House of Representatives, "three fifths of all other [nonfree] Persons" were to be counted. This accommodated southern delegates' twin concerns that when levying taxes the federal government might discriminate against the South in the way it counted slaves and that the South would be underrepresented if slaves were not counted for the purposes of representation. The convention agreed as well to authorize Congress, in Article I, Section 9, to stop the "migration or importation" of slaves, although not before 1808. Finally, without much debate the convention endorsed (in Article IV, Section 2) the return of fugitive slaves to their owners.

Despite the efforts of some at the Constitutional Convention to limit the perpetuation of slavery, the Constitution registered the prejudices and white supremacy of the country.[1] Over a half century later, Chief Justice Roger Taney wrote those prejudices into constitutional law with his sweeping opinion in *Dred Scott v. Sandford* (1857) (see page 1270), denying that blacks (not just slaves and temporarily freed slaves, but all blacks) could be citizens, and striking down the Missouri Compromise of 1850, in which Congress had sought to exclude slavery from federal territories north of the line 36°30'. When holding that blacks were excluded from "We the People of the United States," of which the preamble of the Constitution speaks, Chief Justice Taney laid bare the brute fact of white supremacy, explaining that blacks were "a subordinate and inferior class of beings, who had been subjugated by the dominant race, and, whether emancipated or not, yet remained subject to their authority."

Prior to the Civil War, the Court did little to undermine slavery. In *Prigg v. Pennsylvania,* 41 U.S. 539 (1842), though, the Court struck down a state law requiring masters to present to a magistrate proof of ownership of a runaway slave, and upheld the federal Fugitive Slave Law of 1793, authorizing federal judges to certify a slaveholder's claim over a fugitive slave. In his opinion for the Court, Justice Joseph Story, however, also noted that states were not compelled by Congress to enforce the 1793 law. As a result, northern states were encouraged not to enforce fugitive slave laws, while southern states pushed for more stringent laws to protect their interests.

Although abolitionists attacked the constitutionality of fugitive slave laws, the Taney Court firmly defended the South's interests in slavery. In *Strader v. Graham,* 51 U.S. 83 (1851), for instance, the Taney Court unanimously upheld Kentucky's law making abettors of fugitive slaves liable for damages to slaveowners, even if slaves had been taken into free territory.[2]

With the outbreak of the Civil War in 1861, *Dred Scott*'s impact was limited. After the war, the ruling was technically overturned by the Thirteenth Amendment (in 1865), which abolished slavery and "involuntary servitude," as well as gave Congress the "power to enforce this article by appropriate legislation." The Reconstruction Congress also considered how to ensure the voting rights and the civil rights of newly freed blacks. In 1862, Congress repealed the District of Columbia's "Black Codes," which limited the property rights of blacks and made certain offenses criminal for blacks only. But in 1865 President Andrew Johnson vetoed the passage of further civil rights legislation, contending that the protection of civil rights was a matter for the states, not the federal government. Congress, however, overrode the veto with a two-thirds vote and enacted the Civil Rights Act of 1866. Because controversy remained over the constitutionality of that legislation, one of the objectives of promoters of the Fourteenth Amendment in 1866 was to ensure the constitutional basis for the Civil Rights Act of 1866. The Fifteenth Amendment later specifically aimed at guaranteeing blacks equal voting rights (see Vol. 1, Ch. 8).

Both the Civil Rights Act of 1866 and the Fourteenth Amendment sought to ensure the citizenship of newly freed blacks and the equal protection of the laws. Congress was very explicit about the legal equality extended to blacks in the Civil Rights Act. It specifically guarantees:

> citizens, of every race and color . . . the same right, in every State and Territory . . . to make and enforce contracts, to sue, be parties, and give evidence, to inherit, purchase, lease, sell, hold, and convey real and personal property, and to full and equal benefit of all laws and proceedings for the security of person and property, as is enjoyed by white citizens, and shall be subject to like punishments, pains, and penalties, and to no other.

Although the Fourteenth Amendment's equal protection clause is less detailed, Congress reaffirmed in Section 5 of that amendment its "power to enforce" the amendment with "appropriate legislation," such as the Civil Rights Act of 1866 and the Civil Rights Act of 1875, which barred racial discrimination in public accommodations.

In the face of congressional efforts to legislate away white prejudice, the Court defended and gave constitutional legitimacy to racial segregation. In *The Slaughterhouse Cases* (1973) (see Chapter 3), the Chase Court sharply limited the scope of the Fourteenth Amendment. There and in *Strauder v. West Virginia,* 100 U.S. 303 (1880), the Court gave the amendment narrow scope in eliminating racial discrimination. In *Strauder,* the Waite Court conceded the potential contributions of the Fourteenth Amendment. Strauder, a black, sought to have his case moved from a state to a federal court because West Virginia barred blacks from serving on juries. When affirming his request, the Court observed that,

> [t]he words of the amendment . . . contain a necessary implication of a positive immunity, or right, most valuable to the colored race,—the right to exemption from unfriendly legislation against them distinctively as colored,—exemption from legal distinctions, implying inferiority in civil society, lessening the security of their enjoyment of the rights which others enjoy, and discriminations which are steps towards reducing them to the condition of a subject race. . . . The very fact that colored people are singled out and expressly denied by statute all right to participate in the administration of the law, as jurors, because of their color, though they are citizens, and may be in other respects fully qualified, is practically a brand upon them, affixed by the law, an assertion of their inferiority, and a stimulant to that race prejudice which is an impediment to securing to individuals of that race that equal justice which the law aims to secure to all others.

That same year in *Ex Parte Virginia,* 100 U.S. 313 (1880), the Waite Court again indicated that practices might be made to conform to the promise *"No state* shall . . . deny to any person

. . . the equal protection of the laws." This case involved a Virginia judge charged with violating federal law for excluding blacks from juries. He countered that, because the state had no law excluding blacks from juries, his actions though official did not constitute "state action" in violation of the amendment. Rejecting that argument, the Waite Court held that the amendment barred government "agencies" and "officials" from denying the equal protection of the laws.

Three years later, however, the Waite Court turned state action into a barrier for eliminating racial discrimination. In the *Civil Rights Cases* (1883) (see page 1277), the Court held that Section 5 of the Fourteenth Amendment only authorized Congress to enact legislation barring racial discrimination that resulted from state action—state laws or actions done "under the color of state laws." Congress, in the Court's view, was not authorized to enact the Civil Rights Act of 1875 or to forbid racial discrimination by individuals and corporations in public accommodations.[3] The state action doctrine thus became a vehicle for perpetuating racial discrimination and segregation.

The *Civil Rights Cases* undercut congressional power and legitimated private racial discrimination. The Fuller Court, then, gave legitimacy to the doctrine of "separate but equal" facilities for blacks and whites in *Plessy v. Ferguson* (1896) (see page 1287). Whereas forty years earlier in *Dred Scott* Chief Justice Taney had no doubts about the inferior status of blacks, in *Plessy* Justice Brown denied that the doctrine of separate but equal implied "the inferiority of either race."

The Court's rulings in the late nineteenth century returned control over race relations to the states. By the turn of the twentieth century, the states of the old Confederacy had largely disenfranchised blacks (see Vol. 1, Ch. 8) and erected a system of racial segregation. Blacks were separated from whites in public schools, government office buildings, public parks, and recreational areas, as well as hotels, restaurants, theaters, and other places of public accommodations.

The Court and the country did not begin to change until well into the twentieth century. In a few early cases, the Court led the way, striking down laws aimed at denying blacks' voting rights,[4] some racial zoning laws,[5] and recognizing the inequities of racially segregated educational facilities.[6] But only after the battle over the New Deal in 1937 and the period surrounding World War II did the federal government undertake the long process of dismantling the system of racial segregation. In 1939, Democratic President Franklin Roosevelt created a Civil Liberties Unit within the Department of Justice and later issued an executive order creating a Committee on Fair Employment Practices with authority over businesses working for the federal government.[7] More significant were the executive orders issued by FDR's successor, President Harry Truman. In 1948, he boldly ordered an end to racial segregation in the military,[8] and established the Fair Employment Board and outlawed racial discrimination in the federal government.

Congress remained unwilling to act and the actions of FDR and Truman provoked rebellion within the Democratic party. In 1948 Alabama, Louisiana, Mississippi, and South Carolina left the Democratic party to form the Dixiecrat party. But Roosevelt's and Truman's appointments to the Court contributed to the shifting tide in constitutional politics after World War II. FDR elevated Justice Stone to the chief justiceship and named eight justices between 1937 and 1943: Hugo Black in 1937, Stanley Reed in 1938, Felix Frankfurter and William Douglas in 1939, Frank Murphy in 1940, James Byrnes and Robert Jackson in 1941, and Wiley Rutledge in 1943. Truman then appointed Chief Justice Fred Vinson in 1946 and Justices Harold Burton (in 1945) and Thomas Clark and Sherman Minton (in 1949).[9]

In the 1940s and 1950s, litigation brought by the National Association for the Advancement of Colored People (NAACP) pushed the Court into a leading role in the process of ending racial segregation. When striking down restrictive covenants in *Shelley v. Kraemer* (1948) (see page 1293), the Court turned the state action doctrine into an instrument for prohibiting private racial discrimination.[10] The state action doctrine, which had supported systems of racial discrimination, became a tool for the Court to reach and ban private racial discrimination.

In the two decades following *Shelley*, the Court never denied relief on the grounds that no state action was present. In *Burton v. Willimington Parking Authority*, 365 U.S. 715 (1961), for example, the Warren Court applied the state action doctrine to a restaurant denying service to blacks. It did so on the grounds that the restaurant, although privately owned, was located in a publicly owned parking garage and that public property could not be leased in a manner inconsistent with the Fourteenth Amendment. In *Evans v. Newton,* 382 U.S. 296 (1966) (with Justices Black, Harlan, and Stewart dissenting), the Warren Court held that the equal protection clause was violated by Macon, Georgia's "whites only" public park. The land for the park was deeded to the city in 1911 with the stipulation that it be used for a park "for whites only." Although the city resigned as the trustee for the park, and private trustees were appointed, the Court held that the Fourteenth Amendment applied under its new formulation of the state action doctrine. The Court then unanimously struck down Alabama's system of racially segregated prisons in *Lee v. Washington,* 390 U.S. 1 (1967), and, with only Justice Black dissenting, *Hunter v. Erickson,* 393 U.S. 385 (1969), overturned an ordinance barring fair housing practices.

The civil rights movement gathered momentum in the 1960s. Under the leadership of Dr. Martin Luther King, Jr., thousands of protesting blacks defied segregation in restaurants and other public accommodations. When blacks started sit-ins at luncheon counters and restaurants, they were arrested for trespassing on private property or for breach of the peace. The Warren Court was reluctant to extend the state action doctrine to reach segregated lunch counters. Although overturning convictions of civil rights "sitters-in," it did so without relying on the state action doctrine.[11] In *Bell v. Maryland,* 378 U.S. 226 (1964), for example, the convictions of twelve sit-in protesters were overturned on the grounds that Maryland's newly enacted antidiscrimination law might be applied by state courts to abate the prosecutions. Concurring Chief Justice Warren and Justices Douglas and Goldberg also argued that because the restaurant was "property that is serving the public" it could not discriminate against blacks. But dissenting Justice Black, joined by Justices Harlan and White, contended that Congress, not the Court, had the power under the Fourteenth Amendment to ban segregated public accommodations. Justice Black worried about the scope of the state action doctrine and remained unwilling to extend the equal protection clause to the practice of racial discrimination by owners of restaurants.

The controversy within the Warren Court over whether the state action doctrine applied to restaurants was settled by the president and Congress. Almost a hundred years after the Civil Rights Act of 1875, Congress finally addressed the issue of segregated public accommodations. In response to the massive southern resistance to school desegregation and the violent reactions to the pressures for change brought by the civil rights movement, Democratic President John F. Kennedy proposed new aggressive civil rights legislation.[12] Following Kennedy's assassination, President Lyndon Johnson pushed the Civil Rights Act of 1964 and other legislation through Congress.[13] Besides limiting the use of literacy tests for voters (see Vol. I, Ch. 8), authorizing the Department of Justice to challenge segregated public facilities, the Civil Rights Act of 1964 in Title II forbade racial discrimination in public accommodations and in Title VII outlawed discrimination in employment.

Since the *Civil Rights Cases* had held that the state action limited congressional power under the Fourteenth Amendment, Congress passed the Civil Rights Act of 1964 on its authority under the commerce clause (see, Vol. 1, Ch. 6). When the constitutionality of the Civil Rights Act of 1964 was challenged, the Warren Court upheld it in *Heart of Atlanta Motel, Inc. v. United States* (1964) and *Katzenbach v. McClung* (1964) (both in Vol. I, Ch. 6). The Court upheld as well the Voting Rights Act of 1965, banning racial discrimination in elections, in *South Carolina v. Katzenbach*, 383 U.S. 301 (1965) (see Vol. I, Ch. 8). Ironically, in the year that Congress passed the Civil Rights Act of 1968, forbidding discrimination in the sale, rental, financing and advertising of housing, the Warren Court also construed the Civil Rights Act of 1866 to ban private racial discrimination in housing and affirmed Congress's authority to enact such legislation under the Thirteenth Amendment. In *Jones v. Alfred H. Mayer, Co.*, 392 U.S. 409 (1968), the Court finally accepted the view of Justice Harlan dissenting in the *Civil Rights Cases*, that the Thirteenth Amendment proscribes all "badges and incidents" of slavery. In *McLaughlin v. Florida*, 379 U.S. 184 (1964), and *Loving v. Virginia*, 388 U.S. 1 (1967), the Warren Court struck down state miscegenation laws, which barred interracial marriages.

The civil rights revolution forged by the Warren Court, and Democratic presidents and Congresses, embittered southern Democrats and some Republicans. In the 1968 presidential election, Republican candidate Richard Nixon campaigned against the "egalitarian jurisprudence" of the Warren Court, promising to appoint strict constructionists to the bench as part of his "southern strategy" to win the votes of southern white voters. With his election, a brief and dramatic period of social and legal change gradually came to an end. Nixon made his mark by appointing Chief Justice Warren Burger in 1969 and Justices Harry Blackmun in 1971 and Lewis F. Powell and William Rehnquist in 1972.

With the Burger Court (1969–1986) came changes. It drew the line on further extension of earlier rulings, but it also confronted new controversies (involving, for example, affirmative action programs, as examined in section C, of this chapter) that would not have arisen were it not for the civil rights revolution of the 1960s. In *James v. Valtierra*, 402 U.S. 137 (1971), for instance, a bare majority upheld a law requiring qualified voters to approve low-cost housing projects, over the objection of the dissenters that sanctioned racial segregation in housing. However, in *Hills v. Gautreaux*, 425 U.S. 284 (1976), the Court approved a lower court's order for the adoption of a comprehensive metropolitan plan for desegregating Chicago's public housing system.

The state action doctrine was given new twists and limited during the Burger Court years. The Court held that a restaurant's refusal to serve a white woman in the company of blacks was state action.[14] But *Evans v. Abney*, 396 U.S. 435 (1970), signaled that the Burger Court would limit the scope of the state action doctrine. There, once again the justices confronted the continuing controversy over Macon, Georgia's all-white park. After the Warren Court's ruling in *Evans v. Newton* (1966), the heirs of the donor of the park reclaimed the land on the grounds that the donor's will was not honored, because it expressly conditioned use of the land for whites only. The Burger Court upheld a state court's decision returning the land and found no state action to trigger the Fourteenth Amendment. In 1971, then, a bare majority of the Burger Court upheld the decision of Jackson, Mississippi, to close, rather than desegregate, the city's public swimming pools. Justices Douglas, Brennan, Marshall, and White dissented from that ruling in *Palmer v. Thompson*, 403 U.S. 217 (1971).

In *Moose Lodge No. 107 v. Irvis*, 407 U.S. 163 (1972), the Burger Court refused to apply the state action doctrine to a private club that refused to serve blacks, even though it had a state liquor license. Writing for the majority, Justice Rehnquist explained that

[t]he Court has never held, of course, that discrimination by an otherwise private entity would be violative of the equal protection clause if the private entity receives any sort of benefit or service at all from the State, or if it is subject to state regulation in any degree whatever. Since state-furnished services include such necessities of life as electricity, water, and police and fire protection, such a holding would utterly emasculate the distinction between private as distinguished from State conduct set forth in *The Civil Rights Cases* and adhered to in subsequent decisions. Our holdings indicate that where the impetus for the discrimination is private, the State must have "significantly involved itself with invidious discriminations,". . . in order for the discriminatory action to fall within the ambit of the constitutional prohibition.

Dismissing the argument that by licensing the private club the state became implicated in racial discrimination, Justice Rehnquist observed,

However detailed this type of regulation may be in some particulars, it cannot be said to in any way foster or encourage racial discrimination. Nor can it be said to make the State in any realistic sense a partner or even a joint venturer in the club's enterprise. The limited effect of the prohibition against obtaining additional club licenses when the maximum number of retail licenses allotted to a municipality has been issued, when considered together with the availability of liquor from hotel, restaurant, and retail licensees falls far short of conferring upon club licensees a monopoly in the dispensing of liquor in any given municipality or in the State as a whole. We therefore hold that . . . the operation of the regulatory scheme enforced by the Pennsylvania Liquor Control Board does not sufficiently implicate the State in the discriminatory

THE DEVELOPMENT OF LAW
Other Recent Rulings on State Action

Case	Vote	Ruling
Jackson v. Metropolitan Edison Co., 419 U.S. 345 (1974)	6:3	Held that a privately owned electric company, operating under a state license, which terminated service to a customer was not covered by the state action doctrine, in a suit brought by the customer, claiming a right to notice, a hearing, and the opportunity to pay past electric bills. Justices Douglas, Brennan, and Marshall dissented.
Blum v. Yaretsky, 457 U.S. 991 (1982)	7:2	The Court rejected the argument that state subsidies to a private institution constituted state action and made the institution subject to the limitations of the Fourteenth Amendment; here, patients in a nursing home, who were transferred to another without notice or a hearing, claimed they were denied procedural due process; Justices Brennan and Marshall dissented.
San Francisco Arts & Athletics, Inc. v. United States Olympic Committee (USOC), 483 U.S. 522 (1987)	5:4	Held that the USOC was not a government actor, despite Congress's granting it the right to prohibit commercial and promotional uses of the word *Olympic*, and rejected the equal protection claims of the petitioner who was barred from calling its athletic competitions the "Gay Olympic Games"; Justices Brennan, Marshall, Blackmun and O'Connor dissented.

Case	Vote	Ruling
National Collegiate Athletic Association (NCAA) v. Tarkanian 109 S.Ct. 454 (1988)	5:4	Upheld the University of Nevada, Las Vegas's disciplinary actions against its head basketball coach in accordance with the NCAA's rules, and ruled that the NCAA recommendations for disciplinary actions were not state action, and hence the NCAA was not liable for violating the coach's civil rights; Justice White, a former football player was joined by Justices Brennan, Marshall, and O'Connor in dissent, finding the NCAA to be a state actor because it acted jointly with the University of Nevada.

guest policies of Moose Lodge so as to make the latter "State action" within the ambit of the Equal Protection Clause of the Fourteenth Amendment.

Dissenting Justices Brennan, Marshall, and Douglas took quite a different view of the scope of the state action doctrine. In Justice Brennan's words,

When Moose Lodge obtained its liquor license, the State of Pennsylvania became an active participant in the operation of the Lodge bar. Liquor licensing laws are . . . primarily pervasive regulatory schemes under which the State dictates and continually supervises virtually every detail of the operation of the licensee's business. Very few, if any, other licensed businesses experience such complete state involvement. Yet the Court holds that that involvement does not constitute "state action" making the Lodge's refusal to serve a guest liquor solely because of his race a violation of the Fourteenth Amendment. The vital flaw in the Court's reasoning is its complete disregard of the fundamental value underlying the "state action" concept.

By narrowing the scope of the state action doctrine, the Burger Court enlarged the range of private activities immune from suits under the Fourteenth Amendment. It did so by limiting the public function theory that underlies the doctrine of state action. Whereas the Warren Court looked at the totality of interrelationships between government and private activities, the Burger and Rehnquist Courts tend to scrutinize and then dismiss various arguments for extending the doctrine of state action. With those exceptions already noted, though, the Court has refused to extend the state action doctrine primarily in cases *not* involving claims of racial discrimination.

Despite retrenchment in the state action doctrine, the Burger Court continued to strictly scrutinize claims of racial discrimination, as illustrated by the unanimous ruling in *Palmore v. Sidoti* (1984) (see page 1295). But see Justice Rehnquist's dissenting opinion, joined by Chief Justice Burger, in *Batson v. Kentucky,* 476 U.S. 79 (1986) (see Chapter 9), arguing that "there is simply nothing 'unequal' about the State using its peremptory challenges to strike blacks from" juries trying black defendants. See also the five-to-four ruling that statistical evidence does not establish that capital punishment is inflicted in racially discriminatory ways in *McCleskey v. Kemp,* 481 U.S. 279 (1987) (see Chapter 10).

Notable also is *Bob Jones University v. United States* and *Goldsboro Christian Schools, Inc. v. United States,* 461 U.S. 574 (1983). There the Court upheld the policy decision of the Internal Revenue Service denying tax-exempt status to private schools that racially discriminate. In his opinion for the Court, Chief Justice Burger conceded that the "[d]enial of tax benefits will inevitably have a substantial impact on the operation of private religious schools." But he underscored that

[t]he governmental interest at stake here is compelling. . . . [T]he Government has a fundamental, overriding interest in eradicating racial discrimination in education—discrimination that prevailed, with official approval, for the first 165 years of this Nation's history. That governmental interest substantially outweighs whatever burden denial of tax benefits places on petitioners' exercise of their religious beliefs. The interests asserted by petitioners cannot be accommodated with that compelling governmental interest, . . . and no "less restrictive means,". . . are available to achieve the governmental interest.

However, in *Bazemore v. Friday,* 478 U.S. 385 (1986), speaking for a bare majority Justice White held that the "affirmative duty to desegregate" had no application to 4-H and Homemaker Clubs, which were segregated until 1965 and run by the North Carolina Agricultural Extension Service. He observed that "[w]hile school children must go to school, there is no compulsion to join 4-H or Homemaker Clubs, and . . . there is no statutory or regulatory authority to deny a young person the right to join any Club he or she wishes to join." Dissenting Justice Brennan, joined by Justices Blackmun, Marshall, and Stevens, countered that "[n]othing in our earlier cases suggests that the State's obligation to desegregate is confined only to those activities in which members of the public are compelled to participate."

The state action doctrine, nevertheless, became less important for striking down private racial discrimination after *Jones v. Alfred H. Mayer Co.*, 392 U.S. 409 (1968), held that Congress intended to forbid private racial discrimination in the Civil Rights Act of 1866 and that it had the authority to do so under the Thirteenth Amendment. The Burger Court, furthermore, extended that ruling and reinforced the Civil Rights Act of 1866 as a barrier to private racial discrimination in housing, schools, and employment,[15] whenever there is proof of intentional discrimination.[16]

In an important ruling in *Runyon v. McCrary,* 427 U.S. 160 (1976), the Burger Court held that the Civil Rights Act of 1866 extended to private schools that refuse to admit blacks. "It is now well established," Justice Stewart observed in his opinion for the Court, that the Civil Rights Act of 1866 "prohibits racial discrimination in the making and enforcement of private contracts," emphasizing that "while parents have a constitutional right to send their children to private schools and a constitutional right to select private schools that offer specialized instruction, they have no constitutional right to provide their children with private school education unfettered by reasonable governmental regulations." But dissenting Justice White, joined by Justice Rehnquist, countered by rereading the legislative history of the Civil Rights Act and concluded that "the statute means what it says and no more, i.e., that it outlaws any legal rule disabling any person from making or enforcing a contract, but does not prohibit private racially motivated refusals to contract." In his concurring opinion, the Court's "southern gentleman," Justice Powell, responded, "If the slate were clean I might well be inclined to agree with Mr. Justice White that [the statute] was not intended to restrict private contractual choices. Much of the review of the history and purpose of this statute set forth in his dissenting opinion is quite persuasive. It seems to me, however, that it comes too late." He pointed out that "[a] small kindergarten or music class, operated on the basis of personal invitations extended to a limited number of preidentified students . . . would present a far different case," but here the Runyons had advertised in the yellow pages of the phone book and by mail-order solicitations. Powell concluded "that we must either apply the rationale of *Jones* or overrule that decision." Justice Stevens, also concurring, agreed with the Court's decision because of the "interest in stability and orderly development of the law," adding that "even if *Jones* did not accurately reflect the sentiments of the Reconstruction Congress, it surely accords with the prevailing sense of justice today." Concluding, he cautioned that, "for the

Court now to overrule *Jones* would be a significant step backwards, with effects that would not have arisen from a correct decision in the first instance."

The Rehnquist Court extended the protection of the Civil Rights Act of 1866 to Arabians and Jews upon concluding that "Jews and Arabs were among the people [in 1866] then considered to be distinct races and hence within the protection of the statute."[17] In 1987, however, the Rehnquist Court also indicated a move in more conservative directions by suggesting a willingness in *Patterson v. McLean Credit Union* to reconsider and possibly overturn the 1976 ruling in *Runyon v. McCrary.* Rehnquist and White dissented in *Runyon* and in another decision, *McDonald v. Santa Fe Trail Transportation Co.*, 427 U.S. 273 (1976), which extended liability under the Civil Rights Act of 1866 to employers who racially discriminated in their hiring and firing of employees. Joined on the bench a decade later by President Ronald Reagan's appointees (Justices O'Connor, Scalia, and Kennedy), they appeared prepared to forge a new majority and vindicate their dissenting views in *Runyon.*

The Rehnquist Court (without Justice Kennedy, yet to be nominated and confirmed) heard oral arguments in *Patterson v. McLean Credit Union* in 1987. But shortly after Justice Kennedy's confirmation in 1988, he cast the crucial fifth vote for a bare majority to carry the case over for reargument on the question of "Whether or not the interpretation of [the Civil Rights Act of 1866] adopted by this Court in *Runyon v. McCrary.* . . . should be reconsidered."[18] Dissenting Justice Blackmun, joined by Justices Brennan, Marshall, and Stevens, warned that the new majority on the Court threatened no longer to take precedent seriously and pointed out that Congress could have overruled *Runyon* because it involved statutory, not constitutional, interpretation.

The basic issue in *Patterson* was whether the Civil Rights Act of 1866 made employers liable for not only racial discrimination in hiring and firing workers, but also for racial harassment in the workplace. Brenda Patterson, a black woman, claimed that during ten years of working for the McLean Credit Union of North Carolina, she was treated in a hostile manner, subjected to racist comments, and discriminated against in work assignments. After being laid off, she sued the credit union.

The decision to hear rearguments in *Patterson* and to reconsider *Runyon* set off a storm of political protest. Together, 66 United States senators, 119 United States representatives, 47 state attorneys general, and 112 civic groups joined in briefs opposing the overturning of *Runyon.* Ultimately, in *Patterson v. McLean Credit Union*, 109 S.Ct. 2363 (1989), the Rehnquist Court decided that "no special justification has been shown for overruling

Runyon." In his opinion for the Court, Justice Kennedy explained that

whether *Runyon's* interpretation of [the Civil Rights Act of 1866] as prohibiting racial discrimination in the making and enforcement of private contracts is wrong or right as an original matter, it is certain that it is not inconsistent with the prevailing sense of justice in this country. To the contrary, *Runyon* is entirely consistent with our society's deep commitment to the eradication of discrimination based on a person's race or color of his or her skin.

Still, he refused to hold employers liable for racial harassment and discrimination as a condition of employment. The statute, in Justice Kennedy's words, covers "only conduct at the initial formation of the contract and conduct which impairs the right to enforce contract obligations through [the] legal process." That conclusion provoked dissenting Justice Brennan, joined by Justices Blackmun, Marshall, and Stevens, to complain that

When it comes to deciding whether a civil rights statute should be construed to further our Nation's commitment to the eradication of racial discrimination, the Court adopts a formalistic method of interpretation antithetical to Congress's vision of a society in which contractual opportunities are equal. . . .

In the past, this Court has overruled decision antagonistic to our Nation's commitment to the ideal of a society in which a person's opportunities do not depend on her race, e.g., *Brown v. Board of Education* (1954) (overruling *Plessy v. Ferguson* (1896)), and I find it disturbing that the Court has in this case chosen to reconsider, without any request from the parties, a statutory construction so in harmony with that ideal.

Having decided, however, to reconsider *Runyon,* and now to reaffirm it by appeal to *stare decisis,* the Court glosses over what are in my view two very obvious reasons for refusing to overrule this interpretation [of the statute]: that *Runyon* was correctly decided, and that in any event Congress has ratified our construction of the statute.

Patterson reflects the ongoing struggles in the Court and the country over the exercise of judicial review in ending the last vestiges of racial discrimination.[19]

No less significantly, in *Spallone v. United States,* 110 S.Ct. 625 (1989), a bare majority of the Court upheld federal district court Judge Leonard Sand's finding of contempt of court and imposition of fines on four Yonkers City councilmen for refusing to vote for legislation needed to carry out a public housing plan. After years of litigation, the Yonkers City Council finally agreed to the plan as part of a settlement of a federal housing discrimination suit, brought under Title VIII of the Civil Rights Act of 1968 and the equal protection clause of the Fourteenth Amendment. But four of the seven council members then refused to endorse an ordinance implementing the settlement. On appeal to the Supreme Court, Justice White joined Reagan's four appointees to form a bare majority for upholding, but sharply criticizing, Judge Sand's orders. Writing for the majority, Chief Justice Rehnquist held that Judge Sand's imposition of personal fines on the council members was not a "proper exercise of judicial power." In his view, Judge Sand should have waited before taking such a drastic step until he determined whether fines he also imposed against the city would move the recalcitrant council members to change their minds. In Chief Justice Rehnquist's words,

Sanctions directed against the city for failure to take actions such as required by the consent decree coerce the city legislators and, of course, restrict the freedom of those legislators to act in accordance with their current view of the city's best interests. But we believe there are significant differences between the two types of fines. The imposition of sanctions on individual legislators is designed to cause them to vote, not with a view to the interest of their constituents or of the city, but with a view solely to their own personal interests. . . . Such fines thus encourage legislators, in effect, to declare that they favor an ordinance not in order to avoid bankrupting the city for which they legislate, but in order to avoid bankrupting themselves.

The four dissenters, Justices Brennan, Marshall, Blackmun, and Stevens, objected to the majority's "parsimonious view" of Judge Sand's orders. "The key question," as Justice Brennan put it,

is whether Judge Sand abused his discretion when he decided not to rely on sanctions against the city alone but also to apply coercive pressure to the recalcitrant councilmembers on an individual basis. Given the city council's consistent defiance and the delicate political situation in Yonkers, Judge Sand was justifiably uncertain as to whether city sanctions alone would coerce compliance at all. . . . Under these conditions, Judge Sand's decision to supplement the city sanctions with personal fines was surely a sensible approach. The Court's contrary judgment rests on its refusal to take the fierceness of the councilmembers' defiance seriously, refusal blind to the scourge of racial politics in Yonkers and dismissive of Judge Sand's wisdom borne of his superior vantage point.

Justice Brennan concluded with the admonition that,

[t]he Court's decision today that Judge Sand abused his remedial discretion . . . creates no new principle of law; indeed, it invokes no principle of any sort. But it directs a message to district judges that, despite their repeated and close contact with the various parties and issues, even the most delicate remedial choices by the most conscientious and deliberate judges are subject to being second-guessed by this Court. I hope such a message will not daunt the courage of district courts who,

if ever again faced with such protracted defiance, must carefully yet firmly secure compliance with their remedial orders. But I worry that the Court's message will have the unintended effect of emboldening recalcitrant officials continually to test the ultimate reach of the remedial authority of the federal courts.

NOTES

1. See the excellent collection of writings of the framers of the Constitution on the matter of slavery in Philip Kurland and Ralph Lerner, eds., *The Founders' Constitution* Vol. 1 (Chicago: University of Chicago Press, 1987), 495–576.

2. See also *Ableman v. Booth*, 62 U.S. 506 (1859).

3. See also *United States v. Cruikshank*, 92 U.S. 542 (1876).

4. See, for example, *Guinn v. United States*, 238 U.S. 347 (1915); and *Lane v. Wilson*, 307 U.S. 268 (1939) (striking down grandfather clauses denying voting rights to most blacks). See also Vol. 1, Ch. 8.

5. See *Missouri Ex. Rel. Gaines v. Canada*, 305 U.S. 337 (1938).

6. See *Buchanan v. Warley*, 245 U.S. 60 (1971).

7. Exec. Order 8802, *Federal Register*, Vol. VI (1941), 3109.

8. Exec. Order 9981, *Federal Register*, Vol. XII (1948), 4313.

9. For a discussion of FDR's and Truman's appointments, see David M. O'Brien, *Storm Center: The Supreme Court in American Politics*, 2nd ed., (New York: Norton, 1990), Ch. 2.

10. In *Reitman v. Mulkey*, 387 U.S. 369 (1967), a bare majority of the Warren Court struck down California's restrictive covenant law.

11. See *Garner v. Louisiana*, 368 U.S. 157 (1961); *Bouie v. City of Columbia*, 378 U.S. 342 (1964); and *Barr v. City of Columbia*, 378 U.S. 146 (1964).

12. In 1957 and 1960, Congress enacted two other civil rights laws, but both proved ineffective. See Carl Brauer, *John F. Kennedy and the Second Reconstruction* (New York: Columbia University Press, 1977).

13. See James Harvey, *Black Civil Rights during the Johnson Administration* (Jackson: University and College Press of Mississippi, 1973).

14. *Adickes v. S. H. Kress & Co.*, 398 U.S. 144 (1970).

15. In addition to the cases discussed, see *Griffin v. Breckenridge*, 403 U.S. 88 (1971).

16. See *General Building Constructors Association, Inc. v. Pennsylvania*, 451 U.S. 375 (1982).

17. See *St Francis College v. Al-Khazraji*, 481 U.S. 604 (1987); and *Shaare Tefila Congregation v. Cobb*, 481 U.S. 615 (1987).

18. See *Patterson v. McLean Credit Union*, 485 U.S. 617 (1988).

19. For example, in *Griggs v. Duke Power Company*, 401 U.S. 424 (1971), the Burger Court held that under the Thirteenth Amendment and the Civil Rights Act of 1866 that employers were prohibited from requiring a high-school degree or standardized test for employees when neither was work-related and operated to discriminate against the hiring of blacks. But in *Wards Cove Packing, Inc. v. Atonio*, 109 S.Ct. 2115

(1989), a bare majority of the Rehnquist Court held that workers may not use statistical evidence to show racial discrimination in the workplace and that *Greggs,* in Justice White's words, "should have been understood to mean" that.

SELECTED BIBLIOGRAPHY

Barnes, Catherine. *Journey From Jim Crow: The Desegregation of Southern Transit.* New York: Columbia University Press, 1983.

Eisenberg, Theodore. *Civil Rights Legislation.* Charlottsville, VA: Michie Co., 1981.

Fehrenbacher, Don. *The Dred Scott Case: Its Significance in American Law and Politics.* New York: Oxford University Press, 1978.

Hampton, Henry, and Fayer, Steve. *Voices of Freedom: An Oral History of the Civil Rights Movement from the 1960s through the 1980s.* New York: Bantam Books, 1990.

Hyman, Harold, and Wiecek, William. *Equal Justice Under Law: Constitutional Development 1835–1875.* New York: Harper & Row, 1982.

Lofgren, Charles. *The Plessy Case.* New York: Oxford University Press, 1987.

tenBroek, Jacobus. *The Antislavery Origins of the Fourteenth Amendment.* Berkeley: University of California Press, 1951.

Tushnet, Mark. *The American Law of Slavery, 1810–1860.* Princeton, NJ: Princeton University Press, 1981.

Dred Scott v. Sandford
19 How. (60 U.S.) 393 (1857)

In 1848, a Missouri slave, Dred Scott, sought to win his freedom in a lawsuit against the widow of John Emerson, his owner and an army medical officer. Scott contended that he had been emancipated as a result of Emerson's having taken him to live in military posts in Illinois and in federal territory north of 36°30' where slavery was outlawed by the Missouri Compromise of 1820. In that legislation, Congress admitted Maine into the Union as a free state, Missouri as a slave state, and banned slavery in all federal territories north of the line 36°30'.

The question Scott raised was whether his residence on free soil had changed his status as a slave. Prior to the 1830s, northern and southern states tried to accommodate each others interests. Southerners were permitted to travel with their slaves in the North without interference, while southern courts upheld the rule that a slave temporarily domiciled in a free state became permanently free. But under the pressure of abolitionists in the 1830s and 1840s, this accommodation broke down. Northern states began denying southerners the privilege of traveling with their slaves and holding that slaves, who were not fugitives, became free once they were on free soil. Southern states in turn grew increasingly resentful and retailed by refusing to enforce the antislavery law of other jurisdictions. So it was that after two trials and Scott temporarily won his freedom in 1852, the Missouri state supreme court held that it would no longer enforce the antislavery laws of other states and that Scott's residence on free soil did not change his status as a slave.

In a further effort to win Scott's freedom, his attorneys sought review by a federal circuit court in a lawsuit against Mrs. Emerson's brother and agent in the litigation, John Sanford of New York. (Sanford's name was misspelled as Sandford in the official records.) Since Sanford resided in another state than Scott, attorneys claimed that Scott's case fell within federal court's diversity jurisdiction (jurisdiction over suits brought by citizens of different states). But their legal strategy raised a new issue: to bring a lawsuit in federal court, Scott had to show that he was a citizen. Sanford's attorneys countered that Negroes were not citizens in Missouri and therefore Scott had no standing to sue and the court lacked jurisdiction. The trial judge agreed that Scott's legal status depended on the law in Missouri, not his erstwhile residence in free territory, and a jury decided for Sanford.

Scott's lawyers next appealed to the Supreme Court, which included five southern Democrats, two northern Democrats, one northern Whig, and one Republican. During their oral arguments before the Court in February 1856, Sanford's attorneys raised an additional issue. They argued that not only was Scott a slave, not a citizen, but that he could not have become even temporarily a "freeman" by residing in a free state because the Missouri Compromise was unconstitutional. That was a hotly debated political question sharply dividing the country, and the Court decided to hold the case over and hear rearguments in its next session.

On March 6, 1857, Chief Justice Roger Taney read from the bench his opinion for the Court: Scott lost. The chief justice held that Scott had no standing to sue in federal courts because he was not and could not be a citizen by virtue of the fact that he was a Negro and a slave. Taney proceeded to declare the antislavery provision of the Missouri Compromise unconstitutional. In sharply worded dissenting opinions, Justice John McLean and Benjamin Curtis took strong exception to the chief justice's sweeping opinion.

Chief Justice Taney's decision contributed to the ongoing struggle that erupted four years later in the Civil War. Despite the Court's ruling, Scott was soon freed by his owners, only to die a year and a half later. Two months after the ruling, Sanford also died, in an insane asylum. The constitutional effect of the ruling was also short lived. In 1862, Congress forbid slavery in all federal territories. Following the Civil War, the Thirteenth Amendment (1865), abolishing slavery, and the Fourteenth Amendment (1868) overturned Chief Justice Taney's ruling.

Chief Justice TANEY delivers the opinion of the Court.

[After reviewing the facts, Chief Justice TANEY first addressed the question of whether Scott was a citizen and entitled to bring his lawsuit.]

The question is simply this: can a negro, whose ancestors were imported into this country and sold as slaves, become a member of the political community formed and brought into existence by the Constitution of the United States, and as such become entitled to all the rights, and privileges, and immunities, guarantied by that instrument to the citizen. One of these rights is the privilege of suing in a court of the United States in the cases specified in the Constitution. . . .

The words "people of the United States" and "citizens" are synonymous terms, and mean the same thing. They both describe the political body, who, according to our republican institutions, form the sovereignty, and who hold the power and conduct the government through their representatives. They are what we familiarly call the "sovereign people," and every citizen is one of this people, and a constituent member of this sovereignty. The question before us is, whether the class of persons described in the plea in abatement compose a portion of this people, and are constituent members of this sovereignty. We think they are not, and that they are not included, and were not intended to be included, under the word "citizens" in the Constitution, and can, therefore, claim none of the rights and privileges which that instrument provides for and secures to citizens of the United States. On the contrary, they were at that time considered as a subordinate and inferior class of beings, who had been subjugated by the dominant race, and whether emancipated or not, yet remained subject to their authority, and had no rights or privileges but such as those who held the power and the government might choose to grant them.

It is not the province of the court to decide upon the justice or injustice, the policy or impolicy of these laws. The decision of that question belonged to the political or law-making power; to those who formed the sovereignty and framed the Constitution.

The duty of the court is to interpret the instrument they have framed, with the best lights we can obtain on the subject, and to administer it as we find it, according to its true intent and meaning when it was adopted.

In discussing this question, we must not confound the rights of citizenship which a state may confer within its own limits, and the rights of citizenship as a member of the Union. It does not by any means follow, because he has all the rights and privileges of a citizen of a State, that he must be a citizen of the United States. He may have all the rights and privileges of the citizen of a State, and yet not be entitled to the rights and privileges of a citizen in any other State. For, previous to the adoption of the Constitution of the United States, every State had the undoubted right to confer on whomsoever it pleased the character of a citizen, and to endow him with all its rights. But this character, of course, was confined to the boundaries of the State, and gave him no rights or privileges in other States beyond those secured to him by the laws of nations and the comity of States. Nor have the several States surrendered the power of conferring these rights and privileges by adopting the Constitution of the United States. . . . The Constitution has conferred on Congress the right to establish an uniform rule of naturalization, and this right is evidently exclusive, and has always been held by this court to be so. Consequently, no State, since the adoption of the Constitution, can, by naturalizing an alien, invest him with the rights and privileges secured to a citizen of a State under the federal government, although, so far as the State alone was concerned, he would undoubtedly be entitled to the rights of a citizen, and clothed with all the rights and immunities which the Constitution and laws of the State attached to that character.

It is very clear, therefore, that no State can, by any Act or law of its own, passed, since the adoption of the Constitution, introduce a new member into the political community created by the Constitution of the United States. It cannot make him a member of this community by making him a member of its own. And for the same reason it cannot introduce any person, or description of persons, who were not intended to be embraced in this new political family, which the Constitution brought into existence, but were intended to be excluded from it. . . .

In the opinion of the court, the legislation and histories of the times, and the language used in the Declaration of Independence, show, that neither the class of persons who had been imported as slaves, nor their descendants, whether they had become free or not, were then acknowledged as a part of the people, nor intended to be included in the general words used in that memorable instrument.

It is difficult at this day to realize the state of public opinion in relation to that unfortunate race, which prevailed in the civilized and enlightened portions of the world at the time of the Declaration of Independence, and when the Constitution of the United States was framed and adopted. But the public history of every European nation displays it, in a manner too plain to be mistaken.

They had for more than a century before been regarded as beings of an inferior order; and altogether unfit to associate with the white race, either in social or political relations; and so far inferior, that they had no rights which the white man was bound to respect; and that the negro might justly and lawfully be reduced to slavery for his benefit. He was bought and sold, and treated as an ordinary article of merchandise and traffic, whenever a profit could be made by it. This opinion was at that time fixed and universal in the civilized portion of the white race. It was regarded as an axiom in morals as well as in politics, which no one thought of disputing, or supposed to be open to dispute; and men in every grade and position in society daily and habitually acted upon it in their private pursuits, as well as in matters of public concern, without doubting for a moment the correctness of this opinion. . . .

We refer to these historical facts for the purpose of showing the fixed opinions concerning that race, upon which the statesmen of that day spoke and acted. It is necessary to do this, in order to determine whether the general terms used in the Constitution of the United States, as to the rights of man and the rights of the people, was intended to include them, or to give to them or their posterity the benefit of any of its provisions.

The language of the Declaration of Independence is equally conclusive.

It begins by declaring that, "when in the course of human events it becomes necessary for one people to dissolve the political bands which have connected them with another, and to assume among the powers of the earth the separate and equal station to which the laws of nature and nature's God entitle them, a decent respect for the opinions of mankind requires that they should declare the causes which impel them to the separation."

It then proceeds to say: "We hold these truths to be self-evident: that all men are created equal; that they are endowed by their Creator with certain inalienable rights; that among them is life, liberty, and pursuit of happiness; that to secure these rights, governments are instituted, deriving their just powers from the consent of the governed."

The general words above quoted would seem to embrace the whole human family, and if they were used in a similar instrument at this day, would be so understood. But it is too clear for dispute, that the enslaved African race were not intended to be included, and formed no part of the people who framed and adopted this Declaration; for if the language, as understood in that day, would embrace them, the conduct of the distinguished men who framed the Declaration of Independence would have been utterly and flagrantly inconsistent with the principles they asserted; and instead of the sympathy of mankind, to which they so confidently appealed, they would have deserved and received universal rebuke and reprobation.

Yet the men who framed this Declaration were great men— high in literary acquirements—high in their sense of honor, and incapable of asserting principles inconsistent with those on which they were acting. They perfectly understood the meaning of the language they used, and how it would be understood by others; and they knew that it would not, in any part of the civilized world, be supposed to embrace the negro race. . . .

This state of public opinion had undergone no change when the Constitution was adopted, as is equally evident from its provisions and language. . . .

[T]here are two clauses in the Constitution which point directly and specifically to the negro race as a separate class of persons, and show clearly that they were not regarded as a portion of the people or citizens of the government then formed.

One of these clauses reserves to each of the thirteen States the right to import slaves until the year 1808, if it thinks proper. And the importation which it thus sanctions was unquestionably of persons of the race of which we are speaking, as the traffic in slaves in the United States had always been confined to them. And by the other provision the States pledge themselves to each other to maintain the right of property of the master, by delivering up to him any slave who may have escaped from his service, and be found within their respective territories. By the first above-mentioned clause, therefore, the right to purchase and hold this property is directly sanctioned and authorized for twenty years by the people who framed the Constitution. And by the second, they pledge themselves to maintain and uphold the right of the master in the manner specified, as long as the government they then formed should endure. And these two provisions show, conclusively, that neither the description of persons therein referred to, nor their descendants, were embraced in any of the other provisions of the Constitution; for certainly these two clauses were not intended to confer on them or their posterity the blessings of liberty, or any of the personal rights so carefully provided for the citizen. . . .

[U]pon a full and careful consideration of the subject, the court is of opinion that, upon the facts stated in the plea in abatement, Dred Scott was not a citizen of Missouri within the meaning of the Constitution of the United States, and not entitled as such to sue in its courts; and, consequently, that the Circuit Court had no jurisdiction of the case, and that the judgment on the plea in abatement is erroneous. . . .

[Chief Justice TANEY then turned to the question of whether

Scott remained a slave after his trip into the Louisiana Territory.]

The Act of Congress, upon which the plaintiff relies, declares that slavery and involuntary servitude, except as a punishment for crime, shall be forever prohibited in all that part of that territory ceded by France, under the name of Louisiana, which lies north of thirty-six degrees thirty minutes north latitude, and not included within the limits of Missouri. And the difficulty which meets us at the threshold of this part of the inquiry is, whether Congress was authorized to pass this law under any of the powers granted to it by the Constitution; for if the authority is not given by that instrument, it is the duty of this court to declare it void and inoperative, and incapable of conferring freedom upon one who is held as a slave under the laws of any one of the States. . . .

[T]he power of Congress over the person or property of a citizen can never be a mere discretionary power under our Constitution and form of government. The powers of the government and the rights and privileges of the citizen are regulated and plainly defined by the Constitution itself. And when the territory becomes a part of the United States, the Federal Government enters into possession in the character impressed upon it by those who created it. It enters upon it with its powers over the citizen strictly defined, and limited by the Constitution, from which it derives its own existence, and by virtue of which alone it continues to exist and act as a government and sovereignty. It has no power of any kind beyond it; and it cannot, when it enters a territory of the United States, put off its character, and assume discretionary or despotic powers which the Constitution has denied to it. It cannot create for itself a new character separated from the citizens of the United States, and the duties it owes them under the provisions of the Constitution. The territory being a part of the United States, the government and the citizen both enter it under the authority of the Constitution, with their respective rights defined and marked out; and the Federal Government can exercise no power over his person or property, beyond what that instrument confers, nor lawfully deny any right which it has reserved. . . .

For example, no one, we presume, will contend that Congress can make any law in a territory respecting the establishment of religion or the free exercise thereof, or abridging the freedom of speech or of the press, or the right of the people of the territory peaceably to assemble and to petition the government for the redress of grievances. . . .

These powers, and others in relation to rights of person, which it is not necessary here to enumerate, are, in express and positive terms, denied to the general government; and the rights of private property have been guarded with equal care. Thus the rights of property are united with the rights of person, and placed on the same ground by the fifth amendment to the Constitution, which provides that no person shall be deprived of life, liberty and property, without due process of law. And an Act of Congress which deprives a citizen of the United States of his liberty or property, merely because he came himself or brought his property into a particular Territory of the United States, and who had committed no offense against the laws, could hardly be dignified with the name of due process of law. . . .

Now, as we have already said in an earlier part of this opinion, upon a different point, the right of property in a slave is distinctly and expressly affirmed in the Constitution. The right to traffic in it, like an ordinary article of merchandise and property, was guaranteed to the citizens of the United States, in every State that might desire it, for twenty years. And the government in express terms is pledged to protect it in all future time, if the slave escapes from his owner. This is done in plain words—too plain to be misunderstood. And no word can be found in the Constitution which gives Congress a greater power over slave property, or which entitles property of that kind to less protection than property of any other description. The only power conferred is the power coupled with the duty of guarding and protecting the owner in his rights.

Upon these considerations, it is the opinion of the court that the Act of Congress which prohibited a citizen from holding and owning property of this kind in the territory of the United States north of the line therein mentioned, is not warranted by the Constitution, and is therefore void; and that neither Dred Scott himself, nor any of his family, were made free by being carried into this territory; even if they had been carried there by the owner, with the intention of becoming a permanent resident. . . .

[Finally, Chief Justice TANEY turned to whether Scott was made free by traveling to Illinois, a free state. He held that Scott's status was to be determined by Missouri law, and thus Scott remained a slave.]

Justice WAYNE, Justice NELSON, Justice GRIER, Justice CAMPBELL, and Justice CATRON concurred in separate opinions.

Justice MCLEAN and Justice CURTIS dissented in separate opinions.

The Civil Rights Cases
109 U.S. 3, 3 S.Ct 18 (1883)

At issue in five cases, coming from California, Kansas, Missouri, New Jersey, and Tennessee, which were consolidated and decided together, was the constitutionality of Congress's passage of the Civil Rights Act of 1875. That legislation made it a *federal* crime for owners and operators of any public accommodation—schools, churches, cemeteries, hotels, places of amusement, and common carriers—to "deny the full enjoyment of the accommodations thereof" because of race or religion. Each of the cases involved challenges to the enforcement of the law against innkeepers, theater owners, and a railroad company.

With only Justice John Marshall Harlan dissenting, Justice Joseph Bradley held for the Court that Congress had no authority under the Thirteenth and Fourteenth Amendments to enact the Civil Rights Act of 1875, and had intruded on the powers reserved to the states by the Tenth Amendment. Moreover, Justice Bradley narrowly read the Thirteenth Amendment to only abolish slavery, but not private racial discrimination, and limited the Fourteenth Amendment to bar only racial discrimination backed by state action. By contrast, Justice Harlan pointed out that the Court previously upheld Congress's power to regulate the behavior of private individuals—notably, when upholding fugitive slave laws requiring the return of slaves to their owners. Also, in his view racial discrimination was a badge of servitude abolished by the Thirteenth Amendment and a matter on which Congress could legislate when enforcing the Thirteenth and Fourteenth Amendments. As a result of the majority's ruling, racist attitudes were reinforced and the basis was laid for states to pass Jim Crow laws, requiring the separate treatment of blacks and whites in public accommodations.

Justice BRADLEY delivers the opinion of the Court.

Has congress constitutional power to make [the Civil Rights Act of 1875]? Of course, no one will contend that the power to pass it was contained in the constitution before the adoption of the last three amendments. The power is sought, first, in the fourteenth amendment, and the views and arguments of distinguished senators, advanced while the law was under consideration, claiming authority to pass it by virtue of that amendment, are the principal arguments adduced in favor of the power. . . .

The first section of the fourteenth amendment,—which is the one relied on,—after declaring who shall be citizens of the United States, and of the several states, is prohibitory in its character, and prohibitory upon the states. It declares that "no state shall make or enforce any law which shall abridge the privileges or immunities of citizens of the United States; nor shall any state deprive any person of life, liberty, or property without due process of law; nor deny to any person within its jurisdiction the equal protection of the laws." It is state action of a particular character that is prohibited. Individual invasion of individual rights is not the subject-matter of the amendment. It has a deeper and broader scope. It nullifies and makes void all state legislation, and state action of every kind, which impairs the privileges and immunities of citizens of the United States, or which injures them in life, liberty, or property without due process of law, or which denies to any of them the equal protection of the laws. It not only does this, but, in order that the national will, thus declared, may not be a mere *brutum fulmen*, the last section of the amendment invests congress with power to enforce it by appropriate legislation. To enforce what? To enforce the prohibition. To adopt appropriate legislation for correcting the effects of such prohibited state law and state acts, and thus to render them effectually null, void, and innocuous. This is the legislative power conferred upon congress, and this is the whole of it. It does not invest congress with power to legislate upon subjects which are within the domain of state legislation; but to provide modes of relief against state legislation, or state action, of the kind referred to. It does not authorize congress to create a code of municipal law for the regulation of private rights; but to provide modes of redress against the operation of state laws, and the action of state officers, executive or judicial, when these are subversive of the fundamental rights specified in the amendment. Positive rights and privileges undoubtedly secured by the fourteenth amendment; but they are secured by way of prohibition against state laws and state proceedings affecting those rights and privileges, and power given to congress to legislate for the purpose of carrying such prohibition into effect; and such legislation must necessarily be predicated upon such supposed state laws or state proceedings, and be directed to the correction of their operation and effect. . . .

And so in the present case, until some state law has been passed, or some state action through its officers or agents has been taken, adverse to the rights of citizens sought to be protected by the fourteenth amendment, no legislation of the United States under said amendment, nor any proceeding under such legislation, can be called into activity, for the prohibitions of the amendment are against state laws and acts done under state authority. Of course, legislation may and should be provided in advance to meet the exigency when it arises, but it should be adapted to the mischief and wrong which the amendment was intended to provide against; and that is, state laws or state action of some kind adverse to the rights of the citizen secured by the amendment. . . . In fine, the legislation which congress is authorized to adopt in this behalf is not general legislation upon the rights of the citizen, but corrective legislation; that is, such as may be necessary and proper for counteracting such laws as the states may adopt or enforce, and which by the amendment they are prohibited from making or enforcing, or such acts and proceedings as the states may commit or take, and which by the amendment they are prohibited from committing or taking. It is not necessary for us to state, if we could, what legislation would be proper for congress to adopt. It is sufficient for us to examine whether the law in question is of that character.

An inspection of the law shows that it makes no reference whatever to any supposed or apprehended violation of the fourteenth amendment on the part of the states. It is not predicated on any such view. It proceeds *ex directo* to declare that certain acts committed by individuals shall be deemed offenses, and shall be prosecuted and punished by proceedings in the courts of the United States. It does not profess to be corrective of any constitutional wrong committed by the states; it does not make its operation to depend upon any such wrong committed. It applies equally to cases arising in states which have the justest laws respecting the personal rights of citizens, and whose authorities are ever ready to enforce such laws as to those which arise in states that may have violated the prohibition of the amendment. In other words, it steps into the domain of local jurisprudence, and lays down rules for the conduct of individuals in society towards each other, and imposes sanctions for the enforcement of those rules, without referring in any manner to any supposed action of the state or its authorities.

If this legislation is appropriate for enforcing the prohibitions of the amendment, it is difficult to see where it is to stop. Why may not congress, with equal show of authority, enact a code of laws for the enforcement and vindication of all rights of life, liberty, and property? If it is supposable that the states may deprive persons of life, liberty, and property without due process of law, (and the amendment itself does suppose this,) why should not congress proceed at once to prescribe due process of law for the protection of every one of these fundamental rights, in every possible case, as well as to prescribe equal privileges in inns, public conveyances, and theaters. The truth is that the implication of a power to legislate in this manner is based upon the assumption that if the states are forbidden to legislate or act in a particular way on a particular subject, and power is conferred upon congress to enforce the prohibition, this gives congress power to legislate generally upon that subject, and not merely power to provide modes of redress against such state legislation or action. The assumption is certainly unsound. It is repugnant to the tenth amendment of the constitution, which declares that powers not delegated to the United States by the constitution, nor prohibited by it to the states, are reserved to the states respectively or to the people. . . .

In this connection it is proper to state that civil rights, such as are guaranteed by the constitution against state aggression, cannot be impaired by the wrongful acts of individuals, unsupported by state authority in the shape of laws, customs, or judicial or executive proceedings. The wrongful act of an individual, unsupported by any such authority, is simply a private wrong, or a crime of that individual; an invasion of the rights of the injured party, it is true, whether they affect his person, his property, or his reputation; but if not sanctioned in some way by the state, or not done under state authority, his rights remain in full force, and may presumably be vindicated by resort to the laws of the state for redress. . . .

But the power of congress to adopt direct and primary, as distinguished from corrective, legislation on the subject in hand, is sought, in the second place, from the thirteenth amendment, which abolishes slavery. This amendment declares "that neither slavery, nor involuntary servitude, except as a punishment for crime, whereof the party shall have been duly convicted, shall exist within the United States, or any place subject to their jurisdiction;" and it gives congress power to enforce the amendment by appropriate legislation.

This amendment, as well as the fourteenth, is undoubtedly self-executing without any ancillary legislation, so far as its terms are applicable to any existing state of circumstances. By its own unaided force and effect it abolished slavery, and established universal freedom. Still, legislation may be necessary and proper to meet all the various cases and circumstances to be affected by it, and to prescribe proper modes of redress for its violation in letter or spirit. And such legislation may be primary and direct in its character; for the amendment is not a mere prohibition of state laws establishing or upholding slavery, but an absolute declaration that slavery or involuntary servitude shall not exist in any part of the United States. . . .

After giving to these questions all the consideration which their importance demands, we are forced to the conclusion that such an act of refusal has nothing to do with slavery or involuntary servitude, and that if it is violative of any right of the party, his redress is to be sought under the laws of the state; or, if those laws are adverse to his rights and do not protect him, his remedy will be found in the corrective legislation which congress has adopted, or may adopt, for counteracting the effect of state laws, or state action, prohibited by the fourteenth amendment. It would be running the slavery argument into the ground to make it apply to every act of discrimination which a person may see fit to make as to the guests he will entertain, or as to the people he will take into his coach or cab or car, or admit to his concert or theater, or deal with in other matters of intercourse or business. Innkeepers and public carriers, by the laws of all the states, so far as we are aware, are bound, to the extent of their facilities, to furnish proper accommodation to all unobjectionable persons who in good faith apply for them. If the laws themselves make any unjust discrimination, amenable to the prohibitions of the fourteenth amendment, congress has full power to afford a remedy under that amendment and in accordance with it. . . .

There were thousands of free colored people in this country before the abolition of slavery, enjoying all the essential rights of life, liberty, and property the same as white citizens; yet no one, at that time, thought that it was any invasion of their personal *status* as freemen because they were not admitted to all the privileges enjoyed by white citizens, or because they were subjected to discriminations in the enjoyment of accommodations in inns, public conveyances, and places of amusement. Mere discriminations on account of race or color were not regarded as badges of slavery. If, since that time, the enjoyment of equal rights in all these respects has become established by constitutional enactment, it is not by force of the thirteenth amendment, (which merely abolishes slavery,) but by force of the fourteenth and fifteenth amendments.

On the whole, we are of opinion that no countenance of authority for the passage of the law in question can be found in either the thirteenth or fourteenth amendment of the constitution; and no other ground of authority for its passage being suggested, it must necessarily be declared void, at least so far as its operation in the several states is concerned.

Justice HARLAN dissenting.

The opinion in these cases proceeds, as it seems to me, upon grounds entirely too narrow and artificial. The substance and spirit of the recent amendments of the constitution have been sacrificed by a subtle and ingenious verbal criticism. "It is not the words of the law but the internal sense of it that makes the law. The letter of the law is the body; the sense and reason of the law is the soul." Constitutional provisions, adopted in the interest of liberty, and for the purpose of securing, through national legislation, if need be, rights inhering in a state of freedom, and belonging to American citizenship, have been so construed as to defeat the ends the people desired to accomplish, which they attempted to accomplish, and which they supposed they had accomplished by changes in their fundamental law. By this I do not mean that the determination of these cases should have been materially controlled by considerations of mere expediency or policy. I mean only, in this form, to express an earnest conviction that the court has departed from the familiar rule requiring, in the interpretation of constitutional provisions, that full effect be given to the intent with which they were adopted. . . .

The thirteenth amendment, my brethren concede, did something more than to prohibit slavery as an *institution*, resting upon distinctions of race, and upheld by positive law. They admit that it established and decreed universal *civil freedom* throughout the United States. But did the freedom thus established involve nothing more than exemption from actual slavery? Was nothing more intended than to forbid one man from owning another as property? Was it the purpose of the nation simply to destroy the institution, and then remit the race, theretofore held in bondage, to the several states for such protection, in their civil rights, necessarily growing out of freedom, as those states, in their discretion, choose to provide? Were the states, against whose solemn protest the institution was destroyed, to be left perfectly free, so far as national interference was concerned, to make or allow discriminations against that race, as such, in the enjoyment of those fundamental rights that inhere in a state of freedom? . . .

That there are burdens and disabilities which constitute badges of slavery and servitude, and that the express power delegated to congress to enforce, by appropriate legislation, the thirteenth amendment, may be exerted by legislation of a direct and primary character, for the eradication, not simply of the institution, but of its badges and incidents, are propositions which ought to be deemed indisputable. They lie at the very foundation of the civil rights act of 1866. Whether that act was fully authorized by the thirteenth amendment alone, without the support which it afterwards received from the fourteenth amendment, after the adoption of which it was re-enacted with some additions, the court, in its opinion, says it is unnecessary to inquire. But I submit, with all respect to my brethren, that its constitutionality is conclusively shown by other portions of their opinion. It is expressly conceded by them that the thirteenth amendment established freedom; that there are burdens and disabilities, the necessary incidents of slavery, which constitute its substance and visible form; that congress, by the act of 1866, passed in view of the thirteenth amendment, before the fourteenth was adopted, undertook to remove certain burdens and disabilities, the necessary incidents of slavery, and to secure to all citizens of every race and color, and without regard to previous servitude, those fundamental rights which are the essence of civil freedom, namely, the same right to make and enforce contracts, to sue, be parties, give evidence, and to inherit, purchase, lease, sell, and convey property as is enjoyed by white citizens; that under the thirteenth amendment congress has to do with slavery and its incidents; and that legislation, so far as necessary or proper to eradicate all forms and incidents of slavery and involuntary servitude, may be direct and primary, operating upon the acts of individuals, whether sanctioned by state legislation or not. These propositions being conceded, it is impossible, as it seems to me, to question the constitutional validity of the civil rights act of 1866. I do not contend that the thirteenth amendment invests congress with authority, by legislation, to regulate the entire body of the civil rights which citizens enjoy, or may enjoy, in the several states. But I do hold that since slavery, as the court has repeatedly declared, was the moving or principal cause of the adoption of that amendment, and since that institution rested wholly upon the inferiority, as a race, of those held in bondage, their freedom necessarily involved immunity from, and protection against, all discrimination against them, because of their race, in respect of such civil rights as belong to freemen of other races. . . .

What has been said is sufficient to show that the power of congress under the thirteenth amendment is not necessarily restricted to legislation against slavery as an institution upheld by positive law, but may be exerted to the extent at least of protecting the race, so liberated, against discrimination, in respect of legal rights belonging to freemen, where such discrimination is based upon race. . . .

I also submit whether it can be said—in view of the doctrines of this court as announced in *Munn* v. *Illinois,* [94 U.S. 113 (1877)], that the management of places of public amusement is a purely private matter, with which government has no rightful concern. In the *Munn Case* the question was whether the state of Illinois could fix, by law, the maximum of charges for the storage of grain in certain warehouses in that state—the *private property of individual citizens.* . . .

The doctrines of *Munn* v. *Illinois* have never been modified by this court, and I am justified, upon the authority of that case, in saying that places of public amusement, conducted under the authority of the law, are clothed with a public interest, because used in a manner to make them of public consequence and to affect the community at large. The law may therefore regulate, to some extent, the mode in which they shall be conducted, and consequently the public have rights in respect of such places which may be vindicated by the law. It is consequently not a matter purely of private concern.

Congress has not, in these matters, entered the domain of state control and supervision. It does not assume to prescribe the general conditions and limitations under which inns, public conveyances, and places of public amusement shall be conducted or managed. It simply declares in effect that since the nation has established universal freedom in this country for all time, there shall be no discrimination, based merely upon race or color, in respect of the legal rights in the accommodations and advantages of public conveyances, inns, and places of public amusement.

I am of opinion that such discrimination is a badge of servitude, the imposition of which congress may prevent under its power, through appropriate legislation, to enforce the thirteenth amendment; and consequently, without reference to its enlarged power under the fourteenth amendment, the act of March 1, 1875, is not, in my judgment, repugnant to the constitution.

It remains now to consider these cases with reference to the power congress has possessed since the adoption of the fourteenth amendment. . . .

[To begin,] an essential inquiry [is] what, if any, right, privilege, or immunity was given by the nation to colored persons when they were made citizens of the state in which they reside? Did the national grant of state citizenship to that race, of its own force, invest them with any rights, privileges, and immunities whatever? That they became entitled, upon the adoption of the fourteenth amendment, "to all privileges and immunities of citizens in the several states," within the meaning of section 2 of article 4 of the constitution, no one, I suppose, will for a moment question. What are the privileges and immunities to which, by that clause of the constitution, they became entitled? To this it may be answered, generally, upon the authority of the adjudged cases, that they are those which are fundamental in citizenship in a free government, "common to the citizens in the latter states under their constitutions and laws by virtue of their being citizens." Of that provision it has been said, with the approval of this court, that no other one in the constitution has tended so strongly to constitute the citizens of the United States one people. . . .

But what was secured to colored citizens of the United States— as between them and their respective states—by the grant to them of state citizenship? With what rights, privileges, or immunities did this grant from the nation invest them? There is one, if there be no others—exemption from race discrimination in respect of any civil right belonging to citizens of the white race in the same state. That, surely, is their constitutional privilege when within the jurisdiction of other states. And such must be their constitutional right, in their own state, unless the recent amendments be "splendid baubles," thrown out to delude those who deserved fair and generous treatment at the hands of the nation. Citizenship in this country necessarily imports equality of civil rights among citizens of every race in the same state. It is fundamental in American citizenship that, in respect of such rights, there shall be no discrimination by the state, or its officers, or by individuals, or corporations exercising public functions or authority, against any citizen because of his race or previous condition of servitude. . . .

Much light is thrown upon this part of the discussion by the language of this court in reference to the fifteenth amendment. In *U.S. v. Cruikshank,* [92 U.S. 542 (1876)], it was said:

> In *U.S. v. Reese,* 92 U.S. 214 [(1876)], we held that the fifteenth amendment has invested the citizens of the United States with a new constitutional right, which is exemption from discrimina-

tion in the exercise of the elective franchise on account of race, color, or previous condition of servitude. From this it appears that the right of suffrage is not a necessary attribute of national citizenship, but that exemption from discrimination in the exercise of that right on account of race, etc., is. The right to vote in the states comes from the states; but the right of exemption from the prohibited discrimination comes from the United States. The first has not been granted or secured by the constitution of the United States, but the last has been.

Here, in language at once clear and forcible, is stated the principle for which I contend. It can hardly be claimed that exemption from race discrimination, in respect of civil rights, against those to whom state citizenship was granted by the nation, is any less for the colored race a new constitutional right, derived from and secured by the national constitution, than is exemption from such discrimination in the exercise of the elective franchise. It cannot be that the latter is an attribute of national citizenship, while the other is not essential in national citizenship, or fundamental in state citizenship.

If, then, exemption from discrimination in respect of civil rights is a new constitutional right, secured by the grant of state citizenship to colored citizens of the United States, why may not the nation, by means of its own legislation of a primary direct character, guard, protect, and enforce that right? It is a right and privilege which the nation conferred. It did not come from the states in which those colored citizens reside. It has been the established doctrine of this court during all its history, accepted as vital to the national supremacy, that congress, in the absence of a positive delegation of power to the state legislatures, may by legislation enforce and protect any right derived from or created by the national constitution. . . .

But the court says that congress did not, in the act of 1866, assume, under the authority given by the thirteenth amendment, to adjust what may be called the social rights of men and races in the community. I agree that government has nothing to do with social, as distinguished from technically legal, rights of individuals. No government ever has brought, or ever can bring, its people into social intercourse against their wishes. Whether one person will permit or maintain social relations with another is a matter with which government has no concern. I agree that if one citizen chooses not to hold social intercourse with another, he is not and cannot be made amendable to the law for his conduct in that regard; for no legal right of a citizen is violated by the refusal of others to maintain merely social relations with him, even upon grounds of race. What I affirm is that no state, nor the officers of any state, nor any corporation or individual wielding power under state authority for the public benefit or the public convenience, can, consistently either with the freedom established by the fundamental law, or with that equality of civil rights which now belongs to every citizen, discriminate against freemen or citizens, in their civil rights, because of their race, or because they once labored under disabilities imposed upon them as a race. The rights which congress, by the act of 1875, endeavored to secure and protect are legal, not social, rights. The right, for instance, of a colored citizen to use the accommodations of a public highway upon the same terms as are permitted to white citizens is no more a social right than his right, under the law, to use the public streets of a city, or a town, or a turnpike road, or a public market, or a post-office, or his right to sit in a public building with others, of whatever race, for the purpose of hearing the political questions of the day discussed. . . .

To-day it is the colored race which is denied, by corporations and individuals wielding public authority, rights fundamental in their freedom and citizenship. At some future time it may be some other race that will fall under the ban. If the constitutional amendments be enforced, according to the intent with which, as I conceive, they were adopted, there cannot be, in this republic, any class of human beings in practical subjection to another class, with power in the latter to dole out to the former just such privileges as they may choose to grant. The supreme law of the land has decreed that no authority shall be exercised in this country upon the basis of discrimination, in respect of civil rights, against freemen and citizens because of their race, color, or previous condition of servitude. To that decree—for the due enforcement of which, by appropriate legislation, congress has been invested with express power—every one must bow, whatever may have been, or whatever now are, his individual views as to the wisdom or policy, either of the recent changes in the fundamental law, or of the legislation which has been enacted to give them effect.

For the reasons stated I feel constrained to withhold my assent to the opinion of the court.

Plessy v. Ferguson
163 U.S. 537, 3 S.Ct. 18 (1896)

Four years after the Supreme Court struck down the Civil Rights Act of 1875 in the *Civil Rights Cases* (1883) (see page 1277), Florida enacted the first "Jim Crow" law, requiring separate but equal facilities for blacks and whites in railway passenger cars. Louisiana and other states in the Deep South followed with similar laws. Blacks were embittered by the passage of these laws, but the Court adapted the Constitution to support racial discrimination by white legislative majorities. In *Louisville, New Orleans & Texas Pacific Railroad v. Mississippi,* 133 U.S. 587 (1890), the Court ruled that segregated railroad passenger cars traveling in intrastate commerce did not interfere with Congress's power to regulate interstate commerce under the commerce clause.

Louisiana's "Jim Crow" law was challenged in a test case brought by Homer Plessy, who was one-eighth black. When he boarded a railroad train in New Orleans, which was headed for Covington, Louisiana, he refused to sit in the car reserved for "Colored Only" and sat in one reserved for whites instead. He was arrested, convicted, and appealed to the Supreme Court. Plessy's attorneys contended that Louisiana's law violated the Thirteenth and Fourteenth Amendments.

By a vote of eight to one, the Supreme Court rejected Plessy's arguments. Note the sharply different interpretations of the Constitution and social attitudes in the majority's opinion by Justice Henry Brown and in the sole dissenting opinion by Justice John Harlan. Whereas Justice Brown dismisses the claim the state's action violates the Thirteenth Amendment as "too clear for argument," Justice Harlan has no doubt that compulsory racial segregation imposed precisely the kind of badge of servitude that the amendment aimed to outlaw. Justice Brown's treatment of the Fourteenth Amendment claim is also far from cogent. Although allowing that the amendment "was undoubtedly to enforce the absolute equality of the two races before the law," he adds that "in the nature of things it could not have been intended to abolish distinctions based on color." For the Court's majority, racial segregation was not discriminatory and did not "necessarily imply the inferiority of either race to the other," but rather a reasonable exercise of state police power "for the promotion of the public good, and not for the annoyance or oppression of a particular class." By contrast, Justice Harlan conceived of all forms of racial discrimination to constitute invidious discrimination under the Fourteenth Amendment.

Justice BROWN delivers the opinion of the Court.

This case turns upon the constitutionality of an act of the general assembly of the state of Louisiana, passed in 1890, providing for separate railway carriages for the white and colored races. . . .

The constitutionality of this act is attacked upon the ground that it conflicts both with the thirteenth amendment of the constitution, abolishing slavery, and the fourteenth amendment, which prohibits certain restrictive legislation on the part of the states.

1. That it does not conflict with the thirteenth amendment, which abolished slavery and involuntary servitude, except as a punishment for crime, is too clear for argument. Slavery implies involuntary servitude,—a state of bondage; the ownership of mankind as a chattel, or, at least, the control of the labor and services of one man for the benefit of another, and the absence of a legal right to the disposal of his own person, property, and services. . . .

2. . . . The object of the [Fourteenth] Amendment was undoubtedly to enforce the absolute equality of the two races before the law, but, in the nature of things, it could not have been intended to abolish distinctions based upon color, or to enforce social, as distinguished from political, equality, or a commingling of the two races upon terms unsatisfactory to either. Laws permitting, and even requiring, their separation, in places where they are liable to be brought into contact, do not necessarily imply the inferiority of either race to the other, and have been generally, if not universally, recognized as within the competency of the state legislatures in the exercise of their police power. The most common instance of this is connected with the establishment of separate schools for white and colored children, which have been held to be a valid exercise of the legislative power even by courts of states where the political rights of the colored race have been longest and most earnestly enforced. . . .

In this connection, it is also suggested by the learned counsel for the plaintiff in error that the same argument that will justify the state legislature in requiring railways to provide separate accommodations for the two races will also authorize them to require separate cars to be provided for people whose hair is of a certain color, or who are aliens, or who belong to certain nationalities, or to enact laws requiring colored people to walk upon one side of the street, and white people upon the other, or requiring white men's houses to be painted white, and colored men's black, or their vehicles or business signs to be of different colors, upon the theory that one side of the street is as good as the other, or that a house or vehicle of one color is as good as one of another color. The reply to all this is that every exercise of the police power must be reasonable, and extend only to such laws as are enacted in good faith for the promotion of the public good, and not for the annoyance or oppression of a particular class. . . .

So far, then, as a conflict with the fourteenth amendment is concerned, the case reduces itself to the question whether the statute of Louisiana is a reasonable regulation, and with respect to this there must necessarily be a large discretion on the part of the legislature. In determining the question of reasonableness, it is at liberty to act with reference to the established usages, customs, and traditions of the people, and with a view to the promotion of their comfort, and the preservation of the public peace and good order. Gauged by this standard, we cannot say that a law which authorizes or even requires the separation of the two races in public conveyances is unreasonable, or more obnoxious to the fourteenth amendment than the acts of congress requiring separate schools for colored children in the District of Columbia, the constitutionality of which does not seem to have been questioned, or the corresponding acts of state legislatures.

We consider the underlying fallacy of the plaintiff's argument to consist in the assumption that the enforced separation of the two races stamps the colored race with a badge of inferiority. If this be so, it is not by reason of anything found in the act, but solely because the colored race chooses to put that construction upon it. The argument necessarily assumes that if, as has been more than once the case, and is not unlikely to be so again, the colored race should become the dominant power in the state legislature, and should enact a law in precisely similar terms, it would thereby relegate the white race to an inferior position. We imagine that the white race, at least, would not acquiesce in this assumption. The argument also assumes that social prejudices may be overcome by legislation, and that equal rights cannot be secured to the negro except by an enforced commingling of the two races. We cannot accept this proposition. If the two races are to meet upon terms of social equality, it must be the result of natural affinities, a mutual appreciation of each other's merits, and a voluntary consent of individuals. . . .

Legislation is powerless to eradicate racial instincts, or to abolish distinctions based upon physical differences, and the attempt to do so can only result in accentuating the difficulties of the present situation. If the civil and political rights of both races be equal, one cannot be inferior to the other civilly or politically. If one race be inferior to the other socially, the constitution of the United States cannot put them upon the same plane.

Justice BREWER did not participate in the decision of this case.

Justice HARLAN dissenting.

In respect of civil rights, common to all citizens, the constitution of the United States does not, I think, permit any public authority to know the race of those entitled to be protected in the enjoyment of such rights. Every true man has pride of race, and under appropriate circumstances, when the rights of others, his equals before the law, are not to be affected, it is his privilege to express such pride and to take such action based upon it as to him seems proper. But I deny that any legislative body or judicial tribunal may have regard to the race of citizens when the civil rights of those citizens are involved. Indeed, such legislation as that here in question is inconsistent not only with that equality of rights which pertains to citizenship, national and state, but with the personal liberty enjoyed by every one within the United States. . . .

It was said in argument that the statute of Louisiana does not discriminate against either race, but prescribes a rule applicable alike to white and colored citizens. But this argument does not meet the difficulty. Every one knows that the statute in question had its origin in the purpose, not so much to exclude white persons from railroad cars occupied by blacks, as to exclude colored people from coaches occupied by or assigned to white persons. . . .

It is one thing for railroad carriers to furnish, or to be required by law to furnish, equal accommodations for all whom they are under a legal duty to carry. It is quite another thing for government to forbid citizens of the white and black races from traveling in the same public conveyance, and to punish officers of railroad companies for permitting persons of the two races to occupy the same passenger coach. If a state can prescribe, as a rule of civil conduct, that whites and blacks shall not travel as passengers in the same railroad coach, why may it not so regulate the use of the streets of its cities and towns as to compel white citizens to keep on one side of a street, and black citizens to keep on the other? Why may it not, upon like grounds, punish whites and blacks who ride together in street cars or in open vehicles on a public road or street? Why may it not require sheriffs to assign whites to one side of a court room, and blacks to the other? And why may it not also prohibit the commingling of the two races in the galleries of legislative halls or in public assemblages convened for the consideration of the political questions of the day? Further, if this statute of Louisiana is consistent with the personal liberty of citizens, why may not the state require the separation in railroad coaches of native and naturalized citizens of the United States, or of Protestants and Roman Catholics?

The answer given at the argument to these questions was that regulations of the kind they suggest would be unreasonable, and could not, therefore, stand before the law. Is it meant that the determination of questions of legislative power depends upon the inquiry whether the statute whose validity is questioned is, in the judgment of the courts, a reasonable one, taking all the circumstances into consideration? A statute may be unreasonable merely because a sound public policy forbade its enactment. But I do not understand that the courts have anything to do with the policy or expediency of legislation. . . .

The white race deems itself to be the dominant race in this country. And so it is, in prestige, in achievements, in education, in wealth, and in power. So, I doubt not, it will continue to be for all time, if it remains true to its great heritage, and holds fast to the principles of constitutional liberty. But in view of the constitution, in the eye of the law, there is in this country no superior, dominant, ruling class of citizens. There is no caste here. Our constitution is color-blind, and neither knows nor tolerates classes among citizens. In respect of civil rights, all citizens are equal before the law. The humblest is the peer of the most powerful. The law regards man as man, and takes no account of his surroundings or of his color when his civil rights as guarantied by the supreme law of the land are involved. It is therefore to be regretted that this high tribunal, the final expositor of the fundamental law of the land, has reached the conclusion that it is competent for a state to regulate the enjoyment by citizens of their civil rights solely upon the basis of race.

In my opinion, the judgment this day rendered will, in time, prove to be quite as pernicious as the decision made by this tribunal in the *Dred Scott Case.* . . .

The present decision, it may well be apprehended, will not only stimulate aggressions, more or less brutal and irritating, upon the admitted rights of colored citizens, but will encourage the belief that it is possible, by means of state enactments, to defeat the beneficient purposes which the people of the United States had in view when they adopted the recent amendments of the constitution, by one of which the blacks of this country were made citizens of the United States and of the states in which they respectively reside, and whose privileges and immunities, as citizens, the states are forbidden to abridge. Sixty millions of whites are in no danger from the presence here of eight millions of blacks. The destinies of the two races, in this country, are indissolubly linked together, and the interests of both require that the common government of all shall not permit the seeds of race hate to be planted under the sanction of law. What can more certainly arouse race hate, what more certainly create and perpetuate a feeling of distrust between these races, than state enactments which, in fact, proceed on the ground that colored citizens are so inferior and degraded that they cannot be allowed to sit in public coaches occupied by white citizens? That, as all will admit, is the real meaning of such legislation as was enacted in Louisiana. . . .

I am of opinion that the statute of Louisiana is inconsistent with the personal liberty of citizens, white and black, in that state, and hostile to both the spirit and letter of the constitution of the United States. If laws of like character should be enacted in the several states of the Union, the effect would be in the highest degree mischievous. Slavery, as an institution tolerated by law, would, it is true, have disappeared from our country; but there would remain a power in the states, by sinister legislation, to interfere with the full enjoyment of the blessings of freedom, to regulate civil rights, common to all citizens, upon the basis of race, and to place in a condition of legal inferiority a large body of American citizens, now constituting a part of the political community, called the "People of the United States," for whom, and by whom through representatives, our government is administered. Such a system is inconsistent with the guaranty given by the constitution to each state of a republican form of government, and may be stricken down by congressional action, or by the courts in the discharge of their solemn duty to maintain the supreme law of the land, anything in the constitution or laws of any state to the contrary notwithstanding.

For the reason stated, I am constrained to withhold my assent from the opinion.

Shelley v. Kraemer
334 U.S. 1, 68 S.Ct. 836 (1948)

Louis Kraemer and his wife sought and obtained an injunction against J.D. Shelley, a black, from taking possession of a parcel of land in their St. Louis, Missouri, neighborhood. Shelley bought the land from one of Kraemer's neighbors without knowing that it was covered by a restrictive covenant, barring owners from selling their land to members of "the Negro or Mongolian race." A state trial court found the covenant technically faulty, but was reversed on appeal by the Missouri State Supreme Court, which held that the covenant did not deny Shelley's constitutional rights.

Shelley's appeal to the Supreme Court became a test case for the NAACP and was argued by the NAACP's leading counsel, Charles Houston and Thurgood Marshall. The NAACP sought to persuade the Court to reconsider an earlier ruling, *Corrigan v. Buckley*, 271 U.S. 323 (1926), upholding restrictive covenants. Eighteen *amicus curiae* briefs, including one by Democratic President Harry Truman's solicitor general, supported the NAACP's position.

With three justices (Reed, Jackson, and Rutledge) not participating in the decision, the Court unanimously held that judicial enforcement of restrictive covenants constituted state action and ran afoul of the Fourteenth Amendment. But note that Chief Justice Fred Vinson neither overrules *Corrigan* nor explains why and how far the state action doctrine extends to bar private racial discrimination not forbidden by the states.

Chief Justice VINSON delivers the opinion of the Court.

These cases present for our consideration questions relating to the validity of court enforcement of private agreements, generally described as restrictive covenants, which have as their purpose the exclusion of persons of designated race or color from the ownership or occupancy of real property. Basic constitutional issues of obvious importance have been raised. . . .

It is well, at the outset, to scrutinize the terms of the restrictive agreements involved in these cases. In the Missouri case, the covenant declares that no part of the affected property shall be "occupied by any person not of the Caucasian race, it being intended hereby to restrict the use of said property . . . against the occupancy as owners or tenants of any portion of said property for resident or other purpose by people of the Negro or Mongolian Race." Not only does the restriction seek to proscribe use and occupancy of the affected properties by members of the excluded class, but as construed by the Missouri courts, the agreement requires that title of any person who uses his property in violation of the restriction shall be divested. . . .

It should be observed that these covenants do not seek to proscribe any particular use of the affected properties. Use of the properties for residential occupancy, as such, is not forbidden. The restrictions of these agreements, rather, are directed toward a designated class of persons and seek to determine who may and who may not own or make use of the properties for residential purposes. The excluded class is defined wholly in terms of race or color; "simply that and nothing more."

It cannot be doubted that among the civil rights intended to be protected from discriminatory state action by the Fourteenth Amendment are the rights to acquire, enjoy, own and dispose of property. Equality in the enjoyment of property rights was regarded by the framers of that Amendment as an essential precondition to the realization of other basic civil rights and liberties which the Amendment was intended to guarantee. Thus, § 1978 of the Revised Statutes, derived from § 1 of the Civil Rights Act of 1866 which was enacted by Congress while the Fourteenth Amendment was also under consideration, provides:

> All citizens of the United States shall have the same right, in every State and Territory, as is enjoyed by white citizens thereof to inherit, purchase, lease, sell, hold, and convey real and personal property.". . .

It is likewise clear that restrictions on the right of occupancy of the sort sought to be created by the private agreements in these cases could not be squared with the requirements of the Fourteenth Amendment if imposed by state statute or local ordinance. . . .

But the present cases do not involve action by state legislatures or city councils. Here the particular patterns of discrimination and the areas in which the restrictions are to operate, are determined, in the first instance, by the terms of agreements among private individuals. Participation of the State consists in the enforcement of the restrictions so defined. The crucial issue with which we are here confronted is whether this distinction removes these cases from the operation of the prohibitory provisions of the Fourteenth Amendment.

Since the decision of this Court in the *Civil Rights Cases,* 1883 109 U.S. 3, the principle has become firmly embedded in our constitutional law that the action inhibited by the first section of the Fourteenth Amendment is only such action as may fairly be said to be that of the States. That Amendment erects no shield against merely private conduct, however discriminatory or wrongful.

We conclude, therefore, that the restrictive agreements standing alone cannot be regarded as a violation of any rights guaranteed to petitioners by the Fourteenth Amendment. So long as the purposes of those agreements are effectuated by voluntary adherence to their terms, it would appear clear that there has been no action by the State and the provisions of the Amendment have not been violated. . . .

But here there was more. These are cases in which the purposes of the agreements were secured only by judicial enforcement by state courts of the restrictive teams of the agreement. . . .

That the action of state courts and of judicial officers in their official capacities is to be regarded as action of the State within the meaning of the Fourteenth Amendment, is a proposition which has long been established by decisions of this Court. . . .

We hold that in granting judicial enforcement of the restrictive agreements in these cases, the States have denied petitioners the equal protection of the laws and that, therefore, the action of the state courts cannot stand. We have noted that freedom from discrimination by the States in the enjoyment of property rights was among the basic objectives sought to be effectuated by the framers of the Fourteenth Amendment. That such discrimination has occurred in these cases is clear.

Justice REED, Justice JACKSON, and Justice RUTLEDGE did not participate in the consideration or decision of these cases.

Palmore v. Sidoti
466 U.S. 429, 104 S.Ct. 1879 (1984)

The facts of this case, involving the issue of interracial adoption, are stated at the outset of the opinion for the Court by Chief Justice Warren Burger.

Chief Justice BURGER delivers the opinion of the Court.

When petitioner Linda Sidoti Palmore and respondent Anthony J. Sidoti, both Caucasians, were divorced in May 1980 in Florida, the mother was awarded custody of their three-year-old daughter.

In September 1981 the father sought custody of the child by filing a petition to modify the prior judgment because of changed conditions. The change was that the child's mother was then cohabiting with a Negro, Clarence Palmore, Jr., whom she married two months later. . . .

After hearing testimony from both parties and considering a court counselor's investigative report, the court . . . concluded that the best interests of the child would be served by awarding custody to the father. The court's rationale is contained in the following:

> "The father's evident resentment of the mother's choice of a black partner is not sufficient to wrest custody from the mother. It is of some significance, however, that the mother did see fit to bring a man into her home and carry on a sexual relationship with him without being married to him. Such action tended to place gratification of her own desires ahead of her concern for the child's future welfare. *This Court feels that despite the strides that have been made in bettering relations between the races in this country, it is inevitable that Melanie will, if allowed to remain in her present situation and attains school age and thus more vulnerable to peer pressures, suffer from the social stigmatization that is sure to come."*. . .

The Second District Court of Appeal affirmed. . . . [W]e reverse. . . .

A core purpose of the Fourteenth Amendment was to do away with all governmentally-imposed discrimination based on race. . . .

The State, of course, has a duty of the highest order to protect the interests of minor children, particularly those of tender years. In common with most states, Florida law mandates that custody determinations be made in the best interests of the children involved. The goal of granting custody based on the best interests of the child is indisputably a substantial governmental interest for purposes of the Equal Protection Clause.

It would ignore reality to suggest that racial and ethnic prejudices do not exist or that all manifestations of those prejudices have been eliminated. There is a risk that a child living with a step-parent of a different race may be subject to a variety of pressures and stresses not present if the child were living with parents of the same racial or ethnic origin.

The question, however, is whether the reality of private biases and the possible injury they might inflict are permissible considerations for removal of an infant child from the custody of its natural mother. We have little difficulty concluding that they are not. The Constitution cannot control such prejudices but neither can it tolerate them. Private biases may be outside the reach of the law, but the law cannot, directly or indirectly, give them effect. . . .

The effects of racial prejudice, however real, cannot justify a racial classification removing an infant child from the custody of its natural mother found to be an appropriate person to have such custody.

The judgment of the District Court of Appeal is reversed.

B. RACIAL DISCRIMINATION IN EDUCATION

The process of dismantling a century-old system of segregated schools was long, often violent, and could not be achieved by simple judicial decree. At the turn of the twentieth century, in *Cummings v. Richmond County Board of Education,* 175 U.S. 528 (1899), the Fuller Court upheld a Georgia school board's decision to close its all-black high school, because it needed the buildings for an all-black elementary school. Writing for a unanimous Court, Justice Harlan, who had dissented in the *Civil Rights Cases* and *Plessy v. Ferguson,* stressed that public schools were a subject of state, not federal, control. The White Court (1910–1921) and Taft Court (1921–1930) repeatedly avoided the issue of segregated schools.[1]

Not until the Hughes Court (1930–1941) was there a suggestion that racially segregated schools might be constitutionally suspect. In *Missouri ex rel. Gaines v. Canada,* 305 U.S. 337 (1938), Chief Justice Hughes struck down a portion of Missouri's law that, while denying blacks admission to its law school, provided funding for blacks to attend law schools in other states. Lloyd Gaines, a black citizen of Missouri, qualified for admission into the University of Missouri's law school and argued that as a taxpayer he had a right to attend the law school. By a seven-to-two vote (with Justices McReynolds and Butler dissenting), the Hughes Court held that the equal protection clause was violated because Missouri failed to provide any law school for blacks. Instead, it simply shifted its responsibility to other states. Far from seriously questioning the constitutionality of the separate but equal doctrine as applied to education, Chief Justice Hughes emphasized that states must furnish "equal facilities in separate schools." As a result of the Court's ruling, Missouri established a separate all-black law school at its all-black university, Lincoln University.

The National Association for the Advancement of Colored People (NAACP) financed and argued Gaines's case before the Supreme Court. Encouraged by its small victory, the NAACP mounted a litigation campaign to bring down segregated schools. The NAACP's strategy was twofold. First, it sought to ensure that states in fact provided *equal* educational facilities. Second, it aimed to persuade the Court that "separate but equal" educational facilities were inherently unequal.

A decade after *Gaines*, the NAACP won a first step toward desegregation. In 1948, along with *Shelley v. Kraemer* (see page 1293), in an unsigned *per curiam* opinion, the Vinson Court opinion ordered Oklahoma to provide a qualified black woman with an equal education in the state's law school.[2] Two years later, the NAACP had two more victories. Both rulings were unanimously decided and handed down by Chief Justice Vinson.

In *Sweatt v. Painter*, 339 U.S. 629 (1950), the Court ordered the admission of H. M. Sweatt, a black man, into the University of Texas law school. Sweatt refused to go to the state's separate law school for blacks. And he persuaded the Court that that law school was inferior, and therefore *unequal*, not only in terms of physical facilities but also in the "reputation of the faculty, experience of the administration, position and influence of the alumni, standing in the community, tradition and prestige." In *McLaurin v. Oklahoma State Regents*, 339 U.S. 637 (1950), the Vinson Court went even further. McLaurin, a black, was admitted into the University of Oklahoma's School of Education to work for a Ph.D. But the state legislature mandated that McLaurin, the only black at the university, be treated on a segregated basis; that is, in classes he sat separately from whites, used a special table in the school's library, and ate at a designated table at different times from whites in the school cafeteria. McLaurin contended that this treatment denied him the equal protection of the laws and the Court agreed. In both cases, the Vinson Court acknowledged the intangible elements in education and concluded that separate but equal facilities, at least in higher education, were not equal. But the Court stopped short of overturning the separate but equal doctrine.

The NAACP had prepared the basis for the Court's striking down racially segregated public schools. But when it brought several cases challenging dual educational systems for blacks and whites in 1951, it was far from clear that the Vinson Court would continue to press ahead. *Sweatt* and *McLaurin* involved only higher education and affected a relatively small number of blacks. Yet they ignited political controversy and strong opposition in the South. The Court knew that striking down segregated primary and secondary schools would affect millions of people, that overturning an educational system in place for close to a hundred years would invite widespread opposition; see Justice Jackson's unpublished memorandum concerning *Brown v. Board of Education of Topeka, Kansas* on page 1312.

Brown v. Board of Education of Topeka, Kansas (1954) (see page 1305) handed down three years after arriving on the Court's docket and in the first year of Chief Justice Earl Warren's tenure, marked a turning point for the Court and the country. That unanimous ruling striking down segregated public schools was the culmination and the beginning of new political struggles. Along with *Brown I, Bolling v. Sharpe* (1954) (see page 1315) struck down segregated schools in the District of Columbia. The Fourteenth Amendment only forbids states from denying the equal protection of the laws, and the District of Columbia is under the control of the federal government. In an opinion that would come to have major significance for later rulings on racial and nonracial discrimination, Chief Justice Warren construed the Fifth Amendment's due process clause to incorporate the Fourteenth Amendment's equal protection guarantee and apply it to the federal government.

In *Brown* and *Bolling* the Warren Court did not overrule *Plessy*'s doctrine of separate but equal, nor was anything said about segregation in other public accommodations—hotels, restaurants, and the like. Neither did the Court provide immediate remedial relief. The Court's unanimous rulings were achieved only at cost of compromise among the justices in the face of certain resistance to their ruling. In order to minimize some of the anticipated opposition, *Brown* was carried over to another term for reargument on the question of remedies—how soon should desegregation take place and what kind of order should the Court issue? One year later in *Brown v. Board of Education of Topeka, Kansas (Brown II)* (1955) (see page 1317), the Warren Court issued its mandate for states and local school boards to proceed "with all deliberate speed" in dismantling segregated schools.

Opposition to the Warren Court's rulings led to bitter, sometimes violent confrontations. In 1956, nineteen U.S. senators and 82 members of the House of Representatives denounced *Brown* as unconstitutional in a "Southern Manifesto." The Republican administration of President Dwight D. Eisenhower did little to enforce compliance with *Brown*. The Warren Court, nevertheless, stood firmly behind its ruling, as registered in the controversy over *Cooper v. Aaron* (1958) (see page 1321). In subsequent decisions, the Warren Court reaffirmed that school boards had a positive duty to desegregate. In *Griffin v. County School Board of Prince Edward County*, 391 U.S. 430 (1968), for example, the

Fourteenth Amendment was interpreted to forbid school boards from closing all public schools, rather than desegregating them.[3] Still given the massive resistance toward *Brown*, the Warren Court effectively placed the burden on lower federal courts to oversee its implementation.[4]

Ten years after *Brown* and massive resistance and continuing litigation, Justice Black complained, "There has been entirely too much deliberation and not enough speed" in complying with *Brown*. "The time for mere 'deliberate speed' has run out."[5] *Brown*'s mandate amounted to a moral appeal and an invitation for delay. At the beginning of the school year in 1964, President Johnson was apprised of the piecemeal progress and continuing resistance:

Arkansas: Desegregation expanded in schools in Little Rock and Fort Smith. About 870 Negroes reported in previously white schools, compared to 390 last year. Twenty-one districts desegregated, compared to 13 last year.

Florida: Four counties integrated, bringing to 21 the number admitting Negroes (State has 67 counties). No trouble. Estimated 8,000 Negroes attending all-white schools.

Mississippi: Biloxi—Seventeen Negro children attended integrated classes in four previously all-white elementary schools, after 10 years of angry resistance. *Canton*—Nineteen Negro students attempted to enroll in the all-white high school but left quietly when rejected by school officials. Civil rights workers said earlier they would not oppose school officials if the youngsters were turned away, but would follow with court action later.

Virginia: Virginia will have 25 newly desegregated districts this year—including Prince Edward Country [which had previously closed rather than desegregate its schools]—making 80 of 128 in the State with some integration. About 6,000 Negroes are attending once-white schools.[6]

With no federal leadership, implementation of *Brown* was deliberately slow and uneven. Ruby Martin, an attorney for the U.S. Commission on Civil Rights in the early 1960s, recalls that "the work of the lawyers from 1954 to 1964 resulted in two percent of the Negro kids in the Southern states attending schools with white students."[7] The Department of Justice had little role in ending school segregation before the passage of the Civil Rights Act of 1964. Even after the Department of Justice assumed a role in enforcing school desegregation, little attention was initially given to areas outside of the South or to problems other than ending *de jure* segregation—segregation enforced by laws prohibiting the integration of public schools. The Department of Justice paid almost no attention to *de facto* segregation, due to socioeconomic conditions, such as housing patterns, in the North and West. Eventually, the Department of Health, Education and Welfare (HEW) was given responsibility for ending segregated schools. It had authority to issue guidelines and review plans for integration. More importantly, HEW had the power to cut off federal funding if school districts refused to submit or comply with desegregation plans.

By the mid-1960s the Department of Justice and HEW had assumed leadership in implementing *Brown*. Nevertheless, it took time to build records and evidence of segregation in northern and western school districts, and then to challenge local authorities in the courts. Not until the summer of 1968 did the outgoing Johnson administration initiate the first school desegregation cases in the North and West, and try to achieve the national coverage that the Court envisioned in *Brown*. By the end of the decade, the Court was growing impatient. In Justice Black's words, "there is no longer the slightest excuse, reason, or justification for further postponement of the time when every public school system in the United States will be a unitary one."[8] Progress was made but the Court and the country were also changing.

In Chief Justice Burger's first year on the Court, a brief *per curiam* opinion was handed down in *Alexander v. Holmes County Board of Education*, 396 U.S. 19 (1969). The Court ordered the Fifth Circuit Court of Appeals to deny further requests for delay from southern school districts in ending dual systems of public education and emphasized that the "standard allowing 'all deliberate speed' for desegregation is no longer constitutionally permissible." The message in *Alexander*, like that in *Brown*, remained ambiguous. Justice Thurgood Marshall could not win unanimity on finally setting a cutoff date for school desegregation. Justice Black threatened a dissenting opinion, protesting that "all deliberate speed" connoted delay, not speed. "The duty of this Court and of the others," Black implored, "is too simple to require perpetual litigation and deliberation. That duty is to extirpate all racial discrimination from our system of public schools NOW." But on the bench less than four months, Burger vigorously opposed setting any final cutoff date for desegregation. Justice Brennan sought consensus yet agreement could not be reached on a more precise order than for proceeding with desegregation here and now. *Alexander*, Justice White lamented in an unpublished memo, "neither says the order is to be entered now, within six months or even with deliberate speed." "Hugo," he added, "is convinced that a mistake was made in 1954–1955 with respect to the deliberate speed formula. I am beginning to understand how mistakes like that happen. Nevertheless, I join, expecting the Court of Appeals to make sure that the shortcomings of this order never come to light."⁹

The shortcomings of *Alexander* and the impact of the Court's changing composition came to light when the Court of Appeals delayed yet again. In *Carter v. West Feliciana Parish School Board*, 396 U.S. 290 (1970), the Court scolded the continued failure to proceed with desegregation. This time, though, Chief Justice Burger and Justices Rehnquist and Stewart voiced their disagreement and insistence on maintaining a flexible approach toward desegregation: The Fifth Circuit, they argued, "is far more familiar than we with the various situations of these several school districts, some large, some small, some rural and some metropolitan, and has exhibited responsibility and fidelity to the objectives of our holdings in school desegregation cases."

After two decades the problems of implementing and achieving compliance with *Brown* persisted; some schools remained segregated. Litigation by the NAACP and other civil rights groups forced change, but it was piecemeal, costly, and modest. The judiciary alone could not achieve desegregation. Evasion and resistance were encouraged by the reluctance of presidents and Congress to enforce the mandate. Enforcement and implementation required the cooperation and coordination of all three branches.

But by the 1970s and 1980s, the political controversy touched off by *Brown* primarily revolved around lower courts ordering of gerrymandered school district lines and the busing of schoolchildren to achieve racial balance and integrated schools. Although *Brown*'s bare-bones decree ended up encouraging evasion and continued litigation, over the years *Brown*'s mandate was transformed from one of ending racially separated dual school systems into a mandate for *integrated* public schools—a mandate that some members of the Warren Court would never had agreed to in *Brown*.

The Burger Court thus faced the task of providing guidance for lower federal courts and how far they could go in ordering integrated public schools. The Court's two major rulings on the use of busing to achieve school segregation came in *Swann v. Charlotte-Mecklenburg Board of Education* (1971) (see page 1327) and *Milliken v. Bradley* (1974) (see page 1332). In *Swann* Chief Justice Burger established that where all-black schools exist because of present or past *de jure* discrimination, lower courts were to presume intentional segregation. In such situations, the Court upheld court-ordered busing of schoolchildren to achieve integration. But Chief Justice Burger stressed that courts were not to seek exact racial balance in their desegregation orders. Writing

"Separate but equal" in West Memphis, Tennessee, in the early 1950s. *Ed Clark, Life Magazine © Time Inc.*

for a bare majority in *Milliken*, Chief Justice Burger underscored that the equal protection clause does not reach *de facto* school segregation, resulting from housing patterns, and lower courts may not order busing as a remedy for *de facto* segregation where there is no evidence of an "intent" by school boards to discriminate. Throughout the 1970s and 1980s the Court reviewed numerous challenges to court-ordered busing. The Reagan administration strongly opposed the use of busing to achieve integrated schools. But when the administration asked the Court to reconsider its ruling in *Swann*, the Court unanimously declined to do so in *Metropolitan County Board of Education of Nashville v. Kelley*, 459 U.S. 1183 (1983).

NOTES

1. See *Berea College v. Kentucky*, 211 U.S. 45 (1908); and *Gong Lum v. Rice*, 275 U.S. 78 (1927).

2. See *Spiuel v. Oklahoma,* 322 U.S. 631 (1948); and *Fisher v. Hurst,* 333 U.S. 147 (1948).

3. For other Warren Court rulings, see *Goss v. Board of Education of City of Knoxville,* 373 U.S. 683 (1963) (striking down a transfer plan allowing blacks to go to formally segregated schools); *Green v. County School Board of New Kent County, Virginia,* 391 U.S. 430 (1968) (striking down a freedom of choice plan for desegregation, where no white students attended black schools); and *Monroe v. Board of Commissioners of the City of Jackson, Texas,* 391 U.S. 450 (1968). In *United States v. Montgomery County Board of Education,* 395 U.S. 225 (1969), the Court upheld a lower court's order that schools with less than twelve teachers have at least one of a different race and that schools with twelve or more teachers have one teacher of a different race for every six faculty and staff persons.

4. For a fine study of the role of lower federal court judges in implementing *Brown* and the resistance they faced, see Jack Peltason, *Fifty-Eight Lonely Men* (New York: Harcourt, Brace & World, 1961).

5. *Griffin v. Prince Edward County School Board,* 377 U.S. 218 (1964).

6. "Memorandum, School Openings and Desegregation," Lee White Papers, Box 5, Johnson Presidential Library.

7. Ruby Martin, Oral History Interview, Johnson Presidential Library.

8. *Alexander v. Holmes County Board of Education,* 396 U.S. 1218 (1969).

9. All quotations in this paragraph are from the justices' memo in John M. Harlan Papers, Boxes 487, 565 and 606, Seeley G. Mudd Library, Princeton University; and William J. Brennan Papers, Box 218, Library of Congress.

SELECTED BIBLIOGRAPHY

Bass, Jack. *Unlikely Heroes.* New York: Simon & Schuster, 1981.

Chafe, William. *Civilities and Civil Rights.* New York: Oxford University Press, 1980.

Kluger, Richard. *Simple Justice.* New York: Alfred Knopf, 1976.

Peltason, Jack W. *Fifty-Eight Lonely Men: Southern Federal Judges and School Desegregation.* New York: Harcourt, Brace & World, 1961.

Schwartz, Bernard. *Swann's Way: The School Busing Case and the Supreme Court.* New York: Oxford University Press, 1980.

Wasby, Stephen, D'Amato, Anthony, and Metrailer, Rosemary. *Desegregation from Brown to Alexander.* Carbondale: Southern Illinois University Press, 1977.

Wilkinson, III J. Harvie. *From Brown to Bakke: The Supreme Court and School Integration: 1954–1978.* New York: Oxford University Press, 1979.

Wolf, Eleanor. *Trial and Error: The Detroit School Segregation Case.* Detroit: Wayne State University Press, 1981.

Wolters, Raymond. *The Burden of Brown: Thirty Years of School Desegregation.* Knoxville: University of Tennessee Press, 1984.

Brown v. Board of Education of Topeka, Kansas (Brown I)
347 U.S. 483, 74 S.Ct. 686 (1954)

This case challenging the constitutionality of racially segregated public schools arrived on the Supreme Court's docket in 1951 and was consolidated with three other cases (from Delaware, South Carolina, and Virginia) and another, *Bolling v. Sharpe* (see page 1315), attacking the federal government's segregated school system in the District of Columbia. On such a politically explosive issue, Justice Tom Clark recalled, the Court wanted "to get a national coverage, rather than a sectional one."

Oral arguments were heard in December 1952. Instead of the decision coming down as expected in the spring, however, the Court decided to hear rearguments in its next term. The Vinson Court was split and deeply troubled by the prospect of white southern opposition to its striking down racially segregated public schools. Justice Felix Frankfurter persuaded his colleagues to carry the cases over to the next term because 1952 was an election year. "When you have a major social political issue of this magnitude," timing and public reactions are important considerations, and, Frankfurter told a law clerk, "we do not think this is the time to decide it." By holding the cases over, the Court was able to receive the views in an *amicus curaie* brief of the incoming administration of Republican President Dwight Eisenhower.

Rearguments were scheduled for early November 1953. But then an unexpected turn of events: Chief Justice Fred Vinson died suddenly of a heart attack in the summer and Eisenhower promptly named as his successor, Earl Warren. Warren, a popular governor of California and that state's favorite-son candidate for the Republican party's 1952 presidential nominee, had impressed Eisenhower as having "unimpeachable integrity," "middle of the road views," and a "splendid record during his years of active law work" as a state attorney general.

Rearguments were, again, put off until December, at which time the new chief justice sat back and listened to the arguments for and against ending segregated schools. At the justices' private conference, though, Warren did two strategic things. First, he firmly expressed his conviction that racially segregated schools denied blacks their rights under the Fourteenth Amendment. Second, because a majority of the justices appeared to support his position, Warren proposed that no vote be taken until the case was fully discussed and considered by all. No formal vote was taken until mid-February.

Chief Justice Warren's opinion for the Court is short and to the point; he wanted a brief opinion that could be printed in newspapers so every citizen could read the decision. Warren also sought a unanimous ruling because *Brown* would inevitably spark widespread resistance, and unanimity might help undercut some of the anticipated opposition. Notably, if *Brown* were decided when it first arrived, the vote would probably have been six to three or even five to four. Vinson was still chief justice and Justice Jackson's notes of conference discussions indicate that Justice Reed would uphold segregation as constitutional, as Vinson might have. Justices Clark and Jackson were also inclined to let segregated schools stand. Yet Warren and Frankfurter managed to persuade all of the justices to join the ruling. At the last minute, Warren got Jackson, who was in the hospital recovering from a heart attack, to suppress a potential concurring opinion (see p. 1312). Jackson had a practice of writing memorandums on cases, with a view to clarifying his thinking and bargaining with the others, and then often withholding their publication when the Court's final draft opinion came along. But as Justice Burton noted in his diary, Warren did a "magnificent job in getting a unanimous Court (This would have been impossible a year ago—probably 6 to 3 with the Chief Justice [Vinson] one of the dissenters)."

Chief Justice WARREN delivers the opinion of the Court.

In each of the cases, minors of the Negro race, through their legal representatives, seek the aid of the courts in obtaining admission to the public schools of their community on a nonsegregated basis. In each instance, they have been denied admission to schools attended by white children under laws requiring or permitting segregation according to race. This segregation was alleged to deprive the plaintiffs of the equal protection of the laws under the Fourteenth Amendment. . . .

The plaintiffs contend that segregated public schools are not "equal" and cannot be made "equal," and that hence they are deprived of the equal protection of the laws. Because of the obvious importance of the question presented, the Court took jurisdiction. Argument was heard in the 1952 Term, and reargument was heard this Term on certain questions propounded by the Court.

Reargument was largely devoted to the circumstances surrounding the adoption of the Fourteenth Amendment in 1868. It covered exhaustively consideration of the Amendment in Congress, ratification by the states, then existing practices in racial segregation, and the views of proponents and opponents of the Amendment. This discussion and our own investigation convince us that, although these sources cast some light, it is not enough to resolve the problem with which we are faced. At best, they are inconclusive. The most avid proponents of the post-War Amendments undoubtedly intended them to remove all legal distinctions among "all persons born or naturalized in the United States." Their opponents, just as certainly, were antagonistic to both the letter and the spirit of the Amendments and wished them to have the most limited effect. What others in Congress and the state legislatures had in mind cannot be determined with any degree of certainty.

An additional reason for the inconclusive nature of the Amendment's history, with respect to segregated schools, is the status of public education at that time. In the South, the movement toward free common schools, supported by general taxation, had not yet taken hold. Education of white children was largely in the hands of private groups. Education of Negroes was almost nonexistent, and practically all of the race were illiterate. In fact, any education of Negroes was forbidden by law in some states. Today, in contrast, many Negroes have achieved outstanding success in the arts and sciences as well as in the business and professional world. It is true that public school education at the time of the Amendment had advanced further in the North, but the effect of the Amendment on Northern States was generally ignored in the congressional debates. Even in the North, the conditions of public education did not approximate those existing today. The curriculum was usually rudimentary; ungraded schools were common in rural areas; the school term was but three months a year in many states; and compulsory school attendance was virtually unknown. As a consequence, it is not surprising that there should be so little in the history of the Fourteenth Amendment relating to its intended effect on public education. . . .

In approaching this problem, we cannot turn the clock back to 1868 when the Amendment was adopted, or even to 1896 when *Plessy v. Ferguson,* [163 U.S. 537 (1896)], was written. We must consider public education in the light of its full development and its present place in American life throughout the Nation. Only in this way can it be determined if segregation in public schools deprives these plaintiffs of the equal protection of the laws.

Today, education is perhaps the most important function of

state and local governments. Compulsory school attendance laws and the great expenditures for education both demonstrate our recognition of the importance of education to our democratic society. It is required in the performance of our most basic public responsibilities, even service in the armed forces. It is the very foundation of good citizenship. Today it is a principal instrument in awakening the child to cultural values, in preparing him for later professional training, and in helping him to adjust normally to his environment. In these days, it is doubtful that any child may reasonably be expected to succeed in life if he is denied the opportunity of an education. Such an opportunity, where the state has undertaken to provide it, is a right which must be made available to all on equal terms.

We come then to the question presented: Does segregation of children in public schools solely on the basis of race, even though the physical facilities and other "tangible" factors may be equal, deprive the children of the minority group of equal educational opportunities? We believe that it does.

In *Sweatt v. Painter,* 339 U.S. 629 [(1950)], in finding that a segregated law school for Negroes could not provide them equal educational opportunities, this Court relied in large part on "those qualities which are incapable of objective measurement but which make for greatness in a law school." In *McLaurin v. Oklahoma State Regents,* 339 U.S. 637 [(1958)], the Court, in requiring that a Negro admitted to a white graduate school be treated like all other students, again resorted to intangible considerations: ". . . his ability to study, to engage in discussions and exchange views with other students, and, in general, to learn his profession." Such considerations apply with added force to children in grade and high schools. To separate them from others of similar age and qualifications solely because of their race generates a feeling of inferiority as to their status in the community that may affect their hearts and minds in a way unlikely ever to be undone. The effect of this separation on their educational opportunities was well stated by a finding in the Kansas case by a court which nevertheless felt compelled to rule against the Negro plaintiffs:

> "Segregation of white and colored children in public schools has a detrimental effect upon the colored children. The impact is greater when it has the sanction of the law; for the policy of separating the races is usually interpreted as denoting the inferiority of the negro group. A sense of inferiority affects the motivation of a child to learn. Segregation with the sanction of law, therefore, has a tendency to [retard] the educational and mental development of Negro children and to deprive them of some of the benefits they would receive in a racial[ly] integrated school system."

Linda Brown (later Mrs. Charles D. Smith of Topeka, Kansas], whose father charged that his state's segregated schools were inherently discriminating and whose case led to a landmark school desegregation ruling. *AP/Wide World.*

Whatever may have been the extent of psychological knowledge at the time of *Plessy v. Ferguson*, this finding is amply supported by modern authority.* Any language in *Plessy v. Ferguson* contrary to this finding is rejected.

---

* [Footnote 11:] K. B. Clark, Effect of Prejudice and Discrimination on Personality Development (Midcentury White House Conference on Children and Youth, 1950); Witmer and Kotinsky, Personality in the Making (1952), e. VI; Deutscher and Chein, The Psychological Effects of Enforced Segregation: A Survey of Social Science Opinion, 26 J.Psychol. 259 (1948); Chein, What are the Psychological Effects of Segregation Under Conditions of Equal Facilities?, 3 Int. J. Opinion and Attitude Res. 229 (1949); Brameld, Educational Costs, in Discrimination and National Welfare (MacIver, ed., 1949), 44–48; Frazier, The Negro in the United States (1949), 674–681. And see generally Myrdal, An American Dilemma (1944).

We conclude that in the field of public education the doctrine of "separate but equal" has no place. Separate educational facilities are inherently unequal. Therefore, we hold that the plaintiffs and others similarly situated for whom the actions have been brought are; by reason of the segregation complained of, deprived of the equal protection of the laws guaranteed by the Fourteenth Amendment. This disposition makes unnecessary any discussion whether such segregation also violates the Due Process Clause of the Fourteenth Amendment.

Because these are class actions, because of the wide applicability of this decision, and because of the great variety of local conditions, the formulation of decrees in these cases presents problems of considerable complexity. On reargument, the consideration of appropriate relief was necessarily subordinated to the primary question—the constitutionality of segregation in public education. We have now announced that such segregation is a denial of the equal protection of the laws. In order that we may have the full assistance of the parties in formulating decrees, the cases will be restored to the docket, and the parties are requested to present further argument . . . [on the nature of the remedial decrees this Court should order.] . . .

INSIDE THE COURT

William H. Rehnquist's Memorandum to Justice Robert Jackson on *Brown v. Board of Education*

As a law clerk to Justice Robert Jackson in 1952–1953, William Rehnquist wrote a memorandum to the justice on *Brown v. Board of Education.* Later, at his confirmation hearings on his nomination to the Supreme Court in 1971, Rehnquist claimed that the memo was written at Jackson's request and reflected the justice's views rather than his own. But the content and style of the memo (as well as the fact that Justice Jackson's private papers contain several other memos written by Rehnquist) indicate that the memo reflected Rehnquist's views on the case and the role of the Court.

A Random Thought on the Segregation Cases

One-hundred fifty years ago this Court held that it was the ultimate judge of the restrictions which the Constitution imposed on the various branches of the national and state government. Marbury v. Madison.
This was presumably on the basis that there are standards to be applied
other than the personal predilections of the Justices.

As applied to questions of inter-state or state-federal relations,
as well as to inter departmental disputes within the federal government,
this doctrine of judicial review has worked well. Where theoretically co-ordinate
bodies of government are disputing, the Court is well suited to its role
as arbiter. This is because these problems involve much less emotionally
charged subject matter than do those discussed below. In effect, they determine the skeletal relations of the governments to each other without
influencing the substantive business of those governments.

As applied to relations between the individual and the state, the
system has worked much less well. The Constitution, of course, deals with
indivudal rights, particularly in the First Ten and the Fourteenth Amendments. But as I read the history of this Court, it has seldom been out of
hot water when attempting to interpret these individual rights. Fletcher
v. Peck, in 1810, represented an attempt by Chief Justice Marshall to
extend the protection of the contract clause to infant business. Scott
v. Sanford was the result of Taney's effort to protect slaveholders from
legislative interference.

After the Civil War, business interest came to dominate the Court,
and they in turn ventured into the deep water of protecting certain types
of individuals against legislative interference. Championed first by Field,
then by Peckham and Brewer, the high water mark of the trend in protecting
corporations against legislative influence was probably Lochner v. NY. To
the majority opinion in that case, Holmes replied that the Fourteenth A-
mendment did not enact Herbert Spencer's Social Statics. Other cases coming later in a similar vein were Adkins v. Children's Hospital, Hammer v.
Dagenhart, Tyson v. Banton, Ribnik v. McBride. But eventually the Court
called a halt to this reading of its own economic views into the Constitution. Apparently it recognized that where a legislature was dealing
with its own citizens, it was not part of the judicial function to thwart
public opinion except in extreme cases.

In these cases now before the Court, the Court is, as Davis suggested, being asked to read its own sociological views into the Constitution.
Urging a view palpably at variance with precedent and probably with legislative hsitory, appellants seek to convince the Court of the moral wrong-
ness of the treatment they are receiving. I would suggest that this is a
question the Court need never reach; for regardless of the Justice's individual views on the merits of segregation, it quite clearly is not one of
those extreme cases which commands intervention from one of any conviction.
If this Court, because its members individually are "liberal" and dislike
segregation, now chooses to strike it down, it differs from the McReynolds
court only in the kinds of litigants it favors and the kinds of special
claims it protects. To those who would argue that"personal" rights are
more sacrosanct than "property" rights, the short answer is that the Constitution makes no such distinction. To the argument made by Marshall that
a majority may not deprive a minority of its constitutional right, the answer must be made that while this is sound in theory, in the long run it
is the majority who will determine what the constitutional rights of the
minority are. One hundred and fifty years of attempts on the part of this
Court to protect minority rights of any kind--whether those of business,
slaveholders, or Jehovah's Witnesses--have all met the same fate. One by
one the cases establishing such rights have been sloughed off, and crept
silently to rest. If the present Court is unable to profit by this example,
it must be prepared to see its work fade in time, too, as embodying only
the sentiments of a transient majority of nine men.

I realize that it is an unpopular and unhumanitarian position, for
which I have been excoriated by "liberal" colleagues, but I think Plessy
v. Ferguson was right and should be re-affirmed. If the Fourteenth Amendment did not enact Spencer's Social Statics, it just as surely did not
enact Myrdahl's American Dilemna.

whr

Source: Robert H. Jackson Papers, Library of Congress.

INSIDE THE COURT

Justice Robert H. Jackson's Unpublished Memorandum on *Brown v. Board of Education*

In mid-February, 1954, when the Warren Court finally voted on *Brown v. Board of Education,* Justice Jackson drafted a memorandum to clarify his thoughts and possibly file as a concurring opinion. He never circulated it to the other justices, but had it with him when Chief Justice Warren visited him in the hospital in May, shortly before the Court's final opinion was handed down. In his memorandum Justice Jackson probed the social realities and constitutional issues that Chief Justice Warren's opinion for the Court largely glanced over.

Justice Jackson began by pointing out that

Since the close of the Civil War the United States has been "hesitating between two worlds—one dead—the other powerless to be born." War brought an old order to an end but as usual force proved unequal to founding a new one. Neither North nor South has been willing really to adapt its racial practices to its professions. The race problem would be quickly solved if some way could be found to make us all live up to our hypocracies. . . .

Racial tensions seem to develop wherever the ratio of colored population to white passes a point where the latter vaguely feel themselves, for some reason, insecure. But in the South the Negro not only suffers from racial suspicions and antagonisms present in other states and in other countries, but also I am convinced, has suffered great prejudice from the aftermath of the great American white conflict. The white South retains in historical memory a deep resentment of the forces which, after conquest, imposed a fierce program of reconstruction and the deep humiliation of carpetbag government. The Negro is the visible and reachable beneficiary and symbol of this unhappy experience, on whom many visit their natural desire for retaliation. . . .

Tested by the pace of history, the rise of the Negro in the South, as well as the North, is one of the swiftest and most dramatic advances in the annals of man. Economic and social forces seem to mark discrimination for extinction even faster than legal measures. It is easy, however, to understand that historical process may do the contemporary individual no good for his life moves faster than society. But whether a real abolition of segregation will be accelerated or retarded by what many are likely to regard as a ruthless use of federal judicial power is a question that I cannot and need not answer.

That Negro segregation in the schools has outlived whatever original justification it may have had and is no longer wise or fair public policy is a conclusion congenial to my background and social and political views. Economic, social and political consideration seem to mark it for certain and early, if gradual extinction. Whatever we may say the law is today, I have no doubt that within a generation segregation will be outlawed. As the twin forces of mortality and replacement operate on this bench that seems inevitable unless some dramatic and unforeseeable excess by the Negro and his friends shall cause reversal of present trends.

Jackson then turned to the Court's role in interpreting the Constitution, cautioning that

[W]e cannot oversimplify this decision to be a mere expression of our personal opinion that school segregation is unwise or evil. We have not been chosen as legislators but as judges. Questions of method and standards of constitutional interpretation and of limitation on responsible use of judicial power in our federal system are as far reaching as any that have been before the Court since its establishment. This Court must face the difficulties in the way of honestly saying that the states which have segregated schools have not, until today, been justified in regarding their practice as lawful. And the thoughtful layman, as well as the trained lawyer, must wonder how it is that a supposedly stable organic law of our nation this morning forbids what for three quarters of a century it has allowed. I think we individual justices may not, in justice to this Court as an institution and to our profession, brush off these problems.

Turning to the problems of explaining and justifying the Court's authority to strike down racially segregated schools, Jackson observed:

> Any authority of the judiciary to promulgate this decision has existed in the State cases has existed since 1868 and in the case of the District of Columbia since 1791. The due process and equal protection clauses of the Fourteenth Amendment and the due process clause of the Fifth Amendment are the respective texts for interpretation. Neither of these says anything about education or about segregation. But they are majestic and sweeping generalities which, standing alone can be read to require a full and equal racial partnership. Yet, if these texts had such meaning to the age that wrote them, how could it be that for more than a half century from the adoption of the Fifth Amendment to the Emancipation Proclamation, it was never suggested that the Due Process Clause of the Fifth Amendment even prohibited negro slavery in the District of Columbia? . . .

> There is controversy as old as the Republic as to whether the courts apply constitutional generalities in the sense that they were understood by the age that framed them or by the later age that reads them. It is implied in our questions on which all of the litigants have besowed extensive research that the original public will that struggled for expression in these Constitutional phrases is at least relevant to our decision.

> In searching for the original will and purpose expressed in the Fourteenth Amendment, all that I can fairly get from the legislative debates is that it was a passionate, confused, and deplorable era. . . . The majority stopped at conferring upon the freed man very limited civil rights. Most of leaders and spokesmen for the movement that carried the Civil War Amendments appear never to have reached a point in their thinking where they foresaw either Negro education or Negro segregation as serious or foreseeable problems, let alone any conclusion as to their solution.

> If deeds, rather than words, count as evidence, there is little indeed to show that these Amendments were understood in their own time to condemn the practice here in question. The Congress that proposed the Fourteenth Amendment and all Congresses to this day have established and maintained segregated schools in the District of Columbia. . . .

> This practice of legislators and educators and opinions of the Courts has been reinforced by custom, a powerful lawmaker. Indeed not long ago we decided that custom had nullified the Constitutional plan for independent Presidential electors. But here the custom of segregation is not contrary to any express provision, has prevailed in all Southern and many Northern states, and has been recognized in many judicial decisions. This court, in common with courts everywhere, has recognized the force of long custom and has been reluctant to use judicial power to try to recast social usages. But we decide today that the unwritten law has long been contrary to a custom deeply anchored in our social system. Thus despite my personal satis-

faction with the Court's judgment, I simply cannot find, in surveying all of the usual sources of law, anything which warrants me in saying that it is required by the original purpose and intent of the Fourteenth or Fifth Amendment.

Having reviewed the history and social practices since the adoption of the Fourteenth Amendment, and finding no support for the Court's ruling in a "jurisprudence of original intention," Jackson boldly observed that

> [t]oday's decision can not, with intellectual honesty, be grounded in anything other than the doctrine, of which Judge Cardozo reminded us, that these Constitutional generalities "have a content and a significance that vary from age to age." Certainly no one familiar with his teachings would think this meant, what some people advocate, that we declare new constitutional law with the freedom of a constitutional convention sitting continuously and with no necessity for submitting its innovations for approval of Congress, ratification by the states or approval of the people.

> Of course the Constitution must be a living instrument and cannot be read as if written in a dead language. It is neither novel nor radical doctrine that statutes once constitutional may become invalid by changing conditions and those good in one state of facts may be bad under another. . . .

Still, Jackson was deeply troubled by the fact that the Court's ruling might not appear to have the force of law and he turned to the sociological evidence that had been presented by the NAACP, and which Chief Justice Warren cited in footnote eleven of his opinion. And he sought to underscore that the Court's ruling rested on the Constitution, not social science or sociological jurisprudence:

> But a good many considerations are urged upon us to decree an end to segregation regardless of what the Amendments originally meant or purposed which I do not think appropriate for judicial appraisal or acceptance. Extra-legal criteria from sociological, psychological and political sciences are proposed. Segregation is said to be offensive to the best contemporary opinion here and damaging to our prestige abroad. It is said to be based on a philosophy of inherent inequality of races, and that it creates in young Negro children an inferiority complex which retards their education and embitters their attitudes to life. These are disputed contentions which I have little competence to judge as scientific matters but with which, for purposes of the case, I shall not disagree. . . .

> However that may be, and if all the woes of colored children would be solved by forcing them into white company, I do not think we should import into the concept of equal protection of the law these elusive psychological and subjective factors. They are not determinable with satisfactory objectivity or mensurable [*sic*] with reasonable certainty. If we adhere to objective criteria the judicial process will still be capricious enough.

Concluding, Jackson observed,

> The real question as I see it is whether the Constitution permits any classification or separation of Negro and White merely on the basis of color or racial descent. If not these policy arguments are superfluous and, if so, they are for consideration of the legislatures not the courts.

> I think the change which warrants our decision is not a change in the Constitution but in the Negro population. Certainly in the 1860's and through-

out the nineteenth century the Negro population, as a whole, was a different people than today. Lately freed from bondage, they had no opportunity as yet to show their capacity for education and assimilation, or even a chance to demonstrate that they could be self-supporting or in our public life anything more than a pawn for white exploiters. I cannot say that it was an unreasonable assumption that negro educational problems were elementary, special and peculiar and their mass teaching an experiment not easily tied in which the education of pupils of more favored background. Nor, when we view the progress that has been made under it, can we honestly say that the practice of each race pursuing its education apart was wholly to the Negro's disadvantage. His progress under these conditions has been spectacular.

Whatever may have been true at an earlier period, the mere fact that one is in some degree colored no longer creates a presumption that he is inferior, illiterate, retarded or indigent. Moreover, assimilation is under way to a marked extent. Blush or shudder, as many will, mixture of blood has been making inroads on segregation faster than the courtroom. A line of separation between the races has become unclear and blurred and an increasing part of what is called colored population has as much claim to white as to colored blood. This development baffles any just segregation effort.

Also relevant changes have occurred in the status of the public school. Education, even for the white, was once regarded as a privilege bestowed on those fortunate enough to be able to take advantage of it and often was not compulsory. The concept today has changed. Education is not a privilege but a right and more than that a duty, to be performed not merely for one's own advantage but for the security and stability of the nation. Access to educational facilities has been gradually transformed from a matter of grace into a right which may not be encumbered with unconstitutionally discriminatory or oppressive conditions. And while education was long regarded as at most a local or state concern, far from the reach of federal authority, the federal judicial power especially, and the appropriative power of Congress has moved in to the local problems and made education a national concern.

The Negro is not free of local educational control. He must meet the prescribed standards of learning, discipline and health. He may be treated on his individual merit as a pupil, attend schools set apart for those of his neighborhood. But he may not be included or excluded merely because he has Negro blood wholly or in part.

Source: From the Robert H. Jackson Papers, Library of Congress.

Bolling v. Sharpe
347 U.S. 497, 74 S.Ct. 693 (1954)

Handed down with *Brown v. Board of Education* (see page 1305), this case involved the District of Columbia's segregated schools. The facts are further discussed in the opinion delivered by Chief Justice Earl Warren.

Chief Justice WARREN delivers the opinion of the Court.

This case challenges the validity of segregation in the public schools of the District of Columbia. The petitioners, minors of the Negro race, allege that such segregation deprives them of due process of law under the Fifth Amendment. They were refused admission to a public school attended by white children solely because of their race. They sought the aid of the District Court for the District of Columbia in obtaining admission. That court dismissed their complaint. The Court granted a writ of certiorari before judgment in the Court of Appeals because of the importance of the constitutional question presented.

We have this day held that the Equal Protection Clause of the Fourteenth Amendment prohibits the states from maintaining racially segregated public schools. The legal problem in the District of Columbia is somewhat different, however. The Fifth Amendment, which is applicable in the District of Columbia, does not contain an equal protection clause as does the Fourteenth Amendment which applies only to the states. But the concepts of equal protection and due process, both stemming from our American ideal of fairness, are not mutually exclusive. The "equal protection of the laws" is a more explicit safeguard of prohibited unfairness than "due process of the law," and, therefore, we do not imply that the two are always interchangeable phrases. But, as this Court has recognized, discrimination may be so unjustifiable as to be violative of due process.

Classifications based solely upon race must be scrutinized with particular care, since they are contrary to our traditions and hence constitutionally suspect. As long ago as 1896, this Court declared the principle "that the constitution of the United States, in its present form, forbids, so far as civil and political rights are concerned, discrimination by the general government, or by the states, against any citizen because of his race." And in *Buchanan v. Warley*, 245 U.S. 60 [(1917)], the Court held that a statute which limited the right of a property owner to convey his property to a person of another race was, as an unreasonable discrimination, a denial of due process of law.

Although the Court has not assumed to define "liberty" with any great precision, that term is not confined to mere freedom from bodily restraint. Liberty under law extends to the full range of conduct which the individual is free to pursue, and it cannot be restricted except for a proper governmental objective. Segregation in public education is not reasonably related to any proper governmental objective, and thus it imposes on Negro children of the District of Columbia a burden that constitutes an arbitrary deprivation of their liberty in violation of the Due Process Clause.

In view of our decision that the Constitution prohibits the states from maintaining racially segregated public schools, it would be unthinkable that the same Constitution would impose a lesser duty on the Federal Government. We hold that racial segregation in the public schools of the District of Columbia is a denial of the due process of law guaranteed by the Fifth Amendment to the Constitution.

Brown v. Board of Education of Topeka, Kansas (Brown II)
349 U.S. 294, 75 S.Ct. 753 (1955)

During the rearguments on what kind of remedial decree the Court should issue to enforce *Brown,* Chief Justice Warren confronted the hard fact of southern resistance. The attorney for South Carolina, S. Emory Rogers, pressed for an open-ended decree—one that would not specify when and how desegregation should take place. He boldly proclaimed:

Mr. Chief Justice, to say we will conform depends on the decree handed down. I am frank to tell you, right now [in] our district I do not think that we will send—[that] the white people of the district will send their children to the Negro schools. It would be unfair to tell the Court that we are going to do that. I do not think it is. But I do think that something can be worked out. We hope so.

"It is not a question of attitude," Warren shot back, "it is a question of conforming to the decree." Their heated exchange continued:

Chief Justice Warren: But you are not willing to say here that there would be an honest attempt to conform to this decree, if we did leave it to the district court [to implement]?

Mr. Rogers: No, I am not. Let us get the word "honest" out of there.

Chief Justice Warren: No, leave it in.

Mr. Rogers: No, because I would have to tell you that right now we would not conform—we would not send our white children to the Negro schools.

The exchange reinforced Warren's view "that reasonable attempts to start the integration process is [*sic*] all the court can expect in view of the scope of the problem, and that an order to immediately admit all negroes in white schools would be an absurdity because [it would be] impossible to obey in many areas." Thus while total immediate integration might be a reasonable order for Kansas, it would be unreasonable for Virginia, and the district judge might decide that a grade a year is reasonable compliance in Virginia. Six law clerks were assigned to prepare a Segregation Research Report. They summarized available studies on how school districts in different regions might be desegregated and projected the reactions to various desegregation plans.

The Court's problem, as one of Justice Stanley Reed's law clerks put it, was to frame a decree "so as to allow such divergent results without making it so broad that evasion is encouraged." The clerks agreed that there should be a simple decree, but disagreed on whether there should be guidelines for its implementation. One clerk opposed any guidelines. The others thought that "smacks of indecisiveness, and gives the extremists more time to operate." The problem was how precise a guideline should be established. What would constitute good faith compliance? "Although we think a 12-year gradual desegregation plan permissible," they confessed, "we are not certain that the opinion should explicitly sanction it."

At the justices' private conference, Warren repeated these concerns. Justice Black and Minton thought that a simple decree, without an opinion, was enough. As Black explained, "the less we say the better off we are." The others agreed. A short, simple opinion seemed advisable for reaffirming *Brown* I and providing guidance for dealing with the inevitable problems of compliance. Justice John Harlan wanted *Brown* II to expressly recognize that school desegregation was a local problem to be solved by local authorities. The others also insisted on making clear that school boards and lower courts had flexibility in ending segregation. In Justice Harold Burton's view, "neither this Court nor district courts should act as a school board or formulate the program" for desegregation.

Agreement emerged that the Court should issue a short opinion decree. In a memorandum, Chief Justice Warren summarized the main points of agreement. The opinion should simply state that *Brown* I held unconstitutional racially segregated public schools. *Brown* II should acknowledge that "local school authorities have the primary responsibility for assessing and solving these problems; [and] the courts will have to consider these problems in determining whether the efforts of local school authorities" are in good faith compliance. The cases, he concluded, should be remanded to the lower courts "for such proceedings and decree necessary and proper to carry out this Court's decision." The justices agreed and along these lines Warren drafted the Court's opinion.

The phrase "all deliberate speed" was borrowed from an opinion by Justice Oliver Wendell Holmes, in *Virginia v. West Virginia,* 200 U.S. 1 (1911), a case dealing with how much and when

Virginia ought to receive from the state's public debt at the time West Virginia broke off and became a state. It was inserted in the final opinion of *Brown* II at the suggestion of one of Frankfurter's law clerks. Forced integration might lead to lowering educational standards. Immediate, court-ordered desegregation, Frankfurter warned, "would make a mockery of the Constitutional adjudication designed to vindicate a claim to equal treatment to achieve 'integrated' but lower educational standards." The Court, he insisted, "does its duty if it gets effectively under way the righting of a wrong. When the wrong is deeply rooted state policy the court does its duty if it decrees measures that reverse the direction of the unconstitutional policy so as to uproot it 'with all deliberate speed.' " As much as an apology for not setting precise guidelines as a recognition of the limitations of judicial power, the phrase symbolized the Court's bold moral appeal to the country.[*]

Chief Justice WARREN delivers the opinion of the Court.

These cases were decided on May 17, 1954. The opinions of that date, declaring the fundamental principle that racial discrimination in public education is unconstitutional, are incorporated herein by reference. All provisions of federal, state, or local law requiring or permitting such discrimination must yield to this principle. There remains for consideration the manner in which relief is to be accorded.

Because these cases arose under different local conditions and their disposition will involve a variety of local problems, we requested further argument on the question of relief. In view of the nationwide importance of the decision, we invited the Attorney General of the United States and the Attorneys General of all states requiring or permitting racial discrimination in public education to present their views on that question. The parties, the United States, and the States of Florida, North Carolina, Arkansas, Oklahoma, Maryland, and Texas filed briefs and participated in the oral argument. . . .

Full implementation of these constitutional principles may require solution of varied local school problems. School authorities have the primary responsibility for elucidating, assessing, and solving these problems; courts will have to consider whether the

---

[*] Quotations are from materials in the Stanley Reed Papers, University of Kentucky Library; the Harold Burton Papers, Library of Congress, the Tom Clark Papers, University of Texas Law School Library; the Felix Frankfurter Papers, Harvard Law School; and the Earl Warren Papers, Library of Congress.

action of school authorities constitutes good faith implementation of the governing constitutional principles. Because of their proximity to local conditions and the possible need for further hearings, the courts which originally heard these cases can best perform this judicial appraisal. Accordingly, we believe it appropriate to remand the cases to those courts.

In fashioning and effectuating the decrees, the courts will be guided by equitable principles. Traditionally, equity has been characterized by a practical flexibility in shaping its remedies and by a facility for adjusting and reconciling public and private needs. These cases call for the exercise of these traditional attributes of equity power. At stake is the personal interest of the plaintiffs in admission to public schools as soon as practicable on a nondiscriminatory basis. To effectuate this interest may call for elimination of a variety of obstacles in making the transition to school systems operated in accordance with the constitutional principles set forth in our May 17, 1954, decision. Courts of equity may properly take into account the public interest in the elimination of such obstacles in a systematic and effective manner. But it should go without saying that the vitality of these constitutional principles cannot be allowed to yield simply because of disagreement with them.

While giving weight to these public and private considerations, the courts will require that the defendants make a prompt and reasonable start toward full compliance with our May 17, 1954, ruling. Once such a start has been made, the courts may find that additional time is necessary to carry out the ruling in an effective manner. The burden rests upon the defendants to establish that such time is necessary in the public interest and is consistent with good faith compliance at the earliest practicable date. To that end, the courts may consider problems related to administration, arising from the physical condition of the school plant, the school transportation system, personnel, revision of school districts and attendance areas into compact units to achieve a system of determining admission to the public schools on a non-racial basis, and revision of local laws and regulations which may be necessary in solving the foregoing problems. They will also consider the adequacy of any plans the defendants may propose to meet these problems and to effectuate a transition to a racially nondiscriminatory school system. During this period of transition, the courts will retain jurisdiction of these cases.

The judgements below, except that in the Delaware case, are accordingly reversed and the cases are remanded to the District Courts to take such proceedings and enter such orders and decrees consistent with this opinion as are necessary and proper to admit to public schools on a racially nondiscriminatory basis with all deliberate speed the parties to these cases.

Cooper v. Aaron
358 U.S. 1, 78 S.Ct. 1401 (1958)

In Little Rock, Arkansas, Governor Orval Faubus encouraged disobedience by southern segregationists by calling out the state's National Guard to keep black children from entering Little Rock's Central High School. The attorney general of the United States, Herbert Brownell, got an injunction against the governor's action and eight black children, including John Aaron, were permitted to enter the school. But continued hostility lead the removal of the children and to President Dwight Eisenhower's sending army troops to enforce the court's order and to protect the children.

William Cooper and other members of the Little Rock school board asked a federal district court for a two-and-one-half-year delay in the implementation of its desegregation plans. A federal appellate court, however, reversed the district court's order postponing desegregation. Cooper and the school board immediately appealed that decision to the Supreme Court, which granted review and expedited proceedings. Hearing oral arguments just three days after granting review, the Court handed down the next day a brief order affirming the appellate court's decision. It later published a full opinion (excerpted here).

Justice Brennan's draft of the Court's opinion was worked on by all of the justices in the Court's conference room. Over the strong objections of some of the justices, Justice Felix Frankfurter insisted on writing a concurring opinion because, he said, many of his former students at Harvard Law School were leading members of the southern bar and because ex-Justice (and former Governor of South Carolina) James Byrnes had called on the country to curb the Court. Byrnes had published an attack on *Brown* and an article written by one of Frankfurter's favorite former law clerks, Alexander Bickel. As a clerk, Bickel had prepared a lengthy research report on school desegregation when the Court first considered *Brown*. Later when back at Harvard, Bickel revised and published it in the *Harvard Law Review*. Given Byrnes' attack, Frankfurter felt the need to lecture southern lawyers on the legitimacy of the Court's ruling in *Brown*. But the other justices worried that Frankfurter's opinion might undercut the Court's unanimous decision. For this reason, the justices took the unusual step of noting in the opinion that three—Brennan, Stewart and Whittaker—were not on the bench when *Brown* was handed down but that they would have joined the unanimous decision if they had been. They also agreed to depart from the practice of one justice signing the opinion for the

Court in order to underscore their unanimity and that Frankfurter's opinion was not a "dilution" "of the views expressed in the Court's joint opinion."

Opinion of the Court by the CHIEF JUSTICE, Justice BLACK, Justice FRANKFURTER, Justice DOUGLAS, Justice BURTON, Justice CLARK, Justice HARLAN, Justice BRENNAN, and Justice WHITTAKER.

As this case reaches us it raises questions of the highest importance to the maintenance of our federal system of government. It necessarily involves a claim by the Governor and Legislature of a State that there is no duty on state officials to obey federal court orders resting on this Court's considered interpretation of the United States Constitution. Specifically it involves actions by the Governor and Legislature of Arkansas upon the premise that they are not bound by our holding in *Brown v. Board of Education,* 349 U.S. 483 (1954). That holding was that the Fourteenth Amendment forbids States to use their governmental powers to bar children on racial grounds from attending schools where there is state participation through any arrangement, management, funds or property. We are urged to uphold a suspension of the Little Rock School Board's plan to do away with segregated public schools in Little Rock until state laws and efforts to upset and nullify our holding in *Brown v. Board of Education* have been further challenged and tested in the courts. We reject these contentions. . . .

In affirming the judgment of the Court of Appeals which reversed the District Court we have accepted without reservation the position of the School Board, the Superintendent of Schools, and their counsel that they displayed entire good faith in the conduct of these proceedings and in dealing with the unfortunate and distressing sequence of events which has been outlined. We likewise have accepted the findings of the District Court as to the conditions at Central High School during the 1957–1958 school year, and also the findings that the educational progress of all the students, white and colored, of that school has suffered and will continue to suffer if the conditions which prevailed last year are permitted to continue.

The significance of these findings, however, is to be considered in light of the fact, indisputably revealed by the record before us, that the conditions they depict are directly traceable to the actions of legislators and executive officials of the State of Arkansas, taken in their official capacities, which reflect their own determination to resist this Court's decision in the *Brown* case and which have brought about violent resistance to that decision in Arkansas. In its petition for certiorari filed in this Court, the

School Board itself describes the situation in this language: "The legislative, executive, and judicial departments of the state government opposed the desegregation of Little Rock schools by enacting laws, calling out troops, making statements villifying federal law and federal courts, and failing to utilize state law enforcement agencies and judicial processes to maintain public peace."

One may well sympathize with the position of the Board in the face of the frustrating conditions which have confronted it, but, regardless of the Board's good faith, the actions of the other state agencies responsible for those conditions compel us to reject the Board's legal position. Had Central High School been under the direct management of the State itself, it could hardly be suggested that those immediately in charge of the school should be heard to assert their own good faith as a legal excuse for delay in implementing the constitutional rights of these respondents, when vindication of those rights was rendered difficult or impossible by the actions of other state officials. The situation here is in no different posture because the members of the School Board and the Superintendent of Schools are local officials; from the point of view of the Fourteenth Amendment, they stand in this litigation as the agents of the State.

The constitutional rights of respondents are not to be sacrificed or yielded to the violence and disorder which have followed upon the actions of the Governor and Legislature. As this Court said some 41 years ago in a unanimous opinion in a case involving another aspect of racial segregation: "It is urged that this proposed segregation will promote the public peace by preventing race conflicts. Desirable as this is, and important as is the preservation of the public peace, this aim cannot be accomplished by laws or ordinances which deny rights created or protected by the federal Constitution." *Buchanan v. Warley,* 245 U.S. 60 [(1907)]. Thus law and order are not here to be preserved by depriving the Negro children of their constitutional rights. The record before us clearly establishes that the growth of the Board's difficulties to a magnitude beyond its unaided power to control is the product of state action. Those difficulties, as counsel for the Board forthrightly conceded on the oral argument in this Court, can also be brought under control by state action.

The controlling legal principles are plain. The command of the Fourteenth Amendment is that no "State" shall deny to any person within its jurisdiction the equal protection of the laws. "A State acts by its legislative, its executive, or its judicial authorities. It can act in no other way. The constitutional provision, therefore, must mean that no agency of the State, or of the officers or agents by whom its powers are exerted, shall deny to any person within its jurisdiction the equal protection of the laws. Whoever, by virtue of public position under a State government . . . denies or takes away the equal protection of the laws, violates the constitutional inhibition; and as he acts in the name and for the State, and is clothed with the State's power, his act is that of the State. This must be so, or the constitutional prohibition has no meaning." *Ex parte Virginia,* 100 U.S. 339 [(1880)]. Thus the prohibitions of the Fourteenth Amendment extend to all action of the State denying equal protection of the laws; whatever the agency of the State taking the action. . . .

In short, the constitutional rights of children not to be discriminated against in school admission on grounds of race or color declared by this Court in the *Brown* case can neither be nullified openly and directly by state legislators or state executive or judicial officers, nor nullified indirectly by them through evasive schemes for segregation whether attempted "ingeniously or ingenuously." *Smith v. Texas,* 311 U.S. 128 [(1940)].

What has been said, in the light of the facts developed, is enough to dispose of the case. However, we should answer the premise of the actions of the Governor and Legislature that they are not bound by our holding in the *Brown* case. It is necessary only to recall some basic constitutional propositions which are settled doctrine.

Article VI of the Constitution makes the Constitution the "supreme Law of the Land." In 1803, Chief Justice MARSHALL, speaking for a unanimous Court, referring to the Constitution as "the fundamental and paramount law of the nation," declared in the notable case of *Marbury v. Madison* 1 Cr. 137 [(1803)], that "It is emphatically the province and duty of the judicial department to say what the law is." This decision declared the basic principle that the federal judiciary is supreme in the exposition of the law of the Constitution, and that principle has ever since been respected by this Court and the Country as a permanent and indispensable feature of our constitutional system. It follows that the interpretation of the Fourteenth Amendment enunciated by this Court in the *Brown* case is the supreme law of the land, and Art. VI of the Constitution makes it of binding effect on the States "any Thing in the Constitution or Laws of any State to the Contrary notwithstanding." Every state legislator and executive and judicial officer is solemnly committed by oath taken pursuant to Art. VI, § 3 "to support this Constitution." Chief Justice TANEY, speaking for a unanimous Court in 1859, said that this requirement reflected the framers' "anxiety to preserve it [the Constitution] in full force, in all its powers, and to guard against resistance to or evasion of its authority, on the part of a State. . . ." *Ableman v. Booth,* 21 How. 506 [(1859)].

No state legislator or executive or judicial officer can war against the Constitution without violating his undertaking to support it. Chief Justice MARSHALL spoke for a unanimous Court in saying that: "If the legislatures of the several states may, at will, annul the judgments of the courts of the United States, and destroy the rights acquired under those judgments, the constitution itself becomes a solemn mockery. . . ." *United States v. Peters,* 5 Cranch 115 [(1809)].

It is, of course, quite true that the responsibility for public education is primarily the concern of the States, but it is equally true that such responsibilities, like all other state activity, must be exercised consistently with federal constitutional requirements as they apply to state action. The Constitution created a government dedicated to equal justice under law. The Fourteenth Amendment embodied and emphasized that ideal. State support of segregated schools through any arrangement, management, funds, or property cannot be squared with the Amendment's command that no State shall deny to any person within its jurisdiction the equal protection of the laws. The right of a student not to be segregated on racial grounds in schools so maintained is indeed so fundamental and pervasive that it is embraced in the concept of due process of law. *Bolling v. Sharpe,* 347 U.S. 497 [1954)]. The basic decision in *Brown* was unanimously reached by this Court only after the case had been briefed and twice argued and the issues had been given the most serious consideration. Since the first *Brown* opinion three new Justices have come to the Court. They are at one with the Justices still on the Court who participated in that basic decision as to its correctness, and that decision is now unanimously reaffirmed. The principles announced in that decision and the obedience of the States to them, according to the command of the Constitution, are indispensable for the protection of the freedoms guaranteed by our fundamental charter for all of us. Our constitutional ideal of equal justice under law is thus made a living truth.

Justice FRANKFURTER concurring.

While unreservedly participating with my brethren in our joint opinion, I deem it appropriate also to deal individually with the great issue here at stake. . . .

We are now asked to hold that the illegal, forcible interference by the State of Arkansas with the continuance of what the Constitution commands, and the consequences in disorder that it entrained, should be recognized as justification for undoing what the Board of Education had formulated, what the District Court in 1955 had directed to be carried out, and what was in process of obedience. No explanation that may be offered in support of such a request can obscure the inescapable meaning that law should bow to force. To yield to such a claim would be to enthrone official lawlessness and lawlessness if not checked is the precursor of anarchy. On the few tragic occasions in the history of the Nation, North and South, when law was forcibly resisted or systematically evaded, it has signalled the breakdown of constitutional processes of government on which ultimately rest the liberties of all. Violent resistance to law cannot be made a legal reason for its suspension without loosening the fabric of our society. What could this mean but to acknowledge that disorder under the aegis of a State has moral superiority over the law of the Constitution. For those in authority thus to defy the law of the land is profoundly subversive not only of our constitutional system but of the presuppositions of a democratic society. The State "must. . . yield to an authority that is paramount to the State.". . .

The duty to abstain from resistance to "the supreme Law of the Land," U.S. Const., Art. VI, § 2, as declared by the organ of our Government for ascertaining it, does not require immediate approval of it nor does it deny the right of dissent. Criticism need not be stilled. Active obstruction or defiance is barred. Our kind of society cannot endure if the controlling authority of the Law as derived from the Constitution is not to be the tribunal specially charged with the duty of ascertaining and declaring what is "the supreme Law of the Land." See President Andrew Jackson's Message to Congress of January 16, 1833, 2 Richardson, Messages and Papers of the Presidents, 610, 623. Particularly is this so where the declaration of what "the supreme Law" commands on an underlying moral issue is not the dubious pronouncement of a gravely divided Court but is the unanimous conclusion of a long-matured deliberative process. The Constitution is not the formulation of the merely personal views of the members of this Court, nor can its authority be reduced to the claim that state officials are its controlling interpreters. Local customs, however hardened by time, are not decreed in heaven. Habits and feelings they engender may be counteracted and moderated. Experience attests that such local habits and feelings will yield, gradually though this be, to law and education. And educational influences are exerted not only by explicit teaching. They vigorously flow from the fruitful exercise of the responsibility of those charged with political official power and from the almost unconsciously transforming actualities of living under law.

The process of ending unconstitutional exclusion of pupils from the common school system—"common" meaning shared alike—solely because of color is no doubt not an easy, overnight task in a few States where a drastic alteration in the ways of communities is involved. Deep emotions have, no doubt, been stirred. They will not be calmed by letting violence loose—violence and defiance employed and encouraged by those upon whom the duty of law observance should have the strongest claim—nor by submitting to it under whatever guise employed. Only the constructive use of time will achieve what an advanced civilization demands and the Constitution confirms. . . .

Swann v. Charlotte-Mecklenberg Board of Education

402 U.S. 1, 91 S.Ct. 1267 (1971)

Fifteen years after *Brown,* approximately 60 percent of the black students in Charlotte-Mecklenberg, North Carolina, still attended schools that were 99 percent black, even though 71 percent of all students in the school system were white. James Swann and several others filed a lawsuit in federal district court to modify a 1965 desegregation plan and to achieve further integration. As a result, two proposed desegregation plans were drawn up by the school board and a court-appointed expert, Dr. John Finger, and submitted to district Judge James B. McMillan. He accepted a modified version of the school board's plan for secondary schools but approved Dr. Finger's plans for elementary schools, which provided for more racial balance than acceptable to the school board. On appeal, a federal appellant court vacated that part of Judge McMillan's order dealing with the desegregation of elementary schools and remanded the case. After further proceedings, Judge McMillan issued a sweeping order, incorporating Finger's proposals and requiring districtwide busing.

President Richard Nixon, who appointed Chief Justice Burger in 1969, firmly opposed court-ordered busing. Inside the Court the issue also proved volatile. After oral arguments, Chief Justice Burger led the discussion at conference, suggesting that no votes be taken, just as his predecessor had done when considering *Brown.* At the same time, though, he indicated sympathy with the Nixon administration's opposition to court-ordered busing. Justice Black spoke next and was also unhappy with busing as a judicially fashioned remedy. But then a solid majority emerged for upholding the district court's order; Justices Douglas, Harlan, Brennan, White, and Marshall more or less agreed. Justices Stewart and newly appointed Justice Blackmun were more tentative, but inclined to go along with the majority.

What angered Justice Douglas and troubled some of the others was that Burger decided to draft an opinion for later conference discussion; since Burger had not appeared to be solidly with the views of the majority, the opinion assignment should have gone to Douglas, the senior associate justice in the majority. When Burger later circulated his draft it was indecisive in tone and took a restrictive view of the power of courts to remedy segregated schools, as well as failed to expressly uphold the lower court's order. What happened in the weeks that followed was an exchange of memorandums, various draft opinions, along with threats of dissenting opinions.

In the end, the chief justice incorporated suggestions and revisions put forth by Justices Brennan, Stewart, and Harlan and delivered an opinion for a unanimous Court, approving the lower court's order for districtwide busing.

Chief Justice BURGER delivers the opinion of the Court.

This case and those argued with it arose in States having a long history of maintaining two sets of schools in a single school system deliberately operated to carry out a governmental policy to separate pupils in schools solely on the basis of race. That was what *Brown v. Board of Education,* [349 U.S 294 (1955)], was all about. These cases present us with the problem of defining in more precise terms than heretofore the scope of the duty of school authorities and district courts in implementing *Brown I* and the mandate to eliminate dual systems and establish unitary systems at once. . . .

The objective today remains to eliminate from the public schools all vestiges of state-imposed segregation. . . .

If school authorities fail in their affirmative obligations under these holdings, judicial authority may be invoked. Once a right and a violation have been shown, the scope of a district court's equitable powers to remedy past wrongs is broad, for breadth and flexibility are inherent in equitable remedies. . . .

In seeking to define even in broad and general terms how far this remedial power extends it is important to remember that judicial powers may be exercised only on the basis of a constitutional violation. Remedial judicial authority does not put judges automatically in the shoes of school authorities whose powers are plenary. Judicial authority enters only when local authority defaults.

School authorities are traditionally charged with broad power to formulate and implement educational policy and might well conclude, for example, that in order to prepare students to live in a pluralistic society each school should have a prescribed ratio of Negro to white students reflecting the proportion for the district as a whole. To do this as an educational policy is within the broad discretionary powers of school authorities; absent a finding of a constitutional violation, however, that would not be within the authority of a federal court. As with any equity case, the nature of the violation determines the scope of the remedy. In default by the school authorities of their obligation to proffer acceptable remedies, a district court has broad power to fashion a remedy that will assure a unitary school system. . . .

The central issue in this case is that of student assignment, and there are essentially four problem areas:

(1) to what extent racial balance or racial quotas may be used as an implement in a remedial order to correct a previously segregated system;

(2) whether every all-Negro and all-white school must be eliminated as an indispensable part of a remedial process of desegregation;

(3) what the limits are, if any, on the rearrangement of school districts and attendance zones, as a remedial measure; and

(4) what the limits are, if any, on the use of transportation facilities to correct state-enforced racial school segregation.

(1) RACIAL BALANCES OR RACIAL QUOTAS.

The target of the cases from *Brown I* to the present was the dual school system. The elimination of racial discrimination in public schools is a large task and one that should not be retarded by efforts to achieve broader purposes lying beyond the jurisdiction of school authorities. One vehicle can carry only a limited amount of baggage. It would not serve the important objective of *Brown I* to seek to use school desegregation cases for purposes beyond their scope, although desegregation of schools ultimately will have impact on other forms of discrimination. We do not reach in this case the question whether a showing that school segregation is a consequence of other types of state action, without any discriminatory action by the school authorities, is a constitutional violation requiring remedial action by the school desegregation decree. This case does not present that question and we therefore do not decide it.

Our objective in dealing with the issues presented by these cases is to see that school authorities exclude no pupil of a racial minority from any school, directly or indirectly, on account of race; it does not and cannot embrace all the problems of racial prejudice, even when those problems contribute to disproportionate racial concentrations in some schools. . . .

If we were to read the holding of the District Court to require, as a matter of substantive constitutional right, any particular degree of racial balance or mixing, that approach would be disapproved and we would be obliged to reverse. The constitutional command to desegregate schools does not mean that every school in every community must always reflect the racial composition of the school system as a whole. . . .

[But here] the use made of mathematical ratios was no more than a starting point in the process of shaping a remedy, rather than an inflexible requirement. From that starting point the District Court proceeded to frame a decree that was within its discretionary powers, as an equitable remedy for the particular circumstances. As we said in *Green*, [*v. School Board of New Kent County*, 391 U.S. 430 (1968)], a school authority's remedial plan or a district court's remedial decree is to be judged by its effectiveness.

Awareness of the racial composition of the whole school system is likely to be a useful starting point in shaping a remedy to correct past constitutional violations. In sum, the very limited use made of mathematical ratios was within the equitable remedial discretion of the District Court.

(2) ONE-RACE SCHOOLS.

[I]t should be clear that the existence of some small number of one-race, or virtually one-race, schools within a district is not in and of itself the mark of a system that still practices segregation by law. The district judge or school authorities should make every effort to achieve the greatest possible degree of actual desegregation and will thus necessarily be concerned with the elimination of one-race schools. No *per se* rule can adequately embrace all the difficulties of reconciling the competing interests involved; but in a system with a history of segregation the need for remedial criteria of sufficient specificity to assure a school authority's compliance with its constitutional duty warrants a presumption against schools that are substantially disproportionate in their racial composition. Where the school authority's proposed plan for conversion from a dual to a unitary system contemplates the continued existence of some schools that are all or predominately of one race, they have the burden of showing that such school assignments are genuinely nondiscriminatory. The court should scrutinize such schools, and the burden upon the school authorities will be to satisfy the court that their racial composition is not the result of present or past discriminatory action on their part. . . .

(3) REMEDIAL ALTERING OF ATTENDANCE ZONES.

[O]ne of the principal tools employed by school planners and by courts to break up the dual school system has been a frank—and sometimes drastic—gerrymandering of school districts and attendance zones. An additional step was pairing, "clustering," or "grouping" of schools with attendance assignments made deliberately to accomplish the transfer of Negro students out of formerly segregated Negro schools and transfer of white students to formerly all-Negro schools. More often than not, these zones are neither compact nor contiguous; indeed they may be on opposite ends of the city. As an interim corrective measure, this cannot be said to be beyond the broad remedial powers of a court.

Absent a constitutional violation there would be no basis for judicially ordering assignment of students on a racial basis. All things being equal, with no history of discrimination, it might well be desirable to assign pupils to schools nearest their homes. But all things are not equal in a system that has been deliberately constructed and maintained to enforce racial segregation. The remedy for such segregation may be administratively awkward, inconvenient, and even bizarre in some situations and may impose burdens on some; but all awkwardness and inconvenience cannot be avoided in the interim period when remedial adjustments are being made to eliminate the dual school systems.

No fixed or even substantially fixed guidelines can be established as to how far a court can go, but it must be recognized that there are limits. The objective is to dismantle the dual school system. "Racially neutral" assignment plans proposed by school authorities to a district court may be inadequate; such plans may fail to counteract the continuing effects of past school segregation resulting from discriminatory location of school sites or distortion of school size in order to achieve or maintain an artificial racial separation. When school authorities present a district court with a "loaded game board," affirmative action in the form of remedial altering of attendance zones is proper to achieve truly nondiscriminatory assignments. In short, an assignment plan is not acceptable simply because it appears to be neutral.

In this area, we must of necessity rely to a large extent, as this Court has for more than 16 years, on the informed judgment of the district courts in the first instance and on courts of appeals.

We hold that the pairing and grouping of noncontiguous school zones is a permissible tool and such action is to be considered in light of the objectives sought.

(4) Transportation of Students.

The scope of permissible transportation of students as an implement of a remedial decree has never been defined by this Court and by the very nature of the problem it cannot be defined with precision. No rigid guidelines as to student transportation can be given for application to the infinite variety of problems presented in thousands of situations. Bus transportation has been an integral part of the public education system for years, and was perhaps the single most important factor in the transition from the one-room schoolhouse to the consolidated school. Eighteen million of the Nation's public school children, approximately 39%, were transported to their schools by bus in 1969–1970 in all parts of the country. . . .

The decree provided that the buses used to implement the plan would operate on direct routes. Students would be picked up at schools near their homes and transported to the schools they were to attend. The trips for elementary school pupils average about seven miles and the District Court found that they would take "not over 35 minutes at the most." This system compares favorably with the transportation plan previously operated in Charlotte under which each day 23,600 students on all grade levels were transported an average of 15 miles one way for an average trip requiring over an hour. In these circumstances, we find no basis for holding that the local school authorities may not be required to employ bus transportation as one tool of school desegregation. Desegregation plans cannot be limited to the walk-in school.

An objection to transportation of students may have validity when the time or distance of travel is so great as to either risk the health of the children or significantly impinge on the educational process. District courts must weigh the soundness of any transportation plan in light of what is said in subdivisions (1), (2), and (3) above. It hardly needs stating that the limits on time of travel will vary with many factors, but probably with none more than the age of the students. The reconciliation of competing values in a desegregation case is, of course, a difficult task with many sensitive facets but fundamentally no more so than remedial measures courts of equity have traditionally employed. . . .

On the facts of this case, we are unable to conclude that the order of the District Court is not reasonable, feasible and workable. However, in seeking to define the scope of remedial power or the limits on remedial power of courts in an area as sensitive as we deal with here, words are poor instruments to convey the sense of basic fairness inherent in equity. Substance, not semantics, must govern, and we have sought to suggest the nature of limitations without frustrating the appropriate scope of equity.

At some point, these school authorities and others like them should have achieved full compliance with this Court's decision in *Brown I*. The systems would then be "unitary" in the sense required by our decisions. . . .

For the reasons herein set forth, the judgment of the Court of Appeals is affirmed as to those parts in which it affirmed the judgment of the District Court. The order of the District Court, dated August 7, 1970, is also affirmed. It is so ordered.

Milliken v. Bradley
418 U.S. 717, 94 S.Ct. 3112 (1974)

In the 1970s as pressure grew to desegregate urban school systems in the North and West, the school desegregation controversy took a new twist. In some large metropolitan areas, like Detroit, Michigan, "white flight" to the suburbs left inner city school districts overwhelmingly black. In response, federal district courts began ordering *inter*district remedies, requiring the busing of white children from the suburbs to inner city schools and the busing of blacks students to predominately white suburban schools. When the first challenge to such court-ordered busing reached the Supreme Court, the justices split four to four. Justice

Powell did not participate in that case because it came from Richmond, Virginia, where he had once headed that city's school board. But the next year the Court decided "the Detroit busing case."

Ronald Bradley, along with several other black students and the NAACP, filed a class action suit against Michigan's governor, William Milliken, and other state officials. They charged that school district lines were drawn in racially discriminatory ways. A federal district court agreed, ordering the Detroit school board to draw up a desegregation plan and asking eighty-five surrounding school districts to present evidence relevant to the creation of a comprehensive metropolitan desegregation plan. The court eventually adopted a desegregation proposal, drafted by a panel of experts, mandating the busing of school children to and from Detroit and fifty-three neighboring districts. When a federal appellate court affirmed the substance of that order, Governor Milliken appealed to the Supreme Court.

For a bare majority, Chief Justice Burger ruled that court-ordered *inter*district busing is inappropriate for resolving the *intra*district problems, where suburban districts had not engaged in *de jure* segregation, but were *de facto* segregated due to housing patterns. Justices Brennan, Douglas, Marshall, and White dissented.

Chief Justice BURGER delivers the opinion of the Court.

We granted certiorari in these consolidated cases to determine whether a federal court may impose a multidistrict, areawide remedy to a single-district *de jure* segregation problem absent any finding that the other included school districts have failed to operate unitary school systems within their districts, absent any claim or finding that the boundary lines of any affected school district were established with the purpose of fostering racial segregation in public schools, absent any finding that the included districts committed acts which effected segregation within the other districts, and absent a meaningful opportunity for the included neighboring school districts to present evidence or be heard on the propriety of a multidistrict remedy or on the question of constitutional violations by those neighboring districts. . . .

Viewing the record as a whole, it seems clear that the District Court and the Court of Appeals shifted the primary focus from a Detroit remedy to the metropolitan area only because of their conclusion that total desegregation of Detroit would not produce the racial balance which they perceived as desirable. Both courts proceeded on an assumption that the Detroit schools could not be truly desegregated—in their view of what constituted desegregation—unless the racial composition of the student body of each school substantially reflected the racial composition of the population of the metropolitan area as a whole. The metropolitan area was then defined as Detroit plus 53 of the outlying school districts. . . .

Here the District Court's approach to what constituted "actual desegregation" raises the fundamental question, not presented in *Swann* [*v. Charlotte-Mecklenberg Board of Education*, 402 U.S. 1 (1971)], as to the circumstances in which a federal court may order desegregation relief that embraces more than a single school district. The court's analytical starting point was its conclusion that school district lines are no more than arbitrary lines on a map drawn "for political convenience." Boundary lines may be bridged where there has been a constitutional violation calling for interdistrict relief, but the notion that school district lines may be casually ignored or treated as a mere administrative convenience is contrary to the history of public education in our country. No single tradition in public education is more deeply rooted than local control over the operation of schools; local autonomy has long been thought essential both to the maintenance of community concern and support for public schools and to quality of the plex questions, and then the "school superintendent" for the entire area. This is a task which few, if any, judges are qualified to perform and one which would deprive the people of control of schools through their elected representatives. . . .

The record before us, voluminous as it is, contains evidence of *de jure* segregated conditions only in the Detroit schools; indeed, that was the theory on which the litigation was initially based and on which the District Court took evidence. With no showing of significant violation by the 53 outlying school districts and no evidence of any interdistrict violation or effect, the court went beyond the original theory of the case as framed by the pleadings and mandated a metropolitan area remedy. To approve the remedy ordered by the court would impose on the outlying districts, not shown to have committed any constitutional violation, a wholly impermissible remedy based on a standard not hinted at in *Brown I* and *II* or any holding of this Court.

In dissent, Justice WHITE and Justice MARSHALL undertake to demonstrate that agencies having statewide authority participated in maintaining the dual school system found to exist in Detroit. They are apparently of the view that once such participation is shown, the District Court should have a relatively free hand to reconstruct school districts outside of Detroit in fashioning relief. Our assumption, *arguendo*, that state agencies did participate in the maintenance of the Detroit system, should make it clear that it is not on this point that we part company. The difference between us arises instead from established doctrine laid down by our cases. *Brown, Green* [*v. School Board of New Kent County*, 391 U.S 430 (1968)], *Swann,* [*United States v.*] *Scotland Neck* [*City*

Board of Education, 407 U.S. 484 (1972)], and[*Wright v. City Council of the City of*] *Emporia,* [407 U.S. 451 (1972)], each addressed the issue of constitutional wrong in terms of an established geographic and administrative school system populated by both Negro and white children. In such a context, terms such as "unitary" and "dual" systems, and "racially identifiable schools," have meaning, and the necessary federal authority to remedy the constitutional wrong is firmly established. But the remedy is necessarily designed, as all remedies are, to restore the victims of discriminatory conduct to the position they would have occupied in the absence of such conduct. Disparate treatment of white and Negro students occurred within the Detroit school system, and not elsewhere, and on this record the remedy must be limited to that system. . . .

The constitutional right of the Negro respondents residing in Detroit is to attend a unitary school system in that district. Unless petitioners drew the district lines in a discriminatory fashion, or arranged for white students residing in the Detroit district to attend schools in Oakland and Macomb Counties, they were under no constitutional duty to make provisions for Negro students to do so. The view of the dissenters, that the existence of a dual system in Detroit can be made the basis for a decree requiring cross-district transportation of pupils, cannot be supported on the grounds that it represents merely the devising of a suitably flexible remedy for the violation of rights already established by our prior decisions. It can be supported only by drastic expansion of the constitutional right itself, an expansion without any support in either constitutional principle or precedent.

Accepting, *arguendo*, the correctness of [a] finding of state responsibility for the segregated conditions within the city of Detroit, it does not follow that an interdistrict remedy is constitutionally justified or required. With a single exception, discussed later, there has been no showing that either the State or any of the 85 outlying districts engaged in activity that had a cross-district effect. The boundaries of the Detroit School District, which are coterminous with the boundaries of the city of Detroit, were established over a century ago by neutral legislation when the city was incorporated; there is no evidence in the record, nor is there any suggestion by the respondents, that either the original boundaries of the Detroit School District, or any other school district in Michigan, were established for the purpose of creating, maintaining, or perpetuating segregation of races. There is no claim and there is no evidence hinting that petitioner outlying schools districts and their predecessors, or the 30-odd other school districts in the tricounty area—but outside the District Court's "desegregation area"—have ever maintained or operated anything but unitary school systems. Unitary school systems have been required for more than a century by the Michigan Constitution as implemented by state law. Where the schools of only one district have been affected, there is no constitutional power in the courts to decree relief balancing the racial composition of that district's schools with those of the surrounding districts. . . .

We conclude that the relief ordered by the District Court and affirmed by the Court of Appeals was based upon an erroneous standard and was unsupported by record evidence that acts of the outlying districts effected the discrimination found to exist in the schools of Detroit. Accordingly, the judgment of the Court of Appeals is reversed and the case is remanded for further proceedings consistent with this opinion leading to prompt formulation of a decree directed to eliminating the segregation found to exist in Detroit city schools, a remedy which has been delayed since 1970.

Reversed and remanded.

Justice STEWART concurred.

Justice DOUGLAS dissenting.

When we rule against the metropolitan area remedy we take a step that will likely put the problems of the blacks and our society back to the period that antedated the "separate but equal" regime of *Plessy v. Ferguson,* 163 U.S. 537 [(1896)]. The reason is simple.

The inner core of Detroit is now rather solidly black; and the blacks, we know, in many instances are likely to be poorer, just as were the Chicanos in *San Antonio School District v. Rodriguez,* 411 U.S. 1 [(1973)]. By that decision the poorer school districts must pay their own way. It is therefore a foregone conclusion that we have now given the States a formula whereby the poor must pay their own way.

Today's decision, given *Rodriguez,* means that there is no violation of the Equal Protection Clause though the schools are segregated by race and though the black schools are not only "separate" but "inferior."

So far as equal protection is concerned we are now in a dramatic retreat from the 7-to-1 decision in 1896 that blacks could be segregated in public facilities, provided they received equal treatment.

As I indicated in *Keyes v. School District No. 1, Denver, Colorado,* 413 U.S. [189 (1973)], there is so far as the school cases go no constitutional difference between *de facto* and *de jure* segregation. Each school board performs state action for Fourteenth Amendment purposes when it draws the lines that confine it to a given area, when it builds schools at particular sites, or when it allocates students. The creation of the school districts in Metropolitan Detroit either maintained existing segregation or caused additional segregation. Restrictive covenants maintained by state action or inaction build black ghettos. It is state action when public funds are dispensed by housing agencies to build racial ghettos. Where a community is racially mixed and school authorities segregate schools, or assign black teachers to black schools or close schools in fringe areas and build new schools in black areas and in more distant white areas, the State creates and nurtures a segregated school system, just as surely as did those States involved in *Brown v. Board of Education*, 347 U.S. 483 [(1954)]. when they maintained dual school systems. . . .

It is conceivable that ghettos develop on their own without any hint of state action. But since Michigan by one device or another has over the years created black school districts and white school districts, the task of equity is to provide a unitary system for the affected area where as here, the State washes its hands of its own creations.

Justice WHITE, with whom Justice DOUGLAS, Justice BRENNAN, and Justice MARSHALL join, dissenting.

Regretfully, and for several reasons, I can join neither the Court's judgment nor its opinion. The core of my disagreement is that deliberate acts of segregation and their consequences will go unremedied, not because a remedy would be infeasible or unreasonable in terms of the usual criteria governing school desegregation cases, but because an effective remedy would cause what the Court considers to be undue administrative inconvenience to the State. The result is that the State of Michigan, the entity at which the Fourteenth Amendment is directed, has successfully insulated itself from its duty to provide effective desegregation remedies by vesting sufficient power over its public schools in its local school districts. If this is the case in Michigan, it will be the case in most States. . . .

I am surprised that the Court, sitting at this distance from the State of Michigan, claims better insight than the Court of Appeals and the District Court as to whether an interdistrict remedy for equal protection violations practiced by the State of Michigan would involve undue difficulties for the State in the management of its public schools. In the area of what constitutes an acceptable desegregation plan, "we must of necessity rely to a large extent, as this Court has for more than 16 years, on the informed judgment of the district courts in the first instance and on courts of appeals." *Swann v. Charlotte-Mecklenburg Board of Education*, 402 U.S. 1 (1971). Obviously, whatever difficulties there might be, they are surmountable; for the Court itself concedes that, had there been sufficient evidence of an interdistrict violation, the District Court could have fashioned a single remedy for the districts implicated rather than a different remedy for each district in which the violation had occurred or had an impact.

I am even more mystified as to how the Court can ignore the legal reality that the constitutional violations, even if occurring locally, were committed by governmental entities for which the State is responsible and that it is the State that must respond to the command of the Fourteenth Amendment. An interdistrict remedy for the infringements that occurred in this case is well within the confines and powers of the State, which is the governmental entity ultimately responsible for desegregating its schools.

Finally, I remain wholly unpersuaded by the Court's assertion that "the remedy is necessarily designed, as all remedies are, to restore the victims of discriminatory conduct to the position they would have occupied in the absence of such conduct." In the first place, under this premise the Court's judgment is itself infirm; for had the Detroit school system not followed an official policy of segregation throughout the 1950's and 1960's, Negroes and whites would have been going to school together. There would have been no, or at least not as many, recognizable Negro schools and no, or at least not as many, white schools, but "just schools," and neither Negroes nor whites would have suffered from the effects of segregated education, with all its shortcomings. Surely the Court's remedy will not restore to the Negro community, stigmatized as it was by the dual school system, what it would have enjoyed over all or most of this period if the remedy is confined to present-day Detroit; for the maximum remedy available within that area will leave many of the schools almost totally black, and the system itself will be predominantly black and will become increasingly so. Moreover, when a State has engaged in acts of official segregation over a lengthy period of time, as in the case before us, it is unrealistic to suppose that the children who were victims of the State's unconstitutional conduct could now be provided the benefits of which they were wrongfully deprived. Nor can the benefits which accrue to school systems in which schoolchildren have not been officially segregated, and to the communities supporting such school systems, be fully and immediately restored after a substantial period of unlawful segregation. The education of children of different races in a desegregated environment has unhappily been lost, along with the social, economic, and political advantages which accompany a desegregated school system as compared with an unconstitutionally segregated system. It is for these reasons that the Court has consistently followed the course of requiring the effects of past official segregation to be eliminated "root and branch" by imposing, in the present, the duty to provide a remedy which will achieve "the greatest possible degree of actual desegregation, taking into account the practicalities of the situation." It is also for these reasons that once a constitutional violation has been found, the district judge obligated to provide such a remedy "will thus necessarily be concerned with the elimination of one-race schools." These concerns were properly taken into account by the District Judge in this case. Confining the remedy to the boundaries of the Detroit district is quite unrelated either to the goal of achieving maximum desegregation or to those intensely practical considerations, such as the extent and expense of transportation, that have imposed limits on remedies in cases such as this. The Court's remedy, in the end, is essentially arbitrary and will leave serious violations of the Constitution substantially unremedied.

Justice MARSHALL, with whom Justice DOUGLAS, Justice BRENNAN, and Justice WHITE join, dissenting.

I cannot subscribe to this emasculation of our constitutional guarantee of equal protection of the laws and must respectfully dissent. Our precedents, in my view, firmly establish that where, as here, state-imposed segregation has been demonstrated, it becomes the duty of the State to eliminate root and branch all vestiges of racial discrimination and to achieve the greatest possible degree of actual desegregation. I agree with both the District Court and the Court of Appeals that, under the facts of this case, this duty cannot be fulfilled unless the State of Michigan involves outlying metropolitan area school districts in its desegregation remedy. Furthermore, I perceive no basis either in law or in the practicalities of the situation justifying the State's interposition of school district boundaries as absolute barriers to the implementation of an effective desegregation remedy. Under established and frequently used Michigan procedures, school district lines are both flexible and permeable for a wide variety of purposes, and there is no reason why they must now stand in the way of meaningful desegregation relief. . . .

Nowhere in the Court's opinion does the majority confront, let alone respond to the District Court's conclusion that a remedy limited to the city of Detroit would not effectively desegregate the Detroit city schools. I, for one, find the District Court's conclusion well supported by the record and its analysis compelled by our prior cases. . . .

Under a Detroit-only decree, Detroit's schools will clearly remain racially identifiable in comparison with neighboring schools in the metropolitan community. Schools with 65% and more Negro students will stand in sharp and obvious contrast to schools in neighboring districts with less than 2% Negro enrollment. Negro students will continue to perceive their schools as segregated educational facilities and this perception will only be increased when whites react to a Detroit-only decree by fleeing to the suburbs to avoid integration. School district lines, however innocently drawn, will surely be perceived as fences to separate the races when, under a Detroit-only decree, white parents withdraw their children from the Detroit city schools and move to the suburbs in order to continue them in all-white schools. . . .

Nor can it be said that the State is free from any responsibility for the disparity between the racial makeup of Detroit and its surrounding suburbs. The State's creation, through *de jure* acts of segregation, of a growing core of all-Negro schools inevitably acted as a magnet to attract Negroes to the areas served by such schools and to deter them from settling either in other areas of the city or in the suburbs. By the same token, the growing core of all-Negro schools inevitably helped drive whites to other areas of the city or to the suburbs. . . .

The State must also bear part of the blame for the white flight to the suburbs which would be forthcoming from a Detroit-only decree and would render such a remedy ineffective. Having created a system where whites and Negroes were intentionally kept apart so that they could not become accustomed to learning together, the State is responsible for the fact that many whites will react to the dismantling of that segregated system by attempting to flee to the suburbs. Indeed, by limiting the District Court to a Detroit-only remedy and allowing that flight to the suburbs to succeed, the Court today allows the State to profit from its own wrong and to perpetuate for years to come the separation of the races it achieved in the past by purposeful state action. . . .

Desegregation is not and was never expected to be an easy task. Racial attitudes ingrained in our Nation's childhood and adolescence are not quickly thrown aside in its middle years. But just as the inconvenience of some cannot be allowed to stand in the way of the rights of others, so public opposition, no matter how strident, cannot be permitted to divert this Court from the enforcement of the constitutional principles at issue in this case. Today's holding, I fear, is more a reflection of a perceived public mood that we have gone far enough in enforcing the Constitution's guarantee of equal justice than it is the product of neutral principles of law. In the short run, it may seem to be the easier course to allow our great metropolitan areas to be divided up each into two cities—one white, the other black—but it is a course, I predict, our people will ultimately regret. I dissent.

C. AFFIRMATIVE ACTION AND REVERSE DISCRIMINATION

In the late 1960s, the federal government not only took the lead in ending racial segregation and discrimination in education, housing, and employment. Along with state and local govern-

THE DEVELOPMENT OF LAW
Other Rulings on School Desegregation

Case	Vote	Ruling
North Carolina Board of Education v. Swann, 402 U.S. 43 (1971)	9:0	Struck down a state law forbidding the use of busing to achieve school desegregation.
Wright v. City Council of Emporia, 407 U.S. 451 (1972)	5:4	Held that a city, which had been part of a county school system, could not establish a separate school if it impeded efforts to dismantle a dual school system; Chief Justice Burger and Justices Blackmun, Powell, and Rehnquist dissented.
United States v. Scotland Neck City Board of Education, 407 U.S. 484 (1972)	5:4	Struck down a state law providing for some new school districts that were 57 percent white and 43 percent black, while other districts remained over 89 percent black; Chief Justice Burger and Justices Blackmun, Powell, and Rehnquist dissented.
Keyes v. Denver School District, 413 U.S. 189 (1973)	8:1	Found that intentional segregation by a school system created a *prima facie* case for unlawful segregation in the entire school system; Justice Rehnquist dissented.
Pasadena City Board of Education v. Spangler, 427 U.S. 424 (1976)	6:2	Held that schools need not rearrange attendance zones each year so as to ensure that a racial mix is maintained in perpetuity; Justices Brennan and Marshall dissented.
Columbus Board of Education v. Penick, 443 U.S. 449 (1979); and *Dayton Board of Education v. Brinkman*, 443 U.S. 526 (1979)	7:2 5:4	The Court found intentional discrimination and upheld a lower court's order for massive busing, where in 1976 70 percent of all students attended schools that

Case	Vote	Ruling
		were either 80 percent black or white; in *Penick*, Justices Powell and Rehnquist dissented, and in *Brinkman* they were joined by Chief Justice Burger and Justice Stewart in dissent.
Board of Education of City School v. Harris, 444 U.S. 130 (1979)	6:3	Found discriminatory impact in the allocation of teachers; Justices Stewart, Powell, and Rehnquist dissented.
Washington v. Seattle School District 1, 458 U.S. 457 (1982)	5:4	Struck down an initiative requiring children to attend schools nearest to their homes; Chief Justice Burger and Justices O'Connor, Powell, and Rehnquist dissented.
Crawford v. Bd. of Education of the City of Los Angeles, 458 U.S. 527 (1982)	8:1	Upheld California's amendment to its state constitution limiting state court-ordered busing for the purpose of achieving integrated public schools; Justice Marshall dissented.
Missouri v. Jenkins, 110 S.Ct. 1651 (1990)	5:4	Justice White upheld the authority of a federal judge to order the Kansas City, Missouri, school board to raise taxes to pay for a wide-ranging magnet school plan designed to achieve racial integration. But, in so holding, Justice White was joined by only Justices Brennan, Marshall, Stevens, and Blackmun. In a separate concurring opinion, joined by Chief Justice Rehnquist and Justices O'Connor and Scalia, Justice Kennedy declined to join the Court's holding. Simply put, in Justice Kennedy's words, "The power of taxation is one that the federal judiciary does not possess."

ments and private business, the federal government promoted "affirmative action" programs—programs aimed at increasing opportunities for blacks, women, and other minorities in higher education and employment. Affirmative action programs range from aggressive recruiting and remedial training programs, to setting goals and guidelines, and to set–asides and quotas specifying an exact number or percentage of admissions or jobs for blacks, women, and other minorities. Following the enactment of the Civil Rights Act of 1964, President Johnson issued an executive order (No. 11246) encouraging the use of affirmative action programs to overcome the effects of past and present discrimination. In 1967, the Department of Labor adopted a policy of preferential hiring for minorities and women and the Department of Health, Education and Welfare (HEW, now the Department of Education) assumed responsibility for affirmative action in higher education. By the 1970s, HEW issued guidelines and threatened the withholding of federal funding from colleges and universities that failed to meet its hiring and admissions goals for blacks, women, and other minorities.

Affirmative action programs sparked heated political controversy and posed an explosive issue for the Court and the country. Proponents claimed that such programs remedied the effects of past discrimination and would improve the status of blacks, women and minorities. They pointed out that for a century and a half racial segregation was tolerated; the Constitution had not been color-blind. Moreover, they argued that racial preferences in affirmative action programs were benign; through "positive discrimination" blacks, women, and other minorities would finally achieve an equality of opportunity denied them in the past. As Justice Blackmun, concurring in *Regents of the University of California v. Bakke* (1978) (see page 1348), put it: "In order to get beyond racism, we must first take account of race. There is no other way."

Opponents of affirmative action programs raised numerous objections. Some argued that racial preferences were not benign for blacks or whites. Just as "Jim Crow" laws stigmitized blacks as inferior, so too race-conscious affirmative action programs implied that blacks were not as meritorous as whites. And racial preferences disadvantaged whites. Other critics conceded that preferential recruitment and special training programs might be appropriately and temporarily used to overcome the effects of past discrimination. But they strongly objected to quotas and set aside programs. As a matter of public policy, they argued that it was wrong to accord special benefits to members of groups that had suffered past discrimination because those given special advantages may not have actually been victims of discrimination.

Moreover, programs setting racial quotas inexorably discriminated against whites and invited charges of *reverse discrimination.* Once again dissenting Justice Harlan's opinion in *Plessy* became poignant, as critics of affirmative action charged that "The Constitution is (or ought to be) color-blind."

White males denied admission to higher education, government contracts, and employment opportunities attacked affirmative action programs for denying their rights under the Fourteenth Amendment's equal protection clause and the Civil Rights Act of 1964. The latter in dealing with federal funding of public and private institutions provides in Title VI that "[n]o person in the United States shall, on the ground of race, color, or national origin, be excluded from participation in, be denied the benefits of, or be subjected to discrimination under any program or activity receiving Federal financial assistance." In Title VII of the Civil Rights Act, Congress sought to end racial discrimination in employment in the private sector and specified that

[n]othing contained in this subchapter shall be interpreted to require any employer, employment agency, labor organization, or joint labor-management committee subject to this subchapter to grant preferential treatment to any individual or to any group because of the race, color, religion, sex, national origin of such individual or group on account of an imbalance which may exist with respect to the total number or percentage of persons of any race, color, religion, sex, or national origin employed by any employer, referred or classified for employment by any employment agency or labor organization, admitted to membership or classified in any labor organization, or admitted to, or employed in, any apprenticeship or other training program, in comparison with the total number or percentage of such persons of such race, color, religion, sex, or national origin in any community, State, section, or other area, or in the available work force in any community, State, section or other area.

The Burger Court could not escape the constitutional and statutory challenges to affirmative action programs. A bare majority, however, sought to do so in *DeFunis v. Odegaard*, 416 U.S. 312 (1974). Marco DeFunis, Jr., was one of 1,600 applicants for admission to the University of Washington Law School, but was denied a place in the first-year entering class of 150 students. He sued Charles Odegaard, president of the university, contending that the law school's admission criteria invidiously discriminated against him in violation of the Fourteenth Amendment. A state trial court agreed and ordered DeFunis's admission. On appeal, the Washington State Supreme Court reversed. By this time DeFunis was in his second year of law school and he appealed to the Supreme Court. Justice Douglas, as circuit justice for the ninth circuit, stayed the state court's ruling pending "the final disposition of the case by [the Supreme] Court." DeFunis thus remained in school and was in his third year when the Burger Court dismissed his case as moot. A bare majority vacated the state court decision on concluding that because DeFunis would graduate at the end of the academic year the Court should not address the substantive constitutional issue in this case. Justice Brennan, joined by Justices Douglas, Marshall, and White, dissented and criticized the majority for side-stepping the issue, and warned that the controversy would inevitably return to the Court.

In a separate dissenting opinion in *DeFunis,* Justice Douglas addressed the merits of the case. In his view, the Law School Admissions Test (LSAT) may work hardships on members of minority groups and law schools ought to find other ways to ensure diverse student bodies:

The key to the problem is the consideration of each application *in a racially neutral way.* Since the LSAT reflects questions touching on cultural backgrounds, the Admissions Committee acted properly in my view in setting minority applications apart for separate processing. These minorities have cultural backgrounds that are vastly different from the dominant Caucasian. Many Eskimos, American Indians, Filipinos, Chicanos, Asian Indians, Burmese, and Africans come from such disparate backgrounds that a test sensitively tuned for most applicants would be wide of the mark for many minorities. . . .

The key to the problem is consideration of such applications *in a racially neutral way.* Abolition of the LSAT would be a start. The invention of substitute tests might be made to get a measure of an applicant's cultural background, perception, ability to analyze, and his or her relation to groups. They are highly subjective, but unlike the LSAT they are not concealed, but in the open. A law school is not bound by any legal principle to admit students by mechanical criteria which are insensitive to the potential of such an applicant which may be realized in a more hospitable environment. It will be necessary under such an approach to put more effort into assessing each individual than is required when LSAT scores and undergraduate grades dominate the selection process. Interviews with the applicant and others who know him is a time-honored test. Some schools currently run summer programs in which potential students who likely would be bypassed under conventional admissions criteria are given the opportunity to try their hand at law courses, and certainly their performance in such programs could be weighed heavily. There is, moreover, no bar to considering an individual's prior achievements in light of the racial discrimination that barred his way, as a factor. . . . Nor is there any bar to considering on an individual basis, rather than according to racial classifications, the likelihood that a particular candidate will more likely employ his legal skills to service communities that are not now adequately represented than will competing candidates. . . . Certainly such a program would substantially fulfill the Law School's interest in giving a more diverse group access to the legal profession. Such a program might be less convenient administratively than simply sorting students by race, but we have never held administrative convenience to justify racial discrimination.

Although Justice Douglas favored aggressive recruitment of minorities, he staunchly opposed the use of racial classifications and quotas. In his words:

> The Equal Protection Clause commands the elimination of racial barriers, not their creation in order to satisfy our theory as to how society ought to be organized. The purpose of the University of Washington cannot be to produce black lawyers for blacks, Polish lawyers for Poles, Jewish lawyers for Jews, Irish lawyers for Irish. It should be to produce good lawyers for Americans and not to place First Amendment barriers against anyone. . . . A segregated admissions process creates suggestions of stigma and caste no less than a segregated classroom, and in the end it may produce that result despite its contrary intentions. One other assumption must be clearly disapproved; that blacks or browns cannot make it on their individual merit. That is a stamp of inferiority that a State is not permitted to place on any lawyer.

Four years after *Defunis* and three years after Justice Douglas was replaced by Justice Stevens on the bench, the Burger Court handed down its major ruling on affirmative action programs in higher education in *Regents of the University of California v. Bakke* (1978) (see page 1348). The justices, though, split four to four and (with the exception of a one-paragraph statement of the facts) no other justice joined Justice Powell's opinion announcing the Court's ruling. Note that Justice Powell holds that racial quotas are impermissible, but not affirmative action programs aimed at promoting diverse student bodies. Notably, he relies on an "exacting scrutiny" test, instead of the "strict scrutiny" test, in his narrowly tailored opinion applying only to higher education.

Throughout the 1980s, the Burger Court remained sharply divided over affirmative action programs and claims of reverse discrimination in employment. The justices split five to four and six to three when upholding most programs, and Justice Powell often cast the deciding vote, rebuffing the views pressed by the Reagan administration and opponents of affirmative action. Justices Brennan, Marshall, and Blackmun invariably supported affirmative action programs, while Justices Rehnquist and White generally stood in opposition (see the table on page 1370).

In *United Steelworkers of America v. Weber*, 443 U.S. 193 (1979), with Justices Powell and Stewart not participating, four justices joined Justice Brennan in reading the Civil Rights Act to *permit* (although not require) private voluntary programs designed to achieve racial balance in the workplace through an on-the-job training program set up for blacks. Although Chief Justice

Burger and Justice Rehnquist dissented in *Weber,* the following year Burger delivered the Court's opinion in *Fullilove v. Klutznick,* 448 U.S. 448 (1980), upholding Congress's power to set aside 10 percent of all public-works contracts for minority-owned businesses. In two cases, the Burger Court struck down affirmative action programs. In *Firefighters Local Union No. 1784 v. Stotts,* 467 U.S. 561 (1984), the Court held that under the Civil Rights Act the seniority interests of white workers could not be sacrificed in employment layoffs to preserve jobs for more recently hired blacks. A bare majority in *Wygant v. Jackson Board of Education,* 476 U.S. 267 (1986), then interpreted the Fourteenth Amendment to bar layoffs of white teachers with more seniority than black teachers, where there was no evidence that black teachers had actually suffered past discrimination.

In Chief Justice Burger's last term (1985–1986) on the Court, however, Justice Brennan massed a majority for upholding under the Civil Rights Act a court-ordered affirmative action program setting a "hiring goal" for minority workers, in *Local 28 of the Sheet Metal Workers v. Equal Employment Opportunity Commission,* 478 U.S. 421 (1986), and a judicial consent decree setting hiring goals as a remedy for a union's past discriminatory practices, in *Local No. 93, International Association of Firefighters v. City of Cleveland,* 478 U.S. 501 (1986). Justice Brennan managed to forge majorities in two more 1987 rulings. In *United States v. Paradise,* 480 U.S. 149 (1987), he held that the equal protection clause did not bar a court-ordered quota for the promotion of blacks within the ranks of Alabama's state troopers. And in *Johnson v. Transportation Agency, Santa Clara, California,* 480 U.S. 616 (1987), Justice Brennan upheld a program for promoting minorities and women to positions that were traditionally segregated and where members of those groups had been traditionally underrepresented.

By the end of the 1980s, though, the Rehnquist Court signaled an abrupt shift in analysis and approach toward challenges to affirmative action programs, registering the impact of President Ronald Reagan's appointees to the Court, and in particular Justice Kennedy's appointment in 1988 to the seat previously occupied by Justice Powell. Note that Justice O'Connor's opinion in *City of Richmond v. J. A. Croson* (1989) (see page 1382), when overturning Richmond's set aside program for minority-owned businesses (modeled and adopted after the one approved by the Court in *Fullilove*), substitutes the strict scrutiny test for *Bakke*'s exacting scrutiny test, and indicates that only narrowly tailored affirmative action programs aimed at remedying actual victims of past discrimination will survive constitutional challenge. In addition, writing for a bare majority in *Martin v. Wilks*, 109 S.Ct. 2180 (1989), Chief Justice Rehnquist held that white workers who were not parties to a judicial consent decrees establishing an affirmative action program could nevertheless years later challenge the constitutionality of the program. Defenders of state and local affirmative action programs, then, must meet the Rehnquist Court's heightened standard of judicial review, demonstrating that the programs are narrowly tailored remedies for actual victims of past or present discrimination.

One year after *Croson*, however, Justice Brennan managed to forge a bare majority for upholding affirmative action programs adopted by the *federal* government and mandated by Congress, in *Metro Broadcasting, Inc. v. Federal Communications Commission* (1990) (see page 1401). He and the two other dissenters in *Croson* were joined by Justice White (who voted with the majority in *Croson* but also with the majority in the 1980 *Fullilove* ruling upholding Congress's power to establish affirmative action programs) and Justice Stevens (who concurred in *Croson* yet dissented in *Fullilove*). Chief Justice Rehnquist and Justices O'Connor, Scalia, and Kennedy dissented.

SELECTED BIBLIOGRAPHY

Glazer, Nathan. *Affirmative Discrimination.* New York: Basic Books, 1976.
Rossum, Ralph. *Reverse Discrimination: The Constitutional Debate.* New York: Dekker, 1980.
Sindler, Allan P. *Bakke, Defunis, and Minority Admissions.* New York: Longman, 1978.

Regents of the University of California v. Bakke
438 U.S. 265, 98 S.Ct. 2733 (1978)

Alan Bakke, a white male, applied but was denied admission to the medical school at the University of California at Davis. There were only 100 openings each year, and 16 of them were reserved for "disadvantaged" minority students (blacks, Hispanics, Asians, and American Indians). Bakke had been twice denied admission before, even though minorities who had lower grade point averages and lower scores on the Medical College Admission Test were admitted. And he decided to challenge the constitutionality of the admission policy for minorities, contending that he was denied admission on account of his race.

A state superior court held that Davis's program violated Title VI of the Civil Rights Act, the equal protection clause of the Fourteenth Amendment, and a provision of the state constitution. However, the court declined to order Bakke's admission on the grounds that he would not have been admitted even if Davis did not have its affirmative action program. Subsequently, the state supreme court ordered Bakke's admission and reaffirmed that Davis's program impermissibly used race as a factor in its admissions program, and that it could not survive "strict scrutiny" under the Fourteenth Amendment's equal protection clause because the program was not the least restrictive means of advancing the state's interests in an integrated medical profession and increasing the number of doctors serving minority patients.

The Regents of the University of California appealed the state supreme court's decision to the Supreme Court. The controversy over affirmative action programs and claims of reverse discrimination were politically volatile for the Court and the country. At the time, an unprecedented number (120) of organizations joined fifty-eight *amicus* ("friend of the court") briefs: eighty-three for the university, thirty-two for Bakke, and five urging the Court not to decide the case.

The Court's ruling was announced by Justice Lewis F. Powell in an opinion upholding affirmative action programs (but not quota systems like that at Davis), and admitting Bakke to the medical school. Powell delivered the Court's ruling because the other justices were unwilling to bend on their positions and were divided four to four on the statutory and constitutional issues.

Chief Justice Burger, and Justices Rehnquist and Stewart accepted the view of Justice Stevens that the Court need not address the question of whether affirmative action programs violate the Constitution. They voted to strike down quota systems as an impermissible racial classification under Title VI of the Civil Rights Act of 1964 and to admit Bakke.

Justices White, Marshall, and Blackmun sided with Brennan in reaching the constitutional question and holding that affirmative action programs, including quotas, are constitutionally permissible remedies for past racial discrimination. They would not have admitted Bakke.

Justice Powell massed the votes, but not the justices' support for his opinion, from each bloc on each of the two key issues. His opinion finds that quota systems are invalid and that Bakke should have been admitted, relying on the four votes of the

Stevens bloc. At the same time, Powell upholds affirmative action programs in universities and thereby won the vote of the Brennan bloc. Powell, however, refused to accept Brennan's view that past racial discrimination justified racial quotas. Instead, Powell holds that affirmative action programs, but not quotas, are permissible because under the First Amendment universities need a diverse student body to ensure academic freedom and the educational process. Powell's pragmatic rationalization for the controversial decision thus had the support of no other justice.

Justice POWELL delivers the opinion of the Court.

For the reasons stated in the following opinion, I believe that so much of the judgment of the California court as holds petitioner's special admissions program unlawful and directs that respondent be admitted to the Medical School must be affirmed. For the reasons expressed in a separate opinion, my Brothers the CHIEF JUSTICE, Justice STEWART, Justice REHNQUIST and Justice STEVENS concur in this judgment.

I also conclude for the reasons stated in the following opinion that the portion of the court's judgment enjoining petitioner from according any consideration to race in its admissions process must be reversed. For reasons expressed in separate opinions, my Brothers Justice BRENNAN, Justice WHITE, Justice MARSHALL, and Justice BLACKMUN concur in this judgment.

Affirmed in part and reversed in part. . . .

The guarantees of the Fourteenth Amendment extend to all persons. Its language is explicit: "No State shall . . . deny to any person within its jurisdiction the equal protection of the laws." It is settled beyond question that the "rights created by the first section of the Fourteenth Amendment are, by its terms, guaranteed to the individual. The rights established are personal rights." *Shelley v. Kraemer,* 334 U.S. 1 [(1948)]. The guarantee of equal protection cannot mean one thing when applied to one individual and something else when applied to a person of another color. If both are not accorded the same protection, then it is not equal. . . .

The Court has never questioned the validity of those pronouncements. Racial and ethnic distinctions of any sort are inherently suspect and thus call for the most exacting judicial examination.

This perception of racial and ethnic distinctions is rooted in our Nation's constitutional and demographic history. The Court's initial view of the Fourteenth Amendment was that its "one pervading purpose" was "the freedom of the slave race, the security and firm establishment of that freedom, and the protection of the newly-made freeman and citizen from the oppressions of those who had formerly exercised dominion over him." *Slaughter-*

House Cases, 16 Wall. 36 (1873). The Equal Protection Clause, however, was "[v]irtually strangled in infancy by post-civil-war judicial reactionism." It was relegated to decades of relative desuetude while the Due Process Clause of the Fourteenth Amendment, after a short germinal period, flourished as a cornerstone in the Court's defense of property and liberty of contract. See, *e.g., Mugler v. Kansas,* 123 U.S. 623 (1887); *Allgeyer v. Louisiana,* 165 U.S. 578, [(1897)]; *Lochner v. New York,* 198 U.S. 45 (1905). In that cause, the Fourteenth Amendment's "one pervading purpose" was displaced. See, *e.g., Plessy v. Ferguson,* 163 U.S. 537 (1896). It was only as the era of substantive due process came to a close, see, *e.g., Nebbia v. New York,* 291 U.S. 502 (1934); *West Coast Hotel Co. v. Parrish,* 300 U.S. 379 (1937), that the Equal Protection Clause began to attain a genuine measure of vitality, see, *e.g., United States v. Carolene Products,* 304 U.S. 144 (1938); *Skinner v. Oklahoma ex rel. Williamson,* [316 U.S. 535 (1942)].

By that time it was no longer possible to peg the guarantees of the Fourteenth Amendment to the struggle for equality of one racial minority. During the dormancy of the Equal Protection Clause, the United States had become a Nation of minorities. Each had to struggle—and to some extent struggles still—to overcome the prejudices not of a monolithic majority, but of a "majority" composed of various minority groups of whom it was said—perhaps unfairly in many cases—that a shared characteristic was a willingness to disadvantage other groups. As the Nation filled with the stock of many lands, the reach of the Clause was gradually extended to all ethnic groups seeking protection from official discrimination. See *Strauder v. West Virginia,* 100 U.S. 303 (1880) (Celtic Irishmen) (dictum); *Yick Wo v. Hopkins,* 118 U.S. 356 (1886) (Chinese); *Truax v. Raich,* 239 U.S. 33, (1915) (Austrian resident aliens); *Korematsu,* [*v. United States,* 323 U.S. 214 (1944)] (Japanese); *Hernandez v. Texas,* 347 U.S. 475 (1954) (Mexican-Americans). The guarantees of equal protection, said the Court in *Yick Wo,* "are universal in their application, to all persons within the territorial jurisdiction, without regard to any differences of race, of color, or of nationality; and the equal protection of the laws is a pledge of the protection of equal laws."

Although many of the Framers of the Fourteenth Amendment conceived of its primary function as bridging the vast distance between members of the Negro race and the white "majority," *Slaughter-House Cases, supra,* the Amendment itself was framed in universal terms, without reference to color, ethnic origin, or condition of prior servitude. As this Court recently remarked in interpreting the 1866 Civil Rights Act to extend to claims of racial discrimination against white persons, "the 39th Congress was intent upon establishing in the federal law a broader principle than would have been necessary simply to meet the particular and immediate plight of the newly freed Negro slaves." *McDonald v. Santa Fe Trail Transportation Co.*, 427 U.S. 273 (1976). And that legislation was specifically broadened in 1870 to ensure that "all persons," not merely "citizens," would enjoy equal rights under the law. See *Runyon v. McCrary*, 427 U.S. 160 [(1976)] (WHITE, J., dissenting). Indeed, it is not unlikely that among the Framers were many who would have applauded a reading of the Equal Protection Clause that states a principle of universal application and is responsive to the racial, ethnic, and cultural diversity of the Nation. . . .

Over the past 30 years, this Court has embarked upon the crucial mission of interpreting the Equal Protection Clause with the view of assuring to all persons "the protection of equal laws," *Yick Wo, supra*, in a Nation confronting a legacy of slavery and racial discrimination. . . . Because the landmark decisions in this area arose in response to the continued exclusion of Negroes from the mainstream of American society, they could be characterized as involving discrimination by the "majority" white race against the Negro minority. But they need not be read as depending upon that characterization for their results. It suffices to say that "[o]ver the years, this Court has consistently repudiated '[d]istinctions between citizens solely because of their ancestry' as being 'odious to a free people whose institutions are founded upon the doctrine of equality.'" *Loving v. Virginia*, 388 U.S. 1 (1967), quoting *Hirabayashi*, [*v. United States*], 320 U.S. [81 (1943)].

Petitioner urges us to adopt for the first time a more restrictive view of the Equal Protection Clause and hold that discrimination against members of the white "majority" cannot be suspect if its purpose can be characterized as "benign." The clock of our liberties, however, cannot be turned back to 1868. It is far too late to argue that the guarantee of equal protection to *all* persons permits the recognition of special wards entitled to a degree of protection greater than that accorded others. "The Fourteenth Amendment is not directed solely against discrimination due to a 'two-class theory'—that is, based upon differences between 'white' and Negro." *Hernandez* [*v. Texas*, 47 U.S. 475 (1954)].

Once the artificial line of a "two-class theory" of the Fourteenth Amendment is put aside, the difficulties entailed in varying the level of judicial review according to a perceived "preferred" status of a particular racial or ethnic minority are intractable. The concepts of "majority" and "minority" necessarily reflect temporary arrangements and political judgments. As observed above, the white "majority" itself is composed of various minority groups, most of which can lay claim to a history of prior discrimination at the hands of the State and private individuals. Not all of these groups can receive preferential treatment and corresponding judicial tolerance of distinctions drawn in terms of race and nationality, for then the only "majority" left would be a new minority of white Anglo-Saxon Protestants. There is no principled basis for deciding which groups would merit "heightened judicial solicitude" and which would not. Courts would be asked to evaluate the extent of the prejudice and consequent harm suffered by various minority groups. Those whose societal injury is thought to exceed some arbitrary level of tolerability then would be entitled to preferential classifications at the expense of individuals belonging to other groups. Those classifications would be free from exacting judicial scrutiny. As these preferences began to have their desired effect, and the consequences of past discrimination were undone, new judicial rankings would be necessary. The kind of variable sociological and political analysis necessary to produce such rankings simply does not lie within the judicial competence—even if they otherwise were politically feasible and socially desirable.

Moreover, there are serious problems of justice connected with the idea of preference itself. First, it may not always be clear that a so-called preference is in fact benign. Courts may be asked to validate burdens imposed upon individual members of a particular group in order to advance the group's general interest. Nothing in the Constitution supports the notion that individuals may be asked to suffer otherwise impermissible burdens in order to enhance the societal standing of their ethnic groups. Second, preferential programs may only reinforce common stereotypes holding that certain groups are unable to achieve success without special protection based on a factor having no relationship to individual worth. See *DeFunis v. Odegaard,* 416 U.S. 312 (1974) (DOUGLAS, J., dissenting). Third, there is a measure of inequity in forcing innocent persons in respondent's position to bear the burdens of redressing grievances not of their making.

By hitching the meaning of the Equal Protection Clause to these transitory considerations, we would be holding, as a constitutional principle, that judicial scrutiny of classifications touching on racial and ethnic background may vary with the ebb and flow of political forces. Disparate constitutional tolerance of such classifications well may serve to exacerbate racial and ethnic antagonisms rather than alleviate them. Also, the mutability of a constitutional principle, based upon shifting political and social judgments, undermines the chances for consistent application of the Constitution from one generation to the next, a critical feature of its coherent interpretation. *Pollock v. Farmers' Loan & Trust Co.,* 157 U.S. 429 (1895) (WHITE, J., dissenting). In expounding the Constitution, the Court's role is to discern "principles sufficiently absolute to give them roots throughout the community and continuity over significant periods of time, and to lift them above the level of the pragmatic political judgments of a particular time and place." A. Cox, The Role of the Supreme Court in American Government 114 (1976).

If it is the individual who is entitled to judicial protection against classifications based upon his racial or ethnic background because such distinctions impinge upon personal rights, rather than the individual only because of his membership in a particular group, then constitutional standards may be applied consistently. Political judgments regarding the necessity for the particular classification may be weighed in the constitutional balance, *Korematsu v. United States,* 323 U.S. 194 (1944), but the standard of justification will remain constant. This is as it should be, since those political judgments are the product of rough compromise struck by contending groups within the democratic process. When they touch upon an individual's race or ethnic background, he is entitled to a judicial determination that the burden he is asked to bear on that basis is precisely tailored to serve a compelling governmental interest. The Constitution guarantees that right to every person regardless of his background.

Petitioner contends that on several occasions this Court has approved preferential classifications without applying the most exacting scrutiny. Most of the cases upon which petitioner relies are drawn from three areas: school desegregation, employment discrimination, and sex discrimination. Each of the cases cited presented a situation materially different from the facts of this case.

The school desegregation cases are inapposite. Each involved remedies for clearly determined constitutional violations. . . . Racial classifications thus were designed as remedies for the vindication of constitutional entitlement. Moreover, the scope of the remedies was not permitted to exceed the extent of the violations. . . . Here, there was no judicial determination of constitutional violation as a predicate for the formulation of a remedial classification.

The employment discrimination cases also do not advance petitioner's cause. . . .

In this case . . . there has been no determination by the legislature or a responsible administrative agency that the University engaged in a discriminatory practice requiring remedial efforts. Moreover, the operation of petitioner's special admissions program is quite different from the remedial measures approved in those cases. It prefers the designated minority groups at the expense of other individuals who are totally foreclosed from competition for the 16 special admissions seats in every Medical School class. Because of that foreclosure, some individuals are excluded from enjoyment of a state-provided benefit—admission to the Medical School—they otherwise would receive. When a classification denies an individual opportunities or benefits enjoyed by others solely because of his race or ethnic background, it must be regarded as suspect. *E. g., McLaurin v. Oklahoma State Regents,* 339 U.S. [637 (1950)].

We have held that in "order to justify the use of a suspect

classification, a State must show that its purpose or interest is both constitutionally permissible and substantial, and that its use of the classification is 'necessary . . . to the accomplishment' of its purpose or the safeguarding of its interest." *In re Griffiths*, 413 U.S. 717 (1973) (footnotes omitted); *Loving v. Virginia*, 388 U.S. [1 (1967)]; *McLaughlin v. Florida*, 379 U.S. 184 (1964). The special admissions program purports to serve the purposes of: (i) "reducing the historic deficit of traditionally disfavored minorities in medical schools and in the medical profession," Brief for Petitioner 32; (ii) countering the effects of societal discrimination; (iii) increasing the number of physicians who will practice in communities currently underserved; and (iv) obtaining the educational benefits that flow from an ethnically diverse student body. It is necessary to decide which, if any, of these purposes is substantial enough to support the use of a suspect classification.

If petitioner's purpose is to assure within its student body some specified percentage of a particular group merely because of its race or ethnic origin, such a preferential purpose must be rejected not as insubstantial but as facially invalid. Preferring members of any one group for no reason other than race or ethnic origin is discrimination for its own sake. This the Constitution forbids. . . .

The State certainly has a legitimate and substantial interest in ameliorating, or eliminating where feasible, the disabling effects of identified discrimination. The line of school desegregation cases, commencing with *Brown*, attests to the importance of this state goal and the commitment of the judiciary to affirm all lawful means toward its attainment. In the school cases, the States were required by court order to redress the wrongs worked by specific instances of racial discrimination. That goal was far more focused than the remedying of the effects of "societal discrimination," an amorphous concept of injury that may be ageless in its reach into the past.

We have never approved a classification that aids persons perceived as members of relatively victimized groups at the expense of other innocent individuals in the absence of judicial, legislative, or administrative findings of constitutional or statutory violations. After such findings have been made, the governmental interest in preferring members of the injured groups at the expense of others is substantial, since the legal rights of the victims must be vindicated. In such a case, the extent of the injury and the consequent remedy will have been judicially, legislatively, or administratively defined. Also, the remedial action usually remains subject to continuing oversight to assure that it will work the least harm possible to other innocent persons competing for the benefit. Without such findings of constitutional or statutory violations, it cannot be said that the government has any greater interest in helping one individual than in refraining from harming another. Thus, the government has no compelling justification for inflicting such harm.

Petitioner does not purport to have made, and is in no position to make, such findings. Its broad mission is education, not the formulation of any legislative policy or the adjudication of particular claims of illegality. For reasons similar to those stated [above in] this opinion, isolated segments of our vast governmental structures are not competent to make those decisions, at least in the absence of legislative mandates and legislatively determined criteria. . . . Lacking this capability, petitioner has not carried its burden of justification on this issue.

Hence, the purpose of helping certain groups whom the faculty of the Davis Medical School perceived as victims of "societal discrimination" does not justify a classification that imposes disadvantages upon persons like respondent, who bear no responsibility for whatever harm the beneficiaries of the special admissions program are thought to have suffered. To hold otherwise would be to convert a remedy heretofore reserved for violations of legal rights into a privilege that all institutions throughout the Nation could grant at their pleasure to whatever groups are perceived as victims of societal discrimination. That is a step we have never approved. . . .

Petitioner identifies, as another purpose of its program, improving the delivery of health-care services to communities currently underserved. It may be assumed that in some situations a State's interest in facilitating the health care of its citizens is sufficiently compelling to support the use of a suspect classification. But there is virtually no evidence in the record indicating that petitioner's special admissions program is either needed or geared to promote that goal. . . .

Petitioner simply has not carried its burden of demonstrating that it must prefer members of particular ethnic groups over all other individuals in order to promote better health-care delivery to deprived citizens. Indeed, petitioner has not shown that its preferential classification is likely to have any significant effect on the problem.

The fourth goal asserted by petitioner is the attainment of a diverse student body. This clearly is a constitutionally permissible goal for an institution of higher education. Academic freedom, though not a specifically enumerated constitutional right, long has been viewed as a special concern of the First Amendment. The freedom of a university to make its own judgments as to education includes the selection of its student body. . . .

[In] arguing that its universities must be accorded the right to select those students who will contribute the most to the "robust exchange of ideas," petitioner invokes a countervailing constitutional interest, that of the First Amendment. In this light, petitioner must be viewed as seeking to achieve a goal that is of paramount importance in the fulfillment of its mission. . . .

Physicians serve a heterogeneous population. An otherwise qualified medical student with a particular background—whether it be ethnic, geographic, culturally advantaged or disadvantaged—may bring to a professional school of medicine experiences, outlooks, and ideas that enrich the training of its student body and better equip its graduates to render with understanding their vital service to humanity.

Ethnic diversity, however, is only one element in a range of factors a university properly may consider in attaining the goal of a heterogeneous student body. Although a university must have wide discretion in making the sensitive judgments as to who should be admitted, constitutional limitations protecting individual rights may not be disregarded. Respondent urges—and the courts below have held—that petitioner's dual admissions program is a racial classification that impermissibly infringes his rights under the Fourteenth Amendment. As the interest of diversity is compelling in the context of a university's admissions program, the question remains whether the program's racial classification is necessary to promote this interest.

It may be assumed that the reservation of a specified number of seats in each class for individuals from the preferred ethnic groups would contribute to the attainment of considerable ethnic diversity in the student body. But petitioner's argument that this is the only effective means of serving the interest of diversity is seriously flawed. In a most fundamental sense the argument misconceives the nature of the state interest that would justify consideration of race or ethnic background. It is not an interest in simple ethnic diversity, in which a specified percentage of the student body is in effect guaranteed to be members of selected ethnic groups, with the remaining percentage an undifferentiated aggregation of students. The diversity that furthers a compelling state interest encompasses a far broader array of qualifications and characteristics of which racial or ethnic origin is but a single though important element. Petitioner's special admissions program, focused *solely* on ethnic diversity, would hinder rather than further attainment of genuine diversity.

Nor would the state interest in genuine diversity be served by expanding petitioner's two-track system into a multitrack program with a prescribed number of seats set aside for each identifiable category of applicants. Indeed, it is inconceivable that a university would thus pursue the logic of petitioner's two-track program to the illogical end of insulating each category of applicants with certain desired qualifications from competition with all other applicants.

The experience of other university admissions programs, which take race into account in achieving the educational diversity valued by the First Amendment, demonstrates that the assignment of a fixed number of places to a minority group is not a necessary means toward that end. An illuminating example is found in the Harvard College program:

"In recent years Harvard College has expanded the concept of diversity to include students from disadvantaged economic, racial and ethnic groups. Harvard College now recruits not only Californians or Louisianans but also blacks and Chicanos and other minority students. . . .

"In practice, this new definition of diversity has meant that race has been a factor in some admission decisions. When the Committee on Admissions reviews the large middle group of applicants who are 'admissible' and deemed capable of doing good work in their courses, the race of an applicant may tip the balance in his favor just as geographic origin or a life spent on a farm may tip the balance in other candidates' cases. A farm boy from Idaho can bring something to Harvard College that a Bostonian cannot offer. Similarly, a black student can usually bring something that a white person cannot offer.

"In Harvard College admissions the Committee has not set target-quotas for the number of blacks, or of musicians, football players, physicists or Californians to be admitted in a given year. . . . But that awareness [of the necessity of including more than a token number of black students] does not mean that the Committee sets a minimum number of blacks or of people from west of the Mississippi who are to be admitted. It means only that in choosing among thousands of applicants who are not only 'admissible' academically but have other strong qualities, the Committee, with a number of criteria in mind, pays some attention to distribution among many types and categories of students." App. to Brief for Columbia University, Harvard University, Stanford University, and the University of Pennsylvania, as *Amici Curiae* 2–3.

In such an admissions program, race or ethnic background may be deemed a "plus" in a particular applicant's file, yet it does not insulate the individual from comparison with all other candidates for the available seats. The file of a particular black applicant may be examined for his potential contribution to diversity without the factor of race being decisive when compared, for example, with that of an applicant identified as an Italian-American if the latter is thought to exhibit qualities more likely to promote beneficial educational pluralism. Such qualities could include exceptional personal talents, unique work or service experience, leadership potential, maturity, demonstrated compassion, a history of overcoming disadvantage, ability to communicate with the poor, or other qualifications deemed important. In short, an admissions program operated in that way is flexible enough to consider all pertinent elements of diversity in light of the particular qualifications of each applicant, and to place them on the same footing for consideration, although not necessarily according them the same weight. Indeed the weight attributed to a particular quality may vary from year to year depending upon the "mix" both of the student body and the applicants for the incoming class.

This kind of program treats each applicant as an individual in the admissions process. The applicant who loses out on the last available seat to another candidate receiving a "plus" on the basis of ethnic background will not have been foreclosed from all consideration for that seat simply because he was not the right color or had the wrong surname. It would mean only that his combined qualifications, which may have included similar nonobjective factors, did not outweigh those of the other applicant. His qualifications would have been weighed fairly and competitively, and he would have no basis to complain of unequal treatment under the Fourteenth Amendment. . . .

In summary, it is evident that the Davis special admissions program involves the use of an explicit racial classification never before countenanced by this Court. It tells applicants who are not Negro, Asian, or Chicano that they are totally excluded from a specific percentage of the seats in an entering class. No matter how strong their qualifications, quantitative and extracurricular, including their own potential for contribution to educational diversity, they are never afforded the chance to compete with applicants from the preferred groups for the special admissions seats. At the same time, the preferred applicants have the opportunity to compete for every seat in the class.

The fatal flaw in petitioner's preferential program is its disregard of individual rights as guaranteed by the Fourteenth Amendment. Such rights are not absolute. But when a State's distribution of benefits or imposition of burdens hinges on ancestry or the color of a person's skin, that individual is entitled to a demonstration that the challenged classification is necessary to promote a substantial state interest. Petitioner has failed to carry this burden. For this reason, that portion of the California court's judgment holding petitioner's special admissions program invalid under the Fourteenth Amendment must be affirmed.

In enjoining petitioner from ever considering the race of any applicant, however, the courts below failed to recognize that the State has a substantial interest that legitimately may be served by a properly devised admissions program involving the competitive consideration of race and ethnic origin. For this reason, so much of the California court's judgment as enjoins petitioner from any consideration of the race of any applicant must be reversed.

Justice BRENNAN, Justice WHITE, Justice MARSHALL, and Justice BLACKMUN, concurring in part and dissenting in part.

The Court today, in reversing in part the judgment of the Supreme Court of California, affirms the constitutional power of Federal and State Governments to act affirmatively to achieve equal opportunity for all. The difficulty of the issue presented—whether government may use race-conscious programs to redress the continuing effects of past discrimination—and the mature consideration which each of our Brethren has brought to it have resulted in many opinions, no single one speaking for the Court. But this should not and must not mask the central meaning of today's opinions: Government may take race into account when it acts not to demean or insult any racial group, but to remedy disadvantages cast on minorities by past racial prejudice, at least when appropriate findings have been made by judicial, legislative, or administrative bodies with competence to act in this area. . . .

We agree with Justice POWELL that, as applied to the case before us, Title VI goes no further in prohibiting the use of race than the Equal Protection Clause of the Fourteenth Amendment itself. We also agree that the effect of the California Supreme Court's affirmance of the judgment of the Superior Court of California would be to prohibit the University from establishing in the future affirmative-action programs that take race into account. Since we conclude that the affirmative admissions program at the Davis Medical School is constitutional, we would reverse the judgment below in all respects. Justice POWELL agrees that some uses of race in university admissions are permissible and, therefore, he joins with us to make five votes reversing the judgment below insofar as it prohibits the University from establishing race-conscious programs in the future. . . .

The threshold question we must decide is whether Title VI of the Civil Rights Act of 1964 bars recipients of federal funds from giving preferential consideration to disadvantaged members of racial minorities as part of a program designed to enable such individuals to surmount the obstacles imposed by racial discrimination. We join parts . . . of our Brother POWELL's opinion and three of us agree with his conclusion that this case does not require us to resolve the question whether there is a private right of action under Title VI.

In our view, Title VI prohibits only those uses of racial criteria that would violate the Fourteenth Amendment if employed by a State or its agencies; it does not bar the preferential treatment of racial minorities as a means of remedying past societal discrimination to the extent that such action is consistent with the Fourteenth Amendment. The legislative history of Title VI, administrative regulations interpreting the statute, subsequent congressional and executive action, and the prior decisions of this Court compel this conclusion. None of these sources lends support to the proposition that Congress intended to bar all race-conscious efforts to extend the benefits of federally financed programs to minorities who have been historically excluded from the full benefits of American life. . . .

Congress recognized that Negroes, in some cases with congressional acquiescence, were being discriminated against in the administration of programs and denied the full benefits of activities receiving federal financial support. It was aware that there were many federally funded programs and institutions which discriminated against minorities in a manner inconsistent with the standards of the Fifth and Fourteenth Amendments but whose activities might not involve sufficient state or federal action so as to be in violation of these Amendments. Moreover, Congress believed that it was questionable whether the Executive Branch possessed legal authority to terminate the funding of activities on the ground that they discriminated racially against Negroes in a manner violative of the standards contained in the Fourteenth and Fifth Amendments. Congress' solution was to end the Government's complicity in constitutionally forbidden racial discrimination by providing the Executive Branch with the authority and the obligation to terminate its financial support of any activity which employed racial criteria in a manner condemned by the Constitution.

Of course, it might be argued that the Congress which enacted Title VI understood the Constitution to require strict racial neutrality or color blindness, and then enshrined that concept as a rule of statutory law. Later interpretation and clarification of the Constitution to permit remedial use of race would then not dislodge Title VI's prohibition of race-conscious action. But there are three compelling reasons to reject such a hypothesis.

First, no decision of this Court has ever adopted the proposition that the Constitution must be colorblind.

Second, even if it could be argued in 1964 that the Constitution might conceivably require color blindness, Congress surely would not have chosen to codify such a view unless the Constitution clearly required it. The legislative history of Title VI, as well as the statute itself, reveals a desire to induce voluntary compliance with the requirement of nondiscriminatory treatment. . . . It is inconceivable that Congress intended to encourage voluntary efforts to eliminate the evil of racial discrimination while at the same time forbidding the voluntary use of race-conscious remedies to cure acknowledged or obvious statutory violations. Yet a reading of Title VI as prohibiting all action predicated upon race which adversely affects any individual would require recipients guilty of discrimination to await the imposition of such remedies by the Executive Branch. Indeed, such an interpretation of Title VI would prevent recipients of federal funds from taking race into account even when necessary to bring their programs into compliance with federal constitutional requirements. This would be a remarkable reading of a statute designed to eliminate constitutional violations, especially in light of judicial decisions holding that under certain circumstances the remedial use of racial criteria is not only permissible but is constitutionally required to eradicate constitutional violations. . . .

Third, the legislative history shows that Congress specifically eschewed any static definition of discrimination in favor of broad language that could be shaped by experience, administrative necessity, and evolving judicial doctrine. Although it is clear from the debates that the supporters of Title VI intended to ban uses of race prohibited by the Constitution and, more specifically, the maintenance of segregated facilities, they never precisely defined the term "discrimination," or what constituted an exclusion from participation or a denial of benefits on the ground of race. . . .

Congress' resolve not to incorporate a static definition of discrimination into Title VI is not surprising. In 1963 and 1964, when Title VI was drafted and debated, the courts had only recently applied the Equal Protection Clause to strike down public racial discrimination in America, and the scope of that Clause's nondiscrimination principle was in a state of flux and rapid evolution. Many questions, such as whether the Fourteenth Amendment barred only *de jure* discrimination or in at least some circumstances reached *de facto* discrimination, had not yet received an authoritative judicial resolution. The congressional debate reflects an awareness of the evolutionary change that constitutional law in the area of racial discrimination was undergoing in 1964.

In sum, Congress' equating of Title VI's prohibition with the commands of the Fifth and Fourteenth Amendments, its refusal precisely to define that racial discrimination which it intended to prohibit, and its expectation that the statute would be administered in a flexible manner, compel the conclusion that Congress intended the meaning of the statute's prohibition to evolve with the interpretation of the commands of the Constitution. . . .

Finally, congressional action subsequent to the passage of Title VI eliminates any possible doubt about Congress' views concerning the permissibility of racial preferences for the purpose of assisting disadvantaged racial minorities. It confirms that Congress did not intend to prohibit and does not now believe that Title VI prohibits the consideration of race as part of a remedy for societal discrimination even where there is no showing that the institution extending the preference has been guilty of past discrimination nor any judicial finding that the particular beneficiaries of the racial preference have been adversely affected by societal discrimination.

Just last year Congress enacted legislation explicitly requiring that no grants shall be made "for any local public works project unless the applicant gives satisfactory assurance to the Secretary [of Commerce] that at least 10 per centum of the amount of each grant shall be expended for minority business enterprises." The statute defines the term "minority business enterprise" as "a business, at least 50 per centum of which is owned by minority group members or, in case of a publicly owned business, at least 51 per centum of the stock of which is owned by minority group members." The term "minority group members" is defined in explicitly racial terms: "citizens of the United States who are Negroes, Spanish-speaking, Orientals, Indians, Eskimos, and Aleuts." Although the statute contains an exemption from this requirement "to the extent that the Secretary determines otherwise," this escape clause was provided only to deal with the possibility that certain areas of the country might not contain sufficient qualified "minority business enterprises" to permit compliance with the quota provisions of the legislation. . . .

Prior decisions of this Court also strongly suggest that Title VI does not prohibit the remedial use of race where such action is constitutionally permissible. In *Lau v. Nichols*, 414 U.S. 563 (1974), the Court held that the failure of the San Francisco school system to provide English-language instruction to students of Chinese ancestry who do not speak English, or to provide them with instruction in Chinese, constituted a violation of Title VI. . . .

These prior decisions are indicative of the Court's unwillingness to construe remedial statutes designed to eliminate discrimination against racial minorities in a manner which would impede efforts to attain this objective. There is no justification for departing from this course in the case of Title VI and frustrating the clear judgment of Congress that race-conscious remedial action is permissible. . . .

We conclude, therefore, that racial classifications are not *per se* invalid under the Fourteenth Amendment. Accordingly, we turn to the problem of articulating what our role should be in reviewing state action that expressly classifies by race. . . .

Unquestionably we have held that a government practice or statute which restricts "fundamental rights" or which contains "suspect classifications" is to be subjected to "strict scrutiny" and can be justified only if it furthers a compelling government purpose and, even then, only if no less restrictive alternative is available. See, *e.g., San Antonio Independent School District v. Rodriguez*, 411 U.S. 1 (1973); *Dunn v. Blumstein*, 405 U.S. 330 (1972). But no fundamental right is involved here. See *San Antonio*. Nor do whites as a class have any of the "traditional indicia of suspectness: the class is not saddled with such disabilities, or subjected to such a history of purposeful unequal treatment, or relegated to such a position of political powerlessness as to command extraordinary protection from the majoritarian political process.". . .

On the other hand, the fact that this case does not fit neatly into our prior analytic framework for race cases does not mean that it should be analyzed by applying the very loose rational-basis standard of review that is the very least that is always applied in equal protection cases. " '[t]he mere recitation of a benign, compensatory purpose is not an automatic shield which protects against any inquiry into the actual purposes underlying a statutory scheme.' " *Califano v. Webster,* 430 U.S. 313 (1977), quoting *Weinberger v. Wiesenfeld,* 420 U.S. 636 (1975). Instead, a number of considerations—developed in gender-discrimination cases but which carry even more force when applied to racial classifications—lead us to conclude that racial classifications designed to further remedial purposes " 'must serve important governmental objectives and must be substantially related to achievement of those objectives.' ". . .

First, race, like, "gender-based classifications too often [has] been inexcusably utilized to stereotype and stigmatize politically powerless segments of society." *Kahn v. Shevin,* 416 U.S. 351 (1974) (dissenting opinion). While a carefully tailored statute designed to remedy past discrimination could avoid these vices, we nonetheless have recognized that the line between honest and thoughtful appraisal of the effects of past discrimination and paternalistic stereotyping is not so clear and that a statute based on the latter is patently capable of stigmatizing all women with a badge of inferiority. . . . State programs designed ostensibly to ameliorate the effects of past racial discrimination obviously create the same hazard of stigma, since they may promote racial separatism and reinforce the views of those who believe that members of racial minorities are inherently incapable of succeeding on their own.

Second, race, like gender and illegitimacy, is an immutable characteristic which its possessors are powerless to escape or set aside. While a classification is not *per se* invalid because it divides classes on the basis of an immutable characteristic, it is nevertheless true that such divisions are contrary to our deep belief that "legal burdens should bear some relationship to individual responsibility or wrongdoing," and that advancement sanctioned, sponsored, or approved by the State should ideally be based on individual merit or achievement, or at the least on factors within the control of an individual. . . .

Because this principle is so deeply rooted it might be supposed that it would be considered in the legislative process and weighed against the benefits of programs preferring individuals because of their race. But this is not necessarily so: The "natural consequence of our governing process [may well be] that the most 'discrete and insular' of whites . . . will be called upon to bear the immediate, direct costs of benign discrimination." Moreover, it is clear from our cases that there are limits beyond which majorities may not go when they classify on the basis of immutable characteristics. Thus, even if the concern for individualism is weighed by the political process, that weighing cannot waive the personal rights of individuals under the Fourteenth Amendment.

In sum, because of the significant risk that racial classifications established for ostensibly benign purposes can be misused, causing effects not unlike those created by invidious classifications, it is inappropriate to inquire only whether there is any conceivable basis that might sustain such a classification. Instead, to justify such a classification an important and articulated purpose for its use must be shown. In addition, any statute must be stricken that stigmatizes any group or that singles out those least well represented in the political process to bear the brunt of a benign program. Thus, our review under the Fourteenth Amendment should be strict—not " 'strict' in theory and fatal in fact," because it is stigma that causes fatality—but strict and searching nonetheless. . . .

Certainly, on the basis of the undisputed factual submissions before this Court, Davis had a sound basis for believing that the problem of underrepresentation of minorities was substantial and chronic and that the problem was attributable to handicaps imposed on minority applicants by past and present racial discrimination. Until at least 1973, the practice of medicine in this country was, in fact, if not in law, largely the prerogative of whites. In 1950, for example, while Negroes constituted 10% of the total population, Negro physicians constituted only 2.2% of the total number of physicians. The overwhelming majority of these, moreover, were educated in two predominantly Negro medical schools, Howard and Meharry. By 1970, the gap between the proportion of Negroes in medicine and their proportion in the population had widened: The number of Negroes employed in medicine remained frozen at 2.2% while the Negro population had increased to 11.1%. The number of Negro admittees to predominantly white medical schools, moreover, had declined in absolute numbers during the years 1955 to 1964.

Moreover, Davis had very good reason to believe that the national pattern of underrepresentation of minorities in medicine would be perpetuated if it retained a single admissions standard. For example, the entering classes in 1968 and 1969, the years in which such a standard was used, included only 1 Chicano and 2 Negroes out of the 50 admittees for each year. Nor is there any relief from this pattern of underrepresentation in the statistics for the regular admissions program in later years.

Davis clearly could conclude that the serious and persistent underrepresentation of minorities in medicine depicted by these statistics is the result of handicaps under which minority applicants labor as a consequence of a background of deliberate, purposeful discrimination against minorities in education and in society generally, as well as in the medical profession. . . .

The second prong of our test—whether the Davis program stigmatizes any discrete group or individual and whether race is reasonably used in light of the program's objectives—is clearly satisfied by the Davis program.

It is not even claimed that Davis' program in any way operates to stigmatize or single out any discrete and insular, or even any identifiable, nonminority group. Nor will harm comparable to that imposed upon racial minorities by exclusion or separation on grounds of race be the likely result of the program. It does not, for example, establish an exclusive preserve for minority students apart from and exclusive of whites. Rather, its purpose is to overcome the effects of segregation by bringing the races together. True, whites are excluded from participation in the special admissions program, but this fact only operates to reduce the number of whites to be admitted in the regular admissions program in order to permit admission of a reasonable percentage—less than their proportion of the California population—of otherwise underrepresented qualified minority applicants.

Nor was Bakke in any sense stamped as inferior by the Medical School's rejection of him. Indeed, it is conceded by all that he satisfied those criteria regarded by the school as generally relevant to academic performance better than most of the minority members who were admitted. Moreover, there is absolutely no basis for concluding that Bakke's rejection as a result of Davis' use of racial preference will affect him throughout his life in the same way as the segregation of the Negro schoolchildren in *Brown I* would have affected them. Unlike discrimination against racial minorities, the use of racial preferences for remedial purposes does not inflict a pervasive injury upon individual whites in the sense that wherever they go or whatever they do there is a significant likelihood that they will be treated as second-class citizens because of their color. This distinction does not mean that the exclusion of a white resulting from the preferential use of race is not sufficiently serious to require justification; but it does mean that the injury inflicted by such a policy is not distinguishable from disadvantages caused by a wide range of government actions, none of which has ever been thought impermissible for that reason alone.

In addition, there is simply no evidence that the Davis program discriminates intentionally or unintentionally against any minority group which it purports to benefit. The program does not establish a quota in the invidious sense of a ceiling on the number of minority applicants to be admitted. Nor can the program reasonably be regarded as stigmatizing the program's beneficiaries or their race as inferior. The Davis program does not simply advance less qualified applicants; rather, it compensates applicants, who it is uncontested are fully qualified to study medicine, for educational disadvantages which it was reasonable to conclude were a product of state-fostered discrimination. Once admitted, these students must satisfy the same degree requirements as regularly admitted students; they are taught by the same faculty in the same classes; and their performance is evaluated by the same standards by which regularly admitted students are judged. Under these circumstances, their performance and degrees must be regarded equally with the regularly admitted students with whom they compete for standing. Since minority graduates cannot justifiably be regarded as less well qualified than nonminority graduates by virtue of the special admissions program, there is no reasonable basis to conclude that minority graduates at schools using such programs would be stigmatized as inferior by the existence of such programs. . . .

Finally, Davis' special admissions program cannot be said to violate the Constitution simply because it has set aside a predetermined number of places for qualified minority applicants rather than using minority status as a positive factor to be considered in evaluating the applications of disadvantaged minority applicants. For purposes of constitutional adjudication, there is no difference between the two approaches. In any admissions program which accords special consideration to disadvantaged racial minorities, a determination of the degree of preference to be given is unavoidable, and any given preference that results in the exclusion of a white candidate is no more or less constitutionally acceptable than a program such as that at Davis. Furthermore, the extent of the preference inevitably depends on how many minority applicants the particular school is seeking to admit in any particular year so long as the number of qualified minority applicants exceeds that number. There is no sensible, and certainly no constitutional, distinction between, for example, adding a set number of points to the admissions rating of disadvantaged minority applicants as an expression of the preference with the expectation that this will result in the admission of an approximately determined number of qualified minority applicants and setting a fixed number of places for such applicants as was done here. . . .

Accordingly, we would reverse the judgment of the Supreme Court of California holding the Medical School's special admissions program unconstitutional and directing respondent's admission, as well as that portion of the judgment enjoining the Medical School from according any consideration to race in the admissions process.

Justice WHITE, Justice MARSHALL, and Justice BLACK-MUN concurred in separate opinions.

Justice STEVENS, with whom the CHIEF JUSTICE, Justice STEWART, and Justice REHNQUIST join, concurring in part and dissenting in part.

Both petitioner and respondent have asked us to determine the legality of the University's special admissions program by reference to the Constitution. Our settled practice, however, is to avoid the decision of a constitutional issue if a case can be fairly decided on a statutory ground. "If there is one doctrine more deeply rooted than any other in the process of constitutional adjudication, it is that we ought not to pass on questions of constitutionality . . . unless such adjudication is unavoidable." *Spector Motor Co. v. McLaughlin*, 323 U.S. 101 [(1944)]. The more important the issue, the more force there is to this doctrine. In this case, we are presented with a constitutional question of undoubted and unusual importance. Since, however, a dispositive statutory claim was raised at the very inception of this case, and squarely decided in the portion of the trial court judgment affirmed by the California Supreme Court, it is our plain duty to confront it. Only if petitioner should prevail on the statutory issue would it be necessary to decide whether the University's admissions program violated the Equal Protection Clause of the Fourteenth Amendment.

Section 601 of the Civil Rights Act of 1964, 78 Stat. 252, 42 U.S.C. § 2000d, provides:

> "No person in the United States shall, on the ground of race, color, or national origin, be excluded from participation in, be denied the benefits of, or be subjected to discrimination under any program or activity receiving Federal financial assistance."

The University, through its special admissions policy, excluded Bakke from participation in its program of medical education because of his race. The University also acknowledges that it was, and still is, receiving federal financial assistance. The plain language of the statute therefore requires affirmance of the judgment below. A different result cannot be justified unless that language misstates the actual intent of the Congress that enacted the statute or the statute is not enforceable in a private action. Neither conclusion is warranted.

Title VI is an integral part of the farreaching Civil Rights Act of 1964. No doubt, when this legislation was being debated, Congress was not directly concerned with the legality of "reverse discrimination" or "affirmative action" programs. Its attention was focused on the problem at hand, the "glaring . . . discrimination against Negroes which exists throughout our Nation," and, with respect to Title VI, the federal funding of segregated facilities. The genesis of the legislation, however, did not limit the breadth of the solution adopted. Just as Congress responded to the problem of employment discrimination by enacting a provision that protects all races, see *McDonald v. Santa Fe Trail Transp. Co.,* 427 U.S. 273 [(1976)], so, too, its answer to the problem of federal funding of segregated facilities stands as a broad prohibition against the exclusion of *any* individual from a federally funded program "on the ground of race." In the words of the House Report, Title VI stands for "the general principle that *no person* . . . be excluded from participation . . . on the ground of race, color, or national origin under any program or activity receiving Federal financial assistance." H.R.Rep.No.914, 88th Cong., 1st Sess., pt. 1, p. 25 (1963), U.S. Code Cong. & Admin.News 1964, p. 2401 (emphasis added). This same broad view of Title VI and § 601 was echoed throughout the congressional debate and was stressed by every one of the major spokesmen for the Act.

Petitioner contends, however, that exclusion of applicants on the basis of race does not violate Title VI if the exclusion carries with it no racial stigma. No such qualification or limitation of § 601's categorical prohibition of "exclusion" is justified by the statute or its history. The language of the entire section is perfectly clear; the words that follow "excluded from" do not modify or qualify the explicit outlawing of any exclusion on the stated grounds.

The legislative history reinforces this reading. The only suggestion that § 601 would allow exclusion of nonminority applicants came from opponents of the legislation and then only by way of a discussion of the meaning of the word "discrimination." The opponents feared that the term "discrimination" would be read as mandating racial quotas and "racially balanced" colleges and universities, and they pressed for a specific definition of the term in order to avoid this possibility. In response, the proponents of the legislation gave repeated assurances that the Act would be "colorblind" in its application. Senator Humphrey, the Senate floor manager for the Act, expressed this position as follows:

> "[T]he word 'discrimination' has been used in many a court case. What it really means in the bill is a distinction in treatment . . . given to different individuals because of their different race, religion or national origin. . . . "The answer to this question [what was meant by 'discrimination'] is that if race is not a factor, we do not have to worry about discrimination because of race. . . . The Internal Revenue Code does not provide that colored people do not have to pay taxes, or that they can pay their taxes 6 months later than everyone else." 110 Cong.Rec. 5864 (1964). "[I]f we started to treat Americans as Americans, not as fat ones, thin ones, short ones, tall ones, brown ones, green ones, yellow ones, or white ones, but as Americans. If we did that we would not need to worry about discrimination." *Id.,* at 5866.

In giving answers such as these, it seems clear that the proponents of Title VI assumed that the Constitution itself required a colorblind standard on the part of government, but that does not mean that the legislation only codifies an existing constitutional prohibition. The statutory prohibition against discrimination in federally funded projects contained in § 601 is more than a simple paraphrasing of what the Fifth or Fourteenth Amendment would require. The Act's proponents plainly considered Title VI consistent with their view of the Constitution and they sought to provide an effective weapon to implement that view. As a distillation of what the supporters of the Act believed the Constitution demanded of State and Federal Governments, § 601 has independent force, with language and emphasis in addition to that found in the Constitution. . . .

In short, nothing in the legislative history justifies the conclusion that the broad language of § 601 should not be given its natural meaning. We are dealing with a distinct statutory prohibition, enacted at a particular time with particular concerns in mind; neither its language nor any prior interpretation suggests that its place in the Civil Rights Act, won after long debate, is simply that of a constitutional appendage. In unmistakable terms the Act prohibits the exclusion of individuals from federally funded programs because of their race. As succinctly phrased during the Senate debate, under Title VI it is not "permissible to say 'yes' to one person; but to say 'no' to another person, only because of the color of his skin.". . .

The University's special admissions program violated Title VI of the Civil Rights Act of 1964 by excluding Bakke from the Medical School because of his race. It is therefore our duty to affirm the judgment ordering Bakke admitted to the University.

Accordingly, I concur in the Court's judgment insofar as it affirms the judgment of the Supreme Court of California. To the extent that it purports to do anything else, I respectfully dissent.

THE DEVELOPMENT OF LAW
Other Rulings on Affirmative Action and Reverse Discrimination

Case	Vote	Facts and Ruling
United Steelworkers of America v. Weber, 443 U.S. 193 (1979)	5:2	The United Steelworkers of America and Kaiser Aluminum Chemical Corporation reached agreement on an

Case	Vote	Facts and Ruling
		affirmative action plan to overcome racial imbalances in the company's workforce. It required that at least half of the trainees in an on-the-job training program be set aside for blacks. The plan was to remain in effect until the proportion of black workers matched the proportion of blacks in the local labor force. Brian Weber, a white worker excluded from the program, sued and claimed that the plan violated Title VII of the 1964 Civil Rights Act which prohibits "discriminat[ion]. . . because of . . . race."
		With Justices Powell and Stewart not participating, the majority in an opinion by Justice Brennan held that the affirmative action program was consistent with the spirit, if not the letter, of the Civil Rights Act, despite the wording of Title VII and the legislative history of the act, demonstrating that Congress had not approved of "preferential treatment for any group of citizens. In fact, it specifically forbids it."
		Chief Justice Burger and Justice Rehnquist dissented, criticizing the majority for contradicting both the language of Title VII and its legislative history, and for "totally rewrit[ing] a crucial part" of the law in order to achieve "a good result."
Fullilove v. Klutznick, 448 U.S. 448 (1980)	6:3	In the Public Works Employment Act of 1977, Congress

Case	Vote	Facts and Ruling
		required that 10 percent of a $4 billion public works program be set aside for "minority-controlled businesses" (MCBs), defined as companies in which at least 50 percent interest was held by blacks, Hispanics, Asian-American, American Indians, Eskimos, or Aleuts. The program was challenged as unconstitutional under the equal protection component of the Fifth Amendment's due process clause.

Chief Justice Burger's plurality opinion adopted the exacting scrutiny test used in *Bakke* and found that Congress had an appropriate objective in remedying past discrimination, holding that "the limited use of racial and ethnic criteria, in the context of the case presented, is a constitutionally permissible *means* for achieving the congressional objectives." He also "reject-[ed] the contention that in the remedial context the Congress must act in a wholly 'color-blind' fashion."

Concurring Justice Powell applied the strict scrutiny test and concluded that the set asides were "justified as a remedy that serves the compelling interest in eradicating the continuing effects of past discrimination identified by Congress." Also concurring, Justice Marshall, joined by Justices Brennan and Blackmun, contended that

Case	Vote	Facts and Ruling
		"the racial classifications employed in the set-aside provision are substantially related to the achievement of the important and congressionally articulated goal of remedying the present effects of past racial discrimination."
		Dissenting Justice Stewart, joined by Justice Rehnquist, argued that the set-asides violated the principle that "Our Constitution is colorblind, and neither knows nor tolerates classes among citizens." In another dissenting opinion, Justice Stevens claimed that Congress had failed to consider the different degrees of injury suffered by various minorities (blacks, Indians, Eskimos, etc.) and observed that "because classifications based on race are potentially so harmful to the entire body politic, it is especially important that the reasons for any such classification be clearly identified and unquestionably legitimate."
Firefighters Local Union No. 1784 v. Stotts, 467 U.S. 561 (1984)	6:3	A black member of the Memphis Fire Department sued the department, claiming that race was a factor in hiring and promotion decisions in violation of Title VII of the Civil Rights Act of 1964. That suit resulted in a consent decree requiring at least 50 percent of all new employees be black until two-fifths of the department was black. But when projected budget deficits in 1981 forced a reduc-

Case	Vote	Facts and Ruling
		tion in the number of city employees, the department announced that it would abide by its "last-hired-is-the-first-fired" seniority system. A newly hired black employee challenged the layoff policy and a federal district court ordered the department to honor the consent decree and layoff several white firefighters with more seniority than black firefighters. An appellate court affirmed that decision, and the union appealed to the Supreme Court, which reversed the lower court.
		Justice White's opinion for the majority found the consent decree to only bind the parties to remedy past discriminatory hiring and promotion practices, to contain no agreement to set aside seniority in the event of layoffs, and held that setting aside seniority systems as a remedial measure violated Title VII of the Civil Rights Act.
		Concurring, Justice Stevens concluded that the majority need not have addressed the statutory question because the only issue here was compliance with the consent decree.
		Dissenting Justice Blackmun, joined by Brennan and Marshall, charged that the issue was moot because the layoff had ended and that the majority should have dismissed the case.
Wygant v. Jackson Board of Education, 476 U.S. 267 (1986)	5:4	White teachers with seniority who were laid off sued when

Case	Vote	Facts and Ruling

minority and less senior teachers were retained as a result of a collective bargaining agreement between a school district and a teachers' union, which gave preference to members of minority groups and required the laying off of white teachers before black teachers with less seniority.

In a plurality opinion, joined by Chief Justice Burger and Justices Rehnquist and O'Connor, Justice Powell held that the equal protection clause of the Fourteenth Amendment was violated and that the school had not established a compelling interest or narrowly tailored its use of racial criterion to remedy past discriminatory hiring practices.

In a concurring opinion, Justice White underscored that none of the Court's precedents had suggested support for "the discharge of white teachers to make room for blacks, none of whom has been shown to be a victim of racial discrimination." In another concurring opinion, Justice O'Connor contended that the layoffs were neither narrowly tailored nor bore a relation to remedying employment discrimination.

By contrast, dissenting Justice Marshall, along with Brennan and Blackmun, maintained that the layoffs were "substantially related" to "important governmental objectives." Also dissent-

Case	Vote	Facts and Ruling
		ing, Justice Stevens took the view that the school advanced its interests in educating children by having black teachers as role models for minority students.
Local 28 of the Sheet Metal Workers v. Equal Employment Opportunity Commission, 478 U.S. 421 (1986).	5:4	A federal district court found the union in violation of Title VII of the Civil Rights Act of 1964 for discriminating against minority workers. It ordered a 29 percent minority hiring goal (reflecting the percentage of minorities in the local labor force) as a remedy for the union's past discriminatory practices. When the union refused to comply, it was found in civil contempt and the union appealed the court-imposed affirmative action program on the grounds that it violated Title VII.

In a plurality opinion, Justice Brennan found nothing in Section 706(g) of Title VII to forbid courts from imposing remedies such as "hiring goals" and "timetables" even if they "might incidentally benefit individuals who are not the actual victims of [past] discrimination." He concluded that "the relief ordered in this case . . . is narrowly tailored to further the Government's compelling interest in remedying past discrimination."

In a concurring opinion, Justice Powell thought that here the "particularly egregious conduct" of the union justified the imposition of a racial quota and that ap-

Case	Vote	Facts and Ruling
		peared to be the only effective remedy available to the court.
		In a concurring and dissenting opinion, Justice O'Connor thought that the lower court went too far in establishing an impermissible "quota," rather than a hiring "goal" for minorities.
		In separate dissenting opinions, Justices White and Rehnquist, the latter joined by Chief Justice Burger, maintained that the remedial order went too far and, in Rehnquist's words, Title VII "forbids a court from ordering racial preferences that effectively displace non-minorities except to minority individuals who have been the actual victims of a particular employer's racial discrimination."
Local No. 93, International Ass'n of Firefighters v. City of Cleveland, 478 U.S. 501 (1986)	6:3	An independent, nonunion organization of black and Hispanic firefighters brought a class-action suit alleging discrimination in the hiring, assigning and promoting of the city's firefighters. The union intervened in the suit, but over its objections, the district court handed down a consent decree (between the minority firefighters and the city), which set racial goals and quotas for the hiring and promoting of minority firefighters.
		In his opinion for the majority, Justice Brennan observed that "whether or not [Section] 706(g) [of the Civil Rights Act] precludes a

Case	Vote	Facts and Ruling
		court from imposing certain kinds of race-conscious relief after trial, that provision does not apply to relief awarded in a consent decree. . . . [V]oluntary action available to employers and unions seeking to eradicate racial discrimination may include reasonable race-conscious relief that benefits individuals who were not actual victims of discrimination."
		Dissenting Justice White countered that "Title VII forbids racially discriminatory employment practices." And dissenting Justice Rehnquist, joined by Chief Justice Burger, thought that *Firefighters v. Stotts* was controlling and rejected the majority's attempt to distinguish this case.
United States v. Paradise, 480 U.S. 149 (1987)	5:4	Upon finding that not one of Alabama's 232 state troopers with a rank of corporal or higher was black, a federal district court ordered that half of all promotions to the rank of corporal go to blacks, if qualified blacks were available. An appellate court affirmed the order, as did a bare majority of the Supreme Court.
		In a plurality opinion, joined by Justices Marshall, Blackmun and Powell, Justice Brennan held that the equal protection clause was not violated because the quotas advanced a compelling governmental interest in remedying past and present discrimination, and that

Case	Vote	Facts and Ruling
		the quota was narrowly tailored, further explaining that "The features of the one-for-one requirement and its actual operation indicate that it is flexible in application at all ranks. . . . the requirement may be waived if no qualified black candidates are available. . . . Further, it applies only when the Department needs to make promotions."
		In a separate concurring opinion, however, Justice Stevens took exception with the view that the remedy must be "narrowly tailored to achieve a compelling governmental interest," and claimed that the district court had "broad and flexible authority to remedy the wrongs" here.
		By contrast, dissenting Justice O'Connor, joined by Chief Justice Rehnquist and Scalia, charged that the district court failed to narrowly tailor its remedy and to consider alternatives to using a racial quota. In another dissenting opinion, Justice White rebuffed the district court for "exceed[ing] its equitable powers in devising a remedy in this case."
Johnson v. Transportation Agency, Santa Clara, California, 480 U.S. 616 (1987)	6:3	A white male passed over for a promotion because an equally qualified female was promoted instead, challenged Santa Clara County's program for hiring and promoting minorities and women. Under the program, promotions within a traditionally segregated job

Case	Vote	Facts and Ruling
		classification where women were underrepresented, agencies could consider the gender of a qualified candidate as one factor in making its promotion decisions; but no specific quota or goal was set aside.

Justice Brennan upheld the program over the claim that it violated Title VII of the 1964 Civil Rights Act. Consistent with *Bakke*, he observed that, "The Agency earmarks no positions for anyone; sex is but one of several factors that may be taken into account in evaluating qualified applicants for a position."

In his concurring opinion, Justice Stevens contended that *Bakke* had misconstrued the Civil Rights Act, but explained that he felt compelled to respect it as a precedent because of the "undoubted public interest in 'stability and orderly development of the law.' " For much the same reason, Justice O'Connor concurred, although she lamented the Court's "expansive and ill-defined approach to voluntary affirmative action."

Dissenting Justice Scalia, joined by Chief Justice Rehnquist and Justice White, charged that the Court's prior rulings on affirmative action contradicted the express language of Title VII of the Civil Rights Act; the remedy here was not imposed because of any past discrimination but solely for the purpose of

Case	Vote	Facts and Ruling
		achieving racial balance; and he criticized the majority for failing to distinguish prior rulings upholding private affirmative action programs from public, state-sponsored affirmative action programs, like that of Santa Clara County.
Martin v. Wilks, 109 S.Ct. 2180 (1989)	5:4	Some white firefighters in Birmingham, Alabama, denied promotion in favor of less-qualified blacks, challenged a consent decree mandating goals for the hiring and promoting of blacks, as violation of Title VII of the Civil Rights Act of 1964. A federal district court held that the white firefighters could challenge the affirmative action program, even though they had not been parties to original suit that resulted in a consent decree establishing the program. A federal appellate court reversed and the Supreme Court affirmed that decision.
		Chief Justice Rehnquist held that white firefighters could challenge the legality of affirmative action programs created by consent decrees because, even though not parties to the original litigation, their interests and employment were affected.
		Along with Justices Brennan, Marshall, and Blackmun, Justice Stevens dissented, observing that the white firefighters could have but did not join the initial lawsuit and represented their opposition to

Case	Vote	Facts and Ruling
		the affirmative action consent decree. In his view, "One of the disadvantages of sideline-sitting is that the bystander has no right to appeal from a judgment no matter how harmful it may be. . . . There is nothing unusual about the fact that litigation between adverse parties may, as a practical matter, seriously impair the interests of third parties who elect to sit on the sidelines. Indeed, in complex litigation this Court has held that a sideline-sitter may be bound as firmly as an actual party if he had adequate notice and a fair opportunity to intervene and if the judicial interest in finality is sufficiently strong."

City of Richmond v. J. A. Croson
488 U.S. 469, 109 S.Ct. 706 (1989)

In 1983, the city of Richmond, Virginia, passed an ordinance requiring nonminority building contractors to subcontract 30 percent of all city-awarded projects to minority owned businesses, or Minority Business Enterprises (MBEs). This set aside quota was as much a remedy for past discrimination as a way to help black construction companies penetrate the local building industry. Half of Richmond's population is black, but minority-owned firms won less than 1 percent of the $25 million awarded in city contracts in the preceding five years. The program was patterned after a federal one that the Supreme Court had upheld in *Fullilove v. Klutznick,* 448 U.S. 448 (1980). There the Burger Court was divided six to three, with Justices Stewart, Rehnquist, and Stevens dissenting. The majority in an opinion by Chief Justice Burger upheld Congress's setting aside 10 percent of all federal contracts for minority-owned businesses. That quota was based on roughly half the difference between percentages of minority contractors and minorities in the country. Likewise, Richmond's quota fell about halfway between the city's black population (50 percent) and the number of minority contractors (less than 1 percent) in the city. Opponents, nevertheless, charged that the program created a "racial spoils system." A majority of the city's nine-member council is black and adopted the program six to two, with one abstention.

Before bidding on a $127,000 city contract to install urinals and toilets in the city jail, an Ohio plumbing contractor, J. A. Croson knew it had to meet the 30 percent quota and that meant finding an MBE subcontractor to supply the fixtures, because their cost alone was 75 percent of the contract. Croson won the contract as the only bidder, despite failing to interest MBE subcontractors in the project. After trying again unsuccessfully to find an MBE subcontractor, Croson sought a waiver of the 30 percent set aside. On hearing that, an MBE finally made a bid for the subcontract but it came in $7,000 higher than Croson had estimated. So the company asked the city to raise its contract price accordingly. The city refused and announced it would reopen bidding on the project.

Croson sued. A federal district judge's decision upholding the city's set aside program was reversed on appeal, and Richmond took its case to the highest court in the land. The composition of the Court, however, had dramatically changed since *Fullilove* was handed down. President Ronald Reagan had elevated Justice Rehnquist to the chief justiceship in 1986 and named to the bench Justices Sandra O'Connor (in 1981), Antonin Scalia (in 1986), and Anthony Kennedy (in 1988). Whereas in *Fullilove* the justices voted six to three to uphold a federal set aside program, here the justices split six to three in striking down Richmond's program. Justice O'Connor's opinion for the majority, moreover, registers the Rehnquist Court's shift toward a strict scrutiny of affirmative action programs.

Justice O'CONNOR delivers the opinion of the Court, with whom the CHIEF JUSTICE, Justice WHITE and Justice KENNEDY join in part.

II

The parties and their supporting *amici* fight an initial battle over the scope of the city's power to adopt legislation designed to address the effects of past discrimination. Relying on our decision in *Wygant* [*v. Jackson Board of Education*, 476 U.S. 267 (1986)], appellee argues that the city must limit any race-based remedial efforts to eradicating the effects of its own prior discrimination. This is essentially the position taken by the Court of Appeals below. Appellant argues that our decision in *Fullilove* [*v. Klutznick,* 448 U.S. 448 (1980)], is controlling, and that as a result the city of Richmond enjoys sweeping legislative power to define and attack the effects of prior discrimination in its local construction industry. We find that neither of these two rather stark alternatives can withstand analysis. . . .

Appellant and its supporting *amici* rely heavily on *Fullilove* for the proposition that a city council, like Congress, need not make specific findings of discrimination to engage in race-conscious relief. Thus, appellant argues "[i]t would be a perversion of federalism to hold that the federal government has a compelling interest in remedying the effects of racial discrimination in its own public works program, but a city government does not." Brief for Appellant 32 (footnote omitted).

What appellant ignores is that Congress, unlike any State or political subdivision, has a specific constitutional mandate to enforce the dictates of the Fourteenth Amendment. The power to "enforce" may at times also include the power to define situations which *Congress* determines threaten principles of equality and to adopt prophylactic rules to deal with those situations. . . .

That Congress may identify and redress the effects of society-wide discrimination does not mean that, *a fortiori,* the States and their political subdivisions are free to decide that such remedies are appropriate. Section 1 of the Fourteenth Amendment is an explicit *constraint* on state power, and the States must undertake any remedial efforts in accordance with that provision. To hold otherwise would be to cede control over the content of the Equal Protection Clause to the 50 state legislatures and their myriad political subdivisions. The mere recitation of a benign or compensatory purpose for the use of a racial classification would essentially entitle the States to exercise the full power of Congress under § 5 of the Fourteenth Amendment and insulate any racial classification from judicial scrutiny under § 1. We believe that such a result would be contrary to the intentions of the Framers of the Fourteenth Amendment, who desired to place clear limits on the States' use of race as a criterion for legislative action, and to have the federal courts enforce those limitations. . . .

It would seem equally clear, however, that a state or local subdivision (if delegated the authority from the State) has the authority to eradicate the effects of private discrimination within its own legislative jurisdiction. This authority must, of course, be exercised within the constraints of § 1 of the Fourteenth Amendment. Our decision in *Wygant* is not to the contrary. *Wygant* addressed the constitutionality of the use of racial quotas by local school authorities pursuant to an agreement reached with the local teachers' union. It was in the context of addressing the school board's power to adopt a race-based layoff program affecting its own work force that the *Wygant* plurality indicated that the Equal Protection Clause required "some showing of prior discrimination by the governmental unit involved." *Wygant.* As a matter of state law, the city of Richmond has legislative authority over its procurement policies, and can use its spending powers to remedy private discrimination, if it identifies that discrimination with the particularity required by the Fourteenth Amendment. To this extent, on the question of the city's competence, the Court of Appeals erred in following *Wygant* by rote in a case involving a state entity which has state-law authority to address discriminatory practices within local commerce under its jurisdiction.

Thus, if the city could show that it had essentially become a "passive participant" in a system of racial exclusion practiced by elements of the local construction industry, we think it clear that the city could take affirmative steps to dismantle such a system. It is beyond dispute that any public entity, state or federal, has a compelling interest in assuring that public dollars, drawn from the tax contributions of all citizens, do not serve to finance the evil of private prejudice. . . .

III

A. The Richmond Plan denies certain citizens the opportunity to compete for a fixed percentage of public contracts based solely upon their race. To whatever racial group these citizens belong, their "personal rights" to be treated with equal dignity and respect are implicated by a rigid rule erecting race as the sole criterion in an aspect of public decisionmaking.

Absent searching judicial inquiry into the justification for such race-based measures, there is simply no way of determining what classifications are "benign" or "remedial" and what classifications are in fact motivated by illegitimate notions of racial inferiority or simple racial politics. Indeed, the purpose of strict scrutiny is to "smoke out" illegitimate uses of race by assuring that the legislative body is pursuing a goal important enough to warrant use of a highly suspect tool. The test also ensures that the means chosen "fit" this compelling goal so closely that there is little or no possibility that the motive for the classification was illegitimate racial prejudice or stereotype.

Classifications based on race carry a danger of stigmatic harm. Unless they are strictly reserved for remedial settings, they may in fact promote notions of racial inferiority and lead to a politics of racial hostility. See *University of California Regents v. Bakke* [438 U.S. 265 (1978)] (opinion of POWELL, J.) ("[P]referential programs may only reinforce common stereotypes holding that certain groups are unable to achieve success without special protection based on a factor having no relation to individual worth"). We thus reaffirm the view expressed by the plurality in *Wygant* that the standard of review under the Equal Protection Clause is not dependent on the race of those burdened or benefited by a particular classification. . . .

Under the standard proposed by Justice MARSHALL's dissent, "[r]ace-conscious classifications designed to further remedial goals," are forthwith subject to a relaxed standard of review. How the dissent arrives at the legal conclusion that a racial classification is "designed to further remedial goals," without first engaging in an examination of the factual basis for its enactment and the nexus between its scope and that factual basis we are not told. However, once the "remedial" conclusion is reached, the dissent's standard is singularly deferential, and bears little resemblance to the close examination of legislative purpose we have engaged in when reviewing classifications based either on race or gender. . . . The dissent's watered-down version of equal protection review effectively assures that race will always be relevant in American life, and that the "ultimate goal" of "eliminat[ing] entirely from governmental decisionmaking such irrelevant factors as a human being's race," *Wygant* (STEVENS, J., dissenting) will never be achieved.

Even were we to accept a reading of the guarantee of equal protection under which the level of scrutiny varies according to the ability of different groups to defend their interests in the representative process, heightened scrutiny would still be appropriate in the circumstances of this case. One of the central arguments for applying a less exacting standard to "benign" racial classifications is that such measures essentially involve a choice made by dominant racial groups to disadvantage themselves. If one aspect of the judiciary's role under the Equal Protection Clause is to protect "discrete and insular minorities" from majoritarian prejudice or indifference, see *United States v. Carolene Products Co.*, 304 U.S. 144, 153, n. 4 (1938), some maintain that these concerns are not implicated when the "white majority" places burdens upon itself. See J. Ely, Democracy and Distrust 170 (1980).

In this case, blacks comprise approximately 50% of the population of the city of Richmond. Five of the nine seats on the City Council are held by blacks. The concern that a political majority will more easily act to the disadvantage of a minority based on unwarranted assumptions or incomplete facts would seem to militate for, not against, the application of heightened judicial scrutiny in this case.

III

B. The District Court found the city council's "findings sufficient to ensure that, in adopting the Plan, it was remedying the present effects of past discrimination in the *construction industry.*"

Like the "role model" theory employed in *Wygant,* a generalized assertion that there has been past discrimination in an entire industry provides no guidance for a legislative body to determine the precise scope of the injury it seeks to remedy. It "has no logical stopping point." *Wygant, supra.* "Relief" for such an ill-defined wrong could extend until the percentage of public contracts awarded to MBEs in Richmond mirrored the percentage of minorities in the population as a whole.

Appellant argues that it is attempting to remedy various forms of past discrimination that are alleged to be responsible for the small number of minority businesses in the local contracting industry. Among these the city cites the exclusion of blacks from skilled construction trade unions and training programs. This past discrimination has prevented them "from following the traditional path from laborer to entrepreneur." The city also lists a host of nonracial factors which would seem to face a member of any racial group attempting to establish a new business enterprise, such as deficiencies in working capital, inability to meet bonding requirements, unfamiliarity with bidding procedures, and disability caused by an inadequate track record.

While there is no doubt that the sorry history of both private and public discrimination in this country has contributed to a lack of opportunities for black entrepreneurs, this observation, standing alone, cannot justify a rigid racial quota in the awarding of public contracts in Richmond, Virginia. Like the claim that discrimination in primary and secondary schooling justifies a rigid racial preference in medical school admissions, an amorphous claim that there has been past discrimination in a particular industry cannot justify the use of an unyielding racial quota.

It is sheer speculation how many minority firms there would be in Richmond absent past societal discrimination, just as it was sheer speculation how many minority medical students would have been admitted to the medical school at Davis absent past discrimination in educational opportunities. Defining these sorts of injuries as "identified discrimination" would give local governments license to create a patchwork of racial preferences based on statistical generalizations about any particular field of endeavor.

These defects are readily apparent in this case. The 30% quota cannot in any realistic sense be tied to any injury suffered by anyone. The District Court relied upon five predicate "facts" in reaching its conclusion that there was an adequate basis for the 30% quota: (1) the ordinance declares itself to be remedial; (2) several proponents of the measure stated their views that there had been past discrimination in the construction industry; (3) minority businesses received .67% of prime contracts from the city while minorities constituted 50% of the city's population; (4) there were very few minority contractors in local and state contractors' associations; and (5) in 1977, Congress made a determination that the effects of past discrimination had stifled minority participation in the construction industry nationally.

None of these "findings," singly or together, provide the city of Richmond with a "strong basis in evidence for its conclusion that remedial action was necessary." *Wygant.* There is nothing approaching a prima facie case of a constitutional or statutory violation by *anyone* in the Richmond construction industry.

The District Court accorded great weight to the fact that the city council designated the Plan as "remedial." But the mere recitation of a "benign" or legitimate purpose for a racial classification, is entitled to little or no weight. . . .

The District Court also relied on the highly conclusionary statement of a proponent of the Plan that there was racial discrimination in the construction industry "in this area, and the State, and around the nation." It also noted that the city manager had related his view that racial discrimination still plagued the construction industry in his home city of Pittsburgh (statement of Mr. Deese). These statements are of little probative value in establishing identified discrimination in the Richmond construction industry. The fact-finding process of legislative bodies is generally entitled to a presumption of regularity and deferential review by the judiciary. But when a legislative body chooses to employ a suspect classification, it cannot rest upon a generalized assertion as to the classification's relevance to its goals. . . .

Reliance on the disparity between the number of prime contracts awarded to minority firms and the minority population of the city of Richmond is similarly misplaced. . . .

In the employment context, we have recognized that for certain entry level positions or positions requiring minimal training, statistical comparisons of the racial composition of an employer's workforce to the racial composition of the relevant population may be probative of a pattern of discrimination. . . . But where special qualifications are necessary, the relevant statistical pool for purposes of demonstrating discriminatory exclusion must be the number of minorities qualified to undertake the particular task. . . .

In this case, the city does not even know how many MBEs in the relevant market are qualified to undertake prime or subcontracting work in public construction projects. . . . Nor does the city know what percentage of total city construction dollars minority firms now receive as subcontractors on prime contracts let by the city.

To a large extent, the set-aside of subcontracting dollars seems to rest on the unsupported assumption that white prime contractors simply will not hire minority firms. . . . Without any information on minority participation in subcontracting, it is quite simply impossible to evaluate overall minority representation in the city's construction expenditures.

The city and the District Court also relied on evidence that MBE membership in local contractors' associations was extremely low. Again, standing alone this evidence is not probative of any discrimination in the local construction industry. There are numerous explanations for this dearth of minority participation, including past societal discrimination in education and economic opportunities as well as both black and white career and entrepreneurial choices. Blacks may be disproportionately attracted to industries other than construction. . . . The mere fact that black membership in these trade organizations is low, standing alone, cannot establish a prima facie case of discrimination.

Finally, the city and the District Court relied on Congress' finding in connection with the set-aside approved in *Fullilove* that there had been nationwide discrimination in the construction industry. The probative value of these findings for demonstrating the existence of discrimination in Richmond is extremely limited. By its inclusion of a waiver procedure in the national program addressed in *Fullilove,* Congress explicitly recognized that the scope of the problem would vary from market area to market area. . . .

Moreover, as noted above, Congress was exercising its powers under § 5 of the Fourteenth Amendment in making a finding that past discrimination would cause federal funds to be distributed in a manner which reinforced prior patterns of discrimination. While the States and their subdivisions may take remedial action when they possess evidence that their own spending practices are exacerbating a pattern of prior discrimination, they must identify that discrimination, public or private, with some specificity before they may use race-conscious relief. Congress has made national findings that there has been societal discrimination in a host of fields. If all a state or local government need do is find a congressional report on the subject to enact a set-aside program, the constraints of the Equal Protection Clause will, in effect, have been rendered a nullity. . . .

In sum, none of the evidence presented by the city points to any identified discrimination in the Richmond construction industry. We, therefore, hold that the city has failed to demonstrate a compelling interest in apportioning public contracting opportunities on the basis of race. To accept Richmond's claim that past societal discrimination alone can serve as the basis for rigid racial preferences would be to open the door to competing claims for "remedial relief" for every disadvantaged group. The dream of a Nation of equal citizens in a society where race is irrelevant to personal opportunity and achievement would be lost in a mosaic of shifting preferences based on inherently unmeasurable claims of past wrongs. . . .

The foregoing analysis applies only to the inclusion of blacks within the Richmond set-aside program. There is *absolutely no evidence* of past discrimination against Spanish-speaking, Oriental, Indian, Eskimo, or Aleut persons in any aspect of the Richmond construction industry. The District Court took judicial notice of the fact that the vast majority of "minority" persons in Richmond were black. It may well be that Richmond has never had an Aleut or Eskimo citizen. The random inclusion of racial groups that, as a practical matter, may never have suffered from discrimination in the construction industry in Richmond, suggests that perhaps the city's purpose was not in fact to remedy past discrimination.

If a 30% set-aside was "narrowly tailored" to compensate black contractors for past discrimination, one may legitimately ask why they are forced to share this "remedial relief" with an Aleut citizen who moves to Richmond tomorrow? The gross overinclusiveness of Richmond's racial preference strongly impugns the city's claim of remedial motivation. . . .

IV

As noted by the court below, it is almost impossible to assess whether the Richmond Plan is narrowly tailored to remedy prior discrimination since it is not linked to identified discrimination in any way. We limit ourselves to two observations in this regard.

First, there does not appear to have been any consideration of the use of race-neutral means to increase minority business participation in city contracting. . . . Many of the barriers to minority participation in the construction industry relied upon by the city to justify a racial classification appear to be race neutral. If MBEs disproportionately lack capital or cannot meet bonding requirements, a race-neutral program of city financing for small firms would, *a fortiori*, lead to greater minority participation. The principal opinion in *Fullilove* found that Congress had carefully examined and rejected raceneutral alternatives before enacting the MBE set-aside. . . .

Second, the 30% quota cannot be said to be narrowly tailored to any goal, except perhaps outright racial balancing. It rests upon the "completely unrealistic" assumption that minorities will choose a particular trade in lockstep proportion to their representation in the local population. . . .

Since the city must already consider bids and waivers on a case-by-case basis, it is difficult to see the need for a rigid numerical quota. As noted above, the congressional scheme upheld in *Fullilove* allowed for a waiver of the set-aside provision where an MBE's higher price was not attributable to the effects of past discrimination. Based upon proper findings, such programs are less problematic from an equal protection standpoint because they treat all candidates individually, rather than making the color of an applicant's skin the sole relevant consideration. Unlike the program upheld in *Fullilove*, the Richmond Plan's waiver system focuses solely on the availability of MBEs; there is no inquiry into whether or not the particular MBE seeking a racial preference has suffered from the effects of past discrimination by the city or prime contractors.

Given the existence of an individualized procedure, the city's only interest in maintaining a quota system rather than investigating the need for remedial action in particular cases would seem to be simple administrative convenience. But the interest in avoiding the bureaucratic effort necessary to tailor remedial relief to those who truly have suffered the effects of prior discrimination cannot justify a rigid line drawn on the basis of a suspect classification. . . . Under Richmond's scheme, a successful black, Hispanic, or Oriental entrepreneur from anywhere in the country enjoys an absolute preference over other citizens based solely on their race. We think it obvious that such a program is not narrowly tailored to remedy the effects of prior discrimination.

V

Nothing we say today precludes a state or local entity from taking action to rectify the effects of identified discrimination within its jurisdiction. If the city of Richmond had evidence before it that nonminority contractors were systematically excluding minority businesses from subcontracting opportunities it could take action to end the discriminatory exclusion. Where there is a significant statistical disparity between the number of qualified minority contractors willing and able to perform a particular service and the number of such contractors actually engaged by the locality or the locality's prime contractors, an inference of discriminatory exclusion could arise. Under such circumstances, the city could act to dismantle the closed business system by taking appropriate measures against those who discriminate on the basis of race or other illegitimate criteria. In the extreme case, some form of narrowly tailored racial preference might be necessary to break down patterns of deliberate exclusion. . . .

Proper findings in this regard are necessary to define both the scope of the injury and the extent of the remedy necessary to cure its effects. Such findings also serve to assure all citizens that the deviation from the norm of equal treatment of all racial and ethnic groups is a temporary matter, a measure taken in the service of the goal of equality itself. Absent such findings, there is a danger that a racial classification is merely the product of unthinking stereotypes or a form of racial politics. "[I]f there is no duty to attempt either to measure the recovery by the wrong or to distribute that recovery within the injured class in an even-handed way, our history will adequately support a legislative preference for almost any ethnic, religious, or racial group with the political strength to negotiate 'a piece of the action' for its members." *Fullilove.* (STEVENS, J., dissenting). Because the city of Richmond has failed to identify the need for remedial action in

the awarding of its public construction contracts, its treatment of its citizens on a racial basis violates the dictates of the Equal Protection Clause. Accordingly, the judgment of the Court of Appeals for the Fourth Circuit is
Affirmed.

Justice STEVENS concurring in part.

I believe the Constitution requires us to evaluate our policy decisions—including those that govern the relationships among different racial and ethnic groups—primarily by studying their probable impact on the future. I therefore do not agree with the premise that seems to underlie today's decision, that a governmental decision that rests on a racial classification is never permissible except as a remedy for a past wrong. I do, however, agree with the Court's explanation of why the Richmond ordinance cannot be justified as a remedy for past discrimination, and therefore join Parts I, III-B, and IV of its opinion.

Justice KENNEDY concurring in part.

I join all but Part II of Justice O'CONNOR's opinion and give this further explanation. . . .
The moral imperative of racial neutrality is the driving force of the Equal Protection Clause. Justice SCALIA's opinion underscores that proposition, quite properly in my view. The rule suggested in his opinion, which would strike down all preferences which are not necessary remedies to victims of unlawful discrimination, would serve important structural goals, as it would eliminate the necessity for courts to pass upon each racial preference that is enacted. Structural protections may be necessities if moral imperatives are to be obeyed. His opinion would make it crystal clear to the political branches, at least those of the States, that legislation must be based on criteria other than race.
Nevertheless, given that a rule of automatic invalidity for racial preferences in almost every case would be a significant break with our precedents that require a case-by-case test, I am not convinced we need adopt it at this point. On the assumption that it will vindicate the principle of race neutrality found in the Equal Protection Clause, I accept the less absolute rule contained in Justice O'CONNOR's opinion, a rule based on the proposition that any racial preference must face the most rigorous scrutiny by the courts. My reasons for doing so are as follows. First, I am confident that, in application, the strict scrutiny standard will operate in a manner generally consistent with the imperative of race neutrality, because it forbids the use even of narrowly drawn racial classifications except as a last resort. Second, the

rule against race-conscious remedies is already less than an absolute one, for that relief may be the only adequate remedy after a judicial determination that a State or its instrumentality has violated the Equal Protection Clause. I note, in this connection, that evidence which would support a judicial finding of intentional discrimination may suffice also to justify remedial legislative action, for it diminishes the constitutional responsibilities of the political branches to say they must wait to act until ordered to do so by a court. Third, the strict scrutiny rule is consistent with our precedents, as Justice O'CONNOR's opinion demonstrates.

Justice SCALIA concurring.

I agree with much of the Court's opinion, and, in particular, with its conclusion that strict scrutiny must be applied to all governmental classification by race, whether or not its asserted purpose is "remedial" or "benign." I do not agree, however, with the Court's dicta suggesting that, despite the Fourteenth Amendment, state and local governments may in some circumstances discriminate on the basis of race in order (in a broad sense) "to ameliorate the effects of past discrimination." The benign purpose of compensating for social disadvantages, whether they have been acquired by reason of prior discrimination or otherwise, can no more be pursued by the illegitimate means of racial discrimination than can other assertedly benign purposes we have repeatedly rejected. See, *e.g., Wygant v. Jackson Board of Education,* 476 U.S. 267 [(1986)] (plurality opinion) (discrimination in teacher assignments to provide "role models" for minority students); *Palmore v. Sidoti,* 466 U.S. 429 (1984) (awarding custody of child to father, after divorced mother entered an interracial remarriage, in order to spare child social "pressures and stresses"); *Lee v. Washington,* 390 U.S. 333 (1968) (*per curiam*) (permanent racial segregation of all prison inmates, presumably to reduce possibility of racial conflict). The difficulty of overcoming the effects of past discrimination is as nothing compared with the difficulty of eradicating from our society the source of those effects, which is the tendency—fatal to a nation such as ours—to classify and judge men and women on the basis of their country of origin or the color of their skin. A solution to the first problem that aggravates the second is no solution at all. At least where state or local action is at issue, only a social emergency rising to the level of imminent danger to life and limb can justify an exception to the principle embodied in the Fourteenth Amendment that "[o]ur Constitution is color-blind, and neither knows nor tolerates classes among citizens," *Plessy v. Ferguson,* 163 U.S. 537, (1896) (HARLAN, J., dissenting). . . .

A sound distinction between federal and state (or local) action based on race rests not only upon the substance of the Civil War Amendments, but upon social reality and governmental theory. . . . The struggle for racial justice has historically been a struggle by the national society against oppression in the individual States. . . .

In my view there is only one circumstance in which the States may act *by race* to "undo the effects of past discrimination": where that is necessary to eliminate their own maintenance of a system of unlawful racial classification. . . . We have stressed each school district's constitutional "duty to *dismantle* its dual system," and have found that "[e]ach instance of a failure or refusal to fulfill this affirmative duty *continues the violation* of the Fourteenth Amendment." *Columbus Board of Education v. Penick* [433 U.S. 449 (1979)].

I agree with the Court's dictum that a fundamental distinction must be drawn between the effects of "societal" discrimination and the effects of "identified" discrimination, and that the situation would be different if Richmond's plan were "tailored" to identify those particular bidders who "suffered from the effects of past discrimination by the city or prime contractors." In my view, however, the reason that would make a difference is not, as the Court states, that it would justify race-conscious action but rather that it would enable race-neutral remediation. Nothing prevents Richmond from according a contracting preference to identified victims of discrimination. While most of the beneficiaries might be black, neither the beneficiaries nor those disadvantaged by the preference would be identified *on the basis of their race.* In other words, far from justifying racial classification, identification of actual victims of discrimination makes it less supportable than ever, because more obviously unneeded. . . .

It is plainly true that in our society blacks have suffered discrimination immeasurably greater than any directed at other racial groups. But those who believe that racial preferences can help to "even the score" display, and reinforce, a manner of thinking by race that was the source of the injustice and that will, if it endures within our society, be the source of more injustice still. The relevant proposition is not that it was blacks, or Jews, or Irish who were discriminated against, but that it was individual men and women, "created equal," who were discriminated against. And the relevant resolve is that that should never happen again. Racial preferences appear to "even the score" (in some small degree) only if one embraces the proposition that our society is appropriately viewed as divided into races, making it right that an injustice rendered in the past to a black man should be compensated for by discriminating against a white. Nothing is worth that embrace. Since blacks have been disproportionately disadvantaged by racial discrimination, any race-neutral remedial program aimed at the disadvantaged *as such* will have a disproportionately beneficial impact on blacks. Only such a program, and not one that operates on the basis of race, is in accord with the letter and the spirit of our Constitution.

Justice MARSHALL, with whom Justice BRENNAN and Justice BLACKMUN join, dissenting.

[T]oday's decision marks a deliberate and giant step backward in this Court's affirmative action jurisprudence. Cynical of one municipality's attempt to redress the effects of past racial discrimination in a particular industry, the majority launches a grapeshot attack on race-conscious remedies in general. The majority's unnecessary pronouncements will inevitably discourage or prevent governmental entities, particularly States and localities, from acting to rectify the scourge of past discrimination. This is the harsh reality of the majority's decision, but it is not the Constitution's command. . . .

My view has long been that race-conscious classifications designed to further remedial goals "must serve important governmental objectives and must be substantially related to achievement of those objectives" in order to withstand constitutional scrutiny. . . . Analyzed in terms of this two-prong standard, Richmond's set-aside, like the federal program on which it was modeled, is "plainly constitutional.". . .

Turning first to the governmental interest inquiry, Richmond has two powerful interests in setting aside a portion of public contracting funds for minority-owned enterprises. The first is the city's interest in eradicating the effects of past racial discrimination. It is far too late in the day to doubt that remedying such discrimination is a compelling, let alone an important, interest. . . .

Richmond has a second compelling interest in setting aside, where possible, a portion of its contracting dollars. That interest is the prospective one of preventing the city's own spending decisions from reinforcing and perpetuating the exclusionary effects of past discrimination.

When government channels all its contracting funds to a white-dominated community of established contractors whose racial homogeneity is the product of private discrimination, it does more than place its imprimatur on the practices which forged and which continue to define that community. It also provides a measurable boost to those economic entities that have thrived within it, while denying important economic benefits to those entities which, but for prior discrimination, might well be better qualified to receive valuable government contracts. In my view, the interest in ensuring that the government does not reflect and reinforce prior private discrimination in dispensing public contracts is every bit as strong as the interest in eliminating private discrimination—an interest which this Court has repeatedly deemed compelling.

The remaining question with respect to the "governmental interest" prong of equal protection analysis is whether Richmond has proffered satisfactory proof of past racial discrimination to support its twin interests in remediation and in governmental nonperpetuation. Although the Members of this Court have differed on the appropriate standard of review for race-conscious remedial measures, we have always regarded this factual inquiry as a practical one. Thus, the Court has eschewed rigid tests which require the provision of particular species of evidence, statistical or otherwise. At the same time we have required that government adduce evidence that, taken as a whole, is sufficient to support its claimed interest and to dispel the natural concern that it acted out of mere "paternalistic stereotyping, not on a careful consideration of modern social conditions." *Fullilove v. Klutznick.*

Richmond's reliance on localized, industry-specific findings is a far cry from the reliance on generalized "societal discrimination" which the majority decries as a basis for remedial action. But characterizing the plight of Richmond's minority contractors as mere "societal discrimination" is not the only respect in which the majority's critique shows an unwillingness to come to grips with why construction-contracting in Richmond is essentially a whites-only enterprise. The majority also takes the disingenuous approach of disaggregating Richmond's local evidence, attacking it piecemeal, and thereby concluding that no *single* piece of evidence adduced by the city, "standing alone," suffices to prove past discrimination. But items of evidence do not, of cours, "stan[d] alone" or exist in alien juxtaposition; they necessarily work together, reinforcing or contradicting each other.

In any event, the majority's criticisms of individual items of Richmond's evidence rest on flimsy foundations. The majority states, for example, that reliance on the disparity between the share of city contracts awarded to minority firms (.67%) and the minority population of Richmond (approximately 50%) is "misplaced.". . . First, considering how miniscule the share of Richmond public construction contracting dollars received by minority-owned businesses is, it is hardly unreasonable to conclude that this case involves a "gross statistical disparit[y]." There are roughly equal numbers of minorities and nonminorities in Richmond—yet minority-owned businesses receive *one-seventy-fifth* the public contracting funds that other businesses receive. . . .

Second, and more fundamentally, where the issue is not present discrimination but rather whether *past* discrimination has resulted in the *continuing exclusion* of minorities from an historically tight-knit industry, a contrast between population and work force is entirely appropriate to help gauge the degree of the exclusion. . . . This contrast is especially illuminating in cases like this, where a main avenue of introduction into the work force—here, membership in the trade associations whose members presumably train apprentices and help them procure subcontracting assignments— is itself grossly dominated by nonminorities. The majority's assertion that the city "does not even know how many MBE's in the relevant market are qualified," is thus entirely beside the point. . . . The city's requirement that prime public contractors set aside 30% of their subcontracting assignments for minority-owned enterprises, subject to the ordinance's provision for waivers where minority-owned enterprises are unavailable or unwilling to participate, is designed precisely to ease minority contractors into the industry.

The majority's perfunctory dismissal of the testimony of Richmond's appointed and elected leaders is also deeply disturbing. . . .

Had the majority paused for a moment on the facts of the Richmond experience, it would have discovered that the city's leadership is deeply familiar with what racial discrimination is. The members of the Richmond City Council have spent long years witnessing multifarious acts of discrimination, including, but not limited to, the deliberate diminution of black residents' voting rights, resistance to school desegregation, and publicly sanctioned housing discrimination. Numerous of federal courts chronicle this disgraceful recent history. . . .

When the legislatures and leaders of cities with histories of pervasive discrimination testify that past discrimination has infected one of their industries, armchair cynicism like that exercised by the majority has no place. . . . Disbelief is particularly inappropriate here in light of the fact that appellee Croson, which had the burden of proving unconstitutionality at trial, *Wygant*, (plurality opinion), has *at no point* come forward with *any* direct evidence that the City Council's motives were anything other than sincere.

Finally, I vehemently disagree with the majority's dismissal of the congressional and Executive Branch findings noted in *Fullilove* as having "extremely limited" probative value in this case. The majority concedes that Congress established nothing less than a "presumption" that minority contracting firms have been disadvantaged by prior discrimination. The majority, inexplicably, would forbid Richmond to "share" in this information, and permit only Congress to take note of these ample findings. In thus requiring that Richmond's local evidence be severed from the context in which it was prepared, the majority would require cities seeking to eradicate the effects of past discrimination within their borders to reinvent the evidentiary wheel and engage in unnecessarily duplicative, costly, and time-consuming factfinding.

No principle of federalism or of federal power, however, forbids a state or local government from drawing upon a nationally relevant historical record prepared by the Federal Government. . . .

Of couse, Richmond could have built an even more compendious record of past discrimination, one including additional stark statistics and additional individual accounts of past discrimination. But nothing in the Fourteenth Amendment imposes such onerous documentary obligations upon States and localities once the reality of past discrimination is apparent.

In my judgment, Richmond's set-aside plan also comports with the second prong of the equal protection inquiry, for it is substantially related to the interests it seeks to serve in remedying past discrimination and in ensuring that municipal contract procurement does not perpetuate that discrimination. The most striking aspect of the city's ordinance is the similarity it bears to the "appropriately limited" federal set-aside provision upheld in *Fullilove*. Like the federal provision, Richmond's is limited to five years in duration, and was not renewed when it came up for reconsideration in 1988. Like the federal provision, Richmond's contains a waiver provision freeing from its subcontracting requirements those nonminority firms that demonstrate that they cannot comply with its provisions. Like the federal provision, Richmond's has a minimal impact on innocent third parties. While the measure affects 30% of *public* contracting dollars, that translates to only 3% of overall Richmond area contracting. . . .

Finally, like the federal provision, Richmond's does not interfere with any vested right of a contractor to a particular contract; instead it operates entirely prospectively. . . .

As for Richmond's 30% target, the majority states that this figure "cannot be said to be narrowly tailored to any goal, except perhaps outright racial balancing." The majority ignores two important facts. First, the set-aside measure affects only 3% of overall city contracting; thus, any imprecision in tailoring has far less impact than the majority suggests. But more important, the majority ignores the fact that Richmond's 30% figure was patterned directly on the *Fullilove* precedent. Congress' 10% figure fell "roughly halfway between the present percentage of minority contractors and the percentage of minority group members in the Nation." *Fullilove, supra*. The Richmond City Council's 30% figure similarly falls roughly halfway between the present percentage of Richmond-based minority contractors (almost zero) and the percentage of minorities in Richmond (50%). In faulting Richmond for not presenting a different explanation for its choice of a set-aside figure, the majority honors *Fullilove* only in the breach. . . .

Today, for the first time, a majority of this Court has adopted strict scrutiny as its standard of Equal Protection Clause review of race-conscious remedial measures. This is an unwelcome development. A profound difference separates governmental actions that themselves are racist, and governmental actions that seek to remedy the effects of prior racism or to prevent neutral governmental activity from perpetuating the effects of such racism. . . .

I am also troubled by the majority's assertion that, even if it did not believe generally in strict scrutiny of race-based remedial measures, "the circumstances of this case" require this Court to look upon the Richmond City Council's measure with the strictest scrutiny. The sole such circumstance which the majority cites, however, is the fact that blacks in Richmond are a "dominant racial grou[p]" in the city. In support of this characterization of dominance, the majority observes that "blacks comprise approximately 50% of the population of the city of Richmond" and that "[f]ive of the nine seats on the City Council are held by blacks."

While I agree that the numerical and political supremacy of a given racial group is a factor bearing upon the level of scrutiny to be applied, this Court has never held that numerical inferiority, standing alone, makes a racial group "suspect" and thus entitled to strict scrutiny review. Rather, we have identified *other* "traditional indicia of suspectness": whether a group has been "saddled with such disabilities, or subjected to such a history of purposeful unequal treatment, or relegated to such a position of political powerlessness as to command extraordinary protection from the majoritarian political process." *San Antonio Independent School District v. Rodriguez*, 411 U.S. 1 (1973).

It cannot seriously be suggested that nonminorities in Richmond have any "history of purposeful unequal treatment." *Ibid.* Nor is there any indication that they have any of the disabilities that have characteristically afflicted those groups this Court has deemed suspect. Indeed, the numerical and political dominance of nonminorities within the State of Virginia and the Nation as a whole provide an enormous political check against the "simple racial politics" at the municipal level which the majority fears. If the majority really believes that groups like Richmond's nonminorities, which comprise approximately half the population but which are outnumbered even marginally in political fora, are deserving of suspect class status for these reasons alone, this Court's decisions denying suspect status to women, see *Craig v. Boren*, 429 U.S. 190 (1976), and to persons with below-average incomes, see *San Antonio Independent School Dist.*, *supra*, stand on extremely shaky ground. . . .

In my view, the "circumstances of this case," underscore the importance of *not* subjecting to a strict scrutiny straitjacket the increasing number of cities which have recently come under minority leadership and are eager to rectify, or at least prevent the perpetuation of, past racial discrimination. In many cases, these cities will be the ones with the most in the way of prior discrimination to rectify. . . .

Today's decision, finally, is particularly noteworthy for the daunting standard it imposes upon States and localities contemplating the use of race-conscious measures to eradicate the present effects of prior discrimination and prevent its perpetuation. The majority restricts the use of such measures to situations in which a State or locality can put forth "a prima facie case of a constitutional or statutory violation." In so doing, the majority calls into question the validity of the business set-asides which dozens of municipalities across this Nation have adopted on the authority of *Fullilove.*

Nothing in the Constitution or in the prior decisions of this Court supports limiting state authority to confront the effects of past discrimination to those situations in which a prima facie case of a constitutional or statutory violation can be made out. By its very terms, the majority's standard effectively cedes control of a large component of the content of that constitutional provision to Congress and to state legislatures. If an antecedent Virginia or Richmond law had defined as unlawful the award to nonminorities of an overwhelming share of a city's contracting dollars, for example, Richmond's subsequent set-aside initiative would then satisfy the majority's standard. But without such a law, the initiative might not withstand constitutional scrutiny. The meaning of "equal protection of the laws" thus turns on the happenstance of whether a State or local body has previously defined illegal discrimination. Indeed, given that racially discriminatory cities may be the ones least likely to have tough antidiscrimination laws on their books, the majority's constitutional incorporation of state and local statutes has the perverse effect of inhibiting those States or localities with the worst records of official racism from taking remedial action. . . .

The majority today sounds a full-scale retreat from the Court's longstanding solicitude to race-conscious remedial efforts "directed toward deliverance of the century-old promise of equality of economic opportunity." *Fullilove.* The new and restrictive tests it applies scuttle one city's effort to surmount its discriminatory past, and imperil those of dozens more localities. I, however, profoundly disagree with the cramped vision of the Equal Protection Clause which the majority offers today and with its application of that vision to Richmond, Virginia's, laudable set-aside plan. The battle against pernicious racial discrimination or its effects is nowhere near won. I must dissent.

Justice BLACKMUN, with whom Justice BRENNAN joins, dissenting.

I never thought that I would live to see the day when the city of Richmond, Virginia, the cradle of the Old Confederacy, sought on its own, within a narrow confine, to lessen the stark impact of persistent discrimination. But Richmond, to its great credit, acted. Yet this Court, the supposed bastion of equality, strikes down Richmond's efforts as though discrimination had never existed or was not demonstrated in this particular litigation. Justice MARSHALL convincingly discloses the fallacy and the shallowness of that approach. History is irrefutable, even though one might sympathize with those who—though possibly innocent in themselves—benefit from the wrongs of past decades.

So the Court today regresses. I am confident, however, that, given time, it one day again will do its best to fulfill the great promises of the Constitution's Preamble and of the guarantees embodied in the Bill of Rights—a fulfillment that would make this Nation very special.

Metro Broadcasting Inc. v. Federal Communications Commission

110 S.Ct. 2997 (1990)

In 1982 the Federal Communications Commission (FCC) assigned a new UHF television station channel to Orlando, Florida. Three companies—Metro Broadcasting, Inc.; Winter Park Communications, Inc.; and Rainbow Broadcasting Company—filed competing applications for use of the channel. In awarding television channels, the FCC holds a comparative hearing before an administrative law judge. When the judge awarded the station to Metro Broadcasting, both of the other competitors appealed to the FCC's review board, which overturned the decision and awarded the channel to Rainbow Broadcasting Company. It did so on the basis of the FCC's affirmative action policies, which gave preferences to minority owners of broadcast companies in awarding licenses. The FCC's policies, which Congress had endorsed in legislation over the objections of the Reagan administration, aimed to increase minority ownership in broadcast media and diversity in broadcast programming.

After unsuccessfully appealing the FCC's decision to the Court of Appeals for the District of Columbia, Metro Broadcasting appealed to the Supreme Court. Justice Brennan's opinion announcing the Court's decision was joined by only four justices. Chief Justice Rehnquist and Justices O'Connor, Scalia, and Kennedy dissented.

Justice BRENNAN delivers the opinion of the Court.

The issue in these cases, consolidated for decision today, is whether certain minority preference policies of the Federal Communications Commission violate the equal protection component of the Fifth Amendment. The policies in question are (1) a program awarding an enhancement for minority ownership in comparative proceedings for new licenses, and (2) the minority "distress sale" program, which permits a limited category of existing radio and television broadcast stations to be transferred only to minority-controlled firms. We hold that these policies do not violate equal protection principles.

The policies before us today can best be understood by reference to the history of federal efforts to promote minority participation in the broadcasting industry. In the Communications Act of 1934 as amended, Congress assigned to the Federal Communications Commission (FCC or Commission) exclusive authority to grant licenses, based on "public convenience, interest, or necessity," to persons wishing to construct and operate radio and television broadcast stations in the United States. Although for the past two decades minorities have constituted at least one-fifth of the United States population, during this time relatively few members of minority groups have held broadcast licenses. In 1971, minorities owned only 10 of the approximately 7,500 radio stations in the country and none of the more than 1,000 television stations; in 1978, minorities owned less than 1 percent of the Nation's radio and television stations; and in 1986, they owned just 2.1 percent of the more than 11,000 radio and television stations in the United States. . . .

The Commission has therefore worked to encourage minority participation in the broadcast industry. The FCC began by formulating rules to prohibit licensees from discriminating against minorities in employment. The FCC explained that "broadcasting is an important mass media form which, because it makes use of the airwaves belonging to the public, must obtain a Federal license under a public interest standard and must operate in the public interest in order to obtain periodic renewals of that license." Regulations dealing with employment practices were justified as necessary to enable the FCC to satisfy its obligation under the Communications Act to promote diversity of programming. . . .

It is of overriding significance in these cases that the FCC's minority ownership programs have been specifically approved—indeed, mandated—by Congress. In *Fullilove* v. *Klutznick,* [448 U.S. 448] (1980), Chief Justice BURGER, writing for himself and two other Justices, observed that although "[a] program that employs racial or ethnic criteria . . . calls for close examination," when a program employing a benign racial classification is adopted by an administrative agency at the explicit direction of Congress, we are "bound to approach our task with appropriate deference to the Congress, a co-equal branch charged by the Constitution with the power to 'provide for the . . . general Welfare of the United States' and 'to enforce, by appropriate legislation,' the equal protection guarantees of the Fourteenth Amendment." We explained that deference was appropriate in light of Congress' institutional competence as the national legislature, as well as Congress' powers under the Commerce Clause, the Spending Clause, and the Civil War Amendments.

A majority of the Court in *Fullilove* did not apply strict scrutiny to the race-based classification at issue. . . . We apply that standard today. We hold that benign race-conscious measures mandated by Congress—even if those measures are not "remedial" in the sense of being designed to compensate victims of past governmental or societal discrimination—are constitutionally permissible to the extent that they serve important governmental objectives within the power of Congress and are substantially related to achievement of those objectives.

Our decision last Term in *Richmond v. J. A. Croson Co.,* [488 U.S. 469] (1989), concerning a minority set-aside program adopted by a municipality, does not prescribe the level of scrutiny to be applied to a benign racial classification employed by Congress. As Justice KENNEDY noted, the question of congressional action was not before the Court (opinion concurring in part and concurring in judgment), and so *Croson* cannot be read to undermine our decision in *Fullilove.* In fact, much of the language and reasoning in *Croson* reaffirmed the lesson of *Fullilove* that race-conscious classifications adopted by Congress to address racial and ethnic discrimination are subject to a different standard than such classifications prescribed by state and local governments. . . .

We hold that the FCC minority ownership policies pass muster under the test we announce today. First, we find that they serve the important governmental objective of, broadcast diversity. Second, we conclude that they are substantially related to the achievement of that objective.

Congress found that "the effects of past inequities stemming from racial and ethnic discrimination have resulted in a severe underrepresentation of minorities in the media of mass communications." Congress and the Commission do not justify the minority ownership policies strictly as remedies for victims of this discrimination, however. Rather, Congress and the FCC have selected the minority ownership policies primarily to promote programming diversity, and they urge that such diversity is an important governmental objective that can serve as a constitutional basis for the preference policies. We agree. . . .

We also find that the minority ownership policies are substantially related to the achievement of the Government's interest. One component of this inquiry concerns the relationship between expanded minority ownership and greater broadcast diversity; both the FCC and Congress have determined that such a relationship exists. Although we do not " 'defer' to the judgment of the Congress and the Commission on a constitutional question," and would not "hesitate to invoke the Constitution should we determine that the Commission has not fulfilled its task with appropriate sensitivity" to equal protection principles we must pay close attention to the expertise of the Commission and the factfinding of Congress when analyzing the nexus between minority ownership and programming diversity. With respect to this "complex" empirical question we are required to give "great weight to the decisions of Congress and the experience of the Commission."

The FCC has determined that increased minority participation in broadcasting promotes programming diversity. As the Commission observed in its 1978 Statement of Policy on Minority Ownership of Broadcasting Facilities, "ownership of broadcasting facilities by minorities is [a] significant way of fostering the inclusion of minority views in the area of programming" and "[f]ull minority participation in the ownership and management of broadcast facilities results in a more diverse selection of programming.". . . The FCC's conclusion that there is an empirical nexus between minority ownership and broadcasting diversity is a product of its expertise, and we accord its judgment deference.

Furthermore, the FCC's reasoning with respect to the minority ownership policies is consistent with longstanding practice under the Communications Act. From its inception, public regulation of broadcasting has been premised on the assumption that diversification of ownership will broaden the range of programming available to the broadcast audience. . . .

Congress also has made clear its view that the minority ownership policies advance the goal of diverse programming. In recent years, Congress has specifically required the Commission, through appropriations legislation, to maintain the minority ownership policies without alteration. We would be remiss, however, if we ignored the long history of congressional support for those policies prior to the passage of the appropriations acts because, for the past two decades, Congress has consistently recognized the barriers encountered by minorities in entering the broadcast industry and has expressed emphatic support for the Commission's attempts to promote programming diversity by increasing minority ownership. . . .

Congress has twice extended the prohibition on the use of appropriated funds to modify or repeal minority ownership policies and has continued to focus upon the issue. For example, in the debate on the fiscal year 1989 legislation, Senator Hollings, chair of both the authorizing committee and the appropriations subcommittee for the FCC, presented to the Senate a summary of a June 1988 report prepared by the Congressional Research Service, entitled, Minority Broadcast Station Ownership and Broadcast Programming: Is There a Nexus? The study, Senator Hollings reported, "clearly demonstrates that minority ownership of broadcast stations does increase the diversity of viewpoints presented over the airwaves."

As revealed by the historical evolution of current federal policy, both Congress and the Commission have concluded that the minority ownership programs are critical means of promoting broadcast diversity. We must give great weight to their joint determination.

The judgment that there is a link between expanded minority ownership and broadcast diversity does not rest on impermissible stereotyping. Congressional policy does not assume that in every case minority ownership and management will lead to more minority-oriented programming or to the expression of a discrete "minority viewpoint" on the airwaves. Neither does it pretend that all programming that appeals to minority audiences can be labeled "minority programming" or that programming that might be described as "minority" does not appeal to nonminorities. Rather, both Congress and the FCC maintain simply that expanded minority ownership of broadcast outlets will, in the aggregate, result in greater broadcast diversity. A broadcasting industry with representative minority participation will produce more variation and diversity than will one whose ownership is drawn from a single racially and ethnically homogeneous group. The predictive judgment about the overall result of minority entry into broadcasting is not a rigid assumption about how minority owners will behave in every case but rather is akin to Justice POWELL's conclusion in [*Board of Regents of the University of California v. Bakke*, [438 U.S. 265 (1978)], that greater admission of minorities would contribute, on average, "to the 'robust exchange of ideas.' ". . . To be sure, there is no ironclad guarantee that each minority owner will contribute to diversity. But neither was there an assurance in *Bakke* that minority students would interact with nonminority students or that the particular minority students admitted would have typical or distinct "minority" viewpoints. . . .

Although all station owners are guided to some extent by market demand in their programming decisions, Congress and the Commission have determined that there may be important differences between the broadcasting practices of minority owners and those of their nonminority counterparts. This judgment—and the conclusion that there is a nexus between minority ownership and broadcasting diversity—is corroborated by a host of empirical evidence. Evidence suggests that an owner's minority status influences the selection of topics for news coverage and the presentation of editorial viewpoint, especially on matters of particular concern to minorities. "[M]inority ownership does appear to have specific impact on the presentation of minority images in local news," inasmuch as minority-owned stations tend to devote more news time to topics of minority interest and to avoid racial and ethnic stereotypes in portraying minorities. In addition, studies show that a minority owner is more likely to employ minorities in managerial and other important roles where they can have an impact on station policies. If the FCC's equal employment policies "ensure that . . . licensees' programming fairly reflects the tastes and viewpoints of minority groups," it is difficult to deny that minority-owned stations that follow such employment policies on their own will also contribute to diversity. While we are under no illusion that members of a particular minority group share some cohesive, collective viewpoint, we believe it a legitimate inference for Congress and the Commission to draw that as more minorities gain ownership and policymaking roles in the media, varying perspectives will be more fairly represented on the airwaves. The policies are thus a product of " 'analysis' " rather than a " 'stereotyped reaction' " based on " '[h]abit.' " *Fullilove* (STEVENS, J., dissenting) (citation omitted). . . .

We find that the minority ownership policies are in other relevant respects substantially related to the goal of promoting broadcast diversity. First, the Commission adopted and Congress endorsed minority ownership preferences only after long study and painstaking consideration of all available alternatives. For many years, the FCC attempted to encourage diversity of programming content without consideration of the race of station owners. When it first addressed the issue, in a 1946 report entitled Public Service Responsibility of Broadcast Licensees (Blue Book), the Commission stated that although licensees bore primary responsibility for program service, "[i]n issuing and in renewing the licenses of broadcast stations, the Commission [would] give particular consideration to four program service factors relevant to the public interest." In 1960, the Commission altered course somewhat, announcing that "the principal ingredient of the licensee's obligation to operate his station in the public interest is the diligent, positive and continuing effort . . . to discover and fulfill the tastes, needs, and desires of his community or service area, for broadcast service." Licensees were advised that they could meet this obligation in two ways: by canvassing members of the listening public who could receive the station's signal, and by meeting with "leaders in community life . . . and others who bespeak the interests which make up the community."

By the late 1960's, it had become obvious that these efforts had failed to produce sufficient diversity in programming. The Kerner Commission, for example, warned that the various elements of the media "have not communicated to whites a feeling for the difficulties and frustrations of being a Negro in the United States. They have not shown understanding or appreciation of—and thus have not communicated—a sense of Negro culture, thought, or history. . . . The world that television and newspapers offer to their black audience is almost totally white. . . ."

Report of the National Advisory Commission on Civil Disorders 210 (1968). In response, the Commission promulgated equal employment opportunity regulations, and formal "ascertainment" rules requiring a broadcaster as a condition of license "to ascertain the problems, needs and interests of the residents of his community of license and other areas he undertakes to serve," and to specify "what broadcast matter he proposes to meet those problems, needs and interests." The Commission explained that although it recognized there was "no single answer for all stations," it expected each licensee to devote a " 'significant proportion' " of a station's programming to community concerns. The Commission expressly included "minority and ethnic groups" as segments of the community that licensees were expected to consult. . . .

By 1978, however, the Commission had determined that even these efforts at influencing broadcast content were not effective means of generating adequate programming diversity. The FCC noted that "[w]hile the broadcasting industry has on the whole responded positively to its ascertainment obligations and has made significant strides in its employment practices, we are compelled to observe that the views of racial minorities continue to be inadequately represented in the broadcast media.". . . The Commission concluded that "despite the importance of our equal employment opportunity rules and ascertainment policies in assuring diversity of programming it appears that additional measures are necessary and appropriate. . . .

In short, the Commission established minority ownership preferences only after long experience demonstrated that race-neutral means could not produce adequate broadcasting diversity. The FCC did not act precipitately in devising the programs we uphold today; to the contrary, the Commission undertook thorough evaluations of its policies *three* times—in 1960, 1971, and 1978—before adopting the minority ownership programs. In endorsing the minority ownership preferences, Congress agreed with the Commission's assessment that race-neutral alternatives had failed to achieve the necessary programming diversity. . . .

The minority ownership policies, furthermore, are aimed directly at the barriers that minorities face in entering the broadcasting industry. The Commission's Task Force identified as key factors hampering the growth of minority ownership a lack of adequate financing, paucity of information regarding license availability, and broadcast inexperience. . . . Although it has underscored emphatically its support for the minority ownership policies, Congress has manifested that support through a series of appropriations acts of finite duration, thereby ensuring future reevaluations of the need for the minority ownership program as the number of minority broadcasters increases. In addition, Congress has continued to hold hearings on the subject of minority ownership. . . .

Finally, we do not believe that the minority ownership policies at issue impose impermissible burdens on nonminorities. Although the nonminority challengers in these cases concede that they have not suffered the loss of an already-awarded broadcast license, they claim that they have been handicapped in their ability to obtain one in the first instance. But just as we have determined that "[a]s part of this Nation's dedication to eradicating racial discrimination, innocent persons may be called upon to bear some of the burden of the remedy," *Wygant* [*v. Jackson Board of Education,* 476 U.S. 267 (1986)] (opinion of POWELL, J.), we similarly find that a congressionally mandated benign race-conscious program that is substantially related to the achievement of an important governmental interest is consistent with equal protection principles so long as it does not impose *undue* burdens on nonminorities. . . .

In the context of broadcasting licenses, the burden on nonminorities is slight. The FCC's responsibility is to grant licenses in the "public interest, convenience, or necessity," and the limited number of frequencies on the electromagnetic spectrum means that "[n]o one has a First Amendment right to a license." *Red Lion* [*Broadcasting Co. v. FCC*], 395 U.S. [367 (1969)]. Applicants have no settled expectation that their applications will be granted without consideration of public interest factors such as minority ownership. Award of a preference in a comparative hearing or transfer of a station in a distress sale thus contravenes "no legitimate firmly rooted expectation[s]" of competing applicants.

The Commission's minority ownership policies bear the imprimatur of longstanding congressional support and direction and are substantially related to the achievement of the important governmental objective of broadcast diversity. The judgment . . . is affirmed, and the [case is] remanded for proceedings consistent with this opinion.

It is so ordered.

Justice STEVENS concurring.

Today the Court squarely rejects the proposition that a governmental decision that rests on a racial classification is never permissible except as a remedy for a past wrong. I endorse this focus on the future benefit, rather than the remedial justification, of such decisions.

I remain convinced, of course, that racial or ethnic characteristics provide a relevant basis for disparate treatment only in extremely rare situations and that it is therefore "especially important that the reasons for any such classification be clearly identified and unquestionably legitimate." *Fullilove* v. *Klutznick* (1980) (dissenting opinion). The Court's opinion explains how both elements of that standard are satisfied. Specifically, the reason for the classification—the recognized interest in broadcast diversity—is clearly identified and does not imply any judgment concerning the abilities of owners of different races or the merits of different kinds of programming. Neither the favored nor the disfavored class is stigmatized in any way. In addition, the Court demonstrates that this case falls within the extremely narrow category of governmental decisions for which racial or ethnic heritage may provide a rational basis for differential treatment. The public interest in broadcast diversity—like the interest in an integrated police force, diversity in the composition of a public school faculty or diversity in the student body of a professional school—is in my view unquestionably legitimate.

Therefore, I join both the opinion and the judgment of the Court.

Justice O'CONNOR, with whom the CHIEF JUSTICE, Justice SCALIA, and Justice KENNEDY join, dissenting.

At the heart of the Constitution's guarantee of equal protection lies the simple command that the Government must treat citizens "as *individuals,* not 'as simply components of a racial, religious, sexual or national class.'" *Arizona Governing Committee* v. *Norris,* 463 U.S. 1073 (1983). Social scientists may debate how peoples' thoughts and behavior reflect their background, but the Constitution provides that the Government may not allocate benefits and burdens among individuals based on the assumption that race or ethnicity determines how they act or think. To uphold the challenged programs, the Court departs from these fundamental principles and from our traditional requirement that racial classifications are permissible only if necessary and narrowly tailored to achieve a compelling interest. This departure marks a renewed toleration of racial classifications and a repudiation of our recent affirmation that the Constitution's equal protection guarantees extend equally to all citizens. The Court's application of a lessened equal protection standard to congressional actions finds no support in our cases or in the Constitution. I respectfully dissent.

I

As we recognized last Term, the Constitution requires that the Court apply a strict standard of scrutiny to evaluate racial classifications such as those contained in the challenged FCC distress sale and comparative licensing policies. See *Richmond* v. *J. A. Croson Co.,* [488 U.S. 469] (1989); see also *Bolling* v. *Sharpe,* 347 U.S. 497 (1954). "Strict scrutiny" requires that, to be upheld, racial classifications must be determined to be necessary and narrowly tailored to achieve a compelling state interest. The Court abandons this traditional safeguard against discrimination for a lower standard of review, and in practice applies a standard like that applicable to routine legislation. Yet the Government's different treatment of citizens according to race is no routine concern. This Court's precedents in no way justify the Court's marked departure from our traditional treatment of race classifications and its conclusion that different equal protection principles apply to these federal actions.

In both the challenged policies, the FCC provides benefits to some members of our society and denies benefits to others based on race or ethnicity. Except in the narrowest of circumstances, the Constitution bars such racial classifications as a denial to particular individuals, of any race or ethnicity, of "the equal protection of the laws." The dangers of such classifications are clear. They endorse race-based reasoning and the conception of a Nation divided into racial blocs, thus contributing to an escalation of racial hostility and conflict. See *Croson*; *Korematsu v. United States,* 323 U.S. 214 (1944) (MURPHY, J., dissenting) (upholding treatment of individual based on inference from race is "to destroy the dignity of the individual and to encourage and open the door to discriminatory actions against other minority groups in the passions of tomorrow"). Such policies may embody stereotypes that treat individuals as the product of their race, evaluating their thoughts and efforts—their very worth as citizens—according to a criterion barred to the Government by history and the Constitution. Racial classifications, whether providing benefits to or burdening particular racial or ethnic groups, may stigmatize those groups singled out for different treatment and may create considerable tension with the Nation's widely shared commitment to evaluating individuals upon their individual merit. "Because racial characteristics so seldom provide a relevant basis for disparate treatment, and because classifications based on race are potentially so harmful to the entire body politic, it is especially important that the reasons for any such classifications be clearly identified and unquestionably legitimate." *Fullilove* v. *Klutznick* (STEVENS, J., dissenting) (footnotes omitted).

The Constitution's guarantee of equal protection binds the Federal Government as it does the States, and no lower level of scrutiny applies to the Federal Government's use of race classifications. In *Bolling* v. *Sharpe*, the companion case to *Brown* v. *Board of Education* (1954), the Court held that equal protection principles embedded in the Fifth Amendment's Due Process Clause prohibited the Federal Government from maintaining racially segregated schools in the District of Columbia: "[I]t would be unthinkable that the same Constitution would impose a lesser duty on the Federal Government." Consistent with this view, the Court has repeatedly indicated that "the reach of the equal protection guarantee of the Fifth Amendment is coextensive with that of the Fourteenth." *United States* v. *Paradise*, [480 U.S. 149 (1987)].

Nor does the congressional role in prolonging the FCC's policies justify any lower level of scrutiny. As with all instances of judicial review of federal legislation, the Court does not lightly set aside the considered judgment of a coordinate branch. Nonetheless, the respect due a coordinate branch yields neither less vigilance in defense of equal protection principles nor any corresponding diminution of the standard of review. *Bolling* v. *Sharpe,* itself involved extensive congressional regulation of the segregated District of Columbia public schools. . . .

The Court asserts that *Fullilove* supports its novel application of intermediate scrutiny to "benign" race conscious measures adopted by Congress. Three reasons defeat this claim. First, *Fullilove* concerned an exercise of Congress powers under § 5 of the Fourteenth Amendment. In *Fullilove,* the Court reviewed an act of Congress that had required States to set aside a percentage of federal construction funds for certain minority-owned businesses to remedy past discrimination in the award of construction contracts. Although the various opinions in *Fullilove* referred to several sources of congressional authority, the opinions make clear that it was § 5 that led the Court to apply a different form of review to the challenged program. . . . *Croson* resolved any doubt that might remain regarding this point. In *Croson,* we invalidated a local set-aside for minority contractors. We distinguished *Fullilove,* in which we upheld a similar set-aside enacted by Congress, on the ground that in *Fullilove* "Congress was exercising its powers under § 5 of the Fourteenth Amendment." *Croson* indicated that the decision in *Fullilove* turned on "the unique remedial powers of Congress under § 5," and that the latitude afforded Congress in identifying and redressing past discrimination rested on § 5's "specific constitutional mandate to enforce the dictates of the Fourteenth Amendment." Justice KENNEDY's concurrence in *Croson* likewise provides the majority with no support, for it questioned whether the Court should, as it had in *Fullilove,* afford any particular latitude even to measures undertaken pursuant to § 5.

Second, *Fullilove* applies at most only to congressional measures that seek to remedy identified past discrimination. The Court upheld the challenged measures in *Fullilove* only because Congress had identified discrimination that had particularly affected the construction industry and had carefully constructed corresponding remedial measures. *Fullilove* indicated that careful review was essential to ensure that Congress acted solely for remedial rather than other, illegitimate purposes. The FCC and Congress are clearly not acting for any remedial purpose, and the Court today expressly extends its standard to racial classifications that are not remedial in any sense. . . .

Finally, even if *Fullilove* applied outside a remedial exercise of Congress' § 5 power, it would not support today's adoption of the intermediate standard of review proffered by Justice MAR-SHALL but rejected in *Fullilove*. Under his suggested standard, the Government's use of racial classifications need only be " 'substantially related to achievement' " of important governmental interests. Although the Court correctly observes that a majority did not apply strict scrutiny, six Members of the Court rejected intermediate scrutiny in favor of some more stringent form of review. Three Members of the Court applied strict scrutiny. Chief Justice BURGER's opinion, joined by Justice WHITE and Justice POWELL, declined to adopt a particular standard of review but indicated that the Court must conduct "a most searching examination,". . . and that courts must ensure that "any congressional program that employs racial or ethnic criteria to accomplish the objective of remedying the present effects of past discrimination is narrowly tailored to the achievement of that goal." Justice STE-VENS indicated that "[r]acial classifications are simply too pernicious to permit any but the most exact connection between justification and classification.". . . Even Justice MARSHALL's opinion, joined by Justice BRENNAN and Justice BLACKMUN, undermines the Court's course today: that opinion expressly drew its lower standard of review from the plurality opinion in *Regents of University of Calif.* v. *Bakke* (1978), a case that did not involve congressional action, and stated that the appropriate standard of review for the congressional measure challenged in *Fullilove* "is the same as that under the Fourteenth Amendment." And, of course, *Fullilove* preceded our determination in *Croson* that strict scrutiny applies to preferences that favor members of minority groups, including challenges considered under the Fourteenth Amendment.

The guarantee of equal protection extends to each citizen, regardless of race: the Federal Government, like the States, may not "deny to any person within its jurisdiction the equal protection of the laws." As we observed only last Term in *Croson*, "[a]bsent searching judicial inquiry into the justification for such race-based measures, there is simply no way of determining what classifications are 'benign' or 'remedial' and what classifications are in fact motivated by illegitimate notions of racial inferiority or simple racial politics.". . .

The Court's reliance on "benign racial classifications," is particularly troubling. " 'Benign' racial classification" is a contradiction in terms. Governmental distinctions among citizens based on race or ethnicity, even in the rare circumstances permitted by our cases, exact costs and carry with them substantial dangers. To the person denied an opportunity or right based on race, the classification is hardly benign. The right to equal protection of the laws is a personal right, see *Shelley* v. *Kraemer*, [344 U.S. 1] (1948), securing to *each* individual an immunity from treatment predicated simply on membership in a particular racial or ethnic group. The Court's emphasis on "benign racial classifications" suggests confidence in its ability to distinguish good from harmful governmental uses of racial criteria. History should teach greater humility. Untethered to narrowly confined remedial notions, "benign" carries with it no independent meaning, but reflects only acceptance of the current generation's conclusion that a politically acceptable burden, imposed on particular citizens on the basis of race, is reasonable. The Court provides no basis for determining when a racial classification fails to be "benevolent." By expressly distinguishing "benign" from remedial race-conscious measures, the Court leaves the distinct possibility that any racial measure found to be substantially related to an important governmental objective is also, by definition, "benign." Depending on the preference of the moment, those racial distinctions might be directed expressly or in practice at any racial or ethnic group. We are a Nation not of black and white alone, but one teeming with divergent communities knitted together by various traditions and carried forth, above all, by individuals. Upon that basis, we are governed by one Constitution, providing a single guarantee of equal protection, one that extends equally to all citizens.

This dispute regarding the appropriate standard of review may strike some as a lawyers' quibble over words, but it is not. The standard of review establishes whether and when the Court and Constitution allow the Government to employ racial classifications. A lower standard signals that the Government may resort to racial distinctions more readily. The Court's departure from our cases is disturbing enough, but more disturbing still is the renewed toleration of racial classifications that its new standard of review embodies. . . .

Under the appropriate standard, strict scrutiny, only a compelling interest may support the Government's use of racial classifications. Modern equal protection doctrine has recognized only one such interest: remedying the effects of racial discrimination. The interest in increasing the diversity of broadcast viewpoints is clearly not a compelling interest. It is simply too amorphous, too insubstantial, and too unrelated to any legitimate basis for employing racial classifications. The Court does not claim otherwise. Rather, it employs its novel standard and claims that this asserted interest need only be, and is, "important." This conclusion twice compounds the Court's initial error of reducing its level of scrutiny of a racial classification. First, it too casually extends the justifications that might support racial classifications, beyond that of remedying past discrimination. We have recognized that racial classifications are so harmful that "[u]nless they are strictly reserved for remedial settings, they may in fact promote notions of racial inferiority and lead to a politics of racial hostility." *Croson.* . . .

Second, it has initiated this departure by endorsing an insubstantial interest, one that is certainly insufficiently weighty to justify tolerance of the Government's distinctions among citizens based on race and ethnicity. This endorsement trivializes the constitutional command to guard against such discrimination and has loosed a potentially far-reaching principle disturbingly at odds with our traditional equal protection doctrine.

An interest capable of justifying race-conscious measures must be sufficiently specific and verifiable, such that it supports only limited and carefully defined uses of racial classifications. In *Croson*, we held that an interest in remedying societal discrimination cannot be considered compelling. We determined that a "generalized assertion" of past discrimination "has no logical stopping point" and would support unconstrained uses of race classifications. . . .

Our traditional equal protection doctrine requires, in addition to a compelling state interest, that the Government's chosen means be necessary to accomplish and narrowly tailored to further the asserted interest. This element of strict scrutiny is designed to "ensur[e] that the means chosen 'fit' [the] compelling goal so closely that there is little or no possibility that the motive for the classification was illegitimate racial prejudice or stereotype." *Croson*. The chosen means, resting as they do on stereotyping and so indirectly furthering the asserted end, could not plausibly be deemed narrowly tailored. The Court instead finds the racial classifications to be "substantially related" to achieving the Government's interest, a far less rigorous fit requirement. The FCC's policies fail even this requirement. . . .

The FCC assumes a particularly strong correlation of race and behavior. The FCC justifies its conclusion that insufficiently diverse viewpoints are broadcast by reference to the percentage of minority owned stations. This assumption is correct only to the extent that minority owned stations promote the desired additional views, and that stations owned by individuals not favored by the preferences cannot, or at least do not, broadcast underrepresented programming. Additionally, the FCC's focus on ownership to improve programming assumes that preferences linked to race are so strong that they will dictate the owner's behavior in operating the station, overcoming the owner's personal inclinations and regard for the market. This strong link between race and behavior, especially when mediated by market forces, is the assumption that Justice Powell rejected in his discussion of health care service in *Bakke*. In that case, the state medical school argued that it could prefer members of minority groups because they were more likely to serve communities particularly needing medical care. Justice POWELL rejected this rationale, concluding that the assumption was unsupported and that such individual choices could not be presumed from ethnicity or race.

The majority addresses this point by arguing that the equation of race with distinct views and behavior is not "impermissible" in this particular case. Apart from placing undue faith in the Government and courts' ability to distinguish "good" from "bad" stereotypes, this reasoning repudiates essential equal protection principles that prohibit racial generalizations. The Court embraces the FCC's reasoning that an applicant's race will likely indicate that the applicant possesses a distinct perspective, but notes that the correlation of race to behavior is "not a rigid assumption about how minority owners will behave in every case." The corollary to this notion is plain: individuals of unfavored racial and ethnic backgrounds are unlikely to possess the unique experiences and background that contribute to viewpoint diversity. Both the reasoning and its corollary reveal but disregard what is objectionable about a stereotype: the racial generalization inevitably does not apply to certain individuals, and those persons may legitimately claim that they have been judged according to their race rather than upon a relevant criterion. . . .

Moreover, the FCC's selective focus on viewpoints associated with race illustrates a particular tailoring difficulty. The asserted interest is in advancing the Nation's different "social, political, esthetic, moral, and other ideas and experiences," *Red Lion*, yet of all the varied traditions and ideas shared among our citizens, the FCC has sought to amplify only those particular views it identifies through the classifications most suspect under equal protection doctrine. Even if distinct views could be associated with particular ethnic and racial groups, focusing on this particular aspect of the Nation's views calls into question the Government's genuine commitment to its asserted interest. . . .

Our equal protection doctrine governing intermediate review indicates that the Government may not use race and ethnicity as "a 'proxy for other, more germane bases of classification.' " The FCC has used race as a proxy for whatever views it believes to be underrepresented in the broadcasting spectrum. This reflexive or unthinking use of a suspect classification is the hallmark of an unconstitutional policy. The ill fit of means to end is manifest. The policy is overinclusive: many members of a particular racial or ethnic group will have no interest in advancing the views the FCC believes to be underrepresented, or will find them utterly foreign. The policy is underinclusive: it awards no preference to disfavored individuals who may be particularly well versed in and committed to presenting those views. The FCC has failed to implement a case-by-case determination, and that failure is particularly unjustified when individualized hearings already occur, as in the comparative licensing process. See *Orr v. Orr*, 440 U.S. 268 (1979). Even in the remedial context, we have required that the Government adopt means to ensure that the award of a particular preference advances the asserted interest. In *Fullilove*, even reviewing an exercise of § 5 powers, the Court upheld the challenged set-aside only because it contained a waiver provision that ensured that the program served its remedial function in particular cases. . . .

Moreover, the FCC's programs cannot survive even intermediate scrutiny because race-neutral and untried means of directly accomplishing the governmental interest are readily available. The FCC could directly advance its interest by requiring licensees to provide programming that the FCC believes would add to diversity. The interest the FCC asserts is in programming diversity, yet in adopting the challenged policies, the FCC expressly disclaimed having attempted *any* direct efforts to achieve its asserted goal. The Court suggests that administrative convenience excuses this failure, yet intermediate scrutiny bars the Government from relying upon that excuse to avoid measures that directly further the asserted interest. The FCC and the Court suggest that First Amendment interests in some manner should exempt the FCC from employing this direct, race-neutral means to achieve its asserted interest. They essentially argue that we may bend our equal protection principles to avoid more readily apparent harm to our First Amendment values. But the FCC cannot have it both ways: either the First Amendment bars the FCC from seeking to accomplish indirectly what it may not accomplish directly; or the FCC may pursue the goal, but must do so in a manner that comports with equal protection principles. And if the FCC can direct programming in any fashion, it must employ that direct means before resorting to indirect race-conscious means.

Other race-neutral means also exist, and all are at least as direct as the FCC's racial classifications. The FCC could evaluate applicants upon their ability to provide and commitment to offer whatever programming the FCC believes would reflect underrepresented viewpoints. If the FCC truly seeks diverse programming rather than allocation of goods to persons of particular racial backgrounds, it has little excuse to look to racial background rather than programming to further the programming interest. Additionally, if the FCC believes that certain persons by virtue of their unique experiences will contribute as owners to more diverse broadcasting, the FCC could simply favor applicants whose particular background indicates that they will add to the diversity of programming, rather than rely solely upon suspect classifications. Also, race-neutral means exist to allow access to the broadcasting industry for those persons excluded for financial and related reasons. The Court reasons that various minority preferences, including those reflected in the distress sale, overcome barriers of information, experience, and financing that inhibit minority ownership. Race-neutral financial and informational measures most directly reduce financial and informational barriers. . . .

The FCC has posited a relative absence of "minority viewpoints," yet it has never suggested what those views might be, or what other viewpoints might be absent from the broadcasting spectrum. It has never identified any particular deficiency in programming diversity that should be the subject of greater programming, or that necessitates racial classifications. . . . [T]he FCC has never determined that it has any need to resort to racial classifications to achieve its asserted interest, and it has employed race-conscious means before adopting readily available race-neutral, alternative means.

The FCC seeks to avoid the tailoring difficulties by focusing on minority ownership rather than the asserted interest in diversity of broadcast viewpoints. The Constitution clearly prohibits allocating valuable goods such as broadcast licenses simply on the basis of race. Yet the FCC refers to the lack of minority ownership of stations to support the existence of a lack of diversity of viewpoints, and has fitted its programs to increase ownership. See *1978 Policy Statement,* 68 F. C. C. 2d 979 (1978); *Commission Policy Regarding Advancement of Minority Ownership in Broadcasting,* 92 F. C. C. 2d 849 (1982). This repeated focus on ownership supports the inference that the FCC seeks to allocate licenses based on race, an impermissible end, rather than to increase diversity of viewpoints, the asserted interest. And this justification that links the use of race preferences to minority ownership rather than to diversity of viewpoints ensures that the FCC's programs, like that at issue in *Croson,* "cannot be said to be narrowly tailored to any goal, except perhaps outright racial balancing.". . .

Even apart from these tailoring defects in the FCC's policies, one particular flaw underscores the Government's ill fit of means to end. The FCC's policies assume and rely upon the existence of a tightly bound "nexus" between the owners' race and the resulting programming. The Court's lengthy discussion of this issue, purports to establish only that some relation exists between owners' race and programming: *i.e.,* that the FCC's choice to focus on allocation of licenses is rationally related to the asserted end. The Court understandably makes no stronger claims, because the evidence provides no support and because the requisite deference would so obviously abandon heightened scrutiny. For argument's sake, we can grant that the Court's review of congressional hearings and social science studies establishes the existence of some rational nexus. But even assuming that to be true, the Court's discussion does not begin to establish that the programs are directly and substantially related to the interest in diverse programming. That equal protection issue turns on the degree owners' race is related to programming, rather than whether any relation exists. To the extent that the FCC cannot show the nexus to be nearly complete, that failure confirms that the chosen means do not directly advance the asserted interest, that the policies rest instead upon illegitimate stereotypes, and that individualized determinations must replace the FCC's use of race as a proxy for the desired programming.

Three difficulties suggest that the nexus between owners' race and programming is considerably less than substantial. First, the market shapes programming to a tremendous extent. Members of minority groups who own licenses might be thought, like other owners, to seek to broadcast programs that will attract and retain audiences, rather than programs that reflect the owner's tastes and preferences. Second, station owners have only limited control over the content of programming. The distress sale presents a particularly acute difficulty of this sort. Unlike the comparative licensing program, the distress sale policy provides preferences to minority owners who neither intend nor desire to manage the station in any respect. Whatever distinct programming may attend the race of an owner actively involved in managing the station, an absentee owner would have far less effect on programming.

Third, the FCC had absolutely no factual basis for the nexus when it adopted the policies and has since established none to support its existence. . . .

Even apart from the limited nature of the Court's claims, little can be discerned from the congressional action. First, the Court's survey does not purport to establish that the FCC or Congress has identified any particular deficiency in the viewpoints contained in the broadcast spectrum. Second, no degree of congressional endorsement may transform the equation of race with behavior and thoughts into a permissible basis of governmental action. Even the most express and lavishly documented congressional declaration that members of certain races will as owners produce distinct and superior programming would not allow the Government to employ such reasoning to allocate benefits and burdens among citizens on that basis. Third, we should hesitate before accepting as definitive any declaration regarding even the existence of a nexus. The two legislative reports that claim some nexus to exist refer to sources that provide no support for the proposition. Congress through appropriations measures sought to foreclose examination of an issue that the FCC believed to be entirely unresolved. Especially where Congress rejects the considered judgment of the executive officials possessing particular expertise regarding the matter in issue, courts are hardly bound to accept the congressional declaration. Additionally, the FCC created the challenged policies. Congress has, through the appropriations process, frozen those policies in place by preventing the FCC from reexamining or altering them. That congressional action does not amount to an endorsement of the reasoning and empirical claims originally asserted and then abandoned by the FCC, and does not reflect the same considered judgment embodied in measures crafted through the legislative process and subject to the hearings and deliberation accompanying substantive legislation.

Finally, the Government cannot employ race classifications that unduly burden individuals who are not members of the favored racial and ethnic groups. The challenged policies fail this independent requirement, as well as the other constitutional requirements. The comparative licensing and distress sale programs provide the eventual licensee with an exceptionally valuable property and with a rare and unique opportunity to serve the local community. The distress sale imposes a particularly significant burden. The FCC has at base created a specialized market reserved exclusively for minority controlled applicants. There is no more rigid quota than a 100% set-aside. This fact is not altered by the observation, that the FCC and seller have some discretion over whether stations may be sold through the distress program. For the would-be purchaser or person who seeks to compete for the station, that opportunity depends entirely upon race or ethnicity. The Court's argument that the distress sale allocates only a small percentage of all license sales, also misses the mark. This argument readily supports complete preferences and avoids scrutiny of particular programs: it is no response to a person denied admission at one school, or discharged from one job, solely on the basis of race, that other schools or employers do not discriminate. . . .

In sum, the Government has not met its burden even under the Court's test that approves of racial classifications that are substantially related to an important governmental objective. Of course, the programs even more clearly fail the strict scrutiny that should be applied. The Court has determined, in essence, that Congress and all federal agencies are exempted, to some ill-defined but significant degree, from the Constitution's equal protection requirements. This break with our precedents greatly undermines equal protection guarantees, and permits distinctions among citizens based on race and ethnicity which the Constitution clearly forbids. I respectfully dissent.

Justice KENNEDY, with whom Justice SCALIA joins, dissenting.

Almost 100 years ago in *Plessy* v. *Ferguson*, 163 U.S. 537 (1896), this Court upheld a government-sponsored race-conscious measure, a Louisiana law that required "equal but separate accommodations" for "white" and "colored" railroad passengers. The Court asked whether the measures were "reasonable," and it stated that "[i]n determining the question of reasonableness, [the legislature] is at liberty to act with reference to the established usages, customs and traditions of the people, and with a view to the promotion of their comfort." The *Plessy* Court concluded that the "race-conscious measures" it reviewed were reasonable because they served the governmental interest of increasing the riding pleasure of railroad passengers. The fundamental errors in *Plessy*, its standard of review and its validation of rank racial insult by the State, distorted the law for six decades before the Court announced its apparent demise in *Brown v. Board of Education*, [347 U.S. 483] (1954). *Plessy*'s standard of review and its explication have disturbing parallels to today's majority opinion that should warn us something is amiss here. . . .

I cannot agree with the Court that the Constitution permits the Government to discriminate among its citizens on the basis of race in order to serve interests so trivial as "broadcast diversity." In abandoning strict scrutiny to endorse this interest the Court turns back the clock on the level of scrutiny applicable to federal race-conscious measures. Even strict scrutiny may not have sufficed to invalidate early race based laws of most doubtful validity, as we learned in *Korematsu v. United States*, 323 U.S. 214 (1944). But the relaxed standard of review embraced today would validate that case, and any number of future racial classifications the Government may find useful. Strict scrutiny is the surest test the Court has yet devised for holding true to the constitutional command of racial equality. Under our modern precedents, as Justice O'CONNOR explains, strict scrutiny must be applied to this statute. The approach taken to congressional measures under § 5 of the Fourteenth Amendment in *Fullilove v. Klutznick*, 448 U.S. 448 (1980), even assuming its validity, is not applicable to this case. . . .

The history of governmental reliance on race demonstrates that racial policies defended as benign often are not seen that way by the individuals affected by them. Today's dismissive statements aside, a plan of the type sustained here may impose "stigma on its supposed beneficiaries," and "foster intolerance and antagonism against the entire membership of the favored classes." Although the majority disclaims it, the FCC policy seems based on the demeaning notion that members of the defined racial groups ascribe to certain "minority views" that must be different from those of other citizens. Special preferences also can foster the view that members of the favored groups are inherently less able to compete on their own. And, rightly or wrongly, special preference programs often are perceived as targets for exploitation by opportunists who seek to take advantage of monetary rewards without advancing the stated policy of minority inclusion. . . .

Though the racial composition of this Nation is far more diverse than the first Justice HARLAN foresaw, his warning in dissent is now all the more apposite: "The destinies of the two races, in this country, are indissolubly linked together, and the interests of both require that the common government of all shall not permit the seeds of race hate to be planted under the sanction of law." *Plessy* (dissenting opinion). Perhaps the Court can succeed in its assumed role of case-by-case arbiter of when it is desirable and benign for the Government to disfavor some citizens and favor others based on the color of their skin. Perhaps the tolerance and decency to which our people aspire will let the disfavored rise above hostility and the favored escape condescension. But history suggests much peril in this enterprise, and so the Constitution forbids us to undertake it. I regret that after a century of judicial opinions we interpret the Constitution to do no more than move us from "separate but equal" to "unequal but benign."

D. NONRACIAL CLASSIFICATIONS AND THE EQUAL PROTECTION OF THE LAWS

As noted in the beginning of this chapter, in the 1970s and 1980s the Court sought retrenchment from further expansion of the application of the Warren Court's "two-tiered" approach to the equal protection clause. When confronted with challenges to nonracial classifications, the Burger Court evolved a third, intermediate standard of judicial review—the *exacting scrutiny* or *strict rationality test*—for *quasi-suspect categories* like gender and illegitimacy, as well as refused to extend heightened review to claims of discrimination based on wealth and age.

(1) Gender-Based Discrimination

Social and economic conditions did not make it possible until the mid-twentieth century for political movements and legal developments to push toward guaranteeing equal rights for women. Only in the 1970s did the Supreme Court begin to question gender-based discrimination. For more than a century, the Fourteenth Amendment offered little promise for women as the Court reinforced the second-class status and sexual stereotypes of women in constitutional law. *Bradwell v. State of Illinois*, 83 U.S. 130 (1873), for example, upheld Illinois's denial of women the right to practice law, and *Minor v. Happersett*, 88 U.S. 162 (1875) dismissed out-of-hand the claim that women had a constitutional right to vote. Even after the Nineteenth Amendment (1920), extending the right to vote to women, the Court held that neither that amendment nor the Fourteenth Amendment secured legal equality for women.[1] Sexual stereotypes of women as the "weaker sex," who "looks to her brother and depends on him" in Justice David Brewer's words, undergirded even progressive legislation and rulings, like *Muller v. Oregon*, 208 U.S. 412 (1908). In *Muller*,

Justice Brewer upheld Oregon's law limiting the hours women could work in factories upon taking notice of the fact that

The two sexes differ in structure of body, in the functions to be performed by each, in the amount of physical strength, in the capacity for long-continued labor, particularly when done standing, . . . [in] the self-reliance which enables one to assert full rights, and in the capacity to maintain the struggle for subsistence. This difference justifies a difference in legislation and upholds that which is designed to compensate for some of the burdens which rest upon her.

On much the same rationale the Warren Court unanimously concluded that the equal protection clause did not bar Florida from excluding women from jury service, in *Hoyt v. Florida*, 368 U.S. 57 (1961).

World War II brought about changes in the workforce. An unprecedented number of women worked in industries and factories as a result of wartime mobilization. After the war, economic expansion provided expanded employment opportunities. By the 1960s, the women's movement was revitalized and feminist groups pushed for political and legal changes. Congress responded to that political pressure. In 1963, the Equal Pay Act amended the Fair Labor Standards Act to require equal pay for equal work. The Civil Rights Act of 1964 prohibited sex discrimination by employers, labor organizations, and employment agencies. In 1972, the Civil Rights Act was amended to authorize in Title V the denial of federal funding for public and private programs that discriminated against women, and Title IX specifically requires equal athletic facilities and opportunities for women. Congress also passed in 1972 the Equal Rights Amendment, which after a decade long battle failed to win ratification by three-fourths of the states as required under the Constitution.

CONSTITUTIONAL HISTORY
The Equal Rights Amendment

During the Progressive era after the turn of the century, political pressure began to mount for the adoption of a constitutional amendment to guarantee equal rights for women. Indeed, for almost fifty years (from 1923 to 1972) Congress annually considered one proposal or another for an equal rights amendment.

Finally, in response to the women's movement and lobbying of organizations such as the National Organization for Women (NOW) and the National Women's Political Caucus, in 1972 Congress passed the proposed Equal Rights Amendment, providing that

Section 1. Equality of rights under the law shall not be denied or abridged by the United States or by any State on account of sex.

Section 2. The Congress shall have the power to enforce, by appropriate legislation, the provisions of this article.

Section 3. The Amendment shall take effect two years after the date of ratification.

Within a year of the ERA's proposal, twenty-two states ratified the amendment. But by 1978, one year before the deadline for ratification of the amendment by three-fourths of the states, only thirty-five states had voted for ratification—three votes short of the number needed. Political opposition intensified as organizations such as the National Council of Catholic Women, Mormons, and other religious groups, as well as political activitist Phyllis Schlafly's Eagle Forum, mobilized to defeat the ERA's ratification. Three states voted to rescend their earlier support, and faced with the prospect of the ERA's defeat in 1979 Congress voted to extend the ratification deadline for three more years. In 1982, the ERA was defeated; fifteen states refused ratification and five that had supported the amendment rescinded their votes.

The ERA divided rather than united women politically and culturally. Some women's groups argued that the amendment would not in fact ensure equality in higher education and employment. Others countered that the ERA would do away with protective legislation safeguarding the rights of women in the workplace, requiring marital and child support from divorced husbands, and exempting women from compulsory military registration and service. Still others claimed that the amendment was only symbolic; while some ERA's supporters maintained that even a symbolic affirmation of the constitutional equality of women was important. By the late 1970s, many gender-based classifications that the ERA was originally intended to outlaw had been rendered illegal by Congress, executive orders, and rulings of the Supreme Court, which applied the equal protection clause, the Civil Rights Act of 1964, and other federal legislation.

The Supreme Court signaled that it would take seriously challenges to gender-based classification in *Reed v. Reed*, 404 U.S. 71 (1971). Writing for a unanimous Court there, Chief Justice Burger overturned Idaho's statute giving preference to males over females in interstate proceedings. While finding the statute lacked a rational basis for distinguishing between men and women, he declined to address the claim that gender is a "suspect" category requiring strict scrutiny. Less than two years later in *Frontiero v. Richardson* (1973) (see page 1428), then, Justice Brennan could persuade only three other justices that gender was a suspect category.

Despite the fact that the Court came within one vote of declaring gender a suspect category, *Reed* and *Frontiero* indicated that gender was quasi-suspect category to which the Court would give heightened, if not strict, scrutiny. In *Craig v. Boren* (1976) (see page 1433), the Court further developed its "heightened or 'intermediate' level of scrutiny test." In applying this test the Court considers whether a gender-based distinction bears a substantial relationship to an important governmental interest. As the tables on pages 1424 and 1426 show, the Court has tended to promote gender-neutral classifications, striking down even laws (as in *Craig*) which are defended as "benign" or "compensatory."[2] Note that gender-neutral laws disproporately affecting one gender, though, typically do not receive the same heightened scrutiny accorded explicit gender-based classifications. Moreover, the Court has upheld some gender-based classifications as illustrated in the five-to-four ruling in *Michael M. v. Superior Court of Sonoma County* (1981) (see page 1441).

THE DEVELOPMENT OF LAW
Other Rulings Striking Down Gender-Based Distinctions under the Constitution

Case	Vote	Ruling
Reed v. Reed, 404 U.S. 71 (1971)	9:0	Chief Justice Burger struck down Idaho's statute giving preference to males in intestate proceedings for lacking a rational basis.
Weinberger v. Wiesenfeld, 420 U.S. 636 (1975)	8:0	With Justice Douglas not participating, the Court struck down a section of the Social Security Act that granted survivors benefits to widows and minor children, but not to widowers because the fact that men are more likely to be employed is not a compelling reason for distinguishing between males and females.
Stanton v. Stanton, 421 U.S. 7 (1975)	8:1	With Justice Rehnquist dissenting, the Court overturned as irrational a Utah law requiring child-support payments for males until

Case	Vote	Ruling
		they reach the age of twenty-one and for females until they reach the age of eighteen.
Califano v. Goldfarb, 430 U.S. 199 (1977)	5:4	Struck down a portion of the Social Security Act which provided benefits for widows based on the earnings of deceased husbands, but no benefits for widowers unless they had received half of their financial support from their deceased spouses.
Orr v. Orr, 440 U.S. 268 (1979)	6:3	With Chief Justice Burger and Justices Rehnquist and Powell dissenting, the majority struck down Alabama's law making husbands, but not wives, liable for alimony payments after a divorce.
Caban v. Mohammed, 441 U.S. 380 (1979)	5:4	Overturned New York's law permitting unwed mothers, but not fathers, to withhold consent from the adoption of their children; Chief Justice Burger and Justices Rehnquist, Stewart and Stevens dissented.
Califano v. Westcott, 433 U.S. 2655 (1979)	9:0	Held unconstitutional under the Fifth Amendment due process clause a section of the Social Security Act that provided benefits to families with dependent children because of father's, but not mother's, unemployment.
Wengler v. Druggists Mutual Insurance Co., 446 U.S. 142 (1980)	8:1	With only Justice Rehnquist dissenting, the Court found insufficient support for Missouri's workmen's compensation law, which denied widowers, but not widows, benefits, unless a widower was "either mentally or physically incapacitated" or established a de-

Case	Vote	Ruling
		pendence on his wife's income.
Kirchberg v. Fennstra, 450 U.S. 455 (1981)	9:0	Struck down Louisiana's law giving husbands a right to dispose of jointly owned property without wife's consent as unjustified.
Mississippi University for Women v. Hogan, 458 U.S. 718 (1982)	5:4	With Chief Justice Burger and Justices Blackmun, Powell, and Rehnquist dissenting, a bare majority overturned a nursing school's policy of denying admission to qualified males.

THE DEVELOPMENT OF LAW

Other Rulings Upholding Gender-Based Distinctions under the Constitution

Case	Vote	Ruling
Kahn v. Shavin, 416 U.S. 351 (1974)	6:3	Justice Douglas's opinion upheld Florida's law giving widows, but not widowers, a $500 property tax exemption as rational, given the greater financial difficulties that women face when their spouses die than those facing men whose spouses die; Justices Brennan, Marshall, and White dissented.
Schlesinger v. Ballard, 419 U.S 498 (1975)	5:4	Upheld federal statutes requiring mandatory discharge of women in the Navy after thirteen years, if they have not been promoted, and of men after nine years, because it was a rational distinction based on the different opportunities afforded men and

Case	Vote	Ruling
		women for sea and combat duty.
Geduldig v. Aiello, 417 U.S. 484 (1974)	6:3	Upheld as rational California's program of allowing disability insurance benefits for private employees not covered by workmen's compensation laws, except for pregnancy and certain other disabilities because the cost of extending coverage might jeopardize the program.
Rostker v. Goldberg, 453 U.S. 57 (1981)	6:3	Upheld the Military Selective Service Act's authorization for the president to require males, but not females, to register for potential military service; Justices Brennan, White, and Marshall dissented.
Personnel Administrator of Massachusetts v. Fenney, 442 U.S. 256 (1979)	7:2	Upheld a Massachusetts law giving preference in hiring decisions to veterans who qualify for state civil service positions, over the objections of a qualified woman who was passed over for a position.

The Court has also tended, although not invariably, to affirm claims against gender discrimination under the Civil Rights Act of 1964 and other federal legislation. Notably, in *Meritor Savings Bank, FBD v. Vinson* (1986) (see page 1449) the Court held that Title VII of the Civil Rights Act of 1964 bars "sexual harrassment" in the workplace, and not just gender discrimination in the hiring and firing of employees. See also the table on page 1454.

NOTES

1. See *Fay v. New York,* 332 U.S. 261 (1947). The struggle for women's voting rights is further examined in Vol. 1, ch. 8.

2. See, for example, *Califano v. Goldfarb*, 430 U.S. 199 (1977), *Orr v. Orr*, 440 U.S. 268 (1979), and *Mississippi University for Women v. Hogan*, 458 U.S. 718 (1982).

SELECTED BIBLIOGRAPHY

Babcock, Barbara, Freedman, Ann, Norton, Eleanor, and Ross, Susan, eds. *Sex Discrimination: Causes and Remedies*. Boston: Little, Brown, 1974.

Boles, Janet. *The Politics of the Equal Rights Amendment*. New York: Longman's 1979.

Epstein, Cynthia. *Women in Law*. New York: Basic Books, 1981.

Ginsberg, Ruth. *Constitutional Aspects of Sex-Based Discrimination*. St. Paul, MN: West, 1974.

Harrison, Cynthia. *On Account of Sex: The Politics of Women's Issues, 1945–1968*. Berkeley: University of California Press, 1988.

MacKinnon, Catherine. *Sexual Harassment of Working Women: A Case of Sex Discrimination*. New Haven, CT: Yale University Press, 1978.

O'Connor, Karen. *Women's Organizations' Use of the Courts*. Lexington, MA: Lexington Books, 1980.

Rhode, Deborah. *Justice and Gender*. Cambridge, MA: Harvard University Press, 1989.

Rhode, Deborah. *Theoretical Perspectives on Sexual Differences*. New Haven, CT: Yale University Press, 1990.

Frontiero v. Richardson
411 U.S. 677, 93 S.Ct. 1764 (1973)

Sharron Frontiero and her husband sued U.S. Secretary of State Elliot Richardson and sought an injunction against the enforcement of federal statutes governing the award of benefits for "dependents" of military personnel. Sharron Frontiero was a lieutenant in the U.S. Air Force. She had sought but was denied increased quarters and allowances and health and medical benefits for her husband, who was a full-time student. Because such benefits would automatically be given to the wife of a male military officer, Frontiero argued that the laws unreasonably discriminated against women and violated the due process clause of the Fifth Amendment. Although the Fifth Amendment contains no equal protection clause, *Bolling v. Sharpe* (1954) (see page 1315) and other rulings had held that the amendment bars the discrimination by the federal government that is "so unjustifiable as to be violate of due process."[*]

On appeal to the Supreme Court, the justices agreed with Frontiero eight to one, with Justice Rehnquist dissenting. However, the majority split four to four on the question of whether gender is a suspect classification and what standard the Court should use when reviewing cases challenging gender-based discrimination. Justice Brennan, joined by three others, contended that gender, like race, is a suspect classification; while Justice Powell, writing for three others, disagreed and contended that it would be wrong for the Court to go that far, because at the time the country was debating the ill-fated Equal Rights Amendment.

Justice BRENNAN with whom Justice DOUGLAS, Justice WHITE, and Justice MARSHALL join, delivers the opinion of the Court.

The question before us concerns the right of a female member of the uniformed services to claim her spouse as a "dependent" for the purposes of obtaining increased quarters allowances and medical and dental benefits under 37 U.S.C. §§ 401, 403, and 10 U.S.C. §§ 1072, 1076, on an equal footing with male members. Under these statutes, a serviceman may claim his wife as a "dependent" without regard to whether she is in fact dependent upon him for any part of her support. A servicewoman, on the other hand, may not claim her husband as a "dependent" under these programs unless he is in fact dependent upon her for over one-half of his support. Thus, the question for decision is whether this difference in treatment constitutes an unconstitutional discrimination against servicewomen in violation of the Due Process Clause of the Fifth Amendment. A three-judge District Court for the Middle District of Alabama, one judge dissenting, rejected this contention and sustained the constitutionality of the provisions of the statutes making this distinction. . . . We reverse. . . .

At the outset, appellants contend that classifications based upon sex, like classifications based upon race, alienage, and national origin, are inherently suspect and must therefore be subjected to close judicial scrutiny. We agree and, indeed, find at least implicit support for such an approach in our unanimous decision only last Term in *Reed v. Reed*, 404 U.S. 71 (1971).

In *Reed*, the Court considered the constitutionality of an Idaho statute providing that, when two individuals are otherwise equally entitled to appointment as administrator of an estate, the male

---

[*]   *Schneider v. Rusk*, 377 U.S. 163 (1964).

applicant must be preferred to the female. Appellant, the mother of the deceased, and appellee, the father, filed competing petitions for appointment as administrator of their son's estate. Since the parties, as parents of the deceased, were members of the same entitlement class the statutory preference was invoked and the father's petition was therefore granted. Appellant claimed that this statute, by giving a mandatory preference to males over females without regard to their individual qualifications, violated the Equal Protection Clause of the Fourteenth Amendment.

The Court noted that the Idaho statute, "provides that different treatment be accorded to the applicants on the basis of their sex; it thus establishes a classification subject to scrutiny under the Equal Protection Clause." Under "traditional" equal protection analysis, a legislative classification must be sustained unless it is "patently arbitrary" and bears no rational relationship to a legitimate governmental interest.

In an effort to meet this standard, appellee contended that the statutory scheme was a reasonable measure designed to reduce the workload on probate courts by eliminating one class of contests. Moreover, appellee argued that the mandatory preference for male applicants was in itself reasonable since "men are as a rule more conversant with business affairs than . . . women." Indeed, appellee maintained that "it is a matter of common knowledge, that women still are not engaged in politics, the professions, business or industry to the extent that men are." And the Idaho Supreme Court, in upholding the constitutionality of this statute, suggested that the Idaho Legislature might reasonably have "concluded that in general men are better qualified to act as an administrator than are women."

Despite these contentions, however, the Court held the statutory preference for male applicants unconstitutional. In reaching this result, the Court implicitly rejected appellee's apparently rational explanation of the statutory scheme, and concluded that, by ignoring the individual qualifications of particular applicants, the challenged statute provide "dissimilar treatment for men and women who are . . . similarly situated." The Court therefore held that, even though the State's interest in achieving administrative efficiency "is not without some legitimacy," "[t]o give a mandatory preference to members of either sex over members of the other, merely to accomplish the elimination of hearings on the merits, is to make the very kind of arbitrary legislative choice forbidden by the [Constitution]. . . ." This departure from "traditional" rational-basis analysis with respect to sex-based classifications is clearly justified.

There can be no doubt that our Nation has had a long and unfortunate history of sex discrimination. Traditionally, such discrimination was rationalized by an attitude of "romantic paternalism" which, in practical effect, put women, not on a pedestal, but in a cage. . . .

As a result of notions such as these, our statute books gradually became laden with gross, sterotyped distinctions between the sexes and, indeed, throughout much of the 19th century the position of women in our society was, in many respects, comparable to that of blacks under the pre-Civil War slave codes. Neither slaves nor women could hold office, serve on juries, or bring suit in their own names, and married women traditionally were denied the legal capacity to hold or convey property or to serve as legal guardians of their own children. . . .

Moreover, since sex, like race and national origin, is an immutable characteristic determined solely by the accident of birth, the imposition of special disabilities upon the members of a particular sex because of their sex would seem to violate "the basic concept of our system that legal burdens should bear some relationship to individual responsibility. . . ." *Weber v. Aetna Casualty & Surety Co.*, 406 U.S. 164, 175 (1972). And what differentiates sex from such nonsuspect statuses as intelligence or physical disability, and aligns it with the recognized suspect criteria, is that the sex characteristic frequently bears no relation to ability to perform or contribute to society. As a result, statutory distinctions between the sexes often have the effect of invidiously relegating the entire class of females to inferior legal status without regard to the actual capabilities of its individual members. . . .

With these considerations in mind, we can only conclude that classifications based upon sex, like classifications based upon race, alienage, or national origin, are inherently suspect, and must therefore be subjected to strict judicial scrutiny. Applying the analysis mandated by that stricter standard of review, it is clear that the statutory scheme now before us is constitutionally invalid.

The sole basis of the classification established in the challenged statutes is the sex of the individuals involved. Thus, under 37 U.S.C. §§ 401, 403, and 10 U.S.C. §§ 2072, 2076, a female member of the uniformed services seeking to obtain housing and medical benefits for her spouse must prove his dependency in fact, whereas no such burden is imposed upon male members. In addition, the statutes operate so as to deny benefits to a female member, such as appellant Sharron Frontiero, who provides less than one-half of her spouse's support, while at the same time granting such benefits to a male member who likewise provides less than one-half of his spouse's support. . . .

The Government offers no concrete evidence, however, tending to support its view that such differential treatment in fact saves the Government any money. In order to satisfy the demands of strict judicial scrutiny, the Government must demonstrate, for example, that it is actually cheaper to grant increased benefits with respect to *all* male members, than it is to determine which male members are in fact entitled to such benefits and to grant increased benefits only to those members whose wives actually meet the dependency requirement. Here, however, there is substantial evidence that, if put to the test, many of the wives of male members would fail to qualify for benefits. And in light of the fact that the dependency determination with respect to the husbands of female members is presently made solely on the basis of affidavits rather than through the more costly hearing process, the Government's explanation of the statutory scheme is, to say the least, questionable.

In any case, our prior decisions make clear that, although efficacious administration of governmental programs is not without some importance, "the Constitution recognizes higher values than speed and efficiency." *Stanley v. Illinois,* 405 U.S. 645 (1972). And when we enter the realm of "strict judicial scrutiny," there can be no doubt that "administrative convenience" is not a shibboleth, the mere recitation of which dictates constitutionality. . . . On the contrary, any statutory scheme which draws a sharp line between the sexes, *solely* for the purpose of achieving administrative convenience, necessarily commands "dissimilar treatment for men and women who are . . . similarly situated," and therefore involves the "very kind of arbitrary legislative choice forbidden by the [Constitution]. . . ." *Reed v. Reed,* [404 U.S. 71 (1971)]. We therefore conclude that, by according differential treatment to male and female members of the uniformed services for the sole purpose of achieving administrative convenience, the challenged statutes violate the Due Process Clause of the Fifth Amendment insofar as they require a female member to prove the dependency of her husband.

Reversed.

Justice STEWART concurred.

Justice REHNQUIST dissented.

Justice POWELL, with whom the CHIEF JUSTICE and Justice BLACKMUN join, concurring.

I agree that the challenged statutes constitute an unconstitutional discrimination against servicewomen in violation of the Due Process Clause of the Fifth Amendment, but I cannot join the opinion of Justice BRENNAN, which would hold that all classifications based upon sex, "like classifications based upon race, alienage, and national origin," are "inherently suspect and must therefore be subjected to close judicial scrutiny." It is unnecessary for the Court in this case to characterize sex as a suspect classification, with all of the far-reaching implications of such a holding. . . .

There is another, and I find compelling, reason for deferring a general categorizing of sex classifications as invoking the strictest test of judicial scrutiny. The Equal Rights Amendment, which if adopted will resolve the substance of this precise question, has been approved by the Congress and submitted for ratification by the States. If this Amendment is duly adopted, it will represent the will of the people accomplished in the manner prescribed by the Constitution. By acting prematurely and unnecessarily, as I view it, the Court has assumed a decisional responsibility at the very time when state legislatures, functioning within the traditional democratic process, are debating the proposed Amendment. It seems to me that this reaching out to pre-empt by judicial action a major political decision which is currently in process of resolution does not reflect appropriate respect for duly prescribed legislative processes.

Craig v. Boren

429 U.S. 190, 97 S.Ct. 451 (1976)

Curtis Craig, a male under twenty-one years old, and a female distributor of alcoholic beverages sought in federal district court declaratory and injunctive relief against the enforcement of an Oklahoma statute that forbade the sale of 3.2 beer to males, but not females, under the age of twenty-one. They argued that the law constituted invidious discrimination against males and violated the equal protection clause of the Fourteenth Amendment. After a three-judge district court denied relief, Craig appealed to the Supreme Court, which reversed by a vote of seven to two, with Chief Justice Burger and Justice Rehnquist dissenting.

Justice BRENNAN delivers the opinion of the Court.

The interaction of two sections of an Oklahoma statute, 37 Okla.Stat. §§ 241 and 245, prohibits the sale of "nonintoxicating" 3.2% beer to males under the age of 21 and to females under the age of 18. The question to be decided is whether such a gender-based differential constitutes a denial to males 18–20 years of age of the Equal Protection of the Laws in violation of the Fourteenth Amendment. . . .

Analysis may appropriately begin with the reminder that *Reed v. Reed,* [404 U.S. 71 (1971)], emphasized that statutory classifications that distinguish between males and females are "subject to scrutiny under the Equal Protection Clause." To withstand constitutional challenge, previous cases establish that classifications by gender must serve important governmental objectives and must be substantially related to achievement of those objectives. Thus, in *Reed,* the objectives of "reducing the workload on probate courts,". . . and "avoiding intra-family controversy," were deemed of insufficient importance to sustain use of an overt gender criterion in the appointment of intestate administrators. Decisions following *Reed* similarly have rejected administrative ease and convenience as sufficiently important objectives to justify gender-based classifications. . . .

Reed v. Reed has also provided the underpinning for decisions that have invalidated statutes employing gender as an inaccurate proxy for other, more germane bases of classification. Hence, "archaic and overbroad" generalizations, *Schlesinger v. Ballard* [419 U.S. 498 (1975)], concerning the financial position of servicewomen, *Frontiero v. Richardson,* [411 U.S. 677 (1973), and working women, *Weinberger v. Wiesenfeld,* [420 U.S. 636 (1975)], could not justify use of a gender line in determining eligibility for certain governmental entitlements. Similarly increasingly outdated misconceptions concerning the role of females in the home rather than in the "marketplace and world of ideas" were rejected as loose-fitting characterizations incapable of supporting state statutory schemes that were premised upon their accuracy. . . .

In this case, too, "*Reed* we feel is controlling. . . ." We turn then to the question whether, under *Reed,* the difference between males and females with respect to the purchase of 3.2% beer warrants the differential in age drawn by the Oklahoma statute. We conclude that it does not. . . .

We accept for purposes of discussion the District Court's identification of the objective underlying §§ 241 and 245 as the enhancement of traffic safety. Clearly, the protection of public health and safety represents an important function of state and local governments. However, appellees statistics in our view cannot support the conclusion that the gender-based distinction closely serves to achieve that objective and therefore the distinction cannot under *Reed* withstand equal protection challenge.

The appellees introduced a variety of statistical surveys. First, an analysis of arrest statistics for 1973 demonstrated that 18–20-year-old male arrests for "driving under the influence" and "drunkenness" substantially exceeded female arrests for that same age period. Similarly, youths aged 17–21 were found to be overrepresented among those killed or injured in traffic accidents, with males again numerically exceeding females in this regard. Third, a random roadside survey in Oklahoma City revealed that young males were more inclined to drive and drink beer than were their female counterparts. Fourth, Federal Bureau of Investigation nationwide statistics exhibited a notable increase in arrests for "driving under the influence." Finally, statistical evidence gathered in other jurisdictions, particularly Minnesota and Michigan, was offered to corroborate Oklahoma's experience by indicating the pervasiveness of youthful participation in motor vehicle accidents following the imbibing of alcohol. . . .

Even were this statistical evidence accepted as accurate, it nevertheless offers only a weak answer to the equal protection question presented here. The most focused and relevant of the statistical surveys, arrests of 18–20-year-olds for alcohol-related driving offenses, exemplifies the ultimate unpersuasiveness of this evidentiary record. Viewed in terms of the correlation between sex and the actual activity that Oklahoma seeks to regulate—driving while under the influence of alcohol—the statistics broadly establish that .18% of females and 2% of males in that age group were arrested for that offense. While such a disparity is not trivial in a statistical sense, it hardly can form the basis for employment of a gender line as a classifying device. Certainly if maleness is to serve as a proxy for drinking and driving, a correlation of 2% must be considered an unduly tenuous "fit." Indeed, prior cases have consistently rejected the use of sex as a decisionmaking factor even though the statutes in question certainly rested on far more predictive empirical relationships than this.

Moreover, the statistics exhibit a variety of other shortcomings that seriously impugn their value to equal protection analysis. Setting aside the obvious methodological problems, the surveys do not adequately justify the salient features of Oklahoma's gender-based traffic-safety law. None purports to measure the use and dangerousness of 3.2% beer as opposed to alcohol generally, a detail that is of particular importance since, in light of its low alcohol level, Oklahoma apparently considers the 3.2% beverage to be "non-intoxicating.". . .

There is no reason to belabor this line of analysis. It is unrealistic to expect either members of the judiciary or state officials to be well versed in the rigors of experimental or statistical technique. But this merely illustrates that proving broad sociological propositions by statistics is a dubious business, and one that inevitably is in tension with the normative philosophy that underlies the Equal Protection Clause. Suffice to say that the showing offered by the appellees does not satisfy us that sex represents a legitimate, accurate proxy for the regulation of drinking and driving. In fact, when it is further recognized that Oklahoma's statute prohibits only the selling of 3.2% beer to young males and not their drinking the beverage once acquired (even after purchase by their 18–20-year-old female companions), the relationship between gender and traffic safety becomes far too tenuous to satisfy

Reed's requirement that the gender-based difference be substantially related to achievement of the statutory objective.

We hold, therefore, that under *Reed,* Oklahoma's 3.2% beer statute invidiously discriminates against males 18–20 years of age. . . .

We conclude that the gender-based differential contained in 37 Okla.Stat. § 245 constitutes a denial of the Equal Protection of the Laws to males aged 18–20 and reverse the judgment of the District Court.

Justice POWELL concurring.

I join the opinion of the Court as I am in general agreement with it. I do have reservations as to some of the discussion concerning the appropriate standard for equal protection analysis and the relevance of the statistical evidence. Accordingly, I add this concurring statement. . . .

Reed and subsequent cases involving gender-based classifications make clear that the Court subjects such classifications to a more critical examination than is normally applied when "fundamental" constitutional rights and "suspect classes" are not present.

I view this as a relatively easy case. No one questions the legitimacy or importance of the asserted governmental objective: the promotion of highway safety. The decision of the case turns on whether the state legislature, by the classification it has chosen, had adopted a means that bears a "fair and substantial relation" to this objective. . . .

It seems to me that the statistics offered by the State and relied upon by the District Court do tend generally to support the view that young men drive more, possibly are inclined to drink more, and—for various reasons—are involved in more accidents that young women. Even so, I am not persuaded that these facts and the inferences fairly drawn from them justify this classification based on a three-year age differential between the sexes, and especially one that it so easily circumvented as to be virtually meaningless. Putting it differently, this gender-based classification does not bear a fair and substantial relation to the object of the legislation.

Justice STEVENS concurring.

There is only one Equal Protection Clause. It requires every State to govern impartially. It does not direct the courts to apply one standard of review in some cases and a different standard in other cases. Whatever criticism may be levelled at a judicial opinion implying that there are at least three such standards applies with the same force to a double standard.

I am inclined to believe that what has become known as the two-tiered analysis of equal protection claims does not describe a completely logical method of deciding cases, but rather is a method the Court has employed to explain decisions that actually apply a single standard in a reasonably consistent fashion. I also suspect that a careful explanation of the reasons motivating particular decisions may contribute more to an identification of that standard than an attempt to articulate it in all-encompassing terms. It may therefore be appropriate for me to state the principal reasons which persuaded me to join the Court's opinion.

In this case, the classification is not as obnoxious as some the Court has condemned, nor as inoffensive as some the Court has accepted. It is objectionable because it is based on an accident of birth, because it is a mere remnant of the now almost universally rejected tradition of discriminating against males in this age bracket, and because, to the extent it reflects any physical difference between males and females, it is actually perverse. The question then is whether the traffic safety justification put forward by the State is sufficient to make an otherwise offensive classification acceptable.

The classification is not totally irrational. For the evidence does indicate that there are more males than females in this age bracket who drive and also more who drink. Nevertheless, there are several reasons why I regard the justification as unacceptable. It is difficult to believe that the statute was actually intended to cope with the problem of traffic safety, since it has only a minimal effect on access to a not-very-intoxicating beverage and does not prohibit its consumption. Moreover, the empirical data submitted by the State accentuates the unfairness of treating all 18–21-year-old males as inferior to their female counterparts. The legislation imposes a restraint on one hundred percent of the males in the class allegedly because about 2% of them have probably violated one or more laws relating to the consumption of alcoholic beverages. It is unlikely that this law will have a significant deterrent effect either on that 2% or on the law-abiding 98%. But even assuming some such slight benefit, it does not seem to me that an insult to all of the young men of the State can be justified by visiting the sins of the 2% on the 98%.

Justice BLACKMUN and Justice STEWART concurred.

Justice BURGER dissented.

Justice REHNQUIST dissenting.

The Court's disposition of this case is objectionable on two grounds. First, is its conclusion that *men* challenging a gender-based statute which treats them less favorably than women may invoke a more stringent standard of judicial review than pertains to most other types of classifications. Second is the Court's enunciation of this standard, without citation to any source, as being that "classifications by gender must serve *important* governmental objectives and must be *substantially* related to achievement of those objectives" (emphasis added). The only redeeming feature of the Court's opinion, to my mind, is that it apparently signals a retreat by those who joined the plurality opinion in *Frontiero v. Richardson*, from their view that sex is a "suspect" classification for purposes of equal protection analysis. I think the Oklahoma statute challenged here need pass only the "rational basis" equal protection analysis, and I believe that it is constitutional under that analysis. . . .

Most obviously unavailable to support any kind of special scrutiny in this case is a history or pattern of past discrimination, such as was relied on by the plurality in *Frontiero* to support its invocation of strict scrutiny. There is no suggestion in the Court's opinion that males in this age group are in any way peculiarly disadvantaged, subject to systematic discriminatory treatment, or otherwise in need of special solicitude from the courts. . . .

The Court's conclusion that a law which treats males less favorably than females "must serve important governmental objectives and must be substantially related to achievement of those objectives" apparently comes out of thin air. The Equal Protection Clause contains no such language, and none of our previous cases adopt that standard. I would think we have had enough difficulty with the two standards of review which our cases have recognized—the norm of "rational basis," and the "compelling state interest" required where a "suspect classification" is involved—so as to counsel weightily against the insertion of still another "standard" between those two. How is this Court to divine what objectives are important? How is it to determine whether a particular law is "substantially" related to the achievement of such objective, rather than related in some other way to its achievement? Both of the phrases used are so diaphanous and elastic as to invite subjective judicial preferences or prejudices relating to particular types of legislation, masquerading as judgments whether such legislation is directed at "important" objectives or, whether the relationship to those objectives is "substantial" enough.

I would have thought that if this Court were to leave anything to decision by the popularly elected branches of the Government, where no constitutional claim other than that of equal protection is invoked, it would be the decision as to what governmental objectives to be achieved by law are "important," and which are not. As for the second part of the Court's new test, the Judicial Branch is probably in no worse position than the Legislative or

Executive Branches to determine if there is *any* rational relationship between a classification and the purpose which it might be thought to serve. But the introduction of the adverb "substantially" requires courts to make subjective judgments as to operational effects, for which neither their expertise nor their access to data fits them. And even if we manage to avoid both confusion and the mirroring of our own preferences in the development of this new doctrine, the thousands of judges in other courts who must interpret the Equal Protection Clause may not be so fortunate. . . .

The Court "accept[s] for purposes of discussion" the District Court's finding that the purpose of the provisions in question was traffic safety, and proceeds to examine the statistical evidence in the record in order to decide if "the gender-based distinction *closely* serves to achieve that objective. . . . One need not immerse oneself in the fine-points of statistical analysis, however, in order to see the weaknesses in the Court's attempted denigration of the evidence at hand.

One survey of arrest statistics assembled in 1973 indicated that males in the 18–20 age group were arrested for "driving under the influence" almost 18 times as often as their female counterparts, and for "drunkenness" in a ratio of almost ten-to-one. Accepting, as the Court does, appellants' comparison of the total figures with 1973 Oklahoma census data, this survey indicates a 2% arrest rate among males in the age group, as compared to a .18% rate among females. . . .

The Court's criticism of the statistics relied on by the District Court conveys the impression that a legislature in enacting a new law is to be subjected to the judicial equivalent of a doctoral examination in statistics. Legislatures are not held to any rules of evidence such as those which may govern courts or other administrative bodies, and are entitled to draw factual conclusions on the basis of the determination of probable cause which an arrest by a police officer normally represents. In this situation, they could reasonably infer that the incidence of drunk driving is a good deal higher than the incidence of arrest.

And while, as the Court observes, relying on a report to a presidential commission which it cites in a footnote, such statistics may be distorted as a result of stereotyping, the legislature is not required to prove before a court that its statistics are perfect. In any event, if stereotypes are as pervasive as the Court suggests, they may in turn influence the conduct of the men and women in question, and cause the young men to conform to the wild and reckless image which is their stereotype. . . .

Nor is it unreasonable to conclude from the expressed preference for beer by ⅘ of the age group males that that beverage was a predominant source of their intoxication-related arrests. Taking that as the predicate, the state could reasonably bar those males from any purchases of alcoholic beer, including that of the 3.2% variety. This Court lacks the expertise or the data to evaluate the intoxicating properties of that beverage, and in that posture our only appropriate course is to defer to the reasonable inference supporting the statute—that taken in sufficient quantity this beer has the same effect as any alcoholic beverage.

Quite apart from these alleged methodological deficiencies in the statistical evidence, the Court appears to hold that that evidence, on its face, fails to support the distinction drawn in the statute. The Court notes that only 2% of males (as against .18% of females) in the age group were arrested for drunk driving, and that this very low figure establishes "an unduly tenuous 'fit'" between maleness and drunk driving in the 18–20-year-old group. On this point the Court misconceives the nature of the equal protection inquiry.

The rationality of a statutory classification for equal protection purposes does not depend upon the statistical "fit" between the class and the trait sought to be singled out. It turns on whether there may be a sufficiently higher incidence of the trait within the included class than in the excluded class to justify different treatment. Therefore the present equal protection challenge to this gender-based discrimination poses only the question whether the incidence of drunk driving among young men is sufficiently greater than among young women to justify differential treatment. Notwithstanding the Court's critique of the statistical evidence, that evidence suggests clear differences between the drinking and driving habits of young men and women. Those differences are grounds enough for the State reasonably to conclude that young males pose by far the greater drunk driving hazard, both in terms of sheer numbers and in terms of hazard on a per-driver basis. The gender-based difference in treatment in this case is therefore not irrational.

The Court's argument that a 2% correlation between maleness and drunk driving is constitutionally insufficient therefore does not pose an equal protection issue concerning discrimination between males and females. The clearest demonstration of this is the fact that the precise argument made by the Court would be equally applicable to a flat bar on such purchases by *anyone,* male or female, in the 18–20 age group; in fact it would apply a *fortiori* in that case given the even more "tenuous 'fit'" between drunk driving arrests and femaleness. The statistics indicate that about 1% of the age group population as a whole is arrested. What the Court's argument is relevant to is not equal protection, but due process—whether enough persons in the category drive drunk to justify a bar against purchases by all members of the group. . . .

This is not a case where the classification can only be justified on grounds of administrative convenience. There being no apparent way to single out persons likely to drink and drive, it seems plain that the legislature was faced here with the not atypical legislative problem of legislating in terms of broad categories with regard to the purchase and consumption of alcohol. I trust, especially in light of the Twenty-first Amendment, that there would be no due process violation if no one in this age group were allowed to purchase 3.2% beer. Since males drink and drive at a higher rate than the age group as a whole, I fail to see how a statutory bar with regard only to them can create any due process problem.

Michael M. v. Superior Court of Sonoma County
450 U.S. 464, 101 S.Ct. 1200 (1981)

In the summer of 1978, in the Superior Court of Sonoma County, California, a boy of seventeen and a half, Michael M., was tried and convicted for statutory rape. Under California's law, *statutory rape* is defined as unlawful "sexual intercourse accomplished with a female not the wife of the perpetrator, where the female is under the age of 18 years." At his trial and on an unsuccessful appeal of his conviction, Michael M.'s attorneys argued that the law violated the equal protection clause of the Fourteenth Amendment because only males were criminally liable. On appeal to the Supreme Court, the justices split five to four in upholding the statute, and Justice Rehnquist's opinion announcing the Court's decision was joined by only three other justices. Justices Stewart and Blackmun concurred in separate opinions. Justice Brennan's dissenting opinion was joined by Justices Marshall and White, and Justice Stevens filed a separate dissenting opinion.

Justice REHNQUIST, with whom the CHIEF JUSTICE, Justice STEWART, and Justice POWELL join, delivers the opinion of the Court.

The question presented in this case is whether California's "statutory rape" law, § 261.5 of the Cal.Penal Code Ann. (West Supp.1981), violates the Equal Protection Clause of the Fourteenth Amendment. Section 261.5 defines unlawful sexual intercourse as "an act of sexual intercourse accomplished with a female not the wife of the perpetrator, where the female is under the age of 18 years." The statute thus makes men alone criminally liable for the act of sexual intercourse.

In July 1978, a complaint was filed in the Municipal Court of Sonoma County, Cal., alleging that petitioner, then a 17½-year-old male, had had unlawful sexual intercourse with a female under the age of 18, in violation of § 261.5. The evidence, adduced at a preliminary hearing showed that at approximately midnight on June 3, 1978, petitioner and two friends approached Sharon, a 16½-year-old female, and her sister as they waited at a bus stop. Petitioner and Sharon, who had already been drinking, moved away from the others and began to kiss. After being struck in the face for rebuffing petitioner's initial advances, Sharon submitted to sexual intercourse with petitioner. . . .

As is evident from our opinions, the Court has had some difficulty in agreeing upon the proper approach and analysis in cases involving challenges to gender-based classifications. . . . [W]e have not held that gender-based classifications are "inherently suspect" and thus we do not apply so-called "strict scrutiny" to those classifications. See *Stanton v. Stanton,* 421 U.S. 7 (1975). Our cases have held, however, that the traditional minimum rationality test takes on a somewhat "sharper focus" when gender-based classifications are challenged. See *Craig v. Boren,* 429 U.S. 190 (1976) (POWELL, J., concurring). In *Reed v. Reed,* 404 U.S. 71 (1971), for example, the Court stated that a gender-based classification will be upheld if it bears a "fair and substantial relationship" to legitimate state ends, while in *Craig v. Boren,* Court restated the test to require the classification to bear a "substantial relationship" to "important governmental objectives."

Underlying these decisions is the principle that a legislature may not "make overbroad generalizations based on sex which are entirely unrelated to any differences between men and women or which demean the ability or social status of the affected class." *Parham v. Hughes,* 441 U.S. 347 (1979) (plurality opinion of STEWART, J.). But because the Equal Protection Clause does not "demand that a statute necessarily apply equally to all persons" or require " 'things which are different in fact . . . to be treated in law as though they were the same,' " *Rinaldi v. Yeager,* 384 U.S. 305, (1966), quoting *Tigner v. Texas,* 310 U.S. 141 (1940), this Court has consistently upheld statutes where the gender classification is not invidious, but rather realistically reflects the fact that the sexes are not similarly situated in certain circumstances. *Parham v. Hughes,* [441 U.S. 347 (1979)]; *Califano v. Webster,* 430 U.S. 313, (1977); *Schlesinger v. Ballard,* 419 U.S. 498 (1975); *Kahn v. Shevin,* 416 U.S. 351 (1974). As the Court has stated, a legislature may "provide for the special problems of women." *Weinberger v. Wiesenfeld,* 420 U.S. 636 (1975).

Applying those principles to this case, the fact that the California Legislature criminalized the act of illicit sexual intercourse with a minor female is a sure indication of its intent or purpose to discourage that conduct. Precisely why the legislature desired that result is of course somewhat less clear. . . .

. . . The justification for the statute offered by the State, and accepted by the Supreme Court of California, is that the legislature sought to prevent illegitimate teenage pregnancies. . . .

We are satisfied not only that the prevention of illegitimate pregnancy is at least one of the "purposes" of the statute, but also that the State has a strong interest in preventing such pregnancy. At the risk of stating the obvious, teenage pregnancies, which have increased dramatically over the last two decades, have significant social, medical, and economic consequences for both the mother and her child, and the State. Of particular concern to the State is that approximately half of all teenage pregnancies end in abortion. And of those children who are born, their illegitimacy makes them likely candidates to become wards of the State.

We need not be medical doctors to discern that young men and young women are not similarly situated with respect to the problems and the risks of sexual intercourse. Only women may become pregnant, and they suffer disproportionately the profound physical, emotional and psychological consequences of sexual activity. The statute at issue here protects women from sexual intercourse at an age when those consequences are particularly severe.

The question thus boils down to whether a State may attack the problem of sexual intercourse and teenage pregnancy directly by prohibiting a male from having sexual intercourse with a minor female. We hold that such a statute is sufficiently related to the State's objectives to pass constitutional muster.

Because virtually all of the significant harmful and inescapably identifiable consequences of teenage pregnancy fall on the young female, a legislature acts well within its authority when it elects to punish only the participant who, by nature, suffers few of the consequences of his conduct. It is hardly unreasonable for a legislature acting to protect minor females to exclude them from punishment. Moreover, the risk of pregnancy itself constitutes a substantial deterrence to young females. No similar natural sanctions deter males. A criminal sanction imposed solely on males thus serves to roughly "equalize" the deterrents on the sexes. . . .

[W]e cannot say that a gender-neutral statute would be as effective as the statute California has chosen to enact. The State persuasively contends that a gender-neutral statute would frustrate its interest in effective enforcement. Its view is that a female is surely less likely to report violations of the statute if she herself would be subject to criminal prosecution. In an area already fraught with prosecutorial difficulties, we decline to hold that the Equal Protection Clause requires a legislature to enact a statute so broad that it may well be incapable of enforcement.

We similarly reject petitioner's argument that § 261.5 is impermissibly overbroad because it makes unlawful sexual intercourse with prepubescent females, who are, by definition, incapable of becoming pregnant. Quite apart from the fact that the statute could well be justified on the grounds that very young females are particularly susceptible to physical injury from sexual intercourse, see *Rundlett v. Oliver*, 607 F.2d 495 (CA1 1979), it is ludicrous to suggest that the Constitution requires the California Legislature to limit the scope of its rape statute to older teenagers and exclude young girls.

There remains only petitioner's contention that the statute is unconstitutional as it is applied to him because he, like Sharon, was under 18 at the time of sexual intercourse. Petitioner argues that the statute is flawed because it presumes that as between two persons under 18, the male is the culpable aggressor. We find petitioner's contentions unpersuasive. Contrary to his assertions, the statute does not rest on the assumption that males are generally the aggressors. It is instead an attempt by a legislature to prevent illegitimate teenage pregnancy by providing an additional deterrent for men. The age of the man is irrelevant since young men are as capable as older men of inflicting the harm sought to be prevented. . . .

Accordingly, the judgment of the California Supreme Court is Affirmed.

Justice STEWART concurring.

The Constitution is violated when government, state or federal, invidiously classifies similarly situated people on the basis of the immutable characteristics with which they were born. Thus, detrimental racial classifications by government always violate the Constitution, for the simple reason that, so far as the Constitution is concerned, people of different races are always similarly situated. See *Fullilove v. Klutznick*, 448 U.S. 448 [(1980)] (dissenting opinion); *McLaughlin v. Florida*, 379 U.S. 184 [(1964)] (concurring opinion); *Brown v. Board of Ed.*, 347 U.S. 483 [(1954)]; *Plessy v. Ferguson*, 163 U.S. 537 [(1896)] (dissenting opinion). By contrast, while detrimental gender classifications by government often violate the Constitution, they do not always do so, for the reason that there are differences between males and females that the Constitution necessarily recognizes. In this case we deal with the most basic of these differences: females can become pregnant as the result of sexual intercourse; males cannot. . . .

The fact that males and females are not similarly situated with respect to the risks of sexual intercourse applies with the same force to males under 18 as it does to older males. The risk of pregnancy is a significant deterrent for unwed young females that is not shared by unmarried males, regardless of their age. Experienced observation confirms the commonsense notion that adolescent males disregard the possibility of pregnancy far more than do adolescent females. And to the extent that § 261.5 may punish males for intercourse with prepubescent females, that punishment is justifiable because of the substantial physical risks for prepubescent females that are not shared by their male counterparts.

Justice BLACKMUN concurred.

Justice BRENNAN, with whom Justice WHITE and Justice MARSHALL join, dissenting.

The State of California vigorously asserts that the "important governmental objective" to be served by § 261.5 is the prevention of teenage pregnancy. It claims that its statute furthers this goal by deterring sexual activity by males—the class of persons it considers more responsible for causing those pregnancies. But even assuming that prevention of teenage pregnancy is an important governmental objective and that it is in fact an objective of § 261.5, California still has the burden of proving that there are fewer teenage pregnancies under its gender-based statutory rape law than there would be if the law were gender neutral. To meet this burden, the State must show that because its statutory rape law punishes only males, and not females, it more effectively deters minor females from having sexual intercourse.

The plurality assumes that a gender-neutral statute would be less effective than § 261.5 in deterring sexual activity because a gender-neutral statute would create significant enforcement problems. The plurality thus accepts the State's assertion that

> "a female is surely less likely to report violations of the statute if she herself would be subject to criminal prosecution. In an area already fraught with prosecutorial difficulties, we decline to hold that the Equal Protection Clause requires a legislature to enact a statute so broad that it may well be incapable of enforcement.". . . (footnotes omitted).

However, a State's bare assertion that its gender-based statutory classification substantially furthers an important governmental interest is not enough to meet its burden of proof under *Craig v. Boren*, [429 U.S. 190 (1976)]. Rather, the State must produce evidence that will persuade the court that its assertion is true. See *Craig v. Boren*.

The State has not produced such evidence in this case. Moreover, there are at least two serious flaws in the State's assertion that law enforcement problems created by a gender-neutral statutory rape law would make such a statute less effective than a gender-based statute in deterring sexual activity.

First, the experience of other jurisdictions, and California itself, belies the plurality's conclusion that a gender-neutral statutory rape law "may well be incapable of enforcement." There are now at least 37 States that have enacted gender-neutral statutory rape laws. Although most of these laws protect young persons (of either sex) from the sexual exploitation of older individuals, the laws of Arizona, Florida, and Illinois permit prosecution of both minor females and minor males for engaging in mutual sexual conduct. California has introduced no evidence that those States have been handicapped by the enforcement problems the plurality finds so persuasive. Surely, if those States could provide such evidence, we might expect that California would have introduced it. . . .

The second flaw in the State's assertion is that even assuming that a gender-neutral statute would be more difficult to enforce, the State has still not shown that those enforcement problems would make such a statute less effective than a gender-based statute in deterring minor females from engaging in sexual intercourse. Common sense, however, suggests that a gender-neutral statutory rape law is potentially a *greater* deterrent of sexual activity than a gender-based law, for the simple reason that a gender-neutral law subjects both men and women to criminal sanctions and thus arguably has a deterrent effect on twice as many potential violators. Even if fewer persons were prosecuted under the gender-neutral law, as the State suggests, it would still be true that twice as many persons would be *subject* to arrest. . . .

Until very recently, no California court or commentator had suggested that the purpose of California's statutory rape law was to protect young women from the risk of pregnancy. Indeed, the historical development of § 261.5 demonstrates that the law was initially enacted on the premise that young women, in contrast to young men were to be deemed legally incapable of consenting to an act of sexual intercourse. Because their chastity was considered particularly precious, those young women were felt to be uniquely in need of the State's protection. In contrast, young men were assumed to be capable of making such decisions for themselves; the law therefore did not offer them any special protection. . . .

I would hold that § 261.5 violates the Equal Protection Clause of the Fourteenth Amendment, and I would reverse the judgment of the California Supreme Court.

Justice STEVENS dissenting.

I think the plurality is quite correct in making the assumption that the joint act that this law seeks to prohibit creates a greater risk of harm for the female than for the male. But the plurality surely cannot believe that the risk of pregnancy confronted by the female—any more than the risk of venereal disease confronted by males as well as females—has provided an effective deterrent to voluntary female participation in the risk-creating conduct. Yet the plurality's decision seems to rest on the assumption that the California Legislature acted on the basis of that rather fanciful notion.

In my judgment, the fact that a class of persons is especially vulnerable to a risk that a statute is designed to avoid is a reason for making the statute applicable to that class. The argument that a special need for protection provides a rational explanation for an exemption is one I simply do not comprehend.

In this case, the fact that a female confronts a greater risk of harm than a male is a reason for applying the prohibition to her—not a reason for granting her a license to use her own judgment on whether or not to assume the risk. Surely, if we examine the problem from the point of view of society's interest in preventing the risk-creating conduct from occurring at all, it is irrational to exempt 50% of the potential violators. See dissent of Justice BRENNAN. And, if we view the government's interest as that of a *parens patriae* seeking to protect its subjects from harming themselves, the discrimination is actually perverse. Would a rational parent making rules for the conduct of twin children of opposite sex simultaneously forbid the son and authorize the daughter to engage in conduct that is especially harmful to the daughter? That is the effect of this statutory classification. . . .

In my opinion, the only acceptable justification for a general rule requiring disparate treatment of the two participants in a joint act must be a legislative judgment that one is more guilty than the other. The risk-creating conduct that this statute is designed to prevent requires the participation of two persons—one male and one female. In many situations it is probably true that one is the aggressor and the other is either an unwilling, or at least a less willing, participant in the joint act. If a statute authorized punishment of only one participant and required the prosecutor to prove that that participant had been the aggressor, I assume that the discrimination would be valid. Although the question is less clear, I also assume, for the purpose of deciding this case, that it would be permissible to punish only the male participant, if one element of the offense were proof that he had been the aggressor, or at least in some respects the more responsible participant in the joint act. The statute at issue in this case, however, requires no such proof. The question raised by this statute is whether the State, consistently with the Federal Constitution, may always punish the male and never the female when they are equally responsible or when the female is the more responsible of the two.

Justice Sandra Day O'Connor, the first woman appointed to the Supreme Court, and Chief Justice Warren Burger in 1981. *Timothy Murphy of U.S. News & World Report.*

It would seem to me that an impartial lawmaker could give only one answer to that question. The fact that the California Legislature has decided to apply its prohibition only to the male may reflect a legislative judgment that in the typical case the male is actually the more guilty party. Any such judgment must, in turn, assume that the decision to engage in the risk-creating conduct is always—or at least typically—a male decision. If that assumption is valid, the statutory classification should also be valid. But what is the support for the assumption? It is not contained in the record of this case or in any legislative history or scholarly study that has been called to our attention. I think it is supported to some extent by traditional attitudes toward male-female relationships. But the possibility that such a habitual attitude may reflect nothing more than an irrational prejudice makes it an insufficient justification for discriminatory treatment that is otherwise blatantly unfair. For, as I read this statute, it requires that one, and only one, of two equally guilty wrongdoers be stigmatized by a criminal conviction. . . .

Nor do I find at all persuasive the suggestion that this discrimination is adequately justified by the desire to encourage females to inform against their male partners. Even if the concept of a wholesale informant's exemption were an acceptable enforcement device, what is the justification for defining the exempt class entirely by reference to sex rather than by reference to a more neutral criterion such as relative innocence? Indeed, if the exempt class is to be composed entirely of members of one sex, what is there to support the view that the statutory purpose will be better served by granting the informing license to females rather than to males? If a discarded male partner informs on a promiscuous female, a timely threat of prosecution might well prevent the precise harm the statute is intended to minimize.

Finally, even if my logic is faulty and there actually is some speculative basis for treating equally guilty males and females differently, I still believe that any such speculative justification would be outweighed by the paramount interest in evenhanded enforcement of the law. A rule that authorizes punishment of only one of two equally guilty wrongdoers violates the essence of the constitutional requirement that the sovereign must govern impartially.

I respectfully dissent.

Meritor Savings Bank, FBD v. Vinson
477 U.S. 57, 106 S.Ct. 2399 (1986)

Justice William Rehnquist discussed the facts of this case, involving sexual harassment in the workplace, in his opinion announcing the Court's decision.

Justice REHNQUIST delivers the opinion of the Court.

This case presents important questions concerning claims of workplace "sexual harassment" brought under Title VII of the Civil Rights Act of 1964, 78 Stat. 253, as amended, 42 U.S.C. § 2000e *et seq.*

In 1974, respondent Mechelle Vinson met Sidney Taylor, a vice president of what is now petitioner Meritor Savings Bank (the bank) and manager of one of its branch offices. When respondent asked whether she might obtain employment at the bank,

Taylor gave her an application, which she completed and returned the next day; later that same day Taylor called her to say that she had been hired. With Taylor as her supervisor, respondent started as a teller-trainee, and thereafter was promoted to teller, head teller, and assistant branch manager. She worked at the same branch for four years, and it is undisputed that her advancement there was based on merit alone. In September 1978, respondent notified Taylor that she was taking sick leave for an indefinite period. On November 1, 1978, the bank discharged her for excessive use of that leave.

Respondent brought this action against Taylor and the bank, claiming that during her four years at the bank she had "constantly been subjected to sexual harassment" by Taylor in violation of Title VII. She sought injunctive relief, compensatory and punitive damages against Taylor and the bank, and attorney's fees.

At the 11-day bench trial, the parties presented conflicting testimony about Taylor's behavior during respondent's employment. Respondent testified that during her probationary period as a teller-trainee, Taylor treated her in a fatherly way and made no sexual advances. Shortly thereafter, however, he invited her out to dinner and, during the course of the meal, suggested that they go to a motel to have sexual relations. At first she refused, but out of what she described as fear of losing her job she eventually agreed. According to respondent, Taylor thereafter made repeated demands upon her for sexual favors, usually at the branch, both during and after business hours; she estimated that over the next several years she had intercourse with him some 40 or 50 times. In addition, respondent testified that Taylor fondled her in front of other employees; followed her into the women's restroom when she went there alone, exposed himself to her, and even forcibly raped her on several occasions. These activities ceased after 1977, respondent stated, when she started going with a steady boyfriend. . . .

Taylor denied respondent's allegations of sexual activity, testifying that he never fondled her, never made suggestive remarks to her, never engaged in sexual intercourse with her and never asked her to do so. He contended instead that respondent made her accusations in response to a business-related dispute. The bank also denied respondent's allegations and asserted that any sexual harassment by Taylor was unknown to the bank and engaged in without its consent or approval.

The District Court denied relief, but did not resolve the conflicting testimony about the existence of a sexual relationship between respondent and Taylor. . . .

The Court of Appeals for the District of Columbia Circuit reversed. . . .

We granted certiorari, and now affirm but for different reasons.

Title VII of the Civil Rights Act of 1964 makes it "an unlawful employment practice for an employer . . . to discriminate against any individual with respect to his compensation, terms, conditions, or privileges of employment, because of such individual's race, color, religion, sex, or national origin." 42 U.S.C. § 2000e–2(a)(1). The prohibition against discrimination based on sex was added to Title VII at the last minute on the floor of the House of Representatives. The principal argument in opposition to the amendment was that "sex discrimination" was sufficiently different from other types of discrimination that it ought to receive separate legislative treatment. This argument was defeated, the bill quickly passed as amended, and we are left with little legislative history to guide us in interpreting the Act's prohibition against discrimination based on "sex."

Respondent argues, and the Court of Appeals held, that unwelcome sexual advances that create an offensive or hostile working environment violate Title VII. Without question, when a supervisor sexually harasses a subordinate because of the subordinate's sex, that supervisor "discriminate[s]" on the basis of sex. Petitioner apparently does not challenge this proposition. It contends instead that in prohibiting discrimination with respect to "compensation, terms, conditions, or privileges" of employment, Congress was concerned with what petitioner describes as "tangible loss" of "an economic character," not "purely psychological aspects of the workplace environment." In support of this claim petitioner observes that in both the legislative history of Title VII and this Court's Title VII decisions, the focus has been on tangible, economic barriers erected by discrimination.

We reject petitioner's view. First, the language of Title VII is not limited to "economic" or "tangible" discrimination. The phrase "terms, conditions, or privileges of employment" evinces a congressional intent " 'to strike at the entire spectrum of disparate treatment of men and women' " in employment. . . .

Second, in 1980 the EEOC issued guidelines specifying that "sexual harassment," as there defined, is a form of sex discrimination prohibited by Title VII. As an "administrative interpretation of the Act by the enforcing agency," these guidelines, " 'while not controlling upon the courts by reason of their authority, do constitute a body of experience and informed judgment to which courts and litigants may properly resort for guidance.' " The EEOC guidelines fully support the view that harassment leading to noneconomic injury can violate Title VII.

In defining "sexual harassment," the guidelines first describe the kinds of workplace conduct that may be actionable under Title VII. These include "[u]nwelcome sexual advances, requests for sexual favors, and other verbal or physical conduct of a sexual nature." Relevant to the charges at issue in this case, the guidelines provide that such sexual misconduct constitutes prohibited "sexual harassment," whether or not it is directly linked to the grant or denial of an economic *quid pro quo,* where "such conduct has the purpose or effect of unreasonably interfering with an individual's work performance or creating an intimidating, hostile, or offensive working environment."

In concluding that so-called "hostile environment" (*i.e.,* non *quid pro quo*) harassment violates Title VII, the EEOC drew upon a substantial body of judicial decisions and EEOC precedent holding that Title VII affords employees the right to work in an environment free from discriminatory intimidation, ridicule, and insult. . . .

Since the guidelines were issued, courts have uniformly held, and we agree, that a plaintiff may establish a violation of Title VII by proving that discrimination based on sex has created a hostile or abusive work environment. . . .

Of course, . . . not all workplace conduct that may be described as "harassment" affects a "term, condition, or privilege" of employment within the meaning of Title VII. . . . For sexual harassment to be actionable, it must be sufficiently severe or pervasive "to alter the conditions of [the victim's] employment and create an abusive working environment." Respondent's allegations in this case—which include, not only pervasive harassment but also criminal conduct of the most serious nature—are plainly sufficient to state a claim for "hostile environment" sexual harassment.

The question remains, however, whether the District Court's ultimate finding that respondent "was not the victim of sexual harassment," effectively disposed of respondent's claim. The Court of Appeals recognized, we think correctly, that this ultimate finding was likely based on one or both of two erroneous views of the law. First, the District Court apparently believed that a claim for sexual harassment will not lie absent an *economic* effect on the complainant's employment. . . . Since it appears that the District Court made its findings without ever considering the "hostile environment" theory of sexual harassment, the Court of Appeals' decision to remand was correct.

Second, the District Court's conclusion that no actionable harassment occurred might have rested on its earlier "finding" that "[i]f [respondent] and Taylor did engage in an intimate or sexual relationship . . ., that relationship was a voluntary one." But the fact that sex-related conduct was "voluntary," in the sense that the complainant was not forced to participate against her will, is not a defense to a sexual harassment suit brought under Title VII. The gravamen of any sexual harassment claim is that the alleged sexual advances were "unwelcome." While the question whether particular conduct was indeed unwelcome presents difficult problems of proof and turns largely on credibility determinations committed to the trier of fact, the District Court in this case erroneously focused on the "voluntariness" of respondent's participation in the claimed sexual episodes. The correct inquiry is whether respondent by her conduct indicated that the alleged sexual advances were unwelcome, not whether her actual participation in sexual intercourse was voluntary. . . .

Although the District Court concluded that respondent had not proved a violation of Title VII, it nevertheless went on to consider the question of the bank's liability. Finding that "the bank was without notice" of Taylor's alleged conduct, and that notice to Taylor was not the equivalent of notice to the bank, the court concluded that the bank therefore could not be held liable for Taylor's alleged actions. The Court of Appeals took the opposite view, holding that an employer is strictly liable for a hostile environment created by a supervisor's sexual advances, even though the employer neither knew nor reasonably could have known of the alleged misconduct. The court held that a supervisor, whether or not he possesses the authority to hire, fire, or promote, is necessarily an "agent" of his employer for all Title VII purposes, since "even the appearance" of such authority may enable him to impose himself on his subordinates. . . .

This debate over the appropriate standard for employer liability has a rather abstract quality about it given the state of the record in this case. We do not know at this stage whether Taylor made any sexual advances toward respondent at all, let alone whether those advances were unwelcome, whether they were sufficiently pervasive to constitute a condition of employment, or whether they were "so pervasive and so long continuing . . . that the employer must have become conscious of [them]."

We therefore decline the parties' invitation to issue a definitive rule on employer liability, but we do agree with the EEOC that Congress wanted courts to look to agency principles for guidance in this area. While such common-law principles may not be transferable in all their particulars to Title VII, Congress' decision to define "employer" to include any "agent" of an employer, 42 U.S.C. § 2000e(b), surely evinces an intent to place some limits on the acts of employees for which employers under Title VII are to be held responsible. For this reason, we hold that the Court of Appeals erred in concluding that employers are always automatically liable for sexual harassment by their supervisors. For the same reason, absence of notice to an employer does not necessarily insulate that employer from liability.

Finally, we reject petitioner's view that the mere existence of a grievance procedure and a policy against discrimination, coupled with respondent's failure to invoke that procedure, must insulate petitioner from liability. While those facts are plainly relevant, the situation before us demonstrates why they are not necessarily dispositive. Petitioner's general nondiscrimination policy did not address sexual harassment in particular, and thus did not alert employees to their employer's interest in correcting that form of discrimination. Moreover, the bank's grievance procedure apparently required an employee to complain first to her supervisor, in this case Taylor. Since Taylor was the alleged perpetrator, it is not altogether surprising that respondent failed to invoke the procedure and report her grievance to him. Petitioner's contention that respondent's failure should insulate it from liability might be substantially stronger if its procedures were better calculated to encourage victims of harassment to come forward.

In sum, we hold that a claim of "hostile environment" sex discrimination is actionable under Title VII, that the District Court's findings were insufficient to dispose of respondent's hostile environment claim, and that the District Court did not err in admitting testimony about respondent's sexually provocative speech and dress. As to employer liability, we conclude that the Court of Appeals was wrong to entirely disregard agency principles and impose absolute liability on employers for the acts of their supervisors, regardless of the circumstances of a particular case.

Accordingly, the judgment of the Court of Appeals reversing the judgment of the District Court is affirmed, and the case is remanded for further proceedings consistent with this opinion.

It is so ordered.

Justice MARSHALL, with whom Justice BRENNAN, Justice BLACKMUN, and Justice STEVENS joined, concurred in a separate opinion.

THE DEVELOPMENT OF LAW

Other Rulings Dealing with Gender Discrimination and Statutory Interpretation

Case	Vote	Ruling
General Electric Co. v. Gilbert, 429 U.S. 125 (1976)	6:3	Justice Rehnquist held that the denial of employees' disability benefits for pregnancy disability leave was permissible under Title VII of the Civil Rights Act; Congress subsequently passed legislation overriding the Court's decision.
Nashville Gas Co. v. Satty, 434 U.S. 136 (1977)	9:0	Justice Rehnquist held that women who take pregnancy leaves may not be denied

Case	Vote	Ruling
		their seniority in employment on returning to work, under Title VII of the Civil Rights Act.
Dothard v. Rawlinson, 433 U.S. 321 (1977)	8:1	With Justices Marshall and Brennan concurring and dissenting in part, and Justice White dissenting, the Court held that the assignment of female prison guards in certain areas of a prison did not violate the Civil Rights Act.
City of Los Angeles, Department of Water & Power v. Manhart, 435 U.S. 702 (1978)	6:3	With Chief Justice Burger and Justices Rehnquist and Powell dissenting, the Court struck down under Title VII an ordinance requiring female employees to pay $15 more than male employees into a pension fund, despite evidence that women statistically live longer than men.
Hishon v. King & Spaulding, 467 U.S. 69 (1984)	9:0	Held that Title VII does not reach a law firm's decision on the promotion of "associates" to "partners," rejecting the claim of a female lawyer who was denied a partnership.
Grove City College v. Bell, 465 U.S. 555 (1984)	6:3	Title IX of the Federal Education Act of 1972 authorizes the withholding of federal funds from institutions that impermissibly engage in gender-based discrimination; here, the Court construed the statute to authorize the withholding of funds only from specific programs that discriminated against women and not from the entire institution—in 1988 Congress passed legislation overriding the Court's ruling.
California Federal Savings & Loan Association v. Guerra, 479 U.S. 272 (1987)	6:3	With Justices Rehnquist, White and Powell dissenting, upheld a California law

Case	Vote	Ruling
		requiring employers to provide pregnancy disability leaves, even though such leaves are not required under Title VII.

(2) Wealth, Poverty and Illegitimacy

In *Griffin v. Illinois,* 351 U.S. 12 (1956), when holding that states must provide indigent defendants with transcripts of their trials for appeals on constitutional questions, Justice Black observed that "[i]n criminal trials a State can no more discriminate on account of poverty than on account of religion, race, or color." Justice Black thus suggested that classifications based on wealth might be constitutionally suspect. Subsequently, the Court construed the due process and equal protection clauses to ensure that indigents are not denied the right to vote (see Vol. I, Ch. 8), and that they have an equal right of access to judicial proceedings (see Chapter 9).

Nevertheless, the Court applies the "rational basis" test and refuses to scrutinize laws that disadvantage the poor in the overwhelming majority of cases. See, for example, *Maher v. Roe* (1977) (see page 1180) upholding restrictions on Medicaid funding for women seeking elective abortions.

In *Shapiro v. Thompson* (1969) (see page 1457) however, the Court overturned a state residency requirement for indigents seeking public assistance. It did so, though, on the grounds that the residency requirement denied indigents their "fundamental right to interstate travel," rather than a right to welfare benefits. Other residency requirements have been similarly struck down, but never on the basis that wealth is a suspect classification. In *Dandridge v. Williams,* 397 U.S. 471 (1970), for instance, the Court rejected the claim of a fundamental right to public assistance, when upholding Maryland's law limiting benefits under the Aid-to-Dependent-Children Social Security program to $250 per month, regardless of the needs and size of a family. So too in *San Antonio Independent School District v. Rodriquez* (1973) (see page 1466), the Court rejected the claim that public education is a fundamental right and that states may not discriminate against indigents in public education.

In contrast to claims of discrimination based on wealth and poverty, the Court gives greater scrutiny to challenges of laws discriminating against illegitimate children. The Court has done so under both the "rational basis" test, as in *Levy v. Louisiana,*

391 U.S. 68 (1968), and the slightly higher standard of review, announced in *Matthews v. Lucas*, 427 U.S. 495 (1976), demanding that classifications based on illegitimacy be "substantially related to a permissible state interest" (see also table on page 1480).

SELECTED BIBLIOGRAPHY

Brudno, Barbara. *Poverty, Inequality, and the Law.* St. Paul, MN: West 1976.
Lawrence, Susan. *The Poor in Court.* Princeton, NJ: Princeton University Press, 1990.

Shapiro v. Thompson
394 U.S. 618, 89 S.Ct. 1322 (1969)

Two months after moving from Massachusetts to Connecticut, Vivian Thompson applied for assistance under the Aid to Families with Dependent Children program. She was nineteen years old, pregnant, and the mother of one child. Thompson was denied assistance because she failed to meet Connecticut's one-year residency requirement for receiving assistance. She sued in federal district court Bernard Shapiro, Connecticut's welfare commissioner. That court held that the residency requirement had a "chilling effect on the right to travel" and denied Thompson the equal protection of the law as guaranteed by the Fourteenth Amendment. Shapiro then appealed that ruling to the Supreme Court, which granted review and consolidated the case with others, challenging the constitutionality of residency requirements of Pennsylvania and the District of Columbia.

Justice BRENNAN delivers the opinion of the Court.

[This] is an appeal from a decision of a three-judge District Court holding unconstitutional a State or District of Columbia statutory provision which denies welfare assistance to residents of the State or District who have not resided within their jurisdictions for at least one year immediately preceding their applications for such assistance. We affirm. . . .

There is no dispute that the effect of the waiting-period requirement in each case is to create two classes of needy resident families indistinguishable from each other except that one is composed of residents who have resided a year or more, and the second of residents who have resided less than a year, in the jurisdiction. On the basis of this sole difference the first class is granted and the second class is denied welfare aid upon which may depend the ability of the families to obtain the very means to subsist—food, shelter, and other necessities of life. . . . The interests which appellants assert are promoted by the classification either may not constitutionally be promoted by government or are not compelling governmental interests.

Primarily, appellants justify the waiting-period requirement as a protective device to preserve the fiscal integrity of state public assistance programs. It is asserted that people who require welfare assistance during their first year of residence in a State are likely to become continuing burdens on state welfare programs. Therefore, the argument runs, if such people can be deterred from entering the jurisdiction by denying them welfare benefits during the first year, state programs to assist long-time residents will not be impaired by a substantial influx of indigent newcomers. . . .

We do not doubt that the one-year waiting period device is well suited to discourage the influx of poor families in need of assistance. An indigent who desires to migrate, resettle, find a new job, and start a new life will doubtless hesitate if he knows that he must risk making the move without the possibility of falling back on state welfare assistance during his first year of residence, when his need may be most acute. But the purpose of inhibiting migration by needy persons into the State is constitutionally impermissible.

This Court long ago recognized that the nature of our Federal Union and our constitutional concepts of personal liberty unite to require that all citizens be free to travel throughout the length and breadth of our land uninhibited by statutes, rules, or regulations which unreasonably burden or restrict this movement. That proposition was early stated by Chief Justice TANEY in the *Passenger Cases*, 7 How. (48 U.S.) 283 (1849):

"For all the great purposes for which the Federal government was formed, we are one people, with one common country. We are all citizens of the United States; and, as members of the same community, must have the right to pass and repass through every part of it without interruption, as freely as in our own States."

We have no occasion to ascribe the source of this right to travel interstate to a particular constitutional provision. It suffices that, as Justice STEWART said for the Court in *United States v. Guest*, 383 U.S. 745 (1966):

"The constitutional right to travel from one State to another . . . occupies a position fundamental to the concept of our

Federal Union. It is a right that has been firmly established and repeatedly recognized.

". . . [The] right finds no explicit mention in the Constitution. The reason, it has been suggested, is that a right so elementary was conceived from the beginning to be a necessary concomitant of the stronger Union the Constitution created. In any event, freedom to travel throughout the United States has long been recognized as a basic right under the Constitution."

Thus, the purpose of deterring the immigration of indigents cannot serve as justification for the classification created by the one-year waiting period, since that purpose is constitutionally impermissible. If a law has "no other purpose . . . than to chill the assertion of constitutional rights by penalizing those who choose to exercise them, then it [is] patently unconstitutional."

Alternatively, appellants argue that even if it is impermissible for a State to attempt to deter the entry of all indigents, the challenged classification may be justified as a permissible state attempt to discourage those indigents who would enter the State solely to obtain larger benefits. . . .

[However,] a State may no more try to fence out those indigents who seek higher welfare benefits than it may try to fence out indigents generally. Implicit in any such distinction is the notion that indigents who enter a State with the hope of securing higher welfare benefits are somehow less deserving than indigents who do not take this consideration into account. But we do not perceive why a mother who is seeking to make a new life for herself and her children should be regarded as less deserving because she considers, among others factors, the level of a State's public assistance. Surely such a mother is no less deserving than a mother who moves into a particular State in order to take advantage of its better educational facilities.

Appellants argue further that the challenged classification may be sustained as an attempt to distinguish between new and old residents on the basis of the contribution they have made to the community through the payment of taxes. [But, a]ppellants' reasoning would logically permit the State to bar new residents from schools, parks, and libraries or deprive them of police and fire protection. Indeed it would permit the State to apportion all benefits and services according to the past tax contributions of its citizens. The Equal Protection Clause prohibits such an apportionment of state services.

We recognize that a State has a valid interest in preserving the fiscal integrity of its programs. It may legitimately attempt to limit its expenditures, whether for public assistance, public education, or any other program. But a State may not accomplish such a purpose by invidious distinctions between classes of its citizens. It could not, for example, reduce expenditures for education by barring indigent children from its schools. Similarly, in the cases before us, appellants must do more than show that denying welfare benefits to new residents saves money. The saving of welfare costs cannot justify an otherwise invidious classification.

Appellants next advance as justification certain administrative and related governmental objectives allegedly served by the waiting-period requirement. They argue that the requirement (1) facilitates the planning of the welfare budget; (2) provides an objective test of residency; (3) minimizes the opportunity for recipients fraudulently to receive payments from more than one jurisdiction; and (4) encourages early entry of new residents into the labor force. . . .

The argument that the waiting-period requirement facilitates budget predictability is wholly unfounded. The records [here] are utterly devoid of evidence that either State or the District of Columbia in fact uses the one-year requirement as a means to predict the number of people who will require assistance in the budget year. . . .

The argument that the waiting period serves as an administratively efficient rule of thumb for determining residency similarly will not withstand scrutiny. The residence requirement and the one-year waiting-period requirement are distinct and independent prerequisites for assistance under these three statutes, and the facts relevant to the determination of each are directly examined by the welfare authorities. Before granting an application, the welfare authorities investigate the applicant's employment, housing, and family situation and in the course of the inquiry necessarily learn the facts upon which to determine whether the applicant is a resident. . . .

Similarly, there is no need for a State to use the one-year waiting period as a safeguard against fraudulent receipt of benefits; for less drastic means are available, and are employed, to minimize that hazard. . . .

[Finally, a] state purpose to encourage employment provides no rational basis for imposing a one-year waiting-period restriction on new residents only.

We conclude therefore that appellants in these cases do not use and have no need to use the one-year requirement for the governmental purposes suggested. Thus, even under traditional equal protection tests a classification of welfare applicants according to whether they have lived in the State for one year would seem irrational and unconstitutional. But, of course, the traditional criteria do not apply in these cases. Since the classification here touches on the fundamental right of interstate movement, its constitutionality must be judged by the stricter standard of whether it promotes a *compelling* state interest. Under this standard, the waiting-period requirement clearly violates the Equal Protection Clause.

Justice STEWART concurring.

In joining the opinion of the Court, I add a word in response to the dissent of my Brother HARLAN, who, I think, has quite misapprehended what the Court's opinion says.

The Court today does *not* "pick out particular human activities, characterize them as 'fundamental,' and give them added protection. . . ." To the contrary, the Court simply recognizes, as it must, an established constitutional right, and gives to that right no less protection than the Constitution itself demands.

Chief Justice WARREN, with whom Justice BLACK joins, dissenting.

Congress has imposed a residence requirement in the District of Columbia and authorized the States to impose similar requirements. The issue before us must therefore be framed in terms of whether Congress may create minimal residence requirements, not whether the States, acting alone, may do so. . . .

Congress, pursuant to its commerce power, has enacted a variety of restrictions upon interstate travel. It has taxed air and rail fares and the gasoline needed to power cars and trucks which move interstate. Many of the federal safety regulations of common carriers which cross state lines burden the right to travel. . . . And Congress has prohibited by criminal statute interstate travel for certain purposes. Although these restrictions operate as a limitation upon free interstate movement of persons, their constitutionality appears well settled. . . .

The Court's right-to-travel cases lend little support to the view that congressional action is invalid merely because it burdens the right to travel. Most of our cases fall into two categories: those in which *state*-imposed restrictions were involved, see, *e. g., Edwards v. California,* 314 U.S. 160 (1941); *Crandall v. Nevada,* 6 Wall. 35, (1868), and those concerning congressional decisions to remove impediments to interstate movement, see, *e. g., United States v. Guest,* 383 U.S. 745 (1966). Since the focus of our inquiry must be whether Congress would exceed permissible bounds by imposing residence requirements, neither group of cases offers controlling principles. . . .

[Here,] travel itself is not prohibited. Any burden inheres solely in the fact that a potential welfare recipient might take into consideration the loss of welfare benefits for a limited period of time if he changes his residence. Not only is this burden of uncertain degree, but appellees themselves assert there is evidence that few welfare recipients have in fact been deterred by residence requirements. . . .

The insubstantiality of the restriction imposed by residence requirements must then be evaluated in light of the possible congressional reasons for such requirements. . . .

Our cases require only that Congress have a rational basis for finding that a chosen regulatory scheme is necessary to the furtherance of interstate commerce. Certainly, a congressional finding that residence requirements allowed each State to concentrate its resources upon new and increased programs of rehabilitation ultimately resulting in an enhanced flow of commerce as the economic condition of welfare recipients progressively improved is rational and would justify imposition of residence requirements under the Commerce Clause. And Congress could have also determined that residence requirements fostered personal mobility. An individual no longer dependent upon welfare would be presented with an unfettered range of choices so that a decision to migrate could be made without regard to considerations of possible economic dislocation. . . .

Since the congressional decision is rational and the restriction on travel insubstantial, I conclude that residence requirements can be imposed by Congress as an exercise of its power to control interstate commerce consistent with the constitutionally guaranteed right to travel.

Justice HARLAN dissenting.

In upholding the equal protection argument, the Court has applied an equal protection doctrine of relatively recent vintage: the rule that statutory classifications which either are based upon certain "suspect" criteria or affect "fundamental rights" will be held to deny equal protection unless justified by a "compelling" governmental interest.

The "compelling interest" doctrine, which today is articulated more explicitly than ever before, constitutes an increasingly significant exception to the long-established rule that a statute does not deny equal protection if it is rationally related to a legitimate governmental objective. The "compelling interest" doctrine has two branches. The branch which requires that classifications based upon "suspect" criteria be supported by a compelling interest apparently had its genesis in cases involving racial classifications, which have, at least since *Korematsu v. United States*, 323 U.S. 214 (1944), been regarded as inherently "suspect." The criterion of "wealth" apparently was added to the list of "suspects" as an alternative justification for the rationale in *Harper v. Virginia Bd. of Elections*, 383 U.S. 663, (1966), in which Virginia's poll tax was struck down. . . . Today the list apparently has been further enlarged to include classifications based upon recent interstate movement, and perhaps those based upon the exercise of *any* constitutional right. . . . [However,] I do not consider wealth a "suspect" statutory criterion. . . .

The second branch of the "compelling interest" principle is even more troublesome. For it has been held that a statutory classification is subject to the "compelling interest" test if the result of the classification may be to affect a "fundamental right," regardless of the basis of the classification. . . .

I think this branch of the "compelling interest" doctrine particularly unfortunate and unnecessary. It is unfortunate because it creates an exception which threatens to swallow the standard equal protection rule. Virtually every state statute affects important rights. This Court has repeatedly held, for example, that the traditional equal protection standard is applicable to statutory classifications affecting such fundamental matters as the right to pursue a particular occupation, the right to receive greater or smaller wages or to work more or less hours, and the right to inherit property. Rights such as these are in principle indistinguishable from those involved here, and to extend the "compelling interest" rule to all cases in which such rights are affected would go far toward making this Court a "super-legislature." This branch of the doctrine is also unnecessary. When the right affected is one assured by the Federal Constitution, any infringement can be dealt with under the Due Process Clause. But when a statute affects only matters not mentioned in the Federal Constitution and is not arbitrary or irrational, I must reiterate that I know of nothing which entitles this Court to pick out particular human activities, characterize them as "fundamental," and give them added protection under an unusually stringent equal protection test. . . .

If the issue is regarded purely as one of equal protection, then, for the reasons just set forth, this nonracial classification should be judged by ordinary equal protection standards. The applicable criteria are familiar and well established. A legislative measure will be found to deny equal protection only if "it is without any reasonable basis, and therefore is purely arbitrary.". . .

In light of th[e] undeniable relation of residence requirements to valid legislative aims, it cannot be said that the requirements are "arbitrary" or "lacking in rational justification." Hence, I can find no objection to these residence requirements under the Equal Protection Clause of the Fourteenth Amendment or under the analogous standard embodied in the Due Process Clause of the Fifth Amendment.

The . . . decisive [question is] . . . whether the governmental interests served by residence requirements outweigh the burden imposed upon the right to travel. In my view, a number of considerations militate in favor of constitutionality. First . . . legitimate governmental interests are furthered by residence requirements. Second, the impact of the requirements upon the freedom of individuals to travel interstate is indirect and, according to evidence put forward by the appellees themselves, insubstantial.

Third, these are not cases in which a State or States, acting alone, have attempted to interfere with the right of citizens to travel, but one in which the States have acted within the terms of a limited authorization by the National Government, and in which Congress itself has laid down a like rule for the District of Columbia. Fourth, the legislatures which enacted these statutes have been fully exposed to the arguments of the appellees as to why these residence requirements are unwise, and have rejected them. This is not, therefore, an instance in which legislatures have acted without mature deliberation. . . .

Taking all of these competing considerations into account, I believe that the balance definitely favors constitutionality. In reaching that conclusion, I do not minimize the importance of the right to travel interstate. However, the impact of residence conditions upon that right is indirect and apparently quite insubstantial. On the other hand, the governmental purposes served by the requirements are legitimate and real, and the residence requirements are clearly suited to their accomplishment. To abolish residence requirements might well discourage highly worthwhile experimentation in the welfare field. The statutes come to us clothed with the authority of Congress and attended by a correspondingly heavy presumption of constitutionality. Moreover, although the appellees assert that the same objectives could have been achieved by less restrictive means, this is an area in which the judiciary should be especially slow to fetter the judgment of Congress and of some 46 state legislatures in the choice of methods. Residence requirements have advantages, such as administrative simplicity and relative certainty, which are not shared by the alternative solutions proposed by the appellees. In these circumstances, I cannot find that the burden imposed by residence requirements upon ability to travel outweighs the governmental interests in their continued employment. Nor do I believe that the period of residence required in these cases—one year—is so excessively long as to justify a finding of unconstitutionality on that score.

THE DEVELOPMENT OF LAW
Rulings on Residency Requirements, the Right to Interstate Travel, and Indigency

Case	Vote	Ruling
Dunn v. Blumstein, 405 U.S. 330 (1972)	6:1	Struck down one-year state residency and three-month county residency requirements as a violation of the

Case	Vote	Ruling
		fundamental right to vote (see also Vol. 1, Ch. 8); Chief Justice Burger dissented.
Valdis v. Kline, 412 U.S. 441 (1973)	6:3	Held as violative of the due process clause Connecticut's presumption that out-of-state students attending the state's colleges retain their status as out-of-state students, for tuition purposes, throughout their attendance in college; Chief Justice Burger and Justices Douglas and Rehnquist dissented.
Memorial Hospital v. Maricopa County, 415 U.S. 250 (1974)	8:1	Found that Arizona's one-year residency requirement for nonemergency medical care at the county's expense to violate the right to travel; Justice Rehnquist dissented.
Sosna v. Iowa, 419 U.S. 393 (1975)	6:3	Upheld a one-year residency requirement for initiating divorce proceedings; Justices Brennan, Marshall and White dissented.
Califano v. Aznavorian, 439 U.S. 170 (1978)	9:0	Upheld Congress's withholding of benefits under the Supplemental Security Income program for any month that a recipient spends entirely outside of the United States.
Zobel v. Williams, 457 U.S. 55 (1982)	8:1	Struck down Alaska's system for redistributing state income from mineral deposits to each adult resident, based on the number of years of state residency since 1959, upon finding no rational relationship between the residency requirement and the state's goal of prudent management of the fund; Justice Rehnquist dissented.

Case	Vote	Ruling
Supreme Court of New Hampshire v. Piper, 470 U.S. 274 (1985)	8:1	Struck down, under the privileges and immunities clause, a state supreme court ruling that only state residents were eligible for admission to the state bar.
Supreme Court of Virginia v. Friedman, 487 U.S. 59 (1988)	7:2	Struck down a state supreme court ruling that out-of-state lawyers must become permanent state residents before they may be admitted to the state bar on motion (without taking the state bar examination). The majority found the distinction between resident and nonresident lawyers did not have a close and substantial relationship to the state's interests; Chief Justice Rehnquist and Justice Scalia dissented.

San Antonio Independent School District v. Rodriguez

411 U.S. 1, 93 S.Ct. 1278 (1973)

Demetrio Rodriguez and several other Mexican-Americans sued their school district, the state board of education, the state attorney general and several other government officials. They contended that Texas's system for financing public schools violated the equal protection clause of the Fourteenth Amendment because it discriminated on the basis of wealth. Besides federal funds for education, the state provided for a minimum level of education in all districts by funding a large portion of the cost of teachers' salaries and other operating expenses. In addition, each school district contributed a portion through local property taxes. But because the value of property varied greatly from one school district to another, there were wide disparities in school districts' per-pupil expenditures. At a pretrial conference, the San Antonio Independent School District sided with Rodriguez. But state officials continued to defend the system of financing public schools and appealed to the Supreme Court the ruling of a federal district court, which held that Texas discriminated against students in poor school districts in violation of the Fourteenth Amendment. The Supreme Court split five to four in reversing the lower court and held that wealth is not a suspect classification and found that the state's system of funding public education was rational and constitutional. In 1989, though, the Texas State Supreme Court ruled contrariwise and found that the state discriminated in violation of provision of the *state* constitution.

Justice POWELL delivers the opinion of the Court.

Until recent times, Texas was a predominantly rural State and its population and property wealth were spread relatively evenly across the State. Sizable differences in the value of assessable property between local school districts became increasingly evident as the State became more industrialized and as rural-to-urban population shifts became more pronounced. The location of commercial and industrial property began to play a significant role in determining the amount of tax resources available to each school district. These growing disparities in population and taxable property between districts were responsible in part for increasingly notable differences in levels of local expenditure for education. . . .

The school district in which appellees reside, the Edgewood Independent School District, has been compared throughout this litigation with the Alamo Heights Independent School District. This comparison between the least and most affluent districts in the San Antonio area serves to illustrate the manner in which the dual system of finance operates and to indicate the extent to which substantial disparities exist despite the State's impressive progress in recent years. Edgewood is one of seven public school districts in the metropolitan area. Approximately 22,000 students are enrolled in its 25 elementary and secondary schools. The district is situated in the core-city sector of San Antonio in a residential neighborhood that has little commercial or industrial property. The residents are predominantly of Mexican-American descent: approximately 90% of the student population is Mexican-American and over 6% is Negro. The average assessed property value per pupil is $5,960—the lowest in the metropolitan area—and the median family income ($4,686) is also the lowest. At an equalized tax rate of $1.05 per $100 of assessed property—the highest in the metropolitan area—the district contributed $26 to the education of each child for the 1967–1968 school year above its Local Fund Assignment for the Minimum Foundation Program. The Foundation Program contributed $222 per pupil for a state-local total of $248. Federal funds added another $108 for a total of $356 per pupil.

Alamo Heights is the most affluent school district in San Antonio. Its six schools, housing approximately 5,000 students, are situated in a residential community quite unlike the Edgewood District. The school population is predominantly "Anglo," having only 18% Mexican-Americans and less than 1% Negroes. The assessed property value per pupil exceeds $49,000, and the median family income is $8,001. In 1967–1968 the local tax rate of $.85 per $100 of valuation yielded $333 per pupil over and above its contribution to the Foundation Program. Coupled with the $225 provided from that Program, the district was able to supply $558 per student. Supplemented by a $36 per-pupil grant from federal sources, Alamo Heights spent $594 per pupil. . . .

Texas virtually concedes that its historically rooted dual system of financing education could not withstand the strict judicial scrutiny that this Court has found appropriate in reviewing legislative judgments that interfere with fundamental constitutional rights or that involve suspect classifications. . . .

We must decide, first, whether the Texas system of financing public education operates to the disadvantage of some suspect class or impinges upon a fundamental right explicitly or implicitly protected by the Constitution, thereby requiring strict judicial scrutiny. If so, the judgment of the District Court should be affirmed. If not, the Texas scheme must still be examined to determine whether it rationally furthers some legitimate, articulated state purpose and therefore does not constitute an invidious discrimination in violation of the Equal Protection Clause of the Fourteenth Amendment. . . .

[F]or the several reasons that follow, we find neither the suspect-classification nor the fundamental-interest analysis persuasive.

The wealth discrimination discovered by the District Court in this case, and by several other courts that have recently struck down school-financing laws in other States, is quite unlike any of the forms of wealth discrimination heretofore reviewed by this Court. Rather than focusing on the unique features of the alleged discrimination, the courts in these cases have virtually assumed their findings of a suspect classification through a simplistic process of analysis: since, under the traditional systems of financing public schools, some poorer people receive less expensive educations than other more affluent people, these systems discriminate on the basis of wealth. This approach largely ignores the hard threshold questions, including whether it makes a difference for purposes of consideration under the Constitution that the class of disadvantaged "poor" cannot be identified or defined in customary equal protection terms, and whether the relative—rather than absolute—nature of the asserted deprivation is of significant consequence. Before a State's laws and the justifications for the classifications they create are subjected to strict judicial scrutiny, we think these threshold considerations must be analyzed more closely than they were in the court below.

The case comes to us with no definitive description of the classifying facts or delineation of the disfavored class. . . . The Texas system of school financing might be regarded as discriminating (1) against "poor" persons whose incomes fall below some identifiable level of poverty or who might be characterized as functionally "indigent," or (2) against those who are relatively poorer than others, or (3) against all those who, irrespective of their personal incomes, happen to reside in relatively poorer school districts. Our task must be to ascertain whether, in fact, the Texas system has been shown to discriminate on any of these possible bases and, if so, whether the resulting classification may be regarded as suspect.

The precedents of this Court provide the proper starting point. The individuals, or groups of individuals, who constituted the class discriminated against in our prior cases shared two distinguishing characteristics: because of their impecunity they were completely unable to pay for some desired benefit, and as a consequence, they sustained an absolute deprivation of a meaningful opportunity to enjoy that benefit. In *Griffin v. Illinois*, 351 U.S. 12 (1956), and its progeny, the Court invalidated state laws that prevented an indigent criminal defendant from acquiring a transcript, or an adequate substitute for a transcript, for use at several stages of the trial and appeal process. The payment requirements in each case were found to occasion *de facto* discrimination against those who, because of their indigency, were totally unable to pay for transcripts. . . .

Likewise, in *Douglas v. California*, 372 U.S. 353 (1963), a decision establishing an indigent defendant's right to court-appointed counsel on direct appeal, the Court dealt only with defendants who could not pay for counsel from their own resources and who had no other way of gaining representation. *Douglas* provides no relief for those on whom the burdens of paying for a criminal defense are relatively speaking, great but not insurmountable. Nor does it deal with relative differences in the quality of counsel acquired by the less wealthy.

Williams v. Illinois, 399 U.S. 235 (1970), and *Tate v. Short*, 401 U.S. 395 (1971), struck down criminal penalties that subjected indigents to incarceration simply because of their inability to pay a fine. Again, the disadvantaged class was composed only of persons who were totally unable to pay the demanded sum. Those cases do not touch on the question whether equal protection is denied to persons with relatively less money on whom designated fines impose heavier burdens. . . .

Finally, in *Bullock v. Carter*, 405 U.S. 134 (1972), the Court invalidated the Texas filing-fee requirement for primary elections.

Both of the relevant classifying facts found in the previous cases were present there. The size of the fee, often running into the thousands of dollars and, in at least one case, as high as $8,900, effectively barred all potential candidates who were unable to pay the required fee. As the system provided "no reasonable alternative means of access to the ballot," inability to pay occasioned an absolute denial of a position on the primary ballot.

Only appellees' first possible basis for describing the class disadvantaged by the Texas school-financing system—discrimination against a class of definably "poor" persons—might arguably meet the criteria established in these prior cases. Even a cursory examination, however, demonstrates that neither of the two distinguishing characteristics of wealth classifications can be found here. First, in support of their charge that the system discriminates against the "poor," appellees have made no effort to demonstrate that it operates to the peculiar disadvantage of any class fairly definable as indigent, or as composed of persons whose incomes are beneath any designated poverty level. Indeed, there is reason to believe that the poorest families are not necessarily clustered in the poorest property districts. A recent and exhaustive study of school districts in Connecticut concluded that "[i]t is clearly incorrect . . . to contend that the 'poor' live in 'poor' districts. . . ."

[T]here is no basis on the record in this case for assuming that the poorest people—defined by reference to any level of absolute impecunity—are concentrated in the poorest districts.

Second, neither appellees nor the District Court addressed the fact that, unlike each of the foregoing cases, lack of personal resources has not occasioned an absolute deprivation of the desired benefit. The argument here is not that the children in districts having relatively low assessable property values are receiving no public education; rather, it is that they are receiving a poorer quality education than that available to children in districts having more assessable wealth. Apart from the unsettled and disputed question whether the quality of education may be determined by the amount of money expended for it, a sufficient answer to appellees' argument is that, at least where wealth is involved, the Equal Protection Clause does not require absolute equality or precisely equal advantages. . . .

For these two reasons—the absence of any evidence that the financing system discriminates against any definable category of "poor" people or that it results in the absolute deprivation of education—the disadvantaged class is not susceptible of identification in traditional terms.

As suggested above, appellees and the District Court may have embraced a second or third approach, the second of which might be characterized as a theory of relative or comparative discrimination based on family income. Appellees sought to prove that a direct correlation exists between the wealth of families within each district and the expenditures therein for education. That is, along a continuum, the poorer the family the lower the dollar amount of education received by the family's children. . . .

If, in fact, these correlations could be sustained, then it might be argued that expenditures on education—equated by appellees to the quality of education—are dependent on personal wealth. Appellees' comparative-discrimination theory would still face serious unanswered questions, including whether a bare positive correlation or some higher degree of correlation is necessary to provide a basis for concluding that the financing system is designed to operate to the peculiar disadvantage of the comparatively poor, and whether a class of this size and diversity could ever claim the special protection accorded "suspect" classes. These questions need not be addressed in this case, however, since appellees' proof fails to support their allegations or the District Court's conclusions. . . .

This brings us, then, to the third way in which the classification scheme might be defined—*district* wealth discrimination. . . . Assuming a perfect correlation between district property wealth and expenditures from top to bottom, the disadvantaged class might be viewed as encompassing every child in every district except the district that has the most assessable wealth and spends the most on education. Alternatively, as suggested in Justice MARSHALL'S dissenting opinion the class might be defined more restrictively to include children in districts with assessable property which falls below the statewide average, or median, or below some other artificially defined level.

However described, it is clear that appellees' suit asks this Court to extend its most exacting scrutiny to review a system that allegedly discriminates against a large, diverse, and amorphous class, unified only by the common factor of residence in districts that happen to have less taxable wealth than other districts. The system of alleged discrimination and the class it defines have none of the traditional indicia of suspectness: the class is not saddled with such disabilities, or subjected to such a history of purposeful unequal treatment, or relegated to such a position of political powerlessness as to command extraordinary protection from the majoritarian political process.

We thus conclude that the Texas system does not operate to the peculiar disadvantage of any suspect class. But in recognition of the fact that this Court has never heretofore held that wealth discrimination alone provides an adequate basis for invoking strict scrutiny, appellees have not relied solely on this contention. They also assert that the State's system impermissibly interferes with the exercise of a "fundamental" right and that accordingly the prior decisions of this Court require the application of the strict standard of judicial review. . . .

We are in complete agreement with the conclusion of the three-judge panel below that "the grave significance of education both to the individual and to our society" cannot be doubted. But the importance of a service performed by the State does not determine whether it must be regarded as fundamental for purposes of examination under the Equal Protection Clause. Justice HARLAN, dissenting from the Court's application of strict scrutiny to a law impinging upon the right of interstate travel, admonished that "[v]irtually every state statute affects important rights." *Shapiro v. Thompson*, 394 U.S. 618 (1969). In his view, if the degree of judicial scrutiny of state legislation fluctuated, depending on a majority's view of the importance of the interest affected, we would have gone "far toward making this Court a 'super-legislature.' ". . .

It is not the province of this Court to create substantive constitutional rights in the name of guaranteeing equal protection of the laws. Thus, the key to discovering whether education is "fundamental" is not to be found in comparisons of the relative societal significance of education as opposed to subsistence or housing. Nor is it to be found by weighing whether education is as important as the right to travel. Rather, the answer lies in assessing whether there is a right to education explicitly or implicitly guaranteed by the Constitution. Education, of course, is not among the rights afforded explicit protection under our Federal Constitution. Nor do we find any basis for saying it is implicitly so protected. As we have said, the undisputed importance of education will not alone cause this Court to depart from the usual standard for reviewing a State's social and economic legislation. It is appellees' contention, however, that education is distinguishable from other services and benefits provided by the State because it bears a peculiarly close relationship to other rights and liberties accorded protection under the Constitution. Specifically, they insist that education is itself a fundamental personal right because it is essential to the effective exercise of First Amendment freedoms and to intelligent utilization of the right to vote. In asserting a nexus between speech and education, appellees urge that the right to speak is meaningless unless the speaker is capable of articulating his thoughts intelligently and persuasively. The "marketplace of ideas" is an empty forum for those lacking basic communicative tools. Likewise, they argue that the corollary right to receive information becomes little more than a hollow privilege when the recipient has not been taught to read, assimilate, and utilize available knowledge.

A similar line of reasoning is pursued with respect to the right to vote. Exercise of the franchise, it is contended, cannot be divorced from the educational foundation of the voter. The electoral process, if reality is to conform to the democratic ideal, depends on an informed electorate: a voter cannot cast his ballot intelligently unless his reading skills and thought processes have been adequately developed.

We need not dispute any of these propositions. The Court has long afforded zealous protection against unjustifiable governmental interference with the individual's rights to speak and to vote. Yet we have never presumed to possess either the ability or the authority to guarantee to the citizenry the most *effective* speech or the most *informed* electoral choice. That these may be desirable goals of a system of freedom of expression and of a representative form of government is not to be doubted. These are indeed goals to be pursued by a people whose thoughts and beliefs are freed from governmental interference. But they are not values to be implemented by judicial intrusion into otherwise legitimate state activities.

Even if it were conceded that some identifiable quantum of education is a constitutionally protected prerequisite to the meaningful exercise of either right, we have no indication that the present levels of educational expenditures in Texas provide an education that falls short.

We have carefully considered each of the arguments supportive of the District Court's finding that education is a fundamental right or liberty and have found those arguments unpersuasive. . . .

The foregoing considerations buttress our conclusion that Texas' system of public school finance is an inappropriate candidate for strict judicial scrutiny. These same considerations are relevant to the determination whether that system, with its conceded imperfections, nevertheless bears some rational relationship to a legitimate state purpose. It is to this question that we next turn our attention. . . .

In its reliance on state as well as local resources, the Texas system is comparable to the systems employed in virtually every other State. The power to tax local property for educational purposes has been recognized in Texas at least since 1883. When the growth of commercial and industrial centers and accompanying shifts in population began to create disparities in local resources, Texas undertook a program calling for a considerable investment of state funds. . . .

While assuring a basic education for every child in the State, it permits and encourages a large measure of participation in and control of each district's schools at the local level. In an era that has witnessed a consistent trend toward centralization of the functions of government, local sharing of responsibility for public education has survived. . . .

In part local control means . . . the freedom to devote more money to the education of one's children. Equally important, however, is the opportunity it offers for participation in the decisionmaking process that determines how those local tax dollars will be spent. Each locality is free to tailor local programs to local needs. Pluralism also affords some opportunity for experimentation, innovation, and a healthy competition for educational excellence. An analogy to the Nation-State relationship in our federal system seems uniquely appropriate. Justice BRANDEIS identified as one of the peculiar strengths of our form of government each State's freedom to "serve as a laboratory: and try novel social and economic experiments." No area of social concern stands to profit more from a multiplicity of viewpoints and from a diversity of approaches than does public education.

Appellees do not question the propriety of Texas' dedication to local control of education. To the contrary, they attack the school-financing system precisely because, in their view, it does not provide the same level of local control and fiscal flexibility in all districts. Appellees suggest that local control could be preserved and promoted under other financing systems that resulted in more equality in educational expenditures. While it is no doubt true that reliance on local property taxation for school revenues provides less freedom of choice with respect to expenditures for some districts than for others the existence of "some inequality" in the manner in which the State's rationale is achieved is not alone a sufficient basis for striking down the entire system. . . .

Appellees further urge that the Texas system is unconstitutionally arbitrary because it allows the availability of local taxable resources to turn on "happenstance." They see no justification for a system that allows, as they contend, the quality of education to fluctuate on the basis of the fortuitous positioning of the boundary lines of political subdivisions and the location of valuable commercial and industrial property. But any scheme of local taxation—indeed the very existence of identifiable local governmental units—requires the establishment of jurisdictional boundaries that are inevitably arbitrary. It is equally inevitable that some localities are going to be blessed with more taxable assets than others. . . .

In sum, to the extent that the Texas system of school financing results in unequal expenditures between children who happen to reside in different districts, we cannot say that such disparities are the product of a system that is so irrational as to be invidiously discriminatory.

Justice STEWART concurred in a separate opinion.

Justice BRENNAN dissenting.

Although I agree with my Brother WHITE that the Texas statutory scheme is devoid of any rational basis, and for that reason is violative of the Equal Protection Clause, I also record my disagreement with the Court's rather distressing assertion that a right may be deemed "fundamental" for the purposes of equal protection analysis only if it is "explicitly or implicitly guaranteed by the Constitution." As my Brother MARSHALL convincingly demonstrates, our prior cases stand for the proposition that "fundamentality" is, in large measure, a function of the right's importance in terms of the effectuation of those rights which are in fact constitutionally guaranteed. . . .

Here, there can be no doubt that education is inextricably linked to the right to participate in the electoral process and to the rights of free speech and association guaranteed by the First Amendment. This being so, any classification affecting education must be subjected to strict judicial scrutiny, and since even the State concedes that the statutory scheme now before us cannot pass constitutional muster under this stricter standard of review, I can only conclude that the Texas school-financing scheme is constitutionally invalid.

Justice WHITE, with whom Justice DOUGLAS and Justice BRENNAN join, dissenting.

I cannot disagree with the proposition that local control and local decisionmaking play an important part in our democratic system of government. Much may be left to local option, and this case would be quite different if it were true that the Texas system . . . extended a meaningful option to all local districts to increase their per-pupil expenditures and so to improve their children's education to the extent that increased funding would achieve that goal. The system would then arguably provide a rational and sensible method of achieving the stated aim of preserving an area for local initiative and decision.

The difficulty with the Texas system, however, is that it provides a meaningful option to Alamo Heights and like school districts but almost none to Edgewood and those other districts with a low per-pupil real estate tax base. In these latter districts, no matter how desirous parents are of supporting their schools with greater revenues, it is impossible to do so through the use of the real estate property tax. In these districts, the Texas system utterly fails to extend a realistic choice to parents because the property tax, which is the only revenue-raising mechanism extended to school districts, is practically and legally unavailable. . . .

Both the Edgewood and Alamo Heights districts are located in Bexar County, Texas. Student enrollment in Alamo Heights is 5,432, in Edgewood 22,862. The per-pupil market value of the taxable property in Alamo Heights is $49,078, in Edgewood $5,960. In a typical relevant year, Alamo Heights had a maintenance tax rate of $1.20 and a debt service (bond) tax rate of 20¢ per $100 assessed evaluation, while Edgewood had a maintenance rate of 52¢ and a bond rate of 67¢. These rates, when applied to the respective tax bases, yielded Alamo Heights $1,433,473 in maintenance dollars and $236,074 in bond dollars, and Edgewood $223,034 in maintenance dollars and $279,023 in bond dollars. As is readily apparent, because of the variance in tax bases between the districts, results, in terms of revenues, do not correlate with effort, in terms of tax rate. Thus, Alamo Heights, with a tax base approximately twice the size of Edgewood's base, realized approximately six times as many maintenance dollars as Edgewood by using a tax rate only approximately two and one-half times larger. Similarly, Alamo Heights realized slightly fewer bond dollars by using a bond tax rate less than one-third of that used by Edgewood. . . .

Plainly, were Alamo Heights or North East to apply the Edgewood tax rate to its tax base, it would yield far greater revenues than Edgewood is able to yield applying those same rates to its base. Conversely, were Edgewood to apply the Alamo Heights or North East rates to its base, the yield would be far smaller than the Alamo Heights or North East yields. The disparity is, therefore, currently operative and its impact on Edgewood is undeniably serious. It is evident from statistics in the record that show that, applying an equalized tax rate of 85¢ per $100 assessed valuation, Alamo Heights was able to provide approximately $330 per pupil in local revenues over and above the Local Fund Assignment. In Edgewood, on the other hand, with an equalized tax rate of $1.05 per $100 of assessed valuation, $26 per pupil was raised beyond the Local Fund Assignment. As previously noted in Alamo Heights, total per-pupil revenues from local, state, and federal funds was $594 per pupil, in Edgewood $356.

In order to equal the highest yield in any other Bexar County district, Alamo Heights would be required to tax at the rate of 68¢ per $100 of assessed valuation. Edgewood would be required to tax at the prohibitive rate of $5.76 per $100. But state law places a $1.50 per $100 ceiling on the maintenance tax rate, a limit that would surely be reached long before Edgewood attained an equal yield. Edgewood is thus precluded in law, as well as in fact, from achieving a yield even close to that of some other districts.

The Equal Protection Clause permits discriminations between classes but requires that the classification bear some rational relationship to a permissible object sought to be attained by the statute. It is not enough that the Texas system before us seeks to achieve the valid, rational purpose of maximizing local initiative; the means chosen by the State must also be rationally related to the end sought to be achieved. . . .

If the State aims at maximizing local initiative and local choice, by permitting school districts to resort to the real property tax if they choose to do so, it utterly fails in achieving its purpose in districts with property tax bases so low that there is little if any opportunity for interested parents, rich or poor, to augment school district revenues. Requiring the State to establish only that unequal treatment is in furtherance of a permissible goal, without also requiring the State to show that the means chosen to effectuate that goal are rationally related to its achievement, makes equal protection analysis no more than an empty gesture. In my view, the parents and children in Edgewood, and in like districts, suffer from an invidious discrimination violative of the Equal Protection Clause.

Justice MARSHALL, with whom Justice DOUGLAS concurs, dissenting.

In my judgment, the right of every American to an equal start in life, so far as the provision of a state service as important as education is concerned, is far too vital to permit state discrimination on grounds as tenuous as those presented by this record. Nor can I accept the notion that it is sufficient to remit these appellees to the vagaries of the political process which, contrary to the majority's suggestion, has proved singularly unsuited to the task of providing a remedy for this discrimination. I, for one, am unsatisfied with the hope of an ultimate "political" solution sometime in the indefinite future while in the meantime, countless children unjustifiably receive inferior educations that "may affect their hearts and minds in a way unlikely ever to be undone." *Brown v. Board of Education,* [347 U.S. 483] (1954). I must therefore respectfully dissent. . . .

The Court apparently seeks to establish today that equal protection cases fall into one of two neat categories which dictate the appropriate standard of review—strict scrutiny or mere rationality. But this Court's decisions in the field of equal protection defy such easy categorization. A principled reading of what this Court has done reveals that it has applied a spectrum of standards in reviewing discrimination allegedly violative of the Equal Protection Clause. This spectrum clearly comprehends variations in the degree of care with which the Court will scrutinize particular classifications, depending, I believe, on the constitutional and societal importance of the interest adversely affected and the recognized invidiousness of the basis upon which the particular classification is drawn. . . .

I therefore cannot accept the majority's labored efforts to demonstrate that fundamental interests, which call for strict scrutiny of the challenged classification, encompass only established rights which we are somehow bound to recognize from the text of the Constitution itself. To be sure, some interests which the Court has deemed to be fundamental for purposes of equal protection analysis are themselves constitutionally protected rights. . . . But it will not do to suggest that the "answer" to whether an interest is fundamental for purposes of equal protection analysis is *always* determined by whether that interest "is a right . . . explicitly or implicitly guaranteed by the Constitution."

I would like to know where the Constitution guarantees the right to procreate, *Skinner v. Oklahoma ex rel. Williamson,* 316 U.S. 535 (1942), or the right to vote in state elections, *e. g., Reynolds v. Sims,* 377 U.S. 533 (1964), or the right to an appeal from a criminal conviction, *e. g., Griffin v. Illinois,* 351 U.S. 12 (1956). These are instances in which, due to the importance of the interests at stake, the Court has displayed a strong concern with the existence of discriminatory state treatment. But the Court has never said or indicated that these are interests which independently enjoy full-blown constitutional protection. . . .

The majority is, of course, correct when it suggests that the process of determining which interests are fundamental is a difficult one. But I do not think the problem is insurmountable. And I certainly do not accept the view that the process need necessarily degenerate into an unprincipled, subjective "picking-and-choosing" between various interests or that it must involve this Court in creating "substantive constitutional rights in the name of guaranteeing equal protection of the laws." Although not all fundamental interests are constitutionally guaranteed, the determination of which interests are fundamental should be firmly rooted in the text of the Constitution. The task in every case should be to determine the extent to which constitutionally guaranteed rights are dependent on interests not mentioned in the Constitution. As the nexus between the specific constitutional guarantee and the nonconstitutional interest draws closer, the nonconstitutional interest becomes more fundamental and the degree of judicial scrutiny applied when the interest is infringed on a discriminatory basis must be adjusted accordingly. Thus, it cannot be denied that interests such as procreation, the exercise of the state franchise, and access to criminal appellate processes are not fully guaranteed to the citizen by our Constitution. But these interests have nonetheless been afforded special judicial consideration in the face of discrimination because they are, to some extent, interrelated with constitutional guarantees. Procreation is now understood to be important because of its interaction with the established constitutional right of privacy. The exercise of the state franchise is closely tied to basic civil and political rights inherent in the First Amendment. And access to criminal appellate processes enhances the integrity of the range of rights implicit in the Fourteenth Amendment guarantee of due process of law. Only if we closely protect the related interests from state discrimination do we ultimately ensure the integrity of the constitutional guarantee itself. This is the real lesson that must be taken from our previous decisions involving interests deemed to be fundamental. . . .

It is true that this Court has never deemed the provision of free public education to be required by the Constitution. Indeed, it has on occasion suggested that state-supported education is a privilege bestowed by a State on its citizens. See *Missouri ex rel. Gaines v. Canada,* [305 U.S. 337 (1938)]. Nevertheless, the fundamental importance of education is amply indicated by the prior decisions of this Court, by the unique status accorded public education by our society, and by the close relationship between education and some of our most basic constitutional values. . . .

The nature of our inquiry into the justifications for state discrimination is essentially the same in all equal protection cases: We must consider the substantiality of the state interests sought to be served, and we must scrutinize the reasonableness of the means by which the State has sought to advance its interests. Differences in the application of this test are, in my view, a function of the constitutional importance of the interests at stake and the invidiousness of the particular classification. . . .

Here, both the nature of the interest and the classification dictate close judicial scrutiny of the purposes which Texas seeks to serve with its present educational financing scheme and of the means it has selected to serve that purpose.

The only justification offered by appellants to sustain the discrimination in educational opportunity caused by the Texas financing scheme is local educational control. . . .

I do not question that local control of public education, as an abstract matter, constitutes a very substantial state interest. . . . [But] it is apparent that the State's purported concern with local control is offered primarily as an excuse rather than as a justification for interdistrict inequality.

In Texas, statewide laws regulate in fact the most minute details of local public education. . . .

Moreover, even if we accept Texas' general dedication to local control in educational matters, it is difficult to find any evidence of such dedication with respect to fiscal matters. . . . If Texas had a system truly dedicated to local fiscal control, one would expect the quality of the educational opportunity provided in each district to vary with the decision of the voters in that district as to the level of sacrifice they wish to make for public education. In fact, the Texas scheme produces precisely the opposite result. Local school districts cannot choose to have the best education in the State by imposing the highest tax rate. Instead, the quality of the educational opportunity offered by any particular district is largely determined by the amount of taxable property located in the district—a factor over which local voters can exercise no control. . . .

In my judgment, any substantial degree of scrutiny of the operation of the Texas financing scheme reveals that the State has selected means wholly inappropriate to secure its purported interest in assuring its school districts local fiscal control. At the same time, appellees have pointed out a variety of alternative financing schemes which may serve the State's purported interest in local control as well as, if not better than, the present scheme without the current impairment of the educational opportunity of vast numbers of Texas schoolchildren. I see no need, however, to explore the practical or constitutional merits of those suggested alternatives at this time for, whatever their positive or negative features, experience with the present financing scheme impugns any suggestion that it constitutes a serious effort to provide local fiscal control. . . .

THE DEVELOPMENT OF LAW
Other Rulings Dealing with Illegitimate Children

Case	Vote	Ruling
Levy v. Louisiana, 391 U.S. 68 (1968); and *Glona v. American Guarantee,* 391 U.S. 73 (1968)	6:3	Justice Douglas held that illegitimate children are persons within the meaning of the Fourteenth Amendment's equal protection clause and have a right to recover damages for the wrongful death of their mother, striking down Louisiana's law providing that only legitimate surviving children may sue for damages; Justices Harlan, Black, and Stewart dissented.
Labine v. Vincent, 401 U.S. 532 (1971)	5:4	Justice Black held that the equal protection clause was not violated by Louisiana's statute precluding illegitimate children from making claims of inheritance from their natural father's estate; Justices Brennan, Douglas, White, and Marshall dissented.
Gomez v. Perez, 409 U.S. 535 (1973)	7:2	*Per curiam* decision finding the equal protection clause to be violated by a law distinguishing between legiti-

Case	Vote	Ruling
		mate and illegitimate children in providing for a father's responsibility for child support; Justices Stewart and Rehnquist dissented.
Weber v. Aetna Casualty, 406 U.S. 164 (1972)	8:1	Justice Powell struck down Louisiana's workers' compensation law that forbade recovery for the wrongful death of parent by illegitimate children; Justice Rehnquist dissented.
New Jersey Welfare Rights Organization v. Cahill, 411 U.S. 619 (1973)	8:1	A *per curiam* decision holding that the equal protection clause was violated by a state law distinguishing between legitimate and illegitimate children in the award of state welfare benefits; Justice Rehnquist dissented.
Jimenz v. Weinberger, 417 U.S. 628 (1974)	8:1	Chief Justice Burger held that the denial of federal welfare benefits to illegitimate dependents of disabled persons violated the equal protection component of the Fifth Amendment's due process clause; Justice Rehnquist dissented.
Matthews v. Lucas, 427 U.S. 495 (1976)	6:3	Justice Blackmun upheld the Social Security Act's denial of disability benefits to illegitimate, but not legitimate, children and held that the provision did not require strict judicial scrutiny; Justices Stevens, Marshall, and Brennan dissented.
Trimble v. Gordon, 430 U.S. 762 (1977)	5:4	Justice Powell struck down a statute allowing illegitimate children to inherit only from their mothers, and not fathers, because it was not "substantially related to a permissible state interest"; Chief Justice Burger and Justices Blackmun, Rehn-

Case	Vote	Ruling
		quist, and Stewart dissented.
Lalli v. Lalli, 439 U.S. 259 (1978)	5:4	Despite the ruling in *Trimble,* Justice Powell held for a bare majority that two illegitimate children were not entitled to share in their natural father's estate because during his lifetime he had not obtained a judicial order declaring his paternity; Justices Brennan, Marshall, Stevens, and White dissented.
Fiallo v. Bell, 430 U.S. 787 (1977)	6:3	Justice Powell upheld Congress's denial of preferential status for immigration to the illegitimate children of aliens; Justices Brennan, Marshall, and White dissented.
Quilloin v. Walcott, 434 U.S. 246 (1978)	9:0	Justice Marshall held that a natural father's equal protection claims were not violated by the application of "best interests of a child" standard in adoption proceedings and thus he did not have a veto over the adoption of his child by the natural mother's legal husband.
Parham v. Hughes, 441 U.S. 347 (1979)	5:4	Justice Stevens upheld a Georgia law precluding a father who had not legitimated a child from suing for the child's wrongful death; Justices Brennan, Blackmun, Marshall, and White dissented.
Reed v. Campbell, 476 U.S. 852 (1986)	9:0	Justice Stevens held that illegitimate children are entitled to inherit from the estate of a deceased father.
Michael H. v. Gerald D., 109 S.Ct. 2333 (1989)	5:4	For a plurality, Justice Scalia upheld California's law creating a legal presumption that a child born to a mar-

Case	Vote	Ruling
		ried woman living with her legal husband is a child of the marriage, and rejected arguments that the natural father, under the Fifth Amendment's due process clause, had a right to file a filiation suit to establish paternity and a right to child visitation, as well as dismissed the claim that the statute violated the child's equal protection rights; Justice Stevens concurred; Justices Brennan, Blackmun, Marshall, and White dissented.

(3) Alienage and Age

With the exception of the right to vote, most constitutional rights extend to the "people" or "persons," including citizens and aliens. Aliens, though, do not enjoy the same freedom as citizens when entering the country and their residency in the United States may be conditioned by the government (as with student visas). In contrast to citizens, aliens may also be deported and the property of enemy aliens confiscated by the government during wartime.

Despite the constitutional rights that aliens share with citizens, and the historic waves of immigrants who built the country, state and federal laws since the Alien and Sedition Act of 1798 have discriminated against aliens, frequently denying them various kinds of public benefits and employment. But in *Graham v. Richardson*, 403 U.S. 532 (1971), the Court announced that alienage was a suspect category and that laws discriminating against aliens must survive strict scrutiny. While a series of subsequent rulings overturned other laws denying aliens benefits and employment opportunities, the Court drew back in *Foley v. Connelie*, 435 U.S. 291 (1979), when it came to New York's law barring aliens from being employed as state police officers. There and in *Ambach v. Norwick*, 441 U.S. 68 (1979), and *Cabell v. Chavez-Salido*, 454 U.S. 432 (1982), the Court held that aliens could be disqualified from positions in public employment that required the exercise of discretion in the performance of important governmental functions, such as law enforcement and education. The Court was also sharply split in *Plyler v. Doe* (1982) (see page 1486), when holding that Texas could not deny undocumented aliens a public education.

While giving heightened scrutiny to classifications based on alienage, in *Massachusetts Board of Retirement v. Murgia*, 427 U.S. 307 (1976), the Court held that age is not a suspect category under the equal protection clause. There, the Court upheld a state law requiring uniformed police to retire at age fifty. In *Vance v. Bradley*, 440 U.S. 93 (1979), the Court as well upheld under the rational basis test Congress's requiring members of the Foreign Service to retire at age sixty to promote younger members of the service and because of the risks and rigors of overseas service. However, Congress forbade age discrimination in a number of laws; notably, the Age Discrimination in Employment Act of 1967 prohibits employment discrimination against individuals between the ages of forty and seventy.

THE DEVELOPMENT OF LAW
Rulings on the Classification of Aliens

Case	Vote	Ruling
Graham v. Richardson, 403 U.S. 532 (1971)	9:0	Declared that alienage was a suspect classification and held that Arizona's requirements for state welfare benefits violated the equal protection clause because they conditioned benefits on citizenship and durational residency requirements for aliens.
In re Griffiths, 413 U.S. 717 (1973)	7:2	Overturned a state law barring aliens from practicing law; Chief Justice Burger and Justice Rehnquist dissented.
Sugerman v. Dougall, 413 U.S. 634 (1973)	9:1	Held that New York's prohibition of aliens from being employed as state civil servants violated the equal protection clause; Justice Rehnquist dissented.

Case	Vote	Ruling
Hampton v. Mow Sun Wong, 426 U.S. 88 (1976)	5:4	Justice Stevens held for a bare majority that the concept of equal justice embodied in the due process clause of the Fifth Amendment forbid the exclusion of all persons who are not citizens of the United States, or natives of Samoa, from being employed in the federal civil service; Chief Justice Burger and Justices Rehnquist, Blackmun, and White dissented.
Mathews v. Diaz, 426 U.S. 67 (1976)	9:0	For a unanimous Court, Justice Stevens upheld the denial of Social Security medicare-benefits to aliens who had not resided in the United States for at least five years, observing that the Court should defer to "the strong federal interest in regulating foreign affairs."
Nyquist v. Mauclet, 432 U.S. 1 (1977)	5:4	Struck down a New York law barring resident aliens from eligibility for state financial aid and scholarships; Chief Justice Burger and Justices Powell, Stevens, and Rehnquist dissented.
Foley v. Connelie, 435 U.S. 291 (1978)	6:3	Upheld New York's statute barring aliens from being employed as state police officers on the grounds that police serve important governmental functions; Justices Marshall, Brennan, and Stevens dissented.
Ambach v. Norwick, 441 U.S. 68 (1979)	5:4	Upheld a state law barring aliens from teaching in public schools unless they intended to become citizens of the United States, on the grounds that some state functions are so bound up with the operation of state government as to permit

Case	Vote	Ruling
		the exclusion of those persons from positions in the government who have not yet become part of the process of government; Justices Blackmun, Brennan, Marshall, and Stevens dissented.
Cabell v. Chavez-Salido, 454 U.S. 432 (1982)	5:4	Extended the state functions analysis in *Ambach* to permit California to bar aliens from working as state probation officers. *Ambach's* dissenters renewed their opposition.
Bernal v. Fainter, 467 U.S. 216 (1984)	9:1	Struck down a Texas law requiring a notary public to be an American citizen, holding that laws that discriminate against aliens must survive the Court's strict scrutiny, unless a state demonstrates that its discrimination against aliens is in the service of an important public function; Justice Rehnquist dissented.

SELECTED BIBLIOGRAPHY

Karst, Kenneth. *Belonging to America: Equal Citizenship and the Constitution.* New Haven, CT: Yale University Press, 1989.

Preston, William, Jr. *Aliens and Dissenters: Federal Suppression of Radicals, 1903–1933.* Cambridge, MA: Harvard University Press, 1963.

Plyler v. Doe

457 U.S. 202, 102 S.Ct. 2382 (1982)

In 1975, two years after the Supreme Court's ruling in *San Antonio Independent School District v. Rodriguez* (1973) (see page

1466), the Texas state legislature passed legislation authorizing local school districts to exclude children of undocumented aliens from public schools and to withhold school districts funds for the education of those children. A class action suit for certain school-age Mexican children who illegally entered and resided in Texas was brought against James Plyler, a school superintendent, and other state officials. A federal district court held that the state had violated the equal protection clause of the Fourteenth Amendment. On appeal to the Supreme Court, the lower court's ruling was affirmed by a bare majority in an opinion delivered by Justice William J. Brennan.

Justice BRENNAN delivers the opinion of the Court.

The question presented by these cases is whether, consistent with the Equal Protection Clause of the Fourteenth Amendment, Texas may deny to undocumented school-age children the free public education that it provides to children who are citizens of the United States or legally admitted aliens. . . .

In applying the Equal Protection Clause to most forms of state action, we thus seek only the assurance that the classification at issue bears some fair relationship to a legitimate public purpose.

But we would not be faithful to our obligations under the Fourteenth Amendment if we applied so deferential a standard to every classification. The Equal Protection Clause was intended as a restriction on state legislative action inconsistent with elemental constitutional premises. Thus we have treated as presumptively invidious those classifications that disadvantage a "suspect class," or that impinge upon the exercise of a "fundamental right." With respect to such classifications, it is appropriate to enforce the mandate of equal protection by requiring the State to demonstrate that its classification has been precisely tailored to serve a compelling governmental interest. In addition, we have recognized that certain forms of legislative classification, while not facially invidious, nonetheless give rise to recurring constitutional difficulties; in these limited circumstances we have sought the assurance that the classification reflects a reasoned judgment consistent with the ideal of equal protection by inquiring whether it may fairly be viewed as furthering a substantial interest of the State. We turn to a consideration of the standard appropriate for the evaluation of [the Texas program].

Sheer incapability or lax enforcement of the laws barring entry into this country, coupled with the failure to establish an effective bar to the employment of undocumented aliens, has resulted in the creation of a substantial "shadow population" of illegal migrants—numbering in the millions—within our borders. This situation raises the specter of a permanent caste of undocumented resident aliens, encouraged by some to remain here as a source of cheap labor, but nevertheless denied the benefits that our society makes available to citizens and lawful residents. The existence of such an underclass presents most difficult problems for a Nation that prides itself on adherence to principles of equality under law.

The children who are plaintiffs in these cases are special members of this underclass. Persuasive arguments support the view that a State may withhold its beneficence from those whose very presence within the United States is the product of their own unlawful conduct. These arguments do not apply with the same force to classifications imposing disabilities on the minor *children* of such illegal entrants. At the least, those who elect to enter our territory by stealth and in violation of our law should be prepared to bear the consequences, including, but not limited to, deportation. But the children of those illegal entrants are not comparably situated. Their "parents have the ability to conform their conduct to societal norms," and presumably the ability to remove themselves from the State's jurisdiction; but the children who are plaintiffs in these cases "can affect neither their parents' conduct nor their own status." *Trimble v. Gordon*, 430 U.S. 762 (1977). Even if the State found it expedient to control the conduct of adults by acting against their children, legislation directing the onus of a parent's misconduct against his children does not comport with fundamental conceptions of justice. . . .

Of course, undocumented status is not irrelevant to any proper legislative goal. Nor is undocumented status an absolutely immutable characteristic since it is the product of conscious, indeed unlawful, action. But [Texas's program] is directed against children, and imposes its discriminatory burden on the basis of a legal characteristic over which children can have little control. It is thus difficult to conceive of a rational justification for penalizing these children for their presence within the United States. Yet that appears to be precisely the effect of [the Texas law].

Public education is not a "right" granted to individuals by the Constitution. *San Antonio [Independent] School District, [v. Rodriguez*, 411 U.S. 1 (1973)]. But neither is it merely some governmental "benefit" indistinguishable from other forms of social welfare legislation. Both the importance of education in maintaining our basic institutions, and the lasting impact of its deprivation on the life of the child, mark the distinction. . . . As noted early in our history, "some degree of education is necessary to prepare citizens to participate effectively and intelligently in our open political system if we are to preserve freedom and independence." *Wisconsin v. Yoder*, 406 U.S. 205 (1972). . . . In addition, education provides the basic tools by which individuals might lead economically productive lives to the benefit of us all. In sum, education has a fundamental role in maintaining the fabric of our society.

We cannot ignore the significant social costs borne by our Nation when select groups are denied the means to absorb the values and skills upon which our social order rests.

In addition to the pivotal role of education in sustaining our political and cultural heritage, denial of education to some isolated group of children poses an affront to one of the goals of the Equal Protection Clause: the abolition of governmental barriers presenting unreasonable obstacles to advancement on the basis of individual merit. . . . Illiteracy is an enduring disability. The inability to read and write will handicap the individual deprived of a basic education each and every day of his life. The inestimable toll of that deprivation on the social economic, intellectual and psychological well-being of the individual, and the obstacle it poses to individual achievement, makes it most difficult to reconcile the cost or the principle of a status-based denial of basic education with the framework of equality embodied in the Equal Protection Clause. . . .

These well-settled principles allow us to determine the proper level of deference to be afforded [Texas]. Undocumented aliens cannot be treated as a suspect class because their presence in this country in violation of federal law is not a "constitutional irrelevancy." Nor is education a fundamental right; a State need not justify by compelling necessity every variation in the manner in which education is provided to its population. But more is involved in this case than the abstract question whether [Texas] discriminates against a suspect class, or whether education is a fundamental right. [Texas's program] imposes a lifetime hardship on a discrete class of children not accountable for their disabling status. The stigma of illiteracy will mark them for the rest of their lives. By denying these children a basic education, we deny them the ability to live within the structure of our civic institutions, and foreclose any realistic possibility that they will contribute in even the smallest way to the progress of our Nation. In determining the rationality of [Texas's law] we may appropriately take into account its costs to the Nation and to the innocent children who are its victims. In light of these countervailing costs, the discrimination contained in [Texas's program] can hardly be considered rational unless it furthers some substantial goal of the State.

It is the State's principal argument, and apparently the view of the dissenting Justices, that the undocumented status of these children *vel non* establishes a sufficient rational basis for denying them benefits that a State might choose to afford other residents. The State notes that while other aliens are admitted "on an equality of legal privileges with all citizens under nondiscriminatory laws," the asserted right of these children to an education can claim no implicit congressional imprimatur. Indeed, on the State's view, Congress' apparent disapproval of the presence of these children within the United States, and the evasion of the federal regulatory program that is the mark of undocumented status, provides authority for its decision to impose upon them special disabilities. Faced with an equal protection challenge respecting the treatment of aliens, we agree that the courts must be attentive to congressional policy; the exercise of congressional power might well affect the State's prerogatives to afford differential treatment to a particular class of aliens. But we are unable to find in the congressional immigration scheme any statement of policy that might weigh significantly in arriving at an equal protection balance concerning the State's authority to deprive these children of an education. . . .

To be sure, like all persons who have entered the United States unlawfully, these children are subject to deportation. But there is no assurance that a child subject to deportation will ever be deported. An illegal entrant might be granted federal permission to continue to reside in this country, or even to become a citizen. In light of the discretionary federal power to grant relief from deportation, a State cannot realistically determine that any particular undocumented child will in fact be deported until after deportation proceedings have been completed. . . .

We are reluctant to impute to Congress the intention to withhold from these children, for so long as they are present in this country through no fault of their own, access to a basic education. In other contexts, undocumented status, coupled with some articulable federal policy, might enhance State authority with respect to the treatment of undocumented aliens. But in the area of special constitutional sensitivity presented by this case, and in the absence of any contrary indication fairly discernible in the present legislative record, we perceive no national policy that supports the State in denying these children an elementary education. . . .

Appellants argue that the classification at issue furthers an interest in the "preservation of the state's limited resources for the education of its lawful residents.". . . [But, t]he State must do more than justify its classification with a concise expression of an intention to discriminate. Apart from the asserted state prerogative to act against undocumented children solely on the basis of their undocumented status—an asserted prerogative that carries only minimal force in the circumstances of this case—we discern three colorable state interests that might support [Texas's law].

First, appellants appear to suggest that the State may seek to protect the State from an influx of illegal immigrants. . . . [However, t]here is no evidence in the record suggesting that illegal entrants impose any significant burden on the State's economy. To the contrary, the available evidence suggests that illegal aliens underutilize public services, while contributing their labor to the local economy and tax money to the State fisc. The dominant incentive for illegal entry into the State of Texas is the availability of employment; few if any illegal immigrants come to this country, or presumably to the State of Texas, in order to avail themselves of a free education. . . .

Second, . . . appellants suggest that undocumented children are appropriately singled out for exclusion because of the special burdens they impose on the State's ability to provide high quality public education. But the record in no way supports the claim that exclusion of undocumented children is likely to improve the overall quality of education in the State. . . . Of course, even if improvement in the quality of education were a likely result of barring some number of children from the schools of the State, the State must support its selection of this group as the appropriate target for exclusion. In terms of educational cost and need, however, undocumented children are "basically indistinguishable" from legally resident alien children.

Finally, appellants suggest that undocumented children are appropriately singled out because their unlawful presence within the United States renders them less likely than other children to remain within the boundaries of the State, and to put their education to productive social or political use within the State. Even assuming that such an interest is legitimate, it is an interest that is most difficult to quantify. The State has no assurance that any child, citizen or not, will employ the education provided by the State within the confines of the State's borders. In any event, the record is clear that many of the undocumented children disabled by this classification will remain in this country indefinitely, and that some will become lawful residents or citizens of the United States. It is difficult to understand precisely what the State hopes to achieve by promoting the creation and perpetuation of a subclass of illiterates within our boundaries, surely adding to the problems and costs of unemployment, welfare, and crime. It is thus clear that whatever savings might be achieved by denying these children an education, they are wholly insubstantial in light of the costs involved to these children, the State, and the Nation.

If the State is to deny a discrete group of innocent children the free public education that it offers to other children residing within its borders, that denial must be justified by a showing that it furthers some substantial state interest. No such showing was made here. Accordingly, the judgment of the Court of Appeals in each of these cases is

Affirmed.

Justice MARSHALL concurring.

While I join the Court's opinion . . . I continue to believe that an individual's interest in education is fundamental, and that this view is amply supported "by the unique status accorded public education by our society, and by the close relationship between education and some of our most basic constitutional values."

Justice BLACKMUN, concurring.

[The] Court in *Rodriguez* articulate[d] a firm rule: fundamental rights are those that "explicitly or implicitly [are] guaranteed by the Constitution." It therefore squarely rejected the notion that "an ad hoc determination as to the social or economic importance" of a given interest is relevant to the level of scrutiny accorded classifications involving that interest, and made clear that "[i]t is not the province of this Court to create substantive constitutional rights in the name of guaranteeing equal protection of the laws.". . .

I continue to believe that [*Rodriguez*] provides the appropriate model for resolving most equal protection disputes. . . .

[H]owever, I believe the Court's experience has demonstrated that the *Rodriguez* formulation does not settle every issue of "fundamental rights" arising under the Equal Protection Clause. Only a pedant would insist that there are no meaningful distinctions among the multitude of social and political interests regulated by the States, and *Rodriguez* does not stand for quite so absolute a proposition. To the contrary, *Rodriguez* implicitly acknowledged that certain interests, though not constitutionally guaranteed, must be accorded a special place in equal protection analysis. Thus, the Court's decisions long have accorded strict scrutiny to classifications bearing on the right to vote in state elections, and *Rodriguez* confirmed the "constitutional underpinnings of the right to equal treatment in the voting process.". . . In other words, the right to vote is accorded extraordinary treatment because it is, in equal protection terms, an extraordinary right: a citizen cannot hope to achieve any meaningful degree of individual political equality if granted an inferior right of participation in the political process. Those denied the vote are relegated, by state fiat, in a most basic way to second-class status.

In my view, when the State provides an education to some and denies it to others, it immediately and inevitably creates class distinctions of a type fundamentally inconsistent with those purposes, mentioned above, of the Equal Protection Clause. Children denied an education are placed at a permanent and insurmountable competitive disadvantage, for an uneducated child is denied even the opportunity to achieve. And when those children are members of an identifiable group, that group—through the State's action—will have been converted into a discrete underclass. Other benefits provided by the State, such as housing and public assistance, are of course important; to an individual in immediate need, they may be more desirable than the right to be educated. But classifications involving the complete denial of education are in a sense unique, for they strike at the heart of equal protection values by involving the State in the creation of permanent class distinctions. In a sense, then, denial of an education is the analogue of denial of the right to vote: the former relegates the individual to second-class social status; the latter places him at a permanent political disadvantage.

This conclusion is fully consistent with *Rodriguez*. The Court there reserved judgment on the constitutionality of a state system that "occasioned an absolute denial of educational opportunities to any of its children," noting that "no charge fairly could be made that the system [at issue in *Rodriguez*] fails to provide each child with an opportunity to acquire . . . basic minimal skills.". . .

Because I believe that the Court's carefully worded analysis recognizes the importance of the equal protection and preemption interests I consider crucial, I join its opinion as well as its judgment.

Justice POWELL concurring.

I join the opinion of the Court, and write separately to emphasize the unique character of the case before us. . . .

Although the analogy is not perfect, our holding today does find support in decisions of this Court with respect to the status of illegitimates. . . .

In this case, the State of Texas effectively denies to the school age children of illegal aliens the opportunity to attend the free public schools that the State makes available to all residents. They are excluded only because of a status resulting from the violation by parents or guardians of our immigration laws and the fact that they remain in our country unlawfully. The respondent children are innocent in this respect. They can "affect neither their parents' conduct nor their own status.". . .

The classification at issue deprives a group of children of the opportunity for education afforded all other children simply because they have been assigned a legal status due to a violation of law by their parents. These children thus have been singled out for a lifelong penalty and stigma. A legislative classification that threatens the creation of an underclass of future citizens and residents cannot be reconciled with one of the fundamental purposes of the Fourteenth Amendment. In these unique circumstances, the Court properly may require that the State's interests be substantial and that the means bear a "fair and substantial relation" to these interests. . . .

In my view, the State's denial of education to these children bears no substantial relation to any substantial state interest.

Chief Justice BURGER, with whom Justice WHITE, Justice REHNQUIST, and Justice O'CONNOR join, dissenting.

Were it our business to set the Nation's social policy, I would agree without hesitation that it is senseless for an enlightened society to deprive any children—including illegal aliens—of an elementary education. I fully agree that it would be folly—and wrong—to tolerate creation of a segment of society made up of illiterate persons, many having a limited or no command of our language. However, the Constitution does not constitute us as "Platonic Guardians" nor does it vest in this Court the authority to strike down laws because they do not meet our standards of desirable social policy, "wisdom," or "common sense."

The Court's holding today manifests the justly criticized judicial tendency to attempt speedy and wholesale formulation of "remedies" for the failures—or simply the laggard pace—of the political processes of our system of government. The Court employs, and in my view abuses the Fourteenth Amendment in an effort to become an omnipotent and omniscient problem solver. That the motives for doing so are noble and compassionate does not alter the fact that the Court distorts our constitutional function to make amends for the defaults of others. . . .

[T]he Court expressly—and correctly—rejects any suggestion that illegal aliens are a suspect class, or that education is a fundamental right. Yet by patching together bits and pieces of what might be termed quasi-suspect-class and quasi-fundamental-rights analysis, the Court spins out a theory custom-tailored to the facts of these cases.

In the end, we are told little more than that the level of scrutiny employed to strike down the Texas law applies only when illegal alien children are deprived of a public education. If ever a court was guilty of an unabashedly result-oriented approach, this case is a prime example.

The Court first suggests that these illegal alien children, although not a suspect class, are entitled to special solicitude under the Equal Protection Clause because they lack "control" over or "responsibility" for their unlawful entry into this country. Similarly, the Court appears to take the position that [the Texas law] is presumptively "irrational" because it has the effect of imposing "penalties" on "innocent" children. However, the Equal Protection Clause does not preclude legislators from classifying among persons on the basis of factors and characteristics over which individuals may be said to lack "control." Indeed, in some circumstances persons generally, and children in particular, may have little control over or responsibility for such things as their ill-health, need for public assistance, or place of residence. Yet a state legislature is not barred from considering, for example, relevant differences between the mentally-healthy and the mentally-ill, or between the residents of different counties, simply because these may be factors unrelated to individual choice or to any "wrongdoing." The Equal Protection Clause protects against arbitrary and irrational classifications, and against invidious discrimination stemming from prejudice and hostility; it is not an all-encompassing "equalizer" designed to eradicate every distinction for which persons are not "responsible."

The Court does not presume to suggest that appellees' purported lack of culpability for their illegal status prevents them from being deported or otherwise "penalized" under federal law. Yet would deportation be any less a "penalty" than denial of privileges provided to legal residents? . . .

The Court's analogy to cases involving discrimination against illegitimate children is grossly misleading. The State has not thrust any disabilities upon appellees due to their "status of birth." Rather, appellees' status is predicated upon the circumstances of their concededly illegal presence in this country, and is a direct result of Congress' obviously valid exercise of its "broad constitutional powers" in the field of immigration and naturalization. . . .

The second strand of the Court's analysis rests on the premise that, although public education is not a constitutionally-guaranteed right, "neither is it merely some governmental 'benefit' indistinguishable from other forms of social welfare legislation." Whatever meaning or relevance this opaque observation might have in some other context, it simply has no bearing on the issues at hand. Indeed, it is never made clear what the Court's opinion means on this score.

The importance of education is beyond dispute. Yet we have held repeatedly that the importance of a governmental service does not elevate it to the status of a "fundamental right" for purposes of equal protection analysis. In *San Antonio School District*, Justice POWELL, speaking for the Court, expressly rejected the proposition that state laws dealing with public education are subject to special scrutiny under the Equal Protection Clause. Moreover, the Court points to no meaningful way to distinguish between education and other governmental benefits in this context. Is the Court suggesting that education is more "fundamental" than food, shelter, or medical care? . . .

Once it is conceded—as the Court does—that illegal aliens are not a suspect class, and that education is not a fundamental right, our inquiry should focus on and be limited to whether the legislative classification at issue bears a rational relationship to a legitimate state purpose. . . .

Without laboring what will undoubtedly seem obvious to many, it simply is not "irrational" for a State to conclude that it does not have the same responsibility to provide benefits for persons whose very presence in the State and this country is illegal as it does to provide for persons lawfully present. . . .

Denying a free education to illegal alien children is not a choice
I would make were I a legislator. Apart from compassionate considerations, the long-range costs of excluding any children from
the public schools may well outweigh the costs of educating them.
But that is not the issue; the fact that there are sound *policy*
arguments against the Texas legislature's choice does not render
that choice an unconstitutional one.

Justice William J. Brennan, Jr., in his chambers. During his thirty–
four years on the bench (1956–1990), Justice Brennan had a major
influence on the Court's interpretation and application of the Fourteenth
Amendment. *Supreme Court Historical Society.*

MEMBERS OF
THE SUPREME COURT
OF THE UNITED STATES

	Appointing President	Dates of Service
CHIEF JUSTICES		
Jay, John	Washington	1789–1795
Rutledge, John	Washington	1795–1795
Ellsworth, Oliver	Washington	1796–1800
Marshall, John	Adams, J.	1801–1835
Taney, Roger Brooke	Jackson	1836–1864
Chase, Salmon Portland	Lincoln	1864–1873
Waite, Morrison Remick	Grant	1874–1888
Fuller, Melville Weston	Cleveland	1888–1910
White, Edward Douglass	Taft	1910–1921
Taft, William Howard	Harding	1921–1930
Hughes, Charles Evans	Hoover	1930–1941
Stone, Harlan Fiske	Roosevelt, F.	1941–1946
Vinson, Frederick Moore	Truman	1946–1953
Warren, Earl	Eisenhower	1953–1969
Burger, Warren Earl	Nixon	1969–1986
Rehnquist, William Hubbs	Reagan	1986–
ASSOCIATE JUSTICES		
Rutledge, John	Washington	1790–1791
Cushing, William	Washington	1790–1810
Wilson, James	Washington	1789–1798

	Appointing President	Dates of Service
Blair, John	Washington	1790–1796
Iredell, James	Washington	1790–1799
Johnson, Thomas	Washington	1792–1793
Paterson, William	Washington	1793–1806
Chase, Samuel	Washington	1796–1811
Washington, Bushrod	Adams, J.	1799–1829
Moore, Alfred	Adams, J.	1800–1804
Johnson, William	Jefferson	1804–1834
Livingston, Henry Brockholst	Jefferson	1807–1823
Todd, Thomas	Jefferson	1807–1826
Duvall, Gabriel	Madison	1811–1835
Story, Joseph	Madison	1812–1845
Thompson, Smith	Monroe	1823–1843
Trimble, Robert	Adams, J. Q.	1826–1828
McLean, John	Jackson	1830–1861
Baldwin, Henry	Jackson	1830–1844
Wayne, James Moore	Jackson	1835–1867
Barbour, Philip Pendleton	Jackson	1836–1841
Catron, John	Van Buren	1837–1865
McKinley, John	Van Buren	1838–1852
Daniel, Peter Vivian	Van Buren	1842–1860
Nelson, Samuel	Tyler	1845–1872
Woodbury, Levi	Polk	1845–1851
Grier, Robert Cooper	Polk	1846–1870
Curtis, Benjamin Robbins	Fillmore	1851–1857
Campbell, John Archibald	Pierce	1853–1861
Clifford, Nathan	Buchanan	1858–1881
Swayne, Noah Haynes	Lincoln	1862–1881
Miller, Samuel Freeman	Lincoln	1862–1890
Davis, David	Lincoln	1862–1877
Field, Stephen Johnson	Lincoln	1863–1897
Strong, William	Grant	1870–1880
Bradley, Joseph P.	Grant	1870–1892
Hunt, Ward	Grant	1873–1882
Harlan, John Marshall	Hayes	1877–1911
Woods, William Burnham	Hayes	1881–1887
Matthews, Stanley	Garfield	1881–1889
Gray, Horace	Arthur	1882–1902
Blatchford, Samuel	Arthur	1882–1893
Lamar, Lucius Quintus C.	Cleveland	1888–1893
Brewer, David Josiah	Harrison	1890–1910
Brown, Henry Billings	Harrison	1891–1906

	Appointing President	Dates of Service
Shiras, George, Jr.	Harrison	1892–1903
Jackson, Howell Edmunds	Harrison	1893–1895
White, Edward Douglass	Cleveland	1894–1910
Peckham Rufus Wheeler	Cleveland	1896–1909
McKenna, Joseph	McKinley	1898–1925
Holmes, Oliver Wendell	Roosevelt, T.	1902–1932
Day, William Rufus	Roosevelt, T.	1903–1922
Moody, William Henry	Roosevelt, T.	1906–1910
Lurton, Horace Harmon	Taft	1910–1914
Hughes, Charles Evans	Taft	1910–1916
Van Devanter, Willis	Taft	1911–1937
Lamar, Joseph Rucker	Taft	1911–1916
Pitney, Mahlon	Taft	1912–1922
McReynolds, James Clark	Wilson	1914–1941
Brandeis, Louis Dembitz	Wilson	1916–1939
Clarke, John Hessin	Wilson	1916–1922
Sutherland, George	Harding	1911–1938
Butler, Pierce	Harding	1923–1939
Sanford, Edward Terry	Harding	1923–1930
Stone, Harlan Fiske	Coolidge	1925–1941
Roberts, Owen Josephus	Hoover	1930–1945
Cardozo, Benjamin Nathan	Hoover	1932–1938
Black, Hugo Lafayette	Roosevelt, F.	1937–1971
Reed, Stanley Forman	Roosevelt, F.	1938–1957
Frankfurter, Felix	Roosevelt, F.	1939–1962
Douglas, William Orville	Roosevelt, F.	1939–1975
Murphy, Frank	Roosevelt, F.	1940–1949
Byrnes, James Francis	Roosevelt, F.	1941–1942
Jackson, Robert Houghwout	Roosevelt, F.	1941–1954
Rutledge, Wiley Blount	Roosevelt, F.	1943–1949
Burton, Harold Hitz	Truman	1945–1958
Clark, Thomas Campbell	Truman	1949–1967
Minton, Sherman	Truman	1949–1956
Harlan, John Marshall	Eisenhower	1955–1971
Brennan, William Joseph, Jr.	Eisenhower	1956–1990
Whittaker, Charles Evans	Eisenhower	1957–1962
Stewart, Potter	Eisenhower	1958–1981
White, Byron Raymond	Kennedy	1962–
Goldberg, Arthur Joseph	Kennedy	1962–1965
Fortas, Abe	Johnson, L.	1965–1969
Marshall, Thurgood	Johnson, L.	1967–
Blackmun, Harry A.	Nixon	1970–

	Appointing President	Dates of Service
Powell, Lewis Franklin, Jr.	Nixon	1972–1986
Rehnquist, William Hubbs	Nixon	1972–
Stevens, John Paul	Ford	1975–
O'Connor, Sandra Day	Reagan	1981–
Scalia, Antonin	Reagan	1986–
Kennedy, Anthony	Reagan	1988–
Souter, David Hackett	Bush	1990–

GLOSSARY

Advisory opinion. An opinion or interpretation of law that does not have binding effect. The Court does not give advisory opinions, for example, on hypothetical disputes; it decides only actual cases or controversies.

Affirm. In an appellate court, to reach a decision that agrees with the result reached in a case by the lower court.

Affirmative action programs. Programs required by federal or state laws designed to remedy discriminatory practices by hiring minority-group persons and/or women.

Amicus curiae. A friend of the court, a person not a party to litigation, who volunteers or is invited by the court to give his views on a case.

Appeal. To take a case to a higher court for review. Generally, a party losing in a trial court may appeal once to an appellate court as a matter of right. If the party loses in the appellate court, appeal to a higher court is within the discretion of the higher court. Most appeals to the Supreme Court are within its discretion to deny or grant a hearing.

Appellant. The party that appeals a lower-court decision to a higher court.

Appellee. One who has an interest in upholding the decision of a lower court and is compelled to respond when the case is appealed to a higher court by the appellant.

Brief. A document prepared by counsel to serve as the basis for an argument in court, setting out the facts and legal arguments in support of his case.

Case. A general term for an action, cause, suit, or controversy, at law or equity; a question contested before a court.

Case law. The law as defined by previously decided cases, distinct from statutes and other sources of law.

Certification, writ of. A method of taking a case from appellate court to the Supreme Court in which the lower court asks that some question or interpretation of law be certified, clarified, and made more certain.

Certiorari, writ of. A writ issued from the Supreme Court, at its discretion and at the request of a petitioner, to order a lower court to send the record of a case to the Court for its review.

Civil Law. The body of law dealing with the private rights of individuals, as distinguished from criminal law.

Class action. A lawsuit brought by one person or group on behalf of all persons similarly situated.

Comity. Courtesy, respect; referring to the deference federal courts pay to state court decisions that are based on state law.

Common law. The collection of principles and rules, particularly from unwritten English law, that derive their authority from long-standing usage and custom or from courts recognizing and enforcing those customs.

Compelling state interest. A test used to uphold state action against First Amendment and equal protection challenges because of the serious need for government action.

Concurring opinion. An opinion by a justice that agrees with the result reached by the Court in a case but disagrees with the Court's rationale or reasoning for its decision.

Contempt (civil and criminal). Civil contempt is the failure to do something for the benefit of another party after being ordered to do so by a court. Criminal contempt occurs when a person exhibits disrespect for a court or obstructs the administration of justice.

Controversies. *See* Justiciable controversy.

Criminal law. The body of law that deals with the enforcement of laws and the punishment of persons who, by breaking laws, commit crimes against the state.

Declaratory Judgment. A court pronouncement declaring a legal right or interpretation but not ordering a special action.

De facto. In fact, in reality.

Defendant. In a civil action, the party denying or defending itself against charges brought by a plaintiff. In a criminal action, the person indicted for the commission of a offense.

De jure. As a result of law, as a result of official action.

Dicta. *See* Obiter dictim.

Discretionary jurisdiction. Jurisdiction that a court may accept or reject in particular cases. The Supreme Court has discretionary jurisdiction in over 90 percent of the cases that come to it.

Dismissal. An order diposing of a case without a hearing or trial.

Dissenting opinion. An opinion by a justice that disagrees with the result reached by the Court in a case.

Docket. All cases filed in a court.

Due process. Fair and regular procedure. The Fifth and Fourteenth Amendments guarantee persons that they will not be deprived of life, liberty, or property by the government until fair and usual procedures have been followed.

Error, writ of. A writ issued from an appeals court to a lower court requiring that it send the record of a case so that it may review it for error.

Exclusionary rule. This rule commands that evidence obtained in violation of the rights guaranteed by the Fourth and Fifth Amendments must be excluded at trial.

Executive agreement. A treatylike agreement with another country made by the president.

Executive privilege. Exemption from the disclosure requirements for ordinary citizens because of the executive's need for confidentiality in discharging highly important governmental functions.

Ex parte. From, or on, only on side. Application to a court for some ruling or action on behalf of only one party.

Federalism. The interrelationships among the states and the relationship between the states and the national government.

Federal preemption. The federal government's exclusive power over certain matters such as interstate commerce and sedition to the exclusion of state jurisdiction and law.

Grand jury. A jury of twelve to twenty-three persons that hears in private evidence for serving an indictment.

Habeas corpus. Literally, "you have the body"; a writ issued to inquire whether a person is lawfully imprisoned or detained. The writ demands that the persons holding the prisoner justify his detention or release him.

Immunity. A grant of exemption from prosecution in return for evidence by testimony.

In camera. "In chambers," referring to court hearings in private without spectators.

Indictment. A formal charge of offenses based on evidence presented by a prosecutor from a grand jury.

In forma pauperis. In the manner of a pauper, without liability for the costs of filing cases before a court.

Information. A written set of charges, similar to an indictment, filed by a prosecutor but without a grand jury's consideration of evidence.

Inherent powers. Powers originating from the structure of government or sovereignty that go beyond those expressly granted or which could be construed to have been implied from those expressly granted.

Injunction. A court order prohibiting a person from performing a particular act.

In re. In the affair of, concerning; often used in judicial procedings where there is no adversary but where the matter (such as a bankrupt's estate) requires judicial action.

Judgment. The official decision of a court.

Judicial review. The power to review and strike down any legislation or other government action that is inconsistent with federal or state constitutions. The Supreme Court reviews government action only under the Constitution of the United States and federal laws.

Jurisdiction. The power of a court to hear a case or controversy, which exists when the proper parties are present and when the point to be decided is among the issues authorized to be handled by a particular court.

Justiciable controversy. A controversy in which a claim of right is asserted against another who has an interest in contesting it. Courts will consider only justiciable controversies, as distinguished from hypothetical disputes.

Majority opinion. An opinion in a case that is subscribed to by a majority of the justices who participated in the decision.

Mandamus, writ of. "We command"; an order issued from a superior court directing a lower court or other government authority to perform a particular act.

Mandatory jurisdiction. Jurisdiction that a court must accept. The Supreme Court must decide cases coming under its appellate jurisdiction, though it may avoid giving them plenary consideration.

Moot. Unsettled, undecided. A moot question is also one that is no longer material, or that has already been resolved, and has become hypothetical.

Motion. A written or oral application to a court or judge to obtain a rule or order.

Natural rights. Rights based on the nature of man and independent of those rights secured by positive laws.

Obiter dictum. A statement by a judge or justices expressing an opinion and included with, but not essential to, an opinion resolving a case before the court. Dicta are not necessarily binding in later cases.

Opinion for the court. The opinion announcing the decision of a court.

Original jurisdiction. The jurisdiction of a court of first instance, or trial court. The Supreme Court has original jurisdiction under Article III of the Constitution.

Per curiam. "By the court"; an unsigned opinion of the court.

Petitioner. One who files a petition with a court seeking action or relief, including the plaintiff or appellant. When a writ of certiorari is granted by the Supreme Court, the party seeking review is called the petitioner, and the party responding is called the respondent.

Petit jury. A trial jury, traditionally a common law jury of twelve persons, but since 1970 the Supreme Court has permitted states to use juries composed of less than twelve persons.

Plenary consideration. Full consideration. When the Supreme Court grants a case review, it may give it full consideration, permitting the parties to submit briefs on the merits of the case and to present oral arguments, before the Court reaches its decision.

Plurality opinion. An opinion announcing the decision of the Court, but which has the support of less than a majority of the Court.

Political question. Questions that courts refuse to decide because they are deemed to be essentially political in nature, or because their determination would involve an intrusion on the powers of the executive or legislature, or because courts could not provide a judicial remedy.

Probable cause. Reasonable cause, having more evidence for, rather than against, when establishing the basis for obtaining a search warrant, for example.

Rational basis test.   A test used by appellate courts to uphold legislation if there is evidence of a rational basis for the law's enactment.

Reapportment.   A realignment or change in electoral districts due to changes in population.

Remand.   To send back. After a decision in a case, the case is often sent back by a higher court to the court from which it came for further action in light of its decision.

Respondent.   The party that is compelled to answer the claims or questions posed in a court by a petitioner.

Reverse.   In an appellate court, to reach a decision that disagrees with the result reached in a case by a lower court.

Ripeness.   When a case is ready for adjudication and decision; the issues presented must not be hypothetical, and the parties must have exhausted other avenues of appeal.

Search warrant.   An order issued by a judge or magistrate directing a law enforcement official to search and seize evidence of the commission of a crime, contraband, the fruits of crime, or things otherwise unlawfully possessed.

Separation of powers.   The division of the powers of the national government according to the three branches of government: the legislative, which is empowered to make laws; the executive, which is required to carry out the laws; and the judicial, which has the power to interpret and adjudicate disputes under the law.

Seriatim.   Separately, individually, one by one. The Court's practice was once to have each justice give his opinion on a case separately.

Sovereignty.   Supreme political authority; the absolute and uncontrollable power by which an independent nation-state is governed.

Standing.   Having the appropriate characteristics to bring or participate in a case; in particular, having a personal interest and stake in the outcome.

Stare Decisis.   "Let the decision stand." The principle of adherence to settled cases, the doctrine that principles of law established in earlier cases should be accepted as authoritative in similar subsequent cases.

State action.   Actions undertaken by a state government and those done "under the color of state law"; that is, those actions required or sanctioned by a state.

Statute.   A written law enacted by a legislature.

Subpoena.   An order to present oneself before a grand jury, court, or legislative hearing.

Subpoena duces tecum.   An order to produce specified documents or papers.

Summary decision.   A decision in a case that does not give it full consideration; when the Court decides a case without having the parties submit briefs on the merits of the case or present oral arguments before the Court.

Tort.   An inury or wrong to the person or property of another.

Transactional immunity.   Immunity granted a person in exchange for evidence or testimony, which protects that person from prosecution, regardless of independent evidence against him; *see* Use immunity.

Treaties.   A compact made between two or more independent nations; treaties are made in the United States by the president with the advice and consent of the Senate.

Use immunity.   Immunity granted a person in exchange for evidence or testimony but that only protects that person from prosecution based on the use of his own testimony.

Vacate.   To make void, annul, or rescind the decision of a lower court.

War power.   The power of the national government to wage war; Congress has the power to declare war, while the president, as commander in chief, has authority over the conduct of war.

Writ.   An order commanding someone to perform or not perform acts specified in the order.

INDEX OF CASES

Cases in boldface type are excerpted.

GENERAL INDEX